AF782033

THE EXPERT IN LITIGATION AND ARBITRATION

THE EXPERT

IN LITIGATION AND ARBITRATION

by D Mark Cato

|L|L|P|

LONDON HONG KONG

1999

LLP Professional Publishing
(a trading division of the Informa Publishing Group Ltd)
69–77 Paul Street
London EC2A 4LQ

EAST ASIA
LLP Asia
Sixth Floor, Hollywood Centre
233 Hollywood Road
Hong Kong

First published 1999

© D Mark Cato and contributors 1999

British Library Cataloguing in Publication Data
A catalogue record for this book
is available from the
British Library

ISBN 1–85978–662–6

All rights reserved. No part of this publication may be reproduced, stored in a retrieval system, or transmitted, in any form or by any means, electronic, mechanical, photocopying, recording or otherwise, without the prior written permission of LLP Professional Publishing.

Whilst every effort has been made to ensure that the information contained in this book is correct, neither the editor and contributors nor LLP Professional Publishing can accept any responsibility for any errors or omissions or for any consequences resulting therefrom.

Are you satisfied with our customer service?

These telephone numbers are your service hot lines for questions and queries:

Delivery: +44 (0) 1206 772866
Payment/invoices/renewals: +44 (0) 1206 772114
LLP Products & Services: +44 (0) 1206 772113
e-mail: Publications@LLPLimited.com or fax us on +44 (0) 1206 772771

We welcome your views and comments in order to ease any problems and answer any queries you may have.

LLP Limited, Colchester CO3 3LP, U.K.

Text set in 10/12pt Bembo
by Mendip Communications Limited,
Frome, Somerset
Printed in Great Britain by
MPG Books Limited,
Bodmin, Cornwall

I have gathered a posy of other men's flowers
and nothing but the thread that binds them is my own.

Montaigne

I dedicate this book to my beloved grandson, "Freddy", born on 5 October 1998—may he never require the services of an expert. Also to that legion of friends and colleagues who are Life Members of *The Twisted Arm Club*, of whom a number have contributed to this book

Over the years, since I launched into authorship, I have been proud to enlist the assistance of those very many eminent academics and practising arbitrators and lawyers whom it is my privilege and pleasure to know.

FOREWORD

THE EXPERT IN LITIGATION AND ARBITRATION

by
The Right Honourable The Lord Howe of Aberavon, CH, QC
Former Foreign Secretary and Deputy Prime Minister of the United Kingdom

Kosovo, Tiananmen, Chernobyl, Pinochet, CNN. Increasingly we all share the same worldwide satellite-borne vocabulary. Trade, travel, tourism, television, technology—all these are competing with each other in the demolition of time and distance.

Politics and technology alike have been boosting rather than obstructing the growth of transnational business. Sometimes the obstacles for trade have been demolished by conscious political decision: in the European Union or in NAFTA, for example. Elsewhere the process has been triggered by near-revolutionary upheaval: with the displacement of Maoism by Deng Xiaoping's "socialist" marketplace or with the Gorbachev disintegration of the Soviet Empire. Very often it has been (in Keynes' words) the "animal spirits" of the entrepreneur that have been the driving force for change.

So we have grown used to the idea of a single world marketplace. Not just for goods but for capital and cash as well—whisked across frontiers invisibly and, literally, at the speed of light. We think less often perhaps of the global marketplace of law and legal thinking that must accompany the growth in trade and investment. Yet inevitably there has been a corresponding increase in transnational disputes. So too there has grown a corresponding need for skill and guidance in avoiding and resolving such disputes.

Multinational trade is inevitably multijurisdictional. Very often the choice of jurisdiction is the most difficult question of all. So more and more it makes sense to create what is in effect a unique jurisdiction, through a tailormade pattern of alternative dispute resolution. Sometimes even, in truly "adventurous" territories, one has almost literally to take one's own law with one.

And ADR, in whatever form and in whatever mix of territories, means more work not just for lawyers but for experts of every kind—and in a variety of roles. Perhaps too often we see ourselves as primarily involved in what Sir Mackenzie Chalmers, the Victorian jurist, described as the pathology of trade and commerce—in the forensic determination of head-on conflict. But the expert's role is now seen to be much wider than that. Even where disputation has already broken out, the expert's input to mediation, conciliation, to other means of dispute resolution—very often by the removal of technical or linguistic misunderstandings—will continue to grow.

So too in helping to shape relationships, to settle agreements, to formulate codes of practice that will make disputes less likely. And nowhere more than in the cross-frontier transactions—where often there can be significantly different perceptions of the role and standing of the expert himself. As between the United States, for example, and many other common law jurisdictions, there are differences—or so it is often thought—between the balance that has to be struck between duty to one's client and duty to the court or tribunal. Almost by definition, the scope for misunderstanding between Anglo-Saxon and Continental systems is different again.

And all the more so, when one is concerned with inter-cultural as well as intercontinental relationships. The contributors to this book, drawn as they are from Australasia as well as from China, from Continental Europe as well as from the United States and the United Kingdom itself, offer a broad perspective of advice on all these issues.

Yet even the most eminent professionals, said one commentator the other day, be they accountants, engineers or surgeons, can be reduced to simpletons in the witness box. That is why this is more than a book about experts, by experts, for experts. "The more a man looks at a thing," said G K Chesterton, the master of paradox, "the less he can see it, and the more a man learns about a thing, the less he knows it.... He goes on seeing less and less of its significance. In the same way, alas! we all go on every day, unless we are continually goading ourselves into humility."

This book aims to display humility and commonsense as well as expertise—and is all the better for that.

PREFACE

ETHICS AND THE EXPERT

by
The Right Honourable The Lord Saville of Newdigate
Chairman of the Judicial Committee of The Academy of Experts

"The expert witness is not an advocate employed on behalf of a party."

I take these words from the Guidance Note on Contingency Fees issued by the Judicial Committee of The Academy of Experts. That Committee (of which I was a member and am now Chairman) holds the view that any form of contingency fee arrangement is incompatible with the expert's duty of independence and impartiality.

The job of experts in litigation or arbitration is to give their independent, objective and unbiased opinions on the matter referred to them and falling within their area of expertise.

The job of advocates is to present the best case they properly can on behalf of their clients.

If an expert tries to adopt the advocate's role under the guise of giving expert evidence, then that expert will necessarily not be giving an independent, objective and unbiased opinion.

In truth such an expert will be attempting to deceive the court or tribunal.

Such attempts may succeed or they may fail. If they succeed, then the expert has perverted the course of justice. If they fail (and more often than not it is only too apparent to an experienced judge or arbitrator that the expert is not acting with independence and impartiality) then the result will be that the court or tribunal concerned will be likely heavily to discount the evidence that expert gives, which will mean that, so far from assisting the client, the expert will have done the client a great disservice.

In its Guidance Note the Judicial Committee also observed that "An Expert Witness must not only be independent, but must be seen to be independent". Hence the view of the Committee that contingency fees are not compatible with the duties of a true expert, since such fees could hardly fail to raise suspicions of partiality and lack of independence, even if in fact the expert was able to resist the temptation so to act.

There are those who do not share these views; indeed they regard them as idealistic and impracticable in the real world. However in my opinion unless they form the basis of the proper function and duties of experts, the argument that only court or tribunal appointed experts should be heard becomes very difficult indeed to rebut.

These points (and others of equal importance) are considered and discussed in detail in this book, which I would commend to all concerned with experts in litigation or arbitration.

ACKNOWLEDGEMENTS

- Norman Williams, Barrister—The Incorporated Council of Law Reporting for England and Wales
- *The Times Law Reports*
- *The Solicitors' Journal*
- *Family Law Reports*
- Donald Valentine, Barrister, Atkin Chambers—Commentary on Sandi Murdoch's article—see paras 8—555 to 8—566
- *The Arbitration and Dispute Resolution Law Newsletter*
- *The New Law Journal*

THE CONTRIBUTORS

The following are only brief notes about each of the contributors. For further information see the bibliographical notes at the end of their respective contributions.

The Right Honourable The Lord Howe of Aberavon, CH, QC
President of The Academy of Experts. Former Deputy Prime Minister, Foreign Secretary and Chancellor of the Exchequer of the United Kingdom.

The Right Honourable The Lord Saville of Newdigate
Chairman of the Departmental Advisory Committee on Arbitration Law (advising on the Arbitration Act 1996). Chairman of the Judicial Committee of The Academy of Experts.

Andrew Bartlett, QC, FCIArb
Arbitrator and Queen's Counsel working in building and civil engineering; professional negligence; insurance and reinsurance, and product liability. General editor of Emden's *Construction Law.*

Aldo Berlinguer
Attorney. Arbitrator. Associate Professor of Comparative Private Law at the University of Cagliari. Member of the Italian Association of Comparative Law. Member of the Italian and Spanish Bar.

John Bolton, MSc(Eng), MBA (Hons), FCIArb
Partner in Eversheds, the national law firm of solicitors. International construction lawyer. Lecturer and Assessor for the Woolf Report, *Access to Justice.*

Michel Brisac
An *Expert Agrée* by the *Cour de Cassation. President d'Honneur Fondateur* of the *Compagnie Nationale des Ingenieurs Diplômes Experts près les Cours judiciaires ou administratives d'appel* (CNIDECA).

***Eur Biol* Michael Chapman**
Arbitrator, practising expert and expert witness and arbitrator. *Expert près le Comité Nationale Français de la Chambre de Commerce Internationale.* Chartered Biologist and a European Registered Toxicologist practising in France. Author.

Nicholas Cheffings, FCIArb
Partner and Head of Property Litigation at Lovell White Durrant, City of London solicitors. Specialises in property litigation. Lecturer and author.

Michael Cohen, LLB, FIBA, FCIArb, QDR, FAE, Barrister
Registered arbitrator. Qualified mediator and practising insurance expert. Chairman Emeritus of The Academy of Experts.

Tim Cooper, BSc, FRICS, FCIArb
Senior Partner of North Staffordshire firm of chartered surveyors. Registered arbitrator. Vice-President of the West Midlands Rent Assessment Panel. Experienced lecturer, expert witness and independent expert.

The Honourable Mr Justice Cresswell
High Court Judge, Queen's Bench Division. As the author of what have become known as the *Ikarian Reefer* Rules he has been influential in raising experts' standards.

John Ellison, FCA, FBAE
Chartered accountant. Expert witness. Chairman of KPMG Forensic Accounting.

Tony Ensom, FRICS, FCIArb, MAE
Chartered building surveyor. Specialises in construction law, contract administration and dispute avoidance and resolution. Customer Services Director of Citex Consulting Limited in London. Acts as arbitrator, independent expert and adjudicator.

A A de Fina, OAM, FIArbA, FIE(Aust), FAIM, FRINA
International arbitrator in commercial disputes. Widely experienced expert witness in engineering and naval architecture. Author and lecturer.

Richard Freeman, MA (Cantab), FCA, FCIArb, DipICArb, FAE, QDR
Chartered Accountant. Expert witness, arbitrator and mediator. Head of Litigation Services at Horwath Clark Whitehill. Chairman of The Academy of Experts.

His Honour Judge John Frenkel
Sits at the Bristol Civil Trial Centre and is consulting editor for the *Practical Civil Court Precedents*. He is particularly well placed to comment and speculate on the application of the new Rules to civil proceedings.

Jonathan Gaunt, QC
Joint Head of Falcon Chambers in London. Specialises in property law.

Robert Goldspink
Partner and Head of the International Litigation practice group of Morgan, Lewis & Bockius, LLP, of the USA, London, Brussels, Frankfurt, Tokyo and Singapore.

Marcus Harling
A member of the Committee of TeCSA. He was responsible for the development of the TeCSA Expert Witness Protocol Version 1.0 and currently sits as a representative of TeCSA on the Lord Chancellor's Department's Working Group.

Nigel H Harris, MA, MB, BChir, FRCS, FAE, MCIArb
Consultant orthopaedic surgeon. Experienced expert witness in professional negligence and personal injury. Author.

Gary R Hickinbottom, MA, DipICArb, FCIArb
Partner in Cameron McKenna, City of London firm of solicitors. Specialises in multi-jurisdictional technical litigation, in particular group product liability claims. Recorder in the Crown Court and County Court. Author.

Doug Jones, AM, RFD, BA, LLB, LLM, FCIArb, FIA&MA
International construction lawyer and arbitrator. Partner in Clayton Utz, Australian lawyers. Author.

Dr Albert Knott, PE
Specialist in structural and mechanical failure analysis and accident reconstruction, Colorado, USA.

David Leonard, TD, MA(Cantab), FCIArb, FSIArb, FHKIArb
Former High Court judge, Hong Kong. Non-practising solicitor. Arbitrator and mediator. Lecturer. Panel member of the Hong Kong International Arbitration Centre and of CIETAC.

John Leslie Livingstone, PhD, CPA, CVA, MAE
Expert witness in accounting and economics in many significant cases over the past twenty years. Directs a national litigation consulting practice headquartered in West Palm Beach, Florida, USA.

Dr Roger J Maddrell, BSc, PhD, DiplDelft, FICE, FGS, FAE, QDR
Chief Engineer with consulting civil engineers Halcrow. Specialises in the maritime field. Author.

Simon Morgans
Solicitor and legal adviser to the Legal Aid Board, United Kingdom.

Paul Newman, MA, DipLaw, Barrister, FCIArb, RIBA and CIC Accredited Adjudicator, ADR Net Accredited Mediator
Non-practising barrister and senior construction lawyer with Hugh James Ford Simey solicitors in Cardiff. UK legal adviser to a major national and international firm of claims consultants. Author and formerly a lecturer.

Fei Ning, BSc, LLM
Partner in Haiwen & Partners, Beijing, China. Engineer.

Dr Bernard Peckels
Expert appointed by the French Supreme Court of Appeal. Author.

Graham Perry, JP, MA, FCIArb
Non-practising solicitor. International arbitrator in the commodity field. Fellow of the Chartered Institute of Arbitrators. Panel member, CIETAC, China.

Dr Heiko Plassmeier
Lawyer at Döser Amereller Noack/Baker & McKenzie, Düsseldorf, Germany. Practises in German and international litigation and arbitration, general civil and commercial law and information technology.

Alan Redfern
Barrister and arbitrator. Previously head of litigation and arbitration at Freshfields, international lawyers in the City of London. Specialises in international commercial arbitration.

Professor Faust Rossi
Samuel S Leibowitz Professor of Trial Techniques at Cornell Law School, USA. Lectures internationally. Prolific author.

Phillippa Rowe, MA, FCII, MAE, QDR
Chartered insurance practitioner. Involved in litigation support. Expert witness and adviser, arbitrator and author.

Keith Salmon
Specialises in computer disputes and corporate fraud. Author. Leading UK expert witness.

***Eur Ing* Patrick Sheen, BSc, CEng, FIEE, FIFireE, FAE**
Electrical engineer, UK. Specialises in forensic engineering concerning industrial accidents on the civil side and in criminal cases deals with murder, manslaughter and arson.

George Staple, CB, QC, FCIArb
Solicitor, partner in Clifford Chance, City of London international lawyers. Former Director of the Serious Fraud Office. Chairman of the Fraud Advisory Panel established by the Institute of Chartered Accountants in England and Wales.

Roger Trett, MInstCES, FLLA, ACIArb, FGS, MAssCostEng, FAE
Chairman and Chief Executive of Trett Consulting, an international firm providing contractual services within the construction and engineering industries. Particular expertise in forensic delay analysis and *quantum*. Deputy Chairman of The Academy of Experts.

Dr Volker Triebel, FCIArb
Partner at Boesebeck Droste, Düsseldorf, Germany and of the Inner Temple, Barrister. Practises in German and international arbitration, commercial and corporate law, mergers and acquisitions.

Andrew Tugwell, FRICS, FCIArb
Chartered surveyor and property litigation solicitor with Nabarro Nathanson, City of London. Fellow of the Royal Institution of Chartered Surveyors and the Chartered Institute of Arbitrators.

Professor Vincenzo Vigoriti, FCIArb
Professor of Law at the University of Florence. Author. Attorney. Italian Bar Association, Italian Association for Civil Procedure, Associazione Italiana Arbitrato, Fellow of the Chartered Institute of Arbitrators, American Arbitration Association, WIPO, Fellow of the American Bar Association, American Law Institute.

Ron Vince
Consulting engineer. Director of Edon Liddiard Vince Limited, Marine Surveyors and Naval Architects. Expert witness on all aspects of ship hulls and machinery litigation and damage to refrigerated cargoes.

Lesley Webber
Solicitor. Partner and Head of Property Litigation and Planning at Beachcroft Wansbroughs, City of London. Specialises in landlord and tenant disputes. Member of the Property Advisory Group to the DETR. Co-author,' PACT Scheme. Lecturer.

Peter Wainwright, MA, FRICS
Chartered surveyor. Formerly President of General Practice Division RICS, Manchester. Chairman and Director of Lambert Smith Hampton (Manchester). Specialises in landlord and tenant matters in arbitration, expert determination and acting as an expert witness. Lecturer.

9 December 1998

BIBLIOGRAPHY

Used by co-ordinating author; other contributors include their own Bibliography

A no-win case for Experts, Dr Christopher Pamplin, *The Lawyer*, 25 November 1997.

A Review of Some Recent Cases involving Expert Evidence, B Mahendra, *NLJ Practitioner*, 28 November 1997.

Can I get a Witness? Tony Bingham, *Building*, 12 December 1997.

Official Referees' Solicitors Association, *Expert Witnesses Protocol—Version 1.0.*

What's right and fair?—A report on Arbitrators/Independent Experts and Commercial Property Rent Review, Nabarro Nathanson, Solicitors, February 1997.

Root don't Toot, Tony Bingham, *Building*, 27 February 1998.

Giving Expert Witness? What the judge might throw out, Jeremy Williams and Peter Garcia, *Chartered Surveyor Monthly*, April 1998.

The Expert Witness and his Evidence, Reynolds & King, BSP Oxford Press.

Administration of Justice, A Shilston (1992) 58, JCI Arb 4–251.

Clarifying the Role of Experts in the Courtroom, His Hon Judge Humphrey LLoyd, QC, *Building*, 13 October 1989.

Construction Disputes—Liability and the Expert Witness, Andrea Burns, Butterworths (1989) p. 241.

The Independent Expert, Michael Ludlow, (1993) 59, JCI Arb 4–231.

Guidance on the Form and Content of Experts' Reports, *Counsel Magazine*, October–December 1993.

The Expert Witness (2nd edition) (*The Doctor's Dilemma*), Jean Graham Hall and Gordon D Smith, Barry Rose (1997).

No Duck, no Dinner, Tony Bingham, *Building*, 27 March 1998.

The Importance of the Expert, Construction Edge, Edge & Ellison bulletin, Issue 3, Spring 1998.

Experts and Privilege, Colin Passmore, *New Law Journal*, 18 September 1998.

The Ikarian Reefer revisited, Hon Mr Justice Cresswell, *The Expert*, Winter/Spring 1998.

Expert Evidence under the new Civil Procedure Rules—It's never too late, District Judge Frenkel, *NLJ Practitioner*, February 1999.

CONTENTS

TABLE OF CASES

All references are to paragraph numbers or Appendix numbers. Where an Appendix contains multiple parts, or retains its own internal numbering system, these have been included to make the reference more precise. They follow the Appendix reference in brackets, e.g. App. C(1.6), App. D (Form 1). (MO) = Model Order. (GN) = Guidance Note.

TABLE OF CASES

ITALY

NEW ZEALAND

PEOPLE'S REPUBLIC OF CHINA

UNITED STATES OF AMERICA

TABLE OF LEGISLATION

All references are to paragraph numbers or Appendix numbers. Where an Appendix contains multiple parts, or retains its own internal numbering system, these have been included to make the reference more precise. They follow the Appendix reference in brackets, e.g. App. C(1.6), App. D (Form 1). (MO) = Model Order. (GN) = Guidance Note.

AUSTRALIA

EGYPT

FRANCE

GERMANY

HONG KONG

INTERNATIONAL

ITALY

NETHERLANDS

PEOPLE'S REPUBLIC OF CHINA

SINGAPORE

SWEDEN

THAILAND

UNITED KINGDOM

INTRODUCTION

- Are you an expert? If so, at what?
- Can a party paid expert really be independent and free of partisanship?
- To whom does an expert owe a duty? Can you subpoena an expert?
- What about privilege, professional liability and fraud when it comes to expert evidence?
- What is the expert's position concerning legal aid and would the whole process be improved if there was one expert—tribunal appointed—instead of two or three (one for each party and one possibly to advise the tribunal)?

These are typical of the questions which are dealt with by the "Introductory Articles", reproduced in chapters 1 and 9 of this book. All have been written by leading exponents in their field; most have appeared in learned journals; and all have been reviewed by the original authors and, in almost all instances, updated for the purpose of this book.

When I first conceived the idea of a book on the expert, it was with a view to exploring ways of making the introduction of expert evidence in arbitration and litigation more cost-effective. It was whilst researching what had been written about the subject that I came across most of these Introductory Articles and decided that they were too good to be buried and forgotten in the inevitable pile of such similar articles which we all accumulate over the years—hence their reproduction in this book.

From bitter experience, in my own discipline of construction, I am only too aware that the costs of experts' reports and subsequent giving of expert evidence can form a significant part of a party's total costs. It follows that any procedure which effectively reduces the length of time that experts are being cross-examined—i.e. the most costly part of any case—must be worth exploring.

In order to derive the maximum benefit at the least cost from experts, they need to be clearly and effectively instructed. Get the instructions right and you are well on the way to getting the best out of your expert. Give your expert poor, or too broadly-based, instructions, and you might as well say "Here is a spade, go home, dig a hole in your garden and pour my client's money into it".

It is a short step from these initial concerns to deciding to explore how experts are used in other disciplines and to see if we could improve our own use of experts by adopting procedures followed in these other disciplines. This led to chapters 2–7 in Part I and, when I decided to cover expert determination as well, to chapters 10–14 in Part II.

It was clearly sensible to embrace litigation as well as arbitration and thus consider how experts are currently used in court—again, to see what lessons could be learned. When I first drafted this Introduction, the word "currently" applied to the situation of experts in court as it then was. Shortly after this, the new Civil Procedure Rules were published which completely revised the courts' approach to the use of experts. As a result, publication of this book was deferred and all the UK contributors were sent Parts 27, 32 and 35 of these new Rules and asked to amend their article or chapter where appropriate.

Having decided to include a new short section on the Civil Procedure Rules (Chapter 1/1) and how these rules are likely to affect the role of the expert in court, to avoid undue repetition the contributors have limited their own comments on these rules to those specific changes which may have to be made to their own procedures in relation to their specific discipline and the subject matter on which they are writing.

These Rules have sprung from the Woolf Report, *Access to Justice*—chapter 13 of which is reproduced in full as Appendix A/1 to this book by kind permission of the Lord Chancellor's Department.

Looking at the contents of this book in more detail, Part I commences with a series of seminal articles concerning the expert (Chapters 1/1 to 1/22) which have appeared from time to time in various learned journals. All of the authors were given the opportunity of updating these articles, or amending them, for inclusion in this book, including, as noted above, any additional necessary commentary on the new Civil Procedure Rules.

Although the titles of the contributions from various experts from different disciplines, and various parts of the world, broadly speak for themselves, it is not always obvious from the title of the article exactly what aspect of expertise the author is covering. For this reason, I give below a very brief outline of their contents.

THE NEW CIVIL PROCEDURE RULES AND THE EXPERT WITNESS—
JUDGE JOHN FRENKEL (CHAPTER 1/1)

As consulting editor for the *Practical Civil Court Precedents*, Judge Frenkel is particularly well placed to comment and speculate on the application of these new Rules to civil proceedings, which take effect after 26 April 1999.

He summarises very succinctly the effect of the application of these new Rules to the expert and to expert evidence given in the civil proceedings.

ARE YOU AN EXPERT?—DR ALBERT W KNOTT, PE (CHAPTER 1/2)

Dr Knott is a forensic engineer and in this article he recommends the development of a personal philosophy for anyone giving expert evidence in this extremely important field. He then sets out and discourses on 27 different lessons which he recommends a forensic expert to learn and observe.

INDEPENDENCE, PARTISANSHIP AND THE CONTENT OF EXPERT EVIDENCE—
ANDREW BARTLETT, QC (CHAPTER 1/3)

Here the author deals with the quality of expert witnesses under the headings included in the title and in doing so covers the difficult problem of the tension which arises over the expert's various roles and how an expert should deal with a change of mind.

INDEPENDENCE, AND USE, OF EXPERT WITNESSES—NABARRO NATHANSON
(CHAPTER 1/4)

This article first appeared in a report entitled "What's right and fair?" which dealt with surveyors acting as experts in Commercial Property Rent Review.

The reader may be misled, from the title, into thinking this covers some of the same ground as the previous article, whereas it explores specifically the difficulty experienced by a surveyor acting as an expert witness whilst at the same time representing his client. It goes on to set out guidelines as drawn up by the Royal Institution of Chartered Surveyors in such cases, which are lifted from *The Ikarian Reefer*.

These guidelines appear more than once in various parts of this book, for which I make no apology; apart from not being able to edit them out of individual contributions without perhaps losing the sense of what is being said, these guidelines strike at the epicentre of what giving expert evidence is all about and this cannot be repeated too often in a book dedicated to the subject. (See, in particular, the following article by The Honourable Mr Justice Cresswell.)

THE IKARIAN REEFER REVISITED—THE HONOURABLE MR JUSTICE CRESSWELL (CHAPTER 1/5)

> "Since the decision in the leading case, the need for clear guidance for expert witnesses has been increasingly recognised, and is now reflected in the new Civil Procedure Rules under the Woolf reforms. This article summarises the guidance which will apply to expert evidence, including expert reports and meetings of experts, in relation to Commercial Court Practice."

Logically, Mr Justice Cresswell shows how *The Ikarian Reefer* guidelines relate to the all-important Appendix 12 of *The Guide to Commercial Court Practice*, 5th edition (reproduced as Appendix L to this book).

TO WHOM DOES THE EXPERT OWE A DUTY?—MICHAEL CHAPMAN (CHAPTER 1/6)

Michael Chapman deals with the seemingly conflicting interest of the expert's duty to assist the tribunal and his duty to the client, who is paying his fees. The author cites a number of sources, including some reported cases, in support of his view that there has been much comment but little debate, barring repetition of entrenched opinions, on the subject.

Dr Chapman finally reviews the early draft of his article against the background of the new Civil Procedure Rules and concludes that these Rules "heighten the conflict between those who search for the truth and those who must 'pick a winner' ". In support of his conclusion the author takes the reader through various aspects of these new Rules.

SUBPOENA OF AN EXPERT WITNESS—JOHN BOLTON (CHAPTER 1/7)

The author deals with the topic of subpoenaing an expert witness and how the experience of being subpoenaed is not half so unpleasant as the anticipation of the event. He then explores the motive behind a subpoena and the unwilling witness. He concludes with a useful appendix on "The Defective Subpoena".

HOW PRIVILEGED IN IS AN EXPERT?—GARY HICKINBOTTOM, MA (CHAPTER 1/8)

Having started with the general articles about the expert and his approach to the task, we then have the first of the narrower, but important, articles devoted to various aspects of expert evidence. This one deals with privilege and not only covers the historical case law on the subject, but also includes two 1997 cases where the judge came to opposing conclusions concerning privilege and the expert.

In the *Clough* case it was held that reference to an undisclosed privileged document in a disclosed expert's report waived the privilege in the other document.

In the *Vista Maritime* case the judge expressly rejected a submission that the inclusion in a statement, or report, of references to privilege matters is an irreversible step which necessarily involves a waiver of privilege in all connected material.

Obviously this contradiction is something that hopefully the Court of Appeal will hopefully sort out at the earliest opportunity.

PROFESSIONAL RESPONSIBILITIES AND LIABILITY OF EXPERTS AND EXPERT WITNESSES—PAUL NEWMAN (CHAPTER 1/9)

Apart from some general comments concerning the expert, his skills and his report, this article deals with the duty of care to be expected of an expert, his liability if he makes a negligent mis-statement, and the remedies for such negligent mis-statement, including limitation problems.

THE EXPERT AND THE INVESTIGATION AND PROSECUTION OF SERIOUS FRAUD—GEORGE STAPLE, QC (CHAPTER 1/10)

The title of this article, by a former Director of the Serious Fraud Office (SFO), speaks for itself. Apart from dealing with the special features of serious fraud and how the expert should approach the task of giving evidence in such cases, the author also deals briefly with the function of the SFO as prosecuting authority and concludes with a consideration of the international dimension and extradition.

LEGAL AID—THE EXPERT'S POSITION—SIMON MORGAN (CHAPTER 1/11)

This article explores the controversial topic of legal aid in both criminal and civil cases with particular emphasis on the expert's position *vis-à-vis* his fees. The article is an update of a paper delivered in 1994 to The Academy of Experts and includes verbatim questions and answers which followed it. Specifically, the author deals with how the new Civil Procedure Rules impact on legal aid.

THE "SINGLE JOINT" EXPERT WITNESS—RICHARD FREEMAN (CHAPTER 1/12A)

The topic addressed by the author of this article is particularly apposite at the time of publication being the immediate aftermath of the introduction of the new Civil Procedure Rules.

The general feeling seems to be that the court's power to appoint a single expert is not a favoured option and the parties will appoint their own "technical adviser" willy-nilly. Thus, the objective of cost saving is likely not to be achieved—only time will tell how this laudable objective will work out in practice.

A SINGLE ACCOUNTANCY EXPERT IN MATRIMONIAL PROCEEDINGS—RICHARD FREEMAN (CHAPTER 1/12B)

Again, as with the previous article by this author, the vexed question of appointing a single expert is addressed. However this time, as the article suggests, it concerns the single accountant in matrimonial proceedings.

The article was originally written prior to the implementation of the new Civil Procedure Rules, and suggests that "lawyers should voluntarily and regularly make neutral appointments now and not wait for the proposed rules of civil justice to be enacted". Well, they have been enacted and whether or not lawyers heed Mr Freeman's advice remains to be seen. In any event the author is quite clear that such a single expert should never be forced on the parties although judges certainly have been given this power by the new Rules. The author is in no doubt that an independent accountant would undoubtedly remove much unproductive confrontation and attrition and be employed to advantage in matrimonial cases.

A NEUTRAL EXPERT FOR CRIMINAL CASES?—RICHARD FREEMAN (CHAPTER 1/12C)

In his third article, the author suggests that complex legal issues in criminal cases are best put to juries by a neutral, rather than party-appointed, expert.

Compare this with the extract from the Woolf Report at Appendix A/1, where this report argues for the wider, but not uniform, use of a "single" or neutral expert in both criminal and civil actions

Interestingly, Woolf suggests that "Given the strength of opposition to my proposals, it would not be realistic to expect a significant shift towards a single expert in the short term".

My own experience as an arbitrator confirms this view. Whenever I have suggested the use of a tribunal-appointed expert to deal with such complex issues as computer-generated programming to demonstrate the actual effect of delay on the building project, in every instance the suggestion has been rejected on the grounds of expense, as each party has felt the need to appoint their own expert, in any event, to deal with the report of the neutral expert.

See also Appendix K/3 for a typical agenda item in an arbitration providing for the appointment of a neutral expert.

THE PRACTICAL ROLE OF AN EXPERT IN COMPUTER DISPUTES—KEITH SALMON (CHAPTER 1/13)

Although much of what the author of this article says is, as expected, common ground with the duties and obligations of experts in other disciplines, the value lies in the specific advice given to experts giving evidence in computer disputes. With the growth of IT and system made software such disputes will, undoubtedly, become more prevalent. Even as we go to publication, the UK government is experiencing severe problems with its computer hardware/software involving the issuing of passports, social security cheques and student grants, all of which could end up either in litigation or arbitration.

SOME PRACTICAL POINTS FOR EXPERT WITNESSES—TIM COOPER (CHAPTER 1/14)

The concluding general article in Chapter 1 gives some very useful guidance, from a very experienced rent review arbitrator, to the inexperienced expert witness. Of course, it begs the question as to whether someone really inexperienced in giving evidence is a suitable choice to act as an expert but on the premise that there is always a first time, even for expert witnesses, anyone who may be cautious about accepting an instruction to act will find these guidance notes provide a degree of comfort, as well as covering some of the fundamentals associated with the role.

EXPERTS IN FOREIGN JURISDICTIONS (CHAPTERS 1/15 TO 1/21)

The succeeding six articles are all written by leading academics, or practitioners, in Germany, France, Italy, the USA, Australia and mainland China and Hong Kong.

I started on the exercise of comparing and contrasting the approach in each of these jurisdictions but abandoned the attempt as being a fruitless task—the reader would be far better served to read what each of these distinguished authors have written from their own wide experience and research.

THE ROLE OF THE ACADEMY OF EXPERTS—MICHAEL COHEN (CHAPTER 1/22)

Chapter 1 concludes with a short article by the chairman emeritus of the leading body of experts—Michael Cohen. Mr Cohen tracks the Academy's pursuit of excellence and shows how far the Academy has come in 10 years in raising the standard of experts, both in litigation and arbitration.

EXPERTS IN VARIOUS DISCIPLINES IN THE UK (CHAPTERS 2 TO 7)

The next six chapters are all written by acknowledged leading experts in the following disciplines:

- Medical negligence
- Crime
- Construction disputes
- Insurance and Reinsurance
- Maritime disputes
- Rent Review disputes.

The brief given to the authors of the various chapters on these different disciplines was for them to base their contribution on their most interesting cases and, if they were arbitrations, then sanitise them to a point beyond recognition—and broadly cover the following:

1. General background to the work of the expert in their particular discipline, including headline cases with full quotes from the judgments on those parts where the judge may have commented on the quality etc. of expert evidence.
2. The background facts to a typical case.
3. How you came to be appointed.
4. How you were instructed and, if appropriate and available, a model form of those instructions and/or alternatively how you believe you *should* have been instructed.
5. How you tackled the task.
6. A report or an appropriate extract from a report prepared (to act as a model to other practitioners).

It will be seen that this brief was interpreted differently from one contributor to another but whether or not the brief has been followed to the letter does not detract from the authoritative nature of the sound practices reflected in these chapters.

As with the experts in foreign jurisdictions, my initial intention was to try to draw some common thread from each of these separate disciplines that could possibly be applied universally; however, that simply did not work. Inevitably, I was biased towards practices associated with construction disputes which, frankly, are not necessarily readily adaptable to cases involving other disciplines. So I strongly recommend reading all six chapters, whether or not they cover the same discipline as that in which you, the reader, is engaged and then drawing what lessons you can from the practices of other professionals and applying them to your own practice where appropriate.

CHAPTER 8

All of the following issues, including an introductory piece on the "Expert Generally", are addressed by me in the 70-plus "problems" dealt with in Chapter 8 "Interlocutory and Trial/Hearing Problems" (trial, of course, in litigation and hearing in arbitration):

- Is a doctor any different from any other expert?
- One party appointed an expert and the other party failed to do so.
- Expert omits to deal with material facts.
- When an expert's report consists mainly of hearsay, advocacy and submissions, can it be struck out in its entirety?
- Independent expert or arbitrator?

The introductory piece sets out to deal with the duties, obligation and liability of an expert generally, setting the scene for the problems which follow. I have specifically avoided attempting to amend either this introductory piece or the suggested "Course of Action" in the "problems" speculating on the application of the new Civil Procedure Rules but instead added a short section covering these Rules at paras 8–053 *et seq*. The time to make such amendments, is, I suggest, when these rules have been in operation for a year or two and we see how they work in practice.

This substantial section on problems likely to be encountered by the expert is a little more, I admit, than the "thread" referred to in the quote from Montaigne on the dedication page of this book.

As a construction arbitrator a substantial element of these "problems" arose out of my own experience. However, where possible and practical, I have adapted the facts of the case to cover general application—both litigation and arbitration—as many of the situations are common to both jurisdictions.

The approach of taking some facts, deriving a question and then proposing a "Course of Action" is a style I have previously used, particularly in my book *Arbitration Practice and Procedure—Interlocutory and Hearing Problems* (now in a greatly enlarged second edition) from whence a number of the examples in this book were derived.

In the Preface of the First Edition of that book I said of the "Course of Action":

> "Faced with a new situation to which the solution is not immediately obvious the sensible arbitrator will take time to consider his preferred 'Course of Action' and, of course, there may well be a number of ostensibly satisfactory solutions. In this book we have either used situations drawn from reported and unreported cases, or hypothesised facts in order to illustrate a particular point in a 'Course of Action'. For 'Course of Action' read 'just one reasonable and sound solution to the problem posed by the question'.
>
> ... The facts of individual cases are rarely identical and even where they are very similar, different considerations may apply. The authors entirely accept this reservation however and we trust the good sense of practitioners using this book to realise its limitations.
>
> If they do that and remember that the 'Course of Action' is by no means gospel but merely one possible solution, they should find this book an extremely useful tool.
>
> This conveniently leads me to the question of authorities. The solution suggested to the problems posed in this book could be likened to a party citing authority to a tribunal in support of their contentions except that the 'Courses of Action' given here are *not* authority. As a judge or arbitrator would weigh the authorities given to him, against the facts of the case he was hearing, so readers of this book should view the 'Course of Action' proposed here, against their own particular problem."

It will become immediately obvious to the reader that where the "Course of Action" relates to a procedure to be followed by the tribunal, it is not intended to suggest that judges would adopt a similar "Course of Action". Indeed, as all arbitrators are individuals, and will have their own ideas about how best to proceed, so no two judges will proceed on precisely the same lines. All of which serves to illustrate that although the "Course of Action" proposed illustrates one sound and sensible way of resolving the particular problem, it is precisely that, just one way—possibly of many.

The other feature of these "problems" which may well cause the reader puzzlement at first encounter, is when they suddenly come across Thomasina. This is best explained by the following extract from the Second Edition of *Arbitration Practice and Procedure* where this phenomenon was explained thus:

"Another ploy I have used is to introduce Thomasina (from my other book, *The Sanctuary House Case*). Thomasina, it will be recalled for those of you who have read the other book, was the arbitrator's pupil. She is a dear girl who is very keen to learn and frequently tries the patience of my '*alter ego*', the kindly arbitrator in *The Sanctuary House Case*—Mr D Emsee. By listening to what he has to say on a possible course of action and then asking 'but what if...', Thomasina stands in the shoes of all of us who would like to ask 'what if', but perhaps feel that, either we should know the answer and therefore should not be asking, or we are reticent about putting that question to the person to whom we are talking.

To confuse matters further, Thomasina has a boyfriend called Charley, who is what is known in the trade as a 'rent boy' or, more correctly, the pupil of a rent review arbitrator. Charley occasionally adds his comments to solutions to problems from a rent review arbitrator's perspective. Having said that, let me assure the more serious reader who finds these characters intrusive and distracting that there is very little input into this book by either of these pupils; they have merely been used, *very occasionally*, as a transparent didactic device for exploring situations from different angles. My own reason for even mentioning this is to avoid the reader suffering the same fate as a colleague of mine who, coming across Thomasina for the first time, in one of my examples, asked who on earth she was?"

From the reviews received for both books it is clear that there are those readers who find Thomasina and Charley a "reader-friendly" device and others who consider that even this very occasional "transparent didactic device for exploring situations from different angles" detracts "from the serious quality of a major work". For those readers then who share this criticism, my apologies. The references to these two "characters" are, as I say, scant and really should not detract from this book which, indeed, like my other three books, is meant to be a serious work.

Hopefully, one way or the other, I have covered most of the pitfalls faced by experts and dealt with many of the situations that they could find themselves in, either in court or before an arbitrator.

I know, however, from my own experience, that no matter how long I practise as an arbitrator, entirely new problems arise almost daily in my work. They may well be similar to previous problems but they often present some new point which I have simply never encountered before and is certainly not covered by any text book that I have come across.

For this reason I invite you, dear reader, to send me details of any situation you have faced which is not covered by the examples in this book. Of course, any such problems used will be acknowledged in any future editions of my books and you will have contributed to the nexus of knowledge for future generations of experts.

I reiterate what I said above. What I have specifically not attempted to do is to speculate, in any suggested "Course of Action", where this is likely to change as a result of the publication of the new Civil Procedure Rules and Guidelines.

The reason for this is two-fold.

(a) it would be pure speculation and thus of limited value to the reader; and
(b) the new Rules and their application have been addressed fully by other contributors in both articles and chapters. In subsequent editions of this book (should there be any!) I may well expand on a "Course of Action" where appropriate, to reflect these new Rules, which by that time will be at least partially tried and tested.

Before I delve into the Appendices I should mention the obvious for anyone who has studied the contents pages of this book, and that is that the whole process for the expert witness is repeated in Part II—Expert Determination—but, inevitably, in considerably decreased volume, as expert determination is not practised in as wide a field as that which uses expert witnesses.

Rent review disputes are by far the largest application of expert determination, followed by construction, accountancy, energy and, increasingly, disputes concerning computers.

The fundamental difference between expert determination and arbitration is that for the former there is no statutory system of court review of the experts' decisions. The expert's determination is usually final and binding on the parties and can only be challenged (before determination) on jurisdictional grounds or, less commonly, on grounds of fraud, collusion or mistake.

Inevitably there is overlap between the Introductory Articles in this book and the chapters which follow, as each has been written by leading exponents in their own field who are going to be only too aware of the milestone cases where judges have devoted time and thought to the role and duty of experts. The guidelines for the expert witness from *The Ikarian Reefer* are inevitably repeated a number of times, not only in the text but also in the judgments cited. Similarly, *Jones* v. *Sherwood* inevitably appears on a number of occasions when expert determination is under consideration.

I make no apology for such repetition, or indeed for perhaps occasionally straying onto the same ground once more in my own chapter 8 and chapter 14. Such repetition serves only to reinforce the importance of the cases cited and the lessons to be learned from the judgments which follow.

So much for the substantive element of the book. What of the Appendices, mentioned earlier in this Introduction? Each is worthy of some short comment.

APPENDIX A/1—EXTRACT FROM "ACCESS TO JUSTICE"—THE WOOLF REPORT

The opening paragraph of this report sums up the entire *raison d'être* for this book.

> "It was a basic contention of my interim report that two of the major generators of unnecessary cost in civil litigation were uncontrolled discovery and expert evidence. No one has seriously challenged that contention."

Long before Lord Woolf's Report there was judicial concern about the use of expert witnesses, as is evidenced by Richard Southwell, QC's comment in his judgment in *Burroughs Day* v. *Bristol City Council* [1996] 1 EGLR 167, where he said:

> "Some of the expert witnesses apparently thought that it was an essential part of their function as experts to act as supplementary advocates for their clients."

Commenting on Lord Woolf's Interim Report, in the summer of 1996, Dibb Lupton Broomhead's *Property Newsletter* said this:

> "In preparing his Report, Lord Woolf took account of a 1995 Official Referee's court decision to appoint a court expert. That case has now been heard in the Court of Appeal. The judgment delivered by Sir Thomas Bingham, Master of the Rolls, gives some indication as to whether court appointed experts are likely to receive judicial backing.
>
> *Abbey National Mortgages Plc* v. *Key Surveyors Nationwide Ltd and Others* (1996) EGCS 23.
>
> *Facts:* The plaintiffs alleged negligent valuations of 29 properties in various parts of the country. The defendants sought leave to appoint 29 experts (one for each property) on a basis that local experience would be necessary. The Official Referee made orders that a court valuation expert be appointed (under RSC Order 40) and that expert valuation evidence be limited to one witness for each side.

The defendants appealed, arguing *(inter alia)*, that a court-appointed expert would *not* be an 'expert' as he would necessarily lack personal knowledge of the values in many of the areas upon which he had to report.

Held: The Official Referee had jurisdiction to make these 'bold and innovatory' orders. 'The Judge plainly made them with his eyes open, conscious that he was breaking new ground' said the Master of the Rolls and: 'There can be no purpose in commissioning expensive and far reaching reports on civil procedures if lessons which emerge are not heeded. Exhortations to trial judges to be interventionist and managerial would be futile if every managerial initiative by a trial judge were to be condemned as an unwarranted departure from orthodoxy.'

Sir Thomas Bingham went on to consider whether the court expert was entitled to consider hearsay evidence. In practice, a valuer is 'fully entitled to rely on what reasonably appears to him to be reliable information'. 'We do not accept that any valuation expert is confined to giving evidence based on comparables of which he has direct first-hand knowledge.'

Finally, on the independence of an expert witness compared with that of a court-appointed expert, the Master of the Rolls said that expert witnesses often tend to espouse the cause of those instructing them 'on occasion becoming more partisan than the parties'. 'There must be at least a reasonable chance that an expert appointed by the court, with no axe to grind but a clear obligation to make a careful and objective valuation, may prove a reliable source of expert opinion.'

In the light of these comments, opponents of court-appointed experts may have cause for concern."

In April 1996 in *Construction & Engineering Law*, Richard Fernyhough, QC—Head of Keating Chambers in Essex Street, London—responded to Lord Woolf's Interim Report *Access to Justice* by highlighting problems relevant to the context of the report. In particular he addressed six areas of interest to those who engage or are dependent upon the performance of experts and rely on their advice and evidence.

"Question of Independence

The main problem as I see it is that of the independence, or lack of it, of experts. It has been noticeable over the last 15 years how experts have become more and more partisan.

The trouble is that many experts now make their living out of giving expert evidence and they fear that, if they express views contrary to their client's interest, they may not be instructed again. This may very well be true, but if so, it is a sad reflection on our system. Generally, one finds that experts who are still fully occupied in private practice are more independent than those who are full time experts.

Another major problem is that many experts tend to 'over-investigate' the case. They often expend huge amounts of time and therefore money in investigating every fact of the case. Much of this work is of no value whatsoever yet it considerably increases the costs. If the court kept control of expert evidence and selected the issues upon which it wished to hear such evidence, this mischief could be controlled. Alternatively, the court should be ready to apply costs sanctions if it appears that experts have been guilty of 'over-investigation'.

Court-appointed or neutral experts

The concept of the court-appointed expert is not popular. I understand that the French experience, for example, has not been happy and often the court-appointed expert, because the pay is so bad, is of low quality.

Where there is a legitimate difference of opinion between opposing experts it is difficult to see how a court-appointed expert could help. In most cases he would be likely to come down in favour of one of the parties' experts or the other.

If so, the judge would almost invariably accept his viewpoint. This would hardly be fair to the losing party who would have had the outcome of the case taken out of his hands. But a court-appointed expert might be appropriate where, for example, the sum in dispute was small or neither party had yet appointed an expert.

Similarly a direction to the parties to jointly instruct an expert might very well be helpful provided it was given early in the proceedings.

The best compromise to this problem which I can suggest is as follows: in all ordinary cases the parties should be required, as soon as the matter comes to court, jointly to instruct one expert to give his opinion on the technical issues in the case. If he were jointly instructed the expert would be far more likely to remain truly independent. The jointly instructed expert would then report to the parties and to the court. After consideration of his report and after hearing the parties, the court would then decide whether or not to permit the parties to call their own experts. If the court allowed them to do so then their own experts would give evidence in the ordinary way and the jointly-appointed expert would drop out of sight. But if, on the other hand, the court declined to permit this, then the report of the jointly-instructed expert would be the only expert evidence in the case.

This approach, it is thought, would encourage settlement since both parties would see the view of a truly independent, competent expert at the outset and might well accept it. If not, they would have to persuade the judge that the case was appropriate for a fully developed battle between experts. The court might not incline to this view. Similarly, this system should save costs or, at least, potentially might do so in many cases.

Experts' meetings

I am quite clear that no one but the experts themselves should be present at without prejudice experts' meetings. I am also quite clear that, with a suitably worded direction from the judge, it would be professionally improper for a solicitor to instruct his expert not to agree anything at such a meeting.

The standard direction ought to direct the experts to attempt to agree facts and issues at the meeting and, at the end of the meeting, to draw up a document to be signed by all experts recording the agreements and disagreements (together with the reasons for them) reached at the conclusion of the meeting. The expert must feel free, in accordance with his professional conscience, to agree whatever he feels proper at the meeting. Of course, it should be made clear that any such agreement is not binding on the client who may reject it or ratify it as he wishes. However, any such agreement *is* binding on the expert who should be held to it by his colleagues and the court.

It is usually most helpful for experts to meet both before reports are exchanged and after their exchange. It is not usually a good idea for them first to meet after the exchange of reports since by then the experts will have pinned their colours to their respective masts and may be reluctant to change their views.

Sometimes it is helpful to order the sequential exchange of experts' reports in cases where, for example, one party has a monopoly of knowledge of the facts of the particular case. The classic case is in respect of *quantum* experts.

Usually only the plaintiff knows the details of the sums which he is claiming and how they are calculated. In such cases it is sensible for the plaintiff's expert to produce his report first, then to meet the other parties' experts to explain his report and answer their questions and then for the other parties to serve their reports.

If the court does permit the parties to call their own experts, then I would suggest that those experts should attend before the judge who should instruct them as to the issues which he would find most helpful for them to deal with and, at the same time, the judge should encourage them to keep their reports short and to reach as much agreement as possible.

I am all in favour of the court taking a positive line with experts from an early stage so that the experts feel brought in to the judicial process which should help to reinforce their feeling of independence.

Impartiality of experts

I am not in favour of the waiver of legal professional privilege in relation to experts. I am sure than [*sic*] any such rule would frequently be circumvented in practice and I think it is an unnecessary intrusion into the privacy of the parties.

On the other hand, I do think that experts should be encouraged by the court to be independent. Such encouragement should include a statement within the body of every report in which the expert declares whether he has any and, if so, what, interest in the proceedings. Equally, if the report is addressed to the court and deals with the technical issues which the court has identified, then the expert is more likely to retain his impartiality.

The quality of experts' reports

Broadly speaking in the Official Referee's Courts, I do not think that this is a general problem. Usually the experts' reports are of a high quality even if, sometimes, they are far too long.

Some bodies provide considerable amounts of training for experts which has served to improve the quality over recent years. But I am not in favour of a compulsory system of training and accreditation for experts. This would serve to turn experts into a separate and recognisable profession of its own which I consider would be a retrograde step.

The best experts are usually those who are in full-time practice in their own fields and who only give evidence in court occasionally. Such persons are up to date with developments in their field and retain their impartiality because their expert work only forms a small part of their earnings. It would be a great pity to lose some people from the system by requiring compulsory education and accreditation.

Equally I am not in favour of a standard format for the instruction of experts. In complex cases I do not think this would be practicable and it would unduly hamper the expert's discretion as to the way he approached the investigation and prepared his report. On the other hand I *am* in favour of the court taking close control over the issues upon which the expert should be entitled to give evidence.

Expert's attendance at trial

I quite agree that the present system whereby some experts sit for day after day at the back of the court listening to the evidence is a terrible waste of time and cost. Ordinarily the Taxing Master should, in my view, disallow the costs of an expert who attends court to sit through the evidence. Nowadays with the exchange of detailed statements of the witnesses, it is quite unnecessary for the expert to hear their evidence: he can simply read their statements. There may be cases, however, where it is desirable for the expert to hear the cross-examination of a key factual witness.

On the other hand, when it comes to giving evidence, I consider that experts must attend to give evidence orally and should obviously also attend to hear their counterpart giving evidence. I think this is inevitable. I am not sure that using video conferencing or other methods of recording evidence would in fact be practicable or save very much money.

But since the judge is going to lay down a firm timetable for the trial and will, within that timetable, control the length of cross-examination of all witnesses including experts, then the problem of an expert being in the witness box for day after day should be brought under control.

Last word

I do not think it is sensible to make reforms in the area of Expert Evidence without as [*sic*] the same time considering the related topics of Assessors and Referees for Enquiry and Report (for Special Referees). The court should, ideally, have the full range of expert assistance available when it consists [*sic*] how best the technical issues in a case should be investigated.

Footnote March 1999[—Positively the Last Word]

Now that the Civil Procedure Rules have been published it is clear that they proceed very much along the lines foreseen in 1996. The key question now will be how the rules are used by the court. A lot of discretion in case management is given to the judge who will need to have extensive experience of the type of litigation which he is 'managing'. A 'hands on the wheel' approach is fine so long as the driver is experienced and sensible."

Although I had described Richard Fernyhough's Footnote as positively the last word, of course, in a sense it is a prologue rather than an epilogue. Just how these rules work out in practice remains to be seen, but it is clear that much of what Richard Fernyhough said about the Interim Report *Access to Justice* is still pertinent to these new Civil Procedure Rules.

Despite these comments being made about the Interim Report much of what Mr Fernyhough said is equally applicable to the final published report.

The "over-investigation" point has echoes of my "hole in the garden" illustration, mentioned earlier.

Despite the strong opposition to the "court-appointed expert" Lord Woolf has retained that as a viable alternative which should not be overlooked.

Lord Woolf has stuck to his guns, in that, in the majority of cases he sees no reason why the experts should not meet alone, although he accepts that there are circumstances in which this will not be appropriate. He does not specifically mention "without prejudice" meetings in this regard, but it may well be that in this respect Mr Fernyhough and Lord Woolf agree.

On the impartiality of experts, I like the idea that all experts' reports will, in future, be addressed to the court. I see no reason why the same practice should not be adopted by arbitrators.

On waiver of legal privilege, with which Mr Fernyhough was not in favour, Lord Woolf seems to have softened his approach by suggesting that the draft reports should not be disclosable, but he sees no reason why privilege should apply to the experts' instructions. At least this might avoid experts being given conflicting instructions in the future.

I agree with the Woolf Report, as indeed does Mr Fernyhough, in that the tribunal should control the issues over which the expert is entitled to give evidence. I believe that arbitrators have this power by virtue of s. 34(2)(h) of the Arbitration Act 1996.

THE STATUS OF THE RSC AND THE BODY OF COMMON LAW

It has been said that with the advent of CPR out goes the White Book (and the Green Book) and the body of precedent built up in the common law. Whilst this might be an admirable objective—a clean slate, so to speak—the CPR are far from comprehensive and, where they are deficient, lawyers and judges, I believe, will inevitably turn to the old RSC for guidance.

Similarly, there is far too large a body of authority, for example concerning the courts' interpretation of the rights, duties and obligations of the expert both in litigation and arbitration, not to refer to it from time to time, even if such reference can only be considered to be persuasive rather than binding.

For this reason, references throughout this book to the RSC should be considered against any equivalent in the CPR; if there is none then the old rules may well give guidance. Similarly, for the reasons stated above, I consider that the judgments cited herein are still of seminal importance.

APPENDIX B—OFFICIAL REFEREES' SOLICITORS ASSOCIATION EXPERT WITNESS PROTOCOL—VERSION 1.0

The ORSA protocol arose out of ORSA's response to the Issue Paper on Expert Evidence from the *Access to Justice* team in the hope that it would encourage independence and impartiality of the expert. What changes will occur to this protocol is a matter of speculation, but see the comment on the following page entitled The Technology and Construction Solicitors' Association (TeCSA) Expert Witness Protocol.

In the ORSA protocol it is suggested that the instructing solicitor ensures that the documentation and information made available to the expert is carefully chosen. The "Brief" will normally include:

- Area in which the expert is called upon to give his opinion.
- Specific issues on which the expert is asked to advise.

If these guidelines are observed in every appointment involving an expert, it should go some way to avoid the "over-investigation" justifiably complained of by Richard Fernyhough and also meet my own criticism concerning poor or inadequate instructions.

A secondary point of importance is the recommendation that "the solicitor and the expert should keep the brief under review at all times". It may well be wise in a complex case to set out formal review meetings rather than leaving it to the solicitor or the expert to raise the matter.

The expert should be advised of any hearing or trial date "on which he is likely to be required to attend . . .". I do so agree with Richard Fernyhough when he says that experts sitting "day after day at the back of the court listening to evidence is a terrible waste of time and cost. Ordinarily the Taxing Master should, in my view, disallow the costs of an expert who attends court to sit through the evidence." (As, indeed, I would myself when determining the winning party's recoverable costs.)

ORSA echoes Richard Fernyhough's view that lawyers and clients should not be present at "without prejudice" meetings of experts. However, not all meetings of experts need to be "without prejudice". I have in mind meetings of *quantum* experts and here, particularly in arbitration, it can be fruitful for the arbitrator to sit in on these meetings with the *quantum* experts in an attempt to assist them to reach an agreement on *quantum* for what may be hundreds of individual items, subject, of course, to liability where appropriate, being determined after he has heard and considered the oral evidence.

Note paragraph 28 of this protocol, which, *inter alia*, states:

> "It is not the role of the expert to make a finding of fact which is in issue. Where an opinion depends upon facts which are in issue, this should be clearly stated."

I certainly agree with the guideline in paragraph 32, a budget for the experts' costs and ensuring that the fees charged are proportionate to the value or importance of the matters in issue. "Proportionate" clearly implies to me a percentage of the amount in dispute.

Consider this in relation to an arbitrator's duty under s.33 of the Arbitration Act 1996 to "avoid unnecessary expense" and his powers under s.63 (subject to no agreement otherwise by the parties) to determine, as he sees fit, what costs are recoverable by the winning party. Also, possibly, any agreement by the parties or directions given by the arbitrator under s.65 where the arbitrator may well have directed that the recoverable costs of the arbitration, *or any part of the arbitral proceedings* (i.e. the expert evidence) be limited to a specified amount.

Finally, I was interested to read what ORSA said in paragraph 36 concerning cancellation and commitment fees for expert witnesses. I agree that these should only apply if they have been agreed in advance, and where the expert can establish that he has no other appropriate work to undertake. However, under these circumstances, and bearing in mind the strictures in paragraph 13 to the effect that the "expert shall not take on any new commitment which might interfere with his responsibilities under the appointment" which might well mean that after consultation with his instructing solicitor, the expert has turned down other remunerative work, I question why it would be unreasonable to provide remuneration for the whole of the period cancelled.

THE TECHNOLOGY AND CONSTRUCTION SOLICITORS' ASSOCIATION (TECSA) EXPERT WITNESS PROTOCOL—COMMENTARY BY MARCUS HARLING, BURGES SALMON, BRISTOL

The Technology and Construction Solicitors' Association (formerly known as the Official Referees' Solicitors Association—ORSA) published its Expert Witness Protocol in 1996.

The TeCSA Expert Witness Protocol grew out of the Association's response to the Issue Paper on Expert Evidence from the *Access to Justice* team. The Expert Witness Protocol was developed out of a need to find a way to encourage the legal profession and experts to address key issues early to avoid problems later, or as the Protocol says "... assisting clarity of communication ... to provide a framework within which experts and solicitors are able to operate freely ...".

So, why was the protocol needed, and what is its status after 26 April 1999? What will be the effect of Part 35 of the Civil Procedure Rules on the protocol and what changes are likely to be reflected in Version 2.0 of the TeCSA Expert Witness Protocol?

Why the Protocol? TeCSA is composed of solicitors who satisfy significant and objective tests of experience in construction and technology dispute resolution. TeCSA wanted to communicate better practice to a wider constituency. Early day consultation identified three key problem areas, where guidance would be welcomed by solicitor and expert alike:

- the commercial relationship between solicitor and expert not being dealt with fully and properly at the outset, thereby prejudicing the relationship and potentially the expert's and solicitor's duties to the tribunal;
- misunderstandings about the expert's role at the different stages of a dispute;
- wide range of concerns relating to "without prejudice" meetings.

Whatever the causes of these concerns they were issues where guidance could be given in a general way. The protocol was not prepared so that it should be applied in a rigid way. It exists to encourage issues to be addressed. If expert and solicitor consider the issues in the protocol, but decide to do things differently, then the protocol has achieved its objective. The important thing is that key issues are not ignored.

Woolf Reforms, 26 April 1999—What happens now? The TeCSA Expert Witness Protocol reproduced in Appendix B is Version 1.0 (published as the ORSA Expert Witness Protocol). After 26 April 1999 it should be read together with the Civil Procedure Rules. Do not read only Part 35, "Experts and Assessors". Start with Part 1. Some key words from Part 1 will illustrate the extent to which we now all operate in a different climate.

> "... the overriding objective is to enable the court to deal with cases justly which involves, so far as practicable, putting the parties on an equal footing, saving expense and dealing with the case in ways proportionate to the amount involved, the importance of the case and complexity of the issues and the financial position of each party."

Those who felt that the courts did not provide sufficient control over the use of expert evidence should fear no more. There should be sufficient control mechanisms to prevent a party with resources engaging in what I have heard referred to as "bludgeoning by expert".

In his Foreword to the Civil Procedure Rules the Lord Chancellor emphasises that the Rules are essentially a change of culture. Any culture change has its promoters and detractors. Not one person whom I have talked to pretends the changes will be easy to apply in the area of expert evidence. Some regret the passing of the relevance of much procedural case law, others look forward to delivering a better service.

The Civil Procedure Rules The Civil Procedure Rules create some big issues and make significant changes. The way in which case management conferences are run in the early days will be a significant factor. There will be problems. There will be apparently inconsistent orders made in different courts. The feedback process, both within the Lord Chancellor's Department and through the involvement of lawyers, experts and their respective professional organisations is a valuable part of the implementation of the reform.

The Technology and Construction Court (in its former guise of the Official Referees' Court) has for many years promoted active case management. Those of us familiar with that forum may see less change than others.

Significant areas of tension have been identified. It remains to be seen whether these concerns are justified. Particular issues in relation to Part 35 are:

- the duty to restrict expert evidence and how that is applied by the courts. Will courts be tempted to unduly restrict the disciplines and numbers of experts?;
- the wording of the Statement of Truth in paragraph 1.4 of the Practice Direction: "I believe that the facts I have stated in this report are true and the opinions I have expressed are correct".

When do the provisions of Part 35 begin to bite? Views on this are polarised. Group A (I shall call them the "non-believers") say that until an "expert" is named as such following the case management conference, or is subsequently instructed in terms that he is to be such an expert, the rules do not apply.

Group B (I shall call them the "ever-faithful") believe that the rules should apply in full as soon as any technical person is appointed to consider any matter in relation to any dispute as there will be a possibility that that dispute may result in litigation.

Group C (in which I place myself) accepts that a flexible and positive approach is needed. Once the Civil Procedure Rules begin to bed down and clarification is given, the point at which a person is an "expert who has been instructed to give or prepare evidence for the purpose of court proceedings" may well vary from case to case.

The wording of Part 35 acknowledges that an expert can be an expert outside the remit of Part 35. Imagine, for a moment, the difficulties of applying Part 35 to an expert appointed to support statutory adjudication in the construction industry.

TeCSA Expert Witness Protocol—Version 2.0? The answer to whether TeCSA will produce Version 2.0 is not yet clear. This is not an attempt to back-track on the need to update the existing document, but a wish to reflect:

- actual practice in at least the period to October 1999 so that Version 2.0 can address real and not perceived issues;
- the progress of the Lord Chancellor's Department's working group on expert evidence within Part 35 which is aiming to produce a guidance note later in 1999.

In the meantime the TeCSA Expert Witness Protocol should be read together with the Civil Procedure Rules. TeCSA would welcome comments on particular issues or problems that might be dealt with in Version 2.0. The revised version of the protocol may become a much more straightforward document if the Lord Chancellor's Department's working group produce clear guidance covering all key areas.

It is widely recognised that the *Practice Note* which accompanies Part 35 requires clarification. I sit as a representative of TeCSA on the working group established by the Lord Chancellor's Department. Its terms of reference are:

- to prepare a draft code of guidance for the appointment and use of experts and assessors under Part 35 and the practice direction thereto of the CPR;
- to submit a draft to the Civil Justice Council and the Master of the Rolls for consultation;
- to consult generally with the legal profession and other interested bodies.

We expect to produce consultation material shortly.

APPENDIX C—SURVEYORS ACTING AS EXPERT WITNESSES: PRACTICE STATEMENT & GUIDANCE NOTES (PUBLISHED BY THE ROYAL INSTITUTION OF CHARTERED SURVEYORS)

This is a first-class document which, as the title suggests, is broken down into two parts: the Practice Statement, of which, in the opinion of the RICS, "A Member conforming to the practices recommended in these Guidance Notes should have at least a partial defence to an allegation of negligence by virtue of having followed those practices"; and the Guidance Notes, which provide advice to Members and are recommended for specific professional tasks. "They are intended to embody 'best practice', i.e. procedures which in the opinion of the RICS meet a high standard of professional competence."

Of the Practice Statement the principal message is: "Expert evidence provided by chartered surveyors must be, and must be seen to be, the independent product of the surveyor."

I will not attempt to paraphrase either the Practice Statement or the Guidance Notes, they are well worth reading in their entirety.

Matters which deserve highlighting however are:

- The primary duty of the surveyor is to the Judicial Body.
- The duty applies as much in an arbitration or elsewhere.
- A surveyor must, prior to accepting instructions
  - (a) advise that this Practice Statement will apply;
  - (b) ensure that there is a written record as to the matters on which expert evidence is required;
  - (c) agree Terms of Business.

The experts' reports must:

- Distinguish between matters of plain fact, expert observation and expert inferences.
- Use plain language and explain any technical terms.

The surveyor must notify all concerned if after issue of the evidence he identifies a material inaccuracy or changes his view of the matter material to his stated opinion.

The Guidance Notes set out what is considered "good practice" and are prepared against the background of the Woolf Report *Access to Justice*.

Inevitably they set out the duties and responsibilities of expert witnesses culled from *The Ikarian Reefer*.

I particularly liked the section on written reports where the structure and nature of the content of a typical report was suggested.

Also commendable is "good practice" concerning the meetings between the experts.

Finally, there is an interesting comment on contingency fees which the RICS accept are incompatible with "the duty, impartiality and independence required of an expert ... and accordingly, contingency fees should be avoided if at all possible". (Note: no distinction is drawn between contingency fees and conditional fees. For a discussion of the difference see Tony Bingham's article in *Building*, "No duck, no dinner", 27 March 1998.)

The Guidance Notes goes on to accept that some members charge "on a contingency basis as a matter of normal practice" and "... while the Institution would not expect any of its Members to allow the quality of their evidence to be influenced by the potential fee, should the Judicial Body become aware that such a fee basis has been agreed, that Body may consider that the evidence and opinion proffered is not entirely unbiased".

That surely has to be an understatement. I certainly should be sceptical about an expert who was being wholly and totally remunerated on a contingency fee basis. I strongly advise arbitrators to ask the question of experts who they suspect might well be on contingency fees. In this context, however, note the Court of Appeal decision in *Lusty* v. *Finsbury Securities* (1991) 58 BLR 66 where it was held that even where an expert has an interest in the decision, his evidence as to the value of the work is admissible.

Finally in this Appendix there are some useful sample Terms of Engagement for expert witnesses and a useful note on the changes of hearsay evidence which have occurred as a result of the Civil Evidence Act 1995.

(NOTE: MAY 1999—In relation to the Civil Procedure Rules the RICS have said that they see no reason to change what is there, but suggest adding the following: *"The Practice Statement is in the process of being updated to take into account the new Civil Procedure Rules but the principal change will be the form of wording to be used in the declaration which has to be made at the end of each report. The Guidance Notes are to be expanded."*)

OTHER PROTOCOLS AND GUIDELINES ARISING FROM THE NEW CIVIL PROCEDURE RULES

At the time of publication two protocols have been issued, one on personal injury and the other on clinical negligence. In addition there is a general Practice Direction Protocol. Others will undoubtedly follow. However, it is hoped that these first two protocols should give a broad indication to the reader as to how the these new Civil Procedure Rules are likely to affect all expert evidence in other disciplines.

APPENDIX D—PROFESSIONAL ARBITRATION ON COURT TERMS (PACT)

What, you might ask, is this doing in a book on The Expert?

PACT is a scheme designed and developed by the Royal Institution of Chartered Surveyors and The Law Society as an alternative to the court determining lease renewal terms and rent for commercial property (Landlord and Tenant Act 1954).

The parties may elect to have the rent and terms of their new lease determined by an experienced professional acting as an arbitrator or an independent expert—thus, the inclusion of this relatively new scheme.

The full scheme is included as Appendix D to this book, so I will comment no further than to say that there are four alternative procedures offered through four versions of Consent Order which must be approved by the court on joint application by the landlord and tenant. These are:

- *Model Order 1* For referring all outstanding issues to arbitration.
- *Model Order 2* For referring the initial rent to independent expert determination and interim rent to arbitration.

- *Model Order 3* For referring issues other than rent to arbitration before endeavouring to agree the rental issues, and then, failing agreement, referring the initial rent to independent expert determination and interim rent to arbitration.
- *Model Order 4* For expert drafting of the text of the lease.

Model Orders 1 and 2 are the basic forms which it is anticipated will be of most use to the parties and their advisors.

> "Model Orders 3 and 4 illustrate the extra flexibility which can be built into the basic approach. Form 3 adopts a two-stage approach allowing time for agreement, which may avoid the need for the second stage. Form 4 selects one specific aspect of the process, namely drafting the new lease itself. The parties can therefore agree which matters should be decided by the court and which by an independent professional."

PACT was commented on in an article entitled "The role of the single expert" by Michael R Curry—The Lands Tribunal, Royal Courts of Justice, Belfast, which first appeared in the *New Law Journal—Expert Witness Supplement*, 28 November 1997, and is reproduced below with the kind permission of both author and publisher.

> "There appears to be widespread concern about the proposal to lean heavily towards the use of only a single expert to assist the court to determine expert issues. The recent working paper (*Access to Justice Judicial Case Management Working Paper* (July 1997)) identifies fears about how the role of the single expert might evolve and whether the parties would employ their own experts anyway to review the findings. I have some experience of giving and receiving expert evidence and this article has two purposes. The first is to suggest greater initial flexibility in the proposals. The second is to draw attention to a scheme which may provide an alternative role model. I claim to be relatively neutral as I am not directly affected by either the proposals or the scheme.
>
> As the reform proposals are not a solution recognised as being clearly the best, it may be prudent to keep options open and initially encourage the use of alternatives, even if it means widening the spectrum of solutions available. After review at a later date, which would include practical experience of a wider range of options, either the scope of choice might be reduced generally or particular solutions allocated to the particular types of problem where they worked best.
>
> Clearly, some expert issues will be such that they cannot be severed, and there may be no alternative to having experts assisting within the court.
>
> Useful information may come from experience of the new scheme for arbitrators, who now have a power (s. 37 of the Arbitration Act 1996) to appoint experts to report to them and the parties, or appoint assessors to assist them. There is a simple obligation to give the parties a reasonable opportunity to comment on any information, opinion or advice offered by any such person.
>
> Rather than a single expert assisting the court, one preferred option, in suitable cases, may be to have expert issues finally determined separately by an expert, who may act as an arbitrator or independent expert. Different users will have different views, but the roles and their relative merits are well documented and both have merits which may not have had the consideration they deserve. Both options result in experts determining the issues rather than assisting the court to determine them so there is no confusion about the relationship with the court.
>
> If issues are capable of being severed and put to a single expert, and that is what those who have a stake in the outcome prefer, there should be no great obstacle to putting them to an expert for determination. The machinery to open the door from the court to what is really a range of ADR schemes need not be complex.
>
> The proposed stay for mediation simply could be enlarged to encompass all forms of ADR, i.e. including arbitration and expert determination. Although it is an option for the parties, not the courts, it may be that at a future date, unreasonable refusal to go down that route might be considered in the question of costs."

Of PACT, Mr Curry had this to say:

> "The appointments are made by the RICS or the Law Society in exactly the same way as arbitrators or independent experts are currently and have been for many years, appointed for rent reviews. So the scheme builds on established principles and practice to provide a service which is complementary to, rather than within, the court. Those who have a stake in the outcome have a choice in the method—court or expert, lawyer or surveyor, independent expert or arbitrator, and, if the latter, the parties have the flexibility of the new Act [Arbitration Act 1996]. It is a scheme yet to be tested but it could be a role model for others. In this jurisdiction, commercial lease renewals have been referred to an expert tribunal for more than 30 years (Business Tenancies Act (N.I.) 1964):
>
> > 'The relative speed and informality of proceedings before the Lands Tribunal, and the awareness shown by members of the Tribunal of contemporary commercial life, seem to have gained the confidence of those who deal with business tenancies on a regular basis. By contrast, delays in court proceedings in England, often exploited by tenants, led to the introduction in 1969 of a special procedure for interim rents to be paid pending renewal, a procedure which has been unnecessary—so far—in Northern Ireland.' (Professor Norma Dawson, *Business Tenancies in Northern Ireland* (1994, p. 3).)
>
> The author was referring to my predecessors."

APPENDIX E—COURT OF INTERNATIONAL ARBITRATION AUSTRALIA: EXPERT DETERMINATION RULES

I have included the above Rules in Appendix E firstly because they are Rules which could have a universal application either without amendment or, at least in other cases, only minor amendment, and secondly because these Rules, although directed to international disputes, can also be applied domestically.

The objective of these Rules is summarised by the author—the President of the Court of International Arbitration, Australia, A A de Fina (by whose kind permission these Rules are reproduced)—as follows:

> "These Rules govern a process for the determination of disputes where the subject matter of the dispute relates particularly to an area of expertise such as but not limited to science and technology, computers, finance and accountancy, and shipping and transport.
>
> Particularly these Rules
>
> (i) provide flexibility of process but at all times reliant on specialist expertise;
> (ii) provide a fabric for dealing with transnational matters;
> (iii) allow for the appointment of more than one person or a partnership or corporation as the Expert;
> (iv) allow for submission of a wide range of matters;
> (v) allow in certain circumstances of the application of merchant law;
> (vi) avoid concepts which may be limited to a particular culture or system of law."

APPENDIX F—THE ACADEMY'S MODEL TERMS OF ENGAGEMENT FOR EXPERTS (ON BEHALF OF A PARTY INVOLVED IN A DISPUTE BEFORE ANY COURT OF LAW OR AT ARBITRATION OR ANY OTHER TRIBUNAL)

These Model Terms, compiled by The Academy of Experts (by whose kind permission they are reproduced) are commented on in an article by Dr Roger J Maddrell which precedes them in this Appendix.

APPENDIX G—THE ACADEMY'S MODEL FORM OF EXPERT'S REPORT

In pursuit of raising the standards of expert reports, The Academy of Experts have produced a very useful Model which is reproduced in full in this Appendix.

Experts of any discipline are well advised to follow this recommended format and if they do they are unlikely to miss any important aspects which should be covered by all such reports.

APPENDIX H—THE ACADEMY'S MODEL CODE OF PRACTICE

This Appendix speaks for itself and is a code by which all experts should abide.

APPENDIX J—THE ACADEMY'S FORM OF DECLARATION FOR EXPERTS

This is the recommended form of declaration to be included at the end of every expert's report.

APPENDIX K—MODEL FORMS OF DIRECTION FOR EXPERTS

The first of these directions (Appendix K/1) was drafted by Sir Laurence Street, the former Chief Justice for New South Wales, Australia

Like my own direction which follows (in Appendix K/2), it is designed to substantially reduce the time taken to cross-examine experts at the arbitration hearing and gives the arbitrator/referee the additional role envisaged by the Arbitration Act 1996, in pursuit of the arbitrator's duty *to avoid unnecessary delay and expense.*

Finally, in Appendix K/3, I have included the standard item which I include on all of my agendas for preliminary meetings. It offers two alternatives. The first is a normal direction to experts, but expanded to include an exchange of written questions to be posed by the respective experts to each other following exchange of their respective reports. These questions are to be answered in writing following which the arbitrator himself may require written answers to any questions he may have on the experts' reports.

This form of direction, which I have used from time to time, is designed to reduce to a minimum the time for cross-examining experts at the hearing.

As I said earlier, this direction was developed by me in pursuance of my duty under s. 33 of the Arbitration Act 1996 *to avoid unnecessary delay and expense.*

However, I must confess that it is not frequently adopted by parties, particularly when they are represented by solicitors and I do not believe in imposing this sort of direction on the parties when they are so represented.

Perhaps I can be criticised for not being robust enough—at least on this one occasion!—but there we are. The reader must make up his own mind and try this out or something like it, if it appeals.

An alternative form of direction is also included, where, in consultation with the parties, it seems desirable to use a tribunal-appointed expert.

Then follows a typical direction that I would give in a case where I have convinced the parties, or their representatives, to adopt my earlier direction to exchange written questions.

Unless the parties have agreed otherwise—and as they can rarely agree on the time of day, this is unlikely—the Arbitration Act 1996 gives the arbitrator absolute discretion over such matters as requiring the experts to exchange and answer written questions (s.34(2)(h)) with an eye on his s.33 duty—"to adopt procedures suitable to the circumstances of the particular case, avoiding unnecessary delay and expense . . .".

However, having said that, I prefer persuasion over such matters rather than imposition.

That then brings an end to the summary of the contents of this book on The Expert. Many eminent academics or leading practising experts have contributed to this extremely comprehensive coverage of the subject, for which I am immensely grateful. It is to be hoped that by a judicious use of the full index those elements in which the reader is particularly interested can be readily accessed.

I shall finish with a quotation from Edge & Ellison's newsletter *Construction Edge*—Issue 3 Spring 1998—on "The Importance of the Expert":

> "The importance of identifying the correct expert or experts to deal with the issues arising in the case has been underlined by a recent Court of Appeal authority. The case concerned the alleged negligence of a chartered surveyor. However, the parties chose experts of different disciplines, one a structural engineer and the other a chartered surveyor. On appeal the court considered that it was almost always necessary to hear evidence from an individual within the same profession to ascertain whether there had been failure to meet the required professional standards. Indeed, the court considered that the evidence of an expert from another discipline was not, strictly, admissible. See *Sansum & Another* v. *Metcalf Hambleton & Co* (1997) *The Times*, 19 December."

ABOUT THE AUTHOR

D Mark Cato is a Chartered Surveyor and has worked in many countries of the world, including the USA, Australia, France, Italy, the Southern Republic of the Yemen, Bahrain and throughout the Persian Gulf, Ethiopia and Somalia.

Since the late 1980s he has been a full-time arbitrator and has been appointed in well over 100 references. He lectures at various universities and speaks regularly at seminars and conferences on arbitration in the UK and overseas.

He is a well-known author on arbitration with three other major works to his name:

- *Arbitration Practice and Procedure—Interlocutory and Hearing Problems* (Second Edition)
- *The Sanctuary House Case—An Arbitration Workbook*
- *So You Really Want to be an Arbitrator?*

He is a Registered Arbitrator and, at date of publication, a member of the General Council, member of the Executive Board and Chairman of the Professional Committee of the Chartered Institute of Arbitrators. He took an internal Masters Degree in Construction Law and Arbitration in King's College London in 1993.

He is the Founder President of The Arbitration Club which, together with its off-shoot, The International Arbitration Club, has over 400 members in seven branches.

He is married, with two grown-up children and lives with Alice, his wife, on the Herts/Essex border. In October 1998 he became the very proud grandfather of little Freddy.

PART I

THE EXPERT WITNESS

CHAPTER 1

INTRODUCTORY ARTICLES

CHAPTER 1/1

THE NEW CIVIL PROCEDURE RULES AND THE EXPERT WITNESS

Judge John Frenkel

IT IS NEVER TOO LATE

001 The Civil Procedure Rules 1998 (CPR—not cardio pulmonary resuscitation) and most of the practice directions were published on 29 January 1999. They can be obtained from the Stationery Office (020 7873 9090) (price £250 for two loose-leaf volumes plus service supplements) or from the LCD Website *http://www.open.gov.uk/lcd*. The commencement date is 26 April 1999. You must start planning post-CPR strategy now.

002 In a claim where the court will need to receive expert evidence, the critical path through the preparation stage is making ready the expert evidence. The case management requirements of the CPR need investigation. Although actions issued before 26 April 1999 will generally proceed under the old rules, once a defended pre-April action comes to the notice of a judge, the court will—so far as is practicable—bring the action within the CPR. That means allocation to a procedural track and a timetable order that contains the date of trial. The normal track for a claim worth no more than £5,000 is the small claims track, over £5,000 but no more than £15,000, the fast track and above £15,000, the multi track.

NO COMPROMISE

003 The introduction of the CPR requires a partnership between practitioners, judges and the Court Service. We shall all have to adjust to and accommodate each other's shortcomings. However, there is one principle that cannot be compromised. The court must set the trial date or the period for the trial when it gives directions. The case management practice directions are quite specific. Unless civil disputes can be resolved within the time set by the court, the reforms will fail. The lesson learned from other jurisdictions is that a trial date set at an early stage will cause the claim to manage itself because the parties must complete their preparation within the timetable.

004 In the small claims track the court will give allocation directions that include the hearing date. In fast and multi-track claims the court will give directions at the allocation and listing questionnaire stages. The practice direction encourages paper directions whenever possible. Smart solicitors will manage the claim and set their own timetable rather than leave it to the district judge. Give the court proper information in the allocation questionnaire and you will not generally have to attend a case management conference except, in the heaviest and most complicated claims or, where one of the litigants is in person. A common reason for the district judge to appoint an allocation directions appointment in the multi-track will be the failure to propose a trial period in the proposed timetable order.

005 The principle of the new procedure is: "There should be a fundamental transfer in responsibility for the management of civil litigation from the litigants and their advisors to the court." Part 28 CPR and the fast track practice direction require the court when it allocates a claim to make "allocation directions". A typical fast track timetable will direct the listing questionnaire to be filed within 22 weeks and the trial within 30 weeks. Part 29 CPR and the multi-track case management practice direction state that the court cannot approve allocation directions agreed by the parties unless they include a date for the trial or the trial period. The claim will be included in something like a warned list. It is probably not generally appreciated that set down, as a concept, will disappear. In all three tracks the timetable will always include the date of trial or the period of trial.

EXPERT EVIDENCE—THE WOOLF VIEW

006 Lord Woolf was forthright in his views of expert evidence. They are views which are reflected in the CPR and practice directions. Over to his final report:

> "It was my basic contention of my interim report that two of the major generators of unnecessary cost in civil litigation were uncontrolled discovery and expert evidence. No one has seriously challenged that contention.
>
> A large litigation support industry, generating a multi-million pound fee income, has grown up among professions such as accountants, architects and others, and new professions have developed, such as accident reconstruction and care experts. This goes against all principles of proportionality and access to justice. In my view, its most damaging effect is that it has created an ethos of what is acceptable which has in turn filtered down to smaller cases. Many potential litigants do not even start litigation because of the advice they are given about the costs, and in my view this is as great a social ill as the actual cost of pursuing litigation.
>
> There should be no more than one expert in any one speciality unless this is necessary for some real purpose. The appointment of a neutral expert would not necessarily deprive the parties of the right to cross-examine, or even to call their own experts in addition to the neutral expert if that were justified by the scale of the case.
>
> In fast track cases the exercise of the court's discretion will be more restricted. The principle of proportionality of cost dictates that the scope of expert evidence must be limited. The rules on expert evidence on the fast track will therefore limit the parties generally to one expert per side in any single speciality (with an overall limit of two per side) with no oral evidence. Single experts will be used wherever possible.
>
> The present system has the effect of exaggerating the adversarial role of experts, and this helps neither the court nor the parties. As the Court of Appeal has recently remarked: 'For whatever reason, and whether consciously or unconsciously, the fact is that expert witnesses instructed on behalf of parties to litigation often tend to espouse the cause of those instructing them to a greater or lesser extent. On occasion they become more partisan than the parties' (*Abbey National Mortgages plc* v. *Key Surveyors Nationwide Ltd* [1996] EGCS 23)."

EXPERTS—AND THE RULES

007 Judicial training encourages every judge to try to foster a new approach to the use of expert evidence, particularly the employment of a single expert. It is the very approach which the CPR accommodates. Most district judges deal with family work. We are all aware that in family work no expert evidence may be adduced without the court's permission. The result is that the single expert is customary. Family work is no less contentious and emotional than non-family civil work.

008 Part 35 CPR restricts expert evidence to that which is reasonably required to resolve the proceedings.

009 It is to be the duty of an expert to help the court on the matters within his expertise. This duty is to override any obligation to the person from whom he has received instructions or who pays him.

010 No party may call an expert or put in evidence an expert's report without the court's permission. If permission is granted under Part 35, it shall be in relation only to the expert named or the field identified by the court's direction.

011 The court may limit the amount of the expert's fees and expenses that the party who wishes to rely on the expert may recover from any other party. Where the court gives a direction for a single joint expert to be used, each instructing party may give instructions to the expert.

012 When an instructing party gives instructions to the expert he must, at the same time, send a copy of the instructions to the other instructing parties. The court may give directions about the payment of the expert's fees and expenses; and any inspection, examination or experiments which the expert wishes to carry out.

THE PRACTICE DIRECTION ON EXPERTS

013 Part 35 CPR is complemented by a practice direction. This is how it sets the scene.

> "Part 35 is intended to limit the use of oral expert evidence to that which is reasonably required. In addition, where possible, matters requiring expert evidence should be dealt with by a single expert. Permission of the court is always required either to call an expert or to put an expert's report in evidence."

014 Consider using a single expert before the district judge does so. Questions about why one is not being employed will be another common reason for the district judge to appoint an allocation directions hearing (fast track) or case management conference (multi-track). The burden lies on the party who wants to instruct a separate expert to show why a jointly instructed expert is not in the interests of justice. It is unlikely to be enough to say, in a post-26 April claim, "the expert was instructed before the commencement of the new procedure". Everyone knows that change is coming. If after April the defendant wants an expert's report it is likely that the court will insist on a single expert, jointly instructed. Many judges will consider that it will do no one a kindness if the old system is allowed to continue while everyone gets used to the new one.

015 How will the CPR affect everyday practice? I fully accept that experience may show my remarks to be incautious and that events may prove me wrong.

EXPERT EVIDENCE ON THE FAST TRACK

016 The Part 28-relating fast track practice direction contains directions for expert evidence.

> "On it appearing to the court that expert evidence is necessary on the issue of . . . and that evidence should be given by the report of a single expert instructed jointly by the parties, the . . . shall no later than . . . inform the court whether or not such an expert has been instructed.
>
> The expert evidence on the issue of . . . shall be limited to a single expert jointly instructed by the parties.
>
> If the parties cannot agree by . . . who that expert is to be and about the payment of his fees, either party may apply for further directions.
>
> Unless the parties agree in writing or the court orders otherwise, the fees and expenses of such an expert shall be paid to him by the parties equally [. . .] and be limited to £. . . .
>
> The report of the expert shall be filed at the court no later than . . . .
>
> No party shall be entitled to recover by way of costs from any other party more than £. . . for the fees or expenses of an expert."

Direction on experts at allocation stage

017 There are two questions to be asked about every request for permission to use expert evidence. Is that expert necessary? Why should there not be a joint report? At the allocation stage the court gives permission to prepare expert evidence. At the listing questionnaire stage, after everyone has considered the report, the court decides if the expert will give evidence by report or orally.

PREDICTIONS

018 The LCD guesstimate that there will be 110,000 small claims, 7,300 fast track claims, and 2,700 multi-track claims per year. My remarks apply principally to lower value claims; there are plenty of them.

A NEW START? IS THE "EXPERT" NECESSARY?

019 The conclusions of road traffic accident reconstruction experts differ because each expert must assume that their different instructions are correct. Frequently, an employment expert's report will merely quote the New Earnings Survey, local job advertisements and employment agencies' letters. The judge must decide the plaintiff's capacity for work. In matrimonial ancillary relief proceedings, solicitors produce a bundle of relevant documents to establish earning capacity or the lack of it. Money is never spent on employment experts. Lord Woolf also mentions care consultants and accountants. There is no doubt that in larger claims, experts will be necessary and permitted. In smaller claims the court will ask if the cost of the report outweighs its value. The claimant's solicitor can frequently obtain the evidence to prove damages without outsourcing the enquiries.

020 Rule 32.4 CPR provides "No party may call an expert or put in evidence an expert's report without the court's permission". This is a dramatic inroad into the freedom of litigants to conduct their cases as they wish. Hitherto many judges would not have thought it right to deny a party the right to pursue a particular line of expert evidence. Rule 32.1 puts the court under a duty to restrict the expert evidence "to that which is reasonably required to resolve the proceedings". That will be the law. The burden will lie on the party seeking permission to call an expert witness to justify doing so. There is to be a crucial balance: on one side is the requirement that the cost of the proceedings shall be proportionate to the weight of the claim, on the other side is the need to ensure that justice is not sidelined by a drive for economy.

021 Should expert evidence be given in a single report? Under the present regime, the total cost of calling two orthopaedic experts can be £2,000—20 per cent of a £10,000 claim. In the majority of claims under £15,000 the defendant relies on the plaintiff's medical report. The protocols and the CPR extend this sensible policy.

022 The claimant must now consult the defendant to identify the expert. The future income of all experts will depend on a reputation for impartiality. Recently, whenever I have suggested to parties that a joint expert be instructed, I have been told that there would be no difficulty identifying the expert and agreeing a fee.

023 The Law Society has published in *The Directory of Experts*, a model letter of instruction to medical experts. Another example is to be found in the Pre-Action Protocol for Personal Injury Claims (obtainable from the Civil Justice Division of the Lord Chancellor's Department, 54–60 Victoria Street, London SW1E 6QW—telephone Liam Collingridge on 020 7210 0663.

IMPARTIALITY PLEASE

024 The appointment of the single expert is probably the area of greatest uncertainty in the whole reform package. How can the court make single expert orders until experts have demonstrated that lawyers and court can have confidence in their ability to be impartial? How will experts ever acquire the culture of impartiality unless judges make single expert orders? We will break out of this vicious circle only if judges exercise the power imposed on them by the overriding objectives and make single expert orders whenever possible. It is suggested that the principle of proportionality means that in fast track, an order for a single expert should be the norm, particularly, but not exclusively, in those cases governed by pre-action protocols.

OBJECTIONS

"The use of a single expert will usurp the function of the judge"

025 This suggestion is not made about the reports of court welfare officers in family proceedings.

"My clients have a panel of experts whom they instruct me to use"

026 The aim of the protocols is to prevent the perpetuation of adversarial experts. Although, there is no general litigation pre-action protocol, the personal injury protocol has the capacity to be a model for a wide range of disputes. Rule 3.1(4) CPR requires the court, when it exercises its case management powers, to take into account whether a party has failed to observe a protocol. And Rule 44.3 CPR "General Rules about Costs" requires the court when it assesses the costs to take into account a party's conduct, before, as well as during proceedings.

"The claimant has an expert, why shouldn't I have one?"

027 If the claimant obtains an expert's report without consulting the defendant and the defendant now wants his own expert's advice, what will the court do under the new procedure? In some claims the court will make the normal order and will direct a single expert's report. The claimant will not be permitted to use the earlier report obtained without consulting the defendant. The cost of obtaining the first report will fall on the claimant, come what may. If the defendant unreasonably refused an offer to select an expert, the court may refuse the defendant permission to obtain a separate report. Rule 1 CPR requires the court to consider the overriding principle of proportionality. An order that is appropriate in a smaller claim may be unjust in a larger one. It may be easier to persuade the court to order separate reports on the question of liability, than damages.

"The instruction of a single expert will increase my costs!"

"I shall need to instruct a separate expert to advise my client of the points on which to cross-examine the single expert"

028 The district judge may ask how you know this when you have not yet seen what the jointly instructed expert has to say?

NEW POWERS FOR OLD CLAIMS

029 The practice direction on transitional arrangements provides that if automatic directions (High Court or county court) have begun to apply to existing proceedings, they will continue to have effect after 26 April. When proceedings come before a judge (whether at a hearing or on paper) for the first time after 26 April, he may direct how the CPR are to apply. This practice direction will give the court the same dramatic power to restrict the parties' freedom to call expert evidence in pre-26 April claims as it has in post-26 April claims. It remains to be seen how this power will be exercised. The important point is, the power exists. *Sullivan* v. *West Yorkshire PTE* [1985] 2 All ER 134 heads for the dustbin.

"DO YOU *REALLY* WANT TO BE MY EXPERT?"

030 The practice direction on "Experts" (which complements Part 35 of the CPR) sets out the usual matters that you would expect a competent expert to include in his report. And the report must:

- contain a statement that the expert understands his duty to the court and has complied with that duty and,
- set out the substance of all material instructions and that includes telephone as well as written instructions (privilege will not attach to the instructions) and
- state that the report is true.

CROSS-EXAMINATION BEFORE TRIAL

031 Here is quite an innovation. The CPR allow each party to put one set of pre-trial written questions to the opponent's expert(s) without permission. Questions, whose purpose must be to clarify the report, should be asked not later than 28 days after receipt of the report.

WE MUST MEET, SOME TIME

032 The court now has power to direct separate experts to meet and prepare a statement of their reasons for disagreement. The spirit in which these discussions are held will be a factor for the court to consider when it comes to exercise its discretion on the costs of the case under Rule 44.3. Instructions given to the expert about the conduct of the joint meeting will not be privileged.

DIRECTIONS ON EXPERTS AT LISTING STAGE

033 In the fast track there is a presumption that there will be no oral expert evidence and that the expert's evidence will be given in a report. After all, fast track trial costs are fixed, the trial time estimate does not exceed one day and there is no discretion to allow the costs of a second day. The court has the power to permit expert oral evidence. If the trial will last more than a day the court may transfer the claim to the multi-track. The court must apply the proportionality test. The burden lies on the party wanting to cross-examine an expert to show that the effect on the probative value of the expert evidence outweighs the additional cost to the parties.

034 In the multi-track, because the parties receive permission to instruct separate experts, they will not necessarily be permitted to call their experts at the trial. The court must consider whether any questionnaires to the experts have been answered? Has there been a meeting of the experts? The proportionality test must be applied. Where there are experts of more than one type, the court may permit one class of expert to testify but direct that another class will give evidence by a report.

035 The listing questionnaire directions must confirm the trial date. If the expert evidence is given by report, the "unavailability date" problem disappears. This is important in the fast track with its presumption that the date of trial will be within 30 weeks of the date of the allocation directions.

District Judge John Frenkel *sits at the Bristol Civil Trial Centre and is the consulting editor for the* Practical Civil Court Precedents.

(The above first appeared, as two articles, in the New Law Journal, *12, 19 February 1999 by whose kind permission they are reproduced.)*

CHAPTER 1/2

ARE YOU AN EXPERT?

Dr Albert W. Knott, PE

001 In this article, the author describes the task facing an engineer in providing expert testimony. He discusses and recommends the development of a personal philosophy. Recommendations are made regarding standards of excellence in honesty, thoroughness, and the exploration and elimination of bias. Forensic engineering is a demanding arena requiring personal integrity as well as technical competence.

INTRODUCTION

002 A normal witness in court is allowed to tell the jury what happened, but is not allowed to state opinions. The witness tells the jury the facts but is not allowed to draw conclusions from those facts. The jurors must reach their own conclusions about the relative guilt or innocence of the litigants based on their interpretation of the facts.

003 The court defines an expert witness as a person who has sufficient special knowledge to be allowed to interpret the facts for the jury by expressing opinions and conclusions. A normal witness gives testimony without compensation. An expert witness is paid for his or her work. This is a discussion about experts, and about you.

ARE YOU AN EXPERT?

004 To an engineer, an expert is a practitioner who has risen to a position of pre-eminence in his or her profession by years of education; by extensive design, laboratory, or field experience; and through having his or her work published. To an engineer, a young person with a bachelor's degree in engineering is not an expert. However, to a court, a young person who knows how to design "the beam in question" is an expert, because he or she has sufficient special knowledge above that of the jury to be allowed to express an opinion about the beam. To an engineer, not only in-depth, but broad knowledge is required for a person to become an expert. To a court, in-depth special knowledge is required. It certainly helps to have broad knowledge, and the credentials of a broadly educated person can be impressive to a jury. However, when a lawyer looks at you and asks, "Why do you (of all people) think you are an expert?", your calm, confident answer should be: "Because of my special background, training, and experience." Of course, you had better be prepared to itemise that special background, training and experience and to show how it bears directly on the question at hand.

DO YOU QUALIFY?

005 You probably do qualify as an expert in the eyes of the court, because you do have special knowledge beyond that of the jury sufficient to allow the judge to let the jury hear your opinions. However, having said that, I would like to discuss separating the wheat from the chaff. Being an expert witness allows you to influence justice. This is an awesome responsibility, and one seldom appreciated by engineers preparing for their first court case. What you say will be bitterly contested by your opponents, and what you say will influence the lives, fortunes, and futures of people. This is time for very serious thought.

006 You are a technologist. You are educated in a field that the average person holds in great esteem. What you do is not understood. What you say is important. I would like to talk about you becoming a good expert witness.

Lesson 1: Your purpose in court is succinctly to teach seemingly complex technology to people who do not have a technological background

007 Teaching people you like is great experience for learning to be an expert witness. Teaching, by itself, is not what I am talking about—teaching people you *LIKE*, is. The jury wants to know what you are saying. This experience is unique in their lives. They have a sense of the importance of their task to mete out justice. They want you to teach them the truth. So speak to them. They are your audience. Do not be condescending or pompous. Be genuine in your feeling toward them. Develop a rapport. Speak to them as you would to an intelligent, and enquiring neighbour.

Lesson 2: You must be a good teacher, with an ability to make technology sound simple, and straight-forward

Lesson 3: Learn to speak to, and with, people. Learn to be genuine, and to relate. Learn to teach people as if you like them

008 An important job requirement is to be able to write clearly. I feel that my written report is my most effective selling tool. Each report is turned over to competent people on the other side. If it stands up well under that kind of scrutiny, then I may have impressed a future client, the opposing attorney.

009 Putting down words is not writing. The report must be concise, clear, and correct. A wordy report hides the truth in verbiage, and wastes the time of the reader in ferreting out what you are trying to say. Be concise.

010 Be clear. There is a combination of words that will precisely state what you are thinking. Study what you have written. What do the words really say? How else can someone interpret what you have said? Is each sentence in a paragraph important to that paragraph? Is each sentence in the paragraph on the same topic? If not, your writing may be illustrating to the other side your inability to think and your inability to express yourself. You may be showing opposing attorneys how you can be attacked.

Lesson 4: Learn to write. Nine out of ten of your peers, with your current level of education, cannot

011 To be an expert witness, you should strive to be the pre-eminent practitioner that your peers expect. That is your long-term goal. This means you should have or should get a good education. You should have good design and field experience. You should conduct tests. You should be actively involved in furthering the public image of your profession. You should write, give papers, attend society meetings, hold office, and be aggressive in helping others to learn. You should be active in continuing education. You should take courses, attend lectures and conferences, read extensively in your field, and give seminars. You should place yourself into teaching and oral presentation situations. You should at least occasionally teach a course at your local university.

Lesson 5: Know yourself, and carefully define your area of expertise

Lesson 6: Acquire sound experience in your field

012 To solve a problem in, for example, electrical engineering, I would rather hire a person who can think, than a person with a degree in electrical engineering who can not. It is a fact that good people can change fields in forensic engineering. Broadly educated people make better thinkers.

013 We do not like to have an "expert" who does not have degrees in the field in which he or she is giving testimony. That is a somewhat unfortunate situation. When I hire a person, I do so because that person can think, and then I try to get him or her to think in the field in which he or she holds degrees. However, I do not keep the person in that narrow field; I encourage him or her to branch out.

014 A fundamental characteristic needed in a person working in the field of failure analysis is the ability to reason through a complex set of real-world facts to identify the true cause, the core of the problem. This person must use scientific reasoning and must be able to prove a case to a competent listener. The more broad a person's experience, the more knowledge and experience that person can bring to bear on a problem.

015 I once had a case in which a roofing board made of shredded wood fiber and gypsum (glorified shredded wheat) was used to support normal asphalt shingles on a sloping roof surface. The board material was supported on steel bulb tees, small beams that look much like a railroad rail in cross section. The roof leaked like a sieve. The owner had counted 432 individual leaks one day.

016 The way an asphalt shingle is nailed onto this roofing board is for the nail to be driven in and cleated, or hooked into the material, as it is seated. The nails are built-up sheet metal mechanisms to get themselves to hook. Hence if water gets to the head of the nail, it will pour down through the nail mechanism and leak into the shredded wheat. The shingle overlap keeps the water from getting to the nail head.

017 The expert on the other side disassembled several sections of the roof, found many nails misdriven (the mechanism tends to squash over if not driven squarely), and concluded that the cause of the leakage was improper construction. The expert had been hired by the architect.

018 Logan Donnel, a roofing expert from Boulder, Colorado, whom I had asked to join me in the investigation, came up with the correct answer. The roof will not leak unless water gets to the nail head. If water gets to the head, it makes no difference whether it was correctly driven or not; it will leak. Therefore, the problem was the water getting to the nail head, not whether the nail was misdriven. What could cause water to flow uphill, up under the shingle, to reach the nail head? Normal shingle roofs with a slope of 4-in-12 do not leak.

019 The days of leakage did not correlate with weather data on rain. They did not correlate with wind-driven rain. However, they did correlate well with snow. The roof would leak two or three days after each snowfall.

020 Logan pointed out that the roof board fits between the steel bulb tees, not on top. The board was supported by the bottom flanges of the bulb tee. Hence the head of the bulb tee is up, just under the shingles. Heat from the building interior was conducted up through the metal of the bulb tee, and melted a strip of snow on the roof surface just above it. The resulting water seeped down through the snow into the shingles supported by the roof board; and because the roof board was good insulation, the water froze. This ice dam caused the water to back up under the shingle and reach the nail head—thus the random, generally distributed leakage.

Lesson 7: Be a person who thinks. The real answers are not in your textbooks

Lesson 8: Never base your opinions on judgement alone: Base it on facts, logic, tests, and proof

021 A dishonest expert prostitutes the very concept of justice. However, do not conclude that an opponent is dishonest, merely because you believe you are honest, and he or she is saying something else. Honest men can differ diametrically in their final opinions, because we are asked to distinguish between "reasonable" and "unreasonable". We must decide "yes or no, black or white". We have to make up our minds. Although there is a major difference between black and white, there may be almost no difference between "reasonably dangerous" and "unreasonably dangerous". Where is the dividing line? Does bias play a role?

022 If my daughter had been killed by a drunk driver, I would probably have an unreasoned hatred for such drivers. However, if I killed another man's daughter through my own drinking, I would be deeply sorry, but my feeling toward drunk drivers would be a deep concern for their health, not a hatred against them. These are forms of bias.

023 A remarkable experiment was once conducted at an eastern university. A professor in psychology divided his class into two groups to conduct parallel opinion polls. He met with the first group, passed out packets of photographs of people, and asked the students to go to the *even*-numbered houses in a section of town, knock on the door, and ask the respondent if the pictures were of *successful* or *unsuccessful* people. The professor confided to the group that, oddly enough, people are basically *optimists* and that they would find that statistically the respondents would be found to answer that the photos were of *successful* people. He sent them out to conduct the poll.

024 He then met with the other half of the class, sent them to the *odd*-numbered houses in the same neighbourhood but told them that, oddly enough, people were generally *pessimistic* these days, and that they would find that the majority of the respondents would conclude that the pictures were generally of *unsuccessful* people. He sent the second group out.

025 The class reassembled, compared their results, and found, generally 60 to 40, that their responses matched the special biases the professor had suggested. The first group got 60/40 for *successful* people, and the second got 60/40 for *unsuccessful* people.

026 The class discussed how they could have obtained such results. They concluded that something about the way they had asked the questions must have biased the homeowners to respond in accordance with the bias of the poll taker. Therefore, they decided to mend their ways and take the poll again.

027 They took the poll three times. The third time the students read their question monotonically from a card. They got the spread of results to narrow, but they did *NOT* eliminate the original built-in bias.

028 If bias is that insidious and natal, then how can we be unbiased when we are hired to be right? We are trained to be right; we have staked our professional reputations and our way of life on being right. We are all little children who like to be patted on the head and congratulated. As adults, we like to be paid for our work. We have a build-in bias to be agreeable to, and hence to agree with, our clients. In my own practice, I find that I find *FOR* my clients about 80 per cent of the time. We have a good reputation for calling the shots as we see them, and clearly advising our clients when we can *NOT* find *FOR* them. My clients say they respect me for my candor. They cry a lot, but they say they need it to minimise their losses. In addition it can be argued that there are two sides to every question, and pointing out the good points in my client's case is what my client wants me to do. However, does that justify finding *FOR* my clients on an 80/20 basis? Do I just get the clients with the white hats?

029 An honest person must have, or must develop, the ability to see him or herself as biased. If we admit we are biased, then and only then can we begin to cope with bias. Tell yourself that you are biased and believe it. Develop ways to explore your bias. For example, psyche yourself up to believe that you were, in fact, hired by the other side. Can you say to your "new" client precisely the same thing you are contemplating telling your "old" client? If you cannot, it is bias.

Lesson 9: Tell yourself you are biased, and believe it. Then eliminate it (if you can)

030 By the way, do you speed when the cops are not around? Did you take your son to the movie when he was twelve, and tell the cashier that the kid was really eleven? If you do these things, two things accrue: you are dishonest, and you have taught your son to be a liar also. You will not be an honest expert witness.

031 On the other hand, if someone makes a mistake in your favour when making change, do you point it out? Do you ask the waitress to correct the bill, so that you can pay the full price? If you do, then two things accrue: you are honest, and you have a marvellous time surprising waitresses. You will be a good expert witness.

Lesson 10: Study and practise honesty and professionalism. You do *NOT* have a price

THE INVESTIGATION

032 If your client is an insurance company, it is usually interested in proof that it should or should not pay a claim. For example if a wall blows over in a wind, you may have to distinguish between a collapse due to an unusual wind, or a collapse due simply to ageing of the wall. Ageing is normal and is not covered. Poor construction is the responsibility of the builder and is not covered. Insurance covers the unusual, such as vandalism, extreme wind, or hail. Foundation failure due to normal soil settlement is not covered. If the soil moved because a pipe broke and flooded the basement, then it is covered.

Lesson 11: Learn to identify the problem your client has. Learn to solve *HIS* or *HER* problem

033 The normal process of an investigation leading to the presentation of court testimony is as follows. First, you are hired by an insurance company, a lawyer, a builder, a manufacturer, or an irate or injured citizen. You listen carefully to the assignment and design an investigation. Usually, your work is done on a time-and-materials basis. You give an estimated upper limit of cost, which you agree not to exceed without prior client approval. You are careful to discuss the scope of your work and the potential for changes in scope as the findings come to light. Your work is research in nature, hence you can seldom do it for a fixed price.

034 The work is done to determine the probable cause of a failure or an accident. The lawyer will have to prove the case in court, and a proof in law is *not* the same as a proof in engineering. The law has evolved into distinct arenas. For example, strict liability, negligence, and warranty. You may be able to show that the manufacturer had a first-rate quality control program. This is an excellent defence in negligence but has absolutely no application in strict liability. Hence, as an engineering investigator, you must design the scope of your work around what the lawyer wants to be able to prove.

Lesson 12: Work with the lawyer. Learn what he or she needs to show. Learn proof in law. Learn to listen

035 A common problem is that the insurance representative usually wants a report for his file, so that he or she can show the supervisor the completeness of his or her work and the scientific support for the decision to pay or deny the claim. If you found that the fire was caused by faulty wiring in the coffee maker, the claims adjuster wants the report to justify paying the claim to the homeowner. However, the lawyer for the insurance company does *NOT* want a report, because he or she can sue the manufacturer of the coffee maker and recover the company's money. The lawyer will want your report to support his or her argument in court and has not yet decided what theory or theories of law to use. He or she does not want your report floating around just yet, because it was not written with the law suit in mind. Your report may be an excellent proof in engineering, but it is not a proof in law. The lawyer may wish you to do more work before reaching your final conclusions.

Lesson 13: You must identify the assignment in terms of the end use of your work

036 Never do less than a thorough investigation. You are toying with the lives and fortunes of the people involved in the law suit. As a professional, you have a duty to your client to give proper advice. But you have an equal duty to the people on the opposite side to be fair and honest with that advice.

Lesson 14: Use the scientific method for proof or denial of causal theories. Be thorough. Carefully explore and eliminate your biases

037 You will be asked to critique the report of an opposing expert. Usually your attorney will ask you to suggest questions to ask the expert during the deposition. Your tendency while reading the report will be to denigrate the writer and his or her opinions. That is bias. Study it. Would you be so vocal in downgrading the author if he or she had written the same thing in a technical article published in a national journal? You might not have agreed with the article, but would you have been so adamant about it? Treat you opponent with courtesy and fairness. Be thorough and insightful, clearly identifying the fundamental assumptions the writer is making and clearly explaining to your attorney the agreements and disagreements you may have with the writer's methods or conclusions.

Lesson 15: Be fair to your opponent. Instruct your attorney on where you agree and disagree

038 You may find, if your have defeated your bias, that the other person has some good opinions and may even be right. You may find to your horror that you are wrong. It will do your client a fundamental disservice to hide your findings in order to save face. That is dishonest. If you are truly a professional, you will bring out your findings in time to allow your client to minimise losses. If you do not, the client may have a viable law suit against you.

Lesson 16: Receptively explore the truth of other opinions

039 The federal government has been experimenting with a technique of decision making that has applicability in law. For example, if the authorities want to predict how much grain the Soviets will want to buy next year, they ask five or six experts. The experts furnish their reports. Each report is then circulated to the other experts for their review. Then the experts again are asked for their opinion. The second time, the opinions have coalesced into a more common opinion. This opinion is adopted for making federal policy. It has been found that this coalesced opinion is much better than the original spread of opinions.

040 The operative in this federal decision-making process is flexibility. The experts are allowed to be flexible. If you are professional, you will be open minded and ready to explore the validity of the concepts of others. Knowing the opposition makes you stronger. It is, of course, absolutely disastrous to your attorney's case if you change your mind while on the stand. That would simply be extremely poor preparation on your part. Take the time upstream to find the truth.

Lesson 17: Modify your opinion in the light of new evidence or more thoughtful analysis, but do it early

IN DEPOSITION

041 Usually your report is written after your investigation and after discussing your findings with your client. This report is then made available to the opposing attorneys, assuming suit has been filed, and these attorneys give it to their experts for analysis. Your report is analysed, and the opposing attorney asks you, or subpoenas you, to appear at deposition.

042 Your deposition, taken by the opposing attorney, is a detailed oral response by you to any questions the attorney may ask. You will usually be asked to bring your complete file. The attorney who hired you or who represents your client will attend, and will occasionally object to the way questions are being asked. If your attorney feels you may not have understood the question asked by the opposing counsel, he or she will ask for clarification and, for your benefit, will state the several ways the question could have been interpreted. When an attorney objects, I take it as a signal that I may not have fully thought through my answer. The attorney is giving me time to think again.

043 I have found that there are two philosophies in giving depositions. First, your attorney may suspect that the opposition wants to settle the case out of court. In that case, your attorney may ask you to be talkative, to offer additional supporting evidence, and in short, to thoroughly impress the opposing attorney with the solidity of the engineering arguments given.

044 The second philosophy, based on your attorney's assessment that the opposition has no intention of settling, is to tell no more than is necessary to answer succinctly only the questions asked. Your attorney will want you to give the opponent no more than is required by propriety and honesty. Anything else you say can and will be used against you in a court of law.

045 My own approach is to be honest and complete, or honest and brief, as my attorney wishes. We, as engineers, have an obligation to tell the "whole" truth; we can do that with brevity. But if an opposing attorney does not ask a crucial question, we are not obligated to point out the omission during deposition. Your attorney will be glad to bring it out for the opponents' discomfort during the trial.

046 Your deposition is taken by the opposition for three reasons: first, to explore what you have to say; second, to evaluate you as a witness, and third, to solidify you in a position from which you can not easily stray. Beware of questions like, "Have you told me everything related to your opinion?" or "Is this all the work you intend to do on this case?"

Lesson 18: In giving a deposition, listen carefully to the questions, and answer them truthfully

Lesson 19: In general, do not extend your answers into areas not covered by the question. Be succinct and clear and as complete as the question requires. If your attorney asks you to be a teacher, be one. If not, don't

IN COURT

047 On the day of court, show up early and sit in the courtroom to calm down and get a feeling for the courtroom dynamics. When you take the stand and are sworn in by the judge, the first task of your attorney will be to get you accepted as an expert. Your attorney will ask you to list your education, training, and experience. He or she will ask about your activities in professional and technical societies. The judge is specifically interested in seeing that you are qualified in the specific field at hand.

048 In your pretrial preparation meeting, the attorney should have discussed with you how to state your qualifications. The two of you should have decided on what words to use. For example, one attorney, after finding out that I had expertise in dynamics tried to qualify me as an expert in "physics" simply because dynamics was a topic in physics. The other attorney, older and wiser, did not object to having me qualified to give expert testimony in the case, because I was an expert. But I was not a physicist. You should discuss with your attorney the definition of your branch of engineering and how it applies.

049 The attorney will eventually turn to the judge and offer you as an expert. The opposing attorney will either accept the offer, in which case you will be allowed by the judge to give opinion testimony, or the opposing attorney will ask to *voir dire*, a French phrase meaning to "speak the truth". You should take it to mean "here I come, ready or not". The opposing attorney will try to ask questions that will show that you have limited expertise in the specific field at hand, and therefore your testimony should be limited or disallowed. The attorney is really trying to prevent certain opinions from being introduced and is doing it on the grounds that your expertise does not extend into that area. He or she will ask you questions and, on the basis of your answers, will move to reject you as an expert.

050 Note: You will not be allowed to say anything more in your defence. The judge will assume the answers you gave during *voir dire* were complete. Your own attorney may ask you additional questions to clear up the confusion, but don't count on it. Note that if the opposing attorney is successful, he or she may have destroyed you and your client's case.

Lesson 20: Work with your attorney in the preparation meeting to forestall this counter attack before it starts. Be prepared to show that you are an expert

Lesson 21: Be prepared to explain why you are sufficiently qualified to be classified by the court as an expert in the specific case at hand

051 Finally, you will be asked to present your findings. Your preparation will have included your absorption of the evidence available to you, absorption of the details of your analysis, absorption of your final report, and absorption of the text of the deposition you gave. Be totally prepared on all details in these four pivotal data sets.

052 Your attorney will normally ask to meet with you a few days before trial. If not, seek him or her out. The purpose of the meeting is to have each prepare the other for trial. Your attorney may have his or her questions for you already written out. Help refine them. Your attorney will need to know what opinions you will express and what you will not. Will you say the product was (or was not) defective? Will you say the designer was (or was not) negligent? What specifically are your proofs?

053 You will need from your attorney at least the following:

1. A refresher course in what your attorney wants to prove;
2. The specifics of what the opposing attorney will want to prove;
3. What questions you should expect from the other attorney;
4. How your testimony will fit into the presentation;
5. What if any changes have occurred in the background information or testimony by others since you last talked.

Lesson 22: In preparation for court, never memorise answers but fully understand your opinions and the logic on which they are based

Lesson 23: Know yourself, and know your opposition

Lesson 24: Be a firm and confident proponent of your final opinion

054 One of the fundamental characteristics of being an expert witness is that you are a target; you will be attacked. Your integrity will be questioned in public. You will be told you are wrong. Very competent people will try to prove just that, with varying degrees of success.

055 Most engineers live a very sheltered life. They design things that don't fall down. The neighbours respect them for their competence. Their major concerns in life are doing good work, being honest, collecting their bills, and not getting sued.

056 If one of their buildings ever does collapse, engineers disintegrate, professionally, mentally, and personally. Their lives are shattered. It takes a strong, introspective person to square his or her shoulders, and face the world again when that happens.

057 Being an expert witness has many of the characteristics of facing personal failure. I do not recommend the life for any one who does not tend naturally to be thoroughly prepared.

Lesson 25: Develop a thick skin. Never get angry. Calm down and answer the question confidently, professionally, and helpfully

058 Normally, in giving direct testimony, I like to be allowed to teach the jury. The attorney will ask, "Dr Knott, please tell the jury in your own words what you did to investigate this problem." Then you are off.

059 The other attorney will often object on any basis possible, such as: "Your honour, 'Mr' Knott is going into areas beyond the scope of the question asked. I respectfully request the court to make 'Mr' Knott answer just 'yes or no'." The opposing attorney wants to make your attorney ask all of the questions leading to the proof in law, hoping that he or she will overlook some link that is essential to prove your attorney's case. The opposing attorney wants your attorney and you to bore the jury with the awkwardness of your presentation. You and your attorney have to be prepared to go either route. This gamesmanship is the arena in which a confident, experienced witness is at home. A good attorney and a good witness are a team.

060 After your attorney has brought out the evidence, logic, and proof in support of your opinions, he or she will ask you if you have reached an opinion on the basis of reasonable, scientific probability. Your answer is, "yes, I have". Your attorney will then ask you what it is. You state your opinion to the jury. Your story is now complete.

061 The opposing attorney will then question you to show through well-formulated questions, largely based on your deposition, that you overlooked something, are not telling the truth, that what you said in your deposition is not the same as what you are saying now, and/or you are a paid accomplice of the attorney or client who hired you. If you are fully qualified and have reached sound opinions, the opposing attorney's only area of attack will be: "You are being paid to give the testimony your attorney wants, aren't you?" Your answer is, "I am being paid my normal consulting fee". If he or she asks you your fee, state calmly and confidently what it is. Finally the attorney will finish. Leave the stand with an air of confidence.

Lesson 26: Be professional, courteous, and helpful during cross examination

Lesson 27: Be fundamentally confident in yourself

SHOULD YOU BECOME INVOLVED?

062 Some of my engineering friends have asked why I am involved in court. Somehow, being associated with scheming lawyers, and casting blame on otherwise innocent people, seems to be a degrading occupation. My answer is that I enjoy problem solving; I enjoy debate with good, thoughtful opponents; and the pay is good. That is probably why I stayed in it, once I got started.

063 However, the fundamental reason why you and I should get involved in the presentation of expert testimony is that technology is not understood by lay juries, nor is it understood sufficiently by lawyers and judges. If the truth on engineering subjects is to be found, it must come from engineers. Leaving justice up to the uninformed is not appropriate. The courts have recognised the complexity of the technological problems being litigated. It is for this reason that engineering experts are used.

064 Bringing the truth about technology into court so that a jury can make just decisions is one of the highest callings to which an engineer can aspire. If you are honest with yourself, and are professional, you will be an attribute to the process. Civilisation is built on fairness to others. You will be a gladiator in that arena. (But you will often find yourself up to your neck in lions.)

Albert W Knott *of the Knott Laboratory, Inc., Denver, Colorado, is a specialist in structural and mechanical failure analysis and accident reconstruction.*

This article first appeared in Forensic Engineering, *Vol. 1, 1987, pp. 7–16, and was reproduced in* Arbitration, *May 1993, when Dr Knott confirmed that the paper did not require updating. It is now replicated by kind permission of Pergamon Press's successors Elsevier Science.*

Lesson 26: Be professional, courteous, and helpful during cross-examination.

Lesson 27: Be fundamentally confident in yourself.

[illegible]

CHAPTER 1/3

INDEPENDENCE, PARTISANSHIP AND THE CONTENT OF EXPERT EVIDENCE

Andrew Bartlett

001 It is possible for there to be differing views on the quality of expert witnesses. Reference to an "Academy of Experts" conjures up a lofty image of august and olympian figures qualified to make infallible pronouncements on even the most arcane subjects. At the opposite end of the spectrum, a consultant, referring to forensic scientific witnesses, was recently reported as saying: "There are a lot of people out there talking rubbish" (*The Independent*, 9 September 1994). Most often the truth is somewhere between the two. Most expert witnesses are busy professional people, working under pressure, trying to do their very best, but without any claim to infallibility.

002 Party-appointed experts have an important role to play in litigation and arbitration, that is, in helping to achieve just resolutions of disputes and the attainment of justice. This function requires high standards of conduct, which reduce so far as possible the effects of human fallibility. The promotion of high standards is not helped by unrealistic idealism concerning the role of experts. High standards need to be built on firm foundations, not on unsustainable myths.

NOT FULLY INDEPENDENT

003 The chief unsustainable myth is the complete independence of the expert. There is an idealistic point of view which sees the expert witness as a wholly dispassionate and independent outsider, whose function is to assist the court by offering a reliable and scientific opinion which is totally objective and free of bias.

004 In the legal context the well-known *dictum* of Lord Wilberforce on this topic is more quoted than any other. He stated that expert evidence "should be, and should be seen to be, the independent product of the expert, uninfluenced as to form or content by the exigencies of litigation" (*Whitehouse* v. *Jordan* [1981] 1 WLR 246, 256). This *dictum* has frequently been quoted in articles and lectures, and by judges in subsequent cases. Read too literally, it is incorrect and misleading. It should be understood in its context. In *Whitehouse* v. *Jordan* there were special circumstances concerning the preparation of the experts' reports to which a number of the judges involved in the case took exception. In practice—as everyone involved in litigation or arbitration knows—the *dictum* is honoured more in the breach than in the observance. It would be more satisfactory if the courts were to grasp the nettle and say that the *dictum* is wrong. They would be free to take this course. It was an *obiter dictum*, not necessary for the decision in the case, and therefore not binding in law. In their Lordships' opinions only Lord Fraser expressed agreement with it. Lords Edmund-Davies, Russell and Bridge did not associate themselves with it.

005 Such entirely independent evidence exists only in never-never land. Judges and arbitrators make the difficult task of judging yet more difficult if they pretend that the evidence of reputable experts is as independent as Lord Wilberforce suggested it should be. This idealistic view ignores the practical context in which the expert comes to give evidence to the court. The expert is often not independent, but is appointed by one party. From the very nature of the appointment, he or she is, in a certain sense, partisan, having been engaged by one side to help that side. Pursuant to the appointment, the expert generally fulfils a variety of roles:

- *candid adviser*, expressing frank and possibly adverse opinions to the client,
- *hired gun*, whether in negotiations with the opposing party's expert, or supplying to counsel material with which to shoot down the opposing expert in cross-examination, and
- in writing reports, *justifier or defender* of those parts of the client's case that can properly be justified or defended.

006 Experts are paid by their clients to fulfil these roles, and they often work as part of a team consisting of the clients, the experts, and the lawyers: a team with a common objective of advancing the client's case. When people work in a team, it is normal for team spirit to develop.

007 Giving evidence at trial, experts become professional witnesses, sworn to tell the truth. It is unrealistic to suppose that at trial the experts (however hard they try) can shake off entirely their former roles so as to become wholly independent and perfectly impartial.

008 Dr Knott, an engineer in Colorado, illustrates the insidiousness even of *unconscious* bias by reference to a psychology experiment conducted at a university:

> "... A professor in psychology divided his class into two groups to conduct parallel opinion polls. He met with the first group, passed out packets of photographs of people, and asked the students to go to the *even*-numbered houses in a section of town, knock on the door, and ask the respondent if the pictures were of *successful* or *unsuccessful* people. The professor confided to the group that, oddly enough, people are basically *optimists* and that they would find that statistically respondents would be found to answer that the photos were of *successful* people. He sent them out to conduct the poll.
>
> He then met with the other half of the class, sent them to the *odd*-numbered houses in the same neighbourhood but told them that, oddly enough, people were generally *pessimistic* these days, and that they would find that the majority of the respondents would conclude that the pictures were generally of *unsuccessful* people. He sent the second group out.
>
> The class reassembled, compared their results, and found, generally 60 to 40, that their responses matched the special biases the professor had suggested. The first group got 60/40 for *successful* people, and the second got 60/40 for *unsuccessful* people.
>
> The class discussed how they could have got such results. They concluded that something about the way they had asked the questions must have biased the homeowners to respond in accordance with the bias of the poll taker ...".
>
> Dr Albert W Knott, "Are you an expert?" (1993) 59, JCI Arb 2–111, 113.
> (Reproduced in this book as Chapter 1/2; see paras 1/2–023 to 1/2–026 above.)

009 If unconscious bias can operate in such circumstances, how much more is it likely that an expert witness will be unconsciously biased in favour of his client, who remains his paymaster and (perhaps) his friend?

010 It is better to recognise the reality that experts are not likely to be entirely independent or unbiased. A 1967 *dictum* of Cross J accepted that experts are only human and can hardly avoid having some faint desire that their side should win—simply because it is their side (referred to in the JUSTICE report *Science and the Administration of Justice*: see the article by A Shilston at (1992) 58, JCI Arb 4–251, 256). In the real world the expert's evidence will rarely be exactly the same as it would be if acting for the other side. The closer it is, the stronger it is likely to be. But there will be the inevitable and insidious influence of having approached the problem from the client's side.

011 This is not to suggest that the expert's evidence will not be honest. There are always different ways of expressing facts and ideas, and there are often ranges of legitimate opinions on a given set of facts. But the expert's choice of words and formation of opinions will inevitably be influenced by the one-sided nature of the expert's appointment. The expert is not truly independent.

IF NOT FULLY INDEPENDENT, HOW PARTISAN CAN OR SHOULD THE EXPERT BE?

"Partisan"?

012 "Partisan", as defined in *Chambers' English Dictionary*, means an adherent of a party, especially "a blind or unreasoning adherent". For experts to be partisan in the latter sense is as improper as it is unwise. Even if experts are engaged by one party, it is vital that they remain open-minded and reasonable.

Influenced by the needs of the litigation?

013 Despite Lord Wilberforce's *dictum*, it is permissible, and indeed usual, for the input given by experts to be influenced by the needs of the litigation *in certain respects*. At the very least it must be directed to the particular issues on which the evidence is required. (This is implicitly recognised by rule 35.7(1) of the Civil Procedure Rules which is predicated on the understanding that expert evidence relates only to particular issues in the case.) In some circumstances it may be disastrous for the client if the expert's report is "the independent product of the expert, uninfluenced as to form or content by the exigencies of litigation". Such a report may raise points which have nothing to do with the pleaded case and which provoke a different and damaging claim to be made against the client.

014 That experts' reports ought not to be influenced by the needs of the litigation is unsustainable myth number two. Of course the content of experts' evidence and reports must not be determined by the need to win the litigation. Of course they must not be dishonestly or recklessly devised, slanted, or "massaged" for the purpose of supporting the client's case. Of course the substance of the experts' views must not be modified to suit the client. But, within the limits of propriety, an expert witness is entitled, and ought, to receive guidance from the party's legal advisers as to the form and content of his written evidence, so that it is suitable for the needs of the litigation.

015 The proper contents of such guidance are discussed in the Appendix to this chapter below.

Propriety, as a limit on the duty to the client

016 In *Polivitte Ltd* v. *Commercial Union Assurance Co plc* [1987] 1 Lloyd's Rep 379, 386, Garland J made the somewhat Delphic statement:

> "I have almost considered the role of an expert to be two-fold: first to advance the case of the party calling him, so far as it can properly be advanced on the basis of information available to the expert in the professional exercise of his skill and experience; and, secondly, to assist the court, which does not possess the relevant skill and experience, in determining where the truth lies."

017 The word "almost" was well chosen. Everyone concerned in litigation knows that the purpose of employing an expert is to advance the case of the party calling him. Humphrey LLoyd QC (now one of the judges of the Technology and Construction Court) is on record as having pointed out that in reality "opinion evidence is presented to assist a party rather than the Court" ("Clarifying the Role of Experts in the Courtroom", *Building*, 13 October 1989). Yet if that purpose is baldly stated, without suitable qualification, it gives an incorrect impression of the expert's true role and duties, which require a degree of objectivity and the exercise of independent professional judgement, and above all, propriety. The expert only advances the case of the party calling him as far as that can with propriety be done.

018 The additional concept of "assisting the court" is a noble one, but is not necessarily the most helpful analysis for the purpose of giving experts practical guidance as to their duties. The concept of a duty to the court can be misunderstood. It can tend to take on a life of its own, and make an expert witness feel that he is "piggy-in-the-middle", being pulled in different directions, owing conflicting duties to client and to court, and in difficulty knowing which should prevail in particular situations. As a concept it serves unnecessarily to create an uncomfortable antithesis. Rule 35.3 of the Civil Procedure Rules seeks to resolve the conflict in the most direct fashion, stating:

> "(1) It is the duty of an expert to help the court on the matters within his expertise. (2) This duty overrides any obligation to the person from whom he has received instructions or by whom he is paid."

019 There is another way of looking at this problem. Joseph Molony, QC (a leading advocate and former chairman of the Bar Council) wrote a now famous letter to *The Times* in which he took issue with the concept that expert witnesses have an overriding duty to the court. In his view there was not such a duty. He wrote:

> "The only duty of expert witnesses that I know of is to answer the questions they are asked truthfully and in accordance with their knowledge of the facts, combined with their experience and understanding of the subject. A supplementary duty, I would say, is not to allow to pass any apparent misunderstanding of their evidence which the court or either advocate may entertain."
>
> *The Times*, 28 October 1966 (conveniently reprinted at (1992) 58, JCI Arb 4–257).

020 For the purpose of deciding what to do in borderline situations, it can be more helpful for experts to think of themselves as having only one duty, which is the duty to serve their clients—but only within the limits of proper behaviour. The most important feature of the expert's "duty to the court" is that the expert is required to conform to proper standards of behaviour. What matters is not the idea of the duty, but the requirement of proper behaviour. Propriety can therefore be seen as a limiting factor which helps define the duty to the client. Part of the definition of the duty to the client is that the duty can never in any circumstances oblige the expert to engage in unethical or dishonest behaviour. Adopting this analysis, there is no collision between conflicting duties, and no undue difficulty in making practical decisions.

021 If a yet clearer limit is needed, expert witnesses are unlikely to go wrong if they are guided at all times by the ninth of the Ten Commandments: "You shall not give false testimony".

022 Thus experts can hardly avoid being partisan, in the sense that they are employed to assist their clients, but they must not be partisan if that means acting other than with integrity, probity, and honesty.

Not acting as an advocate

023 "An expert witness in the High Court should never assume the role of an advocate" (*National Justice Compania Naviera SA* v. *Prudential Assurance Company Ltd (The Ikarian Reefer)* [1993] 2 Lloyd's Rep 68, 81 *per* Cresswell J). It is one thing to write a report and give honest evidence with a view to assisting the client and advancing the client's case. It is quite another to adopt the role of advocate.

024 An expert who descends into the arena as a combatant invites personal attack. This happened in *University of Warwick* v. *Sir Robert McAlpine*, where "counsel felt it necessary to challenge not only the reliability but also the credibility of experts with unadorned attacks on their veracity". As the judge said, "This simply should not happen where the court is called upon to decide complex scientific or technical issues" ((1988) 42 BLR 1, 22–23, *per* Garland J).

025 To seek to advance the client's case by giving expert evidence is not the same as promoting it as an advocate. There is a critical difference. An advocate argues the client's case *irrespective of the advocate's personal beliefs as to whether it is well-founded or not.* Barristers or other advocates must not interpose their own judgement between their clients and the court: it is for the court to judge. Hence the duty of barristers to defend those whom they privately believe may well be guilty. In contrast, expert witnesses must put forward only *their own genuinely-held views*. This is the true meaning of the independence of the expert. It is an independence of mind and of judgement. The expert is not a mouthpiece for the client.

Criminal cases

026 The above remarks would need some further qualification in criminal cases. The duty of the prosecution side in a criminal case is not to secure a conviction come what may, but is to place the facts before the jury so that they may decide on the guilt of the accused. Moreover, there is a different burden of proof in criminal cases. In a civil case the court determines the facts in accordance with the balance of probabilities. An expert giving an opinion in a criminal case is doing so in a different context, where the court is concerned not with probabilities but with whether there is certainty or doubt, since criminal charges must be proved beyond a reasonable doubt.

SOME PRACTICAL PROBLEMS

The tension that arises from the experts' varying roles

027 Experts move from being candid advisers, hired guns and justifiers to being professional witnesses, sworn to tell the truth. Although their position is far from independent, and they are under obligation to assist their clients, they must attempt to exercise independent and objective professional judgement.

028 There is often tension here. But there are ways in which it can be reduced:

(1) By being courageously candid with the client from the start. If there are defects in the client's case, it is best to say so plainly and at the first opportunity, so that these can be considered and taken into account. Then, if the case goes to court, experts should never find themselves in the witness box trying to defend the indefensible.

(2) By being open-minded and thoughtful. The expert should consider very carefully the opposing side's point of view. It is not good enough merely to think of arguments to counter it. It must be fully understood and acknowledged. The expert should not be blind and unreasoning but perceptive and reasonable.

(3) By remembering that it is self-defeating to be too opinionated. The opinionated expert is a gift to the opposing side, since such evidence will carry little weight with the tribunal. Therefore part of the expert's duty, for the purpose of assisting the client, is to strive for objectivity.

The problem of omissions

029 What can properly be omitted from the report or from the expert's oral evidence? This is one of the thorniest questions that can arise.

030 Sometimes there are known facts which tend to weigh against the opinion that the expert has formed and the question arises whether these should be omitted from the report. In *The Ikarian Reefer* Cresswell J said that the expert's report should state facts or assumptions on which his opinion was based, together with material facts which could detract from the concluded opinion. This is clearly right. If the expert's opinion is to carry proper weight he must show that he has already taken account of all facts which might tend to weaken his stated conclusions on the issues with which his report is concerned.

031 A more difficult situation arises where there are matters which might be used against the interests of the expert's client, but which are not directly relevant to the pleaded issues. Should these be included in the report? Stated shortly, the traditional position is that there is no duty to include such matters. This is examined more fully in the Appendix below.

032 Nevertheless, while in principle it is legitimate to exclude unfavourable matter by confining the report strictly to the issues raised on the pleadings, an expert witness must not mislead by omission (see *per* Cazalet J in *In re J (a Minor) (Expert Evidence)* [1990] TLR 568). It is therefore necessary, when something is omitted, carefully to avoid forms of expression which may be misinterpreted as carrying undue implications of a favourable view on a matter not expressly dealt with. Misleading selectivity must be avoided: *Cala Homes (South) Ltd* v. *Alfred McAlpine Homes East Ltd* [1995] FSR 818; [1995] CILL 1083.

033 It is important to remember also that the line dividing legitimate from illegitimate omissions is one that may depend on the character of the litigation. Where the proceedings are of an inquisitorial character, the expert's duty to disclose unfavourable material may be a higher one. The foremost example is wardship proceedings, where the interests of any adult parties are made subject to the paramountcy of the welfare of the child. In such cases there are no pleadings to limit the issues; the task of the experts is to assist the court as best they can in a straightforward and objective manner, and they certainly must not omit to mention any factor which does not support their opinion: *In re J (a Minor) (Expert Evidence)* [1990] TLR 568.

034 Evidence given in court or in an arbitration is normally sworn evidence. The witness swears, or solemnly affirms, that his evidence will be "the truth, the whole truth, and nothing but the truth". It is important to appreciate that this does not mean what at first sight it appears to mean. One of the first things a young policeman learns about giving evidence in court is that the very last thing he must do is to tell the whole truth. If he mentions an accused's previous convictions, this usually results in the trial being aborted, the jury discharged, and public money wasted, and he incurs the wrath both of the judge and of his superiors. The witness's answers must be given within the framework of the law of evidence (which excludes much information that common sense would suggest is relevant) and, in a civil case, within the framework of the pleadings (which define the issues to be addressed by the evidence).

035 In *Derby* v. *Weldon (No 9)*, Staughton LJ said: "I do not think that an expert witness, or any other witness, obliges himself to volunteer his views on every issue in the whole case when he takes an oath to tell the whole truth. What he does oblige himself to do is to tell the whole truth about those matters which he is asked about". (This passage in the judgment of Staughton LJ is cited by Simon Carne, (1994) *The Expert* Vol. 1, No. 3, p. 24. It is not included in the shortened *Times* newspaper report, [1990] TLR 712.)

036 Judge Newey wrote in a textbook in 1989: "... since the procedure in both courts and arbitrations is adversarial, an expert is not obliged to speak out, or write in his report, about matters concerning which he has not been asked ..." (*Construction Disputes: Liability and the Expert Witness*, ed. Andrea Burns, Butterworth & Co (Publishers) Ltd (1989) p. 241).

037 The problem of omissions was less acute when it was understood that experts' reports should not cover anything beyond the pleaded issues, and the experts' promise to tell the truth in their oral evidence applied only to those matters which they were asked about. How far the new Civil Procedure Rules have altered this situation remains to be seen.

What if experts change their minds?

038 A candidate for pupillage in my chambers was asked in interview how he would handle a situation where the expert came to him in court as the case was about to start and said he had changed his mind about a critical matter. The interviewee said he would tell him firmly to "get into that witness box and lie, lie, lie". Needless to say, his application for pupillage was unsuccessful.

039 A recent judicial *dictum* proposed: "If after exchange of reports, an expert witness changes his mind on a material matter, then the change of view should be communicated to the other side through legal representatives without delay and, when appropriate, to the court" (*The Ikarian Reefer* [1993] 2 Lloyd's Rep 68, 82, *per* Cresswell J).

040 This *dictum*, although approved *obiter* by the Court of Appeal ([1995] 1 Lloyd's Rep 455, 496), surely requires qualification. The judge's choice of words may have been influenced by the large amount of court time that had been wasted in the particular case on expert evidence which ultimately proved to be irrelevant and useless. The duty of the legal representatives is more complex than appears to be suggested. The *dictum* has been forcefully and convincingly criticised in an article by a highly respected and very experienced solicitor (see Michael Ludlow's excellent article "The independent expert" (1993) 59, JCI Arb 4–231 at 234). Commonly it will be the duty of the lawyers to seek clarification or a second opinion before making any communication to the other side.

041 If the expert changes his view, it may be that he is entitled to communicate the change to the other side without first informing his client (this was the view of Otton LJ in *Stanton* v. *Callaghan* [1998] 4 All ER 961). Whether that is right or not, the wiser course is for him to tell the lawyers on his side, and tell them promptly. It will then be for the lawyers to decide what is proper to be done. It is their duty to give him proper guidance. There can be considerable difficulties in knowing what is the proper course to follow, as illustrated by *Vernon* v. *Bosley (No. 2)* [1997] 1 All ER 614, where counsel acted in accordance with advice received from the Bar Council, and was supported by one member of the Court of Appeal while being criticised by two members of the Court.

***Andrew Bartlett** was called to the Bar in 1974 and was appointed a QC in 1993. He practices from One Paper Buildings (Temple, London EC4). His principal fields of work at the Bar are building and civil engineering, professional negligence, insurance and reinsurance, and product liability. Active as an arbitrator since 1991, he is a member of the London Court of International Arbitration and is on the arbitration panel of the Chartered Institute of Arbitrators. He is the General Editor of* Emden's Construction Law *(Butterworths).*

APPENDIX: GUIDANCE ON THE FORM AND CONTENTS OF EXPERTS' REPORTS

(The following material first appeared in its original form in *Counsel* magazine October 1993 and November/December 1993. It is reproduced by kind permission of the publishers. A few changes have been made in the light of the Civil Procedure Rules introduced as part of the Woolf reforms.)

The *form* of an expert's report should not be left to chance, or to the personal views of the expert. Some experts are well versed in legal matters and have experience of what is required. But many, while true experts in their own fields, will have had no practical experience of litigation, and will need detailed guidance as to a suitable form for their report. If justice is to be done to the client's case, the lawyers' duty is to ensure that the report is in a form which the judge or arbitrator will find helpful and easy to follow. If it is not in such a form, time and costs may be wasted, and the client's case may be unfairly prejudiced. Experts inexperienced in litigation may not be aware of many matters which to a litigation lawyer would seem obvious. For example:

- the report should be dated and signed;
- there should be a table of contents at the beginning;
- the report should commence with an introduction of the author, and his CV should be contained either in the introduction or in an appendix;
- the report should be clearly laid out, preferably in short numbered paragraphs;
- the contents should be presented in a logical order, broken down into whatever separate sections are appropriate for the particular case, covering matters such as background facts, explanation of technical concepts, discussion of the material issues, and conclusions;
- supporting items such as calculation sheets, test results and the like should be contained in appendices;
- the report should be consecutively paginated throughout (including the appendices);
- any photographs contained in the report should be properly reproduced (black and white photocopies are generally useless).

The *Practice Direction* issued to supplement Part 35 of the Civil Procedure Rules also requires that the report be addressed to the court and not to the party from whom the expert has received his instructions. It must say at the end that the expert understands and has complied with his overriding duty to help the court on the matters within his expertise, and it must be verified by the statement: "I believe that the facts I have stated in this report are true and that the opinions I have expressed are correct".

In relation also to the *content* of experts' reports, the lawyers have very important functions to perform. The lawyers should vet the report to ensure that it contains, and contains only, the material that it ought to contain:

1 *Does it clearly indicate the scope of the expert's remit?* The expert should state exactly what he has been asked to report on by indicating the nature of his terms of reference.
2 *Does it adequately identify the material on which it is based?* Differences of opinion between experts often stem from their having been given different facts or assumptions to work from. If the tribunal is to weigh conflicting opinions from different experts it is vital for it to know the factual basis of each opinion (cf. the remarks of Cresswell J in *National Justice Compania Naviera SA* v. *Prudential Assurance Company Ltd (The Ikarian Reefer)* [1993] 2 Lloyd's Rep 68). To comply with the CPR *Practice Direction*, the report must contain a statement setting out the substance of all material instructions (whether written or oral), including a summary of the facts material to the opinions expressed. It must also give details of any literature or other material which the expert has relied on in making the report.
3 *Is it properly researched?* If the data available to the expert are insufficient for him to be confident of his opinion, he should indicate the areas of uncertainty and state explicitly that his opinion is provisional (*In re J* [1990] TLR 568, *The Ikarian Reefer, supra*). Where there is a

range of opinion on the matters dealt with in the report, the CPR *Practice Direction* requires the expert to summarise the range of opinion and give reasons for his own view.

4 *Does the report properly acknowledge the limits of the writer's expertise?* Experts should make clear the extent to which questions considered by them fall within their special expertise. Reports which incorporated argument or comment on facts outside the expert's own field have provoked adverse reaction from the court (*Polivitte Ltd* v. *Commercial Union Assurance Co plc* [1987] 1 Lloyd's Rep 379, 387; *The Ikarian Reefer, supra*). But it is sometimes necessary for an expert to consider wider matters. The Court of Appeal in *The Ikarian Reefer* [1995] 1 Lloyd's Rep. 455, 496 pointed out that it is not always possible to confine an expert to his own area of expertise. For example, an experienced fire expert, when he is assessing the significance of certain evidence, must be entitled to weigh the probabilities and this may involve making use of the skills of other experts or drawing on his general mechanical or chemical knowledge.

5 *Is the report dependent on the research or opinions of others?* Where the report is that of a leader of a team of investigators or research assistants who have acted under his direction or control, it may be sufficient if that fact is merely stated. But in general, if a report contains evidence or expertise contributed by persons other than its apparent author, then those persons and their contributions should be identified so that at the very least they can be tendered for cross-examination (*University of Warwick* v. *Sir Robert McAlpine* (1988) 42 BLR 1, 23). For use in court, the report must say who carried out any test or experiment used for the report, stating their qualifications, and whether they acted under the expert's own supervision.

6 *Has there been any change of view by the expert which requires explanation?* Sometimes experts express one view in experts' meetings or in reports and subsequently change their minds and express a different opinion. Where this occurs, it should be dealt with in their latest report, giving any necessary explanations. Otherwise they may lay themselves open to damaging cross-examination upon their inconsistencies (*University of Warwick, supra*).

7 *Does the report go too far in usurping the role of the judge?* This is a difficult and delicate matter. The traditional wisdom was that in no case was it competent for the expert to express his opinion upon any of the issues, whether of law or fact, which the judge had to determine: see *per* Neville J in *Crosfield & Sons* v. *Techno-Chemical Laboratories Ltd* (1913) 29 TLR 379, which was still cited more than 80 years later in the *Supreme Court Practice 1997*. But times have changed, as has the law of evidence. Expert opinion on an issue in the proceedings was made admissible by section 3 of the Civil Evidence Act 1972. In a professional negligence case it is impossible for the expert to state his opinion without expressing a view on the very issue of negligence that the judge has to decide. Indeed, in *Whitehouse* v. *Jordan, supra*, counsel appear to have been criticised for *deleting* a passage in a report where the expert stated expressly that there had been no negligence (see the report of the proceedings in the Court of Appeal [1980] 1 All ER 650, 655f-g). Nevertheless, judicial sensitivities remain. It is still advisable for the expert to tread warily, and, if he can, to avoid giving the appearance of trespassing unduly into the province of the judge. Even in a professional negligence case, it may be wise for him, instead of saying (for example) "the defendant was negligent", to say "in my opinion the defendant adopted a course which no skilled practitioner acting carefully would have adopted".

8 *Do the words of the report truly reflect the expert's views?* This may seem at first sight an odd question, but engineers, scientists, doctors and other experts are not always accomplished craftsmen with words. It can happen that particular words or phrases which the expert has used in his draft report, when carefully examined, are ambiguous, or do not accurately reflect his real views, but carry unintended meanings or erroneous implications. To the expert the word "possible" may denote something that is more likely than not, or something that is possible but unlikely. When proof of a fact depends on the balance of probabilities, the difference between these shades of meaning becomes fundamental. Such words or phrases should be amended in debate between the lawyers and the expert until both are satisfied that the written words accurately convey the expert's true opinion.

9 *Does the report adequately cover the pleaded allegations?* This is particularly likely to be a problem in complex cases. It is unfair to leave it to the expert to guess which allegations

made in the pleadings he ought to comment on. The lawyers know which allegations are for this expert to deal with, which for another, and which will be matters solely for factual evidence or legal argument. It is important that solicitors or counsel check that every allegation that ought to be dealt with by the expert is clearly covered in the report.

10 *What omissions from the report are legitimate?* The former Rules of the Supreme Court (RSC Order 38, rule 37(1) and Order 25, rule 8(1)(b)) provided for the disclosure of "the substance" of the evidence of an expert whom a party proposes to call. In *Kenning* v. *Eve Construction Ltd* [1989] 1 WLR 1189 an engineer, asked by the defendants to report on an accident, wrote a report refuting the allegations of negligence pleaded in the Statement of Claim. In a separate letter he drew attention to two points, which were not covered in the Statement of Claim or in his report, on which he considered the defendants were at fault. By mistake the defendants' solicitors sent off not merely the report but also the letter, which was greeted with some interest, not to say glee, by the plaintiff's solicitors when they received it. The defendants sought to prevent the plaintiff relying on the letter. The deputy judge acknowledged that it was a widespread practice that anxieties, qualifications or adverse views expressed by expert witnesses were very often communicated to their instructing solicitors by way of a confidential covering letter. He also acknowledged that the letter was privileged. But he held that, if the defendants wished to call the expert, they must disclose not only his report but also his letter, since otherwise they would not be complying with their obligation to disclose "the substance" of his evidence.

This was a wrong decision. In effect, the deputy judge was misled by the simplicity of the case. He evidently felt that the report, which dealt only with the matters raised by the pleadings, concealed by omission the expert's views on what he called "the overall issue of liability": see [1989] 1 WLR 1189 at 1194. This was an understandable reaction in a simple case, but one only has to consider its application to a complex case for it at once to be exposed as fallacious. Suppose in a building case the plaintiff, based on advice from his own expert, pleads 47 criticisms of various parts of a defective structure. The defendants' expert in the course of his investigation comes upon another 15 items where the defendants may be vulnerable to criticism. What should he say in his report? It is the duty of the defendants' lawyers to tell him that his report should not go beyond the pleaded issues. This is the only logical and practical solution in an adversarial system of justice. The plaintiff may not be aware of the 15 further points, or he may have decided not to pursue them in order to avoid more complication or delay or expense or some adverse reflection on some of the 47 points already pleaded. The defendants' expert should not raise in his report points against his own clients which have not been pleaded. Conversely, the plaintiff's expert's report should cover the allegations that are pleaded, and should not raise any additional criticisms, unless they are to be made the subject of an application to amend. Failure by the plaintiff's lawyers to restrict the contents of the report to issues that are pleaded leads to needless expense and confusion as both the judge and the defendants try to determine which passages in the report are relied upon by the plaintiff in support of the pleaded case and which are to be disregarded as irrelevant. The court's task under the adversarial system is to address the "overall issue of liability" not in the abstract but by considering the particular issues which the parties have chosen to raise on their pleadings.

The Court of Appeal had to consider a related situation in *Derby & Co Ltd* v. *Weldon (No 9)* [1990] TLR 712 (not to be confused with separate decisions in the same litigation, reported under the same name and number in WLR and All ER). In that case the defendants' expert accountant had prepared a report, which had been disclosed, on the plaintiffs' "initial conspiracy" claim. The report did not deal with an "alternative initial conspiracy" which had been introduced into the plaintiffs' pleadings by amendment. The court took the view that the rules for disclosure of expert evidence did not override legal professional privilege. Any report that the accountant might have prepared on the "alternative initial conspiracy" was privileged, and, if the defendants did not wish to adduce evidence from him on that issue, they could not be ordered to disclose any report that he might have made upon it. The court confirmed that *Kenning*, *supra*, was wrongly decided. In the Rules of Court the "substance" of the evidence referred only to the evidence it was *intended* the expert should give at trial; it does not mean all the evidence he *could* give.

The new Civil Procedure Rules make no specific alteration in the law in this respect.

A party does not have to disclose a report that is not going to be relied on. But it remains to be seen what the effect will be of Rule 35.3, which lays down the expert's duty to help the court on the matters within his expertise. Under the previous law, while experts had to give their honest opinions on the matters that they were asked to deal with, they were under no obligation to volunteer evidence on topics that they were not asked to deal with: *Cala Homes (South) Ltd* v. *Alfred McAlpine Homes East Ltd* [1995] FSR 818; [1995] CILL 1083. How far that remains the position may be a matter of debate.

CHAPTER 1/4

INDEPENDENCE, AND USE, OF EXPERT WITNESSES

Nabarro Nathanson

001 There has been much discussion and comment recently about the difficulty of a surveyor acting as an expert witness while representing his client. This is commonplace in rent reviews.

002 In July 1996, Lord Woolf's *Report on Proposed Changes in Civil Litigation Procedures* was published. His proposals covering the use of expert evidence are some of the most far reaching and important in the whole of his Report and have significant impact on rent review arbitrations.

003 The overall intention of the Woolf Report was to make expert witnesses understand clearly that their first duty is to provide an objective, impartial report and that they are not to be influenced by whichever side instructed them. It was recommended that codes of practice, providing guidance as to the practice in relation to expert witnesses, should be drawn up jointly with the appropriate professional bodies representing the expert witnesses and the legal profession.

004 In response, the Royal Institution of Chartered Surveyors (RICS) produced a "practice statement and guidance notes for surveyors acting as expert witnesses", effective from March 1997. (See Appendix C.)

005 The general guiding principles to be followed by an expert witness giving evidence, which the RICS document encompasses, were set out in a case in 1993 (known as *The Ikarian Reefer* (see Chapter 1/5)):

- Expert evidence presented to the court should be, and be seen to be, the independent product of the expert uninfluenced as to form or content by the exigencies of litigation.
- An expert witness should provide independent assistance to the court by way of objective, unbiased opinion in relation to matters within his expertise. An expert witness in the High Court should never assume the role of advocate.
- Expert witnesses should state the facts or assumptions upon which their opinion is based. They should not omit to consider material facts which could detract from their concluded opinion.
- Expert witnesses should make it clear when a particular question or issue falls outside their expertise.
- In cases where an expert witness has prepared a report and could not assert that the report contained the truth, the whole truth and nothing but the truth without some qualification, then that qualification should be stated in the report.

006 Somewhat starkly, around half of those interviewed felt that an expert witness could be independent and represent a client at the same time, while the other half felt that they could not. There is clear polarisation amongst participants on this issue and it is an area where the courts are going to be paying much greater attention in the future.

007 It is a very difficult area. The RICS has very much taken on board the comments of Lord Woolf, and the principles laid down in *The Ikarian Reefer* to produce guidelines that are clear. For example, the document states clearly that it is imperative that its members appreciate that, while an instruction will originate from a particular client, the duty to that client becomes secondary once the surveyor is instructed as an expert witness to produce evidence for a judicial body, such as an arbitrator. This should be made clear to the client at the time. In some cases, the RICS notes, this change of emphasis may not be acceptable to the client and, in such instances, instructions to act should be declined.

008 There is little more that the RICS can do. It is for its members to take on board the message which is now being delivered very forcibly by all concerned with the integrity of the process. This is an education process for the surveying profession and clients alike.

Extract from the publication "What's right and fair?" A Report on Arbitrators/Independent Experts and Commercial Property Rent Review 1997 *reproduced with the kind permission of Nabarro Nathanson, Solicitors.*

CHAPTER 1/5

THE IKARIAN REEFER REVISITED

The Hon Mr Justice Cresswell

001 In *The Ikarian Reefer* [1993] 2 Lloyd's Rep 68 I summarised some of the duties and responsibilities of expert witnesses in civil cases. Since that decision there has been a growing recognition of the need for the courts and the profession to identify in clear terms what is expected of expert witnesses. Expert evidence has a critical function to play in civil and criminal litigation. The interests of justice require that expert witnesses should receive clear guidance as to their duties and responsibilities.

WOOLF REFORMS

002 Lord Woolf's far reaching and visionary reforms reflect the need for clear guidance to expert witnesses. I refer to how such guidance appears in the fifth edition of the *Guide to Commercial Court Practice*. The requirements of Appendix 12 (reproduced as Appendix L of this book) apply in relation to all aspects of expert evidence (including expert reports, meetings of experts and expert evidence given orally) unless the court orders otherwise. Legal representatives are required to ensure that Appendix 12 is at the earliest point drawn to the attention of an expert retained by a party.

GENERAL PROVISIONS

003 The general provisions in Appendix 12 as to expert evidence in cases in the Commercial Court are as follows:

"**1.** It is the duty of an expert to help the court on the matters within his expertise (CPR 35.3(1)). This duty is paramount and overrides any obligation to the person from whom the expert has received instructions or by whom he is paid (CPR 35.3(2)).

2. Expert evidence presented to the court should be, and should be seen to be, the independent product of the expert uninfluenced by the exigencies of litigation.

3. An expert witness should provide independent assistance to the court by way of objective unbiased opinion in relation to matters within his expertise. An expert witness should never assume the role of an advocate.

4. An expert witness should not omit to consider material facts which could detract from his concluded opinion.

5. An expert witness should make it clear when a particular question or issue falls outside his expertise.

6. If an expert's opinion is not properly researched because he considers that insufficient data is available, then this must be stated with an indication that the opinion is no more than a provisional one.

7. In a case where an expert witness who has prepared a report could not assert that the report contained the truth, the whole truth and nothing but the truth without some qualification, that qualification should be stated in the report.

8. If, after exchange of reports, an expert witness changes his view on a material matter having read another expert's report or for any other reason, such change of view should be communicated in writing (through legal representatives) to the other side without delay, and when appropriate to the court."

COMMENT

004 It will be seen from the above that these general provisions reflect what I said in *The Ikarian Reefer.*

REPORTS

005 As to reports, the Guide provides:

"**H2.10** The requirements at paragraphs 1.1 and 1.2 of the practice direction supplementing CPR Part 35 should be followed. Paragraphs 1.3 and 1.4 of the practice direction are addressed at paragraphs H2.14 and H2.15 below.

H2.11 The expert should take care always to state clearly the questions or issues with which he is dealing in his report.

H2.12 In stating the substance of all material instructions on the basis of which his report is written (see CPR 35.10(3) and paragraph 1.2(8) of the practice direction supplementing CPR Part 35) an expert witness should state the facts or assumptions upon which his opinion is based. If any of the facts stated are within his own direct knowledge he should make clear which those are. If a stated assumption is, in the opinion of the expert witness, unreasonable or unlikely he should state that clearly.

H2.13 It is useful if a report contains a glossary of significant technical terms.

H2.14 At the end of the expert's report there must be a statement that:

a. the expert understands his duty to the Court and has complied with that duty (see CPR 35.10(2));
b. the expert has read and understood Appendix 12 to the Commercial Court Guide;
c. he has complied and will continue to comply with Appendix 12 at all stages of his involvement in the case;
d. the assumptions upon which his opinion is based are not in his opinion unreasonable or unlikely assumptions (or, where in his opinion any assumption is unreasonable or unlikely, that is clearly stated);
e. the facts stated in his report that are facts within his own direct knowledge have been identified as such and are true;
f. the opinions expressed in his report represent his true professional opinion.

The report must be signed by the expert."

COMMENT

006 I strongly favour the above. Good practice requires that an expert witness should confirm at the end of his or her report that he/she has read and understood a clear statement from the court as to the duties and responsibilities of expert witnesses and has complied and will continue to comply with the same at all stages of his/her involvement in the case.

MEETINGS

007 As to meetings of experts, the Guide provides:

"**H2.19** A meeting or meetings of expert witnesses before trial will normally be ordered. Sometimes it may be useful for there to be further meetings during the trial itself.

H2.20 The purposes of meetings of experts are to give experts the opportunity:

a. to discuss the expert issues;

b. to decide, with the benefit of that discussion, on which expert issues they share or can come to agree the same expert opinion and on which expert issues there remains a difference of expert opinion between them (and what that difference is).

(In the Commercial Court this description of the purpose of the meetings takes the place of the description at CPR 35.12(1).)

H2.21 Subject to paragraph H2.24 below, the content of the discussion between the experts at or in connection with a meeting is without prejudice, and in particular (in accordance with CPR 35.12(4)) shall not be referred to at the trial unless the parties agree.

H2.22 Subject to any directions of the court, the procedure to be adopted at these meetings is a matter for the experts, not the parties or their legal representatives.

H2.23 Neither the parties nor their legal representatives should seek to restrict the freedom of experts to identify and acknowledge the expert issues on which they agree (i.e. on which they share the same expert opinion) at (or following further consideration after) meetings of experts.

H2.24 At or following their meetings the experts should prepare a joint memorandum for the court recording:

a. the fact that they have met and discussed the expert issues;

b. the expert issues on which they agree (i.e. on which they share the same expert opinion);

c. the expert issues where there is a difference of expert opinion between them, and a summary of what that difference of opinion is.

(In the Commercial Court this automatic requirement applies notwithstanding the court's powers under CPR 35.12(3).)

H2.25 Where experts reach agreement on an expert issue during (or, following further consideration after) their meetings the agreement shall not bind the parties unless the parties expressly agree to be bound by the agreement.

H2.26 Following the preparation of the joint memorandum each expert may prepare a short supplemental report highlighting the reasons why the expert adheres to the views he does on the expert issues recorded in the memorandum as being issues where there is a difference of expert opinion."

COMMENT

008 In the past meetings between experts have not always been as productive as they might be. It is to be hoped that these new provisions will result in meetings of experts proving more productive!

The Hon Mr Justice Cresswell *is a High Court Judge, Queen's Bench Division. As the author of what have become known as the* Ikarian Reefer *Rules, he has been influential in raising experts' standards.*

This article first appeared in The Expert, *Winter/Spring 1999 and is reproduced here with kind permission of The Academy of Experts.*

CHAPTER 1/6

TO WHOM DOES THE EXPERT OWE A DUTY?

Michael Chapman

001 The ambiguity of the role of the expert witness has been the subject of some comment over the years. Unfortunately whilst there has been comment there seems to have been little debate, more the repeating of entrenched opinions.

002 There is an aphorism that "when two learned schools of thought reach conclusions that are apparently contradictory, then it is usually the case that they are both wrong, or both right". In the present situation the differences undoubtedly originate from the point of view of their authors. The danger is when a statement that may be reasonable in context becomes transposed out of that context as a universal truism.

003 Anthony Speaight ("Expert Evidence—Seven Pillars of Wisdom, but are they sound?", (1996) 62, JCIArb 4–269–271) referred to the "unresolved contradictions in the role of the expert in litigation". Four years previously Alan Shilston ("Some Reflections on the Role of the Expert Witness", (1992) 58, JCIArb 4–251–258) had stated "the role of the expert witness in Anglo-Saxon common law jurisdictions remains ambiguous".

004 However there seems to be a growing mood that somehow the expert witness is the servant of the court, or even society at large. If this is the *one* aspect of continental (European) expertise to be imported into England it would be a pity. Expertise is a wider concept than the work of expert witnesses. It is too easy to confuse the role of the expert and that of the expert witness, or if not confuse, then at least to mix their respective duties. The Association of European Recognised Experts (AEXEA) has published a proposed *Professional Ethics of a European Expert*. (AEXEA is the *Association des Experts Européens Agrés*, c/o Michèle Agrapart-Delmas, 28 Rue du Château, 77000 Melun, France. It published the proposed *Professional Ethics of a European Expert* in a six language edition by the author Dr Michel Olivier.) Article 2.2.3 of this document suggests that "an expert is not anybody's agent or representative. He should be devoted not to a party, but only to the truth and *work for the benefit of all*" (emphasis added).

005 Shilston (*op. cit.*) commented on and reproduced a letter of the late Sir Joseph Molony QC, published in *The Times* of 28 October 1966 ("the only duty of expert witnesses that I know is to answer the questions they are asked truthfully and in accordance with their knowledge of the facts, combined with their experience and understanding of the subject . . ."). He referred to Molony's letter as a "beacon", in particular noting that there had been no follow-up correspondence, and mindful "that as most members of the Bar (and the judiciary) probably read *The Times*, I assumed that the renowned (Sir) Joseph Molony, who from his obituary notices in *The Times* was said to be a man of great learning and towering intellectual powers, had very probably stated the position correctly".

006 The present author waited with interest to see if there would be any argument against

Molony's thesis, but saw none. The editor of *Arbitration* (JCIArb, Shilston) also reported that there was none (*pers. comm.*). Molony's position was cited in the pages of the *Journal of the Royal Society of Medicine* in response to a discussion on expert witnesses (Chapman, 1994, *JRSM*, 87(3), 186). The only commentary received on the latter was a verbal "ticking off" by an elderly member of the Bar who told the author he was "totally wrong" but did not have the time to explain why. He never found the time subsequently.

007 Andrew Bartlett in a fascinating talk (reproduced in *The Expert* as "Independence and Partisanship" and in this book as Chapter 1/3) in September 1994, went over much of the same ground in a far more thorough way than this present note. He is quite trenchant in suggesting that "even Homer may nod" and that judicial opinions (many of them in any event *obiter dicta*) might be wrong, or that in one difficult case "a number of the judges ... over-reacted". He describes the "chief unsustainable myth [as] the complete independence of the expert". When first published the journal's editor was moved to write "his approach is based on reality and, however uncomfortable, his arguments need to be developed rather than rejected".

008 To ensure that there had been no lost chance for a debate, much of the above history was repeated in a postscript to an article in *Arbitration* (Chapman (1997) 63, JCIArb 2–141) concluding with the statement:

> "So is the 'unambiguous view' anything more than the outpouring of overworked lecturers at law schools which has gathered credence by frequent repetition? I would hope it has a greater intellectual foundation. If so would somebody please 'come out' and state what it is? Otherwise I fear I, for one, am tempted to characterise the Law Society's *Code of Practice: Expert Witnesses engaged by Solicitors* as being 'motherhood and apple pie' when it states 'When giving evidence at court the role of ... an expert witness, is to assist the court ...'"

009 Sir Joseph Molony's argument (as reproduced in 58, JCIArb 4–25) was in reply to a letter from the MP S C Silkin, QC. Molony wrote:

> "'There will be widespread agreement with your leader', writes Mr S C Silkin, QC, MP (25 October 1966) claiming to interpret the reaction of barristers to your criticism of the decision of the Court of Appeal in *Rondel* v. *Worsley*. I would say the contrary, and that there is general approval of the judgement and endorsement of the reasoning underlying it.
>
> However, this is a matter of opinion. When Mr Silkin proceeds to discuss the implications of the judgement, he advances some strange contentions in support of his disapproval. He says that 'professional men acting as expert witnesses ... have an overriding duty to the court and to justice'.
>
> What is the authority for this proposition? The only duty of expert witnesses that I know of is to answer the questions they are asked truthfully and in accordance with their knowledge of the facts, combined with their experience and understanding of the subject. A supplementary duty, I would say, is not to allow to pass any apparent misunderstanding of their evidence which the court or either advocate may entertain. This latter duty is shared with all witnesses but the professionally qualified witness should be better able to recognise the occasion when it arises.
>
> Mr Silkin then asks two long forensic questions, which proceed on the assumption that professional witnesses and advocates owe a *duty to the court* to be competent and that the Barrister's exemption from liability to his client is coterminous with breach of duty *to the court*. These are completely fallacious propositions."

010 The recent work of Lord Woolf has reopened these issues, though in his main report (Chapter 13, "Expert Evidence", reproduced as Appendix A/1 of this book) there seems little acknowledgement of views such as those traced here. He does suggest "experts would welcome some formal recognition of their role as advisers to the court rather than advocates of the parties" (paragraph 28) and "expert witnesses need a basic understanding of the legal system and their roles within it" (paragraph 54). Respectfully, I disagree. It would obviously be extreme to suggest that a totally (forensically) naïve witness is the ideal. But, if the witness's duty is just to answer questions (whether orally or in a report) about his area of expertise, why should he need to know anything about the system within which his answers are to be used? (Bartlett, *op. cit.*, gives some good answers to that point.)

011 Recent court cases seem to have followed this line rather than refined the argument (e.g. *Stanton* v. *Callaghan*, which, though very supportive of experts on liability, does so on the basis of an overriding duty to the court).

012 One example from my own experience is a situation where I found I could not "help the court". Despite repeated pressure from the bench I held to my opinion that on the basis of the facts relating to one of the matters in dispute, it was my opinion that neither I nor any similarly experienced professional could come to a useful opinion. Courts, it has perhaps unfairly been said, "pick winners". A court-appointed expert may find himself having to do what is familiar to anyone who has sat as an arbitrator: having to "choose" one or the other. A party's expert has undoubtedly to decide, but his decision is not restricted to a binary one.

013 Present suggestions are obviously not that extreme, but they might leave the expert betwixt Bartlett's "justifier or defender" and a full "decider" (for a discussion of the latter see Chapman (1997) 63, JCIArb 138–144). How should an expert who feels it is his duty to assist the court give evidence in a child abuse case? To protect the child, in the interests of society, he could say the child should have weighed half as much again. Looking paternalistically on a young mother who has erred, but about whose future conduct he is optimistic, he might say the child was a third underweight. The example is trite for the sake of simplicity. In a complex technical matter the court will not have the ability to see the nuance between the half full and the half empty description—that is not to denigrate the court, it is quite simply a truism of why the court in the first place needed the assistance of experts.

014 One court judgment (*Cala Homes* [1995] CILL 1083) has fallen notoriously against a party which had the temerity to engage an expert who had previously, in print, dared to suggest his duty was more than to the court.

015 The courts though—it is most respectfully suggested—are not, except in the very long term, a good place to ventilate issues such as this. It requires parties with long pockets to continue the debate to the House of Lords.

016 More curiously, whilst the judicial system is probably the best we can hope for as a system of resolving disputes, it is *ab initio* not suited to resolving arguments about itself. The judicial principle of *nemo judex in re sua* is a good one. Without entering into who, if anyone, might fill the role better, there is undoubtedly a danger in members of the judiciary reaching decisions on procedural matters. That has been seen in many countries regarding arbitration (too often glossed over as "judicial jealousy", but usually a far more subtle—and in some cases hazardous—problem). It must also apply to any decision on how experts are to operate.

017 Any judicial ruling on an expert's duty is bound to have suffered the temptation to over-emphasise any duty to the court to the detriment of highlighting duties to other parties.

THE CIVIL PROCEDURE RULES

018 Since the above piece was written the Civil Procedure Rules and their associated Practice Directions have been published (HMSO, London, February 1999, £250—the most relevant parts are reproduced in this book). These implement results of the "Woolf Process", including the consultations that took place on drafts of these Rules.

019 The Rules, in this author's opinion, heighten the conflict between those who search for truth and those who must "pick a winner". That conflict is eternal. It cannot be avoided. All that we can achieve is that firstly the conflict is minimised and secondly that the processes used help both sides achieve the desire of doing justice. The author should clearly state, at this stage (admitting to being a practising arbitrator) that "picking a winner" is not said disparagingly—when a dispute exists, it is undoubtedly he who decides, rather than he who gives evidence that is being the more useful member of society. A decision has to be made.

020 It also has to be said that there is a parallel conflict with regard to the parties. A party may, quite naturally, be more interested in "winning" than in seeing justice done. The current Rules, though, state: "The parties are required to *help the court* further the overriding objective" (emphasis added) (Rule 1.3). It must be queried how realistic this can be.

021 It can be argued that this is merely a standard by which the court can assess a party's conduct, a standard that the court can use to bring the party's behaviour under control. It would be nice to think so, but to the outsider "justice" can sometimes seem introverted. One of the clearest examples of that is perhaps the relative weight that legal scholars give to "law" and "fact" in arbitration. That a court-based system needs to develop case law is generally accepted, but the differing attitudes that are exhibited (not least in statute) as to what should happen if an arbitral tribunal is "wrong in law" as compared with if it makes an incorrect finding of fact is interesting. A commercial man is likely to greet an error in law with more equanimity than he is to accept a finding in favour of a lying witness if the facts are ones of which he has first hand experience. Yet statutes frequently seem to view the furtherance and/or preservation of law as more important than the resolution of the dispute to which the law must be applied. Those who come to a tribunal for the resolution of their dispute must accept some rules of conduct, but the process must not become—nor be allowed to seem to become—more important than either the dispute or the disputing parties.

022 It is Part 35 of the Rules that relates to Experts. The six pages of "rules" are supplemented by three pages of Practice Directions. Unfortunately the latter in many places merely duplicate what the Rules have already said.

023 This duplication is demonstrated by Rule 35.10(2) and Direction 1.2(7) (the system of numbering sub-sub-paragraphs is not consistent between the Rules and the Directions):

> "35.10(2) At the end of the expert's report there must be a statement that—
> (a) the expert understands his duty to the court; and
> (b) he has complied with that duty."

> "1.2(7) [An expert's report must:] contain a statement that the expert understands his duty to the court and has complied with that duty (rule 35.10(2)), . . ."

If the latter is meant to be a summary of the former (it does list requirements for a report) it seems odd that it omits to state that the statement "must" occur, according to the Rules, at the end of the report.

024 Rule 35.3 states "It is the duty of an expert to help the court on matters within his expertise". The question of whether experts should "help" or whether they should tell the truth (or both?) has been discussed in detail in the original article above.

025 Rule 35.4 allows the court to restrict expert evidence. There must be an implicit power of any tribunal to restrict the calling of witnesses (and, once called, what evidence they can give). The wording of this sub-rule, though, is interesting. Firstly (35.4(1)) it commences in the negative ("no party may call . . . without permission"), it then continues (35.4(2)) that when applying for permission the party must identify the field of expertise and "where practicable the expert" himself. So, the court needs to know not only what type of evidence it is wished to call, but ("where practicable") the name of the witness before deciding whether to allow them to be called. There are undoubtedly rogue experts in circulation—some seem immune to having their notions destroyed in the witness box—but is the way to stop them to allow the judiciary to decide (in advance of a hearing) who are "good" experts and who are "bad" experts? (If that indeed is the purpose of this section? But it is difficult to see what other purpose it could serve.) The history of science is littered with people who tenaciously hung on to "rogue" ideas to be eventually proved right. The market place has generally weeded out "bad" experts from among the crowd (and the market place generally—and with the greatest respect—has better intelligence gathering than the judiciary). The rogue expert was in any event to a large degree a creation of the market distortion itself created by profuse legal aid for civil claims. That is now, for better or worse, a thing of the past.

026 Rule 35.6 requires experts to respond to written questions on their written reports—a not unreasonable requirement. Rule 35.6(4)(b) deals with the situation where "the expert does not answer that question", without defining what not answering consists of. The consequences are draconian: the court may order that none of the expert's evidence can be used and/or that expert's fees are not recoverable. Having witnessed the advocate–witness "dance" of "Answer the question", "But I have", so often in verbal exchanges, the present author sees the above rule offering scope for some disputes. (There is no opportunity for dialogue as, perhaps reasonably, written questions "may only be put once" (Rule 35.6(2)(a)).)

027 The proposal for the use of a joint expert has moved considerably from the position initially advocated in the Woolf Report. John Lord (1998, in *Your Witness*, 14, p. 5) commenting on a draft of these rules, remarked that one should "note, however, that the emphasis is on the use of an expert appointed jointly by the parties rather than by the court, which was the method recommended initially by Lord Woolf". The result is a peculiar attempt to move away from party experts, but without arriving at the continental system (see the chapter in the present volume on the French system). It is almost as if, in admiration of the role of the *ministère public*, England had proposed that parties should engage a joint advocate(!).

028 Interestingly the Rule is bland: "the court may direct that . . . evidence . . . is . . . given by one expert only", but when one turns to the Practice Direction the matter of desirability of a joint expert is not dealt with in the actual numbered directions, but rather in the preamble. Here it states "In addition, where possible, matters . . . should be dealt with by a single expert". This seems considerably stronger than the text of the Rules. On the one hand it seems unfortunate that this matter has not been better resolved, but maybe the result is preferable and what we will in fact see is some experimentation and in the end experience will dictate in which direction this particular aspect of civil procedure will travel.

029 Rule 35.14 allows experts to seek guidance ("directions") directly from the court "without giving notice to any party".

030 The Directions, as noted above, on the subject of experts, largely repeat the Rules, but they do introduce a few points.

031 Direction 1.2 sets out a list of "musts" for a report.

> **Point 2** is that it must "give details of any literature or other material . . . relied on in making the report". A rather wide requirement, but it probably was intended to say that the expert should give a full citation for any material referred to in the report.
>
> **Point 5** requires the expert to "summarise the range of opinion" on a topic. The author, like many others, has always tried to do this. It is much easier to deal with

conflicting opinions head-on at an early stage than in court in the witness box. But it is not always easy to summarise opinions with which one is not enamoured. Many experts will not be that well briefed on schools of thought that they have little time for. The present situation does also allow the expert to address opinions he feels will be fielded against him, the proposal requires him to address "the range". Should medical reports in future deal with homoeopathy?

Point 6 makes it a ("must") requirement that all reports "contain a summary of the conclusions reached". The author has usually tended to do this in his own reports (surely any report writer would?). In occasional reports there may only be one "conclusion", clearly stated in the penultimate paragraph ... will it now be necessary to add a section headed "Summary of Conclusions"?

Point 7 has been dealt with above. The wording of the statement will have to be *circum loquacious*. Presumably "I understand my duty to the court and have complied with that duty" will be preferable to "I have helped the court on the matters within my expertise" (the latter is rendered from Rule 35.3(1)). The whole matter begs the question of whether the expert (a witness of opinion) is entitled to express an opinion on whether he has been helpful.

032 Direction 1.4 requires the expert to declare "I believe the facts I have stated in this report are true and that the opinions I have expressed are correct".

033 The author cannot be alone in having frequently written reports based upon "facts" about which he had the gravest doubts. A report could state that "if A is the case, then my opinion is B". It has been up to the party and their advocate to prove (or not) that "A" was the case. The first half of this new declaration does not seem to countenance the hypothetical opinion. If it is purely designed to deal with facts introduced by the expert it does so rather weakly (hardly "the truth, the whole truth ...").

034 The second part begs the question of whether one can believe that an opinion is "correct". Often an opinion may be just "more likely". The fact that it is *an opinion* often is due to the range of opinions that are possible!

035 Interestingly the International Centre for the Settlement of Investment Disputes is one of the few bodies that seems to have also developed a declaration specifically for experts (in their Arbitration Rules at Rule 35 (see Chapman, *Commercial & Consumer Arbitration Statutes and Rules*, Blackstone, 1997, pp. 480–481)). This is: "I solemnly declare upon my honour and conscience that my statement will be in accordance with my sincere belief". (For other witnesses the declaration is: "I solemnly declare upon my honour and conscience that I shall speak the truth, the whole truth and nothing but the truth".)

036 Opinions are, surely, sincerely held, not "believed to be correct"?

Shadow experts

037 Previously in Part 1 ("Overriding Objective") of the Rules emphasis is given to dealing with the case justly, and it is stated (Rule 1.1(2)): "Dealing with a case justly includes, so far as is practicable ... ensuring the parties are on an equal footing ... dealing with the case in ways which are proportionate ... to the financial position of each party."

038 The present author sees the possibility of these Rules pushing expertise in a direction that further advantages the better-off client. Realistically the richer party is always going to have the advantage, but anything that promotes that advantage is not to be encouraged.

039 The example is from current practice in criminal cases, but the point applies to civil cases under the new rules. It is frequently the case that in criminal cases all the experts with "hands on" day-to-day expertise of any particular technique are government scientists. Another expert can appear and give a theoretical commentary on the technique, its advantages and disadvantages or whatever, but at the end of the day any dispute over the technical evidence will usually be decided in the state's favour as their expert is "more expert". Indeed the present author knows of a distinguished NHS consultant biochemist who had a blood alcohol analysis rejected by the court in favour of the forensic science laboratory's result on the other half of the divided sample, on the basis that he did so few such analyses that the laboratory's result was to be preferred. If a private expert gives evidence, then under cross examination he is likely to be led to support the prosecution by a series of bland questions about whether he agrees that "such and such" a technique is widely used, etc.

040 The better approach, in the interests of seeing the evidence presented is "properly tested", is for the expert to suggest he does not give evidence. Instead he can brief the advocate in writing, or even sit behind the advocate in court, and suggest lines of questioning that will determine whether the prosecution expert is *au fait* with his subject, whether he carried out tests correctly, etc.

041 The present Rules would seem to encourage the rise of such a "shadow expert". Perhaps his fees will not be recoverable, but he could be a valuable member of the team.

042 The nightmare scenario is one where a party (or their advocates) engage a "master expert" to oversee the case. He advises, he drafts questions (perhaps "live" in court) to be put to other experts. He marshals the evidence. He, having seen all the papers and knowing what opinion is required, selects a suitably credible, but perhaps not over-intelligent, colleague to be the actual "stand up" expert, who will give the required opinions in court. The latter will ideally not have over-wide knowledge or experience and so will give scant attention to the "range of opinion". He will be blinkered without being offensively dogmatic.

043 Of course there is nothing stopping such a situation happening at the present time. Some may even feel that in some specialised areas (perhaps some of the defences conducted by medical defence bodies, protecting their members against accusations of negligence) there are already flavours of this.

044 The new Rules did not create this possibility, but will they encourage it?

Michael Chapman *(mchapman@mchapman.com; http://www.mchapman.com/mc/) is a practising expert, expert witness and arbitrator. He is based in France, some 60 kilometres from Geneva, but routinely practises across Europe.*

He is a Eur. Biol., specialising in the assessment of chemical safety and the regulation of medicines. As a European Registered Toxicologist he is involved in the preparation of expert reports for applications for marketing authorisations and product licences for pharmaceuticals as well as preparing reports or appearing in the courts to give evidence on medicines, poisoning, drugs of abuse and related topics. As a senior member of an international consultancy group he is involved with the project management of the development and licensing of ranges of pharmaceutical products for leading healthcare companies.

He was appointed Expert près le Comité National Française de la Chambre de Commerce Internationale *in 1995.*

Michael Chapman has interests in electronic commerce as a publisher. he is listed as an arbitrator and mediator by the World Intellectual Property Organisation (WIPO, Geneva) and has attended their training on Internet-related dispute resolution procedures.

This article is developed from a note: "Is there anybody to argue in favour of expert witnesses in England and Wales having an unambiguous duty?" *first published in* Arbitration, *the Journal of the Chartered Institute of Arbitrators (May 1997, 63, JCIArb 2–141).*

CHAPTER 1/7

SUBPOENA OF AN EXPERT WITNESS

John Bolton

"THE FEAR IS GREATER THAN THE PAIN"

001 Did you ever have to go to a dentist for a filling and dread the dentist's drill? Or have you had to go to a doctor for an injection and have fear of the hypodermic needle?

002 The fear and anticipation of the real event is always greater than the pain itself. Being served with a subpoena to attend at court is really not half as unpleasant an event as the anticipation of it may seem. If you are an expert witness you will even be paid for your time to attend court and so a subpoena may be a blessing in disguise.

003 A witness may be summoned by subpoena to a court or arbitration. There are two types of subpoena:

(a) Writ of subpoena *ad testificandum*—this is where a witness may be forced to attend court or an arbitration.

(b) writ of subpoena *duces tecum*—this is the method by which a witness is compelled to bring before the court any documents that could be obtained at the trial of the action.

004 Any party to the proceedings may issue a writ of subpoena *ad testificandum*. This ensures that the witness is required to attend the hearing. A master or judge may order the issue of a writ of subpoena to compel the attendance of an expert before a court or arbitrator, provided the witness is anywhere within the United Kingdom at the time. The subpoena ensures the presence at the hearing of the witness. A subpoena *duces tecum* compels the witness to bring before the court any relevant document that could be useful on the trial of the action. Wilful disobedience to the writ by a person within the jurisdiction of the United Kingdom is a contempt of court. A contempt of court renders the witness liable to committal and imprisonment provided a reasonable sum has been tendered for conduct money and expenses.

005 Experts should not be overly concerned if they cannot attend court; the court often looks favourably upon a witness who has requirements which make his attendance either impossible or requires attendance for a limited time only. Lord Woolf in his *Access to Justice* Report proposed to limit the experts to written testimony. This should reduce the time wasted by experts in court.

DEFECTIVE SUBPOENAS

006 Defective subpoenas are also another way to avoid going to court, although as noted below a certain amount of care should be taken with them. Examples of defective subpoenas include those which have not complied with the technical requirements such as layout, font size and margins. If an expert considers that the subpoena is defective on technical grounds he should ensure he has notified the serving party if he does not intend to attend, because the court may choose to ignore such technical defects.

007 A subpoena may be technically defective if the print font is too small. All documents prepared for use in the Supreme Court must use not smaller than 11 point type for printing (RSC Order 66, rule 2(3)). In addition, a margin of not less than 1½ inches must be allowed to the left-hand side (RSC Order 66, rule 1(1)). These, of course, are highly technical defects and if this is the point that is going to be taken by the witness it would be advisable to notify the person serving the subpoena that the subpoena is defective and that you intend to rely on this point.

008 However, a subpoena may be defective in a number of other ways. These are more substantive reasons but it is still advisable to notify the serving party that you do not intend to attend court on the basis of the defective subpoena.

009 Writ of subpoena has a life of 12 weeks from the date of issue. It must be served within those 12 weeks and if not properly served within that time, it lapses and a fresh subpoena must be obtained by the solicitor.

010 In addition, sufficient time must be allowed between the service of the subpoena and the date that attendance is required at court. A subpoena must be served not less than four days (excluding weekends) before the date on which attendance at court is demanded (RSC Order 38, rule 17).

011 Service on your own expert by post is common procedure and if the expert witness does not intend to take a point on the method of service then that will not become an issue. However, proper service of a subpoena must be done personally on the individual named in it. Service by post is not permitted except where the object of the service has been avoiding personal service and the court specifically orders substituted service such as by post or fax communication (RSC Order 13, rule 17).

012 A subpoena which calls for a hearing in chambers requires leave of the court prior to issue. Subpoenas cannot be issued without the necessary leave.

EXPENSES

013 At the time of service of a subpoena the witness should be offered a sufficient sum to cover the reasonable costs of his travel to and from court to give the evidence. If a number of days are required, only the first days of travel expense need to be provided at the time of service as for subsequent days additional cash may be tendered at the court.

MOTIVE BEHIND A SUBPOENA

014 In addition, a subpoena which is motivated by a hope that the witness holds something useful but is not based on good grounds for believing that witness in fact can provide the evidence will be set aside as an improper fishing expedition. See the case of *Macmillan* v. *Bishopsgate Investment Management (No 1)* [1993] 1 WLR 1372. In this case, during the cross-examination of a witness called on behalf of the defendant in the action, the plaintiff applied for an order requiring the witness to produce transcripts of his private examination conducted under the Insolvency Act by the liquidators of a company which was not a party to the action. The trial judge refused the application and on appeal the appeal was dismissed on the basis that the production of the documents by the witness was not necessary for disposing fairly of the cause of action and therefore the plaintiff's application to require the transcripts should have been refused.

015 Another decision the grounds of which experts should be aware is *London and Leeds Estates Ltd* v. *Paribas Ltd (No 2)* [1995] 2 EG 134. The principle of the case is that an expert witness can be forced by subpoena to reveal evidence he has given in a valuation of comparable premises if it is relevant to his valuation of the disputed property. The expert can be required by the subpoena to produce his file, but the court's powers do not extend to allow the serving party to "go fishing" to find if there is any prejudicial paperwork to the expert's case.

016 Thus, a subpoena may be oppressive. When a subpoena is issued in an effort to gain discovery against an unwilling witness, or for the motive of compelling inspection of documents to see whether a party issuing the subpoena might have a cause of action against the witness, there are arguments for viewing it as an abuse of process and for setting the subpoena aside. (*Senior* v. *Holdsworth* [1975] 2 WLR 987.)

017 In the 1979 Court of Appeal case of *Harmony Shipping Co SA* v. *Davis* [1981] 1 Lloyd's Rep 377 an expert witness on handwriting was approached by the plaintiffs in an action to advise on the authenticity of a document. He was only one of a few such experts capable of advising. The expert advice was that the document was not genuine. In discussing his advice the expert stated that it was his rule not to give advice to both sides of an action. Subsequently the expert was approached by the defendants to advise them on the document's authenticity. Not realising that he had already advised the plaintiffs on the matter, he advised the defendants that the document was not genuine. He later realised that he had advised both sides and told the defendant's solicitor that he could accept no further instructions from them. The defendants who wished the expert to give evidence on their behalf issued a subpoena *ad testificandum* requiring him to attend and give such evidence. The plaintiffs applied to the trial judge to set aside the subpoena but the judge ruled that the expert was a compellable witness and ought to give the evidence as to his opinion of the document. The Court of Appeal decided that there was an underlying principle that no party had any property in the evidence of a witness of fact and that the expert could be compelled by the court to give evidence because the same principle applied to an expert witness. The court was therefore entitled to compel an expert witness to give evidence both of the facts that he observed and of his opinion on those facts subject only to a claim of legal professional privilege. (*Harmony Shipping Co SA* v. *Davis* [1981] 1 Lloyd's Rep 377.)

018 The obvious point for the expert here is that he must be wary if he has acted on the other side in any comparable case, since he may be subpoenaed to bring along the proofs of evidence from that case. If the expert expressed the same opinion in the former case there will be no problem. However if the evidence of the expert in the former case shows marked differences from his evidence in the current case his or her overall credibility will be damaged.

UNWILLING WITNESS

019 In a later case, *The Society of Lloyd's* v. *Clementson (No 2)* [1996] CLC 1205 heard in February 1996 the Court of Appeal held that the court had a discretion as to whether to compel an expert to appear against his wishes as a witness. It could take into account whether his attendance at court would disrupt or impede other important work that the expert had to do.

020 Lord Justice Staughton said that the court had a discretion to compel an expert to appear as a witness and that it should take into account the following:

(i) That the court was *prime facie* entitled to every man's evidence whether of fact or opinion;
(ii) Whether the expert had some connection with the case in question;
(iii) Whether the expert was willing to come provided that his image was protected by subpoena;
(iv) Whether the attendance at court would disrupt or impede other important work that the expert had to do; and
(v) Whether another expert of equal calibre was available.

021 The court held that Mr Clementson should not be required to spend days in court giving evidence, not to mention the preparation time, unless it was absolutely essential. No doubt the judge would treat him with consideration and try to confine his evidence but who knew if such was possible.

022 Solicitors often use the subpoena as a method of requiring their experts to appear in court. This is because many expert witnesses find it difficult to schedule the days in their calendar. The use of a subpoena is of benefit to both the witness and the instructing party because it freezes those days on which the expert's presence is required.

023 However, expert witnesses should not be concerned if they cannot comply provided they have a proper excuse for not attending. The court often looks favourably upon a witness who has requirements which make his attendance either impossible or require attendance be for a limited time only.

024 Lord Woolf, in his *Access to Justice* Report, proposed to limit the experts to written testimony. Should his reforms materialise, this will greatly reduce the wasted time spent by experts in court waiting to give their evidence. Hopefully this, likewise, will reduce the cost of justice.

025 An expert witness who has two conflicting summonses should immediately draw the attention of both parties who have subpoenaed him to the fact that there is a date in conflict. It may well be that on that basis one or other hearing may be limited or adjusted so that the expert can comply with both subpoenas. Failing that, the expert should make an application to have the subpoena set aside for the case for which he will not be able to attend at court. It may well be that the court will reschedule the hearing.

EFFECT OF THE WOOLF CHANGES TO CIVIL PROCEDURE

026 Basically the changes initiated by Lord Woolf's *Access to Justice* do not materially affect the subpoena process. However it should be noted that Woolf's basic strategy is to reduce the cost of expert witnesses and in particular to reinforce their duty to the court. As a result Lord Woolf has sought to instigate a single expert witness process and where possible to allow the one expert to give evidence for both parties. In addition, he has reminded the experts that their first duty is to the court and that they may contact the court directly in order to seek guidance on their instructions. This may open a whole new arena for experts being directed to appear before the judge. Only time and the evolution of the new detailed rules in this regard will be able to assist us in determining the expert's liability in the future. The expert to respond to a summons for subpoena before the judge alone.

027 Finally, under the system of fast track (cases where the amount of damages sought is less than £15,000 although in the future the limit may be increased to £50,000) it is not anticipated that experts give oral evidence in court but rather submit written reports and responses to questions. As a result of this change, it is likely that subpoenas will be less frequently issued for experts to appear before the court. This should result in a saving of expert's time and consequently of the costs of expert evidence.

SUMMARY

028 Subpoenas attempt to ensure that the best evidence is before the court. An attempt should be made to comply with a subpoena but if this is not possible punitive measures will always follow.

029 In summary, subpoenas are tools which assist the court and the parties in administering civil justice. They should not be thought of as oppressive devices and witnesses should not hold them in fear.

John F Bolton BSc, MSc (Eng), MBA (Hons), FCIArb, Solicitor *is an international construction lawyer with extensive experience in construction management formulations. He has prepared detailed claims for disruption and delay. He has advised on contractual arrangements for construction firms, in particular FIDIC Conditions of Contract.*

He graduated from Canisus College in Buffalo, New York, with an MBA. He also has a MS in Engineering and is admitted as a solicitor in England and Wales, is a member of the International Bar Association and a Fellow of the Chartered Institute of Arbitrators.

He is a Partner at Eversheds, the national firm specialising in construction and a frequent lecturer on court procedure. He was also an assessor for Lord Woolf.

APPENDIX

The Defective Subpoena

1. **Writ of subpoena has expired by the time service is attempted**
   Subpoena has a life of 12 weeks from date of issue: *RSC Order 38, rule 17*.
2. **Service is short**
   Subpoena must be served not less than four days (excluding weekends) before the day on which attendance at court is demanded.
3. **Method of service is invalid**
   A subpoena must be served *personally* on the individual named in it: *RSC Order 38, rule 17*.
4. **No conduct money has been tendered**
   At time of service the witness should be offered reasonable costs of his travel to and from court: *Supreme Court Act 1981, s.36(4)*.
5. **Subpoena may have been issued without the necessary leave**
   For a hearing in chambers rather than the full trial, leave of the court should be obtained: *RSC Order 32, rule 7(1)*.
6. **The subpoena may be a mere fishing expedition**
   Subpoenas motivated by a hope that the witness holds something useful, but without good grounds will often be set aside as improper fishing expeditions: *Macmillan* v. *Bishopsgate Investment Management (No 1)* [1993] 1 WLR 1372.
7. **The subpoena may be oppressive**
   Where a subpoena is issued in efforts to gain pre-trial discovery against an unwilling mere witness: *Senior* v. *Holdsworth* [1975] 2 WLR 987.

CHAPTER 1/8

HOW PRIVILEGED IS AN EXPERT?

Gary R Hickinbottom

001 "[Our law] recognises that proper mutual discovery in litigation and arbitration is in the public interest in that it promotes settlements: it reduces [the risk of] a party being taken by surprise: and enables the judge to decide the case in the light of contemporary documentary material which is often more valuable than oral testimony" (*Sunderland Steamship P & I Association* v. *Gatoil International Inc (The Lorenzo Halcoussi)* [1988] 1 Lloyd's Rep 180 at 184, *per* Steyn J).

THE BASIS OF DISCOVERY

002 Although something of an over-simplification, it is sometimes said that in civil law jurisdictions each party to a dispute has to construct its own case, based on the evidence it has in its possession. It is restricted to that evidence. Traditionally, discovery is unknown, as is cross-examination. The judge simply has the task of weighing the two cases, and declaring which he considers the better. He has no objective truth to search for. On the other hand, in common law jurisdictions there is the concept of an objective truth in each dispute that everyone is searching for. Even in a large building dispute based entirely on *quantum*, theoretically the official referee or arbitrator is searching for the (objectively) right answer: as are the parties and their advisers. This is why traditionally each side has had to disclose to the other relevant documents which harm its case, as well as those which support it. It is also why cross-examination is allowed. Discovery has consequently been a fundamental plank of public policy in dispute resolution in England and Wales: in the search for the objective truth, it is a matter of public policy that each side bares its evidential soul.

003 On the basis of such public policy considerations, the courts have insisted upon the fullest and best relevant documentary evidence on any issue being made available by the parties, by the process of discovery, to ensure so far as possible that the judge arrives at a true decision: and "relevance" has been construed widely by the courts. Disclosure of documents has not been limited to those that would prove or disprove any matter in question in the dispute: any document "which it is reasonable to suppose contains information which may enable the party applying for discovery either to advance his own case or to damage that of his adversary, or which may fairly lead him to a train of enquiry which may have either of these two consequences" has had to be disclosed (*Compagnie Financière du Pacifique* v. *Peruvian Guano Co* (1882) 11 QBD 55 at 62–63, *per* Brett LJ). The principle has been consistently reiterated over the years (see, e.g., *Shaw* v. *The National Trust* (1989) *The Independent*, 13 February and *The Captain Gregos* (1990) *The Times*, 21 December).

004 However, it has always been accepted that there are circumstances in which this general rule should be ousted by other public policy considerations. For example, the courts have not allowed oppressive discovery to be sought, but only discovery that is necessary for the saving of costs or fair adjudication of the issues between the parties (RSC Order 24, rule 8: see also *West Midlands Passenger Transport Executive* v. *Singh* [1988] 1 WLR 730, and *Mölnlycke AB* v. *Proctor & Gamble Ltd (No 3)* [1990] RPC 498). By implication, the same has been applied to arbitrations (*Dolling-Baker* v. *Merrett* [1990] 1 WLR 1205).

005 The failure properly to appreciate that the relevance test for "discoverability" was effectively limited by Order 24, rule 8 resulted in general over-disclosure of documents, particularly in technical disputes. This problem has now been addressed. In 1994, the Lord Chancellor appointed Lord Woolf to review the rules and procedure of the civil courts. Following an Interim Report in June 1995, Lord Woolf published his Final Report in July 1996 ("the Woolf Report"). Of discovery, Lord Woolf indicated that he considered that "the process had become disproportionate, especially in larger cases where large numbers of documents may have to be searched for and disclosed, though only a small number turn out to be significant": and, although he "considered that disclosure contributes to the just resolution of disputes and should therefore be retained", he said it should be "in a more limited form" (Woolf Report, Section III, Paragraph 37). Therefore, the Woolf Report proposed as a matter of principle to restrict full discovery (which public policy tends to dictate in the interests of coming to a correct decision), because of the competing public policy interest in making dispute resolution cost-effective. Effect has been given to these proposals in the new Civil Procedure Rules 1998 ("CPR") (effective from April 1999), which apply to all civil courts, and which, with limited exceptions, have taken over from the old White Book of the High Court, and Green Book of the County Court, which have ceased to apply. The mechanics of disclosure under the new provisions are dealt with below but, briefly, a party is only obliged to disclose documents upon which he relies, and those which adversely affect his own or another party's case, or which support another party's case. The breadth of disclosure required by *Peruvian Guano* has gone. "Standard disclosure" in most cases will be fairly restricted: and it is unlikely to be easy for a party to persuade a court that further "specific disclosure" is necessary. Precisely how these provisions will be applied by the courts in practice is not yet known. The breadth of the court's discretion suggests that there may be a lack of consistency. However, certainly, disclosure of documents in proceedings in England and Wales will in the future generally be more restricted, on public policy grounds. It is interesting to note that, at the same time as Lord Woolf was reporting in England, a similar review of procedure in Scotland (a civil law jurisdiction) recognised the important public policy benefits of compulsory disclosure of documents so far as justice was concerned, and proposed mandatory discovery on a basis as wide as that under the *Peruvian Guano* case (*Review of Business of the Outer House of the Court of Session*, chaired by Lord Cullen (1995), paragraph 5.13), although those proposals have yet to be implemented and, indeed, they appear to have been shelved indefinitely. However, the proposals of Lord Cullen show that the public policy balance between justice (in the sense of optimising the chances of a court coming to the correct result) and cost-effectiveness is difficult, and more than one view can legitimately be held.

006 The general disclosure rules may of course be limited by public policy factors other than cost-effectiveness. Certain communications have never had to be disclosed for production: they are "privileged" from production. These include documents passing between a person and his solicitors ("legal professional privilege") and documents passing between a solicitor and third parties (or between persons with a common interest, such as potential co-defendants or insured/insurer) which come into existence after litigation is pending and made with a view to such litigation ("litigation privilege"). Generally, the CPR do not alter the law relating to the well-established privileges. Contrary to the traditional rule that all instructions to, discussions with and draft reports from experts made with a view to litigation are privileged, under this head, the Interim Woolf Report (paragraph 33) proposed that all instructions to experts—written or oral—be disclosable. However, the Final Report backed away from the proposal that *all* communications passing to and from experts be disclosable: and the CPR respects the traditional privilege. An expert is now required to state in his report the substance of all material instructions (oral or written) on the basis of which the report was written (Rule 35.10(3) and Practice Direction to Part 35, Paragraph 1.2(8)): but not any specific document, and there is a bar on the expert being cross-examined on his instructions, unless there are reasonable grounds to consider the statements of instructions given is inaccurate or incomplete (Rule 35.10(4) and Practice Direction to Part 35, Paragraph 3). Because an opinion is worthless without knowledge of the facts upon which it is based (and, consequently, experts' reports have always had to include the full factual basis for the opinion evidence given, if that evidence is to be compelling), this rule is unlikely to result in a significant change in practice for many experts.

007 Documents passing between parties for the *bona fide* purpose of resolving a dispute ("without prejudice") form a separate class that, whilst not being confidential or privileged (in the true sense of that word), are not disclosable and cannot be relied upon in proceedings because it is in the public interest to encourage frankness in discussions between parties in dispute that may lead to compromise or settlement.

008 Because public policy is involved, these exceptions may themselves be ousted. For example, the courts will not allow privilege or the "without prejudice" tag to protect a document which has been produced in furtherance of a criminal or fraudulent purpose. Further, although this article is restricted to a consideration of disclosure and privilege in the context of adversarial proceedings, in the context of proceedings under the Children Act 1989, experts' reports are not the subject of privilege (*In re L (A Minor) (Police Investigation: Privilege)* [1997] AC 16), but are subject to statutory confidentiality such that reports cannot be disclosed even to other parties without the leave of the court (Family Proceedings Rules 1991, rule 4.23). Therefore, in the different context of proceedings relating to the welfare of children, the public policy issues are dealt with in a different way. (For a general discussion of the relationship between privilege in adversarial proceedings and the Children Act scheme, see *Vernon* v. *Bosley (No 2)* [1997] 3 WLR 683.)

MECHANICS

009 The mechanics of disclosure are set out in CPR Part 31. Disclosure may be sought pre-action (Rule 31.16) or against a non-party (Rule 31.17) in any action. So far as disclosure between parties to an action is concerned, each party is required to give standard disclosure of documents, by preparing and serving on the other parties a list of all documents which exist or have existed, and which are or have been in the control of that party. The party is required to disclose only

(a) the documents on which he relies;
(b) the documents which adversely affect his own (or another party's) case, or support another party's case; and

(c) documents he is specifically required to disclose by a relevant practice direction.

010 Prior to preparing the list, a party is required to make a reasonable search for documents falling into these categories. In determining the scope of the search, certain specific factors have to be taken into account, namely:

(a) the number of documents involved;
(b) the nature and complexity of the proceedings;
(c) the ease and expense of retrieval of any particular documents; and
(d) the significance of any document which is likely to be located during the search.

011 As can be seen from these criteria, there is a considerable subjective element involved. Standard disclosure very much depends upon the honesty of the party. However, every party personally (rather than by way of his solicitor) must make a formal statement setting out the extent of the search which has been made, and certifying both that he understands the duty to disclose documents and that he has carried out that duty.

012 If a party is not satisfied with the standard disclosure given, he may seek an order for specific disclosure of documents (Rule 31.12). In considering what further disclosure is appropriate, the court will have in mind "the overriding objective" of the Rules set out in Rule 1.1. The Rules are to enable the court to deal with cases justly, including, so far as practicable:

(a) ensuring that the parties are on an equal footing;
(b) saving expense;
(c) dealing with a case in ways which are proportionate to the amount involved, the importance of the case, the complexity of the issues and the financial position of each party;
(d) ensuring that it is dealt with expeditiously and fairly; and
(e) allotting to it an appropriate share of the court's resources (Rule 1.1(2)).

013 With regard to the specific role of experts, they are not often directly involved in collecting contemporaneous documents for the purposes of disclosure and, where they are, no particular problems arise. Difficult questions can, however, arise in respect of documents in the hands of a contemporaneous adviser/consultant of a party. Such documents will be disclosable by a party if that party has the right to call for them. Although it will depend on the facts of the individual case and the profession involved, generally it is considered that working papers cannot usually be called for and are consequently not disclosable. However, under the CPR, there is general provision for order for disclosure against a non-party (Rule 31.17) and, where an adviser's documents are particularly pertinent to the issues between the parties, it is open to the court to order disclosure under these new provisions.

014 It can of course be of great assistance to have an expert help with inspecting the other side's technical documents. A party is allowed (by agreement or express court sanction) to use an expert to assist in the inspection, but that expert may be the subject of specific conditions, e.g. as to confidentiality. For example in *Davies* v. *Eli Lilly & Co* [1987] 1 WLR 428, a case arising out of the *Opren* litigation, the expert involved was also a medical journalist, and his assistance to the plaintiffs in inspection was made subject to specific express terms as to the maintenance of confidentiality.

DUAL PURPOSE REPORTS

015 "Litigation privilege" covers, for example, communications between a party or his solicitor on the one hand and an expert on the other, where the communications relate to the preparation of an expert's report for use in the litigation—an expert's report, even if prepared for exchange, remains privileged until it is actually exchanged (*Derby* v. *Weldon (No 9)* [1991] 1 WLR 652) and it does not now seem that that principle has been significantly eroded as a result of the Woolf Report. Proceedings need not have been commenced for the privilege to arise: the correct test is whether litigation is "in reasonable prospect" (*Waugh* v. *British Railways Board* [1980] AC 521 and *Guinness Peat Properties Ltd* v. *Fitzroy Robinson Partnership* [1987] 1 WLR 1027).

016 There may be specific difficulties in determining the status of documents coming into existence for more than one purpose. It is not sufficient that *one* of the purposes for which the document came into existence was to obtain legal advice in litigation: that must be the sole, or at least dominant, purpose. Before 1980, the position was unclear. In 1976, the influential High Court of Australia held by a majority that legal professional privilege was confined to documents brought into existence for the sole purpose of use in legal proceedings, Barwick CJ dissenting by stating the test in terms of dominant purpose (*Grant* v. *Downs* (1976) 135 CLR 674). So far as England and Wales were concerned, the position was clarified in *Waugh* v. *British Railways Board* (*supra*). An internal inquiry report to the railway inspectorate incorporating statements of witnesses was prepared for equal dual purposes: first for safety purposes, and second "to enable [the Board's chief solicitor] to advise the Board on its legal liability and if necessary conduct its defence". Expressly following the view of Barwick CJ in *Grant* v. *Downs*, Lord Wilberforce said (at page 533C): "It appears to me that unless the purpose of submission to the legal adviser in view of litigation is at least the dominant purpose for which the relevant document was prepared, the reasons which require privilege to be extended to it cannot apply. On the other hand to hold that the purpose, as above, must be the sole purpose would, apart from difficulties of proof, in my opinion, be too strict a requirement, and would confine the privilege too narrowly." He went on to hold that obtaining the legal advice was consequently not the dominant purpose (because there was another, equal purpose), and the report was not privileged. The facts in *Waugh* itself were literally "borderline".

017 *Waugh* is still good law. However, where there is the possibility of litigation following an incident, the courts do not try to draw fine lines between taking advice about one's position in the light of that incident, and taking advice in respect of the potential claim. In *Hellenic Mutual War Risks Association (Bermuda) Ltd* v. *Harrison (The Sagheera)* [1997] 1 Lloyd's Rep 160), in the context of such a situation, Rix J said (at page 166):

> "It may well have been, of course, that in the first instance the hope would be that litigation would be unnecessary: but I do not think that it is possible to distinguish between the purpose of taking legal advice concerning one's rights or obligations, where that necessitates acquiring information from third parties, and the additional purpose of using that information in aid of litigation, should litigation be necessary, so long as litigation is reasonably in prospect. That is not in my judgement an example of a dual purpose which prevents the purpose of using information in aid of litigation from being dominant as required by the test formulated in *Waugh* . . . In that case the other purpose with which the report in question had been prepared had nothing to do with legal advice, but the operation and safety of the railways . . ."

018 *Guinness Peat Properties Ltd* v. *Fitzroy Robinson Partnership* (*supra*) was a case concerning insured/insurer common interest privilege, but it shed useful light on the purpose rule generally. A letter was written by architects to their professional indemnity brokers giving the insurers notice of a claim. Slade LJ (giving the judgment of the court) said (at page 1037B): "[T]he dominant purpose of the ... letter must be viewed objectively on the evidence, particularly by reference to the intentions of the insurers who procured its genesis ... [S]o viewed, the dominant purpose was to produce a letter of notification which would be used in order to obtain legal advice or to conduct or aid in the conduct of litigation which was at the time of its production in reasonable prospect."

019 The court held that the purpose had to be ascertained objectively, rather than confining the test to a narrow subjective examination of the purpose of the writer of the letter, which was of course simply to give notice to the insurers.

020 These cases show that a number of difficulties can arise when a document is, or may be, written for more than one purpose. It is consequently good practice for an expert to be clear in his own mind as to the purpose of his report, and to make this purpose clear on the face of his report.

SELECTION OF MATERIALS

021 An expert may fortify his opinion by referring to books and other publications relating to research (*H* v. *Schering Chemicals Ltd* [1983] 1 WLR 143). Where an expert puts together particular texts and articles for the assistance of the lawyers conducting the case, the selection will be privileged (*Lyell* v. *Kennedy* (1884) 27 ChD 1).

LOSS OF CONFIDENTIALITY AND MISTAKEN DISCLOSURE

022 The position with regard to mistaken disclosure is somewhat more difficult. Legal professional privilege belongs to the client, and a lawyer owes his client a duty to assert privilege in the absence of instructions to the contrary. On the other hand, solicitors on the record and counsel instructed by them have ostensible authority to waive privilege or, to put it in a more precise way, to waive the confidentiality in the documents that founds the privilege. As a matter of principle, the waiver will be not less effective if done without instructions and/or mistakenly. Consequently, care has to be taken not to waive privilege accidentally.

023 This is particularly so because, where privilege is waived in a document or part document, the courts and opposing party have usually allowed an opportunity to see that disclosure in context, and to satisfy themselves that the extract in respect of which privilege has been waived represents the whole of the material relevant to the question in issue. Therefore, waiver of privilege over part of a document can lead to the whole of that document being disclosable, together with any other related documents (*Nea Karteria Maritime Company Ltd* v. *Atlantic & Great Lakes Steamship Corporation and Cape Breton Development Corporation (No 2)* [1981] Com LR 138; *Great Atlantic Insurance Co* v. *Home Insurance Co* [1981] 1 WLR 529; *Pozzi* v. *Eli Lilly & Co* (1986) *The Times*, 3 December; and *Vista Maritime Inc* v. *Sesa Goa* [1997] CLC 1600), unless the extract is severable (*The Sagheera, supra*). In *Nea Karteria Maritime Company Ltd*, in dealing with the assertion that the plaintiffs had waived privilege in respect of certain documents, Mustill J said (at page 139): "I believe that the principle underlying the rule of practice . . . is that where a party is deploying in court material which would otherwise be privileged, the opposite party and the court must have an opportunity of satisfying themselves that what the party has chosen to release from privilege represents the whole of the material relevant to the issue in question. To allow an individual item to be plucked out of context would be to risk injustice through its real weight or meaning being misunderstood."

024 However, mere reference to a privileged document in a pleading, affidavit, witness statement or expert's report does not constitute waiver: on the issue of whether confidentiality has been waived, the courts have indicated that they will look at the matter flexibly and in the light of considerations of fairness, rather than by reference to mechanistic tests (*Vista Maritime Inc* v. *Sesa Goa, supra* and *R* v. *The Secretary of State for Transport, ex parte Factortame Ltd* (1997) 9 Admin LR 591). Nevertheless, although the test is dependent upon the circumstances of the particular case (and the reported cases are not entirely consistent) if, in coming to his opinion in a report which is ultimately exchanged, an expert has relied in substance upon any document (e.g. the statement from a party by whom he has been instructed), privilege in that document is likely to be waived in practice. Just as it has been said that extracts from a counsel's opinion are usually valueless ("or worse") without the rest of the opinion and the instructions on which it was based to show upon what the opinion was founded and any reservations and qualifications (*Gleeson* v. *J Wippell & Co* [1977] 1 WLR 510 at 519, *per* Sir Robert Megarry V-C), it has been held that the court is entitled to have adduced before it the facts and material which the expert has found and observed, and upon which his opinion is based (*Harmony Shipping Co Ltd* v. *Saudi Europe Line* [1979] 1 WLR 1380). This is particularly so because of the expert's duty to the court to be full and frank, and not to withhold a relevant opinion (see, e.g., *National Justice Compania Naviera SA* v. *Prudential Assurance Co (The Ikarian Reefer)* [1993] 2 Lloyd's Rep 68). The Woolf Report proposed that this duty owed to the court be reiterated and strengthened, and to ensure that it expressly overrides the expert's duty to his own client: and the CPR implement this in terms (Rule 35.3).

025 As indicated above, the CPR require an expert to state the substance of his material instructions, although (unless there are reasonable grounds to consider this statement inaccurate or incomplete) the court will not order specific disclosure of any document, or permit cross-examination on the issue of instructions. However, generally, if the expert in fact relied upon a document in coming to his opinion then that document should be disclosed (whether or not it is referred to in the report): and if he did not rely upon a document, then it need not be disclosed, again whether or not it is referred to in the opinion. Of course, if a document is referred to in a report, there is an assumption that the expert considered it and took it into account in coming to his opinion. It may be difficult for reliance upon that document to be disowned (as suggested in *Vista Maritime*), without undermining the opinion based upon it. Furthermore, because of the principles arising out of waiver of privilege, if there is reference to part of a document (or a document in a chain), an expert must be particularly careful, although he or his client may be able to save disclosure of the balance by relying on the provisions of Rule 35.10 and revealing precisely upon what he is relying without the need to disclose the document itself. Nevertheless, there is a risk that the court will order full disclosure. In difficult cases, the expert may need to be guided by those solicitors instructing him.

026 The relevant principles—and the obligations falling upon experts—were reviewed in *Clough* v. *Tameside & Glossop Health Authority* [1998] PIQR P219, a recent case but one heard before the introduction of the CPR. In that case, an expert had referred to an earlier (undisclosed) expert's report in his own written evidence, and an issue arose as to the disclosability of that earlier report. It was held that it was disclosable. Bracewell J said (at page P224):

> "Experts are in a special and indeed unique category of witness, in that, under the Civil Evidence Act 1972, s.3, an opinion on any relevant matter on which an expert is qualified to give expert evidence, shall be admissible. The duties of experts are clearly laid down in [*The Ikarian Reefer*]. Those duties apply to all the courts in all divisions and require experts to give independent assistance to the courts by way of objective, unbiased opinion in relation to matters within their expertise. An expert must state the facts or assumptions on which the opinion was based and should not omit to consider material facts which detract from any concluded opinion. An essential element of the process is for a party to know and to be able to test in evidence the information supplied to the experts in order to ascertain if the opinion is based on a sound factual basis or on disputed matters or hypothetical facts yet to be determined by the courts.
>
> If an expert has discounted some evidence supplied to him, he may, at the conclusion of the case, be held wrong to have done so and his opinion may thereby be invalidated. Equally, he may have assumed an incorrect significance for a particular piece of material. It is only by proper and full disclosure to all parties, that an expert's opinion can be tested in court: in order to ascertain whether all appropriate information was supplied and how the expert would deal with it. It is not for one party to keep their cards face down on the table so that the other party does not know the full extent of information supplied. Fairness dictates that a party should not be forced to meet a case pleaded or an expert opinion on the basis of documents he cannot see. Although civil litigation is adversarial, it is not a matter of withholding relevant information if you can get away with it.
>
> The Commercial Courts and the Family Division have been in the forefront of developing procedures whereby experts give unbiased opinions based on instructions and on information disclosed and known to all parties.
>
> This is, in my judgement, essential if experts are to be of any assistance to the court. The report of Lord Woolf, *Access to Justice*, specifically commends this approach to expert evidence and the trend in the Queen's Bench Division is developing to require candour, particularly in professional negligence cases."

027 Therefore, a solicitor must take care in selecting documents to go to an expert: and an expert must take care in the documents to which he refers in any report for service. Unfortunately, sometimes insufficient care is taken. In particular, there are a number of cases in which materials prepared by an expert have been accidentally disclosed by a solicitor, e.g. a confidential covering letter or even an entire report (*Kenning* v. *Eve Construction* [1989] 1 WLR 1189 (covering letter); *Webster* v. *James Chapman & Co* [1989] 3 All ER 939; and *Pizzey* v. *Ford Motor Company Ltd* [1994] PIQR P15 (whole report)). The general common law rule is that, once a document has been disclosed, confidentiality is lost and it is too late to assert privilege based upon that confidentiality, unless the disclosure has been by way of an obvious mistake. CPR Rule 31.20 provides that, where a party inadvertently allows a privileged document to be inspected, the party who has inspected the document may only use it or its contents with the permission of the court: but the new Rule does not give guidance as to the principles upon which the court will give permission, except that the court will of course take into account "the overriding objective" set out in Rule 1.1. It is likely that they will tend to follow the common law rule. Because of the increasing duties upon an expert to be full and frank (see above), it is possible that the courts may be less willing to hold that expert materials have been disclosed in obvious error. Other than the usual care which an expert takes (for example, marking all drafts prior to finalising a report for service with suitable rubric making it clear that that version is confidential and not for disclosure to the other side), there is little he can do about this himself: it is a matter for those instructing him.

WITHOUT PREJUDICE

028 The public policy basis of "without prejudice" privilege is that *bona fide* communications between parties to effect a compromise should not be admissible in evidence, thereby encouraging parties to reach settlement by allowing them to speak their minds fully and frankly. It is based on the sensible proposition that "it is better to settle than to fight" (*Norwich Union Life Insurance Society* v. *Tony Waller Ltd* (1984) 128 SJ 300).

029 Experts may be involved in "without prejudice" discussions between parties. Indeed, it was common for "without prejudice" meetings of experts to be ordered under RSC Order 38, rule 38, a rule originally developed by those judges sitting as official referees, which provided:

> "In any cause or matter the court may, if it thinks fit, direct that there be a meeting 'without prejudice' of such experts within such periods before or after discussion of their reports as the court may specify, for the purpose of identifying those parts of their evidence which are in issue. Where such a meeting takes place, the experts may prepare a joint statement indicating those parts of their evidence on which they are, and those on which they are not, in agreement."

030 It is clearly important to encourage experts at such meetings to be as full and frank as possible, and for them not to have to look over their shoulder all the time. As a matter of principle, it is therefore important that what goes on in these meetings should be confidential and not admissible in evidence. However, where a court orders experts to meet on a "without prejudice" basis, it does so so that the experts can assist the court by trying to narrow the issues and agree facts, and record points of agreement and disagreement in a joint statement. Therefore, again, there is a balance to be made between two different public interests, namely that in narrowing issues and that in full disclosure between parties to litigation. The courts have rationalised these interests by holding that experts' meetings and communications associated with them are protected by privilege: but any agreement between the experts as a result of the meetings is not privileged. However, Lord Woolf considered the balance that had been struck was not optimal: in particular, in both of his Reports, Lord Woolf expressed concern about parties and their lawyers attempting to restrict the ability of experts to come to any agreement in a joint meeting, and he recommended that it should be unprofessional conduct for an expert to be given or to accept instructions not to agree.

031 The relevant RSC Rule—and Lord Woolf's concerns—have been considered in two recent cases, *Stanton* v. *Brian F Callaghan* (1999) 15 Const LJ 50 and *Robin Ellis Ltd* v. *Malwright Ltd* [1999] BLR 81. As matters of principle, these cases held:

(i) Experts' meetings and the communications associated with them are "without prejudice" and protected by privilege. Evidence of them is not admissible in court.
(ii) That which is agreed as a result of without prejudice meetings between experts is not privileged, and is admissible in court.
(iii) The purpose of these meetings between experts is not to achieve a settlement of the proceedings or to produce agreements binding on the parties: and any agreement between the experts resulting from the meetings is not binding on the parties. The purpose of such meetings is to narrow issues of fact, including opinion.
(iv) After an expert "begins to take part in the management and conduct of the trial in advance of proceedings in court", if he changes his opinion in the form of a joint statement, he is immune from being sued by the party that has employed him.

032 These principles regarding "without prejudice" meetings of experts ordered by the court under RSC Order 38, rule 38 are to a very large extent reflected by the new provisions of the CPR. Rule 35.12 states:

"(1) The court may, at any stage, direct a discussion between experts for the purpose of requiring the experts to
  (a) identify the issues in the proceedings; and
  (b) where possible, reach agreement on an issue.
(2) The court may specify the issues which the experts must discuss.
(3) The court may direct that following a discussion with the experts they must prepare a statement for the court showing:
  (a) those issues on which they agree;
  (b) those issues on which they disagree and a summary of their reasons for disagreeing.
(4) The content of the discussion between the experts shall not be referred to at the trial unless the parties agree.
(5) Where experts reach agreement on an issue during their discussion, their agreement shall not bind the parties unless the parties expressly agree to be bound by the agreement."

033 However, despite Rule 35.12(5) (and the identical common law principle enunciated in *Robin Ellis Ltd* v. *Malwright Ltd*), if the experts do in fact come to an agreement, the parties may find it difficult in practice not to adopt that agreement. As Judge Newey QC put it in *Richard Roberts Holding Ltd* v. *Douglas Smith Stimson Partnership (No 3)* (1990) 47 BLR 113 at 125–126):

"If, of course, during or at the conclusion of a meeting an expert is persuaded of the correctness of another expert's views and states as much in writing or even orally, he cannot subsequently give evidence truthfully to the contrary. The only exception to this is when fresh information, such as the result of new laboratory tests, or a growth in scientific knowledge, has caused him again to change his mind.

If, in the absence of any new developments, an expert were to give evidence contrary to that which he had agreed, he could not be cross-examined about what had happened at the meeting because it was 'without prejudice', but other sanctions might be invoked against him. If he is a member of a profession, complaint might be made to its governing body; further or alternatively if he is a member of an association of consultants or of experts he might be reported to it.

In practice a party whose expert witness has at a 'without prejudice' meeting held before trial agreed matters which are contrary to that party's case, is in a difficulty. He can either accept as binding upon himself the agreement made by the expert, or he can replace the expert. If a party adopts the latter course, he will have to apply to the court to order a further experts' meeting and will almost certainly be ordered to pay the costs of the first one."

CONCLUSION

034 Therefore, although the principles of discovery (now, disclosure) of documents and privilege are based on sound public policy criteria, the detailed rules governing the procedure are technical. The courts have not always been confident and consistent in construing them, and the discretion given to the courts by the CPR is not likely to lead to greater consistency. These rules are currently evolving rapidly, and they have taken another evolutionary leap with the introduction of the CPR. Consequently, there are areas of disclosure in which an expert may become involved where particular care and consideration (and, on occasions, perhaps professional advice) are required.

Gary Hickinbottom *is a partner in Cameron McKenna, where he deals with multi-jurisdictional technical litigation, including a variety of trade and public law disputes, but particularly group product liability claims such as those involving contraceptives and antibiotics. He led the team that successfully defended the main defendant in the benzodiazepine litigation, which is the largest product liability claim to have been brought in England. In addition, he has a* pro bono *practice, acting for condemned men on death row in the West Indies. He sits as a traffic adjudicator under the Road Traffic Act 1991, and a Recorder sitting in the Crown Court and County Court on criminal, civil and private family cases. He is a council member of The Academy of Experts, and a Fellow of the Chartered Institute of Arbitrators. He has written widely on procedural matters and is on the editorial board of* The Litigator *and* Personal Injury.

CHAPTER 1/9

PROFESSIONAL RESPONSIBILITIES AND LIABILITY OF EXPERTS AND EXPERT WITNESSES

Paul Newman, Barrister

SECTION A

The expert and his skills

What is an expert?

001 There is no case law or statute in which the term "expert" is expressly defined. Therefore, for practical purposes an expert must be taken to be someone who, by his training or experience or combination of both, has developed certain skills in a specialism, whether that be architecture, civil engineering or the analysis of handwriting. Because of professional or statutory criteria, aimed at the setting of appropriate standards, certain professions, such as architecture, require specific formal qualifications.

002 The English courts appear to value in an expert the ability to use knowledge by virtue of training and/or experience in a particular specialism rather than to give excessive weight to the route or method by which the expertise was obtained: *R* v. *Silverlock* [1894] 2 QB 766. In that particular case a solicitor was permitted to give expert evidence in the science of handwriting.

003 A similar flexibility in defining an expert emerges from section 4(1) of the Civil Evidence Act 1972. Although this is concerned solely with the question of proof of foreign law in English courts (a matter for expert evidence) it suggests that the requisite level of expertise can be gained from *either* "knowledge *or* experience".

004 The unique distinction between an expert witness and the lay witness in the context of court or arbitration proceedings is that the former, unlike the latter, is expressly permitted to give opinion evidence. Lay witnesses must, in general, limit themselves to the facts.

What is a specialism?

005 Conventionally an expert will give advice, an opinion or evidence in regard to matters that fall within a specific branch of knowledge, whether that be architecture, French law or the analysis of handwriting. The simple proposition that an expert should limit himself to specific narrow questions within a single specialism breaks down in the conduct of construction cases. There are many specialisms contained within the apparently unitary professions of civil engineer, architect and surveyor. The fact that a witness has no direct experience of a particular specialism does not automatically disqualify him from being an expert. The modern construction industry has given rise to the now well known creature, the "claims consultant". More often than not a claims consultant is professionally qualified as a quantity surveyor and should not, on the face of it, be able to give expert evidence in regard to the causes of delay in the completion of building works. Such evidence would more conventionally fall within the specialism of an architect. However, in at least one case, the judge took the robust view that the experienced claims consultant could properly be regarded as a multi-disciplinary expert in the assessment of the ordinary consequences of carrying out building works.

006 So far as the choice of expert witnesses is concerned, there is no pecking order of excellence and it is always a question of choosing "horses for courses". It is better to have one *relevant* expert than three rival experts whose expertise is derived from a similar but not directly relevant field. Given that many factual situations do not fall neatly within a given specialism the lay client, *via* his legal advisers, should give careful thought to the choice of a relevant expert. It may often be the case that it is better to have an adequate generalist than another expert who has professional experience within an extremely narrow specialism.

The duty of care to be expected of a professional

007 A professional may incur liability for the quality of his written or oral advice or opinion in contract, negligence or under statute and these are the actual or perceived failings upon which the expert witnesses will be asked to report.

008 Contractually a professional's duty at common law is to exercise reasonable skill and care (whether such a term is express or implied). This is also reflected in section 3 of the Supply of Goods and Services Act 1982. In the tort of negligence a professional will be judged by the same criteria of reasonable skill and care but subject to the normal tortious requirements of duty of care, foreseeability and remoteness of damage.

009 In negligence and contractual cases concerning alleged breach of professional standards the defendant professional is judged by the standard of conduct to be expected from a prudent and competent person practising that particular specialism. He is not automatically and necessarily pilloried for coming to the wrong conclusion:

> "No matter what profession it may be, the common law does not impose on those who practise it any liability for damage resulting from what in the result turn out to have been errors of judgement, unless the error was such as no reasonable well-informed and competent member of that profession could have made: *Saif Ali and Another* v. *Sydney Mitchell & Co (A Firm) and Others* [1980] AC 198 at 220."

010 The expert's level of competence is judged by the standards prevailing at the time of the alleged negligence and not with the benefit of hindsight.

011 The courts have on a number of occasions defined the standard of care required. In *T E Eckersley and Others* v. *Binnie and Partners and Others* (1988) 18 Con LR 1 Bingham LJ stated in the Court of Appeal at pages 80–81:

> "The law requires of a professional man that he live up in practice to the standards of the ordinary skilled man exercising and professing to have his special professional skill. He need not possess the highest expert skill; it is enough if he exercises the ordinary skill of an ordinary competent man exercising his particular art. So much is established by *Bolam* v. *Friern Hospital Management Committee* [1957] 2 All ER 118; [1957] 1 WLR 582, which has been applied and approved time without number . . .

From these general statements it follows that a professional man should command the *corpus* of knowledge which forms part of the professional equipment of the ordinary member of his profession. He should not lag behind other ordinary assiduous and intelligent members of his profession in knowledge of new advances, discoveries and developments in his field. He should have such awareness as an ordinarily competent practitioner would have of the deficiencies in his knowledge and the limitations on his skill. He should be alert to the hazards and risks inherent in any professional task he undertakes to the extent that other ordinary competent members of his profession would be alert. He must bring to any professional task he undertakes no less expertise, skill and care than any other ordinarily competent members of his profession would bring, but need bring no more. The standard is that of the reasonable average. The law does not require of a professional man that he be a paragon, combining the qualities of polymath and prophet . . .

In deciding whether a professional man has fallen short of the standards observed by ordinarily skilled and competent members of his profession, it is the standards prevailing at the time of his acts or omissions which provide the relevant yardstick. He is not . . . to be judged by the wisdom of hindsight. This of course means that knowledge of an event which happened later should not be applied when judging acts and omissions which took place before that event, . . . It is necessary, if the defendants' conduct is to be judged fairly, that the making of this detailed retrospective assessment should not of itself have the effect of magnifying the significance of the methane risk as it appeared or should reasonably have appeared to ordinarily competent men with a job to do at the time."

"State of the art"

012 It has frequently been stated by the courts that negligence or contractual breaches of professional standards are to be determined by reference to what could reasonably have been expected of the professional at the time of the alleged breach.

013 In *Kimbell* v. *Hart District Council* (1986) 9 Con LR 118 the Official Referee was concerned with suspect soil which proved to be unsuitable in extreme weather conditions. The judge needed to assess what warning was available in the early 1960s which put or should have put the local authority on notice as to the possible dangers inherent in construction on sub-soil of this type and to what extent, if at all, construction in such circumstances was in contravention of relevant bye-laws.

014 Although the courts do not wish to fetter the development of new techniques in technology and increased knowledge in particular fields the professional who over enthusiastically embraces new techniques may not be able to rely on "state of the art" defences. This particularly applies to the use of new techniques for their own sake when they may be still little researched and tested.

015 In *Victoria University, Manchester* v. *Hugh Wilson & Lewis Womersley and Another* (1984) 2 Con LR 43, the Official Referee, His Honour Judge Newey, QC, decided at page 74:

"For the architects to use untried, or relatively untried materials or techniques could not in itself be wrong, as otherwise the construction industry could never make any progress. I think, however, that architects who are venturing into the untried or little tried would be wise to warn their clients specifically of what they are doing and to obtain their express approval."

How to avoid being negligent

016 If there are relevant codes of practice for a particular professional body or a British Standard, any breach by a professional would establish a strong *prima facie* case of negligence but, in the final analysis, in the words beloved of all lawyers, each case will be decided on "its own facts".

017 Although in cases of alleged professional negligence the courts will seek to assess what a reasonably competent professional would have done in similar circumstances this does not mean that it will necessarily be entirely swayed by simple evidence as to the ordinary practice of a professional in the particular specialism. Although such evidence may materially assist the court it is for the court to decide whether in the circumstances there was a sufficient breach of duty.

018 However, the professional's knowledge of particular needs of his client may affect the degree of skill and care he is required to exercise. In *Greaves & Co (Contractors) Ltd* v. *Baynham Meikle & Partners* (1975) 4 BLR 56, an engineer was held liable when a warehouse he designed failed under the weight of oil drums being stored there. The Court of Appeal held that there was an implied term that the structure would be fit for its purpose. Again, in *Stormont Main Working Men's Club & Institute Ltd* v. *J Roscoe Milne Partnership* (1988) 13 Con LR 127 the architect, who was particularly experienced in designing working men's clubs, including snooker facilities, was sued by his clients when it became apparent that there was insufficient space for competitions. The judge found that "The expectations of the client, so far as the architect can be expected to be aware of them, are relevant when considering the duty of the architect to seek clarification of his brief" (page 133) and that "an architect has a duty to exercise due care to ensure that the design should be reasonably effective to achieve the client's purpose" (page 133); so that "if the client has expressed his instructions in terms which leave the architect in no doubt as to what his purpose is, the architect has a duty to ascertain what is the purpose he is instructed to achieve" (page 133). On the facts of the particular case the judge decided that it was reasonable for the architect to have assumed only recreational use of the working men's club. Therefore, it is essential for all professionals to assess the terms of their appointment and although they may have indicated to the client, by means of a standard form appointment or otherwise, that they are only taking on a due skill care and diligence obligation they must ensure that they have not unwittingly put themselves in a position where they are agreeing to comply with a fitness for purpose obligation.

SECTION B

The professional's liability for negligent misstatement

The Hedley Byrne principle

019 The law of negligence requires:

- a duty of care by one party owed to another party;
- a breach of that duty of care so that the innocent party is injured;
- loss and damage suffered by the innocent party as a result of that breach of duty of care.

020 The law clearly recognises that party A is liable to be sued by party B for the consequences of the former's negligence which causes physical harm to party B. A simple example would be the negligent car driver who, in knocking down a pedestrian, causes the latter personal injuries. When the scenario changes to one where the harm caused to party B by party A is pure financial loss, the courts have struggled for consistency and a coherent response. This type of claim is often referred to as "pure economic loss" and would include the case of the contractor and the negligent certifier. In recent years courts first took a restrictive view of those financial losses that are recoverable and then began to relax once more. This may be a major reason why *Pacific Associates infra* may appear to have been illogical. The decision may simply have coincided with a period when the courts vacillated in their approach to economic loss claims. *Pacific Associates* may erroneously have been caught up in the climate created by the cases of negligently constructed buildings which neither caused physical harm nor produced a threat of physical harm.

021 In *Murphy* v. *Brentwood District Council* [1991] 1 AC 398 the House of Lords completed the task commenced by a differently constituted House of Lords in *D & F Estates Ltd and Others* v. *Church Commissioners for England and Others* [1989] AC 177. *Murphy*, where the claim was brought against the local authority in respect of negligent inspection of defectively designed foundations to a domestic dwelling house, established that a plaintiff under English law could not recover the cost of repairing a defective item where damage did not extend beyond the item itself. Interestingly in Canada the Supreme Court decided by a 4:3 majority in *Norsk Steamship Company Ltd* v. *Canadian National Railway Co* (1992) not to follow *Murphy*, as has been the case in other jurisdictions.

022 The cases of so-called negligent misstatement, which include the negligent certifier and contractor situation in the construction industry, represent the major exception to the *Murphy* principle. Negligent misstatement is a relatively recent creation and finds its roots in the decision of the House of Lords in *Hedley Byrne and Co Ltd* v. *Heller and Partners Ltd* [1964] AC 465, where the plaintiff had suffered financial losses because of negligent financial advice given to him by the defendant. The House of Lords was satisfied that the defendant was aware that his advice would be relied upon and it was foreseeable that, if the advice was bad, the plaintiff would suffer loss. On the facts of the particular case the defendant was saved from the consequences of his own negligence because he had qualified his advice with a disclaimer of responsibility. Since *Hedley Byrne* the courts have consistently held that a plaintiff is entitled to recover his financial losses in circumstances where he relied on the oral or written advice or other written statement of a party, and the party knew that the advice or written statement in question would be relied upon.

023 An important restatement of the *Hedley Byrne* principle was that of the House of Lords in *Caparo Industries plc* v. *Dickman and Others* [1990] 2 AC 605. Touche Ross, the accountants, were auditors of Fidelity, a public company. Caparo made a successful bid for Fidelity in reliance, it alleged, on Fidelity's audited accounts. Caparo commenced proceedings against Touche Ross, alleging negligence in certifying the accounts. The argument advanced was that Touche Ross owed a duty of care to investors and potential investors in respect of the audit. The House of Lords took the opportunity to re-emphasise that at the heart of all negligent misstatement cases was the need for reliance by party A on party B. It was always necessary to prove that a defendant knew that his statement would be communicated to the plaintiff, either as an individual or as a member of an identifiable class, for a specific purpose and that the plaintiff was very likely to rely upon it.

024 What is difficult to assess is the construction industry conundrum of an architect's potential liability to the contractor if the architect is incompetent in the discharge of his duties. Here the law is unfortunately in a muddle. It would seem only fair that the architect should have a duty to the contractor to exercise reasonable skill and care when issuing payment certificates (including any ascertainment of loss and expense) or granting extensions of time. There is certainly some case law to support this proposition, including favourable judicial comments in *Lubenham Fidelities and Investment Co Ltd* v. *South Pembrokeshire District Council and Another* (1986) 33 BLR 39 and *Shui On Constructions Ltd* v. *Shui Kai Co Ltd* (1985) 4 Const LJ 305. Most pertinent is the decision in *Michael Salliss & Co Ltd* v. *Carlil and William F*

Newman & Associates (1987) 13 Con LR 68, where the Official Referee, His Honour Judge Fox-Andrews, QC, concluded at page 78 that a contractor had a right to recover damages against an unfair architect:

> "If the architect unfairly promotes the building employer's interest by low certification or merely fails properly to exercise reasonable care and skill in his certification it is reasonable that the contractor should not only have the right as against the owner to have the certificate reviewed in arbitration but should also have the right to recover damages against the unfair architect."

025 Following the simple and uncomplicated approach of *Michael Salliss*, the law was unfortunately thrown into confusion by the decision of the Court of Appeal in *Pacific Associates Inc and Another* v. *Baxter and Others* (1988) 44 BLR 33. The contractor was employed under an amended FIDIC form for international civil engineering works. The contractor made a "hard materials" claim for the costs resulting from alleged errors in the borehole reports. The engineer refused to certify any additional payments. In subsequent litigation the contractor alleged that the engineer had been negligent and had failed to act impartially when certifying. The Court of Appeal decided on the facts presented to it that the contractor had established no duty of care between the engineer and him. Two arguments were crucial in reaching that conclusion. First, there was a disclaimer in the contract between the employer and the contractor. This excluded any personal liability on the part of the engineer and his staff. Even on the most superficial analysis and with no disrespect to the Court of Appeal, the ready acceptance by the Court of Appeal of the engineer's right to rely on a disclaimer in a contract to which he was not a party was a legal nonsense. Second, and of greater general importance given the traditional prevalence of arbitration provisions in all standard form building and civil engineering contracts, the Court of Appeal concluded (without the apparent benefit of previous legal authority) that the existence of an arbitration provision in the contract between employer and contractor was effective to exclude the creation of any direct duty upon the engineer towards the contractor.

026 Without recourse to the intellectual sleight of accepting that *Pacific Associates* was decided upon its own particular facts, it is extremely difficult to reconcile the Court of Appeal's decision with that of a superior court, the House of Lords, in the slightly later case of *Caparo*. The retreat from *Pacific Associates* is clearly seen in the unreported Australian case, *R W Miller and Co Pty Ltd* v. *Krupp (Australia) Pty Ltd* (1992). Although the plaintiff's claim in negligence was dismissed in accordance with the *Pacific Associates* principle, the judge concluded that *Pacific Associates* clearly "turned on the particular circumstances" in which the "contractual framework" had applied.

027 What was not discussed by the Court of Appeal, being irrelevant on the facts of the actual case, was the nature of the relationship between architect or engineer and contractor in the absence of any arbitration clause or specific disclaimer. In choosing not to discuss more fully and generally the architect's or engineer's duty of care to a contractor, the Court of Appeal left room for fresh analysis of the problem in future cases. To that extent, *Pacific Associates* may not offer the negligent certifier total protection against contractors' claims. Courts may decide to distinguish *Pacific Associates*, if necessary, as having been decided on its own particular facts. This device is used by lawyers to explain away problematic decisions of the courts which seem to defy an ordinary understanding of the law. Leaving to one side the slightly unusual contract form in *Pacific Associates*, which included a specific disclaimer about the certifier's duty to the contractor, the principle established does appear to be otherwise relevant to the architect's position under unamended contracts of the JCT and ICE families.

028 The return to a more realistic approach is found in *Davy Offshore Ltd* v. *Emerald Field*

Contracting Ltd (1991) 27 Con LR 138. In the words of the Official Referee, His Honour Judge Thayne Forbes, QC:

> "In my judgement, it is clear that the obligation to act fairly is concerned with those duties of the architect/engineer which require him to use his professional judgement in holding the balance between his client and the contractor. Such duties are those where the architect/engineer is obliged to make a decision or form an opinion which affects the rights of the parties to the contract, for example, valuations of work, ascertaining direct loss and expense, granting extensions of time, etc. When making such decisions pursuant to his duties under the contract, the architect/engineer is obliged to act fairly" (page 146).

029 The 1990s have seen some significant economic loss cases, with a greatly increased tendency on the part of the courts to find that party A owes to party B a duty of care in negligence (in the absence of a contractual link) and to hold that financial loss is recoverable. As such, it is now less than clear if an architect or engineer when certifying owes a duty of care to the contractor. The relaxation of the courts' position was evident in the House of Lords' decision in *Henderson* v. *Merrett Syndicates* [1994] 3 All ER 506 *(infra)*. A further important development was the decision of the House of Lords in *White and Another* v. *Jones and Others* [1995] 1 All ER 691. This case involved a negligent solicitor who delayed the preparation of a new will on behalf of a client whereby the client's daughters were denied the inheritance they would otherwise have received. The House of Lords felt that the solicitor owed a duty of care to the intended beneficiaries under the will and that the principle in *Hedley Byrne & Co Ltd* v. *Heller & Partners Ltd* [1964] AC 465 was applicable. The negligent solicitor could reasonably foresee that an intended beneficiary would be deprived of a benefit under a will if he carried out his duties negligently. Lord Nolan thought that the principle was of wide application. As he stated at page 735: ". . . a professional man or an artisan who undertakes to exercise his skill in a manner which, to his knowledge, may cause loss to others if carelessly performed, may thereby implicitly assume a legal responsibility towards them. The fact that he is doing so in pursuance of a contractual duty or a statutory function cannot of itself exclude that responsibility."

030 Lord Nolan referred to an Australian case, *Voli* v. *Inglewood Shire Council* (1963) 110 CLR 74, in which the architect of the Shire Hall was held to have owed a duty to visitors to the hall to make the stage safe for the burden reasonably expected to be placed on it. In the words of Windeyer J at page 84:

> "Whatever might have been thought to be the position before the broad principles of the law of negligence stated in modern form in *Donoghue* v. *Stevenson*, it is now beyond doubt that, for the reasonably foreseeable consequences of careless or unskilful conduct, an architect is liable to anyone whom it could reasonably have been expected might be injured as a result of his negligence. To such a person he owes a duty of care quite independently of his contract of employment."

031 There is a modest grain of comfort for the engineer or architect in the sense that the Australian decision in *Voli* concerned personal injuries. It might be possible for a construction professional in other situations to exclude or limit his liability to third parties by some provision in his appointment. The House of Lords did not choose to deal with the particular question. Therefore, at the moment it is at least arguable that an architect, who negligently over-certifies monies due to the contractor, may not only owe a duty of care to the developer of a building but also to the funder. In the design context, it may now be arguable that the designer owes a duty of care to the end user of a builder, not merely to avoid physical harm to the occupants or visitors to the building, but also to avoid economic loss to an end user.

032 It should be noted that the decision in *White* v. *Jones* was not unanimous with Lords Keith and Mustill dissenting. Lord Mustill was particularly concerned with the construction industry but felt that this area of the law was far from fully developed and would potentially give rise to more cases. However, the lesson to be learnt is that no professional nowadays can assume that the existence of a contractual duty with the direct employer necessarily precludes the existence of a concurrent duty to third parties and it is essential that all professionals, who are at risk, carry appropriate insurance.

033 The mood of the English courts may now be sufficiently liberal to provide the opportunity for important overseas decisions, particularly from Canada and Australia, to be argued before them.

034 In *Edgworth Construction Ltd* v. *N D Lea & Associates* (1993) 66 BLR 64, the Supreme Court of Canada held that engineers who negligently prepared tender information for contractors had a duty of care to contractors who might rely upon the information provided. Edgworth Construction was engaged in the construction of roads in British Columbia. In 1977 it bid on a contract to build a section of highway. Its bid was successful and it entered into a contract with the provincial government. Edgworth alleged that it had lost money on the project due to errors in the specification and drawings. It commenced proceedings for negligent misrepresentation against the engineers who prepared drawings as well as the individual engineers who affixed their seals to the drawings. The contractor did not sue the provincial government as there was an exemption clause excluding the provincial government from liability.

035 In its analysis, the court held that the engineers undertook to provide the tender information for use by a definable group of people with whom it did not have any contractual relationship. The purposes of supplying the information was to allow tenderers to prepare a price to be submitted. The engineers knew this. The plaintiff contractor was one of the tenderers and relied upon the information provided by the engineers in preparing its bid. Its reliance upon the engineers' work was reasonable and it had suffered loss as a consequence. The court also found that the engineers could have taken steps to protect themselves from liability by an appropriate disclaimer of responsibility. If that had been the case the contractor could not have relied upon the documents in the way in which he did. Although individual engineers had fixed their seals to the drawings, the court held at page 70, according to McLachlin J, "… this is insufficient to establish a duty of care between the individual engineers and Edgworth. The seal attests that a qualified engineer prepared the drawing. It is not a guarantee of accuracy. The affixation of a seal, without more, is insufficient to found liability for negligent misrepresentation." Further, the court held that the engineers could not rely upon the exclusion clause in the principal agreement between the provincial government and the contractor. This decision was contrary to that of the English Court of Appeal in *Pacific Associates.*

SECTION C

Limitation of actions

036 Litigation or arbitration must ordinarily be commenced within the limitation period (i.e. the time limit set for bringing claims). This means that old and stale claims cannot be pursued. This protects a defendant from uncertainty and forces a plaintiff to bring his claim when it is at its most fresh and, in theory at least, witnesses are available.

Limitation periods in contract

037 In contract the cause of action (i.e. the right to sue) accrues on the date of the breach of contract. The fact that damage is suffered later does not give the plaintiff any further or other cause of action. The date upon which a breach occurs may not be limited to the date upon which the acts complained of were carried out. Although defective work may create one cause of action when carried out, a further breach and a further cause of action may arise when an attempt to remedy earlier defective work also fails. In the case of a contract which is executed as a deed the limitation period is 12 years from the date of breach, rather than six years.

Limitation periods in tort

038 In tort the cause of action accrues only when damage is suffered. The cause of action may not arise until long after the relevant work was carried out. If a builder negligently erects a chimney stack the cause of action in contract arises when the work is done, or when the builder purports to finish. If the work remains in place and there is no diminution in the structural integrity of the chimney stack any right of action in contract will be lost after six years. If after 10 years the chimney stack collapses and causes personal injuries, death or property damage the injured party then has an immediate right of action in tort.

039 Buildings which suffer latent damage obviously present particular difficulties. For a number of years the courts took a practical line and decided that the cause of action in tort could only arise when a building owner/occupier became aware or ought reasonably to have become aware of the existence of damage.

040 The law was thrown into confusion by the decision in *Pirelli General Cable Works Ltd* v. *Oscar Faber and Partners (A Firm)* [1983] 2 AC 1. The defendant consulting engineers advised on the design of a chimney, built in 1969. Cracks developed near the top of the chimney not later than 1970. They remained undiscovered until 1977 with legal proceedings being commenced in 1978.

041 The House of Lords (Lord Fraser of Tullybelton) held that the cause of action accrued when the damage came into existence rather than when it was discovered (page 16):

> "The plaintiff's cause of action will not accrue until *damage* occurs, which will commonly consist of cracks coming into existence as a result of the defect even though the cracks or the defect may be undiscovered and undiscoverable. There may perhaps be cases where the defect is so gross that the building is doomed from the start, and where the owner's cause of action will accrue as soon as it is built, but it seems unlikely that such a defect would not be discovered within the limitation period. Such cases, if they exist, would be exceptional."

042 The difficulties caused by the *Pirelli* decision led to the Latent Damage Act 1986.

The Latent Damage Act 1986

043 The Act introduced two main changes into the law:

(i) *The concept of "discoverability"*. An action may be commenced after the end of the six-year limitation period, provided that it is brought within three years after the plaintiff's "date of knowledge", as defined in the Act.

(ii) There is an overriding 15-year "long-stop" limitation period, after which (subject to the exceptions contained in sections 2(2) and 4 of the Act) all negligence actions will be statute barred.

(iii) After some initial uncertainty, the Act is only applicable to cases brought in tort.

044 The "date of knowledge" itself is defined in subsections (5) to (9) of section 14A. This sets out a comprehensive series of tests in order to establish when the plaintiff "knew or ought to have known" of the damage. Thus, before the extended limitation period will come into operation, the plaintiff must have "knowledge" of the following matters:

(i) That the damage which he has suffered is sufficiently serious that a reasonable person, assuming a defendant who had admitted liability and who was able to pay the damages claimed, would consider the issue of proceedings to be justified (subsection (6));

(ii) That the damage was attributable to the act complained of (subsection (7)(*a*));

(iii) Who should be named as defendant (subsection (7)(*b*));

(iv) If the negligent act is alleged to have been committed by someone other than the defendant, the identity of that person and the reasons for bringing an action against the defendant (subsection (7)(*c*)).

045 The word "knowledge" is not defined. It is clear, however, from subsection (9) that it is intended to include not only actual knowledge but also such knowledge as the plaintiff would have been able to obtain by proper observation or, in cases where it was reasonable for him to have done so, by seeking appropriate expert advice. If such expert advice does not reveal the damage, the plaintiff will not be imputed with knowledge of it, provided he took all reasonable steps to obtain appropriate advice.

046 The problem of fixing the date of knowledge for the purposes of section 14A of the Act was considered in *Joan Horbury* v. *Craig Hall and Rutley* [1991] CILL 692. The *onus* was on the plaintiff, following the decision of the Court of Appeal in *London Congregational Union Inc* v. *Harriss and Harriss*, to establish that her claim was not statute-barred and not for the defendant to disprove it. Mrs Horbury argued that the earliest possible date to activate the three year "knowledge period" was July 1985 when she first discovered the *extent* of dry rot, damp and woodworm at her property after an independent surveyor's report. Dry rot had been discovered in 1982 but the seriousness of the problem had not been appreciated even though money had to be spent on repairs. A chimney, also found to be unsafe in early 1984, was made good when the loft was converted. The judge concluded that it was irrelevant that the plaintiff had discovered the extent of defects on a piecemeal basis over a number of years. Her state of knowledge in 1982 was such that a reasonable person would have considered the damage sufficiently serious to justify instituting proceedings against the defendant.

047 There is one exception (section 1) to the rule that a plaintiff has three years from his "date of knowledge" in which to bring an action. Where a person acquires already damaged property and his predecessor in title knew or ought to have known of the damage at the time when he held an interest in the property, the knowledge of the predecessor will be imputed to his successor and the three-year extension of the limitation period will run against the latter as from the former's "date of knowledge". A person who buys a defective dwelling-house may find that he is unable to bring an action in respect of damage because his predecessor failed to take advantage of the extended limitation period.

048 Section 14B is designed to mitigate the hardship which could result to potential defendants under the "discoverability test". Subject to sections 2(2) and 4, no action may be brought after the expiration of 15 years from the date of the defendant's breach of duty.

Fraud and deliberate concealment

049 Where the plaintiff's claim is based on fraud, the ordinary limitation provisions will not apply. The plaintiff will have six years from the date when he discovered or could reasonably have discovered the fraud in which to bring an action. The 15-year-long stop does not apply to cases of fraud. The defendant's liability remains indefinite. Section 32 of the Limitation Act 1980 also extends to "deliberate concealment" which is defined in subsection (2) as "the deliberate commission of a breach of duty in circumstances in which it is unlikely to be discovered for some time".

050 An illustrative example of this principle was *Gray and Others (The Special Trustees of the London Hospital)* v. *T P Bennett & Son (A Firm) and Others Ltd* (1987) 43 BLR 63. The limitation period did not run due to the deliberate concealment of some "butchered" concrete nibs in a hospital built in 1962. The bulging brickwork which resulted from the concealment was not discovered until 1979 when time began to run. The plaintiff had until 1985 to serve legal proceedings.

051 Where a person acquires a building which is already damaged at the time of the acquisition, but where the damage is not by that time "discoverable" within the meaning of section 14A, the rule in *Pirelli* is preserved. Although a fresh cause of action will accrue to the successor in title on the date when he acquires the property, the cause of action will be deemed to have accrued on the date when the original cause of action arose. Therefore, the "basic" six-year limitation period will run against the successor in title from the date when damage first occurred, and a 15-year long-stop from the date of the breach of duty.

Practical problems

052 The 15-year long-stop runs from the date of the breach of duty. In practice it will frequently be extremely difficult to establish the precise date (many years later) when a specific breach of duty occurred.

053 There may also be the possibility of claims under the Civil Liability (Contribution) Act 1978. A defendant, against whom judgment has been awarded in legal proceedings, may recover a contribution towards the damages from a third party who is wholly or partly to blame for the plaintiff's loss. A defendant may commence a contribution action at any time up to two years after judgment is entered against him. Therefore, given that most legal actions will take several years to come to trial, contractors may be vulnerable to third party actions for a period in excess of the normal long-stop of 15 years.

Limitation problems in negligent misstatement cases

054 The case of *Peter John Hiron and Others* v. *Pynford South Ltd and Others* (1991) 60 BLR 78 combines the complex areas of negligent misstatement; concurrent rights to sue in contract and in negligence and limitation of actions.

055 Structural damage to Mr and Mrs Hiron's house occurred in October 1976. In

September 1977 they retained Leo Lewis as their consultant. On 17 February 1978 Mr and Mrs Hiron made a claim on Legal and General (their insurers) who, in September 1978, retained an engineer, Peter Olley, to advise. In early 1980 Pynford carried out an investigation for Mr and Mrs Hiron and later reported. Peter Olley recommended the report to Legal and General (subject to minor qualification) and also had the tacit approval of Mr and Mrs Hiron's consultant. The recommended works were then carried out and completed in 1981. In 1983 the house, which was unstable, suffered further physical damage. Further remedial works were required.

056 In subsequent legal proceedings Mr and Mrs Hiron alleged that the two consultants, by endorsing Pynford's report, had been negligent. The court was satisfied that:

(i) Peter Olley owed no duty of care in negligence to Mr and Mrs Hiron. They had retained their own expert, Leo Lewis.

(ii) So far as concurrent responsibilities in contract and negligence were concerned, the mere existence of a contract did not preclude liability in tort. According to the Official Referee, His Honour Judge Newey, QC at page 89:

> "I think that the correct approach is that when there was a contract between plaintiffs and defendants it should be treated as a very important consideration in deciding whether there was sufficient proximity between them and whether it is just and reasonable that the defendant should owe a duty in tort."

(iii) So far as any claims that Mr and Mrs Hiron might have against their consultant, and Legal and General might have against their consultant, were concerned, both Mr and Mrs Hiron and Legal and General had the benefit of a contract with their consultant under which the contractual rights mirrored those that would otherwise have existed in tort. The situation might have been different if contractual and tortious duties had not precisely coincided.

(iv) The limitation period for negligent misstatement was triggered when damage was suffered and not when the damage was discovered. It might be that the cause of action would arise virtually simultaneously with any rights to sue in contract.

SECTION D

Remedies for professional negligence

Liability in contract and negligence

057 In the event of an expert providing his client with incompetent advice he may ordinarily be sued in contract and/or negligence. Contract and negligence provide a claimant potentially with *two* rights to sue for damages out of a single incident (without, of course, creating a right to two awards of damages). At times, the courts have responded in different ways to claims based on tort and contract.

058 Although A and B may be in contract, in some situations it is more attractive for A to set out his case in negligence (where the scope of duties would be similar to those in contract) because of potential limitation problems. Subject to the specific application of the Limitation Act 1980 and the Latent Damage Act 1986, the prescribed periods (but not the trigger date) during which legal actions can be commenced are the same for both contract and tort. With the exception of personal injury claims, where the limitation period is ordinarily three years from the date of injury, other tortious wrongs and claims for breach of contract, other than those where the contract was executed under seal, have a six-year limitation period. The limitation period for contracts under seal is 12 years. Although the Latent Damage Act 1986, which does not apply to contractual claims, may provide a 15-year long-stop limitation period in tort, the real distinction between actions in tort and contract is the date when the cause of action arises. In contract, the limitation period runs from the date the breach of contract occurred. In tort, the limitation period ordinarily commences on the date when damage resulted, although statute provides that the "trigger date" for limitation purposes might be the first date on which the damage was reasonably discoverable. Obviously the date of resultant damage can be later than the date when the initial breach of contract occurred. One well known example of a party's reliance on tort, as opposed to contract, to avoid limitation problems was *Pirelli General Cable Works Ltd* v. *Oscar Faber and Partners (supra).*

059 Traditionally, lawyers have prepared legal pleadings arguing the plaintiff's case both under any relevant contract and in tort. Unfortunately, words of Lord Scarman in *Tai Hing Cotton Mill Ltd* v. *Liu Chong Hing Bank Ltd* [1986] AC 80 at page 107 introduced an element of confusion into established practice, although they were part of a Privy Council decision and as such not of binding effect in England: "Their Lordships do not believe that there is anything to the advantage of the law's development in searching for a liability in tort where the parties are in a contractual relationship. This is particularly so in a commercial relationship."

060 To some extent Lord Scarman's comments were merely a reflection of what he felt the legal position should be. It was illogical for there to be any tortious liability in circumstances where the parties had the benefit of a contract. Such is consistent with the position in France where the doctrine of *non cumul* specifically prevents the concurrence of claims in contract and tort. Unfortunately the English approach has been a switchback of uncertainties. A significant modern decision was a first instance one of Oliver J in *Midland Bank Trust Co Ltd* v. *Hett, Stubbs and Kemp* [1978] 3 All ER 571. The case concerned a negligent solicitor who, in drawing up an option to purchase a parcel of land, failed to register the option as an estate contract. Although the contrary was argued by the defendant solicitor, the existence of a detailed written contract was no bar to tortious recovery. In the words of Oliver J at page 598: "There is not and never has been any rule of law that a person having alternative claims must frame his action in one or the other. If I have a contract with my dentist to extract a tooth, I am not thereby precluded from suing him in tort if he negligently shatters my jaw . . ."

061 The case was significant; the judge rejected the proposition that a professional who had a contract with the client was thereby freed from any possible liability in negligence, a proposition apparently accepted in earlier cases.

062 At Court of Appeal stage in *National Bank of Greece* v. *Pinios Co No 1* [1990] 1 AC 637 Lloyd LJ said at page 650: "But so far as I know it has never been the law that a plaintiff who has the choice of suing in contract or in tort can fail in contract yet nevertheless succeed in tort; . . ."

063 He went on to state at page 651: "The position would be different if the contract and the tort lay in different fields. Thus, if, to take a simple example, I give my employee a lift home, and injure him by my careless driving, then obviously he will not be prevented from recovering from me in tort, because of the existence between us of a contract of employment . . ."

064 In *Bell* v. *Peter Browne & Co* [1990] 2 QB 495, a case concerning solicitors' negligence in the transfer of the former matrimonial home by the plaintiff to his wife subject to an interest in the proceeds of sale, Mustill LJ thought it a pity that English law recognised concurrent duties in contract and negligence which he considered to be an anomaly and unnecessary. At page 511 he stated:

> "... I think it a pity that English law has elected to recognise concurrent rights of action in contract and tort. Other legal systems seem to manage quite well by limiting attention to the contractual obligations which are, after all, the foundation of the relationship between the professional man and his client: as for example, in the case of French law, *via* the doctrine of *non cumul*. That precisely the same breach of precisely the same organisation should be capable of generating causes of action which arise at different times is in my judgement an anomaly which our law could well do without. Nevertheless the law is clear and we must apply it."

065 Again, the reluctance to identify a tortious cause of action in circumstances where there was a written contract, was reflected in the decision of the Official Referee, His Honour Judge Newey, QC, in *Hiron and Others* v. *Pynford South Ltd and Others* (1991) 60 BLR 78 at page 89:

> "In view of the cases, while it may be that the courts are moving towards a restrictive view of duties in tort when there is a contract between the parties, it seems clear that at present the mere existence of a contract does not preclude liability in tort.
>
> I think that the correct approach is that when there was a contract between plaintiffs and defendants it should be treated as a very important consideration in deciding whether there was sufficient proximity between them and whether it is to be just and reasonable that the defendant should owe a duty in tort."

066 Surprisingly 1993 and 1994 brought a spate of decisions on the question of concurrent liability. First, His Honour Judge Michael Kershaw, QC, sitting as an Official Referee, considered the issue in *Lancashire and Cheshire Associations of Baptist Churches Inc* v. *Howard and Seddon Partnership* [1993] 3 All ER 467. Here, the plaintiff's claim against a firm of architects resulted from alleged defects in the design of a new church sanctuary which caused ventilation and condensation problems. A writ was issued against the architects claiming damages for breach of contract and negligence. The judge concluded at page 477: "... there can be a duty in tort despite the existence of a contract for professional services, albeit that the implied as well as the express terms of a contract will regulate the extent of that duty ... It cannot be said that there is a duty in tort in all cases where the parties are in a contractual relationship."

067 The judge had in mind that a party's claim in tort might ultimately be defeated because it constituted a head of loss not recognised by the general law of tort, such as pure economic loss in circumstances where the facts did not fall within the *Hedley Byrne* principle as developed by the courts. Here, the designs submitted by the defendants were to enable the plaintiff to consider the accommodation and appearance of the proposed building. The architects had made no express statement as to the building's technical adequacy *via* the design work; there was no reliance and therefore no right to recover the simple cost of correcting defects.

068 The Limitation Act 1980 operated quite separately from a party's general legal rights as defined by the appropriate law:

> "in my judgement the flaw in [counsel's] reasoning is to treat the right given to a defendant by the Limitation Act 1980 as a right derived from a contract, whether from express or from implied terms of the contract. It is not. It is derived from the 1980 Act. That Act does not imply a term into a contract. On the contrary, it has rightly been said that the successive statutes of limitation merely bar a plaintiff's remedy, and not his cause of action. In my judgement the principle that where the

parties choose to regulate their rights by contract tort cannot alter those rights applies only to rights created by the terms of the contract, and not to rights resulting from the application of the 1980 Act" (at page 475).

069 The question of concurrence then arose in other cases, including *Conway* v. *Crowe Kelsey Partner and Another* [1994] CILL 927 and the seminal decision of the House of Lords in *Henderson* v. *Merrett Syndicates Ltd* [1994] 3 All ER 506 *(infra)*. In *Conway* the plaintiffs engaged the defendant consulting engineers in relation to structural damage caused to their property by heave. Subsequently when any cause of action in contract was statute barred, they sued the defendant in tort. The judge, His Honour Judge Newman, QC, an Official Referee, analysed the legal position. He concluded that orthodoxy dictated that the two causes of action, in contract and tort, existed independent of each other despite the paradox that a defendant might use a defence under the Limitation Act 1980 to defeat a claim in contract. Consistent with His Honour Judge Kershaw, QC in *Lancashire and Cheshire Associations of Baptist Churches (supra)* the judge concluded at page 928:

"The defence of limitation is a creature of statute; it is procedural in its effect; it gives a defendant the right to plead the statute if he wishes; he will not always wish to do so . . .

"If Parliament has therefore enacted different limitation periods for contract and tort it is not unfair or unreasonable to the defendant that the defence of limitation has not arisen against the plaintiffs' claim in tort."

070 His Honour Judge Fox-Andrews, QC had adopted a similar approach in the slightly earlier case of *Wessex Regional Health Authority* v. *HLM Design Ltd* [1993] CILL 907. In the words of the judge at page 909:

"I am satisfied that where there is a contractual relationship between a person and someone professing to special skills for which professional qualifications are necessary and the contract relates to the exercise of those skills and the case falls within the principles of *Hedley Byrne* as explained in *Caparo* and *Murphy* there may be a concurrent duty to take reasonable care to prevent or avoid economic loss so long as it is fair and reasonable."

071 These first instance decisions were then complemented by the seminal decision of the House of Lords in *Henderson* v. *Merrett Syndicates Ltd* [1994] 3 All ER 506. The case related to an action by Lloyd's Names who were members of syndicates managed by the defendant underwriting agents. In some instances the Names' underwriting was managed by an agent with whom he had a contract while in others the Names' business was managed by a sub-agent with whom he had no contract. As far as the contracts were concerned it was agreed that there was an implied duty on behalf of the agents to exercise reasonable skill and care. Two questions arose. First, did primary or sub-agents owe a duty of care in tort to Names? Second, could an agent who was in contract with a Name owe concurrently a duty of care in tort? After a detailed consideration of the law, primarily found in the speech of Lord Goff, the issues were resolved in favour of the Names. Lord Goff thoroughly endorsed the first instance decision, *Midland Bank Trust Co Ltd* v. *Hett, Stubbs and Kemp (supra)* and found *Hedley Byrne & Co* v. *Heller and Partners Ltd* [1964] AC 465 applicable to establish a duty of care in favour of the Names.

072 On whether or not professional men could have a concurrent liability in tort if they caused economic loss, clearly since the decision in *Hedley Byrne & Co (supra)* professional men were potentially liable in tort for negligent misstatement. At pages 524–525 he commented as follows:

"At first, as is shown in particular by cases concerned with liability for solicitors' negligence, the courts adopted something very like the French solution, holding that a claim against a solicitor for negligence must be pursued in contract, and not in tort . . . Furthermore when, in *Bagot* v. *Stevens Scanlan & Co Ltd* . . . Diplock LJ adopted a similar approach in the case of a claim against a firm of architects, he felt compelled to recognise that a different conclusion might be reached in cases where the law in the old days recognised either something in the nature of a status like a public calling (such as common carrier, common innkeeper, or a bailor and bailee) or the status of master and servant.

. . . I must confess to finding it startling that, in the second half of the twentieth century, a problem of considerable practical importance should fall to be solved by reference to such an outmoded form of categorisation as this.

. . . If concurrent liability in tort is not recognised, a claimant may find his claim barred at a time when he is unaware of its existence. This must moreover be a real possibility in the case of claims against professional men, such as solicitors or architects, since the consequences of their negligence may well not come to light until long after the lapse of six years from the date when the relevant breach of contract occurred. Moreover the benefits of the Latent Damage Act 1986, under which the time of the accrual of the cause of action may be postponed until after the plaintiff has the relevant knowledge, are limited to actions in tortious negligence. This leads to the startling possibility that a client who has had the benefit of gratuitous advice from his solicitor may in this respect be better off than a client who has paid a fee. Other practical problems arise, for example, from the absence of a right to contribution between negligent contract-breakers; from the rules as to remoteness of damage, which are less restricted in tort than they are in contract; and from the availability of the opportunity to obtain leave to serve proceedings out of the jurisdiction."

073 Further on in his judgment he stated at pages 529–530:

"Attempts have been made to explain how doctors and dentists may be concurrently liable in tort while other professional men may not be so liable, on the basis that the former cause physical damage whereas the latter cause pure economic loss . . . But this explanation is not acceptable, if only because some professional men, such as architects, may also be responsible for physical damage. As a matter of principle, it is difficult to see why concurrent remedies in tort and contract, if available against the medical profession, should not also be available against members of other professions, whatever form the relevant damage may take."

074 The New Zealand decision *Rowlands* v. *Collow* [1992] 1 NZLR 178 was quoted by Lord Goff at page 531: "The issue is now virtually incontestable; a person who has performed professional services may be held liable concurrently in contract and in negligence, unless the terms of the contract preclude the tortious liability."

075 On the basis a professional may have concurrent liability in tort and contract, how does he best protect himself? The obvious response is for the professional to put an exclusion clause in his appointment with the client limiting the latter's right to seek any remedies for deficient performance by the professional to those arising in contract rather than tort. This was the approach of His Honour Judge Newman, QC in *Conway* v. *Crowe Kelsey (supra)* at page 928:

"If professional practitioners wish to avoid the longer limitation period afforded to their clients in tort resulting from their special relationship or proximity, they have, perhaps with the exception of National Health hospital doctors and dentists whose position is even more complicated today, only to include an express term in their contract excluding any liability in tort."

076 Despite Lord Goff's similar indication that the concurrent obligation in tort might be avoided by a suitable contractual provision in that the law of tort was not "supplementary to the law of contract" but "the general law, out of which the parties can, if they wish, contract" any exclusion clause must be read subject to the test of reasonableness under the Unfair Contract Terms Act 1977.

SECTION E

Third party liability under someone else's contract

077 The deliberations of the House of Lords in *Linden Gardens Trust* v. *Lenesta Sludge Disposals; St Martin's Property Corporation* v. *Sir Robert McAlpine & Sons* [1994] 1 AC 85 considered not only the proper interpretation to be placed upon the assignment provisions in JCT contracts but also raised a further point of interest on the use of collateral warranties for commercial developments as the main vehicle to ensure recovery of third party loss.

078 The standard JCT assignment provision prevents any assignment of rights without the consent of the other party. Traditionally, third party users of a development have taken the benefit of the building contract and relating consultancy appointments by way of assignment at practical completion stage. In *St Martin's*, the House of Lords held that, provided certain conditions are met, the original employer under a building contract can claim *substantial damages* from the contractor for defects, even if he has sold the building at full value and is under no liability for repairs. It is not open to the contractor to argue that, because the employer has suffered no actual loss, the employer's entitlement is limited to nominal damages. The judgment was based on an old principle dating from *Dunlop* v. *Lambert* (1839) 6 Cl & F 600 that a consignor of goods who had parted with the property in the goods before the date of breach could even so recover substantial damages for the failure to deliver the goods. In the words of Lord Browne-Wilkinson in *St Martin's* at pages 114–115:

> "In my judgement the present case falls within the rationale of the exceptions to the general rule that a plaintiff can only recover damages for his own loss. The contract was for a large development of property which, to the knowledge of both the Corporation and McAlpine, was going to be occupied, and possibly purchased, by third parties and not by Corporation itself. Therefore it could be foreseen that damage caused by a breach would cause loss to a later owner and not merely to the original contracting party, Corporation. As in contracts for the carriage of goods by land, there would be no automatic vesting in the occupier or owners of the property for the time being who sustained the loss of any right of suit against McAlpine. On the contrary, McAlpine had specifically contracted that the rights of action under the building contract *could* not without McAlpine's consent be transferred to third parties who became owners or occupiers and might suffer loss. In such a case, it seems to me proper, as in the case of the carriage of goods by land to treat the parties as having entered into the contract on the footing that Corporation would be entitled to enforce contractual rights for the benefit of those who suffered from defective performance but who, under the terms of the contract, could not acquire any right to hold McAlpine liable for breach. It is truly a case in which the rule provides 'a remedy where no other would be available to a person sustaining loss which under a rational legal system ought to be compensated by the person who has caused it'."

079 The decision in *St Martin's* begged a number of questions. First, in what circumstances will parties be held to have contemplated a future sale or letting? The answer may be obvious in the case of a large multi-unit shopping centre, but what about an industrial warehouse or office block, particularly of the speculative kind? Secondly, the Law Lords did not need to answer what happens if the sale occurs after the defective work was done and not before, as in *St Martin's*. Thirdly, the decision left open the amount of damages recoverable. The Law

Lords assumed that the employer's claim would be for the cost of repairs. What of the traditional approach of adopting the difference in value between the development as it should have been and as it was built? Similarly, the Court of Appeal decision in *Darlington Borough Council* v. *Wiltshier Northern Ltd* (1994) 69 BLR 1 is of interest in extending the tentacles of liability. More recently the question was considered, again by the Court of Appeal, in *Alfred McAlpine Construction Ltd* v. *Panatown Ltd* [1998] CILL 1353. Panatown engaged McAlpine to design and build an office block and multi-storey car park. On completion, Panatown alleged defective performance of the building contract and served notice of termination on the contractor. The site owner and effective developer was an associated company of Panatown, Unex, which also had the benefit of a duty of care warranty. In arbitration, McAlpine argued Panatown could only recover nominal losses, not being the owner. The arbitrator, unlike the Official Referee on appeal, held Panatown could recover substantial losses. The Court of Appeal held Panatown were entitled to substantial losses notwithstanding the existence of a warranty.

080 The more relaxed views of the courts in permitting recovery of losses for the benefit of a third party can also be seen in *Phillips Petroleum Co (UK) Ltd and Norsea Pipeline Ltd* v. *IT Corporation Ltd and Flaretec Alloys and Equipment Ltd* [1998] CILL 1366. The first plaintiff, Phillips, operated a North Sea oil terminal. Phillips sued IT Corporation over the design, manufacture and delivery of a flare tip which was alleged to be defective in various regards. Much of the defence related to arguments that Phillips had suffered no loss because it had been fully reimbursed by Norsea under an internal funding arrangement. According to the Official Referee, His Honour Judge Newman, QC, the case fell within the exception to the rule in *Dunlop* v. *Lambert.* The Official Referee quoted from counsel's submission on behalf of Phillips at page 1367: "In a world of increasingly complex transactional structures, the courts are not willing to countenance genuine loss disappearing into a black hole as a side wind of an otherwise sensible commercial arrangement."

081 On 30 March 1998, the Court of Appeal delivered its second judgment in *Alfred McAlpine Ltd* v. *Panatown Ltd* which was reported in [1998] CILL 1383. This judgment, which extended the principle of third party recovery of loss even further, concerned Panatown's rights to recover damages for delay. Here, counsel for McAlpine submitted that the judgment in *Darlington Borough Council* v. *Wiltshier Northern Ltd* [1995] 1 WLR 68 precluded such recovery.

082 The question of a party which had not incurred a loss recovering on behalf of another party which had suffered a loss arose in *John Harris Partnership (A Firm)* v. *Groveworld Ltd* [1999] CILL 1485. Groveworld was a property developer. John Harris was the architect which, following non-payment, sued Groveworld as employer. Groveworld counterclaimed damages for breach of contract. The case was heard in the Technology and Construction Court, formerly the Official Referees' Court. John Harris argued, as part of its defence, that Groveworld had not incurred all the losses claimed. Groveworld had a joint venture partner and under the joint venture Groveworld only had to fund 45 per cent of the loss and expenditure which was at the heart of the claim. Based on established case law, His Honour Judge Anthony Thornton, QC held Groveworld could recover the full extent of losses. At page 1486 he stated:

> "[Recovery on behalf of Frogmore, the joint venture partner] is adumbrated by two of the judgments in *Darlington.* In summary, Dillon LJ and Waite LJ, at pages 17 and 25 respectively, affirmed the principle established in the much earlier Court of Appeal decision in *Lloyd's* v. *Harper* 16 ChD 290 that where a party holds a claim for another's loss on trust for that other party, the first party, as trustee, can pursue the loss in its own name and then hold the recovered damages on trust

for the party who suffered the loss. This ability to recover arises where the parties to the contract under which the claim is brought contemplated that the plaintiff would have a right to recover the third party's loss."

083 Concern at the sometimes harsh effect of the privity of contract doctrine may become less common following legislative change. The Law Commission published its proposals in a consultative document, *Consultative Paper on Third Party Rights*, Law Commission Paper No 242, 31 July 1996. At the date of writing, the Contracts (Rights of Third Parties) Bill is before Parliament. It is almost certain to become law. At its heart, which was vigorously opposed in particular in sectors of the construction industry, the Bill provides for a partial statutory abolition of the common law doctrine of privity of contract. Under clause 1, parties will be able to enforce contractual terms, if either a party to them, or those terms purport to confer a benefit on them. The editors of *Construction Industry Law Letter* argue at [1999] CILL, pages 1481–1482 that "these principles do not translate very happily into the context of a construction contract" and then pose a number of hypothetical situations which might lead to a greater number of potential liabilities because of the subjective element in interpreting the Bill. One example they pose is of the sub-contractor providing craneage to the main contractor who effectively is providing craneage for the lifting of other sub-contractors' materials.

084 Under section 2 where a third party has rights under a contract, the others may not ordinarily "cancel the contract, or vary it in such a way as to extinguish or alter his entitlement under that right". There are complex provisions to make this work, including appeals to the High Court to dispense with third party consent. However, it is anticipated parties will be able to exclude the operation of the Act and thereby remove the clear-cut simplicity some commentators advocated.

SECTION F

Courts, the expert witness and his report

085 Subject to disclaimers, an expert is usually liable to his client for advice given in breach of the contractual duty to use reasonable skill and care or given negligently. In certain circumstances an expert will not be liable for his advice: *Palmer and Another* v. *Durnford Ford and Another* [1992] 2 All ER 122. The expert had given pre-litigation advice with the client commencing proceedings in reliance on the expert's report. The claim subsequently proved to be unsustainable when the report prepared by the other side's expert was received. Was the expert witness liable for his advice given before the commencement of the litigation? The judge concluded that it was well established that a witness was not generally liable in regard to evidence given during proceedings. That immunity also extended to the preparation of evidence to be given in court. However, the judge held that immunity only extended to what could fairly be said to be preliminary to the giving of evidence in court, judged perhaps by the principal purpose for which the work was done. The production or approval of a report for exchange would be immune but work done for the principal purpose of advising a client as to the merits of a case was not. At the end of the day each case "depends on its own facts" and the application of the judge's broad principles may be difficult.

086 The principle in *Durnford Ford and Another* was followed by Sir Thomas Bingham MR in *M (a Minor)* v. *Newham London Borough Council and Others; X and Others (Minors)* v.

Bedfordshire County Council [1994] 4 All ER 602. At pages 617–618 the Master of the Rolls stated:

> "The public interest which these authorities [cases referred to earlier in the judgment] recognised and protected was the proper administration of justice: to that end witnesses must be immune from civil action arising from what they say in court; and that protection must not be circumvented by allowing civil actions based on the earlier stages of preparation of a witness's evidence. But the cases do not indicate that those who have never become involved in the administration of justice enjoy immunity. The immunity of a witness has in the past been treated as analogous to the immunity accorded to those involved in the conduct of proceedings, and were the immunity as wide as was claimed, a barrister or a solicitor advising a client whether to proceed, or an expert advising a client on a factual question with a view to proceedings, would be immune from actions for negligence . . ."

087 *X and Others (Minors) Ltd* v. *Bedfordshire County Council; M (A Minor) and Another* v. *Newham London Borough Council and Others; E (A Minor)* v. *Dorset County Council (supra)* were the subject of a consolidated appeal from the Court of Appeal to the House of Lords. The House of Lords decision can be found at [1995] 3 All ER 353. Lord Browne-Wilkinson considered the question of witness immunity at pages 384–386. He stated at page 385:

> "The immunity of witnesses from any action founded on their evidence was originally designed to ensure in the public interest that witnesses would not, through fear of later civil proceedings, be inhibited from giving frank evidence in court. This immunity was widened by this House in *Watson* v. *M'Ewan, Watson* v. *Jones* [1905] AC 480, . . . to cover information and reports given by a potential witness to the legal advisers of a party for the purpose of preparing a proof."

088 His Lordship then quoted from the judgment of Drake J in *Evans* v. *London Hospital Medical College* [1981] 1 All ER 715 at page 720:

> "The immunity given to a witness or potential witness is because—'the administration of justice would be greatly impeded if witnesses were to be in fear that persons against whom they gave evidence might subsequently involve them in costly litigation' . . . If this object is to be achieved I think it essential that the immunity given to a witness should also extend to cover statements he makes prior to the issue of a writ or commencement of a prosecution, provided that the statement is made for the purpose of a possible action or prosecution and at a time when a possible action or prosecution is being considered . . . If immunity did not extend to such statements it would mean that the immunity attaching to the giving of evidence in court or the formal statements made in preparation for the court hearing could easily be outflanked and rendered of little use. For the same reason I think the immunity must extend also to the acts of a witness in collecting or considering material on which he may later be called to give evidence."

089 It was his considered opinion, at page 385, ". . . in my judgment the Court of Appeal decision placed too narrow a limit on the principle of witness immunity". However, *X (Minors)* v. *Bedfordshire County Council* may be distinguishable from "ordinary" civil litigation. In the words of Lord Browne-Wilkinson at page 386:

> ". . . I find the reasoning of Drake J compelling at least in relation to the investigation and preparation of evidence in criminal proceedings. In my judgement exactly similar considerations apply where, in performance of a public duty, the local authority is investigating whether or not there is evidence on which to bring proceedings for the protection of the child from abuse, such abuse frequently being a criminal offence. I express no view as to the position in relation to ordinary civil proceedings but nothing I have said casts any doubt on the decision of Mr Simon Tuckey QC in *Palmer* v. *Durnford Ford (A Firm)* [1992] 2 All ER 122."

090 The decision in *Landall* v. *Dennis Faulkner and Alsop* [1994] 5 Med LR 268 is an interesting one for expert witnesses and lawyers alike. It confirms:

- there is immunity for a witness in respect of evidence given in court;
- such immunity extends to reports for trial prepared by a witness.

091 An application before Holland J tried unsuccessfully to separate the early pre-trial advice from the report which would have removed the expert's immunity. Holland J did remind experts they must decline to give advice outside their expertise and they have a duty to the court to limit the contentious matters to be dealt with at the hearing.

092 The question of an expert's immunity from suit was considered by the Court of Appeal in *Stanton and Another* v. *Callaghan and Others* [1998] 4 All ER 961. Here, the Court of Appeal held that an action for negligence and breach of contract was not to be brought against an expert witness by the party retaining him in respect of work done preparing a report and adjoined statement prior to, and in contemplation of a trial where the trial never took place and the expert did not give evidence. The expert's immunity from suit was founded on the requirement of public policy that in the interests of the administration of justice a witness should not be inhibited from giving frank and fearless evidence.

How honest is an expert to be?

093 The overriding duty of any expert retained for litigation purposes is not to be a partisan champion of his client's case. Whatever the inducement, the expert should not adopt an argument which the party instructing him may wish the expert to advance, unless the expert is satisfied that it is a proper argument. The expert witness is *not* his client's advocate and any temptation to be unfairly partisan may, subject to what was stated above, subsequently result in a negligence claim against the relevant expert.

094 The courts and other tribunals have, on a number of occasions, analysed the true nature of expert evidence. The general message appears to be that "expert evidence presented to the court should be, and should be seen to be, the *independent* product of the expert, uninfluenced as to form or content by the exigencies of litigation. To the extent that it is not, the evidence is likely to be not only incorrect but also self-defeating" (*infra*). The expert can do worse than to model the layout of his report on the Model Form of Expert's Report prepared by the British Academy of Experts (see Appendix G).

095 The classic formulation of the expert's role is that of Lord Wilberforce in *Whitehouse* v. *Jordan* [1981] 1 WLR 246 at page 256:

> "Whilst some degree of consultation between experts and legal advisers is entirely proper, it is necessary that expert evidence presented to the court should be, and should be seen to be, the independent product of the expert, uninfluenced as to form or content by the exigencies of litigation. To the extent that it is not, the evidence is likely to be not only incorrect but self-defeating."

096 In a family law case, *In Re J (a Minor) (Expert Evidence)* (1990) *The Times*, 31 July, it was stated:

> "His Lordship said that the expert witnesses were in a privileged position in that they were permitted to given an opinion in evidence. Such experts had to express only genuinely held opinions which were not biased in favour of one party ... Opinions could differ but such

differences were usually in a legitimate area of disagreement ... An expert witness should not mislead by omission. A report should provide a straightforward not misleading opinion, be objective, should not admit facts which did not support the opinion and should have been researched properly ... If the expert considered that the data available were insufficient, then it had to be indicated to the court that the opinion was only provisional ... An expert witness should avoid providing a report which sought to promote a particular case as that would be an abuse of the expert's proper function and would render the report an argument not an opinion ... A misleading opinion would cause costs to be increased because competing evidence would have to be called. In all cases, costs could be reduced if the expert witnesses on each side could discuss together their reports in advance of the hearing."

097 The responsibilities of expert witnesses were reviewed in *National Justice Compania Naviera SA* v. *Prudential Assurance Company Ltd (The Ikarian Reefer)* [1993] CILL 838. Cresswell J reaffirmed that an expert witness was obliged to give independent and unbiased evidence. If he lacked expertise in a particular area or had insufficient information to reach a properly researched conclusion he was obliged to say so. The judge set out a number of useful propositions which should greatly assist expert witnesses in the preparation of their reports:

(i) Expert evidence should be, and should be seen by the court to be, the independent product of the expert. It should not be influenced as to form or content by the exigencies of litigation. *Dicta* of Lord Wilberforce in *Whitehouse* v. *Jordan* [1981] were approved.

(ii) The expert was to provide independent assistance to the court by way of objective unbiased opinion on matters within his expertise. The expert witness in the High Court should never assume the role of advocate. *Dicta* of Garland J in *Polivitte Ltd* v. *Commercial Union Assurance Co plc* [1987] 1 Lloyd's Rep 379 and of Cazalet J in *Re J* [1990] FCR 193 were approved.

(iii) Facts or assumptions upon which the opinion was based should be stated together with any material facts which could detract from the concluded opinion.

(iv) An expert witness should make it clear when any question or issue fell outside his expertise.

(v) If the expert witness had access to insufficient data it had to be made clear that his opinion was provisional. Any qualification in regard to the contents of the expert's report needed to be expressly stated. *Dicta* of Staughton LJ in *Derby and Co Ltd and Others* v. *Weldon and Others (No 9)* (1990) *The Times*, 9 November were approved.

(vi) If, after exchange of reports, an expert witness changed his mind on any material issue, such change of mind should be made known to the other party without delay.

(vii) All ancillary materials, including photographs, plans and surveys, referred to in the report should be provided to the other party at the date of exchange of reports.

The form and content of expert's reports is considered in the Practice Direction (Experts and Assessors) to the Civil Procedure Rules.

098 The duty of the expert witness to be measured, non-partisan, and to avoid usurping the role of the courts was considered in *Autospin (Oil Seals) Ltd* v. *Beehive Spinning (A Firm)*, (1995) *The Times*, 9 August. This was a decision of Laddie J in the Chancery Division in an action for breach of copyright of, *inter alia*, a code numbering system devised and used by the plaintiff for the purpose of precision manufacture for its range of oil seal products.

Apparently the plaintiff's expert had, after describing the system, said: "As far as I am aware no other seal manufacturer has used such a system." The clear purpose of that had been to support the plaintiff's claim that its system was unique.

099 In his column in *Building*, 8 September 1995, Tony Bingham discussed a further decision of Laddie J in *Cala Homes (South) and Others* v. *Alfred McAlpine Homes (East)* which was subsequently reported at [1995] CILL 1083. According to Laddie J when an expert witness sits down to write his report, he "should not consider that it is his job to stand shoulder to shoulder through thick and thin with the side which is paying his bill". According to Bingham:

> "What Laddie J highlighted was the difficulty of an expert witness compiling a report that rehearses the strengths of a party's position while using a 'precisely delicate touch' in interpreting the things the expert would rather not have to deal with at all. [One expert] describes this process as 'sleight of mind', whereby an expert presents data in a way that suggests an interpretation favourable to the side instructing him, even going as far as playing down or omitting some material consideration."

100 RSC Order 38, rule 37(1) and Order 25, rule 8(1)(b) provided for the disclosure of "the substance" of the evidence of an expert whom a party proposed to call. In *Kenning* v. *Eve Construction Ltd* [1989] 1 WLR 1189 an engineer, asked by the defendant to report on an accident, wrote a report refuting the allegations of negligence pleaded in the statement of claim. In a separate letter he drew attention to two points, which were not covered in the statement of claim or in his report, on which he considered that the defendant was at fault. By mistake the defendant's solicitors sent the report and the letter to the plaintiff's solicitors. The defendant sought to prevent the plaintiff from relying on the letter. The deputy judge acknowledged that it was a widespread practice that anxieties, qualifications or adverse views expressed by expert witnesses were very often communicated to instructing solicitors by way of a confidential covering letter. Although the letter would have ordinarily been privileged he held, perhaps somewhat strangely, that if the defendant wished to call this particular expert, he must disclose not only his report but also his letter. Otherwise he would not be complying with his obligation to disclose "the substance" of his evidence. Although perhaps morally correct, the decision of the deputy judge was illogical. It was not for the expert to deal with the overall issue of liability. It is never the defendant's responsibility to improve or make the plaintiff's case. Conversely, the plaintiff's expert report should only cover the allegations pleaded in the statement of claim and not other matters. It is not the role of the plaintiff's expert to improve the plaintiff's pleaded case.

101 The Court of Appeal considered a related situation in *Derby & Co Ltd* v. *Weldon (No 9)* (1990) TLR 712. The defendant's expert accountant prepared his report, which had been disclosed on the plaintiff's "initial conspiracy" claim. The report did not deal with an "alternative initial conspiracy" which had been introduced into the plaintiff's pleadings by amendments. The court took the view that the rules for disclosure of expert evidence did not ordinarily provide legal professional privilege. Any report which the accountant might have been prepared on the "alternative initial conspiracy" was privileged, and, if the defendant did not wish to adduce evidence from him on that issue, he could not be ordered to disclose any report that he might have made upon it. The court confirmed that *Kenning* was wrongly decided. In the rules of court "the substance" of the evidence refers only to the evidence it is intended the expert should give at trial. It does not mean all the evidence he could give.

102 With increasingly fickle, or perhaps astute, clients for whom relationships are less important than competence, and the expert having often been appointed on his fee bid, the incidents of dissatisfaction are probably growing and more claims are being made against professionals. The re-emergence of the law of negligence over recent years, with potentially different and extended limitation periods over those operating in contract, has made the professional expert more vulnerable. Again, experts want to know when they are and are not at risk. So often, experts give pre-litigation or arbitration advice and the point at which they pass from one role to another is unclear. Neither clients nor experts consider the changed relationship until problems arise.

103 The Civil Procedure Rules, for use in both the County and High Courts, came into force on 26 April 1999. The rules relating to expert witnesses are found in Part 35 and the accompanying Practice Direction 35. Gone are the days of the plea for pious good practice to be found in *The Ikarian Reefer* [1993] CILL 838, where Cresswell J set out some ground rules for the preparation of expert's reports, warning experts not to become the partisan champion of the paying party and dealing with issues outside their field of expertise. Under Rule 35.3 the expert has an overriding duty to the court and is obliged to help the court on matters within his expertise. Rule 35.3(2) states that the expert's duty overrides any obligation that he owes to his client. Experts cannot be called to give evidence without the court's permission; read Rule 35.4(4) carefully. Under Rule 35.5(2), the court will never direct the expert to attend a hearing to give oral evidence in fast track claims. Under Rule 35.6 parties can put to an expert written questions about his report. Those questions can only be put once and within 28 days of service of the expert's report. To focus the minds of expert witnesses, Practice Direction 35 paragraphs 1.3 and 1.4 require the expert to include in his report a statement of truth in the prescribed format with the consequences of the making of false statements dealt with in Rule 32.14 (being the possible instigation of proceedings).

This contribution is the substantially revised version of a lecture given at a Chartered Institute of Arbitrators' training course held in Cardiff on the role of the expert witness, and was originally published in Arbitration.

CHAPTER 1/10

THE EXPERT AND THE INVESTIGATION AND PROSECUTION OF SERIOUS FRAUD

George Staple

001 A former chairman of the bar once said "The SFO, by the very nature of their office, make cases long. Whenever they get their hands on a case it becomes of inordinate length"—and I suppose, by implication, difficult for a jury to cope with.

002 We must begin by asking ourselves why the Serious Fraud Office was created in the first place. What was so special about serious fraud that it was necessary to set up an independent government department, exclusively devoted to this particular crime? Why not simply leave it to be handled by the police and Crown Prosecution Service alongside all other serious crime.

003 History shows us many examples of fraud on the grand scale from the South Sea Bubble to the great railway and banking frauds of the mid-nineteenth century. Both Dickens and Trollope offer a glimpse of serious fraud on a par with anything we have experienced from the 1980s. So serious fraud is not a new phenomenon, and yet previous generations have apparently not needed an SFO. Why do we?

THE SPECIAL FEATURES OF SERIOUS FRAUD

004 In the early 1980s there was increasing public concern that those who were committing serious fraud were not being brought expeditiously and effectively to book. The government was encouraging ordinary families to invest their savings in the equity markets. It was, therefore, its duty to ensure that markets were honestly managed and that transgressors in those markets were swiftly discovered, convicted and punished.

005 The City of London is an important component, not only of the UK's financial system, but also of the international financial system. Its reputation is a precious thing, and it behoves us all not to take it for granted. Without a reputation for fair dealing the City's standing as a world financial centre would wither. It needs strong and effective guardians.

006 These factors alone make serious fraud a special crime. But there is also a number of features of that category of serious offences we call "fraud" which do not generally apply to other crime. First, fraud is largely document-based. All cases dealt with by the SFO involve the analysis of thousands—indeed hundreds of thousands, if not millions—of documents. The handling of these documents from their acquisition by the SFO through to their being made available to the defence and being used as evidence, requires adherence to a strict code.

007 Secondly, the victims of an offence of serious fraud are normally very numerous. Unhappily they are often people who can least afford to lose money. They may, of course, be institutions, but frequently they are pensioners or small investors who have lost their life savings.

008 Thirdly, serious fraud usually has a foreign dimension. Since the abolition of exchange control in 1979, it has been possible to transfer money of any amount and denomination to a different jurisdiction at the touch of a button. The successful investigation and prosecution of fraud is, therefore, a process which is reliant on treaties and conventions which impose a further legal *régime* not usually encountered in the prosecution of other crime.

009 Fourthly (and perhaps it goes without saying), cases of serious fraud are very complex. They involve commercial transactions which have taken place over long periods of time. Fraud is not accidental and is rarely the activity of one person. Those involved use international networks of companies, trusts and bank accounts to conceal their activities.

010 All these factors set serious fraud apart from other crime. They mean that the authorities who have to deal with it need to be equipped with special skills and powers. They were identified by the Fraud Trials Committee under the chairmanship of Lord Roskill in the mid-1980s and led directly to the government setting up the SFO.

011 Contrary to the view reported in the opening paragraph, therefore, the cases investigated and prosecuted by the SFO are by their nature likely to be long and complicated. It is not the SFO that makes them so. The task of the SFO is to render them into a manageable form for a jury of 12 ordinary people to understand in court.

SHAPE OF THE CASE

012 Of course there is a danger that enthusiastic case teams will find it hard to abandon a particular avenue of investigation, particularly if it provides compelling evidence of guilt. It requires great courage and confidence to present a pared-down case to a jury, knowing that you have left out other strong evidence of guilt. There is a risk that cases take on a momentum of their own and that case teams, who are immersed in an investigation, risk not fully appreciating the immensity of the task with which they are confronting 12 ordinary people. But prosecutors must be courageous in trying to steer a course between the twin duties of prosecuting to a reasonable extent the criminality involved while at the same time avoiding the overloaded indictment.

TOO MANY DEFENDANTS

013 It is also said that the net is thrown too wide; that too many defendants are put in the dock. Although rare, there may have been instances of that happening in the past. It does not happen now. The Code for Crown Prosecutors requires prosecutors to charge only those whose involvement goes to the heart of the case.

014 On the other hand, it has to be recognised that, in most cases of corporate fraud, the criminal conduct has existed and has become institutionalised over several years. It is very often the case that the fraud could not have grown unchecked without the active participation of fellow directors, and sometimes professional advisers, such as lawyers, accountants and brokers. Indeed the fraudster is usually skilled at selecting and surrounding himself with people who can be bought and corrupted. There is a real danger that by casting the net too narrowly and targeting only the principal players, the case is not adequately prosecuted. Serious fraud can often only flourish in an atmosphere where others, particularly professional men, are prepared to tag along. There is a danger that by only prosecuting the central figures, we create a climate where those on the fringes of very serious fraud can expect to go scot-free. Whereas similarly placed players in, let us say, a medium-sized, but relatively simple mortgage or long firm fraud, would expect to be tried and convicted. However, although the criminal justice system cannot abdicate responsibility for the prosecution of serious criminal conduct, some of those on the periphery can now be adequately dealt with before regulatory tribunals.

SEVERANCE

015 Under the heading of severance of the indictment I include evidence pruning because the two are so frequently linked. One of the difficulties is that crucial decisions on severance, which often have the effect of excluding much compelling evidence of guilt, are made at the preparatory hearing, when the judge is still new to the case. I appreciate that it is impossible for judges to be as steeped in the facts and their ramifications as prosecuting counsel, who will have lived with the case for anything up to two-and-a-half years. But it is at the preparatory hearing that the critical decisions on severance and pruning the evidence have to be taken. The court is stuck with those decisions from then on.

016 Another difficulty is that, although the court, in the interests of manageability, may refuse to allow the prosecution to adduce a large section of the evidence, it does not necessarily follow that the defence will wish to obliterate all references to it. The defendant himself, or a co-defendant, may consider it in his interests to introduce part of it in a manner which reflects credit on him, and can be claimed as proof of honest intent or belief. This can lead to real unfairness, with the defence inviting the jury to regard certain facts as proof of its client's honesty, although, unbeknown to the jury, the prosecution has earlier been prevented from putting all the evidence before them as yet further proof of dishonesty.

017 Judges must, I think, be ready to contemplate the possibility that severance and pruning decisions that may appear at an early stage superficially logical are not in fact viable. I would also suggest that there may be room for some healthy scepticism when the prosecution's time assessment is doubled—or even trebled—by the defence in an attempt to encourage the judge, in order to ensure a manageable trial, to make radical severance and pruning decisions. Better defence disclosure at an earlier stage would certainly inform the judge's decisions on severance and evidence pruning.

FUNCTION OF THE PROSECUTING AUTHORITY

018 In looking at the SFO's performance we should start by reminding ourselves of the role of a prosecuting authority. The objective is not to win at all costs. A prosecuting authority has a duty as much to deliver a fair trial as to secure a conviction. Unlike the Crown

Prosecution Service, the SFO has the additional responsibility of conducting a fair and thorough investigation.

019 After carrying out an investigation the SFO has to decide whether to bring charges. That judgement is made on the fullest possible information to ensure that it has the complete picture. Unlike other investigators, the SFO has the power to compel people on pain of criminal sanction to answer questions and produce documents. The transcripts of such interviews are not admissible in evidence. But the power, necessary though it is, in essentially document-based cases, does not make the SFO popular. They are repeatedly urged not to investigate too widely due to the time and huge resources these investigations inevitably involve. But if they do not, there is the constant threat that cases will fail because they have not established some essential fact. They cannot sacrifice thoroughness for expediency—cases will only collapse if they do.

020 It is not the SFO's function to decide whether someone is guilty of fraud: that is for the jury. Where they think there is a case to answer, as required by the Code for Crown Prosecutors, they only prosecute someone if there is a realistic prospect of conviction, and where it is in the public interest to do so.

021 It is a fact of life that when the evidence comes to be reviewed, some cases are found to be stronger than others. An undoubted problem is that the defence, under the present system in the UK, is not obliged to disclose its hand until a late stage. Usually advantage is taken of this and the prosecution is often still unaware of the precise nature of the defence case when counsel sits down after presenting the Crown's case. Until then it has to proceed on the basis of what it considers the defence is likely to be.

022 To my mind this does not enhance the criminal justice system. Much earlier defence disclosure is needed if these cases are going to be rendered manageable. I shall address this question later.

023 So the judgment of whether to bring charges, and whom to charge, is taken on the best view the Crown can form after a painstaking investigation: but it is a judgement. Often this judgement involves considerations of whether witnesses are likely to come up to proof or, because they are so often overseas, whether they are going to be available at all.

024 If the defence considers the prosecution have got the charging decision wrong, there is ample opportunity for the case to be dismissed on transfer to the Crown Court or, alternatively, at the close of the prosecution case. In the end, of course, assuming the case surmounts those hurdles, the prosecution has to satisfy a jury so they are sure that the defendant is guilty as charged. It is rightly a very high standard. But in a serious fraud, often dependent on complex accountancy evidence and many documents, it is not that difficult for a seed of doubt to be sown in a jury's mind. I have never made any complaint about that—far from it—but it is right that the system is understood.

025 If cases were being dismissed after transfer, or at the close of the prosecution case, there might have been some justification for criticism of the SFO. I will not say it has never happened, but it is a rarity for cases to be dismissed after transfer or at the close of the prosecution case. Over the ten years of the SFO's existence, it has been responsible for 192 trials involving 437 defendants, 296 of whom have been convicted. That represents an overall conviction rate of about 68 per cent. In over 75 per cent of its cases at least one defendant has been convicted, and that has usually been the principal defendant. These are not minor cases. They are all serious and complex frauds usually committed on an international scale.

026 The conviction rate is not by any means a prosecuting authority's only performance indicator, although I recognise that much emphasis will always be placed upon it. That being so, is the conviction rate acceptable? Does it represent the real deterrent the SFO was set up to achieve? In an adversarial system, the whole purpose of which is to ensure that only where it can be said there is no reasonable doubt will a defendant be convicted, the answer, I think, must be "yes".

TOWARDS BETTER DISCLOSURE

027 In serious fraud a prosecution case statement will be provided at an early stage, together with witness statements and all the documentary evidence on which the prosecution relies. In addition, the defence has the right to inspect all unused material available to the prosecution.

028 Although the defence, since the Criminal Justice Act 1987, may be required to deliver a case statement, it has usually been fairly brief, and the defence has not in general been obliged to give much away until trial. The prosecution must, of course, prove its case, but has it served the ends of justice for the defence to keep its own case more or less up its sleeve until as late as the trial itself—indeed sometimes until after the prosecution has presented its case in court?

029 Both the civil and criminal systems have the same purpose. Although some cynics might disagree, they are intended to arrive at the truth. They get there by very different routes. Should not the criminal system, like the civil system, ensure that everyone arrives in court knowing what each side's case is going to be? If the defence were known at an earlier stage the scope for agreement of what is in issue would be greatly increased. The prosecution in a serious fraud case would be able to gauge much more precisely which of the huge volume of documents in its possession would be likely to be relevant to the defence, and often it would be possible to dispense with many witnesses. The saving in court time would be enormous.

030 The Roskill Committee recognised that the time had come in fraud trials to move away a little from the strong culture of the criminal justice system and to reduce to a limited extent the right of silence. Lord Runciman's Royal Commission on Criminal Justice recognised that it was not enough for the defence simply to disclose the general nature of its case. Defendants needed to indicate in some detail the points on which they disagreed with the prosecution case.

031 The Runciman recommendations have now led to a new *régime* of disclosure being provided for in the Criminal Procedure and Investigations Act 1996. The prosecution, having served a case statement and disclosed all the witness statements and documentary evidence upon which it relies, is obliged to make further disclosure. It must disclose previously undisclosed prosecution material that might undermine the prosecution case. This is known as "primary disclosure". At the same time the defence will receive from the prosecution a schedule of all unused material, except material for which public interest immunity is claimed. The defence will have no right at this stage to see any of the primary disclosure and will be required to provide a statement of its own case.

032 Having seen the defence case, the prosecution will next disclose additional prosecution material which might reasonably assist the defence as disclosed in the defence statement. This is known as "secondary disclosure". The defence will then be able to apply for disclosure of material not previously disclosed and which it believes will assist the defence. During the course of the proceedings the prosecution will be obliged to keep under review the question of whether further prosecution material needs to be disclosed because it undermines the prosecution case or assists the defence as disclosed. The Act also provides that inferences may be drawn from certain failures in relation to disclosure by the defence, or a departure at trial from the defence previously disclosed. However, it is not possible for the defendant to be convicted solely on the drawing of such an inference.

033 It is to be hoped that by means of the system of primary and secondary prosecution disclosure the defence will be drawn out into the open so that a realistic idea can be obtained of what are the issues in the case. If the new legislation achieves its purpose it will hugely reduce the time taken pre-trial in the inspection by the defence of unused material. It will define the issues for the trial and, as a result, will save much time in court.

THE INTERNATIONAL DIMENSION

034 Although many of the cases that have attracted so much attention are City frauds, the SFO is dealing increasingly with very determined international criminals who have taken to fraud as an easy way of making money. Their activities usually span several different jurisdictions. They have no respect for international frontiers; indeed they are adept at exploiting the territorial nature of our laws. There is ample scope for the commission of offences partly in one jurisdiction and partly in others. Often witnesses and documentary evidence are to be found in a number of different jurisdictions. Suspects, of course, are frequently not in the jurisdiction in which they should be brought to trial.

035 International trade having been a feature of life for many centuries has led to the development of a body of private international law which has ensured the efficient disposal of commercial disputes. But large-scale international fraud is a relatively new development, which got under way in the early 1980s. I have no need to underline the economic advantages of the abolition of exchange control. But how prepared were we to deal with the huge expansion in international fraud that came with it? On the whole, we were probably rather ill-prepared.

036 In Europe the Convention on Mutual Legal Assistance in Criminal Matters of 1959 enabled evidence to be gathered in one contracting state for use in the criminal courts of another. It was not ratified by the United Kingdom until 1991, but it has enormously improved the response to international fraud in Europe.

037 Although many countries now have modern mutual assistance laws, others—particularly in the Commonwealth—still rely on old British legislation not designed to help with fraud investigation. Where the relationship between the United Kingdom and the overseas territories is closest, the mutual assistance arrangements may be most constrained. If, for example, the UK authorities request help from Switzerland, it will be acted upon swiftly under the European Convention. But if a similar request goes to certain UK Dependent Territories—often significant off-shore financial centres—it is rejected unless and until a defendant has been charged. Some investigations have had to be abandoned as a result.

038 Paradoxically some Caribbean Dependent Territories have entered into treaties (negotiated by the Foreign and Commonwealth Office) to share information with, and provide mutual assistance to, the United States, but have been unwilling to change their domestic legislation to render the same assistance to the United Kingdom and others.

039 Little will be achieved in international affairs without goodwill and reciprocity. To this end the United Kingdom has done much to improve its own legal *régime*. It has tried to ensure a rapid response to the requests of other states. The powers under section 2 of the

Criminal Justice Act 1987, which enable the Director of the SFO to compel the production of information, have now been extended so that the SFO can assist fraud investigations in England, Wales and Northern Ireland, being conducted by foreign authorities.

040 There are also difficulties when cases come on for trial. Bankers and others often have to be brought from abroad to explain the intricacies of financial transactions involving networks of bank accounts and the use of off-shore companies, trusts and administrators. But such witnesses cannot be made to attend our courts. They may even be subject to strict secrecy laws with penal sanctions in their own country, if they do. It is difficult to imagine a greater inhibition to successful prosecution than that.

041 Where it is not possible to bring witnesses to the UK from abroad or to take their evidence by satellite link, there are provisions in the Criminal Justice Act 1988 which allow the admission of hearsay in the form of business and other records. Unfortunately insufficient use has been made of these provisions, probably due to the strength of the oral tradition in English courts.

042 English criminal law must also recognise new forms of evidence. It takes no account of changes in computer technology. But a technological revolution has been occurring. It is increasingly hard to determine in which country a "transaction", and therefore an offence, has taken place. In the fight against international fraud, close co-operation between governments is essential and they must recognise the urgent need to modernise their laws in this field, if that fight is to be effective.

EXTRADITION

043 Lastly, the law of extradition needs constant vigilance. There are too many countries which refuse to extradite their own nationals. Sometimes they refuse to extradite because they assert worldwide jurisdiction over their nationals on the principle that they will deal with them wherever they commit their crimes. But is the reluctance to extradite really appropriate when so many legal systems have incorporated universally recognised safeguards of human rights? There is no reason to fear that an accused will not receive a fair trial in most countries. There may be some where that will not be the case and a refusal to extradite may still be appropriate, but they will not be many.

CONCLUSION

044 The investigation and prosecution of serious fraud will never be easy, and I have referred to only some of the problems which confront the prosecutor. But, in spite of all the criticism of the present system, there is no doubt that much fraud which, prior to the Roskill Committee and the setting-up of the SFO went unreported, uninvestigated and un-prosecuted, is now being effectively dealt with.

This article first appeared in Butterworth's Journal of International Banking and Finance Law *(Vol II, No 3, March 1996) under the title of "The Investigation and Prosecution of Serious Fraud: The Serious Fraud Office", when* ***George Staple*** *was director of the Serious Fraud Office (SFO). Although the article was not specifically written, in the first instance, for the expert witness, it has subsequently been redrafted for this book and contains much useful guidance for those appearing in fraud cases as experts. Mr Staple is now a partner in Clifford Chance, and heads this firm's Investigation, Fraud and Regulatory Matters group. He is also chairman of the Fraud Advisory Panel which is an independent body established by the Institute of Chartered Accountants in England and Wales.*

CHAPTER 1/11

LEGAL AID—THE EXPERT'S POSITION

Simon Morgans

001 I will briefly describe the development of the legal aid system. However, the main part of this evening will be the detail of working in a legally aided case as an expert, about prior approval authorities and about differences between civil and criminal cases. I will refer to payment rates, the fixed and recommended rates for experts in Crown Court cases and about taxation and delays in payment.

002 Now I do not know why payment of experts' fees should be delayed. I have some ideas but I simply do not know why in general it happens. May I ask those of you who are experts, have you ever suffered delayed payment in excess of a year? (On seeing the number of positive responses) *Good heavens.* In excess of usual terms of business? *Well, I am surprised.*

003 Now perhaps a question to the solicitors here. Have you ever delayed payment to an expert because you wanted to delay payment, or because of some inefficiency or error on your part? *Absolutely not!* And have you ever delayed payment to an expert because you had to, because of something to do with the system? *Yes.*

004 It does appear that if there are any delays in payment it is not through any wilful action of the solicitor trying to keep you out of money you are entitled to. So perhaps it is something to do with the system.

THE DEVELOPMENT OF LEGAL AID

005 The Legal Aid Act 1949 was one of the social reforms introduced after the Second World War. Litigation was much rarer then. It is since then that the public has become more aware of its rights and has sought to enforce them through the courts. Similarly divorce was much rarer because it was only the wealthy who could afford to separate as spouses and live separately.

006 The Law Society was asked to run the scheme. It had in place local law societies, members of which could act on assessing committees to determine on a case-by-case basis whether or not legal aid should be granted. Later for administrative purposes the country was divided into 15 legal aid areas, a general committee to decide on the grant and refusal of legal aid, and an area committee to hear appeals against refusals of legal aid and to deal with costs.

007 Since then the administration has been streamlined, there are now 13 areas, only one type of committee and the system is run by the Legal Aid Board. Under the anticipated Access to Justice Act, administration will, in 2000, be taken over by a new Legal Services Commission based on the board's present staff and offices.

EXPLANATION OF TERMS

008 First costs. Costs means the charges in a solicitor's bill. Perhaps only solicitors could think of calling their charges costs, it gives the impression that they are something they are suffering rather than benefiting from. It has been said that costs are the last thing solicitors ever think about—every night before they go to bed.

009 The term *costs* is generally used to mean all the charging components in a solicitor's bill, usually a number of pages itemising all the work done and all the expenses incurred. The term *profit costs*, or solicitor's costs, means the charges for the solicitor's own work as distinct from any barrister's fees or expert's charges or any out of pocket expenses such as train fares.

010 Costs in civil cases may be described as *inter partes* which means costs between the parties in the litigation. For example, where the losing party is ordered to pay some or all of the winning party's solicitor's costs the *inter partes* costs are those costs which have to be paid by, generally, the loser. Costs may also be *legal aid costs* which will almost always mean all the amount of the charges in a legally aided case whether or not an opponent has been ordered to pay them, or *legal aid only costs* which means those charges of a solicitor payable from the legal aid fund which no losing opponent has been ordered to pay. *Central funds* are the Lord Chancellor's funds available in criminal cases for paying witnesses, including expert witnesses, for attending court to give evidence. Such witnesses cannot be paid out of the legal aid fund unless it is a very rare case where the court makes a direction.

THE PRESENT SYSTEM

011 The present legal aid system has the following components:

- the Legal Aid Board;
- the Crown Court and magistrates' courts;
- the county courts and Supreme Court taxing departments;
- the Judicial Office of the House of Lords.

The Legal Aid Board

012 This (among other things) deals with:

- all applications for civil legal aid
- everything connected with the advice and assistance scheme including assistance by way of representation, which is known as ABWOR
- the assessment of claims for costs, i.e. solicitors' bills (under £1,000) in legally aided civil cases
- the assessment of all claims for costs for legally aided civil and criminal proceedings in the magistrates' courts

- the granting and refusing (in civil and criminal cases) of prior authority for expenditure on, e.g. experts' fees (but not for prior authority for the giving of evidence at court in criminal cases because the board has power only to grant authorities for expenditure under legal aid certificates or orders. Payment for expert witnesses giving evidence at court in criminal proceedings is made from central funds and not under the legal aid order).

The Crown Court and magistrates' courts

013 These courts can grant criminal legal aid. The Crown Court, through its determining officers, also assesses or "determines" lawyers' bills for legally aided criminal work in the Crown Court and payment for such work is made by the Crown Court. The Legal Aid Board, therefore, does not have any part in Crown Court proceedings except when it is asked for prior authorities for expenditure, e.g. on experts' fees.

The county courts and Supreme Court taxing departments

014 These tax all solicitors' legal aid bills in civil cases (except those which are assessed by the Legal Aid Board). They also tax bills where legal aid is not involved if there has been an *inter partes* order for costs, e.g. the loser has to pay the winner's costs and taxation will decide how much of them the loser actually has to pay.

015 "Tax" or "taxation"[1] are more legal "jargon". Taxing a bill means the same as assessing or determining it. That is allowing for payment by the legal aid fund (or by the opposing party) an appropriate amount of the lawyer's bill.

016 Under the new Civil Procedure Rules the term "taxation" is replaced by "assessment" as part of a drive to remove jargon from the legal process. (Other sensible changes include "plaintiff" becoming "claimant", "summons" and "writ" becoming "claim form" and "pleadings" becoming "statement of case".)

017 Such a "taxation" will result in an *allocatur*, which will show the amount to be paid by the Legal Aid Board and the amount (if any) of that payable by the opponent. I say "of that" because the whole bill is payable by the Legal Aid Board but some of it may also be payable by the opponent. If the opponent can be made to pay, either the Legal Aid Board or the assisted person will benefit. The assisted person may benefit because, if he has recovered money or property in the proceedings, the Legal Aid Board will have a charge on it to the extent that the opponent has not paid the amount which has to be paid out of the legal aid fund.

018 Although I say "of that", regulations governing legal aid costs do provide that, in some cases, more is recoverable from an opponent under an *inter partes* order for costs than can be recovered from the Legal Aid Board. But this has little impact so far as experts' fees are concerned.

THE EXPERT'S INTERFACE WITH THE LEGAL AID SYSTEM

019 I do not know the reasons for delayed payment but I have a theory that there are three culprits:

- Regulation 64 (the "hermetic hypothesis");
- Terms of business; and
- Errors.

020 Errors speak for themselves. They occur on occasion in all human activity and with a legal system as diverse as the one we have, it is, perhaps not so surprising that they should occur from time to time. Terms of business and what I have called the "hermetic hypothesis" go rather deeper. And there is room for argument here.

021 In my view, how and when experts should be paid in all civil, criminal and advice and assistance cases depends upon the expert's contract with the solicitor. Except in the case of an expert instructed to give evidence at court in a criminal matter—you will remember that payment for that work comes from central funds and is not made under the legal aid order. This sounds pretty unobjectionable. And, if this is the case, what is the problem? Why should not everything be straightforward? Things are the same in a legal aid case as in any other. Well I will come back to the problem and the possible *contra* argument in a minute. First, I will describe how I see the position, in a bit more detail.

022 My view is this: If the solicitor has agreed with the expert the timing of the payment to him (e.g. within 14 days of receiving the expert's bill or within a reasonable time of the solicitor being paid on account by the Legal Aid Board) the solicitor should pay the expert within that time. If the solicitor has agreed with the expert the fee he will pay him the solicitor should pay the expert that agreed fee. This is so even if less than this amount is eventually paid to the solicitor from legal aid. So that covers agreements on timing and amount of fees.

023 If the solicitor has not agreed the timing and/or the amount then, subject to any other relevant factors which may affect the position (e.g. whether the amount claimed is reasonable having regard to the work done), the solicitor should pay the expert the amount stated in his bill within a reasonable time. In my view, there are no implied terms that the expert will either

(a) be prepared to accept what is allowed on taxation, assessment or determination, and/or

(b) be prepared to wait for payment (e.g. until the solicitor's bill has been taxed or the solicitor has received a payment on account of disbursements)[2].

024 Indeed on taxation, the taxing officers will often require proof that an expert's fees have been paid before they will allow them on taxation.

LEGISLATION

025 Legislation[3] ensures that, in legal aid cases, experts are paid only by the solicitors who instruct them (or out of the legal aid fund or by the Lord Chancellor).[4] It enables solicitors to pay experts[5] whom they instruct. It prohibits solicitors from assisting or requiring their clients, or any third parties, to pay them.[6] Therefore, if a solicitor instructs an expert for an agreed fee and the fee, or the full amount of it, is not allowed, the solicitor must bear the deficit. The expert should not bear it (the solicitor should pay him the agreed fee) and the solicitor must not be a party to payment of it, or any part of it, by his client or a third party, except the legal aid fund or the Lord Chancellor.[7]

AUTHORITIES

026 Now, unsurprisingly, many experts prefer to agree their fees in advance and do not like doing work on the basis that the solicitor will pay them whatever is allowed on taxation or assessment. Taxation[8] and assessment are outside the experience of most experts (and my suggestion to the experts reading this is to keep it that way). When the solicitor does agree a fee with an expert he faces the risk that less than the agreed fee will be allowed on taxation, determination or assessment. What can he do to reduce this risk?

027 In many civil and criminal cases the solicitor can eliminate this risk by applying in advance[9] to the legal aid area office for an authority to instruct the expert.[10] Authority will be granted if the office is satisfied that instructing the expert is necessary for the proper conduct of the proceedings and the proposed fee is reasonable.[11] If an authority is granted, it will state the amount of expenditure authorised. Up to this amount, the solicitor is guaranteed payment unelss he (in civil cases, he or his client) knew or ought reasonably to have known that the purpose for which the authority was given had failed or become irrelevant or unnecessary before the costs were incurred.[12]

028 If an authority is refused, there is no right of appeal but the solicitor can reapply with further information. (In my experience the biggest cause of delay in dealing with applications for prior authority is insufficient information—often because the lawyer and the expert have not discussed what is required and why—and unusually high fees without any evidence of the lawyer having sought quotes from other experts.) If an authority is granted but, e.g. after preliminary work, the expert informs the solicitor that the job will take significantly longer because of factors which have only now become apparent to the expert, so he wishes to charge more, the solicitor should consider whether it is reasonable to agree an increased fee with the expert and, if so, he may apply again to the area office for an authority at an increased fee.

029 In ABWOR cases, the solicitor must obtain prior permission from the area office before obtaining an expert's report or opinion. If prior permission is not obtained, the Legal Aid Board will not pay the solicitor for the expert's report or opinion. In advice and assistance cases, there is no provision for authorities. Because the advice and assistance scheme is a basic advice scheme, it is for the solicitor to judge whether it is reasonable to obtain an expert's advice.

PAYMENTS ON ACCOUNT

030 If solicitors have to pay experts without undue delay but the case may drag on for years, how do they avoid losing or paying interest on the money? In civil and ABWOR cases regulations provide that solicitors can apply to the legal aid area office for payments on account of disbursements (including experts' fees) incurred or about to be incurred.[13] This now applies in the Crown Court too. In Crown Court criminal cases, regulations[14] provide that, for criminal legal aid orders granted after 26 April 1993, where a solicitor has obtained prior authority from the legal aid area office to incur a disbursement of £100 or more and then has incurred a liabilty to pay £100 or more in respect of that disbursement, he may apply to the Crown Court (with the authority and the invoice) for an interim payment of that disbursement. If the Crown Court determining officer approves the application, payment will be made to the solicitor and notification of the payment will be given to the expert.

031 Therefore, in most cases solicitors do not have to carry the cost of instructing experts until the solicitors' bills are paid by the Legal Aid Board or the Lord Chancellor's department. But whether or not a solicitor has received, or can receive, a payment on account does not affect his liabilty to pay any expert he has instructed in accordance with his agreement with the expert.

032 It is worth emphasising that a payment on account is just that. If, e.g., £150 is paid by the Legal Aid Board to the solicitor on account of an expert's bill for £150, but only £100 is later allowed on taxation, the overpayment by the board of £50 will be deducted when the board pays the solicitor's final bill.

WITNESSES AT COURT—EXPERT AND PROFESSIONAL

033 The position so far as witnesses at court, expert and professional, are concerned is a little more complex. In civil and ABWOR cases, the solicitor is responsible for paying all the witnesses he instructs on behalf of his client to attend court to give evidence. In civil cases the solicitor can apply for authorities and payments on account. In ABWOR cases, he must apply for prior permission and can apply for payments on account.

034 However, in criminal cases the position is different. First, prior authority cannot be obtained. Secondly, unless the court makes a contrary direction (and this is unusual), payment to witnesses attending to give evidence is made from central funds, i.e. the Lord Chancellor, not from the legal aid fund. I understand that the reason for this is because witnesses are seen as assisting the court. For professional witnesses, i.e. witnesses who attend to give factual evidence (e.g. of the fact that the defendant attended the witness for treatment for a broken arm) the allowances used to be fixed by the Treasury and are now fixed by the Lord Chancellor's department. For expert witnesses, a reasonable amount will be allowed having regard to the nature and difficulty of the case, the work necessarily involved and such factors as whether there is a reasonable choice of experts available. There are no prescribed scales of allowance for expert witnesses though there are recommended rates which are available from the Lord Chancellor's department. They can also be found in *Stones Justices Manual.*

035 Professional witnesses' (like other factual witnesses') allowances are intended simply to compensate for expenses/losses incurred in attending court to give evidence.[15] Expert witnesses' payments are intended to reflect the fact that they are attending court in their line of business. They are not, therefore, simply compensation payments.

036 Witnesses at court in criminal cases are paid not by the solicitors who instruct them but from central funds. In many cases they can receive payment by attending at the court cash office when they have finished giving their evidence. If an expert witness's hourly rate is in the region of the rates usually charged by similar experts and is deemed reasonable, there should be no delay in payment. The amount allowed will generally include a notional hour's preparation for the hearing.

037 Although an expert cannot set (or agree) his fee for attending court to give evidence in a criminal case, he will not be able to avoid attending if the solicitor requires his attendance. The solicitor may oblige him to attend by issuing a witness summons. If the expert does not then attend he will be in contempt of court and liable to imprisonment.[16]

038 In criminal cases, an expert warned to attend court may sometimes be cancelled at relatively short notice, for example because of a change of plea or change of date. Where this happens central funds will not pay the expert a fee as of right for the cancelled attendance. However, if the expert has reasonably prepared for the hearing and/or reasonably incurred expenses an appropriate fee may be paid. The case of *Reynolds* v. *Meston* (1986) (unreported, 24 February) confirmed that whether such a fee is allowed and, if so, the amount depends on the particular facts of each case.

039 The position here is similar in ABWOR and civil cases. In all cases, the expert will be expected to show that he has attempted to mitigate his loss. For example, if a doctor has had to cancel appointments, he may be expected to try either to uncancel them, to fix other ones or to do other work.

REGULATION 64 ETC.

040 Now I said that, in my view, what and when a solicitor should pay an expert is the same in a private case as a legally aided one. It is governed by the contract between them. But this is not totally free from doubt. I referred to regulation 64 of the Civil Legal Aid (General) Regulations 1989 (and regulation 55 of the Legal Aid in Criminal and Care Proceedings (General) Regulations 1989 is fairly similar) and what I feel driven to call the "hermetic hypothesis".

041 Regulation 64 is headed "Restriction on payment otherwise than from the fund" and provides:

> "Where a certificate has been issued in connection with any proceedings, the assisted person's solicitor or counsel shall not receive or be a party to the making of any payment for work done in those proceedings during the currency of that certificate (whether within the scope of the certificate or othewise) except such payments as may be made out of the fund."

042 If you take this as meaning that, once a legal aid certificate has been issued, you have a hermetically sealed system in which, for example, an expert can be paid only what is allowed after taxation or assessment to be payable to him out of the legal aid fund, it is impossible for a solicitor to agree fees with an expert other than on the basis that the expert will receive only what is allowed on taxation. Furthermore, a logical extension of this approach would be that solicitors could only make a payment to an expert once they, themselves, had received from the Legal Aid Board a final payment or a payment on account of disbursements. And what if, after making such a payment, the expert's fee was disallowed on taxation?

043 Even obtaining an authority for expenditure on the expert's fees could not fully cover the position because in (admittedly unusual) circumstances such as where it has become irrelevant to obtain the expert's report, the expert's fees can still be disallowed even though an authority has been obtained.

044 And then again, what is meant by "such payments as may be made out of the fund"? Does it mean "may, from time to time" so that the payment has actually to be made out of the fund before the solicitor can pass it on or does it mean "may in the future" or does it mean merely that the payments need only be of a nature that are payable from the fund, i.e. they are in principle payable? And what about the need to produce receipted invoices on taxation?

045 It seems to me that we need to look at the purpose of the regulation. I guess that it is designed to protect assisted persons (and their families etc.) from being pressured to pay extra. It also seems to me that, if a solicitor has to stand any shortfall between what he has agreed to pay an expert and what is allowed for the expert's fee on taxation, that is not "receiving or being a party to the making of any payment for work done in (the) proceedings". The solicitor is actually making the payment, not being a party to making it. It would have been an easy matter for the draftsman to have said "shall not make, receive or be a party to the making".

046 And, if the regulation is hermetic, the lawyer is in a bind. He may not be able to find an expert who will agree to accept whatever is allowed on taxation, especially as there may be some risk of the whole fee being disallowed because the solicitor should not have commissioned the work at all. That said, because there are contrary arguments, I believe some solicitors may be wary of paying experts until after the conclusion of a case because of concern that they may be in breach of a regulation.

047 Apart from errors and regulation 64, I suggested that terms of engagement could also cause problems. By this, I mean that the solicitor should be clear (and make it clear to the expert) why he is instructing the expert and what he requires of him, should be clear as to the payment terms and should ensure that he is obtaining value for money, preferably (where the fees are likely to be significant) obtaining two or three quotations first. "Terms of engagement" includes not only the solicitor's contract with the expert but his "contract", if I can call it that, with the Legal Aid Board to spend taxpayers' money wisely.

FRANCHISING

048 Legal Aid Franchising was introduced by the Legal Aid Board on 1 August 1994. It is not "High Street Franchising" in the way that for example, McDonalds is a franchise. It is more akin to the British Standard BS5750 (ISO 9001) quality standard approach.

049 A firm of solicitors which wants a franchise must have in place systems and procedures which meet the board's Quality Assurance Standard and must contract with the board to continue to meet them. Compliance with the Quality Assurance Standard will provide quality assurance for the legal services which the firm provides. In return, franchised firms will be able to display the board's franchise logo in the same way that firms meeting BS5750 (ISO 9001) can display the kite mark, will have devolved to them some of the board's powers to exercise on the board's behalf and will receive better payments on account.

050 One of the requirements of the Quality Assurance Standard is that firms must have a central register and written procedure for using experts which must include provision for the following:

- use of clear selection and evaluation criteria
- where appropriate, consultation with the client prior to selection
- maintenance of records of experts used
- giving of instructions which clearly describe what is required
- checking of opinions and reports received to ensure they adequately provide the information or service sought
- arrangements for the payment of fees
- a record of any expert who fails to meet the Service Standards was used
- if an expert is used for the first time, a record of why they were used.

051 The board will expect franchised firms to use only those experts who have been assessed by the firm as being capable of meeting their requirements. That assessment could be based on one or more of a number of factors including particular expertise or experience, recommendation, speed of response, value for money, flexibility etc.

THE FUTURE

052 Lots of things are changing! In 2000 the Legal Aid Board is expected to be replaced by a Legal Services Commission based on the board's current administrative structure. The Commission is expected to assume responsibility for criminal legal aid as well as civil legal aid and to establish a Community Legal Service.

053 Also in 2000, the Legal Aid Board (and subsequently the Commission) will be contracting with firms of solicitors and advice agencies for the provision of advice and assistance in civil matters and for the provision of representation in matrimonial/family matters. Contracts will be made only with firms and agencies which are (or are about to become) franchised. Within a year or two after this, it is expected that all civil advice, assistance and representation will be provided under contracts. And, from 2000, a grant of representation will be made only if a case meets rigorous criteria in a new Funding Code.

054 From 26 April 1999 the new Civil Procedure Rules replace the two sets of court rules previously covering civil proceedings. They provide for court-appointed experts in what are called "fast track" cases. But how often this facility will be used remains to be seen.

055 Perhaps more significantly for experts the rules require costs to be proportionate to the size of the claim if they are to be recoverable from the opposing party. This is likely to lead to downward pressure on experts' fees, particularly in smaller value claims.

056 Of course, in a legally aided case, any costs not recovered may be taken out of any damages recovered by the legally aided client.

WHAT DOES THIS MEAN FOR EXPERTS?

057 As I see it, firms will be assessing the services you provide in a more structured way than they have in the past. It will not be enough for a firm merely to say that any expert accredited by another body, such as The Academy of Experts, is automatically "approved" by them, too. A recommendation might be sufficient for the first use of an expert but the expectation is that the firm itself will then make an assessment of the expert and form its own views.

058 Furthermore, the delivery of publicly funded legal services under contracts is likely to lead to solicitors requiring greater value for money from the experts they instruct and the new Civil Procedure Rules are likely to lead to fewer experts being instructed. It is, however, too soon to say how or whether any of the principles outlined earlier in this article will be affected.

059 I am, however, sure that whatever changes there may be in the law, in government or in legal aid, the pursuit of better quality, including better value for money will be (or become) a feature of both privately and publicly funded legal services. This will apply as much to experts as to lawyers.

QUESTION TIME

060 **Ann Protheroe:** "You referred to solicitors who should pay their experts within a reasonable time. What do you consider reasonable? Secondly, if we are dissatisfied with the speed at which the solicitor is dealing with our account can we get in touch with the Legal Aid Board ourselves?"

061 Author: "What is reasonable would be for argument between you and the solicitor. I cannot help you on that; it depends on the facts. I suspect that a court might approach it on the basis of what were industry standards in the absence of any agreement at all between you and the lawyer. If a solicitor is slow in paying and if he blames the Legal Aid Board, there is nothing to stop you writing to the board."

062 [This answer was expanded upon afterwards in discussion with the editor as follows:

> "Any letter should be to the area office and not to head office; the Legal Aid Board does not deal with criminal cases at the Crown Court; the board would not deal substantively with the expert but might in appropriate cases bring the matter up with the solicitor; in situations of serious complaint there may be a reason for the board to refer it to the Law Society."]

063 Jan Stuart, Engineer: "In a prior approval case can you apply for an upfront payment for the expert?"

064 Author: "I have never come across a case where the expert requires payment before doing the work. I suppose it would essentially be a matter for the solicitor to decide whether or not it is reasonable to contract with an expert who wants to proceed on that basis."

065 Chairman: "One of the problems is that many of our members are just individuals who have to incur quite an expense in order to prepare that initial report. So it is not even really a question of being paid for their work but being paid for their out of pocket expenses."

066 Author: "I cannot see any objection in principle because there is nothing different about a legal aided case from a private case. The solicitor's responsibility would be to decide. He has a duty to the legal aid fund money in the same way as he has a duty to his client and his client's money. If the solicitor feels that is a sensible way of proceeding then I cannot see any objection to legal aid operating in the same way. It is slightly novel and if that fact were known to the area legal aid office they would want some sort of reassurance that the solicitor had considered whether this is the right expert to use if somebody else would wait. I cannot really see it as a problem."

067 Jean Graham Hall, a former circuit judge: "I would like to know how much you monitor the number of experts that are needed. I raise this because I have just met a number of court welfare officers who talked to me about the expert gravy train. In one case they had a dozen experts."

068 Author: "Our difficulty is that in a case like that we would not carry out the taxation, it would be the court that would tax the bill. If we were asked for prior authority and so that way get in the case earlier on we would question the continued use of the number of experts. Children Act cases do seem to pull in many experts: each one follows the opinion of counsel saying it is needed. It is quite difficult for the board to say when it only has the information about the case that the solicitor has provided, although in some cases we can. Clearing the terms of business at the start must be a good way forward. This point about somebody bearing the risk and not bearing the risk is also a useful point to sort out. There are some cases where the whole of an expert's fee might be disallowed because the court on taxation takes the view that the solicitor should never have instructed them in the first place, but the expert would never know that. In cases like that one would expect the solicitor to pay the shortfall but if it is a case where the expert is taxed down because he has been charging 50 per cent higher than any other similar expert then I cannot see why an agreement cannot be reached."

069 James Stanbury, accountant: "This question relates back to the original instructions and quoting to a solicitor. Sometimes we are not privy to the facts of the case, which makes it difficult to itemise what work will be done for the quotation given. What expectation is there at the Legal Aid Board for details of the work we are expected to do for the fee requested to be itemised?"

070 Author: "My guess is the level of detail point will depend upon the amount of work which is envisaged is going to be done. This relates to the amount of the fee and the reason why the work is going to be done. It might be a little bit diffcult to give a blanket explanation but the best way of looking at it is to imagine that it is a private case and you put yourself in the position of a client, what sort of questions would you want to consider and what would you want your solicitor to discuss with the expert before deciding what the expert was going to do and how much he was going to charge for it. Again it comes down to clarifying the terms of business."

071 Chairman: "The initial difficulty in giving an estimate is mainly because the amount of material available to the expert is not sufficient to enable him to do a fully detailed quote and very often the amount of work would be the bulk of the work anyway. But given that stage has taken place and he has his prior approval he then receives the papers. As he is going through them the case fundamentally changes. Now the moan that comes to me is that when he goes back to the solicitor and says I quoted you this for the job but that is not the job you now want me to do. At that stage the common comment appears to be 'sorry but it is almost impossible to get the legal aid board to allow you to revamp your quote once you have given it'."

072 Author: "I think this is a communication point again. There is less risk of this happening if the instructions are clear at first. But if it does happen then the expert needs to communicate clearly with the solicitor so that the solicitor understands why the expert is going to have to do more work. When the solicitor understands that he needs to pass it on clearly to the Legal Aid Board."

073 Name not given: "We know about our duty to our client, and our duties to the court. Do we also have a duty to Legal Aid Board?"

074 Author: "The primary duty of the solicitors and the barristers is to the Legal Aid Board. They have a duty to the board in the same way as they have to a private client to obtain value for money when they are instructing an expert. An expert instructed by a lawyer has got a duty to the lay client: as a case of general law it would apply equally in a legal aid case. Legal aid is really just a public funding of legal services, it is not intended to distort normal relationships."

075 Monica Bond, accountant. "In the context of prior authority, recently increasingly instructing solicitors say that they are going to get three quotes. First is that mandatory now and secondly what factors do you take into account?"

076 Author: "Three quotes are not mandatory. It seems to me that if it is a large disbursement it would be very sensible for a lawyer to get, for example, three quotes. It can be quite a useful thing for a legal aid area office to suggest that it is done. What I would expect is that the solicitor would not simply send the Legal Aid Board under a compliments slip the three quotes, but send in the quotes and say I am happy to take the cheapest or I want to take the middle one or the dearest because . . ."

077 Chairman: "It is interesting to hear somebody making some solid points and actually giving answers. We may not like the answers but my previous experience of all legal aid matters is that there was never an answer. Simon, thank you very much indeed."

Postscript

078 New Rules of Civil Procedure were introduced in April 1999. They do not impact directly on legal aid but they do provide that the court may limit the amount of an expert's fees that the party instructing the expert may recover from the other party. And, in a legally aided case, if the full amount of an expert's fees are not recovered from the other party, the balance must be borne by the legal aid fund or, if any damages are recovered by the legally assisted person, taken out of those damages.

079 Under the new rules, the court may also direct that evidence is to be given by a single expert instructed by the parties jointly, may give directions about the expert's fees and expenses and may limit the amount that can be paid, by way of fees and expenses, to the expert. If asked to grant an authority for expenditure in such cases, the Legal Aid Board would limit the amount authorised to the appropriate proportion of the expert's fees prescribed by the court.

080 Finally, the Legal Aid Board has recently published its exclusive contracting proposals for legal aid. Under these proposals (which are anticipated to come into effect in January 2000 for advice and assistance and for representation in family/matrimonial cases) the board has reserved to itself the power to set maximum rates for experts' fees.

081 The new Rules of Civil Procedure and legal aid exclusive contracting are likely to bear down on the rates experts can charge. In future, value for money will be an even greater imperative.

End Notes

1. At the end of legal aid cases, solicitors must prepare detailed bills setting out all the work done. The bills are then examined and, broadly, reasonable payment is allowed for work actually and reasonably done. (In some cases solicitors' hourly rates are set by regulations.) If the person examining a bill considers, e.g., that the solicitors' hourly rate, or the rate or amount charged by an expert he has instructed, is too high, a lesser sum will be allowed. If the work was not actually and reasonably done, the whole amount may be disallowed.

   In civil courts this procedure has been known as "taxation" but is now known as "assessment" and is a judicial function. In the Crown Court it is known as "determination" and is an administrative function. The Legal Aid Board examines advice and ABWOR bills, bills for criminal proceedings in magistrates' courts and some civil bills. This is also known as "assessment", which is an administrative function but which, in some categories of civil case, must ensure that what is allowed is what would have been allowed following a taxation. In all cases, it is the solicitor's bill (not the expert's fee) which is taxed, determined or assessed. Whatever amount is allowed, the solicitor remains liable to pay the expert in accordance with his agreement with him.

   The case of *Cementation Construction* v. *James D Keaveney, A firm* (1988) *The Times*, 21 July, confirmed that an expert has no *locus standi* on a taxation and that, if the expert has been engaged by a solicitor on the basis that he will be paid whatever is allowed on taxation, the solicitor should, at the taxation, use his best endeavours to secure the allowance of a proper fee.
2. In any event, the solicitor will usually be required to produce a receipted voucher in respect of the disbursement for it to be allowed on taxation.
3. The relevant provisions are sections 6(2), 25 and 31(3) of the Legal Aid Act 1988; regulation 64 of the Civil Legal Aid (General) Regulations 1989, and regulation 55 of the Legal Aid in Criminal and Care Proceedings (General) Regulations 1989.

   Section 6(2) provides that (subject to regulations) there must be paid out of the Legal Aid Fund:

   > "such sums as are, by virtue of any provisions of or made under this Act, due from the Board in respect of remuneration and expenses properly incurred in connection with the provision, under this Act, of advice, assistance, mediation or representation."

   Section 25 provides:

   > "(1) Where representation under this Part has been granted to any person the costs of representing him shall be paid—
   > (a) by the Lord Chancellor; or
   > (b) by the Board;
   > as the Lord Chancellor may direct.

(2) Subject to regulations, the costs of representing any person under this Part shall include sums on account of the fees payable to his legal representative and disbursements reasonably incurred by his legal representative for or in connection with his representation.

(3) The costs required by this section to be paid in respect of representing him shall not include any sum in respect of allowances to witnesses attending to give evidence in the proceedings for the purposes of which he is represented in any case where such allowances are payable under any other enactment."

Section 31(3) provides:

"A person who provides advice, assistance or representation under this Act shall not take any payment in respect of the advice, assistance or representation except such payment as is made by the Board or authorised by, or by regulations under, this Act."

Regulation 64 of the Civil Legal Aid (General) Regulations 1989 provides:

"Where a certificate has been issued in connection with any proceedings, the assisted person's solicitor or counsel shall not receive or be a party to the making of any payment for work done in those proceedings during the currency of that certificate (whether within the scope of the certificate or otherwise) except such payments as may be made out of the fund."

Regulation 55 of the Legal Aid in Criminal and Care Proceedings (General) Regulations 1989 provides:

"Where a legal aid order has been made, the legally assisted person's solictior or counsel shall not receive or be a party to the making of any payment for work done in connection with the proceedings in respect of which the legal aid order was made except such payments as may be made—

(a) out of the Legal Aid Fund or by the Lord Chancellor, or

(b) in respect of any expenses or fees incurred in—

(i) preparing, obtaining or considering any report, opinion or further evidence, whether provided by an expert witness or otherwise; or

(ii) bespeaking transcripts of shorthand notes or tape recordings of any proceedings, including police questioning of suspects;

where an application under Regulation 54 for authority to incur such expenses or fees has been refused by the Area Committee."

4. The legislation protects the assisted person by ensuring that he is not under pressure to make any payment in connection with his case except his assessed contribution under the relevant regulations. Similarly, the assisted person is protected by section 31(3) of the Legal Aid Act 1988 from any potential pressure to pay his solicitor money (see note 3). The only exception to this is found in criminal proceedings (see note 6).

5. The solicitor can make the payment whether or not he has received any payment on account of the disbursement from the legal aid fund.

Regulation 64 of the Civil Legal Aid (General) Regulations 1989 and regulation 55 of the Legal Aid in Criminal and Care Proceedings (General) Regulations 1989 (see note 3) are to prevent "topping up". They do not prevent the solicitor from meeting his contractual liabilities to experts whom he has instructed.

6. The only exception to this rule is found in regulation 55 of the Legal Aid in Criminal and Care Proceedings (General) Regulations which enables certain payments, in criminal cases, where an application to the area office for prior authority has been made and refused.

7. Unless the specific exemption in regulation 55 of the Legal Aid in Criminal and Care Proceedings (General) Regulations 1989 applies (see note 6). If the expert's fee (or the full amount of it) is not paid by the assisted person's opponent (under an order or agreement for costs) the assisted person will end up paying for the expert's fees if the statutory charge arises on property recovered or preserved for him.

8. Broadly, the purpose of taxation is to allow a reasonable fee for work actually and reasonably done. While the expert may be expected to know whether his fees are broadly similar to those of other experts of similar standing, he could not be expected to know, e.g., either whether an expert's report is required at all or whether such a senior expert's report, or such a detailed report, is required.

9. The solicitor must make the application in advance—see *Wallace* v. *Freeman Heating Co Ltd* [1955] 1 WLR 172 (for civil cases) and Legal Aid in Criminal and Care Proceedings (General) Regulations 1989, regulation 54(1) (for criminal cases) which refers to a "prior" authority.

10. Application is made on form APP6 (ABWOR and Civil) and APP7 (Criminal).

11. Further details of the Legal Aid Board's approach may be found in Notes for Guidance 10 and 17-15 in the *Legal Aid Handbook*, which is published by Sweet & Maxwell.

12. In criminal cases, even where authority has been granted, for the full amount of payment to be allowed, the expenditure must have been "reasonably" incurred (regulation 7(5) of the Legal Aid in Criminal and Care Proceedings (Costs) Regulations 1989). This is not so in civil cases (Civil Legal Aid (General) Regulations 1989, regulation 63(2)).

13. The relevant provisions are: regulation 30A of the Legal Advice and Assistance Regulations 1989 and regulation 101(1)(a) of the Civil Legal Aid (General) Regulations 1989.
14. Regulation 4A, Legal Aid in Criminal and Care Proceedings (Costs) Regulations 1989.
15. For example where the witness is a doctor in general practice, this includes the cost of hiring a *locum*.
16. Criminal Procedure (Attendance of Witnesses) Act 1965.

An article based on a talk given to The Academy of Experts by ***Simon Morgans, LLB, LLM, MBA****, solicitor and legal adviser to the Legal Aid Board.*

CHAPTER 1/12

SINGLE AND/OR NEUTRAL EXPERTS

Richard Freeman

CHAPTER 1/12A

THE "SINGLE JOINT" EXPERT WITNESS

001 Expert witnesses in England in recent years have almost invariably been appointed by the parties to give evidence *on their behalf*. Experts appointed in this way owe a primary duty to the court and are obliged to give objective evidence of their honest opinion. But they are paid by one party, receive their instructions and influence from that party and its lawyers and they cannot be genuinely impartial, whatever their level of integrity. A simple test that demonstrates this is that the expert is bound to be pleased if he finds evidence that favours his party's position. He may deal with adverse evidence properly but cannot obtain pleasure from it.

002 The current employment of court experts and assessors in civil law countries is well known but their occasionally widespread application in common law jurisdictions in the past was something of a surprise to me. Carol Jones (*Expert Witnesses—Science, Medicine and the Practice of Law* (Clarendon Press, Oxford)) reports that court experts enjoyed an immense but brief popularity in the United States between 1880 and 1920 when scientists were described as men of sincerity, simplicity, fidelity, and generosity of character, noble in their aims and in their efforts. They were seen as totally objective, altruistic and impartial but problems arose when they could not agree amongst themselves, even when they were not paid hirelings. In England, Ms Jones says that the idea of making experts more powerful by placing them alongside the judge was not welcome and that the legal system had spent several hundred years moving experts away from that position. Even if this history is not wholly accurate, it perfectly describes some of the current fears that must be addressed.

003 Lord Mackay, the former Lord Chancellor, may reside in memory and press cuttings as a mean Scot more interested in cost than justice but his enduring legacy is very different. Lord Bingham of Cornhill and Lord Woolf, both great reforming judges, were appointed by Lord Mackay to positions of great influence (eventually, to Lord Chief Justice and Master of the Rolls respectively). The current concentration on reducing costs results from the proposition that a fully argued determination at unaffordable cost and excessive delay is incompatible with justice. This proposition is treated as self-evident by the users of the litigation system but regarded by many professionals simply as an attack on their financial interests.

004 *Access to Justice* (Lord Woolf's comprehensive report on the civil justice system) concluded that the excessive and incorrect use of expert evidence was one of the major factors in the unacceptable level of cost. The *Report*'s main recommendation on this aspect was for the introduction of a single expert and, as with any major change, there was and still is strong opposition. However, this complex subject was not treated as carefully as it might have been and the result is that the recently announced Civil Procedure Rules (the "Rules") take a far more limited approach than the original report.

005 There are important benefits to be obtained from the proper use of neutral, genuinely impartial, experts. The key to obtaining benefits and not being saddled with the reverse is to pick the correct circumstances for these appointments. At first this will have to be driven by the tribunal but the best neutral appointments will come once the party's lawyers actively embrace the procedure. There is a parallel with the way that the legal profession was initially forced to consider mediation but is increasingly pleased with its advantages in the right circumstances.

006 In past years, I have written several somewhat futuristic articles which explored the way in which neutral experts might be used. Two of them are reproduced here, relating to matrimonial actions (Chapter 1/12B) and criminal cases (Chapter 1/12C). The use of a neutral expert in criminal matters is not a topic under current consideration, rather unfortunately, as there are major advantages in respect of both justice and cost. However, the article on matrimonial cases summarises points of general importance and continued relevance to the new civil system.

007 At the time of writing (July 1999) the CPR have been in operation for three months but there has been very little action. Litigation work is well down and The Academy has not heard of any material appointments as a single joint expert. The Commercial Court Guide and some authoritative guides on the CPR say that there is "no presumption in favour of a single joint expert". Many lawyers think that the use of the single expert will be very limited.

008 The CPR, however, are very clear and judges have both the power and the duty to impose the single joint expert where it is correct and cost effective to do so. The duty is set out in the overriding principles in Part 1. The extent of the use of such experts is in the hands of the judges. I hope that they will be quite forthright in imposing this principle. If so, lawyers will eventually embrace the idea in the same way as they are now embracing mediation.

009 Since April 1999 the debate on how single joint experts will operate seems to have polarised. Solicitors require the expert to be tightly under control. Judges want the expert to feel free to report to the court as they think fit. Experts generally consider that they can carry out the role but are nervous of being placed in compromising positions. They are also concerned about their fees.

010 Practice Direction 35 paragraph 1.6 referred to an approved expert's protocol. This has proved particularly difficult to produce with any degree of consensus, particularly regarding the single joint expert. The "protocol" has been replaced by a "code of guidance" and the intention is that a first version will be approved for use by 1 January 2000.

011 It is too early to be specific as to how the codes of guidance will develop regarding the various operational issues that I refer to in Chapter 1/12B. A key aim is that good experts must not be discouraged. Mutual trust between expert and lawyers and between expert and court is essential. The expert's fees and the work required of the expert must be proportional to the value of the dispute.

012 A neutral expert or assessor is not an arbitrator but he is in a very similar position in effect. The more the parties trust that person, and the more the rules engender that trust, the more cost effective will be the procedure. To be properly effective the neutral expert should be better and more experienced than the party appointed expert, who has a solicitor to advise and instruct him on points of difficulty. Unless the parties can agree on a particular expert, such a neutral is *imposed* on them and the integrity and expertise of that person is vital. Currently a party's advising lawyers do not test an expert's suitability for a party appointment just by reading his CV; they either know him from past cases or make detailed enquiries and interview him. Therefore, when Practice Direction 35 paragraph 1.2(1) merely obliges the expert to give details of his "qualifications" at the time of his report it is insufficient to generate trust. I would like to see this greatly expanded and disclosed before the expert is selected.

013 It is cost-saving, both to litigants and the public purse, that has generated this interest in the single joint expert and changes must truly save costs. The fear must be that instances of false economy will occur. Moreover, it would certainly be counterproductive if costs were brutally capped without a general acceptance that the expert's duties also have to be proportionate to the amount at issue.

014 *Balancing Justice and Cost* has been the banner statement for London Scheme Arbitration. I was the main author of this scheme which was launched at the Law Society on 3 November 1998 (but still has a way to go before it is adopted). This scheme aims to limit overall costs to 20 per cent of the value of the dispute. Precisely the same principles of proportionality have to apply for the use of neutral experts and I see nothing wrong in the court limiting the amount that can be spent on experts to a percentage of such value.

015 The court has the power to limit the expert's fees but it would be counterproductive for an expert to be so harshly limited that he has to gloss over real counter arguments that might be put. There will have to be some balance so that the case management of the judges allows the expert to tailor his report to the fee allocated.

016 With a party appointed expert, there is a natural reference to the instructing solicitors in case of difficulty. The equivalent for a single joint expert is to refer to the court for directions, not something to be taken lightly. In my opinion he must always be allowed to report that this is a case where party appointed experts are more suitable.

017 Even with all the obvious difficulties, I remain convinced that a neutral expert is an important feature that should be encouraged. There is a real need for a code of practice far more detailed and carefully considered than the Rules.

CHAPTER 1/12B

A SINGLE ACCOUNTANCY EXPERT IN MATRIMONIAL PROCEEDINGS

This article was first published in Family Law *in December 1997, after* Access to Justice *but before the Civil Procedure Rules were published. The Family Division is not directly affected by the CPR. It has a long track record of using single experts in matters affecting children and in valuations but has yet to embrace the procedure for accountancy.*

The procedural difficulties set out in this article remain at large and they remain my checklist of matters to consider with lawyers when taking instructions as a single joint expert.

RICHARD FREEMAN

001 Lord Woolf's proposed rules will take time to implement but they are already having a persuasive effect on judges' directions and orders for costs. Many of the proposed changes may never be enacted at all and the expert witness section is as contentious as any, but while there are serious difficulties with a single expert for issues of liability, many issues of *quantum* or financial presentation would be more rationally and cost effectively addressed by a truly impartial appointment. This is particularly so in matrimonial actions (and other personal matters, injury, and employment). This article suggests that lawyers should voluntarily and regularly make neutral appointments now and not wait for the proposed rules of civil justice to be enacted. Indeed, the family court should encourage this, although I consider that the use of RSC Order 40 to force the issue is cumbersome and unnecessary.

VOLUNTARY RATHER THAN ENFORCED SINGLE EXPERTS

002 The single expert for all types of evidence in all courts may, and I think should, never be forced on the parties. Rather than have blanket rules there should be persuasion applied, with different types of court applying relevant procedures, and with experts for *quantum* being far more involved in this position than experts for liability. The voluntary choice of a single accountant could easily be considered, discussed, and agreed between solicitors, suggested to the court, or possibly put in a *Calderbank* (*Calderbank* v. *Calderbank* [1976] Fam Law 93) letter. It could become a simple part of a standard checklist in the same way as mediation.

UNNECESSARY COSTS IN THE MEETING OF EXPERTS' PROCEDURES

003 In major commercial claims the best way to resolve complex *quantum* issues is for two accountants to be engaged to consider the position from their client's point of view, report accordingly, and then meet, discuss, and narrow differences. Good experts welcome the criticism of an experienced opposing expert as it helps to form a definitive opinion. A single expert would have an almost impossible task; determining an expert opinion might be possible but presenting an opinion for cross-examination by all parties does not sound like fun. The procedure of experts meeting to establish points of agreement and disagreement was born in the Official Referees' courts. It reduces court time even though the series of meetings to get to that stage might still be very attritional and costly.

004 However, an individual's affairs are almost invariably less complicated than those of a large company. A single *quantum* expert in matrimonial cases can more easily present a balanced view with a range of possibilities, with the court unlikely to be misled. A series of costly reports and meetings between accountants can be avoided. As with witness statements, a theoretically sensible procedure sometimes wastes money.

OBJECTIVE FINANCIAL STATEMENT

005 There is every reason for the courts to want a definitive and objective statement of the financial position of the marital estate to be available as close to the commencement of every divorce as possible. The only question to be answered is how best to achieve this. Parties cannot be prevented from engaging whatever professional assistance they want and, where there are serious concerns about hidden assets, such assistance may be a justifiable cost. Yet, even in such a case, an independent accountant would undoubtedly remove much unproductive confrontation and attrition.

006 Currently, solicitors in most cases, even quite large ones, do not use expert accountants at all, or they engage them late in the case when an early settlement cannot be found, invariably with increased costs. There are excellent practical reasons for this with party appointed experts and I do not need to expand, but good reasons almost disappear once an independent expert is considered. Only occasionally might there be minimal additional cost; in general an independent accountant, with appropriate training and experience, would be a valuable catalyst.

"IMPARTIAL" PARTY APPOINTED EXPERTS

007 Lord Woolf's review, *Access to Justice* (HMSO, 1996), recommends that party appointed experts must be impartial, reporting to the court not the party. Would this achieve the same result? There can be little confidence in that recommendation as there has been quite sufficient case law around to that end but without universal effect. Indeed, there is a serious practical and theoretical difficulty when the expert cannot communicate directly with the opposing party and advisers except through the opposing expert. It is a strange task to be asked to prepare, on behalf of a husband, a budget for a wife whom one is not allowed to meet. In

F v. *F* (*Ancillary Relief: Substantial Assets*) [1995] 2 FLR 45 Thorpe LJ used the word "objective", which is preferable. Instead of Lord Woolf trying to force experts into unnatural points of view, true impartiality should be sought from a single witness.

APPOINTMENT OF A SINGLE EXPERT

008 Undoubtedly, there are difficult questions to address as to how such a single expert should be appointed and the extent of his instructions and authority. A Fellows' Forum at The Academy of Experts, under the chairmanship of Rodney Broom, is considering this very thorny problem and I am a prime mover in this work. The views that I now express are mainly my own, but I have been influenced by others. I should say that on each point there is a body of opposing opinion.

THE MAIN ISSUES

009 I see the main issues for single experts (taken as a whole, rather than just *quantum* in matrimonial actions) as set out below. For completeness I deal with them all even though some are almost irrelevant to matrimonial cases.

010 To what extent should a single expert:

(1) Define (or influence) his own instructions?
(2) Disclose information received?
(3) Determine specific matters?
(4) Be able to propose and use supplementary expert advice?
(5) Have to explain views that he does not support?
(6) Write a fully comprehensive report?
(7) Be liable to be discredited?
(8) Be able to set charging rates in advance?

011 Some of these issues, considered across the board, raise almost impossible problems when a court has to apply a formal structure, laid down in rules of civil justice. However, looking at these issues in particular for accountancy investigation and quantification in matrimonial cases, the problems are relatively easily resolved. It would be a pity if sensible action were held up because the rules do not easily work for some unrelated field (for example liability in medical negligence).

Define (or influence) his own instructions

012 Solicitors may feel that they, with the court, should define the expert's brief, possibly without his input, but this would be counterproductive and ignore the experience and expertise of the expert. The expert's instructions should be agreed by the lawyers and court but the expert should have an unfettered right to propose what they should be.

013 A single expert accountant must be under a duty to investigate suspected hidden funds and consider what might be hidden even if not instructed in any specific area. Assuming that the husband has complex financial affairs, the single expert must be able to act as he would for a wife who might have no real knowledge. The alternative would be for the wife to feel that she must engage her own expert, thus defeating some of the object of cost saving.

Disclose information received

014 There is a strong body of opinion that a single expert should act like an arbitrator in the sense of making sure that he discloses everything heard from one party to the other. I believe that that would increase costs unnecessarily and, indeed, I do not think that the Arbitration Act 1996 (ss.33 and 34) requires this level of formality in future in any event. So I would have the single expert acting in the same way as in an expert determination with reasoned award, disclosing those parts of his investigation that he considers relevant. There is no reason for a single expert to disclose that a wife has suggested that she wants 20 fur coats if that is absurd. Why discredit her unless she insists?

Determine specific matters

015 I believe that an expert should be able to say "I consider this point to be a fact and I determine it to be so. Such determination will become final and conclusive unless there is objection within [specify the period]." Lord Woolf's rules allow for examination of the single expert in court but as much as can be eliminated from argument beforehand the better.

Be able to propose and use supplementary expert advice

016 I only foresee this as a possible problem when an expert is forced to act as a single expert under instructions agreed between lawyers without his involvement. If the accountant has a duty to investigate for possible hidden funds, then he might want to use an investigator and should be allowed to do so (subject to agreement over costs).

Have to explain views that he does not support

017 The consensus is that this is vitally important, although I do have a reservation, relating to costs, when it comes to fast track cases. In all cases I would write to the solicitor whose client suggests something with which I do not agree as "I do not agree [xxx]. If you accept my opinion without more explanation please write to me acordingly, otherwise I will set out full reasons in my report." This gives an opportunity for cost saving that should not be overlooked.

Write a fully comprehensive report

018 Again, the consensus is that this is vitally important, but I have the same points regarding the potential for avoiding costs.

Be liable to be discredited

019 The sort of scenario where this would be a disaster is in medical negligence and is probably the most important reason why single experts reporting on liability should not be forced on the litigation process. I think that parties should be asked to state those parts of a single expert's report that they want to challenge and those parts they accept (in much the same way as experts are asked to state their points of agreement and disagreement in advance of trial). However, I cannot see that there would be especial concern with matrimonial accountancy evidence and where parties have chosen an expert, rather than having him imposed, there is less sympathy for their position if they then do not agree with him.

Be able to set charging rates in advance

020 The issue that is most likely to cause trouble is the proposed provision that courts will set fees for experts. The obligations on a single expert are significantly greater than those on a party appointed expert, who can always ask his instructing solicitor for advice. Indeed, he can hide behind his instructing solicitor (for better or for worse). The single expert will be in a very lonely position, detached from what is happening in the case, with the prospect of being cross-examined by the parties and incurring the wrath of the court if things go wrong.

021 I believe that such a position calls for considerable experience and training in providing a neutral view. Experience and training as an arbitrator, expert determinator, or mediator should be relevant and fees should be set according to that experience. Unfortunately, the Woolf recommendations seem to concentrate on small cases carried out cheaply and it is only too easy to feel that this will result in a fair measure of chaos and rough justice. A voluntary arrangement with a sensible fee agreement would avoid that.

CONCLUSION

022 Everyone has doubts as to how the proposed rules for civil justice will work in respect of single or neutral experts. There are various studies afoot apart from The Academy of Experts', particularly within the construction industry and others involved in the Official Referees' court. One area where a single expert can be effectively employed to advantage before any formal rules come into place is in accountancy evidence in matrimonial cases.

A NEUTRAL EXPERT FOR CRIMINAL CASES?

This article was first published in The Expert *in Volume 2, No 2, June 1997. The subject is not under current consideration at all, as far as I know. However, with the CPR breaking the ice on single experts in our current litigation system, the article may not be as futuristic as it was when written. It may be the general pressure on legal aid costs that is the catalyst but it should still be considered an aid to justice.*

RICHARD FREEMAN

CONFLICTING TECHNICAL EVIDENCE SHOULD BE ASSESSED BY SOMEONE TECHNICALLY COMPETENT TO DO SO. IT SHOULD NOT BE LEFT TO JUDGE AND JURY

001 The major miscarriages of justice that stain our system all stem from actions that took place many years ago. It is easy to assume that the prosecution will now take greater care to ensure that the evidence of technical prosecution witnesses does not create an injustice. However, my current experience, albeit in cases of fraud rather than murder, is that there is little change. Unduly prejudicial prosecution evidence continues to make a lottery of cases with a high technical content.

002 The sight of an investigator literally dancing in the street, after "getting a result" that is plainly unjust, is obscene. It may be understandable once one considers the three years that it took the team to investigate and prosecute and the effect on their future careers. There is little chance of objectivity under such pressure.

003 At a meeting of The Academy I put to George Staple, then Director of the Serious Fraud Office, that it was wrong for investigators to give what is, in effect, expert evidence. He disagreed, saying that the decision to prosecute was taken by others. But those "others", unseen and unheard, probably authorised the expenditure on the investigation in the first place. Again this is not an objective view.

004 Yet the system can be used to restrict defence experts to only part of the evidence. They are also suspected of bias, often rightly so, whether they know it or not.

005 The medieval principle, that an individual should be judged by his peers, still works well on matters within the competence of the main players, counsel, judge, and jury. Truthfulness, motive and intentions can be determined in a way that, for all the arguments, has stood the test of time. I think it is wrong to scrap the jury for not being able to handle something that it was not designed to do.

006 It is ridiculous to add to the duties of a jury, or to the duties of a non-technical judge for that matter, a decision on a conflict of technical evidence. If an individual is to be judged by his peers so should the experts submit to some form of assessment by someone who knows what they are talking about.

007 In *The Expert* (Volume 2, No 1 at page 4) a psychoneurologist was quoted as saying "This man's brain is like a Swiss cheese"—favourably quoted, because the system requires KISS: "Keep It Simple, Stupid". But how does the layman decide if the opposing expert describes the brain as like "Danish Blue"? Or like the moon, with the appearance of cheese but actually rock solid? On such nonsense people can go to jail and sometimes, as a consequence, lose their marriages and business in the process.

008 Recently I went to Wormwood Scrubs to see someone who, in my expert opinion, should not have been there. The next day, I was immersed in something new and any feeling of repugnance was somewhat sublimated. It is so much easier for all of us to get on with the system but it is just wrong.

009 Lord Howe quotes G K Chesterton:

> "Now it is a terrible business to mark a man out for the vengeance of men. But it is a thing to which a man can grow accustomed . . . And the horrible thing about all legal officials, even the best, about all judges, magistrates, barristers, detectives and policemen is not that they are wicked . . . or . . . stupid . . . it is simply that they have got used to it . . . They do not see the awful court of judgment; they only see their own workshop."

010 As experts, we cannot take control or responsibility of the whole system, but we should be able to find a way to ensure that technical evidence is put forward in a wholly neutral and objective manner that does not in itself mislead and cause an injustice.

***Richard Freeman, MA (Cantab), FCA, FCIArb, DipICArb, FAE, QDR** is a chartered accountant, expert witness, arbitrator and mediator. He has considerable experience, as witness or advocate, in a wide range of different courts and tribunals in the United Kingdom and in Michigan and New York. He is Chairman of The Academy of Experts and was the founding editor of* The Expert. *He has arbitrated since 1994, is a member of the Accountants in Arbitration committee and chaired the sub-committee of the London branch of the Chartered Institute of Arbitrators that devised the London Scheme. He is Head of Litigation Services at Horwath Clark Whitehill.*

CHAPTER 1/13

THE PRACTICAL ROLE OF AN EXPERT IN COMPUTER DISPUTES

Keith Salmon

001 It does seem to me that a confused view of what experts should and should not do is developing. Many people seem quite confused about what experts are and this confusion seems to arise from a lack of practical experience of litigious matters involving experts. When I last looked at the profession, there were in excess of 1,000 computer dispute expert witnesses. Only 19 had ever been appointed as expert witnesses; presumably the others had read books or attended training courses about it. Lack of experience did not stop experts from stating what we should or should not do. The most vociferous experts were those without practical experience.

002 Therefore, I would suggest that we arrive at a central requirement for an expert witness: practical expertise derived from instruction. Without practical experience derived from actual instruction, an expert's view of his duties is quite probably wrong, possibly seriously. I enjoy the experience derived from successfully acting in 650 computer disputes for FMC's clients. Initially, I had some very strange views. Now, of course, I am quite certain of my responsibilities and capabilities.

003 It has been said that an expert must *not always* "tell the truth, the whole truth and nothing but the truth". What nonsense! The truth is as binding upon an expert witness as it is upon anyone giving evidence. If there are points of procedure that prohibit certain evidence being given, then this is a matter for the trial judge to decide at the time of the hearing. It is not for an expert or The Academy to predetermine. This is an aspect of *decided* legal procedure with which I have no problem.

004 Moreover, it cannot pose a problem to a jury, as has been suggested in the past, because civil cases are no longer heard by a jury. It cannot pose a problem for counsel because experts only answer the questions asked by counsel. If counsel finds that he does not receive the answers he requires, then I suggest he spends more time in preparation so that he asks the correct questions (a common fault in my experience).

005 It has been said that the case of *Whitehouse* v. *Jordan* [1981] 1 WLR 246 dictates that experts must or must not do a whole variety of things—sometimes very strange things. I think most lawyers and experts would do well to read a transcript of that case. In simple terms, the case involved doctors who allowed counsel to delete and rewrite parts of their reports in a personal injury case. In the end, the doctors thought out and produced very little of their reports. That is why the court wisely ruled that an expert report must be the product of an expert's endeavours and experience.

006 Most people would agree that this is a proper and logical decision:

Proper—because unless the report comes from the expert's experience (of the matter in hand, not of matters in general), it is hearsay evidence and, in practical terms, worthless.
Logical—because how otherwise can the expert perform in court? He needs to form a view that he can support.

007 The decision in *Whitehouse* v. *Jordan* and the new Civil Procedure Rules (CPR) are often misconstrued:

1. They do not mean that an expert is an *officer of the court*. He is not an officer.
2. They do not mean that an expert has a *sole and exclusive duty to the court which extinguishes his duty to his client*. An expert has a duty to the court which, in times of conflict, overrides his duty to his client. However, an expert's duty to his client still exists, firstly in contract law, if he was instructed directly by the client, and secondly in the tort of negligence, under which he has a duty of care to his client to perform his tasks competently. There are certain circumstances in which the expert can claim immunity from suit and these chiefly relate to his giving evidence in court but at certain other stages of his dealings with his client an expert can be liable in contract or negligence.
3. They do not mean that the expert is under a duty to the other parties. Even if the court appoints a person to be the single joint expert in a matter, that expert's duty is to the court as it always was when such a procedure was invoked in the past (Order 40 RSC).
4. They do not mean that each expert must state points which go against their client's cause of action. This is not stated anywhere in the CPR, Practice Directions, Civil Procedure Act 1997 or Lord Woolf's Final Report. In an adversarial legal system it is inequitable to insist that the opposing parties should take measures to prove each other's cause of action and thus it is with regard to this point. Experts should tell the truth, be accurate, be authoritative, be assertive and be cooperative. If they do this then they shall rely upon points of expert evidence which are essential to the just and satisfactory resolution of the parties' civil dispute. By doing so they will address all of the relevant points in their clients' pleadings and this is all that is required by the civil justice system of the United Kingdom.

008 Simplistic statements concerning expert evidence can produce quite confusing results. So what should an expert witness do? Well, under the new CPR the law recognises that experts can and do perform various roles at different stages of the litigation. That is why Part 35 of the CPR addresses the roles of *experts and assessors*. There are perhaps two things which above all an expert should do. They are:

1. He should thoroughly examine the computer system, the contractual documentation between the parties and establish what the evidence will and will not support. If the client's evidence indicates a valid cause of action, he should advise the client's lawyers accordingly. However, if the evidence does not show a cause of action, then he should advise the client and his lawyer to settle the matter. (Support for my views can be found in the Overriding Objective of Lord Woolf's Final Report on Access to Justice.) I am firmly of the opinion that too many litigations are initiated when the issues have not been investigated thoroughly. This wastes court time and places an increased tax burden upon the public.
2. Once he has assessed the matter, he should initiate steps designed to secure a settlement meeting with his opponents. He should negotiate, explaining his client's cause of action and remedy. These attempts at settlement are proposed by Lord Woolf's Final Report and are highly desirable before inordinate amounts of cost and delay (which are largely imposed by the court upon litigants) occur.

In addition, the following procedures are usually necessary:

1. To advise on the strength of a client's cause of action early in a matter, such strength accruing to the relevance and seriousness of technical defects and deficiencies to the terms of the client's contract with his supplier or customer.

2. To advise on mitigation and damage limitation.
3. To translate computer terminology into legal and financial terminology.
4. To advise on strategy in promoting settlement measures or speedy litigation procedure.
5. To reveal technical evidence from the examination of the client's computer to show actual, not theoretical, faults and lack of function.
6. To disclose financial evidence accruing to the various chains of causation so that a decision can be made about whether the matter is "worth the candle".
7. To assist the client's solicitor in explaining to the client the necessity for the complexity, cost and delays accruing to the execution of litigation procedure, the need and nature of mitigation and the cost-effectiveness of a satisfactory settlement rather than a marvellous case fought to exhaustion.
8. To aid the client's solicitor to institute procedural steps to force the opposing party, its solicitor and expert out of lethargy and into the meaningful progression of a matter (courts could be far more helpful in this respect).

009 In many matters that have established history, the legal profession is quite able to handle experts without the anxiety currently being expressed. In personal injury matters, judges can identify those doctors who did not try to familiarise themselves with the matter, who have allowed counsel to write their reports, who are not experts in a particular branch of medicine, or who have little idea of their duties as expert witnesses.

010 Just because computers are relatively new (they have been around since 1955 in commerce), or because they cause much financial damage to companies, or have a strange terminology associated with them, or are promoted enthusiastically by counsel as required knowledge, I do not think that judges should abandon their tried and tested ways of assessing experts. The silent questions: "Does he make any sense to me?"; "Does he appear to know what he is talking about?"; "Has he done his homework in this matter?" are still as valid in the assessment of a computer-dispute expert witness today as they were in the assessment of a doctor in a personal injury matter 30 years ago.

011 If expert witnesses need to change, (and I think they do), they need to:

1. Know the computer system in dispute.
2. Examine the system in detail to reveal the full extent of the defects and deficiencies in that system.
3. Establish the theoretical financial damage caused by those defects and deficiencies based on substantive law.
4. Learn most aspects of civil law and apply them to any objective assessment of the results of the computer examination or financial investigation.
5. Explain to the client, the client's solicitor and counsel what the expert evidence will and will not support in law.
6. Translate the expert evidence into its congruent principles of substantive law so that everyone knows what he is considering.
7. Explain, by means of pertinent examples (perhaps best found in some leading decisions), the meaning of various aspects of the computer's lack of performance and the directly-arising, naturally-occurring financial results of those aspects.
8. Experts should be experts and not merely people without practical experience or knowledge of the matter in hand.

012 I am not suggesting that expert witnesses try to be advocates, a task they have always performed badly and embarrassingly. However, they should translate what they have found into the disciplines used in civil law (cf. law and corporate finance). In this way experts can achieve that most desirable, and least achieved, aspect of any complex commercial matter, namely competently to advise the court on the meaning and relevance of the complexities of the matter.

013 The Academy, for all its valuable advice in many areas, is not immune from misunderstanding some of the practical and legal details involved in expert evidence.

014 If UK law needs to change towards civil disputes (which I believe is long overdue), then the following changes are necessary, in my opinion:

1. Suppliers need to carry professional indemnity insurance with a minimum cover of £2,000,000. Failure to do so should be a criminal offence and give rise to directors' liabilities.
2. Courts need to award sensible levels of damages. At present, litigation in the UK is much a game of logical thought. Monetary compensation is considered to be a minor necessity and a rather grubby subject.
3. Courts need to manage their case load. Despite Woolf, it is not happening.
4. Courts need to recognise that in a civil litigation neither of the parties should be given latitude for missing deadlines. Defendants should be given no flexibility: they are not participants in a criminal case facing the weight of the judiciary and the moral condemnation of society. The parties are simply involved in a squalid commercial argument revolving around money. Three missed deadlines during the progress of the entire litigation should strike out the party.
5. The taxation of costs should be abolished. If you lose your action you deserve all you get.
6. Awards of legal costs should be abolished. They can easily be embraced within a client's damages if properly awarded.
7. Each litigant should be under a duty to account for the disposal of corporate assets once formal proceedings start. The duty should be one to show that an asset disposal was proper, not for the other party to try to show that it was not.

***Keith Salmon** read law at London University and has spent 23 years in the computer industry. He is co-chairman of FMC, a company that specialises in computer disputes and corporate fraud. He is co-author with Richard Mawrey QC of* Computers and the Law.

CHAPTER 1/14

SOME PRACTICAL POINTS FOR EXPERT WITNESSES

Tim Cooper

001 What follows is some guidance to inexperienced expert witnesses who may be cautious in acting. Hopefully it will give them some confidence in pursuing the discipline.

002 The problem centres on a failure to understand the task entrusted, the background to it, usual practice: what, why, how? The answer lies in understanding and appreciating the practical aspects and having good communication skills.

003 An expert is someone who by means of a previous course of study or habit has obtained knowledge in a particular field which surpasses that of an inexperienced person or layman and, therefore, makes him or her better equipped to express an informed opinion: *R* v. *Silverlock* [1894] 2 QB 766.

004 When accepting an instruction to advise, an expert should always remember that when acting in an advisory capacity the expert is under a duty to explain the whole thing to his client in simple terms. In *CIL Securities Ltd* v. *Briant Champion Long* [1993] 2 EGLR 164 an allegation of negligence succeeded against an expert surveyor. The surveyor had failed to obtain sufficient evidence of comparable transactions before advising settlement of a rent review. At 167L the court decided that "a surveyor [in the position of an expert advising the client on a rent review] is under a duty to explain the whole thing to his client in simple terms".

005 If an expert is instructed to prepare a report in contemplation of litigation/a dispute it is essential to distinguish between

(i) a report to give advice, to which legal professional privilege/litigation privilege should attach, to the effect that the report would not be disclosed to the opposing party, and

(ii) a witness statement to be exchanged by the parties.

The importance of the distinction is that privilege should attach to an expert's report to advise, so that it will not be subject to inspection in the discovery process, whereas a witness statement is provided specifically for exchange.

006 A colour co-ordinated Microsoft originated document looks good. If the terminology used is wrong credibility will be diluted. Some accepted terminology is emphasised in italics in what follows.

007 Persons acting in a judicial capacity make *holdings* on the *submissions* on issues of law, and *findings* on the *evidence* on issues of fact; sometimes they *hold and find* or *decide* when law and fact are mixed. *Feelings* are not part of the decision-making process, nor appropriate to experts.

Courts make *judgments* including *orders, determinations* and *declarations.*
Tribunals make *determinations.*
Arbitrators make *awards.*
Independent experts make *determinations.*
Contentions are *admitted, not admitted* (i.e. putting the other side on proof), *denied.*
Witnesses, including expert witnesses, write *[expert] witness statements,* sometimes called *expert reports* (hence the requirement to distinguish a report to give evidence and the statement for exchange), usually for exchange after consideration by legal advisers.
Advocates make *submissions* and should not seek to persuade witnesses to advance a party's case.
Expert witnesses give *evidence.*
Expert witnesses provide *proofs of evidence* to assist advocates/the tribunal.

008 *Expert witness statements/reports* must, in court proceedings, comply with the requirements in the relevant practice direction. At the end of the statement there must be a "Statement of Truth" per the Part 35 Practice Direction of the CPR:

> "I believe that the facts I have stated in this report are true and that the opinions I have expressed are correct."

The statement must also state the substance of all material instructions, whether written or oral, on the basis of which the statement was written; also that the expert understands his duty to the court.

Practising expert witnesses should ensure they comply with the relevant current court practice directions to avoid embarrassment at trial and to their client. If there is any doubt on the requirements it is essential to identify them and comply with them. Be warned—in April 1999 very wide-ranging practice direction changes were introduced. Ignorance of them will be at your peril! The instructing solicitor should tell you what is currently required, but do not assume his silence or lack of guidance is your excuse not to comply. Remember your duty is to the court.

009 Written representations procedure on documents only is usually by *statements of case,* i.e. a written statement to include facts, evidence, propositions of law and submissions: prepared by the advocate with the assistance of (expert) witness(es). Sometimes a party's representative acts as both the advocate and expert witness. The statement of case is followed by *reply to statement of case,* and possibly a reply thereto on a point of law.

010 Prior to a hearing before an expert tribunal (e.g. arbitration, lands tribunal) parties exchange *statements of case,* either a full exposition or a skeleton.

But no matter upon which a party places reliance must be left out. It is essential to establish the extent of the *statement* (full exposition or skeleton) to ensure both parties prepare a similar type document.

011 The new Civil Procedure Rules, effective from 26 April 1999, now set out the requirements and terminology in civil proceedings in the courts. Significant changes in terminology are:

RSC/CCR	**CPR**
Plaintiff	Claimant
Writ	Claim Form
Pleadings	Statements of Case
Discovery	Disclosure
Calderbank Offer	Part 36 Offer
Summons for Directions	Case Management Conference
Leave	Permission
Subpoena	Witness Summons
Taxation	Detailed Assessment

However, the terminology which follows in this paragraph and paras 012 and 013 is retained to assist readers in understanding what has been used in the old Rules of the Supreme Court and County Court Rules. In formal proceedings (e.g. the court) the normal route is exchange of *pleadings*. The action in court is commenced by issuing a *writ* in the High Court, a *summons* in the county court. Disputes of pure law are often begun without pleadings (as both parties know the issue(s) in dispute), using an *originating summons*. The first *pleading* (as a *statement of claim* in the High Court, as *particulars of claim* in the county court, as *points of claim* in an arbitration) is a written statement of facts which the party intends to prove in support of its contention. It should contain the history, the facts (not arguments, evidence or propositions of law, unless a statutory defence in a reply), the claim, the remedy sought. The respondent will wish to serve a *reply* and *counterclaim*, if any; followed by a *reply to the respondent's reply* and *defence to counterclaim* etc. *Amendments* are usually allowed with a compensatory costs order to the aggrieved party. *Further and better particulars* (to the pleadings) are usual; applications will be allowed if the pleading is uninformative, ambiguous or vague, e.g. bald statements do not usually sufficiently identify, itemise or otherwise describe the allegation. The essential purpose of pleadings is to define the issues and thereby to inform the parties in advance of the case they have to meet.

012 Following close of pleadings *discovery* takes place whereby both parties have to list all documents which are or have been in their possession, custody or power relating to matters in question. This can be a very expensive and lengthy exercise. Discovery applies to the parties, not third parties. The *list* is in three schedules

(i) a list of documents in the possession or power of the author of the list,
(ii) documents which a party has in his possession or power but which he objects to produce for inspection—the ground of objection must be stated,
(iii) documents which the party once had but no longer has in his possession or power (often the same as in list (i) e.g. originals, copies of which are contained in list (i)).

013 Following listing of documents *inspection* takes place which is the looking at and taking copies of documents that the opposing party has disclosed. Inspection is limited to those documents which are not privileged. Inspection is usually to find markings on the originals but in practice a party usually telephones and asks for copies of whichever documents it seeks from the lists and pays for them. An order for *specific discovery* is an order to *disclose* a document or a class/group of documents. It does not require listing and inspection as the documents exist. The parties (usually the claimant) then put together *paginated bundles* of documents intended to be relied upon—minimum of four copies (one each for the tribunal, claimant, respondent, the witness stand).

014 *Privilege* means that the other party cannot produce or rely on that privileged document in any proceedings. Privilege includes:

1. Legal professional privilege: covers documents passing between solicitor and client for the purposes of obtaining legal advice whether or not litigation is in contemplation. The privilege attaches to the client, not the solicitor.
2. Privilege against self-incrimination: i.e. a real risk of criminal charge or penalty.
3. Privilege against disclosing documents contrary to the public interest: e.g. national security, public documents.
4. Privilege attaching to without-prejudice communications: i.e. communications passing between the parties to a dispute for the purposes of negotiations to compromise the dispute; the document does not need to be marked "without prejudice" for the privilege to attach.
5. Litigation privilege: this can only be claimed when the dominant purpose of producing that document was that litigation was definitely in prospect; not a mere vague anticipation of it—see below.

015 Advisers/witnesses should ensure they clearly understand the difference between *subject to contract* and *without prejudice*. Subject to contract means the document so marked is not an offer which can be accepted, whereas a without prejudice offer, not subject to contract, can be accepted and form a binding contract subject to land law on transfers of interests in land in writing/by deed. As an example a *Calderbank* offer marked subject to contract is of no effect as it cannot be accepted as a binding agreement/contract.

016 The status of the expert may be any of the following: adviser, negotiator, expert, witness of fact, expert witness, advocate, independent expert, arbitrator.

017 An *adviser* advises a client of the strengths and weaknesses of a case and should give an honest opinion. An adviser is not protected from an allegation of negligence.

018 A *negotiator* is entitled to ignore the weaknesses of his case; its strengths can be exaggerated and any flaws are for the other side to point out. A negotiator is not protected from an allegation of negligence: see *CIL Securities Ltd* v. *Briant Champion Long* [1993] 2 EGLR 164—failure of survey or failure to obtain sufficient evidence of comparable transactions before advising settlement is negligence.

019 The opinion of an *expert* is sought in order that the protagonists can evaluate their chances of success and measure the possible returns against the likely costs. Litigation privilege may attach (see above) but there is merit in providing the opinion to the client's legal adviser to seek to attract legal professional privilege, in which case the advice should clearly state that the advice is given to assist the legal adviser to advise the client.

020 A *witness of fact* gives evidence of facts.

021 An *expert witness* gives opinion evidence on facts or matters within his expertise. An expert witness is protected from an allegation of negligence: *Palmer* v. *Durnford Ford* (1991) *The Times*, 11 November.

022 An *advocate* presents and argues a party's case both generally and specifically. He has a duty to introduce all relevant law both for and against his case.

023 An expert witness giving evidence should understand the task and duty of the tribunal (whether as judge, arbitrator, or tribunal). The duty is to arrive at the correct answer *on the evidence and the submissions:* a tribunal is not appointed to investigate the truth of the matter but to say who has adduced the heavier evidence and/or the most convincing arguments on law. A tribunal does not develop rival arguments or fill deficiencies. It must not take on the role of an *independent expert.* Its knowledge and experience is limited to understanding the parties' contentions. The parties must not suppose that the tribunal will do their work for them. It is expected to receive the evidence of witnesses and the submissions of advocates and to be guided by them in reaching its conclusion.

024 With acknowledgment and thanks to Ronald Bernstein, QC, FCIArb (*Journal of The Chartered Institute of Arbitrators* 1992, Vol 58, p. 12), here is his list of ways to lose a case:

(i) If you haven't the relevant experience—take the job on and hope for the best.
(ii) Always give the client the opinion he wants to hear.
(iii) Don't worry at telling lies as long as they are little ones.
(iv) Don't investigate everything—your experience will win the case.
(v) Never admit that you are uncertain about anything.
(vi) Never change your mind from your original opinion having heard the other party.
(vii) Before answering any question in cross-examination pause to work out why it is being asked. If you can't work it out ask why it is being asked.
(viii) Take every opportunity of showing how superior your knowledge is to that of everyone else, including the tribunal and the advocate.

025 The costs of contesting a dispute are often a significant factor and it is not unusual for the total costs to exceed the amount in dispute. In applying the principle that *costs follow the event,* the event is the resolution of the dispute; the issues giving rise to the dispute may be issues of law and/or fact. In the absence of special circumstances the issues giving rise to the dispute are not relevant in considering the event. Both parties' costs will be running. Significant costs will have accrued prior to a hearing: the sequence of pleadings, further and better particulars, discovery, witness/expert witness reports, counsel—all of which are likely to be logged on an hourly basis.

026 A party will be liable to pay his solicitor's costs (to include counsel's fees and fees of expert witnesses) on a solicitor-client basis *(indemnity basis)* i.e. that which has been agreed or is sustainable. If a party wins that party will recover its costs, i.e. the loser will pay the winning party's costs (and its own costs). Accordingly the costs' risk can be very significant.

027 In the event that the winning party obtains an order for its costs, the losing party may object to the level of those costs. If so, the winning party's costs will be referred for *taxation* (an assessment of the level of costs). However, taxation (in the absence of unusual circumstances) will be on a party–party basis *(standard basis).* This means that the costs allowed shall be a reasonable amount in respect of all costs reasonably incurred and any doubts shall be resolved in favour of the paying party: RSC Order 62, rule 12. Accordingly a winning party may only receive a proportion of its costs despite a costs order in its favour. In any event a successful party cannot recover more than its actual costs which it has agreed with its advisers (the indemnity principle).

028 The costs of an expert witness may be included in the taxation of the successful party's costs. The Supreme Court Taxing Office Practice Direction 2 of 1992 at para. 1.12 says

> "In the case of witness expenses and professional fees the account should be accompanied by details showing the work done, the time spent, by whom and when and the computation of the charge. Copies of those details should be annexed to the copy bill served on the paying party. The importance of this rule of practice is stressed. Failure to comply may result in a reduction in or the disallowance of such items."

Compliance with this direction means that the bill must be itemised, i.e. details showing itemised details of the work done, the time spent, by whom and when, computation of the charge. Detailed rules and Practice Directions are now contained in the CPR.

029 Waiting time may be charged at the full rate. Travelling time is not chargeable unless a significant distance, say more than ten miles. If counsel/the advocate wishes the expert witness to be present to assist in cross-examination, or the solicitor requires advice on possible settlement terms during the hearing, hourly fees are sustainable and the hours spent should be allowed on a taxation.

030 Costs, allowed as the costs of items of work which were reasonably required for the proper conduct of the case, will be allowed irrespective of when those items of work were performed: see *Gibson's Settlement Trusts* [1981] Ch 179.

031 The following are some practical points which should assist an inexperienced expert witness.

Always: Seek to improve/develop writing skills. Bad grammar, spelling, presentation are not authoritative. Use short sentences for clarity. Date and sign the report/statement.

Advice report: Should be a systematic presentation to enable a client to assess the strengths and weaknesses of his case. Seek to ensure privilege attaches, by addressing it to the solicitor. Three copies should be provided: for the solicitor, client, counsel. It may be presented on the author's stationery but should be double spaced to enable other advisers to make notes on it.

Witness statement: Should not be on the author's stationery. It should be on A4 white paper with double spacing and a wide right hand margin. It should not be "bound". It should be stapled at the top left hand corner, have numbered paragraphs and be paginated. The appendix may include the author's letterhead stationery. Keep it simple; it is essential to ensure the tribunal understands the evidence. Sign and date it. Provide six copies (two solicitors, two counsel, witness stand, tribunal). Put as much as possible in appendices.

Arrival at court: Tell the usher/clerk which case it is. He will direct you to the parties/the court. It is likely a discussion on terms of settlement will take place. Communicate with the solicitor; only counsel if counsel involves you.

The bundle/notes: There will be a *bundle* in the witness stand. The tribunal and the two advocates will have the same bundle. It should contain the pleadings, documents intended to be relied upon, witness/expert witness statements previously exchanged. A witness is not usually entitled to look at notes made, since his evidence is first hand evidence. An expert witness is entitled to look at his notes but always ask the tribunal before doing so, e.g. "may I refer to my notes?".

Notes (contemporaneous): Contemporaneous notes are more persuasive than a recollection. Therefore, in appropriate files, make contemporaneous notes, especially dates and times.

Advice/discussions: An expert witness when not giving evidence may advise the client/solicitor/counsel. Credibility will be enhanced if an intelligent pro-active interest in the case is taken, but be polite and cautious. An expert does not have conduct of the case. An expert giving evidence must not speak to or communicate with anyone privately when giving evidence including during an adjournment, e.g. lunch break, overnight. If there is doubt whether evidence is still being given, e.g. having left the witness stand, ask the tribunal whether you have been released or ask your counsel to enquire from the tribunal whether you have been released.

Examination: An expert witness will be examined by his side's advocate as *examination* *in chief*. This may involve trawling through the whole of your witness statement, or it may be taken as read and you will be asked whether it still stands and you wish to add anything. In examination in chief leading questions cannot be asked. A *leading question* is one that anticipates or assumes the answer, e.g. when did you stop beating your grandmother? The reason leading questions are not allowed is that no evidential weight will be attached to the answers by the judge as the answer is not the independent opinion of the witness. It is your opportunity to give your evidence but let counsel guide you in what you say. The next stage is *cross-examination* when counsel on the opposite side can ask any questions relevant to the issue in dispute and your expertise. Best advice to an expert under cross-examination is to keep the answers as short as possible: "yes" or "no" will suffice. This will make it more difficult for opposing counsel but do not overlook your duty to the tribunal. Following cross-examination your counsel may wish to *re-examine* you (again leading questions cannot be asked); you will have to remember what you have said so that your evidence is consistent. If evidence in re-examination is inconsistent with examination in chief without good cause the credibility of the whole of the evidence may be thrown into doubt. This is perhaps why counsel often avoid re-examination.

Conduct in the witness stand: It will be the advocate asking questions. The expert provides his answers to the tribunal, not the advocate. Watch the tribunal. If the tribunal is writing it is not listening, so wait until it has stopped writing. It is likely the tribunal will ask you questions to enable it to understand the evidence you are giving. Do not be afraid to go back to basics, e.g. principles appropriate to your discipline. Be polite. Ensure you make eye contact with the tribunal. Do not under any circumstances argue with either the tribunal or counsel even though the adrenaline has started to run.

Assisting counsel: If counsel has asked you to be available for his cross-examination of the other side's expert you will sit behind counsel. He may turn round at any time and ask you for comment or advice on his conduct of your side's case. If you believe there is an important point counsel has missed jot a note down on a piece of paper (take a notebook with you) and pass it to him (on the desk in front of him); make sure he can read it. But be careful not to interrupt his flow of presentation by being a nuisance.

Awareness: Keep your eye on the tribunal at all times. You are seeking to convince the tribunal, not counsel.

When to stop: The tribunal will indicate if it is bored or readily understands the evidence by saying, e.g. "I understand the point, I hear what you say".

When to keep going: If the tribunal is showing an interest in what you say, help it to understand. You might say "do you wish me to assist you further on this point, to explain my evidence, my Lord/your Honour/Sir?".

Confidence: If you have a genuine and honest belief in the figures you are speaking to, and a thorough understanding of the methods used by convention to achieve the end result, you are in with a very good chance of pushing the result your way.

Consistency: If an expert's evidence is inconsistent or shown to be inconsistent the whole of that evidence may be thrown in doubt. Do not be tempted to add a bit or subtract a bit if it is not your truthful opinion; you will have fallen into a trap, the trap of discrediting your other evidence. This other evidence may be your evidence derived from experience upon which you are relying heavily. You have shot yourself in the foot.

Honesty: If you can honestly say that your opinion would have been the same if you had been instructed by the other side you are well on the way to achieving the objective.

Change of mind: Reject a suggestion, in cross-examination, that your figure is "in the region of" (a tactic of counsel), e.g. in speaking to £100,000, counsel says your opinion is an art, why not £95,000? Do not fall for this. As an expert you are entitled to give expert opinion evidence. If £100,000 is your honest opinion, stick to your honest opinion but acknowledge it is an opinion. If new evidence is revealed after your written witness statement do not be afraid to adjust your figure; tell your counsel/solicitors (and the tribunal) immediately. Your credibility will be enhanced as you have recognised your duty to the tribunal.

Knowledge and experience: Stress your knowledge and experience but this may be wasted if the evidence is not consistent, honest and credible. Often more weight is likely to be attached to experience than qualifications. When faced with two opposing witnesses of equal experience qualifications and plausibility the tribunal will prefer the evidence which seems more probable.

Advocate/expert: When acting as advocate and expert ensure the tribunal understands which mode you are in at all times to avoid discrediting your honest and truthful opinion as an expert witness. An expert witness should not seek to advance his client's case; he should be seen to be genuinely independent and neither partial nor committed to a party's case. An advocate's job is to argue the case. It is not the tribunal's job to do the work for you. It should be helpful to dissect your and the opposing party's case, identify the differences, present the differences and summarise your contentions thereon in closings. If you cannot meet the responsibilities of an expert witness or advocate you are probably better not dealing with the matter.

Appearance: Make sure you turn up looking the part, appropriately dressed. Watch your body language.

Listening: Take your time. If the tribunal is writing it is unlikely to be listening.

Uncertain: If you are unsure on any matter do not be afraid to ask. A tribunal has a duty to ensure the parties understand the procedure. However, a tribunal, assisting a party or an unrepresented party suggests partiality.

Apparent uncertainty of the tribunal: If you doubt the experience of the tribunal outline your case clearly and unequivocally, politely pointing it in the right direction. If the tribunal is a lay person suggest by implication he is accountable for his decision on each of the issues you have identified. You must ensure the tribunal understands your contentions.

Different evidential methods: If opposing parties adopt different methods ensure you give your opinion as an expert on the figures appropriate to the other party's method even though you do not accept that method. If you do not there is a danger a tribunal might not accept your method, adopting the other party's method and if the other party's figures have not been contested they might be adopted in their entirety in which case your side loses completely.

Omission: Do not overlook the merit in saying that you have taken into account all of the facts which might tend to weaken your case and identify those facts. You should not mislead by omission.

Legal submission: If you are going to make a legal submission and cite any authority for it do read the whole of a recognised report and provide a copy, possibly appropriately highlighted. Custom in court dictates that if you rely on any legal authority a copy of the material on which you rely must be provided to the other side: the principle that no party shall be taken by surprise.

Precedent: *Holdings* of law in previous cases provide judicial principles which should be observed. *Findings* of fact in previous cases are not precedent and are not evidence.

Litigation privilege: Privilege can only be claimed for reports when the dominant purpose of producing the document was that litigation was definitely in prospect; not a mere vague anticipation of it: see *Waugh* v. *British Railways Board* [1979] 2 All ER 1169; *M & W Grazebrook Ltd* v. *Wallens* [1978] 2 All ER 868; *Alfred Crompton Amusement Machines Ltd* v. *Cmrs of Customs & Excise (No 2)* [1972] 2 All ER 353. There is greater protection if the report is addressed to the solicitor (not the client) to attract legal professional privilege. State the report is provided to assist in giving legal advice to the client.

Unchallenged evidence: A tribunal will not draw inferences from alleged facts. The evidence must be presented. Unchallenged evidence is accepted unless it falls short of establishing the contention in support of which it is made: see *Lewis Emanuel & Son Ltd* v. *Sammut* [1959] 2 Lloyd's Rep 629 at p. 634, col. 2.

Objective: Is to concentrate the tribunal's mind on the issue in dispute and its subordinate issues.

Content of statement of case: If an expert is entrusted with the conduct of a case the statement of case should not be a rambling statement. It must be structured. The object is to concentrate the tribunal's mind on the issues within the dispute, as the holdings and findings on them will inevitably lead to the result.

Reply to statement of case: should deal with *all* points contested as a failure to contest will imply an admission.

Inspections: At an inspection ensure you show the tribunal all the evidence on which you rely. Make sure the tribunal understands your contentions. Look at any evidence introduced by the other side.

Applications and directions: If you have conduct of the case read the tribunal's directions and seek to comply. If you cannot comply contact the other side first and seek to obtain agreement to a consent application; thereby reducing costs. If an interlocutory application (with reasons) is made which is likely to be contested serve it simultaneously on the other side and introduce a reasonable time limit for the other side to respond; requesting the tribunal to "proceed in the absence of the other party" if the time limit is not adhered to.

Late evidence: Eleventh hour relevant evidence may be put in but there is a risk of a costs' sanction. Relevance is based on the question of whether it might or could be reasonably be expected to provoke a line of enquiry which would be of assistance to a party.

Liability having conduct of the case: If, on behalf of your client, you are receiving correspondence, notices from a tribunal, you have a duty of care to your client to ensure he knows the effect of what is going on.

***Calderbank* offer:** A *Calderbank* offer must have teeth to be effective. It should be an unequivocal open offer "without prejudice save as to costs". Costs and any interest terms must be referred to, to compare like with like. The offer (if it beats the substantive decision) protects costs and is effective from the date it may reasonably have been expected to have been accepted (usually 7–21 days). Proof of delivery of the offer may be required. The CPR refers to a *Calderbank* offer as a "Part 36" offer.

Self Assessment: Have the humility to try and identify your strengths and weaknesses after an appearance. This will identify areas for improvement. Examples include: appearance, attitude, voice, communication, confidence, persuasiveness, professionalism.

***Tim Cooper, BSc, FRICS, FCIArb** has over 25 years' experience as a valuation expert adviser to disputants and as an expert witness to judicial bodies including the courts. His professional experience dates from 1965 in London, with subsequent experience in the Midlands for 25 years. He is joint senior partner in Charles Butters & Sons, an independent practice of chartered valuation surveyors in North Staffordshire. He is a practising Registered Arbitrator, regularly accepting consensual and nominated appointments from the RICS and the CIArb. He is Vice-President (since 1988) of the West Midlands Rent Assessment Panel, entailing acting as Chairman Member of Leasehold Valuation Tribunals with,* inter alia, *leasehold enfranchisement and service charge jurisdictions. He is also a visiting lecturer and tutor to the College of Estate Management Diploma in Arbitration.*

CHAPTER 1/15

THE EXPERT WITNESS IN INTERNATIONAL LITIGATION

Robert Goldspink

001 "An expert witness is like a flea collar. When your case is a dog, you need something that will chase the fleas away, something that will keep your case from scratching and biting itself in front of a jury." This American lawyer's practical if injudicious description of the role of the expert stands in marked contrast with the role of the expert in English litigation, as set out *Whitehouse* v. *Jordan* [1981] 1 WLR 246: "When an expert is preparing evidence for potential use in court proceedings or is giving evidence in court, his responsibility is to help the court impartially on the matters within his expertise; and this overrides his duty to the client."

002 The purpose of expert evidence in all jurisdictions is essentially the same. It is to provide the judge or jury with information on matters which are too difficult for the normal man to be able to master. It is not the expert's job to decide cases, or to decide issues in cases.

003 There are wide variations on how to become qualified to give expert evidence; and in how experts give their evidence. These differences reflect, in part, different methods of litigation in each of the countries concerned.

004 At this time, when in England we are looking at the possibility of greater use of court-appointed (as opposed to party-appointed) experts, and when some are calling for a system of accreditation of expert witnesses, it is instructive to look at three other countries' ways of dealing with these issues; France, Germany and the US. France uses court-appointed experts and has a system of accreditation; Germany has a dualist system of court-appointed experts and of party-appointed experts, plus a system of accreditation; the US normally uses party-appointed experts, and has tests for qualifying experts as court witnesses, but not of accreditation.

005 We will conclude that within the wide spectrum of ways in which experts give evidence, the US, party-appointed, expert system is at one end of the spectrum; the French and German court-appointed systems of experts are at the other; and the English system stands somewhere in the middle.

006 In this article, I will cover the following matters:

- France:
  - (a) selection and accreditation of expert witnesses;
  - (b) types of expert evidence; and
  - (c) challenges to the appointment of an expert.
- Germany:
  - (a) selection and accreditation of expert witnesses; and
  - (b) challenges to the appointment and evidence of an expert.

- How experts give evidence in France and Germany
- France, Germany: whether expert witnesses may be sued
- How experts are paid in France and Germany
- US:
  - (a) who may be an expert witness; and
  - (b) discovery and depositions of experts.
- Finally, a review of some issues of expert evidence arising in multi-jurisdiction litigation in England, the US, France and Germany.

THE COURT-APPOINTED EXPERTS

France

Selection and accreditation

007 There are differences between the English and French concepts of an expert witness. In France, an expert is a profession in its own right. The very title "expert" is protected: someone who falsely claims to be an *expert près de la cour d'appel* or *agrée par la cour de cassation* is liable to criminal penalty. His or her task is as assistant to the judge.

008 In France the judge has the power to appoint "any person of his choice" to examine a question of fact which requires clarification by a technical expert (a *technicien*)—*Nouveau code de procedure civile* (NCPC), Art 232; and to determine the way in which the procedure is to be carried out. The judge has a wide discretion whether to appoint an expert, and can do so on his or her own initiative, but normally does so on the request of the parties. If the judge appoints an expert, the reasons for doing so must be given, and the precise terms of reference set out.

009 A single court-appointed expert is the norm, though there are provisions for appointing more if needed. Ordinarily a cab-rank basis applies, and the court appoints the next accredited expert on the list. Generally speaking the parties accept the choice without argument. It is common practice to suggest the names of experts informally to the court, but the court is not obliged to accept that choice.

010 Normally the expert will come from an approved list. Every year a national list of approved experts is drawn up by the *cour de cassation* (Supreme Court in Civil Matters); and a list is drawn up for each regional *cour d'appel* (Court of Appeal) of which there are 30 in metropolitan France.

011 To get on the court of appeal list, the expert must apply before 1 March to the public prosecutor in the *Tribunal de Grande Instance* (High Court). He or she must show expertise in a particular specialty, and set out his or her titles, qualifications, scientific, technical, or professional credentials, and other matters. There are a number of other requirements. For example, the expert cannot have committed a crime of dishonesty, immorality or dishonour; must not have been sanctioned or disciplined by their institute; cannot be a bankrupt, or involved in some way with bankrupt companies; cannot have acted in a way which compromises their independence; must have been practising for a sufficiently long time (the precise time is not specified); and must be younger than 70.

012 The public prosecutor then checks out the applicant, and sends the application for review by the High Court, the presidents of the Commercial Courts and others; thereafter it is sent to the regional court of appeal which prepares the list in the first week of November. Someone who gets on to this list could expect to remain there indefinitely.

013 To get on the Supreme Court list, an expert must normally have been on one of the national lists for the last three years. He or she then has to apply to the *procureur general* of the Supreme Court. Lists of the accredited experts are maintained, and are publicly-accessible, in each area.

014 Upon entry to the list for the court of appeal, the expert must swear an oath in front of the court of appeal to assist the pursuit of justice, to accomplish the appointed task, to complete the necessary reports in the allotted time, and to prepare advice with honour and in good conscience.

015 There are disciplinary provisions for those who misconduct themselves, e.g. for dishonourable acts, lack of probity, offences against accepted standards of good behaviour; and serious faults in the execution of assignments including failing to meet deadlines.

Types of expert evidence

016 Once a judge has decided to have an expert witness, he or she decides between four types of investigative measures:

(a) Inspection by consent (*expertise amiable*). This is a voluntary process and is described by one commentator as "often a cause of major problems". No final decision is arrived at.
(b) Reports (*constatations*).
(c) Consultations, and
(d) Expert Opinions. This is the fullest type of report. The New Code of Civil Procedure sought to limit the use of full expert enquiries because of the delays and costs involved.

017 Reports (*constatations*) are simple measures providing reports on something without the expert being required to express any opinion at all on the *de facto* or *de jure* consequences of the matter. Usually a written report is provided unless the judge requires otherwise. The judge sets the amount of remuneration which the expert may receive, following completion of the job, directly from the person ordered to pay the expert's fees.

018 Consultations arise where there is no need for a complex investigation but the judge is seeking an opinion from the expert on a specific technical issue. Again, the judge sets the amount of remuneration which the expert may receive, following completion of the job—again, directly from the person under investigation.

019 Expert opinions arise only if *constatations* or consultations are not sufficient to clarify matters for the judge. In practice, judges continue to have wide recourses to expert enquiries even though they should only do so in respect of complex cases for which a *constatation* or consultation is insufficient. The judge must describe the circumstances requiring the expert opinion, define the task and set the deadline for it.

020 The expert, in turn, must give notice of acceptance, and cannot start work till advised by the court clerk that a proper retainer has been deposited, and registered. If the expert jumps the gun, his or her expert assignment may be null and void, unless the court orders otherwise. The expert then notifies the parties by registered letter. Any problems are referred back to the judge.

021 The expert is entitled to commission a specialist opinion from someone else in an area outside his or her own speciality. This concept is strange to English minds.

Challenges to the appointment of experts

022 The judge's appointment of an expert is open to challenge on the same grounds as are available to challenge the selection of a judge, i.e. personal relationship—subordinate, friend, enemy, interest in the outcome of the case. And the expert himself or herself may object to his or her appointment, but would have to have a legitimate reason. The expert is obliged to complete the court's mission in good conscience, with independence, and to take a neutral position with the parties (NCPC, Art 237).

023 So in summary, in France we have:

- a regulated system of accreditation
- an oath of office
- four types of assignment
- the judge setting parameters, timetable and deadline
- the judge picking the expert in his discretion, possibly on the basis of Buggins's Turn
- the expert getting on with the job, because this is their profession and they are subject to penal and professional discipline if they fail.

Germany

Selection and accreditation

024 Germany has a dual system of court-appointed experts and party-appointed experts. Germany tends towards appointing court-appointed experts. Certainly, the court decides if it is necessary to have an expert, even if both parties suggest that a particular fact be proved by an expert.

025 Like France, Germany has a system of accreditation.

026 Under the German Civil Code, the court should prefer, when selecting an expert, someone who is a publicly-certified and sworn expert. One gets this accreditation following an administrative proceedings (unrelated to the litigation) and the expert has to be sworn in by the administrative body issuing the certificate.

027 Experts may apply and be certified and sworn in as experts by a local chamber of commerce, a local government agency or certain other administrative bodies specified in the German Small Businesses Act. That Act contains a list of areas of expertise for which experts may be certified. The relevant authority may from time to time certify experts for additional areas of expertise if a need arises. To become accredited applicants must produce evidence to the satisfaction of the relevant authority of their knowledge and experience in the relevant area.

028 Anyone who is to become accredited as an expert must swear that if appointed for a particular case he or she will personally review the relevant facts, prepare a written report, conduct himself or herself in an independent manner and not accept instructions from any party involved in the litigation.

029 If there is to be a court-appointed expert, the court frequently tries to reach agreement with the parties on the selection of the court appointee, failing which it will select one of the parties' choice or find its own. If the parties agree on an expert, the court is bound to take him or her.

Challenges to the expert's appointment

030 The court then makes a formal ruling appointing the expert and determining the object, scope and time frame of the expert's assignment. Exceptionally, the parties can object to the court's selection, e.g. if there is reason to believe that the expert will not be impartial, because of a relationship with the parties or an interest in the outcome of the dispute.

031 So in Germany:

- there is a dual system of experts;
- courts try to get the parties to agree who should be appointed;
- if the parties agree on the expert, the court must appoint that person;
- the courts are statutorily bound to prefer accredited experts; and
- the court determines the scope object and time frame, as in France.

032 Let us now turn to how the expert does his job in these countries.

HOW EXPERTS GIVE EVIDENCE

France

033 I will deal here with expert opinions as opposed to *constatations* and consultations. The principle of *contradiction* is applicable. This means that the parties and their *avocats* are entitled to be informed of the investigations and to be present when they are carried out (where appropriate); they may also comment on the investigations that are being effected and on the final report of the expert. The principle also enables any party to challenge the statements and arguments put forward by the other parties; and requires that any papers or correspondence remitted by one party to the expert must be disclosed to the other parties.

034 Generally speaking, the expert will summon the parties and their lawyers to a series of technical meetings, and will invite submissions of technical, but not usually legal, arguments. The expert may ask the parties or third parties for documents and go back to the judge in case of difficulty: NCPC, Art 243. The expert is not entitled to get discovery from the parties. But if a party refuses to give documents then the expert may seek an injunction from the court requiring the disclosure of documents.

035 The parties may make oral and written submissions to the expert. Mostly they do so on a written basis—French litigation is mostly written.

036 The expert must take account of the observations of the parties or their counsel and if they are in writing (when they are known as "dues" or "statements") must attach them to the final opinion, if asked to do so. In any event, the expert, must state the result of any such submission from the parties.

037 Judges may be present during the expert's investigations, but in practice they rarely exercise this privilege. The expert has to keep the judge informed of the progress of his/her investigations: NCPC, Art 273. The expert has to work confidentially. The expert's opinion may not be divulged outside the court except with the permission of the judge or the party concerned.

038 Experts normally provide a written report. An expert can also give oral expert evidence to the trial court (NCPC, Art 282). If necessary, the expert must appear before the judge to clarify questions raised by his findings, in which case the parties must be summoned.

039 So, in France, the expert gets instructions from the judge, and just gets on with it. The judge probably will not attend during the expert's work, including meetings between the experts and the parties. The parties have the right to know what is going on and to make submissions to the expert as things proceed. The expert must append parties' written statements to the final report. If the expert wants documents or information or facts, those must be asked for from the person with that document etc., and the court can reinforce such requests as needed. If the expert wants to get another expert aboard in an area outside his own, then that is permissible.

Germany

040 The expert may establish personal contacts with a party, a witness or any other person involved in the case, e.g. if a medical doctor is appointed in a malpractice case, he or she may see the patient. There is no rule which requires the expert only to see one party in the presence of the other party, and typically a medical doctor would not see anyone other than the injured party, with neither party's counsel nor the judge around; this is in contrast with the French system which basically provides for mutuality of access.

041 In Germany, the court provides the expert with the necessary documents and other information for the expert to analyse for relevancy and use in preparation of a written report. The court can supplement the instructions later if need be.

042 Although no specific rule exists saying so, it is accepted that parties and their counsel should not contact or try to interfere with or influence the expert during the preparation of the report.

043 The opportunity to question the expert arises *after* he or she has reported. The expert's report will normally be a written one. The parties and their counsel can then question the expert's findings. They may attack an unfavourable opinion by submitting a brief; by demanding that the expert appear at a hearing where he or she may be questioned; by applying for the appointment of a second expert; by submitting their own report; or by offering the oral testimony of a party-appointed expert.

044 But this questioning of an expert by the parties is not comparable to English cross examination. One can't grill the expert for a couple of hours, followed by a grilling by the other side. Instead, the questioning is an informal, question-and-answer session with the opportunity for both the parties and the judges to join in.

045 The expert's evidence is, typically, not transcribed by a court reporter but, rather, summarised by the judge in the presence of the parties, except where one of the parties insists that the evidence is recorded *verbatim.*

046 So, under the German system, the expert does not have a roving investigative brief, but provides a written report to the court, and is then open to question-and-answer sessions under the guidance of the court, when the parties can attack his or her findings with the assistance of their own appointed expert witnesses.

047 In neither Germany nor France is the judge bound by the expert's reports or conclusions; this may not come as a total surprise.

CAN THE EXPERT BE SUED?

048 Broadly speaking in France and Germany, the expert's duty is to report to the court. In France there is no duty as I understand it to hand over to the court all his or her papers and findings, and these remain privileged in the course of his or her mission. In Germany, the court may ask the expert to turn over any notes, documents or other material related to the preparation of the expert report. In neither France nor Germany is there provision to make the expert turn over or discover his or her papers to the parties.

049 In Germany the expert's duty is to prepare a report in an impartial way and using his or her best efforts and knowledge. Otherwise there are no minimum standards set forth in the law applying to the expert's work: the selection process is intended to deal with this. The expert is not subject to a contractual liability to the parties, but it is thought that one could be liable in tort in an exceptional case if he or she intentionally distorts facts or findings; but I know no case in which this came up. If evidence is given under oath and the expert violates the oath, this would be perjury, a criminal offence.

050 In France, experts must accomplish their tasks conscientiously, objectively and impartially (NCPC, Art 237) and answer only those questions which have been asked, without ever giving a legal assessment. There is a deadline. It is not possible for the expert to be a conciliator between the parties. Nor may they receive any remuneration directly from a party in the case, even as reimbursement of expenses unless the judge permits it. I am advised by Triplet et Associés that an expert may be civilly liable to a party in France if three conditions are satisfied: negligence or "faute", proof of loss or damage, and the causal nexus between the expert's fault and the court's decision. These hurdles are not easily overcome. An expert may be liable for criminal penalties, notably if he breaks his obligations of confidentiality surrounding his investigation, or if he falsifies the data or results of his enquiry.

HOW EXPERTS ARE PAID IN FRANCE AND GERMANY

051 In Germany the Expert Witness Compensation Act provides for an hourly rate of DM50 ($90)–DM100, which in exceptional cases may be increased by up to 50 per cent. For certain categories of experts such as doctors there is a specific fee schedule. But if the expert is late in submitting the report, remuneration may be forfeited and a fine applied.

052 In France, the fees are set by the court. The costs of the expertise are usually paid for by the party who requested it, or jointly by the parties in such proportions as the judge determines (NCPC, Art 269). These costs will be borne ultimately by the party paying the costs of the action, usually the loser.

US

053 Things are very different in the US. In the US disputes on facts are often determined by juries, not judges; trials are often much shorter than in the UK; and in the US there is wider pre-trial discovery by depositions and interrogatories, whereby the evidence and potential sources of evidence can be "discovered" by the lawyers preparing for trial. Expert evidence in the US is given by party-appointed experts.

054 There is a huge amount of written learning on the subject of expert evidence, both as to the law and the strategy of how to deal with expert evidence.

055 Litigation can become a war of attrition given the time and invasiveness of discovery, which often lasts years. The manner of cross examination can be very aggressive to English sensibilities. The amount of damages awarded far exceeds anything awarded elsewhere and can be ruinous to the defeated party. One of the most famous American judges of this century, Judge Learned Hand, said in 1926: "As a litigant I should dread a lawsuit beyond almost anything short of sickness and death".

Who may be an expert in an American case?

056 The American common law did not like experts. The courts were wary of charlatans claiming knowledge no one could have. So, unless the field were generally recognised in judicial circles, experts were not allowed to testify. Secondly, experts are explainers. The question therefore arose: did a jury really need something explained to them? If the matter was within the ken of an average layman expert evidence was not going to be allowed. Thus once, experts were not allowed to testify on whether a vehicle would leave its tracks on the earth; or how fast people walked. Thirdly, experts were tested on whether they were in fact properly qualified, or whether their opinion really helps the judge or jury decide what the facts were.

057 A codification of the law on expert evidence then took place at Federal level in the Federal Rules of Evidence. Each state has its own rules on expert evidence which need to be understood, but many of these tend to be similar to the Federal Rules.

058 Under Rule 702 of the Federal Rules of Evidence, expert opinions are admissible where the expert's "scientific technical or other specialised knowledge will assist the trier of fact to understand the evidence or to determine a fact in issue". Thus there are two threshold questions:

(1) does the witness possess sufficient "scientific technical or other specialised knowledge?"; and
(2) will that evidence assist the trier of fact?

059 By *Frye* v. *United States* (293 F 1013), a 1923 case, scientific testimony was admissible only if the tests or procedures had gained "general acceptance"; this test has been used to keep out evidence of novel or innovative processes until they have been adopted by the scientific community. There has been some relaxation of this, but there is still a reaction against junk science which has produced a plethora of experts in every area imaginable.

Discovery and depositions of experts

060 How do experts get brought into a case? Under the Federal Rules of Civil Procedure experts get introduced at the discovery stage.

061 Discovery encompasses (*inter alia*, see Rule 26(5) Federal Rules):

- disclosure of the name and, if known, the address and phone number of each individual likely to have discoverable information relevant to the disputed facts, identifying the subject of the information;

- a computation of any category of damages claimed by the disclosing party, not privileged or protected from disclosure, making available for inspection and copying the documents on which such commutation is based, including materials bearing on the nature and extent of the injuries suffered;
- the identity of any person used at trial to present evidence under rules 702, 703, or 705 of the rules of evidence (these are provisions relating to expert witnesses); and
- "except as otherwise stipulated or directed by the court, this disclosure shall with respect to a witness who is retained or specially employed to provide expert testimony in the case or whose duties as an employee of the party regularly involved in giving expert testimony, be accompanied by a written report prepared and signed by the witness. The report shall contain a complete statement of all opinions to be expressed and the basis and reasons therefor; the date or other information considered by the witness in forming the opinions; any exhibits to be used as a summary of, or support for, the opinions; the qualifications of the witness, including a list of all publications authored by the witness within the preceding 10 years; the compensation to be paid for the study and testimony; and a listing of any other cases in which the witness has testified as an expert at trial or by deposition within the preceding four years" (Rule 26(B)).

062 Extensive discovery is therefore given about the expert and his background, as well as his opinion well before trial. The express purpose of this is to enable "opposing parties [to] have a reasonable opportunity to prepare effective cross examination and perhaps arrange for expert testimony from other witnesses".

063 An expert may be deposed by an opponent before trial, after he or she has delivered their report (Rule 26(b)(4)(A)). There are limits on what may be asked as to privileged documents or information in the expert's possession; and there are provisions which allow for the partial penetration of this privilege: see Rule 26(b)(3), set out below.

064 The court has a power to limit what it perceives to be too much discovery if it perceives that it is

> . . . unreasonably cumulative or duplicative, or is obtainable from some other source that is more convenient, less burdensome or less expensive;
> (ii) the party seeking discovery has had ample opportunity by discovery to obtain the information sought; or
> (iii) the burden or expense of the proposed discovery outweighs its likely benefit . . .". (Rule 26(b)(2)).

But still the ambit of discovery is very wide in contrast with English practice.

065 Nor is it uncommon for American lawyers to seek the opinions of several experts at an early stage to find the one whose theories best suit the case which his client wishes to advance. Some of these lawyers distinguish between expert "witnesses" who will eventually go to trial and expert "advisers" who are consulted but who are not destined to be called, e.g. the views expressed were incompatible to this client's case, or to prevent the other side from retaining that expert.

066 But Rule 26(b)(4) also provides for depositions of expert "advisers" in limited circumstances, e.g. as provided in Rule 35(b) or upon a showing of exceptional circumstances under which it is impracticable for the party seeking discovery to obtain facts or opinion on the same subject by other means. The party seeking to get a deposition of the other side's expert may have to pay for it. Rule 26(4)(C):

"Unless manifest injustice would result,

(i) the court shall require that a party seeking discovery pay the expert a reasonable fee for time spent in responding to discovery under this subdivision; and

(ii) with respect to discovery obtained under subdivision (b)(4)(B) of this rule the court shall require the party seeking discovery to pay the other party a fair portion of the fees and expenses reasonably incurred by the latter party in obtaining facts and opinions from the expert."

067 There are extensive tomes written on the strategy of whether it is a good idea to depose the other side's expert. Sometimes it would be a strategic mistake to do so.

068 What are the stages of questioning experts go through? First, they have to be proved by their client's lawyer as *qualified* to testify as an expert; I have already referred to Rule 702 of the Federal Rules of Evidence. Under Rule 702, expert opinions are admissible where the expert's "scientific technical or other specialized knowledge will assist the trier of fact to understand the evidence or to determine a fact in issue", and that expert is "qualified as an expert by knowledge, skill, experience, training or education".

069 Thus "qualifying" the witness is the first step. Some states also require a formal "tendering" of the expert as an expert. So the evidence that will be sought by the expert's own side will go to *curriculum vitae*, but in practice either the expert's own counsel or the other side will get into every nook and cranny of their past. The books suggest, for instance, going into the expert's family background, length of residence, hobbies, clubs, social organisations, charitable organisations; prior jobs and responsibilities there; education and training; membership of professional organisations; professional achievements; not to mention articles written, and previous occasions on which the person has been an expert witness; and fees for testifying. One of my American partners claims to have used his opponent expert's doctoral thesis to good effect in cross-examining him! If you don't qualify, you don't testify.

070 The books, naturally, give all sorts of hints about how to deal with particular difficulties. For instance, if you were merely to speak to your CV, it might sound as if you were boasting. Note, we are dealing not with truth, but with whether a jury believes your truth is better than your opposing expert's truth. So, for instance, the lawyer will seek to hand up your CV, and only ask you highlighted questions. Or he will seek to avoid boring the jury by going through the boring bits.

071 Then, after qualifying, may come a pretty common opening question:

Q: "Dr X. Do you have an opinion based upon a reasonable degree of medical certainty?"
A: "Yes."
Q: "Dr X—what is that opinion?"

072 A summary outline of direct examination ordinarily includes:

- the subject matter of the opinion;
- the theories or principles behind it;
- the sources of information relied on by the expert;
- any standard tests or routine procedures used in this area;
- specific tests or procedures used in this case;
- other bases for the opinion;
- the opinion or conclusion; and

- an explanation of the opinion.

073 The expert's sources of information can be problematical. Some may be first hand, some second or third hand or more remote.

074 One common procedure is to ask the expert for his opinion as a hypothetical question: "If the facts were shown to be such and such, what would our opinion be?" This question could become very complex and contain myriad permutations so as to cope with all the other hypotheses that the opposing expert could put forward.

075 Whatever method, the source of information must be *reasonably* relied on. This, and the rules on hearsay evidence, are a fruitful, if bemusing and technical, source of the opposing counsel objecting at regular intervals to a particular piece of evidence on the grounds that it is inadmissible as, e.g., hearsay.

076 For instance, Dr X may have relied on a blood test performed by a different doctor, say Dr Y. If Dr X is asked what Dr Y said in his blood test report, the opposing counsel may object on the grounds of hearsay. The question is whether the information Dr X relied on was a reasonable thing for other experts in the field also to rely on and reach the same conclusions. Dr X might, therefore, reasonably rely on information from Dr Y, but not on what Dr Y said in his report. So you would get the question: "Is the information in Dr Y's report information of a type which experts in your field normally rely on to reach a conclusion?" If the answer is yes, then the next question is: "Based upon that information, and your experience, training and education, do you have an opinion about the nature of the P's injuries? If yes, what is that opinion?"

077 It was once considered improper for the expert to offer an opinion on the "ultimate issue" in the case, which, as a matter of procedure, is reserved for the decision of the judge or jury. But this led to elliptical testimony, with the expert testifying to a series of inferences and opinions but not drawing the most obvious factual conclusions. So this has been relaxed to some extent. An expert in a medical malpractice case would not be stopped therefore from saying that certain tests were indicated and that the defendant did not undertake them. And some judges will allow an expert to say that failure to carry out the tests fell below the standard of care generally exercised by practitioners in the relevant community; but some would balk at this. Most judges would balk at the idea of the expert testifying that the defendant's conduct was malpractice, on the theory that malpractice is a legal conclusion which is not within the specialised knowledge of a doctor.

A problem of privilege in the US

078 An expert witness in England may prepare a draft, privileged proof of evidence. In some circumstances, a US court could require discovery of it, under the US doctrine of Work Product Penetration Rule 26(b)(3).

> "Subject to the provisions of subdivision (b)(4) of this rule, a party may obtain discovery of documents and tangible things otherwise discoverable under subdivision (b)(1) of this rule and prepared in anticipation of litigation or for trial by or for another party or by or for that other party's representative (including the other party's attorney, consultant, surety, indemnitor, insurer or agent) only upon showing that the party seeking discovery has substantial need of the materials in the preparation of the party's case and that the party is unable without undue hardship to obtain the

substantial equivalent of the materials by other means. In ordering discovery of such materials when the required showing has been made, the court shall protect against disclosure of the mental impressions, conclusions, opinions or legal theories of an attorney or other representative of a party concerning the litigation."

079 Many US lawyers consider that proofs evidence are discoverable, because of the rule that a party may obtain without the required showing a statement concerning the action or its subject matter previously made by that party. If the request is refused, the person may move for a court order. For purposes of this paragraph, a statement previously made is

(a) a written statement signed or otherwise adopted or approved by the person making it or
(b) a stenographic, mechanical, electrical or other recording, or a transcription thereof, which is a substantially *verbatim* recital of an oral statement by the person making it and contemporaneously recorded.

080 One must thus always bear in mind that the rules of privilege are subtly different between England and the US and that indeed there are different rules in each state; there are different rules on the waiver of privilege, too.

MULTI-JURISDICTIONAL LITIGATION

081 This final section addresses the practical question of whether a party may use the service of the same expert witness in multi-jurisdiction litigation; in our example in the US, England, France and Germany. The types of case where this could arise include:

- international personal injury cases: tobacco; breast implants; drugs cases;
- international asset tracing cases, perhaps;
- cases where there are chains of claims, e.g. buying/selling/resale cases; and
- cases where strategically one party is fighting to get the jurisdiction taken away from another jurisdiction.

082 Several issues arise:

(1) If the case is really based in England or the US, the clash of cultures is going to make it difficult, or impossible, for a party-appointed expert also to act as expert in France or Germany. In Germany he might also give evidence but the chances are that there will be a court-appointed expert in any event. The converse is not necessarily true. If the case starts in Germany or France, that expert could perhaps also be appointed as a court-appointed expert in England and the US; but the chances are that you will want a separate expert in the US and England (subject to whatever the trends are when the Woolf Report comes into operation).
(2) When selecting experts, you choose them irrespective of nationality, because they will help win your case. This could be controversial but it is true.

083 It by no means follows that the most eminent expert in England or the US will be the man for the court in, say, France. Anecdotally it is sometimes said that in the south of France, if you introduce a Parisian expert, you may be starting one step behind. What this means is, you may need several experts—one (court-appointed) expert for the civil law countries and party-appointed experts for the common law countries. This means there is the opportunity for different results in the different territories, but this is unavoidable.

084 There is some difficulty in theory in having party-appointed experts dealing with court-appointed experts. If one has a case of US litigation in which the evidence of a court-appointed European expert was relevant, it would be an interesting question whether you could use the US deposition process to get at his workings and then leverage up on that to mount an attack in Europe on the findings of the expert. I have seen neither situation myself and should be grateful to hear from those who have.

***Robert Goldspink** is a litigation partner at Morgan, Lewis & Bockius LLP's London office.* *He would like to thank partners in the US and Germany, and Triplet et Associés in France for their help on this article.* *Mr Goldspink can be contacted on e-mail at Gold5517@mlb.com and by telephone on 020 7710 5500.* *This article was published in June 1998 and the law is stated as at that date.*

CHAPTER 1/16

THE USE OF EXPERTS IN LITIGATION AND ARBITRATION IN GERMANY

Dr Volker Triebel and Dr Heiko Plassmeier

001 Not only the substantive laws, but also the Anglo-American rules of procedure differ fundamentally from the German ones. To understand the rules and usages concerning the use of experts in litigation and arbitration in Germany, it is necessary to set out some differences between the German and Anglo-American systems of conducting such proceedings. This introduction will be followed by an outline of the statutory regulations applicable to the use of experts in litigation; the equivalent rules of German arbitration law—which has only recently been the subject of a major reform when the UNCITRAL model law was implemented into sections 1025 *et seq.* of the German Code of Civil Procedure (*ZPO*)—will only be dealt with in so far as they differ from the regulations applicable to court proceedings.

THE USE OF EXPERTS IN LITIGATION

Introduction and outline of differences between the German and Anglo-American system

Adversarial trial

002 The basic difference between the German rules and usages regarding expert evidence and the corresponding Anglo-American regulations can be explained by the different understanding of an "adversarial trial" for instance in England and Germany. In both countries, court proceedings are in principle "adversarial", but to a different extent: in German courts, the parties are only supposed to present the facts upon which they wish to rely in support of their respective case (*da mihi factum, dabo titi ius*, the old Roman maxim is incorporated in section 293 ZPO). This implies that the parties do not normally provide their cases' legal framework as the court is supposed to know the law (*iura novit curia*, this maxim applies only to a limited extent where foreign law is concerned: see below).

Written pleadings v. *advocacy*

003 While the English technique of pleading is highly developed and its main objective is to define the issues and warn the other side of the main aspects of the case, no such art of drafting pleadings exists in Germany. Because of the different role of the judge, the objective of written pleadings in Germany is to convince the judge. A German lawyer drafting pleadings will throw all rules of English pleadings overboard; he will set out the facts, not merely in summary form but often in great detail. He may dwell on immaterial points, as he is afraid that these may be material to the judge. A German lawyer will also plead law—although he is not obliged to do so—and it is not unusual for the pleadings to contain elaborate theses as to a particular point of law. Further, pleadings contain not merely facts, but also the evidence by which these facts are to be proven. It is good practice to divide the facts into paragraphs and indicate after each paragraph the means of evidence, i.e. the names and addresses of witnesses, the documentary evidence (which is usually attached to the pleadings) and also indicate whether experts should be heard. German lawyers are thus accustomed to indicating the evidence before it is decided whether the facts are in dispute. German lawyers thus leap before they come to the style.

004 Such elaborate written pleadings severely reduce the need for oral argument. German judges read written pleadings. Often they are impatient and do not allow oral repetition of what has already been submitted in writing. However, by law they are required to pay lip service to oral hearings. Yet, in oral hearings there is hardly any room for oral argument. Court hearings in Germany are—at least in civil cases—not understandable to a third party attending, as the lawyers will normally present their case merely by reference to their written submissions made beforehand. Rumour has it that a lawyer from Munich once bet DM 100 that he could win a case in court—the hearing even involved the taking of evidence from the parties—without saying a single word only by nodding or shaking his head in the right places and placing documents in front of the judge when so required (cf. Gritschneder, *Anwaltsgeschichten*, pp. 118 *et seq.*). He won.

Role of the German judge

005 Even if this little story is part of the myths and fairy tales surrounding German court proceedings (and it is well conceivable to a German lawyer that it is genuine), it speaks volumes for both the importance of written submissions and the role of the judge during a hearing and, indeed, in the entire process of law-finding in Germany. At least in theory, the English trial system is based on the idea of an "ignorant judge" who only learns the facts of the case (and the applicable rules of law) in the course of counsels' elaborations in court with which the judge does not normally interfere except to adjudicate on the relevance of evidence. German judges take a very dominant part in the proceedings: they also do work done in England by the Masters, Registrars and sometimes by the clerks. German judges prepare the oral hearings. They are supposed to know the law; they will set down time limits for filing defences and replies and punish those who do not comply. They will set down the case for an oral hearing. Most importantly, they themselves will decide whether, and if so, what evidence is taken and in which order. They will have studied the pleadings carefully and often will have made up their minds before the oral hearing.

006 Perhaps the most striking difference in practice is that in proceedings in England, the parties adduce their evidence and present their witnesses, expert witnesses, etc. at trial, while in German proceedings, the parties merely offer evidence and it is for the court to decide whether such evidence is taken. In many cases the judge will not hear witnesses at all, even if the lawyers insist, if he thinks their testimony irrelevant. Judges question the witnesses first and only then give the lawyers a chance to put their questions. The lawyers should easily recognise what is material in the eyes of the judge and not be tempted to ask unnecessary questions. The hearing of witnesses is thus much shorter than in England, often lasting only a couple of hours, seldom more than a day. Hence, proceedings are much shorter.

007 The position of a German judge is best characterised by section 139 ZPO. That section imposes a duty upon the judge to see that the parties plead all their allegations of relevant facts completely and further make all suitable applications in the circumstances. He is under a duty to discuss the facts and the relevant law with the parties; also to refer to legal points which the judge will consider. A person should not be taken by surprise when later reading the judgment.

Influence on expert evidence

008 The German way of conducting court proceedings in turn influences the use of experts:

- In the ordinary way, only one expert will be appointed by the court—not the parties—to determine decisive questions of fact. He is supposed to be an independent supporter of the court in coming to the right decision. This, again, shows the different understanding of an "adversarial" trial: even though he has the power to do so on the application of any party under RSC Order 40 (the procedure prescribed in this Order is very similar to the German rules), an English judge would never in practice appoint an expert himself, as the Anglo-American belief is that it is preferable to have two party-appointed experts for the judge to make up his mind about whose expert's evidence he finds more convincing.
- Where the parties appoint an expert, he will not normally be taken as impartial in German proceedings. It follows that where both parties' experts come to opposite conclusions, the court will appoint its own expert (*Obergutachter*) and base its judgment on this expert's evidence. The costs of appointing a party expert will not normally be reimbursed to the appointing party even though it wins the case entirely.
- Contrary to the English system where the expert is a true "expert witness" in that he will normally have to give his report in open court subject to examination, cross-examination and re-examination by counsel, the German expert normally only presents his report in writing to the court and the court will pass on copies of the report to the parties for their comments. Only in exceptional cases where either the factual basis of an expert's report is uncertain or the conclusions he draws are not comprehensible will the expert have to stand witness in court to answer the court's and counsel's questions.
- The German expert is not an "expert witness" within the meaning attributed to the term in English procedural law. There is a difference both in practice and in terminology: as we have seen, the German expert hardly ever gives oral evidence in court. Furthermore, the equivalent German term to "expert witness" (*sachverständige Zeuge*) is used not to denote an expert within the meaning of "expert witness" but a witness who as a matter of mere coincidence happens to have expert knowledge on the issues on which he is asked to testify. The *sachverständige Zeuge* is therefore merely a witness with expert knowledge. He is heard as a witness in open court and merely testifies on issues of fact without evaluating them with his expert knowledge. The judge will not normally attach to his testimony the special weight of an expert opinion.

009 Besides these differences, there are also important similarities between the German expert and the English expert witness: in both countries he will be heard on issues of fact (as to questions of law, see below) the assessment of which is beyond both the understanding of the parties and the court. Expert evidence will therefore normally be required where specialist knowledge is necessary, for instance in cases of medical malpractice or construction cases where the facts cannot be determined without a surgeon's or architect's opinion. However, a German court is free not to appoint an expert in such cases and even to deny a party's application for appointment of an expert where the court thinks itself fit to determine issues which normally require expert knowledge itself. Specialised courts will sometimes act in this way even though it will expose their judgment to an increased risk of being overturned on appeal.

German law on expert evidence in detail

The role of the expert

010 Under German law, the expert is treated as an assistant of the court (BVerwG NJW 1986, 2268) whose duty it is to:

- convey to the court his experience and expert knowledge in areas of science, technology or particular professions;
- apply non-legal rules of science or a particular trade to the instant case (BGH MDR 1974, 382);
- determine questions of fact which the judge as a layman cannot ascertain himself (BGHZ 37, 389).

011 Except for the special procedural rules in sections 402 *et seq.* ZPO summarised below, the expert is treated in the same way as a witness in court proceedings.

Appointment of an expert

012 An expert may be appointed either upon application of one of the parties or by the court *ex officio*. A party's application for appointment of an expert is not binding upon the court, i.e. the court may in its own discretion deny such application if it holds that it has sufficient knowledge of its own to determine the issue in question. However, the refusal of the court to appoint an expert is subject to review upon appeal and its judgment may be overturned if the superior court holds that—contrary to the lower court's assessment—this court did not have sufficient knowledge and that an expert should have been appointed.

013 The choice of a particular expert to be appointed to determine issues of fact designated either by the applicant party or the court is in practice carried out according to lists kept by professional bodies such as a chamber of industry and commerce or a chamber of crafts (section 404, para. 2 ZPO). These lists include sworn experts who besides their particular knowledge in their field of expertise also have forensic experience and are in principle obliged to give their opinion if so requested (section 407, para. 1 ZPO). In areas where no such lists exist, the court has to appoint an expert with sufficient knowledge and will often nominate a person known from the court's past experience to be a reliable expert. Where after submission of a written expert opinion doubts arise as to the expert's competence, the court may in some cases be obliged to ask another expert to give a second opinion. This decision is within the court's discretion yet subject to review on appeal.

Subject matter of expert opinions

014 The expert gives his opinion on the issues identified in one party's application for appointment of an expert and/or the court order of appointment. The extent of the court order defines the limits to the scope of the expert's opinion. The court is under a duty to supervise the expert's activities and can if necessary give additional orders as to the extent of his opinion (section 404a ZPO). Should the expert in the course of drafting his opinion find it necessary to include additional issues or conduct his own investigations, he has to apply to the court to have the scope of his opinion extended. The expert will not normally be given the power to examine witnesses, yet he can be granted a right of examination in hearings before the court. Where the expert intends to examine the subject matter of the proceedings on which he is supposed to testify he must give the parties a reasonable opportunity to attend such examination.

015 Besides issues of fact, the court can also request expert evidence on questions of foreign law applicable to the instant case. In this respect, the position is similar in German and English courts even though the theory is slightly different: whereas under English procedural law, questions of foreign law are openly treated as questions of fact, they take an intermediate position between fact and law under the German rules. Under section 293 ZPO:

- *Iura novit curia* does not apply, i.e. the court is not supposed to know foreign law;
- the court is obliged to examine what the applicable foreign law is on a point at issue, and its judgment will be overturned on appeal if it fails to do so (BGHZ 36, 348 (353); BGH NJW 1988, 647; 1995, 1032; NJW-RR 1995, 766);
- the court is free with respect to the method of ascertaining the contents of foreign law: it may find the relevant provisions itself or with the aid of a foreign court under international treaties such as the 1968 European Convention on Information on Foreign Law: it may also appoint an expert, normally a professor or an expert from one of the Max-Planck-Institutes to ascertain foreign law or leave it to the parties to give evidence on foreign law in whatever way they choose. Where the parties disagree on the contents of the applicable law (and, in fact, sometimes even where they agree, but the court does not find the evidence convincing), the court can still ask for an expert's opinion.

Experts' duties and remuneration

DUTIES

016 Once appointed, the expert has to

- submit his opinion in writing (section 407a ZPO): immediately upon appointment the expert has to verify whether he has sufficient knowledge to answer the questions addressed in the court order of his appointment. Where this is not the case, he has to notify the appointing court immediately. Where the expert has doubts as to the contents and scope of his appointment, he has to seek clarification from the appointing court. An expert may not delegate his duties to another expert and only be assisted in so far as he assumes full responsibility for the final contents of his opinion. An expert may only refuse to submit his written opinion and testify in open court where circumstances are prevailing which would free a witness from his obligation to testify, i.e. where the expert is married or otherwise related to one of the parties, due to the rules of his trade or profession has to keep confidential certain information on the issues on which he is asked to testify or where the testimony would put the expert himself or a member of his family in jeopardy of either financial losses or criminal prosecution. Where no such grounds are present and the expert fails to submit his written opinion or submits it with undue delay, the court may order him to pay a fine and in addition bear the costs caused by his delay (sections 409, 411 ZPO);

- appear in court to explain his written opinion (section 411 para. 3 ZPO) if the court orders him to do so either upon application of one of the parties or on its own initiative;
- submit his opinion anew if the court considers an opinion previously rendered unsatisfactory (section 412 ZPO). However, the court must normally give the expert an opportunity to explain his opinion in open court and clarify uncertainties in his written submission before ordering the expert to submit a new opinion or appointing another expert;
- swear that he has given his written or oral testimony impartially and according to the best of his knowledge (sections 410, 402, 391 ZPO). Contrary to proceedings before courts in Anglo-American countries, a *witness* takes the oath *after* his testimony and is only ordered to do so upon the party's express application which is hardly ever made in practice. Contrary to the position of a witness, an expert may be sworn in before or after his testimony, yet again this hardly ever happens in practice; where the expert is a sworn expert, he may rely on his general oath and not take an oath in every individual case.

REMUNERATION

017 Regarding the expert's remuneration, a distinction needs to be drawn between experts appointed by the court and party-appointed experts: experts appointed by the court do not have a contractual relationship with the parties to the proceedings and the remuneration for their services is fixed by statute (Act on Reimbursement of Witnesses and Experts, *Gesetz über die Entschädigung von Zeugen und Sachverständigen, ZSEG*). Where one party appoints its own expert, the contract between the party and the expert determines both the services to be rendered and the expert's remuneration which can be freely negotiated and is not subject to the limitations of the ZSEG.

018 The distinction between a court-appointed expert and an expert chosen by one party also has its bearing on the costs of the proceedings: while the successful party can recover the costs and expenses paid under court order for a court-appointed expert in the ratio of its relative success at trial, the costs and expenses paid to a party-appointed expert cannot normally be recovered, even if the appointing party succeeds in full.

019 A few remarks on the statutory regime for remuneration of court-appointed experts under the ZSEG are required. The Act's understanding of an expert's remuneration is akin to compensation rather than a just salary for the expert's services. As the hourly rates a court-appointed expert is entitled to charge under the Act are fixed at a very low level, it is disputed whether the ZSEG's rates are in accordance with the German constitution (*Grundgesetz*). However, the Federal Constitutional Court has held in 1972 (NJW 1972, 1891) that the Act is generally in accordance with constitutional principles even though certain doubts still remain. The current statutory rate for an hour of a court-appointed expert's work is fixed in section 3 para. 2 ZSEG at between DM 50 and DM 100. The precise amount to be paid out to the expert is determined by the appointing court's taxation officer taking into account the degree of expertise required for the expert's services, the complexity of the issues involved, expenses incurred for technical equipment and the particular circumstances of the expert's services. For the highest hourly rate of DM 100 to be fixed, it is not required that all these factors justify a higher than average remuneration; fulfilment of one of these factors can suffice. In exceptional cases, the expert's remuneration can be increased by 50 per cent of the basic rate (section 3 para. 3 ZSEG). Besides this compensation, the expert can claim reimbursement of expenses incurred in the course of performing his services.

Experts' liability

020 As with respect to remuneration, the basis for an expert's liability, for instance for mistakes in his opinion, differ according to whether he was appointed by the court or as a party expert by one of the parties to the proceedings: for court-appointed experts who perform their services as part of a public law duty, liability can only arise from statute law, while the primary basis of liability for a party-appointed expert is the contract concluded with the appointing party.

COURT-APPOINTED EXPERTS

021 *Limited scope of liability* In the absence of a contractual relationship between a court-appointed expert and the court as well as the parties to the proceedings in which the expert is asked to testify, the expert's liability can only be based on tort, i.e. sections 823 *et seq.* of the German Civil Code (*BGB*) and certain special provisions on tortious liability in other statutes. However, liability in tort under German law does not normally cover instances of "purely economic loss"; tortious liability under section 823 BGB only arises in cases of damage intentionally or negligently caused to the life, body, health, freedom, property or any "other right", including among others privacy or intellectual property rights, but not in cases of damage to a person's purely financial interests. As damage caused by wrongful expert's opinions will normally be "purely economic", for instance where due to an expert's mistake the plaintiff is awarded lower damages than he is entitled to, the scope of court-appointed expert's liability is therefore rather limited.

022 In the absence of a contractual relationship or at least negotiations for conclusion of a contract between the parties to civil proceedings and a court-appointed expert, there is also no liability under German law for careless false statements as it is for instance known in English law under the rule in *Hedley Byrne* v. *Heller & Partners* ([1964] AC 465).

023 *Experts' privilege* In addition to the limited scope of liability, German courts have under a long-standing line of authority recognised another privilege of a court-appointed expert: where liability is based on an expert's wrongful opinion, he can only be held liable in cases of intentional misconduct or gross negligence, but not for "simple" negligence (*leichte Fahrlässigkeit*). In earlier judgments of the Federal Supreme Court (e.g. BGHZ 62, 54), an expert's liability for negligence was excluded completely. However, the Federal Constitutional Court in BVerfG NJW 1979, 305 subsequently reduced the expert's exemption from tortious liability, holding that an expert remains responsible at least in cases of gross negligence.

024 The rationale behind this privilege—which is disputed in academic writing—is that the expert as an assistant to the court should not be upset and his independence jeopardised by a higher risk of liability than the risk which the judge himself has to bear. As judges are independent and not liable for acts done in the course of performing their office unless such acts amount to a perversion of the course of justice (*Rechtsbeugung*)—which requires intentional breach of duty—the same should in principle apply to their assistants.

PARTY-APPOINTED EXPERTS

025 Contrary to a court-appointed expert, the liability of a "party expert" can besides tort be based on breach of contract or pre-contractual duty. As far as tortious liability is concerned, the situation of the two kinds of experts does not differ, yet on the basis of contractual liability, a party-appointed expert can be held liable for purely economic as well as other losses the appointing party suffers due to mistakes in the expert's opinion or other instances of breach of contract.

026 *Nature of the contract* The contract concluded between the expert and the appointing party will normally be a contract for works and services, not a contract for pure services: as part of his contractual obligations, the party-appointed expert undertakes to produce an end result, most prominently a written opinion, so that his duties are not confined to pure services. Where the promised end product is defective, i.e. where the expert's opinion is wrong because he has failed to consider certain material facts, analysed these facts in a wrongful way or where there are errors in his calculation, such mistakes will give rise to the expert's liability. The same applies where an expert's opinion is correct, but incomplete or inconceivable.

027 *Remedies for breach* In all these cases, the appointing party has several remedies: as the contract is normally characterised as a contract for works and services, the expert is only taken to have performed his contractual duties in full as soon as the appointing party has declared acceptance of the end product (section 640 para. 1 BGB) as conforming with the terms of the contract. Until acceptance is declared, the expert has to rectify mistakes and if necessary render an entirely new opinion (section 633 BGB). The appointing party is also free to set a deadline for rectification of mistakes and either cancel the contract or reduce the expert's remuneration if this deadline expires without rectification (section 634 para. 1 BGB). After acceptance, the expert—subject to the short limitation period of six months (section 638 para. 1 BGB)—remains liable to rectify mistakes, yet he can no longer be obliged to render his opinion anew.

028 While the above remedies apply regardless of any fault on the expert's part, the appointing party will only have a claim in damages where the mistake in the expert's opinion was caused by his intentional breach or negligence (section 635 BGB).

029 *Breach of a pre-contractual duty* The party-appointed expert's liability in damages can also arise from the doctrine of *culpa in contrahendo*, i.e. breach of a pre-contractual duty, regardless of whether a contract subsequently materialises or not. An instance of *culpa in contrahendo* would for instance be present where in the course of negotiations for conclusion of a contract with the appointing party, the expert gives wrongful advice which induces investigations into the facts of the case that do not further the appointing party's cause and therefore lead to financial losses. As in a contractual situation, fault on the expert's part (intentional breach or negligence) is a necessary requirement of the appointing party's claim in damages.

THE USE OF EXPERTS IN ARBITRATION

Reform of German arbitration law

030 With effect as from 1 January 1998 and after six years of preparation, Germany adopted the UNCITRAL Model Law on International Commercial Arbitration of 1985 and thereby brought its statutory arbitration law into line with modern legislation in many other countries. It had long been recognised that reform of the provisions concerning arbitration included in the ZPO originating in 1877 was overdue. The new law (sections 1025 *et seq.* ZPO, BGBl. 1997 I, p. 3224) is an attempt not only to unify arbitration law, but also to increase the attraction of Germany as a venue for international arbitration proceedings, as the former outdated legislation accounted for the fact that according to the ICC statistic for 1995, only 4 per cent of all arbitration proceedings under the ICC rules took place in Germany.

031 The new statutory provisions are almost a wholesale incorporation of the UNCITRAL Model Law. However, in two important respects they deviate from the Model Law: there is no distinction between domestic and international arbitration proceedings, i.e. the same set of rules applies to both kinds of proceedings. Contrary to the UNCITRAL Model Law, the scope of application of the new German law is not limited to "commercial" arbitration proceedings; the new law (like its predecessor) thereby avoids this distinction in determining whether its provisions apply.

032 Most of the new provisions can be contracted out (section 1042 para. 3 ZPO). Among others, the parties may decide on the arbitral tribunal's competence to appoint experts (section 1049 para. 1 ZPO).

The Role of the expert in arbitration

Freedom of the parties to exclude expert evidence

033 In arbitration proceedings, the role of the expert naturally differs from his position in proceedings before a state court due to the fundamental difference between trial before judges appointed by the state and party chosen arbitrators. The increased possibilities for the parties to influence the course of arbitration proceedings are demonstrated for instance by the power conferred upon them by the new section 1049 para. 1 ZPO (which adopts Art. 26, para. 2 of the UNCITRAL Model Law) to restrain the arbitrators from appointing experts at all. Whether expert evidence is taken and, if so, what procedure the arbitral tribunal has to follow is left entirely to the parties' discretion; they are free to agree either before or during the proceedings and may also change their original agreement in the course of the proceedings.

034 The reason for allowing the parties to exclude expert evidence as laid down in the government's official reasoning (BT-Drs. 13/5274, p. 50) is that in Anglo-American systems, it is unusual to have an expert appointed by the court or arbitral tribunal against the parties' intention and that the parties' trust and confidence in the arbitrators does not necessarily extend to an expert so appointed.

Contractual position of the expert in arbitration

APPOINTMENT

035 Whereas a court-appointed expert does not have any contractual relationship with the parties to the proceedings, the expert in arbitration is seen as the parties' contract partner with the appointing arbitrators acting as the parties' agents in concluding the contract between them and the expert. The arbitrators' right to represent the parties is in turn derived from the contract which forms the basis of their appointment and obliges them to investigate the facts of the instant case to the extent appropriate for rendering an award (RGZ 74, 321 at pp. 323 *et seq.*; BGHZ 42, 313 at p. 315).

DUTIES

036 The contract between the expert and the parties will only rarely contain detailed provisions as to the performance of the expert's duties, yet the duties of a court-appointed expert in court proceedings are normally taken to become contract terms unless specific differences can be derived from the different sets of procedural rules. It follows that the expert is free to accept his appointment, yet once he has accepted it, he will be subject to the procedural rules of the ZPO as described above (unless the parties have agreed within the powers conferred upon them by the Act on another set of rules to apply to the arbitration proceedings, in which case the expert's duties will be derived from these rules).

037 Unless otherwise agreed, the parties or their representatives can apply for examination of the expert in a hearing before the arbitral tribunal after he has given his written opinion and retain their own experts to give evidence (section 1049 para. 2 ZPO). The role of party-appointed experts in arbitration does not differ from their counterparts in litigation.

038 The expert's remuneration will only in rare cases—where the parties expressly so agree—be limited to the low rates provided for in the ZSEG. In the ordinary case, it will be contractually agreed along with his appointment.

LIABILITY

039 As regards his liability, the expert in arbitration is in principle in the same position as a party-appointed expert in litigation before state courts: even though he is independent and contractually bound not only to one, but to both parties, his liability—for instance for mistakes in the opinion rendered to the arbitral tribunal—can be based on tort as well as on breach of contractual or pre-contractual duty. The remedies available to the parties and the measure of damages recoverable are also the same as for malperformance of a party-appointed expert in litigation.

040 However, it is firmly established in judgments of the Federal Supreme Court (cf. e.g. BGHZ 42, 313) that the privilege of a court-appointed expert in litigation also applies to liability of an expert in arbitration: regardless of whether his liability is contractual or tortious, the expert in arbitration will only be held liable in damages for mistakes in his opinion if the injured party can show a grossly negligent breach of duty on the expert's part. The rationale behind this extension of the privilege is that arbitration proceedings are a surrogate to court proceedings so that an expert retained in arbitration must not be held liable to a greater extent than a court-appointed expert in litigation (BGHZ 42, 313 at p. 316).

041 The court-appointed expert in litigation and arbitration governed by German procedural rules is under the domain of the court or the arbitral tribunal: it is for the court or tribunal to decide whether expert evidence is taken and how this is done, when experts are to be appointed and who is to be appointed. This practice not only shortens the proceedings, but it also cuts the costs.

Volker Triebel *was born in 1941 in Hildburghausen/Thuringia. He studied German law at the Universities of Würzburg, Bonn, Munich and English law at Jesus College, Oxford and the Law School of the Inns of Court, London. Between 1969 and 1972, he worked as an Academic Assistant at the Institute of Comparative Law, University of Würzburg. He was admitted in Düsseldorf, Germany in 1972 and called to the Bar for England and Wales as a Barrister of the Inner Temple in 1976. His main areas of practice are German and international arbitration, commercial and corporate law and mergers and acquisitions. Volker Triebel is a Fellow of the Chartered Institute of Arbitration; between 1985 and 1990, he was the German delegate to the International Arbitration Court of the International Chamber of Commerce.*

Heiko Plassmeier *was born in Hameln/Lower Saxony in 1966. He studied law at the University of Göttingen and at Jesus College, Cambridge (LLM). Between 1991 and 1995, he worked as an Assistant to the Chair for Private International and Comparative Law, University of Göttingen and was admitted in Düsseldorf, Germany in 1996. His main areas of practice are German and international litigation and arbitration, general civil and commercial law and the law of information technology.*

CHAPTER 1/17

THE EXPERT IN FRANCE

CHAPTER 1/17A

EXPERTS IN FRENCH LITIGATION

Michel Brisac

THE ROLE OF THE EXPERT IN THE FRENCH COURT OF APPEAL BEARS MANY SIMILARITIES TO THE UK SYSTEM

001 Reliable certainly, but too slow and too expensive. We have all heard these accusations levelled at expert witnesses and, in a wider context, at the whole French system of conflict resolution.

002 The system contributes, for its part, modest but often impossible to get round, to the difficulty of settling disputes through the courts, which are snowed under by an increase in the number of cases and bogged down in procedure. Some people think this can be overcome by recourse to alternative procedures, such as arbitration, regulated by the Code of Civil Procedure so that it becomes a "mini-trial" (a phrase which, in the absence for the time being of a regulated formula in France, has still not been translated), mediation or more simply conciliation.

003 But, it seems, if some experts in the French Appeal Court have asked themselves what their place would be in these new, in a sense privatised, procedures, few have reflected on the probably essential role that they could play leading up to the traditional trial, to alleviate some of the faults criticised here, while still helping the litigants. After all, to contribute to the acceleration of the trial, to cut out the dead wood, to identify those paths that lead nowhere and to throw light on the debate, would be doing a service both to the justice system and to the public.

004 We are all familiar with the process of inspection by consent (*expertise amiable*); it has its role to play and some of the procedures have recently been formalised. However, it often causes major problems: there is no final decision imposed on all parties, only a non-binding agreement reached from suggested conclusions, and unfortunately all too infrequently account is taken of the severity of the conflict and the importance of the issues at stake. So how can court-appointed experts contribute, within their competence, to the freeing-up of the courts and tribunals and to the reduction in costs and delays which, paradoxically, they are often accused of increasing?

005 If one admits that sifting through the technical facts of the matter under investigation before handing over to the courts the task of settling the dispute is a step in the right direction, experts' contribution in a variety of fields such as building, industry, business management or finance can be vital. How? Because their training, their experience in litigation and their knowledge of the procedures seen from the point of view of their technical speciality, and the trust which lawyers and litigants put in them, makes them particularly able to shed light on the technical facts, both before the start of the trial and during the trial, if it ever takes place.

006 In addition, they will find in court a new field of activity (at least for some of them, since there are already some who are experienced in this field) for their particular expertise in which they could prove invaluable.

007 Whether the circumstances of the case lead an action to be referred or to be heard straight away, in court or at arbitration, there will be in most cases (one will always find an exception, if only that the proceedings are difficult to justify technically!) an enormous interest in what one has previously:

- analysed, understood, brought together and finally, set out the real problem;
- formulated the technical arguments objectively, in a way that will be easily understood by others;
- set out all the economic considerations;
- made a list of documents and papers to gather or prepare;
- identified, exhaustively if possible, all the players whose expert testimony would be necessary or merely useful to the proceedings, while avoiding involving others;
- in this way, tried to bring together all the necessary conditions for a fair debate to take place later.

008 To see to it that, basically, at this preliminary stage, probably without any research into the liabilities of each party, if there are several, one will know as far as possible, "what happened" or "how it happened" according to the chosen formula.

009 If one proceeds in this way, everyone can manage, without neglecting his own interests, to advance the subsequent trial as quickly as possible and at as little cost as possible, rather than deploying one's talent in such a way as will delay the proceedings. This would also be the way, as we have already said, for a quality justice system, where integrity takes its rightful place. In any respect, within this scope and at this stage of a trial, the role of the expert in the French Court of Appeal will be vital.

010 A recognised technical expert, up to date (a rare characteristic among technicians who do not have this particular skill) with the significance of words and the meaning of the concepts being manipulated by counsel and with the subject, has a role at an early stage, first at the opening of the trial then, probably more discreetly, during the course of the trial. On all these points, by reason of their competence, their experience and their code of ethics, the role experts play can and must prove itself indispensable in controlling costs and delay.

011 From then on, they have the right to consider their role as complementary to that which they exercise as assistants to the judge—and perhaps the only role, at least in the jurisdiction of the principal courts and for the better informed among them, that they can carry out without ethical conflicts as, if only to preserve their credibility, the technical advice which they offer in their role as consultant to their clients will be the same as that they give to the judge who has designated them.

012 By contrast, and this could be beneficial in these respects, the methods by which this activity will be carried out, whether the advising expert acts alone or in a group, within an informal or a structured team, in collaboration, if the case calls for it, with his peers in other member states of the EU, will be much more varied than simply carrying out his role as an expert witness in the true sense of the term.

013 Whatever form it takes, fulfilling this function of bringing clarity to the debate will contribute to the reduction in costs and delays and so to the ultimate aim.

014 Faced with the anxiety of his client who is often worried about:

- the competence of the court appointed expert who will be designated;

- the expert's professional connections and his independence;
- the cost and delay in carrying out his instructions

the lawyer will find in the technical advice that the expert will have offered almost as soon as he has been assigned the case, the replies that will allow him to fine-tune his own opinion of the best way to serve their mutual client.

015 Perhaps, to take a precise if narrow example, the lawyer will find in the technical opinion expressed the reasons for settling, or trying to settle a number of points of law, even before commissioning the expert witness and defining precisely his mission.

016 I would add that, in the face of the traditional cost of expert witnesses, our colleagues will find the legitimate diversification they need in this parallel activity. A law of 1971 and subsequent amendments requires them to provide certain services for the state, the cost of which can only be partially covered by providing technical expertise.

CONCLUSIONS

017 The shortest and most efficient way to reduce *ab initio* costs and delays of a trial, whatever the type of litigation, comes back to clarifying the problem from the start, in all its elements, technical, financial and human. The methods are well known and an attempt has been made here to summarise them.

018 If the technical causes of the application, the financial stake and the parties concerned are well defined, specified and identified, the judge and the expert witness he will have designated will be able to fulfil their vital functions in the shortest possible time and at as little cost as possible, according, of course, to the nature of the problem.

***Michel Brisac** is an expert agrée by the Cour de Cassation and President d'Honneur Fondateur of the Compagnie Nationale des Ingenieurs Diplômes Experts près les Cours judiciaires ou administratives d'appel (CNIDECA). This article, translated by Alison Bucknall, first appeared in the* Gazette du Palais, *6 March 1997, was reproduced in* The Expert *June 1997 and is reproduced here by kind permission of the author.*

CHAPTER 1/17B

THE EXPERT

Bernard Peckels

001 A report from an expert is an investigative measure requested by the judge to clarify certain specific technical aspects in order that the court may arrive at the production of evidence in full knowledge of the facts.

002 The use of an expert is governed by strict rules enacted by the Civil and Penal Codes.

003 In the civil court the proceedings are governed by the *principe du contradictoire*—the principle of due hearing of both parties—which is applicable both to the expert and the judge. Article 16 of the New Code of Civil Procedure (NCPC) requires the observation of this principle and an insistence on its observation by others, which means one may not, when making a decision, rely on any means, explanation or document emanating from the parties to the case unless they have, in effect, been cross-examined about it. Non-compliance with this basic principle by the technical expert can result in the invalidation of his report.

004 It is the judge who decides whether to call for an expert opinion in a civil case and the judge who orders such a report; though a party or his advocate may request the judge to order one.

005 The judge may appoint any person of his choice, a natural person or a legal entity, to carry out the expert assignment. This person is then invested with powers as a result of his assignment, which confers on him the status of expert witness until it is finished.

006 The expert must carry out his assignment personally; when a legal entity has been appointed, it is the duty of its legal representative to appoint the natural person or persons who will carry out the expertise and to inform the judge of their appointment. The expert must accomplish his task conscientiously, objectively and impartially and answer only those questions which have been asked him without making any decision as to the legal merits of the case. It is also essential that he comply with the deadlines which have been given him. The judge may not give him the task of conciliating the parties.

007 The expert appointed may be challenged by the parties. The grounds for a valid challenge are the same as those provided by law for the judge himself; as in the case of the judge, they concern the expert or his spouse. It may be a matter, for example, of a personal interest or a personal relationship, whether familial, as a subordinate, friend or enemy. Apart from being challenged, the technical expert may also be replaced if he refuses to accept the assignment by reason of a legitimate impediment.

008 The expert may collect oral or written information from any person, but he must specify their identity, profession and address, as well as any relationship, whether familial, as a subordinate or due to a common interest. He may also ask the parties and third parties to send him all the documents which he considers necessary; in the event of non-compliance, this may be ordered by the judge.

009 The judge is not bound by the expert's reports and conclusions. If the report adversely affects the private life or the legitimate interests of any person, it may not be divulged outside the court, except with the permission of the judge or the party concerned.

010 The expert may not receive any remuneration directly from a party to the case, even as reimbursement of expenses, unless the judge has ruled to the contrary.

011 Three types of investigative measure may be requested: reports, consultations and expert opinions. In practice, the expert opinion is the most frequently requested. Reports are a simple measure intended solely to provide a report on something, without the expert being able to express any opinion at all on the *de facto* or *de jure* consequences which might result from it; unless the judge rules to the contrary, reports are given in writing.

012 A consultation is provided when the technical question being asked does not require complex investigations. Unless the judge rules to the contrary, it will be given orally at the hearing. As with the reports, the judge sets the amount of remuneration which the technical expert may then receive directly from the person under jurisdiction. This remuneration will be paid following proof of the completion of the task.

013 Lastly, the expert opinion itself, which according to the Code should not be ordered unless the preceding measures would be insufficient to clarify matters for the judge.

014 In nominating an expert, the circumstances which led to the requirement to make such a nomination must be stated, together with the task to be dealt with by that expert and the deadline by which that task is to be completed.

015 One expert is the norm although occasionally more are necessary. The expert must formally accept the appointment. An estimate of the final total of the expert's fee has to be made and that amount registered at the Clerk's Office. The expert may not start work until he has been advised by the Clerk's Office that this retainer has been deposited. If the retainer is not paid, the expert's assignment becomes null and void; unless the judge orders an extension to the deadline or lifts the nullity and the hearing then continues.

016 Expert opinions are prepared following notification to the parties by registered letter; only counsel may be notified by ordinary letter. Failure to comply with these provisions may result in the expert opinion being deemed to be invalid.

017 During preparation of the expert opinion, account must be taken of the parties' submissions or those of their counsel and if these are in writing (they are then known as "statements") he must give his opinion to them if the parties so request and, in any case, state the effect on his opinion of these submissions.

018 If the expert experiences any difficulties over completing the task assigned to him, he should refer them to the judge. If he needs an opinion on a technical issue he may request one, but only from a specialist in a speciality other than his own.

019 A deadline is set by the court for the filing of the expert's opinion and if, for justifiable reason, the expert is unable to meet this date, he must inform the judge. During the preparation of the expert opinion, the expert may, for good reason, request an additional fee or an advance on the sum deposited. Following the filing of his opinion he presents the judge with a request for remuneration, for which the latter will set the total amount, which will be paid to him by the Clerk's Office up to the amount of the sums deposited; any additional amount, where the court awards, will then be paid to him directly by the court.

CRIMINAL CASES

020 In criminal cases, there are aspects of the expert report or opinion which vary from civil cases and therefore are worthy of note. For example the sacrosanct principle of hearing of both parties does not have to be observed. With the exception, of the person directly concerned by the expert's opinion, he does not, therefore, have to notify the parties of that opinion.

021 In the criminal court, as in the civil court, each time a technical question is raised, an expert opinion can be requested by any examining or sentencing court of law, either by the court itself or by a party. However, if the examining magistrate does not intend to pursue the question he must justify his decision by a ruling.

022 Experts must be chosen from a list of the *cour d'appel* (Court of Appeal) or from the national list of the *cour de cassation* (Supreme Court of Appeal). It is only in exceptional circumstances, in contrast to the civil court, that the judge may appoint an expert who is not on a list; again, if he does so he must justify his decison and such expert must swear an oath before undertaking his assignment. As in the civil court, more than one technical expert may be appointed if necessary.

023 Again, as in civil cases, a deadline is imposed for the lodging of the opinion. Once the opinion has been filed all documentation, objects etc. which may have been given to the expert to assist him in his task must be returned within 48 hours of the completion of his assignment.

024 The expert may, if he finds it necessary, ask an opinion of someone from a speciality other than his own, but in contrast to the civil court, it is mandatory for him to first obtain the judge's permission to seek such advice.

025 If any sealed documents have been given to the expert he must, if he has had recourse to such documents, mention the fact in his opinion.

026 If he considers it necessary, the expert may hear persons other than the one under investigation, either at his own volition or at the request of a party. So far as the person under investigation is concerned, the expert may not question him except in the presence of the judge, unless the person renounces his right to this provision or if the expert is a doctor or psychologist.

027 During preparation of the expert's opinion a party to the case may request that particular areas of research be carried out by that expert.

028 Having completed his written opinion, the expert may be required to appear and give evidence in court; in which case he must attend the hearing unless the President of the court decides otherwise.

029 In criminal cases, where the total amount of the expert's expenses and fees exceed 1,000 francs, he must always inform the Public Prosecutor, of this fact before commencing his work. The Public Prosecutor then has three days in which to comment on the level of the fees requested if he considers them to be too high. For some disciplines however—for example, commercial fraud, forensic medicine, toxicology, biology, radiography and mechanical engineering—the fees are laid down by the code for penal proceedings and thus reference to the Public Prosecutor should be unnecessary.

THE EXPERTS

030 One of the special characteristics of the use of expert witnesses in France derives from the fact that these experts are selected from lists drawn up by the *cours d'appel* or the *cour de cassation*. These lists were established by a law of 29 June 1971 and brought into effect by a decree of 31 December 1974.

031 With the exception of members of certain professions (magistrates, barristers, solicitors), all natural persons or legal entities may, subject to certain conditions, apply to be included on these lists. These conditions include *inter alia* such matters as age; professional expertise and time served in the profession, carrying out an activity which is not compatible with the independence required to fulfil expert witness assignments. This latter test might include such things as charges of immorality, a criminal record for dishonourable acts, a lack of probity or offences against accepted standards of good behaviour, or any disciplinary or administrative penalty which has been levied against the expert.

032 Experts may be struck off the list in the event of legal incapacity or of conviction for dishonourable acts, lack of probity or offences against accepted standards of good behaviour, but also for serious faults in the execution of their assignments (for example the refusal of an assignment without a legitimate reason or non-completion of the assignment within the prescribed deadline following a formal notice). Striking off and non-statement in the lists can be appealed against.

033 The age limit for inclusion on the list of experts is 70. After that, and on condition of having been on a list for at least 10 years, the title of honorary expert can be awarded.

034 Following examination of the applicant's record, successful applicants are accepted by the General Assembly of each *cour d'appel* during the first fortnight of November or by the Office of the *cour de cassation* in the first fortnight of December of each year.

035 Inclusion on the court's list is for one year, after which the expert should be re-listed annually without formality provided no grievance against that expert has been made in the preceding year although it must be stressed that re-listing is by no means automatic.

036 The title of "*expert près de la cour d'appel de* . . . (expert at the Court of Appeal of . . .)" or "*agrée" par la cour de cassation* (appointed by the Supreme Court of Appeal)" is a protected title. Its misuse can result in criminal sanctions. Experts are not permitted to advertise.

037 In return for being formally listed, the experts have certain obligations. They must swear an oath to support the law, to accept the assignments given them, to fulfil them within the prescribed deadlines, to produce the necessary reports and to give their opinion honourably and honestly.

038 Working as an expert is deemed by the French state to be a profession. This has social security and tax implications. In terms of social security, even if the expert is already liable for similar contributions in the context of another activity, for example, as an employee, contributions to sickness insurance schemes for non-salaried workers, family income support schemes and pension schemes associated with his main profession are compulsory.

039 Income from work as an expert is taxed as a non-commercial profit; to this is added the payment of other taxes—*Contribution Sociale Generalisée* (generalised social tax), *Remboursement de la Dette Sociale* (contribution to pay off the national social security deficit), *Taxe Professionelle* (business licence) and VAT—doctors and translators-interpreters being spared the last one!

040 One of the major problems associated with experts is that of training, both in professional and procedural terms. This is generally organised by the academies of experts registered with the *cours d'appel* with the participation of magistrates and barristers. This training, which unfortunately is neither compulsory nor continuing, usually takes place following admission to the lists.

041 There are also academies of experts which exist within each *cour d'appel* to provide training for and to defend the legitimate interests of experts. These academies are associations and membership is not compulsory. In practice 50 per cent to 60 per cent of experts registered on the lists belong to one or other of these academies. Alongside these multi-disciplinary academies, associated with each *cour d'appel* and the *cour de cassation*, there exist national academies for individual professions (health, construction, chartered accountancy etc.). All of these operate under the umbrella of the *Fédération Nationale des Compagnies Judiciares* (National Federation of Academies of Experts) which has a membership of over 8,000 experts. This federation is therefore wholly representative and perfectly qualified to speak for its members and to discuss the important problems which concern the expert in a wider sense, or the problems raised by expert opinion in court cases.

THE PLACE OF EXPERT OPINION

042 What place does expert opinion occupy in France in the context of all categories of dispute, both in number and percentages?

043 It is very difficult, if not impossible, to reply to this question at the moment. To be able to do so with certainty it would be necessary, year on year, to know the number of disputes and occasions that expert opinions of all types are sought. Unfortunately, as far as we know, no statistics currently exist which would be able to provide this information.

044 So far as cases which reach court are concerned some statistical information is available. This comes from the study carried out by P Migeot, reported at the 15th Congress of the *Fédération Française des Compagnies* at Lille in October 1996. This report analyses the number of expert opinions sought by sector, as follows:

- for property, in 1992, out of 202,890 claims, 60,000 went to court;
- cases concerning motoring, also in 1992 (accidents to property and the person), out of 200,000 victims of personal injury, 30,000 went to court;
- in the domain of health (medical liability) there were 1,300 claims made in 1991 to insurance companies but the number which received compensation is not recorded;
- for personal injury out of 5,081 cases between 1987 and 1991, 25 per cent of the victims received compensation of which 66 per cent was by amicable settlement and 34 per cent were through court settlement.

045 Five per cent of all court cases 1991, where expert opinions were ordered, were for civil cases. That is that 5 per cent of all cases required expert opinion but fewer than one third of these went to court. 5 per cent of 33⅓ per cent = 1.7 per cent; therefore less than 2 per cent of all cases which go to court require an expert opinion.

CONCLUSION

046 The current problems of overloading in the French courts is likely to lead to some of their work being given to the *Société Civile* (non-trading company). That would mean that the number of expert witnesses currently used in French courts would diminish even further in future years to the benefit of the insurance companies and be replaced by privately commissioned expert reports or by expert opinions requested in the context of conciliations, mediations, arbitrations or by Alternative Dispute Resolution (ADR) which has been introduced into France from the United States.

***Dr Bernard Peckels** is an expert appointed by the French Supreme Court of Appeal and editor of* Experts *magazine, 5 rue Carnot, 78000 Versailles, France. Tel 00 +33–1 30 21 79 22.*

This article first appeared in The Expert, *September 1997 and is reproduced here by kind permission of the author. The text of the original article has been subsequently edited jointly by D Mark Cato and Dr Michael Chapman, who accept full responsibility for it.*

CHAPTER 1/17C

THE EXPERT IN FRANCE—WITNESS OR DECIDER?

Michael Chapman

001 It is the example of France that is usually cited in England as a situation where the expert is appointed by the court from a limited list of "agreed experts". This is something of an oversimplification.

THE TITLE

002 In general the title of "expert" is not protected. Those whose names appear on "the lists" (see below) may use the titles "*expert près de la cour d'appel de . . .*" or "*expert agrée par la cour de cassation*" as is appropriate. These titles may be used on professional stationery and are considered a significant accolade. Professions that in their codes of conduct (*codes de déontologie*) restrict material that may appear on letterheads, etc., do specifically permit the use of these two titles.

003 Experts who have served at least 10 years on a list and have reached the age of 70 may be granted honorary status in which case the suffix "*honoraire*" is added to the relevant title.

004 It is illegal to imply that one is on a court list if one is not. There however seem to have been no cases on this matter and thus the area is a grey one. The title "*expert près les tribunaux*" is used by some non-listed persons who nevertheless serve as expert witnesses. It causes no confusion to advocates but, like "*expert judiciaire*", is perhaps sufficiently confusing to the layman that its usage should not occur.

005 Interestingly there is a *Compagnie des Experts près le Comité National Français de la Chambre de Commerce Internationale* which maintains a list of persons for nomination by the French national committee of the International Chamber of Commerce, in referrals under the ICC's Centre for Expertise procedures. The *Compagnie* normally takes listing by a court as a precondition for listing by themselves (Compagnie des Experts près le CNF, 9 boulevard Malesherbes, 75008 Paris; ICC International Centre for Expertise, 38 cours Albert 1er, 75008 Paris).

THE LISTS

006 Lists are prepared annually. There is one national list (the list of the *cour de cassation*) and one list for each *cour d'appel* (there are some 30 *cours d'appel* in France).

007 No formal qualification is required for one's name to be entered on a list. The applicant must be engaged in (or have been engaged in) the profession, or an activity connected with the speciality, for a sufficient time. He must also have practised that profession or activity in conditions that confer sufficient expertise. Beyond this, the matter is very much for each court to decide. The *cour de cassation* did issue a notice, which in practice is perhaps of little aid to the reader, that having practised for three days is insufficient experience(!).

008 There is an upper age limit to being accepted onto the lists. This is 70 years. There is, in theory, no lower age limit. Between 1944 and 1975 listed experts had to be French nationals. This is no longer the case, but foreign nationals are still a rarity.

009 It is possible to be listed on both the national and a local list. Listing by more than one *cour d'appel* though is not permitted. An expert can be listed either in the area of his home or of his professional address.

010 On first being listed (but not each year) the expert must take an oath (the *serment*) "*d'apporter leur concours à la Justice, d'accomplir leur mission, de faire leur rapport et de donner leur avis en leur honneur et en leur conscience*". Whilst the oath remains most important, the ceremony surrounding its taking is now greatly diminished. Indeed it is now possible to make the declaration to the court in writing.

011 Removal from the list is possible in the case of legal incapacity, grave professional misconduct, or when there is a finding against an expert which is contrary to honour, to probity or to good morals.

NON-LISTED EXPERTS

012 Since the *loi du 29 juin 1971* there have been two "types" of experts in the French courts: listed and non-listed. Very many experts are not listed. Indeed, it is a myth that all French experts are listed. The citing of France by those who wish to see some restriction placed on who may be an expert witness before the English courts is invalid. The French situation shows (if it is explained fully) how a system with official lists can adapt to use the widest possible range of experts, whether listed or not.

013 Article 1 of that law makes the choice of expert in civil cases entirely free.

014 In criminal cases, however the court must always (in principle) nominate an expert from the list. The use of a non-listed expert in a criminal case must always "have a reason" (be "motivated").

015 Experience shows that it is listed experts who are most frequently utilised in both civil and criminal cases. The non-listed expert has not taken an oath before the court. He used to be obliged to make such a declaration. In civil matters this has fallen into total disuse. In criminal matters, though, unless the expert report includes the *serment* (again it may be made in writing, and thus form part of each report) the report is a nullity. (As the non-listed expert has to make the *serment* afresh in each report he makes, it has been suggested that the strongest reason for using listed experts in criminal cases was the following. When selecting experts at the beginning of a case it was easy to recall these potential problems, whilst at a late date when all the documents (which, as is so often the case, have been submitted at the last minute) were being assembled, it was easy to overlook whether a report did or did not contain the *serment*. If it did not the case could quite easily collapse.)

016 One advantage of using non-listed experts is that there is no upper age limit. The limit of 70 years is a bar to listing, not to giving expert evidence. Thus a person of considerable experience can be used.

NUMBER OF EXPERTS

017 Just as in England a case can involve a variety of specialities (e.g. a road traffic accident expert/engineer and a medical expert on personal injuries). As the experts are appointed by the courts the interesting question arises as to whether more than one expert can be appointed within the one speciality.

018 In civil matters the principle is that only one expert should be appointed unless the judge decides a greater number is preferable. Three experts are occasionally appointed if the case is considered particularly complex or important; or, in some rare cases where this is required by law (e.g. the verification of handwriting).

019 The experts (of the same speciality) are to work collectively. This does not require each to be present at every stage of their work. They can delegate minor tasks among themselves (taking measurements, consulting official records, etc.).

020 In criminal matters the judge has to decide if the expert will go "to the heart of the matter", or whether it is merely ancillary. If it is deemed to be fundamental, then at least two experts must be appointed (unless exceptional circumstances justify the designation of only one expert). As in so many matters relating to judicial decisions, the law gives what to a large degree is clear advice but then leaves wide (often total) discretion to the judge if the circumstances are in some way out of the ordinary. (A similar situation was noted previously as to whether listed experts had to be used in criminal cases.) However in this situation if it is the *juge d'instruction* (investigating magistrate) who decides to proceed with only one expert, they must first notify that intention to the *ministère public* and to the parties. A procedural objection on the grounds of failure to notify cannot be made unless it is argued that, due to it, there has been a failure to establish the truth. In urgent cases, the expert can start his work before the notifications are made.

021 The expert may consult another expert, provided the latter's expertise is in a different field from his own (this does not exclude a general medical expert from consulting say a radiographer). He may then adopt this opinion as his own. Such a person is generally termed a *sapiteur.*

HOW THE EXPERT CARRIES OUT HIS FUNCTIONS

022 The expert has his role clearly defined by the tribunal (*la mission*). This gives him the point(s) he must answer in his report. The way he sets about this is defined in rules laid down in the penal and civil codes (articles 156 to 169 of the *Code de procédure pénale*, and articles 232 to 248 and 263 to 284-1 of the *Nouveau code de procédure civile*).

023 He will typically be sent the files and documents the parties wish him to consider. He will then call a meeting (*une convocation*) of the parties. This meeting is the first essential act of his role. Failure to summon a party properly to such a meeting is liable to cause the expertise to be declared a nullity. There is no statutory period of notice that has to be given prior to a meeting. A period of eight days is stated for court ordered meetings of witnesses and this may serve as a guide. Except in urgent cases it would be normal for an expert to give, say, 15 days' notice of a meeting. The expert fixes the date, though if parties are represented he will usually try and agree a date with their advocates. The meeting may be held at the expert's offices, or more commonly on "site".

024 The form of calling the meeting is most important (and typifies much of French official notifications). Failure to comply with "form" becomes problematic if the expert decides to continue with a meeting *ex parte*. Notification should be made by registered letter with advice of receipt. If he then proceeds *ex parte* the expert should append the "advice of receipt" of his registered letter (which gave notice of the meeting) to his report. In practice normal post is often used, as is notice *via* a party's advocate or verbal notice. The last is particularly common and is adequate for arranging meetings subsequent to the first.

025 Under the French system civil expertise has the *caractère contradictoire*. This is fundamental, a close approximation in meaning being that the expert is meant to conduct an adversarial investigation. One may, or may not, argue that the role is inquisitorial, but whatever it is, the expert is to supervise an adversarial enquiry into the facts. To classify the French system of judicial experts as non-adversarial is as false a generalisation as to presume all experts are listed. It is this *caractère contradictoire* that places such a great onus on the expert if he decides to proceed *ex parte* (again similarities with the English arbitrator spring readily to mind).

026 Parties may represent themselves at meetings or they may be represented. As the expert's meeting is not a hearing, there is no monopoly of representation given to advocates; and parties may have lay representatives. The expert will initially take details of those present (their names, positions, etc.). He will notify them of his *mission* and tell them how he intends to proceed. He will ask for documents relating to the matters under dispute (invoices, medical certificates, accounts and so on). He may make a site inspection and/or take measurements. He may fix the date, time and place of a subsequent meeting. He will ask the parties for names of persons they intend to act as *sachants* (see below).

027 Finally he will ask the parties or their representatives to address him with an assertion (a *dire*) on the points in dispute. (In a civil dispute the parties themselves, if real persons, or their senior executives will often not be able to give sworn testimony before the tribunal itself. Their interest in the outcome making their testimony inadmissible. The expert's meeting is a useful way for their statements to be introduced into the judicial process.)

028 The *caractère contradictoire* of his appointment in a civil case means that the expert should perform most of his functions before the two parties. He may perform accessory or secondary operations alone, but he must ensure that these really are in such category. Medical examinations are an obvious exception to such rule though the other party should be given opportunity to have a doctor of their choice in attendance.

029 If, however, e.g. a chemist performs an analysis in his laboratory, he must communicate the results to the parties and give them an opportunity to comment upon them.

030 Either party can communicate with the expert and make suggestions or assertions as to the matters under investigation (these are called *dires*). They may be written or oral. A written *dire* should be appended to his report and have been copied to the other party. Failure to address a point raised in a *dire* will cause the report to become a nullity. Responses, though, need not be direct.

031 The expert may take evidence from any person. The role of the *sapiteur* is addressed above. He need not be heard before the parties. It is sufficient that his advice is communicated to the parties for their comment. The expert may also hear non-experts (e.g. witnesses to an event). These are not (or rather should not be, but mistakenly are on occasions) called witnesses (*témoins*). The correct term is *sachants*. The expert has absolute discretion as to which *sachants* he will hear, even when these are nominated by the parties.

032 *Sachants* are not sworn. This has the advantage that the expert can hear persons who could not give sworn testimony due to having too close an interest in the matter in dispute. (Interestingly for arbitrations the NCPC, article 1461 states "Third parties shall be heard without being sworn".) A hearing of *sachants* should, in principle, be adversarial but parties can and do authorise experts to hear them in their absence.

033 An expert may also sit with a judge. This particular situation is not considered in this short article. An expert may also be summoned to a court hearing (which is on a case he has not previously been concerned with) to be consulted by the judge. In such circumstances the parties may also question the expert.

034 In criminal cases the principle of the *caractère contradictoire* does not apply. In a civil case the philosophy is that the parties are equal and thus they must be treated on an equal footing. In a criminal case the question is whether it can be proved that there has been a breach of the law. It would be easy to parody these differences as some absence of *audi alteram partem*, which it certainly is not. It could be analysed as civil expertise being more adversarial and criminal expertise more inquisitorial: this is certainly arguable. Equally, one could merely view it as a reflection of English standards of proof.

035 In civil cases absolute even-handedness is essential; as the parties are equal. The decision is based on "the balance of probabilities". In criminal cases the assertion has to be proved "beyond reasonable doubt". There is no interest in criminal cases in probable, but still doubtful conclusions (in Scotland with the "not proven" verdict possible as well as "guilty" and "not guilty", obviously different arguments apply).

036 Only if the experts determine it would be of use to their work, will the defendant be examined by them. This will typically be as a hearing (*un interrogatoire*) before the judge with lawyers in attendance. The defendant may be examined alone but if he elects to see the experts, without his lawyers, he must make a written statement to this effect. This must then be appended to the experts' report. Medical examinations are invariably held without judge or lawyers present.

037 This is not to say that the *caractère contradictoire* never has a place in criminal expertise. The experts may proceed to confront a party if they feel this will be more effective. In matters related to fraud and false accounting it is a requirement. The scope for the criminal expert to take the initiative is considerably less than for the civil expert. For example if he wishes to consult another specialist (*un spécialiste adjoint*), in a role akin to his civil colleague consulting a *sapiteur*, he must first obtain the authorisation of the judge and the resulting report must be appended to that of the expert.

THE REPORT

038 The report and the required number of copies is sent by the expert to the court. There is no obligation, but it is considered a courtesy, to notify the parties' lawyers when this takes place. Some judges request their experts to send a "pre-report" to the parties (in civil cases). This may cause a settlement (by inducing the parties to conciliate or compromise their claims). If not, it is likely to enable the parties to ensure that any errors in the report are corrected. Like many such procedural developments this has obvious advantages in theory; in practice, though, it may only serve to delay final judgment, increasing costs in the meantime.

039 The report is generally in writing, though a verbal report is possible if very rarely used. (It is more used in minor criminal cases.) The only essential element to a report is the signature(!). If there is more than one expert they must prepare a common report, in which, if their opinions differ, each indicates his own opinion.

THE EXPERT AS CONCILIATOR

040 It is very much expected that the expert should seek to conciliate the parties. Even if he does not achieve a conciliation during his work, then his final reporting on the facts in dispute will often cause the parties to negotiate their own settlement.

041 The judge cannot give an expert the taste of acting as mediator (NCPC, article 240). One learned author has described this as "quite inexplicable". An alternative view is that whilst the judge cannot give this task to the expert, nothing prevents him from carrying it out. Perhaps this is not an unwise framework. The expert should not be burdened with attempting to conciliate the irreconcilable when his primary duty is to report; nevertheless he should (like a good arbitrator) attempt it within his own discretion.

OBTAINING COPIES OF JUDGMENTS

042 The expert not being appointed by either party does not have the relationship of a common law expert with his instructing lawyer. He will not therefore readily know the outcome of the cases in which he is involved.

043 Judgments may not be obtained by the public. It is, though, permissible for an expert to request copies of those relating to his cases (though it is unclear who pays for production of this extra copy). The expert can only request the copy after the judgment has been made. As he has no way of knowing when that is, he usually has to rely on the advocates to notify him of the date of judgment.

EXPERT: AN EXPERT WITNESS OR A "DECIDER"?

044 From the above it may be seen that the French *expert* is in many ways more akin to one possible role for a court-appointed arbitrator in sixteenth-century England. Mustill and Boyd (*Commercial Arbitration*, 2nd edition, 1989, at page 432) describe how

> "Instead of being subject to intermittent supervision from outside, the arbitration took place within the structure of the legal process itself. Where an action was pending in a court of common law or

equity, the parties could by consent obtain an order referring some or all of the matters in dispute to the decision of *an arbitrator who was in effect substituted for the jury as the tribunal of fact* ... The parties were free to choose a tribunal better suited than a jury for dealing with technical issues or complex matters of account. But the action remained in being. Although the court delegated part of its function to the arbitrator, it retained the remainder" (emphasis added).

045 In practice the *expert* may act as a tribunal of fact for the matters referred to him, but no decision is finally his. The court not only has the only word on any point of law, but also the last word on any matter of fact. The comparison though is an interesting one, and made point by point in the author's paper "Is the French Civil Expert a 'Decider'?" ((1997) 63, JCIArb 2, 138–144).

End Notes

Sources

Loi du 29 juin 1971 (no 71–498) *relative aux experts judiciaires.*
Décret du 31 décembre 1974 (no 74–1184) *relatif aux experts judiciares.*
Nouveau code de procédure civile (NCPC), arts 232 to 284-1.
Code de procédure penale, arts 154–169-1.
Circulaire du 15 janvier 1985 du Garde de Sceaux, Ministre de la Justice relative à l'expertise civile. (Reproduced in J. Voulet & J. Boulez's *Expertises Judiciares* (10th edition), Paris, Delmas, pp. 239–242.)
Caratini, M. 1984 *Gazette du Palais*, nos 120, 121 & 122 of 29, 30 April and 1 May 1984.

Acknowledgments

The author would like to express his thanks to those who kindly helped with the preparation of this article or the papers upon which it is based: *Mme le juge* Beatrice Thony of the *Tribunal de grande instance*, Lyon; *M le professeur* Gérard Keck, *Expert près la cour d'appel de Lyon*; Alan Shilston, editor, *Arbitration*, London; and, Claude Bessard, *ancien Président, Tribunal de commerce*, Paris. Any errors of fact and all statements of interpretation or opinion are the sole responsibility of the author.

The origin of the word "decider" may be obvious, but I make grateful acknowledgement to the role of Uncumber's father in *A Very Private Life* by Michael Frayn (Collins, London, 1968, page 24).

Michael Chapman *(mchapman@mchapman.com; http://www.mchapman.com/mc/) is a practising expert, expert witness and arbitrator. He is based in France, some 60 kilometres from Geneva, but routinely practises across Europe.*

He is a Eur.Biol., specialising in the assessment of chemical safety and the regulation of medicines. As a European Registered Toxicologist he is involved in the preparation of expert reports for applications for marketing authorisations and product licences for pharmaceuticals as well as preparing reports or appearing in the courts to give evidence on medicines, poisoning, drugs of abuse and related topics. As a senior member of an international consultancy group he is involved with the project management of the development and licensing of ranges of pharmaceutical products for leading healthcare companies.

He was appointed Expert près le Comité National Français de la Chambre de Commerce Internationale *in 1995.*

Michael Chapman has interests in electronic commerce as a publisher. He is listed as an arbitrator and mediator by the World Intellectual Property Organisation (WIPO, Geneva) and has attended their training on Internet-related dispute resolution procedures.

This article is based on an article which originally appeared in Arbitration, *the Journal of the Chartered Institute of Arbitrators (November 1995, 61, JCIArb 4, pp. 264–268).*

THE EXPERT WITNESS IN ITALIAN LITIGATION AND ARBITRATION

Aldo Berlinguer and Vincenzo Vigoriti

Translation edited by A D R Colvin, University of Florence

TECHNICAL CONSULTANCY (EXPERT EVIDENCE) IN CIVIL PROCEEDINGS AND ARBITRATION

Nature and functions

001 It is not an accident that in the Italian civil justice system the activity of an expert is called technical consultancy (*Consulenza tecnica*) since such a name is intended to bring into relief two particular aspects of this figure. There is the auxiliary nature of the consultant with respect to the judge, and there is the level of technical competence which distinguishes him.

002 Technical consultancy is governed by the first and second book of the Civil Procedure Code (CPC), i.e. the part relating to the judicial bodies (Arts 61 *et seq.*) and in that relating to the examination of evidence (Arts 191 *et seq.*) in an *ad hoc* section prior to that relating to evidence (see Appendix to this chapter).

003 There is thus a change of direction in the CPC (1941) compared with the Code of 1865, which characterised this activity as an appraisal (*perizia*), and placed it amongst the instruments of proof. Article 264 of the 1865 CPC provided "appraisers shall make a single report, in which they must express a single motivated opinion by majority vote".

004 The report for the 1865 Code thus made a distinction between testimonial proof and opinion in the sense that testimonial proof would assess transient facts, whilst the opinion would assess permanent facts. This was due to the fact that the prevailing opinion was that this activity did not consist, at least directly, in determining the decision of the judge concerning the truth or falsity of determined facts, but rather in offering to him the assistance of technical understanding which the judge himself does not normally possess (Franchi, 1973 at 682 *et seq.*; Vellani, at 525).

005 Under the present CPC, the activity of the expert witness, by its variety and breadth, has a juridical nature different from an instrument of proof, varying between ascertainment of a fact and evaluation of the same. Thus it may merely be a verification of an existing situation or a rational decision on a technical issue. This decision supplements the judge's activity itself and may be adopted by him.

006 The Court of Cassation summarised the position:

> "While the 1865 Civil Procedure Code brought in as evidence the work of the expert, that is the opinion which it considered as one of the instruments of proof, the current Civil Procedure Code considers instead the work of the consultant as an auxiliary supplied to the judge as a team worker,

> so that the expert's proof should not be considered evidence in itself, but constitutes a method for checking the evidence."
>
> (Cassation 24 November 1973, No 3187, *Massimario della Giurisprudenza Italiana*, 1973, 1090.)

007 For this reason, in civil proceedings technical consultancy is amongst those measures which the judge can order of his own motion. Thus the parties, cannot agree to exclude it where the judge considers it necessary (Carnacini at 768 *et seq*.; Vellani, at 526.)

008 Case law is partially directed to the recognition of consultancy as a form of evidence only where "it becomes a technical evaluation or assessment of situations of fact such as to be elucidated solely by reference to set technical understandings" (Court of Cassation, 26 March 1986, no 2171, in *Rep.Foro.It.* 1986, under the heading of "Consulente tecnico, No 7"). In other words:

> "The judge may entrust the expert not only with the task of evaluating the facts ascertained by himself or given as existing (deductive consultancy), but also that of assessing the facts themselves (the consultant as observer). In the first case the consultancy supposes the previous completion of the taking of evidence and has as its purpose the evaluation of facts whose features have been completely proved by the parties. In the second case the consultancy may constitute itself an objective source of evidence, without this signifying that the parties may escape from their burden of proof and remit the assessment of their rights to the activity of the consultant. In this second case it is necessary, in fact, that the party at least presents in evidence the fact which is the basis of its claim, and that the judge considers that his finding requires technical knowledge which he does not possess or that there are other reasons which prevent or make it inadvisable to proceed directly to the decision."
>
> (Cassation 4 November 1996, No 9522, in *Danno e Responsabilita*, 1997, 15, with a note by Carbone. See also Cassation, 13 October 1986, No 5990, in *Rep.Foro.It.* 1986, Consulente technico, No 5; Bernardini at 614.)

009 On the other hand the task of evaluating the legal aspects of the dispute must not be entrusted to the expert nor may he be allowed to venture into the domain of judicial assessment of the facts (cf. Cassation, 7 June 1989, No 2765, in *Foro.pad*. 1990, I, 278, with a note by Rubino Sammartano; Fazzalari at 70).

010 Similar considerations apply also to arbitration whether in its *rituale* or *irrituale* form (formal or informal; for the distinction between *rituale* and *irrituale* arbitration, see Vigoriti, 1992 at 251; *id*. 1990 at 77; Fazzalari at 9 *et seq*.; Alpa at 655 *et seq*.).

011 Formal arbitration is governed by the CPC, with the proceedings conducted as a trial culminating with the issue of an award that is immediately binding on the parties. Such an award can be enforced as a judgment after it has been registered with the court (*exequatur*).

012 Informal arbitration, on the other hand, is essentially a contractual procedure, by which the parties agree in advance to settle all possible controversies in a manner to be decided by the arbitrators. The process need only protect the parties' fundamental rights, and although the award is only contractually binding it cannot be deposited with a court nor can an *exequatur* be issued. In informal arbitration it is not uncommon to have recourse to experts.

013 Some arbitral rules—such as those applying to commodity disputes—provide for the arbitrator to act as his own expert although the more common practice is to appoint an independent expert.

014 Obviously the freer and more informal nature of the informal proceedings, which the parties can regulate as they think best, affects the manner of performance of the technical consultancy to the extent to which the parties themselves may increase or diminish the inquisitorial role of the arbitrator. In addition, the distinction between technical consultancy and proof will be more subtle, as one can see from the tendency in case law to consider the technical consultancy as a sufficient motive to justify an extension of the period of time laid down for issue of the award even though not strictly part of the evidence (cf. Cassation, 14 December 1971, No 3633, in *Giustizia Civile* 1972, I, 1104; Cassation, 7 March 1967, No 532, in *Giustizia Civile* 1967, I, 891; Vigoriti, 1993 at 188 *et seq.*).

015 This extension can apply where the Code provides that this is only possible "when the taking of evidence is necessary" (Art 820, para. 2, CPC).

SELECTION AND APPOINTMENT OF THE EXPERT

016 Methods of selection of experts are governed differently in the case of judicial proceedings and that of arbitration. In litigation the criteria, methods and timing of the choice of the expert are rigidly defined, in view also of the importance which this consultant comes to assume in the exercise of the judicial function. Thus selection of the expert must take place "normally" from amongst those persons registered in the appropriate lists held at each court, as set out in the CPC Implementation Provisions:

> "All judges who have their seat in the district of the court must normally entrust the functions of technical consultant to those registered on the list of the same court." (Art 22, para. 1.)
>
> "In each court shall be established a list of technical consultants. The list is divided by category. There must always be included in the list the categories:
> 1. Medical/Surgical;
> 2. Industrial;
> 3. Commercial;
> 4. Agricultural;
> 5. Banking;
> 6. Insurance." (Art 13.)

017 And Article 15 adds:

> "those who are equipped with a special technical competence in a determined subject may obtain registration on the list, provided that they have unblemished moral character and are registered in the respective professional associations."

018 The list is kept by a committee of three persons, chaired by the president of the court. The other two members comprise the Public Prosecutor (*Procuratore Della Repubblica*) and a professional person registered in the professional list designated, as appropriate, by the Bar Council or the council of the professional category to which the applicant belongs for registration in the list of experts (Art 14, CPC Implementation Provisions).

019 The committee decides, by majority, on the registrations in the list once all the necessary information has been gathered by the judicial police on the public and private conduct of the candidate (Art 18, CPC Implementation Provisions). Every four years there is a revision of the list to exclude consultants who no longer meet the criteria provided at Article 15 or Article 18, CPC Implementation Provisions.

020 The appointment of the expert in civil proceedings normally occurs from amongst professionals registered on the appropriate list, except where the investigating judge considers it necessary to appoint someone with a specific expertise who is not on a court list from another area. In this case "he must consult the President of his own court and indicate in the Order, the grounds for his choice" (Art 22, para. 2, CPC Implementation Provisions).

021 The court will normally nominate a single expert, except in cases "of grave necessity, or when the law expressly so provides" (Art 191, para. 2, CPC). The appointment is covered by an order, by which is fixed a hearing for appearance and a time limit given to the parties by which they may nominate their own expert by way of a declaration given to the court registrar (Art 201, CPC).

022 The president of the court is required to supervise the distribution of appointments, from the lists, to ensure that they are made in a fair and equitable manner. The registrar is charged with keeping a register on which is noted all appointments made and the amount of payment allowed by each judge (Art 23, CPC Implementation Provisions).

023 Any expert registered on the appropriate list, is obliged to render his services, when so requested by the court, unless there is a reasonable excuse, which the judge will evaluate summarily without challenge, and with wide discretion. The lack of a justified reason constitutes a punishable offence. An expert commits an offence who avoids the appointment by fraudulent means:

> "Anyone appointed by the judicial authorities as an expert, interpreter, or guardian of objects submitted to sequestration by the criminal judge, who obtains by fraudulent means exemption from the obligation to appear or to render his services, shall be punished by imprisonment for up to six months ..."
>
> (Art 366 of the Criminal Code). (See *infra*, paras 065 *et seq*., "Liability of the expert in civil proceedings".)
>
> "Where the expert intends to accept the appointment he must swear, at the preliminary hearing, well and faithfully to fulfil the functions ascribed to him, for the sole purpose of bearing the truth to the judge. Refusal to swear is the same as refusal to accept the appointment."
>
> (Art 193, CPC.) (Vellani at 530.)

024 As for the aspect of impartiality and independence of the expert, Article 192 of the CPC provides that:

> "the consultant who does not wish to accept the appointment or who intends to abstain from it must make a declaration of this, or a petition to the judge who appointed him, at least three days prior to the preliminary hearing. In the same period the parties must set down their petitions of recusation by depositing a summons to the examining judge in the registry."

025 In contrast to a judge, the expert does not thus have a legal obligation to refuse an appointment in particular circumstances of lack of impartiality or independence, identified by the law. There is only a duty to refuse, which case law has tended to confine into the same limits as are envisaged against the consultant expert for recusation by the parties (imposition of objection or appeal grounded on a judge's relationship with, or possible antagonism to, a party in a law suit). For example, if his conduct has been such as to cause his suspension or striking off from his professional body (Protetti at 45 *et seq*.).

026 Both petitions for such suspension and recusation are normally presented in writing to the same judge who appointed the consultant, but in theory it is accepted that the abstention petition may also be presented orally to the registrar who would accept them by taking a minute (Protetti at 44; Vellani at 338).

027 According to Article 51 of the CPC

> "the Judge has the duty to refuse to hear a case:
> 1. If he has an interest in the case or in another turning on the same question of law;
> 2. If he himself or his wife is related up to the fourth degree, or cohabits with or is the habitual table companion of one of the parties or any of their representatives;

3. If he or his wife has a pending case or a serious enmity or relations of credit or debit with one of the parties or any of their representatives;
4. If he has given advice or lent his support to the case, or has given evidence in it as witness, or else has had cognisance of it as magistrate at a different level of the trial or as an arbitrator or has provided assistance as an expert;
5. If he is the tutor, guardian, factor, agent or employer of one of the parties; if, further, he is the director or manager of an entity, an association (whether or not legally recognised), a committee, a company or establishment which has an interest in the case.

In any other case in which there are serious risks of impropriety, the judge may request authorisation to abstain from his superior in rank. When the reason for this request concerns that superior, authorisation shall be requested of a superior of higher grade."

028 In arbitration, on the other hand, the procedure is freer, as there is no obligation to select consultants from the appropriate lists, nor any predetermination as to the number of experts. Moreover there is no equivalent to the preliminary hearing, given that in the world of arbitration the expert is not bound to give evidence under oath. Also the parties are not bound by the same strict time limits, imposed by court procedures, for the appointment of their own experts by the parties.

029 The appointment of all experts in arbitration, and the procedure to be followed, is therefore a matter for the parties and the discretion of the arbitrators themselves. "The parties may establish the procedure to be followed either in the arbitration agreement, or in the arbitration clause, or by a separate written deed (provided that such deed is drawn up prior to commencement of the arbitral proceedings) (Art 816, para. 2, CPC).

030 For the aspect of impartiality of the arbitrator, as an essential element of any adjudicating activity, see Fazzalari 1998 at 1 *et seq.*; Berlinguer 1995 at 339. An arbitrator is bound by the same Article 51 guidelines, concerning impartiality and independence, as is a judge, (see above) and the procedural route towards recusation is similar, although less restrictive over time limits and formalities.

031 The parties must present their petitions within three days of acceptance of a tribunal expert's appointment since once it has commenced the consultancy may no longer be challenged, and the failure to raise timeously, what would otherwise be substantive grounds for recusation, cannot annul the work accomplished by the expert (Bernardini at 620). (For the basis of challenge to arbitrators see Vigoriti, "A Common Law of Arbitration: Arbitral Awards and Appeals", 1995 at 29; *id.* "Homologation and challenge of arbitral awards in Italy", 1991 at 350.)

ACTIVITY OF THE EXPERT IN CIVIL PROCEEDINGS AND IN ARBITRATION

032 The current CPC has appreciably lessened the limitations which previously existed governing the method of working for experts. The working method of the expert is no longer limited, as was the case in the repealed code, only to the drafting of a written appraisal, but now the expert takes a full part in the proceedings (Vellani at 531).

033 At the preliminary hearing, in the presence of the parties, the expert will be given his brief, often in the form of questions to which he must respond. How he goes about his investigations is entirely up to him, although he may seek guidance, or assistance in his investigations, from the examining judge (Art 194, CPC).

034 Whenever the examining judge takes part in these investigations, these will be documented with minutes, or noted in a written report drafted by the expert (Art 195, para. 2, CPC).

035 It is interesting to note that there is no obligation on the expert to commit his findings to writing in the form of a report, although where a judge considers this necessary he may order such a report and lay down a time limit within which it must be lodged with the registry (Art 195, para. 3, CPC).

036 During the whole period of the trial, the expert may be invited to take part in hearings, to supply clarifications, to request explanations from the parties, to take information from third parties, to execute plans, models and designs etc. (Art 194, para. 1, CPC). Moreover, "when he considers it appropriate the president shall invite the expert to assist in discussions and express his opinion in the presence of the parties, who may clarify those opinions through their representatives" (Art 197, CPC).

037 Obviously the expert, not being one of judges, cannot take any part in the decision, nor may he be present in the discussion and deliberations between the judges, but he may only offer further clarification requested to the activity he was instructed to perform and the report which he presented.

038 Although the law is silent on the point, practice dictates that in assessments which are particularly complex or burdensome, the expert may be assisted by others of his choice and trust (Protetti at 62 *et seq.*).

039 This practice has been judicially approved in cases in which the judge has authorised it, or in those cases in which, even without authorisation, it is necessary to bring in other persons. In this regard the Court of Cassation stated: "The expert may officially have recourse to the work of assistants in the performance of the material duties relating to the appointment received" (Cassation, 11 February 1976, No 456, in *Rep.Foro.It.* 1976, 10).

040 In that case, it was a matter of carrying out the measurements of a piece of land. However, the consultant may never entirely entrust his duties to other persons. The work of the assistants can never be a substitute for those of the appointed expert. This is so also on the level of payment. Case law has established that:

> "the expert appointed by the judge may not assign to others the performance of the duties entrusted to him, with the consequence that wherever he may be authorised to make use of assistants, he may not claim the additional reimbursement paid by him to those assistants, . . ."
>
> (Cassation, 7 July 1981, No 4435, in *Massimario della Giustizia Civile* 1981, 7).

041 Obviously, problems will arise wherever the appointed expert does not share the opinion of his assistants (Cassation, 27 March 1984, No 2005, in *Massimario della Giustizia Giurisprudenza Italiana*, 1984, 405). On this it has been said that the expert report is only valid if the expert himself "took responsibility to evaluate the written and other conclusions, of the assistants, referring to them in his own report, with approval and with the assumption of all moral and scientific responsibility" (Cassation, 5 December 1985, No 6099, in *Massimario della Giustizia Civile*, 1985, 12; Protetti at 63).

042 Similar considerations also apply to arbitration given that the law does not lay down the procedure to be followed by the expert, so this can be decided by the parties "In the absence of any procedure agreed between the parties arbitrators have complete discretion over the most appropriate procedure" (Art 816, para. 5, CPC).

043 Moreover, even in arbitration proceedings, the principle of free deliberation of the tribunal, to a certain extent, removes the work of the expert from the complete freedom of the parties. In the sense that wherever arbitrators consider it necessary, they may indubitably arrange for technical assessments by third parties, even if these contradict the will of the parties.

It also remains a constant that there is a need in the arbitral process, as in ordinary proceedings, that examination and assessments should be carried out with the concurrent participation of the parties. This is to allow each of these to be able to be present at the same, to make their own observations, and to contradict those of others, for which there is the legally provided necessity for arbitrators to "assign to the parties time periods for presentation of documents and memoranda, and to set forth their replies" (Art 816, para. 4, CPC).

The expert witness and the right to a fair hearing

044 What is essential, whether in civil court proceedings or in arbitration, is to ensure the principle of a fair hearing, or *audi alteram partem*, meaning the positive right of participation in the proceedings accorded to the parties in the case and characterised as a positive right to verify the assessment of facts, to make representations concerning the evaluation of the same and to propose different conclusions to those coming from the opponent (Vigoriti, 1993, 2,188), on the basis of "symmetrical parity", to borrow an expression from Fazzalari, 1997, 52.

045 The problem is thus again that of respect for fundamental guarantees which require the definition of the limits of the principle of *audi alteram partem* firstly in arbitration proceedings, and secondly for expert witnesses.

046 It can be said that the concept of the fair hearing is deeply rooted in Italian arbitral culture, and the most authoritative learned writers define it as a notion which is elementary in that it comes from time immemorial (Fazzalari, 1994, 1). Arbitration is a form of proceeding to which apply all the fundamental principles which give it a judicial characteristic, including that of *audi alteram partem*, independently from the particular procedural rules adopted. The principle applies to all types of arbitration, legal or equitable, formal or free, although this may be through different procedural mechanisms. One judgement observed "arbitrations in ritual proceedings, charged with deciding in equity and without procedural formality are bound nevertheless still to respect the principle of *audi alteram partem*" (Cassation, 29 January 1992, No 923, in *Foro.Italiano* 1992, I, 1385; App Milan, 18 September 1990, No 1807, with a note by Vigoriti, 1991, 560-1; Berlinguer, 1994, 4, 759 *et seq*.).

047 Some doubts persist on the other hand mainly as a matter of interpretation, which arise from the conflict which tends to oppose freedom of form on the one side and fundamental procedural principles on the other.

048 At this level, there are some obvious easily identifiable constants in the procedural rules to which at least formal arbitration should generally conform. Amongst these is the duty to allot a time period for the parties to appoint their own technical consultants. Article 201, CPC states "the examining judge, in the order for appointment of the consultant, ascribes the parties a time limit by which they can appoint their own technical consultant, with a declaration received at the registry". There is an obligation to give notice of the day, time and place of the appraisal operations for the purpose of allowing the parties to be present at the operations themselves (Arts 90, 91 of the CPC Implementation Provisions). The Court of Cassation in its decision of the 11 June 1990 (*Rep.Foro.It.* 1990, heading *Consulente tecnico*, No 11) states notification of commencement of appraisal operations must be made to the party the object of the proceedings by the registry (as also to the parties' experts). This is by means of notice governed by Article 45 of the Civil Code Implementation Provisions. If not received personally by the addressee, who for the purpose signs a receipt to be kept in the official file, it must be notified, pursuant to Law No 59 of 1979 (Art 8), under the responsibility of the judicial official, who may, in those cases allowed, use registered post with receipt of delivery.

049 Omission of such a formality of notice is grounds for nullity of the technical consultancy, in that it implies violation of the principle of *audi alteram partem*, without considering the nature of the activities performed. Moreover, Article 157, second paragraph, CPC, states that only the parties for whose interest a requirement has been established may raise nullity of the act for lack of the requirement itself, but must do so in the first plea or defence subsequent to the act or to the notice of it: Bernardini, 1993, 617.

050 Another requirement is to keep the parties' experts copied with the same invitations and notices intended for the court-appointed consultant (Art 91, CPC Implementation Provisions), and again to give the possibility for the parties to examine documents obtained. Article 76 of the CPC Implementation Provisions provides: "the parties and their properly instructed representatives may examine the acts and documents on the official file and in those of the other parties and have copies made by the registry, subject to observance of the stamp duty laws". In the case of an accounting consultancy, the Court of Cassation has established that the court expert to whom the task has been delegated of conducting an accounting enquiry, must necessarily place the parties themselves in a position, through their representatives and experts, to be present at the main work of co-ordination, assessment and verification of the content of the said acts. This is in order that they may contemporaneously evaluate the documents of which the expert is the custodian, have copies taken, and opportunely raise observations and notes in the course of each operation. The obligation does not require him to call the parties in any preliminary phase to the appraisal operations proper, where this is a matter of a first reading for purposes of perusing the acts to be examined (Cassation, 8 October 1979, No 5190 in *Massimario della Giurisprudenza Italiana*, 1979, 1294). Another constant is to allow the parties to clarify and develop their reasons through their representatives on the opinion of the expert expressed in the deliberating chamber in the presence of the panel of judges (Art 197 of the CPC).

051 These are all elements which in a certain manner relate to the discipline of arbitration, but none of them are expressly referred to. This is not an attempt by the legislator to diminish respect for the underlying guarantees, but is an aspect of safeguard exercised in different forms, more discretionary and flexible, but no less onerous for that. Rather it is out of respect for the peculiar nature of the institution which supports it (V. Vigoriti, 1993, 191; at a comparative level see also the observations of Recchia, 1991, 3,405).

052 In this context, the contribution of case law has been decisive. In relation to the problem of the right to a fair hearing in technical consultancy, there is no point in analysing different principles for the various types of arbitration, but in substance there remains that irreducible bundle of guarantees which is the "hard core" of all the principles (Cassation No 3189/1989). There is a lowest common multiple of guarantees, leaving as a purely procedural matter the choice of formal or free arbitration. For examination of the principle of the right to be heard in *irrituale* arbitration see V. Vigoriti, 1991, 561; Berlinguer 1994, 766.

053 Having said that, the principle of *audi alteram partem* is considered to have been maintained where a time period has been allowed for the parties to present notes and pleadings, after completion of the taking of evidence and without any requirement to allow the parties to appoint technical consultants (Cassation 923/1992, *cit.*). Similarly, the duty is satisfied "when the arbitrators have allowed the parties to set forth their arguments, to adduce evidence, to present pleadings and replies within an established period and to have notice timeously of the petitions and claims of the other party" (Cassation, 11 January 1988, No 64 in *Rep.Foro.It.* 1988; *Arbitrato*, No 87). The principle is also respected when "notwithstanding the failure to fix an appropriate time period, the parties have in any case had the possibility to arrange for the protection of their interests through the accomplishment of their activities in defence" (Cassation, 18 March 1981, No 1595 in *Foro.It.Massimario* 1981; *Arbitrato* No 94).

054 Failure to observe the principle of *audi alteram partem*, expressly listed amongst the motives for appealing an arbitral award by the reform of Law No 25 of 1994, means nullity of the arbitral decision in the case of formal arbitration. Article 829, first paragraph No 9 of the CPC provides: "quashing on the grounds of nullity is allowed, notwithstanding any waiver . . . if the principle of *audi alteram partem* has not been observed in the arbitral proceedings". For free arbitration there is no similar provision of law, but given that this principle is a matter of public policy, it should be considered that even a free arbitration award rendered in violation of the principle must be considered null, regardless of the intent of the parties (Vigoriti 1991; Bernini 1993, 338–9).

055 Beyond any distinction between *rituale* or *irrituale* procedure, Article 5 of the 1958 New York Convention approves this principle for purposes of recognition of foreign awards in Italy, in that it provides that an award made contrary to internal public policy is a sufficient ground for refusing execution of the award (see Berlinguer, "Capacity of the Parties and respect of *audi alteram partem* as Conditions for recognition of the foreign award in Italy", *Foro. Italiano* 1998, I, 293 *et seq.*).

THE EXPERT'S REPORT

056 The report is the written development of his work which the expert is bound to present to the judge within the prescribed period. The law does not specify what requirements must be observed or what method must be followed for the drafting of the report, so the practice has been to develop a certain type of format and decided cases underline those elements which must be considered as essential or otherwise.

057 Normally this should be in the form of an essay to be delivered in italian (Art 122, CPC), save for any special rules which relate to other linguistic communities and those for the Alto Adige region which in some cases allow the expert to express himself in his own mother tongue and in others to make the report simultaneously in two languages (cf. DPR 15 July 1988, No 574).

058 It is commonly held that the report is a public deed, as Article 744 of the CPC provides that "Registrars and keepers of public registers are obliged, except as provided by law, to send copies and extracts of judicial acts held by them to whomsoever may request them, under penalty of damages and expenses" (see Cerino-Canova, 1980, 433). As for other judicial deeds, the report is also received by the registrar, so anybody may request to be given a copy of the appraisal report in order to inspect it. Contrary opinion is that the report is a privileged document for the parties to the case and their representatives on the basis of Article 76 of the CPC Implementation Provisions. Only the parties and their representatives may examine the deeds and documents contained in the official file and in the files of the other parties, but this view is held by a minority, unsupported by case law (see Satta, 1971, IV, 54; Teresi-Trojano, "La Pubblicita' degli atti giudiziali e dei Registri di cancelleria", in *Giurisprudenza Italiana* 1984, IV, 343).

059 The report is normally divided into several parts, following a typical format which includes a heading, a preamble, scope, development of investigations, verification of facts, technical evaluation, conclusions (see Protetti–Protetti 1997, 77). The expert applies his own technical experience to analyse and decipher determined factual circumstances, introducing in the process rules of experience, well known facts, and also to a limited extent, judicial rules. There is in fact no need for the well known facts to be inserted in the questions to be submitted to the technical advisor. These belong to common knowledge and thus can be shared by all, including the judge. Similarly, the keys to interpretation which allow them to be understood do not constitute elements of the judge's private knowledge. They are thus elements which he may not use in support of the decision, but given facts of common experience, indispensable in the activity of judgement.

060 Without wanting to enter into too much detail concerning evidential proof or semantic discussions outside the scope of this work, it is sufficient to refer to the definition which case law has given of well known facts and lessons of experience, that is:

> "A well known fact is understood to mean that occurrence which takes place in a determined and defined form, whose knowledge is part of the culture itself of a circle of persons. Lessons of common experience on the other hand can be identified as those definitions or hypothetical judgments of general content, independent of the case in question on which the judge is called to decide, acquired by experience, but autonomous with respect to the individual case by observations which are deduced and which must also be of value for other cases."
>
> (Cassation 25 January 1970, No 2006, *Rep.Foro.It.* 1971, *Procedimento Civile*, No 208.)

061 Having examined the facts, carried out verifications, and, if appropriate, taken evidence from the parties or other persons, the expert concludes his report by formulating replies to the questions set forth. The judge must take account of these in the decision, and still more so where he considers that he does not agree with the report itself.

> "Although the judge of the merits must take account in giving reasons for the judgment of the technical consultant's report, even when he adheres to its conclusions, he may not simply make a reference to the report. In any case, when the judge adopts a report of a strictly accounting nature (characterised by the fact of using only an accounting analysis, once the basic criteria have been established) then the requirement for giving reasons has been satisfied by the affirmation of the judge concerning the correctness of procedure followed by the CTU (official technical consultant) and the conclusions reached."
>
> (Cassation, 13 May 1990, No 3678, in *Rep.Foro.It.* 1990, *Consulente tecnico*, No 15.)

062 It should be borne in mind that wherever the report is considered not to be exhaustive or to be defective, in any aspect, the judge will have the power to supplement it by a request for clarifications which he may ask of the expert at any time. In more serious cases, including those in which a liability of the expert may emerge, the judge may equally order, at any time, a fresh start to the appraisal investigations.

EXAMINATION OF ACCOUNTS

063 Special rules are set forth in the Civil Procedure Code for a case of technical consultancy where the purpose is to examine the accounts in documents and registers ("when it is necessary to examine accounting documents and registers, the examining judge may charge the expert with this task, entrusting to him the task of attempting a conciliation between the parties": Art 188, CPC). This is the frequent case, in which the dispute turns on a breach of contract which can only be ascertained through examination of certain accounting records. In such a case the powers of the expert are appropriately extended, and range from the power to meet together with parties for definition of the appraisal, to the possibility, with their prior consent, to examine even documents and registers which were not produced for the case. The expert's powers also extend to the possibility of attempting conciliation between the parties themselves. If then the conciliation succeeds, the examining judge may approve the minutes in an unchallengeable order, and give that the effect of a writ of execution (Art 199, second paragraph, CPC).

064 In arbitration on the other hand, nothing is provided for such a case. This is perhaps because the arbitrators themselves in such situations are usually selected from amongst experts in the subject, who perfectly well know their way around the intricacies of reading and understanding accounting documents and balance sheets. The prevailing view is thus that for arbitration there does not need to be a technical accounting consultant, and that it would be superfluous in such proceedings to delegate to third persons the task of attempting conciliation between the parties ("that such a task falls to the consultant appointed by the arbitrator must be excluded, given the very structure and limits of the arbitration proceeding": Bernardini, 1992, 623).

LIABILITY OF THE EXPERT IN CIVIL PROCEEDINGS

065 At the level of liability, Article 64 of the Civil Procedure Code applies to experts in civil proceedings the provisions of the Penal Code relating to appraisals. The old formulation of this law, which gave the judge the power to sentence an expert to a financial penalty where the latter had committed a serious fault in fulfilment of his duty has now been substituted by a different punishment. This requires the examining judge not to impose the punishment himself, but to report the expert to the penal judge (on this, see Vellani 1988, 536).

066 The expert must thus answer a charge for offences under Article 366 of the Penal Code, for "refusal of legally imposed duties", first when by fraudulent means he obtains exemption from rendering his services, that is "by artifices, tricks, pretence or lies" he escapes from the task ascribed to him. The proof for this offence is not satisfied by mere "allegations of incompatibility, sickness or other impediment which, as they can be checked by the judicial authorities, are not sufficient to deceive them" (Cassation, 3 January 1939 in *Giust. pen.* 1939, II, 1150). The offence is secondly committed by refusal to carry out duties, to give his personal details or to swear the required oath. Case law shows that it is sufficient for purposes of committing the offence that the expert failed to appear before the judge (see Cassation, 13 November 1948 in *Giurisprudenza completa della Cassazione penale*, 1948, II, 3579; for a contrary view, Manzini, 1950, IV, 676).

067 The expert is also responsible for the truth of his affirmations and his investigations. In case of falsehood, he risks liability pursuant to Article 373 of the Penal Code for the offence of false testimony. Case law in fact establishes that:

> "The provisions for examination of witnesses, applicable pursuant to Article 501, para. 1 of the Civil Procedure Code to expert witnesses, include Article 497 of the Penal Procedure Code with its standard form of obligation to speak the truth. Indeed, in that article it deals with moral and judicial responsibility, going beyond the obligation to speak the whole truth, which may well be understood as the intention of the legislator in relation to the expert that the same should be inspired by the principles of loyalty and sincerity which are at the basis of the establishment of proof

in criminal proceedings. This is the more so because the contribution of understanding of the expert is not limited to the exposition of valuations, but in most cases also involves the establishment of objective facts."

(Court of Turin, 20 March 1991 in *Giurisprudenza Italiana* 1994, II, 77 with a note by Marini.)

068 The offence may concern both the affirmations made by the expert in the presence of the judge, and those contained in the final report presented by the expert. What counts for the purposes of application of the criminal penalty (imprisonment from two to six years and prohibition from public office and the relevant profession) is that the unfaithful consultancy report constitutes the basis for the judgment. The expert is not however punishable in the case of retraction of evidence. Article 376, second paragraph of the Penal Code in fact provides that

"wherever falsehood has occurred in a civil proceeding, the person responsible shall not be punished if he withdraws the false evidence and demonstrates the true evidence prior to definitive judgment being pronounced upon request of the judge, even if the judgment is not irrevocable".

069 The liability of the professional person is thus based on his formal qualification as a judicial auxiliary and on his substantial characterisation as a public officer. The more authoritative judgments have sought to reject the private law concept of the relationship between the parties and the expert and accept instead the opposite according to which:

"ideas of private law may not be applied to the expert in considering compliance or breach, almost as if he were linked to the parties by a relationship of rendering services, since he performs in the ambit of proceedings a public function as an auxiliary of the judge in the public and superior interest of justice, with civil liability, as well as criminal or disciplinary liability, which implies the duty to compensate for loss which as a public officer he may have caused in violation of the duties connected with his office."

(Cassation, 25 May 1973, No 1545 in *Foro.Italiano* 1975, I, 684, with a note by Pezzano. On this see also Vigoriti, "Liability of the Judge" in *Enciclopedia giuridica*, Rome 1991, 11.)

070 Criminal liability of the expert goes together with other forms of liability. These can be of a disciplinary nature, which the expert may incur pursuant to Articles 14–21 of the Implementation Provisions of the Civil Procedure Code. They may also be a matter of professional discipline to which the person is subject through the sole fact of being listed on a professional register, and thus being subject to the powers of self-regulation of the institutional bodies of that profession. The liability may be of a civil nature, in which case it is of a non-contractual tortious type.

071 In relation to the first type of liability, the elements of the offence listed in the Procedural Code are two: "not to have maintained impeccable political and moral conduct", a provision which is now almost devoid of meaning so far as concerns political conduct and in any case of very general effect and difficult to apply; the second and overriding criterion is "not to have complied with the obligations arising from appointments received" (Art 19)—see Franchi, 1973, 719. Sanctions are a warning, suspension or removal from the register (Art 20).

072 The law does not set forth the relationship between types of conduct and the relative sanctions, thus leaving the judge ample powers of discretion in considering whether there is liability.

073 The meting out of the sanction is the responsibility of the committee (Art 14), which proceeds in two phases. In the first, the chairman raises the failure and receives the reply from the person concerned (Art 21, first paragraph). In the second phase, wherever the chairman considers that he must proceed with a trial, the expert is summoned in front of the disciplinary committee which then decides after having heard him. An appeal is allowed to the Court of

Appeal (Art 21). It seems that further appeal to the Council of State is possible against the decision of the latter upon the grounds of legitimacy pursuant to Article 113 on the Constitution (Franchi 1973, 721).

074 Disciplinary responsibility pursuant to Article 19 of the Implementation Provisions is different from the similar responsibility to which the expert may be submitted on the basis of his registration in a professional list. Disciplinary professional responsibility may derive from the same facts or from different facts and must be ascertained according to the rules of the order or association to which the expert belongs. For some reflections on disciplinary and professional sanctions for the responsibility of the expert pursuant to Article 19, see Franchi 1973, 722.

075 Different considerations arise at the level of civil liability. Article 64, paragraph two of the Civil Procedure Code as modified by Article 25, of Law No 281 of 4 June 1985, provides that

> "in any event, wherever the expert incurs serious blame for the performance of the acts required of him, he shall be punished by detention for up to a year and a fine up to 20 million Lira. Article 35 of the Penal Code applies. In any event he shall be liable for damages caused to the parties."

076 One is in fact dealing with a rule which is not completely explicit and comprehensible, whose extent is not clear. It is commonly considered that this type of liability, measured against a high degree of blameworthiness or fraud, is equally applicable to experts both in penal and civil procedure. One is actually dealing with the same type of liability as for the work of the judge or any employee of the State to whom the expert may be easily compared in terms of function. This criterion allows the construction of a *régime* of unitary and coherent liability for the expert: see Vigoriti, 1993, 11; Protetti-Protetti, 137.

077 There is of course no lack of dissenting opinions by those who consider the law governing contractual obligations to be applicable in these circumstances. This is set forth in Article 1176 of the Civil Code, which ascribes the liability of the expert according to the degree of difficulty of the activity performed (see Vellani). There are also those who consider that the expert's liability must vary according to the fact which the judge may or may not have accepted and established according to the results of his investigation. In the more positive case the expert would actually be exempt of liability, whereas if against him there would be a contrary presumption (Franchi 1973, 719). In both cases these are just minority opinions which have not been reflected in the cases. Where the expert has committed fraud or a serious fault in the performance of his duties he may thus be obliged to compensate the losses unfairly incurred by the parties. Such a finding must however take place in separate proceedings. Article 162, paragraph 2 of the Civil Procedure Code is not applicable to such a case. Article 162 provides:

> "if the nullity of the procedural acts is due to the registrar, an official of the court or the lawyer, the judge, by an order declaring the imposition of costs for redoing the work to be charged to the person liable, and upon a petition by the party, may order the person liable to compensation of the loss caused by the nullity, pursuant to Article 60, no 2, made at the same time as the judgment of the case."

078 So far as concerns final liability towards third parties, who may have been caused loss by performance of the consultancy, there are no distinctions with the general *régime* at law.

Auxiliaries of the court are liable pursuant to Article 2043 of the Civil Code (Franchi, 1973, 718).

079 To conclude, the qualification of the expert as a public officer does not seem to have substantial implications at the level of civil liability of such auxiliaries in relation to the parties to the action and third parties. The expert's limit of liability for acts performed with fraud or serious blame is similar to the provisions referred to in Article 22 of the Consolidated Law for Provisions Concerning the Status of Civil Employees of the State, but also reflects Article 2236 of the Civil Code. Otherwise, the *régime* of Article 64 of the Civil Procedure Code does not depart from that of common rule of law.

080 In any case the State is not liable pursuant to Article 28 of the Constitution, which provides that "civil servants and employees and public entities shall be directly liable, according to penal, civil and administrative laws, for acts performed in violation of law. In such cases civil liability shall extend to the State and public entities". Nor is the State liable on any other ground for losses unfairly caused by the expert. The State though is bound to compensate the expert for losses which he may have sustained in the performance of duties conferred on him on account of the erroneousness or insufficiency of instructions given to him by the judge. The Court of Cassation has confirmed that:

> "the expert who, by complying with the instructions of the judge pursuant to Article 317 of the Penal Procedure Code during the performance of the appointment, suffers loss in consequence of erroneous or insufficient instructions, has the right to compensation for this by the public administration. There is no application for the principle of independent liability of the public administration, given the binding nature of the instructions by the judge. There is no derogation or restriction in consequence of the limitations established on account of personality in order to assert the personal liability of the magistrates."
>
> (Cassation, 24 March 1982, No 1879, in *Giustizia civile* 1982, I, 3105.)

In arbitration

081 In arbitration, the private law character of the appointment conferred upon the expert and the nature of the relationship with arbitrators do not allow that professional person to be considered as equivalent to a public service appointment, so it is not appropriate to consider criminal liability (see Bernardini, 625). There are however various possibilities of disciplinary responsibility (see Cassation, 25 May 1973, no 1545, in *Foro.Italiano* 1975, I, 684 with note by Pezzano) and civil liability. For the latter it is mainly a matter of emphasising that this is a contractual relationship between arbitrator and expert which does not directly involve the parties. There are no reciprocal implications of obligation, and there is no fiduciary element which normally characterises such a service, and so it is clear that the expert is only subject to tort liability (see Cassation, 25 May 1973, no 1545).

082 Thus, here too one needs to evaluate which threshold of liability should apply to the expert. Should it be that generally envisaged by Article 2043 of the Civil Code? Article 2043 constitutes the keystone of extra-contractual liability, providing: "Any wilful or blameworthy act, which causes wrongful damage to others, obliges the person who committed the act to compensate the damage". Should the liability be that of the agent? This is set forth in Article 1710 of the Civil Code: "the agent is bound to follow the terms of his agency with the diligence of a good family father"—a concept close to the reasonable man—together with Article 1176 of the Civil Code. Article 1176 provides: "In the fulfilment of an obligation the debtor must use the diligence of the good family father. In fulfilment of obligations arising in the conduct of professional business, the diligence must be assessed with regard to the nature of the activity undertaken".

083 Another possibility could be the liability determined by Article 64 of the Civil Procedure Code applied to fraud and serious negligence? Here too, the tendency of the cases has been in the latter direction, that is towards consideration of experts as civilly liable to the parties only where the expert has acted without the least degree of technical appraisal which could be described as professional, and in violation of the fundamental rules of the profession (for a definition of serious negligence, see Cassation, 20 October 1970, No 2260, in *Massimario della Giurisprudenza Italiana*, 1970, 901). There is thus less stringent liability for the technical consultant either compared to that of the agent or compared to that of the person committing a tort. The situation is closer to the category of the undertaker of work subject to certain distinctions.

084 As for the relationship of causation necessary to give rise to the expert's liability, case law tends to attribute all foreseeable and avoidable events which have resulted from his conduct, and it does not suffice that there has been a mere sequence between the blameworthy conduct of the expert and the incident of damage, but such a relationship must have a consequential chain, according to a calculation of statistical regularity (cf. Cassation, 15 October 1971, No 2918, in *Massimario della Giurisprudenza Italiana*, 1971, 1572). On the other hand where the expert's appointment has been annulled, the Supreme Court affirmed that:

> "a request intended to obtain from the expert the return of sums paid to him, in relation to a consultancy which was then annulled, gives rise to a right by the party to repayment of that which was not due without being precluded, directly or indirectly, from using the provisions of Article 64 of the Civil Procedure Code—which concern the aquiline liability of the expert for damages caused by a delict—and is subject to the ordinary rules of jurisdiction according to value."
>
> (Cassation, 21 October 1992, no 11474, in *Massimario della Giustizia Civile*, 1992, 10.)

085 The lack of direct relations between the expert and the parties does not then prevent an arbitrator from having indirect liability for the acts of others by virtue of the agency relationship which binds them to the parties in the case. More precisely there is a liability pursuant to Article 1228 of the Civil Code which provides: "Save as otherwise agreed by the parties, the debtor, who in the performance of an obligation uses the work of third parties, is liable also for the wilful and negligent acts of them".

086 Besides, as has been properly deplored by most recent academic writers: "it is the arbitrator who chooses the expert, and between those two there is a private relationship for the performance of work for which the expert is bound in relation to the arbitrators and it is they who are liable to pay their fees" (see Fabbrini Tombari, *Arbitrato irrituale*, in a comment on Cassation, 7 December 1996, No 10923, in *Rivista dell'arbitrato*, 1997, 2, 337 *et seq.* at 343).

087 An aspect of liability may thus emerge during the course of arbitration, when the expert has caused delay to the arbitrators in the issue of the award, for the consequential causation of liability on the part of the arbitrators towards the parties. In a case of free arbitration for example, the Court of Cassation has managed to confirm that where the arbitrators consider that they should use an expert "there can be no dispute that they are bound to answer for the fraudulent or blameworthy acts of the expert, who takes the role of an auxiliary, given that his service is merely instrumental, and thus not autonomous, by reference to the work of the arbitrators" (Cassation, 27 March 1987, No 3005, in *Foro.padano* 1987, 404, quoted by Bernardini, 626).

088 Similar considerations concerned a panel of arbitrators when they maintained that:

"wherever the parties do not provide at the request of the arbitrators for compensation of the expenses of the consultancy, the arbitrators may decide on the basis of the documents without nominating an expert, since the consultant who has been chosen and instructed as to his appointment could claim from the arbitrators payment of his own dues."

(Arbitral Panel of Ancona, 13 June 1990 in *Rivista dell'arbitrato*, 1992, 577. See also Fabbrini Tombari, 337.)

EXPENSES, FEES AND COMPENSATION OF THE EXPERT

089 As for the costs, Law No. 319 of 8 July 1980 deals expressly with the payment of remuneration for the technical consultant by providing a complex system of classification linked to professional tariffs. Article 1 of the said Law subdivides the payments into two categories: fees and compensation, qualifying the first as emoluments directly due to the expert for the professional activity performed, and the second expenses for travel and subsistence incurred by the same expert in the performance of his duties. In reality there exists also another type of expense which the Law envisages, that incurred by the technical consultant for the performance of tests which he has effected, and for the co-operation of other experts (Art 7).

090 Law 319/1980 comprehensively governs each emolument according to tables of expenditure in which are set forth the fixed fees for the professional person, by reference to typical services of the same and pegged to professional rates. There are also variable fee amounts, determined in relation to the particular appointment according to a valuation which fluctuates between a maximum and a minimum, or which is fixed on a percentage basis of the value of the dispute. Where neither of the two criteria mentioned appears appropriate to determine the payment for the expert for the service performed, "the fees shall be proportionate to the time spent and shall be determined on the basis of days" (Art 4).

091 The Law further provides that: "if the judicial authority declares, with a recent order, the urgency of the work by fixing a time less than that normally considered necessary, the fixed and variable fees may be increased by up to twenty per cent" (Art 2, para. 3). Whilst "for services of exceptional importance, complexity and difficulty the fees may be increased up to double" (Art 5).

092 The payment of fees to the expert takes place by a reasoned order of the examining judge or the Public Attorney, and relates to the future as it is not linked to the result of the dispute. The activity of the expert, prior to appointment of the same, in fact represents a burden which falls upon the party in whose interest it is to establish certain findings in order to obtain a favourable result. This is solely on the ground that "in the course of the trial each of the parties must provide for the costs of the acts which it performs and those which it requests, and must pay in advance for other acts necessary for the trial when the advance is placed at its charge by law or by the judge" (Art 90 of the Civil Procedure Code). From the moment at which the consultancy is requested it becomes an integral part of the procedural structure of the trial, so that all relevant expenses become necessary just as those relating to the judge, the registry, or other organs of the judicial apparatus. It follows that all parties to the trial are bound to meet these independently of their procedural and substantive position, up to the final settlement between them of the expense of the case on the basis of the principle that the loser pays. Case law maintains that:

"Payment of the costs of the official technical consultancy, effected by the examining judge in the course of the judgment pursuant to Article 90 of the Civil Procedure Code, shall not have the value and content of a judgment for payment, but only of an order for provisional advance, and is intended to be superseded by the dispositions of the judgment concerning the relevant burden, taking account that such advance is governed by the basis of procedural interest to request the act to which the expenses relate, where the definitive decision on their attribution is governed by the principle that the loser of the entire dispute pays, save for payments pursuant to Article 92 of the Civil Procedure Code."

(Cassation, 15 March 1984, No 1753, in *Massimario della Giustizia Civile*, 1984, 3–4.)

093 The order for payment of the costs of the technical consultancy constitutes a provisional writ for execution of payment in relation to the parties whose obligation it is (Art 11, fourth paragraph) and may be appealed within 20 days of receipt of notice. The right of appeal belongs both to the expert and to each party and the time limit is peremptory, notwithstanding that the Law says nothing on this (see Cassation, 13 June 1995, No 6684, in *Massimario della Giustizia Civile*, 1995, 6; Cassation, 27 July 1988, No 4777, in *Massimario della Giurisprudenza Italiana*, 1988, 644). In any challenge proceedings all parties interested participate with complete rights for each to be heard. Time periods are reduced by half. The expert may act in person, without the aid of an attorney. An attempt at conciliation must be made, and in case of failure the bench decides by an unchallengeable decree, even if case law allows that recourse may be made to Cassation for validation of legitimacy of the decision (see Cassation, 4 August 1995, No 8608, in *Giurisprudenza del bollettino della legislazione tecnica* 1996, 3684; Cassation, 17 May 1995, No 5431, in *Massimario della Giustizia Civile*, 1995, 1019).

094 In the appeal decision no evaluation will be made of the utility or result of the consultancy, but only considerations of fairness and adequacy of the payment. The cases in fact maintain:

"In an appeal judgment against the order for a payment of the fees to the expert, pursuant to Article 11 of Law No 319 of 8 July 1980, the judge must limit his examination to checking the payment itself and establishing whether this occurred according to appropriate criteria for the totality of the work performed, to the exclusion of any evaluation of the influence and the utility of the technical consultancy, which is reserved to the judge of the merits for the case in which the expert report was produced."

(Cassation, 8 February 1996, No 1014, in *Massimario della Giustizia Civile*, 1996, 177.)

095 Independently of the procedure just explained, and of the efficacy given by the Law to the appointment, the expert may in any case choose to sue for his payment by way of originating proceedings, or by obtaining a lien according to Article 633, paragraph 1 of the Civil Procedure Code which allows "whoever has performed his work in the course of a trial" to obtain injunctive protection for his debt, as it is unanimously considered that the full meaning of the Law includes also the fees of the technical consultant (see Vellani, 540). The object of the action of the expert may be any of the parties in the case since they are severally liable for payment. As already remarked, the costs of consultancy are actually part of the costs of the trial and are therefore to be borne by all those who took part in the trial, unless otherwise expressly ordered by the judge. The award of costs, which is defined in the judgment, cannot be made against the technical consultant, since the principle that the loser pays relates only to the parties (Cassation, 25 May 1973, No 1545, in *Foro.Italiano* 1975, I, 684, with a note by Pezzano).

096 Different considerations govern arbitration, again on account of the private nature of the relations between the persons concerned. The costs *régime* assumes the nature of a bargain and exclusively governed by party autonomy and the powers of discretion of the adjudicating body.

097 Normally, the practice is that the arbitrators, in the appointment order for the expert, provide for the parties to establish an expenditure fund to include the costs of the professional and an approximate figure corresponding to the expenses which the expert himself must incur in the performance of his appointment. This is also out of a need for caution, so as to enable the arbitrators themselves to be protected against any future claims by experts who have not been properly paid.

098 In any event, the expert may use his entitlement as a writ for execution of payment against the person who appointed him at any time subsequent to performance of the appointment, even before the trial has reached its term, and independently of its result (Cassation, 2 March 1973, No 573, in *Foro.Italiano* 1973, 158).

***Aldo Berlinguer** is an attorney and arbitrator, and Associate Professor of Comparative Private Law at the University of Cagliari. He is a Member of the Italian Association of Comparative Law and a Member of the Italian and Spanish Bar.*

***Vincenzo Vigoriti** has been Professor of Law at the University of Florence since 1970 and an attorney in private practice since 1977, as well as holding numerous visiting professorships and lectureships at overseas law schools.*

He is a member of the Italian Bar Association, the Italian Association for Comparative Law, the Italian Association for Civil Procedure and the American Law Institute, and is a Fellow of the American Bar Association. Since 1995 he has sat on the comitato scientifico *of the Rivista dell'Arbitrato. He specialises in civil and commercial law, international trade, construction, arbitration and litigation.*

BIBLIOGRAPHY

BERNARDINI, "Arbitrato e Consulenza tecnica", in *Riv. trimestrale diritto e procedura civile* 1993, 614.

CARNACINI, "Tutela giurisdizionale e tecnica del processo", in *Studi in onore di Enrico Redenti,* II, Milan 1951.

ALPA, "La dualita' dell' arbitrato nel diritto comparato", in *Riv. arbitrato* 1991, 655.

BERLINGUER, "Impartiality and Independence of Arbitrators in International Practice", in 6(4) Am.Rev.Int'l. Arb. 339 (1995).

BERLINGUER, "Contraddittorio e consulenza tecnica", in *Riv. arbitrato* 1994, 4, 759.

BERNINI, *L'arbitrato,* Bologna 1993.

CERINO–CANOVA, in E. Allorio, *Commentario del Codice di Procedura civile,* Turin 1980.

FAZZALARI, *L'arbitrato,* Turin 1997.

FAZZALARI, "Ancora sull imparzialita dell'arbitro", in *Riv. arbitrato* 1998.

FRANCHI, *La perizia civile,* Padua 1959.

FRANCHI, "Consulente tecnico" in E. Allorio, *Commentario al codice di procedura civile,* I, Turin 1973.

FAZZALARI, "La riforma dell arbitrato", in *Riv. arbitrato* 1994, 1.

MANZINI, *Trattato di diritto penale,* Turin 1950.

E PROTETTI–M T PROTETTI, *La Consulenza tecnica nel processo civile,* Milan 1997.

RECCHIA, "Riforme Legislative Straniere sull' arbitrato", in *Riv. arbitrato* 1991, 3, 405.

SATTA, *Commentario al codice di procedura civile,* Milan 1971.

VELLANI, "Consulenza tecnica nel diritto processuale civile", in *Digesto Discipline privatistiche,* III, Turin, 1988.

VIGORITI, "Arbitrato e consulenza tecnica", in *Riv. arbitrato* 1993, 2.

VIGORITI, "Quale contraddittorio par l'arbitrato libero?" in *Riv. arbitrato* 1991.

VIGORITI, "The Long March of Italian Law Towards International Arbitration", in Am.Rev.Int'l.Arb I 1992, 251, Essays in Honour of Hans Smit.

VIGORITI, "International Arbitration in Italy", in Am.Rev.Int'l.Arb I 1990, 7.

VIGORITI, "A Common Law of Arbitration: Arbitral Capital Awards and Appeals", in 6(1) Am.Rev.Int'l.Arb. 29 (1995).

VIGORITI, "Homologation and challenge of arbitral awards in Italy", in 2 Am.Rev.Int'l.Arb. 350 (1991).

APPENDIX

1. RULES OF CIVIL PROCEDURE WHERE APPLICABLE TO EXPERT WITNESSES

Art 61 (*Expert witness*)—If necessary, the judge can request the assistance, in order to complete single acts or throughout the entire trial, of one or more expert witnesses having specific competence in the matter concerned. The expert witnesses shall be chosen from those listed in specific registers in accordance with the provisions implementing this Code.

Art 62 (*Services provided by the expert witness*)—The expert witness carries out the researches as commissioned by the judge and gives, in the hearing and in chambers, all the information and explanations requested by the judge according to arts 193 and following, and arts 441 and 463.

Art 63 (*Duty to take up the task and challenging of the expert witness*)—The expert witness chosen from those registered is under obligation to provide his services, unless the judge states that a proper reason for the abstention is given. The expert witness can be challenged by the parties for the reasons provided for by Art 51.[1] The judge who appointed the expert witness shall treat the matter of his challenge.

Art 64 (*Liability of the expert witness*)—The rules provided for by the Penal Code concerning experts are also applied to the expert witnesses. In any case, the expert witness who is liable for gross negligence in the execution of the services requested, is punished by imprisonment for up to one year or to pay a fine up to Lire 20,000,000. Art 35 of the Penal Code applies. In any case damages suffered by the parties have to be paid.[2]

Art 87 (*Assistance provided by lawyers and expert witnesses*)—The party can be assisted by one or more lawyers and by an expert witness, in the cases and the conditions provided for by this code (of civil procedure).

Art 92 (*Costs order for single acts. Costs compensation*)—The judge, in making an order on the basis of the provisions set forth above, can exclude the reimbursement of the costs met by the winning party, where they are excessive or unnecessary. The judge can order a party, whether or not the loser, to reimburse the costs caused to the other party—even those not in the refundable category, where they could not be subject to repetition—because of the breach of art 88. Where both parties lose or for other good reasons, the judge can order the apportionment, partially or totally, of the costs between the parties. Where the parties have settled, the costs are supposed to be included in the settlement, unless the parties have otherwise agreed in the record of settlement.

Art 177 (*Effects and revocation of court orders*)—The court orders, howsoever justified, may never prejudice the final judgment.

Except as provided in the following paragraph, court orders may always be modified or revoked by the judge who pronounced them.

The following cannot be modified or revoked by the judge who pronounced them:

(1) court orders given on the basis of the parties' agreement, where the matter concerned can be the subject of free determination by the parties; anyway, these orders can also be revoked by the examining magistrate or by the full court, where all the parties agree;
(2) court orders which by law are not subject to appeal;
(3) court orders which can be appealed through a specific type of claim[3];
(4) court orders which have been appealed on the basis of the following article.[4]

Art 191 (*Designation of an expert witness*)—In the cases provided for by arts 61 and following, the examining magistrate by court order—as provided by art 187, last para—or by another subsequent order appoints an expert witness and fixes the hearing at which the witness must appear. Several expert witnesses can be appointed only in cases of serious necessity or where it is expressly required by law.

Art 192 (*Abstention and recusation of the expert witness*)—The order is served on the expert witness by the justice's clerk, together with the invitation to appear before the court in the hearing fixed by the judge.

Where the expert witness does not accept the task or, although obliged to provide the service, intends to abstain, he must file a report or a petition to the judge by whom he has been appointed at least three days before the first trial hearing; within the same time limit the parties must present their petitions of recusation by depositing a complaint to the judge in the chancery of the court. The judge provides by court order not subject to appeal.

Art 193 (*Oath of the expert witness*)—In the first trial hearing the examining magistrate reminds the expert witness of the importance of the office which he is requested to carry out and receives from him the oath to fulfil thoroughly and faithfully the task which he has been entrusted with in order to make the truth known to the judge.

Art 194 (*Services provided for by the expert witness*)—The expert witness is present at the hearings he has been invited to by the judge; even out of his district, he carries out by himself or in co-operation with the judge—according to the decision of the latter—the enquiries described by art 62. The expert witness can be authorised to ask for explanations from the parties, to make enquiries from others and to execute plans, copies and surveys.

Even where the judge gives orders to the expert witness to make enquiries by himself, the parties can take part in the operations in person or through their own expert witnesses and lawyers and can make written and oral remarks and petitions to the expert witness.

Art 195 (*Minutes and report*)—Where the enquiries carried out by the expert witness were made in co-operation with the judge, minutes should be kept. The judge can also order the expert witness to draft a written report.

Where the enquiries are carried out without the assistance of the judge, the expert witness must draw a report containing the remarks and questions made by the parties. The report must be deposited in the chancery of the court within the deadline fixed by the judge.

Art 196 (*Renewal of the enquiries and substitution of the expert witness*)—The judge always has the power to order the renewal of enquiries and on serious grounds the substitution of the expert witness.

Art 197 (*Assistance in hearing and in chamber*)—Where he considers it appropriate, the chief justice invites the expert witness to be present at the oral pleading before the court and to give his opinion in chamber in presence of the parties, who can explain and develop their arguments through their lawyers.

Art 198 (*Auditing of accounts*)—Where the examination of accounting records and books is needed, the examining magistrate can assign the expert witness to choose and entrust him with the task of attempting to conciliate the parties.

The expert witness hears the parties and, upon their unanimous approval, can also examine records and books not exhibited for the case. Where the approval of the parties is not previously and unanimously given, the results of the examination cannot be mentioned by the expert witness in the minutes and report provided for by art 195.

Art 199 (*Minutes of conciliation*)—Where the parties came to a conciliation, a minute is drawn and signed by the parties and the expert witness and is enclosed in the litigation file. By decree, the examining magistrate gives binding effect of execution to the minute.

Art 200 (*Failure of conciliation*)—If conciliation between the parties does not succeed, the expert witness sets forth in a report the results of his enquiries and his opinion, and deposits it in the chancery of the court within the deadline fixed by the examining magistrate.

The statements of the parties recorded by the expert witness in his report can be taken into consideration by the judge according to art 116, para 2.

Art 201 (*Expert witness appointed by a party*)—With the same court writ appointing the court expert witness, the examining magistrate gives the parties a time limit to designate their own expert witnesses. The justice's clerk must be informed.

Pursuant to art 194, the expert witness appointed by the party is present at the enquiries carried out by the court expert witness and participates in the hearing and in chambers whenever the court expert witness does, in order to clarify and develop, with the leave of the court, his remarks concerning the results of the enquiries.

Art 259 (*Mode of inspection*)—The examining magistrate leads the inspection personally, and is supported, where needed, by an expert witness even where the inspection has to be done outside of the court's district, unless he cannot leave his court because of his duties. In such event the judge delegates the magistrate pursuant to article 203.

Art 260 (*Inspection of the body*)—The examining magistrate can abstain from taking part in inspection of the body and order the expert witness to carry it out by himself. During the inspection of the body all the precautions to guarantee the respect of the person shall be taken.

Art 261 (*Reproductions, copies and experiments*)—The examining judge can order execution models, mouldings, photographic and other reproductions of objects, documents and places, and, where needed, film, surveys or other requiring the use of mechanical means, instruments or procedures.

In order to ascertain whether or not an event did or could have happened in a certain way, the judge can order a re-enactment of the same event and, if necessary, execute a photographic or a film survey of it.

The judge directs the experiments and, if needed, entrusts the execution to an expert witness, who takes an oath according to art 193.

2. L.11/8/1973 N.533—DISCIPLINE ON INDIVIDUAL JOB DISPUTES AND ON SOCIAL SECURITY AND PUBLIC ASSISTANCE DISPUTES (MODIFYING TITLE IV, BOOK II OF THE CODE OF CIVIL PROCEDURE)

Section I
Job Disputes

Art 424 (*Assistance given by an expert witness*)—Where it is required by the nature of the dispute the judge, in any moment, appoints one or more expert witnesses, chosen from special directories in accordance with art 61. To this end, the judge can give directions in accordance with art 420, para 6.

The expert witness can be authorised to make a verbal report and in such case his statements are completely recorded in his minutes, except as provided for by the previous art 422.

Where the expert witness asks to a written report, the judge fixes a time limit not longer than 20 days, not subject to extension, and he adjourns the hearing.

Art 441 (*Expert witness in appeal*)—The trial judges, in the hearing described by art 437, para 1, can appoint an expert witness adjourning to the next hearing, which has to be fixed within the following 30 days. In this event, the trial judges by the same order can take steps in accordance with art 432. The expert witness has to deposit his opinions at least 10 days before the new hearing.

Section II
Social Security and Public Assistance Disputes

Art 445 (*Expert witness*)—In the proceedings, governed by this section, concerning claims for social security and assistancial services, which require technical assessment, the judge appoints one or more expert witnesses chosen from special directories in accordance with art 424. In cases of extreme complexity, the time limit provided for by art 424 can be extended up to 60 days.

4. PROVISIONS IMPLEMENTING THE CODE OF CIVIL PROCEDURE (CPC)

Section IV
Provisions Concerning Job, Social Security and Assistance Disputes

Art 145 (*Deadline to appoint the expert witness*)—In the disputes concerning job, social security and assistance matters, the deadline provided for by art 201 CPC cannot be longer than six days.

Art 146 (*Expert witnesses directory*)—There shall be included in the expert witnesses directory set up in any court, a list of forensic, employment and insurance doctors for proceedings concerning claims for social security and welfare services.

5. PROVISIONS IMPLEMENTING THE CODE OF CIVIL PROCEDURE AND TRANSITIONAL MEASURES

Art 5 (*Institution of a register*)—The register is kept by the Court of Appeal chief justice and it is created by a committee presided over by him and composed of the Public Prosecutor and of the residing judge of the court's division sitting as a labour tribunal.

The committee secretary position is held by the clerk of the court.

Art 13 (*Expert witnesses register*)—A register of expert witnesses shall be set up in every court. The register is divided into categories. The following categories must be always included in the directory:

(1) medical-surgical;
(2) industrial;
(3) commercial;
(4) agricultural;
(5) banking;
(6) insurance.

Art 14 (*Preparation of the register*)—The register is kept by the Chief Justice and is set up by a committee presided over by him and composed of the Public Prosecutor and of a professional registered in the expert witness register. Where appropriate, the above mentioned council can appoint a professional, registered in the directory of another association or other district, after notification to the council which holds the register to which the professional belongs.

Where the applications are submitted by surveyors, the appointment is done by the chamber of commerce, industry and agriculture. The committee secretary position is held by the clerk of the court.

Art 15 (*Entry in the Register*)—Those having specialist technical ability in specific matters, moral and [political] of good standing and registered in their own professional directories can successfully apply for registration.

Nobody can be registered in more than one directory. The committee mentioned above by art 14 decides on the applications for registration. The decision can be appealed to the committee provided for by art 15 within 15 days from the notification.

Art 16 (*Application for the registration*)—Persons who intend to be registered in the directory shall make applications to the Chief Justice.

The following documents must be enclosed with the application:

(1) a birth certificate extract
(2) a certificate of the court records and of the police files dated not earlier than three months before the application;
(3) a certificate of residence in the court district;
(4) a certificate of registration in the professional directory;
(5) the qualifications and documents which according to the opinion of the applicant can show his specialist technical ability.

Art 17 (*Information*)—The Chief Justice has the responsibility to ask the police authorities for specific and appropriate information about the political and civil conduct of the applicant.

Art 18 (*Revision of the register*)—The register is permanent. Every four years the committee referred to in art 14 has the duty to carry out a review of the register in order to remove from it those witnesses who do not meet anymore the requirements requested by art 15 or have an impediment to practise.

Art 19 (*Discipline*)—The supervision over the expert witnesses shall be carried out by the Chief Justice, who can promote, officially or on request made by the public prosecutor or by the chairman of the professional association, disciplinary proceedings against those expert witnesses who have failed to maintain moral (and political) good standing or to comply with the obligations which the appointments given would require. The committee referred to by art 14 is qualified to make disciplinary decisions.

Art 20 (*Disciplinary sanctions*)—The expert witness, who fails to comply with obligations indicated by previous article, can be punished with the following disciplinary sanctions:

(1) a formal warning;
(2) suspension from the register for a period no longer than one year;
(3) removal from the register;

Art 21 (*Disciplinary proceedings*)—Before starting the disciplinary proceedings, the Chief Justice charges the expert witness with the accusation and takes his written reply. Where the Chief Justice, after the charge has been made, intends to proceed, he summons the expert witness to appear before the disciplinary committee. After the expert witness has been heard the committee shall decide. The witness is entitled to challenge the measure on the basis of art 15, last para.

Art 22 (*Assignment of appointments*)—Any judge, whose office falls within the court district, has normally the duty to entrust those listed in the court register with the appointment as witness.

The examining judge who confers an appointment on an expert witness registered in the directory of another court or others not registered in any directory, has the duty to consult the Chief Justice and to explain by decree the reason of his choice.

The office of expert witness to the Court of Appeal is normally given to those listed in the court district registers. Where the office is given to persons listed in other registers or to persons not listed in any register the Chief Justice (higher in grade) must be heard and the reasons of the choice must be indicated.

Art 23 (*Supervision of the assignment of appointments*)—The Chief Justice makes sure that appointments are fairly distributed to those registered in the directory, without the justice the administration of justice running.

In order to carry out this supervision the Chief Justice requires the chancellor to maintain a list in all appointments to expert witnesses and the fees paid by each judge must be written.

The chancellor has the duty to inform the Chief Justice of the court where the expert witness is registered, about the assigned appointments and the fees paid.

The first President of the Court of Appeal carries out the supervision (provided for by para 1) concerning the assigned by that court.

Art 89 (*Order for appointments abstention or recusation of the expert witness*)—The order for abstention or recusation of the expert witness provided for by art 92 CPC is written at the foot of expert witness or party challenge.

The challenge and the order are included in the office dossier.

Art 90 (*Expert witness enquiries without the presence of the judge*)—The expert witness, who is authorised, in accordance with art 194 CPC, to make enquiries without the presence of the judge must inform the parties about the day the hour and the place the operations will be started, by notice enclosed with the minutes of the hearing or by notification from the chancellor.

The expert witness cannot receive documents of pleading other than those including observations and motions of the party, in accordance with art 194 CPC. In any case a copy of the documents of pleading are served on the adverse parties.

Art 91 (*Communications to the expert witnesses appointed by the party*)—In the declaration, referred to in art 201, para 1 CPC, must be indicated the domicile and the address of the expert witness appointed by the party.

The chancellor must give notice to the expert witness properly appointed by the party, about the enquiries scheduled by the court-appointed expert, in order to make it possible for the former to participate in accordance with arts 194 and 201 CPC.

Art 92 (*Disputes arising during the enquiries of the expert witness*)—Where, during the enquiries carried out by the expert witness himself, disputes arise concerning his powers or the limits of the appointment conferred on him, the expert witness shall inform the judge, unless the interested party does this by way of appeal. The appeal proposed by the party does not suspend the enquiries of the expert witness.

After the parties' hearing the judge takes the appropriate measures.

Art 150 (*Calculation of the inflation*)—For purposes of the calculation referred to by art 429, last para CPC, the judge applies the price index calculated by ISTAT for the index-linked pay scale of industrial workers.

6. PENAL CODE

Art 366 (*Refusal of compulsory services*)—Whoever, appointed expert or interpreter or custodian of goods under sequestration by order of a penal court, obtains through fraudulent means exemption from the duty to appear before the court or to provide his services, shall be punished by imprisonment up to six months or payment of a fine of Lire 60,000 to Lire 1,000,000. The same penalty applies to anyone who summoned to provide the above mentioned services, refuses to give his name and address, or to take or carry out the services referred.

The provisions set out above also apply to those summoned to testify as witness or to play any other role in the trial.

Where an expert or an interpreter is found guilty, the sentence implies the disqualification from their debarment of them.

Art 373 (*False expert opinion or interpretation*)—Where the expert appointed by the court gives false opinions or interpretations, or affirms facts not fitting the truth, the same punishment provided for by the previous article applies [imprisonment from two to six years in accordance with art 11, para 2, Act 7/8/1992 n.35].

The sentence implies both the prohibition from public offices and debarment from the profession.

11. L. 8/7/1980 N.319—FEES FOR EXPERTS, EXPERT WITNESSES, INTERPRETERS' AND TRANSLATORS' FEES FOR THE SERVICES PROVIDED ON REQUEST OF THE JUDICIAL AUTHORITIES

Art 1 (*Classification of the fees*)—Fees for experts, expert witnesses, interpreters' and translators' fees for the operations carried out by order of the judicial authorities and concerning both civil and penal matters are divided into remunerations and allowances. Remunerations can be fixed, variable or proportionate to time.

Art 2 (*Fixed and variable remunerations*)—The extent of fixed and variable remunerations is determined according to lists drawn up on the basis of the professional tariffs, concerning similar matters as appropriate, and adapted to the public nature of the appointment and approved by decree of the President of the Republic, on proposal of the Minister of Justice with the consent of the Minister of Treasury.

In order to determine the extent of a variable remuneration, the judge must take into consideration the difficulty of the enquiries and the comprehensiveness and value of the service.

Where, by reasoned decree, the judge requires an urgent performance and gives a deadline shorter than the ordinary one, fixed and variable remunerations can rise up to 20 per cent.

Art 3 (*Application of fixed and variable remuneration by analogy*)—Fixed and variable remunerations also apply to services similar to those expressly provided for by tariff lists.

Art 4 (*Remunerations measured in time*)—The remunerations concerning services which are not provided for by the tariff lists and which do not fall under the application of the previous article have to be proportionate to time and are determined according to the vacations.

The vacation is two hours long. The remuneration amounts to Lire 18,000 for the first vacation and to Lire 10,000 for the following ones.

The remuneration for the vacation can be doubled where the services have to be carried out within five days; it can be increased up to half where a time limit less than 15 days is given.

The remuneration for the vacation can be split in two, where one hour and a quarter has passed, the remuneration has to be paid in full.

The judge cannot settle more than four vacations per day for each appointment.

This restriction does not apply where the tasks are carried out in the presence of the judge: in this case the number of the variations must appear in the judicial acts and the hearing returns.

In compliance with art 455 RD 23/5/1924 n.827, the judge has the duty, at his personal liability, to calculate the number of the vacations to be paid with strict reference to the number of hours needed for the task to be carried out, independently from the deadline for filing the report or translation.

Art 5 (*Increase of the remunerations*)—Where the tasks to be carried out are extremely onerous, complex and difficult, remunerations can be increased up to double.

Art 6 (*Collective appointments*)—Where the task is given to several experts, expert witnesses, interpreters or translators as a body, the overall remuneration is determined on the basis of the payment due to only one expert or expert witness increased by the 40 per cent for each member of the panel, unless the judge ordered each delegate the personal and full execution of the appointment respectively assigned.

Art 7 (*Costs*)—Experts, expert witnesses and translators must submit a specific bill of the costs borne in order to carry out their tasks and enclose the corresponding documents.

The judge examines the costs incurred and excludes those considered not essential from refund.

Where experts and expert witnesses were authorised by the judge to have recourse to the co-operation of other professionals providing auxiliary services for the solution of the questions posed from the appointment, the costs concerned are determined on a scale in accordance with the criteria provided for by this Act and on the basis of the tariffs in force and of the local usages.

Where the auxiliary intellectual or technical job is independent from the task given to the expert or the expert witness, the judge gives the auxiliary himself a specific appointment.

Art 8 (*Duration of the appointment*)—Where the task given to the expert, expert witness, translator or interpreter is not completed within the original term or within that extended because of occurrence of fresh events which cannot be attributed to them, the vacations are determined by not taking into consideration the period following the expiry of the term and remunerations are reduced by the 25 per cent. The sanctions provided for by the Rules of Penal and Civil procedures apply.

Art 9 (*Allowance*)—Where the expert, the expert witness, the interpreter and the translator need to move away from their residence in order to carry out their task, Law 26/7/1978 n.417 applies, as a consequence, the expert, the expert witness, the interpreter and the translator holding a university degree or an equivalent title are made equal to the supervisory executive, and all the others to the executive post grade. Where the expert, expert witness, translator and interpreter are state employees, any possible larger allowance shall be maintained.

Even where no documentary evidence is given, travelling expenses are settled on the basis of first class fares means of transport regularly supplying a public service, other than by air.

Travelling expenses by air or special means of transport are refunded only where previously authorised by the judge and properly recorded.

Art 10 (*Periodical adjustment of remuneration*)—Every three years, by decree of the President of the Republic, on proposal of the Minister of Justice, with the consent of the Minister of Treasury, honorariums referred to by arts 2 and 4 can be modified in accordance with the change, ascertained by ISTAT, in the retail price index for workers' and employees' families as compared with three years previously.

Art 11 (*Settlement of remuneration and objections*)—By motivated decree, the judge or the state prosecutor orders payment of the remuneration to the expert, expert witness, interpreter and translator appointed by him.

The payment is sent to the expert, expert witness, interpreter, translator and to the parties.

In penal proceedings, the information is given by notice advising deposit of the decree in the chancery of the court; a copy of the payment order issued by the magistrate is also sent to the public prosecutor.

In civil proceedings, the payment order constitutes a provisional enforceable title against the party who is due to pay.

The expert, expert witness, interpreter, translator, state prosecutor and the private parties involved can appeal within 20 days from the information received against the payment order to the tribunal or to the Court of Appeal to which the judge belongs or in which the state prosecutor performs his duties or in the administrative district of the magistrate who issued the order.

The procedure is governed by art 29 L.13/6/1942, n.794.[5] Where serious reasons are given, the tribunal or the Court of Appeal, at the objector's request, can order by decree not subject to appeal the suspension of enforcement of payment order. The tribunal or the Court of Appeal can ask for all the acts, documents and information essential to the decision from the judge or the state prosecutor who provided for payment, or the legal office which holds them, except those covered by the obligation to maintain secrecy of disclosures in legal hearings.

Art 12 (*Temporary determination of remuneration*)—Until the decrees provided for by art 2 are issued, the remunerations of experts, expert witnesses, interpreters and translators' honorariums are determined in accordance with the provisions listed in art 4.

Art 13 (*Repeals*)—L.1/12/1956 n.1426 is repealed; art 23 RD 28/5/1931, n.602 which contains provisions implementing the Code of Penal Procedure, art 24 RD 18/12/1941, n.1368, which contains provisions implementing the Code of Civil Procedure and temporary rules, and any other provision not compatible to this Act are repealed.

Art 18—Expert or expert witness is due a remuneration from Lire 150,000 up to Lire 178,000 at the first exhibit for the opinion or the advice on the subject of explosives, weapons, bullets and similar. Where the exhibit is represented by a gun, cartridge cases and bullets are part of it.

Expert or expert witness is due an honorarium from Lire 119,000 to Lire 470,000 at the first exhibit for the opinion or advice on the subject of ballistics. Where the enquiry referred to by first and third paragraphs concerns several exhibits the honorarium for any following exhibit is reduced by 1/3 to 2/3.

Art 19—Expert or expert witness is due an honorarium from Lire 297,000 up to Lire 5,950,000 for the opinion or the advice on the subject of applied geomorphology, hydrogeology, applied geology and slopes stability.

Art 20—For the opinion on legal-medical matters immediately given in the hearing and placed on records, the expert is due the following honorariums, not subject to mutual conjunction:

legal-medical examination	Lire 24,000
corpse external inspection	Lire 24,000

post-mortem examination .... Lire 83,000
post-mortem examination on exhumed corpse .... Lire 119,000

Where the opinion cannot be immediately given and a written report is submitted, for the same tasks the expert is due an honorarium:

from Lire 59,000 to Lire 178,000 for legal-medical examinations
from Lire 143,000 to 476,000 for corpse assessment.

Art 21—The expert witness is due an honorarium from Lire 59,000 to Lire 357,000 for the advice concerning medical and diagnostic assessments and pathology identifications on humans.

Art 22—The expert or the expert witness is due a Lire 18,000 honorarium *per* sample for the opinion or advice concerning the alcohol test.

Art 23—The expert or expert witness is due a Lire 36,000 honorarium *per* sample for the opinion or advice concerning the enquiry of the carbossiemoglobinemico percentage.

Art 24—The expert or expert witness is due an honorarium from Lire 119,000 to Lire 476,000 for the opinion or advice on psychiatric or criminological matters.

Art 25—The expert or expert witness is due an honorarium from Lire 36,000 to Lire 357,000 for the opinion or advice concerning biological material or biological traces diagnosis or biological enquiries or evaluations on laboratory survey results. Where the exhibits or marquetry under examination are several, the honorarium for each of those following the first is reduced by 50 per cent.

Art 26—For the opinion or advice immediately given and placed on records concerning diagnostic assessment on animals, the expert or expert witness is due the following not subject to mutual conjunction honorariums:

clinical examination .... Lire 24,000
necroscopic examination .... Lire 83,000

Where the opinion cannot be immediately given and a written report is submitted, for the same tasks the expert or expert witness is due an honorarium:

from Lire 59,000 to Lire 178,000 for clinical examinations
from Lire 119,000 to 357,000 for necroscopic examinations.

In the case of infectious, epidemic or endemic, diseases which concerned more heads of the same flock, or herd, or breeding, honorariums referred to by the paragraphs set out above are doubled.

Art 27—For the toxicological opinion or advice on non-biological exhibit, the expert or the expert witness is due an honorarium from Lire 59,000 to Lire 178,000 *per* sample for the qualitative search of a substance, from Lire 83,000 to Lire 238,000 for the quantitative analysis.

Where the substances or samples under examination are more than one, the honorarium to be settled for each substance or following sample has to be reduced by 50 per cent.

Art 28—The expert or expert witness is due an honorarium from Lire 59,000 to Lire 178,000 for the chemical-toxicological opinion or advice, concerning the qualitative or quantitative complete general unknown search of the inorganic, volatile organic and non-volatile organic substances, and of pathogens.

The expert or expert witness is due an honorarium from Lire 59,000 to Lire 500,000 for the eco-toxicological opinion or advice directed to show the alterations and impurities of any substances or to identify the infecting, infesting and polluting pathogens. The expert or expert witness is due an honorarium from Lire 59,000 to Lire 595,000 for the opinion or advice on the subject of acoustic pollution.

Art 29—Unless it is differently provided for by these lists, all the honorariums are inclusive of: the report on the task results, the judicial acts examination, the participation to the hearings and of any other activity concerning the questions.

Acknowledgement is made to Studio Legale Internazionale Lombardo for providing a translation of the above Laws.

End Notes

1. Art 51 (Abstention of the judge)—The judge has the duty to abstain:
   (1) if he has an interest in the case concerned or in others for the same law issue;

(2) if the judge himself or his wife is relative up to fourth degree of kin, or is bound on the basis of an affiliation, or cohabits or is usual table companion of any of the parties or any of the lawyers;
(3) if the judge himself or his wife has a pending case or has a heavy animosity or is a creditor or a debtor of any of the parties or any of the lawyers;
(4) if he gave suggestions or assisted any of the parties in the case concerned, or testified as witness in it, or dealt with it as judge, or arbiter, or expert witness in a different instance of the trial;
(5) if he is the guardian, curator, proctor, agent or employer of any of the parties; if, moreover, he is manager of a corporation, of an unincorporated association, of a committee, of a company or a factory which is interested in the case.

In any other case when grave reasons of convenience are given, the judge may request to the head of the office the permission to abstain; where the abstention concerns the head of the office the permission shall be requested to the head of the office higher in grade.

2. Art 61, para 2, as it stands now, has been introduced by art 25, Act 4/6/1985, n.281, providing the Statute of the National Board for companies and stock exchange. The previous text was: "*In any case, where the expert witness who is liable of gross negligence for the execution of the services requested, is punished to pay a fine up to LIRE 20,000. Moreover, the expert witness has the duty to pay damages suffered by the parties.*"
3. The provision contained in this line has been introduced by art 14, Act 26/11/1990, n.353.
4. Para 3, line (4) has been repealed by art 14, Act 26/11/1990, n.353.
5. Art 29 (settlement procedure).

CHAPTER 1/19

THE EXPERT IN THE USA

CHAPTER 1/19A

THE LAW OF EXPERT WITNESSES IN THE UNITED STATES: PAST, PRESENT AND FUTURE

Professor Faust F Rossi

GENERALLY

001 The expert witness is a far more prominent figure in United States litigation than is the case in other nations. The explanation lies in several distinctive features of the American legal system.

002 First there is the adversary system which relies heavily on the parties and their attorneys to find, assemble, shape and present issues and facts. That means that testifying experts are sought out, hired, briefed, presented and paid by the parties themselves. Any time a litigant believes his case will be aided by presenting an expert, he is likely to seek one out if it is economically feasible. If one side in litigation uses an expert on an issue, the other party is likely to reciprocate by finding an opposing expert. In complicated multi-issue litigation, it is not unusual to have as many as six experts on each side. There is no difficulty in finding experts since in most cases the compensation is substantial and private companies exist to provide specialists on demand in a wide variety of disciplines. Although trial judges have the power to appoint neutral experts, most judges are reluctant to substitute their choice for that of the parties.

003 Another consideration is the prevalence of litigation in the United States. Easy access to the court system, coupled with laws that encourage enforcement of substantive rights by private litigation, present many occasions for the use of expert testimony. An active, aggressive and innovative bar, fuelled in part by contingent fees, is adept at pursuing remedies in a wide range of cases. As a result, American courts are required to handle a plethora of sophisticated technical issues in cases involving toxic torts, products liability, malpractice, discrimination, antitrust violations, securities fraud and environmental damage. In many of these cases, testimony by experts is essential because it is legally required if the plaintiff is to meet its burden of presenting sufficient evidence to allow the action to be decided by the jury.

004 An added factor which affects the use of experts is the enormous role played by lay juries as triers of fact. No matter how complex the issues, the litigants have a constitutional right to a jury trial in most cases. The need for experts to explain, simplify and clarify technical issues is likely to be more important when the fact-finder is a lay jury rather than a trained judge who may have had prior experience with the issues presented. Indeed, one of the concerns about the prevalent use of experts is the fear that lay jurors may abdicate their role as fact-finders and give undue weight to the opinions of testifying experts. For this reason, one of the most difficult roles of the trial judge is to filter out unreliable expertise by finding it inadmissible. Much of the uncertainty over evidence rules governing expert testimony concerns the extent of the judge's gatekeeper role. How much scrutiny should the trial judge apply in assessing the admissibility of the expert opinion? If there are defects in the data underlying the opinion or in the methodology used by a qualified expert, should the judge exclude the opinion or admit it and leave it for the jury to assess?

005 This article describes the law of expert testimony as it has developed in the United States during the last 40 years. Two major sources have shaped evidence law governing experts. The first was the adoption by Congress of the Federal Rules of Evidence in 1975. These rules govern evidence in federal courts. However, they have been copied in the individual state courts and now represent mainstream American evidence law. These rules represent a substantial loosening of earlier restrictions on expert witnesses and they ushered in a period of expanded admissibility. The second significant legal authority is the United States Supreme Court decision in *Daubert* v. *Merrell Dow Pharmaceuticals, Inc*, in which the court for the first time laid out principles governing the admissibility of scientific evidence. The *Daubert* decision, although concerned with expertise of a scientific nature, has had a major restraining effect on all forms of expert testimony. The focus of the discussion is on these two major sources of United States law.

006 Over the last 40 years, the law of expert testimony has undergone three periods of development. First came the era of liberality in admitting expert opinions which was fashioned by adoption of the Federal Rules of Evidence and modern state evidence codes patterned on these rules. Next came a short period of strict scrutiny or backlash against liberal admissibility. Courts began to retreat from expansive acceptance of expertise; especially in toxic tort and pharmaceutical drug products liability cases. Now we are in a third stage of development that resulted from the United States Supreme Court decision in *Daubert* v. *Merrell Dow Pharmaceuticals, Inc* 509 US 579 (1993), an opinion which has had a profound effect on many aspects of expert testimony. This current stage may be called an era of uncertainty as courts work through the impact, effect and scope of the *Daubert* case. The text which follows discusses each of the three stages of development in the courts of the United States.

007 Before undertaking a discussion of the law regarding experts in United States courts, some mention should be made about experts in arbitration. The use of expert testimony in arbitration proceedings in the United States is not appreciably different from procedures utilised in most other countries. Two basic principles apply. First, the arbitration agreement, to the extent that it specifies procedures, controls the process. Secondly, unless otherwise provided in the agreement or submission, formal rules of evidence do not apply. This is not to say that exclusionary evidence rules are totally irrelevant to the proceedings. The policies underlying court rules of evidence are considered by the arbitrator in assessing the weight of the evidence. Thus, the arbitrator may admit hearsay in the form of affidavits and reports. Nevertheless, the arbitrator may find this hearsay unpersuasive in the face of more direct live testimony which has been subject to cross-examination.

008 Since most agreements do not require the parties to follow formal rules of evidence, experts in arbitration proceedings may be used in situations that would not be permitted in court litigation. So, for example, experts can be used to opine in areas that could not be the subjects of expert opinion in federal courts. Thus, experts in arbitration can give opinions on matters of law and on whether remedies beyond those available in courts of law can resolve the dispute. The expert's evidence may be received in ways that would not be permitted in formal litigation. Written expert reports may be admitted. The arbitrator may have competing experts testify simultaneously in a conference mode with witnesses directing questions to each other in an effort to jointly resolve disputed issues.

009 Unless otherwise provided in the arbitration agreement, pre-hearing discovery of experts is either non-existent or severely limited. This is a major difference between arbitration and federal court procedure. In the federal courts of the United States, rule 26 of the Federal Rules of Procedure provides for elaborate and expensive pre-trial discovery of a testifying expert. The expert must supply the opposing party with a complete written report of

> "all opinions to be expressed and the basis and reasons therefor; the data or other information considered by the witness in forming the opinions; any exhibits to be used as a summary of or support for the opinions; the qualifications of the witness, including a list of all publications authored by the witness within the preceding ten years; the compensation to be paid for the study and testimony; and a listing of any other cases in which the witness has testified as an expert at trial or by deposition within the preceding four years".

The report must be signed by the expert and submission of the report will usually be followed by an oral pre-trial deposition at which the expert will be questioned at length by opposing counsel. Arbitration avoids these burdensome procedures. It allows experts to be used in more creative, flexible and less costly ways than is possible in the law courts.

THE ERA OF LIBERAL ADMISSIBILITY

010 One of the most significant developments in evidence law has been the acceptance that has been accorded expert opinion testimony under modern codes of evidence. Evidence Rules 702–705 laid the groundwork for expanded admissibility. Decisions interpreting the rules and codes within the last 20 years emphasise the presumption in favour of expert testimony. Longstanding doctrinal barriers have evaporated. As a result, the litigator's options in selecting, using and presenting lay and expert opinion have increased manyfold.

011 The rules favouring admissibility operate on several levels. When a qualified expert seeks to give an opinion related to his expertise, there are three essential questions.

1. About what can the expert testify?—the subject matter question.
2. Upon what kinds of facts must the opinion be grounded?—the proper basis requirement.
3. How, or in what form, is the opinion to be given?—the inquiry into foundation formalities.

012 Modern rules have eased restrictions in each of these areas. The test for determining what subject matter is appropriate for expert testimony has been liberalised. The permissible basis for expert opinion has been expanded. And traditional foundation formalities restricting the manner of presentation have been eliminated. We consider each of these developments in turn.

Appropriate subject matter

013 What subject matter is appropriate for expert testimony? The traditional requirements were two. The expertise must concern matters sufficiently complex as to be beyond the ken of the ordinary lay person. Yet it cannot be so complex, novel or speculative as to be outside the scope of general acceptance within its recognised scientific or professional sphere.

014 A frequently litigated fact pattern demonstrates both aspects. The accused is identified as the culprit by several prosecution witnesses. In rebuttal, the defence calls a cognitive psychologist, an expert in the field of human perception and memory. She seeks to explain the dangers, the problems and the inherent unreliability of eyewitness identifications. Should this evidence be received? Courts divide in result but agree on the issues presented.

015 The first concern is that such testimony is not sufficiently beyond the ken of ordinary jurors. It seeks to apply a body of specialised knowledge to a problem that lay people are accustomed to dealing with. It involves an assessment of the credibility and reliability of testifying eyewitnesses—matters which are arguably well within common experience and, therefore, not a fit subject for expert testimony.

016 The second concern attacks the reliability of the expertise itself. Some would exclude it on the ground that there is not a reliable scientific basis for this kind of testimony. They argue that the field of eyewitness identification has not been sufficiently established as a science. The claim is that studies which question the accuracy of eyewitness identification do not have "general acceptance in the scientific community".

017 Modern evidence codes have affected both these limitations on the scope of expert testimony. For example Federal Rule of Evidence 702 provides that: "If scientific, technical, or other specialised knowledge will assist the trier of fact to understand the evidence or to determine a fact in issue, a witness qualified as an expert by knowledge, skill, experience, training, or education, may testify thereto in the form of an opinion or otherwise."

018 The "beyond the ken of the ordinary juror" standard has all but disappeared. The criterion of "general acceptance" as the sole test of the reliability of expertise is fading.

Elimination of beyond the ken standard: helpfulness is enough

019 Before the enactment of modern evidence codes, expert testimony was admissible only if its subject matter was "so distinctively related to some science, profession, business or occupation as to be beyond the ken of laymen" (*McCormick on Evidence* § 13, p.13 (3rd ed. 1984)). The touchstone was necessity. Only if the testimony was necessary to enable the jury to understand the issue would the expert's opinion be admitted.

020 Federal Rule 702 provides a one sentence definition of when expert testimony is appropriate. It imposes no requirement that the matter be beyond lay comprehension. Helpfulness is the modern touchstone. If the expert's opinion "will assist the trier of fact to understand the evidence or to determine a fact in issue" the subject matter is appropriate.

021 The Third Circuit has joined many other courts and commentators in adopting this liberalised standard. *In re Japanese Electronic Products Antitrust Litigation* 723 F.2d 238 (3d Cir. 1983) reversed on other grounds *sub nom, Matsushita Electric Industrial Co, Ltd* v. *Zenith Radio Corp*, 475 US 574; 106 S.Ct. 1348; 89 L.Ed.2d 538 (1986) involved a massive antitrust action brought by Zenith Radio Corporation and other American companies against major Japanese manufacturers of consumer electronic products. One of the many evidentiary issues was the admissibility of opinions by the plaintiff's economist. The expert based his conclusion largely on the plaintiff's own litigation documents and sought to give his opinion that the defendants had conspired to violate antitrust laws. The district court found that this kind of opinion did not involve any special economic expertise. The expert was doing exactly what the jury is supposed to do—sift through materials provided by the plaintiffs, analyse them factually and reach conclusions regarding culpability. Characterising the expert as no more than an "oath helper", the court rejected the opinion saying that it added an unwarranted aura of scientific reliability and that it was not "beyond the jury's sphere of knowledge".

022 The Court of Appeals found that the lower court had taken too narrow a view of the appropriateness of the expert testimony. The Third Circuit put it this way: "The requirement . . . that expert testimony be 'beyond the jury's sphere of knowledge' adopts a formulation which was rejected by drafters of Rule 702: While that formulation applied prior to the adoption of evidence rules, it no longer applies. Such a test is incompatible with the standard of helpfulness." The court went on to embrace a "presumption that expert testimony will be helpful", a presumption founded on case law favouring admissibility under Rule 702: *In re Japanese Electronic Products Antitrust Litigation* 723 F.2d 238, 279–280 (3d Cir. 1983) reversed on other grounds *sub nom*, *Matsushita Electric Industrial Co, Ltd* v. *Zenith Radio Corp*, 475 US 574; 106 S.Ct. 1348; 89 L.Ed.2d 538 (1986).

023 The point being made is that even when jurors are well equipped to decide a matter based on their experience, an expert still may have specialised knowledge bearing on that same matter which would be helpful. Such an expert should be heard. Trial judges, operating in an area of abundant discretion, now welcome expert assistance which, before evidence codification, would have been rejected as an invasion of the jury function.

024 *United States* v. *Roark* 753 F.2d 991 (11th Cir. 1985) is a case in point. The accused confessed to authorities that, while working as a bank teller, she participated in stealing money from her employer. The confession was offered by the government and duly received in evidence. At this point the defence offered an expert psychological witness to testify in support of the accused's claim that her admissions were involuntary. The psychiatrist sought to testify that the defendant was extremely susceptible to suggestion, that the conditions of her interrogation made it likely she would create stories to please her questioners and that she would "have to comply" with suggestions put forth by authority figures. All this was too much for the trial court. The judge saw it as an issue of who to believe—a credibility choice for the jury and, therefore, a matter on which the expert could provide no assistance. The Eleventh Circuit reversed and held that the expert's testimony should be received since it would help the jury determine the weight to be given to the defendant's incriminating statements.

025 Similar examples of liberalised treatment of experts are easy to find. *United States* v. *Barrett* 703 F.2d 1076 (9th Cir. 1983) involved a bank robbery prosecution in which identity was an issue. A surveillance photograph of the robber was in evidence along with clothes seized from the defendant. The jury was fully competent to view the clothes worn by the robber in the photograph and compare them with those which belonged to the defendant. Nevertheless, the government's photographic expert was allowed to point out similarities in the two pieces of evidence and conclude that the clothes were the same.

026 Abandonment of the traditional "beyond the ken" limitation is eroding judicial hostility to expert testimony that does no more than sharpen the jury's commonsense evaluation of the evidence. So, for example, *Holiday Inns, Inc* v. *Shelburne* 576 So.2d 322 (Fla.Dist.Ct.App.), review dismissed, 589 So.2d 291 (Fla.Sup.Ct. 1991), an expert on "grief and bereavement" was allowed to explain to the jury the nature of the parents' grief in response to their son's death; a matter that everyone would think was well within the experience of jurors.

027 The approach of many of these decisions makes it clear that even if jurors have knowledge of the subject area, that knowledge can be deepened by the expert.

The "general acceptance" standard: Frye v. *United States*

028 One of the traditional subject matter barriers, the "beyond the ken" hurdle, has been destroyed by evidence codification. But there is another; a barrier that has been weakened but that still survives in some state jurisdictions. It requires that the subject matter of expert testimony be of a type generally accepted within its recognised professional sphere. It applies specially to scientific evidence. The American commitment to science and technology over the last generation has forced courts to rule on the admissibility of many new discoveries or applications from the sciences. Thus, this limitation takes on special importance in modern litigation.

HISTORY AND DEVELOPMENT OF THE FRYE "GENERAL ACCEPTANCE" TEST

029 How should a court react when it is presented with a novel form of expertise which has not yet been judicially recognised as a proper subject for expert testimony in the jurisdiction? With caution, is the traditional answer. For many years courts encountering this problem applied the well known *Frye* standard. Derived from language in *Frye* v. *United States* 293 F.2d 1013, 1014 (DC Cir. 1923) the test is whether the process, system or theory upon which the evidence is based is "sufficiently established to have gained general acceptance in the particular field in which it belongs".

030 The *Frye* or "general acceptance" test is a restrictive standard for admissibility of scientific evidence. It means that even if the trial judge believes that some novel form of expertise is reliable enough to be heard by the jury, the court must exclude it if the scientific community has not yet developed a consensus on its accuracy. This test has been used at various times and in various courts to exclude polygraph test results, voiceprints, DNA evidence and its statistical calculations, hypnotically enhanced testimony, opinions on the unreliability of eyewitness identification and many other kinds of scientific opinion or tests. Historically, the *Frye* standard has been applied almost exclusively in criminal cases. In one sense it served as an added protection for the accused. Since many new scientific developments were developed by law enforcement agencies and since defendants often lacked the resources to assess accuracy of government tests, the conservative *Frye* standard assures the accused that only the most reliable scientific expertise will be used against him.

RISING CRITICISM OF THE FRYE "GENERAL ACCEPTANCE" TEST

031 At one time, *Frye* was applied in criminal cases in almost all federal and state courts. However, in the last 20 years, the *Frye* standard has been criticised for

(1) being too conservative and keeping out too much helpful expertise;
(2) assuming more definiteness in science than actually exists;
(3) the "general acceptance" standard is too vague; and
(4) the inability to define the particular field or discipline in which "general acceptance" should exist renders the test ineffective.

As a result, many states began to abandon the *Frye* standard. Today the federal courts and about half the states have rejected this "general acceptance" test. Ironically, just as *Frye* began to be abandoned in the criminal cases where it was born, some courts began to apply it in civil cases as a means of controlling speculative expertise in complicated toxic tort or pharmaceutical products liability cases.

Rejection of the Frye "general acceptance" standard in federal courts—the Supreme Court decision in Daubert

032 Federal Rule 702 says nothing about general acceptance or the *Frye* test. Does this case law doctrine survive enactment of the Federal Rules of Evidence? Until recently, this question plagued the federal courts and led to a sharp conflict in the lower courts. The United States Supreme Court has now put to rest the controversy over whether *Frye* should apply in federal courts.

033 *Daubert* v. *Merrell Dow Pharmaceuticals, Inc* 509 US 579; 113 S.Ct. 2786; 125 L.Ed.2d 469 (1993), rejected the 70-year-old "general acceptance" test on the ground that this rigid admissibility test was at odds with the "liberal thrust of the Federal Rules of Evidence" and "their general approach of relaxing traditional barriers to opinion testimony". The court noted that Federal Rule 702 speaks specifically to the issue of admissibility of expert testimony. That specific rule makes no mention of "general acceptance". *Frye* made "general acceptance" the exclusive test. "That austere standard," said the court, "absent from and incompatible with the Federal Rules of Evidence, should not be applied in Federal trials."

034 *Daubert* is a non-constitutional interpretation of Federal Rule 702. As such, it has no direct effect on states that adhere to *Frye*. Since the Supreme Court's decision in *Daubert*, several state courts have adhered to the *Frye* standard. New York, California and Illinois, among others, continue to adhere to *Frye*. Nonetheless, the trend in the states continues to be one of erosion.

The basis for expert testimony

035 Consider the second significant issue—the permissible foundation for expert testimony. Upon what kinds of facts must the opinion be grounded? What constitutes a proper basis for expert opinion?

036 Here, too, changes wrought by the federal rules and modern codes enhance the power of the expert. In this instance the change is explicit. Federal Rule 703 and similar state provisions expressly expand the permissible basis for expert opinion.

037 Rule 703 provides:

> "The facts or data in the particular case upon which an expert bases an opinion or inference may be those perceived by or made known to the expert at or before the hearing. If of a type reasonably relied upon by experts in the particular field in forming opinions or inferences upon the subject, the facts or data need not be admissible in evidence."

038 Pre-codification law required that an expert's opinion be based upon one or both of two possible sources of information. One acceptable basis consisted of facts which the expert knew from first hand observation. The other acceptable basis included facts which the expert did not know but which facts were supplied to him in court by the evidence, usually through use of the hypothetical question. The data underlying an opinion had to be in the record or personally known to the witness.

039 Rule 703 accepts these standard foundations but adds a third acceptable basis. It provides that an expert may base an opinion on facts presented to him before trial. It states further that "if of a type reasonably relied upon by experts in the particular field . . . the facts or data need not be admissible in evidence". In other words, the expert now may base an opinion upon facts which he does not personally know. He may base his opinion on facts which are not in evidence. Indeed he may base his conclusion on facts which would not be admissible even if offered. The sole requirement is that these facts be of a type "reasonably relied upon" by experts in his field in making out-of-court professional decisions.

040 Thus the expert opinion may rely upon data or documents which constitute inadmissible hearsay or which violate other exclusionary rules as long as the reliance is reasonable.

041 Judicial acceptance of expertise based on non-evidence facts and inadmissible data has been enthusiastic.Thus, in *United States* v. *Gresham* 118 F.3d 258 (5th Cir. 1997), alcohol, tobacco and firearms experts were allowed to conclude that explosives were made outside the State of Texas to show the bomb had moved in interstate commerce—an essential predicate for federal jurisdiction. The opinions were based upon discussions with manufacturers, corporate literature, AFT reference materials, distinctive markings and their law enforcement experience. Similarly, in *Mannino* v. *International Mfg Co* 650 F.2d 846 (6th Cir. 1981) was a suit alleging defects in design of an infant car seat. The plaintiff's expert offered opinions based in part upon "literature and information furnished by the plaintiff's attorney", upon "a seminar sponsored by General Motors", upon "papers on automobile accidents prepared by the Society of Automotive Engineers", and upon "a whole body of literature in the area of bio-mechanics". The trial court excluded the opinion finding its basis improper. The Sixth Circuit reversed. The fact that much of the basis was hearsay which could not be admitted was irrelevant. The underlying data was proper since it was the type of material that experts often rely upon in forming opinions. The court concluded by saying that "great liberality is allowed the expert in determining the basis of his opinions under Rule 703", 650 F.2d at 853.

What is "reasonable reliance" and who decides?

042 If an expert may rely upon media accounts, library research and other inadmissible hearsay, the obvious question is: what are the limits of "reasonable reliance"? If experts of a particular type normally and customarily rely upon certain data in making determinations, is that *per se* "reasonable reliance"?

043 The answer turns on another question. Who determines whether the expert's reliance is reasonable? Do we leave it to the experts or does the judge have a say?

044 Some courts give the trial judge an independent controlling role. A finding that the expert and others in his field regularly rely and act upon certain sources in their working lives is influential but not binding on the court. The reliance may be customary but it is for the judge to decide whether the custom is reasonable.

045 This approach is consistent with the language of Rule 703 which speaks of data "reasonably" not "commonly" relied upon.

046 The assumption that Rule 703 requires application of a separate judicial standard to determine reasonable reliance was expressly and elaborately repudiated by an early Third Circuit case of *In re Japanese Electronic Products Antitrust Litigation* 723 F.2d 238 (3d Cir. 1983) reversed on other grounds *sub nom Matsushita Electric Industrial Co Ltd* v. *Zenith Radio Corp* 475 US 574; 106 S.Ct. 1348; 89 L.Ed.2d 538 (1986).

047 The massive *Japanese Electronics Antitrust* action dealt squarely with the issue. The defendant Japanese manufacturers moved for summary judgment claiming that much of the documentary evidence relied on by the plaintiffs to establish an alleged conspiracy was inadmissible. The trial court agreed that many of the documents were hearsay and insufficiently trustworthy to qualify as business or public records. The court then turned its attention to the expert opinions offered by the plaintiffs. The plaintiffs' experts relied upon many of the very materials which had already been found inadmissible. Judge Becker excluded the opinions on a finding that experts could not reasonably rely on materials inadmissible because of untrustworthiness. Summary judgment for the defendants was granted.

048 It made no difference that uncontested affidavits from the plaintiff's experts proclaimed that the data upon which they relied was of a type generally relied upon by experts in their fields. Instead, the court developed its own set of judicial standards for determining whether the experts' customary reliance was reasonable. Judge Becker assumed that trustworthiness is an independent factor which Rule 703 requires the judge to verify before the expert's opinion may pass the threshold of admissibility. *Zenith Radio Corp* v. *Matsushita Elec Indus Co* 505 F.Supp. 1190, 1325–1330 (E.D. Pa. 1980).

049 For three years the decision was hailed by many as a well-reasoned opinion setting forth the role of the trial judge in controlling expert testimony. Then the Third Circuit reversed.

050 The Court of Appeals rejected the notion of an independent judicial test of reasonable reliance. "The proper inquiry is not what the court deems reliable, but what experts in the relevant discipline deem it to be." The Third Circuit went on to say that "In substituting its own opinion as to what constitutes reasonable reliance for that of the experts in the relevant fields the trial court misinterpreted Rule 703." The Court of Appeals explained that the rule was intended to broaden the basis for expert opinions by focusing on what *experts* deem reliable. Therefore, once the court finds that the data is such that experts in the field rely upon it, the test of Rule 703 is met and concerns about trustworthiness are left to exploration by cross-examination. *In re Japanese Electronic Products Antitrust Litigation* 723 F.2d 238, 276–278 (3d Cir. 1983) reversed on other grounds *sub nom, Matsushita Electric Industrial Co Ltd* v. *Zenith Radio Corp* 475 US 574; 106 S.Ct. 1348; 89 L.Ed.2d 538 (1986).

051 Then, in 1993, the United States Supreme Court decided in *Daubert* v. *Merrell Dow Pharmaceuticals Inc* 509 US 579; 113 S.Ct. 2786 (1993) that the trial judge must perform a "gatekeeper" function and must assure, as a condition of admissibility, that the scientific methodology upon which the expert opinion is founded is scientifically valid. In other words, the expert's conclusions must be based upon "good grounds". In a subsequent decision following *Daubert*, a Third Circuit panel abandoned its position in *In re Japanese Electronics Products Antitrust Litigation* and concluded that "the principal arbiters of the reasonableness of reliance [under Rule 703] are the trial judges and not the experts".

052 *In re Paoli R R Yard PCB Litigation* 35 F.3d 717 (3d Cir. 1994), *cert. denied sub nom, General Elec Co* v. *Ingram* 513 US 1190 (1995) held that the precept that "the proper inquiry is not what the court deems reliable but what experts in the relevant discipline deem it to be" could not survive *Daubert*. The Third Circuit panel now takes the position that:

> "Our former view is no longer tenable in view of *Daubert* . . . *Daubert* makes clear for the first time at the Supreme Court level that courts have to play a gatekeeping role with regard to experts. . . . By requiring the judge to look to the views of other experts rather than allowing the judge to exercise independent judgment, current Third Circuit case law eviscerates the judge's gatekeeping role with respect to an expert's data and instead gives that role to other experts. . . .
>
> We now make clear that it is the judge who makes the determination of reasonable reliance, and that for the judge to make the factual determination under Rule 104(a) that an expert is basing his or her opinion on a type of data reasonably relied upon by experts, the judge must conduct an independent evaluation into reasonableness. The judge can of course take into account the

particular expert's opinion that experts reasonably rely on that type of data, as well as the opinions of other experts as to its reliability, but the judge can also take into account other factors he or she deems relevant."

Is the basis admissible? A back door exception to the exclusionary rules?

053 There is another issue which further enhances the power of the expert. We have seen that courts are generous in allowing opinions based upon otherwise inadmissible evidence. The opinion comes in. May the inadmissible data supporting it also come in? The expert, having reasonably relied upon inadmissible hearsay, is allowed to give his opinion. May he now go further and describe the hearsay basis during direct examination?

054 Rule 703 says nothing on this point. Nor is Rule 705 helpful. It allows the expert to express an opinion on direct examination without necessarily disclosing the basis. But our concern is not with the expert who gives an opinion and says little else. We treat the usual situation of the expert who wants to fully and completely describe the facts, including inadmissible ones, which underlie his opinion. On this question the rules give no answer.

055 Common litigation sense suggests that if an expert gives an opinion, he should be allowed to explain how and why he arrived at it. A full explanation of the basis for the opinion in the usual case allows the jury to effectively assess the validity of the expert's conclusions.

056 The cases, especially in recent years, also approve disclosure on direct examination of the expert witness. In *American Universal Ins Co* v. *Falzone* 644 F.2d 65 (1st Cir. 1981), the fire marshall testified that the fire was of human origin. He based his opinion in part upon statements by his co-workers that they had found no difficulties with an oil burner on the premises. During the marshall's direct examination he not only gave his opinion, he recited the basis for it and over objection described his conversations with his colleagues. The First Circuit found no fault with this procedure. The same conclusion was reached by the Fifth Circuit when it said, "Rules 703 and 705 codify the approach of this and other circuits that permits disclosure of otherwise hearsay evidence for the purpose of illustrating the basis for the expert witness' opinion": *Bryan* v. *John Bean Div of FMC Corp* 566 F.2d 541 (5th Cir. 1978).

057 The issue was recently raised in one of the Bendectin cases. In *Wilson by and through Wilson* v. *Merrell Dow Pharmaceuticals* 893 F.2d 1149 (10th Cir. 1990), the plaintiff alleged that her son's birth defects resulted from her taking Bendectin for morning sickness. Dr Goddard, formerly with the Food and Drug Administration (FDA), testified that from 1980 to 1984, Bendectin sales increased for a time and then decreased to zero; that during this period of fluctuating sales, the rate of limb defects remained "remarkably constant". The expert therefore concluded that Bendectin does not cause birth defects in general or limb reduction defects in particular. Dr Goddard based his figures and his opinion on a chart which he had prepared comparing the rate of sales and the number of limb defects. The defendant's epidemiological expert, Dr Lamm, also testified and based his opinion on a chart comparing sales and defects from 1970 to 1984. Both experts compiled their charts from information they obtained from various drug companies and from the Federal Center for Disease Control. The charts upon which the experts relied were admitted into evidence.

058 The issue was explored in an Arizona state case. In *State* v. *Lundstrom* 161 Ariz. 141; 776 P.2d 1067 (1989), the defendant was convicted of manslaughter for killing his wife. At trial, his defence was that he was suffering from "a brief reactive psychosis", a form of insanity. This defence was offered through the testimony of Bayless, an expert psychologist who was permitted to give his opinion. On direct examination, the defence expert, Bayless, testified that his practice was to consult with physicians and other psychologists when evaluating patients; that he had discussed the defendant's condition with one Dr Garcia, the chief psychiatrist at the correctional facility where the defendant was imprisoned after the killing; and that in reaching his opinion, Bayless relied in part on the fact that Garcia "substantiated" his opinion that the defendant "had suffered a loss of contact with reality". The trial court refused, however, to allow the defence expert witness to recite what Dr Garcia (who did not testify) had told the defence expert about the defendant. On appeal, the defendant's conviction was reversed. In a well-reasoned opinion, the Arizona Supreme Court held that the defence expert witness, Bayless, should have been permitted to explain that Garcia's opinion was the same as his and, moreover, should have been permitted to state the content of Garcia's opinion. The court stated at 161 Ariz. 147; 776 P.2d 1073:

> "One objective of the expert opinion rules is to conform court practice to reality . . . Experts in all professions sometimes rely on the opinions of other experts. In the real world, the surgeon at the operating table may rely on the nurse's report of the pathologist's opinion of the frozen section of tissue before deciding on the type of procedure necessary to complete the surgery. Surely, then, the doctor in the courtroom may rely on his colleagues' opinions in completing his trial testimony. Triers of fact must have foundational information to assess adequately the weight to be given an expert opinion. We agree that under most circumstances an expert may testify as to the substance of another expert's opinion if the testifying expert reasonably relied on that other opinion in forming his own opinion.
>
> The fact that Garcia's diagnosis either paralleled or diverged from Bayless's is crucial. Garcia saw, observed, and evaluated Lundstrom at the county jail the day after the shooting and assigned him to a psychiatric ward. Bayless, retained as an expert long after the event, was subject to attack on the retrospective nature of his opinion. Thus, on cross-examination, when the prosecutor challenged Bayless's high degree of certainty about his diagnosis, Bayless properly invoked Garcia's concurrence as support for that certainty.
>
> Moreover, to reveal the substance of Garcia's opinion is not to reveal hearsay. Facts or data underlying the testifying expert's opinion are admissible for the limited purpose of showing the bases of that opinion, not to prove the truth of the matter asserted. Thus Bayless's testimony that Garcia concurred in his diagnosis was not evidence that Lundstrom was insane, but only a partial basis for Bayless's opinion."

059 The court in *Lundstrom* recognised the risks in its position. It noted at 161 Ariz. 148; 776 P.2d 1074 that:

> "We note the dangers lurking in our interpretation of Rule 703 and we add, therefore, that the right to disclose the bases of an expert opinion on direct examination is not absolute. Under Rule 403, a trial court may weigh the value of admitting the facts or data sought to be disclosed as a basis of an expert opinion against the dangers of unfair prejudice arising from such disclosure. The record does not indicate the trial judge precluded Bayless's references pursuant to the balancing test found in Rule 403. Nor apparently was he asked to do so. Instead, the trial judge appears to have enunciated an unyielding rule of law.
>
> We caution also that if the testifying expert merely acts as a conduit for another non-testifying expert's opinion, the 'expert opinion' is hearsay and is inadmissible, Rule 703 notwithstanding. See also *United States* v. *Williams*, 431 F.2d 1168, 1172 (5th Cir. 1970) (applying pre-Rule 703 law, an expert who consults and merely summarises the content of a hearsay source without applying his own expertise is merely a hearsay witness)."

060 Finally, the *Lundstrom* court observed that "this was not a case in which an expert is retained, reaches an opinion, and then commences an expedition to look for and invite the opinions of other experts who may reinforce his position" *Id.* at 161 Ariz. 148; 776 P.2d 1074.

061 Many have called Rule 703 a "back door exception" to hearsay and other exclusionary rules. This overstates it a bit. So far, the decisions make clear that the hearsay or other inadmissible data is admitted only to explain the opinion and not as substantive evidence. There is no express hearsay exception authorising receipt of "data underlying expert opinion". So courts generally admit such data for the limited purpose of supporting the expert's conclusion and not for the truth of any statements or reports which constitute sources for the opinion.

062 The subtlety of this distinction is likely to escape the trier of fact. The proponent who lays underlying facts before the jury is not likely to fear a limiting instruction. Indeed, a skilful advocate may not have to tolerate even this limitation. There are, after all, good arguments for full substantive admissibility of the hearsay basis.

063 Guarantees of reliability exist by definition since experts in the field rely on this kind of data. Moreover, the expert is present in court, subject to cross-examination and available to analyse and interpret the underlying data. Taken together these reliability factors may be sufficient to qualify the hearsay basis as admissible under the residual hearsay exceptions embodied in Federal Evidence Rule 807 which admits hearsay which the trial court in its discretion deems to be reliable even though it does not fit into one of the traditional exceptions.

064 No one suggests that an expert can recite the contents of inadmissible sources in every instance. In some situations full exploration of the basis would create sufficient prejudice to justify exclusion under Federal Evidence Rule 403 which excludes evidence when its probative value is substantially outweighed "by the danger of unfair prejudice or confusion of the issues".

Elimination of foundation formalities

065 It remains to consider our third and final question. How and in what form may the expert testify? Here again the expert has been liberated; this time by removal of restrictions on the form and manner in which expertise may be presented.

Abandonment of the ultimate issue prohibition: Rule 704

066 A favourite limitation of the older cases was the well known but frequently disregarded "ultimate opinion" rule. It was common to prohibit the expert from testifying directly about the ultimate issue to be decided on the now discredited ground that such testimony would invade the province of the jury. Federal Rule 704(a) states in pertinent part: ". . . testimony in the form of an opinion or inference otherwise admissible is not objectionable because it embraces an ultimate issue to be decided by the trier of fact".

067 Rule 704 makes express the rule of modern decisions when it provides that "testimony in the form of an opinion or inference otherwise admissible is not objectionable because it embraces an ultimate issue to be decided by the trier of fact". Does this mean that experts may now give a bold legal opinion on matters that will decide the case? Not quite. The opinion must be "otherwise admissible" which means it still must be helpful under Rule 702.

068 The assumption seems to be that although opinions on ultimate facts are permissible, opinions on questions of law are not. Therefore, the witness still cannot testify that a particular legal criteria has or has not been met. But even this remaining limitation has been ignored by many courts.

069 The liberality with which ultimate issue testimony is greeted is demonstrated in *Jones* v. *Garnes* 395 S.E.2d 548 (W.Va. 1990). The plaintiff's and defendant's cars collided. The sheriff's deputy arrived at the scene after the accident and conducted an investigation. At trial, the plaintiff offered the deposition of this now unavailable expert. In his deposition the deputy testified that upon arriving at the scene of the accident he secured the area, took statements from witnesses and measurements of the accident site, and determined that the defendant had failed to yield the right of way. The trial court ruled that the expert would be permitted to testify only on matters involving point of impact, skidmarks and vehicle speed. The court sustained the defendant's objection that testimony on who failed to yield the right of way was improper because it went to the "ultimate issue". The appellate court disagreed and reversed the decision below. The West Virginia court noted that testimony, if otherwise admissible, may embrace the ultimate issue according to W.Va. Evidence Rule 704. Therefore, the question is whether the opinion on who failed to yield is "otherwise admissible". The conclusion was that such an opinion by this qualified expert should have been received because the "clear import of the rules of evidence indicates the officer should have been permitted to render the opinion in question" *Id.* at 550.

070 Similarly, in *Tolliver* v. *Consolidated Rail Corp* 463 N.E.2d 389 (Ohio 1984), a damage action arising out of a grade crossing automobile-train, the plaintiff's accidentologist was allowed to testify that the plaintiff "had acted as a reasonable and prudent person given the circumstances of the accident". The opinion was approved by the Ohio Supreme Court since it "assisted the jury in its determination".

071 *United States* v. *Young*, 745 F.2d 733 (2d Cir. 1984), *cert. denied sub nom*, *Myers* v. *United States*, 470 US 1084; 105 S.Ct. 1842; 85 L.Ed.23 142 (1985) is also instructive. In this drug conspiracy prosecution, the narcotics agent who observed the defendant's apparently ambiguous conduct was allowed to give his expert opinion that the accused was engaged in a narcotics transaction. Similarly, experts have been allowed to testify that age discrimination occurred in an age discrimination case, *Davis* v. *Combustion Engineering Inc* 742 F.2d 916 (6th Cir. 1984), and that certain sales were taxable under a section of the Internal Revenue Code: *United States* v. *Garber* 607 F.2d 92, 94–95 (5th Cir. 1979).

072 Perhaps the most elaborate treatment of the ultimate issue problem appears in *United States* v. *Scop* 846 F.2d 135 (2d Cir. 1988). This decision explores the difficulty of distinguishing between opinions on ultimate issues of fact which are permissible and opinions on ultimate issues of law which are not. In this prosecution for securities fraud, the expert testimony of the SEC investigator that the defendants engaged in "manipulation", a "scheme to defraud" and "fraud" was held to have exceeded the permissible bounds of expert opinion. The government's expert witness had spent over 1,000 hours during four years working on the case, had interviewed about 70 witnesses and had helped prepare the indictment. He did not testify at the trial as a witness with personal knowledge but based his opinions solely on the testimony and documentary evidence introduced at trial. Asked whether in his opinion there was a scheme to defraud investors, he answered: "It is my opinion that the stock . . . was manipulated and that certain individuals were active participants and material participants in the manipulation of that stock." He repeatedly described defendants as "active participants" and "material participants" in the manipulation. He admitted that his positive assessment of the testimony of the government witnesses was a basis for his opinions. The court held that Rule 704 does not permit opinions phrased in terms of inadequately explored legal criteria. Here the expert drew directly upon the language of the statute and accompanying regulations concerning "manipulation" and "fraud". These are not self-defining terms but rather have been the subject of diverse judicial interpretations. They are virtually terms of art under the security laws.

073 These decisions reflect the difficulty of distinguishing between impermissible ultimate legal opinions and testimony on ultimate issues of fact or issues of mixed fact and law. Rule 704, by expressly eliminating the ultimate issue objection, has encouraged courts to resolve doubts in favour of allowing expert testimony.

Elimination of the need to explain the basis for expert testimony

074 There is another limiting formality that has evaporated. As recently as a decade ago, many jurisdictions required that every essential basis had to be specified during the direct examination before the opinion could be given. The facts underlying the opinion typically would be testified to by the expert or included in a hypothetical question.

075 Federal Rule 705 removes this technical requirement by stating:

> "The expert may testify in terms of opinion or inference and give reasons therefor without prior disclosure of the underlying facts or data, unless the court requires otherwise. The expert may in any event be required to disclose the underlying facts or data on cross-examination."

076 Thus, Rule 705 permits the expert to testify without prior disclosure of the facts underlying the opinion. Cross-examination is considered sufficient to expose the underlying facts. The hypothetical question is no longer necessary, not even when the expert bases his opinion on facts outside his personal knowledge. The consequence of Rule 705 is that the full burden of exploration of the facts and assumptions underlying the testimony of an expert witness rests squarely on the shoulders of opposing counsel's cross-examination.

077 The practical value of Rule 705 is that it allows the advocate to streamline the way in which expert testimony is given. The proponent may order his examination as he wishes. Prior disclosure of the basis forces the actual opinion to come in the middle of the direct examination. Now the lawyer can get right to the point. Once qualified, the expert may state his opinion first, when the jury is more attentive. The explanation and basis may follow.

078 Moreover, the hypothetical question, when used, can be simple and straightforward. There will be no quibbles over its content. The advocate no longer need fear the once standard objection that facts included in the hypothetical question were insufficient to justify the opinion.

Summary and recapitulation

079 Until very recently, modern evidence codes produced an unmistakable tendency toward admitting expert testimony. The proper scope, permissible basis, and forms of presentation all had been broadened. This liberality was said to reflect greater confidence in juries and in the adversary system. To be sure, there was concern over the unreliability of some expertise and over the false aura of infallibility that it sometimes projects. Nevertheless, the tendency was to admit, leaving exposure of weaknesses to cross-examination and refutation.

080 This basic philosophy toward expert testimony was expressed several times in recent years by the United States Supreme Court. *Beech Aircraft Corp* v. *Rainey* 488 US 153; 109 S.Ct. 439 (1988) involved the scope of the public record exception to the rule against hearsay. Rule 803(8)(c) admits "factual findings resulting from an investigation made pursuant to authority granted by law". Do such admissible "factual findings" include evaluative opinions contained in reports of official investigations? The court said yes and approved admission under Rule 803(18) of a Judge Advocate report which stated that "the most probable cause" of a plane crash was pilot error. The court recognised that this broad approach to Rule 803(18) was "consistent with the Federal Rules' general approach of relaxing the traditional barriers to opinion testimony" *Id.* at 450.

081 The point also was made in dramatic fashion in *Barefoot* v. *Estelle*, 463 US 880; 77 L.Ed.2d 1090; 103 S.Ct. 3383 (1983). This case involved a sentencing hearing to determine whether the death penalty should be imposed upon a convicted murderer. State law required the jury to determine whether there was a probability that the defendant would commit future criminal acts and be a threat to society. Two psychiatrists testified for the state that the defendant "would probably commit further acts of violence and represent a continuing threat to society". The death penalty was imposed.

082 The petitioner urged that psychiatric testimony predicting future dangerousness was so unreliable that its admission in evidence was unconstitutional. The American Psychiatric Association in an *amicus* brief asserted that "the unreliability of psychiatric predictions of long-term dangerousness is by now an established fact within the profession"; that "two out of three predictions of long-term future violence made by psychiatrists are wrong" and that "a layman with access to relevant statistics can do at least as well and possibly better" than psychiatrists in making such predictions.

083 The psychiatric testimony in *Barefoot* v. *Estelle* is vulnerable on many of the issues we have discussed. Arguably it is neither beyond the ken nor even helpful to the trier of fact under Rule 702. Nor, apparently, would it now pass the *Frye* test of general acceptance within the scientific community. Clearly the opinions were conclusions on the ultimate issue, but the Supreme Court affirmed. It was concerned with the constitutionality of the procedures and not directly with the narrower admissibility issue. Nevertheless, the majority made approving reference to rules which admit such psychiatric testimony regardless of questions concerning its reliability.

084 The court noted that modern rules of evidence anticipate that relevant unprivileged evidence should be admitted and its weight left to the fact finder who would have the benefit of cross-examination and contrary evidence. Therefore, said the court at 103 S.Ct. 3397:

> "Psychiatric testimony predicting dangerousness may be construed not only as erroneous in a particular case but as generally so unreliable that it should be ignored. If a jury may make up its own mind about future dangerousness unaided by psychiatric testimony, jurors should not be barred from hearing views of the state psychiatrists along with opposing views of defendant's doctors."

085 The court's assumption was that the jury can screen out unreliable evidence and remain unmoved by the aura of expertise. That assumption began to be severely questioned in the late 1980s and early 1990s.

THE ERA OF RETRENCHMENT: SOME SECOND THOUGHTS

086 Starting approximately ten years ago, courts, commentators and legislators began to express dissatisfaction over the power granted to experts in modern litigation. Controversy centred upon expert testimony offered by plaintiffs' experts on the causation issue in toxic tort or pharmaceutical drug products liability cases. It was on this battlefield that the war between the liberal and restrictive attitudes was waged.

087 In simple terms the issue may be presented in this way. The plaintiff seeks damages for a birth defect or disease allegedly caused by the defendant's drug or chemical. The aetiology of the disease or cause of the birth defect is currently unknown. The plaintiff bears the burden of proof on the issue of causation, both general (can the product cause this kind of infirmity) and specific (did it cause the malady of this plaintiff in this case). The plaintiff's expert seeks to testify that such causation exists. Without this expert's opinion, the plaintiff will not be allowed to reach the jury. The plaintiff expert's opinion is based on animal studies, the patient's history, the literature and a number of other sources. These sources, from which he reasoned to a conclusion favouring the plaintiff, are the kinds of data that scientists in the field consider in assessing possible harmful effects of a drug or chemical. However, the causation question lies at the frontier of scientific inquiry and the answer may be for now, scientifically unknowable. Therefore, there is no scientific consensus as to whether the particular drug or chemical can cause birth defects or disease. In this climate of uncertainty how should the expert testimony of the plaintiff's expert be evaluated?

088 The liberal (sometimes called passive) school would defer to the expert and in many cases would find the evidence of causation sufficient to allow the issue to be determined by the jury. These courts would see the test for evaluating the expert's testimony as one of legal sufficiency ("more likely than not") rather than scientific sufficiency—a standard that approaches certainty. As long as the expert is qualified; as long as the data on which he relied is of a type that experts in his field might reasonably consider; as long as the opinion is in words of sufficient probability; the opinion should be admitted and will be sufficient to meet the plaintiff's burden of production on the causation issue. In other words, the matter is left for the jury.

089 Many, perhaps most, other experts might reject this expert's conclusion. Others, while accepting the reliability of the data used, might dispute the way he reasoned from the data to his conclusion. Still others might conclude that the data used, while worthy of consideration, is not by itself a sufficient foundation for the causation conclusion. Under the liberal view, all these concerns would affect the weight but not the admissibility of the opinion. Weaknesses in the opinion will be exposed on cross-examination and through the testimony of competing experts. In this battle of experts, it is for the jury to declare the winner. Judges, after all, have no special competence to resolve complex scientific issues.

090 The restrictive (sometimes called active) technique is one of strict scrutiny. Under this method the trial judge or appellate court would

- (i) critically evaluate the adequacy of the underlying foundation for the opinion,
- (ii) carefully weigh the reasoning process used by the expert in arriving at his conclusion from the underlying data, and
- (iii) assess the value and accuracy of the opinion in light of the existing scientific literature.

If the opinion is found wanting in one of these areas, it may be excluded. Even if admitted, its meagre value may be insufficient to justify submitting the issue to the jury. In that case the plaintiff would lose through the grant of summary judgment; directed verdict; judgment notwithstanding the verdict, or dismissal on appeal.

091 The language of the Federal Rules of Evidence is sufficiently vague to support either the liberal or restrictive view.

092 What evolved out of this controversy was a high-stakes, politically charged, so-called "junk science" debate with much well-publicised criticism by corporate interests that acceptance of the plaintiffs' invalid scientific theories were hurting American business, discouraging the manufacture of useful products and promoting wasteful litigation. During this period, rules governing pre-trial discovery of the testifying expert were expanded in order to aid the opponent's ability to expose defects in the expert's opinion. Rules of procedure were amended in 1993 so as to entitle the opposing party to an elaborate detailed written report signed by the expert and to be provided well in advance of trial. Parties were given the right to follow up this report by deposing the expert. Some courts also accomplished their desire to rein in expert testimony by reading the *Frye* "general acceptance" standard into Federal Evidence Rules 702 and 703. Thus, unless the plaintiff's expert's methodology was generally accepted in the scientific community, his opinion would be inadmissible.

DAUBERT AND BEYOND: A PERIOD OF UNCERTAINTY

093 As the controversy over "junk science" in the courtroom and "strict scrutiny" was growing, the United States Supreme Court entered the arena and decided the *Daubert* case. Its opinion has been cited thereafter in a host of cases involving all manner of expertise. *Daubert* and the cases interpreting its mandate bring us into the current period of considerable uncertainty.

The Supreme Court speaks in Daubert v. Merrell Dow Pharmaceuticals

094 In June 1993, for the first time in its history, the United States Supreme Court ruled on the standards appropriate for admitting expert scientific evidence. *Daubert* v. *Merrell Dow Pharmaceuticals Inc* 509 US 579; 113 S.Ct. 2786; 125 L.Ed.2d 469 (1993), was another of the recurring lawsuits claiming that the anti-nausea drug, Bendectin, caused birth defects. The issue again presented was whether the plaintiffs' controversial expert testimony of causation should be admitted in the face of uniformly contradictory scientific studies. It is a decision that may eventually have a far-reaching impact on businesses, consumers and society. It immediately affects toxic tort, environmental, pharmaceutical product liability litigation and any other case involving novel or disputable scientific testimony.

095 Announcement of the High Court's decision brought claims of success from both sides. This is not surprising since *Daubert* is really two opinions. The court in one breath rejected the 70-year-old *Frye* "general acceptance" standard on the ground that this rigid admissibility test was at odds with the "liberal thrust" of the Federal Rules of Evidence and "their general approach of relaxing traditional barriers to opinion testimony". In its next breath, it announced that under the Rules supplanting "general acceptance", the trial judge must ensure, as a condition to admissibility, that any and all scientific evidence is reliable. This entails a judicial assessment of "whether the reasoning or methodology underlying the expert opinion is scientifically valid".

096 The result is a partial victory for both injured plaintiffs and for defendant businesses. In the long run, however, defendants came out ahead. The opinion has thwarted plaintiffs in their difficult quest to prove causation whenever the aetiology of the disease or defect is scientifically uncertain. By inviting judges to be active gatekeepers in screening out speculative theories, the court has accelerated the recent trend toward "strict scrutiny" of expert testimony.

097 We examine first the nature and scope of the decision. Then we consider what strategic lessons may be drawn from it. Finally, we speculate on its likely impact in future cases.

098 The plaintiffs in *Daubert* are parents who contended that their children were born with limb-reduction birth defects caused by their mothers' use during pregnancy of the prescription morning sickness drug, Bendectin. Merrell Dow, the maker of Bendectin has defended itself successfully in all but a few of more than 2,000 birth defect suits. Over 30 published epidemiological studies involving over 130,000 patients uniformly found that there was no statistically significant association between Bendectin and birth defects. No published study had found Bendectin to be a human teratogen. The Food and Drug Administration concluded that "available data do not demonstrate an association between birth defects and Bendectin".

099 On this undisputed published record, the defendant moved for summary judgment. The plaintiffs responded with the testimony of eight impressively credentialled experts who concluded that, more likely than not, Bendectin can cause birth defects. These opinions were based upon *in vitro* and *in vivo* animal studies that showed a link between the drug and malformations; chemical composition studies which showed similarities between the structure of Bendectin and that of other substances known to cause birth defects; and, most importantly, on a "reanalysis" and "recalculation" of the data provided by the previously published epidemiological studies which had failed to find a scientific link to birth defects.

100 The trial court granted summary judgment for the defendant and the Ninth Circuit affirmed in a cursory opinion on the ground that the plaintiffs' expert testimony could not be admitted because the foundation for the opinions was not "generally accepted" in the scientific community.

101 This "general acceptance" test was first articulated in 1923 in *Frye* v. *United States* 293 F. 1013, 1014 (DC Cir. 1923) when the court stated that scientific expertise should be admitted only if its foundation was "sufficiently established to have gained general acceptance in the particular field in which it belongs".

102 The Ninth Circuit in *Daubert* held that the "reanalysis" of epidemiological data relied upon by the plaintiffs' experts had not achieved general acceptance in the scientific community because it was unpublished and, therefore, not subjected to the normal peer review process. As a result, the Court of Appeals concluded that the plaintiffs could not satisfy their burden of proving causation at trial.

103 A unanimous Supreme Court reversed, holding that the uncompromising standard of "general acceptance" as the sole criteria for admitting expert testimony had been superseded by enactment of the Federal Rules of Evidence. The court noted that neither language nor history indicates that the "general acceptance" standard was incorporated into the Federal Rules. Accordingly, the court held that the austere *Frye* standard is "absent from and incompatible with the Federal Rules of Evidence and should not be applied in federal trials".

104 If *Frye* is not the standard for admissibility, what is? Seven of the nine justices proceeded to answer this question. Their answer was to establish the trial courts as "gatekeepers" to exclude any evidence that is not scientifically reliable. The question is: how active a role should the judge play in screening expert testimony? On this issue, it was the plaintiffs who found themselves advocating an extreme position.

105 The plaintiffs reasoned as follows. Under Rules 702 and 703 of the Federal Rules of Evidence, the judge's screening role is limited. As long as the expert is qualified; as long as the expertise is in an area that would be helpful to the jury; as long as he looked at data that scientists would think useful in reaching a conclusion; it comes in. The fact that most scientists or the court would reach a different conclusion; the fact that many would disagree with the adequacy of his foundation or his method of reasoning; these weaknesses are matters of weight, not admissibility. Plaintiffs conceded only that in extreme situations the trial judge could exclude under Rule 403 on the ground that probative value was substantially outweighed by dangers of prejudice or jury confusion. And, of course, the court, in passing on the sufficiency of evidence, may find that an expert opinion is too weak to support the plaintiffs' burden of production on the issue of causation. But beyond these safeguards, plaintiffs contended that there is nothing in Rules 702 or 703 that requires a judicial finding of reliability as a condition to admissibility. This is a plausible reading of the language of the rules. After all, there is no express mention of "reliability" in Rules 702 or 703. But neither policy nor precedent supports such an approach.

106 In rejecting the plaintiffs' argument, the court parsed the language of Rule 702. It provides in part that "If scientific, technical, or other specialised knowledge will assist the trier of fact . . ." an expert "may testify thereto". Thus, the subject of the expert's testimony must be "scientific knowledge". To qualify as "scientific knowledge" an inference or assertion must be derived by the scientific method. The requirement that an expert's testimony pertain to "scientific knowledge" establishes a standard of evidentiary reliability. Therefore, the trial judge must determine at the outset "whether the reasoning or methodology underlying the testimony is scientifically valid".

107 There are a number of practical lessons and predictions that can be gleaned from the *Daubert* opinion.

108 The court provides a non-exclusive list of criteria to help the trial judge determine whether the expert's theory or technique is "scientifically valid". These include

(1) whether the theory is testable (does it set forth a hypothesis which is capable of being proven false through observation and experiment and is the data produced by the theory capable of replication?);
(2) whether the scientific claim has been tested (evidence of acceptance in the scientific community or of peer review should raise a presumption that the theory was tested and found methodologically sound; otherwise, the judge would look to other indicators);
(3) whether the theory or technique has been subjected to peer review and publication (submission to the scrutiny of the scientific community through publication or other methods is not an essential condition for admissibility but it is a component of "good science");
(4) the known or potential rate of error of the particular scientific technique and the existence and maintenance of standards controlling the technique's operation;
(5) the degree of acceptance of the theory or technique within the scientific community ("general acceptance", though rejected as the sole test of reliability remains significant as one of the relevant factors. A technique which has attracted little or no support may properly be greeted with scepticism).

109 In addition to *Daubert*'s five criteria for assessing the reliability of expert testimony (testable and tested, peer review and publication, rate of error and standards for controlling error, degree of acceptance in the scientific community), the Advisory Committee for the Federal Rules of Evidence has assembled a list of five other factors which various courts have found relevant. These include:

(1) Whether experts are "proposing to testify about matters growing naturally and directly out of research they have conducted independent of the litigation, or whether they have developed their opinions expressly for the purposes of testifying" *Daubert* v. *Merrell Dow Pharmaceuticals, Inc* 43 F.3d 1311, 1317 (9th Cir. 1995).
(2) Whether the expert has unjustifiably extrapolated from an accepted premise to an unfounded conclusion. See *General Elec Co* v. *Joiner*, 118 S.Ct. 512, 519 (1997)

(noting that in some cases a court "may conclude that there is simply too great an analytical gap between the data and the opinion proffered").

(3) Whether the expert has adequately accounted for obvious alternative explanations. See *Claar* v. *Burlington NRR* 29 F.3d 499 (9th Cir. 1994) (testimony excluded where the expert failed to consider other obvious causes for the plaintiff's condition). Compare *Ambrosini* v. *Labarraque* 101 F.3d 129 (DC Cir. 1996) (the possibility of some uneliminated causes presented a question of weight, so long as the most obvious causes had been considered and reasonably ruled out by the expert).

(4) Whether the expert "is being as careful as he would be in his regular professional work outside his paid litigation consulting": *Sheehan* v. *Daily Racing Form, Inc* 104 F.3d 940, 942 (7th Cir. 1997). See also *Braun* v. *Lorillard Inc* 84 F.3d 230, 234 (7th Cir. 1996) (*Daubert* requires the trial court to assure itself that the expert "adheres to the same standards of intellectual rigour that are demanded in his professional work").

(5) Whether the field of expertise claimed by the expert is known to reach reliable results. See *Sterling* v. *Velsicol Chem Corp* 855 F.2d 1188 (6th Cir. 1988) (rejecting testimony based on "clinical ecology" as unfounded and unreliable).

110 The task imposed on the trial judge by the *Daubert* opinion is a daunting one. It requires the judge, who may be a scientific illiterate, to determine whether the reasoning and methodology of an expert who may be eminently qualified is "scientifically valid". The court will need help and lawyers for the parties must provide it. That means that the issue of scientific reliability must be raised well before trial in order to guarantee adequate exploration. The 1993 Amendments to Federal Rule of Civil Procedure 26 require that experts submit a written signed report containing a complete statement of all opinions, and the basis and reasons underlying the opinions, along with the data considered by the witness in forming the opinions. This expansive pre-trial report, along with any necessary depositions, can form the basis for attack or defence of the validity of the expert's theory.

The neutral expert

111 The court appointment of a neutral expert under Federal Evidence Rule 706 to advise the court is a useful tool. The witness need not be qualified on the substantive area in dispute. It is enough if the court appointed expert is knowledgeable about the field's methodological requirements. In many cases it may be better to have an expert on scientific methodology who has not been involved or taken sides on the controverted substantive issue. Speaking to this issue in *Joiner* v. *General Electric Co* 78 F.3d 524 (11th Cir. 1996), Judge Birch stated in his concurring opinion at 78 F.3d 535:

> "In discharging the *Daubert* mandate, the trial court can enhance the record for appellate review by appointing an expert, under Fed.R.Evid. 706, to assist the court in evaluating proffered scientific evidence. Augmentation of the record with the testimony of a competent, independent and philosophically neutral Rule 706 expert focused upon evaluating the reliability of the proffered expert evidence will likely promote a more comprehensive and adequate ruling by the trial court. As complex scientific and technical evidence becomes more commonplace, in this ever-advancing computer age, the need for the trial court generalist to seek expertise in discharging *Daubert* responsibilities becomes increasingly evident and compelling."

Courts have begun to use Rule 706 experts more frequently in applying the *Daubert* test. See, e.g., *Hall* v. *Baxter Healthcare Corp* 947 F.Supp. 1387 (D. Or. 1996) and *Mediger* v. *Liquid Air Corp* 926 F. Supp. 152 (D. Or. 1995).

112 The analysis of the Federal Rules undertaken in the *Daubert* opinion also provides lawyers and lower courts with a catalogue of six major possible objections to expert testimony. These include discrete challenges involving qualifications, relevance, reliability, proper underlying data, danger of prejudice or confusion, and sufficiency.

113 The first three are found in Rule 702. The expert must be qualified not just generally but on the specific topic on which the opinion is given. The requirement in Rule 702 that the expert testimony "assist the trier of fact" goes to its relevance. Expert testimony which does not relate to any issue in the case is not relevant and, therefore, unhelpful. The relevance concept itself involves a requirement of scientific validity. Certain studies may be useful predictors of birth defects in animals. However, if they tell us nothing about birth defects in humans, they are not relevant in cases like *Daubert*. Beyond relevance, there is the essential requirement of reliability which *Daubert* locates in Rule 702 and which necessitates that the reasoning and foundation for the opinion be "scientifically valid". Rule 703 carries the requirement that the data underlying the opinion be "of a type reasonably relied upon by experts in the particular field in forming opinions or inferences upon the subject".

114 Even if the opinion meets these tests, there remains the hurdle of Rule 403. The otherwise admissible opinion of a qualified witness may still be excluded if the court finds the danger of prejudice or jury confusion too great. In many ways this is a "last resort" objection. An opinion which survives attacks on qualifications, relevance, reliability and proper underlying data and which opinion is essential to meet the burden of proof on causation, is not likely to fail the test of Rule 403. Moreover, as in *Daubert*, the causation question often is litigated with affidavits in motions for summary judgment. Some courts regard exclusion under Rule 403 as inappropriate in summary judgment cases. The balancing of probativeness against prejudice and confusion requires a review of all the evidence. For that reason, Rule 403 is regarded by many as an objection to be made at trial.

115 Finally, even if the opinion is received in evidence, defects in probative value which normally affect weight rather than admissibility may be substantial. In such a situation, an opinion which is the sole basis for proving causation may be found insufficient, especially if countervailing opinions are strong.

116 The Supreme Court majority made no effort to apply its criteria of scientific validity or its analysis of the Federal Rules to the specific facts of *Daubert*. Its observations were general.

117 Plaintiffs cannot take much consolation from the experience of the most recent Bendectin cases. In *DeLuca by DeLuca* v. *Merrell Dow Pharmaceuticals, Inc* 911 F.2d 941 (3d Cir. 1990), the Third Circuit, regarded by some as the most liberal circuit in admitting expert testimony, reversed a grant of summary judgment and remanded to the district court under guidelines similar to those promulgated in *Daubert*. The Third Circuit cautioned the lower court to apply its criteria with "sensitivity" to the policy judgments reflected in the Federal Rules which "embody a strong and undeniable preference for admitting any evidence that has some potential for assisting the trier of fact and a preference for dealing with the risk of error through the adversary process". On remand, the district court, after a five-day hearing, dismissed the plaintiffs' action. It concluded that the opinion of the plaintiffs' expert was inadmissible under Rules 702 and 703: *DeLuca by DeLuca* v. *Merrell Dow Pharmaceuticals, Inc* 791 F. Supp. 1042 (D.N.J. 1992). Similarly, on remand, the plaintiffs' expert testimony was rejected in the Ninth Circuit in *Daubert* itself. See *Daubert* v. *Merrell Dow Pharmaceuticals, Inc* 43 F.3d 1311 (9th Cir. 1995). But see the different and more liberal approach taken in *Ambrosini*

v. *Labarraque* 101 F.3d 129 (DC Cir. 1996) (expert testimony of plaintiff's epidemiologist and teratologist upheld).

118 *Daubert* imposes on federal trial judges the onerous responsibility of evaluating the content and methodology of extremely complex scientific evidence. The anchor of the *Frye* test has been removed. Judges will no longer have the luxury of letting mainstream science make the decision. Nor will they easily be able to pass the problem to juries. How well are courts likely to handle the challenge?

119 A likely answer is that trial judges will screen expert testimony much more carefully than before. The *Daubert* decision mandates a "gatekeeper" role for trial judges and that means a more restrictive approach to admissibility.

Post Daubert decisions

120 The plaintiffs' victory in *Daubert* was short-lived. After the Supreme Court reversed the grant of summary judgment for the defendant, the case was reconsidered on remand by the Ninth Circuit. Once again, summary judgment was granted for the defendant and the plaintiffs' claims were dismissed: *Daubert* v. *Merrell Dow Pharmaceuticals, Inc* 43 F.3d 1311 (9th Cir. 1995). The Court of Appeals applied the *Daubert* standards and concluded that the plaintiffs' experts' testimony did not reflect "scientific knowledge". One "very significant factor" to consider, said the Ninth Circuit is whether the expert is proposing to testify about research conducted independently of the litigation or whether the expert's opinion was developed just for the purpose of testifying. Here, the court said, the plaintiffs' experts developed their theories solely for the purpose of litigation and had never subjected their research to peer review. Moreover, the court reasoned that the experts were seeking to testify only that it was "statistically possible" that the drug, Bendectin, caused birth defects. This was insufficient the court said. To be admissible, the testimony must assert that causation was "more likely than not".

The scope of Daubert—to what kind of expert testimony does it apply?

121 The first question that comes to mind after *Daubert* is to ask when is it applicable? Rule 702 of the Federal Rules of Evidence governs the admissibility of "scientific, technical or other specialised knowledge". It is unclear whether *Daubert* provides, or was intended to provide, useful guidance for "technical or other specialised knowledge" or whether its impact is limited to purely "scientific knowledge".

122 There are four distinct approaches courts have taken regarding the application of *Daubert* to expert witness testimony:

(1) *Daubert* applies only to scientific expert testimony;
(2) *Daubert* applies to all expert testimony;
(3) *Daubert* analysis applies only where the expert's conclusions are based upon methodology or technique, as opposed to experience or training; and
(4) *Daubert* applies only to scientific, technical or specialised expert testimony which is novel or unique.

123 Some courts have taken the position that *Daubert* does not reach beyond the scientific branch of Rule 702 and, therefore, imposes no special reliability requirements on "technical or other specialised knowledge".

124 *United States* v. *Starzecpyzel* 880 F.Supp. 1027 (S.D.N.Y. 1995) involved expert testimony from a Forensic Document Examiner (FDE) seeking to testify regarding the alleged forgery of a signature on two documents. The defendants moved to exclude the opinion, citing the evidentiary reliability requirements of *Daubert*. The court held, however,

(1) that *Daubert* applied only to "scientific knowledge" and
(2) that evidence from an FDE was more in the nature of specialised knowledge derived mostly from experience.

Therefore, the special restrictions of *Daubert*, which the court stated were "irrelevant for many categories of expert testimony", were inapplicable. The result in *Starzecpyzel* was followed by the Sixth Circuit in *United States* v. *Jones* 107 F.3d 1147 (6th Cir. 1997). In *United States* v. *14.38 Acres of Land* 80 F.3d 1074 (5th Cir. 1996) the Fifth Circuit reversed a lower court ruling which excluded expert testimony regarding land value because it was "not based on reliable foundations". The Fifth Circuit stated that aside from eliminating the *Frye* standard for judging the admissibility of novel scientific evidence, *Daubert* "did not otherwise work a seachange over federal evidence law" and noted that *Daubert* expressly limited its discussion to scientific expert testimony. See also *Thomas* v. *Newton Intern Enterprises* 42 F.3d 1266 (9th Cir. 1994) (stating that *Daubert* is confined to scientific expert testimony); *Iacobelli Constr Inc* v. *County of Monroe* 32 F.3d 19 (2d Cir. 1994) (rejecting the application of *Daubert* to construction-litigation experts because such experts "do not present the kind of 'junk science' problem that *Daubert* meant to address"); *US* v. *Sinclair* 74 F.3d 753 (7th Cir. 1996) (stating *Daubert* only provides a method for "evaluating the reliability of witnesses who claim scientific expertise"); *Miller* v. *Chicago and Northwestern Transportation Co* 1996 WL 137658 (N.D. Ill. 1996) ("*Daubert* did not purport to establish the ground rules for the potential admissibility or inadmissibility of 'technical' or 'other specialised knowledge'"). Some state courts have followed this approach when applying their own evidence rules. See, e.g., *Gentry* v. *Magnum* 466 S.E.2d 171 (W.Va. 1995) (refusing to apply the *Daubert/ Wilt* test where the testimony does not deal with "scientific knowledge").

125 Other courts have explicitly stated that *Daubert* applies to all Rule 702 expert testimony. In *United States* v. *Thomas* 74 F.3d 676 (6th Cir. 1996) the Sixth Circuit cites its earlier decision in *Berry* v. *City of Detroit* 25 F.3d 1342 (1994) and reaffirms that "although *Daubert* dealt with scientific experts ... [*Daubert*] is applicable to all expert testimony offered under Rule 702". The court in *State of Ohio* v. *Louis Trauth Dairy Inc* 925 F.Supp. 1247; 1996 WL 263352 (S.D. Ohio 1996) states that "the general framework of *Daubert* applies to all expert testimony", adding the *caveat* that "the *Daubert* factors were devised specifically for scientific testimony ... *Daubert* analysis should be modified in the case of social science or other non-scientific expertise". See also *United States* v. *Velasquez* 64 F.3d 844 (3d Cir. 1995) (acknowledging that many courts have shunned *Daubert* in non-scientific contexts, the court, "in an exercise of caution", applies the *Daubert* factors); *In re Aluminum Phosphide Antitrust Litigation* 893 F.Supp. 1497 (D. Kan. 1995) ("To the extent that *Daubert* factors are relevant to non-scientific or social science subjects . . . the court considers them. . . .").

126 The confusion among district courts over the applicability of *Daubert* is evident in product liability cases. Thus, in *Thornton* v. *Caterpillar Inc* 951 F. Supp. 575 (D.S.C. 1997), the court held that the *Daubert* standard does not apply to the expert testimomy of a mechanical engineer. *Daubert*, said the court, applies only to "novel scientific testimony" and is simply "not applicable, nor was it intended to apply to [for example] auto mechanics . . . accountants, attorneys, DEA agents, IRS agents, real estate appraisers, and the like". Engineers possess technical or other specialised knowledge but, by this court's reasoning, they cannot be called scientists. Thus, the court applied the more liberal helpfulness standard of Rule 702 and admitted the engineer's opinion over the defendants' objections that he had never designed or developed the type of system at issue. Rule 702, concluded the trial judge, does not require the expert to construct an alternative design as a prerequisite to his testimony.

127 Similarly, in approving the expert testimony of an engineer, the court in *Safrani* v. *The Werner Co.* ___ F.Supp. ___; 1997 WL 729110 (S.D.N.Y. 1997) stated that defendant's heavy reliance on *Daubert* is misplaced because *Daubert*'s narrow focus is on the admissibility of "novel scientific evidence". Here the engineer's testimony "did not involve so-called junk science, and thus *Daubert*'s structures are not implicated". The court distinguished "forensic science from such discredited ventures as hedonic damages, clinical ecology, trauma-cancer expertise or the Bendectin plaintiffs' statistical machinations".

128 To this same effect is *McKendall* v. *Crown Control Corp* 122 F.3d 803 (9th Cir. 1997) refusing to apply *Daubert* criteria to exclude the plaintiff's product design expert. However, in *Rogers* v. *Ford Motor Co* 952 F.Supp. 606 (N.D. Ind. 1997), another district court held that testimony by the plaintiff's professional engineer to support the claim of design defect was inadmissible under *Daubert*. The Court in *Rogers* expressly held that *Daubert* is not limited to cases involving "novel scientific theories or methodologies" but rather is appropriate for all kinds of expert testimony. Similarly, a Fifth Circuit panel in *Watkins* v. *Telsmith* 121 F.3d 984 (5th Cir. 1997) also held that *Daubert* is not limited to novel scientific techniques and that the opinion of an expert civil engineer must meet *Daubert* criteria of reliability. It stated that while *Daubert* dealt with expert scientific evidence, the decision's criteria are "equally applicable to technical or other specialised knowledge".

129 The trend in the majority of courts today is to utilise *Daubert*'s criteria without addressing the question of its applicability of non-scientific testimony, apparently assuming that *Daubert* applies to all expert testimony. See, e.g., *Stecyk* v. *Bell Helicopter Textron, Inc* ___ F.Supp. ___; 1998 WL 42302 (E.D. Pa. 1/5/98) ("the better reasoned approach to assessing the reliability of technical testimony under Rule 702 is to apply the *Daubert* factors, taking into account any relevant differences between . . . technical evidence and scientific evidence"). To date, the *Daubert* analysis has been cited and applied to real estate expertise, *Frymire-Brinati* v. *KPMG Peat Marwick* 2 F.3d 183 (7th Cir. 1993), *FDIC* v. *Suna Associates, Inc* 80 F.3d 681 (2nd Cir. 1996); and to economic experts, *Joy* v. *Bell Helicopter Textron, Inc* 999 F.2d 549 (DC Cir. 1993), *Ventura* v. *Titan Sports, Inc* 65 F.3d 725 (8th Cir. 1995); to a fire chief giving an opinion regarding the cause of a fire, *United States* v. *Markum*, 4 F.3d 891 (10th Cir. 1993); to testimony of an FBI agent regarding the structure of organised crime families, *United States* v. *Locascio*, 6 F.3d 924 (2d Cir. 1993); to a vocational rehabilitation expert's opinion on jobs a disabled plaintiff might obtain, *Waldorf* v. *Shuta* 916 F.Supp. 423 (D.N.J. 1996); and to statistical evidence given in a challenge by contractors to minority "set-asides" in the construction industry, *Contractors' Association of Eastern Pennsylvania, Inc* v. *City of Philadelphia* 893 F. Supp. 419 (E.D. Penn. 1995). *In re Executive Telecard, Ltd Securities Litigation* 979 1021 (S.D.N.Y. 1997) involved expert testimony regarding valuation of damages in a securities fraud class action. The court noted that this kind of expertise did not appear to be the sort of "hard science" covered by *Daubert*. But then it analysed the expertise by reference to *Daubert*'s analysis.

130 Some courts have shunned the traditional scientific/non-scientific distinctions in favour of alternative formulations of when the *Daubert* test should apply. *Carmichael* v. *Samyang Tire, Inc* ___ F.3d ___; 1997 WL 786208 (11th Cir. 12/23/97) is an example. Here the 11th Circuit panel reversed the exclusion of the plaintiff's tyre expert's opinion. It held that *Daubert* did not apply to skill or experienced based expertise. The court conceded that the law of physics and chemistry were implicated in the alleged tyre defect. But it concluded that the expert "makes no pretence of basing his opinion on any scientific theory of physics or chemistry". Instead, he utilised his personal experience and skill with failed tyres to conclude that the blowout at issue was caused by either a design or manufacturing defect. The expert claimed that after years of looking at mangled carcasses of blown out tyres, he can identify whether a tyre failed because of abuse or defect. Therefore, such testimony falls outside the scope of *Daubert* and the "skill or experienced based observations" need not satisfy *Daubert*'s standards for the reliability of scientific evidence.

131 Similarly, in *Compton* v. *Subaru of America Inc* 82 F.3d 1513 (10th Cir. 1996) the Tenth Circuit focuses instead upon whether the expert testimony is based upon experience or training. If so, regardless of the scientific context of the testimony, the court states "application of the *Daubert* factors is unwarranted". Applying this test to the instant case, the court concludes that it need not address the plaintiff's contention that *Daubert* was not meant to apply to non-scientific evidence because the testimony given by the expert regarding the safety of a particular automobile roof was not based upon a particular methodology or technique, despite the fact that the court admits that "there is some scientific knowledge involved in the testimony". *Cf. United States* v. *Markum*, 4 F.3d 891 (10th Cir. 1993) (where expert testimony was based upon personal observation and not methodology or technique, the court used traditional Rule 702 analysis). Drawing the same distinction is *McKendall* v. *Crown Control Corp*, 122 F.3d 803 (9th Cir. 1997) (expertise of mechanical engineer on forklift defect was not subject to *Daubert* analysis since based on experience and training). But see *Watkins* v. *Telsmith Inc* 121 F.3d 984 (5th Cir. 1997) (rejecting the *Compton* approach and holding that *Daubert* applies not only to scientific evidence but also to "technical or other specialized knowledge").

132 The *Compton* court also states that subsequent to *Daubert*, the Tenth Circuit has essentially applied the same Rule 702 analysis except in cases involving "unique, untested, or controversial methodologies or techniques". Other courts have similarly restricted their application of *Daubert*. In *Liriano* v. *Hobart Corporation* 1996 WL 304337 (S.D.N.Y. 1996), Judge Scheindlin cited *Compton* approvingly when she stated that "the *Daubert* analysis applies best to cases involving unique, untested or controversial methodologies or techniques" and subsequently applied the traditional Rule 702 analysis, admitting testimony from an expert on safety warnings which was based upon experience and training, not novel scientific method. See also *Roback* v. *VIP Transport Inc* 1996 WL 394164 (7th Cir. 1996) (reversing trial court's exclusion of expert's opinion regarding malfunction of vehicle's cruise control, court states "gathering and compiling data during a test run is hardly novel methodology"); *Edwards* v. *ATRO SpA* 891 F. Supp. 1074 (E.D.N.C. 1995) (*Daubert* not applicable where expert testimony is not "novel scientific evidence" despite court's admission that the opinions are based upon "weak factual foundations"); *Lappe* v. *American Honda Motor Co* 857 F.Supp. 222 (N.D.N.Y. 1994) ("*Daubert* only prescribes judicial intervention for expert testimony approaching the outer boundaries of traditional scientific and technical knowledge"). Several state courts have also adopted this approach when applying their own evidence rules to expert testimony. See *State* v. *Cline* 909 P.2d 1171 (Mont. 1996) ("certainly all scientific expert testimony is not subject to the *Daubert* standard . . . the *Daubert* test should only be used to determine the admissibility of novel scientific evidence"); *Hartman* v. *State* 917 S.W.2d 115 (Tex. Ct. App. 1996) ("the procedures and burden of persuasion . . . do not apply unless the proffered testimony is indeed novel").

133 The confusion over the scope of *Daubert* is dramatically demonstrated by *Moore* v.

Ashland Chemical, Inc 126 F.3d 679 (5th Cir. 1997) where the panel held that *Daubert* only applied to "hard science" and therefore did not apply to causation testimony of a clinical physician. This decision has been scheduled for *en banc* review.

134 Consider also the decision in *United States* v. *Bighead*, 128 F.3d 1329 (9th Cir. 1997), a prosecution for sexual abuse of a minor. The district court allowed the testimony of a child abuse expert who purported to explain why the complainant had waited until four years after the abuse had ended to report it. She explained that delayed disclosure was a typical characteristic she had observed among more than 1,300 persons she had interviewed who said they had been victims of child abuse. Over a strong dissent, the majority held that the testimony did not violate *Daubert* because *Daubert*'s tests apply only to scientific expertise and not to expertise that involves only specialised knowledge.

135 In one of the most recent cases, the Seventh Circuit panel stated expressly that the *Daubert* framework for assessing admissibility of expert testimony is not limited to testimony that involves novel scientific theories or methodologies but is appropriate for all kinds of expert testimony. This view was espoused in *Tyus* v. *Urban Search Management* 102 F.3d 256 (7th Cir. 1997) a Fair Housing Act case. The court held that the plaintiff's expert psychologist and sociologist should have been permitted to testify about the history and patterns of housing discrimination in Chicago and about how advertising sends a message to its target market and how an all-white advertising campaign affects African-Americans. The Seventh Circuit expressly stated its disagreement with the Tenth Circuit decision in *Compton* v. *Subaru of America* 82 F.3d 1513, 1518–19 (10th Cir. 1996) which held *Daubert* applicable only to cases of novel scientific theories or methodologies. In 1999, the United States Supreme Court decided the scope of *Daubert* for the federal courts. It ruled in *Kumho Tire Co* v. *Carmichael* 119 S.Ct. 1167 (1999) that the "gatekeeping" obligation established in the *Daubert* decision applies not only to "scientific" experts but also to those whose testimony is based on "technical" or "other specialized knowledge". The court noted that Rule 702 makes no relevant distinction between scientific knowledge and other types of expert knowledge. It is the word "knowledge", not its modifying adjectives (like "scientific" or "technical"), that establishes the standard of evidentiary reliability.

The standard and procedures used by trial judges in applying Daubert

136 In the aftermath of *Daubert*, there are indications that Rule 104(a) hearings to evaluate the methodology and foundations for expert testimony have become more frequent. As a result, all expert testimony is being screened more carefully in federal courts.

137 In part this is because *Daubert* requires the trial judge to make a preliminary determination as to whether the foundation and the methodology is reliable (scientifically valid). The judge must make this determination at the outset, when the party first offers the evidence. See *Gruca* v. *Alpha Therapeutic Corp* 51 F.3d 638 (7th Cir. 1995). In *Gruca*, the trial court refused to do the *Daubert* analysis and allowed the plaintiff's proffered expert testimony even though the defendant asserted that the evidence should not be admitted. The court later directed a verdict for the defendant; however, the 7th Circuit reversed, finding that the jury could have found for the plaintiff from circumstantial evidence. Moreover, the court held that it was error for the trial court to decline to undertake a *Daubert* analysis. The court held that the judge's ultimate decision about the sufficiency or insufficiency of the evidence for sending the case to the jury does not free the district court from "determining the admissibility of the plaintiff's expert testimony in the first instance, as *Daubert* contemplates", 51 F.3d. at 643.

138 A court may perform its *Daubert* "gatekeeping" duties in three ways. First, if a party objects to the testimony, the court often undertakes a Rule 104(a) hearing to evaluate the reliability and relevancy of the proffered testimony. Secondly, "theories that are so firmly established as to have attained the status of scientific law . . . properly are subject to judicial notice", *Daubert*, 509 US at 592 n.11. Finally, in the absence of an objection to the testimony, the judge may make the analysis *sub silentio* throughout the trial with respect to all testimony and need not make explicit on-the-record rulings regarding admissibility. See *Hoult* v. *Hoult* 57 F.3d 1 (1st Cir. 1995).

139 When the judge is considering proffered expert testimony in a Rule 104(a) hearing, the proponent of scientific expertise must convince the *judge*, not the jury by a preponderance of the evidence that the foundation and methodology are reliable. It is not a *prima facie* evidence standard. It is not enough to present "sufficient evidence" to justify a jury finding under Rule 104(b). This is a Rule 104(a) issue. The proponent must persuade the trial judge by a preponderance of the evidence as a condition of admissibility. Does this mean then that the proponent must prove reliability twice; once to the judge and then again to the jury? Almost, but not quite. The proponent need not prove to the judge that the conclusions are correct; only that they are reliably based. Reliability means the proponent must show "good grounds". It is possible, in other words, to have a well-grounded opinion that reaches the wrong conclusion because "good grounds" does not mean the "best grounds" or "perfect grounds".

140 This subtle distinction is contained in a lengthy and scholarly opinion by the Third Circuit which seeks to explain how *Daubert* should be applied, *In re Paoli Railroad Yard Litigation II* 35 F.3d 717; 743–745 (3d Cir. 1994).

How much scrutiny does Daubert require?

141 The level of scrutiny *Daubert* requires continues to be a source of controversy. Is it enough if the expert relies as a basis for an opinion upon the kind of studies that are *generally* looked at? Or is the trial judge required to review the *specifics* of the studies themselves to determine their reliability before admitting the expert's opinion? In *Joiner* v. *General Electric Co* 78 F.3d 524 (11th Cir. 1996) *reversed* ______ US ______; 1997 WL 764563 (12/15/97) a bitterly divided panel of the 11th Circuit was at odds over the extensiveness of the courts' "gatekeeping" role under *Daubert*. The trial court had excluded expert testimony that the plaintiff's lung cancer was caused by exposure to polychlorinated biphenyls (PCBs) during the plaintiff's employment working with electrical transformers.

142 The Court of Appeals majority in *Joiner* ruled that the plaintiff's expert testimony was erroneously excluded, using a more permissive interpretation of *Daubert*: "[I]t is important for trial courts to keep in mind the separate functions of judge and jury, and the intent of *Daubert* to loosen the strictures of *Frye* and make it easier to present legitimate conflicting views of experts for the jury's consideration" (78 F.3d at 529). Taking a big picture approach to assessing the basis for the experts' opinion, the majority states that "opinions are derived from individual pieces of evidence, each of which by itself may not be conclusive, but when viewed in their entirety are the building blocks of a perfectly reasonable conclusion" (78 F.3d at 532). The majority specifically attacks the trial court's rejection of two animal studies as a partial basis for the experts' testimony, contending that *Daubert* intended courts to rule only whether the expert's use of such studies in forming his or her opinion was methodologically sound, not make independent judgments *vis-à-vis* the studies themselves. The majority stated that dismissal amounted to "an independent scientific judgment on the basis of an individual study" *Id.*

143 The dissent castigated the majority's abstract view of the evidence, instead reading the judges' role expansively, stating "the requirement of reliability extends to each step in an expert's analysis . . . [A]ny step which renders the analysis unreliable under the *Daubert* factors renders the expert's testimony inadmissible" 78 F.3d 537 (quoting *Paoli*, 35 F.3d at 745). Defending the trial court's treatment of the two animal studies, the dissent counters that the trial court's rejection of the studies went to the relevance or "fitness" prong of *Daubert*—in effect, the trial court had found that the studies did not "fit" the particular case. The dissent cites the *Paoli* court's description of the fine line between ruling on "fit" and ruling on the experts' conclusions themselves and insists that "fitness" was the basis for this ruling, unlike the majority's view that the trial judge ruled on the conclusions themselves.

144 The Court of Appeals concurring opinion suggests a possible solution to such disputes: increased use of court-appointed Rule 706 experts. The concurrence states that "as complex scientific and technical evidence becomes more commonplace . . . the need for the trial court generalist to seek expertise in discharging *Daubert* responsibilities becomes increasingly evident and compelling" (78 F.3d at 534).

145 The position of the Court of Appeals dissenting judges prevailed when the *Joiner* case reached the United States Supreme Court. In *General Electric Co* v. *Joiner* 118 S.Ct. 512; ____ US ____ (1997) the Supreme Court reversed and upheld the trial court's decision to exclude the expert testimony. The court held that the animal studies cited by the respondent's experts were so dissimilar to the facts presented here—i.e. the studies involved infant mice that developed alveologenic adenomas after highly concentrated, massive doses of PCBs were injected directly into their peritoneums or stomachs, whereas Joiner was an adult human whose small-cell carcinomas allegedly resulted from exposure on a much smaller scale—that it was not an abuse of discretion for the district court to have rejected the experts' reliance on those studies. Nor did the court abuse its discretion in concluding that the four epidemiological studies on which *Joiner* relied were not a sufficient basis for the experts' opinions, since the authors of two of those studies ultimately were unwilling to suggest a link between increases in lung cancer and PCB exposure among the workers they examined; the third study involved exposure to a particular type of mineral oil not necessarily relevant here; and the fourth involved exposure to numerous potential carcinogens in addition to PCBs.

146 The Supreme Court's decision in *Joiner* is significant for several reasons. It makes clear that each basis underlying the expert's opinion must be examined specifically for reliability and that its connection to the expert's conclusion must satisfy the trial judge. The court rejected the plaintiff's contention that *Daubert*'s focus was solely on the reliability of the underlying data, not on the reliability of the expert's conclusions. The court noted that "conclusions and methodology are not entirely distinct from one another". It concluded that "nothing either in *Daubert* or the Federal Rules of Evidence requires a district court to admit opinion evidence which is connected to existing data only by the *ipse dixit* of the expert. A court may conclude that there is simply too great an analytical gap between the data and the opinion proffered."

147 *Joiner* adds to the growing sense that *Daubert* has restricted rather than expanded the admissibility of scientific evidence.

Daubert's restrictive effect in civil cases

148 Applying *Daubert*, courts have demonstrated a new cautious approach toward admission of expert testimony. An increasing number of decisions demonstrate a restrictive attitude, with courts taking their "gatekeeping" role seriously.

149 Cases which demonstrate a restrictive attitude under *Daubert*'s reliability prong fall into several broad categories: toxic tort, psychological diagnosis, hedonic damage, design defect, damages experts, and other miscellaneous cases.

Toxic tort cases

150 As one might expect, restrictive uses of *Daubert* are more numerous in the toxic tort category than in any other. In excluding this testimony, courts routinely apply the reliability factors outlined in *Daubert* to reach a conclusion, using various combinations of the factors to exclude testimony. The factors most often cited are a lack of adequate testing, publication on the subject, and peer review of the expert's theory. In this toxic tort setting, *Daubert* has been applied rather strictly; however, at least one court laments that "the price paid for this seemingly stringent standard of reliability is that, unavoidably, some legitimate injuries will be left unredressed" (*Cavallo* v. *Star Enterprise* 892 F.Supp. 756, 773 (E.D. Va. 1995)).

151 One of the most striking recent decisions in the toxic tort arena is the breast implant case of *Hall* v. *Baxter Healthcare Corp* 947 F.Supp. 1387 (D. Or. 1996). In this decision, Federal District Judge Robert E. Jones applied *Daubert* gatekeeper standards and ruled inadmissible the plaintiffs' expert testimony seeking to establish that silicone gel implants caused a systemic illness or syndrome or autoimmune disorder of any kind. *Hall* is a momentous decision for several reasons. First, if upheld on appeal, it is likely to have a major impact on tens of thousands of other breast implant cases awaiting trial across the country. Secondly, the pre-trial process used by Judge Jones in evaluating the scientific evidence was unique in its thoroughness and procedural fairness. And, finally, the decision was accompanied by a powerfully reasoned opinion.

152 The plaintiffs in *Hall* sued various breast implant manufacturers asserting that silicone from the implants had migrated and degraded in the bodies of the women victims, thus causing systemic syndrome or illness called "atypical connective tissue disease". On the defendants' motion to exclude the plaintiffs' expert testimony, a Rule 104(a) hearing was scheduled. Narrative written statements of expert testimony were submitted by the parties. Judge Jones invoked his inherent authority and appointed four unbiased and uncommitted experts to act as judicial advisors in the fields of epidemiology, rheumatology, immunology, toxicology and polymer chemistry. These technical advisors reviewed all the written materials. The Rule 104(a) hearing lasted four days. No evidentiary objections were allowed. Experts on both sides were questioned by counsel, the court and the technical advisors. The parties then submitted videotaped summations which the court and the advisors reviewed. The parties were allowed to submit proposed questions to guide the technical advisors in evaluating the testimony used in preparing their reports. The court submitted its own questions to the advisors. The technical advisors submitted their report about one month after the hearing and the court then gave counsel on both sides an opportunity to question them. The court granted the defendants' motion to exclude the plaintiffs' expert testimony concerning causation of any systemic disease or syndrome. It conceded that its opinion "goes further in evaluating and in eliminating the plaintiffs' claims than any other opinion in breast implant litigation pending in this country". But the court explained that "litigation over the ability of silicone breast implants to cause disease in women has been chaotic in its results in part because . . . the interjection of *Daubert* standards into the screening process for proposed scientific evidence has substantially heightened the scrutiny through which such evidence must pass". The court concluded that exclusion of the plaintiffs' expert testimony was commanded by *Daubert* and its progeny.

Psychological diagnosis cases

153 Under *Daubert*, courts have occasionally excluded expert testimony about psychological conditions. Perhaps the best example is *Gier* v. *Educational Service Unit No 16*, 66 F.3d 940 (8th Cir. 1995). In *Gier* psychologists determined that children had been emotionally, physically, or sexually abused at school. The 8th Circuit held that even if the methodology used for diagnosis might be reliable enough to choose a course of therapy (the purpose the methodology was designed to serve), it is not reliable enough to use in legal proceedings. The experts must rely upon only their opinion for psychological classification; thus, the validity of the expert's judgment cannot be established. In addition, the reliability of their judgments has not been established in public reports.

154 *United States* v. *Rouse* 100 F.3d 560 (8th Cir. 1996) suggests that *Daubert* principles may not fully apply to social science. In the majority opinion of an eight circuit panel, the court stated that "soft" science research, theories and opinions cannot have the exactness of "hard" science methodologies. In this child sex abuse case, the trial court excluded expert testimony by the defendant that the interrogation procedures used by government agencies on the children were suggestive. The Court of Appeals reversed the defendant's conviction, finding that *Daubert* was misapplied and that the defence expert's opinion would have helped the jury because psychological research in the area of suggestibility is beyond the knowledge or experience of the average person.

Hedonic damage cases

155 Expert testimony by economists on the monetary value of the "joy of living" was for a time prominent in wrongful death cases. This so-called "hedonic damage" testimony sought to place a value on the "loss of enjoyment of life" by assessing what premiums government, consumers and employers would be willing to pay extra in order to safeguard lives. At first hedonic damage testimony was met with some approval: *Sherrod* v. *Berry* 629 F.Supp. 159, 163–164 (N.D. Ill. 1985); *aff'd*, 827 F.2d 195 (7th Cir. 1987). Today, this expertise has been largely discredited; often by the application of *Daubert* criteria: *Ayers* v. *Robinson* 887 F. Supp. 1049 (N.D. Ill. 1995); *Kurnez* v. *Honda North America, Inc* 166 F.R.D. 386 (W.D. Mich. 1996); *McGuire* v. *City of Santa Fe* 954 F.Supp. 230 (D.N. Mexico 1996).

Design defect cases

156 In design defect cases, courts exclude expert testimony under *Daubert* if the expert's opinion is perceived as pure speculation unsupported by testing. See *Redman* v. *John D Brush and Co.* 111 F.3d 1174 (4th Cir. 1997) (metallurgical expert lacked adequate foundation for his testimony that the defendant's safe was not "burglar deterrent"); *Cummings* v. *Lyle Industries* 93 F.3d 362 (7th Cir. 1996) (expert's opinion that alternative design of trim press would have avoided accident that severed worker's fingers was excluded because it was based upon untested observations); *Tucker* v. *Nike, Inc* 919 F.Supp. 1192 (N.D. Ind. 1995) (doctor failed to conduct tests to determine whether a sneaker's back tab pull caused the plaintiff's Achilles tendon injury, rendering his causation testimony unsupported speculation); *Deimer* v. *Cincinnati Sub-Zero Products, Inc* 58 F.3d 341 (7th Cir. 1995) (rejecting expert testimony that a machine's defective cord-storage wrap device caused the plaintiff's injury, finding that the opinion was based only on personal observation and was therefore unsubstantiated); *Pestel* v. *Vermeer Manufacturing Co* 64 F.3d 382 (8th Cir. 1995) (excluded testimony that a different guard on a stump cutter would have prevented the plaintiff's injury, as the guard designed by the expert had not been tested and the expert had not subjected the guard to the scrutiny of others); *Duffee* v. *Murray Ohio Mfg Co* 879 F.Supp. 1078 (D. Kan. 1995) (opinion on defects in bicycle brake system excluded as unreliable when expert failed to consider any of the information available concerning relevant factors in choosing a brake system and based his opinion merely on personal experience and one conversation with a bicycle dealer); *Stanczyk* v. *Black & Decker, Inc* 836 F.Supp. 565 (N.D. Ill. 1993) (rejecting testimony of mechanical engineer who failed to offer a testable design to support his testimony that an alternative design of a mitre saw would have produced a safer product); *Surace* v. *Caterpillar, Inc* 1995 WL 303895 (E.D. Pa 1995) (electrical engineer's opinion that different alarms were needed because workers could become "immune" to single auditory alarm, excluded partially because of a lack of research on the expert's part); *Bogosian* v. *Mercedes-Benz of North America, Inc* 104 F.3d 472 (1st Cir. 1997) (automobile technician with Bachelor of Science degree in industrial and vocational education not allowed to testify for plaintiff about defect in automobile transmission because his expertise as master mechanic did not extend to defect in issue. He had extensive experience in automobile repair but had never designed a transmission. In addition, the court questioned the reliability of his methodology). These restrictive rules in design defect cases establish that mere personal observation by an expert witness, without further testing or substantiation, will probably not withstand the scrutiny of a *Daubert* analysis.

Damages expert cases

157 Some damages experts have also had some difficulty testifying after *Daubert*. The reason can be similar to that of the design defect cases. Consider *Henry* v. *Hess Oil Virgin Islands Corp.* 163 FRD 237 (D.V.I. 1995), where the plaintiff was injured after slipping on oil while working at a refinery owned by the defendant. As a result, the plaintiff would allegedly be limited to minimum wage-paying jobs. An economic expert testified about the plaintiff's total wage loss. On the defendant's motion, the court ordered a new trial on the issue of damages because the expert did not fully test his opinion, failing both to consider whether the plaintiff could still work for his former employer (who had made an offer) and to contact any government source to substantiate the claim that the plaintiff would be able to obtain only minimum wage.

Miscellaneous cases

158 Finally, courts exclude expert testimony for unreliability where the expert lacks sufficient precision in some important aspect of his or her methodology, rendering it speculative, and hence, unreliable. For example, see *Pomella* v. *Regency Coach Lines Ltd* 899 F.Supp. 335 (E.D. Mich. 1995). There, the court excluded testimony which relied on an assumed value for the coefficient of friction. The plaintiff claimed that the bus driver could have avoided a collision with the plaintiff if the bus had been travelling more slowly on the snowy road. The plaintiff's expert "eyeballed" the coefficient of friction to determine whether the bus would have slipped had it been moving more slowly, rendering his opinion speculative and unscientific. In *Marcel* v. *Placid Oil Co* 11 F.3d 563 (5th Cir. 1994), the 5th

Circuit affirmed exclusion of an economist's testimony based upon a study of the life expectancy of oil workers. The defendant oil company failed to use any evidence comparing work life in the particular oilfield at issue with the national average or with the work life of any other occupation, and therefore failed to demonstrate why the plaintiff would likely have a shorter work life and should therefore not receive damages based on an average work life. See also *In re TMI Litigation Cases Consolidated II* 911 F.Supp. 775 (M.D. Pa. 1995) (where the court excluded one expert's water model of dispersion of radioactive gases partially because his methodology included eyeballing of figures and speculation).

159 Many cases again make the point that personal observation without testing is insufficient. For example, in *Cook* v. *American Steamship Co* 53 F.3d 733 (6th Cir. 1995), a seaman sustained injuries when a line supporting his chair broke, causing him to fall to the deck. The trial court allowed an expert to testify that the line broke because it burned. The 6th Circuit held that it was error to allow the testimony, since the expert merely looked at the rope and saw char marks. This, said the court, the jury could do. The expert did no testing of the rope to scientifically discover why the rope broke.

160 Even doctors' testimony which results from only their personal observation of the patient may be excluded. In *Zarecki* v. *National Railroad Passenger Corp* 914 F.Supp. 1566 (N.D. Ill. 1996), the court rejected a doctor's testimony about the cause of the plaintiff's carpal tunnel syndrome, holding that his "conclusions are based simply on his own observations, which are insufficient in this case to establish that his views are corroborated by the scientific method": 914 F.Supp. at 1574. In rejecting the testimony, this case asserts that whether the theory has been tested is the most important of the *Daubert* factors for reliability. Similarly, in *O'Connor* v. *Commonwealth Edison Co* 13 F.3d 1090 (7th Cir. 1994), a physician's testimony that he could tell whether the plaintiff's cataract was caused by radiation just by looking at it was held inadmissible as contrary to valid scientific methodology.

Daubert's effect in criminal cases

161 In criminal cases, *Daubert* eliminated the restrictive *Frye* "general acceptance" requirement and, in its place, imposed a "gatekeeper" requirement which mandates federal judges to find scientific validity. What is the likely effect of this change on admissibility? In some cases, it makes no difference. Thus, in *United States* v. *Rincon* 28 F.3d 921 (9th Cir. 1994), the Court of Appeals affirmed exclusion of expert testimony on eyewitness identification. The initial exclusion preceded *Daubert* and was based on *Frye*. After *Daubert*, the court reconsidered its ruling and reached the same conclusion.

Polygraph evidence

162 However, in some areas, *Daubert* has proven to be less restrictive than *Frye*. For polygraph evidence, *Daubert* standards have loosened previous restrictions in some courts. The 5th Circuit ruled that in light of *Daubert*, polygraph results could no longer be *per se* inadmissible: *United States* v. *Posado* 57 F.3d 428 (5th Cir. 1995). Following *Posado*'s command to evaluate polygraph testimony according to *Daubert* standards, two district courts within the 5th Circuit found that the offered polygraph testimony met *Daubert*'s reliability and relevancy requirements. One was a criminal case, *United States* v. *Dominguez* 902 F.Supp. 737 (S.D. Tex. 1995); the other, a civil case, *Ulmer* v. *State Farm Fire & Casualty Company* 897 F.Supp. 299 (W.D. La. 1995). In *Ulmer*, polygraph evidence was admitted to corroborate the plaintiffs' denial of involvement in a fire destroying their residence.

163 Re-examination of polygraph evidence has continued in a series of recent decisions.

164 In *United States* v. *Cordoba* 104 F.3d 225 (9th Cir. 1997), the Ninth Circuit held that *Daubert* overruled its *per se* rule of inadmissibility of polygraph evidence. The court felt that a rule of *per se* inadmissibility was inconsistent with the "flexible" Rule 702 inquiry governing admissibility that was assigned to the trial judge by *Daubert* (*Id.* at 227). The court also held that *Daubert* overruled any *per se* rule that polygraph evidence is always inadmissible under Rule 403, as the trial judge is required to conduct the Rule 403 analysis (*Id.* at 228). On remand, however, the district court held that the polygraph evidence offered by the defendant failed the *Daubert* criteria because it had not achieved general acceptance; its error rate is unknown and there are no controlling standards for polygraphy: *United States* v. *Cordoba* ______ F. Supp. ______; 1998 WL 25723 (C.D. Cal. 1/22/98).

165 One state supreme court that addressed this issue held that a *per se* rule of polygraph inadmissibility is not violative of *Daubert*. In an extraordinarily thorough opinion, the Connecticut Supreme Court ruled in *State* v. *Porter* 241 Conn. 57, 698 A.2d 739 (1997) that *Daubert* was the proper standard to apply to determine admissibility of scientific evidence in that state, and that under *Daubert* a *per se* rule against admission of polygraph evidence should be applied.

166 The court assumed, without deciding, that polygraph evidence satisfies the admissibility threshold set out by *Daubert* (*Id.* at 93). However, the court concluded that the prejudicial impact of polygraph evidence greatly exceeds its probative value (*Id.*). The court feared that admitted polygraph evidence would usurp the fact-finding responsibility of the jury (*Id.* at 115–116). The court felt that "[I]n view of the importance of maintaining the role of the jury . . . polygraph evidence so directly abrogates the jury's function that its admission is offensive to our tradition of trial by jury" (*Id.* at 117–118).

167 The court also explained that admission of polygraph results would result in immensely time-consuming "battles of the experts" (*Id.* at 120–121). The court noted that even polygraph advocates admit that many polygraph examiners lack sufficient training and competence (*Id.* at 121). Since there is also little standardisation of polygraph test procedures, the court felt that battles over expert qualifications and proper procedures would flourish in cases where polygraph evidence is admitted (*Id.*).

168 Another worry for the court was that juries would come to expect polygraph evidence with regard to all witnesses. The court wondered whether juries would draw adverse inferences against a witness whenever polygraph evidence supporting the witness was absent (*Id.* at 123–124).

169 The court also pointed out that several states, after experimenting with the admission of polygraph evidence for a few years, rejected its admissibility and returned to a *per se* rule of inadmissibility (*Id.* at 127). The court felt it noteworthy that these four states (Massachusetts, Wisconsin, North Carolina and Oklahoma) rethought and rejected their policy of polygraph evidence admissibility.

170 Finally, the court rejected the defendant's argument that the *per se* inadmissibility rule violated his Sixth Amendment right to present a defence. According to the court, rules for the admission or exclusion of evidence offend the Constitution only when

(1) they disadvantage the defendant more than the State without a rational basis or
(2) they arbitrarily exclude reliable defensive evidence without achieving a superior social benefit

(*Id.* at 134 (citing *Perkins* v. *State*, 902 S.W.2d 88, 94 (Tex. App. 1995))). The court felt that "there is a very strong basis for excluding polygraph evidence, and such exclusion is not arbitrary given the polygraph test's demonstrated lack of probative value" (*Id.* at 134). Accordingly, the *per se* inadmissibility rule did not violate the defendant's right to present a defence.

171 In *United States* v. *Scheffer* ______ US ______; 1998 WL 141151 (3/31/98) the United States Supreme Court was presented with a constitutional challenge to the *per se* exclusion of polygraph evidence when offered by the accused in a criminal case. The Court of Appeals for the Armed Forces, relying on *Rock* v. *Arkansas* 483 US 44 (1987) had held that Military Rule of Evidence 707's categorical exclusion of polygraph evidence violated the defendant's Fifth or Sixth Amendment right to present a defence. The Supreme Court reversed. It noted that a defendant's right to present evidence is subject to reasonable restrictions and that he did not have a constitutional right to present polygraph evidence. The *per se* exclusion of Military Rule 707 serves the legitimate interest of insuring that only reliable evidence is introduced. In this case the rule did not preclude the defendant from introducing any factual evidence. It merely barred him from introducing expert opinion to bolster his own credibility.

DNA evidence

172 *Daubert* has loosened admissibility requirements for expert testimony about DNA. For example, in *United States* v. *Martinez* 3 F.3d 1191 (8th Cir. 1993), the court held that, after *Daubert*, district courts may take judicial notice of the reliability of certain kinds of DNA testing. However, this is not the end of this issue. As the *Galbreath* court ruled for polygraph testimony, the *Martinez* court ruled that even though DNA testing is reliable in the abstract, courts must make a case-by-case determination that a reliable methodology was followed in a particular case. In *United States* v. *Johnson* 56 F.3d 947 (8th Cir. 1995), the defendant contended that the DNA protocol used by the police varied substantially from the generally accepted FBI protocol on which the police protocol was based, and was therefore unreliable. The 8th Circuit held that the minor variations did not negate the basis for reliability, but noted that the party seeking to introduce DNA expert testimony must make a preliminary showing that the expert properly performed a reliable methodology in arriving at his opinion. Also following *Galbreath* and *Martinez*, the district court in *United States* v. *Coronado-Cervantes* 912 F.Supp. 497 (D.N.M. 1996), scrutinised the expert's compliance with standard DNA testing protocol as a condition of admissibility, and not of weight.

173 Another common issue in the admissibility of testimony about DNA testimony concerns the reliability of the statistical probability of a coincidental match. In *United States* v. *Chischilly* 30 F.3d 1144 (9th Cir. 1994), involving the admissibility of DNA evidence of a match between the defendant's blood sample and semen found on the victim's clothing, the issue was whether testimony regarding the statistical probability of a coincidental match should be received. The court conceded that the testimony might be excluded under the *Frye* test, but "under *Daubert*'s more liberal admissibility test", evidence of "opposing views arrayed in virtual scholarly equipoise" shows that both positions have scientific merit and that neither view has the kind of minimal support within the community that would cause a court to view the technique with scepticism under the *Daubert* criteria. Accordingly, the court upheld admissibility. Similarly, the *Coronado-Cervantes* court deemed the frequency calculations reliable. Despite a database of only 200 Native American individuals, the court ruled that the conservativeness of the probabilities calculated was sufficient to admit DNA testimony about the Native American defendant. The evidence had a "tendency" to show that the defendant may be the source of DNA at the crime scene.

Eye witness identification

174 A final area where *Daubert* may have loosened admissibility restrictions is expert testimony on the weaknesses of eye witness identification. *United States* v. *Brien* 59 F.3d 274 (1st Cir. 1995), involved eyewitness identification of an alleged bank robber. Although the 1st Circuit affirmed the district court's exclusion of the defendant's proffered expert testimony, it ruled that such testimony is not inadmissible as a matter of law, but rather is admissible on a case-by-case basis. The court may demand data or literature underlying the expert's assumptions and conclusions to determine reliability under *Daubert*.

CONCLUSION

175 The effect of *Daubert* is to impose, at least on scientific expertise, a level of judicial scrutiny beyond what was thought to be required by the liberal language of the Federal Rules of Evidence. As has been suggested, one way to escape the rigours of *Daubert* is to limit its scope to only opinions that involve novel or hard science. Some courts have done that. Many others have not. The current trend is to apply careful judicial scrutiny to all forms of expertise as a condition of admissibility. Not many courts or commentators are willing to tolerate a strict standard for scientific expertise and a relaxed liberal test for expertise that is "technical" or "specialised". The days of easy admissibility and "leave it to the jury" are gone.

176 An indication that all expert testimony, scientific or not, should meet similar strict scrutiny from the trial judge is reflected in a recently proposed amendment to Federal Evidence Rule 702. In 1998, the Advisory Committee on the Federal Rules of Evidence has submitted to the Judicial Conference Standing Committee on Rules of Practice and Procedure, a proposal that would change Rule 702 as follows (new language in italics):

> "If scientific, technical, or other specialised knowledge will assist the trier of fact to understand the evidence or to determine a fact in issue, a witness qualified as an expert by knowledge, skill, experience, training, or education, may testify thereto in the form of an opinion or otherwise,
> *provided that*
> *(1) the testimony is sufficiently based upon reliable facts or data,*
> *(2) the testimony is the product of reliable principles and methods, and*
> *(3) the witness has applied the principles and methods reliably to the facts of the case."*

177 This obvious purpose and effect of this amendment is to ensure that *Daubert* type reliability standards would apply to all forms of expert testimony.

178 In explaining its proposal, the Advisory Committee explained that the amendment is a response to the *Daubert* decision; is intended to affirm the trial judge's role as gatekeeper and provides standards that the trial judge must use to assess the reliability of proffered expert testimony. The Advisory Committee makes clear that the amendment does not distinguish between scientific and other forms of expert testimony because the trial judge's gatekeeper function must apply to testimony by any expert. In its explanation the Advisory Committee notes that "the amendment rejects the premise that an expert's testimony should be treated more permissively simply because it is outside the realm of science". It concludes that "an opinion from an expert who is not a scientist should receive the same degree of scrutiny for reliability as an opinion from an expert who purports to be a scientist".

179 The extent of the change that *Daubert* has wrought is reflected in the language that would be added by the proposed amendment. As it now reads, Rule 702 does not even mention the word "reliability". As changed by the proposed amendment, the word appears in one form or another reportedly and somewhat redundantly. This proposal, which purports to state existing law, requires the trial judge to determine by a preponderance of the evidence that the opinion is "*sufficiently based*" upon "*reliable facts or data*"; that the opinion is the "product of *reliable principles and methods*"; and that the expert has applied those principles and methods *reliably* to the facts of the case. This approach, if adopted and applied uniformly to all expertise represents a sea change from the previous era of liberal admissibility.

Faust F Rossi *is the Samuel S Leibowitz Professor of Trial Techniques at Cornell Law School. He received his AB degree from the University of Toronto in Ontario, Canada, and his JD with distinction from Cornell Law School. After six years of law practice specialising in litigation, he joined the Cornell Law School where he has taught courses in evidence, civil procedure, trial advocacy, torts and insurance. From 1973 to 1975, Professor Rossi served as Associate Dean for Academic Affairs at the Law School. He has been a Visiting Professor at New York University, San Diego and Emory law schools. In 1987 he was a Visiting Fellow at Wadham College at Oxford University. He also lectured in 1988 as an academic visitor at the University of Siena, Italy. Professor Rossi teaches regularly in the Legal Studies Department of Central European University in Budapest, Hungary. In 1992, he was the national winner of the Jacobson Award for Teaching Excellence. He has lectured on evidence and procedure to judges, lawyers and students throughout the United States and in Europe. Professor Rossi is the author of a book on* Expert Witnesses, *has co-authored a treatise on evidence and has written numerous monographs and articles. He is a member of the American Jurisprudence Editorial Advisory Board and of the faculty of the National Institute for Trial Advocacy. He served as a consultant on the Federal Rules of Evidence for the American College of Trial Lawyers, for the New York State Law Revision Commission and for other federal and state associations.*

CHAPTER 1/19B

EXPERT TESTIMONY IN THE UNITED STATES: SOME DO'S AND DON'TS

John Leslie Livingstone

001 *This article deals with practice in the United States. But a UK barrister has commented that much of it is relevant also to practice in Great Britain and other English-speaking countries. Therefore it is hoped that readers, wherever they are located, may find it useful. The overall message is to be thorough in one's work, diligent in one's preparation, and honest in one's testimony.*

002 In the United States, expert testimony may take the form of:

- An expert report
- An expert affidavit
- Testimony at deposition
- Testimony at trial, arbitration, mediation or other forum.

AN EXPERT REPORT

003 Since 1 December 1993, US federal rules of discovery have required experts to submit written reports. Similar rules have also been adopted to various degrees by about 20 states. In the remaining states, the equivalent of a written expert report may to a certain extent be obtained by means of expert interrogatories.

004 The federal rules of discovery require written expert reports to contain the following information:

(1) A complete statement of all opinions;
(2) The bases and reasons for those opinion;
(3) A description of the data considered in forming the opinions;
(4) Exhibits that support or summarise the opinions;
(5) The qualifications of the expert;
(6) A list of the expert's publications during the last 10 years;
(7) A list of testimony given by the expert in the last four years;
(8) The compensation being received by the expert.

005 These requirements are quite comprehensive, and they raise some important issues with respect to expert reports. They may also provide scope for rigorous cross-examination of the expert by opposing counsel. Examples of this scope will be discussed shortly.

006 Another issue is the style in which the report should be written. Traditional expert style is often laden with technical jargon, densely packed with descriptions of data and methodology, and impenetrable to lay understanding.

007 It is advisable to consider carefully the audience for the report. From the view-point of legal strategy, the most important reader is probably the judge. Also critically important is the jury (if a jury trial is involved). For these key audiences, it is wise for the expert report to be written in clear non-technical fashion, relegating complex or arcane material to appendices. Judges are confronted by mountains of paper, and tend to give short shrift to any lengthy document. However, most judges will gratefully read clear, brief material which sheds light on major problems and helps the court to cut through crucial technical issues. When there is a jury trial, most jurors will welcome a straightforward explanation of expert opinion. Ideally, the expert report should be written in such a helpful manner that the jurors will want to take it with them into the jury room to aid their deliberation of the case.

008 A related consideration refers to how well the expert report sets out detailed sources for the information it contains, and specific citations for all authorities relied upon. To my continuing surprise, I frequently see expert reports that contain few, if any, sources and citations. Also lacking in many cases are the details of intermediate steps of calculations. Presumably, this is because an expert does not wish to aid the other side in understanding his or her report (or has been instructed by counsel to withhold source, citation and calculation information in order to confound the opposition).

009 This tactic is shortsighted. Omitting helpful information deprives not only the opposition but also the judge (and possibly a jury) of useful assistance. In addition, it lowers the credibility of the expert report: competent experts who have made a sound study should be glad to assist lay readers to understand their conclusions. Only experts lacking confidence in their studies would wish to hide their tracks.

010 Further, by obscuring the trails of sources, authorities and calculations, the expert makes his or her own task much more difficult when it comes to testifying in deposition or in court. The testimony may be given long after the report has been written, and the expert may not easily or fully recall all of the sources, authorities and calculations which have been relied upon. Also, the expert may have worked on other engagements subsequent to the one in question, and be unable to recall details which had seemed familiar way back then, but which have since faded. Not only does this put pressure upon the expert's memory, but it will enable a skilled cross-examiner to undermine the expert's poise, the quality of the work performed, and the validity of the conclusions reached.

011 My preferred practice is always to provide a detailed and complete road map in my expert reports, showing every source, authority, and calculation step. It undoubtedly helps the opposition. But it helps my client and myself much more. I want to face cross-examination with no pressure to remember obscure details from work done in the past, and with full confidence that every item in my expert report is fully sourced and supported by competent authority, and that all calculations are easily followed by a lay audience.

012 The considerations discussed above go a long way toward meeting the mandatory standards which the American Institute of Certified Public Accountants (AICPA) requires its members to abide by in all professional engagements. Of course, these standards apply only to AICPA members. But it is still worthwhile to review them here. Briefly, the standards may be summarised as follows:

(1) Undertake only those engagements within your *technical competence*;
(2) Utilise *proper planning and supervision* during the engagement;
(3) Exercise *due care* throughout the engagement;
(4) Ensure that all conclusions are supported by *sufficient relevant data*.

013 These standards are no more than basic common sense, and are eminently reasonable. Certainly, they are not too much to ask in regard to professional work. Yet I am surprised to continue seeing expert reports by AICPA members that fail to meet one or more of the standards. Failure to meet the standards will clearly discredit the testimony of the expert in question when it comes to trial.

014 In fact, since the standards are such reasonable common sense, it would appear advisable for experts in *all fields* to comply with them. Failure to do so exposes an expert to the following type of cross-examination:

Q: I have read you the four AICPA standards. Do you believe that any of these standards is unreasonable to apply to your field of expertise?
A: No, I suppose not. (The expert will find it difficult indeed to argue unreasonableness.)
Q: Since you accept these standards as reasonable in regard to your field, does your report in fact conform with them? (The trap is sprung: the expert has endorsed the standards even though they do not formally govern the field in question. Now, woe betide this expert if he or she has contravened any of these standards—even if the expert had never even heard of these standards until now!)

015 Therefore, an astute cross examiner may compel *any* expert to accept the AICPA standards, even though the expert happens to be in a field far outside AICPA jurisdiction.

EXPERT AFFIDAVITS

016 Expert affidavits are often submitted in support of legal motions, such as summary judgment, or in responses to the motions of the opposition.

017 For the expert, the considerations involved in submitting an affidavit are similar to those discussed above in relation to expert reports. However, client attorneys often instruct the expert to limit the affidavit to stating conclusions, and not include the bases and reasons for opinions, nor the supporting data. In that case, the expert should prepare well-organised workpapers that reflect the bases and reasons for opinions, the supporting data, and details of any calculations. The workpapers would serve to support any testimony that may be given in deposition or trial by the expert, and would provide documentation that AICPA standards had been observed.

TESTIMONY AT DEPOSITION

018 Depositions of experts are examinations under oath which are an integral part of the legal discovery process. Several purposes may be fulfilled by expert depositions.

019 The basic purpose is to explore in depth the opinions to be offered by the expert, and the bases, support and data underlying those opinions. Opposing counsel will want to ascertain the crucial facts, assumptions, and methods relied upon by the expert, and to assess how firm the opinions are.

020 Also, the deposition offers the opportunity to see how well the expert can communicate, how convincing the tesimony may be, and how the expert stands up under cross-examination pressure. The objective is to gain information from the expert, but not to give away the cross-examination of the expert that will be made at trial (unless opposing counsel prefers to put some cards on the table, perhaps to induce a settlement of the case before trial).

021 Another important purpose of the deposition is to pin down the expert testimony. If an expert gives answers to cross-examination at trial that differ from the answers given at deposition, opposing counsel will confront the expert with the deposition testimony. This process will impeach expert testimony, unless the expert has valid and convincing reason for the changed answer—such as receiving important new information subsequent to deposition.

022 In sum, the overall objective of the deposition is to find the strengths and weaknesses of the expert testimony in order to develop appropriate strategies and tactics for trial. These strategies and tactics will probably be directed at diminishing the force of the expert testimony, and discrediting the expert.

023 The deposition will be used by opposing counsel to probe for weaknesses of various kinds in regard to the expert testimony. Possible areas of weakness may include the following.

QUALIFICATIONS OF THE EXPERT

024 These qualifications are:

- Does the expert appear to be a theorist lacking in practical experience?
- Is the expert's knowledge broad rather than specific to the relevant issues? For example, the expert may be well versed in valuing businesses, but has he or she ever valued the particular type of business involved in *this* case—which happens to be a tattoo parlour?
- Is the expert a specialist in an area different from that concerned in the case at hand? For example, is a medical pathologist offering expert testimony with respect to obstetrics?
- Is the expert's professional record mediocre, or flawed?
- Has the expert given any prior testimony or published works inconsistent with expert opinions offered in this case?
- Has any prior testimony or publication by this expert been rebutted or severely criticised?

OBJECTIVITY OF THE EXPERT

025 This can be determined as follows:

- Is the report of a "hired gun" suggested by possible signs such as repeatedly being retained by the same law firm, or continuously being retained by the plaintiff (or defendant) side, or working full-time on litigation matters as an expert?

- Are the expert's opinions based upon sound, independent investigation or do they appear to tilt conveniently to the client's views?
- Did the expert obtain information only from the client, or were outside sources used?
- How soon after being engaged did the expert form opinons?
- What are the fees being charged by the expert, how much has been billed to date, and how much has been paid on these bills?
- Are any fees contingent upon the outcome of the case?

QUALITY OF THE EXPERT REPORT

026 Criteria determining quality are:

- What part of the work was done by persons other than the expert, who are these persons, what are their experience and qualifications, how were they guided and supervised, and how was their work checked?
- Were there earlier drafts of some portions of the expert report, how did these prior drafts differ from the final draft, why were changes made, where are these prior drafts, why were they destroyed instead of being saved?
- What portions of the work did the expert personally perform, did these portions go through several draft stages, what errors were corrected in successive drafts?
- Was a generally accepted methodology employed, were any alternate methods considered, what are the strengths and weaknesses of the methods used, what was done to validate the results obtained, were repeated trials made in order to test the consistency of outcomes, and what was done to guard against errors and to check for accuracy?
- What data were obtained and from which sources, how and by whom were the data collected, how were the data protected from contamination, controlled for consistency and checked for comparability?

027 Overleaf are a number of strategies and tactics that the expert may employ in self-defence:

DO

✔ Listen carefully to each question, and be sure you understand it;

✔ Ask that compound questions be broken down into their individual component parts. If the questioner does not do so, the expert should proceed to do this task;

✔ Request that the questioner define any technical terms used in questions;

✔ Take time to think before answering;

✔ Ask to refer to documents if needed, especially if a question refers to one or more specific documents;

✔ Make each answer stand alone—it may be read back out of context at trial;

✔ Be polite, even if the questioner provokes or insults you;

✔ Beware of hypotheticals—often they are traps. Make sure that the questioner clearly states all assumptions in the hypothetical, write them down, and then carefully repeat all of the assumptions in your answer. It is also worth stating in your answer that these assumptions do not correspond with the facts of the case at hand;

✔ Beware of questions dealing in extremes with terms such as "always", "never", "certain" or "possible". The question may be designed to paint you into a corner;

✔ Hold firm to your opinions, but be open to new data. Make it clear that you keep an open mind.

DON'T

Don't volunteer—just answer the question asked; ✘

Don't guess—if unsure, say so; ✘

Don't bring any documents with you—your briefcase can be inspected; ✘

Don't let yourself be speeded up or rattled—some opposing counsel will subtly increase the tempo of the questioning in order to induce the expert to answer hastily; ✘

Don't try to stretch your qualifications or your opinions; ✘

Don't accept implicit assumptions in questions—ask that assumptions be made explicit; ✘

Don't accept as true, assumptions made by the questioner—a document may not state exactly what a lawyer says it states, and "isn't it true?" does not mean that it *is* true; ✘

Don't be reluctant to admit that you have discussed things with client counsel—that is not objectionable; ✘

Don't simply agree if you are asked "do you agree with the following ... ?". You may wish to qualify your answer to allow for exceptions or special cases; ✘

Don't display inappropriate or distracting mannerisms. If you must fidget, wiggle your toes inside your shoes where they are safely out of sight; ✘

Don't agree that your work is complete—state that you will continue to check and review your work until the time of the trial, and that, if new information comes to your attention, it will be taken into account; ✘

CREDIBILITY OF THE EXPERT

028 Counsel must decide whether or not to attack the methods and the conclusions of the opposing expert. In cases involving substantial complex expertise, a direct attack by counsel may be a daunting prospect. Few lawyers relish hand to hand conflict with a strong expert on the expert's own technical turf. On occasion, lawyers who have acquired the relevant knowledge, or who have experts of their own for support, may be able to prevail. But frequently lawyers will prefer not to make a frontal attack, and to adopt the safer course of a flank assault upon the qualifications or objectivity of the expert. Therefore experts are well advised to be prepared for a direct technical attack, but also to be ready for the lawyer who chooses to whittle away at qualifications or objectivity.

029 In this regard, the expert should obviously not play into the hands of the opposing attorney by making the mistake of exaggerating qualifications, or surrendering objectivity or becoming defensive, impatient or impolite. Nothing is more important than the demeanour of the expert: it is essential not to be arrogant or pompous. It is best to be frank and direct, and not to be evasive. Above all, the expert should be authentic—pretentiousness will be readily apparent and will reduce the expert's credibility.

DIRECT TESTIMONY AT TRIAL

030 Expert testimony at trial starts with direct examination by client counsel, after which comes the cross-examination by opposing counsel, which is limited to matters raised in the direct testimony. Next follows re-examination, which is limited to topics raised in cross-examination, and recross, which is limited to matters dealt with in re-examination.

031 Since the direct examination is friendly, and the cross-examination may be hostile, it is natural both for experts and friendly counsel to give prime attention to preparation for cross-examination. Of course cross-examination merits diligent preparation, but direct examination is equally important. Some points to consider are outlined below.

032 The court's first impression of the expert witness will be obtained at the start of his or her direct testimony. First impressions are significant: there is no second chance to make a first impression. Direct testimony of an expert usually commences by presenting the expert's qualifications, including education and experience. This should not be the customary recitation of degrees earned and punch marks in one's professional ticket. Rather, education and experience should be stated in a manner relevant to issues in the case.

033 For example, the author served as an expert in an antitrust case brought by a gasoline retailer against the large oil company which supplied it with gasoline, oil, and related goods. When stating qualifications in direct examination, it was brought out that the author had more than theoretical knowledge: he had actually worked in a gasoline station.

034 Also, qualifications should be meaningfully explained. For instance, it may not be sufficient to state that the expert occupies the distinguished professorial chair in fluid mechanics at Oxbridge University. Few people really understand what a professorial chair is. Therefore it is wise to explain the nature of an endowed chair, and just how and why the incumbent was selected for it.

035 The direct examination is the time when any weaknesses in the qualifications or the report of the expert should be dealt with. Some counsel and some experts may prefer to wait for the cross-examination and see whether or not the other side finds the flaws. However, it would seem wiser to take the initiative and bring out weaknesses. First, being frank wins credit for honesty, and establishes credibility for the remaining testimony. Secondly, admitting flaws under friendly examination allows full explanations to be given, whereas a skilled questioner will prevent full explanations being given for flaws brought out under cross-examination, thus rendering them more damaging. All in all, it takes the sting out of weaknesses if they are brought out voluntarily.

036 After stating expert qualifications, the direct examination usually presents the opinions of the expert, and the reasons and data supporting these opinions. At this stage, it is customary for the expert to display exhibits to illustrate the technical analysis performed and the results obtained. If the expert is an accountant or economist, it is likely that one or more computer spreadsheets will be shown and explained. In many instances, and especially in jury trials, this may be inadvisable.

037 In my experience, most people dislike numbers and have a fear of finance. At the sight of a spreadsheet, especially if there are many rows and columns, people simply tend to tune out. Therefore, it may be wise to avoid spreadsheets, and to use clearly understandable graphs and charts instead. If it is strongly believed that only a spreadsheet will do, then it would be helpful to begin by advancing a compelling reason for the court to grapple with the sea of numbers. For instance, the direct testimony might be as follows:

> Q: Was this fraud restricted to New York, or did it extend over a larger geographic area?
>
> A: The fraud extended to most of the stores operated by the company, not only in the US but also in many other countries. This spreadsheet shows how much money was stolen from each of the 500 stores operated by the company.

038 Courtroom exhibits relating to expert testimony are best shown as overhead transparencies, slides, or "blowup" posters. In any case, hard copy handouts should be provided for the judge and each member of the jury. Exhibits should be designed to be taken into the jury room, so that jurors can refresh their recollections of the expert testimony. My preference is to prepare exhibits with light colour messages on black backgrounds, so that opposing counsel cannot write on them. It is helpful to pull the exhibits together on a master summary chart. This demonstrates the collective impact of the testimony as a whole. It also allows the expert cogently to restate and synthesise the main themes of the testimony.

CROSS-EXAMINATION

039 As mentioned earlier, the expert should be prepared for challenges to qualifications, objectivity, methodology, data, validity of conclusions, and consistency with prior testimony (given at deposition or in previous cases), publications, and generally accepted standards. The attacks may be courteous or downright nasty. The expert should at all times remain polite, and not be drawn into defensive replies, anger, sarcasm, or evasiveness. It is helpful to bear in mind that opposing counsel with a strong case need not resort to dirty tactics. Therefore nastiness is the sure sign that opposing counsel lacks confidence in the merit of his or her case.

040 Experts who are well versed in scientific inquiry and the scholastic tradition are more likely to be shaken by legal tactics that appear shady in comparison with the more civil behaviour of academia. It is fundamental in scientific and scholarly circles to be impartial and open and to avoid *ad hominem* attacks. Some academics are thrown into disbelief and dismay when confronted by partisan, aggressive advocacy, and need to be well prepared beforehand in order to deal with a hostile style of cross-examination.

041 The expert should be prepared under cross-examination to be asked how the expert opinions might be altered by different data, methodology, assumptions, or alternative conclusions from the results of analysis. By these means, opposing counsel may be trying to render the expert testimony less clear cut and more diffuse. Therefore, when answering, the expert should carefully point out any alternatives posed by the questioner which do not apply to the instant case. It is still necessary to answer the question. But the expert can clearly state that the matter is hypothetical, and does not relate to the case at hand. By this means, the expert can prevent the cross-examination from blurring the direct testimony.

***John Leslie Livingstone** PhD, CPA, MAE has served as an expert accountant and economist in many significant cases over the past 20 years. He directs a nationwide management consulting practice headquartered in West Palm Beach, Florida. He is an Adjunct Professor at Babson College, and the author of numerous professional books and articles, some of which have been translated into Chinese, French, German, Indonesian, Portuguese and Spanish. This article first appeared in* The Expert, *March 1997, and is reproduced here by kind permission of the author.*

CHAPTER 1/20

THE EXPERT WITNESS IN AUSTRALIA

A A de Fina

INTRODUCTION

The court system

001 The Commonwealth of Australia is a federation of states and territories.[1]

002 The legal fabric of Australia provides *inter alia* for federal law (that is, law promulgated by the Commonwealth) to be applied uniformly throughout Australia and administered by a system of federal courts[2] of Australia.

003 The High Court, as the most senior Australian court, is established by the Commonwealth Constitution and has both appellate and original jurisdiction either by the Australian Constitution or by conferring by the Commonwealth Parliament.[3]

004 In its original jurisdiction the High Court is empowered, among other things, to deal with matters arising between residents of different states of the Commonwealth,[4] where the Commonwealth or a person being sued on behalf of the Commonwealth is a party[5] or matters between states or between a state and a resident of another state.[6]

005 In each state or territory, with the exception of external territories, there is established by enacting laws a Supreme Court[7] generally with unlimited jurisdiction in respect of matters arising in that state or territory except for matters expressly excluded by statute or invested in the High Court. There is normally a right of appeal from the judgment of a Supreme Court to the court's Court of Appeal[8] or Full Court[9] or, in some circumstances, directly to the High Court.

006 By cross vesting legislation[10] matters arising in some federal jurisdictions may be brought before state or territorial Supreme Courts,[11] and conversely some matters of state or territorial jurisdiction may be brought before a federal court.

007 Within states there are established intermediate courts which have statutory limitations on jurisdiction.[12] Such limitation is in respect of the value of money or property in dispute, or to subject matter.

008 The intermediate courts are variously titled county, district and local courts.[13] The lowest courts in the hierarchy are those presided over by magistrates and are known as magistrates' courts or local courts.[14] These courts have an extremely limited jurisdiction in civil cases and may deal only with minor offences or committal proceedings in criminal cases.

009 There are a number of other courts in Australia with differing specialist jurisdictions[15] as well as specialist tribunals or quasi-judicial bodies established by statute.[16]

The law of evidence

General

010 The municipal law of Australia is the common law derived from and formulated to a significant extent by the British common law system. The legal system is thus what may be loosely described as adversarial[17] and based upon precedent.[18]

011 In both civil and criminal proceedings trials in superior first instance courts may be conducted before a judge alone or a judge and jury. However, there is increasingly a tendency by legislators in some states to limit the use of juries.[19]

012 The modern law of evidence in Australia was created essentially by 19th and 20th century British case law and moulded by Australian case law.

013 Whilst a number of statutory reforms have been enacted over the past 100 years decisions of common law judges have dictated the form in which much of the law of evidence as it presently exists can be stated. Essentially, the modern day law of evidence consists substantially of exclusionary rules, that is, the rules provide for that which might not be allowed rather than that which might. For example, these rules require that certain matters of evidence of fact which might reasonably be accepted by specialist tribunals or quasi-judicial bodies may not be accepted by courts.

014 However, over recent years there has been an increasing tendency, particularly in civil cases, to water down but not to totally exclude the exclusionary rules relating to expert evidence and the weight which may be placed upon such evidence.[20]

Statutory provisions

015 The most important modern statutory reform is that introduced by the Evidence Act 1995 (Cth). This Act has been mirrored in legislation by one state[21] and has been foreshadowed for adoption in the balance of states of the Commonwealth.[22] In those states and territories where mirror legislation has not yet been introduced the Commonwealth provisions in respect of specified provisions within the Act itself apply.[23] Further, in any event, some of those provisions of the Act not expressly stated may apply by virtue of section 109 of the Constitution. This section in effect provides that where there is any conflict or inconsistency between the laws of a state or territory and the laws of the Commonwealth then the federal law shall prevail.

016 The amplitude of jurisdiction of the Evidence Act is extremely wide[24] and extends far beyond traditional courts.[25] However, the Act excludes application to appeals from a court of a state (including appeals from a court of a state exercising federal jurisdiction) and certain other courts. Where adopted by mirror state legislation, the State Acts are also extremely wide in granting jurisdiction.[26]

017 Different courts often apply the rules of evidence with differing emphasis. This may come about by express legislation in the statute establishing the court. However, if a statute is silent on the rules of evidence it does not follow that the rules of evidence are excluded.

018 Unless there is clear wording in an enabling statute or compelling context to the contrary in a particular jurisdiction or matter the rules of evidence shall apply.[27]

General application of rules of evidence

019 In the ordinary superior courts differences still exist between the rules which apply to the finding of facts at different stages within those proceedings. For example, variations apply prior to trial in respect of issues of fact which arise in relation to the admissibility of evidence, and after trial to those which arise on questions of sentence or on appeal. There are a large number of proceedings of a *quasi* judicial, administrative or legislative nature in which issues of fact require authoritative determination. Many of these proceedings are under the supervision or control by courts of law—for example in commercial arbitration,[28] but are not necessarily governed by the rules of evidence.[29]

020 However, even when the formal rules of evidence apply to a non-judicial tribunal the courts of most jurisdictions in Australia in review are less likely to require strict adherence to the rules of evidence by that tribunal.

EXPERT EVIDENCE

The role of the expert witness

021 The role of the expert was addressed by the Full Court of the Federal Court of Australia in *Arnotts Ltd* v. *Trade Practices Commission*[30] adopting the analysis of Sir Richard Eggleston in *R* v. *Parker*[31] who proposed that an expert has four functions as a witness: "[g]eneralising from experience, acting as a librarian, acting as a statistician, and acting as an advocate". An expert might properly generalise from training and experience to arrive at assertions of fact or of opinion.

022 The librarian function is explained in the following:

> "In many cases the expert does not himself know the answer to the problem from his own study or experience. But being trained in the relevant discipline, he is able to refer to works of authority in which the answer is given. In such a case the expert himself is not generalising, but is making available the fruits of generalisations by other people, either from their own experience or from the experience of others whose writings form part of the literature. The expert witness here is not giving evidence of his own opinion, except to say that in his expert opinion the books to which he is making reference are of sufficient standing to be accepted by the court."

The expert may also apply statistical methods to the material available from other sources to draw significant conclusions.[32]

023 Overall those propositions raise serious difficulties, particularly in distinguishing what might or might not be appropriate. An expert may have a proper role in advocacy in that having given to a tribunal the rules that the expert perceives to be applicable to a case, in such circumstances the evidence given by the witness may consist of argument amounting to advocacy as to what conclusions should be drawn from the facts interpreted in the light of the rules.

024 A difficulty can arise

> "[b]ecause the expert often finds it difficult to distinguish between arguments on the assumption that the 'facts' put forward by his side are the correct ones, and telling the judge or jury which facts they should accept as true. If he makes his assumptions clear, there is no objection to his arguing what the consequences of accepting those assumptions should be; but he is not to do the jury's fact finding for it, where this depends on accepting one or the other set of contradictory witnesses."[33]

025 There is also general acceptance in Australia as adopted in learned texts and by some judges in admitting expert evidence of the description of the expert's role as enunciated in an

English case and being "their duty is to furnish the judge or jury with the necessary scientific criteria for testing the accuracy of their conclusions, so as to enable the judge or jury to form their own independent judgement by the application of these criteria to the facts proved in evidence".[34]

Rules of expert evidence

General

026 The distinction to be drawn between the evidence of an expert witness and that of a lay witness is that an expert witness is extended the facility of giving evidence in the form of opinions and inferences although that facility is not necessarily absolute.

027 Australian and English courts, both of first instance and those of review, have continually expressed concern in respect of expert evidence on the grounds that might be generally categorised as follows:

(a) the role and function of juries might be unduly affected by expert evidence going to matters which are those properly and exclusively before the jury;
(b) where complex and conflicting expert evidence is given in a trial a jury may not be equipped to comprehend and evaluate such evidence appropriately;
(c) if an expert fails to disclose partisanship or bias a jury may be misled by the evidence given by that expert;
(d) the trier of fact, whether judge or jury, may not be assisted by expert evidence, the presentation of which may, among other things, unduly prolong litigation.

General position on expert evidence

028 The general Australian common law position applying to the admission of evidence and leading to the establishing of evidence which may be adduced by an expert is that precluding the giving of opinion and thus is exclusionary.

029 The provisions encompass five rules of law applicable to a witness as an expert and the evidence an expert witness may give. The provisions were stated in *Clark* v. *Ryan*[35] in the following terms:

> "A witness may not give his opinion on matters calling for the special skill or knowledge of an expert unless he is an expert in such matters, and he may not give his opinion on other matters if the facts upon which it is based can be stated without reference to it in a manner equally conducive to the ascertainment of the truth, or if it would not assist the court in coming to a conclusion. The expert will not be permitted to point out to the jury matters which the jury could determine for themselves or to formulate his empirical knowledge as a universal law."

030 This presumes the possibility of drawing a sharp distinction between inferences and the facts upon which such inferences are based. The common law system presumes the drawing of inferences as being a function of the judge or jury and the role of the witness is to state facts. However, notwithstanding the reservations expressed by courts as to the possible distortions arising from the use of expert witnesses, the fundamental principle appears to be an assumption that where special knowledge or skill is required judges and jurors are not necessarily properly equipped to draw appropriate inferences from the facts established.

031 The preliminary question of whether the matter at issue and for which expert evidence is sought to be called is one in which expert evidence can be called was dealt with in *R* v. *Bonython*[36] in the following terms:

"(a) whether the subject matter of the opinion is such that a person without instruction or experience in the area of knowledge or human experience would be able to form a sound judgement on the matter without the assistance of witnesses possessing special knowledge or experience in the area, and

(b) whether the subject matter of the opinion forms part of a body of knowledge or experience which is sufficiently organised or recognised to be accepted as a reliable body of knowledge or experience, a special acquaintance with which by the witness would render his opinion of assistance to the court."

032 In the common law context "opinion" is taken to mean "any inference from observed facts".

033 Although there is currently in Australia a great utilisation and reliance upon expert witnesses and the facility afforded such witnesses to draw inferences, the courts draw a distinction between inference and speculation. Where a qualified person enters into the field of mere speculation in evidence such evidence will be rejected as being speculation.[37]

034 Restrictions to expert evidence have been applied by the courts in reducing the areas in which it can be given. The corollary of being an expert is the principle that "what is generally known ought not be the subject of expert evidence". The concern that a juror may be overwhelmed by the impressiveness of an expert resulted in the common law rule that expert evidence may not be given on the ultimate issue. The difficulties in the ultimate issue rule in making the fine distinctions between those matters and circumstances upon which the ultimate issue may be determined and the ultimate issue itself was partially but not satisfactorily resolved by courts preventing expert witnesses using legal terminology or purporting to interpret legal standards.

035 Expert opinion going beyond or not necessarily relying upon inferences from fact need not be excluded.

036 A highly controversial judgment of the High Court of Australia on the existence or otherwise of confidentiality in arbitral proceedings[38] resulted from an appeal from a Court of Appeal judgment in review of first instance proceedings where opinion evidence of many recognised experts in the law and practice of arbitration from around the world on the matter of confidentiality in commercial arbitration was admitted.

037 In many areas of expertise which may be relevant to curial proceedings (given that many areas of skill and knowledge which may be the subject of expert evidence are continually developing) there may and, in some instances, will inevitably be contesting opinions among experts, particularly in areas that are yet to be generally accepted as valid and reliable. Contesting positions of expert witnesses on matters at issue involving well settled or accepted principles also consistently or sometimes inevitably occurs. Australian courts are more rigorously applying the view that expert opinions based upon the findings or theories of others are not susceptible of meaningful evaluation. That the originator of a theory or hypothesis or research, experimentation or evaluation does not present for testing by cross-examination and the expert witness relying on such findings or theories is in effect only a vehicle for transferring such knowledge is argued as not permitting appropriate evaluation or testing by triers of fact.

038 Australian courts, either at the instigation of a party and now more frequently on their own instigation, are querying the sufficiency of an expert's expertise for the particular case before them. As a consequence, courts have limited experts significantly. For example, a psychologist's qualifications in psycho-linguistics,[39] the ability of an eminent scientist to give evidence involving statistics,[40] a motor vehicle repairer's ability to give evidence about the causation of accidents,[41] a psychologist's qualifications and experience as being sufficient to give psycho-pharmacologic evidence on the effects of ingestion of drugs on an accused person's capacity to form a criminal intent[42] and the expertise of a psychologist to perform and interpret tests and diagnosis establishing that a person suffers from "post-concussion syndrome".[43]

039 Courts are, for the most part, now rigorous in preventing experts giving evidence beyond the boundaries of their expertise. Any such evidence may be declared inadmissible or perceived as lacking in credibility.

040 The responsibility of ensuring that inexpert evidence does not go before a jury lies solely with the judge or tribunal.[44] As a general observation, courts are expanding the areas in which expertise is accepted and in which expert evidence may be given. However, combined with that expansion is greater scrutiny and testing of an expert's qualifications and the nature of the expert's evidence which may be influential or possibly influential in determining a case.

Common law rules

041 Prior to the implementation of the Evidence Act 1995 (Cth) there were generally identified and recognised as effective five "rules of expert evidence" together with a further provision which if broadly interpreted becomes a *de facto* rule of expert evidence and which is described as "judicial notice".

042 The five general rules were described as

The expertise rule
The common knowledge rule
The area of expertise rule
The ultimate issue rule
The basis rule.

Effect of Evidence Act on common law rules

043 By the Evidence Act the ultimate issue and common knowledge rules have been abolished.[45]

044 These provisions of section 80 of the Act are not inconsistent with the position previously adopted by some courts in respect of the ultimate issue rule—for example, in determining similarity of an original design of a house with an alleged copy in a copyright action brought before the Supreme Court in New South Wales.[46]

045 The Act does not affect the operation of any other Act[47] nor does it affect principles of rules of common law or equity except as expressly provided.[48] Accordingly, the expertise rule, the area of expertise rule and the basis rule remain unaffected.

046 Judicial notice is also an express provision.[49]

047 Some general provisions of the Act include

(a) requiring a witness to take an oath or make an affirmation before giving evidence[50];
(b) empowering the court to make such orders as it considers just in relation to[51];
  (i) the way in which witnesses are to be questioned;

(ii) the production and use of documents and things in connection with the questioning of witnesses.

048 But the Act does not affect the common law position in relation to calling and examination of witnesses by the court whether expert or otherwise.[52]

THE EVIDENCE ACT

The Evidence Act 1995 (Cth)

The opinion rule

049 The Evidence Act provides as follows[53]: "The opinion rule—evidence of an opinion is not admissible to prove the existence of a fact about the existence of which the opinion was expressed".

050 But there are exemptions provided in the Act of themselves giving some credence to a view that the rule in strict terms does not exist or is of limited effect.[54] Specific exemptions are:

(i) summaries of voluminous or complex documents[55];
(ii) evidence relevant otherwise than as opinion evidence[56];
(iii) lay opinion[57];
(iv) expert opinion[58];
(v) admissions[59];
(vi) exceptions to the rule excluding evidence of judgments and convictions[60];
(vii) character of and expert opinion about accused persons.[61]

Exceptions to the opinion rule

EXCEPTION: EVIDENCE RELEVANT OTHERWISE THAN AS OPINION EVIDENCE

051 The exception in respect of evidence relevant otherwise than as opinion evidence is stated in the following terms: "s.77: the opinion rule does not apply to evidence of an opinion that is admitted because it is relevant for a purpose other than proof of the existence of a fact about the existence of which the opinion was expressed".

052 This provision allows the admission of evidence to be used to establish the facts in question. That is, to allow admitted evidence to be used for purposes other than that for which it was originally admissible. However the Act imposes discretionary limitations to the use to which such evidence might be put.[62] Such limiting might be imposed if there is a danger that a particular use of the evidence might:

(a) be unfairly prejudicial to a party, or
(b) be misleading or confusing.

053 There is also the exception in respect of evidence relevant for non-hearsay purposes[63] which excludes the application of the hearsay rule[64]: "[t]o evidence of a previous representation that is admitted because it is relevant for a purpose other than proof of a fact intended to be asserted by the representation".

EXCEPTION: LAY OPINIONS

054 Section 78 provides as follows:

"The opinion rule does not apply to evidence of an opinion expressed by a person if:
(a) the opinion is based on what the person saw, heard or otherwise perceived about a matter or event, and
(b) evidence of the opinion is necessary to obtain an adequate account or understanding of the person's perception of the matter or event."

055 It is sometimes difficult to draw the distinction between fact and opinion. Non-expert opinions on such matters as identification,[65] speed, weather, temperature, handwriting and age[66] are permitted as in general terms they are not matters which call for special knowledge,[67] and also as it would be almost impossible to separate inferences from those facts upon which the inferences are based. Lay evidence may be given to establish that a person has consumed alcohol although no objective tests may have been carried out to confirm the nature of the consumed beverage.[68] This rule also allows a witness to answer hypothetical questions related to issues of reliance.[69]

056 Non-experts may be asked to give evidence on whether they consider a person with whom they are well acquainted to be sane.[70]

EXCEPTION: OPINIONS BASED ON SPECIALISED KNOWLEDGE (EXPERT OPINION)

057 By section 79 of the Act an effectively expansive definition of what tests are to be applied to categorise a person who may give opinion evidence is provided: "if a person has specialised knowledge based on the person's training, study or experience, the opinion rule does not apply to evidence of an opinion of that person that is wholly or substantially based on that knowledge."

Limitation on application of opinion rule

Application of opinion rules to admissions

058 By section 81 of the Evidence Act *inter alia* the opinion rule does not apply to evidence of an admission,[71] nor to evidence of a previous representation[72]

"(a) [t]hat was made in relation to an admission at the time the admission was made, or shortly before or after that time, and
(b) to which it is reasonably necessary to refer in order to understand the admission."

059 This exclusion is consistent with the common law position which allows as admissible as against the party making such admissions. The provision applies even if the person making the admission had no direct knowledge of the fact admitted.[73]

Exceptions to the rule—excluding evidence of judgments and convictions

060 In civil proceedings, the provisions of section 91(1) allows admission or use of evidence of grant of probate, letters of administration or a similar order of a court to prove

"(a) the death, or date of death, of a person, or
(b) the due execution of a testamentary document".[74]

061 Section 92(3) allows the admission or use of evidence that a party, subject to limitation, seeks to adduce in respect of another party being convicted of an offence.

> "In a civil proceeding, section 91(1) does not prevent the admission or use of evidence that a party, or a person through or under whom a party claims, has been convicted of an offence, not being a conviction:
> (a) in respect of which a review or appeal (however described) has been instituted but not finally determined, or
> (b) that has been quashed or set aside, or
> (c) in respect of which a pardon has been given."[75]

062 By section 92(3) *inter alia* the opinion rule does not apply to evidence of a kind referred to in section 92(1) and (2).

Exceptions to the rule—excluding expert opinion about accused persons

063 These provisions of the Act apply only in criminal proceedings. By section 110 *inter alia* the opinion rule does not apply:

(a) To evidence adduced by a defendant to prove (whether directly or by implication) that the "[d]efendant is, either generally or in a particular respect, a person of good character".[76]

(b) Where evidence adduced to prove (directly or by implication) that a defendant is generally a person of good character has been admitted, *inter alia* the opinion rule does not apply to "evidence adduced to prove (directly or by implication) that the defendant is not generally a person of good character".[77]

(c) Where evidence adduced to prove (directly or by implication) that a defendant is a person of good character in a particular respect has been admitted, *inter alia* the opinion rule does not apply to evidence adduced to prove (directly or by implication) "that the defendant is not a person of good character in that respect".[78]

064 These provisions follow the common law as it applies to an accused person raising by evidence alleged prior good character. However, by these provisions, limitations existing at common law of the prosecution to raise bad character of the accused[79] is less fettered.

Exception to the rule—Evidence about character of co-accused

065 These provisions apply only in criminal proceedings.

066 By section 111 of the Act where evidence of an opinion about a defendant is adduced by another defendant; and the person expressing the opinion has specialised knowledge based on the person's training, study, or experience; and the opinion is wholly or substantially based on that knowledge,[80] then if such evidence has been admitted *inter alia* the opinion rule does not apply to "[e]vidence adduced to prove that that evidence should not be accepted".[81]

General exclusionary powers in respect of opinion evidence

067 If opinion evidence is otherwise admissible under section 59 of the Act, it may still be excluded by the exercise of the courts' discretionary powers in particular circumstances.[82] In exercising the discretion, relevant factors include:

(a) the nature of the "specialised knowledge";
(b) the affect of its admission on the conduct of the proceedings;
(c) the nature of the issue to which the "specialised knowledge" relates;
(d) whether by admission there will be a risk that the evidence will shift the focus of the proceedings "[f]rom the evidence of the facts in dispute to the conflict between competing theories".[83]

Waiver of the rules of evidence

068 Having established detailed and in some instances expansive provisions in relation to evidence and conduct of proceedings, the Evidence Act at section 190 empowers a court, subject to the agreement of the parties, to dispense with many of the other provisions of the Act in the following terms:

"(1) The court may, if the parties consent, by order dispense with the application of any one or more of the provisions of:
(a) Division 3, 4 or 5 of Part 2.1, or
(b) Parts 2.2 or 2.3, or
(c) Parts 3.2–3.8,
in relation to particular evidence or generally.
(2) In a criminal proceeding, a defendant's consent is not effective for the purposes of subsection (1) unless:
(a) the defendant has been advised do so by his or her lawyer, or
(b) the court is satisfied that the defendant understands the consequences of giving the consent.
(3) In a civil proceeding, the court may order that any one or more of the provisions mentioned in subsection (1) do not apply in relation to evidence if:
(a) the matter to which the evidence relates is not genuinely in dispute, or
(b) the application of those provisions would cause or involve unnecessary expense or delay.
(4) Without limiting the matters that the court may take into account in deciding whether to exercise the power conferred by subsection (3), it is to take into account:
(a) the importance of the evidence in the proceeding, and
(b) the nature of the cause of action or defence and the nature of the subject-matter of the proceeding, and
(c) the probative value of the evidence, and
(d) the powers of the court (if any) to adjourn the hearing, to make another order or to give a direction in relation to the evidence."

069 By section 190(3)(b) in civil proceedings parties would appear *inter alia* to be empowered to agree not to call expert evidence over a view by the court that such evidence might be helpful or even determinative if the parties or either one of them succeed in arguing that the cost of experts is an unnecessary expense in all circumstances.

Power of courts to conduct proceedings

070 As well as the application of common law and equity as provided by section 9 and discussed above section 11(1) of the Act provides that the general "[p]ower of a court to control the conduct of a proceeding is not affected by this Act, except so far as this Act provides otherwise expressly or by necessary intendment".

071 Additionally, by section 26 the courts' control over the questioning of witnesses is maintained in the following terms:

"The court may make such orders as it considers just in relation to:
(a) the way in which witnesses are to be questioned, and
(b) the production and use of documents and things in connection with the questioning of witnesses, and
(c) the order in which parties may question a witness, and
(d) the presence and behaviour of any person in connection with the questioning of witnesses."

EXPERTISE

What constitutes expertise

Formal qualifications

072 In the common law context there is, and remains, controversy on whether expertise that is acquired in a non-academic or informal way by an accumulation of skills is sufficient to designate a person as expert. To that extent the law in Australia appears confused and uncertain. The categorisation under the Evidence Act and rules of court where such rules do provide positive guidance would appear clear and unequivocal but are not limiting.

073 Given the settled law as to the test to be applied for admission as an expert, the question of who may be admitted as an expert should lead to a simple answer, but this is not the case.

074 Such difficulty as might arise flows from the express provision in the Evidence Act partially limiting its application to the operation of a principle or rule of common law or equity and preserving the written and unwritten laws of a state or territory.[84]

075 The seminal common law case in respect of expert witnesses generally is that of *Clark* v. *Ryan.*[85] In that case before the High Court of Australia the appeal point was the admissibility of opinion evidence relating to the causes of a highway collision between an articulated semi-trailer vehicle and a motorvan. A witness at the first instance trial gave evidence to the effect that an articulated semi-trailer vehicle had a characteristic of swinging out when taking a bend and that special care was needed. The witness had no engineering diploma or certificate but had, for some 50 years, been engaged in investigating road accidents for insurance companies and others and in assessing losses. Variously the judges of the High Court observed that to give evidence on how semi-trailers might behave witnesses experienced in their use might give evidence of fact, that the expert's evidence was partly evidence of opinion that lay outside any qualifications that the witness could be said to possess, that the witness expressed conjectures which paraded as scientific opinion and that to describe the witness as an expert was for the purposes of enlisting the witness as an advocate.

076 The divergent opinions expressed by members of the High Court are reflected in judgments in state courts. Courts in New South Wales and South Australia have admitted as expert evidence opinions in areas in which there is no formal study or qualification, for example, sufficiency of a representation on business being done in a hotel in supporting a representation made as observed by an experienced hotelier attending the hotel over a period of time[86] and dissenting views on whether a police officer with 12 years' experience in investigating traffic accidents was qualified as an expert to express an opinion in respect of a traffic accident.[87]

077 The question of being an expert on foreign law was addressed in a single Australian decision involving alleged liability for taxation.[88] In this case, the taxpayer himself claimed the right to give expert evidence concerning the formation of a particular entity in the Principality of Liechtenstein and the law in respect of that entity and whether or not that entity had appointed him to act as agent on its behalf. In this case the court allowed the taxpayer as an expert in some of the matters but not in others. Perhaps an indication as to the possible future might be reflected in the judgment of *Luder* v. *Luder*[89] where the trial judge held that "Expert evidence as to foreign law may be given by witnesses who have acquired a special experience therein. It is not necessary that they should be professional lawyers, but it is sufficient if they occupy a post which gives them experience in the law of the foreign country".

Source of expertise

078 It would appear that under the modern Evidence Acts of Australia the source of an expert's expertise assumes substantially diminished importance compared to the common law requirements as existed prior to the implementation of current statute, and may arguably be now of no importance at all. A simple statement of the current position in Australia may be that provided there is specialised knowledge held by a witness and that knowledge is relevant to the proceedings then the witness's opinions will be admissible provided they are substantially referrable to that knowledge.

079 Where an expert's opinion is based upon facts or alleged facts then those facts must be available for scrutiny by the court. A court must require an explanation of the basis upon which an expert expresses an opinion.[90]

080 It is not sufficient for the opinion of an expert to be based upon material that the expert has read, or evidence given in court and heard by the expert without express identification given by the expert as to those matters[91] and for such matters to be proved.[92]

Field of expertise

081 The admissibility of expert opinion evidence at common law generally required that the witness's opinion relate to and be based upon a recognised field of expertise. Why this should be the position is unclear from the authorities but appears to be the result of partially pragmatic approaches by courts in certain matters.

082 One position adopted by the courts required that the area of expertise purported to be held by an expert witness was "[s]ufficiently established to have gained general acceptance in the particular field to which it belongs".[93] A differing and perhaps more lenient position arose where a court was satisfied that there was a reliable basis for the opinion.[94]

083 The more lenient approach to the admissibility of expert evidence in areas or subjects with which members of the public can expect to have knowledge has been exhibited more frequently in non-jury cases. For example, in a trade practices and negligence case in a trial before a judge alone, the judge was prepared to admit expert evidence on a question in which understanding did not require a special study.[95] The court held: "One difficulty about the view that opinions from experts will not be received except where the field of study is one which requires expertise for understanding is [that] much useful evidence may be lost by such a rule."

084 The judge pointed out that where a question concerns the likely human reactions to particular forms of words, studies may have been done which enable those familiar with the studies "to help the court, even though the court may reach a sound opinion without reference to such studies". The test of whether a particular field of knowledge is a sufficiently organised and recognised branch of science for the purposes of a particular case will depend upon the evidence led in support of the conclusion and the express question upon which the expert's opinion is sought.[96]

COMMON LAW RULES

Common law rules remaining in effect

085 The Evidence Act by its terms does not restrict the application of a number of common law rules developed and existing prior to the introduction of the Evidence Act other than as expressly provided by the terms of the Act.[97]

086 Common law rules remaining totally or substantially effective are the expertise rule, area of expertise rule, and the basis rule.

Expertise rule

087 Simply stated, the expertise rule provides that a witness cannot give opinion evidence if not properly qualified by the court as being an expert. Such qualification does not necessarily turn upon any strict definition but often upon adequacy and particularly relevance of specialised skills or knowledge held by the witness.

088 However, to be so qualified as an expert does not require that a witness be a leading or senior practitioner in the particular field.[98]

089 An expert witness may be permitted to give evidence in the form of facts among other things based upon the application of expertise, for example in the conduct of experiments, or on matters observed.

Area of expertise rule

General

090 Whether or not the evidentiary rule of exclusion applies to prevent expert evidence on areas that are not defined as ones of expertise, irrespective of the expert's skills and training, is presently not settled. The rapid development of areas which were once not considered areas of expertise but have then become accepted as such is commonplace in areas of science and technology, medicine and like areas. Finger printing, voice identification, stylometry evidence, polygraph evidence, DNA profiling, consistently become more and more refined and more and more accepted as having a testable scientific basis.

091 The question of what might be novel scientific evidence today but accepted scientific evidence tomorrow can never be appropriately resolved. Essentially, courts require to be satisfied that techniques or technology have a sufficient scientific basis to render results arrived at by that means as being part of a field of knowledge which is a proper subject of expert evidence.[99] In 1985 a court in Victoria[100] found that "stylistic analysis of documents is a science" and "in appropriate cases expert opinion based on such analysis could be received in evidence when disputes had arisen concerning the authenticity of documents and in particular whether or not words appearing in a document were the words of a particular person".

092 Australian courts would appear to be following some of the principles laid down by United States courts in dealing with what might otherwise be considered esoteric areas. For example, in *R* v. *Runjanjic*[101] the judge applied the United States *Frye*[102] principles as a criteria for the admissibility of novel psychological evidence in relation to a battered wife syndrome case. However, the adoption of the *Frye* test has and remains the subject of judicial controversy, particularly as it is not adopted uniformly in the United States.

093 However, whatever the position adopted by the courts, evidence was not necessarily ruled as inadmissible only because the opinions proffered were based on a particular unproven theory that was not supported by the weight of scientific opinion.[103] The requirement of the Evidence Act that the opinion be based upon an area of "specialised knowledge" would appear to be more expansive than the common law position.

094 Given the qualifying wording of section 79 of the Act it would appear still open to argument as to what the term "specialised knowledge" means.[104] The position appears to be that what "specialised knowledge" is turns upon the circumstances and issues in each particular case.

095 Where the issues are of a scientific, technical, medical or like discipline the predominant view is that appropriate expertise could not be acquired other than by some formal and extensive education and satisfactory qualification or training as part of such education. However, where matters at issue cannot be so categorised and the specialised knowledge may arise from experience, provided such experience is relevant and is otherwise admissible, lack of formal peer recognition, or the lack of existence of a peer group at all, should not prevent opinion evidence based on such specialised knowledge to be admitted.

096 Courts have admitted opinion evidence from a store detective as to conduct,[105] viewing video films,[106] and experience of adolescent girls.[107]

097 An important test applied is the capacity of a tribunal of fact to arrive at appropriate conclusions without expert assistance in deciding the admission of expert evidence. If the issues can be competently approached without expert evidence courts are more likely to limit the admission of such evidence.[108] The corollary of this position was stated in *Cameron* v. *The Queen*[109] in the following terms—"expert evidence is admissible if the relevant facts cannot be made known to the jury without the aid of expert opinion".

098 It would appear that the underlying assumption applied by many judges in allowing or disallowing expert evidence is that there is an area of matters in which juries need no assistance. The difficulty with this position is that there is no clear dividing line and the dividing line, if it exists, will depend upon the facts and circumstances of each particular case. These facts and circumstances may not be disclosed until all of the evidence is on and premature limiting or denying expert evidence may act to the detriment of an appropriate outcome.

Relevance

099 A fundamental test to be applied by courts at all times is that of relevance. At common law opinion evidence was not admissible unless its factual basis was established.[110] The Evidence Act does not impose such a requirement. However the Act does require the admission only of relevant evidence by section 56 as follows:

"(1) Except as otherwise provided by this Act, evidence that is relevant in a proceeding is admissible in the proceeding.
(2) Evidence that is not relevant in the proceeding is not admissible."

100 Whilst section 56(2) is a restatement of the common law rules of evidence, the provisions of section 56(1) appear to remove all of the common law restrictions on admissibility but this is not clear.

101 The exclusion of relevant evidence under the provisions of the Act is governed by specific exclusionary and procedural rules. However, it is open to argument as to whether an expert opinion is advanced without supporting basis, the requirement of relevance can in any event be satisfied.

Definitions

102 The provisions of the Evidence Act giving an effective definition of an expert[111] can be distinguished for example from the express definition of an expert as provided in Australian Corporations Law which provides that "expert, in relation to a matter, means a person whose professional reputation gives authority to a statement made by him or her in relation to that matter".

103 The extent to which this definition might be applied in litigation involving Corporations Law and its effect upon the admission of expert witnesses and expert evidence in such litigation remains to be tested.

104 Court rules in some jurisdictions do provide a definition for the purposes of proceedings before those courts. For example, Order 39, rule 1 of the Australian High Court Rules provides that an "expert" includes "a scientific person, a lawyer, a medical man, an engineer, an accountant, an actuary, an architect, surveyor or other skilled person whose opinion on a question relevant to the issues involved would be received by the court". However, this rule is not limiting in its amplitude.

105 In the Australian Federal Court Rules[112] an effective definition of an expert is provided in the following terms: "An expert, in relation to any question, means a person who has knowledge or experience of, or in connection with, that question, or questions of the character of that question, that his opinion would be admissible in evidence".

106 As a general observation there appears to be no inconsistency between the definitions or effective definitions of who may be admitted as an expert in differing jurisdictions within Australia.

The basis rule

General

107 In addition to being permitted to give evidence of opinion experts may give evidence of fact. Much of the evidence given by experts is in the form of descriptions of what they have perceived. In this form such evidence is subject to the same rules as apply to lay witnesses, thus, subject to permitted exceptions, experts cannot give evidence which is hearsay. However, when they are giving evidence of opinion the hearsay rule is not necessarily strictly applied and to this extent has created problems.

108 In the Australian context, the most controversial and the most litigated issue in expert evidence law has related to the status of expert opinion evidence when not all of the factual basis upon which the opinion is given has been proved to the court. That is, that the opinion evidence is wholly or partly based on hearsay. The basis rule requires that the basis upon which an opinion is expressed must of itself be proved by admissible evidence. If that is not so, then the question before the court becomes one merely of weight to be given to evidence that relies upon material not adduced before the court.

109 As with other rules applying to expert witnesses there is and continues debate as to the very existence of a basis rule which would prevent the giving of opinion evidence unless its bases were admitted in evidence.

110 Objectively, almost all expert witnesses employ hearsay to some degree in forming their views. Where too much hearsay has been adopted by the expert in forming an opinion it becomes effectively impossible to evaluate such opinion.

111 Courts in Australia have not tended to insist upon proof of the extrinsic material normally employed by experts to carry out their work, for example, understanding obtained from the use of professional libraries and knowledge acquired in the discharge of professional duties.[113] The distinction drawn has been categorised as an insistence that when a particular passage of another person's work is cited basis evidence must be adduced.

112 However, psychologists and psychiatrists have been held able to give evidence of what a client said to them in order to explain why they reached certain opinions about the client's state of mind or behaviour. This is because it is evidence not of the truth of what was said but merely of the basis of the opinion formed.[114]

Distinctions in different proceedings

113 Judgments from the New South Wales, Queensland and Victorian Supreme Courts tend towards the position that while flexibility is applied in civil proceedings where a jury is absent, the presence of a jury in criminal proceedings has led to the development of an exclusionary rule of admissibility when expert opinion evidence is proffered to the court without its basis having been proved to the requisite degree.[115]

114 The apparent leniency extended in civil cases is exampled in *Pysch* v. *Hunter*.[116] The trial judge excluded opinion evidence based on what a psychiatrist had learned from the plaintiff's mother who was not called to give evidence. In a valuation case[117] in the Supreme Court of New South Wales the trial judge held that an expert could give evidence on sales of comparable land only if other direct evidence was provided.

115 In criminal cases the more rigorous application of the rule and its terms was stated in *R* v. *Perry*[118] as follows: "since opinion evidence involves the drawing of inferences and conclusions from facts, the admissibility of such evidence depends upon proof or admission of the facts upon which the opinion is based".

116 An example of judicial thinking of admitting a basis evidence but potentially mistrusting the outcome was given in *Milirrpum* v. *Nabalco Pty Ltd*[119] in the federal court in which the trial judge had occasion to consider the basis upon which an anthropologist had given his expert evidence.

> "The anthropologist should be able to give his opinion based on his investigation by processes normal to his field of study just as any other expert does. To rule out any conclusion based to any extent upon hearsay—the statements of other persons—would be to make a distinction, for the purposes of the law of evidence, before a field of knowledge directly concerned with the behaviour of human beings, such as anthropology. A chemist can give an account of the behaviour of inanimate substances in reaction, but an anthropologist must limit his evidence to that based upon what he has seen the aboriginals doing, and not upon what they have said to him."

117 Having admitted the evidence the trial judge then adopted a position which allowed a degree of avoidance by the following: "It seems to me that the question is one of weight, rather than of admissibility, of the evidence, and the court must be astute to enquire how far any conclusion proffered by an expert is indeed based upon facts and to weigh it accordingly."

118 In *Marinovich* v. *The Queen*[120] an Appeals Court in Western Australia applied similar principles in relation to evidence given by police officers concerning the values, purities and nomenclature of various forms of illegal drugs.

119 The High Court of Australia interpreted its earlier pronouncements in *Paric* v. *John Holland (Constructions) Pty Ltd*[121] in the following terms: "It is trite law that for an expert medical opinion to be of any value the facts upon which it is based must be proved by admissible evidence".

Difficulty of application

120 Essentially the difficulty remains that whilst an expert might properly rely upon accumulated knowledge acquired in the usual maintenance of development of his professional position the boundaries of such knowledge and permissible use of it for evidence are not easy to fix. An expert is permitted to rely upon general training and skills which have rendered her or him an expert.[122] The Court of Appeal in *R* v. *Abadom*[123] acknowledged that when an expert is required to consider the likelihood or unlikelihood of some occurrence or factual association in forming a conclusion the statistical results of the work of others must inevitably form an important ingredient in the cogency or probity value of the expert's conclusions in a particular case.

121 The difficulty of limitation and categorisation was addressed in *Borowski* v. *Quayle*[124] where the trial judge referred at length to *Wigmore on Evidence* (1961–1979) in the following terms:

> "The data of every science are enormous in scope and variety. No one professional man can know from personal observation more than a minute fraction of the data which he must every day treat as working truths. Hence a reliance on the reported data of fellow scientists, learned by pursuing their reports in books and journals. The law must and does accept this kind of knowledge from scientific men. On the one hand, a mere layman, who comes to the court and alleges a fact which he has learned only by reading a medical or mathematical book, cannot be heard. On the other hand, to reject a professional physician or mathematician because the fact or some facts to which he testifies are known to him only upon the authority of others would be to ignore the accepted methods of professional work and to insist on finical and impossible standards."

Judicial notice

General

122 Australian courts may take "judicial notice" of a variety of matters which might otherwise have to be proved by expert or lay evidence. A statement made by Lord Sumner J as to the meaning of judicial notice was adopted in *Commonwealth Shipping Representative* v. *P&O Branch Service*[125] in the following terms:

> "At the stage when evidence of material facts can be properly received, certain facts may be deemed

to be established, although not proved by sworn testimony, or by the production, out of the proper custody, of documents, which speak for themselves. Judicial notice refers to facts which a judge may be called upon to receive and act upon, either from his own general knowledge of them or from enquiries to be made by himself and for his own information from sources for which it is proper for him to refer."

123 In *Holland* v. *Jones*,[126] when considering judicial notice, the trial judge held in the following terms:

> "The only guiding principle—apart from statute—as to judicial notice which emerges from the various reported cases, appears to be that wherever a fact is so generally known that every ordinary person may be reasonably presumed to be aware of it, the court 'notices' it, either *simpliciter* if it is once satisfied of the fact without more, or after information or investigation as it considers reliable and necessary in order to eliminate any reasonable doubt."

124 However, as observed by the Australian Law Commission[127] there appear to be many cases departing from the principle in pursuit of convenience or pragmatism. The result is that "as to purely factual matters, the scope of the power of the court is in doubt with decisions departing from the original formulations or principles. Also the mandatory and discretionary aspects of the power are unclear".

Statutory provisions

125 By section 144 of the Evidence Act there is provided:

> "(1) Proof is not required about knowledge that is not reasonably open to question and is:
> (a) common knowledge in the locality in which the proceeding is being held or generally, or
> (b) capable of verification by reference to a document the authority of which cannot reasonably be questioned.
> (2) The judge may acquire knowledge of that kind in any way the judge thinks fit.
> (3) The court (including, if there is a jury, the jury) is to take knowledge of that kind into account.
> (4) The judge is to give a party such opportunity to make submissions, and to refer to relevant information, relating to the acquiring or taking into account of knowledge of that kind as is necessary to ensure that the party is not unfairly prejudiced."

Common knowledge

126 Both the statutory provisions and the common law insofar as it might apply depends in the facility for judicial notice upon "common knowledge". By section 80 of the Evidence Act the previous rule preventing the receival of expert evidence on matters of common knowledge was abolished as a separate basis and eliminated what might otherwise be argued as an anomaly in the position in respect of judges on the one hand and experts on the other. What may or may not be common knowledge, whether for the purposes of evidence or judicial notice, will depend upon the nature of the matter and the particular circumstances.[128] However, by the rules of some courts, matters which are not reasonably open to question may be admitted whether or not they are common knowledge.[129]

Examples of judicial notice

127 Some examples of judicial notice in Australian law are the identity of the Minister for Defence,[130] the standards of weight and measure, the public coin and currency.[131] There are examples of other matters which *prima facie* would appear to have required expert evidence but nevertheless have been treated in the same way. For example:

1. The fact that venereal disease may lie dormant for a long time[132];
2. The construction of a crayfish catching pot[133];
3. The fact that bushland was cleared and occupied with claims made on behalf of the clearers' families[134];
4. The individuality of the corrugations of the skin of the fingers on a human hand (fingerprints)[135];
5. The fact that in South Australia the same farmland may be cropped only once every third year.[136]

Limitations

128 The difficulty in distinguishing that which is within the realm of common knowledge from that which is not and then to establish a definitive statement as to what constitutes or might constitute judicial notice in Australian law is effectively impossible. An important test required under the provisions of section 114(1) is that the knowledge is "[n]ot reasonably open to question". To the extent that this issue might be arguable there would appear no limitation to admitting expert evidence going to reasonableness or otherwise. If there is expert or other disputation about a matter which is sufficiently within the public domain to be classified as general knowledge then it is arguable that it ought not be the subject of judicial notice.

REFORM AND COURT INITIATIVES

Australian Law Reform Commission

129 Cognisant of mounting community criticism of the cost of justice in Australia and the complexity and difficulty apparent in the legal system, in 1995 the then Attorney-General of the Commonwealth of Australia, Michael Lavarch, referred to the Law Reform Commission[137] a review of the adversarial system of litigation.[138] By its preamble, the reference stated:

> "[H]aving regard to:
> - the need for a simpler, cheaper and more accessible legal system;
> - The Justice Statement; and
> - recent and proposed reforms to courts and tribunals",

and, by its terms of reference, required the Commission to enquire and report upon

> "(a) the advantages and disadvantages of the present adversarial system of conducting civil, administrative review and family law proceedings before courts and tribunals exercising federal jurisdiction;
>
> (b) whether any changes should be made to the practices and procedures used in those proceedings; and

(c) any related matter"

and to consider among other matters

"• civil litigation and administrative law procedures in civil code jurisdictions;
• the procedures and case management schemes used by courts and tribunals to control the conduct of proceedings that come before them;
• the relationship between courts and tribunals;
• mechanisms for identifying the issues in dispute;
• means of gathering, testing and examining evidence;
• the use of court-based and community alternative dispute resolution schemes;
• the significance of legal education and professional training to the legal process;
• the training, functions, duties and role of judicial officers as managers of the litigation process;
• appellate court processes".

130 In examining the cost of civil litigation, the Australian Institute of Judicial Administration in its study of the District Court of Queensland and the County Court of Victoria[139] found that the costs of medical reports and medical experts constituted a significant proportion of total costs in litigation in Victoria, ranging from 27 per cent of costs of cases settled pre-trial and 16 per cent of costs where a matter went to verdict, with lesser but still significant costs in Queensland.

131 The report suggested restrictions on the adversarial use of medical evidence, including:

• Compelling early disclosure of all medical reports;
• Restricting witnesses;
• The use of court-appointed experts;
• Altering the rules on taxing of costs bills to minimise experts costs recovery.

132 In its background paper the Law Reform Commission recognised that complex issues of science and technology are increasingly coming before the courts resulting in an increased use of expert witnesses.[140] An increasingly influential body of thought argues that experts are not now so much providers of expert opinions but as skilled guides to lead the court to understand matters of fact which take an expert to discern them.[141]

133 In its discussion reform proposals, the paper refers significantly to the report of Lord Woolf on the civil justice system in England and Wales,[142] particularly the reference to "fast-track" cases and providing power in the court to direct

"• that no expert evidence is to be adduced at all, or no expert evidence of a particular type or relating to a particular issue;
• that the number of expert witnesses *per* party be limited, either generally or in a given speciality;
• that evidence is to be given by one or more experts chosen by agreement between the parties or appointed by the court;
• that expert evidence is to be given in written form without the expert's attendance at court".

134 Significant discussion on the court appointment of experts has arisen. Some Australian courts have powers to so appoint.[143] This power is however rarely used apparently as it is additional to the rights of the parties to call expert witnesses, and would, in most circumstances, only arise for consideration after parties have had experts prepare reports in support or defence of their case.

135 The Queensland Litigation Reform Commission has proposed a provision allowing only for court-appointed expert witnesses.[144] Parties would not have a right to call expert witnesses, the expert's fees would be set by the trial judge according to a scale and that fee would be borne equally by the parties in first instance subject to a judgment award.

136 The benefits proposed under this system are suggested as:

"• the expert is not being paid by any one party and therefore is more likely to be impartial
• if the expert reports early in the proceedings this may result in an early resolution of the dispute
• expert witnesses will not be placed in an adversarial role and the court will not be forced to choose between two opposing experts
• time and money will be saved by the reduction in the number of experts, the reduction in time spent giving expert evidence and the fact that the court has some control over experts' fees."

Parties would still have the right to question the expert, and the judge will have power to appoint another expert in certain instances.

137 The Commission paper also canvasses the desirability of the establishment and maintenance of registers of recognised experts from which the courts and lawyers could draw witnesses, in a system similar to that of many European courts. The Australian Medical Association has undertaken investigation of such a proposal but no implementation has as yet occurred.

Federal Court of Australia

138 In 1997 the Chief Justice of the Federal Court of Australia[145] sought views of interested parties upon proposals relating to the use of experts in technical cases coming before that court. The elements of the proposals were:

"1. Although the court will be very concerned that experts be used in a case quickly and efficiently, the calling of expert evidence would usually be subject to the control of the parties, with the court taking some control in exceptional cases. The exceptions might include limitations on the number of experts called in any field of speciality.
2. Experts should be given clear guidance that, when preparing their evidence or actually giving evidence to a court, their first responsibility is not to their clients but is to be open and truthful to the court.
3. To reinforce the responsibility in item 2 above, any report and draft report prepared for the purpose of giving evidence to a court and delivered to a client will be addressed to the court.
4. Such a report should end with a declaration by the expert that the expert has made inquiries which the expert believes are appropriate and that the matters of significance which the expert regards as materially relevant have not, to the expert's knowledge, been withheld from the expert or by him or her to the court.
5. If experts instructed by the parties meet at the direction of the court, it would be improper conduct for an expert to be given or to accept instructions not to reach agreement. If the experts cannot reach agreement on matters of expert opinion, they should specify their reasons for being unable to do so.
6. Once an expert has been instructed to prepare a report for the use of a court, any communication between the expert and the client, or his or her advisers, related to the subject matter of the report should no longer be the subject of legal privilege.
7. Codes of practice providing guidance as to the practice in relation to experts should be drawn up jointly by the appropriate professional bodies representing the experts and the legal profession (the Law Council of Australia) and an expert should state whether his or her report has been prepared in accordance with a relevant code of practice.
8. Often the evidence of experts will be given at the conclusion of all other evidence in the case.
9. Careful experimentation would be conducted by the court, in appropriate cases, to determine what procedures are the most effective and appropriate to achieve the objective that expert

evidence is presented quickly, efficiently and in the manner most likely to assist the court to understand and apply it.

10. The court would, in appropriate cases, empanel experts in the manner successfully trialled by the Australian Competition Tribunal." (See attachment titled "Reception and Role of Expert Evidence from Economists in the Australian Competition Tribunal" below.)

139 Element 10 relied upon a document prepared by the Australian Competition Tribunal[146] titled "Reception and Role of Expert Evidence from Economists in the Australian Competition Tribunal" which is in the following terms:

"The practice, which has now become the usual practice in the Australian Competition Tribunal concerning the reception of evidence from expert economists is as follows:

1. Economists submit written statements prior to the oral proceedings, but after the reception of written non-expert evidence and documentary material.
2. The witness box is, of course, too limited a space for all experts to be in at the one time, so they usually sit at one end of the bar table.
3. The tribunal informs the experts before they give evidence that they should be free to modify the views expressed by them in their reports as little or as much as they wish, because the tribunal wishes to receive the benefit of their present views, having had access to all of the evidence. It is the experience of the tribunal that some experts modify their views in varying degrees.
4. At the conclusion of all the evidence (other than the evidence of the experts) and before the commencement of addresses, each expert is sworn immediately after the other.
5. Each expert in turn gives an oral exposition of his or her opinion with respect to the relevant issues arising from the evidence.
6. Each expert then in turn expresses his or her opinion about the opinions expressed by the other experts.
7. Counsel then cross examines the experts, being at liberty to cross examine on the basis:
   (a) either that questions could be put to each expert in the customary fashion, one after the other, completing the cross examination of one before proceeding to the next, or
   (b) that questions may be put to all or any of the experts, one after the other in respect of a particular subject; then proceeding to the next subject.
8. Re-examination is conducted on the same basis.
9. Members of the tribunal sometimes intervene with their questions.

The advantages of this system are as follows:

(a) Experts are required to prepare written submissions which are set down as a connected argument and, when giving oral evidence, the same connected thread runs through it, rather than being a series of disconnected responses to questions by counsel.
(b) It achieves the result of the experts defining for their purposes points of agreement and disagreement.
(c) It takes the expert as far away from the adversarial field as possible.

The above practice is recorded generally in *QIW (re Queensland Independent Wholesalers Ltd* (1995) ATPR 41–438 at 40,925) and in other decisions of the tribunal. In *QIW*, four economists appeared. The total time required for their evidence was only 3½ hours."

140 Following public comment, the court in April of 1998 promulgated guidelines under the title "Draft Practice Direction—Guidelines for Expert Witnesses in proceedings in the Federal Court of Australia" as follows

"*Purpose of this Document*

The purpose of this document is to provide general guidelines to expert witnesses of all professions.

It is not intended to address exhaustively all questions that an expert witness may have regarding the provision of evidence and it is suggested that any questions be addressed to the legal representative who has engaged your services.

Practitioners should give a copy of these guidelines to any expert witness they propose to retain for the purpose of giving a report and giving evidence in the proceeding.

GUIDELINES

General Duty to the Court[147]

- An expert witness has an overriding duty to assist the court on matters relevant to his or her area of expertise.
- An expert witness is not an advocate for a party.
- The expert witness's paramount duty is to the court and not to the person retaining the expert.

The Form of the Expert Evidence[148]

- An expert's written report must give details of the expert's qualifications, and of material or literature used in making the report.
- All assumptions made by the expert should be clearly and fully stated.
- The report should identify who carried out any tests or experiments upon which the expert relied in compiling the report, and give details of the qualifications of the person who carried out any such test or experiment.
- Where a number of opinions are provided in the report, the expert should summarise them.
- The expert should give reasons for each opinion.
- At the end of the report the expert should declare that '[the expert] *has made all the inquiries which* [the expert] *believes are desirable and appropriate and that no matters of significance which* [the expert] *regards as relevant have not, to* [the expert's] *knowledge, been withheld from the court'*.
- There should be attached to the report a copy of all written instructions (original and supplementary) given to the expert, as well as a note containing a summary of any oral instructions received.
- If, after exchange of reports or at any other stage, an expert witness changes his or her view on a material matter, having read another expert's report or for any other reason, such change of view should be communicated in writing (through legal representatives) without delay to each party to whom the expert witness's report has been provided and, when appropriate, to the court.[149]
- If an expert's opinion is not fully researched because he or she considers that insufficent data is available or for any other reasons, this must be stated with an indication that the opinion is no more than a provisional one. Where an expert witness, who has prepared a report, believes that it may be incomplete or inaccurate, without some qualification, that qualification must be stated in the report.[150]
- The expert witness should make it clear when a particular question or issue falls outside his or her expertise.
- Where expert evidence refers to photographs, plans, calculations, analyses, measurements, survey reports or other extrinsic matter, these must be provided to the opposite party at the same time as the exchange of reports.[151]

Experts' Conference

- If experts retained by the parties meet at the direction of the court, it would be improper conduct for an expert to be given or to accept instructions not to reach agreement. If the experts cannot reach agreement on matters of expert opinion, they should specify their reasons for being unable to do so."

141 The elements originally proposed covered both the conduct of experts as witnesses as well as procedures to be adopted or applied in dealing with a matter both in respect of a witness and the court. As such the elements recognised that both court procedure and case management were a significant aspect of any reforms that might be introduced. The proposals to date do not deal with changes to court procedure.

EXPERTS IN NON-CURIAL PROCEEDINGS

General

142 In Australia the use of expert witnesses is not limited to court proceedings. The Evidence Act jurisdiction extends to encompass the greater flexibility afforded non-curial tribunals in governing conduct of matters before them[152] and the appointment of tribunals which of themselves have a degree of expertise has allowed procedures which at first instance may appear in conflict with the fundamental philosophy of the Australian common law adversarial system.

Commercial arbitration and court references

143 In commercial disputes of factual complexity (and occasionally legal complexity) two commonly utilised procedures are:

(a) commercial arbitration governed by Commercial Arbitration Acts or Ordinances in all states and territories of the Commonwealth[153]; and

(b) court annexed processes known as special references heard before a court-appointed referee who is required to submit an opinion to the court on the matter referred. The authority for a court to refer matters to a referee derives from relevant rules of court.[154]

144 Ordinarily, the referee appointed will be a person having expertise in the subject matter referred which may be the entire dispute or discrete aspects of the dispute.

145 In arbitration, by section 19(3) of the "Uniform" Acts, subject to agreement by the parties otherwise, the arbitrator "[i]s not bound by the rules of evidence . . ." apparently giving the arbitrator significant discretion in respect of the receiving of evidence. However, by section 22(1) of the "Uniform" Acts the arbitrator is required to determine "[a]ny question that arises for determination in the course of proceedings under the agreement shall be determined according to law". This section provides that the parties to the arbitration may agree to opt out of this provision and allow any matter arising to be determined at the arbitrator's discretion "[b]y reference to considerations of general justice and fairness".[155] Whether or not this latter provision remains effective under the Evidence Act remains untested.

146 There would appear no inconsistency in an obligation upon an arbitrator to determine admissibility and relevance of expert evidence according to law as required by section 22(1) and the discretion in application of the rules of evidence under section 17 of the "Uniform" Acts. However, the exercise of discretion under both sections 14 and 19(3) must be in accordance with the law and is not affected by an agreement made under the provisions of section 22(2) in relation to manner of determination of questions arising in the course of an arbitration. An arbitrator determining with equity and good conscience under the provisions of section 22(2) cannot disregard the law and determine a matter according to personal feelings.[156]

147 Section 22(2) of the Act

1. does not allow arbitrators to disregard all law and be arbitrary in their dealings with the parties;

2. does allow arbitrators freedom to some extent from strict rules and they may use their own knowledge and commercial expertise without formal proof;
3. permits non-observance of the rules of law if it results in no more than irregularities;
4. permits disregard of such rules as the parol evidence rule, the rule that contracts by speciality cannot be varied by oral contract and the rule that one cannot look to subsequent conduct to construe a contract. The rule that collateral contracts cannot be inconsistent with the main contract can similarly be disregarded;

and also

5. allows principles of rectification to be applied and may permit supplementation of contract where the parties have not addressed their minds to all areas.

148 By section 14 of the "Uniform" Acts it is provided that "subject to this Act and to the arbitration agreement, the arbitrator or umpire may conduct proceedings under that agreement in such manner as the arbitrator or umpire thinks fit".

149 In special references, whilst there is no uniform approach in all jurisdictions, the manner of conduct of a reference is ordinarily established by the court in orders made referring the matter to a referee. For example, the Supreme Court of New South Wales is empowered to direct matters to a referee under the provisions of court rules.[157] A standard form order issued by that court requires that conduct of the proceedings shall comply with Part 72, rule 8 which is as follows:

"[72.8] Conduct of proceedings under the reference

8(1) Where the court makes an order under rule 2, the court may give directions with respect to the conduct of proceedings under the reference.

(2) Subject to any direction under subrule (1)—

(a) the referee may conduct the proceedings under the reference in such manner as the referee thinks fit;

(b) the referee, in conducting proceedings under the reference, is not bound by rules of evidence but may inform himself or herself in relation to any matter in such manner as the referee thinks fit.

(3) Evidence before the referee—

(i) may be given orally or in writing; and

(ii) shall, if the referee so requires, be given on oath or affirmation or by affidavit.

(4) A referee may take the examination of any person.

(5) Each party shall, within a time fixed by the referee but in any event before the conclusion of evidence on the enquiry, give to the referee and each other party a brief statement of the findings of fact and law for which the party contends.

(6) The parties shall at all times do all things which the referee requires to enable a just opinion to be reached and no party shall wilfully do or cause to be done any act to delay or prevent an opinion being reached."

150 An order may also include such terms as

"Subject to the provisions of Part 72 the proceedings will be conducted in such manner as ... [t]he referee considers and implements such manner of conducting proceedings under the reference as will without undue formality or delay enable a just determination to be made including if the referee sees fit the making of inquiries by telephone, site inspection, communication with experts retain (sic) on behalf of the parties";

and

"[a]ny evidence in chief before the referee shall unless the referee otherwise permits be by way of written statement signed by the maker of the statement".

151 This and like provisions extend considerable discretion to a referee in the conduct of proceedings and as a consequence to the receipt of expert evidence. However, at all times, as in arbitration, discretion must be exercised according to law.

Developments in procedures involving expert witnesses

Rules for conduct of complex non-curial proceedings

152 Within the context of the discretionary powers extended to arbitrators and referees special rules or procedures have been developed for conduct of complex proceedings. Whilst an arbitrator or a referee might arguably have power to impose rules of conduct the current position in Australia is that agreement of the parties is sought as a precondition to adoption.

153 An example of such procedures and the rationale of their development and supporting their use is given in "Standard Form Rules for Expert Witness Case Management in complex disputes"[158]:

"*Preamble*

The following procedures are suggested as in general terms appropriately drawing together procedures fitting comfortably with and adopting common law and civil law concepts of adversarial and inquisitorial processes, but are advanced in the context of common law proceedings.

The procedures are intended to significantly reduce hearing time by the resolving, refining or defining of some or all of the issues in dispute.

The procedures are contemplated as being potentially directly applicable in non-curial processes but may, in certain circumstances with variation, also be used in court hearings.

The almost inevitable directly opposing positions adopted by experts called by the respective disputants and the tendency of parties to counter or attempt to counter in equal numbers the number of experts called by the opposition gives rise to consideration of limitations or procedures that might be applied by a court or tribunal to appropriately provide efficiency of hearing without deleteriously affecting procedural fairness.

Whilst an expert may give evidence appropriately both as to fact and opinion, it is principally in the area of opinion that considerable time may be expended in the common law adversarial system in the parties establishing or testing opinion evidence.

In various jurisdictions, both within Australia and in other countries, recommended procedures or rules of court have been proposed or established to better facilitate the use of experts.[159] Principally these include some limitation on numbers of experts called to give evidence, the exchange of expert witness statements at some time prior to the commencement of a hearing or the calling of the first expert witness, and/or a requirement for common position and opposing position joint reports prior to adducing of evidence.

Overall the following procedures or appropriate variations of these procedures should significantly reduce hearing time and costs in a particular matter even though the out of hearing meetings or dialogue between experts may involve substantial time.

Success of the processes depends totally upon clear and relevant definition of matters or questions referred and sufficient understanding by the tribunal of the report or answers given in first instance by the experts to enable the inquisitorial process to be conducted by the tribunal with precision and expedition.

Standard Form Rules

1. The tribunal shall be made aware, prior to dealing with expert witness issues and in sufficient detail, of the facts agreed or alleged and the nature, extent and express form of the issues to which expert evidence is intended to be directed.

   This may take the form of outlines or the like of claims and defences including specific reference to and relevance of expert evidence which shall be submitted to the tribunal at directions hearings or preliminary conferences or at the commencement of the full hearing.

2. The tribunal shall deal with challenges to admission as an expert and qualification as to the general admission as an expert within the context of the evidence intended to be adduced from such witness as early as possible, desirably at directions hearings or preliminary conferences.
3. The tribunal shall also determine on the basis of the parties' submissions and the subject matter of the evidence to be adduced from proposed expert witnesses, the number of expert witnesses permitted to give evidence for each party on each discrete and identifiable issue (if capable of such distinction).
   Other than by leave, one expert from each party only shall be allowed.
   An unlimited number will not be allowed.
   Such limitation shall not preclude the later admission, with leave, of further or new expert witnesses to deal with new matters admitted or arising in the course of a hearing.
4. Where expert evidence of opinion is dependent upon agreed or established facts, or where factual issues are in contention between the parties, the tribunal shall be expressly informed by the parties or by each party as to those facts or of the competing contentions of fact before dealing with opinion issues or evidence. This may be achieved appropriately by witness statements or, if in contention, by preliminary or separate issue determination by the directing of the order of evidence including, if appropriate, ordering the splitting of the case.
5. The tribunal shall order the convening of a meeting or meetings or other appropriate form of dialogue or communication between experts relied upon by the parties. Such meeting or dialogue shall be for the purposes of preparing and submitting a report to the tribunal in answer to questions or otherwise.
   This process shall not, unless otherwise ordered, take place or be conducted as part of the formal hearing of the dispute.
6. The purpose of the meeting or dialogue is to prepare and submit to the tribunal a report or answers to questions referred as
   (a) agreed common response or report by all experts
   (b) agreed common response or report as between the common experts for each party but dissented by the common experts for the other party or parties
   (c) differing responses or report where no such commonality.
   In the case of (a) above a brief but express statement of the agreed position and reasons therefor and for (b) and (c) above a detailed, as appropriate, jointly or individually express statement including reasons for disagreement is to be delivered up to the tribunal. Reasons for (a) above will not be required if the issue dealt with does not thereafter remain in contest between the parties.
7. The responses or reports, including reasons and all responses, explanation or commentary given in subsequent inquisitorial appearance before the tribunal (whether given in response to an issue raised by the tribunal or otherwise) shall stand as evidence in chief individually and respectively of each of the witness participants.
8. Within the context of competing positions, the parties shall agree or, if no agreement, be ordered to submit to the tribunal independent questions or matters to be dealt with by the experts in this process.
9. The questions, whether or not agreed by the parties, shall be, as far as possible, clear, unequivocal and relevant. The tribunal shall approve of the questions to be referred and may refer questions of its own formulation, whether or not agreed by the parties.
10. The tribunal shall limit the number of experts for each party taking part in the meeting or dialogue and reporting process either generally or in respect to each discrete question referred.
11. The tribunal may order, limit or identify expressly material upon which the experts may or must rely in this process, or establish any hypothesis, principles or criteria that should be taken into account or utilised by the experts in the process.
12. The experts, or any of them, may, of their own volition, call for any matter or thing identified by them or any one of them during the course of the process and considered necessary by the expert or experts for the proper consideration or reporting on the matter

referred. Should such matter or thing not be within the scope previously imposed by the tribunal, then this shall only be provided by order of the tribunal.

13. In the course of their deliberations, the experts as a group may come or be called before the tribunal for guidance, instruction, clarification, enquiry or direction.
14. Upon the delivery up of the report or answers, the tribunal may, in the event of non-unanimous answers or report or otherwise, order that all experts taking part in the process and subscribing to the answers or report appear collectively or otherwise before the tribunal.
15. The tribunal may make enquiries or seek clarification or explanation of any issue arising by its own inquisition of the experts or any one of them or direct or order further dialogue, meeting or report.
16. During the course of such inquisition the parties or their representatives may elect to be present but, otherwise than by leave, shall not take part in the process. This provision does not prevent objection by a party or parties to particular questions or line of questions or particular interrogation by the tribunal.
17. Following the close of this inquisitorial process by the tribunal, parties may cross-examine an opposing expert witness upon any matter arising from that expert's joint or individual answer or report as delivered to the tribunal or as given during the inquisitorial process, and the party calling the witness may re-examine on such cross-examination.
18. After completion of the inquisitorial process, other than by leave, no expert witness shall be permitted to give evidence on any matter dealt with in the joint or inquisitorial process unless that witness took part in the process or to give further evidence in chief in addition to that already given by report or answer.
    This provision does not act to prevent an expert taking part in the process or any other expert from giving evidence as to other matters.
19. The tribunal may, following submissions, adopt by way of interim, preliminary or final determination, or for the direction of future conduct, any agreed, conceded or determined issue arising out of the report or inquisitorial process."

154 These procedures have proved cost effective, reducing time taken in reducing expert evidence dramatically and arriving at appropriate conclusions in a transparent manner without prejudicing the rights of parties. Major cases involving the use of these processes have subsequently been the subject of curial review without attracting adverse criticism.[160]

Australian Law Reform Commission Enquiry

155 The Australian Law Reform Commission has been conducting an in-depth review of the adversarial system within Australia. Included in that review are considerations of a more inquisitorial system generally. The Law Reform Commission published an Issues Paper in part dealing with the use of experts and expert evidence,[161] and is intending to publish a discussion paper dealing expressly with the expert witness and expert evidence as part of its overall enquiry.

GUIDELINES FOR EXPERT WITNESSES

Australian Council of Professions

156 In June 1998, apparently in part encouraged by proposals emanating from the Federal Court of Australia (see above) the Australian Council of Professions of Australia[162] promulgated a guidelines document titled "The Role and Duties of an Expert Witness in Litigation" in the following terms:

"1. The role of the expert witness in litigation is to assist a court in the administration of justice by providing an opinion or factual information based on the expert's competence in a subject which is outside the knowledge, skill or experience of most people. It is founded in the need for a court charged with the resolution of a matter for access to knowledge relevant to the matter which it does not possess of itself.

2. It follows that the opinion is only useful if it is based on the expert's area of competence, includes all relevant matters and is impartial and dispassionate. Thus the primary duty of an expert is to the court because of his or her role in the process as defined above. An expert is subject to the normal duty in respect of evidence of fact to be complete, accurate and truthful.

3. The expert owes a second duty to the body of knowledge and understanding from which his or her expertise is drawn. This implies recognition of its limitations and the humility which should flow from such recognition, since the outcome of litigation is likely to influence the practical application of such knowledge and understanding in the future. It also implies dealing with the opinions of other competent experts in a respectful manner. It is important to the overall process that the integrity of the processes by which knowledge is acquired and understanding developed should not be degraded. Thus the secondary duty of the expert witness is to the body of knowledge and understanding..

4. The expert witness owes a third duty to the party which has sought his or her advice. That duty is to provide the advice in the context of the first and second duties above, which implies that the expert should not be an advocate for a party. This is a tertiary duty."

157 The expressed intent of the constituent members of the Australian Council of Professions in developing the guidelines is for them to be adopted by the member organisations in appropriate ways particularly by incorporation in codes of ethics or rules governing conduct of members of those organisations.

158 Codes of ethics, rules of professional conduct or codes of practice of many professional organisations within Australia have some provisions which go to matters which might be considered to affect the giving of expert evidence. In some instances these provisions are mandatory as a condition of membership.

159 Such codes variously impose duties such as

"members shall express opinions, make statements or give evidence with fairness and honesty and on the basis of adequate knowledge"[163];

"when giving evidence, recognise your responsibility to assist the court in arriving at a just decision"[164];

"All Corporate and Associate members of the Institute shall observe and be bound by the following Code of Ethics:

[A] member shall issue or publish only such reports or statements as are an accurate record of soundly based observation and experiment and of logical deductions therefrom."[165]

160 To the extent that the particular guidelines for an expert witness in litigation have been created by the Council of the Professions it is understandable that the terms should be couched in the context of professional disciplines established and recognised in and by academic studies and training, and also to some degree within a commercial context involving engagement of the expert by a party.

161 Whilst it might be argued that in the context of the modern law of evidence in Australia that the provisions of paragraph 1 of the guidelines defining the role of the expert are overly simplistic and possibly misleading, generally the role as stated in that paragraph is unexceptional.[166] However, the proposition that as a consequence of the effective definition of the role there is established a hierarchical order of different duties applicable to the expert arguably does not and cannot stand scrutiny.

162 Accepting that on a generous reading paragraphs 1 and 2 of the guidelines do properly set out the role and duty of the expert as a witness to the court whether or not of appropriate amplitude, the further provisions of paragraphs 3 and 4 which create a diminishing hierarchy of duty not relevant to the court are arguably ill-conceived and do not, as stated, reasonably or at all "flow" from what is proposed as the role of the expert.

163 As general statements of philosophy or principle in the conduct of or involvement in a professional discipline no objection might reasonably be taken to these provisions. Apart from the order of standing provided in the guidelines most codes of ethics or rules of conduct of professional organisations make such provisions[167] but may also conflict with some provisions[168] of the guidelines. An expert will normally be liable to a client for advice given in breach of a contractual duty of care.[169]

164 However, in the context of the role and duties of an expert witness in litigation, where admission as an expert witness is at the discretion of the court, the diminishing order of duties of the guidelines are arguably superfluous and further, by their terms, require of the expert a weighting of importance that is not relevant to or necessary for proper satisfaction of the role and duty of the expert as a witness. As written these subservient duties may conflict or potentially conflict with the duty of the expert to the court. The guidelines infer a capacity in an expert witness to determine relevance both of the witness's own special knowledge and the evidence to be adduced by some form of pre-judgment made by the witness.

165 At law, the tests to be applied to allow a witness to give opinion evidence as an expert are essentially those of the sufficiency and relevance of specialised skills, knowledge or experience of the witness, and the relevance of such opinion evidence to the matter at issue, but these tests are to be and can only be applied and determined by the courts. In any event, whether or not the expert is either in a position to or capable of objectively arriving at conclusions of relevance and capacity remote from knowledge of all matters at issue in a particular case is highly arguable even if the expert was aware of all such matters. Additionally, the adoption or existence of this document may open a productive line of cross-examination to attack the credibility of an expert witness or the validity of an opinion.[170]

Australian and New Zealand Forensic Society

166 Presently the only organisation which has a code of ethics dedicated essentially exclusively to matters relating to expert evidence is the Australian and New Zealand Forensic Society. This code of ethics is advanced as being a guide to the practice of forensic science and is an extensive document covering issues of scientific method, reporting and conduct, pre-trial and in court.[171]

167 At sections titled "Pre-trial Conduct" and "Conduct in Court" the code states as follows:

"*Pre-trial Conduct*

(1) Every endeavour should be made to produce the report in sufficient time before the relevant legal proceedings so as to enable proper consideration of it, provided that sufficient notification of the date of legal proceedings has been received.

(2) On the understanding that there is no property in expert scientific witnesses, the prospective witness should be reasonably available for discussion with professional representatives of all parties involved in the proceedings.

(3) Any retainer offered should be refused if it is suspected that a purpose of the offer is to prevent relevant evidence being presented to a court."

"Conduct in Court

(1) As far as possible, simple terms should be used when giving evidence.
(2) Any attempt made to press the witness to testify as to matters beyond and/or outside his/her expertise should be firmly resisted.
(3) An objective and moderate manner in giving evidence should be cultivated.
(4) In the conduct of giving evidence the witness, upon request, is under an obligation to disclose all tests and experiments performed, subject to the directions of the presiding judicial officer.
(5) The witness should plainly state opinion as such and take care to distinguish them from statements of fact.
(6) The witness should appeal to the presiding judicial officer (in the absence of the jury if the trial be by judge and jury) if he or she believes that the manner in which evidence is being elicited is such as to prevent the disclosure of a significant relevant matter or circumstance."

Legal effect of codes of ethics or rules of conduct

168 Whilst there have not been in Australia decisions following the line of reasoning in the United States that codes of ethics and rules of conduct are highly persuasive or "due the utmost consideration by courts in determining whether professionals have acted competently"[172] codes of ethics, rules of conduct, rules of ethics and the like have not been totally ignored as irrelevant in Australian jurisprudence.

169 In part relying on codes of practice in some professional disciplines significant criticism was directed to various experts by the Commissioner in the Royal Commission of Enquiry into the Chamberlain convictions.[173] Commissioner Morling found that various expert witnesses had failed to exhibit appropriate professional detachment in their work. It is suggested that "[f]ailure to comply with a Code of Ethics can be portrayed as indifference to ethical proprieties, a lack of commitment to accepted protocols and procedures, and a preparedness to flout standards that have been formulated, and are adhered to, by peers"[174] and can seriously detract from the credibility of a witness.

LIABILITY OF THE EXPERT WITNESS

General

170 There presently exists no definitive position under Australian law on certain aspects of liability or potential liability of experts acting as witnesses and the potential extension to the preparatory work carried out by the expert for the purposes of giving evidence.

171 Although distinguishable, an analogy might be drawn between the role of the expert in preparing for and giving evidence to a court as being to assist the court, and the conduct of an advocate in preparing for and prosecuting a matter on behalf of a client but in a position as admitted to the court. An action brought by a client against a barrister alleging negligence, breach of contract and breach of duty of care failed.[175] Such a comparison as between an advocate and an expert witness was considered in England and, to some extent, held as being consistent in role and duty.[176]

172 Consideration of liability of expert witnesses raises issues of public policy not yet addressed, as well as issues of contractual and common law duties and obligations.

Civil liability

Evidence

173 Following the well-established precedent of the English common law[177] the position in Australia is that witnesses, whether lay or expert, will have immunity from suit in respect of any civil action brought in relation to evidence given in court proceedings. This will apply even if such evidence is defamatory.[178]

Preparatory work

174 No Australian authority presently exists in respect of immunity or otherwise for experts in the preparatory work for expert testimony. It would appear likely that Australian courts would follow the general principles of immunity protecting witnesses in a courtroom extending to preparation of evidence as established under English law.[179] However, the distinction between what might constitute preparatory work and initial advice may be difficult to establish and will depend upon the facts and circumstances of each case.

Initial advice

175 Where an expert is engaged by a client to act as a witness in court proceedings actually on foot, subject to the *caveats* expressed in para 174 above, the advice given may reasonably be categorised as preparatory work and be the subject of immunity even if negligently given. However, where such initial advice is sought prior to the institution of proceedings the expert will likely be subject to the common law duty of care as well as such contractual obligations as might arise from engagement by a client and in circumstances where no immunity from suit exists.

Criminal liability

176 Where an expert witness deliberately misleads a court immunity which may exist in respect of civil actions is unlikely to extend to such conduct. As a matter of public policy, deliberate or wilful dishonesty in evidence and constituting perjury would appear unlikely to be affected by justifications of immunity for negligence. However, confusion or inadvertent mistake might reasonably be raised as a defence.[180]

End Notes

1. States: Victoria, New South Wales, Tasmania, South Australia, Queensland, Western Australia; Territories: Australian Capital Territory, Northern Territory and the external territories of Norfolk Island, Cocos (Keeling) Islands and Christmas Island.
2. Judiciary Act 1939; Commonwealth of Australia Constitution, s.77.
3. Commonwealth Constitution, ss.75, 76.
4. Commonwealth Constitution, s.75(iv).
5. Commonwealth Constitution, s.75(iii).
6. Commonwealth Constitution, s.75(iv).
7. Supreme Court Act 1993 (Cth); Supreme Court Act 1979 (NT); Supreme Court Act 1935 (WA); Supreme Court Act 1932 (Tas); Supreme Court Act 1970 (NSW); Supreme Court Act 1967 (Qld); Supreme Court Act 1986 (Vic); Supreme Court Act 1935 (SA).
8. Established in NSW in 1965, Victoria in 1996 and Queensland in 1994 as separate divisions with appointed judges of appeal.
9. The Full Court of a jurisdiction consists of a number of judges of the Supreme Court sitting together.
10. Jurisdiction of Courts (Cross-Vesting) Act 1987 (Cth); Jurisdiction of Courts (Cross-Vesting) Act 1988 (Qld); Jurisdiction of Courts (Cross-Vesting) Act 1987 (SA); Jurisdiction of Courts (Cross-Vesting) Act 1987 (Vic);

Jurisdiction of Courts (Cross-Vesting) Act 1987 (NSW); Jurisdiction of Courts (Cross-Vesting) Act 1988 (WA); Jurisdiction of Courts (Cross-Vesting) Act 1987 (Tas); Jurisdiction of Courts (Cross-Vesting) Act 1987 (NT); Jurisdiction of Courts (Cross-Vesting) Act 1987 (ACT).

11. Limited only to areas covered by sections 75 and 76 of the Constitution.
12. There are no intermediate courts in the ACT or NT.
13. District courts in New South Wales, Western Australia, South Australia, Queensland; county courts in Victoria, Tasmania.
14. Magistrates' courts in Victoria, Queensland, South Australia and Australian Capital Territory; local courts in Western Australia, New South Wales and Northern Territory.
15. E.g. Federal Court of Bankruptcy, Federal Industrial Court, Land and Valuation Court (NSW).
16. E.g. Administrative Appeals Tribunal, Taxation Board of Review, Australian Competition Tribunal.
17. That is, generally allows parties through counsel to adduce evidence in chief, to cross-examine and to re-examine witnesses.
18. That is, generally relying upon a line of previous judgments.
19. For example, 1997 amendments to court rules of both the Supreme Court and county court.
20. See later discussion on Evidence Act 1995 (Cth).
21. Evidence Act 1995 (NSW).
22. The Act applies in the Australian Capital Territory by virtue of section 4 of the Commonwealth legislation.
23. Evidence Act 1995 (Cth): section 5 Extended Application of Certain Provisions; section 70(2) Evidence of tags and labels in Customs prosecutions and Excise prosecutions; section 143 Matters of law; section 150 Seals and signatures; section 153 Gazettes and other official documents; section 154 Documents published by authority of Parliaments etc; section 155 Official records; section 157 Public documents relating to court processes; section 158 Evidence of certain public documents; section 159 Official statistics; section 163 Proof of letters having been sent by Commonwealth agencies; section 182 Commonwealth records.
24. Evidence Act 1995 (Cth) Part 1: Definitions means "[(d)] a judge, justice or arbitrator under an Australian law, or (e) a person or body authorised by an Australian law, or by consent of parties, to hear, receive and examine evidence, ... 'Australian law' means a law of the Commonwealth, a State or a Territory."
25. Evidence Act 1995 (Cth), ss.5, 185, 186 and 187.
26. For example, Evidence Act 1995 (NSW), s.4.

    "(1) This Act applies in relation to all proceedings in a NSW court, including proceedings that:
    (a) relate to bail, or
    (b) are interlocutory proceedings or proceedings of a similar kind, or
    (c) are heard in chambers, or
    (d) subject to subsection (2), relate to sentencing.

    (2) If such a proceeding relates to sentencing:
    (a) this act applies only if the court directs that the law of evidence applies in the proceeding, and
    (b) if the court specifies in the direction that the law of evidence applies only in relation to specified matters—the direction has effect accordingly.

    (3) The court must make a direction if:
    (a) a party to the proceeding applies for such a direction in relation to the proof of a fact, and
    (b) in the court's opinion, the proceeding involves proof of that fact, and that fact is or will be significant in determining a sentence to be imposed in the proceeding.

    (4) The court must make a direction if the court considers it appropriate to make such a direction in the interests of justice."
27. *Geschke* v. *Del-Monte Home Furnishers Ltd* [1981] VR 856 at 863 delivered in construing a provision of the Market Court Act 1978, s.23(2) which expressly provided that "The court may inform itself in such manner as it thinks fit and is not required to conduct any proceeding in a formal manner."
28. See Australian "Uniform" Arbitration Acts generally at Part V—Powers of the Court:

    s.38 Judicial review of awards
    s.39 Determination of preliminary point of law by Supreme Court
    s.42 Power to set aside award
    s.44 Removal of arbitrator or umpire
    s.47 General power of the court to make interlocutory orders
    s.48 Extension of time
    s.49 Power to impose terms on orders, etc.
29. See "Uniform" Arbitration Acts generally at Part III—Conduct of Arbitration Proceedings:

    s.14 Procedure of arbitrator or umpire
    s.19 Evidence before arbitrator or umpire.
30. (1990) 97 ALR 555 at 594 *et seq.*
31. [1912] VLR 152.
32. See *Trade Practices Commission* v. *Australian Meat Holdings Pty Ltd* (1988) 83 ALR 299.
33. *R* v. *Parker* [1912] VLR 152 at 154; see also *Clark* v. *Ryan* (1960) 103 CLR 486.
34. *Davie* v. *Magistrates of Edinburgh* 1953 SC 34 at 40.
35. (1960) 103 CLR 486 at 491; see also *Mattioli* v. *Parker (No 2)* [1973] Qd R 499.

36. (1984) 38 SASR 45 at 46–47 per King CJ.
37. For example, *Straker* v. *R* (1977) 15 ALR 103.
38. *Esso Australia Resources Ltd and Others* v. *The Hon Sidney James Plowman (The Minister for Energy and Minerals) and Others* (1995) 128 ALR 391 finding in effect that absent an express agreement between parties to an arbitration on confidentiality no confidentiality exists and a term to that effect could not be implied into the particular agreement to arbitrate.
39. *Murphy* v. *The Queen* (1989) 167 CLR 94.
40. *R* v. *Lucas* [1992] 2 VR 109.
41. *Bugg* v. *Day* (1949) 79 CLR 442.
42. *R* v. *Darrington & McGauley* [1980] VR 353.
43. *Klimoskiv* v. *Water Authority of Western Australia* (1989) 5 SR (WA) 148.
44. *R* v. *Inch* (1990) 91 Cr App R 51.
45. Evidence Act 1995 (Cth), s.80:

    "[E]vidence of an opinion is not admissible only because it is about

    (a) a fact in issue or an ultimate issue, or

    (b) a matter of common knowledge."
46. *Archer Mortlock Murray & Woolley Pty Ltd* v. *Hooker Homes Pty Ltd* [1971] 2 NSWLR 278.
47. Evidence Act 1995 (Cth), s.8.
48. Evidence Act 1995 (Cth), s.9.
49. Evidence Act 1995 (Cth) Part 4.2—Judicial Notice, ss.143, 144, 145.
50. Evidence Act 1995 (Cth), s.21.
51. Evidence Act 1995 (Cth), s.26.
52. Evidence Act 1995 (Cth), s.9.
53. Evidence Act 1995 (Cth), s.76.
54. See *Australian Law Reform Commission Evidence Reference Research Paper* No 13 at p. 35.
55. Evidence Act 1995 (Cth), s.50(3).
56. Evidence Act 1995 (Cth), s.77.
57. Evidence Act 1995 (Cth), s.78.
58. Evidence Act 1995 (Cth), s.79.
59. Evidence Act 1995 (Cth), s.81.
60. Evidence Act 1995 (Cth), s.92(3).
61. Evidence Act 1995 (Cth), ss.110, 111.
62. Evidence Act 1995 (Cth), s.136.
63. Evidence Act 1995 (Cth), s.60.
64. Evidence Act 1995 (Cth), s.59(1).
65. *Lucas* v. *Williams and Sons* [1982] 2 QB 113 (CA).
66. *R* v. *Cox* [1898] 1 QB 179.
67. *R* v. *Beckett* (1913) 8 Cr App R 204.
68. *R* v. *Davies* [1962] 3 All ER 97.
69. *Mansell* v. *Clements* (1874) LR 9 CP 139.
70. *Thomas* v. *R (No 2)* [1960] WAR 129.
71. Evidence Act 1995 (Cth), s.81(1).
72. Evidence Act 1995 (Cth), s.81(2).
73. *Lustre Hosiery Pty Ltd* v. *York* (1936) 54 CLR 134; *Grey* v. *Australian Motorists & General Insurance Co Pty Ltd* [1976] 1 NSWLR 669 at 684–685 (CA).
74. Evidence Act 1995 (Cth), s.91(1).
75. Evidence Act 1995 (Cth), s.92(2).
76. Evidence Act 1995 (Cth), s.110(1).
77. Evidence Act 1995 (Cth), s.110(2).
78. Evidence Act 1995 (Cth), s.110(3).
79. See generally: *R* v. *Stalder* (1981) 3 A Crim R 87 at 95; *R* v. *Attwood* (1960) 102 CLR 353.
80. Evidence Act 1995 (Cth), s.111(1).
81. Evidence Act 1995 (Cth), s.111(2).
82. Evidence Act 1995 (Cth), ss.135–139.
83. *Murphy* v. *The Queen* (1989) 167 CLR 94 at 130–131.
84. Evidence Act 1995 (Cth), s.9.
85. (1960) 103 CLR 486.
86. *McAllister* v. *Richmond Brewing Co (NSW) Pty Ltd* (1942) 42 SR (NSW) 187.
87. *Weal* v. *Bottom* (1966) 40 ALJR 436 (HC).
88. *Klein* v. *Federal Commissioner of Taxation* (1981) 12 ATR 557.
89. (1963) 4 FLR 292 at 295.
90. *R* v. *Jenkins; ex parte Morrison* [1949] VLR 277 at 303; *Steffan* v. *Ruban* [1966] 2 NSWR 622 (CA).
91. *TPC* v. *Arnotts Ltd* (1990) 92 ALR 527.
92. *Paric* v. *John Holland (Constructions) Pty Ltd* (1985) 62 ALR 85 at 87–88.

93. See *R* v. *Gilmore* [1977] 2 NSWLR 935; *R* v. *Runjanjic* (1991) 56 SASR 114 at 119; *R* v. *Lucas* [1992] 2 VR 109 at 115; *R* v. *Lewis* (1987) 29 A Crim R 267 at 269.
94. See *Clark* v. *Ryan* (1960) 103 CLR 486.
95. *E* v. *Australian Red Cross Society* (1991) 105 ALR 53.
96. *Fisher* v. *Brown* [1968] SASR 64.
97. See "Effects of Evidence Act on common law rules", paras 043 *et seq*. above.
98. *R* v. *Morgentaler (No 2)* (1973) 14 CCC (2d) 450 at 452.
99. *R* v. *Bonython* (1984) 15 A Crim R 364.
100. *R* v. *Tilly* [1985] VR 505.
101. (1991) 53 A Crim R 352.
102. *Frye* v. *United States* 293 F 1013 (1923).
103. *Commissioner for Government Transport* v. *Adamcik* (1961) 106 CLR 292 at 306.
104. *Daubert* v. *Merrell Dow Pharmaceuticals* (1993) 61 USLW 4805 at 4808.
105. *R* v. *Shephard* [1993] AC 380.
106. *R* v. *Clare* [1995] ACL Rep 195 UK 12.
107. *Transport Publishing Co Ltd* v. *The Literature Board of Review* (1956) 99 CLR 111.
108. *Burger King Corp* v. *Registrar of Trade Marks* (1973) 128 CLR 417.
109. (1990) 2 WAR 1.
110. *Arnotts Ltd* v. *Trade Practices Commission* (1990) 97 ALR 555.
111. Evidence Act 1995 (Cth), s.79 and s.85.
112. Order 34, Rule 2(2).
113. For example, *Borowski* v. *Quayle* [1966] VR 382; and *PQ* v. *Australian Red Cross Society* [1992] 1 VR 19.
114. *Ratten* v. *The Queen* [1972] AC 378.
115. *R* v. *Perry* (1990) 49 A Crim R 243.
116. (1974) 8 SASR 118.
117. *Wright* v. *Sydney Municipal Council* (1916) 16 SR (NSW) 348.
118. (1990) 49 A Crim R 243.
119. (1971) 17 FLR 141.
120. (1990) 46 A Crim R 282.
121. (1985) 62 ALR 85.
122. *Menday* v. *Protes Assurance Co Ltd* (1976) 1 SA 565.
123. (1983) 76 Crim App R 48.
124. [1966] VR 382 at 386.
125. [1923] AC 191.
126. (1917) 23 CLR 149.
127. 1985 Vol 2, p. 312.
128. See generally *Malone* v. *Smith* (1945) 63 WN (NSW) (Pt 1) 54; *Dougherty* v. *Nationwide News Pty Ltd* (1976) 86 WN (Pt 1) 181.
129. For example, section 82, Supreme Court Act 1970 (NSW).
130. *Holland* v. *Jones* (1917) 23 CLR 149.
131. *Saul* v. *Menon* [1980] 2 NSWLR 314.
132. *Glenister* v. *Glenister* [1945] P 30.
133. *Saint Leger* v. *Bailey* [1962] Tas SR 131.
134. *Toomata* v. *Vea* (1950) 2 ASR 564.
135. *Parker* v. *The King* (1912) 14 CLR 681.
136. *Re Schwerdt* [1939] SASR 333.
137. Established under the provisions of the Law Reform Commission Act 1973 (Cth).
138. Referred on 29 November 1995.
139. *The Cost of civil litigation before intermediate Courts in Australia*: Australian Institute of Judicial Administration Melbourne 1992.
140. Australian Law Reform Commission Background Paper No 5 Dec 1996, s.4 "Expert Evidence".
141. *Working with Experts and Experts' Reports* LAMMS Publications 1992 Badgery-Parker, Seminar in Expert Evidence 2.
142. Lord Woolf *Access to Justice: Final Report to the Lord Chancellor on the civil justice system in England and Wales* 1996, 137.
143. For example, Federal Court of Australia, Order 34, rule 2, empowering a court on its own motion or on application by a party or the registrar to appoint an expert: *Supreme Court of NSW Supreme Court Rules* P39 R2.
144. G Davies & S Sheldon "Some proposed changes in civil procedure", (1993–1994) 3 *Journal of Judicial Administration* 120.
145. The Honourable Mr Justice Michael E Black CJ.
146. A statutory *quasi*-judicial body established under the provisions of the Trade Practices Act 1975.
147. See *Access to Justice: Draft Civil Proceedings Rules*, The Rt Hon Lord Woolf, July 1996 at Pt 32.1; see also Lord Woolf "Medics, Lawyers and the Courts", [1977] 16 CJQ 302 at 313.
148. See *Access to Justice: Draft Civil Proceedings Rules*, The Rt Hon Lord Woolf, July 1996 at Pt 32.9.

149. *The Ikarian Reefer* [1993] 20 FSR 563 at 565.
150. *The Ikarian Reefer* [1993] 20 FSR 563 at 565.
151. *The Ikarian Reefer* [1993] 20 FSR at 565–566. See also Ormrod "Scientific Evidence in Court" [1968] Crim LR 240.
152. For example, "Uniform" Commercial Arbitration Acts, section 14. Subject to this Act and to the arbitration agreement, the arbitrator or umpire may conduct proceedings under that agreement in such manner as the arbitrator or umpire thinks fit. By section 19(3) unless otherwise agreed in writing by the parties to an arbitration agreement, an arbitrator or umpire in conducting proceedings under an arbitration agreement is not bound by rules of evidence but may inform himself or herself in relation to any matter in such manner as the arbitrator or umpire thinks fit.
153. Commercial Arbitration Act 1984 (Amended) (Vic); Commercial Arbitration Act 1985 (Amended) (NSW); Commercial Arbitration Act 1985 (Amended) (NT); Commercial Arbitration Act 1986 (WA); Commercial Arbitration Act 1986 (Amended) (SA); Commercial Arbitration Act 1986 (Amended) (Tas); Commercial Arbitration Act 1990 (Qld); Commercial Arbitration Act 1986 (Amended) (ACT); collectively called the "Uniform Acts" (although there are some differences between some sections of some Acts).
154. NSW—Pt 72 Reference by Court to a Referee (Supreme Court); Part 28B Reference by Court to a Referee (District Court).
    Vic—Chapter 1 Order 50 Special Referee (Supreme Court).
    SA—Rule 76 Assessors, Commissioners and Referees (Supreme Court).
    Qld—Order 97 Reference to Arbitration (Supreme Court).
    WA—Order 35 Assessors and Referees (Supreme Court).
    Tas—Order 39A(1) Power to refer to a referee (Supreme Court).
    ACT—Div 2 Order 83 Court Appointed Referees (Supreme Court).
    NT—Order 50 Special Referee (Supreme Court).
155. "Uniform" Arbitration Acts, s.22(2).
156. *Woodbud Pty Ltd* v. *Warea Pty Ltd* Supreme Court of NSW Young J unreported 15 June 1995 (see (1996) BCL p. 29).
157. Part 72—Reference by the Court to Referee.
158. A A de Fina 1995.
159. For example: Rules of Supreme Courts in Australia: Victoria Ch 1, 0.33; Queensland 0.39; Western Australia 0.36A; Australian Capital Territory 0.39; Northern Territory 0.44; New South Wales P6 36; Civil Evidence Act 1972 (UK); Supreme Court Rules Order 38 (UK); Code of Civil Procedure (Germany), Article 404a; Sir Laurence Street "Standard Direction on Expert Evidence"—66 ALJ 861.
160. *Multicon Engineering Pty Ltd* v. *Federal Airports Corporation* (unreported) Supreme Court of NSW 1995 Rolfe J; *Multiplex Constructions Pty Ltd* v. *Epworth Hospital* (unreported) Supreme Court of Victoria Court of Appeal November 1996.
161. Civil Litigation Background Paper 5, Practice and Procedure.
162. The Council comprises members representing the following professional organisations: The Institution of Engineers Australia; Australian Medical Association; The Royal Australian Institute of Architects; Australian Dental Association Inc; The Australian Veterinary Association Ltd; Australian Society of Certified Practising Accountants; The Institute of Chartered Accountants in Australia; The Institute of Surveyors, Australia Inc; Pharmaceutical Society of Australia; The Institute of Actuaries Australia; The Australian Institute of Quantity Surveyors; Australian Physiotherapy Association; The New South Wales Council of Professions.
163. Tenet No 7, The Institution of Engineers Australia Code of Ethics.
164. Code 3(e), Australian Medical Association Code of Ethics.
165. Bye-law 26.6, The Royal Australian Chemical Institute.
166. Cf. The Role of the Expert Witness, Section 2.1 *above*.
167. For example, see The Institution of Engineers Australia Code of Ethics, Tenets 2, 3 and 8:
    "2. members shall act in order to merit the trust of the community and membership in the honour, integrity and dignity of the members and the profession;
    3. members shall offer services, or advise on or undertake engineering assignments, only in areas of their competence and shall practise in a careful and diligent manner;
    8. members shall take all reasonable steps to inform themselves, their clients and employers and the community of the social and environmental consequences of the actions and projects in which they are involved."
168. For example, The Institution of Engineers Australia Code of Ethics, Tenet 5: "members shall apply their skill and knowledge in the interest of their employer or client for whom they shall act as faithful agents or advisers, without compromising the welfare, health and safety of the community".
169. *Palmer* v. *Durnford Ford* [1992] 2 WLR 407 at 411.
170. See Freckleton and Selby *Expert Evidence* The Law Book Company Ltd, Vol 1 [3.350] at p. 1–594.
171. Australian and New Zealand Forensic Science Society Code of Ethics—extracted from Freckelton Selby *Expert Evidence* The Law Book Co Ltd, Vol 1, p. 1–6535.
172. *Woods* v. *Covington County Bank* 537 F 2d 804 (1976).

173. (1987), pp. 91 and 192. An enquiry commissioned to examine the conviction of Mrs L Chamberlain for the murder of her baby daughter Azaria against an allegation that the daughter had been taken by a dingo (an Australian native wild dog).
174. Freckelton and Selby *Expert Evidence* The Law Book Co Ltd, Vol 1, p. 1–6534; Section 2240, Section 3.350.
175. *Gianarelli* v. *Wraith* (1988) 64 CLR 130 at 140.
176. *Palmer* v. *Durnford Ford* [1992] 2 WLR 407 at 411.
177. For example, see: *R* v. *Skinner* (1772) Lofft 55; *Revis* v. *Smith* (1856) 18 CB 126 at 140; *Hargreaves* v. *Bretherton* [1959] 1 QB 45; *Roy* v. *Prior* [1971] AC 470 at 480.
178. *Cabasi* v. *Vila* (1940) 64 CLR 130 at 140.
179. *Marrinan* v. *Vibart* [1963] 1 QB 528; *Evans* v. *London Hospital Medical College (University of London)* [1981] 1 WLR 184.
180. See Freckelton and Selby *Expert Evidence* The Law Book Company Ltd, Vol 1 [21.10] at p. 1–6031.

***A A de Fina** is widely recognised as one of the world's leading experts in the law and practice of commercial arbitration. Procedures and principles developed by Mr de Fina in respect of expert witness, both in domestic and international arbitrations and in court annexed referee procedures under Australian law, are regarded as significant developments in the use of experts. From acting as an expert witness over 20 years of professional practice as a consulting engineer and naval architect, he now provides worldwide consultancy and tactical advice in major disputes. He has lectured widely and written a number of authoritative texts on experts and expert evidence.*

Mr de Fina's main practice now consists of sitting as a tribunal in international commercial arbitrations principally where matters of science and technology are involved and where experts are almost invariably called to give evidence.

CHAPTER 1/21

THE EXPERT IN MAINLAND CHINA AND HONG KONG

CHAPTER 1/21A

THE PROCEDURE AND PRACTICE OF CALLING EXPERT EVIDENCE IN CHINA IN CIETAC ARBITRATION

Fei Ning

INTRODUCTION

001 In the late 1970s, China began the process of opening its door to the outside world. Twenty years on, China is one of the biggest markets in the world. Increasingly, international business is looking to develop its share of this market. Not surprisingly, practitioners are not far behind trying to understand the Chinese legal framework. Since the bulk of commercial disputes in the People's Republic of China (PRC) are resolved by way of arbitration, the practice of China International Economic and Trade Arbitration Commission (CIETAC) is of particular interest to foreign practitioners and foreign business people. In fact, in the past ten years, hundreds of articles regarding CIETAC practice have been published both by foreigners and Chinese.

002 Since the end of 1979, against the background of China's economic reforms, CIETAC's role in the field of international commercial arbitration became increasingly prominent. In the middle of the 1990s, average case load reached about 600.[1] In 1988, to improve the quality of its services and establish its international reputation, CIETAC amended and adjusted its arbitration rules. There were four versions, the latest, which came into effect on 1 May 1998,[2] is in many aspects considerably more international and modern.

003 On the whole, articles regarding CIETAC practices provide a comprehensive introduction to its organisation and the way it operates. This article will focus on a more narrow aspect of CIETAC practice which, to the author's knowledge, is absent from previous discussions namely, the practice of and procedure for adducing expert evidence. The importance of this issue is particularly obvious in relation to the enforceability of CIETAC's awards. According to an unofficial estimate, from the late 1980s, not less than 80 arbitration awards rendered by CIETAC were submitted to the Hong Kong court for enforcement.[3] Two were refused. In both cases, the reasons for the refusal were related to experts' evidence procedure.

004 The aim of this article is to introduce some of the more important aspects of the procedure governing the expert evidence in CIETAC practice, and in particular, those relating to the experts appointed by the tribunal, e.g. the legal basis for the selection and appointment of experts, the powers of experts, the relationship between the expert and the arbitrators, the rules governing experts' conduct and the admissibility and the finality of experts' opinion. This article will also seek to highlight some problems existing in CIETAC's practice and discuss some possible solutions.

THE LEGAL FRAMEWORK

005 It is usual for an arbitration tribunal to be given express power to appoint experts where it considers this necessary. This power of appointment of experts is generally found in the arbitration agreement, either as an express term or through the incorporation of international or institutional rules of arbitration.[4] Sometimes, the arbitration tribunal can exercise its power to appoint experts under the law governing the arbitration.[5]

Civil and common law jurisdiction

006 In theory, the position of the experts is different in civil law and common law jurisdictions. "A 'neutral' expert appointed by the arbitration tribunal is seldom used in common law jurisdictions because the parties control the proceedings and the production of the evidence. It is the parties who appoint their own experts, known as expert witnesses."[6] In relation to expert witnesses, it is argued that they "frequently lose sight of the truth and only put forward views which enhance their own client's case"[7] and are playing a role "somewhere between that of witness of fact and the party's counsel".[8] Consequently, the opinions given by expert witnesses are often contrary to each other. The role of expert witnesses in common law jurisdictions has to be examined against the background of the discovery and cross-examination procedure. The judge or arbitrator can find the facts through this procedure. This may be one of the reasons why in common law jurisdictions, the judge or arbitrator rarely uses independent experts.

007 In contrast, most of the civil law jurisdictions do not have either discovery or cross-examination procedures and the judge or arbitrator tends to be somewhat suspicious of an expert appointed by the parties. Therefore, they tend to appoint their own experts. "The role of the expert here becomes a duty to either the tribunal or the court, not the parties. The expert is independent, and has to give an independent report."[9]

008 "In arbitration in a civil law context, the tribunal usually calls its own experts, even where the parties have called expert witnesses".[10] "Where the two systems part is in the extent of the initiative which the parties can take in relation to the conduct of the proceedings. The parties' control over the proceedings in common law systems is almost total. It is restricted in civil law countries."[11] However, from a practitioner's point of view, the difference between the two systems in their approach to expert evidence does not necessarily result in fundamental differences in practice. "The US Federal Rules of Evidence, for example, stipulate that an expert witness not only assists the trier of fact to understand the evidence but also to determine a fact in issue."[12] "In international arbitration, the arbitrator is expected to provide a vigorous active solution, one involving clear, concerted procedural initiatives. This is especially true when the parties, as is usually the case in international arbitration, have different legal traditions."[13]

009 China is a civil law country since its legal system originally came from Germany.[14] The process of "discovery" does not exist, either in judicial or in arbitration proceedings. The parties can appoint their own experts. But it is the tribunal which conducts the proceedings. The tribunal is free to select its own expert where it believes it necessary. The function of the tribunal's expert is to provide an opinion in relation to matters which are not in the experience of the tribunal.

The national legislation

The Rules of the People's Court

010 Presently, there is not a separate "Evidence Act" in China. The only rules regarding expert evidence can be found in Chapter VI of China's "Civil Procedure Law" (hereinafter called the "CPL").[15]

011 Article 63 of the CPL provides that:

> "Evidence shall be classified as follows:
> - Documentary evidence;
> - Material evidence;
> - Audio-visual materials;
> - Testimony of witnesses;
> - Statements of the parties;
> - Expert conclusions; and
> - Records of inspection."

012 The above-mentioned evidence must be verified before it can be taken as a basis for ascertaining a fact.[16]

013 Article 64 of CPL provides that:

> "It is the duty of a party to an action to provide evidence in support of his allegation. If, for objective reasons, a party and his agent are unable to collect the evidence by themselves or if the people's court considers the evidence necessary for the trial of the case, the people's court shall investigate and collect it."[17]

014 Article 72 of CPL provides that:

> "1. When the people's court deems it necessary to make an expert evaluation of a problem of a technical nature, it shall refer the problem to a department authorised by the law for evaluation. In the absence of such a department, the people's court shall appoint one to make such evaluation.
> 2. The authorised department and the expert designated by the department shall have the right to consult the case materials necessary for the evaluation and to question the parties and witnesses when circumstances so require.
> 3. The authorised department and the expert designated shall present a written conclusion of the evaluation duly sealed or signed by both. If the evaluation is made by an expert alone, the unit to which the expert belongs shall certify his status by affixing its seal to the expert's conclusion."[18]

015 From the above-mentioned articles it can be seen first, that Chinese law allows the production of expert evidence in litigation. Secondly, the expert can be either appointed by the parties or by the judicial body. Thirdly, the judicial body has the power to appoint its own independent expert.

China's Arbitration Law

016 China's Arbitration Law is relatively new, having come into effect as recently as 1 September 1995.[19] Prior to the implementation of China's Arbitration Law, China had two arbitration systems, domestic and international. The former was conducted by arbitration commissions which came under a government administrative body (the State Administration for Industry and Commerce). The latter was conducted by CIETAC or the China Maritime

Arbitration Commission (CMAC).[20] The effect of the Arbitration Law was to bring the two systems of arbitration together by virtue of a single piece of legislation which applied to both and to provide basic requirements for arbitration agreements and rules for the conducts of arbitration. It is the most important law governing arbitration in China.

017 Article 43 of the Arbitration Law provides that: "Parties shall provide evidence in support of their own positions. The arbitration tribunal may of its own motion collect such evidence as it considers necessary".[21]

018 Article 44 of the Arbitration Law provides that:

> "If the arbitration tribunal considers that a specialised issue requires expert evaluation, it may refer the issue for evaluation to an expert evaluation department agreed on by the parties; alternatively, an expert evaluation of the issue may be given by an expert evaluation department designated by the arbitration tribunal. If requested by a party or required by the arbitration tribunal, the expert evaluation department shall send the expert evaluators to attend the hearing. Subject to the permission of the arbitration tribunal, the parties may put questions to the expert evaluators."[22]

019 Looking at the wording of the statute, it seems that there is no big difference between the CPL and the Arbitration Law regarding expert evidence. In practice, however, the People's Court usually gives more credit to the expert's opinion where the expert was selected by the court. The reason for this may be that in most situations, the expert designated by the court comes from a department authorised by law or recognised by an official authority. This may leave little opportunity for the parties to challenge or question the expert's opinion even though they are entitled to do so under the CPL. Unlike litigation, arbitration offers a much more flexible and informal procedure. The experts appointed by the tribunal are usually professionals. Most of them do not come from official departments. The tribunal, following the international practice, must give the parties reasonable opportunities to question the expert's reports or conclusions.

CIETAC Rules

Historical development (1954–1988)

020 An institution for arbitrating international commercial disputes existed in China as early as 1954. It was named the "Foreign and Trade Arbitration Commission" (FTAC) and was established under the "China Council for the Promotion of International Trade" (CCPIT). But from 1954 to the late 1970s, only a handful of cases was heard by FTAC.[23] The reason for this was that at that time, foreign trade in China was still strongly controlled by the central government and the Chinese partners preferred to avoid disputes with their foreign partners. Administrative methods for settling disputes were preferred to legal action. In the early 1980s, China introduced its "open door policy". The continuous deepening of economic reforms, the opening up to the outside world and the rapid increase in foreign economic and trade transactions, meant that international arbitration in China could develop quickly and without interruption.

021 On 26 February 1980, the State Council noted that: "In order to meet the needs of the constant development of China's economic and trade relations with foreign countries, it is hereby decided that the Foreign Trade Arbitration Commission shall be renamed the Foreign Economic and Trade Arbitration Commission (FETAC)".[24]

022 On 21 June 1988, the State Council replied to CCPIT that

> "the State Council approves the renaming of the Foreign Economic and Trade Arbitration Commission of your Council as the China International Economic and Trade Arbitration Commission (CIETAC). The existing relationship of its subordination remains unchanged and its scope of handling cases covers all disputes arising from international economic and trade transactions. The Arbitration Rules of the China International Economic and Trade Arbitration Commission shall be amended by your Council in accordance with China's law and the international treaties concluded or acceded to by China and with reference to international practice, and then promulgated for implementation after adoption by your Council. Hereafter, any amendments to the Arbitration Rules shall be made by your council's own Decision."[25]

023 Prior to 1988, the Provisional Rules of Procedure of the Foreign Trade Arbitration Commission (hereinafter cited the "Provisional Rules") had governed the practice of FTAC and subsequently FETAC for more than 30 years. Articles 25, 26 and 27 governed questions relating to expert evidence.

024 Article 25 of the Provisional Rules states that: "The parties shall produce evidence in support of the facts upon which their claims or pleadings are based."[26]

025 Article 26 of the Provisional Rules states: "The examination and appraisal of evidence shall be performed by the Arbitration Tribunal at its discretion. An Arbitration Tribunal sitting in a body may decide to entrust one of its members with the work of the examination of evidence."[27]

026 Article 27 of the Provisional Rules states: "The Arbitration Tribunal may consult experts for the clarification of any questions concerning technical or special matters or business practices. Such expert may be designated from among citizens of the People's Republic of China or foreign citizens."[28]

027 From a foreign practitioner's point of view, the main principles of the above articles may be summarised as follows:

1. the parties were primarily responsible for adducing factual evidence necessary to support their claims;
2. the tribunal was given broad powers to independently conduct investigations, gather evidence, and require the production of documents by the parties;
3. the tribunal itself determined the admissibility and validity of evidence, normally without strict reference to the formal rules of evidence contained in the Civil Procedure Law;
4. arbitrators in CIETAC were vested with wide power to obtain evidence from experts.

028 "The rules are silent as to whether parties to the arbitration have any right to be presented with the expert evidence they solicited or gathered by the arbitrators themselves, or to comment on or dispute such evidence."[29]

029 Following the State Council's reply on 21 June 1988, CCPIT acting for the first time without reference to the State Council, amended the Provisional Rules on 12 September 1988. The new Rules (hereinafter referred to as the "1988 Rules") were effected from 1 January 1989. However, the 1988 Rules did not introduce any changes to Articles 25, 26 and 27 of the Provisional Rules with the exception of some adjustments to the wording. The new Rules did not mention any rights of the parties to comment on or dispute on independent expert evidence or the evidence gathered by the arbitrators themselves. In fact, it was not long before CIETAC had to pay the price for such silence: See paragraphs 040–075 below.

The current position—the New Rules

030 In March of 1994, CIETAC amended its rules for the second time (hereinafter referred to as the "New Rules"). The reasons for this second amendment could be identified as follows:

(a) Through five years of extensive practice (from 1989 to 1994), CIETAC established a professional reputation in the field of international commercial arbitration. The number of new cases under its jurisdiction exceeded 200 in the years between 1990 and 1992.[30] In 1993, 486 new cases were filed with CIETAC, which represented an 82 per cent increase compared with 1992.[31] At the same time, the nature of the disputes became more varied, the amounts in dispute even larger, and the cases became increasingly complex. These developments led CIETAC to conclude that a higher standard of professional services was required.

(b) Based on amendments to the previous Civil Procedure Law of the People's Republic of China (For Trial Implementation),[32] China's Civil Procedure Law came into effect on 9 April 1991. The CPL, for the first time in China's legal history, provided some legal rules to supervise CIETAC proceedings.[33] Violation of such rules would result in the court setting aside the award. Therefore, the requirements of law and practice relating to the arbitration procedure became stricter.

(c) Based on its own theoretical research into and practice of arbitration, CIETAC concluded that not all of the current rules could meet the high standards maintained in the international arbitration field. Also, some provisions were not in conformity with the new CPL.[34]

031 The New Rules added 38 new articles, one third of which were modified or added to such an extent as CIETAC deemed proper. CIETAC believed that the New Rules had four characteristics[35]:

(1) they further reflected the principle of the autonomy of the parties;
(2) they strongly reflected the international practices;
(3) they were more complete than the 1988 Rules;
(4) they were easy to understand and simple to apply in practice.

032 Regarding the issues of investigation and evidence gathering by the arbitration tribunal, and the expert's as well as the appraiser's report, the New Rules made the following amendments:

033 Article 38 of the New Rules states:

> "The parties shall produce evidence for the facts on which their claim, defence and counterclaims are based. The arbitration tribunal may undertake investigation and collect evidence on its own initiative, if it deems it necessary.
>
> If the arbitration tribunal investigates and collects evidence on its own initiative, it shall accordingly timely inform the parties to be present at the place where the arbitration tribunal deems it necessary. Should one party or both parties fail to appear at the place directed, the investigation and collection of evidence shall by no means be affected."[36]

034 Article 39 of the New Rules states:

> "The arbitration tribunal may consult an expert or appoint an appraiser for the clarification of

special questions relating to the case. Such an expert and appraiser can be an organisation or a citizen, Chinese or foreign.

The arbitration tribunal has the power to order the parties and the parties are also obliged to submit or produce to the expert or appraiser any materials, documents, properties or goods related to the case for checking, inspection and/or appraisal."[37]

035 Article 40 of the New Rules states:

"The expert's report and the appraiser's report shall be copied to the parties so that they may have the opportunity to give their opinions thereon. At the request of any party to the case and with the approval of the arbitration tribunal, the expert and appraiser may be present at the hearing and give explanations of their reports when the arbitration tribunal deems it necessary and appropriate."[38]

036 Article 41 of the New Rules states: "The evidence submitted by the parties shall be examined and decided by the arbitration tribunal. The expert's report and the appraiser's report shall be determined by the arbitration tribunal whether to be adopted or not."[39]

037 Compared with the 1988 Rules, the most significant change was that the New Rules broke the silence as to the parties' rights to comment on or dispute the opinion of the expert appointed by the tribunal or the evidence gathered by the tribunal. Such supplementary provisions were formulated with reference to the requirements of the actual situation in China and the relevant international practices, e.g. the UNCITRAL Arbitration Rules[40]; the AAA International Arbitration Rules[41]; the London Court of International Arbitration Rules.[42] The purpose of such change was to improve CIETAC procedures, provide the parties with sufficient opportunities to give their opinions, and protect the parties' rights and interests more effectively.

038 After 1994, CCPIT amended the CIETAC Arbitration Rules twice, namely in October 1995 and in May 1998, respectively.[43] However, these amendments did not change the New Rules in respect of evidence in general and expert evidence in particular.[44]

039 From an objective point of view, the articles in the New Rules regarding experts are quite comprehensive. Similar rules and principles can be found in the arbitration laws or the rules of arbitration institutes in most other countries.[45] For example, Article 27 of the UNCITRAL Arbitration Rules; article 23 of the AAA International Arbitration Rules; Articles 22 and 23 of the Singapore International Arbitration Centre Rules; Article 1042 of the Netherlands Civil Procedure Code; Article 12 of the London Court of International Arbitration Rules and Article 38 of the Arbitration Act 1996.[46]

CIETAC PRACTICE

General principle

040 "The principle of 'seeking truth from facts' is not only emphasised by Chinese judicial activities, but also is the most often-repeated by CIETAC practice. This means that the arbitration tribunal must use investigation and thus, through fact-finding draw a clear line between right and wrong, to ascertain liability, to be fair and reasonable."[47]

041 Since the late 1980s, CIETAC has started to use independent experts to assist the tribunal in finding the truth or solving technical problems. From that time, Chinese trade with foreign partners was no longer limited to simple and traditional commodity trade. More and more contracts relating to production lines, high-tech equipment, technology transfer, joint ventures and construction work were concluded. As a consequence, also the disputes became more complex than ever before. Sometimes, these disputes could not be solved without the help of an expert. CIETAC had to improve its services if it was enhance its reputation.

042 In general, the process of fact-finding by a CIETAC arbitrator is carried out at three levels[48]:

(1) examination of the written submissions and evidence produced by the parties;
(2) direct examination of the parties and witnesses at the hearing;
(3) direct investigation of the dispute, either by appointing independent experts or conducting on-site visits.

The required qualifications

043 Article 13 of China's Arbitration Law stipulates what requirements a person to be eligible as an arbitrator must satisfy.[49] But as in other countries, there are no express rules regarding the qualifications an expert has to have, either in China's Arbitration Law or in CIETAC Rules. Generally speaking, an expert should satisfy the following standards[50]:

(1) have significant industry practice, skills, experience and technical abilities;
(2) should have no conflict of interest with any of the parties involved;
(3) have the ability to express his or her opinion.

044 The above elements are common to many jurisdictions.[51]

045 Usually the tribunal will mainly consider the following aspects when selecting the expert:

- no direct or indirect conflict of interest with either party;
- academic background and research ability;
- practical experience and familiarity with the specific issue in dispute;
- foreign language ability and foreign training and/or working background (for Chinese citizens only);
- senior academic and/or professional title/s.

046 According to Article 39 of CIETAC Rules, an expert can be either an organisation or a citizen, Chinese or foreign. But in practice, cases in which a foreign expert was selected are rare. The tribunal prefers to select Chinese experts based on its own survey of available candidates. The reason for this practice may arise out of the following concerns:

- the cost of using a foreign expert is much higher;
- a Chinese expert presumably has a better understanding of the local industrial environment[52];
- communication between the tribunal and a Chinese expert is more convenient.

047 Foreign-party practitioners are sometimes unhappy about such preference. They may even lack confidence in CIETAC's appointment of a local expert. They often wonder whether the Chinese expert has sufficient experience, whether he might favour the Chinese party, whether he is able to communicate with the foreign party, whether the Chinese expert is able to understand the equipment produced by foreign manufacturers or whether he knows the specific technical issues. Those questions and doubts will remain in their minds throughout the entire procedure.

048 CIETAC is aware of these concerns. However, CIETAC has its own concerns regarding the nationality of the expert. Commercial arbitration is tailored for business people. Business people on the whole do not like costly and time-consuming litigation proceedings. They prefer to invite professionals who understand the transaction as well as their business philosophy, and who will help them to settle the dispute in an efficient and fair way. Sometimes, justice is not their main consideration. In this respect, the parties and the tribunal share the same approach: "cost-effectiveness". It is for these reasons that where the tribunal can find a suitable local Chinese expert, it will not consider selecting a foreign one, even though it is aware of the foreign party's concerns.

049 Notwithstanding the above, the possibility that CIETAC will appoint a foreigner as its independent expert cannot be ruled out. In 1989, CIETAC started to accept foreigners as its arbitrators. But it was not until the autumn of 1995, that a CIETAC tribunal was composed of a majority of foreign arbitrators.[53] This novelty happened because the parties had agreed in their arbitration agreement that the tribunal shall be formed of a majority of non-Chinese arbitrators and CIETAC respected the parties' choice.[54] It is conceivable that CIETAC would also agree on a foreign expert in case of such mutual consent by the parties.

050 In August 1996, CIETAC, for the first time, appointed a foreign company (SGS International Controle Maatsschappij (ICM) BV) to perform an investigation on behalf of the tribunal.[55] The reason for this appointment may have been that the investigation had to be carried out outside of China, namely in Rotterdam (NL). This case, however, proves the point made above: cost-effectiveness is one of CIETAC's main guidelines regarding the appointment of an expert. Hence, it can be said that CIETAC will agree to select a foreign expert either on grounds of costs or if there is no Chinese expert available.

Selection of experts

051 The tribunal is given the power to consult an expert where it deems it necessary.[56] The parties can put forward their proposal. However, if they fail to agree on who should be selected as an independent expert, the tribunal has full discretion to make the decision.

052 Where the parties do reach an agreement and the proposed candidate satisfies the tribunal's conditions, it will arrange an interview with the proposed expert in order to form its own opinion.

053 Once the tribunal has made a decision, the arbitrator will give the expert instructions as to what is wanted from him and will direct him as to the rules of conduct during the arbitration proceedings. The parties will receive a notice from the tribunal regarding the expert appointment.

054 It is seldom heard of a candidate refusing such an appointment. Most people will be happy to accept the tribunal's appointment, since such an appointment is considered an honour and will contribute to the person's reputation.

Challenging CIETAC's appointment of an expert

055 In some jurisdictions the parties can challenge the appointment of an expert, e.g. in America this can be done in two ways[57]:

(1) by examining the expert's background and his qualifications, particularly his publications;
(2) by questioning his neutrality.

056 However, most foreign laws are silent on this point. China is no different. The parties may make representations as to whether they agree or object to the proposed appointment. However, once the appointment has been made, in the absence of a clear procedure, there is almost nothing the parties can do about it. Nor can they apply to the court for provisional measures to interfere with the appointment made by the tribunal. The appointment of an expert is completely at the tribunal's discretion. This is so unless a party can prove that the expert is guilty of misconduct during the selection procedure (misconduct in this context covers questions of neutrality, not professional qualifications). In such a case the tribunal will have to consider dismissing the expert. Otherwise, it will risk its final award being set aside by a court in the enforcement procedure on the ground of a procedural defect.

Powers, duties and conduct of experts

057 In CIETAC arbitration, the party-appointed expert, acting as an expert witness, is free to submit his opinion during the arbitration proceeding. On the one hand, his role is to assist the arbitrators to understand a specific issue. On the other hand, he acts as a counsel to the party that appointed him. He gives advice and prepares documents for his client. In relation to the role of an advisor to the tribunal, the tribunal often prefers to appoint its own expert to determine specific issues, e.g. the value of a real estate property, the market price, an engineering or equipment problem. The expert appointed by a tribunal actively participates in the arbitration proceedings only after the tribunal has been composed. In many cases, the tribunal may not determine whether or not it is necessary to use an independent expert until the end of the first oral hearing.

058 The tribunal-appointed expert has the right to review the documents provided by the parties. He may question the parties with the tribunal's approval. He also has the right to participate in the hearing if the tribunal deems it necessary. According to the tribunal's instructions, the expert can carry out on-the-spot-examinations or on-site visits on behalf of the tribunal. The most important duty of the expert is to provide his written opinion to the tribunal based on the information provided by the parties or collected by examination or inspection.[58] Since June 1994, CIETAC Rules require that the expert's report/opinion be sent to the parties and the parties have a reasonable opportunity to give their comments or dispute it.

059 As a general rule: "the arbitrator will not consult the expert or gather information himself without the knowledge of the parties. All facts on which the arbitrator intends to base his award must first be submitted to both parties." CIETAC has an "Ethical Rule" which governs not only the conduct of arbitrators but also the relationship between the arbitrators and the parties.[59] No such rules govern the relationship between the arbitrators and the tribunal's expert. There is nothing to limit the contact between the tribunal and its expert. In fact, it often happened in the past that the tribunal consulted its expert without giving prior notice to the parties. The situation may have now changed. According to Quiet's Secretariat, the tribunal is advised not to contact its expert without the parties' knowledge. It is further advised that information or opinion provided by its expert should be in writing and should be sent to the parties. However, in the absence of express rules regarding this issue, it may be too early to view this advice as a statement of the true position.

060 There are no specific rules governing the expert's conduct except the general principles of independence and impartiality. Usually the expert will be advised by CIETAC about these two principles. To ensure the proper and impartial performance by the expert of his assignment, a member of the tribunal or a secretary from the Secretariat of CIETAC may sometimes accompany the expert in the performance of his mission. This assignment is particularly so when the tribunal decides to carry out on-the-spot-examination or inspection. Where the expert fails to observe his duty of impartiality, the tribunal can discharge the expert. However, no CIETAC tribunal has ever exercised this sanction.

The parties' rights to comment on the expert evidence

061 The New Rules put an express obligation on the tribunal to provide the parties with a copy of the expert's report. The parties also have the right to comment on the report. The New Rules confer on the parties the right to challenge the expert report. Such challenge can either be made in writing or at an especially arranged hearing.[60]

062 As mentioned above, before 1 October 1994, CIETAC Arbitration Rules were silent on the issue of the parties' rights in relation to the opinion produced by the expert. Before too long, the effect of enforceability became evident. On 15 January 1993 Mr Neil Kaplan, the Justice of the High Court of Hong Kong, refused to enforce an arbitration award rendered by CIETAC on 15 November 1990 on the ground of procedural irregularity.[61] Between 1990 and 1992, approximately 40 CIETAC awards were enforced by the High Court of Hong Kong and this was the first refusal in the history of the High Court of Hong Kong.[62] This case is very important, not only because it is a leading case with respect to refusal to enforcement of a CIETAC award, but also because it shows a foreign judicial body's attitude towards the parties' rights to have an opportunity to comment on evidence given by a tribunal-appointed expert.

063 The summary of the case is as follows[63]:

> The arbitration case before CIETAC was a dispute arising out of a sale of steel contract between Paklito Investment Ltd (the plaintiff) and Klockner East Asia Ltd (the defendant). An oral hearing was held by a CIETAC tribunal on 25 April 1990. After the hearing, on 31 July 1990, the tribunal notified the defendant of its decision to appoint its own expert to carry out investigations. Although the defendant objected to such appointment, the expert was employed by the tribunal on 12 September 1990 and the expert report was issued on 31 October 1990 and received by the defendant's lawyer on 8 November 1990. On 12 November the defendant wrote to the tribunal stating its intention to submit a further defence in answer to the expert and questions arising from it. On 15 November 1990 the tribunal rendered the final award in favour of the plaintiff. On 8 January 1991 the defendant wrote to CIETAC that it expected to have an opportunity to adduce further evidence at an oral hearing. No reply was ever received from CIETAC.
>
> On 12 August 1991 *ex parte* leave was granted by a Master to the plaintiff to enforce this award. However, on 11 February 1992 the Master, after an *inter partes* hearing, set aside her order dated 12 August 1991 and the case was subsequently appealed before the Justice Neil Kaplan.
>
> Before the High Court of Hong Kong, the plaintiff stated that under the Chinese law and/or CIETAC's Arbitration Rules (1988), there is no right to cross-examination. In support of this, the plaintiff produced an affidavit from Mr Xi Xiao Tam, a PRC lawyer as well as a letter from the Secretariat of CIETAC. Mr Xi stated that the Chinese system is an inquisitorial one and that

the common law notion of cross-examination of witnesses is "totally absent". The tribunal may conduct its own enquiries and accept the evidence so obtained. The parties are not allowed to challenge evidence obtained in such a manner unless the tribunal invites them to do so. The letter of the Secretariat of CIETAC affirmed Mr Xi's view. The letter confirmed that "any party to the proceedings cannot raise any objection to the expert's report prepared by the independent expert employed by the arbitration tribunal. This is because the expert's report is compiled by an independent and impartial third person. It is a practical and scientific report and is authoritative".

The defendant answered with an opinion from Professor An Chen, Dean of the School of Law and Politics at Xiamen University, who is also a member and arbitrator of CIETAC, and an affirmation from Mr Anthony Neoh QC, who is also a member of CIETAC's panel of arbitrators and has been an active arbitrator for the past three years.

In his opinion, Professor An Chen stated that the most important purpose of the PRC Civil Procedure Law is "to protect the exercise by the parties of their procedure rights". The Civil Procedure Law allows the questioning of witnesses with the approval of the court. The new Civil Procedure Law (the new CPL came into effect on 9 April 1991) even states that "evidence shall be presented in court and examined by the parties".[64] The new provisions of the CPL state that all evidence, including expert conclusions, must be collected and examined "comprehensively and objectively". In fact, the court will always approve a proper request and even encourages such requests because "these greatly assist the clarification of facts and the ascertainment of the truth". Since the CPL is one of the basic laws in China, the Professor also confirmed that the same principles should be observed by CIETAC in its arbitration proceedings even though at that time, under the CIETAC's Arbitration Rules (1988), there were no specific provisions allowing the parties to raise objections to the tribunal's expert reports. Furthermore, "The State Council's Reply" stated that CIETAC rules should comply with China's laws and the international treaties.[65] This means that CIETAC Rules should not be read to breach either China's laws regarding fundamental legal principles, or international treaties to which the PRC has acceded (China acceded to the New York Convention on 22 April 1987).[66] "In this case, the expert report was delivered too late, and the award was issued too soon." In other words, the party against whom the application was made did not have any opportunity to plead or be able to state its opinion.[67] This was contrary to the CPL and the New York Convention.

Other than reconfirming Professor An Chen's opinion, Mr Anthony Neoh QC concluded that

> "I cannot agree with the opinion expressed by the Secretariat that no-one has the right to disagree with the findings of the tribunal's expert. As I have already stated above, the Rules are to be interpreted against the background of the New York Convention in the light if the State Council's direction that the CCPIT shall enact rules in accordance with the international treaties and practice. To comply with the New York Convention, it is necessary in my view that any finding that is adverse to any party must be given to that party to allow that party to answer the case against him/her/it. Perhaps that accounts for the fact that the expert's reports were sent to and received by the defendant's legal representatives in the PRC, otherwise, if the defendant had no right to comment on the expert's report, there would have been no point in sending them at all."[68]

Kaplan J finished with

> "having concluded that a serious breach of due process has occurred I cannot see that it would be right or proper to exercise my discretion in favour of enforcement. I am quite satisfied that even when one takes into account that the parties have chosen an arbitral law and practice which differs to that practised in Hong Kong there is still a minimum requirement below which an enforcing court, taking heed of its own principles of fairness and due process, cannot be expected to approve. Regrettably, this case is a classic example of such a situation."[69]

The appeal was dismissed and the award set aside.

064 This case indicates that, in enforcement proceedings, where CIETAC rules are silent or unclear, the foreign judicial body will take into consideration not only CIETAC's rules, but also the relevant Chinese laws, international treaties to which China has acceded as well as international arbitration practices. Therefore, it is important that CIETAC's rules should comply with international standards. The expert performance in the proceedings should be given due care.

Admissibility of the expert evidence

065 "Where expert evidence is introduced by the parties, the rules regarding the admissibility of the expert evidence applied by arbitration tribunals are in general the same as those applied to other forms of evidence in the same arbitration."[70] From this, it could be assumed that there is no difference between the evidence provided by the parties and the evidence prepared by the tribunal's expert. Both should be submitted to the parties for examination and both can be challenged.

066 In many civil law jurisdictions, the expert's report is evidence that can be freely evaluated by the judge, and thus the arbitrator. "The judge determines the facts independently in accordance with his conviction. It is a general principle of (Swiss) national private law that the judge is not bound by an expert opinion."[71] It is commonly accepted that in international arbitration, the arbitrators are not bound by national rules of procedure. It is therefore completely free to accept all or part of the expert's report's findings.

067 In England, however,

> "if the parties agree to refer [an issue] to the final and conclusive judgment of an expert [. . .], the expert's decision will be final and conclusive, and therefore not open to review or treatment by the court as a nullity on the ground that the expert's decision [on the issue] was erroneous in law, unless it can be shown that the expert has not performed the task assigned to him.[72] This principle was established in *Jones* v. *Sherwood Computer Services Ltd.*[73] And later on, this principle was applied in the *Nikko* case.[74] In both cases, the question was whether the expert had assessed the wrong subject matter as a result of a mistake or whether he carried out the very task which was entrusted to him. 'These two cases not only mark a distinct shift to the finality of expert decision, but also a new emphasis on the contractual basis of an expert's jurisdiction."[75]

068 Despite the free evaluation of expert evidence as mentioned above, some practitioners in civil law jurisdictions support the principle established in *Jones* v. *Sherwood*. According to a Swiss lawyer, for example "one should clarify carefully if and to what extent the finding of the expert should be final and binding for the arbitrators or whether the arbitrators may have a discretion to evaluate and weigh the findings of the expert in the overall context of the arbitration. [. . .] Expert determination [. . .] is a means by which parties agree to jointly instruct a third party (i.e. an expert) to decide a specific issue [. . .] in a binding manner. [The] parties should be aware that it is quite difficult to challenge the expert's determination".[76]

069 To the author's knowledge, there is no such principle in China. It is not expressly stated in any legislation nor is it referred to in case law. The general principle is that the judge or the arbitrator are free to evaluate the evidence provided either by a party-appointed expert or an independent expert appointed by the tribunal. Article 41 of CIETAC's Arbitration Rules (1998) states that: "The evidence submitted by the parties shall be examined and decided by the arbitration tribunal. The adoption of the expert's report and the appraiser's report shall be determined by the arbitration tribunal." Even though there is no similar rule in the CPL, the People's Court implements the principle. However, the CPL gives some special weight to evidence which has been notarised. Article 67 of the CPL stipulates that: "The People's Court shall take the acts, facts and documents legalised by notarisation according to legal procedures as the basis for ascertaining facts, unless there is evidence to the contrary sufficient to invalidate the notarisation." At the same time, as seen in paragraphs 010–019 above, the People's Court may give more credit or respect to the tribunal-appointed expert which usually comes from the department authorised by law. Against this background, it can be assumed that even in arbitration proceedings, some arbitrators may be influenced by the People's Court practice when evaluating an expert report.

070 The second time a CIETAC award was set aside by the Court of Appeal of Hong Kong is a good example of this influence[77]:

> In May 1992, Apex Tech Investment Ltd (the plaintiff) agreed to purchase from Chuang's Development (China) Ltd (the defendant) a block of flats in Dan Shui Hui Yan County in the PRC for HK$ 30,357,300. The plaintiff made two payments but refused to pay the final instalment and therefore, the defendant forfeited the two previous payments.
>
> In accordance with the arbitration clause contained in the contract, the plaintiff initiated arbitration proceedings before CIETAC. The issue the tribunal had to determine was whether the contract was valid. In particular, the tribunal had to decide whether the defendant had acquired the right to sell premises to a foreign company under the land use certificate it had received from the Hui Yan County State-Owned Land Bureau. The use permitted according to the certificate was "industrial estate by foreign investors solely".
>
> The arbitrators reviewed the evidence presented by the parties and conducted their investigation. On 28 March 1994 they were officially informed by the Guangdong Province State-Owned Land Department that the "industrial estate to be established and financed solely by foreign investment" did not include land for "commodity real properties" destined to be sold abroad. In addition, in order to change the land use, the defendant had to obtain additional consents from the proper authorities. This reply had on its face the official register issuing number. On 10 December 1994, based on this official reply, the tribunal rendered its final award in favour of the plaintiff.
>
> The plaintiff sought to enforce the award in Hong Kong. On 24 May 1995 the plaintiff obtained an *ex parte* order from J Leonard, judge of the first instance court, to enforce this award in Hong Kong. The defendant argued that he should have been made aware of the arbitrators' independent investigation and should have been allowed to make further submissions and, if necessary, call further evidence. On 8 September 1995 the judge dismissed the defendant's application to set aside his *ex parte* order. The judge concluded that the result of the arbitration could not have been different even if the defendant had been given the opportunity to be heard. The defendant subsequently appealed before the Court of Appeal of Hong Kong.
>
> The issue on this appeal was whether the judge was wrong in his assumption that it was clear that, if an opportunity to be heard further had been given to the defendant, it could have had no effect upon the tribunal's award.[78]
>
> On 4 January 1995 the defendant sent an inquiry letter to the State-Owned Land Department of Guangdong province and received their reply letter on 5 January 1995. On 11 February 1995, the defendant also received a letter from the Hui Yang County State-Owned Land Bureau.
>
> Having compared these two letters as well as the previous reply to the tribunal, the justice of the Appeals Court concluded that they "were consistent". "However, this consistency also demonstrates without question that there is considerable uncertainty about the meaning of the words in the certificate of use."[79]
>
> > "Having regard to the uncertainty on the meaning of the permission granted to the defendant demonstrated by the award itself and the letters which both preceded and followed it, I am unable to say that if the defendant had been given the opportunity to make further representations to the arbitral tribunal after it had made its own inquiries, that it could not have affected the outcome of the award. As we were rightly reminded by Mr Tang [QC for the defendant] in the course of his submissions this is particularly so when the applicable law is that of the People's Republic of China."[80]
>
> On 15 March 1996, CIETAC's award was set aside by the Court of Appeal of Hong Kong.

071 This is the second case to be set aside by the Hong Kong courts on the ground of irregularity in the arbitration procedure.[81] Again, this "irregularity" was due to the tribunal's independent investigation on a special issue. As mentioned above, since 1994, CIETAC has expressly stipulated in its Arbitration Rules that the parties shall have the opportunity to comment on the tribunal expert's report/opinion.[82] In addition, since the first case (*Paklito Investment Ltd* v. *Klockner East Asia Ltd*) of its award being set aside by the Hong Kong court, CIETAC has adopted a more vigorous approach to observing procedural rules. The question is why (as it appears) the same mistake happened again. A possible explanation could be seen in the fact that the tribunal's attitude towards evidence is different, depending on whether it was provided by an individual (i.e. an expert) or by an administrative department. The issue in the abovementioned case on which the tribunal had to decide, was the legal effect of a certificate issued by a local land administrative body.

072 According to the Chinese vertical administration system, a higher level land administrative body has the power to review a lower level administrative body's activities and to interpret the administration rules.

073 This may be the reason why the tribunal neither informed the parties about its own investigation nor invited them to give their comments on the official reply to the tribunal's inquiries. In fact, the tribunal did not treat this reply as an expert report/opinion, but as an authoritative reply with binding force.

074 The author is of the opinion that in this case the tribunal was wrong in two respects:

- First of all, the official reply was evidence, should have been treated as such and therefore should have been given to the parties for their comments.
- Secondly, the tribunal should have given its reasons why it believed that the official reply from Guangdong Province State-Owned Land Department had superseding power over the certificate issued by the Yui Yang County State-Owned Land Bureau. Since, when two contradicting pieces of evidences are presented to a foreign judicial body, both issued by a Chinese governmental authority, it cannot be expected to be familiar with the Chinese administrative system and know which department has superseding power. Unfortunately, this problem was never addressed, either in the CIETAC award or before the Court of Appeal of Hong Kong.

075 If either of those two mistakes were avoided in the arbitration proceedings, the Court of Appeal of Hong Kong might have come to a different conclusion.

PROBLEMS REGARDING THE EXPERT EVIDENCE

076 In general, CIETAC arbitration has proved to be fair.[83] Nevertheless, some foreign practitioners comment that "CIETAC emphasises arriving at fair results in the light of the facts of the dispute, with apparently less concern for analysis of applicable legal principles".[84] From the author's point of view, the main problems arising out of the use of experts are as follows:

- The current CIETAC Rules confer on the tribunal a broad discretion to decide the main issues regarding experts. Decisions, such as whether or not to initiate an investigation, selection and assignment of specific tasks to particular experts as well as the decision whether to accept or refuse an expert's report or opinion, are all left to the tribunal. However, CIETAC Rules are not clear with regard to the parties' rights in this respect. They do not mention, for example, whether the parties have the right to arrange an investigation, whether they can jointly select an expert to give his opinion on a particular issue and whether they can agree to accept this expert's report as final.
- Another problem is the lack of transparency in CIETAC's practice regarding the use of experts. The scope of the assignment of an expert, the exact issue to be determined and the procedure for the investigations is important information which should be made

available to the parties. In *Paklito Investment* v. *Klockner East Asia* Kaplan J said: "it seems to me that an arbitral authority should have nothing to hide [ ]".[85] Unfortunately, this is not always the case in CIETAC arbitration. Even now, according to Article 43 of CIETAC Rules, the record of the oral hearing in writing or by tape-recording is only for the use and reference of the arbitration tribunal.[86]

- Furthermore, there are no express rules governing the communication between the tribunal and the expert. However, it is commonly accepted that "the arbitrator will not consult the expert or gather information himself without the knowledge of the parties. All facts on which the arbitrator intends to base his award must first be submitted to both parties."[87]

077 It is clear that if these problems are not given proper consideration, they will undoubtedly slow down the development of CIETAC's arbitration. CIETAC would be well advised to introduce a more sophisticated set of rules regarding the use of experts. To the author's knowledge, presently, only the "ICC International Centre for Expertises" provides a separate set of rules to govern the expert, the parties as well as the tribunal in arbitration procedures.[88]

078 Taking into account its present stage of development and, in particularly, the level of its legal expertise and the maturity of its legal understanding, it is not likely that CIETAC will establish, in the near future, a set of comprehensive rules. However, relating to expert evidence, even under its present rules, CIETAC could still improve its practice by adopting the following measures:

1. Give the parties more autonomy to decide by themselves issues such as the nationality of the expert, the investigation procedures, expert expenses, the finality of the expert's report.
2. Ensure that the parties are fully informed of the expert's tasks so as to increase the degree of the transparency of his work. This could be achieved by disclosing the communications between the tribunal and its expert and informing the parties of the expert's plans and procedure for carrying out his assignment.
3. Observe to the full the parties' right to comment on or dispute the expert's report/opinion.

079 In short, the parties should be given more autonomy to participate in the proceedings relating to the expert's evidence. Furthermore, CIETAC may prepare a list of recommended experts for the parties' reference. The experts' list should include foreigners. A regular legal training programme for experts may be necessary. An expert who has at least some basic legal understanding is more likely to conduct himself in a way which does not breach the requirements of proceedings and justice.

CONCLUSION

080 In 40 years of continuous development, and in particular in the course of the last 15 years, a period when its practice became very active, CIETAC has matured considerably and overcome many of its earlier shortcomings. As a consequence, CIETAC's practice is now being evaluated against high international standards and criteria.

081 The challenges facing CIETAC are twofold. First of all, compared with other international arbitration institutes of high repute, such as the International Court of Arbitration of the International Chamber of Commerce (ICC), the Arbitration Institute of the Stockholm Chamber of Commerce (SCC) and the London Court of International Arbitration (LCIA), most of which have been established for many years, CIETAC still needs to gain more experience. To be able to present an alternative to these foreign arbitration institutions and their sophisticated services, CIETAC has to further improve its services.

082 Secondly, CIETAC is increasingly exposed to the challenge presented by domestic arbitration bodies. In June 1996, the General Office of the State Council issued a notice in which it expressly stated that domestic arbitration commissions are allowed to accept foreign-related arbitration disputes.[89] Since then, CIETAC has lost its previous statutory monopoly on arbitration involving foreign parties in China. By June 1997, more than 130 local or provincial arbitration commissions have been set up, e.g. the Beijing Arbitration Commission, the Tianjin Arbitration Commission and the Shanghai Arbitration Commission.[90] Some of them have already accepted foreign-related disputes. Even though those domestic arbitration bodies are still lacking in experience in dealing with foreign-related disputes, it can be assumed that they will seek to catch up and compete with CIETAC, using their own advantages, such as geographical convenience, and more flexible and reasonable rules and fees.

083 As mentioned above, CIETAC revised its rules once again as late as May of this year. Although, the new version does not directly address the articles regarding expert evidence, Article 7 of CIETAC Rules (1998) has the effect of creating a more flexible and comfortable atmosphere for the parties and their legal advisers.

084 Article 7 of the Rules states that: "Once the parties agree to submit their dispute to the Arbitration Commission for arbitration, it shall be deemed that they have agreed to conduct the arbitration under these Rules. *In case the parties have agreed otherwise which is also agreed by the Arbitration Commission, the parties' agreement shall prevail.*"

085 It can be seen from the italicised sentence above, that in the future, the parties will have more autonomy to agreed procedure issues in a CIETAC arbitration. It is not surprising that the problems discussed in this article are not unique to CIETAC. They can even be found outside of China. However, CIETAC must address these problems and look at ways by which it can enhance its credibility and its effectiveness if it is to face the challenges to its position.

End Notes

1. *Yearbook of China International Commercial Arbitration* (1992), p. 4.
2. CIETAC Arbitration Rules (1998).
3. Judith O'Hare, "Enforcement of Foreign Arbitral Award".
4. See, e.g. UNCITRAL Arbitration Rules, Art 27; ICC Rules, Art 14.2; and LCIA Rules, Art 12.
5. See, e.g. the draft of Sweden Arbitration Act, Art 25 (1995); Egypt International Commercial Arbitration Act, Art 39; Thailand Arbitration Act, Art 17.
6. *Arbitration and Expertise*, ICC Dossier of the Institute of International Business Law and Practice, 1994, p. 30.
7. Ronald Bernstein, John Tackaberry, Arthur L. Marriott, Derek Wood, *Handbook of Arbitration Practice*, p. 252.
8. *Arbitration and Expertise*, ICC Dossier of the Institute of International Business Law and Practice, 1994, p. 84.
9. *Ibid.*, p. 117.
10. *Ibid.*, p. 30.
11. *Ibid.*, p. 30.
12. Art 702 of US Federal Rules of Evidence.
13. *Arbitration and Expertise*, ICC Dossier of the Institute of International Business Law and Practice, 1994, p. 31.
14. Zhang Yulin, *China's Drive for International Arbitration*, p. 6.
15. The full text of CPL is published in *China Law and Practice*, Vol 5, 5, pp. 15–61.
16. CPL, Art 63.
17. CPL, Art 64.
18. CPL, Art 72.

19. English translation by Baker & McKenzie, American Law Firm, in 1994.
20. China Maritime Arbitration Commission, established in 1959 under the China Council for the Promotion of International Trade (CCPIT).
21. China's Arbitration Law, Art 43.
22. *Ibid.*, Art 44.
23. Stanley Lubman and Gregory Wajnowski, "International Commercial Dispute Resolution in China", *The American Review of International Arbitration 1993*, Vol 4, No 2, p. 114.
24. Attachment to China Foreign Economic and Trade Arbitration Commission, Rules of Arbitration.
25. Attachment to CIETAC's Rules of Arbitration, 12 September 1988.
26. Provisional Rules of Procedure of the Foreign Trade Arbitration Commission, Art 25.
27. *Ibid.*, Art 26.
28. *Ibid.*, Art 27.
29. Neil Kaplan, Jill Spruce and Michael J Moser, *Hong Kong and China Arbitration,* Cases and Materials, 1994, pp. 325, 326.
30. Cheng Dejun, "Report on the Amendment to the Arbitration Rule of the CIETAC", *Yearbook of China International Commercial Arbitration (1993–1994)*, pp. 76–77.
31. Cheng Dejun, *ibid.*, pp. 76–77.
32. Laws and Regulations of the People's Republic of China Governing Foreign-Related Matters, p. 304.
33. CPL, Art 260.
34. Cheng Dejun, "Report on the Amendment to the Arbitration Rule of the CIETAC", *Yearbook of China International Commercial Arbitration (1993–1994)*, p. 77.
35. Cheng Dejun, *ibid.*, pp. 78–79.
36. CIETAC Arbitration Rules (1994), Art 38.
37. *Ibid.*, Art 39.
38. *Ibid.*, Art 40.
39. *Ibid.*, Art 41.
40. UNCITRAL Arbitration Rules, Art 27.
41. AAA International Arbitration Rules, Art 23.
42. London Court of International Arbitration Rules, Art 12.
43. 1995 and 1998 CIETAC Rules.
44. Arts 38, 39, 40 and 41 of CIETAC Arbitration Rules (effective as from 1 October 1995); Arts 38, 39, 40 and 41 of CIETAC Arbitration Rules (effective as from 10 May 1998).
45. UNCITRAL Arbitration Rules, Art 27; AAA International Arbitration Rules, Art 23; London Court of International Arbitration Rules, Art 12.
46. *China Arbitration Handbook*, pp. 663, 706, 776.
47. Stanley Lubman and Gregory Wajnowski, "International Commercial Dispute Resolution in China", *The American Review of International Arbitration 1993*, Vol 4, No 2, p. 28.
48. See *Business Law in China*, published by the International Chamber of Commerce, p. 435.
49. China's Arbitration Law, Art 13.
50. *Arbitration and Expertise*, ICC Dossier of the Institute of International Business Law and Practice, 1994, p. 48.
51. *Ibid.*, p. 48.
52. Stanley Lubman and Gregory Wajnowski, "International Commercial Dispute Resolution in China", *The American Review of International Arbitration 1993*, Vol 4, No 2, p. 141.
53. CIETAC Arbitration Rules, Art 39.
54. First occasion: case M94209. See Justin Hughes, "Foreign *lis alibi pendens*, Non-Chinese Majority Tribunals and Other Problems of Neutrality in CIETAC Arbitration" in: *Arbitration International*, 1997, Vol 13, No 1, p. 63.
55. *Ibid.*
56. CIETAC Case No G 95531.
57. *Arbitration and Expertise*, ICC Dossier of the Institute of International Business Law and Practice, 1994, p. 50.
58. CIETAC Arbitration Rules 1998, Arts 39 and 40.
59. "Ethical Rules for Arbitrators of the China International Economic and Trade Arbitration Commission" (adopted on 6 April 1993), *Yearbook of CIETAC and CMAC*, p. 180.
60. Art 40 of CIETAC Rules 1994, 1995, 1998.
61. See [1993] 2 HKLR 39.
62. Neil Kaplan, Jill Spruce and Michael J Moser, *Hong Kong and China Arbitration,* Cases and Materials, 1994, p. 281.
63. The summary is digested from [1993] 2 HKLR 39, pp. 271–282.
64. CPL, Art 66.
65. "The State Council's Official Reply Concerning the Renaming of the Foreign Economic and Trade Arbitration Commission as the China International Economic and Trade Arbitration Commission and the Amendment of its Arbitration Rules."
66. "The People's Supreme Court Notice Regarding the Implementation of New York Convention."
67. See [1993] 2 HKLR 39, p. 280.
68. *Ibid.*, p. 281.
69. *Ibid.*, p. 277.

70. D Mark Cato, *Arbitration Practice and Procedure*, p. 342.
71. See Mr F Knoepfler, *Swiss Report*, pp. 8 and 17.
72. Ronald Bernstein, John Tackaberry, Arthur L Marriott, Derek Wood, *Handbook of Arbitration Practice*, p. 216.
73. See *Jones* v. *Sherwood* [1989] EGCS 172.
74. See *Nikko Hotels (UK) Ltd* v. *MEPC plc* (1991) 28 EG 86.
75. Ronald Bernstein, John Tackaberry, Arthur L Marriott, Derek Wood, *Handbook of Arbitration Practice*, p. 218.
76. Marc Blessing "Drafting an Arbitration Clause", *ASA Special Series No 8*, pp. 66–67.
77. See *Apex Tech Investment Ltd* v. *Chuang's Development (China) Ltd* [1996] 2 HKLR 155 Civil Appeal No 231 of 1995.
78. *Ibid.*
79. "Order Enforcing Award Set Aside By Appeals Court in Hong Kong", *Mealey's International Arbitration Report*, February 1997, Vol 12, No 2, p. 12.
80. See *Apex Tech Investment Ltd* v. *Chuang's Development (China) Ltd* [1996] 2 HKLR 155 Civil Appeal No 231 of 1995.
81. See [1993] 2 HKLR 39.
82. CIETAC Arbitration Rules 1994, Arts 40 and 41.
83. Michael J Moser, *Arbitration in China*, p. 45; Thomas Peele and Marsha A, *Dispute Resolution in China*, p. 49.
84. Stanley Lubman and Gregory Wajnowski, "International Commercial Dispute Resolution in China", *The American Review of International Arbitration 1993*, Vol 4, No 2, p. 128.
85. "It seems to me that an arbitral authority should have nothing to hide [...]", Neil Kaplan, Jill Spruce and Michael J Moser, *Hong Kong and China Arbitration*, Cases and Materials, 1994, p. 276.
86. CIETAC Arbitration Rules 1998, Art 43.
87. *Arbitration and Expertise*, ICC Dossier of the Institute of International Business Law and Practice, 1994, p. 142.
88. See *The Rules for the ICC International Centre for Expertise*.
89. Daniel A Laprès and Yuejiao Zhang, *Business Law in China—Trade, Investment and Finance*, 1997.
90. See Zhang Yulin, "*Domestic Commission foreign power leave CIETAC defending its turf*", Chin Joint Venturer 1997, Vol 3, p. 17.

BIBLIOGRAPHY

Books

BARRINGTON, Louise (editor): *Arbitration and Expertise*, ICC Dossier of the Institute of International Business Law and Practice, 1994 (English translation).

BERNSTEIN, Ronald; TACKABERRY, John; MARRIOTT, Arthur L; WOOD, Derek: *Handbook of Arbitration Practice*.

BLESSING, Marc (editor): *The Arbitration Agreement—Its Multifold Critical Aspects*, ASA Special Series No 8, December 1994.

CATO, D Mark: *Arbitration Practice and Procedure*.

CHENG Dejun, WANG Shengzhang (editors): *Foreign Arbitration and Laws*, Beijing 1994 (Chinese only).

CIETAC Research Institute (publisher): *Collection of Foreign Arbitration Documents*, ARI Special Series No 2, Beijing, March 1995 (Chinese only).

CIETAC Research Institute (publisher): *Forty Years of Foreign Arbitration*, ARI Special Series No 2, Beijing, March 1995 (Chinese only).

HU Kangsheng, CHENG Dejun (editors): *China Arbitration Handbook*, Publishing House of Law, Beijing 1995 (Chinese only).

KAPLAN, Neil, SPRUCE, Jill, MOSER, Michael J: *Hong Kong and China Arbitration*, Cases and Materials, Butterworths Hong Kong, Singapore, Malaysia 1994.

LAPRÈS, Daniel A, ZHANG, Yuejiao (editors): *Business Law in China—Trade, Investment and Finance*, ICC Publication No 576, Paris 1997.

MA, Yuan, TANG, Dehua (editors): *Amendments and Implementation of the Civil Procedure Law*, published by People's Court Publications, Beijing 1991 (Chinese only).

REDFERN, Alan, HUNTER, Martin: *Law and Practice of International Commercial Arbitration*.

MUSTILL, Sir Michael, BOYD, Stewart C: *Commercial Arbitration*.

Periodicals

Arbitration and Law Newsletter: Published by CIETAC, CMAC and CCPIT Legal Department (Chinese only).

China International Commercial Arbitration: Yearbook of CIETAC and CMAC.

Articles

CHEN, Luming: "Some Reflections on International Commercial Arbitration in China", in *Journal of International Arbitration*, June 1996, Vol 13, No 2, pp. 121–162.

HUGHES, Justin: "Foreign *lis alibi pendens*, non-Chinese majority Tribunals and Other Problems of Neutrality in CIETAC Arbitration", in *Arbitration International*, LCIA 1997, Vol 13, No 1, pp. 63–83.

LUBMAN, Stanley B, WAINOWSKI Gregory C: "International Commercial Dispute Resolution in China: A Practical Assessment", in *The American Review of International Arbitration* (Columbia University), 1993, Vol 4, No 2, pp. 107–166.

O'HARE, Judith: "Enforcement of a Foreign Arbitral Award".

SONG, Dihuang: "A valid arbitration agreement, or is it? A Perspective under Chinese Law", in *The Arbitration and Dispute Resolution Law Journal*, pp. 78–87.

ZHANG, Yulin: "China's Drive for International Arbitration" (unpublished essay written for the University of British Columbia, Vancouver).

Legislation, Regulations and Rules

AAA International Arbitration Rules
Arbitration Act (1996)
CIETAC Arbitration Rules (12 September 1988, 1 June 1994, 1 October 1995, 10 May 1998)
Draft of Sweden Arbitration Act (1995)
Hamburg—International Place of Arbitration, Hamburg Chamber of Commerce (1990)
Hong Kong International Arbitration Centre Rules
ICC International Centre for Expertise Rules
ICC Rules (1 January 1988)
International Arbitration Rules of Zurich Chamber of Commerce (1989)
London Court of International Arbitration Rules (1 January 1998)
PRC Arbitration Law (September 1995)
PRC Civil Procedure Law (9 April 1991), English version published in *China Law and Practice*, Vol 5, No 5, pp. 15–61
Rules of the Arbitration Institute of the Stockholm Chamber of Commerce (1 January 1988)
US Federal Rules of Evidence
Thailand Arbitration Act (1987)
Egypt International Commercial Arbitration Act (1988)
UNCITRAL Arbitration Rules

Fei Ning, BSc, LLM *is a partner of Haiwen & Partners (H & P) in Beijing, China.*

From 1983 to 1988, he worked as an engineer with Beijing Building Materials Bureau and the Research Institute of Technical Information, the State Administration Bureau for Building Materials. Since then, he was employed as a staff member with the Secretariat of China International Economic and Trade Arbitration Commission (CIETAC).

In 1993, he became a member and 1995 a partner of the Chinese law firm H & P from December 1995 until March 1997. He then joined the Swiss law firm Schellenberg & Haissly (S & H), and then from April 1997 to October 1997 the English law firm Dibb Lupton Alsop, as associated foreign lawyer. After that, he participated in the LLM programme in the School of Oriental and African Studies (SOAS), London University.

CHAPTER 1/21B

THE EXPERT IN HONG KONG AND MAINLAND CHINA

David Leonard

THE EXPERT IN HONG KONG

The legal and constitutional background

001 During the Opium War in 1840 Britain occupied Hong Kong which became a British Colony and remained so until 1997 and the common law of England generally applied in the absence of local legislation.

002 On 1 July 1997, following the Sino-British Joint Declaration of 19 December 1984 Hong Kong became a Special Administrative Region (SAR) of the People's Republic of China (PRC), in accordance with the provisions of Article 31 of the Constitution of the People's Republic of China. Under the Basic Law, which sets out the constitutional position of Hong Kong as an SAR, the common law system is to continue in Hong Kong. Articles 5 and 8 of the Basic Law are in the following terms:

> "Article 5: The socialist system and policies shall not be practised in the Hong Kong Special Administrative Region, and the previous capitalist system and way of life shall remain unchanged for 50 years."
>
> "Article 8: The laws previously in force in Hong Kong, that is, the common law, rules of equity, ordinances, subordinate legislation and customary law shall be maintained, except for any that contravene this Law, and subject to any amendment by the legislature of the Hong Kong Special Administrative Region."

003 Thus in relation to expert evidence the common law continues to apply, subject to any relevant legislation. The fundamental legal principles and authorities which form the basis of the law of Hong Kong governing expert evidence will therefore be familiar to many readers and it is not proposed here to describe them comprehensively but some English authorities will be referred to, as well as local legislation and decided cases.

Judicial independence

004 Article 85 of the Basic Law provides that "the courts of the Special Administrative Region shall exercise judicial power independently, free from any interference. Members of the judiciary shall be immune from legal action in the performance of their judicial functions".

005 Experience of the first year of the existence of the SAR shows that the independence of the judiciary has been maintained. The High Court is now called the Court of First

Instance. The Court of Final Appeal, based in Hong Kong, has replaced the Privy Council. There are some changes in nomenclature but the basic system is unchanged.

Admissibility of expert evidence

006 The opinion of an expert is admissible in civil and criminal proceedings, provided that it relates to matters outside the general experience of the court and is within the scope of his expertise and, of course, is relevant.

007 It is well-settled law that expert evidence is admissible in criminal cases.

008 With regard to civil proceedings, section 58 of the Evidence Ordinance provides that: "Where a person is called as a witness in any civil proceedings his opinion on any relevant matter on which he is qualified to give expert evidence shall be admissible in evidence".

The expert's duty to the court

009 The guideline case in England on the duties and responsibilities of an expert witness, *The Ikarian Reefer; National Justice Compania Naviera SA* v. *Prudential Assurance Co* [1993] 2 Lloyd's Rep 68, is followed in Hong Kong. See e.g. *UBC (Construction) Ltd* v. *Sung Foo Kee Ltd* [1993] 2 HKC 458, where the principles stated in the former case were repeated by Kaplan J. They are:

(1) Expert evidence presented to the court should be, and should be seen to be, the independent product of the expert uninfluenced as to form and content by the exigencies of litigation: see *Whitehouse* v. *Jordan* [1981] 1 WLR 246, 256, *per* Lord Wilberforce.

(2) Independent assistance should be provided to the court by way of objective unbiased opinion regarding matters within the expertise of the expert witness; see *Polivitte Ltd* v. *Commercial Union Insurance Co plc* [1987] 1 Lloyd's Rep 379, 386 *per* Garland J and *Re J* [1990] FCR 193 *per* Cazalet J. An expert witness in the High Court should never assume the role of advocate.

(3) Facts or assumptions upon which the opinion was based should be stated together with material facts which could detract from the concluded opinion.

(4) An expert witness should make it clear when a question or issue fell outside his expertise.

(5) If the opinion was not properly researched because it was considered that insufficient data was available, then that had to be stated with an indication that the opinion was provisional (*Re J, supra*). If the witness could not assert that the report contained the truth, the whole truth and nothing but the truth then that qualification should be stated on the report; see *Derby & Co Ltd and Others* v. *Weldon and Others (No 9)* (1990) *The Times*, 9 November *per* Staughton LJ.

(6) If after exchange of reports, an expert witness changed his mind on a material matter then the change of view should be communicated to the other side through legal representatives without delay and, when appropriate, to the court.

010 Kaplan J, after saying that an expert witness in the case he was trying had completely lost his confidence said: "An expert gives evidence to assist the court. Of course, he wishes to advance his client's case and that is why he has been retained, but at all times, it is vital for an expert to stand back and take a wider perspective of events if he is to be of assistance to the court and continue to enjoy the confidence of the court."

011 The judge added that it was pertinent to note that the additional guidelines of the British Academy of Experts (which has since been renamed the Academy of Experts) stated: "It is the overriding duty of members to act at all times with integrity, fairness and impartiality."

012 In one case, an expert arbitrator, appointed because he was an expert, was accused of bias and misconduct by the party choosing him because he declined to accept an opinion expressed by that party's expert. The case was *Carl International (HK) Ltd* v. *Ernst Komrowski & Co*, Con List 5 of 1996 (unreported). There, Carl International (HK) Ltd (the applicant) was in dispute with Ernst Komrowski & Co (the respondent) over the condition of steel coils, which were allegedly corroded, and over the cause of any such corrosion. The applicant nominated Dr Greene, one of two arbitrators, because he was a steel expert. The other arbitrator was a solicitor who was an experienced and well-known arbitrator in Hong Kong.

013 There was an expert's inspection report, which favoured the applicant whose advisers thought their client was bound to win, because the report was admitted in evidence by consent. They were very concerned when Dr Greene made it clear that he intended to enquire into the circumstances and to make up his own mind upon the evidence about the technical issues. The applicant began but then abandoned an attempt to remove Dr Greene as arbitrator on the ground that he had made up his mind in advance. Finding for the respondent, the arbitrators said that the findings by the expert as to the condition of the goods were binding but the opinions expressed in his report as to the cause of the condition were not. It was observed in the award that it was difficult to see why a full arbitration by a steel expert and a lawyer could be thought necessary if the claimant was correct in thinking that they were bound by the opinion in the expert's report.

014 The applicant sought leave to appeal on grounds of misconduct on the part of both arbitrators though the specific complaints of bias were directed only against Dr Greene. It was held by the judge that the complaints came nowhere near to satisfying the requirements for obtaining leave to appeal. Though the applicant complained that Dr Greene had given evidence to himself, it was apparent from the award that the two arbitrators had subjected the evidence to critical analysis.

Qualification as an expert

015 A witness put forward as an expert must have acquired knowledge by study or experience of his subject and it is for the court to decide on the evidence whether he is qualified to give expert evidence. The matters which the court may take into account were listed by Bruce and McCoy in *Criminal Evidence in Hong Kong* as follows:

"(1) The academic qualifications of the witness—the degrees, diplomas, associateships or certificates held by the expert which are relevant to the topic under consideration. The time and place at which the qualifications were obtained are also relevant.

(2) The extent to which the expert has made a special study of his subject and the diligence with which he keeps 'up-to-date' with recent developments in the field.

(3) The practical experience gained by the expert in exercising his knowledge in his special field and the degree of authority and responsibility exercised by the expert in doing so.

(4) The number of times that the expert has been permitted by other tribunals to give expert

evidence on the subject and the extent to which those other tribunals have accepted him as an expert.

(5) The extent to which the expert has published learned articles or books or other works on the topic."

016 It is not obligatory to fulfil all those requirements. Some experts may have gained their expertise through practical experience; may not have academic qualifications and may not have published books on the subject in question. The fact that an expert has never given evidence before does not indicate a lack of expertise in his field. A witness may nevertheless be accepted as an expert if he is found to be qualified as such. A former Hong Kong governor was accepted in *Cooper-King* v. *Cooper-King* [1900] P 65, as an expert on the marriage laws of Hong Kong notwithstanding the fact that he was not a qualified lawyer.

017 *In Chan Kim-hung* [1977] HKLR 479 at p. 418 Trainor J said that "A witness may express an opinion on an issue before the court if that issue requires special skill or knowledge to resolve it, and the witness possesses special skill or knowledge of the issue. The opinion is not automatically accepted by the court . . ., one of the first things the witness has to do is to satisfy the court that he has special skill or knowledge." In that case, the evidence of a person holding himself out as an expert was rejected because there was insufficient proof of his expertise.

018 It may be that the expertise of the witness is not in issue, in which case it may be established by very brief oral evidence or admitted as a fact. A written statement of his expertise may be admitted by consent under the provisions of the Criminal Procedure Ordinance.

019 There must be a finding by the court that the witness is an expert: *Lo Hung* v. *R* Cr App No 340 of 1983; *Yim Chor-man* v. *R* [1975] HKLR 546. Where there is a dispute about it, the issue should be resolved at the outset of his evidence. If there is a jury, a *voir dire* should be held but if there is a trial by a judge or magistrate sitting alone, it would appear that the evidence may be led at any stage: *Chan Yau-foon* v. *R* [1977] HKLR 486.

There must be a need for expert evidence before it may be adduced

020 In *British Celanese Ltd* v. *Courtaulds Ltd* (1935) 52 RPC 171, Lord Tomlin, commenting on the calling of unnecessary evidence, said, at p. 198:

> "In the first place, time is wasted and money spent on what is not legitimate. In the second place there accumulates a mass of material which so far from assisting the judge renders his task the more difficult, because he has to sift the grain from an unnecessary amount of chaff. In my opinion, the trial court should make strenuous efforts to put a check on this undesirable and growing practice."

021 With that remark in mind, firm guidance was given *obiter* by two judges in the Court of Appeal in *Chen Paul and Another* v. *Lord Energy Ltd* [1998] 1 HKC, a conveyancing case, to the effect that it was a waste of time to call experts to express opinions where expert evidence was not necessary. Rogers JA said this:

> "An expert may give evidence as to a term of art but he is not entitled to say nor is his counsel entitled to ask him what a document means nor what a letter or an agreement or conditions of sale or an assignment mean. The construction of a document is a matter for the court. Still less is an expert witness entitled to give evidence as to what the law is.
>
> In this case, the plaintiff's expert in his witness statement took one page to give his experience, half a page to explain the meaning of one of the sections in one of the Ordinances, one and a half

pages in setting out history primarily of the correspondence and the remaining two pages discussing what a conveyancer would do. All this, in my view, was inadmissible in this case. The defendant's expert was basically a mirror image in a more condensed form of the plaintiff's expert.

The oral evidence was no better . . . .

In my view the so-called expert evidence in this case was a complete waste of time and it should never have been called or admitted . . . ."

022 In *R* v. *Turner* [1975] QB 834 an attempt was made to lead evidence from a psychiatrist to the effect that an accused person was likely to be telling the truth and was likely to have been provoked into committing an offence. There was no evidence that the accused had any mental disability. The evidence was not permitted and Lawton LJ said at p. 841:

". . . an expert's evidence is admissible to furnish the court with scientific information, which is likely to be outside the experience and knowledge of a judge or jury. If on the proven facts a judge or jury can form their own conclusions without help, then the opinion of an expert is unnecessary. . . .

Jurors do not need psychiatrists to tell them how ordinary folk who are not suffering from any mental illness are likely to react to the stresses and strains of life. It follows that the proposed evidence was not admissible to establish that the accused was likely to have been provoked."

023 The Court of Appeal in Hong Kong held, in the case of *Lau Man-cheung* v. *R* [1986] HKLR 1172 that a defence of diminished responsibility under section 3 of the Homicide Ordinance must be based upon expert evidence (following *R* v. *Dix* (1982) 74 Cr App R 306).

024 In *Choi Hon-ping* v. *R* [1965] HKLR 540 a judge permitted a police officer to give evidence that a person was a drug addict when there was no evidence to establish his expertise in assessing drug addiction. On appeal, the judge was criticised but it is implicit that if his expertise had been established, the police officer could have testified on such a matter.

An expert must show how he reached his opinion

025 It is not enough for an expert merely to state his conclusions. He must back them up with evidence of the facts on which he relies.

026 It is his duty "to furnish the judge or jury with the necessary scientific criteria to form their own independent judgement by the application of these criteria to the facts proved in evidence": *Davie* v. *Edinburgh Magistrates* 1953 SC 34. That principle was applied in *Ngai man* (1990) Mag App No 1373 of 1989 (High Court), where an opinion was expressed as to the speed of a vehicle based upon the length of some skid marks. There was no evidence to explain how the speed had been calculated from the marks and it was held that in the circumstances the opinion could be given little weight.

027 In *Chan Kam Tak* (1987) Cr App No 204 of 1987, where a fingerprint expert gave evidence and the court only saw a very small photograph of the fingerprint in question, a conviction was quashed. Similarly in *Tam Wing Hung* [1988] 2 HKLR 44 (CA) a fingerprint expert was given a small photograph, taken by a police photographer, of a fingerprint found on the wrapping of some drugs. He was not given the wrapping bearing the print, but compared the photograph with prints taken from the accused. At the trial he produced the small photograph and drew a sketch to show how he identified matching characteristics in the photograph and the prints of the accused. No enlargement was exhibited. The court found that the expert should have been given the print on the wrapper and photographed it himself.

He should have enlarged the photograph and produced it at the trial. Then the court could have been in a position to form its own judgement on the basis of his expert evidence and the facts proved. Without the enlargement, the expert's evidence was a bare assertion and carried little weight. The conviction was quashed.

028 The same principle was illustrated in *R* v. *Yeung Kwok Fai* [1996] 1 HKC 754 where there was no evidence to show how an expert witness arrived at his conclusions that some watch parts were fake and some were genuine.

029 Likewise, in *Tai Muk-kwai t/a Nan Lien Pharmaceutical Co* Cr App No 1129 of 1979 (CA) the Court of Appeal stated that where he gave opinion evidence about substances submitted for examination, the government chemist should produce to the court the documents providing the basic data upon which he formed his opinion. In *Leung Chi-yuen* (1989) Cr App No 576 of 1987 (CA), expert witnesses gave evidence for the prosecution as to whether certain cartridges had been fired from a certain pistol. No photographs had been taken of markings, which they had seen on the cartridges and pistol barrel, though they could have been taken. The court indicated that the pistol and cartridges should have been available for examination by the defence so that they might be in a position to test the opinions of the prosecution experts. In the absence of photographic evidence, a very careful direction to the jury was required as to how to approach the evidence.

030 In *HKSAR* v. *Lo Yan Kan* [1997] 3 HKC 430 it was submitted on behalf of the appellant that there had been no ground for the trial judge to accept an expert's opinion as to the value of drugs, as the expert had not mentioned the source of his information or explained in detail how much the drugs would have cost when sold retail. The Court of Appeal held that the evidence was properly admitted. As the issue was sensitive, the expert could not have given evidence in detail about the source of the information. It had been clear in the judgment of the trial judge that the information came from drug dealers and undercover agents and therefore the evidence was reliable. Comment: as in England and Wales, the courts will not, as a matter of policy, allow an accused person to elicit evidence in cross-examination from a police officer which would reveal the identity of an informant or expose a police officer acting as an undercover investigator but that is far from allowing what the informant said to be put in as evidence.

031 It is a frequent practice in Hong Kong for an experienced police officer to give evidence in a criminal trial as to the current price of a particular type of drug and as to the methods of drug dealers and addicts. He will, for example, explain the ways in which addicts consume dangerous drugs and the jargon they use.

032 There is a real difficulty for a defendant faced with evidence from a police officer, based on hearsay, as to the current street price of a drug, for he cannot properly test its reliability by cross-examination. He can hardly call a drug dealer to give rebutting evidence. It then becomes a question of his word, allegedly from his own personal knowledge and experience, against the word of a policeman who is repeating what he has allegedly been told. If the Court of Appeal will describe evidence as reliable because it comes from a police officer who says he has heard it from unidentified sources an accused person can only hope that the judge or jury trying him may take a different view.

033 In a civil case, not only must the expert show in court how he reached his conclusion but also it is required that his report, which must be disclosed before trial (Rules of the Supreme Court Order 38, rule 38(1)), must contain a detailed explanation of his reasons for his finding. In *Herman Iskandar* v. *Bonardy Leo* [1988] HKLR 583 (CA) an expert whose report contained his opinion unsupported by an explanation of how he formed it, that a will was a forgery, was not allowed to testify at the trial.

Rules of Court

034 Order 38 of the Hong Kong Rules of the Supreme Court contains detailed provisions relating to expert witnesses.

035 The aim of the rules, as in England, is pre-trial disclosure of expert evidence in order to save time and expense The court has power to limit the number of expert witnesses called and to order the exchange of experts' reports so as to identify the live issues and to avoid the necessity of adjournments which might have to be granted if a party were to be taken by surprise at the trial. Expert evidence may not be adduced except by agreement or with leave of the court or where directions have been applied for or given and complied with, or where it is permitted to be given on affidavit.

036 If a party fails at the right time to disclose the contents of an expert's report to his opponent, the evidence which his expert is to give may be limited or excluded: *Ng Yeung Lai Lin* v. *Fung Shui Kwan* (1989) Probate Case No 1 of 1987 (High Court); *In re the Estate* of *Ng Shum (No 1)* [1990] 1 HKLR 63 (High Court).

037 There are detailed provisions, some of general application and some relating to particular types of claim (e.g. personal injuries) as to the directions which the court may give in relation to expert evidence.

038 The court may direct that experts meet in order to discover where they agree and where they differ. The experts may then issue joint reports showing where they are agreed and where they are not. Discussion at such meetings is "without prejudice" at least until the experts have jointly agreed about some issue. The writer has not in practice come across a case where experts produced the type of joint report contemplated. A solicitor might not take kindly to seeing an expert retained for his client agreeing matters with the expert retained for the other side and might well seek to discourage such an agreement. Another type of pressure exerted by solicitors on experts is to try to persuade them to act on a contingency basis. The Academy of Experts forbids its members so to act, since an expert whose fee depends upon a judgment for the person retaining him will be under pressure to forget his duty to the court to be impartial and objective.

Practice Directions

039 Two types of civil case in which expert evidence is frequently given in the High Court are those assigned to the Personal Injuries list and the Construction and Arbitration list respectively. Practice Directions have been issued setting out standard directions in such cases.

PERSONAL INJURIES

040 In the High Court Personal Injuries List Practice Direction it is provided that a medical report (or reports) within the meaning of Order 18, rule 1C must be served with the statement of claim or counterclaim where a claim or counterclaim is made for damages for death or personal injuries. In a fatal case, a *post mortem* report must also be served, if available. It is also provided that a Master may, at the summons for directions hearing (known as a Check List Hearing) make orders for the exchange of experts' reports and any supplemental experts' reports under Order 38, rule 36.

CONSTRUCTION AND ARBITRATION

041 The business covered by this list is:

(a) Civil or mechanical engineering.

(b) Building or other construction work.

(c) Claims by and against engineers, architects, surveyors and other professional persons or bodies specialising in practice related to the construction industry.

(d) Applications under the Arbitration Ordinance, Cap 341, and Order 73, Rules of the Supreme Court. Some examples of the types of business are applications for stay of proceedings in favour of arbitration; applications for leave to appeal an arbitral award or remit it to the arbitral tribunal; applications to enforce awards etc.

Court-appointed experts

042 As in England, the court may appoint, on the application of a party, an expert (called a "court expert") or experts to assist it in any cause or matter which is to be tried without a jury. The court expert inquires into and reports on any question of fact or opinion, which is not a question of law or construction. If the parties cannot agree on an expert, the court must nominate him. If they cannot agree on the question for the expert or the instructions he is to be given, the court must settle the form of the question and the instructions. In any cause or matter, the court has an inherent power to appoint an expert.

043 The writer does not know of a case where there was a court-appointed expert. In *Nguyen Ho* v. *Director of Immigration* (1990) Civil Appeal No 135 of 1990 (CA) the Court of Appeal was invited to appoint a court expert to test whether certain interpreters were competent. The invitation was declined.

Experts and the ultimate issue

044 The traditional rule is that an expert may not purport to decide the ultimate issue. Once he has been accepted as such by the court, his evidence is admissible but, generally speaking, he may not give his opinion on an issue of fact or law which it is the duty of the court to decide: *Davie* v. *Lord Provost* 1953 SC 34; *Li Lam* [1966] HKLR 809 (Full Court). This rule is more strictly applied in criminal than in civil proceedings and rarely causes any difficulty in practice: it is often found convenient to allow questions to be asked of an expert witness which are not strictly permissible and a judge will direct himself or the jury as to how to approach the expert evidence.

045 It has been suggested that the ultimate issue in the case, e.g. whether a defendant has been negligent, is a "relevant matter", so that expert opinion may by virtue of section 58 of the Evidence Ordinance (*supra*) be adduced as to that question. The flaw in the suggestion is that it appears to disregard the requirement that the witness must be qualified. Only the court is qualified to decide issues of guilt or liability, which must involve issues of law as well as fact. However, evidence of expert opinion as to the facts, if accepted, may lead the tribunal to an inevitable conclusion on the ultimate issue in the case.

046 In *Pang Bing-yee* [1984] HKLR 298 (CA), a murder case, expert psychiatric evidence that the accused had no intention to kill was not admitted. Testimony that the accused had an abnormality or a disease of the mind that could affect his capacity to form an intention would have been admissible. In *Li Lam* [1966] HKLR 809 (Full Court), evidence as to whether an accused had the capacity to form an intention to kill was admitted, but it was for the court to decide whether or not he did form such an intention.

047 A Deputy District Judge held in *Leung Pak Chung*, Case No DCCC 1048 of 1996, 22 April 1997, that the recent authority—*R* v. *Stockwell* (1993) 97 Cr App R 260—suggested that when an expert is called to give his opinion he should be allowed to do so even if his opinion was on the ultimate issue. It was, however, important for the judge to direct himself or the jury that the opinion of the expert was not binding.

048 An expert witness does sometimes think he is there to decide the ultimate issue in the case rather than to give to the court, which is the fact-finding tribunal, the benefit of his expert knowledge and experience. One example is the case of *Easio Garments Ltd* v. *Miles (Hong Kong) Ltd* HCA 12661 of 1994, 11 August 1995 (unreported). There a German professor of law made an affidavit purporting to decide the case in favour of one party instead of limiting himself simply to stating the relevant German law. The judge accepted his evidence as to what the foreign law was and, applying it to the facts which he, the judge, had found, decided the case for the opposite party.

The expert and hearsay

049 As an exception to the hearsay rule, an expert may express an opinion using information, usually in written form, received from other experts. The relevant information has to be of a type generally and reasonably relied on and falling for evaluation within the relevant field of expertise. It was so held in *R* v. *Wan Pui-hay* [1994] 2 HKLR 47 (following *R* v. *Abadom* [1983] 1 WLR 126) and *Reid* v. *Kerr* (1974) 9 SASR 367. The Court of Appeal cited with approval the following passage in *Leung Chi-kin* [1970] HKLR 25 at pp. 39–40: "In chemical matters as well as in other scientific and technical matters those concerned must inevitably place some reliance on the work of others."

When is an expert needed?

050 In *R* v. *Cheung Shing-wai* [1993] 1 HKCLR 311, Sir T L Yang, CJ, heard an appeal against a conviction of careless driving. At the trial, the defendant had sought to call a witness with six years' experience of driving articulated vehicles of the type concerned in the case. The intention had been to adduce from him evidence of the weight of the vehicle and its capability for speed. The magistrate had declined to hear the witness, observing that the weight of the vehicle was irrelevant and unless the witness possessed expert technical knowledge about the mechanics of the vehicle, his evidence was of no weight. The Chief Justice held that a person with the experience of the witness could testify as to the speed which the vehicle was capable of doing. Expert evidence was not needed on such a simple point and the evidence of the witness should have been admitted.

051 In *R* v. *Chan Hon Wai* [1993] 1 HKC 531, a clinical forensic pathologist had been allowed to testify as an expert that it was unlikely for the top of the head to be injured during a struggle for a gun between two men in standing positions since they would be pulling against each other. The trial magistrate had accepted that evidence. On appeal against conviction, it was held that the expert should not have been allowed to theorise about how the injury had occurred. That was a question of fact. Bewley J cited the following passage from the judgment in *R* v. *Turner (Terence)* [1975] QB 834:

> "An expert's opinion is admissible to furnish the court with scientific information which is likely to be outside the experience and knowledge of a judge or jury. If, on the proven facts, a judge or jury can form their own conclusions without help, then the opinion of an expert is unnecessary. In such a case, if it is given dressed up in scientific jargon, it may make judgement more difficult. The fact that an expert witness has impressive qualifications does not by that fact alone make his opinion on

> matters of human nature and behaviour within the limits of normality any more helpful than that of the jurors themselves; but there is a danger that they may think it does."

Topics for expert evidence

052 Some of the topics in relation to which the court has considered the question of expert evidence in Hong Kong are set out below.

Construction, trade and finance

053 Architects, engineers and surveyors testify in the many disputes, which arise in the construction industry. There is no official referee: the judge in charge of the Construction and Arbitration list normally tries construction cases in the High Court. As stated above, there is a Practice Direction governing the procedure in such cases.

Customary law

054 Experts often give evidence on questions of Chinese customary law where it falls to be applied in Hong Kong, e.g. where a party claims to have contracted a valid marriage under that law. To the extent that customary law is part of the law of Hong Kong, the courts are entitled in theory to take judicial notice of it without evidence: *Lui Yuk Ping* v. *Chow To* [1962] HKLR 515. However, because of the paucity of written authority on the subject, expert evidence is received. This was the reason given by Huggins J in *Ng Ying Ho* v. *Tam Suen-yu* [1963] HKLR 923.

055 Sometimes, a person, usually a wife, will seek a declaration from the court that she entered into a valid customary marriage, recognised by the law of Hong Kong. Armed with such a declaration she can register the marriage at the marriage registry. The object of the exercise is to be able to institute divorce proceedings with a view to obtaining ancillary relief in terms of property, maintenance etc. An expert testifies, usually by affidavit, as to the ceremonies required for a customary marriage and the necessary factual evidence is given.

056 In the New Territories, the northern part of what is now the Hong Kong SAR, the Chinese Law as it stood when the land was leased from China in 1898 continued to apply and affect rights of property and inheritance. Expert evidence is necessary when disputes arise in relation to such matters.

Damages in personal injury cases

057 In *Chan Pui Ki and Another* v. *the Kowloon Motor Bus Co (1933) Ltd* Civil Appeal No 263 of 1995, the Court of Appeal in Hong Kong firmly squashed an attempt to introduce the expert evidence of actuaries and economists to prove future loss in actions for damages in personal injuries cases and come down in favour of the conventional method illustrated in *Cookson* v. *Knowles* [1979] AC 556.

058 Giving the judgment of the court, Litton V-P said:

> "... the trial judge entertained evidence (both written and oral) from five non-medical experts and eight medical experts. The non-medical experts comprised two actuaries (Mr Quant and Mr Baxter) and three economists (Mr Wyatt, Dr Busche and Dr Huang). It was regarded as a test case.

Exceptionally, therefore, the evidence of the non-medical experts was justified, even though some of the expressions of opinion ranged far too wide.

Now that all outstanding issues have been resolved by this judgment, there should be no need in the future for non-medical evidence of that kind to be adduced. We would hope that personal injuries litigation will now be much simplified. For the foreseeable future, the only evidence of an economic nature which needs to be put before a court would be the incidence of general inflation: something which can be done by the production of government published statistics. Occasions for opinion evidence from experts on economic matters should be rare indeed."

Engineers

059 An engineer's evidence is admissible to show contributory negligence in failing to wear a seatbelt: *Leung Ni Wing* v. *Hsing Kieng Shing* (1985) Civil Action No 8451 of 1984. In *Ngai-man* (1990) Mag App No 1373 of 1989, expert evidence was given to establish the speed of a motor vehicle by reference to the length of its skid marks.

Disputed writings

060 The Government Chemist and other experts give evidence about suspected forgeries. Such evidence does not require corroboration. See *Kung Wong Sau-hing* v. *Kung kwok-sun* [1985] HKLR 303

061 In a case which went to the Court of Appeal in Hong Kong, experts gave evidence of their opinion that of three possible scenarios, the true one was that certain signatures had been forged. The trial judge came to the same conclusion and convicted. It was held on appeal that the judge should have considered, but had not considered the whole of the evidence upon which he had to answer the ultimate question for him, namely whether the signatures in question had been forged. Expert evidence was to be considered not *in vacuo* but in the context of the whole of the evidence. The convictions were unsafe and unsatisfactory. *R* v. *Chong Kwok wah and Another* Cr App No 549 of 1996, 9 May 1997.

Financial matters

062 As Hong Kong is a centre of international commerce and finance, financial experts often give evidence for the parties in civil and criminal cases. They are generally impressive witnesses, experienced in court work.

Fingerprints

063 The procedure to be followed in relation to expert evidence on fingerprints has been laid down by the Court of Appeal: see *Tam Wing Hung* (1988) Cr App No 511 of 1987 (CA) and *Chan Kam Tak* (1987) Cr App No 204 of 1987 (CA). These cases illustrate the principle that the expert must show how he arrived at his opinion. It is not enough for the expert to say that fingerprints match. He must show the jury how they match so that it may decide the issue for itself.

Food

064 A senior Health Inspector (a government servant) may give expert evidence as to the fitness of meat for consumption: *Chan Yau-foon* (1977) HKLR 486.

Foreign law

065 Section 51 of the Evidence Ordinance provides that a suitably qualified person may, in civil proceedings, give expert evidence as to the law of any country or territory outside Hong Kong. Foreign law is a question of fact, to be proved by evidence, unless the question has already been decided in a previous case in the High Court or Court of Appeal.

Gambling

066 In *Leung Pak Chung* Case No DCCC 1048 of 1996, heard on 22 April 1997, a Deputy District Judge was trying three charges, two of which alleged conspiracy to cheat contrary to common law and to section 16(1)(a) of the Gambling Ordinance, the third alleging conspiracy to cheat contrary to common law. The defendants were alleged to have subjected their victim to a type of confidence trick known as a *tin sin kuk*, according to the prosecution. The victim was taught how to cheat at a game called *chong yuen tan*, being led to believe that he would be able to win money from another player. In fact, the prosecution's case was that the victim was the person who was the object of a conspiracy to steal and he was cheated out of Hong Kong $400,000.

067 A gambling expert testified that the style, *modus operandi* and setting of the case was more or less the same as those of a *tin sin kuk*. He described the gambling method as *chong yuen tan*.

068 The judge held that the mode and details of the game of *chong yuen tan* were outside the ordinary knowledge and experience of ordinary people so that the expert evidence was admissible. It helped the judge to understand how the game was played and how a person setting out to cheat could himself be cheated (*Yim Chor-man, supra*, followed). Furthermore, even if the witness had touched upon the ultimate issue, recent authority suggested that when an expert was called to give his opinion, he should be allowed to do so even if it was on the ultimate issue (*R* v. *Stockwell* (1993) 97 Cr App R 260 followed). It was, however, important for the judge to direct himself or the jury that the opinion of the expert was not binding.

Indecency, obscenity etc.

069 The general common law rule is that an expert witness is not needed where the tribunal is deciding whether or not something is obscene: *DPP* v. *Jordan* [1977] AC 699, 718. In *Yeung Kam-tsuen* v. *R* [1962] HKLR 663 it was held that evidence of opinion as to whether a photograph was indecent was inadmissible. Hogan CJ said that for the purpose of deciding whether a photograph was indecent, revolting or offensive, the court must exercise the community's conscience and treat itself as representing the feelings of the community.

070 However, the Control of Obscene and Indecent Articles Ordinance (Cap 390), section 10(1)(a) provides that in determining whether an article is indecent, the Obscene Articles Tribunal "shall have regard to . . . standards of morality, decency and propriety that are generally accepted by reasonable members of the community". Subsection (2) provides that: "The opinion of an expert as to any of the matters to which a tribunal must have regard under subs.(1) may be admitted in any proceedings before a tribunal either to establish or negative that matter."

071 In *Next Magazine Publishing Ltd* v. *Commissioner for Television and Entertainment Licensing Authority* [1995] 2 HKLR 119 (CA), the facts were that a young man and a young woman had made it their practice to climb upon the roof of Queensway Plaza in the Central

District in Hong Kong every afternoon for the purpose of sexual activities. Persons in adjoining buildings could see the couple through the curtain walls though the couple could not see them. An article about them appeared in a Chinese language periodical known as *Next Magazine* and with it were some photographs. One showed the roof in question seen from a distance. Five showed the couple fully clothed and with their faces blanked out. The Obscene Articles Tribunal classified the article as indecent.

072 *Next Magazine* called a psychiatrist before the tribunal, which accepted him as an expert. He gave it as his opinion that the article was not indecent by the standards of morality, decency and propriety that are generally accepted by reasonable members of the community. The tribunal formed a different view. Its decision was appealed on the basis that the tribunal had failed to have regard to the expert evidence.

073 It was held that whilst the tribunal was bound to have regard to expert evidence admitted under section 10(2), and had had regard to it, it was not bound to accept that evidence. Nazareth V-P pointed out that experts must not usurp the tribunal's function: section 2 (1) provides, *inter alia*, that: "A tribunal shall have exclusive jurisdiction to determine whether (a) Any article is obscene or indecent."

074 In upholding the decision of the tribunal, Bokhary JA said this:

> "There was an element in the article which justified the tribunal in its view that it was indecent, even though a fictional account to the same effect might not have been. Some people may say—and I would not criticise them for saying it—that there was a 'peeping Tom' element in the article. For my own part, I prefer to put it like this. There are standards of privacy which decent people in Hong Kong value as a human right. And the privacy of the naïve couple concerned, who did not seem to understand curtain walls or have contemplated telephoto lenses, was invaded and, not to put too fine a point on it, *sold* in circumstances which branded the result as indecent."

075 In a multi-cultural community such as that of Hong Kong, opinions as to matters of indecency differ in different cultural groups. Generally speaking, the European community is more liberal in such matters than the majority Chinese community and there have been some controversial decisions.

Marine cases

076 There is much marine traffic in and around the famous Hong Kong harbour. Experts in such matters as navigation and engineering have given evidence in cases of marine collisions, accidental groundings and the like.

Medical, psychological etc. issues

077 Medical experts and psychologists frequently give evidence in Hong Kong, in civil and criminal cases, paternity suits, inquests, cases involving the welfare of children etc. It was held in *Lee Kam-chuen* Cr App No 347 of 1976 (CA) that the prosecution has a duty to adduce medical evidence in wounding cases in order to show that the injury falls within the legal definition of a wound.

078 Medical, neurological and psychological experts have given evidence in support of applications for a stay of proceedings on the grounds that an accused has suffered mental deterioration as a result of delay. Defendants have had mixed fortunes. See *R* v. *Cheung Wai-bun* [1993] 1 HKCLR 189; *R* v. *Deacon Chiu* [1993] 2 HKCLR 21 and *R* v. *George Tan Soon-gin* HC Case No 443 of 1993 and 50 of 1994.

Triad societies

079 From the founding of the Colony until the present day, criminal gangs known as triad societies have flourished in Hong Kong. They are organised secret societies with initiation ceremonies; oaths; hierarchical offices and special writings. Under the Societies Ordinance it is an offence to be or profess to be a member or an office bearer of a triad society or to possess triad writings. Through fear of revenge, ordinary citizens are afraid to testify against triad members and one triad member will not normally testify against another because of the oath he has taken, breach of which may well have fatal consequences.

080 In order to make it possible to prove triad offences, evidence is often received from police officers who have gained expert knowledge of triads by study and experience. See *Chan Kim-hung* v. *R* [1997] HKLR 479; *A-G* v. *Ho Wai-chuen* [1965] HKLR 259.

Valuation

081 Surveyors and valuers frequently give evidence in Hong Kong. In *English Exporters (London)* v. *Eldonwall* [1973] Ch 415 it was said that a valuer giving expert evidence may not give hearsay evidence about transactions not within his personal knowledge. That does not apply in the Lands Tribunal in Hong Kong, where valuation evidence is frequently given. In *Union Carbide Asia Ltd* v. *The Hong Kong Land Co Ltd* [1982] HKDCLR 75, the Lands Tribunal held that by virtue of section 10(6) of the Lands Tribunal Ordinance, the strict rules of evidence were relaxed so that virtually any evidence which either side considered of help to the tribunal could be submitted. It was up to the tribunal to decide what should be accepted and what weight to attach to each submission. There was a similar decision in *Financial Secretary Incorporated* v. *True Act Ltd* [1988] HKC 534.

Experts in government service

082 It is common in Hong Kong for the prosecution in criminal cases to adduce expert evidence about such matters as ballistics, fingerprints etc. from persons who are in the employ of the government. For example, the Government Chemist often provides evidence as to dangerous drugs; factory inspectors deal with technical issues arising out of industrial accidents; health inspectors testify about food quality; government surveyors and architects appear in planning cases; police officers with expert knowledge testify about gambling, triad societies, ballistics, dangerous drugs etc.

083 In *Leung Chi-yuen* (1989) Cr App No 576 of 1987 (CA) it was held that a ballistics officer employed by the police might give evidence concerning ballistics.

084 Duffy J in *R* v. *Tai Kai Construction Engineering Co Ltd* [1996] HKC 645 held that it could not be right for the Labour Department to call its own officers as expert witnesses to give opinion evidence about the reason for an accident. He found that the convicting magistrate was wrong to place any reliance on the evidence of such an officer because he could hardly have been described as an independent and impartial witness.

085 Shortly afterwards, however, in *R* v. *Chung Chen-Hsin*, Case No 397 of 1995, objection was taken at a High Court criminal trial to the calling by the prosecution of a police ballistics officer on the ground that there was no evidence that he was not independent of the police investigating team. Stuart Moore J, declining to follow the decision of Duffy J, held that:

(1) from time immemorial, there had never been a requirement that an expert witness must be independent of the prosecution authority or, if called by the defence, of an accused, and

(2) the question of admissibility did not arise in the case where the prosecution had to choose, as its expert, the officer who was in charge of that particular prosecution, provided that the prosecution was able to lay the foundation for him to be accepted as such. The danger in such a case was that if an expert came too close to the facts about which he may have an interest, this might colour his judgement to produce a biased opinion. This would be a matter for the tribunal, which would have to judge the weight to be attached to the evidence.

086 The judge pointed out that in the case he was trying, the witness, a police superintendent and a ballistics officer with 20 years' experience, was accepted to be highly qualified to give evidence in the field of ballistics. His evidence was admitted on the basis that the jury would be directed that a possible lack of independence was only relevant to the weight to be attached to that evidence.

The Government Chemist

087 The Government Chemist in Hong Kong frequently provides evidence on scientific issues in criminal proceedings involving drugs, forgery, etc. By virtue of section 25(1) of the Evidence Ordinance he can give evidence by way of certificate in drug cases. He may rely upon work done by his staff in forming his opinions. He may also rely, like all experts, upon information provided by other experts. It was said in *Leung Chi-kin* [1970] HKLR 25 (Full Court):

> "In chemical matters as in other scientific and technical matters those concerned must inevitably place some measure of reliance on the work of others. As Blair-Kerr J has pointed out in *R* v. *Ma Wai-fun (No 2)* [1962] HKLR 61, a nurse taking a temperature relies on the efficacy of the thermometer and is not usually required to prove its accuracy or the manner in which it works. A chemist using different substances to carry out his tests will normally rely on the labels attached to these substances in his laboratory and, unless there is some special reason for raising the issue, will not normally be required to establish that he had personally tested each of these substances beforehand in order to show that they were what he thought them to be. A chemist or doctor who says that he took, say chloroform, from a bottle so labelled is not normally required to prove that he had personally examined and tested the contents beforehand, any more than he would be asked to prove from his personal knowledge that a glass slide was in fact made from glass before being allowed to refer to it as such."

088 The Court of Appeal in *Wan Pui-hay* (1987) Cr App No 471 of 1986 (CA) considered a case where the Government Chemist compared a substance found in the possession of a suspect with a substance provided by the United States Pharmacopoeia warranted to constitute cannabinol. He issued a certificate in due form under section 25(1)(b) of the Evidence Ordinance to the effect that the suspect substance was terahydrocannabinol. At the trial the defence had objected to the admission of the certificate on the ground that it would be a breach of the hearsay rule. The court saw no ground in law or logic for distinguishing between words caused to be published by an expert in a textbook and those which he wrote or caused to be written on a label then affixed to a bottle or substance. Citing with approval the above passage from *Leung Chi-kin* it held that the trial judge had been right in directing the jury that the chemist's certificate constituted *prima facie* evidence of the nature of the substance found in the possession of the applicant.

Prosecution to give samples to the defence

089 Though it is not a statutory requirement, it has been said that it is the duty of the prosecution to provide samples of exhibits to the defence so that a defence expert may examine and test them: *Tai Muk-kwai t/a Nan Lien Pharmaceutical Co* (1980) Cr App No 1129 of 1979 (CA); and see *Leung Chi-yuen* (1989) Cr App No 576 of 1987 (CA) (*supra*).

Conflicts of expert evidence

090 The court must resolve any conflict of expert evidence. *In Leung Chi-kin* v. *R* [1970] HKLR 25 it was indicated that to take the view that the conflict itself raised a reasonable doubt would be to "open a broad road to the evasion of responsibility".

Arbitration, mediation and conciliation

091 Many disputes involving Hong Kong parties are referred to arbitration and mediation/conciliation. (Under the Arbitration Ordinance, s.2(1) "conciliation" includes "mediation".) Expert witnesses are often involved and individuals with professional qualifications are employed as expert adjudicators, arbitrators and mediators/conciliators.

092 Hong Kong has adopted the UNCITRAL Model law in its Arbitration Ordinance.

093 The Hong Kong International Arbitration Centre has published its own arbitration and mediation rules. It provides a forum for international and domestic arbitration, hosts international conferences and enjoys a high reputation.

"Hired guns"

094 Of course there are still experts in Hong Kong as in England who see themselves as "hired guns", whose primary aim is to win for the parties they see as their clients. They take a partisan line which I usually find all too obvious. The judges do not hesitate to discard their evidence, reminding them of their proper duty.

095 The United Kingdom based Academy of Experts, which educates and gives accreditation to experts, spreads the gospel of impartiality, objectivity and independence. It has a growing membership in Hong Kong. One of its vice-presidents is Daniel Fung QC SC, the former Hong Kong Solicitor General and it enjoys the encouragement and approval of the Chief Justice, Andrew Li, who has made courtrooms available in the High Court for use in the training of experts in the giving of evidence.

Refusal in Hong Kong to enforce CIETAC awards on grounds of procedural error regarding expert witnesses

096 One of the functions of the High Court of Hong Kong prior to the resumption of sovereignty by the PRC was to hear applications, under the New York Convention 1958, for the enforcement of foreign arbitral awards. Many such applications concerned awards delivered in China by the China International Economic and Trade Arbitration Commission (CIETAC), the body established in the PRC to arbitrate disputes arising from international commercial transactions. Now that Hong Kong is an SAR of the PRC the jurisdiction has disappeared, at least until new arrangements have been worked out, for the New York Convention does not operate between two parts of the same state. During the period when the jurisdiction did exist it was sometimes necessary for the court to consider the way in which expert evidence was treated by CIETAC. That is because one of the grounds for refusing to enforce an award under the Convention is that in the arbitration the person against whom the award is invoked "was ... unable to present his case".

097 The exercise of the jurisdiction led to refusals to enforce awards where the arbitral tribunal had failed to give parties an opportunity to deal with the evidence of expert witnesses appointed by the tribunal. Such cases had the effect of causing CIETAC to improve its procedures with the aim of avoiding such refusals. Two relevant cases are mentioned below and the topic is dealt with in detail in paragraphs 108 *et seq.*

098 It was held in *Paklito Investments Ltd* v. *Klockner (East Asia) Ltd* [1993] 2 HKLR 39 that where the (CIETAC) arbitration tribunal had received evidence from tribunal-appointed experts and a party had not been given an opportunity to cross-examine them, adduce contrary evidence and comment upon their evidence, he had been "unable to present his case". The court refused to enforce the award. There is in the judgment of Kaplan J delivered on 15 January 1993 a review of the CIETAC procedure relating to expert evidence, as a result of which the judge concludes that a party has a right to cross-examine and to comment upon the reports of such experts.

099 In another case, *Apex Tech Investment Ltd* v. *Chuang's Development (China) Ltd* [1996] 2 HKC 293, where there was a similar procedural error, an order enforcing the award was quashed by the Hong Kong Court of Appeal, which disagreed with the judge's finding that the result could not have been different, had the irregularity in procedure not occurred.

100 The only other case in which there has been a refusal in Hong Kong to enforce a CIETAC award is *Hebei Import and Export Corporation* v. *Polytek Engineering Company Ltd* Civil Appeal Number 116 of 1997. Chan CJHC (Chief Judge of the High Court) gave the judgment of the Court of Appeal of Hong Kong on 16 January 1998. Interestingly, the court gave an indication, *obiter*, that it was arguable, for reasons which do not require to be discussed here, that a CIETAC award made after the handover of sovereignty might still be enforced in Hong Kong under the New York Convention, but it said that in order to put the matter beyond doubt, it was desirable that the relevant authority should consider appropriate amendments to the Arbitration Ordinance.

101 The facts of the case are that a defendant, a Hong Kong company, applied to the High Court in Hong Kong for the setting aside of an order for the enforcement of a CIETAC award, judgment having been entered before 1 July 1997. The plaintiff was a company in the PRC. A dispute had arisen between the parties out of the sale by the defendant to the plaintiff of allegedly defective equipment for the making of rubber powder.

102 One of the grounds raised by the defendant in the Court of Appeal was that the defendant had not been given proper notice of an inspection which took place in the defendant's factory, attended by the Chief Arbitrator and three experts in the presence of the plaintiff's representative but in the absence of the defendant's representatives. It was submitted that in the circumstances the defendant was deprived of an opportunity to present its case properly to the arbitrators, a ground for refusal of enforcement under section 44(2)(c) of the Arbitration Ordinance.

103 It was also submitted that it would be contrary to public policy to enforce the award, a ground for refusal under section 44(3) of the same Ordinance. The complaint was that

(1) CIETAC was in breach of its undertaking to invite the parties to be present at the inspection of the equipment;
(2) the Chief Arbitrator went with experts to the plaintiff's factory to inspect the equipment in the absence of the defendant; and
(3) the Chief Arbitrator received communications from only one party, i.e. briefing in the form of seminars by the plaintiff's technicians and staff.

It was submitted that as a result of what happened, there was a serious breach of natural justice and a strong case of apparent bias. The tribunal, particularly the Chief Arbitrator, was guilty of misconduct. In view of such a breach of natural justice, misconduct and apparent bias against the defendant, it would be contrary to public policy to enforce the award.

104 The Court of Appeal held that the defendant should have been notified of the inspection and allowed to be present. It noted that only the Chief Arbitrator out of a panel of three arbitrators had been present. The court found that there had been seminars given by the plaintiff's technicians to the inspectors, including the Chief Arbitrator, so that the tribunal had in the course of its proceedings and deliberation received communications from one party in the absence of the other. The defendant did not know what had been communicated and had no opportunity to comment on what had been said. The court held that there was a danger or possibility of bias, applying the test in *R* v. *Gough* [1993] AC 646 and *Re Otis Elevator Co (HK) Ltd* [1994] 1 HKC 740.

105 The court adopted the statement made in the USA case *Parsons & Whittemore RAKTA* 508 F.2d 969 and accepted in *Paklito (supra)* that enforcement under the New York Convention of foreign arbitral awards may be denied on public policy grounds only "where enforcement would violate the forum State's most basic notions of morality and justice". It went on to hold that the defendant had established that there was a serious breach of natural justice and a strong case of apparent bias. What had happened fell short of the Hong Kong court's standard of fairness. It would be against public policy to enforce the award. It also upheld the complaint that the defendant had not had an opportunity to present its case to the tribunal after the inspection and the compilation of experts' reports.

106 On appeal to the Court of Final Appeal the decision of the Court of Appeal was reversed. It was held that there was no evidence to show that the respondent had been unable to present its case. With regard to complaints of procedural irregularities, the court held that the circumstances were such that it was justified in exercising its discretion under section 44(1) of the Arbitration Ordinance to allow enforcement of the award. The respondent had failed to act in good faith, had failed to object promptly to the alleged irregularities and had failed to take steps to explore the significance of what had happened in order to cure the irregularities. The judgments contain a valuable discussion of the principles relating to the enforcement of foreign arbitral awards. See *Hebei Import and Export Corporation* v. *Polytek Engineering Company Ltd (No 2)* (1999) 2 HKCFAR 111; [1999] 1 HKLRD 665; [1999] HKC 205.

Conclusion

107 The law and practice relating to experts in Hong Kong is rooted in the common law and closely resembles the law and practice in England and Wales, with some local variations. There is reason to believe that the similarity will remain until at least 2047 and probably well beyond that date. It may well be that the law and practice in Hong Kong relating to expert evidence may have a formative effect, perhaps through its influence on CIETAC, on the developing legal system in the PRC.

THE EXPERT IN MAINLAND CHINA

Experts in the courts of the PRC

108 The PRC has a developing legal and judicial system and there are few public sources from which details of the current law and practice in the civil courts concerning experts may be ascertained.

The court system of the PRC

109 According to Article 124 of the PRC Constitution, there are four levels of court set in the PRC: the Supreme People's Court, the Higher People's Courts, the Intermediate People's Courts and the Basic (District) People's Courts. Under the Supreme People's Court, the State also set up Special People's Courts such as the Maritime Courts and the Military Courts.

110 The Civil Procedure Law is the primary piece of legislation in China governing civil litigation. The Law is divided into four parts: general provisions, trial procedure, enforcement procedure and special provisions for civil procedures involving foreign parties. The Law sets forth jurisdictional limits for the different levels in China's court system.

111 The Supreme People's Court is the highest judicial organ of the state and is responsible for supervising the administration of justice by the lower level People's Courts and by the Special People's Courts. The Supreme People's Court is also responsible for interpretation of questions concerning a specific application of laws and decrees in judicial practice. The Supreme People's Court has jurisdiction over cases of great impact to the whole nation and cases which the court deems should be tried and adjudicated by itself.

112 The Higher People's Courts are set up at the provincial level for provinces, autonomous regions and municipalities directly under the central government. The Higher People's Courts have jurisdiction as courts of first instance over cases with significant impact in the areas over which they exercise jurisdiction.

113 The Intermediate People's Courts are established at the prefectures of a province or autonomous region. Intermediate People's Courts have jurisdiction as courts of first instance assigned by laws and decrees to their jurisdiction.

114 The Basic People's Courts are established at the local levels throughout the country. Unless otherwise stipulated, the Basic People's Courts have jurisdiction to hear civil cases as courts of first instance.

115 In accordance with the Law of Organisation of the People's Court of the PRC, the People's Courts have established various divisions covering crime; civil; economic; administrative; intellectual; and transportation issues. Different kinds of cases are tried in the light of relevant entity law and procedure.

116 The Civil Procedure Law of the PRC lays down general principles for the conduct of lawsuits but does not go into detailed matters of procedure. There is no Chinese equivalent to the *White Book*. Sometimes the Supreme People's Court issues published written guidance to the lower courts. Three examples relating to technical matters are given below.

Classified number 1371319902. 27 March 1990

CIVIL PROCEDURE AT SECOND INSTANCE

117 The High Court of Jiangxi province wrote to the Economic bench of the Supreme Court asking for an indication as to whether or not technicians can be invited to assess in the procedure of second instance (i.e. in appeals) in economic cases. The case before that court involved technical problems concerning the design and equipment of a glassworks. Referring to a notice concerning the trial of patent cases, the court said that it had decided not to make the technical evaluation, but to invite glass experts from the glass manufacturing authorities to act as assessors to deal with the technical problems and jointly form a collegiate bench to hear the case. It was noted, however, that in Article 36 of the Interim Civil Procedure Code that a people's court, when trying a civil case as a court of second instance, should cause a collegiate bench composed of judges to be formed. The court asked whether it could treat this a special case for the organisation of the trial and it asked for advice and an official reply.

118 The reply was as follows:

> "It is provided in Article 10 of the Law for Organisation of People's Courts that a people's court, when trying a civil case at second instance, should cause a collegiate bench composed of judges alone to be formed. It is also provided in Article 36 of the Interim Civil Procedure Code that a people's court, when trying a civil case as a court of second instance, should cause a collegiate bench composed of judges to be formed. Therefore it is not in accordance with the law to form a collegiate bench of judges and assessors to hear an economic case at second instance. However, according to Article 63 of the Interim Civil Procedure Code when the specific problems involved need to be settled, a people's court may ask for covering authority to appoint persons with professional knowledge to make a technical evaluation."

119 That leaves open the question of the status of the evaluator's report. Another example is as follows:

Classified Number 113311198501. Supreme Court's Notice Concerning the Trial of Patents Cases, 16 February 1985

CLASSIFICATION: ECONOMICS

120 After giving guidance as to the need in patent cases to appoint judicial officers with trial experience especially those having knowledge of science, engineering and foreign languages, the Supreme Court said: "When trying patent cases, the people's court shall cooperate with authorities, give full play to the professional knowledge of the experts or scholars of science research or manufacturing units. The courts can invite them to act as temporary or long-term technical consultants or to conduct technical evaluation, or invite them to act as assessors to try patent cases directly."

Classified Number 113201199501. 2 April 1995. Supreme Court Notice on Printing and Distributing

CLASSIFICATION: CIVIL

121 This is an opinion concerning the correct trial of technology cases.

> "X With respect to the technical evaluation of technology contracts . . . .
>
> "59. In litigation or arbitration of disputes relating to technology contracts, when evaluating the technology involved, the contents of technical results or technical services rendered . . . shall be the subject of evaluation and shall be examined with respect to principle,

design, process, necessary technology materials and so on, according to the inspection and acceptance measures and standards agreed in the contract.

60. If the parties have not agreed on inspection and acceptance in technology contracts, and no state standards or professional standards can be adopted, experts can be organised to make a conclusion as to whether the technology involved in the contracts conforms with the practical and general requirements of the industry.

61. If the parties have not agreed on inspection and acceptance measures or standards in a technology contract, the people's court or arbitration panel can, based on the details of a case, adopt a normally used or practical inspection and acceptance measure and standard which is stipulated by that industry in order to conduct an inspection, appraisal or evaluation. If there is a definite inspection standard agreed in the contract and the technical results are not complicated, the parties can evaluate the technical results by means of on-the-spot demonstration, operation, production and so on.

62. An appraisal authority can be jointly recommended by the parties other than the official appraisal authority. In the absence of a joint recommendation by the parties, the people's court or arbitration panel can appoint the appraisal authority recommended by the appropriate science commission or invite experts to form a group to conduct the evaluation.

63. In case the parties have disputes over the evaluation of the technical results, which have been evaluated according to state provisions, or have been proved to be mature and reliable technical results, people's courts or arbitration panels will not re-evaluate them.

64. A patent certificate cannot replace the conclusion of technical evaluation in case of disputes on licences for the evaluation of patents.

65. The evaluation of technical results should be strictly conducted pursuant to Article 72 of the Civil Procedure Code. The appraisal authority should try to grasp the materials needed in the evaluation in an all-round way and make enquiry of the parties and should not simply make the evaluation according to the appraisal opinions of one or two experts."

122 Paragraph 65 of the above notice provides an answer to the question as to how the court in Jianxi province should treat the evaluator's report in the glassworks appeal which was the subject of the first of the Supreme Court guidelines quoted above.

123 Such a system of general and *ad hoc* guidance to lower courts is clearly necessary where the legal system is evolving and disputes are increasingly technical. Judges come from many different backgrounds and have varying levels of experience. There is a shortage of experienced lawyers in China and a court may not be able to rely on the assistance of an experienced advocate. The concept of private practice, referred to as partnership practice, only began in 1992. Great efforts are being made to train judges and the number of qualified lawyers is increasing. Already there are about five hundred firms in Beijing.

124 Where the broad guidelines of the legislation have to be applied to different situations, the correct course to take must be found by way of interpretation and extrapolation, which affords an opportunity to the advocate to influence the outcome of the case but it also makes for a degree of uncertainty as to what the outcome is likely to be.

125 Experts on the law of the PRC differ when it comes to detail as to the rights of litigants. For example, in the Hong Kong case of *Paklito Investment Ltd* v. *Klockner (East Asia) Ltd* [1993] 2 HKLR 39, there was an issue before the Hong Kong judge as to whether in the PRC there was a right to cross-examination either under Chinese law or under the CIETAC Arbitration Rules and whether there was a right to challenge the evidence of an expert appointed by CIETAC. The judge heard evidence from both sides. His conclusion was that whereas there is indeed no right to cross-examination in a common law sense, both CIETAC Arbitration Rules and the PRC civil law give the parties opportunity to challenge expert evidence collected by the tribunal.

126 As will be seen below, the Arbitration Law of the PRC now makes it clear that a party may, subject to the permission of the arbitration tribunal, test the opinion of a CIETAC appointed appraiser (i.e. an expert)

127 Though there is provision for the tribunal to appoint an expert /appraiser, the parties to an arbitration can and often do engage an expert to give evidence, where there is a technical issue such as the quality of goods or the functioning of machinery.

The Arbitration Law of the PRC

128 Expert witnesses are dealt with in Article 44 of the Arbitration Law of the PRC, effective from 1 September 1995, as follows:

> "Article 44:
>
> If the arbitration tribunal considers that a special issue requires appraisal, it may refer the issue to an appraisal department agreed on by the parties or to an appraisal department designated by the arbitration tribunal.
>
> If requested by a party or required by the arbitration tribunal, the appraisal department shall send its appraiser to attend the hearing. Subject to the permission of the arbitration tribunal, the parties may question the appraiser."

129 An "appraiser" is treated by CIETAC as equivalent to "an expert". This is evident from Articles 39, 40 and 41 of the CIETAC rules quoted below. Article 41 of the rules shows that CIETAC is not bound by the findings of an expert or appraiser. The Arbitration Guide published by CIETAC states at p. 33: "The adoption of the evidence, including the evidence submitted by the parties and the expert's report and the appraiser's report shall be decided by the arbitration tribunal after examination. And the arbitration tribunal has the right to make decision on the relevance, importance and effectiveness of evidence."

Setting aside an arbitral award in the PRC

130 One of the grounds upon which a CIETAC award may be set aside on application by one of the parties to the Intermediate People's Court is that the arbitration procedure was not in conformity with the arbitration rules, so that a failure to follow the rules concerning experts could be fatal to an award.

131 Article 217 of the Civil Procedure Law provides that a ground for refusal of enforcement by the People's Court is that "(3) ... the arbitration procedure was not in conformity with statutory procedure".

132 Article 260 provides that:

> "If the party against whom enforcement is sought presents evidence which proves that the arbitration award made by the foreign-related arbitration institution of the People's Republic of China involves one of the following circumstances, the People's Court shall, after examination and verification by a collegial bench formed by the People's Court, rule to refuse the enforcement of the award:
>
> (1) ...
>
> (2) ...
>
> (3) the formation of the arbitral tribunation (*sic*) or the arbitral procedure was not in conformity with the rules of arbitration."

133 A failure to treat expert evidence properly in accordance with the rules could be a ground for setting aside or refusing to enforce an award.

134 However, though great efforts are being made to train the PRC judiciary in judicial skills and to foster judicial independence, the judges are subject to local pressures which have, at any rate in the past, influenced their decisions. Foreign parties, having agreed upon arbitration in order to be able to avoid litigation in the PRC courts, will normally wait until an attempt is made to enforce an award in a jurisdiction outside the PRC and then resist enforcement in that jurisdiction, rather than challenge the award in the People's Court.

Expert evidence in CIETAC arbitrations

135 Expert evidence is a common feature of arbitration in Mainland China.

136 The Chinese authorities are always seeking to improve CIETAC's procedures in the light of experience and regularly update the CIETAC Arbitration Rules. The version effective from 1 October, 1995 contains the following articles:

> "**Article 38** The parties shall produce evidence for the facts on which their claim, defence or counterclaim is based.
>
> The arbitration tribunal may undertake investigations and collect evidence on its own initiative, if it deems it necessary.
>
> If the arbitration tribunal investigates and collects evidence on its own initiative, it shall give notice and inform the parties to be present on the spot if it deems it necessary. Should one party or both parties fail to appear on the spot, the investigation and collection of evidence shall by no means be affected.
>
> **Article 39** The arbitration tribunal may consult an expert or appoint an appraiser for the clarification of special questions relating to the case. Such an expert or appraiser can be an organisation or a citizen, Chinese or foreign. The arbitration tribunal has the power to order the parties and the parties are also obliged to submit or produce to the expert or appraiser any materials, documents, properties or goods related to the case for checking, inspection and/or appraisal.
>
> **Article 40** The expert's report and the appraiser's report shall be copied to the parties so that the parties may have the opportunity to give their opinions thereon. At the request of any party to the case and with the approval of the arbitration tribunal, the expert and appraiser may be present at the hearing and give explanations of their reports when the arbitration tribunal deems it necessary and appropriate.
>
> **Article 41** The evidence submitted by the parties shall be examined and decided by the arbitration tribunal. The adoption of the expert's report and the appraiser's report shall be determined by the arbitration tribunal."

137 A detailed exposition of practice and procedure in CIETAC where experts are concerned is found in Chapter 1/21A.

David Leonard *was a High Court judge in Hong Kong until 1997. He is a non-practising solicitor; Arbitrator; Mediator; Fellow of the Chartered Institute of Arbitrators; Fellow of the Singapore Institute of Arbitrators; Fellow of the Hong Kong Institute of Arbitrators; Member of CIETAC panel, Beijing, China; Member of Panel of Arbitrators, Hong Kong International Arbitration Centre; CEDR trained Mediator; Qualified Dispute Resolver (QDR), Academy of Experts.*

CHAPTER 1/22

THE ROLE OF THE ACADEMY OF EXPERTS

Michael Cohen

001 To describe the role of most organisations is relatively easy, from which statement it will be apparent that is not so for The Academy. When they reached the decision to proceed 11 years ago, the founders of The Academy of Experts had little idea of what they were starting. They wanted to help bring the standards of the many up to those of the few acknowledged top experts. There were no standards, the courts were being critical, there was no forum available for discussion and no way they could make their collective voice heard.

002 There was, however, a common aim—excellence. The problem was how it could be achieved. The desire was to create a Centre for Excellence to encourage excellence. During a radio interview I coined the phrase "cost efficient dispute resolution". As it came into existence the interviewer adopted it and it has been in use ever since. This immediately became one of The Academy's principal objectives. Although (or because) it is a simple concept it has been adopted by many others around the world.

003 The pursuit of excellence is difficult enough to achieve when one knows excellence. Eleven years ago, the new or budding expert had nowhere to turn. The first mission was therefore to establish a range of standards. This was necessary in most areas of expert work. The Lord Chancellor gave his support with the appointment of the Judicial Committee consisting of senior judges from England, Scotland and Northern Ireland. The Judicial Committee soon agreed Guidance Notes for the conduct of meetings of experts and the Model Form of Expert's Report. Not surprisingly their work has been regarded as extremely persuasive and adopted in many parts of the world, for example permission has been granted for the Model Report to be translated into both Russian and Arabic.

004 At the same time, high-powered multi-disciplinary groups were hard at work. A Member's Handbook was produced. This was to be a working tool or "bible". It contains detailed notes on a wide variety of experts' problems. It has a bibliography, codes of practice and much more. It is constantly supplemented and updated. Later, Guidance Notes for Forensic Scientists and Model Forms of Engagement for Experts were produced, shaping standards even further. An interesting by-product of the Model Form Terms of Engagement has been to concentrate the minds of those appointing experts on their joint duties and responsibilities. This has brought in its wake both higher standards and "disputes" between appointers and their experts on the standards to be applied. (On a personal note, I have now added "Experts" to my expertise and have given testimony on the standards and practice for experts and those using them.)

005 Early on it was agreed that technical meetings should be held throughout the year at which judges, lawyers and experts of all professions would come together to raise their personal sights and standards by discussing their mutual needs and experiences. Ten years on, they are of even greater importance and value. One interesting aspect is that although the "expertise problems" exist, many members report the real benefit is to discuss "expert problems" across disciplines.

006 At a very early stage, The Academy, unlike so much of the legal and professional world, decided against advocating any specific method of dispute resolution. It decided to promote in individual circumstances litigation, arbitration, mediation, expert determination, early neutral evaluation or other formats from the many available. At any given time in a dispute there will be a "best" method and that should be chosen. That the "best" method would change during a dispute merely meant that members could be even more flexible. Experts believe that they can help in most areas and accordingly The Academy has taken a broad perspective.

007 With the awakening came the demand from both experienced experts and aspirants, for training. As this did not exist a further group devised and implemented the initial training programme that has expanded and grown over the years. Today, The Academy has a sophisticated training programme that is used around the world. It covers most aspects of an expert's work with the exception of rehearsing and preparing actual cases which must be the individual's own uncoached work.

008 Vetting may not appear remarkable until it is considered alongside the vetting processes. All of the founders were determined that the Groucho Marx gibe should not be levelled at them or The Academy. To ensure that this did not happen, a complex vetting system was devised for applicants. The first members only gained "interim" membership until the vetting system was in place so that they could go through the process. The Chairman of the Vetting Committee is always a senior practising solicitor and he is supported by assessors and experienced experts and lawyers. More importantly, references are sought on a solicitor-to-solicitor basis. They are often very revealing!

009 It is only after an exhaustive investigation that the grade of Full Member is granted and with it the status of "Accredited Expert". For Accredited Experts the apogee is to be elected a Fellow. Unlike most organisations where Fellows abound, a Fellow of The Academy is a rare creature. At the time of writing there are fewer than 60 of them around the world.

010 When we started the founders did not contemplate "around the world". There were many discussions on the thorny problem of "English" or "British", bearing in mind the differences between English and Scots Law. "British" won. It came as a surprise to us all when applications for membership started arriving from far-flung places. Today we have members in many countries all working to the same standards and using the same tools. It is not uncommon to receive requests for copies of the Model Form of Expert's Report from lawyers and experts continents apart. The spread is not just geographic. There are wide variations in jurisdictions and systems. Although most members come from common law jurisdictions we have a growing number in the civil law countries.

011 This all confirms our philosophy that "an expert is an expert" whatever the territory and jurisdiction. Excellence is recognised and this results in many members being instructed to work and appear before courts in jurisdictions far from their homes.

012 I believe the reason for this is that The Academy's role and philosophy is still to be found in the twin intertwined principles of excellence and cost efficient dispute resolution. This is achieved by accreditation, which can be as an Expert Witness or as a Dispute Resolver.

013 For experts the process has been in place since The Academy's birth. It is still not understood by all, there are still lawyers who will not "on principle" give a report on an expert he has utilised. Sadly it is often the same lawyers who complain that the standards are not high enough! Accreditation in itself is not sufficient if standards are to be maintained. It requires continuing monitoring of standards backed by extensive programmes. Without re-vetting all that is known is that on a given date, maybe years earlier, somebody was at a certain standard. Although with the passage of time, experience and maturity should follow, sadly degenerating standards do likewise. Academy accreditation is recognised by bodies such as the Law Society of England and Wales and an increasing number of lawyers and judges. As one leading advocate told me recently, it is always possible to pick out an Academy member by their approach and standards. Experts also report the tremendous benefit of having an accredited expert on the other side which enables the expert aspects to be dealt with more efficiently.

014 A similar situation exists with Alternative Dispute Resolution (ADR). When The Academy embraced ADR and mediation in particular, there were no widely recognised standards. It came as a great surprise when I discovered that there was not even an agreed language. Within a relatively short time we published "The language of ADR—an international glossary". We had input from individuals and institutions around the world and despite previously established positions, the end result was welcomed unanimously, almost! Years later there is still a demand for it. Following the glossary came the need for a proper standard to be established for assessments and training. This ultimately brought the qualification QDR which is now widely respected, with Qualified Dispute Resolvers (QDR) located in the United States and Hong Kong as well as the United Kingdom and the rest of Europe. Working with other bodies and governments, we believe we have helped to change the climate and aided the increasing use of a wide range of alternatives to traditional litigation. Signs of our achievements can be found in the work of the courts, for example the Central London County Court Mediation Scheme and with the changing attitude of arbitrators to ADR. Even if mediation should have been the preferred dispute resolution method, if the parties have chosen arbitration, the arbitrator can be in a difficult position. If he is pro-active and a settlement results, it is relatively unlikely that there will be any repercussions. If however, it does not succeed there can be many problems for the unwary arbitrator. Can he continue? What (if anything) does he have to disclose? If he has to disclose, what, to whom and when?

015 "One stop" shopping is, we are told, one of the greatest boons to the consumer. At the same time we are told that it is destroying choice for the consumer and it is therefore an act of ritual consumer suicide! Many of these considerations will undoubtedly apply to the "Medarb" procedure which is apparently so popular in the United States. The subject is one that will undoubtedly be explored and debated for some time, as arbitrators consider the ethical and practical considerations.

016 Why has The Academy succeeded? I believe it is because it has achieved what it set out to do. Having established its reputation, The Academy's views are now sought on important issues, which helps it to influence change. A good example of this was the attempt to have experts paid on a contingency basis. Some thought the Code of Practice should be eased. However this was not the view of the Judicial Committee who having carefully considered the subject issued a Guidance Note for Experts (and those who use them) firmly outlawing the practice. It is now widely quoted as the authority against this pernicious practice. With the Vice Chancellor's approval Expert Declarations, which should be an integral part of every Expert Report, now contains a clear statement on the subject from the expert.

017 The Academy, which works with professional bodies around the world, also provides many services for lawyers, the parties and of course arbitrators and arbitral institutions. It will "match" the right accredited expert to the case, which sometimes means transporting them thousands of miles. It gives similar services with the appointment of Qualified Mediators and other Dispute Resolvers. By providing a forum for experts, lawyers, judges and interested bodies, it helps to maintain awareness of the need to achieve and maintain standards. It also serves as a reminder of the experts' two "I"s: the fundamental need for Independence and Impartiality—or, in a word, integrity.

018 The Academy is both a professional society and a qualifying body. As such it is a world-wide source of qualified independent Experts and Dispute Resolvers who are experienced in a wide range of professional, commercial and industrial disciplines. This is by a body owned and run by its members where the motivation is not commerce and profit but service and standards.

__Michael Cohen LLB, FIBA, FCIArb, QDR, FAE, Barrister__ is deeply involved in the world of dispute resolution. He is a Registered Arbitrator, a qualified mediator and a practising insurance expert.

As Chairman of The Academy of Experts he was responsible for the professional standards and training of Experts and Dispute Resolvers around the world. He is a regular course tutor across Europe, the Far East and the Caribbean, as well as being an established contributor to professional journals and a frequent conference speaker.

A practising arbitrator, he is on a variety of panels in the UK and other countries. In addition to general commercial work, he specialises in insurance disputes and marine industry disputes. His mediation practice is even more widely based, including personal injury, inter-company disputes and many other areas.

CHAPTER 2

THE EXPERT WITNESS IN MEDICAL CASES

Nigel H Harris

001 "Expert knowledge, however indispensable, is no substitute for a generous and comprehending outlook upon the human story, with all its sadness and all its unquenchable hope."—Winston Churchill.

INTRODUCTION

002 Although the author of this chapter is an orthopaedic surgeon, the principles and advice are applicable to all disciplines.

003 There is no satisfactory definition of an expert. It is usually understood to mean a person of any professional discipline whose special knowledge or skill gained by training and practice, causes him or her to be an authority. On the other hand, the term expert witness clearly has a legal connotation.

004 It is not always appreciated that possession of appropriate expertise in a particular discipline does not necessarily mean that the person can perform adequately as an expert witness, especially in court; hence the need for education and training.

005 The court requires the assistance of the expert witness in cases of medical malpractice and personal injury litigation. All civil litigation cases generally cannot be mounted and brought to a just conclusion without using expert opinion. The medical expert however is unique because the issues are concerned with patients, and the very nature of the subject is an art and not a science. The latter is not always appreciated by lawyers and patients whose claim cannot be supported. Napley (1975, *The Technique of Persuasion*, Sweet and Maxwell) explained it thus: "Doctors by comparison (with witness as to fact), are dealing within the realms of informal opinion, with subject matter of an art which is neither exact nor necessarily scientific."

006 The advice of medical experts on each side is required throughout all stages of the adversarial system of the litigation process, namely providing advice on the issues involved, writing reports, attending conferences with counsel, meeting with the other side's experts to narrow down the issues and giving evidence at trial.

007 The medical expert provides an opinion in personal injury and medical malpractice cases. In the former the claimant and defendant—usually an insurance company—requires expert opinion on the effect of the accident, whether or not the injury sustained was caused by the accident, and the prognosis. In the latter, both sides require experts to decide on the merits of the claim and whether or not it should be defended.

008 The nature of medical litigation cases is enormously variable so it is not really possible to illustrate relevant matter by reference to a single case, but where appropriate case material will be used. What follows is based on the author's experience with 9,000 cases over the last 15 years.

WHO IS A MEDICAL EXPERT?

009 Lawyers generally representing both claimant and defendant are faced with the dilemma when selecting an expert in a particular case. The principal reason is that, perhaps surprisingly, there are no conditions or criteria imposed on doctors who profess to be experts in medico-legal matters. There are no requirements as to the level of expertise before a doctor can appear in court to criticise the skills of another doctor; it is not even necessary to practise in the same discipline as the doctor being sued.

010 These matters are referred to in order to highlight a fundamental defect which lawyers experienced in medico-legal cases will have little difficulty in circumventing. However, the inexperienced lawyer may instruct an inappropriate expert; the combination is likely to be a disaster, leading to expensive and unnecessary litigation which is not in the best interests of either profession, claimant or defendant.

011 The other difficulty is that on occasion some experts are prepared to write reports and give evidence on matters which are strictly speaking outside their field of competence.

012 For example, the author was giving evidence on behalf of a claimant in a medical negligence claim concerning an injury to a major peripheral nerve which occurred during the course of an operation to repair a recurrent dislocation of the shoulder. The defendants relied heavily on the expertise of the neurosurgeon. The court could not be persuaded of the fact that neurosurgeons have no experience in treating peripheral nerve injuries; their practice concerns the condition of the brain and spinal cord. He was nevertheless prepared to say in evidence that he supported the orthopaedic surgeon's advice and treatment, and went on to comment on nerve repair of which he had no experience. The judge accepted the neurosurgeon's evidence and the claimant's action was unsuccessful.

013 Lawyers need to be aware that in the treatment of disc prolapse and cervical and lumbar spines, operations are regularly performed by both orthopaedic and neurosurgeons. Nevertheless, the chosen expert should be of the same discipline as the operating surgeon. It is self-evident that the principle applies to all disciplines.

014 There have been instances in the past, fortunately now less common, where a general surgeon (an almost extinct species) has given evidence on musculo-skeletal matters such as fractures, or on urological conditions.

015 If proper standards are to be achieved and maintained, diligence and honesty of potential expert witnesses are required combined with a lawyer having knowledge of how the differing medical disciplines function.

016 A recent instruction received by the author illustrates an unexpected, and what must be a very rare, event. An orthopaedic surgeon performed an operation on a congenital abnormality involving a thoracic vertebra which resulted in damage to the spinal cord and consequential lower limb paralysis. It would be accepted by orthopaedic surgeons that such an operation should be performed either by a neurosurgeon, or by a spinal surgeon of which there are very few in the country. The author was unable to accept instructions because of lack of experience in the field, and a spinal surgeon would not accept instructions because the operation had been performed by an orthopaedic surgeon; needless to say, the neurosurgeon would not accept instructions for the same reason. There must be a danger that the unfortunate claimant will not obtain expert medical advice in support of his claim.

017 On a lighter note this section can be summarised by reference to an exchange which took place between a doctor and Mr Justice Stable some years ago.

> "The Judge: 'Doctor, I recall you appeared before me some time ago in a matrimonial case as an expert in psychiatry, and I seem to remember you appearing before me in a road traffic case as an expert in orthopaedic surgery. Now you are today appearing in a medical negligence case as an expert in cardiology. I would like to know precisely what it is you are an expert in?'
>
> The doctor replied without hesitation: 'I am an expert in giving evidence in a court of law, my Lord.'"

QUALITIES OF THE MEDICAL EXPERT WITNESS

018 An expert should be willing to appear for a defendant or claimant and by so doing he is more likely to provide objective testimony. Objectivity is paramount and the courts rely on this quality, in addition to the expert's skill and knowledge. A witness whose testimony is biased in favour of the side from whom instructions have been received (the so called "hired gun"), but who is not supported by personal experience or the medical literature, is unlikely to receive the court's approval. A witness who behaves in this way is doing a disservice to the defendant or claimant as the case may be.

019 The author's experience is that all too often the courts accept expert evidence on behalf of the defendant who puts forward unsupported theories on causation, and with regard to treatment states that they would have dealt with the case in exactly the same way. It is of course a matter for counsel and the judge to test such witness statements, but this is not always done adequately and sometimes not at all.

020 The medical profession has come to recognise in recent years, given the economic climate in the NHS, that much more objective information should be provided on the outcome of therapeutic procedures. Increasingly medical practice will be evidence based, and it is hoped that this will include comments on therapeutic procedures, including operations, which should no longer be performed.

021 In this context, increasing use is being made of protocols, but there is no general agreement in the profession that they are always beneficial for patients. Nevertheless, they are of value to the courts when assessing the merits of expert evidence, and will discourage the non-objective expert.

022 Protocols are generally accepted as useful in accident and emergency departments which are staffed by relatively junior and inexperienced doctors. By way of example, protocols are used for the management of certain fractures, and for trauma to neuro-vascular structures. It is inevitable that such developments will in due course be reflected by medical expert evidence in the courts.

023 There are other essential qualities, namely honesty and integrity. The expert must have the courage to maintain an opinion in spite of strong opposing views, providing always, and this is most important, that it is supported by knowledge, personal experience and reference to the medical literature.

024 Notwithstanding a strongly held opinion, supported by appropriate evidence, the expert must indicate that there is an understanding and appreciation of opposing medical opinions. Such flexibility of mind combined with the willingness to modify and change an opinion if confronted with new and persuasive evidence (either before or during a trial) will be looked on favourably by the court.

025 The essential qualities to which reference has been made cannot be acquired; they are natural attributes which can be developed by experience and training in report writing and giving evidence in court. Without these qualities the true role of the medical expert witness is doomed to failure.

DUTIES AND RESPONSIBILITIES

026 Although the following may be considered guidance for the expert witness, over the years established agreed practice could almost be described as a set of rules.

027 Lawyers accept that the independent expert should not be involved in the treatment of the claimant. However, there can be no objection to a treating doctor being called to give evidence as factual witness.

028 It is appropriate to say a word here about the age of the expert, and whether or not he/she is retired from clinical practice—that is the National Health Service and private practice.

029 The matter was raised by Mr Justice Brooke (*Scott* v. *Bloomsbury Health Authority* [1991] MLR 214.) The case concerned a highly complex orthopaedic and neurosurgical problem. He stated that the allegations of negligence were entirely founded on the opinion of a long-retired neurosurgeon. The claimant's claim was dismissed and he said that something should be done, "To prevent complex claims from being supported in future at the public's expense on the uncorroborated evidence of a consultant who had retired from practice so long ago".

030 It would be reasonable to suggest that age is irrelevant if a doctor who is retired from the National Health Service continues to practice privately. The fully retired expert certainly has a role to play in cases which concern mundane practical matters about which his experience may be invaluable.

031 It will be generally agreed that fully retired doctors should not agree to act as expert witnesses if the case involved complex technology and recently introduced procedures with which they are not familiar.

032 It is not always appreciated by doctors that when preparing reports and giving evidence, their duty is to the court and not the side instructing them; they must provide an objective unbiased opinion within the confines of their expertise. The expert must not assume the role of an advocate. In fact a rule has been recently introduced by the Inland Revenue stating that if so doing, VAT has to be paid!

033 In the course of a House of Lords judgment in 1981 (*Whitehouse* v. *Jordan* [1981] 1 All ER 267 at 276, HL) Lord Wilberforce said, "While some degree of consultation between experts and legal advisors is entirely proper, it is necessary that expert evidence presented to the court should be, and be seen to be, the independent product of the expert, uninfluenced as to form or content by the exigencies of litigation". This judgment was made because a lawyer in the case caused an expert report to be altered in such a way that it reflected more the opinion of the lawyer rather than the medical expert.

034 Experts must of course appreciate that counsel has sometimes the difficult task of settling the expert's report to make it more suitable for exchange, and it may have to be altered in order to reflect certain legal principles about which the inexperienced medical expert is unaware.

035 The author has had to resist pressure from counsel on numerous occasions to change a report by leaving out some fact in the clinical notes which is unfavourable to the client. There may be subtle attempts to persuade the expert to change an opinion. Such pressures must be resisted, especially so if the opinion cannot be substantiated under cross-examination.

036 The medical expert witness who regularly engages in this type of work will be confronted by this problem from time to time. In order to present a balanced picture, a need to amend a medical report in certain circumstances can best be illustrated by an example which makes clear the importance of considering causation as well as liability. Unless the expert can say that on the balance of probabilities an injury was caused by the alleged negligence, the action cannot succeed. The law requires proof of fault causing damage as a basis of liability in tort (Lord Bridge, *Wiltshire* v. *Essex Area Health Authority* [1988] 1 All ER 87, HL).

037 The House of Lords stated: "Where a defendant's negligence was one of several different factors which could have caused a plaintiff's injury, the occurrence of the injury following the defendant's negligence provided no evidence and raised no presumption that it was the defendant's negligence rather that one or more of the other factors which caused the plaintiff's injury."

038 If there was conflicting expert evidence as to whether the defendant's negligence could have caused or contributed to the claimant's condition and the trial judge had failed to raise relevant findings on that question, the issue of causation must be retried before a different judge.

039 The case concerned a premature infant who developed retrolental fibrosis (causing blindness), and it was pleaded that excess oxygen administered to the baby was the causative factor. However, it became clear that this could not be sustained as there were five other possible explanations. If in preparing this case the defendant had not made this clear in the expert's medical report, it would have been reasonable (and as it turned out in this case it was of crucial importance), for counsel to request that the report be altered so as to reflect this significant piece of medical evidence.

040 Facts or assumptions upon which the expert's opinion is based should be clearly stated, together with material facts which could detract from the considered opinions.

041 The expert must make clear when an issue falls outside his field of experience. This does sometimes present difficulties. For example, it seems reasonable to comment on a patient's emotional state such as anxiety or any inappropriate or bizarre reaction to clinical examination which may signify exaggeration of the disability. Any experienced clinician is capable of reporting on such matters without necessarily requesting the opinion of a psychiatrist.

042 It is a common experience for orthopaedic surgeons to give an opinion on the cause of chronic pain following musculo-skeletal injuries. However, many of these patients are referred to pain clinics for treatment. It is probably sensible in such circumstances to obtain the opinion of a pain expert—usually an anaesthetist.

043 Sometimes it is the case that the opinion given in the expert report is based on inadequate data. For example, X-rays may not have been provided or relevant pathology and prescription sheets may be missing. The expert can reasonably decide not to prepare a report until the missing information is provided. However, the expert may be urged to provide a report because of the limitation period. In such instances, the expert should make it clear which documents are missing and mark the report as provisional.

044 After reports are exchanged, some new documents may arrive, and the expert may wish to modify or change the opinion on some material matters.

045 The amendment must be promptly conveyed to instructing solicitors so that the other side's solicitors can be informed. It is good practice for the expert to be prepared if necessary to modify an opinion if confronted in court with new facts.

INSTRUCTING THE EXPERT MEDICAL WITNESS

046 The author's experience is that instructing solicitors use a variety of methods for obtaining the name of a suitable expert. The first step for the solicitor acting for a plaintiff in medical negligence cases after taking a statement, is to obtain the medical records. Instructing the wrong expert is likely if they do not first study the records.

047 The author receives instructions from solicitors who obtain the name from their lists, on the recommendation of counsel, from the *Law Society Directory*, the *Directory of Expert Witnesses*, The Academy of Experts and AVMA (Association for Victims of Medical Accidents).

048 The quality of instruction varies enormously from a few lines asking for an examination and report and without details to several pages including explicit instructions, and if it is a potential medical negligence claim, a brief account of the law and how the report should be set out. Much will depend on whether or not the solicitors are on the personal injury and medical litigation panels.

049 It is common practice for experts to receive a preliminary letter in medical negligence cases, setting out a few essential facts and asking if they are prepared to accept instructions. It may be possible to respond to such an enquiry; on the other hand the expert is entitled to first look at the records before accepting instructions. It certainly can reasonably be argued that the expert should always first look through the records but this may present certain practical difficulties, including unacceptably long delays.

050 In other instances, the expert is asked (usually in medical negligence cases) to provide a report from the records without examining the patient. This in fact may be the only way the expert can assist if there is a serious problem with limitation ("Urgent requests for expert medical opinion", Nigel H Harris, *The Expert* June 1997).

051 To summarise, adequate instructions for the expert should cover the following points, whether it be personal injury or a medical negligence case, and irrespective of whether the expert is to act on behalf of the claimant or defendant.

052 Dates of accident or operation, types of expertise required, reason for requesting a report—that is personal injury or medical negligence or both and whether or not it is to be used in court. List any matters to be particularly addressed and questions which the solicitor considers are relevant and require answers. For example, a pre-existing condition such as osteoarthritis may be important, and solicitors will reasonably ask if the current condition would have occurred in the absence of the relevant accident, has the accident affected the natural history of the pre-existing condition, and in the light of the latter, by how many years have the current symptoms been brought forward? In matters of medical negligence, solicitors may ask the expert to state if the current symptoms and disability are the result of malpractice, or would have occurred in any event.

053 It is of considerable assistance to provide an outline of the case in any matters that may be in dispute. An indication of the limitation period and the last date for receiving the report should be provided. A list of documents should be provided, including X-rays and scans. If appropriate, signed authorities for obtaining medical records should be sent to the expert. It is necessary to indicate if prior authority to incur the fees has been obtained or will be requested. Previously obtained medical reports may be provided and it is essential that the expert be notified whether or not they may be referred to in the report.

054 It should of course be made clear to the expert in the case of medical negligence cases whether or not the request is for a report and opinion based on documents alone. On receipt of the records the expert may decide that he cannot provide even a provisional opinion without examining the patient and the solicitor of course must be so informed.

WHAT THE MEDICAL EXPERT EXPECTS FROM INSTRUCTING SOLICITORS

Personal accident work

055 Solicitors representing claimants usually instruct the expert, and insurance companies request opinions on behalf of defendants. The information required is relatively straightforward. The date of the accident and a brief account of the circumstances are essential. The claimant's solicitor will usually indicate that the symptoms are continuing and that the employment prospects have been affected.

056 It is always helpful if the expert receives an up-to-date statement by the claimant, indicating the current complaints and how they are affected during daily living activities.

057 The defendant's advisers on the other hand will sometimes emphasise in the letter of instruction that as a result of their enquiries they believe the patient is exaggerating their disability, but do not provide evidence for this suspicion. It is unfortunate when experts are prejudiced in this way but it is difficult to think how it could be avoided.

058 The expert does not necessarily require the hospital records and they should be advised to use their discretion as to requesting them. The GP records are however probably essential because the expert needs to objectively assess any relevant past medical history. The commonest example is in the case of neck and low back (lumbar) pain when pre-accident complaint of pain or evidence of degenerative change may be of critical importance with regard to the claim.

059 Solicitors generally provide the expert with a signed authority for obtaining records. However, a strong case could be made for suggesting that all necessary documents ought to be provided for the expert. As stated earlier, solicitors should have inspected and paginated the records before passing them to the expert. Not only will the solicitor have a better understanding of the case and the chronology of events, but much time will be saved.

060 The ideal is for the expert to have the records available at the time of consultation. However, the latter takes place some months after receipt of the instructions. If the expert sends off for the GP records at this time, he receives them (often the originals) with a request to return them within two weeks. To avoid this inconvenience it is necessary to defer sending for the records until after the consultation. A much better or more useful arrangement would be for instructing solicitors and insurance companies to request the GP to send copy records in time for the consultation date.

Medical negligence cases

061 It is obligatory for the instructing solicitor to provide all hospital records including X-rays and the GP records. An outline of the claimant's allegations is essential; it is not sufficient simply to refer the expert to the claimant's statement. The expert requires the solicitor's summary of the points at issue. The solicitor should have obtained the records, studied them and arranged for pagination before passing them to the expert. Unpaginated records can be returned to the solicitor, or alternatively the expert may sort them out and the fee will necessarily reflect the additional work involved.

062 If the solicitor studies the records first there will be a better understanding of the claimant's complaint, the chronology of events can be checked and the expert can be provided with clearer and more precise instructions.

063 The claimant's allegations will usually include one or more of the following—failure to make the correct diagnosis, leading to a late correct diagnosis, failure to obtain informed consent to the treatment (usually an operation), or an invasive investigation, failure to perform an operation competently and failure to recognise and treat complications. The solicitor should clearly indicate the allegations to be investigated.

064 The expert should however appreciate that the allegations may be inaccurate or without substance, but other deficiencies may be revealed about which neither the claimant nor solicitor is aware. The author well remembers a patient who had complained for more than two years of shoulder pain following an accident. He had been seen by numerous doctors, including two orthopaedic consultant surgeons, and had had a variety of treatments without benefit. The examination revealed an irreducible posterior dislocation of the shoulders confirmed by X-rays. This was a case in which a personal injury claim became also one of negligence.

065 Although it is not common practice, the instructions should contain information on the recognised legal standards of proof required, namely the balance of probabilities. It should state that the competence of the clinician is judged by the prevailing standards at the time, and is based on the *Bolam* principle.

066 It is important that medical experts should be familiar with the legal principles involved in medical negligence litigation. In the United Kingdom the law imposes a duty of care but the standard of care is a matter of medical judgement. In other words, standards of medical practice are determined by the medical profession, not the courts. This is exemplified by the *Bolam* test (*Bolam* v. *Friern Hospital Management Committee*) [1957] 1 WLR 582, Mr Justice McNair). The test applies to every aspect of the duty of care, namely diagnosis, advice, consent and treatment owed by a doctor to his patient in the exercise of his function in respect of that patient.

067 The test is the standard of the ordinary skilled man exercising or professing to have that particular skill. It is sufficient if he exercises the ordinary skill of an ordinary competent man exercising that particular art. A doctor is not guilty of negligence if he has acted in accordance with the practice accepted as proper by a responsible body of medical men skilled in that particular art—a doctor is not negligent if he is acting in accordance with such practice merely because there is a body of opinion which takes a contrary view.

068 The expert will be aware therefore that in determining whether or not a doctor has fallen below the required standard of care, the *Bolam* test looks to responsible medical opinion.

069 The author has expressed his concern that the *Bolam* principle puts claimants at a disadvantage ("Standards of Practice" in Expert Witness Supplement, *Solicitors Journal*, 29 July

1997). More accurately it is the correct application of the principle which I question, rather than the principle itself. In this context, clarification of the application of *Bolam* was provided by the House of Lords judgment in *Bolitho* v. *City and Hackney Health Authority* [1997] 4 All ER 771; (1997) *The Times*, 27 November.

070 The whole of this important judgment should be studied, but the following passage may be quoted to indicate that the courts should qualify defendant's expert evidence which is said to represent "a responsible body of medical men", or "standard of practice recognised as proper by a competent reasonable body of opinion", or "a respectable body of professional opinion". Their Lordships stated: "A court was not bound to hold that a defendant doctor escaped liability for negligent treatment or diagnosis just because he had evidence from a number of medical experts who were genuinely of the opinion that his treatment or diagnosis accorded with sound medical practice."

071 The court had to be satisfied that the exponents of the body of opinion relied on could demonstrate that such opinion had a logical basis, in particular concerning, as it often did, the weighing of risks against benefits. The judge, before accepting a body of opinion as being responsible, reasonable or respectable, would need to be satisfied that, in forming their views, the experts had directed their minds to the question of comparative risks and benefits and had reached a defensible conclusion on the matter.

072 There are three other legal pronouncements with which the expert should have knowledge.

In 1985, Lord Clyde said (*Hunter* v. *Haley*, SLT 213)

> "in the realms of diagnosis and treatment there is ample room for genuine differences of opinion, and one man is clearly not negligent because his conclusions differ from that of another professional man, nor because he has displayed less skill or knowledge than others would have shown. The true test for establishing negligence in diagnosis or treatment on the part of a doctor is whether he has proved to be guilty of such failure that no doctor of ordinary skill would be guilty of acting with ordinary care."

073 In a House of Lords judgment (*Maynard* v. *West Midlands RHA* [1985] 1 All ER 635) Lord Scarman said: "Differences of opinion and practice exist, and will always exist, in medical and other professions. There is seldom any one answer exclusive to all the problems of professional judgement, but that is no basis for a conclusion of negligence." It has been common practice in the past for medical experts to conclude that a doctor has committed an error of clinical judgement and was therefore negligent. It is not necessarily appropriate to draw such a conclusion as was made clear by Lord Edmund-Davies (*Whitehouse* v. *Jordan* [1981] 1 All ER 267): "To say that a surgeon committed an error of clinical judgement is wholly ambiguous for, while some such error may be completely consistent with the exercise of professional skill, others may be so glaringly below proper standards to make the findings of negligence inevitable."

074 *Bolam* and the recent House of Lords' judgment notwithstanding, it will continue to be very difficult for claimants to succeed while judges close their minds to the possibility of the bending of expert evidence.

075 Having received appropriate instructions and armed with the information set out above, the expert should be in no doubt as to what is required of him.

MODEL TERMS OF ENGAGEMENT FOR THE EMPLOYMENT OF EXPERTS

076 Appropriate instructions have been referred to and together with the expert's response the details can best be summarised by reference to The Academy of Experts' document on the subject (see Appendix F of this book).

PREPARATION OF THE MEDICAL REPORT

077 The report is a useful document and is provided for the benefit of the court, not the side instructing the expert.

078 In the case of personal injury one report is required; for medical negligence purposes two reports are necessary, a condition and prognosis report, and a second separate report on causation and liability. These reports are exchanged at different times.

079 Reports are usually based on a clinical examination of the patient and careful study of the hospital and GP records. Occasionally, the expert may agree to do a report on liability from a study from the records. Clearly the examination of the patient allows the expert to clarify the chronology of events and fill in the gaps which frequently exist in woefully inadequate medical records. The current condition and causation cannot be established without a clinical examination. There is a less obvious but no less important advantage, namely to provide an atmosphere from which the claimant gains confidence that the expert is objective and understands precisely what took place. There is frequently a lack of correlation between the records and the patient's recollection of events, and this cannot always be resolved. It should be noted along with any deficiencies in the records.

080 There is no standard format for preparing a medical report which must clearly set out the material facts and chronology of events; where appropriate reference should be made to the page number of the records. From experience in discussing reports with counsel and solicitors the following guidance is put forward.

081 Whenever possible medical terms should be avoided or defined. The front sheet should give essential details such as name, address, date of birth and occupation of the claimant; the name, degrees and speciality of the expert; the name and address of the instructing solicitor; date of the accident and the consultation or a statement that the report is based on the records.

082 The report should have an introduction which can be used to state the purpose for which the report is provided and the documents, X-rays and any other reports which have been made available.

083 There then follows a detailed chronology of events. It should be made clear which information has been obtained from the records and which is the claimant's account.

084 The information extracted from the records should detail the results of investigations, including X-rays and operations performed. Medical records may contain some adverse comments, such as the patient did not co-operate with the treatment or failed to keep appointments; this information should be put into the report.

085 Present condition can now be presented. It will include a list of symptoms set out as precisely as possible. It is important to establish the relationship between the accident and the various complaints. Careful questioning may reveal for example that following a road traffic accident the patient complained of neck and shoulder pain. At the consultation, there may also be a complaint of low back pain. It is clearly important to establish the date of onset of the back pain which may turn out to be months after the accident and therefore would not be caused by it. If the neck or back were injured in an accident, symptoms will arise within 48 hours.

086 In medical negligence cases, it is essential to establish whether the current symptoms, continuing severe pain, are related in time to a previous operation, allegedly performed negligently.

087 State with examples how the symptoms are affecting daily living activities and work. With regard to the latter all periods of absence from work must be stated, and, if work has not been resumed, if that is because of continuing symptoms, or perhaps because they have been retired on medical grounds or made redundant. It is useful to record that they are in receipt of benefits. Almost all those in receipt of incapacity benefit for musculo-skeletal injury are found to be fit for alternative, perhaps more sedentary type work, and the benefit award which precludes them registering unemployed and seeking work is therefore inappropriate. Careful questioning may give a clue with regard to motivation for return to work.

088 Indicate if treatment such as physiotherapy or osteopathy is continuing and if not when it finished. How much analgesia is being consumed may indicate the severity and frequency of the pain, and whether or not further operations are planned.

089 It is useful to conclude this section with a general statement as to whether the patient considers their condition is static, improving or deteriorating.

090 The results of the clinical examination may now be set out. In addition to providing objective evidence of physical disability, the examination offers the expert an opportunity to assess the personality of the individual. Anxiety, bizarre behaviour and the presence of inappropriate signs will be noted. At the conclusion of the examination it is appropriate to comment on the X-rays and scans.

091 A separate section should refer to relevant information in the GP records. For example, there may be reference to similar symptoms prior to the accident, previous accidents or a psychiatric history.

092 Having assembled the facts, the expert is in a position to express an opinion on the medical issues involved. It must not be expressed in such a way that the expert is determining the merits of the case, which is a matter for the lawyers. An opinion is required on the facts as stated, not an opinion of the facts.

093 A brief account of the nature of medical condition should be given and its natural history, and the expected outcome from treatment.

094 In personal injury cases it is helpful to correlate the current symptoms and disability with the nature of the injury sustained. The effect of the injury on daily living activities must be set out in some detail.

095 Fitness for work, either the pre-accident job or modified employment, is clearly important. If it has been established that a pre-accident condition such as joint degeneration (osteoarthritis) existed but was symptomless, lawyers will need to know if in the absence of the accident, symptoms would have developed in any event, and about when they would have occurred.

096 If pre-accident symptoms existed an opinion is required as to whether or not the current symptoms are the result of the accident or due to the pre-accident condition. A good example is the very common condition of degenerative change in the cervical and lumbar spines. Such age changes are present in some degree in all adults over 40 years, sometimes earlier. Persistent neck and/or low back pain following trauma some years earlier (an acceleration/extension strain or "whiplash" is the most common mechanism) present the expert with the difficult problem of deciding whether or not symptoms would have developed in any event, and if so how much the accident brought forward the symptoms.

097 Prognosis must include an estimate as to whether or not the current symptoms will improve or deteriorate, whether or not treatment is likely to be necessary, and if work will continue until the normal retirement age and the effects on their prospects on the open job market.

098 If a joint has been injured it will be necessary to give an estimate in percentage terms of the risk of developing secondary osteoarthritis, and if and when it will become symptomatic and possible treatment that may be necessary.

099 For matters concerning allegations of medical negligence, a somewhat different approach and emphasis is required. The first part of the report dealing with condition and prognosis is similar and will include details about loss of amenities and the amount of pain and suffering arising. The second and separate part of the report will discuss causation and liability.

100 First some general guidance. It is well to remember that the report will be used as evidence in court, and therefore statements which cannot be defended or substantiated under cross-examination must be avoided. The evidence must be presented in an objective manner and hyperbole avoided. If the expert is clear as to what occurred it is sensible to be forthright. If the expert considers there has been a departure from accepted practice, supporting evidence must be given including reference to the medical literature.

101 The following declaration should be provided above the signature at the end of the report:

DECLARATION

I, ... DECLARE THAT:

1. I understand that my primary duty in written reports and giving evidence is to the Court, rather than the party who engaged me;
2. I have endeavoured in my reports and in my opinions to be accurate and to have covered all relevant issues concerning the matters stated which I have been asked to address;
3. I have endeavoured to include in my report those matters, which I have knowledge of or of which I have been made aware, that might adversely affect the validity of my opinion;
4. I have indicated the sources of all information I have used;
5. I have not without forming an independent view included, or excluded, anything which has been suggested to me by others (in particular my instructing lawyers);
6. I will notify those instructing me immediately and confirm in writing if for any reason my existing report requires any correction or qualification;
7. I understand that;
   a) my report, subject to any corrections before swearing as to its correctness, will form the evidence to be given under oath or affirmation;
   b) I may be cross-examined on my report by a cross-examiner assisted by an expert;
   c) I am likely to be the subject of public adverse criticism by the judge if the Court concludes that I have not taken reasonable care in trying to meet the standards set out above.

I confirm that I have not entered into any arrangement where the amount or payment of my fees is in any way dependent on the outcome of the case.

The contents of this report are true to the best of my knowledge and belief.

102 In reaching a conclusion, the expert will bear in mind the *Bolam* test and standard of proof which were referred to earlier. Argument in support of the other side should be deployed and commented upon. In this way the expert will indicate that a balanced objective opinion has been provided.

103 Causation: In order to succeed in a negligence claim the plaintiff, in addition to showing there has been a breach of duty by the doctor, must establish on the balance of probabilities that it caused damage or loss (see para 036 above: *Wiltshire* v. *Essex Area Health Authority*). The test is, but for the negligence, would the harm to the claimant have occurred in any event? Notwithstanding the failure in the duty of care, it may be very difficult to establish causation. This is well illustrated by *Hotson* v. *East Berkshire Area Health Authority* ([1987] 2 All ER 909). A child fell from a tree and sustained a hip injury, namely a traumatic displacement of the proximal femoral epiphysis. The condition is known to lead to a 75 per cent risk of developing avascular necrosis of the epiphysis even with prompt diagnosis and treatment. The diagnosis in this case was delayed and it was claimed this was responsible for the subsequent development of necrosis. After going to the House of Lords for a final decision, the claim failed because it was not possible to establish on the balance of probabilities that the delayed diagnosis had caused loss; in other words, it could not be shown that it fell within the 25 per cent of cases which would have made a full recovery had the condition been properly diagnosed.

104 The House of Lords (2 July 1987) stated as follows:

> "Where there has been a 75 per cent risk that an injury sustained by the plaintiff would have led to the same medical consequences even if the defendant Health Authority had not treated him negligently, the judge had erred in awarding 25 per cent chance of making a nearly full recovery."

Lord Mackay stated:

> "It would, however be unwise to lay it down as a rule that a plaintiff could never succeed by proving loss of a chance in a medical negligence case."

LIABILITY

105 A leading article in *The Times*, 13 December 1988, regarding a public inquiry into a rail crash, stated "While negligence should be discovered and made answerable if it has taken place, the enquirers into cause and effect have to remember that there are accidents which no human agency can foresee or prevent". In medical negligence cases claimants have to appreciate that not all treatments (operations for example) are always successful however skilfully performed; similarly complications such as post-operative wound infection are a natural hazard.

106 After analysis of the events, the expert in most cases will be in a position to state that there has been a failure in the duty of care by the doctor and this is the cause of the residual symptoms and disability. The term negligence should not be used in the report because it is in fact a legal concept.

107 The errors should be listed and an indication given as to the course that would have been followed by a substantial body of medical practitioners in the same speciality, and in the year that the treatment took place, and under similar circumstances. As stated earlier, the expressed opinion should be, where possible, supported by the personal experience of the expert and the medical literature.

CASE HISTORY

108 Some of the points discussed with regard to receiving instructions, and preparing a report and providing an opinion on liability in a matter of medical malpractice are illustrated by the following case.

109 A letter of instruction indicated that a 41-year-old operational fire fighter injured his low back at work and developed left sciatica. He was subsequently referred to a hospital orthopaedic department where a CT scan revealed a lumbar 4–5 disc prolapse, with compression of the 5th lumbar nerve root. The letter went on to state that operative treatment was undertaken, following which he complained of symptoms in the right leg with some degree of paralysis of the below knee muscles.

110 He was subsequently referred to a neurosurgeon who explored the spine and found that the operation had been performed on the left lumbar 3–4 level instead of lumbar 4–5 and the right 5th lumbar nerve root had been severed. As a result of these events his employment had to be terminated.

111 This was a full and clear letter of instruction which left no doubt as to the matters which have to be considered. All the relevant medical records and X-rays were provided. Two reports were prepared, namely condition and prognosis (Appendix 1 of this Chapter) and an opinion on causation and liability (Appendix 2 of this chapter). They illustrate how this type of report should be set out for the benefit of the court. Not surprisingly this case was settled in the claimant's favour without coming to trial.

IS THE PATIENT EXAGGERATING THE SYMPTOMS AND ASSOCIATED DISABILITY?

112 The expert will frequently be faced with this dilemma, which is never easy to resolve, and it deserves separate consideration. The problem arises particularly after injury to the musculo-skeletal system, and there is no better example than persistent neck and low back pain many years after the relevant accident.

113 The expert should attempt to give an estimate of the expected recovery time and if possible give an explanation as to why it has not occurred.

114 The claim will concern fitness to return to pre-accident job, and the need to receive incapacity and other benefits. The expert should make it clear whether the patient is fit to return to alternative or modified work. Few injured people in fact are totally and permanently unfit for any form of work.

115 An insurance company and their solicitors may well have the suspicion that continued complaints and absence from work are not genuine; details may have been provided for the expert who will then find it more difficult to provide an objective opinion. It is especially difficult for the expert when there is an absence of physical signs with negative investigations, in other words, if there is little or no correlation between the patient's complaint and the clinical picture.

116 In these circumstances it is more appropriate for the expert to record any suspicions about the genuineness of the disability in a confidential covering letter with the report. However, if the expert has confidence in the opinion and supporting evidence can be provided, the information should be included in the report.

117 In circumstances which I have outlined, an expert instructed by the defendant should suggest possible ways of resolving the dilemma. The first advice should be to not consider settlement until a further examination of the claimant has taken place in six or 12 months time.

118 It may be clear from the history and the reaction of the patient at the consultation that a psychiatric opinion should be obtained. This should only be advisable if mental illness is suspected or there is some evidence of a post-traumatic stress disorder. In all other instances it would seem to be reasonable for the expert (other than a psychiatrist) to express an opinion about a patient's emotional state such as anxiety, hysterical behaviour and apparent depression.

119 In the case of musculo-skeletal disabilities the expert instructed by the defendant may suggest that a video of the patient's daily activities be obtained, preferably after the clinical examination which will have recorded in detail the complaints and inability to undertake certain activities. If a claimant's expert is sent a video for comment, he must do so objectively and make it clear whether or not it can be correlated with a previously expressed opinion.

120 An example is the man who claimed he was disabled and unfit to work following an injury which caused low back pain. He had been receiving numerous state benefits for a number of years. No medical problem was revealed at the clinical examination, but his behaviour was consistent with deliberate exaggeration, including inability to bend forwards, lift or carry objects. The video recording clearly demonstrated that he was undertaking gardening activities, lifting and carrying heavy loads, climbing ladders, and for recreation running about the park with his dog, the existence of which he had denied during cross-examination!

CONFERENCES

121 A meeting with counsel and other experts is a most important and rewarding exercise. The expert is able to explain the nature of the medical condition and clarify anatomical points if appropriate.

122 A first conference is best held after the expert has submitted his report. This gives an opportunity for any necessary amendments to be made before exchange, and it enables counsel to settle the statement of claim.

123 It is usual to hold a pre-trial conference, especially in malpractice cases. On this occasion the expert will have received the other side's expert opinion, and the strength of each side's case can be tested. The expert must now confirm that in the light of all the evidence, he holds to his original opinion. It is possible that the expert may be asked to make further amendments to his report.

MEETING OF EXPERTS

124 Until recently, it was a matter for either side to suggest a meeting of experts. It is now increasingly the case that the court requests such a meeting takes place and within a rigid time scale.

125 The purpose of a without prejudice meeting is to narrow down the issues. It is usually possible to reach agreement on most of them, and indeed many cases will settle out of court as a result of such a meeting.

126 There have been occasions when an expert has received instructions to meet and discuss but not reach any agreement. It is important for experts to understand that they should not take part in such an unacceptable practice. If they are so instructed it should be reported to the court.

127 There are a number of prerequisites if the meeting is to be useful. A fixed agenda agreed by both sides is essential. Some experts prefer the two sides' solicitors to be present but not take part in the discussion. This is a matter for the two sides to discuss. The meeting should take place after exchange of reports but well before the trial date. One or other expert will prepare a draft statement, indicating areas of agreement and disagreement. A final document signed by both experts can then be submitted to the court.

128 In personal injury cases, it appears not to be normal practice for the medical experts to meet before trial. The nature of these cases is such that in the vast majority medical evidence can be agreed, with an obvious saving on costs. The reluctance of solicitors and insurance companies to encourage such meetings is hard to understand. There is however reason to be optimistic that conduct of these cases will change in the future following the implementation of Lord Woolf's recommendations for civil justice reforms.

EVIDENCE IN COURT

129 Although instructed either by the claimant or defendant, the expert nevertheless should provide an entirely objective opinion for the benefit of the court. Some experts do not find it an easy role to play and as a result there may be a tendency to bend their evidence. It is a matter for judges and counsel to expose such activities. In this context experts must appreciate that if they are persuaded by solicitors to enter into conditional fee arrangements their objectivity will be compromised and they must expect it to be exposed in court.

130 The expert must avoid hyperbole and bias and only answer questions put to him. He must show a willingness to change his opinion if confronted with appropriate evidence.

131 In medical malpractice cases it may be necessary for the expert to explain to the court what advice and treatment he would have provided in similar circumstances. It is simply not good enough to say "I would have treated the patient exactly the same way" or alternatively "The treatment provided was of a very inferior standard". The expert should be asked to provide details from his own practice, and indicate supporting evidence in the literature. The expert must expect, but sadly it is not always forthcoming, a searching examination of his opinion both from the judge and opposing counsel. Only in this way is it possible to test and establish the objectivity of the expert's testimony.

132 A further role for the expert is to listen to the opposing side's evidence, and provide counsel with any necessary assistance for the purposes of cross examination.

SUMMARY AND CONCLUSIONS

133 An attempt has been made to provide guidance for not only those doctors who wish to undertake regular medico-legal work, but also those who have been actively engaged in the practice for some years. There is certainly room for flexibility in the way experts approach a particular case.

134 Undoubtedly a number of senior doctors engaged in medico-legal work assume that because they are recognised as experienced in their particular field, they are also capable of providing expert testimony in court; an expert in medical practice is not necessarily an expert medical witness, and they will soon learn from experience that this is so.

135 There is an important place for training in court procedures, including giving evidence and preparing reports, and indeed education on the relevant aspect of the law. It can be reasonably argued that judges who hear medico-legal cases should receive some basic medical training, but further discussion on this aspect is beyond the scope of this chapter.

***Nigel H Harris, MA, MB, BChir, FRCS, FAE, MCI, Arb** has been a consultant orthopaedic surgeon for more than 30 years. He is the author of a post-graduate textbook,* Clinical Orthopaedics *(first published 1983, second edition June 1995, Blackwell Science) and Joint Editor of* Medical Negligence *(first edition 1990, second edition 1994, Butterworths Law). He is an experienced Expert Witness in medical negligence/professional negligence and personal injury. He averages 300 new instructions from solicitors annually.*

APPENDIX 1

Condition and prognosis report

Introduction

I have had available the records and X-rays, and medical reports prepared by Mr WT dated 28.1.95, 7.1.97 and 13.5.97.

History

He had some sort of injury at work and the medical records give a variable description. Thus, there is a statement to say that he strained his back bending, another saying he was standing up from the stoop position and a third saying that he strained his back lifting. Which of these is correct, I do not know. Notwithstanding the mechanism, he developed progressively increasing low back pain and left sciatica and he had to stop work. He first attended his General Practitioner and rested at home with analgesics but the symptoms did not settle and so he was referred to the Orthopaedic Department at Bedford Hospital. He first attended the clinic on the 17 December and it was noted that he had some neurological signs in the left leg, namely some weakness of the extensor *hallucis longus* tendon and a weakness of the peronei, some reduced sensation on the outer border of the foot and an absent ankle jerk. Straight-leg-raising on the left was significantly restricted. A CT scan was requested and this unequivocally confirmed he had a disc prolapse at the L4/5 level compressing the 5th lumbar nerve root on the left side. There was a bulge at the L5/S1 level impinging on but not compressing the first sacral nerve roots and this was not thought to be of great significance.

He was admitted to hospital on 31 December 1993 and had a period of conservative treatment—namely bed rest and traction but his condition did not improve. He was then advised operative treatment to remove the left sided L4/5 disc prolapse.

Operation took place on 10 January 1994. The operation note indicates that the surgeon removed a disc at what he thought was the L4/5 level. The operation note itself is rather difficult to decipher. It looks as if it states that there was a tight canal with nerve root scarred densely down on to bulging disc which was decompressed and the bony canal was de-roofed. No reference is made to dural puncture or CSF leakage. The following day, the right leg was numb from the knee downwards and he was unable to move his right foot. He did not have any bowel or micturition problems. He had a lot of backache and the left sciatica had not been relieved. Examination confirmed the presence of a foot drop on the right and L5 sensory loss.

He was transferred to the care of a Neurosurgeon on 13 January 1994.

After admission, examination confirmed the right foot drop and hyperaesthesia in the right L5 distribution. It also confirmed continuing left sciatica and very limited left straight-leg-raising. A repeat CT scan was undertaken and showed no change from the first scan.

A further operation was performed on 13 January 1994. The principal findings were as follows:

1. The first operation had been performed at the L3/4 level on the left not the supposed L4/5 level.
2. There was a two centimetre dural tear just to the right of the mid-line at the L3/4 level.
3. There was noted to be a severed L5 nerve root on the right side.
4. The L4/5 disc prolapse was found and removed. The dural tear was repaired. The L4/5 disc prolapse was described as substantial.

Following this operation, he obtained complete relief of the left sciatica but some backache persisted. No change occurred in the right foot drop.

Present condition

He was medically retired from his job in June 1994 and has not been able to work since then.

He complains of numbness on the outer side of the right calf and medial side of the dorsum of the foot and adjacent plantar surface. He still has a foot drop which has not changed. He is aware of electric shock sensations running down the right leg. Some backache persists but it is less than it was. He has to take analgesics when necessary. Walking distance is up to a mile and he can drive depending on the type of car.

Examination

He has a gross limp due to the foot drop on the right. He is not wearing a splint. As far as the spine is concerned, extension is much reduced and he can flex forward without tilting to about the proximal tibia. Straight-leg-raising is 80 degrees on each side and there are no nerve root tension signs. Both ankle reflexes are absent. On the left side there is no below knee muscle weakness. On the right side the following muscles were tested:

EHL 3. EDL 1. Tibialis posterior 3 plus or 4. Peronei 0. Calf 5. Tibialis anterior 0. Normal power is grade 5. There is L5 sensory loss.

Opinion

PRESENT CONDITION

He has a very serious disability due to the neurological deficit which I have described in his right lower leg. There will be no change in the condition. In other words, it is a permanent functional deficit. He has some residual low back pain which is to be expected in view of the degenerative change in the low lumbar region. As long as he is not undertaking heavy physical work this is unlikely to trouble him very much now or in the foreseeable future.

Prognosis

There will be no improvement in the neurological status of the right lower leg. Some functional improvement could be produced by an operation to transfer one of the normal acting muscles to replace one of the weaker ones and so improve the foot drop. I have suggested, that he might like to consult his General Practitioner with a view to obtaining an orthopaedic opinion about this.

Periodic backache will continue for the rest of his life.

Work

He is permanently unfit to resume work as an Operational Fire Fighter. He is however perfectly fit to undertake a sedentary type job—mainly sitting but he also could do a certain amount of walking. He must always avoid bending, lifting and carrying things.

He is very severely restricted on the open job market because of his present medical condition which I have described.

The contents of this report are true to the best of my knowledge and belief.

Nigel H Harris, MA, MB, BChir, FRCS, FAE, MCI, Arb
Consultant Orthopaedic Surgeon

APPENDIX 2

Opinion on liability

The operation

The patient is either placed prone with the spine flexed or on the side with as much flexion as possible. It is the surgeon's responsibility to position the patient accurately.

A standard procedure was carried out—namely an *inter lamina* approach. The operation does not say if any bone was removed. Very often a portion of the lamina is removed. If necessary a hemi laminectomy is performed in order to obtain adequate access.

It is suggested that access was made more difficult by extension of the back on the operating table. I have no idea what is meant by this statement. In any event, it must be emphasised that if the position on the operating table made access difficult the fault is in the positioning of the patient, and this is clearly avoidable.

Having obtained adequate access, the nerve root is carefully located and gently retracted to expose the prolapsing discs. It is quite wrong to suggest that, "The view of the spinal cord was poor". The fact is that the spinal cord does not extend more distally than the lower border of the 2nd lumbar vertebrae so it would certainly not reach the level at which the operation was performed.

The nerve root indeed may be tight and bound down by adhesions. I would not expect this to occur in the presence of a normal disc.

The surgeon will ensure he has a good view of the nerve root; if necessary as I have said, bone may have to be removed. Very careful manipulation and retraction of nerve root should never be done unless it can be clearly seen.

In the course of retracting the nerve root, it very occasionally happens that the dural sheath is punctured. A small puncture can be left untouched, but a significant tear is usually sutured.

The operation note makes it clear that the surgeon was unaware that the dura had been torn. This I find surprising because the leakage of Cerebro-Spinal Fluid (CSF) which follows is quite obvious.

He assumed he was operating at the L4/5 level. A subsequent CT scan and exploratory operation confirmed that in fact he operated at the L3/4 level and therefore failed to find and remove the prolapsing L4/5 disc on the left side.

It is very important for a surgeon to check the levels he is exploring either by counting up from the sacrum combined with inspection of the X-rays, or with the aid of a skin marker and X-ray before operation. If exploration at the supposed correct level fails to reveal a significant prolapse (a bulge is not a significant prolapse) (as indicated by the CT scan) the surgeon should be alerted to the possibility that he is operating at the wrong levels. He should then re-check the levels, and if necessary explore a space above or below according to the particular circumstances.

He did not find a disc prolapse, only what he describes as a bulge. He should have checked the levels again and proceeded as I have indicated.

Conclusion

There can be no excuse for poor exposure of the operation field, and in particular the nerve root. The operation note makes no mention of poor exposure but if it occurred, this is the fault of the surgeon. Either he positioned the patient inappropriately and/or he did not remove sufficient bone to expose the nerve root.

There can be no excuse either for operating at the wrong level and not appreciating the fact at the time.

The operative technique employed was wholly inadequate, and fell far short of the standard expected of a reasonably competent consultant orthopaedic surgeon. The patient was entitled to expect a significantly higher standard of expertise than was provided.

DIVISION OF THE RIGHT L5 NERVE ROOT

I refer to this as a separate matter because it is such a grotesque occurrence and far removed from any normal complication of this type of operation. I have never heard of or read of such an occurrence.

It very occasionally happens as a normal hazard in certain circumstances or as a result of carelessness, that a nerve root on the site of operation—that is within the field of operation—is damaged; severance of a root is excessively rare.

I cannot begin to understand how it was possible to divide the fifth lumbar nerve root on the opposite side while operating at the L3/4 level on the left. All I can say is that the surgeon was excessively careless and strayed well beyond the area of direct vision. The root must have been divided either by a knife or scissors, neither of which should be used once the nerve root and disc have been exposed.

Conclusion

There is no possible excuse for the occurrence of this extremely serious error. It is unequivocally indefensible.

The allegation of poor exposure and/or tight structures in the operation field is simply not an acceptable reason for such careless operative technique. No reasonable or competent orthopaedic surgeon would condone such an error under any circumstances.

THE OUTCOME FOLLOWING OPERATION WITHOUT COMPLICATIONS

If the first operation had effectively removed the L4/5 disc prolapse without neurological complications then there is a more than 90 per cent chance that he would be totally relieved of the left leg sciatica. A certain amount of backache would continue but would not necessarily be disabling.

The question arises as to whether after a period of two to three months he would have been capable of returning to work as an operational fireman.

I am bound to say that theoretically he could have attempted to return and might well have been successful for a period of time. However, I think any reasonable orthopaedic surgeon under such circumstances would have advised him and his employer that it would be unwise to return to such work because of the risk of aggravating his backache. With this knowledge, I doubt if his employers would have approved him returning to work as an operational fireman. He certainly could have returned to administrative duties perhaps involving a certain amount of teaching if such a job existed in the Fire Service.

The contents of this report are true to the best of my knowledge and belief.

CHAPTER 3

THE EXPERT WITNESS IN CRIMINAL CASES

P A D Sheen

INTRODUCTION

001 My consultancy deals with a mixed bag of civil and criminal work, the criminal work being at the "messier" end of the range of criminal cases, that is to say suspect insurance claims, arson, arson with intent to endanger human life, murder by petrol, murder concealed by fire and so on.

002 This means that my perspective of the processes of the criminal justice system is coloured by the nature of my work and fellow expert witnesses whose work is at the "cleaner", white collar crime, end of the spectrum may not always agree with what I have to say. At the outset it is, in my opinion, necessary to discuss job titles. The Academy of Experts uses the general term "expert witness" as a generic term to cover the work done by its members. In criminal cases the role of the expert witness is more usually performed by a person who would describe himself as a "forensic scientist" (or in my case as a forensic engineer). Nevertheless no matter how they describe themselves the law tends to treat them all as expert witnesses and this is the term which I shall use.

PART 1: THE ROLE AND RESPONSIBILITIES OF THE EXPERT WITNESS IN CRIMINAL CASES

003 Fundamental to the proper workings of the criminal justice system is that all of those who are working within it have a clear concept of their role within the system, their duties, and to whom they are ultimately responsible for the proper discharge of those duties. In addition, they must have an understanding of the ethical principles which must underpin their work and guide their actions. Given the importance of forensic evidence in most criminal trials this background of understanding of role and the professional duties which go with that role are of particular importance to the expert witness working in the field of criminal law and The Academy has recognised this with the publication of the *Additional Guidelines for Forensic Scientists* (in Appendix 1 to this Chapter). In reading these guidelines it is important to keep in mind that they are *additional* guidelines and have to be read along with the Code of Practice of The Academy.

The House of Lords Select Committee Report on forensic science

004 The House of Lords Select Committee on Science and Technology carried out an inquiry into forensic science mainly as a result of public unease at a long string of miscarriages of justice in high profile cases, especially as in many of them the problem had been that the use or misuse of forensic evidence was a factor. I list these cases as it seems to me that we should have them constantly in the back of our minds as an aid to ensuring that such cases do not recur:

John Preece

005 *John Preece was convicted in 1973 of rape and murder. Central to the prosecution case was that the accused secreted blood in his body fluids and that blood of the same group was found in semen on the clothing of the victim. The fact that the victim was also a secretor and a secretor of blood of the same group as the accused was suppressed.*

006 After a long fight the case was finally referred back to the High Court of Justiciary by the Secretary of State for Scotland in 1981. In their judgment the court said that the forensic scientist involved was "discredited not only as a scientist but as a witness upon the accuracy, fairness and objectivity of whose evidence reliance could be placed". It is fair to point out that the deficiencies in the work of this forensic scientist was discovered by the Forensic Science Service when they introduced the new quality assurance procedures into their laboratories.

The Birmingham Six

007 *The Birmingham Six were convicted in 1975 of the Birmingham pub bombings on the basis of a forensic test which, it was stated at the trial, showed that two of them had been handling explosives. The test used could in fact give a false positive result with common materials such as playing cards, cigarette wrappers and sticky tape.*

008 It is fair to say that the ultimate acquittals of these men was due to careful forensic work on the part of other forensic scientists whose work on electrostatic document analysis (ESDA) made it possible to show that the notes of the interviews made by the police had been tampered with, that four pages had been added and that there were other discrepancies which led the Court of Appeal to come to the conclusion that at the original trial four police officers had misled the court.

009 The Court of Appeal noted in its judgment that: "A disadvantage of the adversarial system may be that the parties are not evenly matched in resources . . . But the inequality of resources is ameliorated by the obligation on the part of the prosecution to make available all material which might prove helpful to the defence"—a point discussed in detail later in paras 092 *et seq.*

The Guildford Four

010 *The Guildford Four were not wrongfully convicted as a result of defective forensic evidence; indeed it was forensic evidence (ESDA test on documents) which was instrumental in having the convictions overturned.*

The Maguire Seven

011 *The Maguire Seven were convicted in 1976 largely as a result of forensic evidence that they had been handling explosives. The convictions were quashed because of the possibility that their hands had been innocently contaminated.*

012 In its judgment the Court of Appeal stated:

> "We are of the opinion that a forensic scientist who is an adviser to the prosecuting authority is under a duty to disclose material of which he knows and which may have some bearing on the offence charged and the surrounding circumstances of the case. The disclosure will be to the authority which retains him and which must in turn (subject to sensitivity) disclose the information to the defence. . . . We can see no cause to distinguish between members of the prosecuting authority and those advising it in the capacity of a forensic scientist. Such a distinction could involve difficult and contested enquiries as to where the knowledge stopped but, most importantly, would be entirely counter to the desirability of ameliorating the disparity of scientific resources as between the Crown and the subject."

Stephen Kiszko

013 *Stephen Kiszko was convicted of murder in 1976. Semen stains on the clothing of the victim could not have come from Mr Kiszko, who was sterile. It appears that this fact was known to the police before the original trial but was not disclosed to the defence (and possibly not disclosed to the prosecuting counsel).*

Judith Ward

014 *Judith Ward was convicted in 1974 of three bombings. The conviction was quashed in 1992. It is worth quoting extensively from the House of Lords report:*

> ". . . the scientist's written statements were 'uninformative', 'economical' and 'calculated to discourage investigation'; results recorded as 'faint' were baldly reported as 'positive'; the existence of substances found in shoe polish which gave the same test result in thin layer chromatography as nitro-glycerine was concealed from both sides by the scientists; and further tests . . . to see if innocent contamination could be caused by *débris* from an explosion, were either misreported or not disclosed at all. Medical evidence had also been suppressed."

015 The court concluded: "Three senior RARDE scientists took the law into their own hands, and concealed from the prosecution, the defence and the court, matters which might have changed the course of the trial. . . . They became partisan. It is the clear duty of government forensic scientists to assist in a neutral and impartial way in criminal investigations. They must act in the cause of justice. That duty should be spelt out to all engaged or to be engaged in forensic services in the clearest terms."

016 It has to be said that these cases are now many years old and the Forensic Science Service has put enormous efforts into ensuring that the quality of the work done in its laboratories and the impartiality and integrity of its staff are all of the highest order. However, from time to time there are pressures on the system to increase the "success" rate of the criminal justice system, often by politicians who wish to prove their "law and order" credentials by being seen to be "tough on crime"; and especially when the crime is a terrorist act, there is tremendous public pressure on those investigating the crime to get a result. Equally there are dangers which arise from the fact that as the police now have to pay the Forensic Science Service for each item of work done police forces are putting forensic investigations in the hands of private practitioners who are not subject to the quality control checks now built into the services provided by the Forensic Science Service.

017 I do not argue that such "private" work is wrong—I could hardly do so as a proportion of the work of my own consultancy is acting as an expert witness for the prosecution in cases including murder. What I am suggesting is that we need to be aware of the potential dangers of this "privatisation" and to set up the mechanisms necessary to monitor and regulate the work of all who present forensic science evidence to the courts.

018 The results of the study by the House of Lords Committee were set out in the report *Forensic Science* (House of Lords Session 1992, 93 5th report HL Paper 24). Although this report is now some years old not all of its recommendations have been carried out and almost everything in the report is valid today and I make no excuses for quoting extensively from the report for it is still the most comprehensive survey of the role and methods of the expert witness in the criminal courts which has been attempted.

The role and duties of the expert witness in the criminal trial

019 The Committee make an interesting comment at paragraph 1.12: "1.12. Forensic science is not a concept recognised by either English or Scottish Law. The law treats a forensic scientist no differently from any other expert witness . . ." (In passing it is well at this point to quote the next part of this paragraph: "(There is one exception to this: the Criminal Justice (Scotland) Act 1980, section 26, allows persons authorised as forensic scientists by the Secretary of State to give evidence under special conditions in certain cases)" and to comment that as with almost everything which is written about the law there has to be the rider that what is being described is the criminal justice process of England and Wales. Scottish methods are different (and in my view better!) and Scottish procedures will be covered later.)

020 As seen by the Committee the role is set out in a paragraph in the Executive Summary to the Report:

> "**1.2.** The task of a forensic scientist is to provide evidence to the courts, based upon scientific examination of chemical or biological specimens. The quality of that evidence depends on the care with which the exhibits are collected, the accuracy of the scientific work, and the clarity with which the findings are presented. All of these depend crucially upon the competence and integrity of the scientific staff, and the adequacy of their experimental resources."

021 I would comment that in the first sentence of this paragraph the Committee seem not to have fully understood the whole scope of forensic science as it embraces much more than the "scientific examination of chemical or biological specimens". That said the second sentence is true and must be kept in mind all the time.

022 In a later paragraph the Committee set out with the utmost clarity the ground rules within which forensic scientists must work:

> "**1.9.** The first duty of any forensic scientist is to justice and to the court."

In the same paragraph the Committee distinguish between three roles for forensic science within the context of criminal trials:

> "(a) Forensic science for the investigator, before anyone has been charged and sometimes before it is even clear that a crime has taken place; in this role, the scientist's job is to help the investigator establish what has happened.

(b) Forensic science for the prosecution; here the scientist is helping to prove 'beyond reasonable doubt' that an offence has been committed and that the accused was responsible.
(c) Forensic science for the defence; here all that is required is to sustain 'reasonable doubt'."

023 With the greatest respect to their Lordships I feel that in (b) and (c) they are so immersed in the adversarial traditions of English law that they do not see that (b) and (c), if taken as guidelines by practising forensic scientists, can all too easily lead to them forgetting that their *primary* duty is "to justice and to the court", and back to thinking that they are "a part of a team". It seems to me to follow from the statement that my primary duty is "to justice and to the court" that my role as a defence expert is *not* to work to ensure that my client is acquitted but to ensure that justice is done. In my view therefore my role is not to "sustain reasonable doubt" but to act as an independent quality control inspector examining the work of the prosecution experts and, if it "passes inspection" to back it in my report and in my evidence. Equally when I am a prosecution expert I am not simply "helping to prove 'beyond reasonable doubt' that an offence has been committed and that the accused was responsible", but am, or should be, looking for evidence that may help the accused or, which should be the same thing, to assist the court in a neutral and impartial way. The greatest danger is when the prosecution expert consciously or subconsciously ignores evidence which "does not fit".

024 In Chapter 1/12C *supra*, "A neutral expert for criminal cases?", Richard Freeman discusses the possibility of a court-appointed "neutral" expert. Mr Freeman deals with what is called "white collar" crime in fraud, accountancy and VAT and in this field I can see the merits of his proposal, especially as so many of the issues in a fraud trial are difficult for a lay jury to understand. However, from my perspective matters are not so clear. In the sort of crime with which I deal—arson, murder and so on—the issues are clear for the jury to understand but there is scope for genuine differences of opinion between experts. For example in a murder trial in which the allegation is that the victim was killed and then the building set alight to conceal the crime it was of crucial importance to establish how fast the fire spread. As prosecution expert my view was that there was insufficient time for the fire to spread as rapidly as it had done and so it seemed to me that there was evidence of two seats of fire which of course points to the fire having been deliberately set. The defence expert felt that if there were defects in the construction of the building then it might be possible for the fire to spread as quickly as it did. In this I agreed with him but felt that, taking into account all of the facts which I had found at the scene, I was still of the opinion that the fire was deliberate. A neutral expert could, I suppose, put both views and indeed in one arson case in which I was the prosecution expert the defence did not call their expert to give evidence because in my own evidence I had done just that, to explain the problems and the different possibilities of how the fire developed and explained the difficulties of interpreting some of the evidence and in doing so had covered all of the ground which the defence wished to cover. However, in the end an expert has to jump off the fence and give an opinion and it may well be that justice is better served by letting the jury hear two reasoned views as to how the incident which is at the centre of the trial might have occurred and leave it to the jury to weigh the conflicting expert opinion along with all of the other evidence with which they have been presented.

025 In saying this I do not advocate experts deliberately differing and indeed later I support the establishment of pre-trial meetings of experts to see if a greater degree of common ground can be found.

026 The best way to see my approach of the defence expert witness as the "quality control inspector" at work is to follow through a case from start to finish. The case which follows is in fact an amalgam of two cases as I wanted certain features in the case to make my points and this I could only achieve by putting together features from two cases in my case book.

Case study—arson

027 Mr Kay was not a happy man. His shop was not doing well. He owed his bank a lot of money, his suppliers were cutting off supplies, writs were arriving and bailiffs were on the horizon. The final straw came when his shop assistant told him that she was pregnant and he was to become a daddy. He locked up the shop at five and at five past five, flames were seen coming from the upstairs windows.

028 The fire brigade arrived and put out the fire and in putting out the fire found some petrol soaked rags. In a small market town the local police (and everyone else!) tend to know who is in financial trouble—as well as who is pregnant (and who is the father!) so Mr Kay was interviewed that evening and charged with arson. I was instructed by his solicitor to work on the case. As usual by the time I had instructions we were some distance in time from the fire but fortunately soon enough after the fire for the burnt out remains of the shop still to be available for inspection.

029 As soon as I am involved in a fire investigation I start a Fire Analysis Report in a pre-printed booklet which puts down in a standardised form every detail relating to the fire and acts as an *aide mémoire* to ensure that I never forget to check and record some detail relating to the fire, and also acts as an index to all of the reports and case papers. (Two typical pages of the eight-page Fire Analysis Report are in Appendix 2 to this chapter.)

030 Going through the report I will highlight those sections which are of special relevance to the "quality control" role discussed earlier, while remarking that the document is also of great use when I am the expert for the prosecution to assist me in ensuring that everything I do is done "by the book".

(1) Were multiple seats of fire found? Two or more seats of fire are indicative of, but not conclusive evidence of, arson and it is essential not to jump to conclusions and to check that the fire investigator did not jump to conclusions so the next question is:

(2) Did the investigator consider possible innocent causes of multiple seats? Consideration of this may well lead to the establishment of a possible line of defence.

(3) Did the investigator have lawful authority to be on the premises? And did the Forensic Scientist/Scene Of Crime Officer (SOCO) have lawful authority to be on the premises?

This is a muddy area! While the fire is burning the fire brigade have a statutory right to enter the building given to them by section 30 of the Fire Services Act 1947 which provides that:

> "**s.30.** Any member of a fire brigade . . . on duty . . . or any constable, may enter and if necessary break into any premises or place in which a fire has or is reasonably believed to have broken out . . . without the consent of the owner or occupier thereof, and may do all such things as he may deem necessary for extinguishing the fire or for protecting from fire . . . any such premises or place or for rescuing any person or property therein."

Now this was passed 50 years ago in an era when World War II had just finished and the population at large were to a very large extent used to obeying orders and to deferring to authority; and, although I have no doubt that even today with the emphasis on "right" and in an increasingly litigious society there would still be general support for the enactment of such a section of an Act, it is worth pointing out that the powers given in section 30 do not extend to a fire investigator even during the fire. He is not doing "all such things as he may deem necessary for extinguishing the fire or for protecting from fire . . . [in] any such premises or place or for rescuing any person or property therein", and in any case it seems to me that any power of entry which the fire investigator might possibly have had to enter the premises while the fire was burning is, as it were, extinguished when the fire is extinguished. There would therefore be no power to enter the premises if he wished to come back the next day to investigate the causes of the fire.

Interestingly, the parallel legislation in Singapore, which has an Act based on (and is almost word for word identical to) the UK 1947 Act, differs from the UK Act in giving a specific right of entry to fire investigators. I have made much of this particular aspect because it is of great importance to the expert witness in criminal work, especially in some countries. The courts in England take, in my view, a very lax attitude to the admission in a criminal trial of illegally obtained evidence. Contrast the attitude of the English courts, which leaves it to the discretion of the courts whether or not to admit evidence which has been illegally obtained, with the much more robust attitude of the courts in many states in America which take the view that illegally obtained material is tainted and hence inadmissible *per se*. Depending therefore upon the jurisdiction in which the trial is to be held, it is worth the while of an expert witness retained by the defence to ask the questions about the rights of the prosecution experts to have been on the premises to gather the evidence which they propose to put before the court.

(4) Were accelerants found? An accelerant such as petrol or kerosene *may* be indicative of the fire having been started deliberately but only if the investigator has considered and eliminated all innocent explanations for the presence of the accelerant. However, if they were found (or were alleged to have been found!) then the evidence to be placed before the court must be subject to a detailed scrutiny by the expert for the defence in his role of providing "quality control", and satisfactory answers need to be obtained to the questions:

(a) Was a sample taken?
(b) By whom?
(c) When?
(d) How was the sample taken?
(e) Is the method of taking the sample likely to contaminate the sample?
(f) How was the sample stored?
(g) Is there any chance that the method of storage could lead to deterioration/contamination of the sample?
(h) Who analysed the sample?
(i) In which laboratory?
(j) What method of analysis was used?
(k) Was this an appropriate method?
(l) Are the results claimed consistent with the method of analysis used?
(m) Is a sample available for the defence to have analysed independently? (I have had a judge accept the argument that as in drink driving cases a duplicate sample is

made available to the defence then the same procedure could and should be followed in an arson trial.)

(n) Chain of evidence—Is the chain of evidence complete? It is central to the production of items of evidence in a criminal trial that there should be a written record accompanying the exhibit which, through a series of signatures, can prove that the exhibit has been properly kept free of any possibility of tampering and/or contamination from the instant at which it was seized at the crime scene to the instant at which it is produced in court. All police forces have procedures and specialist officers to ensure that this is done—but it is always something which the defence expert needs to check as "quality controller".

Then of course if an accelerant was used it must have been brought to the scene in a container or have already been at the scene in a container and so all of the above questions have to be asked about the container or containers.

This is especially true of the question "Is there any evidence of a link between the containers to the accused?".

Equally, many arsons involve the use of a timing device so we ask all the above questions about timing devices alleged to have been found.

(5) Finally we come to the accused. Again the "quality control" questions:

(a) At what time was he interviewed by the police.
(b) Did they take possession of any items of his clothing?
(c) Was the clothing sent for forensic examination?
(d) How was the clothing packaged and stored?
(e) Is there any chance that the method of packaging and/or storage could lead to deterioration/contamination of evidence from the clothing?
(f) Who examined the clothing?
(g) In which laboratory?
(h) What method of analysis was used?
(i) Was this an appropriate method?
(j) Are the results claimed consistent with the method of analysis used? In particular are the findings of residues of accelerants on the clothing consistent with the time interval between the fire and the time at which the police took possession of the clothing?
(k) Chain of evidence—Is the chain of evidence complete?

031 What is being done by this process is to examine everything which has been done in the investigation against a yardstick of good practice and, where appropriate, the law. If the investigation has been properly carried out then its findings will be supported by me. If, however, there are shortcomings then these will be highlighted. I say again that it is not a part of my job to "ensure" that my client is acquitted but to ensure, so far as I am able that he is tried with "due process", a term which does not appear in my law dictionary but a concept from American law which to me represents what a criminal justice system should guarantee to all defendants.

"The truth, the whole truth and nothing . . ."

032 From time to time all expert witnesses have a problem with the oath which they take in the witness box. In civil trials the problems of the literal interpretation of the oath can to a very large extent be resolved by the expert understanding that his role in giving evidence is confined to those matters which have been pleaded. (Although I have to say that this gloss still gives me moral problems. To me if the oath has to have a gloss put on it then there is something wrong with the oath—I am not swearing to the court or to the judge but to Almighty God and I am not too sure that he approves of glosses or of mental reservations applied to oaths sworn in his name!)

033 In giving evidence to the House of Lords Committee Mr Ashken, Director of the Crown Prosecution Service Policy Group, said: "The adversarial system puts an enormous premium on witnesses being able to communicate clearly and convincingly in the witness box so the jury may be persuaded of the value of their evidence."

034 The committee quote this in their *Report* and comment:

> ". . . it is our impression that the scope for a scientific witness to tell his story in his own way is limited. His oath binds him to tell 'The whole truth'. Yet in practice he is required only to answer the questions put to him by counsel; he is not allowed to interact with his audience, as a good teacher sometimes does, to establish whether (or how) they understand what he has said and he sometimes steps out of the witness box feeling that he has not left the court with the impressions which he intended to convey."

035 The committee recommend that the judge should ask an expert witness, when counsel has finished with him but before he steps down, whether he has anything more to say to fulfil the terms of his oath. This would be a great step forward but it is still very rare that such an invitation is given and in my view the problem will not be fully resolved until the recommendation of the committee for pre-trial reviews is implemented (this recommendation is discussed later).

036 Meanwhile all that an expert witness can do if he thinks that an important matter is in danger of being passed over is to extend the scope of his answers to questions so that the neglected matter is gradually brought out—and risk the wrath of counsel!

PART 2: THE PRACTICAL PROBLEMS OF PRACTISING AS AN EXPERT WITNESS IN CRIMINAL CASES

A footnote—a brief introduction to the criminal justice system

037 Many expert witnesses have practices which are wholly concerned with civil litigation and then find that events conspire against them and they find that they are having to give evidence in a criminal case for the first time. This footnote is intended as a short briefing on the system and how it works.

038 Between the point at which the police believe that they have evidence that a crime has been committed and subsequently arrest a person and charge him with having committed the crime the procedure is covered by the Police and Criminal Evidence Act 1984 (PACE). Under PACE there are four codes of practice covering:

(a) The exercise by police officers of statutory powers of stop and search.
(b) The searching of premises by police officers and the seizure of property found by police officers on persons or premises.

(c) The detention, treatment and questioning of persons by police officers.

(d) The identification of persons by police officers.

039 There are circumstances, albeit unusual, in which it is possible that a defence expert witness may, during the course of his gathering of evidence or during his analysis of the evidence put to him, become aware that it is possible that there has been a breach of the Code of Practice and if this is the case he should immediately notify his instructing solicitor and not wait for the facts to be put into his report.

040 Once the accused has been charged the nature of the charge will decide the next step in the process. Offences are divided into three categories: summary only; triable either way; triable on indictment only.

041 The summary offences are those which are relatively minor and of which the trial can only be before the magistrates. The process starts with a summons sent to the accused requiring him to appear at a given date before the magistrates, usually of the place in which the offence is alleged to have been committed. Typical of such offences are the more minor motoring offences and, in general, expert witnesses are rarely involved in such cases although offences under the Health and Safety at Work Act are criminal offences and most trials of such offences take place in magistrates' courts and it is quite common for expert witnesses to be involved in such hearings.

042 The procedure in the more serious cases is undergoing very considerable changes as a result of the coming into force of the Criminal Procedure and Investigations Act 1996 (CPIA) and what follows outlines the procedures for the trial of crimes which fall within the ambit of the Act.

043 For the more serious offences the decision to prosecute will have been made by the Crown Prosecution Service and an indictment will be prepared and served on the accused. The indictment sets out the charges and is accompanied by a copy of the set of documents containing the evidence which is the basis of the charge. Under CPIA the prosecutor has to disclose to the defence all material in his possession which in his opinion might undermine the prosecution case (CPIA, s.3(1)(a)). This is referred to as "primary disclosure".

044 The defence now has to disclose to the court and to the prosecution the essence of their defence especially alibi defences (this is considered in more detail later).

045 In the light of the defence statement the prosecutor has to consider any material in his possession which has not been disclosed to the defence in the primary disclosure and under section 7(2)(a) disclose anything which "might reasonably be expected to assist the accused's defence as disclosed by the defence statement".

046 The actual trial is very similar to the procedure of a civil case so experienced experts appearing for the first time as expert witnesses in a criminal case will be reasonably familiar with the way the court works with, however, the major difference that an expert witness who has only appeared in civil courts may well never have met a jury! (dealing with juries is discussed later in paras 056 *et seq.*).

047 As in civil trials, it is normally not necessary for an expert witness who has had a part of the work upon which his evidence is based done by assistants to call those assistants to give evidence at the trial (*R* v. *Jackson* (1996) *The Times*, 21 May, CA).

048 It has however to be kept in mind that the whole basis upon which the outcome of the trial will be decided is different. In a civil trial the outcome will depend upon the "balance of probabilities" whereas in the criminal trial what is alleged has to be proved "beyond reasonable doubt". This standard was defined in *Miller* v. *Ministry of Pensions* in which Denning J (later Lord Denning) said:

"The degree is well settled. It need not reach certainty, but must carry a high degree of probability. Proof beyond reasonable doubt is not proof beyond the shadow of a doubt. The law would fail to protect the community if it admitted fanciful possibilities to deflect the course of justice. If the evidence is so strong against a man as to leave only a remote possibility in his favour, which can be dismissed with the sentence 'of course it's possible but not in the least probable', the case is proved beyond reasonable doubt, but nothing less short of that will suffice."

049 It has also to be kept in mind that the rules as to what is and what is not admissible in evidence are much more tightly drawn in a criminal trial as compared with a civil trial. This is especially true of hearsay evidence which is accepted in civil proceedings through the various Civil Evidence Acts but the use of which is still very restricted in the criminal courts. As it was put in *Teper* v. *The Queen* [1952] AC 480: "The truthfulness and accuracy of a person whose words are spoken by another witness cannot be tested by cross examination and the light which his demeanour would throw on his testimony is lost."

050 Finally, even though you are an expert (or think that you are!) the judge may not agree with you (*R* v. *Smith (Leonard)* [1997] Crim LR 614, CA). This was a case in which a forensic psychiatrist gave an opinion that the defendant would not pose a threat to the victim if he were released—the judge did not agree.

051 Equally, your opinion must be founded in facts (*R* v. *Turner* [1975] QB 834).

Practical problems

Legal aid for the defence

052 Criminal legal aid will meet the costs of obtaining expert evidence once the defendant has been given a legal aid order from the court and the expense is authorised in advance by the Legal Aid Board Area Committee. (It can also be authorised after the trial but few experts would happily take the risks involved in waiting until after the trial for authorisation.)

053 Because of this system it is rare for an expert to be given instructions until some time after the accused has been charged and by then much which the defence expert could and should have commented upon has already been done. In one murder case in which I was defence expert the police had carried out a reconstruction of the events which led up to the death of the victim. All that was available for me was a very poor quality video recording of the reconstruction which revealed a number of flaws in the methods used in setting up the reconstruction and which, were it possible for me to have been present, could have been commented on and probably had alterations made to make the reconstruction fairer to the accused.

Expert reports

054 Most experts in practice in the civil courts use the "Model Form of Expert's Report" of The Academy of Experts. In criminal cases this format is often not helpful and it is easier to separate the text of the report from its photographs and drawings so that these can be given to the jury in a separate bundle. Each photograph or booklet of photographs and each drawing or book of drawings along with any other object, such as a piece of physical evidence or a model, should be identified with a reference number. This is usually your initials followed by a number, thus I would use PADS1, PADS2 and so on. In the report you would make statements such as: "I took a series of photographs of the scene which I produce as exhibit PADS1"—making certain that the cover of the book of photographs is indeed labelled

PADS1. Referring to the evidence label in Appendix 3 to this chapter, this is the reference which is put into the box labelled "Identification reference number". As such exhibits will probably have been found during your examination of the scene it is well to emphasise at this point the importance of keeping an accurate contemporaneous note of everything done while at the scene with very precise details of where and when every piece of evidence was found and the identification reference number assigned to it. This is best *not* done on loose sheets of paper but in a proper notebook which you are later able to produce in court. My own consultancy uses specially printed notebooks in which times, mileages and expenses relevant to the visit to the scene can be recorded for transfer later to the case time and expenses sheets.

055 It is usually convenient to put your report in the form of a "CJA statement" in which most of the statements used at the trial are. This is the formal statement made under the Criminal Justice Act and an example of such a statement is to be found in Appendix 4 to this chapter. (If you are involved in much criminal work it is convenient to set this up as a template in your computer.) This is the statement which both counsel will have in their bundle and upon which your examination in chief and cross examination will be based. In civil cases the report will need to be clear enough to be understandable by the lawyers and the judge. In criminal cases it always has to be kept in mind that what you say in your report, and subsequently give as evidence in the witness box, must be understandable by the jury—if they do not understand you then all is lost for it is upon what they understand when they finally retire to the jury room that they will decide their verdict. This puts not just a premium on clarity but means that the structure of the report needs to be carefully considered. The structure of the report set out in the Academy's "Model Form" is designed for civil litigation and in criminal cases the first change from the "Model Form" format is that it is still customary in a report for a criminal trial to give details of your qualifications and experience first, as this will form the opening questions from your side's counsel when you give evidence so that the jury can get an impression of how qualified and experienced you are. This is why the specimen CJA Statement in Appendix 4 to this chapter starts with these details. (One important point is the phrase "I reside at the address given overleaf". This address is only on the master copy of the statement and not on any of the copies used at the trial which means that you can keep your address confidential—remember that in a criminal trial you may well be dealing with some very nasty people who have nasty friends.) The "Model Form" format of a clear separation between facts and comment on or discussion of those facts is still valid but the reality that in the end all of the evidence will be given verbally by you and listened to (and understood by) the jury needs to be taken into account. This means two things: clarity and simplicity. Clarity is vital and has to come, at least in part, from the structure of the report. In a civil case report it would be normal to have a section which sets out all of the facts followed by the commentary and discussion. If the case permits it is, in my opinion, far better in preparing a report for a jury to break the whole down into short logical sections, still maintaining the separation of facts and comment/discussion, but allowing the jury to hear the whole divided into "slices" which do not tax them unduly. For example, in an arson case I would consider the evidence as to where the fire started, list the factual evidence and discuss it, ending with my opinion as to the seat of the fire and then move on to the same sequence in considering what ignited the fire and so on.

Juries

056 In civil cases juries are rare. They are used in trials of libel, slander, malicious prosecution, false imprisonment and in exceptional personal injury cases (Supreme Court Act

1981, s.69(3)). The judge can decide if a case is "exceptional"; normally on the grounds that exemplary damages are being claimed.

057 In the majority of criminal cases of sufficient seriousness to merit the appointment of an expert witness the case will be heard by a jury and this alters the way in which you need to produce and present your evidence.

058 The basic advice to the expert in a civil case is to address your answers to the judge. In a criminal case you have to look two ways. The most important set of people in the court is the jury, so give your answers to them while keeping an eye on the judge's pen ensuring you do not get ahead of his written note. Eye contact with the jury is vital. If you see the "glazed shutters" go up, you have lost them—they do not understand what you have said usually because you have not put the technicalities in language they can understand. Once in the witness box there is little you can do about this. Counsel may (should) have noticed the warning signs and asked the same question in a slightly different form so as to give you an opportunity to rephrase your answer, but essentially this is a problem which should have been sorted out before you got to court. All experts need a layperson to read their reports, so that a report can be tested on a typical jury member and revised and simplified until your guinea pig understands it. There is, however, a tight-rope for the expert—make your report simple enough for the jury to understand but never give the impression that you are patronising them!

Instructions

059 As in any branch of the law instructions received by an expert witness range from the terse to the detailed and helpful. In my consultancy this is a range from a telephone call from a Detective Chief Inspector saying "We have had a suspicious death. Can you come and investigate?" through to a series of very detailed questions from counsel.

060 An example is an attempted murder by petrol bomb. The facts are that the defendant was accused of four counts of attempted murder, having allegedly thrown a petrol bomb at a car containing four occupants. The occupants were also allegedly equipped with petrol bombs which they intended to use on the accused. The whole affair stemmed from a dispute over £200 and a used van. The questions from counsel in the instructions were:

(1) Is it possible to say scientifically that the car was burned out by a petrol bomb being flung at a window?

(2) Is it possible to exclude the possibility of the fire having been started accidentally by a petrol bomb being lit inside the car (as there is evidence to suggest that the occupants themselves were equipped with petrol bombs)?

(3) Would a bottle consistent with the fragments found inside the car be likely to smash the side window?

(4) Where in the car did the fire start?

(5) Is the fire damage to the house consistent with a petrol bombing?

(6) What is the significance of the findings of the forensic scientist at page 157 in the bundle?

(7) Is it possible to state what type and colour of bottle the fragments in the car in Exhibit xxx relate to?

(8) Whether the markings on the road outside the accused home are consistent with a petrol bomb explosion and is it possible to tell the direction of flight?

(9) The significance of the petrol contamination to the accused's lower clothing—would a man filling bottles from a baked bean can and subsequently throwing lighted petrol bombs be likely to suffer contamination to his upper clothing?

(10) Would there be evidence of spillage outside the vehicle if the petrol bomb was thrown from outside?

(11) Would such evidence survive?

(12) Is there any evidence to suggest that the bottle found in the vehicle could have been a petrol bomb which ignited in the vehicle and did not enter from outside? Or is the lack of expected spillage on the outside of the vehicle (if that be so) sufficient to support the suggestion?

(13) Would there be any benefit in your having sight of the vehicle?

(14) If you are allowed to look at the accused's clothes, are you able to state whether the presence of petrol on the jeans and/or boots are consistent with its dribbling and/or falling onto the jeans and/or boots while filling up a car with petrol?

(15) There was a fire in the accused's garden a few days before the incident where petrol had been used. Is it possible to say how old the petrol stains were, and if they could have remained on the jeans and/or boots for that period of time?

061 Now this represents the best sort of instructions. Counsel has a clear view of what are the major planks of his case and has posed the questions to which he wants answers.

062 At the other end of the spectrum is a case in which the defendant was charged with manslaughter and arson with intent to endanger human life. After a preliminary telephone conversation the written instructions arrived. These consisted of:

(1) the outline of allegation and issues;

(2) a report from a forensic scientist;

(3) a small bundle of statements from a fire officer and a gas company engineer, and a letter which said "we would be most obliged if you could complete a report and return it to us as soon as possible".

063 This shows, unfortunately, that experts who work in the field of criminal law are just as likely to get inadequate instruction as are their colleagues whose work is in the civil courts.

064 It cannot be stressed too highly that inadequate instructions lead to inadequate reports. From the point of view of the expert there are I suggest only two solutions: to engage in a dialogue with the instructing solicitor and preferably also with counsel so that eventually the matters which are crucial become clear; to proceed with the investigation without finding out what line the defence are proposing to take and simply to establish those facts which are supported by the forensic evidence. This latter approach has the advantage that the expert will be carrying out his investigation with an open mind uncoloured by any knowledge of what defence counsel has in mind.

065 If the expert is instructed early enough there is merit in this approach especially with the new rules on disclosure (paras 069 *et seq.*) as under the new procedure the prosecution will only pass to the defence unused material which is seen by them to be relevant to the defence put forward by the accused and the report of the expert may well suggest possible defences.

Problems for the defence expert witness

066 The major problem for the defence expert witness is that he is normally so late on the scene. I have been instructed in arson cases where the building involved in the fire has been rebuilt before I was instructed. In these circumstances the defence expert is critically dependent upon the Scene Of Crime Officer (SOCO) who attended the fire and upon the reports of fire brigade investigating officers. This is true of course for the defence expert in crimes other than arson in which he will not even have the impartial view of the fire brigade to assist him. In the report of the research study carried out for the Royal Commission on Criminal Justice and published as "The Role of Forensic Science in Criminal Proceedings" (Research Study No 11, HMSO 1993, ISBN 0 11 341064 6) there are a few paragraphs which illustrate the problem of the defence expert.

067 Paragraph 2.3.:

> "In conjunction with the initial decision to use forensic evidence, the police, or more rarely the CPS, must decide what material of potential evidential value to collect, and, from this, which items to send to the laboratory. As with the initial decision to seek forensic evidence, this is a highly selective process. The police will usually have a suspect in mind before any items are sent to the laboratory, so that the forensic scientist is then called upon to confirm or deny the police hypothesis that the suspect is guilty of one or more offences."

and later

> "The obvious consequence of this approach is that the police tend to collect evidence which is thought likely to prove their initial hypothesis and incriminate the subject, rather than disprove that hypothesis by exculpating him or her. As defence solicitor K put it: 'The police have got their man, and they build the case from that.' Indeed, it is difficult to see how it could be otherwise since any investigation must adopt a goal-oriented approach, even if it were not constrained by the limits on resources which circumscribe the operations of the police. The point is not to criticise the police for what is an inevitable aspect of their role, but to recognise that at each stage of the pre-trial process forensic science is utilised by prosecution agencies as a tool for case construction. Its evidential products reflect these demands, rather than being the fruits of a disinterested scientific inquiry . . ."

068 Later still, commenting on the fact that now the Forensic Science Service is an agency and that the police have to pay for each item sent to a FSS laboratory, the study quoted a leading defence expert as saying to the inquiry team:

> "The police, now, because they are paying on the basis of items sent to the laboratory, will be very selective in what they send. In the past the forensic scientist has had the option to decide which items he wished to examine. He had more or less a free hand. In the future, we, the defence experts, are going to have to look at the list of exhibits in a lot of cases and say 'but that should have been examined, and that should have been examined. The police have obviously excluded these things, but we want to examine them.' "

(In passing it is as well to link this comment with the later discussion on the recent changes in the law governing the disclosure of unused evidence by the prosecution to the defence, for it is possible that it may not be possible, in every case, to be able to say "but that should have been examined".)

Assembly of evidence

The police investigation

069 On the prosecution side the Criminal Procedure and Investigations Act also produces changes. Section 23 requires the preparation of a code of practice for criminal investigations and this section is of such importance that it is set out in full below:

> "**s.23(1)** The Secretary of State shall prepare a code of practice containing provisions designed to secure—
>
> (a) that where a criminal investigation is conducted all reasonable steps are taken for the purposes of the investigation and, in particular, all reasonable lines of inquiry are pursued;
>
> (b) that information which is obtained in the course of a criminal investigation and may be relevant to the investigation is recorded;
>
> (c) that any record of such information is retained;
>
> (d) that any other material which is obtained in the course of a criminal investigation and may be relevant to the investigation is retained;
>
> (e) that information falling within paragraph (b) and material falling within paragraph (d) is revealed to a person who is involved in the prosecution of criminal proceedings arising out of or relating to the investigation and who is identified in accordance with prescribed provisions;
>
> (f) that where such a person inspects information or other material in pursuance of a requirement that it be revealed to him, and he requests that it be disclosed to the accused the accused is allowed to inspect it or is given a copy of it;
>
> (g) that where such a person is given a document indicating the nature of information or other material in pursuance of a requirement that it be revealed to him, and he requests that it be disclosed to the accused, the accused is allowed to inspect it or given a copy of it;
>
> (h) that the person who is to allow the accused to inspect information or other material or to give him a copy of it shall decide which of those (inspecting or giving a copy) is appropriate;
>
> (i) that where the accused is allowed to inspect material as mentioned in paragraph (f) or (g) and he requests a copy, he is given one unless the person allowing the inspection is of opinion that it is not practicable or not desirable to give him one;
>
> (j) that a person mentioned in paragraph (e) is given a written statement that prescribed activities which the code requires have been carried out."

070 There are also provisions in section 23(5) and section 24 to allow certain classes of information to be withheld from the accused.

071 The provisions of the code will be brought into effect after the Secretary of State has considered representations made to him about the draft code and has laid the final version of the code before Parliament. He then brings the code into effect by designating an "appointed day". The code will only apply to suspected or alleged offences for which "no criminal investigation has begun before the day so appointed" (section 25(3)). The code was in fact brought into operation on 1 April 1997 (Code: HMSO ISBN 0 11 341163 4).

072 It is almost impossible to predict the effect the Act and the code will have upon the workings of the criminal justice system and in particular upon the work of expert witnesses in criminal cases. Because the code is just that, a code, and does not have the force of law, any breach of the code cannot result in criminal or civil action and although a breach of the code is admissible in evidence it will be for the court to decide what effect the breach of the code has on the matter before the court.

073 From the point of view of the expert witness whether employed by the Forensic Science Service or as an independent forensic consultant called in by the police the effects of the code are indirect. Section 22 defines a criminal investigation as "an investigation conducted by police officers" and so it is their responsibility to treat the information produced by the expert witness in accordance with the code.

074 The interesting question is the effect of section 23(1)(a) which requires that in an investigation "all reasonable lines of inquiry are pursued". This is reinforced by paragraph 3.4 of the code: "In conducting an investigation, the investigator should pursue all reasonable lines of inquiry, whether these point towards or away from the suspect. What is reasonable in each case will depend upon the particular circumstances."

075 Now in many cases information and evidence about possible "reasonable lines of inquiry" are produced by a SOCO or a forensic scientist. How should (or could) such a person act if it becomes clear that the evidence he has found is being ignored as it does not fit the case which the investigating officer has in mind?

076 Paragraph 3.5 of the code rules that:

> "**3.5.** If the officer in charge of an investigation believes that other persons may be in possession of material that may be relevant to the investigation, and if this has not been obtained under paragraph 3.4. above, he should ask the disclosure officer to inform them of the existence of the investigation and to invite them to retain the material in case they receive a request for its disclosure. The disclosure officer should inform the prosecutor that they may have such material. However the officer in charge of an investigation is not required to make speculative inquiries of other persons: there must be some reason to believe that they may have relevant material. That reason may come from information provided to thé police by the accused or from other inquiries made or from some other source."

077 The practical effects of this paragraph are not yet apparent but the possibility certainly seems to exist for the defence to use it to point the investigator towards material which they need for their case and defence expert witnesses need to keep the paragraph in mind.

078 The requirements in section 23(1)(a) and (b) as to the recording and retention of information should be normal practice for any expert witness and indeed the "Additional Guidelines for Forensic Scientists" of The Academy have specific requirements as to the length of time for which materials have to be retained.

Pre trial—the preparation of material for the prosecution

079 As the investigation progresses the code lays down how material collected in the course of the investigation is to be dealt with. Decisions have to be taken as to which material is relevant to the investigation and so has to be disclosed and which material, if any, is "sensitive" and so can be withheld from the defence. These are decisions which are not always easy to make and so the code provides for the asking for and receiving of advice:

> "**6.1.** The officer in charge of the investigation, the disclosure officer or an investigator may seek advice from the prosecutor about whether any particular item of material may be relevant to the investigation."

080 The parallel routes to the prosecutor for this advice may in practice be a cause of tension between officer in charge, disclosure officer and investigators.

THE SCHEDULES

081 The method by which disclosable material and sensitive material is identified to the prosecutor and to the défence is by way of schedules of evidence. These are prepared for all trials upon indictment and for summary trials where it seems likely that the accused will plead not guilty. The code calls for three schedules to be produced:

(1) A schedule of material which is not going to be used by the prosecution

> "**6.2.** Material which may be relevant to an investigation, and which has been retained in accordance with this code, and which the disclosure officer believes will not form part of the prosecution case, must be listed on a schedule."

(2) A schedule of non-sensitive material. Sensitive material is any material which the disclosure officer believes it is not in the public interest to disclose.
(3) A schedule of sensitive material.

The process of keeping the defence informed of what evidence is to be used and what is not to be used by the prosecution is now done largly by pro forma letters produced by the CPS and sent to the solicitors to the defendant. A typical set from a case of arson with intent to endanger life is in Appendix 6 of this chapter. These procedures are in a way the criminal law counterparts of the changes brought about by the 1999 changes to civil procedure.

WHAT IS "SENSITIVE MATERIAL"?

082 Sensitive material is material which the disclosure officer believes that it is "not in the public interest to disclose" and paragraph 6.8 give examples of typical sensitive material:

> "**6.8.** Depending upon the circumstances, examples of such material may include the following among others:
> - material relating to national security;
> - material received from the intelligence and security agencies;
> - material relating to intelligence from foreign sources which reveals sensitive intelligence gathering methods;
> - material given in confidence;
> - material which relates to the use of a telephone system and which is supplied to the investigator for intelligence purposes only;
> - material relating to the identity or activities of informants or undercover police officers;
> - material revealing the location of premises—used for police surveillance or the identity of any person allowing a police officer to use them for surveillance;
> - material revealing . . . techniques and methods relied upon by a police officer in the course of a criminal investigation;
> - material whose disclosure might facilitate the commission of other offences or hinder the prevention and detection of crime;
> - internal police communications such as management minutes;
> - material upon the strength of which search warrants were obtained;
> - material containing details of persons taking part in identification parades;
> - material supplied to an investigator during a criminal investigation which has been generated by . . . a body concerned with the regulation . . . of bodies corporate or of persons engaged in financial activities;
> - material . . . which relates to a child or young person and which has been generated by a local authority social services department; . . ."

083 Now this is a formidable list which covers all of the concerns expressed by investigators after the 1981 Guidelines for the disclosure of unused material that the disclosure rule gave too much scope to the defence, a matter which is discussed later.

084 Equally, it is doubtful how much of this is consistent with the European Convention on Human Rights, again a matter discussed later. Some of the exclusions such as those relating to social services' reports in cases relating to children are probably sensible but the identity of an informant may well be central to the defence case if the defence is that the information given to the police was false and malicious. The category "material relating to national security" has to be considered in the light of the words of Sir Humphrey in "Yes Prime Minister"—"you have to remember, Prime Minister, that the purpose of the Official Secrets Act is not to protect secrets but to protect officials".

THE LAYOUT AND CONTENTS OF THE SCHEDULES

085 The various items of material have to be listed as separate items and numbered consecutively. Each item has to be described in sufficient detail "to enable the prosecutor to decide whether he needs to inspect the material before deciding whether or not it should be disclosed".

INFORMATION FROM THE DISCLOSURE OFFICER TO PROSECUTOR

086 The disclosure officer sends the schedules to the prosecutor normally at the same time as he sends the file with the prosecution case and, in addition, must send the prosecutor further information outlined in paragraph 7.3 of the code:

- records of the first description of a suspect given to the police by a potential witness, whether or not the description differs from that of the alleged offender;
- information provided by an accused person which indicates an explanation for the offence for which he has been charged;
- any material casting doubt on the reliability of a confession;
- any material casting doubt on the reliability of a witness;
- any other material which the investigator believes may fall within the test for primary disclosure.

087 Some of these requirements would have gone a long way towards preventing a number of miscarriages of justice which have had to be put right later by the Court of Appeal especially a batch of cases in which witness statements indicated that the person convicted of the offence bore no resemblance to the description as provided by the witnesses.

The defence expert

088 Obviously in most cases the defence expert will have little or no chance of looking for evidence because he is called in so late in the day. However, it is always possible that an expert called in to investigate matters in, for example, an insurance claim may, during his investigation, discover evidence that a crime might have been committed. On a number of occasions I have investigated apparently accidental fire on behalf of insurers and found evidence during my examination of the scene of the fire which indicated that the fire was suspicious or in other words that the cause was probably a deliberate ignition. Obviously, at this point the police have to be informed as it is for them to investigate crime.

089 The discovery of evidence suggesting that a crime has been committed brings with it problems for the expert. Firstly, should he report his discovery direct to the police or pass the information to those who gave him instructions and leave it to them to notify the police? It may well be that they do not wish the police to be involved—does that relieve the expert of his duty in law to inform the police if he is aware that a crime might have been committed? In my view not—there can be nothing in any code of conduct or any expression of my duty to a client which can override my duty as a citizen to report to the police any evidence which I have which suggests that a crime has been committed.

090 The second and much easier problem is that the rules for dealing with evidence in criminal cases are stringent. Previously, mention has been made of the "chain of evidence". This means that an exhibit to be produced at a criminal trial must be accompanied by a written record which proves that it has been in the custody of a named person from the moment it was picked up at a crime scene to the moment it is produced in court as an exhibit.

091 Practice in civil cases is much more relaxed and therein lies the problem if the fact that the incident being investigated was a crime did not become apparent until some time into the investigation. My own solution to the problem is to adopt criminal investigation standards to the handling of all items of evidence which I collect at scenes of incidents whether the purpose of the investigation is a civil action or not. This is to some extent "overkill" but the discipline of placing each item found in an evidence bag, sealing the bag and tagging it with an evidence label means that if the case turns out to have been a crime then my procedures are appropriate while if it eventually remains a civil matter there is no possibility of any problems in court or in "Rule 38" (now Rule 32.11 of the Civil Procedure Rules) meetings as the provenance of every item has been carefully and systematically logged. A specimen evidence label is illustrated in Appendix 3 to this chapter and it is important to remember that if, at any time, the item of evidence leaves your possession then the person who takes control of it must sign the label and there is provision on the back of the evidence label in Appendix 3 for this record to be made.

Disclosure in the criminal trial

092 The most striking difference between the processes in criminal cases and the comparable processes in civil cases is that the criminal justice system is very much more adversarial than are the civil courts. There is for example no criminal equivalent to a civil "Rule 38" meeting in which the experts meet pre-trial without lawyers present with a brief "to identify those parts of their evidence which are at issue" and, as we shall see later, recent changes in the rules for the disclosure of evidence to the defence by the prosecution take criminal procedure even further away from the norms of the civil courts as regards discovery. The House of Lords Committee came something close to a "Rule 38" meeting in recommending at paragraph 5.20 that there should be a "pre-trial review":

> "**5.20** . . . where scientific evidence is in dispute, the two sides' experts should be brought together in a 'pre-trial review', in the presence of trial counsel and supervised by the trial judge, to seek to resolve the disagreement, or at least to define it as narrowly as possible, in terms to which they will be bound at the trial."

Unfortunately, in my view, this recommendation has never been acted upon.

093 Insofar as the work and crucially the responsibility of the expert witness is concerned the more adversarial nature of the process must not be allowed to affect the work or the thinking of the expert witness. If you take the not unreasonable view that your client is the person or organisation who is paying you to carry out your role then in almost all criminal trials the two expert witnesses, defence and prosecution, have the same client for both are paid by the taxpayers. The prosecution expert witness normally (but not always) works for the Forensic Science Service (an agency under the Home Office which recoups its costs from the police forces which use its services) and the other, the defence expert witness is paid by criminal legal aid. There is always, however, a temptation for one or both of them to see themselves as a part of a team. This belief that the expert is "a part of the team" or, as it has been put, the "hired gun" has led in the past to grave miscarriages of justice and has constantly to be guarded against lest similar miscarriages happen in the future.

In summary proceedings

094 Although it is less usual for an expert to appear at a court of summary jurisdiction than at the higher level courts there are, nonetheless, occasions when expert evidence is necessary at a summary trial. The magistrates have the power to require that the expert evidence is disclosed in advance of the hearing. This power is given to them under the Criminal Procedure and Investigations Act 1996 in which a part of section 20 states:

> "**s.20**(3) Without prejudice to the generality of section 144(1) of the Magistrates' Courts Act 1980 the power to make rules under that section includes the power to make, with regard to any proceedings before a magistrates' court which relate to an alleged offence, provision for—
> (a) requiring any party to the proceedings to disclose to the other party any expert evidence which he proposes to adduce in the proceedings;
> (b) prohibiting a party who fails to comply in respect of any evidence with any requirement imposed by virtue of paragraph (a) from adducing that evidence without the leave of the court.
> (4) Rules made by virtue of subsection (3)
> (a) may specify the kinds of expert evidence to which they apply;
> (b) may exempt facts or matters of any description specified in the rules."

095 It should be noted that the prosecution does not, in law, have to disclose its case to the defendant in advance of the trial (*R* v. *Kingston upon Hull Magistrates ex parte McCann* (1991) 155 JP 569):

> "I am clear that there is no general obligation on a prosecutor to disclose such statements in advance of a summary trial. There may be cases where fairness requires such a disclosure; I say nothing about that one way or another. The fact that many prosecutors chose in a high proportion of cases to give advance disclosure of statements in summary cases is not the point."

At committal hearings

096 Originally the committal hearing was an opportunity for the defendant to have set out before him the case of the prosecution, and hear the evidence of the prosecution witnesses and for his lawyers to cross-examine those as the case had to be presented to the magistrates so that they could decide, at the committal hearing whether there was a case to answer.

097 The Magistrates' Courts Act 1980 allowed the committal hearing to proceed without hearing the evidence of the prosecution witnesses but by considering their written witness statements. Very few defendants contested the committal but the defendant still had access to all of the evidence to be presented by the prosecution including the physical evidence and the statements of the witnesses which they would call at the subsequent Crown Court hearing.

098 The Criminal Procedure and Investigations Act 1996 abolished the right to have prosecution witnesses cross-examined at committal and made the committal hearing a matter wholly of the consideration of witness statements.

In trials on indictment

099 The most contentious part of criminal proceedings since the Criminal Procedure and Investigations Act 1996 is the extent to which the Act requires the defence to inform the court and the prosecution of the defence upon which they will rely at the trial, and also the extent to which it is left to the prosecution to make the decision as to what material in the possession of the prosecution and which would be helpful to the defence, the prosecution should in fact supply.

100 In paras 004 *et seq. supra*, I referred briefly to the series of miscarriages of justice which had caused the House of Lords Committee to carry out their inquiry and to produce their report. In 1981 the Attorney-General issued *Guidelines for the disclosure of "unused" material to defence in cases to be tried by indictment.* "Unused material" was defined in these guidelines as—witness statements and documents referred to in such statements not already served on the defence in the committal bundle and the unedited versions of statements which the defence had already had in their edited form. Later in *R* v. *Saunders* (unreported) the trial judge ruled that this list extended to cover any relevant material not already disclosed.

101 The guidelines provided safeguards so that some classes of information need not be disclosed especially where the information could lead to the intimidation of witnesses. For "sensitive" material the guidelines state that "A balance must be struck between the degree of sensitivity and the extent to which the information might help the defence—any doubt should always be in favour of disclosure."

102 Later case law extended these guidelines. In the appeal of the *Maguire Seven* the court, in its judgment said: ". . . a prosecution scientist must disclose anything relevant to the case to the prosecutor, who must disclose it to the defence. If the scientist keeps anything back, a subsequent conviction may be declared unsafe, even though the prosecutor himself was not at fault."

103 Later still, in the *Judith Ward* appeal, the court widened this responsibility still further:

> "The prosecutor must make 'full and proper inquiries from forensic scientists in order to ascertain whether there is any disclosable material' and the prosecutor must offer material to the defence without waiting for the defence to ask for it. This duty of disclosure operates all the time until the trial is over. If the prosecutor forms the view that it would not be in the public interest to disclose then he has to claim public interest immunity and the defence are to be informed. The matter is then decided by the court (with the jury out) and if the prosecutor does not wish to defend his claim he has to abandon the prosecution."

104 The guidelines, especially as extended by the *Maguire* and the *Ward* rulings caused problems to prosecutors. There were claims that in some cases the defence were making demands for very large volumes of documents as a strategy to put pressure on the prosecution to abandon the case. There were also fears expressed that the disclosure rules might put informers' lives at risk; even though the guidelines made it possible for such information to be withheld there was a fear that through what could properly be required to be disclosed the informer could be identified. These and other pressures caused the government to introduce, through Acts of Parliament, major changes to the way in which criminal investigations and trials are conducted and to make substantial changes to the requirements for disclosure both as regards the prosecution and, critically, as regards the defendant.

105 The changes produce problems for both defence and prosecution expert witnesses and the matter is complicated by the fact that the procedures for the early, committal, stages of the criminal justice process are in the middle of major change and, with these changes, come concomitant changes to the extent to which the prosecution has to disclose materials to the defence. It is not possible to cover in detail the law relating to disclosure in its totality, nor would such a course be sensible, given that the field has already been covered in detail by others (Corker, David *Disclosure in Criminal Proceedings*, Sweet & Maxwell, London 1996 ISBN 0 421 568 100).

PRE-TRIAL—THE PROSECUTION "PRIMARY DISCLOSURE"

106 Section 3(a)(1) of CPIA requires the prosecutor to disclose to the defence all material in his possession which might undermine the prosecution case.

107 Most of the physical evidence and many of the statements are actually in the possession and control of not the prosecutor but the investigator, and obviously to comply with CPIA and the code under it will require a very close liaison between prosecutor and investigator. In practice most of the work is done by a "Disclosure Officer" a role defined in the code of practice as: "the person responsible for examining the records created during the investigation, revealing material to the prosecutor during the investigation and any criminal proceedings resulting from it, disclosing it to the accused, and certifying where necessary that action has been taken in accordance with the requirements of this code".

PRE-TRIAL—THE DEFENCE STATEMENT

108 The major provision of CPIA which extends the law as it relates to the accused is in section 5 which requires the accused to provide a "defence statement". This statement is required to be given after the accused has been served with the indictment and a copy of the set of documents containing the evidence which is the basis of the charge (s.5(4)):

> "**s.5**(5) Where this section applies the accused must give a defence statement to the court and to the prosecutor
> (6) . . . a defence statement is a written statement—
> (a) setting out in general terms the nature of the accused's defence,
> (b) indicating the matters on which he takes issue with the prosecution, and
> (c) setting out, in the case of each such matter, the reason why he takes issue with the prosecution.
> (7) If the defence statement discloses an alibi the accused must give particulars of the alibi in the statement, including—
> (a) the name and address of any witness the accused believes is able to give evidence in support of the alibi, if the name and address are known to the accused when the statement is given;
> (b) any information in the accused's possession which might be of material assistance in finding such a witness, if the name or address is not known to the accused when the statement is given."

PRE-TRIAL—THE PROSECUTION'S "SECONDARY DISCLOSURE"

109 Section 7(2) of CPIA requires the prosecutor, having received the defence statement to carry out a second round of disclosure of material in his possession:

> "**s.7**(2) The prosecutor must—
> (a) disclose to the accused any prosecution material which has not previously been disclosed to the accused and which might reasonably be expected to assist the accused's defence as disclosed by the defence statement . . . or
> (b) give to the accused a written statement that there is no material of a description mentioned in paragraph (a)."

110 The most controversial aspect in the changes in the law brought in by CPIA are these requirements relating to the disclosure of "unused material". In the course of the investigation the prosecution will have amassed a large quantity of material which is, in their opinion, not relevant to the case which they intend to put before the court. Some of this will include statements and some items of evidential value taken from the scene for forensic examination. The *Ward* case, outlined in paras 014–015 above, resulted in the House of Lords laying down in the clearest possible terms the duty of the prosecution to disclose: "A duty exists irrespective of any request by the defence . . . it is a positive duty, which in the context of scientific evidence obliges the prosecution to make full and proper inquiries from forensic scientists in order to ascertain whether there is disclosable material" (Glidewell LJ).

111 Again in the *Maguire* case we have: "A forensic scientist who is an adviser to the prosecuting authority is under a duty to disclose material of which he knows and which may have 'some bearing on the offence charged and the surrounding circumstances of the case'" (Stuart-Smith LJ).

112 He went on to say that such disclosure was desirable because it would help to ameliorate: "the disparity of scientific resources as between the Crown and the subject".

113 CPIA stemmed from the Royal Commission on Criminal Justice (1993) which set out the argument that:

> "The defence can require the police and prosecution to comb through large masses of material in the hope either of causing delay or of chancing upon something which will induce the prosecution to drop the case, rather than have to disclose the material concerned. The defence may do this by successive requests for more material, far beyond the stage at which it could reasonably be claimed that the information was likely to cast a doubt upon the prosecution case. Although it may be time consuming and wasteful of the resources for the police to check all the materials requested, they may have to do so if they are to be sure that it can properly be released."

114 From the point of view of the expert witness for the defence it seems to me that it will be essential for the expert to have instruction as early as is possible in the case because the framing of the defence statement is obviously critical in "flushing out" unused material which might be relevant to a defence which an expert could see reviewing the version of events as given to him by the accused, and considering the material disclosed in the primary disclosure by the prosecution. If however this additional defence is not included in the defence statement then any material which might support it will not be disclosed.

PRE-TRIAL—EXPERTS' REPORTS

115 The prosecution has to disclose to the defendant the case he is to face including the reports of any expert witnesses to be called. This duty is a statutory duty and applies both to the prosecution and to the defence. The statutory duties are set out in a statutory instrument—the Crown Court (Advance Notice of Expert Evidence) Rules 1987 (SI 1987 No 716):

> "[1 and 2 are citation and date of coming into effect.]
>
> **3.**(1) Following the committal for trial of any person . . . if any party to the proceedings proposes to adduce expert evidence (whether of fact or opinion) in the proceedings (otherwise than in relation to sentence) he shall as soon as practicable—
>
> (a) furnish the other party with a statement in writing of any findings or opinion which he proposes to adduce by way of such evidence; and
>
> (b) where a request in writing is made to him in that behalf by any other party, provide that party also with a copy of it (or if it appears to the party proposing to adduce the evidence to be more practicable, a reasonable opportunity to examine) the record of any observation, test, calculation or other procedure on which such finding or opinion is based and any

document or other thing or substance in respect of which such procedure has been carried out.

(2) A party may by notice in writing waive his right to be furnished with any of the matters mentioned in paragraph (1) above and, in particular, may agree that the statement mentioned in subparagraph (a) thereof may be furnished to him orally and not in writing.

(3) In paragraph (1) above, "document" has the same meaning as in Part 1 of the Civil Evidence Act 1968.

4.(1) If a party has reasonable grounds for believing that disclosure of any evidence in compliance with rule 3 above might lead to intimidation or attempted intimidation, of any person on whose evidence he intends to rely in the proceedings, or otherwise to the course of justice being interfered with, he shall not be obliged to comply with those requirements in relation to that evidence.

(2) Where, in accordance with paragraph (1) above, a party considers he is not obliged to comply with the requirements imposed by rule 3 above with regard to any evidence in relation to any other party, he shall give notice in writing to that party to the effect that the evidence is being withheld and the grounds therefor.

5. A party who seeks to adduce expert evidence in any proceedings and who fails to comply with rule 3 above shall not adduce that evidence in those proceedings without leave of the court."

The European Convention on Human Rights

116 The government has announced its intention to incorporate the European Convention on Human Rights into UK law and indeed the Convention is already binding as the government signed the Convention in 1953 and all UK legislation has to conform to the decisions made by the European Court of Human Rights. It seems very likely, to put it no higher, that CPIA will not conform to the Convention and to decisions already made by the European Court of Human Rights and if this be so then the Act will have to be amended.

The Scottish system

117 Expert witnesses whose experience has been wholly within the criminal justice system of England and Wales will find themselves in what is to them uncharted waters if asked to take on a case in Scotland. Scots law is different and Scottish courts and procedures are different, and taking on a Scottish case needs care and preparation.

118 Before the Act of Union in 1707 Scots law had developed from two roots: Scots customary (or common law) and Roman Dutch law. Roman Dutch law was not imported in total but was looked to by Scottish judges when they found lacunae in Scots customary law. This gave Scots law a very different base from the law as it developed in England and Wales and these differences are still very marked even now nearly 300 years after the Act of Union and extend throughout the system in both civil and criminal law and procedure. The influence of Roman Dutch law can be found in the great similarities between Scottish law and South African law.

The Scottish courts

119 The bottom tier of courts are the Local Sheriff courts in the principal market towns, which try minor offences and which are administered by the local authorities with lay justices on the bench (there are stipendary magistrates in Glasgow).

120 Above these are the Sheriff courts which can try cases either summarily or upon indictment. There are six sheriffdoms in Scotland with a Sheriff Principal in charge, each sheriffdom being subdivided into a series of District Sheriff courts. When hearing the more serious cases brought upon indictment the sheriff sits with a jury of 15 but sits alone to hear the lesser offences charged summarily.

121 The High Court of Justiciary is the supreme criminal court, a court which consists of the judges of the Court of Session sitting as Lords Commissioners of Justiciary which tries cases on indictment with a jury and also acts as the appellate court from the lower courts. At first instance a judge sits with a jury of 15. As an appellate court three or more judges decide the appeal. There is no further appeal to the House of Lords in criminal cases.

Precognition

122 Precognition is a process unknown in English law. All witnesses whom it is proposed should be led in evidence (what would in an English court be called "produced") can be interviewed in private before the trial. Normally the interview is conducted by the Procurator Fiscal (PF) and a written record of the interview kept (this document is also called a "precognition"). During the interview the PF may well ask the prospective witness about any documents or exhibits which the witness will be producing at the trial (in Scots terminology these are "Productions").

123 The interview is not normally conducted under oath and what is said is confidential between witness and interviewer, and by and large, is not normally referred to at the trial. (The phrase "by and large" is there to allow for a gradual change in procedure—to quote a Scottish solicitor: ". . . daily in the courts now we are finding that it is quite commonplace to refer to precognitions at the subsequent trial particularly where there is an element of 'prevarication' or loss of memory of the witness.")

124 However if a prospective witness fails to attend the precognition interview or having attended refuses to answer the questions of the interviewer then he may be arrested and the precognition carried out under oath in front of the sheriff. In these circumstances if the witness then gives evidence at the trial which differs from his precognition then the precognition may be referred to at the trial and the witness is liable to be punished.

125 Precognition is a process open to both sides. The PF will precognose the witness produced by the police as a result of their investigation and can also precognose the defence witnesses as the defence has to inform the PF of the names and addresses of its witnesses before the trial. Equally the defence solicitor will be supplied with the names and addresses of the prosecution witnesses by the PF and can carry out the precognition interviews on them. Precognition is a procedure which can be used for trials at any level but is normally only used for witnesses in trials by indictment and is also used in civil trials.

126 As an expert witness is no different from a witness of fact experts need to be aware that they may well have to go through a precognition interview (and possibly two such interviews).

127 The precognition interviews carried out by the PF form an important part of the information which he will take into account in making the decision as to whether the case is strong enough to send for trial and also is of great assistance in his role as prosecutor in shaping his examination in chief.

The prosecution process

128 Fundamental to the Scottish system is a complete separation of the investigation of crime and the decision to prosecute. The decision to prosecute is taken under the direction of the Lord Advocate and indictments are headed "*HMA* v." rather than "*R* v.".

129 The Crown Office in Edinburgh acts on behalf of the Lord Advocate and makes the decision to prosecute and conducts the prosecution in the High Court of Justiciary with either an advocate-depute or a solicitor advocate from the staff of the Crown Office as prosecutor. The Crown Office is also responsible for the Procurator Fiscal Service which is headed by a civil servant, the Crown Agent (who is legally qualified).

THE PROCURATOR FISCAL

130 The Procurator Fiscal (often referred to in conversation as "the PF") is a full-time, legally-qualified, civil servant. The PF is responsible for investigating a crime which is committed within his district, for making the decision to institute proceedings and for acting as prosecutor when the case comes to court. The PF also acts in a similar fashion to a coroner in England and Wales in that he will inquire into sudden and/or suspicious deaths by holding Fatal Accident Inquiries.

131 It should be noted that a Fatal Accident Inquiry is also held to inquire into the death of a person engaged in any industrial employment or occupation where the death is due to an accident occurring in the course of employment.

CLASSES OF OFFENCES

132 The major difference between Scottish practice and that in England and Wales is that a trial upon indictment is referred to as "solemn procedure" and is held before either a judge of the High Court of Justiciary or a sheriff.

133 A summary trial is held without a jury before either a sheriff, magistrate or justice of the peace and is based upon a "complaint".

Procedure—serious crime—solemn procedure

PETITION BY THE PROCURATOR FISCAL (PF)

134 The PF, having received and considered information about a crime which has been committed, presents a petition to a sheriff. The petition:

1. Names the accused.
2. States the charge(s).
3. Requests warrants to:
   - 3.1. Arrest the accused.
   - 3.2. Search the accused and any premises he owns or occupies.
4. Cites the witnesses in the case.

ARREST AND INTERVIEW—THE FIRST EXAMINATION

135 The post-arrest procedures are very similar to those in England and Wales although section 66 of the Police and Criminal Evidence Act 1984 relating to the PACE codes only applies in England and Wales. However, the basic rights and procedures are in essence similar with the right of the accused to have an interview with a solicitor. As soon as possible after arrest the accused has to be brought before a sheriff for examination. This is a brief, formal, appearance which is held in private. The charge is read to the accused who does not normally, at this stage, enter a plea. However, if he does make a plea the plea is taken down in writing and the copy signed by the accused and by the sheriff. After the First Examination the accused can be committed to prison to await the next stage of the process; be committed for trial; or released on bail.

THE JUDICIAL EXAMINATION

136 If the PF thinks that it is appropriate he can bring the accused to court for a "Judicial Examination". The questions from the PF will be aimed at finding out if the accused has any explanation of his involvement in the matters which are the subject of the charge. The accused in not on oath and does not have to answer questions (a right which is explained to him at the beginning of proceedings) and can have his solicitor with him and can consult during the proceedings. The transcript of the Judicial Examination can be used at the subsequent trial.

THE INDICTMENT

137 The PF now has sufficient evidence amassed to be able to send the case to the Crown Office who prepare an indictment. The indictment is, as stated earlier, in the name of the Lord Advocate or "Her Majesty's Advocate" (HMA). The indictment differs in some respects from the indictments in England and Wales and sets out not only the charges but lists the witnesses who will be called and also lists the documents and exhibits which will be produced in evidence at the trial (these are the "Productions"). The accused cannot be held in custody for more than 80 days without being served with an indictment being served upon him and if this time limit is exceeded the accused must be released from custody.

138 The accused now has a definitive statement of the case which the Crown will be putting and will need to prepare his defence. To do this he may need access to documents in the possession of others and he can apply to the court for powers to get access to them *via* a "commission and diligence". A diligence is a decree of the court which, in this case requires the accused to be given access to the documents he needs.

THE 110-DAY RULE

139 Scottish law sets fixed time limits for the trial process and the most important of these is the "110-day rule". In para 134 above the process whereby the PF asks a sheriff for a "petition" was outlined. The petition results in the arrest of the accused. Scottish law is that after this arrest the accused cannot be held in custody for more than 110 days without being brought to trial. These strict time limits, the 80-day and the 110-day rules have implications for expert witnesses for it can result in pressure to complete investigations and to prepare and deliver reports to time.

140 Even if the accused is not in custody but on bail a trial upon indictment must start no more than a year from the arrest on petition.

THE PRELIMINARY DIET

141 The preliminary diet used to be a formal appearance by the accused but is now carried out by the presentation of arguments to the court by the accused. The arguments will be making one or both of two main groups of submissions: matters of law; matters which make the trial impossible.

142 The first group, the matters of law cover such submissions as that the charge is not good in law. The submissions concerning the trial would include the submissions that the accused is insane and unable to plead.

143 At the preliminary diet the accused must put forward any "special defences" upon which he is going to rely at the main trial such as, again, insanity, or that the crime was committed not by the accused but by another person whom he names in his special defence, or "alibi"—that he was elsewhere when the crime was alleged to have been committed.

THE TRIAL DIET

144 This is the trial proper held before a jury of 15. The accused is now called "the panel". The major difference between trial procedure in Scotland and that in England and Wales is that in the Scottish courts there are no opening speeches from counsel and after the charges have been read to the jury counsel for the Crown calls his first witness. Examination in chief, cross-examination and re-examination all follow the procedures in the courts of England and Wales.

145 Perhaps the most significant difference in procedure is not in the way in which witnesses are examined and cross-examined but in the way in which Scots law requires that all material evidence is corroborated. That is to say that every material fact produced in evidence at the trial must be supported either by the independent evidence of another witness or that the corroboration can be inferred from other facts before the court. This has the important consequence that it is not possible to convict solely upon the confession of the accused but the Crown must produce some corroborative evidence which supports the confession. This corroboration may be quite slim—in one case a confession by a young man that he had drowned a small boy in a stream, and in which there was no other evidence at all, was held to be corroborated by the fact that the bottoms of the young man's trousers were wet when he was arrested.

146 The corroboration rule applies equally to the evidence of an expert witness, and two doctors must perform a post-mortem. To quote from *The Courts and the Doctor* (D J Gee and J K Mason, Oxford University Press, 1990, ISBN 0 19 261967 5):

> "Corroboration is of fact, not necessarily of opinion but . . . the two doctors cannot normally appear on opposing sides—the defence must produce their own experts. Even so, the fact that two doctors, who may not listen to each other's evidence, can be examined and cross-examined, does a great deal to modify the concept of the 'expert witness' as opposed to that of the expert who gives evidence."

147 It should be noted that it is not essential for the expert who is corroborating the work of a fellow expert necessarily to appear in court although he may of course have to do so.

148 The jury can give a majority verdict and eight to seven is acceptable. The verdicts, as well as the "guilty" and "not guilty" can also include "not proven". After a "not guilty" or "not proven" verdict "the panel" is "assoilzied" (see para 151).

DISCLOSURE

149 The position as regards the disclosure to the defence by the prosecution of material useful to the defence discussed above in paras 069 *et seq.* (which applies to England and Wales) does not apply to Scotland. In Scotland after the process of precognition and the making of the productions (exhibits) to be produced at the trial available for inspection by the defence the prosecution has no duty to make any further disclosures to the defence. The relevant law is contained in the Prisoners and Criminal Proceedings (Scotland) Act 1992. The position as regards disclosure in Scotland was set out by the then Lord Advocate, Lord Rodger of Earlsferry in the debate on the Bill when he said:

> "The position in Scotland at present is that there is no legal duty to disclose information to the defence. However what matters is not the legal position but what the Crown sees as its duty in practice, whatever the law may provide. The overriding principle is that the Crown must always act in the interests of justice. As part of that general approach, all members of the Procurator Fiscal service are reminded that they must disclose to the defence any information which supports the defence case even though it may be damaging to the Crown case. They are also instructed that they

should provide assistance to the defence if it is necessary to enable a defence witness to be traced, the overall aim should be to try to ensure that the true facts of any case are laid before the judge or jury."

150 Nothing there to quarrel with or to raise any worries except to comment that our colleagues in the United States could not and would not accept the concept that "what matters is not the legal position but what the Crown sees as its duty in practice . . ." and that as in paras 069 *et seq.* above the effects of the European Convention on Human Rights have yet to be felt.

Differences in nomenclature

151 Scottish legal terms are very different from those in use in England and Wales.

Assoilzied—found not guilty and discharged.
Complaint—the initiating document issued by the PF in a summary criminal case.
Diet—a stage in the criminal trial process.
Petition—a document produced by the PF to a sheriff asking for an arrest warrant.
Production—an exhibit.

Note 1—When it is not possible to produce something at the Bar of the Court, e.g. a motor car, then a "label" is lodged in the productions *in lieu* and the judge, jury and parties and lawyers often adjourn to view it outside or elsewhere.

Note 2—It is not uncommon for expert witnesses to have to give or to repeat their evidence elsewhere than in court, e.g. if the court adjourns to examine premises or a car, perhaps burnt out, where the flavour of the expert testimony can be better demonstrated. The lawyers and the court will still, however, "lead" the evidence.

Tholed an assize—has already been tried in relation to the matters charged—*autrefois acquit* or *autrefois convict.*

***P A D Sheen**, an Electrical Engineer and a Fire Engineer, runs a forensic engineering consultancy which covers both civil and criminal cases. On the civil side, personal injury cases (especially electric shock), fire investigations for loss adjusters and insurers and the investigation of suspect insurance claims are the major fields. On the criminal side his work is about evenly divided between being expert witness for the defence and for the prosecution. Cases are mostly in the fields of murder (eight murders to date), manslaughter and arson.*

APPENDIX 1

Academy of Experts

Additional guidelines for forensic scientists

1. The Guidelines apply where members of the Academy are approached to do work or provide an expert opinion in any matter which could lead to court proceedings.
2. It is the overriding duty of members to act at all times with integrity fairness and impartiality. All of the rules which follow should be interpreted in the light of this overriding duty.
3. Members must satisfy themselves at all times that they have the competence and expertise to do the work or to give the opinion sought. This duty involves ensuring that such competence and expertise is up to date with relevant current standards and knowledge. This is not just a personal duty. Members of a firm or partnership must satisfy themselves about these matters with respect to any partner, associate or employee who is asked to give an opinion.
4. Members must ensure that they have all the information necessary to do the work or to give an opinion.
5. Members must ensure that they have access to such facilities or equipment as may be necessary to do the work or to give the opinion. If they have not then it is their duty to decline to act.
6. Where members carry out tests or any form of investigatory work, whether in a laboratory or otherwise, they must ensure that the results of all tests are fully, contemporaneously and accurately recorded and are in such a form that the contents can be reviewed for reliability and accuracy by another expert in the same speciality. In all cases, the relevant protocol used must be identified.
7. All records must include the results of all tests or investigatory work whether or not:
   (a) they were relied upon in doing the work or giving the opinion;
   (b) they were carried out or performed personally, or by someone else.
8. All records must be retained in safe custody for such period as is specifically required by a court, tribunal or the client. In any event, the following are the minimum periods for retention. Where the work or opinion relates to:
   (a) Cases involving homicide, riot, Official Secrets Acts, treason, and other offences against the State, terrorist offences, class 1 offenders involving serious criminal cases, kidnapping and all cases in which a sentence of life imprisonment has been imposed; 20 years.
   (b) Other cases tried and indictment; 10 years.
   (c) All cases tried summarily; 1 year.
   (d) All other cases; 1 year.

   The times referred to above date from the time when the case was finally disposed of by a court or tribunal.
9. Members may give an opinion based on tests or other work carried out by others subject to the following:
   (a) they must be satisfied of the competence and expertise of the person concerned to carry out tests or work required;
   (b) they must have identified specifically to the person concerned the nature of the tests or work to be undertaken and where appropriate the protocol to be used;
   (c) the whole process must have been effected under their real and effective supervision so that they can vouch for the propriety of the procedures used and support the results;
   (d) where the tests or work are undertaken by others, the records must clearly show such tests or work, their date and identify the persons who carried them out.
10. Members may on request provide preliminary advice, including an opinion, orally. Any opinion which will or may be used in the course of court proceedings must be expressed in writing and observe the following rules:
    (a) to set out all qualifications and experience relevant to the matters in issue;
    (b) to indicate and distinguish between facts supplied to them by others, facts they have been asked to assume and facts they have discovered or ascertained themselves. Where they have verified facts supplied by others, this should be stated;
    (c) to indicate the tests and work done upon which they have relied and where records of the same are kept;

(d) to identify by name anyone else involved in the tests and work;
(e) to bear in mind at all times that they alone must determine the wording or any opinion given;
(f) to consider carefully the words they use which indicate the degree of certainty with which it is possible to express an opinion;
(g) to refer to and on request to supply or provide access to any other papers or results recorded in any journal or elsewhere which they have taken into account in reaching an opinion;
(h) to bring to the notice of the instructing solicitor records of all experiments and tests or other work which might tend to disprove or cast any doubt upon an opinion they are expressing in order that the solicitor may consider disclosure to other parties.

11. Members may meet with other experts instructed in connection with the possible court proceedings, and may discuss matters relevant to their tests, work or opinion, subject to the following conditions:
(a) they must first obtain the express consent of the client or instructing solicitor;
(b) in the case of possible criminal proceedings such meetings must not be on a "without prejudice" basis;
(c) notes of the meetings must be kept and where possible agreed with those taking part;
(d) meetings should be attended only by experts unless expressly agreed otherwise.

Introduction

Following the preparation of the Code of Practice and the Guidelines, the need for guidance related specifically to the use of forensic expert evidence in criminal proceedings was recognised. These additional guidelines have been prepared by a British Academy of Experts Working Party chaired by Anthony Scrivener QC. All members are strongly recommended to read the additional guidelines as well as the main section of Guidance Notes in order to broaden their general understanding of the field. Members who are, or who may be, instructed in the context of criminal proceedings should make a point of familiarising themselves with its contents. If there is perceived to be any conflict between the existing Code of Practice, Guidelines and these additional guidelines then these shall prevail.

The brief for the Working Party was to consider the desirability of having a special code or guidelines for forensic scientists and if appropriate to prepare recommendations.

Although the observance of these additional guidelines is mandatory for all members of the British Academy of Experts it is anticipated that they will be taken as establishing general good practice for all forensic science experts.

The Members of the Working Party which prepared these additional guidelines:

Anthony Scrivener QC, *Chairman of Working Party and Vice-President of BAE*
Dr W Allen, *Vice-President BAE, Chairman of Original Guidelines Working Party*
Dr David Anton, *RAF Institute of Aviation Medicine*
Michael Birnbaum QC, *Criminal Bar Association*
Dr Peter Clark, *Home Office Forensic Science Service*
Roger Daw, *Crown Prosecution Service*
Mr Stephen Dawson, *Solicitor—Reynolds Dawson*
Jeffrey Foote QC, *Crown Prosecutor, Crumlin Road, Belfast*
Miss Catherine Mather, *Secretary to Working Party, Solicitor—Stephenson Harwood*
Ron McQuaker, *British Computer Society*
Miss Margaret Pereira CBE, *President of Forensic Science Society*
Dr Brian Sheard, *Metropolitan Police Forensic Science Laboratory*
Miss Joanna Smith, *Assistant Secretary to Working Party, Barrister*
Dr Karen Sullivan, *Dundee Institute of Technology*

The Academy

The British Academy of Experts* is a multi-disciplinary body established in 1987 to ensure high professional standards amongst experts and to promote their use in litigation, dispute resolution and advisory roles.

The Academy adheres to a strict code of practice and members, all of whom are vetted before entry, are drawn from a wide range of disciplines.

The Academy also works closely with the judiciary and many professional bodies including The Law Society, The Home Office Forensic Service, The Royal College of Nursing, The Association of Consulting Engineers of Australia, The American Arbitration Association and The British Marine Industries Federation.

President

The Rt. Hon. The Lord Howe

Vice Presidents

Prof. Dr Jur Karl-Heinz Bückstiegel
Daniel R Fung QC, SC
Sir Donald Harrison MD, MS, PhD, FRSC, FRSM
Prof. Pierre Lalive, Lic.jur., Lic. Litt (Geneva), PhD (Cantab)
His Honour Judge Esyr Lewis QC
Sir Francis McWilliams GBE, BSc(Eng), FEng, DCL
The Rt. Hon Sir Bryan Neill
Rodger Pannone MAE
Norman Royce, OBE, FRIBA, PPCIArb, FBAE
HE Judge Stephen Schwebel
Anthony Scrivener QC

Chairman

Michael Cohen, LLB, FBSC, FCIArb, FBAE, Barrister

Further details can be obtained from:
The Secretary, 2 South Square, Gray's Inn, London WC1R 5HP (Telephone: +44 (0) 171 637 0333; Fax: +44 (0) 171 637 1893; e-mail: ara@atlas.co.uk).

* The British Academy of Experts is now The Academy of Experts.

APPENDIX 2

Two specimen pages from the "Fire Analysis Report"

Fire analysis report

EVIDENCE **TIMES**

Time of Ignition ....

Time of Discovery ....

Time of Call ....

In Attendance ....

Make Up ....

....

....

Stop ....

Extinguished ....

NOTES ON SIGNIFICANCE OF TIMES

PAGE 1

THE FIRE **EVIDENCE**

Size at Time of Discovery [at .... hrs] ....

....

Size at time of Arrival of First Attendance [at .... hrs] ....

....

Maximum Size [at .... hrs] ....

....

Special Features of Fire Development ....

....

Supposed Cause ....

....

....

Is Supposed Cause Consistent with Evidence? ....

....

....

Is Supposed Cause Relevant to
Guilt or Innocence of Accused? ....

....

....

Multiple Seats of Fire Found? ....

Location 1 ....

Location 2 ....

Location 3 ....

Location 4 ....

Did Investigator Consider Possible Innocent Causes of Multiple Seats? ....

....

COMMENT ON LOCATIONS ....

PAGE 3

APPENDIX 3

A specimen evidence label

NORTHERN
FORENSIC
INVESTIGATIONS

EVIDENCE LABEL

Identification ref. Nr. [ ]

Court exhibit Nr. [ ]

CASE ....
....
....

DESCRIPTION
....
....
....
....
....

Time and date seized or produced
....

Seized or produced by
....

CONTINUITY RECORD

Name ....
Job descriptn./ Rank & Nr. ....
....
Date .... / .... / ....

PASSED ON TO

Name ....
Job descriptn./ Rank & Nr. ....
....
Date .... / .... / ....

PASSED ON TO

Name ....
Job descriptn./ Rank & Nr. ....
....
Date .... / .... / ....

PASSED ON TO

Name ....
Job descriptn./ Rank & Nr. ....
....
Date .... / .... / ....

PASSED ON TO

Name ....
Job descriptn./ Rank & Nr. ....
....
Date .... / .... / ....

APPENDIX 4

Criminal Justice Act statement form

STATEMENT OF WITNESS

STATEMENT OF Patrick Anthony David SHEEN

Age of witness (if over 21 enter "over 21")—OVER 21

Occupation of witness—Consulting Forensic Engineer

This statement (consisting of .... pages) each signed by me is true to the best of my knowledge and belief and I make it knowing that, if it is tendered in evidence, I shall be liable to prosecution if I have wilfully stated anything in it which I know to be false or do not believe to be true.

(*Criminal Justice Act 1967, s.9, Magistrates' Courts Act 1980, s.102, Magistrates' Courts Rules 1981, r.70*)

Dated the .... *day of* .... *Signature* ....

I am Patrick Anthony David Sheen and I reside at the address given overleaf.

My qualifications are:

Eur. Ing.—European Engineer—a Professional Engineer qualified to operate in all countries of Europe.

BSc—Bachelor of Science (Electrical Engineering) University of Leeds

CEng—Chartered Engineer

FIEE—Fellow of the Institution of Electrical Engineers

FIFireE—Fellow of the Institution of Fire Engineers (Past President)

FAE—Fellow of the Academy of Experts

I have been in practice as a Consulting Engineer for more than 30 years, for most of that time the practice was run in parallel with my academic career. For the last 15 years I have concentrated on the forensic aspects of engineering, specialising in the investigation of industrial accidents, electric shock and ....

Signature ....

APPENDIX 5

A typical report in a criminal case

Background to the case

Three youths, Smith, Jones and Robinson were petrol sniffing. They had a plastic five-litre petrol container which Smith was sniffing. He was overcome by the fumes and collapsed. As he collapsed the petrol from the container poured over him. He recovered consciousness and stood up. Jones flicked his lighter claiming later that he intended no harm to Smith but wished to frighten him. Smith's clothing ignited and Smith died. Jones was charged with murder. In his defence he stated that his lighter was at least a foot away from Smith's back. I was asked to examine the evidence and to report to defence counsel.

Although it is possible to calculate the probable distribution of petrol in air around a petrol-soaked body the mathematics involved are complex and I was of the opinion that if I did the work by the theoretical route there would be a very real danger that there would only be two people in court who understood what I had done and what were the significance of my results, and those two would be me and the forensic scientist for the prosecution. I therefore decided to carry out real life tests on a life size dummy dressed in clothing identical to that worn by the victim. To this end a shop window dummy was purchased and unfortunately the only dummy quickly available was a female dummy but some work with a power saw soon converted Wilhelmina into Wally. The dummy was modified so that its joints could be moved to allow it to sit or stand and when standing it was supported from a gallows by a rope—my neighbours are used to seeing very odd sights at my property!

THE REPORT

This was in the format of a Criminal Justice Act statement as described earlier and page 1 is shown in Appendix 4. The report proper is then:

I have been asked to determine whether there would be a petroleum vapour/air mixture capable of being ignited by the spark from a cigarette lighter at a distance of one foot from a person whose clothing was soaked in petrol in the way in which the clothing of Mr Smith would have been soaked from the descriptions of the incident in the witness statements.

To answer this question a series of full-size dummy tests were carried out. The witness statements indicate that the victim was seated on the floor sniffing petrol from a petrol container when he was overcome by the fumes and let go of the container which fell and spilt thus drenching him in petrol. This sequence would result in almost all of the petrol being spilt on the region of the abdomen, crutch and thighs, with considerable quantities of petrol being absorbed by the material of the backs of the legs of the jeans and the material around the buttocks as the victim sat in the pool of petrol which resulted from the spill.

Three series of tests were carried out:

TEST 1 Open air in a sheltered alcove wind speed very low (two tests carried out in succession).

TEST 2 As Test 1 but with a higher wind speed so that eddies of the wind were blowing from the dummy towards the sampling probe.

TEST 3 In a very large enclosed building so that there was no wind at all.

In Test 1 an industrial explosimeter was used while in Tests 2 and 3 a precision digital explosimeter was used.

A video record was made of all tests.

The dummy was a modified shop window display dummy dressed in clothing which was as nearly as possible identical to the clothes worn by the victim.

The details of the clothing are:

TOP—Adidas "Torsion" Shell Suit Top in Black/Yellow—identical to that described by the witnesses. Tee shirt.

LOWER PORTION OF DUMMY—Wrangler jeans (new to ensure maximum absorption of petrol), Blue rather than black/red as described. Nylon underpants. Wool/nylon socks. Trainers.

The dummy is 1760 mm (5 foot 9¼ inch) high when standing and has been adapted so that it can be seated and then pulled into a standing position and supported in this position.

The petrol (ESSO Unleaded) was contained in a DUCO petrol container identical to the one described in the witness statements and filled to the same extent (50 mm or two inches of petrol) as described in the statements. This corresponds to just over two litres of petrol.

NOTE ON THE FLAMMABILITY OF PETROL VAPOUR/AIR MIXTURES

Not all mixtures of flammable gases with air can be ignited. If the concentration of the flammable gas is low then the mixture cannot be ignited as it does not contain sufficient fuel to burn—it is too lean a mixture. Conversely if there is a very high concentration of the flammable gas there may not be sufficient oxygen in the mixture to support the combustion—it is too rich a mixture. The range of concentrations between which a flammable gas/air mixture is capable of being ignited is called the *flammable limits*. The lower limit, at which there is insufficient flammable gas is the *lower flammable limit (abbreviation LFL)* and the higher limit, at which there is insufficient oxygen is the *upper flammable limit (abbreviation UFL)*.

For petrol vapour the range is from 1.4 per cent to 7.6 per cent of petrol vapour in air, percentages which vary slightly with different petrols (these are percentages by volume not by weight), and it should be noted that the range is quite small. This is why there can be problems with a car engine as a fuel blockage or an air leak can easily prevent the carburettor from delivering a mixture to the engine with less than 1.4 per cent of petrol in it so the engine cannot run. Equally if the choke is pulled out too far or left out for too long then there is too much petrol vapour in the intake, the concentration is above 7.6 per cent and the engine will not run as it is "flooded".

The mixture is not equally easily ignited across the whole flammable range of 1.4 to 7.6 per cent. It is more difficult to ignite a mixture which is at the ends of the range than a mixture in the middle of the range.

To ignite the petrol/air mixture heat energy has to be put into the mixture to raise its temperature to the point at which ignition will take place. This heat energy can be supplied to the mixture in two main ways:

(a) raising the temperature of the whole gas mixture to the point at which combustion starts;
(b) applying a high energy source such as a spark to the mixture which is at normal temperatures.

Typical of the first method is the diesel engine in which the compression of the air in the cylinder raises it to a temperature high enough to ignite the diesel oil when it is injected. The temperature necessary to ignite the gas/air mixture simply by raising the temperature is called the *Auto-ignition Temperature* which for petrol is between 250 and 400°C.

Typical of the second method is the ignition of a petrol vapour/air mixture in the cylinder of a car engine by a high voltage spark. If the mixture is ignited with a spark then the energy required is quite small.

In summary, if a petrol vapour/air mixture is to be ignited then a spark of sufficient energy must be applied to the mixture AT A TIME AT WHICH THE CONCENTRATION OF THE MIXTURE IS BETWEEN 1.4 AND 7.6 PER CENT OF PETROL VAPOUR IN AIR.

FULL SIZE DUMMY TESTS

The tests were conducted using a full-size dummy which was dressed in clothing which was as nearly as possible identical to the clothing of the victim. The dummy was articulated so that it could be placed in a sitting position and arranged so that it could be hoisted into a standing position and supported in this position. In the standing position the sampling probe of an explosimeter (a device for measuring the concentration of petrol vapour in air) was fixed to a rigid support so that it was at all times held 12 inches away from the lower back of the dummy as this is the position at which the accused was alleged to have been holding his lighter when he operated it.

TEST 1

Test conditions: Outdoors in an alcove sheltered from the wind. Wind slight from west. Test site sheltered from wind (see drawing of test site). (NOTE This drawing has not been reproduced in this book.)

Concentration of petrol vapour measured with a MSA explosimeter. The instrument was overhauled and recalibrated by an instrument calibration company before the tests and recalibrated immediately after the tests. The test certificate is at the end of this report marked "Document 1" (NOTE This document has not been reproduced in this book.)

The calibration was carried out with methane but the petrol vapour is essentially pentane. In order to obtain the concentration of petrol vapour the explosimeter readings (if calibrated for methane) have to be multiplied by two.

Because the MSA explosimeter is designed for work in the field of industrial safety it tends to **over estimate** the concentration of the flammable mixture it is measuring so that there is a safety margin in the readings obtained.

Test Results

Event	Time (min. sec.)	Reading of explosimeter %	Gas %
Petrol applied	0.00		
Dummy upright	0.34		
First reading	1.22	10	0.28
Second reading	2.18	10	0.28
Third reading	3.14	6	0.17
Sampling probe moved to within 50 mm (2 inches) of clothing of dummy	3.56	20	0.56
Sampling probe moved to calf level, close to clothing	5.03	22	0.62
Sampling probe moved back to main test position	5.58	Under 5	Under 0.14
Test concluded	6.05		

NOTE—The explosimeter readings are percentages of the lower flammable limit, in other words percentages of 1.4 per cent of petrol vapour in air by volume. Thus a 10 per cent explosimeter reading is the equivalent of 10 × 2 = 20 per cent of the lower explosive limit for petrol or 0.28 per cent of petrol vapour in air by volume (remember that the explosimeter is calibrated for methane and the readings have to be multiplied by two to calibrate it for petrol).

TEST 1—REPEAT TEST

Conditions as before but petrol split higher on abdomen of dummy (NOTE The test results have not been reproduced in this book).

TEST 2

Test conditions. As Test 1 except that wind speed was higher but the test site was still sheltered from the wind. Eddies of wind were blowing from the dummy towards the sampling probe.

The concentration of petrol vapour in air was measured with a precision digital explosimeter the details of which are:

CROWCON TRIPLE Type 84TR Serial Number 84–0578 Calibrated for pentane, hydrogen sulphide and oxygen. Used on the pentane setting. (The manufacturers have confirmed that readings obtained on this instrument on its pentane setting will be accurate for petrol vapours.)

The instrument was used with its aspirator attachment which allows the gas/air mixture which is to be measured to be drawn into the instrument through a flexible tube. This flexible tube (the sampling probe) was attached to a rigid measuring rod as in Test 1 so that the end could be positioned accurately 300 mm (12 inches) away from the back of the dummy at waist level.

At the conclusion of the tests the explosimeter was returned to its supplier and recalibrated.

The test certificate for this calibration is at the end of this report marked "Document 2" (NOTE This document has not been reproduced in this book). (NOTE The test results have not been reproduced in this book.)

TEST 3

Test conditions. This test was carried out in a large aircraft hanger at Teeside International Airport so that there was no wind at all on the dummy. All other test conditions were identical to those of Test 2 (NOTE The test results have not been reproduced in this book).

DISCUSSION OF TEST RESULTS

No matter whether the tests were carried out out-of-doors or inside a large building in still air at no time was there a flammable gas/air mixture at one foot behind the back of the dummy. This is not surprising on theoretical grounds for the vapour of petrol is very much heavier than air and so the vapour would tend to flow downwards close to the body. The highest reading obtained with the probe held a foot away from the dummy was only 13 per cent of the lower flammable limit and even at two inches from the back of the dummy the mixture was at only at 40 per cent of the lower flammable limit. The outdoor tests showed that the only effect wind had on the readings was to reduce the percentage of petrol vapour in the mixture as the wind dispersed the petrol vapours and diluted them so making ignition even more unlikely.

CONCLUSIONS

The test results are not consistent with the version of events put forward by the defendant and, in my opinion, it is almost certain that the lighter was very much closer to the victim when the defendant flicked it and indeed was probably less than 50 mm or two inches from the back of the victim.

POSTSCRIPT

The accused considered the evidence and pleaded guilty to manslaughter and the prosecution dropped the charge of murder.

APPENDIX 6

Pro formas used by CPS in a typical case

No. T98 1169

CROWN COURT.

Regina

—v—

ADDITIONAL EVIDENCE.

TAKE NOTICE that upon your trial
additional evidence will be called
of which the following is a copy:—

P/c Leeman + KPL/6.

Chief Crown Prosecutor
Mersey/Lancashire

Printed in the UK for HMSO, 59803

CPS

199

Facsimile:
DX No:

Direct Line: 8531

Our Reference: CA/CE

Your Reference: T98 1169
16/07/98

Dear Sirs

NOTICE OF FURTHER EVIDENCE

DEFENDANT:
(D.O.B.)

OPERATIONAL REF. NO./PTI URN:

COURT AND HEARING DATE: Trial @ LCC 21/09/98

I enclose a copy Notice of Further Evidence.

Please acknowledge receipt and confirm that you accept service of the Notice and accompanying statement(s).

Yours faithfully

NFR/NFE 4/(07.96)

CPS

Switchboard:
Facsimile:
DX No:

Solicitors

Direct Line: 8532

Our Reference: CE/A Team.

Your Reference:

29 May 1998

Dear Sirs

DISCLOSURE OF PROSECUTION MATERIAL UNDER SECTION 3 CRIMINAL PROCEDURE AND INVESTIGATIONS ACT 1996

R v
URN:

COURT AND HEARING DATE: No Date—Transfer.

I am required by Section 3 Criminal Procedure and Investigations Act 1996 (CPIA) to disclose to you any Prosecution material which has not previously been disclosed, and which in my opinion might undermine the case for the Prosecution against you/your client.

Attached to this letter is a copy of a schedule of non-sensitive unused material prepared by the police in compliance with their duty under Part II CPIA and the provisions of the Code of Practice. The schedule has been prepared by the Police Disclosure Officer, who in this case is DC

Unless the word "evidence" appears alongside any item, all the items listed on the schedule are not intended to be used as part of the Prosecution case. You will receive a written notice should the position change.

Where indicated, copies of the items listed are attached. Material marked as available for inspection can be viewed by arrangement with the ASU.

In addition, the following material not listed on the schedule is disclosed to you in accordance with the provisions of the CPIA:

STATEMENT OF —MG6c

Crown Prosecution Service · Working in the interests of justice

This material is disclosed to you in accordance with the provisions of the CPIA, and you must not use or disclose it, or any information recorded in it, for any purpose other than in connection with these criminal proceedings. If you do so without the permission of the Court, you may commit an offence.

If you supply a written Defence Statement to me and to the Court within 14 days, material which has not been disclosed at this stage will be further reviewed in the light of that statement.

A Defence Statement is required by Section 5 CPIA in Crown Court cases. In Magistrates' Court cases, Section 6 CPIA makes a Defence Statement optional. Please bear in mind that we will rely upon the information you provide in the statement to identify any remaining material which has not already been disclosed but which might reasonably assist the defence case as you have described it. The statement will also be relied on by the Court if you later make an application under Section 8 CPIA.

If you do not make a Defence Statement where one is required, or provide one late, the Court may permit comment and/or draw an adverse inference.

If you request access to any item which is marked for disclosure by inspection, it is essential that you preserve this schedule in its present form, as access will only be granted upon production of the schedule to the person supervising access.

Also enclosed with this letter for your information is an explanation of the rights and duties of accused persons under the CPIA.

If you have a query in connection with this letter, please contact the writer.

Yours faithfully

SENIOR CROWN PROSECUTOR

Continuation Sheet

Form MG 6C(c)

POLICE SCHEDULE OF NON-SENSITIVE UNUSED MATERIAL

Page No. /

R v ....

Item No.	DESCRIPTION	LOCATION
1	WITNESS STATEMENT	WITH CPS

Continuation Sheet:

Yes ☐ No ☑

FOR CPS USE	
	COMMENT

D = Disclose to defence
I = Defence may inspect

April 97

CPS

Facsimile:
DX No:

Direct Line: 8532

Our Reference: HEC/AC

Your Reference: MC-BH-817-98
30 April 1998

Dear Sirs

DEFENDANT

URN

COURT AND HEARING DATE: 1.5.98— Magistrates' Court

This case is listed for committal on the date referred to above. The committal papers, enclosed herewith, have been prepared in accordance with the MCA 1980 and the Practice Direction of 1986.

In order to further assist, we enclose a Committal Information Form.

Any enquiries about these committal papers should be addressed to the writer, who can be contacted at the above address.

Yours faithfully

SENIOR CROWN PROSECUTOR

NFR/CCCP 08/(01.98)

Crown Prosecution Service · Working in the interests of justice

COMMITTAL INFORMATION

Committal papers have been prepared in relation to the above defendant(s). This "Committal Information" is produced by the Crown Prosecution Service to assist the Crown Prosecution Service advocate at the committal proceedings, the magistrates' court, the defence and police.

TYPE OF COMMITTAL FILE

The committal papers have been prepared in the format which reflects the changes brought about by the CPIA 1996.

INDICTMENT/CHARGES

Please seek committal on the charge(s) as set out in the draft indictment which represent amended versions of charge(s) originally preferred and will involve an application to amend the original charge/summons in so far as concerns count(s):—

COUNT 1

SECTION 40/41 OFFENCES

nil ....

N.B. This document is not to be printed post-committal.

Outline of Allegation and issues for judge and defence

The Crown Court, Sitting at

URN:

R –v–

BRIEF OUTLINE OF ALLEGATION AND ISSUES:

CHARGE(S):

Arson Being Reckless as to whether life is endangered.

PROSECUTION ALLEGATIONS AND ISSUES:

The defendant and his partner obtained a tenancy upon which is owned by in February 1998. They renovated the house and moved in around mid March 1998. The defendant's partner then told him their relationship was over. This greatly distressed the defendant and on the day of the fire he was displaying irrational, emotional and aggressive behaviour. His car was seen by occupants of number on the evening of the fire and he made calls from the house to his partner (who was at her parents). He admitted to the Police he had damaged furnishings at the house that evening in anger and may have dropped a cigarette downstairs. There were accelerants in the house due to the decorating he was doing. A fire began at 10pm, there being several seats in an upstairs bedroom. The Fire Brigade entered and put out the fire. The fire officer states the fire was started deliberately upstairs. The lives of the family present at number were endangered along with those of the Fire Service.

LIKELY ISSUES:

Factual—whether defendant set the fire—if so, whether he was reckless as to lives of others.

AGGRAVATING FEATURES:

Lives of several adults and children endangered.

N.B. This outline (which has been copied to the defence) has been prepared by the Crown Prosecution Service prior to the prosecuting advocate being instructed in order to facilitate the efficient allocation of work at the Crown Court. It is NOT intended to serve any other purpose.

BRIEFING TO PROSECUTION ADVOCATE

CRIMINAL PROCEDURE AND INVESTIGATIONS ACT 1996
DISCLOSURE OF UNUSED MATERIAL

IN FORCE 1 APRIL 1997

The following rules are set out in order that prosecuting advocate can assist the Court when considering disclosure:

1. Primary disclosure of unused material must take place as soon as reasonably practicable after committal.

2. Primary disclosure is material, which in the prosecutor's opinion might undermine the Prosecution case. If the advocate takes a different view, these concerns must be promptly discussed with the CPS before any further disclosure is made.

3. Following primary disclosure, the Defence have 14 days to provide a Defence statement or to apply for an extension to the time limit in order to do so. (Section 5(9) CPIA and Regulation 3(2) Defence (Disclosure) Time Limit Regulations.)

4. Secondary disclosure will take place as soon as reasonably practicable after receipt of the Defence statement. It can only take place after provision of the Defence statement, because the material will consist of anything which might reasonably be expected to assist the accused's defence as set out in the Defence statement. **If a Defence statement is not provided, there can be no secondary disclosure.**

5. It is only after secondary disclosure has taken place that the Defence can apply for the disclosure of additional material (Section 8 CPIA and Rule 7 Crown Court (Disclosure) Rules). **The advocate should firmly resist any application for the disclosure of additional material before the Defence statement has been provided.**

6. Enquiries and requests from the Defence for additional disclosure should be discussed with a CPS representative before disclosure is made. If the advocate has any concerns regarding the material which may require disclosure, these should be conveyed promptly to the CPS.

NFR/CCCP 08/(01.98)

URN:

R v

Form 14A. Notice to accused: right to object to written statement or deposition being read out at trial without further proof (CPI Act 1996, s.68, Sched. 2 paragraphs 1(3)(c) and 2(3)(c): MC Rules 1981, r 4B (as inserted by MC (Amendment) Rules 1997).

To
of

If you are committed for trial, the Crown Court may try you in respect of the charge or charges on which you are committed or in respect of any other charge arising out of the same transaction or set of circumstances which may, with the leave of the Court, be put to you.

[Written statements] [and] [depositions] have been made by the witnesses named below and copies of their [statements] [and] [depositions] are enclosed. Each of these [statements] [and] [depositions] will be read out at the trial without oral evidence being given by the witness who has made the [statement] [or] [deposition] unless you want the witness to give oral evidence and to be cross-examined on such oral evidence. If you want any of these witnesses to give oral evidence, and be cross-examined if necessary, you should inform the Crown Court and me in writing within 14 days of being committed for trial. If you do not do so you will lose your right to prevent the [statement] [or] [deposition] being read out without any oral evidence being given by the witness in question and to require the attendance of that witness unless the Court gives you leave to do so, but that will not prevent the prosecutor from exercising his discretion to call that witness to give oral evidence, and be cross-examined, at the trial if the prosecutor so wishes.

[*[Pre-paid] reply forms [and pre-paid envelopes] are enclosed and if you object to any [statement] [or] [deposition] being read out at the trial without oral evidence being given by the witness who made it you must let the Crown Court and me know within 14 days of being committed for trial, and at the same time indicate which of these witnesses you want to give oral evidence at the trial.

[*If you have a solicitor acting for you in your case you should hand this notice and the [statements] [and] [depositions] to him at once, so that he may deal with them.]

Name of witnesses whose [statements] [and] [depositions] are enclosed

Address any reply to: Crown Prosecution Service

W (Signed) ______________
[On behalf of the Prosecutor]
NFR/CCCP 24/(04.97)

*Omit if documents are sent to accused's solicitor

NFR/CCCP 08/(01.98)

INDICTMENT No.

IN THE CROWN COURT AT

THE QUEEN –v–

is charged as follows:

STATEMENT OF OFFENCE

ARSON BEING RECKLESS AS TO WHETHER LIFE IS ENDANGERED, contrary to Section 1(2) and (3) of the Criminal Damage Act 1971.

PARTICULARS OF OFFENCE

on the 26th day of March 1998 without lawful excuse damaged by fire part of a dwelling house known as belonging to Council intending to destroy or damage such property or being reckless as to whether such property would be destroyed or damaged and being reckless as to whether the life of and other members of the Fire Brigade would thereby be endangered.

Committal Date: Officer of the Court.

LIST OF STATEMENTS

Crown Court at:
URN:
Regina
v

No.	Name of witness	Date/ Statement(s)	Page No.(s)
1		27.3.98	1–5
2		27.3.98	6–8
3		1.4.98	9–11
4		1.4.98	12–14
5		1.4.98	15
6		27.3.98	16–17
7		6.4.98	18–20
8		27.3.98	21
9		20.4.98	22–23
10		21.4.98	24
11			
12			
13			
14			
15			
16			
17			
18			
19			
20			

At the committal proceedings in this matter, the prosecution will not adduce evidence of those portions of those witness statements that are bracketed [ ] and/or deleted, nor will the prosecution seek to adduce that evidence at the trial unless a Notice of Additional Evidence is served.

NFR/CCCP 09/(04.97)

LIST OF EXHIBITS

Crown Court at:
URN:
Regina
v

No.	Exhibit Ref No.s	Description	Page No.(s)
1	SBD/1	PHOTOCOPY OF HOUSING APPLICATION FORM	1–7
2	KPL/2	TRANSCRIPT OF FIRST INTERVIEW WITH	8–50
3	KPL/4	TRANSCRIPT OF SECOND INTERVIEW WITH	51–92
4			
5			
6			
7			
8			
9			
10			
11			
12			
13			
14			
15			
16			
17			
18			
19			
20			
21			
22			

NFR/CCCP 29/(01.97)

CPS

Switchboard:
Facsimile:
DX No:

Solicitors

Direct Line: 8532

Our Reference: HEC/AC

Your Reference: MC-BH-817-98

Date ______________

Dear Sirs

DISCLOSURE OF PROSECUTION MATERIAL UNDER SECTION 3 CRIMINAL PROCEDURE AND INVESTIGATIONS ACT 1996

DEFENDANT:

URN:

COURT AND HEARING DATE: 1.5.98— Magistrates' Court

I am required by Section 3 Criminal Procedure and Investigations Act 1996 (CPIA) to disclose to you any Prosecution material which has not previously been disclosed, and which in my opinion might undermine the case for the Prosecution against you/your client.

Attached to this letter is a copy of a schedule of non-sensitive unused material prepared by the Police in compliance with their duty under Part II CPIA and the provisions of the Code of Practice. The schedule has been prepared by the Police Disclosure Officer, who in this case is ______________________.

Unless the word "evidence" appears alongside any item, all the items listed on the schedule are not intended to be used as part of the Prosecution case. You will receive a written notice should the position change.

At this stage, it is my opinion that there is no Prosecution material which requires disclosure to you.

If you supply a written Defence statement to me and to the Court within 14 days, the material will be further reviewed in the light of that statement.

NFR/CCCP 08/(01.98)

Crown Prosecution Service · Working in the interests of justice

A Defence statement is required by Section 5 CPIA in Crown Court cases. In Magistrates' Court cases, Section 6 CPIA makes a Defence statement optional. Please bear in mind that we will rely upon the information you provide in the statement to identify any remaining material which has not already been disclosed but which might reasonably assist the Defence case as you have described it. The statement will also be relied on by the Court if you later make an application under Section 8 CPIA.

If you do not make a Defence statement where one is required, or provide one late, the Court may permit comment and/or draw an adverse inference.

Also enclosed with this letter for your information is an explanation of the rights and duties of accused persons under the CPIA.

If you have a query in connection with this letter, please contact the writer.

Yours faithfully

SENIOR CROWN PROSECUTOR

NFR/CCCP 08/(01.98)

POLICE SCHEDULE OF NON-SENSITIVE UNUSED MATERIAL

Form MG 6C
Page No. 1

R v ....

The Disclosure Officer believes that the following material which does not form part of the prosecution case is NOT SENSITIVE

Item No.	DESCRIPTION	LOCATION
1.	Copy of tenancy agreement rights and responsibilities of tenant. (Ref SBD/2)	With OIC
2.	Copy of police incident log.	With OIC
3.	Clothing of removed whilst in custody at police station	
4.	Police incident log re	Control Room

Date:	Continuation Sheet:
20.4.98	Yes ☐ No ☒

	FOR CPS USE
*	COMMENT

Reviewing Lawyer:
HEC

* Enter
D = Disclose to defence
I = Defence may inspect

April 97

CHAPTER 4

THE EXPERT WITNESS IN CONSTRUCTION DISPUTE CASES

Roger Trett

001 The expert topic dealt with in this chapter relates to Forensic Delay Analysis (cause and effect) and *quantum* dealing with The Appointment; The Instructions; The Investigation; Discovery; The Draft Report; The Meeting of Experts; The Expert Report; Supplementary Report(s); The Hearing.

THE APPOINTMENT

002 *"I'm late, I'm late"*, cried the White Rabbit in Alice in Wonderland. *"Too late, too late"* is often the cry given by expert witnesses in construction. There is a preponderance of late appointments in construction cases primarily, I believe, because the lawyers believe that the matter will settle and the costs of the expert can be saved. When the matter is not settled and it is realised that expert opinion is required then a flurry of activity takes place to find an expert.

003 Quite often had the expert been appointed much earlier and the evidence tested then the case may well have been settled in a shorter time and at a much reduced cost. What is perceived early as to be the quickest way is almost invariably the longest way and the highest cost.

004 The problem, of course, with expert witness work in construction, particularly delay cases, is the amount of work that has to be undertaken to analyse events and prepare reports. Major projects whether they are building, civil engineering, heavy engineering, offshore etc. will potentially have many hundreds, if not thousands of activities that are all interrelated and which may have to be looked at before the expert can reach a conclusion.

005 As a consequence the appointment of the expert should be made timeously so that there is sufficient time to analyse events and to be a constructive part of the litigation/arbitration team.

006 Before accepting an appointment to act the expert must make sure that there are no conflicts of interest. Any previous work for either party should be disclosed to the instructing solicitors. Even if the expert has worked for the opposing party before it should not necessarily be a bar to acting as expert in this appointment. In fact my experience shows that parties sometimes welcome such an appointment because they respect your integrity and know that you won't be a "hired gun".

THE INSTRUCTIONS

007 Instructions from lawyers are getting better but in many cases verbal instructions only have been given and then not very clearly. This is perhaps because in some instances the lawyers themselves, whilst being fully aware of the law and the procedures, are not always aware of the intricacies of construction cases. Similarly the timing of the appointment can have a bearing on the instructions. If the appointment is made early on in the process then the expert may well, and to my mind, should assist the legal team in the preparation of the "pleadings" following his initial review of the project. As an expert I have assisted in the preparation of these "pleadings" and also in the preparation of requests for further and better particulars.

008 As is more often the case, the expert is appointed after "pleadings" have been served and the instructions normally follow that he/she will address the pleadings that relate to his/her expertise. If the instructions are not concise I would, as an expert, confirm to the lawyers the matters that I am to consider and include in my report.

009 The case that I have decided to sanitise and use as the basis of this chapter is one in which I was involved in 1990. It is a case which illustrates a number of problems that arose and how I dealt with them in my Report. It also illustrates how a narrow instruction may have to be widened to include such other matters as the investigation progresses.

010 This particular case had been running for a period when I was invited to a meeting. The case was explained to me and the instructions given to "prepare a report to allow us to get away with paying as little as possible"—not the best set of instructions! My response, of course, was that I would evaluate the issues as I saw them and not as someone else wanted me to see them. I would be the only one giving evidence, not the lawyers, and I had a duty to the court as well as the client.

011 It can be gleaned from the conversation that the plaintiff and the plaintiff's solicitors had accepted that they were liable (but not admitted it) and that the sole remit of the expert was to minimise the amount payable in compensation. Effectively the instructions were to look at *quantum* only.

012 A brief outline of the claims should set the scene for the investigation. The plaintiff was a manufacturer and erector of precast concrete framed buildings, and had suffered a set-off by the main contractor as a result of alleged delay and out-of-sequence erection of the frame with the consequential delay to the completion date. The main contractor was the defendant.

013 A substantial element of the set-off related to the additional costs of the main contractor and his many other subcontractors for the extended period of completing the work.

014 I could have, and perhaps should have, taken on board the *quantum* only which was my instructions. This would have meant my checking that the additional costs of the contractor and my client were correct and, if not, evaluating them accordingly.

015 However and, perhaps swayed slightly by the instructions, I felt that it would be appropriate that I considered the delay aspects to the project to determine what the real effect of my client's alleged delay was to the project. The main contractor had assumed that the lateness of my client was responsible for the complete overrun of the project period. Thus, if my client was responsible for the complete delay then the evaluation would be for the full period. However if my client was not responsible for the complete delay then the evaluation would be for a lesser period. There was therefore a direct connection between the delay to the project and my *quantum* instructions. Thus my brief was amended to include the necessary forensic delay analysis.

016 Starting from the premise that the erection of the frame was delayed I asked a very simple question "Why was the erection late?". Neither my client's manager nor the company lawyers could answer the question. I then requested a meeting with the erection team. After explaining to them that I wanted to know exactly what happened, especially any of their own actions which caused the delay, I again asked the same question. The response was because the precast members were delivered late and out-of-sequence. The lawyer stepped in and said "you can see the problems why we [my client] were late". This obviously prompted another question: "Why were the precast members late?". Nobody knew the answer. The question had never previously been asked.

017 As my client was also responsible for the manufacture of the precast frame members I suggested a meeting with the manufacturing manager to find the answer as to why the units were late. The manufacturing manager advised me that it was because the drawings were late! In addition by the time the drawings had arrived the capacity to manufacture the beams was committed elsewhere and a number of the units had to be subcontracted. The manufacturing manager did not know the reasons why the drawings were late.

018 It transpired that my client had sublet the detailed drawings to a draughting subcontractor. My immediate thoughts were that if the draughting subcontractor had not performed that there may well be a claim that could be set against them. The first position was, of course, to determine why the draughting subcontractor was late with the drawings.

019 Upon investigation, and examining the draughting subcontractor's records which had not been disclosed, I found that the draughting subcontractor was late with the drawings because the consulting engineer had not released the necessary information to allow the draughtsman to complete the manufacturing drawings—and in turn the consulting engineer was reliant upon the architect releasing the necessary information.

020 An investigation of the release of the information showed that the architect had for six consecutive months put back the release of information to the consulting engineer, who consequently had not been able to release the necessary information to the draughting subcontractor and onto the manufacturing manager. One of the simplest pieces of information outstanding was that of the brickwork support (the construction was of precast frame clad with traditional brickwork). The brickwork support was to be "cast in" to the precast members, then until such time that the support detail was available the drawings could not be released.

021 The consequence of such a position is that when the drawings were eventually made available, the manufacturing capacity was no longer available and the plaintiff had to subcontract the manufacture of a number of the beams to another subcontractor whilst at the same time trying to manufacture as much in-house as possible. As a consequence of the delay the precast frames were late and, due to the necessity to subcontract, out of sequence.

022 Having determined that the reasons for the delay in manufacture were not the responsibility of the plaintiff, it was necessary to look at the progress of the works as it occurred to see whether the allegation of the main contractor was sustainable.

023 As in many cases the main contractor had taken an isolated approach to the progress of the work. The physical aspect of the frame not being erected in accordance with the original programme was the main issue that it could see, and perhaps also that which the client could see. The main contractor therefore concentrated upon the lack of frame without considering the prime cause of delay. The lack of frame was in fact a consequence of the prime cause.

024 Having established that the plaintiff was not the cause of the delay to the project it was then necessary to consider the other aspects of the set-off claim.

025 The main contractor had not only sought to claim the overall delays to the completion date from my client, but had also sought to set-off claims of other subcontractors that flowed from the alleged delay. I examined the subsequent delays to the project and formed the opinion that they could not, on the evidence available, have resulted from the alleged delay of the precast frame and therefore the consequences of which could not be passed on to the plaintiff.

026 The above example of investigation is typical of most construction contracts whether they be building, civil engineering, heavy engineering or offshore. Although some contracts are far more complex than others, a thorough investigation into all the drawings, correspondence, daily diaries, allocation sheets, progress reports etc. is essential to painting the complete picture of a project.

027 Preparing many schedules from the information gleaned is thus necessary to allow the information to be data-based and subsequently interrogated. Many contracts have vast numbers of activities and it is necessary to show the real effects arising from the alleged causes. It is also fundamental, in delay analysis, that the progress of the work at the time the alleged event occurred is considered before the impact of any event can be demonstrated. It is of no value to take a base programme and say, for example, that the client supplied the information late if the contractor was in no position to act upon it.

DISCOVERY

028 In litigation and arbitration under English law the discovery process, i.e. the listing of each party's documents, is a source of information which can hold great potential for one party and perhaps undermine the credibility of the evidence for another.

029 In my opinion it is essential that the expert is involved in the inspection of listed documents. The expert knows which documents to look for and where they are likely to be. In the case considered here substantial information relating to other subcontractors came to light. Information which, in the normal course of events, would have not been available to my client. Had I been unable to refute the alleged delay from the in-house evidence and the plaintiff therefore deemed to have been late, as alleged, it would have been difficult to refute the delay costs in their entirety.

030 In addition the expert should have sufficient experience to identify documents that should have been listed but are not, thus providing the solicitor with the ammunition to request them.

THE DRAFT REPORT

031 After having the benefit of viewing the evidence and discussions with the parties, and preferably discovery, the expert prepares a draft report setting out the basis of the allegation, i.e. the pleadings and addressing the issues to opinion.

032 The legal team would of course, have been aware of your initial views/opinions early on although they may have been drawn prior to perusing all the evidence. It is essential that the expert keeps an open mind to the impact of additional evidence and if it means that as a result your opinion changes then the legal team must be informed immediately. The expert has to have the confidence to stand up and be counted.

033 On completion of the draft report it would be circulated to the legal team and the client so that they are able to see the expert's opinion and the reasons for it. The reason this is done is so that your conclusion can be tested on the basis of the evidence that is available and the client's knowledge of the project. It is not to get the expert to change his mind. The opinions have to be those of the expert and nobody else. It is of no benefit to anybody giving an opinion which is not the expert's own for when it comes to cross-examination the expert will be found out and his/her creditability and the client's case will be questioned.

034 On many occasions I have differed with the case as submitted and had to advise the team accordingly—it is of no use playing the role of a hired gun. Similarly it is of no use in the long term to your client to concentrate solely on the strengths of the case. It is as important that the weaknesses are addressed as well. Whether or not you address the weaknesses in the report is a matter of opinion but they need to be addressed in any event. I would personally prefer to consider them in the report to show that they have been dealt with. It is then more difficult for the opposing counsel to deal with them.

035 Having reviewed the position with your legal team and client but not changed your opinion, unless of course you have seen new evidence that has a material effect upon your original view, the next step is the meeting of experts.

THE MEETING OF EXPERTS

036 The objective of the meeting between the experts is to narrow the issues between the parties such that any subsequent hearing is limited to real matters in dispute and to save time and costs in the hearing.

037 In many cases the expert can be the catalyst to the parties settling the matter before the hearing. Whilst the lawyers are in a procedural battle the ability of the expert to maintain a relationship with the other expert and perhaps the opposing party can bear fruit in moving the matter forward.

038 If the experts disagree on matters of principle the meeting can still be productive in that agreement of figures as figures can save lots of time in any hearing. Although the principle is not agreed the costs that flow in the event that the principle is accepted by the judge or arbitrator can be agreed. In the expert report discussed in this chapter it can be seen that the agreement was reached between the experts on figures as figures and reported accordingly.

039 Whilst the meeting of experts can be productive, it will only be so if the experts are acting correctly and not as hired guns where they are just advocating their client's case regardless of the facts. If one of the experts' minds is made up and it is not going to change then the meetings can be a complete waste of time. Nevertheless you will be able to detect the situation fairly quickly and this will be of use to your legal team because you will be able to convey that the other expert will be suspect under cross-examination. Some lawyers unfortunately request that the experts should not agree anything—this also leads to unproductive meetings. The problem is of course, that to sustain an opinion in the face of evidence to the contrary will not help the case settle, and in the longer term is counter-productive.

040 I have been to a meeting of experts and been confronted by evidence that has necessitated my changing my opinion. If such a situation arises it is essential that your legal team is informed immediately so that they can assess the impact.

041 Another problem that arises on occasions is the "budding" lawyer. That is an expert who has just obtained a law degree and believes that it is the expert's duty to consider matters of law as well: an example being the expert who was insistent upon considering whether the correct notices had been given and within the time constraints set out in the contract. Such matters are for the judge or arbitrator to decide and not for the expert.

042 If the experts can agree on certain matters within their area of expertise then such agreement should be documented at the meeting and a copy given to each of the parties' legal team for verification. The reason for documenting any agreement at the meeting is to provide a joint record of any agreements made so that there is no doubt when reporting back to the parties as to what has been agreed. There obviously have been cases where the parties have not ratified the experts' agreements. Such a position is to be avoided if at all possible as it will put the expert into a position which cannot be sustained. How would the expert respond in cross-examination? However, I would have expected the expert to get the measure of his legal team before compromising his own position. This again points to the need for the expert to be "his own man".

043 A further important point is to restrict the meetings to expert attendance only, lawyers' attendance will stifle any meaningful discussions. Although some lawyers have insisted that they be allowed to sit in, I have always refused to comply with any such request.

THE EXPERT REPORT

044 The Expert Report can now be produced in its final format. The knowledge gained from discovery and meetings of experts will allow the expert to report findings and opinions. Whilst the report is to be the one for exchange there will usually be a draft sent to the legal teams prior to the final issue. The reason that the draft is sent is so that everyone is aware of its content but mainly as a proof read. Some counsel have particular preference as to the way certain opinions are expressed. Provided that the method of expression does not change that which I am trying to convey, then I do not have a problem in agreeing to change. I always say that I am employed as an expert because of my experience in construction matters. I will not however change my opinion simply because it does not suit.

045 Subsequent to finalising the report it will be simultaneously exchanged with the expert report of the other party.

046 Since the preparation of the report discussed in this chapter was originally 1990 (see the note to the Appendix following para 061) one important change which is now included is the declaration which follows the *Ikarian Reefer* case when Mr Justice Cresswell set out the list of duties and responsibilities of the expert witness. At the end of chapter there is a copy of such a declaration from a recent report.

047 In reading the declaration it will be noted that I refer to assistance provided to me by my colleagues. In construction cases there is a large amount of information to be handled and it is impossible for one person to be able to deal with it all and I therefore will give directions and seek assistance in scheduling etc. It is also far more cost effective for the client as a lot of the data management is of a clerical nature. However the expert has to maintain responsibility for that work and therefore must be satisfied that it is completed correctly, but it is essential to acknowledge that assistance has been provided.

SUPPLEMENTARY REPORT(S)

048 It is quite common that after the exchange of reports a supplementary report will be commissioned to deal with difference of opinions between the experts and to perhaps consider fresh evidence that may have come to light *via* the reports. Again the procedure for dealing with the supplementary reports will be the same as that for the initial report.

049 If progress is being made then there is not any reason to stop the experts meeting once the reports have been exchanged. It is the duty of the experts to continue to seek to narrow the issues prior to any hearing.

THE HEARING

050 In a number of cases I have been required to attend the whole of the hearing where I have been part of "the team" with a full input. The expert having considered in detail all the evidence will have a knowledge that is useful to counsel. A contribution can be made in relation to cross-examination as to what questions to ask and to advise on the responses given by the witness of fact and the expert. At the end of the day, with the rest of the team, the expert will sit in on the debriefing and may be required to consider matters that have been brought up during the day and to have responses ready for the following day.

051 It is not always necessary to have the expert in attendance full time. However it is essential that the expert is in attendance when his opposite number is being examined.

052 As for giving evidence, there are many people who have written about posture, speech and the best way to impress the judge or arbitrator, but in my opinion the best way is to have a full and detailed knowledge of the case, a full grasp of the facts and above all an honest opinion. I am not prepared to prepare a report and/or support a case that I do not believe in. Nevertheless one must not enter the witness box with a closed mind. If new evidence is provided the expert must be prepared to consider its impact. It must not be dismissed out of hand. Similarly if one has made a mistake, admit it; your credibility will remain intact.

053 In addition, remain calm. If counsel is trying to question your expertise with personal attacks it means that your report must be fairly sound otherwise your evidence rather than your expertise would be attacked.

054 The ultimate hope, of course, is that your report will be sufficient to allow the parties to reach an agreement so that you do not have to give evidence.

055 I stated above that you should not give an opinion that you do not believe in. It is more productive to advise clients on what they "need to know" rather than what they "want to hear". This basic honesty often leads to matters being settled quicker and at much less expense. The duty of the expert is not to perpetuate his fees but to assist in the early resolution of disputes.

THE NEW COURT RULES

056 The new Court Rules reflecting the Woolf Reforms were published in January 1999 and become effective from 26 April 1999 and contain sections relating to evidence and to experts and assessors; they are found in Parts 32 and 35 respectively. The rules will have an effect upon the expert but not upon the expert's overriding duty to the court. The rules spell out unequivocally that the expert has an overriding duty to the court.

057 The new rules require the parties, at the outset, to name the field in which expert evidence is to be relied upon and where practicable to name the expert in that field at the same time. This will mean that the parties will have to consider their expert appointment much earlier, which should help to avoid several of the problems explained above which arise from late appointment. In fact, the strict management of the timetable by the judge will mean that the parties should have the majority of their case prepared before proceeding, in order that they can meet the timetable. The benefit of an early appointment is that the expert will be able to have some input into the way the case is pleaded if he is to support it. The appointing party will also have the early warning as to whether the expert can support the case. With earlier expert advice the parties may be more realistic in their claims and aspirations.

058 The opportunity, under Rule 35.6, for the opposing party to put written questions to the opposing party's expert and to the *Single Joint Expert* is new. If an expert fails to respond this may bring his evidence and costs into question. The court may decide that his evidence may not be relied upon or that his costs may not be recovered by the party who has instructed him. This may solve some of the problems of experts who are not prepared to answer questions in *without prejudice* meetings.

059 Under Rule 35.7, the court has the power to direct the parties to instruct a *Single Joint Expert* where both parties wish to submit expert evidence on a particular issue. If the parties are unable to agree a Single Joint Expert then the court may direct how the expert is selected. Both parties are entitled to give instructions to the Single Joint Expert. On the face of it, this appears to be a positive move because the expert's first duty has always been to the court or tribunal. I have always been of the opinion that because of that duty, an expert should always be able to act in a capacity as a Single Joint Expert. However, my experience is that on occasions, an opposing view can have merit. If such a situation occurs then it is known about before the trial and appropriate action taken, particularly if it can have an effect upon the outcome. This could be a problem with the Single Joint Expert. It is possible that the Single Joint Expert would be able to determine the conflicts from the relevant party's instructions or from written questions and thus report accordingly. On the other hand, one party may not wish to ask questions but instead deal with any points in cross examination hence leaving the matter until trial. In other words they may seek to discredit the Single Joint Expert's view in the witness box.

060 The other issues that arise from the new Court Rules is the power of the court to determine or limit the amount of expert's fees and expenses under Rule 35.4. Will a judge necessarily understand the level of work that has to be put in where the matters are quite complex, particularly in determining cause and effect in major construction projects? I speculate whether the parties will seek to restrict their fees to experts to the limits provided by the courts, or whether the issue of costs will be dealt with more effectively by robust taxation. This is no doubt a potential area of concern between experts and their clients.

061 The new rules contained in Parts 32 and 35 in relation to evidence and experts do not, in my opinion, change the fundamental role of the expert. The expert's overriding duty is quite clear and has not changed; the primary duty of the expert still being to the court or tribunal. The main differences are potentially:

(a) The naming of the expert in directions.
(b) The Single Joint Expert.
(c) Written questions to the expert.
(d) Limitation on fees.

***Roger Trett** is the Chairman and Chief Executive of Trett Consulting, a company he founded in 1977. Trett Consulting has grown to become a recognised leader in providing commercial and contractual services aimed at investigating contractual, financial and management problems within the construction and engineering industries with 11 offices worldwide. Mr Trett's particular expertise is in forensic delay analysis (cause and effect) and* quantum. *He is Deputy Chairman of The Academy of Experts, Associate of the Chartered Institute of Arbitrators, Member of The Institution of Civil Engineering Surveyors, Fellow of the Association of Lawyers, Fellow of the Institute of Directors, Fellow of the Guild of Surveyors, Member of the Association of Cost Engineers, Member of the London Court of International Arbitration, a representative member of the Joint Consultative Committee of the London Court of International Arbitration, Member of the Indian Society of Arbitrators, Member of the Bahrain Arbitration Panel, an Accredited Mediator and Adjudicator to the Centre for Dispute Resolution, and an Accredited Mediator on the Panel of The Academy of Experts. His experience covers all aspects of construction from building through to shipbuilding.*

Note to the Appendix

In the following sanitised report there are references to documents that were in Volume 2 as appendices. In addition other references to "attached" appendices occur.

Volume 2 has not been reproduced on the basis that it is not necessary in reaching an understanding on the approach but primarily because it would identify the parties.

For the purpose of timescale the dates in the sanitised report have been updated by eight years. Such an update does not have a material effect upon the substance of the report.

APPENDIX

In the High Court of Justice — 1990 No ABCD
Queen's Bench Division
Official Referees Business

IN THE MATTER BETWEEN

JONES & JONES LIMITED Plaintiffs

AND

CASTLE LIMITED Defendants

Expert Report upon the dispute between the parties in relation to the project for the construction of new offices for the Institution of Fund Managers

---

Volume 1 of 2

Prepared by:-

Roger T Trett
4th Floor
CAP House
9/12 Long Lane
London
EC1A 9HA

Tel: (0171) 600 2211
Fax: (0171) 600 3818

This report has been prepared by RT Trett of Trett Consulting.

This report is based upon my understanding of the pleadings and the documents available to me upon discovery in this matter and on the understanding of the obligations imposed upon the parties in this matter.

The contents of this report are as follows:-

Volume 1

Part V	5.0	Review of *Castle Quantum* Claim
Part VI	6.0	Detailed review of *Castle Quantum* Claim
Part VII	7.0	Review of *J&J* final account (as pleaded)
Part VIII	8.0	Conclusion

Part I

1.1 Introduction

1.1.1 This report has been commissioned by Edwards Solicitors (Edwards) on behalf of Jones & Jones (J&J) in the matter of *Jones & Jones Limited* and *Castle Limited* (CASTLE) with regard to work undertaken by J&J for/or under sub-contract to CASTLE in the construction of a new headquarters for the Institution of Fund Managers (the IFM) in Hertfordshire.

1.1.2 A dispute has arisen where CASTLE allege that delays by J&J in carrying out their works occasioned delay to the overall project completion date such that as a direct result CASTLE incurred additional costs and suffered the imposition of liquidated damages by the client the IFM. CASTLE have claimed from J&J these alleged additional costs including where applicable liquidated damages and have "set off" the monies from J&J's measured account.

1.1.3 The matter is the subject of an action in the High Court of Justice, Queen's Bench Division and is being dealt with under Official Referee business before Judge X. Jones & Jones are the Plaintiffs and Castle Limited are the Defendants.

1.2 Parties Referred to in this Report

1.2.1 In this report certain parties, in addition to the Plaintiff and the Defendant, may be referred to, a brief description of the parties, their activities and relationship with the Plaintiff and/or Defendant in this matter are set out below.

1.2.2 *Castle Limited* (CASTLE) (Defendant) are builders and estate developers, based in Hertfordshire and were contracted by the Institution of Fund Managers to construct a new headquarters at Stevenage Hertfordshire.

1.2.3 *Jones & Jones Limited* (J&J) (Plaintiff) trading as Jones Structures (JS), based in Hertfordshire, are precast concrete manufacturers and erectors.

1.2.4 The Institution of Fund Managers (the IFM) Client.

1.2.5 Volume & Gear (VG) are Architects and were employed by CASTLE as Architects for the project.

1.2.6 Brown-Smith (BS) are Consulting Civil & Structural Engineers and were employed by CASTLE for foundation design and brickwork stability.

1.2.7 Smith Associates (SA) Structural Engineers, employed by J&J to undertake design and detail drawing of J&J's scope of work.

1.2.8 Arch Green (AG) are Consulting Engineers employed by CASTLE in that capacity.

1.2.9 PPP Management Services (PPP) are Management Consultants employed by the IFM to project manage the project on behalf of the IFM.

1.2.10 ABC Son, (ABC) are Tiling Contractors employed by CASTLE as a domestic sub-contractor.

1.2.11 James Burn Aluminium (JB) were the Domestic Window and Patent Glazing sub-contractor to CASTLE.

1.2.12 Giles Boot Limited (GBL) are Kitchen Manufacturers and installers and employed as a domestic sub-contractor by CASTLE.

1.2.13 Baird and Form (BF) are Building Service Engineers and employed by CASTLE as a domestic sub-contractor.

1.3 *Brief Description and History of the Project*

1.3.1 CASTLE, in 1994, entered into negotiations with the IFM to design and build a new headquarters for the IFM in Lincolnshire.

1.3.2 The new headquarters consists of a precast structural concrete frame with steel roof, precast concrete floors and traditional block and brick cladding.

1.3.3 The gross external floor area of the building is 70,167 sq. ft. divided:

Ground floor	21,994 sq. ft.
First floor	21,994 sq. ft.
Second floor	21,994 sq. ft.
Plant room	4,185 sq. ft.

1.3.4 Prior to CASTLE entering into a contract with the IFM, and as part of their tender process, CASTLE requested that J&J quote for the supply and erection of the planned precast reinforced concrete frame and steel roof.

(Note: I have not had sight of any formal invitation to tender documentation and I am advised by J&J (Mr Brown) that as far as he could recall no formal invitation was ever given. This being consistent with the good relations that the parties had had over many years. The only item of pre-tender documentation appears (as it is undated) to be a conceptual proposal for the design requirements of the whole project. (A copy is attached at Appendix "2".)

1.3.5 On 19 December 1994 J&J offered to:-

> *"supply, deliver, offload and erect onto foundations prepared by others, a Jones precast reinforced concrete framed structure with steel framed roof, all to dimensions as shown on attached sketches Nos F17378/101–6 inclusive."*

1.3.6 The quotation stated that "Terms and Conditions are attached" which consisted of Jones Structures Standard Terms and Conditions consisting of 5 pages. At page 2 of 5 these terms and conditions refer to:

> *"Contracts: this quotation is based on Jones Structures being employed in accordance with the terms of the JCT Dom 1 form of sub-contract (except where varied by our terms and conditions) no amendments will be accepted except by written agreement."*

1.3.7 From the correspondence it is evident that subsequent to J&J's offer discussions took place between CASTLE and J&J culminating in a confirmation of offer by J&J on 25 February 1995, which offer contained variations to the original offer of 19 December.

Jones's terms and conditions as set-out on 19 December were again included with this confirmation.

1.3.8 Also on 25 February 1995 J&J quoted to CASTLE to supply and erect galvanised hollow section bracing.

1.3.9 On 27 February 1995 CASTLE advised J&J by letter that the figures quoted in J&J's letter of 25 February:-

> *". . . meet with our approval and that in the fullness of time it is our intention to place an order with you for the structural element of the contract."*

The letter went on to add

"... at the time of writing contracts have still to be exchanged although we expect this to be imminent. We are obviously not able to issue formal instructions/orders until such time as this has taken place and any work carried out in advance must therefore be considered 'at risk'. On this understanding we would be pleased if you would proceed with such preliminary drawings and calculations in order to provide column loadings and hence foundation design may progress at all possible haste."

1.3.10 On 5 March 1995 J&J quoted for the roof decking, insulation and gutters for the project.

1.3.11 On 12 March 1995 J&J issued instructions to Smith Associates (SA) to commence the design and detailing of the structural concrete frame and design of steelwork. These instructions contained the date of 18 May 1995 for all manufacturing details to be completed.

1.3.12 The Main Contract was signed on 20 March 1995.

1.3.13 Site erection commenced on 30 September 1995 with the frame being substantially complete on 20 January 1996 and the roofing complete by 18 March 1996.

1.3.14 The Main Contract works were completed in February 1997.

1.4 Basis of J & J Allegations

1.4.1 J&J allege that work was carried out for CASTLE as against the quotation plus variations, and that monies are owing in respect of that work. In seeking to recover monies on behalf of J&J it was argued that no contract existed between J&J and CASTLE and that J&J were entitled to pursue recovery on a "*quantum meruit*" basis.

1.5 Basis of Castle Allegations

1.5.1 CASTLE allege that J&J proceeded tardily and without due diligence such that their (J&J) delay in erection caused the entire overrun of the project as a whole.

1.5.2 CASTLE allege that there was not an agreement (i.e. there was not a contract) between the parties when J&J commenced work on the site on 30 September 1995, CASTLE further allege that J&J and CASTLE entered into a contract on or about 7 October 1995 and by virtue of that contract CASTLE are entitled to "set-off" additional costs and damages for late completion by J&J.

Part II—Delays to Programmed Works

2.1 Approach

2.1.1 In view of the allegations of the parties there are four possible scenarios that have to be considered:-

a) No Contract.
b) Contract at 26 March 1995 (Simple).
c) Contract 26 March 1995 (DOM 1 as amended by J&J conditions).
d) Contract at 7 October 1995.

2.1.2 In order to investigate and form an opinion as to the relevant allegations of the parties I have examined the project from the commencement of design to the completion of the works.

2.1.3 CASTLE have in pursuing their alleged entitlement to costs addressed only the erection period of the works undertaken by J&J and have given no cognisance to the whole of the works that J&J undertook which consisted of an element of design, manufacture and erection.

2.1.4 In addition to examining the progress of the work of J&J it is further necessary to examine the progress of the remaining works being undertaken. The counterclaim of CASTLE is based upon the foundation that the delay to the completion of the works and the additional costs were as a direct result of the alleged lateness of J&J (to sustain that foundation it has to be shown that J&J were solely responsible for a delay that was critical to achieving the completion date of the project).

2.1.5 As a consequence the following sections deal with design, manufacture and erection, and with the progress of other trades.

2.2 Design

2.2.1 The quotation accepted by Castle Limited from J&J was for the "supply, delivery, offload and erect onto foundations prepared by others, a Jones precast reinforced concrete framed structure with steel framed roof, all to dimensions as shown on attached sketches Nos F.17378/101/-6 inclusive". These sketches were A4 sheets identifying typical floor plans, sections and frame details (see Appendix "3").

The price quoted covered "framework, flooring units and precast r.c. stairs".

The quotation went on to list the component parts included, e.g. column sizes, beams etc.

2.2.2 Whilst the quotation was for supply of a "Jones reinforced concrete structure" there is inevitably an element of design and/or design modification required from J&J to take account of the client's requirements. However in order for the precast frame to be designed to fulfil the overall requirements of the project it is essential that sufficient information is available to complete the design and detail drawings. Sufficient information in the case of a precast structure is all information that may have a subsequent bearing on the loadings and movements of the structure, i.e. it is not possible to design a PC frame building storey by storey. As such all details to full height will be required.

2.2.3 SA were instructed by J&J on 12 March 1995, to undertake the design and detailing of the PC frame and the design of steelwork, i.e. subsequent to CASTLE's letter of intent, and were provided with a design/detailing programme requiring final details for manufacture by 18 May 1987 (see Appendix "4").

2.2.4 Also on the basis of the "intent" wherein J&J were asked to commence works at their "risk" J&J prepared a preliminary programme dated 12 March 1995 showing a programme for the works ST 4009A (see Appendix "5") with manufacture commencing 18 May 1995 and erection commencing 22 June 1995.

2.2.5 At a meeting held at VG's office on 16 March 1995 the minutes show that further investigation and design had to be undertaken by VG before sufficient information could be provided to SA to allow preparation of calculations and general arrangement drawings (see Appendix "6").

2.2.6 In particular decisions on:

1. Basement area which would affect column heights.
2. Whether the site would be piled requiring column base plates and holding down bolts as opposed to originally intended pocket details.
3. Depth of p.c. beams and brick support angles.
4. Density of slab to plant room floor.
5. Details of purlins to run over roof rafters.
6. Possibility of provision for future staircase.
7. Whether or not staircase to be taken down to basement level.

2.2.7 At a further meeting between the Contractor and Consultants, entitled pre-contract meeting No 1 held on 26 March 1995. (All meetings prior to commencement on site were entitled pre-contract meetings—see Appendix "7"). CASTLE announced that the formal contract documents had been signed on 20 March 1995 and as a consequence the key dates were:-

a) Date of Contract 20th March 1995.
b) Possession of site 8 June 1995 (although consent to enter and carry out preparatory works in advance of 8 June had been given).
c) Completion date 8 December 1996.

2.2.8 SA informed the meeting that preliminary schematics had been prepared including core areas but no further useful work could be carried out until a decision had been made on:

i) Column bases, pocket or base plate.
ii) Brickwork supports, stainless steel or galvanised.
iii) First-floor perimeter beam, increased depth.
iv) Basement and access location to determine column lengths.
v) Confirmation of design loadings.

2.2.9 In response to the question of the plant room floor SA offered a suggestion that to avoid sound transmission the plant room floor should consist of 75 mm thick PC slab, supported whilst casting 225 mm *in situ* concrete slab.

2.2.10 SA stated that to finalise the GA drawings by next week (3 April 1995) as they would like, the above principles and decisions are urgently required.

2.2.11 Discussion regarding the erection programme took place and J&J advised that erection could commence as required by mid-July 1995 provided the necessary design information decisions were made by 10 April 1995.

2.2.12 The effect of this meeting is to recognise a slippage of approximately four weeks in the overall programme from that originally set-out by J&J following the letter of intent.

2.2.13 A further effect of this meeting was to set-down the parameters of the contract and other key dates, in particular commencement of erection by mid-July 1995.

2.2.14 Having established the mid-July date for erection and by making the relevant adjustments to the duration's pre-erection as set-out in J&J's original programme ST 4009A the relevant dates by which J&J design and detail work had to be carried out to effect erection, can be determined, these were:

1. Design decision 10 April 1995.
2. Calculation and GA's for approval by 17 April 1995.
3. J&J check on 1 by 24 April 1995.
4. Client check on GA by 24 April 1995.
5. Concrete and steel details by 29 May 1995.
6. J&J check on 4 by 5 June 1995.
7. Manufacture commencement by 1 June 1995. Manufacture completion by 31 July 1995.
8. Site erection commencement by 20 July 1995. Site erection completion by 9 October 1995.

2.2.15 These details were incorporated in J&J's programme ST 4009/B which were sent to CASTLE under cover of letter Ref GW/AF/St 4009 (see Appendix "8") dated 10 April 1995.

The letter also pointed out that to achieve this programme all outstanding details must be resolved immediately.

2.2.16 On 13 April 1995 J&J by letter Ref AC/RB/S7 4009 BS requested instructions on 14 points to enable the general arrangement drawings to be finalised.

2.2.17 On 21 April 1995 CASTLE responded to J&J's programme ST 4009/B advising that VG are not scheduled to complete brickwork detailing until the end of week commencing 27 April 1995:

"On this basis you will be unable to complete your (J&J's) general arrangement drawings before this date. We (CASTLE) have produced our own pre-contract programme, copy enclosed, which builds in this two-week delay. All other durations are as your ST 4009/B" (see Appendix "9").

Note: This programme puts frame erection to commence on 10 August 1995.

2.2.18 At pre-contract meeting No 2 on 23 April 1995 (which J&J did not attend on the advice of CASTLE) CASTLE stated at minute 3b that they have been unable to give instructions requested by J&J "but hope to following this meeting". (See Appendix "10".)

2.2.19 At this meeting discussion took place on numerous matters which affected or could affect the p.c. frame design e.g.:

1. Basement location.
2. Foundations.
3. Lift Pits.
4. Fourth staircase (core area).
5. Third-floor plant layout.
6. Sub-Station location.
7. Electrical intake room.
8. Meeting to be held between West & Partners (lifts) to discuss basic principles of design.
9. Meetings to be held to discuss brickwork fixings.
10. VG to mark up JS drawings to indicate service holes.
11. Changes to water tank size and plant area.

2.2.20 At minute 10 the Architect issued a programme that concurred with the CASTLE programme issued to J&J on 21 April 1995.

2.2.21 Pre-Contract meeting No 3 on 28 May 1995 (see Appendix "11") continues to deal with design parameters which were necessary to facilitate the completion of J&J design and detail.

1) JS to omit additional tie beams introduced at grid line E to 1st and 2nd floor (no requirement now for lift out slabs).
2) VG now have a layout drawing of the basement available and will forward copy to JS.
3) BS to forward copy of foundation layout and levels to JS.
4) Roof ceiling load confirmed as 0.5KN/M1.
5) Full Architectural drawings to be issued at end of week.
6) VG to resolve core details by end of next week.
7) BS to investigate method of brick stability to be employed. Could require intermediate columns.
8) Position of service holes to be shown on Architect's drawing.
9) "Keying" to p.c. stairs to receive screed finish.
10) Details to balcony will be made available by VG using either concrete or steel columns.
11) Plant room area may be reduced.

2.2.22 At the meeting J&J advised that a three-week extension (to the design period) was required to account for revised design and detail work concerning loadings to the ceiling at roof level. The design of VG was still not "frozen". In addition JS advised that due to lack of drawings showing service "holes" p.c. planks could not be ordered.

2.2.23 At this meeting a further programme was issued by VG providing a frame erection commencement date of 7 September, this is a four-week slippage to the previous programme. I have concluded that this arises as a result of VG's recognition of the late information emanating from them and/or their consultants, and to cover the three-week extension requested by J&J.

2.2.24 On 29 May 1995 by letter Ref PPP/EG/2081 (received by J&J on 3 June 1995) the Architects advised JS that a Halfen brickwork support system *in lieu* of stainless steel angle should be incorporated.

(Note: This is a decision in principle leaving a number of matters to be resolved before finalisation and inclusion in J&J design (e.g. bearings, cast-in requirements). As a consequence J&J drawings cannot be completed.)

2.2.25 In a letter dated 4 June 1995 reference MDB/AKF/ST.4009 BS CASTLE/VG confirmed that 1st and 2nd floor loadings had been agreed on 19 May 1995.

2.2.26 Letter Ref PPP/EG/2081 dated 5 June 1995 (received by JS 10 June 1995) provides copies of VG latest drawings incorporating elevation sketches with the Halfen inserts and slots shown to the perimeter beams.

2.2.27 On 9 June 1995 BS were advised that the drawings received for the layouts of the "core" areas from VG were not "Preliminary" as marked but "frozen" layouts for structural purposes.

2.2.28 On 11 June 1995 by letter, CASTLE confirmed instructions that the site *datum* level was adjusted thus requiring all drawings and levels to be adjusted, accordingly the letter also gave notification that the piling contractor should commence on 17 June 1995.

2.2.29 On 17 June 1995 J&J received from VG *via* letter Ref PPP/CMG/2081(05) updated sketches taking account of the site *datum* adjustment to beam/column inserts.

2.2.30 Pre-Contract meeting No 4 was held on 25 June 1995 (see Appendix "12") and matters allowing J&J to prepare the detailed drawings were still required to be resolved:

1) Work on lift pit area stopped awaiting determination on size of lifts.
2) JS still require some details in relation to core 3.
3) The weight of louvres is still being investigated—information needed by J&J to finalise roof design.
4) Plant room layout still not frozen.
5) JS have received some drawings that show holes in floor planks to be incorporated in JS drawings.
6) Due to variations a complete basement re-draw is required.
7) JS advise that outstanding core details are critical to the detailing programme.
8) Halfen supports to bay type E still to be finalised.

2.2.31 On 2 July 1995 J&J provided calculations to VG and advised that these should complete the calculations on "the structure". This comment was based upon the knowledge of SA at that time, subsequent paragraphs show that information continued to be subject to change and certain design, e.g. balcony beams was still taking place as late as October 1995.

2.2.32 On 8 July J&J advise CASTLE that due to discussion re-brick restraints and further Halfen supports that some beams are not designed to take the resultant additional load with regard to their reinforcement and connection to the columns. This will result in re-design and detail to beams and columns, JS are therefore holding units until instructed.

(Note: According to the programme issued by VG at pre-contract meeting No 4. Design and detail should have been completed by week ending 12 June 1995 and casting should have commenced on week commencing 13 July 1995.)

2.2.33 At the fifth pre-contract meeting (see Appendix "13") held on 16 July 1995 information was still outstanding regarding J&J's work, limiting their ability to complete the drawings, e.g.:

1) Some details of core 3.
2) Details of louvre to finalise roof design.

3) Potential change to balcony beam.
4) Beam details being amended to incorporate Halfen channel etc.
5) BS received further drawings showing more service holes in floors.

2.2.34 Letter received 22 July 1995 (dated 17 July) CASTLE to J&J requests calculation criteria for bay D-E third floor level (in response to J&J letter of 8 July). Halfen are re-assessing their requirements and VG will progress the matter. CASTLE acknowledge the urgency of finding a resolution.

2.2.35 By CASTLE letter 24 July 1995, PPP, acting for the client IFM, require clarification on matters, some of which affect the columns. CASTLE consider JS would be ill-advised to commence casting until cleared.

2.2.36 At the site progress meeting number 3 dated 28 July 1995 (see Appendix "14") it is minuted that the fabrication of reinforcement, fixings, etc. had commenced for the pre-cast concrete frame and casting of concrete was imminent.

2.2.37 The Architect reported to the meeting that the Architectural progress of "the frame and envelope are basically complete", i.e. 6 weeks later than his envelope works should have been completed and 13 weeks later than the details should have been available to J&J according to the Architect's own programme issued on 27 April 1995.

2.2.38 4 August 1995 SA were instructed to proceed with the necessary revisions on the 3rd floor beams to grids 1 and 7 D&E together with relevant column connections to take account of additional brickwork support required.

2.2.39 On 6 August 1995 meeting No 6 (see Appendix "15") now entitled Design Team meeting again deals with matters affecting finalisation of JS drawings, e.g.:

1) JS have not received details of the angle brickwork restraint posts.
2) Halfen details still awaited.
3) Louvre details passed to SA.
4) Size of balcony beam to be resolved with SA.
5) Stair details received by SA and being progressed.
6) Decisions on plant room floor required to enable design and detailing to proceed.
7) Entrance grid line ID-E to be held until agreement reached.

2.2.40 At site progress meeting number 4 dated 25 August 1995 (see Appendix "16") it is minuted that the design of "the pre-cast concrete frame is complete apart from various details" and that casting of the pre-cast concrete frame has commenced.

2.2.41 To illustrate as far as possible the effect upon the overall progress of the works resulting from the lack of design information from the Architect, I have prepared a bar-chart format programme P1 figure 1.

2.2.42 From the illustration it can be deduced that programme 1 was issued by J&J, programme 2 by CASTLE, programme 3–5 inclusive by the Architect, VG, and that item 6 reflects the achieved dates in respect of calculations, detail drawings, manufacture and erection commencement.

2.2.43 The programmes 3–5 do not make any changes to the frame calculation and detail durations but programme 4 puts back the manufacture and erection dates to take account, I assume, of the Architect's delays.

2.2.44 Programme 5 however, one month later, makes no adjustment to the manufacture and erection dates to take account of the continued late information.

2.2.45 Programme 6, prepared by me shows the achieved dates with the broken line showing the manufacturing date and erection commencement date that would be applicable if the original programme parameters had been maintained.

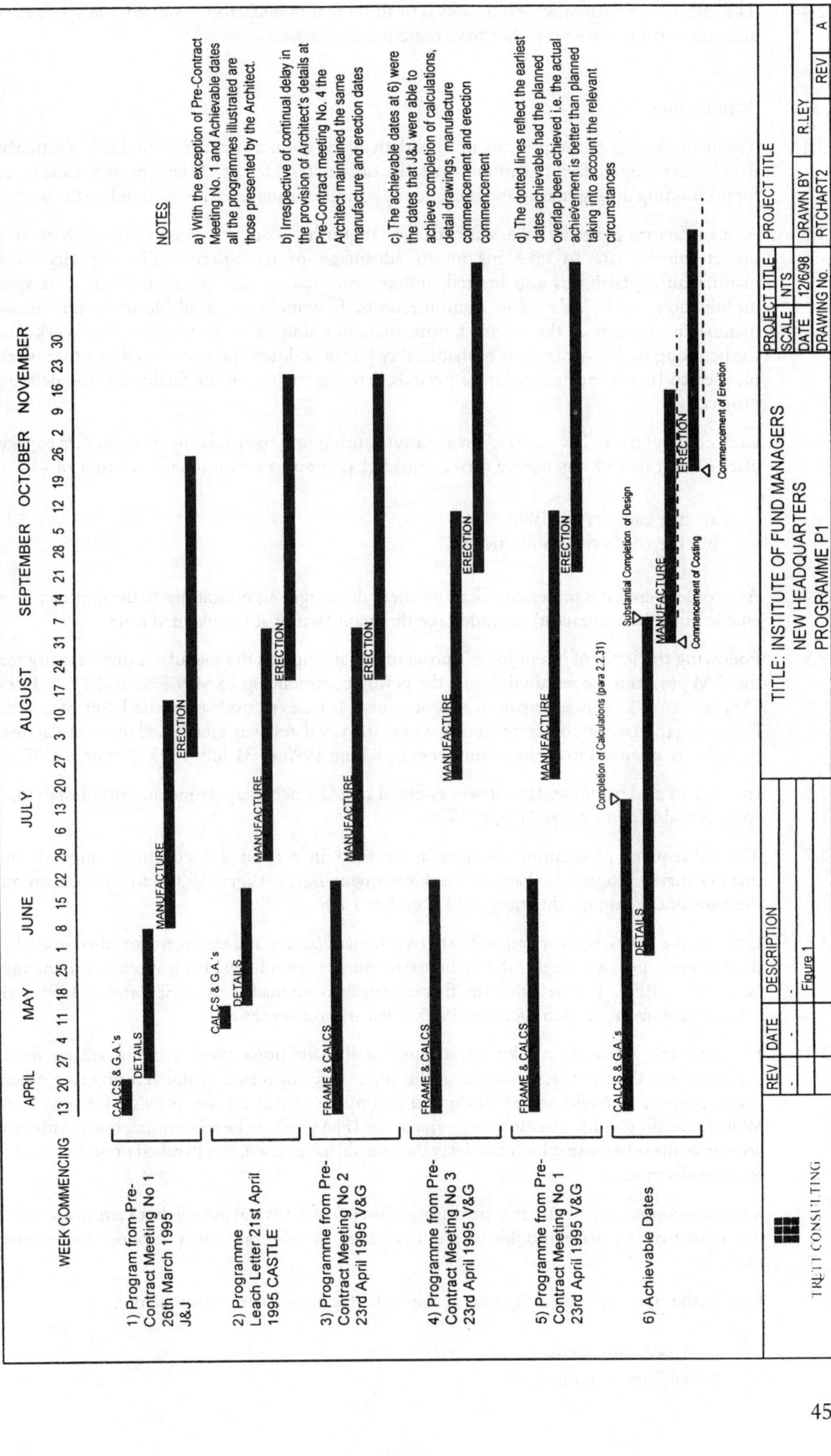
WEEK COMMENCING
APRIL 13 20 27
MAY 4 11 18 25
JUNE 1 8 15 22 29
JULY 6 13 20 27
AUGUST 3 10 17 24 31
SEPTEMBER 7 14 21 28
OCTOBER 5 12 19 26
NOVEMBER 2 9 16 23 30
1) Program from Pre-Contract Meeting No 1 26th March 1995 J&J
CALCS & G.A.'s
DETAILS
MANUFACTURE
ERECTION
2) Programme Leach Letter 21st April 1995 CASTLE
CALCS & G.A.'s
DETAILS
MANUFACTURE
ERECTION
3) Programme from Pre-Contract Meeting No 2 23rd April 1995 V&G
FRAME & CALCS
MANUFACTURE
ERECTION
4) Programme from Pre-Contract Meeting No 3 23rd April 1995 V&G
FRAME & CALCS
MANUFACTURE
ERECTION
5) Programme from Pre-Contract Meeting No 1 23rd April 1995 V&G
FRAME & CALCS
MANUFACTURE
ERECTION
6) Achievable Dates
CALCS & G.A.'s
DETAILS
Completion of Calculations (para 2.2.31)
Substantial Completion of Design
MANUFACTURE
Commencement of Costing
Commencement of Erection
ERECTION
Commencement of Erection
NOTES
a) With the exception of Pre-Contract Meeting No 1 and Achievable dates all the programmes illustrated are those presented by the Architect.
b) Irrespective of continual delay in the provision of Architect's details at Pre-Contract meeting No. 4 the Architect maintained the same manufacture and erection dates
c) The achievable dates at 6) were the dates that J&J were able to achieve completion of calculations, detail drawings, manufacture commencement and erection commencement
d) The dotted lines reflect the earliest dates achievable had the planned overlap been achieved i.e. the actual achievement is better than planned taking into account the relevant circumstances
TRETT CONSULTING
REV | DATE | DESCRIPTION
- | - | Figure 1
TITLE: INSTITUTE OF FUND MANAGERS
NEW HEADQUARTERS
PROGRAMME P1
PROJECT TITLE | PROJECT TITLE
SCALE | NTS | DRAWN BY | R.LEY
DATE | 12/6/98
DRAWING No. | RTCHART2 | REV | A

2.2.46 The effect of the actual achieved dates is to show that manufacturing started one week early and erection three weeks earlier than these projected dates.

2.3 Manufacture

2.3.1 The manufacture of the pre-cast units is dependent upon a number of items, in particular detailed drawings to facilitate mould-making, cast-in items for attachment prior to casting, or for positioning during casting and importantly manufacturing capacity to complete the works.

2.3.2 A manufacturing facility is a static facility requiring work to progress through it at a predetermined rate to take maximum advantage of its capacity. The capacity of a manufacturing facility is also limited, unlike construction sites where if work is delayed mobilisation can be delayed to minimise costs. If work is not available to be put into a manufacturing unit at the planned time then not only is revenue from that work not forthcoming to defray the costs of that facility but in addition there may well be other work planned to be undertaken in future periods denying the use of the facility for the delayed project.

2.3.3 Each contract has to have a "slot" in a manufacturing unit to enable the manufacture to take place—this capacity is generally forward loaded at contract award to take account of:-

a) the capacity available
b) the contractual obligations.

2.3.4 As a consequence it is imperative that the client discharges his obligations to the contractor to enable him (the contractor) to undertake the manufacture at the planned time.

2.3.5 Following the letter of intent Jones's programme anticipated the manufacturing capacity for the IFM project to be required during the period commencing 18 May 1995 to 17 July 1995 (Appendix "5"). This anticipation was of course at Jones's "risk" as *per* the letter of intent. Following the 1st pre-contract meeting where the key dates were established the manufacture period was amended to period commencing 1 June 1995 to 31 July 1995 (Appendix "8").

2.3.6 In order to achieve these dates it was essential that the necessary design and detail drawings were available at the latest 31 May 1995.

2.3.7 The subsequent programme changes as detailed in section 2.2 effectively moved the manufacturing programme back to week commencing 17 August 1995 and completion on the basis of the original duration at 23 October 1995.

2.3.8 Utilising the same overlap relationship between manufacture and erection as detailed in all the programmes, i.e. two weeks, the earliest start on site would have been week commencing 26 October 1995. The date that the first deliveries were made was 30 September 1995 and erection commenced on 5 October 1995. That is three weeks early.

2.3.9 However the above dates take no account of the additional work content arising from variations nor the fact that the works at this time were engaged in manufacturing two other major projects of Multi-Storey beam and column construction, i.e. Roy's Aylesbury and Williams at Weybridge, necessitating parts of the IFM works to be sub-contracted in order to accelerate the otherwise substantial delay that would have arisen, had JS relied upon the works for manufacture.

2.3.10 Such sub-contracting would require organisation of materials and moulds but I am advised the movement of J&J made moulds was also required to sub-contractors' facilities to achieve progress.

2.3.11 I am of the opinion that taking into account the factors affecting manufacture, i.e.

1. late design details
2. additional works

3. committed capacity
4. sub-contracting

that 30 September for the delivery of the first casting to site was reasonable.

2.4 *Erection*

2.4.1 The Architect's programme provided at pre-contract meeting No. 4 (Appendix "12") took no account of the lack of finalisation of the information required to finalise the design and detail drawing for the pre-cast concrete frame, and steel roof, see section 2.2.30 of this report.

2.4.2 The erection of the frame, however, was not solely dependent upon design and manufacture but required the necessary circumstances to allow the frame to be physically erected, e.g. foundations, etc., had to be in position.

2.4.3 The Architects' programme had the structural frame due to commence erection on the 7 September 1995, after the completion of piling, pile caps, ground beams, basement and drainage.

2.4.4 At site progress meeting No. 2 (site progress meetings started when work on site had commenced) held on 30 June 1995 it was minuted at 3.01 (see Appendix "17") that piling was 50% complete and should be complete by 10 July 1995. This represented a one-week delay to the revised programme.

2.4.5 At site progress meeting Nó. 3 held on 28 July 1995 CASTLE minuted at 3.01 that

"a) piling is complete"
"b) basement excavation has commenced and pile cap excavation would probably start later that day".

This represented a 5-week delay to the revised programme and a 10-week delay to the programme issued at Pre-Contract meeting No. 2.

2.4.6 Applying the 5-week delay to the Architects' programme would result in a commencement date of 12 October for the erection of the pre-cast concrete frame.

2.4.7 The records show that J&J commenced delivery of pre-cast units on 30 September, i.e. 2 weeks earlier.

2.4.8 By applying the duration of 12 weeks for the pre-cast frame to the resultant commencement date of 12 October, a completion date for the frame of 22 January 1996 would apply.

2.4.9 The date of 22 January does not take into account:

a) inclement weather
b) variations
c) winter working
d) site conditions
e) restricted mobility
f) late foundations for stairs.

2.4.9.1 INCLEMENT WEATHER
CASTLE were awarded an extension of time of three days in respect of time lost due to inclement weather during the period of frame erection.

2.4.9.2 WINTER WORKING
J&J originally anticipated working during the summer months of 1995, i.e. erection commencement 20 July to 9 October (based upon pre-contract meeting No. 1), thus it is my view that lower productivity would have been achieved during the winter period in which the work was carried out.

2.4.9.3 SITE CONDITIONS

J&J's accepted tender required a hard-cored drained surface over the full extent of the working site. CASTLE provided a site topped by hoggin which J&J allege could be described as a "quagmire" within three weeks of commencing. Thus progress would be hindered. This is confirmed by CASTLE's counterclaim which includes cost of levelling and additional hoggin.

2.4.9.4 RESTRICTED MOBILITY

J&J's accepted prices were qualified in that a hard core road through the centre of the structure for the mobile crane to carry out efficient erection was required. The introduction of the basement pit was not envisaged in J&J's sketches accompanying their quote and this basement precluded the mobile crane from working from the most advantageous erection point. As a consequence I am of the view that the works would have been less efficient.

2.4.9.5 LATE FOUNDATIONS FOR STAIRS

J&J allege that CASTLE originally intended to complete the drainage and foundation slabs in the core areas to allow the stairs to be erected as the work progressed as shown on CASTLE's P1 programme. J&J allege that CASTLE failed to complete the foundation slabs accordingly such that J&J had to refrain from completing the roof steelwork until the pre-cast concrete stairs had been lowered in. The CASTLE daily reports show that the concrete to core 3 base was not poured until 6 January 1996. That the concrete to core 1 was not put in until 20 January 1996 and that the blinding to core 2 base was not commenced until 12 January 1996. The daily reports also show that the stairs were placed three working days later, i.e. 25 January 1996. CASTLE programmed for these slabs to be completed by 28 August 1995 thus there was a delay of 21 weeks by CASTLE in this area. This would have become a delaying factor in itself and more expensive, but would also have denied J&J the opportunity to use the stairs for ease of access during erection.

2.4.9.6 VARIATIONS

The application of the 12-week erection duration does not take into account the variations to the works—some issued after January 1996, the effect of such variations is to increase the workscope of the pre-cast frame by approx. 16%.

(Note: It is recognised that a 16% increase is not necessarily a linear increase in the time required to erect the frame.)

2.4.10 In addition to the variations to the pre-cast frame J&J were awarded the work of roof decking. CASTLE admit in the pleadings that a six-week period for fixing the roof decking was allowed—in addition to the period for erecting the pre-cast frame.

2.4.11 The work to the frame in fact commenced on 5 October, 1 week earlier than the effect of the "on-site" delay caused by CASTLE and was substantially complete by 20 January 1996. Taking the above factors into account I would consider such date to be more than reasonable in all the circumstances.

i.e. 5 October + 12 weeks	= 1 January 1996
+ 3 days inclement weather	= 6 January 1995
+ 12 days' construction Xmas break	= 18 January 1996

Giving cognisance to the points made at 2.4.9 would add considerably to the completion period exceeding the 20 January. In effect J&J accelerated the progress of the works, which is evidenced by the introduction of additional resources.

2.4.12 The roof works were not shown on the Architect's programmes referred to above and no date for completion can be deduced. However CASTLE's programme reference FARA/c/P.I.A dated 1 July 1995 provides a 6-week duration for the roof cladding—this duration has an overlap on the frame erection of 3 weeks. By taking the same overlap period using the

20 January as a completion date for the frame the roof decking should have been complete by 10 February.

2.4.13 The actual roof cladding was completed by 4 March 1996 and it could be argued that such completion was three weeks late in the circumstances. Such argument however rests upon the fact that no disruptive factors occurred during this period, and for CASTLE's allegations and counterclaim to have any substance it would have to be shown that such delay extended the completion date of the project and affected the progress of other works. For information and visual appreciation of the theoretical completion date of J&J had acceleration measures not been taken, I have prepared Figure 2 which incorporates information from the minutes of progress meetings together with the inclement weather plus linear increase in workscope. This visual aid does not take into account the effect of the other contributing items dealt with in 2.4.9.

2.4.14 The result of this theoretical exercise shows that the completion of the frame would have been delayed until week commencing 22 February 1996.

Part III

Review of CASTLE's Counterclaim

3.1 The previous sections of this report have dealt with the matters affecting progress from the information available to J&J at the time, and I am of the opinion that in the circumstances the time taken for J&J to complete their works were reasonable.

3.2 At disclosure, further documentation became available to J&J which enables this report to look at other factors that determined the progress of the works and to form an opinion as to whether CASTLE's counterclaim in my view, can be sustained.

3.3 At the commencement of this report I stated that CASTLE's counterclaim as presented depended upon the fact that J&J's alleged lateness was the reason that the completion date could not be met. I also stated that to prove such a position CASTLE would have to show that the critical path of the project had been affected by J&J's alleged lateness.

3.4 In examining CASTLE's position I have reviewed CASTLE's own programmes, the minutes of meetings and other relevant correspondence.

3.4.1 PROGRAMMES

3.4.1.1 The first full construction programme prepared by CASTLE was dated 1 July 1995 referenced FARA/C/P.I.A and depicted the various work disciplines. It is this programme that CASTLE allege determines the contractual obligations of J&J.

I understand that the first opportunity J&J had of possessing a copy of this programme was following discovery. (A reproduction is included at Appendix "18".)

3.4.1.2 The "front-end" of this programme in respect of on-site activities reflects the revised Architect issued programme at pre-contract meeting No. 3 of 28 May 1995. Such programme will therefore not reflect the lateness of design information subsequent to that meeting.

3.4.1.3 The programme provides for a commencement date of frame erection on 7 September 1995. Irrespective of the programme not giving cognisance to later design information an investigation as to basic progress provides the following:

a) That the erection of the frame follows the completion of piling, construction of basement and lift pits and construction of pile caps and ground beams.
b) That piling was due to commence on 22 June 1995 and be completed on 10 July 1995.

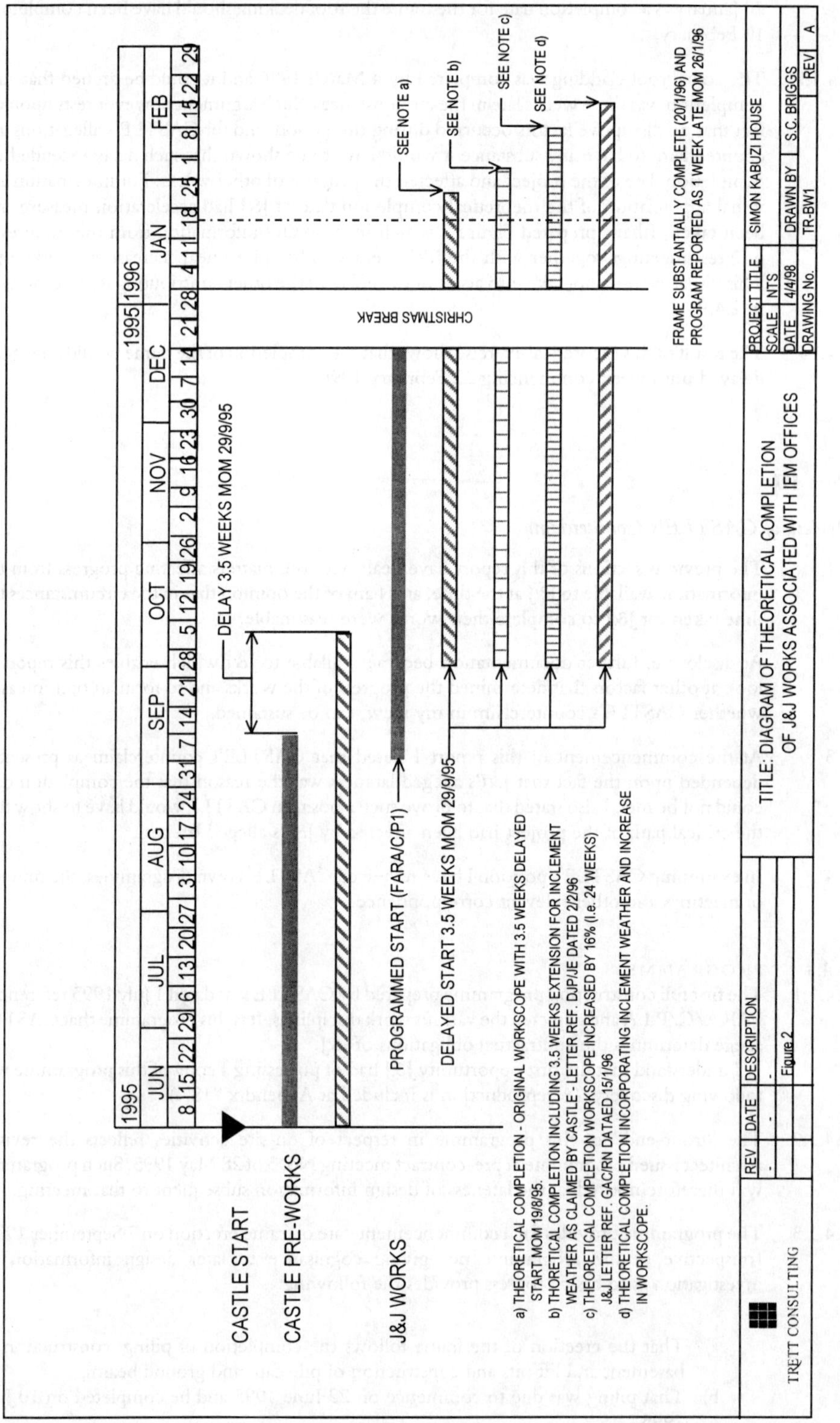

1995
JUN JUL AUG SEP OCT NOV DEC
1995 1996
JAN FEB
8 15 22 29 6 13 20 27 3 10 17 24 31 7 14 21 28 5 12 19 26 2 9 16 23 30 7 14 21 28 4 11 18 25 1 8 15 22 29
CASTLE START
CASTLE PRE-WORKS
J&J WORKS
DELAY 3.5 WEEKS MOM 29/9/95
PROGRAMMED START (FARA/C/P1)
DELAYED START 3.5 WEEKS MOM 29/9/95
CHRISTMAS BREAK
SEE NOTE a)
SEE NOTE b)
SEE NOTE c)
SEE NOTE d)
FRAME SUBSTANTIALLY COMPLETE (20/1/96) AND
PROGRAM REPORTED AS 1 WEEK LATE MOM 26/1/96
a) THEORETICAL COMPLETION - ORIGINAL WORKSCOPE WITH 3.5 WEEKS DELAYED START MOM 19/8/95.
b) THEORETICAL COMPLETION INCLUDING 3.5 WEEKS EXTENSION FOR INCLEMENT WEATHER AS CLAIMED BY CASTLE - LETTER REF. DJP/JE DATED 2/2/96
c) THEORETICAL COMPLETION WORKSCOPE INCREASED BY 16% (I.e. 24 WEEKS) J&J LETTER REF. GAC/RN DATAED 15/1/96
d) THEORETICAL COMPLETION INCORPORATING INCLEMENT WEATHER AND INCREASE IN WORKSCOPE.
TRETT CONSULTING
REV DATE DESCRIPTION
- - -
Figure 2
TITLE: DIAGRAM OF THEORETICAL COMPLETION
OF J&J WORKS ASSOCIATED WITH IFM OFFICES
PROJECT TITLE SIMON KABUZI HOUSE
SCALE NTS
DATE 4/4/98 DRAWN BY S.C. BRIGGS
DRAWING No. TR-BW1 REV A

c) That basement and lift pits were due to commence on 13 July 1995 and be completed by 28 August 1995.
d) That pile caps and ground beams were due to commence on 20 July 1995 and be completed on 10 September 1995.

3.4.1.4 The contemporary evidence (i.e. CASTLE's Daily Reports) shows that:

a) Piling was completed according to programme.
b) Basement and lift pits commenced on 22 July 1995 (1½ weeks late) and were completed on 19 October 1995 (7½ weeks late) which equates to a 6-week overrun in duration.
c) Pile caps and ground beams commenced on 30 July 1995 (1½ weeks late) and were completed on 19 October 1995 (6½ weeks late) which equates to a 6-week overrun in duration.
d) The frame commenced erection on 5 October 1995 (4 weeks late) and was completed on 20 January 1996 (5½ weeks late) which equates to a 1½-week overrun in duration. (See Appendix 37 for illustration.)

3.4.1.5 The above dates show that the frame was not the main item of delay, and that taking the literal relationships of CASTLE's programme activities the dates for commencement of erection of the frame (based upon completion of ground beams and pile caps) would have been 12 October 1995—actual erection commenced on 5 October 1995, 1 week early.

3.4.1.6 The overrun of 1½ weeks of the frame (5½ weeks late in completion—4 weeks late in commencement) compares favourably with the overrun in the duration of the previous activities, i.e. basement and lift pits (7½–1½) 6 weeks, pile caps and ground beams (6½–1½) 5 weeks.

3.4.1.7 Whilst the above indicates that the frame was not the largest delay in terms of overrun, and I am of the opinion the overrun of 1½ weeks is reasonable when taking into account the other prevailing factors as detailed in previous sections, it is necessary to determine whether the frame overrun had an effect upon the completion date, i.e. whether it affected the critical path of the project.

3.4.1.8 In any event the maximum effect the frame could have had upon the project based upon the July 1 programme would be 1½ weeks, before taking cognisance of the other governing factors, and then only if the frame was critical to meeting the completion date. Without the benefit of a contemporary network analysis it is not possible to determine such a position.

3.4.1.9 The unavailability of a contemporary network analysis makes it necessary to consider other relevant information to be able to draw a reasoned conclusion as to the overall effect of the allegations against J&J.

3.4.1.10 The fact that the basement and lift pits were completed 7½ weeks later than planned and were sequenced before the frame may be construed to be the item causing the overall delay.

3.4.1.11 The fact that the pile caps and ground beams were 6½ weeks late could also be construed to be the item causing the overall delay.

3.4.1.12 Of extreme importance is the fact that the lack of information provided by CASTLE's Architect created a "front-end" delay of 7 weeks to the start of planned erection. Utilising CASTLE's own programme of 1 July 1995 (i.e. 20 July 1995 Pre-Contract Meeting No. 1, to 7 September 1995) and that and other factors as described create an overall 12-week delay to commencement of erection (20 July 1995 to 5 October 1995).

3.5 Progress reports

3.5.1 In addition to the above factors the progress reports make the following observations against the programme of 1 July.

a) Progress Meeting No 3 held 28 July 1995 (Appendix "14"). Sub-structure excavations are approximately one week behind programme (i.e. one week lost in the first 3 weeks of programme).
b) Progress Meeting No 4 held 25 August 1995 (Appendix "16"). "The works on site are currently 2 weeks behind programme due to delay in completing the design and sub-letting the works" (i.e. 2 weeks lost in 7 weeks of programme).
c) Progress Meeting held 29 September 1995 (Appendix "19"). "The delay to contract is now 3½ weeks."
d) Progress Meeting held 27 October 1995 (Appendix "20"). "The pre-cast concrete frame erection commenced 3½ weeks late due to the design and problems at Jones's works is now 5 weeks behind programme."
e) Progress Meeting held 24 November 1995 (Appendix "21"). "Mr Pear reported that the delay against programme FARA cp/1 is now 7 weeks."

Progress Meeting held 15 December 1995 (Appendix "22"). "The current delay to the contract is 7 weeks."

3.5.2 In January 1996 CASTLE (see Appendix "38") issued a revised programme which programme maintained the 8 December 1996 completion date. By the issue of this programme maintaining the same completion date CASTLE prove that the delays to date are not critical to achieving that completion date.

a) Progress Meeting held 26 January 1996 (Appendix "23").
It is assessed that the works were about one week behind the revised programme.
b) Progress Meeting held 23 February 1996 (Appendix "24").
"Mr Pear reported that the works are currently about 2 weeks behind programme but the mechanical and electrical services will commence as programme on 29 February. He also pointed out that window installation would take longer than programmed but this would not delay the works overall." (Note the frame was substantially complete on 20 January 1996.)
c) Progress Meeting held 31 March 1996 (Appendix "25").
"Mr Hatch reported that the works were 4 weeks behind programme overall due to the problems with the frame and the brickwork taking longer. He said that the works would again be re-programmed in an effort to achieve completion by the extended date of 14 December 1996. Though this will be tight." (Note 1 the extension covered a period of inclement weather during frame erection period.) (Note 2. The works were re-programmed in January taking account of the position of the progress at that time.) This further delay we consider should not result from the frame activities.
d) Progress Meeting held 28 April 1996 (Appendix "26").
"Mr Pear stated that the brickwork, windows and plasterwork are approx. 6 weeks behind programme. The other critical operations are the mechanical and electrical services and whilst the first fixings were on programme the plant room installations were delayed. A further revised programme will now be prepared and issued by Friday 6 May."

3.5.3 A further programme was issued dated 29 April 1996 (see Appendix "39"). This programme maintained a 14 December 1996 completion date, taking into account extension of time for inclement weather. This programme was prepared in the full knowledge that J&J had left the site totally in March and therefore it must be the case that irrespective of the allegations as to J&J's delay such delay, if any, was not the reason that the completion date was subsequently overrun.

a) Progress Meeting held 28 June 1996 (Appendix "27").
"Mr Pear reported that certain works, especially the external brickwork, were up to 2 weeks behind the revised programme."

b) Progress Meeting held 26 July 1996 (Appendix "28").
"Mr Pear reported some trades up to 5 weeks behind programme but overall 2/3 weeks delay on project. Completion by 14 December 1996 looking very difficult to achieve."

c) Progress Meeting held 30 August 1996 (Appendix "29").
"Mr Pear reported that certain trades are about five weeks behind programme. A new finishings programme will be prepared to attempt to minimise delay."

3.5.4 A further programme P4 was issued in September 1996 (See Appendix "40"). This programme maintained the 14 December completion date.

a) Progress Meeting held 27 September 1996 (Appendix "30").
"Mr Pear stated that work was generally in accordance with the recently issued finishing programme. Completion date by 14 December, however, will be difficult to achieve."

b) Progress Meeting held 31 October 1996 (Appendix "31").
"Mr Pear reported that work was 1 to 2 weeks behind the finishings programme. Completion date by 14 December 1996 is now most unlikely and a more realistic date is 21 December 1996."

c) Progress Meeting held 29 November 1996. (Appendix "32").
"Mr Pear reported that he was aiming for completion by 23 December but this may prove impossibly tight and certain works may be carried out during the Christmas holiday period."
The Client stated: "in view of the Contractor's statement he will inspect the works on Tuesday 3 January 1997 but can be available before this date if the Contractor achieves early completion".

d) Progress Meeting held 14 December 1996 (Appendix "33").
"Mr Pear reported that he was trying to complete by 23 December but it was likely that the following works would be incomplete at that date and he will endeavour to have these carried out during the Christmas holiday period":

1. Carpet installation.
2. Decorations.
3. Mirrors.
4. Kitchen installation

The hut area would not be completed.

e) Progress Meeting held 3 January 1997 (Appendix "34").
"Mr Pear forecast that the works would be completed by 16 January 1997 with the possible exception of:

- Grass seeding.
- Hut area.
- Meeting room screed.
- Additional rim door in core 3 of S. F.
- Replacement damaged doors.

f) Progress Meeting held 12 January 1997 (Appendix "35"). "Mr Pear forecast handover on the morning of 23rd January."

g) Progress Meeting held 19 January 1997 (Appendix "36").
"Mr Pear forecast handover at 09.00 hours on Monday 23 January 1997."

3.6 *Daily Reports*

3.6.1 CASTLE's daily diary reports show further areas of delay subsequent to J&J's work.

a) Superstructure brickwork, according to the January revised programme, was due for completion on 22 April 1996 but was not complete until 27 July 1996 a delay of 14 weeks.
b) Plastering, according to the January revised programme, was due for completion on 13 May 1996, but was not complete until 16 November 1996 a delay of 27 weeks, with making good of bad workmanship taking until 22 January 1997.
c) Car park construction in accordance with the January revised programme was due to be completed by 2 September 1996 but was still being undertaken on 16 November 1996.
Many more instances of delays are available from an investigation of the daily report sheets against the programmes.

3.7 *Other Contributory Delays*

3.7.1 In addition to the review of the progress meetings and revised programmes their exists other contemporary evidence to question the validity of CASTLE's allegation as to the liability for the contract overrun.

a) Letter reference JCH/JEG dated 16 June 1995 provides dates from CASTLE to PPP for "preliminary dates for issue of information" and incorporates dates for superstructure and roof as being week ending 26 June 1995, as opposed to week commencing 27 April as per CASTLE's programme to J&J of 21 April 1995 i.e. a delay of 9 weeks.
The letter also advises PPP of frame erection commencement of 6 September 1995 i.e. a delay of 7 weeks from 20 July, the date set at Pre-Contract Meeting No 1.
b) Letter ref DJP/JCG dated 21 October 1995 CASTLE to JS CASTLE advise JS that the basement storage tanks are subject to a nine-week delivery thus requiring JS to refrain from placing the PC concrete roof planks into position until the tanks have been lowered through the frame.
c) 8 February 1996 CASTLE in a letter to VG state:

> *"We regret the need to write yet again concerning the outstanding information relative to the above project . . ."*

The letter lists 10 points upon which information is outstanding and adds:

> *"Due to delays in erection by Jones Structures, the project is currently running 11 weeks behind the original programme. The delay in issue of the aforementioned information, it could be construed, is a similar period."*

d) Letter 19 August 1996 CASTLE to ABC Ltd (Tiling Contractor).

> *"You did not start work on Monday 15 August 1996, as agreed, but have advised our site management of a revised start date of Tuesday 30 August 1996. Despite this delay, you have assured us that you will complete your works on or before the programmed completion date of 28 October 1996."*

e) Letter 19 September 1996. CASTLE to James Burn Aluminium Ltd. (Window Contractor)

"We understand that certain items are still being manufactured, and that you now propose to return to complete your outstanding work on the following dates:
W/C 26.09.96.
W/C 17.10.96.
We must point out that the foregoing works are delaying the sealing of the building and thus preventing us achieving the environmental control necessary for the installation of the suspended ceiling tiles. To enable this work to proceed, we must now consider erecting temporary screens to seal the building, the cost of which will be contra-charged to yourselves."

Note: i) In the January revised programme this work was of a duration of 6 weeks incorporated with window installation and was due to be completed on 29 April 1996.

ii) In the April revised programme this work changed to a 14-week duration with an additional overlap duration of 10 weeks for patent glazing due to be completed on 19 August 1996.

iii) In the September revised programme this work was due to be complete by 1 October.

i.e. a delay of 22 weeks from the revised January programme.

On 28 September 1996 by letter, James Burn Aluminium advised CASTLE that they could not get-on with their works for various reasons.

"Main entrance doors and frames. We are unable to proceed until the two lintels over the frames are inserted. Core 2 ... we are unable to proceed further due to blockwork awaiting revision to the Architect's latest details. East electric substation. Frame on site, doors and louvres are being manufactured.
Bays D & E 1st floor. We are attempting to improve on the week commencing 17 October 1996 date.
We cannot accept your contention that we are delaying the sealing of the building. The main entrance, core 2 entrance and courtyard are delayed by main contract works which are still to be completed by yourselves ... Finally we would like to record that the heating services are not complete and without the introduction of portable humidifiers it is impossible for you to control the environment in the building to the satisfaction of the suspended ceiling specialists ..."

g) On 15 November 1996 by letter to BF, CASTLE advises:

"... considers that the electrical work should be further advanced and anticipate that there may be some difficulty in completing within the contract period".

h) On 29 November 1996 by letter to B&F CASTLE advises that:

"... the 0 and M manuals and As Installed Drawings are required to be in the hands of the client by the practical completion date, i.e. the 14 December 1996".

Note: Practical completion being forecast in 15 days' time.

i) On 12 December 1996 by letter to BF, CASTLE issue a variation order

"... to supply and install suspended ceilings to the bulkheads in the core areas".

j) On 12 December 1996 by letter to VG, CASTLE comment as to late changes and liquidated damages:

"We are in receipt of a copy of a letter dated 8 December 1996 sent to Mr AV Phelps of the IFM by Station Officer Pennyfather of Hertfordshire County Council Fire Brigade.

We are astounded at the contents and the number of areas where major alterations are being suggested particularly at such a late stage in the project. Surely such items should have been cleared at the initial design stage and as drawing work has proceeded! We are particularly concerned not only at the probable additional costs of construction but also the effects of the comments contained within the letter in respect of practical completion. As you are aware the contract has a liquidated and ascertained damages provision in the sum of £15,000 per week and we would need to look to your practice to cover such amounts that may be directly attributable to your lack of care and attention.

We are aware that at the present time monies are being withheld from you and this is as a direct result of our dissatisfaction with the manner in which you have dealt with various co-ordination matters. We are prompted to ask what other items will come to light before we successfully hand over the building."

k) Letter 23 December 1996 to Giles Boot Ltd (Kitchen Installers).

"Although commencement of your installation was delayed, the area became available on 5 December but you did not commence work until 15 December. We are therefore extremely concerned with your progress and completion in time for handover to the client by 9 January at the latest."

On 11 January 1997 CASTLE in a letter to VG states:

"We are due to meet Mr Smedley of PPP Management Services on Thursday 12 January 1997 to carry out our inspection of the works with a view to agreeing a practical completion date of Monday 16 January 1997.

Mr Smedley has requested that a statement from the Fire Officer is available at this meeting, in response to your letter in reply to the list following his inspection. Before practical completion is agreed, assurances are required that all of these points have been satisfied by either work having been carried out or put in hand, or the Fire Officer's agreement with your argument that the work is not necessary . . . ."

l) By letter to VG on 13 January 1997 CASTLE advises:

"Further to our letter dated 11 January 1997 in connection with the Fire Officer's requirements, we have met with Mr Smedley who requires a definitive response to the items detailed in the letter to the Institution of Fund Managers dated the 8 December 1996. These fall into three categories as follows:

1. *Work incomplete at the date of site inspection*

   ....

2. *Work agreed to be incorporated.*

   ....

3. *F.O. recommendations rejected.*

   ....

Handover has been arranged for Monday 23 January 1996 subject to a satisfactory comprehensive reply to the foregoing . . ."

PART IV

4.0 Summary & Opinion

4.1 At 2.1.1 I stated that there were four possible scenarios to be considered; Parts II and III provide me with sufficient information to allow me to form an opinion in respect of each scenario:

4.2 In my investigations of this matter for the preparation of this report, I have ignored, until this summary and conclusion, the various scenarios and have considered the matter from the point of the requirements and the effect upon those requirements for J&J to fulfil a design, manufacture and erection commitment to CASTLE.

4.3 No Contract

4.3.1 J&J have pleaded that a contract does not exist. This is based on the position, as I understand it, that CASTLE's letter of intent expressed that the works would be "at risk" and made the statement "and that in the fullness of time it is our intention to place an order with you for the structural element of the contract". No formal order was placed.

4.3.2 On the premiss that no formal contract exists between the parties for this work I am advised by the Solicitor that no grounds for a counterclaim from CASTLE exists. Similarly no grounds exist for J&J to pursue extension of time and/or loss and expense claims.

4.3.3 In any event and in the light of the evidence available I am of the opinion that J&J acted in a reasonable manner and that they were not responsible for the overrun alleged by CASTLE.

4.4 Contract at 26 March 1995

J&J have, in the alternative, pleaded that a contract came into existence on or about the 26 March 1995 as either a simple contract or a contract governed by the terms of "DOM 1" as amended by J&J's standard conditions. (See 1.3.6.)

4.4.1 The potential for contract formation at 26 March 1995 arises as follows:

4.4.2 J&J's offer of 19 December 1994, as amended by their letter of 25 February 1995 formed the basis of CASTLE's letter of "intent" of 27 February 1995. Such letter of intent stated:

> *"... at the time of writing contracts still have to be exchanged although we expect this to be imminent. We are obviously not able to issue formal instructions/orders until such time as this has taken place and any work carried out in advance must therefore be considered 'at risk'. On this understanding we would be pleased if you would proceed with such preliminary drawings and calculations in order to provide column loadings and hence foundation design may progress at all possible haste."*

4.4.3 Whilst this was a letter of "intent" and the works were expressly at "risk" I am of the opinion that the "risk" element was limited by the qualifications that formal instructions could not be issued until the main contract was exchanged and that "any work carried out in advance must therefore be considered 'at risk' ".

4.4.4 At Pre-Contract meeting No. 1 held on 26 March 1995, attended by J&J, CASTLE informed that the formal contract documents had been signed on 20 March 1995, and that the key dates were:

a) Date of Contract 20 March 1995.
b) Possession of site 8 June 1995.
c) Completion date 8 December 1996.

The meeting discussed, amongst other things, a mid July erection commencement by J&J.

4.4.5 The reason for J&J being put "at risk" had been overcome by the signing of the main contract, thus the scenario is possibly that J&J were no longer "at risk" and a contract between the parties existed.

4.4.6 At and subsequent to this meeting J&J were involved in all meetings and continued their design and manufacture and accorded with instructions given by CASTLE.

4.4.7 On the premiss that a contract came into existence, or existed at 26 March 1995 it is my view that pre-contract meeting No. 1 set-out the requirements as regards dates for the erection of the frame, i.e. mid-July 1995 (this date being subsequently incorporated in J&J's programme ST 4009/B. This was confirmed by CASTLE's programme in their response to J&J on 21 April which also built in a 2-week delay due to their architect not being able to meet the information dates required to accommodate the frame calculations).

Such erection being clearly dependent upon design and manufacture taking place within sufficient time to accommodate these dates. The sequence of work resulting from pre-contract meeting No. 1 would have resulted in a commencement date for frame erection of 20 July 1995 and a completion date of 6 October 1995.

4.4.8 As a consequence of the delay in the supply of information to accommodate the finalisation of the design the commencement of erection was delayed from 20 July 1995 to 5 October 1995 a delay of 11 weeks, and the erection of the mainframe extended by 1½ weeks.

4.4.9 I account for the extended duration of the main frame of 1½ weeks by the fact that:

a) a three-day period of inclement weather during the period of frame erection was experienced and awarded to the main contractor
b) variations increased the overall work content requiring erection
c) the site conditions impeded progress
d) the introduction of the basement impeded planned erection methods
e) the work was undertaken in a winter instead of a summer period with the inevitable reduction in productivity.

4.4.10 The overall completion date by CASTLE, that is, practical completion was achieved on 13 February 1997, an overrun of 8 weeks 4 days. This overrun alleged by CASTLE to be as a direct result of J&J failures.

4.4.11 The evidence shows that CASTLE have taken no account of the delays caused by the Architect *pre* or *post* J&J site erection nor of the contribution to delays by other factors.

4.4.12 I am of the opinion that the evidence also shows that throughout the progress of the works CASTLE re-programmed maintaining the 14 December completion date long after J&J had left the site. CASTLE continually failed to perform to those programmes. A bar chart illustration of the continued failure is included at Figure 3. Even as late as 29 November CASTLE were forecasting completion by 14 December.

4.4.13 I have not yet had sight of all the sub-contracts let by CASTLE. My review of the CASTLE *Quantum* claim leads me to believe that a number of the sub-contracts were let subsequent to J&J leaving the site, which were let, I believe, with contract dates and durations taking account of the maintained completion date. There is clearly the possibility that these sub-contractors may have been in breach of their sub-contracts thus contributing to the subsequent overrun.

4.4.14 On the basis that a contract existed or came into existence on 26 March 1995 I am of the opinion that the allegation of CASTLE as to J&J liability for the contract overrun cannot be sustained. As a consequence it is my opinion that there are no grounds for the monetary claim submitted in respect of those allegations.

(Note: A response to the heads of CASTLE's counterclaim has been included at Part V of this report.)

4.4.15 On the premiss that a contract existed or came into existence on 26 March 1995 and as a consequence of the delay in the supply of information to accommodate the finalisation of the design the commencement of erection was delayed from 20 July 1995 to 5 October 1995, a delay of 11 weeks, and the erection of the main frame, due to other contributory factors, extended by 1½ weeks, I am of the opinion that J&J were delayed and/or disrupted in the regular progress of the works by reasons outwith J&J control such that additional expense was incurred for which no recovery was forthcoming within the prices to defray such expense.

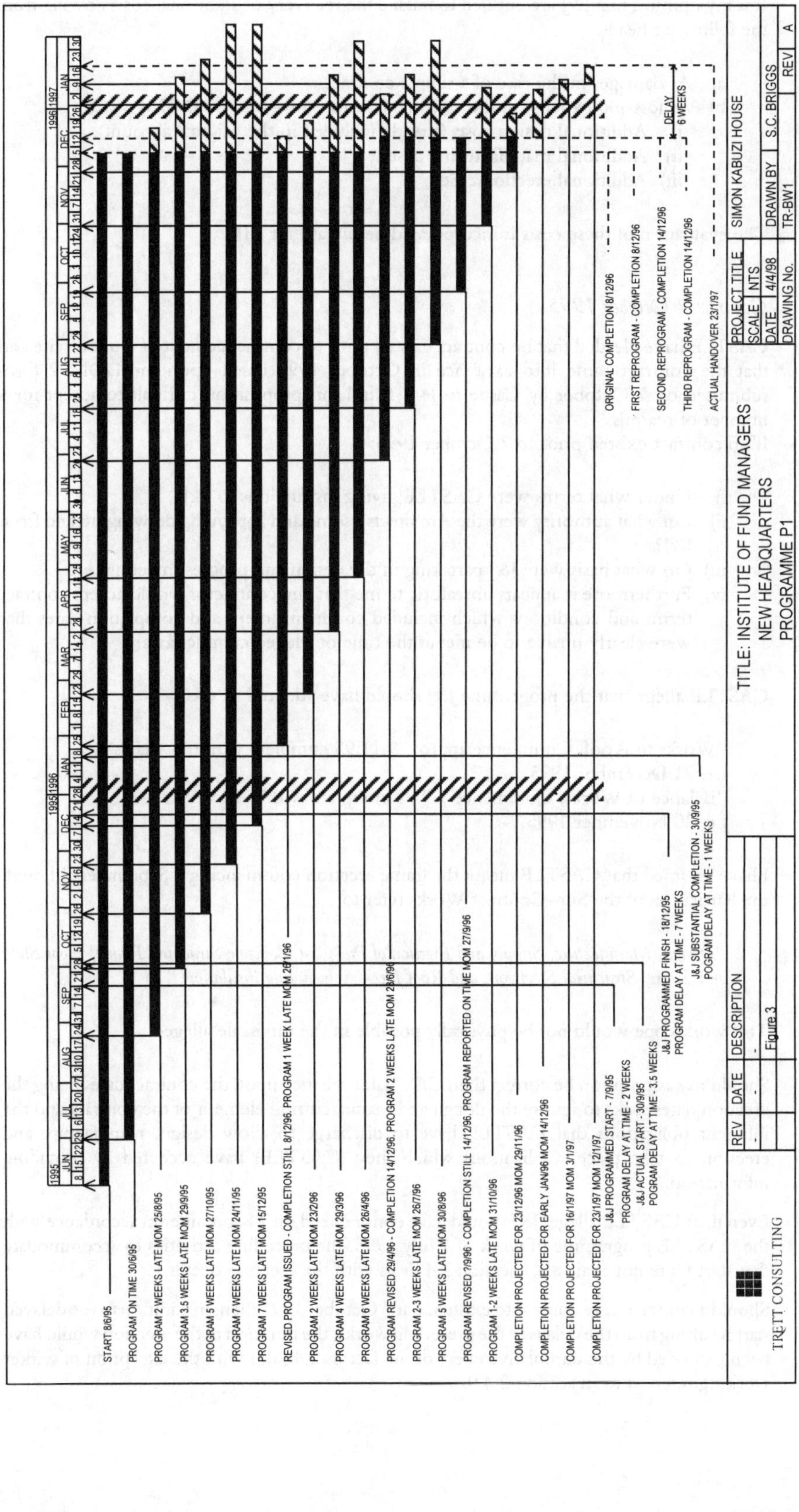
1995 1996 1997
JUN JUL AUG SEP OCT NOV DEC JAN FEB MAR APR MAY JUN JUL AUG SEP OCT NOV DEC JAN
START 8/6/95
PROGRAM ON TIME 30/6/95
PROGRAM 2 WEEKS LATE MOM 25/8/95
PROGRAM 3.5 WEEKS LATE MOM 29/9/95
PROGRAM 5 WEEKS LATE MOM 27/10/95
PROGRAM 7 WEEKS LATE MOM 24/11/95
PROGRAM 7 WEEKS LATE MOM 15/12/95
REVISED PROGRAM ISSUED - COMPLETION STILL 8/12/96. PROGRAM 1 WEEK LATE MOM 26/1/96
PROGRAM 2 WEEKS LATE MOM 23/2/96
PROGRAM 4 WEEKS LATE MOM 29/3/96
PROGRAM 6 WEEKS LATE MOM 26/4/96
PROGRAM REVISED 29/4/96 - COMPLETION 14/12/96. PROGRAM 2 WEEKS LATE MOM 28/6/96
PROGRAM 2-3 WEEKS LATE MOM 26/7/96
PROGRAM 5 WEEKS LATE MOM 30/8/96
PROGRAM REVISED 7/9/96 - COMPLETION STILL 14/12/96. PROGRAM REPORTED ON TIME MOM 27/9/96
PROGRAM 1-2 WEEKS LATE MOM 31/10/96
COMPLETION PROJECTED FOR 23/12/96 MOM 29/11/96
COMPLETION PROJECTED FOR EARLY JAN/96 MOM 14/12/96
COMPLETION PROJECTED FOR 16/1/97 MOM 3/1/97
COMPLETION PROJECTED FOR 23/1/97 MOM 12/1/97
J&J PROGRAMMED START - 7/9/95
PROGRAM DELAY AT TIME - 2 WEEKS
J&J ACTUAL START - 30/9/95
POGRAM DELAY AT TIME - 3.5 WEEKS
J&J PROGRAMMED FINISH - 18/12/95
PROGRAM DELAY AT TIME - 7 WEEKS
J&J SUBSTANTIAL COMPLETION - 30/9/95
POGRAM DELAY AT TIME - 1 WEEKS
ORIGINAL COMPLETION 8/12/96
FIRST REPROGRAM - COMPLETION 8/12/96
SECOND REPROGRAM - COMPLETION 14/12/96
THIRD REPROGRAM - COMPLETION 14/12/96
ACTUAL HANDOVER 23/1/97
DELAY
6 WEEKS
TRETT CONSULTING
REV DATE DESCRIPTION
Figure 3
TITLE: INSTITUTE OF FUND MANAGERS
NEW HEADQUARTERS
PROGRAMME P1
PROJECT TITLE SIMON KABUZI HOUSE
SCALE NTS
DATE 4/4/98
DRAWN BY S.C. BRIGGS
DRAWING No. TR-BW1
REV A

4.4.16 It is my opinion that J&J are entitled to pursue the recovery of additional costs flowing from the following heads:

a) As damages in the case of a simple contract.
b) As loss and expense in the case of a contract governed by DOM1.
   i) Additional design costs (already included in the original account).
   ii) Additional manufacturing costs.
   iii) Additional erection costs.

4.4.17 The evaluation of these costs is incorporated herein at Part VII.

4.5 Contract 7 October 1995

4.5.1 CASTLE have pleaded that no contract existed prior to commencement of work on site and that the contract came into existence in October 1995 based upon the DOM 2 form submitted on 7 October by Castle to J&J. I find this proposition difficult to accept for a number of reasons:
If no contract existed prior to 7 October 1996:

i) Under what terms were CASTLE giving instructions to J&J?
ii) On what authority were the Architects issuing and approving drawings to and from J&J?
iii) On what basis were J&J partaking in the design and progress meetings etc.?
iv) Furthermore it appears unrealistic to me that any contractor would accept contract terms and conditions which included commencement and completion dates that were clearly unable to be met at the time of alleged contract award.

4.5.2 CASTLE allege that the programme J&J should have adhered to was:

"Works to Roof. Commence approx. 9.11.95 complete within 6 weeks"
i.e. 21 December 1995.
"Balance of Works. Commence 7.9.95 complete within 12 weeks"
i.e. 30 November 1995.

4.5.3 I have assumed that CASTLE meant the frame erection commencing 7 September although the Particulars of the Sub-Contract Works refer to:

"Design, Manufacture, Supply and Erection of Pre-Cast Concrete Structural Frame, Floor Slabs and Stairs, Structural Steelwork and Roof Decking including insulation."

This workscope would not be physically possible in the timescale alleged.

4.5.4 Should my assumption be correct then CASTLE's reliance upon the contract dates being the erection dates seeks to ignore the design and manufacturing element of the contract and the inherent obligations that CASTLE have to discharge to allow design, manufacture and erection to take place. Obligations which they (CASTLE) have accepted by providing information.

4.5.5 Even if, as CASTLE allege, J&J should have commenced on 7 September in accordance with the CASTLE programme of work of 1 July 1995, the preceding activities to accommodate that start were not available. (Section 2.4 deals with the erection details.)

4.5.6 Should a contract have come into existence at 7 October 1995 then, in addition to the delayed start resulting from the delays to the preceding works, the duration of the erection would have been extended by the cumulative effect of the factors a, b, d, f with the exception of winter working referred to in section 2.4.9.

4.5.7 In view of the above I am of the opinion that taking into account the relevant circumstances that J&J were not late in the completion of the frame erection.

4.5.8 Furthermore the matter subsequent to frame erection as detailed in Part III shows that even if J&J had been responsible for a delay such delay was not the cause of the eventual overrun.

Part V

5.0 *Review of Castle* Quantum *Claim £293,647*

5.1 Castle have provided a schedule of loss and expense allegedly arising from J&J's alleged failure to complete their sub-contract works within the period set-down by CASTLE. This claim amounts to £293,647.

As a consequence CASTLE allege that as a consequence of 14 weeks overrun on J&J works the main contract period was extended by 8 weeks 4 days.

5.2 I have examined the heads of CASTLE's schedule and make the following observations.

5.2.1 LIQUIDATED & ASCERTAINED DAMAGES £86,650.98

5.2.1.1 CASTLE claim a total of £86,650.98 in respect of liquidated and ascertained damages deducted by the IFM under the terms of the Main Contract for late completion.

5.2.1.2 I have formed the opinion as stated in the previous sections of this report that the responsibility for the overrun of the contract completion date does not rest with J&J. I am of the opinion this head of claim therefore to be unsupportable.

5.2.2 PROLONGATION COSTS £88,746.00

5.2.2.1 CASTLE's claim under this head is for the extended period of CASTLE site and overhead commitments.

5.2.2.2 This head of claim as in 5.2.1 relies upon CASTLE proving that the responsibility for the main contract overrun rests with J&J.

5.2.2.3 It is my opinion that upon this premiss this head of claim is also unsupportable.

5.2.3 WINTER WORKING £10,593.00

5.2.3.1 This claim relies upon the premiss that J&J's late completion on site resulted in CASTLE requiring additional work, plant and protection as a result of the consequent winter working incurred by CASTLE.

5.2.3.2 In addition to my opinion that the commencement on site by J&J resulted from delays caused by the Architect and pre-activity progress on site (which in fact pushed J&J's activities from a summer period to a winter period) I am of the opinion that had J&J been completed on 9 October 1995 then CASTLE would have been required to work through the winter period in any event.

5.2.3.3 The activities planned for the period of October to March on CASTLE's programme of 1 July 1995 are:

a) Internal drains and services 15 October to 7 November.
b) Brickwork sub-structure 12 October to 14 November.
c) Ground floor slab 19 October to 21 November.
d) Brickwork superstructure 2 November to 19 March.

5.2.3.4 None of these items show a dependence upon the frame being complete before commencement and are planned as part parallel activities, although frame completion is required before completion.

Activities a, b, c, d would have suffered the same delays in commencement as the frame due to previous delayed activities on site—pushing them into the later period as was the frame.

5.2.3.5 Activity d) superstructure brickwork was planned to be undertaken throughout the entire winter period. It could be reasonably argued that the alleged delay brought part of such activity into a less inclement period thus increasing expected output.

5.2.3.6 It is my view that the additional costs of winter working alleged in the 1996 winter arose from performance other than J&J's and therefore CASTLE's claim cannot be supported.

5.3 *Disruption/Acceleration Costs—Sub-contractors*

5.3.1 The monetary claim under this head covers for payments made to sub-contractors for alleged disruption—acceleration.

There has been no substantiation of the need to pay disruption or acceleration charges as a result of the alleged delay of J&J.

5.3.2 CASTLE re-programmed the works following completion of J&J's work such that the end date was maintained. The contemporary evidence shows that progress was not achieved in accordance with the programme set-out and that if any disruption or acceleration occurred it was as a result of events subsequent to J&J's presence on site.

5.3.3 A large number of the sub-contracts I believe were not let until after J&J's erection work—which sub-contracts I understand were let to meet the completion dates and in accordance with the programme current at that time, any disruption and acceleration must therefore arise as a result of either breach by CASTLE or the sub-contractor in not performing to the contractual requirements.

5.3.4 It is to be noted that a substantial amount of the costs in respect of this head of claim arise from repairing bad workmanship.

5.3.5 In view of the above it is my opinion that CASTLE's claim cannot be supported.

5.4 *Contra-Charges £4,271.00*

5.4.1 In principle if such works are remedial works as alleged then I would support CASTLE's entitlement to be paid for such work. However, sufficient details have not been provided to fully support this claim (see Part 6).

5.5 *Acceleration Costs—CASTLE*

5.5.1 I understand that CASTLE had not planned to have a finishing foreman and that this item is not for an additional finishing foreman but for a finishing foreman.

5.5.2 If the works were accelerated as stated by CASTLE then the effect should be to reduce the period of time for carrying out these works that were accelerated. In which case an effective reduction in the period of time would reduce the preliminary charges in relation to the accelerated activities, which reduction should be set against any additional cost of resources.

5.5.3 I am of the opinion that CASTLE have not shown that the need to introduce a finishing foreman was as a direct result of J&J's alleged delay. I am of the opinion therefore that CASTLE's claim under this head cannot be supported.

5.6 *Increased Costs of Labour & Materials £25,105.00*

5.6.1 The basis of these charges is the charge of inflation arising as a result of a 14-week alleged delay by J&J.

5.6.2 In principle if J&J had been liable for delay an element of these costs would be claimable by CASTLE. However sufficient details to substantiate that such costs have been incurred have not been provided.

5.6.3 It is my stated view however that the liability for the delays do not rest with J&J and as such their (CASTLE's) claim cannot be supported.

5.6.4 Of some interest however is the light that this section of charges shows upon the work subsequent to J&J's frame completion. In particular in relation to the sub-contract works.

5.6.4.1 CASTLE have taken the published inflation rate for the period and, in respect of sub-contract works have multiplied the value of the sub-contract works by the annual inflation rate *per annum* divided by 52 weeks, multiplied by the number of weeks between the programmed date taken from 1 July 1995 programme, and the agreed contract start date of each sub-contractor. I do not know however whether such costs have actually been incurred.

5.6.4.2 There are two points to consider in respect of these calculations:

a) If the sub-contract was let with a commencement date as set-out by CASTLE in accordance with the programme of 1 July 1995, and was subsequently delayed leading to CASTLE making payments in respect of inflation then evidence should be available to prove that payment was made.
b) If the sub-contract was let subsequent to Jan 96 with the agreed contract start dates as set-out by CASTLE then no additional inflation charges would occur. However CASTLE could argue that due to the agreed sub-contract start dates being later than programmed then the sub-contract quotes were higher because of inflation. If this argument is pursued then the calculations prepared by CASTLE are incorrect. That is, the sub-contract prices are grossed to include inflation and represent 100%+. E.g. Sub-Contract awarded *post* January, agreed contract start 1 March planned contract start 1 Jan.

   Sub-Contract sum for 1 March = £5,000 which sum includes inflation between January and March

   Assume inflation 5% between Jan/March (8 weeks)

   Increased costs $5\% \times \frac{5{,}000}{105} = £238.00$

   and not 5% of £5,000 = £250

   CASTLE's calculations have been based upon the latter calculation.

5.6.4.3 Of fundamental importance are CASTLE's statements in respect of sub-contractors of "agreed contract date of commencement of their sub-contract works" all these agreed dates are subsequent to the dates of the 1 July programme such that the contracts have been let taking into account the progress of the works and the re-programming.

In other words the performance to the agreed contractual dates between CASTLE and their sub-contractors has not been affected by any alleged delays of J&J.

If the programme to which these sub-contractors were due to perform has not been met then such failure must be a matter between CASTLE and the sub-contractor and does not arise from any failure of J&J, such a position goes to support my view that CASTLE's claims against J&J cannot be substantiated.

Part VI

6.0 *Detailed Review of Castle* Quantum *Claim*

6.1 Part V of this report has dealt with the *Quantum* claim of CASTLE by dealing with the general heads of claim. However investigation in detail of their (CASTLE's) claim indicates that a number of the claims made, when looked at in detail, relate to items that, even if J&J were liable for delay, would not fall, in my view, into the category of a counterclaim arising from such liability.

The following paragraphs deal with such items.

6.1.1 (ITEM 1) LIQUIDATED AND ASCERTAINED DAMAGES

These have been dealt with in Part V.

6.1.2 (ITEM 2) PROLONGATION COSTS

The Experts have agreed that the figure of £86,650 was deducted from J&J's accounts, although the final account has not yet been signed off.

a) **Protection of the Works £173.00 (2d(v))**

CASTLE's claim for protection of the works is five times their original estimate. CASTLE would be required to protect the works in any event, a common requirement particularly when different finishing trades are working in the same building.

b) **Hand Tools £200.00 (2d(vi))**

The work content did not increase as a result of any actions of J&J thus I consider that additional hand tools should not be required. CASTLE's counter-claim is five times their original allowance.

I do not consider that items such as paint scrapers, fillers, extension leads etc. arise as a direct cost of any alleged delay by J&J.

c) **Plant Hire £3,573.00 (2e)**

CASTLE have claimed for plant hire from December 1996 through to the February 1997 completion. Any plant hire calculation should be based upon the plant that was hired for an extended period as a result of any delays. Not the hire of plant in the overrun period. The alleged delays of J&J would have, if anything, delayed the bringing onto site of plant for subsequent activities and not necessarily have extended the duration.

d) **Extended Scaffold Hire £8,387.00 (2g)**

CASTLE have based their claim for extended scaffold hire upon unsubstantiated durations from the final account of their scaffolding contractor.

The effect, if any, of the late completion of the frame would not, in my view, be to extend the scaffold hire but would delay the erection of scaffold.

e) **Castle Overheads £56,913.00 (2h)**

No credits have been made in respect of overhead recovery from variations.

6.1.3 (ITEM 3) WINTER WORKING £10,593.00

6.1.3.1 I have preferred the view that CASTLE would have been required to undertake winter working in any event and that the costs of such alleged working do not arise as a result of the actions of J&J. Further investigation of this item shows that:

i) the sum claimed is 4 times the total sum estimated by CASTLE.

ii) items a, b, c, & d claimed by CASTLE have no supporting evidence.

iii) items e & f refer to levelling, excavating and maintaining ground conditions which I am of the opinion would always have been a requirement and obligation of CASTLE. In particular CASTLE refer to contemporary documents in support:

Document No. 87 refers to levelling area to take scaffold. This does not arise from J&J actions.

Document 88 refers to making up ground levels with hoggin for J&J crane. J&J quotation required from CASTLE adequate ground facilities to accommodate their erection crane.

Document 89 is for cleaning roads. An obligation of CASTLE not J&J.

Document 90 is for protection to concrete slab. CASTLE's programme indicated the slab being laid in the winter period thus protection would have been required in any event.

Documents 91–113 inclusive, similarly refer to activities as described above and consist of either activities that were CASTLE's responsibility and which do not arise from actions of J&J.

iv) Item g. CASTLE seek to charge J&J for temperature and humidity control to facilitate suspended ceiling erection. Reasons in addition to my earlier view as to responsibilities for delay, and which question any validity in this charge are:

1. The extended duration for the window installation.
2. The allegation of CASTLE against JB that CASTLE held JB responsible for the lack of CASTLE's ability to seal the building.

It is worth noting that the costs are three times CASTLE's alleged estimate, but which information also shows that CASTLE planned to expend money maintaining temperature and humidity. I can see no reasons emanating from J&J's work that increased the expenditure of this planned operation.

It is also clear from the invoices provided in support of this item that charges have been made by the supplier for items that should have been returned at the cessation of their need by CASTLE.

6.1.4 DISRUPTION/ACCELERATION COSTS—SUB-CONTRACTORS £69,952.00

6.1.4.1 CASTLE have based their claim on Claims from Sub-Contractor for loss and/or expense suffered or incurred as a result of a reduced contract period, loss of production, evening, weekend and Christmas holiday working.

6.1.4.2 Prior to providing a response to individual claims, and to reiterate the previous opinions as to liability of J&J in respect of these claims, it is of importance that an understanding of the manner and timing with which CASTLE let the sub-contracts is understood.

6.1.4.3 CASTLE state that the claims, in part, arise from "a reduced contract period". I have yet to find a sub-contract period, or duration, that was reduced, such that disruption or acceleration for a "reduced contract period" cannot be sustained (See Appendix "41").

6.1.4.4 I have established by a review of the programmes that a shortfall in performance arose, not from the activities of J&J but from subsequent events, not all identified. Thus "loss of production, evening and weekend working" cannot fall, in my opinion, to J&J's account.

6.1.4.5 I have further stated that, from the counterclaim of CASTLE, sub-contracts were let subsequent to the activities of J&J such that the sub-contract programmed dates were not reliant upon the activities of J&J, consequently no counterclaim in respect thereof can be, in my view, sustained.

6.1.4.6 Particular investigation into the counterclaims show:

i) *Plastering* Daywork sheets 121–136 inclusive refer to making good after other trades, i.e fixing of fire hoses, finishing to windows, reveals, etc.

Fire hose reels would not normally be fixed prior to plastering thus there would always be a subsequent requirement to make good.

Similarly any making good of window reveals would be a requirement of the plasterer if damage caused. In this instance however and as detailed in earlier sections of this report, the window manufacturer and installer was late in performance, even though the planned programme duration was substantially extended from that to which CASTLE allege J&J failed to perform.

ii) *Plastering* Daywork sheets 137–156 deal with making good plastering.

138 No claim.
139 Make good on staircase No. 2. (after fire stopping carried out to HV risers).
140 No claim.
141 a) Filling under window cills 2nd floor.
b) Make good to lift areas (door opening after fixing of entrance doors).
c) Make good after electricians and carpenters.
d) Make good to windows. (Scaffold tied through window preventing earlier completion.)

142 No claim.
143 Make good to staircase and bulkheads.
144 No claim.
145 a) Make good to ground floor reveals.
b) Make good to access traps in ducts (after fixing of access plates). Not fixed before plastering (no information on fire dampers).
146 No claim.
147 Finishing off the making good in reception after electricians and window fixers.
148 No claim.
149 Make good after electricians, ground floor toilet area. (Fire alarm panel not fixed at time of plastering.)
150 No claim.
151 a) Make good to stud columns on 2nd floor at ceiling line. (Ducts out of sequence.)
b) Make good to window reveals on south first floor.
c) Make good to door frame south wall (hoist opening).
152 —
153 General making good after other trades.
154 No claim.
155 Making good after other trades.
156 Making good to pipes, door frame after removal of temporary frame. (Pipes not in earlier. Access had to be made to duct.)

I am of the opinion the above work to be part of the normal making good on a project of this nature. Furthermore the allegations of CASTLE as to the lateness of the window and electrical contractors together with the allegations of lack of information from the Architect, and the bad workmanship of the plasterer make it very difficult for me to consider that such costs arise from the alleged lateness of J&J. The daywork sheets in support of this head also contain information that refer to *contra* charges to other contractors for some of these items.
CASTLE's monetary claim for this head amounts to 4 times the sum that they estimate the work should have cost at contract rates. No support for their assessment has been provided but such admission means that they did anticipate a making good requirement.

6.1.4.6(B) *Brickwork & Blockwork*

i) Daywork: Additional cost as a result of working out of sequence.
157 a) Repair blockwork.
b) Making good pump room area (around pipes).
c) General making good.
158 Making good, cutting lintel openings, indents and rebuilding round H&V ducts.
159 Making good round H&V ducts cutting indents, inserting lintels.
160 Ditto.
161 Ditto + b) make good brickwork in courtyard after scaffolding (where tubes went through brickwork). Wall demolished for access to basement. Rebuild blockwork.
162 Make good brickwork, inserting lintels around H&V.
163 Ditto.
164 a) Cleaning brickwork with acid.
b) Make good H&V ducts and general making good.
c) Cutting out damaged cill brick and replace.
165 a) Making good around H&V/clearing rubble
b) Making good damaged brickwork.
c) Making good H&V kitchen area.

d) Making good H&V core 1, cut out blockwork.

166 a) Making good around H&V.

b) Cut out damaged brick to front of building and replace.

c) General cleaning of brickwork.

Similar to the additional costs for plastering I find it difficult to understand how the above items can result from the activities of J&J. Lintels are a requirement of the building regulations and are not cut in late simply because of the alleged lateness of J&J.

ii) *Acceleration Cost* This head of claim revolves around the premiss that it was necessary to work through Easter and accelerate the brickwork as a result of J&J lateness.

I am of the opinion that such a requirement did not arise as a consequence of J&J, due to the reasons provided elsewhere in this report.

iii) *Loss of Production* CASTLE have based this head of claim on the following:

"Brick deliveries were postponed until the precast concrete superstructure had progressed to a stage that warranted their delivery.

It was subsequently found impossible to obtain bricks in sufficient quantities to maintain production."

The *quantum* support for this claim purports to be a claim from the brickwork contractor and the principle stated above. There are other points to consider.

a) A review of the brickwork contractor's claim gives no reference to brickwork unavailability but refers to lack of access due to other trades.

b) The bricks were decided upon very late, however if CASTLE had postponed delivery then the bricks would have been available when called up. One presupposes that the bricks were ordered within sufficient time and that had delivery been put back CASTLE would have advised a further delivery date.

c) If the alleged delay of J&J had the effect of moving the programme back then the later start of the brickwork contractor would not have been subject to any disruption arising from J&J activities and furthermore the work would have moved into a better weather period.

d) It was not necessary for the precast frame to be complete for the brickwork contractor to start. The programme showed an overlap of 4 weeks. The daily diary records show that the superstructure brickwork commenced 6 weeks late, i.e. week commencing 14 December 1995. As such bricks must have been delivered to accommodate this commencement. The claim for loss of productivity by the brickwork contractor covers the period from March 1996 to July 1996.

In view of the claim it is my opinion that the alleged grounds for this head of claim cannot be supported.

6.1.4.6(C) *Asphalt* CASTLE allege that repairs to asphalt roofing work arose as a result of J&J lateness and that asphalt work had to be undertaken out of sequence to allow other trades to progress.

I cannot determine why the asphalt was carried out "out of sequence" as it was always planned for it to follow the frame and roof. If it was carried out as planned prior to other trades then a risk of damage from following trades will always be inherent.

6.1.4.6(D) *Lightning Protection* This claim arises from alleged additional visits to complete the work.

No reasons have been provided as to why such additional visits were necessary and how they are a consequence of J&J's activities.

6.1.4.6(E) *Aluminium Windows* The claim is for glazing repairs arising from working out of sequence.

From the records it has been established that the window contractor's duration was extended and he was late in performing. Those facts do not arise, in my view, from J&J activities.

If he was late in performing then the probability of damage should have been less as the glass would have been in place for a shorter period.

CASTLE have reduced their claim by £700.00 for "normal breakages". No substantiation of such allowance is provided.

6.1.4.6(F) *Floor & Wall Tiling* The claim is for making good as a result of trades working out of sequence.

The claim covers items from:

a) "Re-tile due to poor plastering."
b) "Re-tile panels to sides of vanity unit."
c) "Replace damaged cuts to ceiling line."
d) "Re-tile left hand and right hand sides of vanity unit."
e) "Re-tile left hand . . . of vanity unit to make straight plasterers' rendering."

I am of the opinion that such items of claim are not a consequence of J&J activities.

6.1.4.6(G) *Carpet Tiles* Claim for repairs and making good as a result of trades working out of sequence.

This head of claim covers:

a) Providing 11 No. door bars to various openings.
b) Latex to screed for vinyl.
c) Making good vinyl after revised conduit position.
d) Carry out latex of services area.

Note: Latex is a floor levelling compound.

I am of the opinion that none of these items arise from the activities of J&J.

6.1.4.6(H) *Terrazo* Claim for repairs and making good as a result of trades working out of sequence.

CASTLE claim for general repairs to stairs and cleaning off plastering.

According to the July 1995 and January 1996 programme the plastering should have been finished before the Terrazo commenced, thus there would be no plaster to clear off. No explanation as to why the sequence did not happen as planned has been provided.

6.1.4.6(J) *Kitchen Installation* CASTLE allege that this head of claim arises as "equipment supplied and installed out of sequence to avoid storage charges".

This claim is for cleaning off stainless steel kitchen equipment as an extra—over cost to normal cleaning.

Giles Boot Limited (kitchen installers) did not commence on site until 15 December 1996 and I therefore fail to understand the principle behind this claim, i.e. the contract was planned to be completed by 14 December.

In the event Giles Boot complained to CASTLE that proper protection had not been given to their equipment.

I am of the opinion that this claim does not arise as a result of J&J activities.

6.1.4.6(K) *Suspended Ceilings* There are three items in this claim.

i) Replacement ceiling tiles. Original tiles damaged by water as a result of being stored outside the building.
CASTLE allege that their was no area within the building to store the tiles. I find this extremely difficult to accept. A 77,000 sq. ft building with no room?
In any event it was the responsibility of CASTLE or the ceiling contractor to ensure that proper storage took place. This does not arise from J&J activities.

ii) Acceleration Charge
The acceleration charge includes:
a) Acceleration.
b) Handling damaged tiles.
No substantiation to support either head has been provided.

iii) Damage to the completed ceiling as a result of other trades working out of sequence.
Although a credit has been allowed against the overall claim for "element of repairs not applicable" no details or substantiation of those applicable and/or those not applicable has been provided.
I am of the opinion that the above claim does not arise as a result of J&J activities.

6.1.4.6(L) *Mechanical & Electrical Installation*
Baird & Form Limited The claim is made up of costs for the

i) "storage, handling and transport of electrical floor boxes" and
ii) "additional costs to accelerate the programme. The suspended timber floor was laid without the electrical floor boxes being installed. At a later date they were installed by an electrician."

I have difficulty in coming to terms with this claim. It would seem prudent that if the electrical boxes were in store awaiting installation then that installation should have taken place in the correct sequence. Unless of course there was a lack of co-ordination by CASTLE and their sub-contractors.

I am of the opinion that this head of claim does not arise as a result of J&J activities.

6.1.4.6(M) *Carpentry* Costs are claimed:

i) As a result of trades working out of sequence to accelerate the programme.
Daywork sheets presented in support of this item refer to providing access under floor for electricians.
The July 1995 programme provides for M&E first fix to commence prior to and completion after flooring, thus co-ordination is essential to make sure that flooring is completed in the right sequence.
I am of the view also that an element of access is normally required subsequent to planned activities to finalise various works.
It is my opinion that this claim does not arise as a result of J&J activities.

ii) "Additional protection to enable trades to progress their works out of normal sequence."
Daywork sheet 279 refers to sealing door entrances ready for ceiling tiles (polythene over doors/windows). Previous sections of this report establish that the window contractor was late in installation of windows and certain doors, also that CASTLE advised them (JB) that they (CASTLE) would have to seal the building and *contra*-charge the costs to them. CASTLE letter 19 September 1996 ref DJ P/J E.
Daywork sheets 280 and 281 refer to protection of doors with polythene. This I consider to be a normal requirement on a project of this nature.
Daywork sheet 282 refers (January 1997) to protecting kitchen units. This I consider to be a normal requirement on a project of this nature. Although from Giles Boot's claim this was not done properly or at all.

I am of the opinion that none of the alleged costs of this claim arise as a result of alleged acceleration or as a result of J&J activities.

iii) Extra over payment for operatives to work during the Christmas Holiday.

iv) Payment as an incentive to complete their contract works after the contract period had expired.

On the basis that I am of the opinion that the delay to the works is not the liability of J&J I am also of the opinion that the above charges (iii) (iv) cannot be supported. In addition I fail to see why J&J should be charged with an incentive payment to the carpenters to complete their contract works after the contract period has expired.

It is of note that to provide substantiation CASTLE have provided a copy of the sub-contract between themselves and Mitre carpentry. The contract was signed on 21 September 1996 with a date of main contract completion of 8 December 1996 and the following durations for the carpentry works.

1st Fix "Commence approx. March 1996. Complete within 6 weeks".

2nd Fix "Commence approx. August 1996 Complete within 8 weeks".

The periods are compatible with those shown on the January 1996 re-programme, which took into account the date for completion of the main frame. Thus the programme dates were set subsequent to the knowledge available as to frame progress and therefore were not reliant upon J&J's completion.

The daily diary reports indicate that the carpenters started on site in February 1996.

6.1.4.6(N) *Suspended Timber Floor* This claim is based upon:

"i) To accelerate the programme, areas of flooring were completed before the building was watertight."

The support for this item actually refers to replacement due to dampness. I am of the view that CASTLE should have provided adequate protection.

"ii) Replace flooring as a result of working out of sequence to accelerate the progress of works." (Flooring removed for pipe access.)

In neither case have CASTLE provided information as to the change in sequence nor I find, provided adequate support as to why the pipe access was late (if it was late) or whether such access was a normal expectation in this type of work.

It is my opinion that these costs do not arise as a result of J&J activities.

6.1.4.6(P) *Painting & Decorating; M & J Mnn; Dayworks* This claim is for:

"i) Additional costs as a direct result of working out of sequence to accelerate the programme of works."

The daywork sheets in support of this claim refer to "remove rubbish" touch up and re-decorate in various areas.

In my experience it is not unusual for the painter and decorator to have to return to touch up various areas following other trades.

I am of the opinion that these costs are not excessive for a project of this nature and could well have been anticipated by CASTLE.

ii) Extra over payment for operatives to work during the Christmas Holiday.

This claim is for working outside the contract period and arises as a result of the delays to the programme subsequent to J&J's work.

It is my opinion that in both i) and ii) the costs cannot be shown to arise as a result of J&J activities.

6.1.4.6(Q) *Preliminaries*

i) GKC Services

"Re-clean areas completed out of sequence letter dated 24 January 1997."

The support sheet refers to "re-clean all areas of glass thoroughly inside and out".

It is normal practice to leave the glass clean on a project of this nature. No indication of "out of sequence" reason or sequence has been provided.

ii) FLJ (General Labourer)

a) "Extra over normal attendance on sub-contractors to accelerate their work".
Daywork sheets 345–366 inclusive refer to activities of
"Offloading materials"
"Clear away rubbish"
"General clean up"
"Clear rubbish and sweep up office block".
I am of the opinion that such activities are either a general responsibility of CASTLE or a matter between CASTLE and their sub-contractors.

b) Extra over normal attendance on sub-contractors to accelerate their works. Castle employees.
CASTLE have alleged £4,500 but provided no substantiation whatsoever. A credit of £1,500 on the whole of item Q as an estimate of normal allowance has been allowed. No substantiation of the figure has been provided.
It is my opinion that the above charges do not, or cannot, be shown to arise as a result of J&J activities

6.1.4.7 *Contra Charges*

1a) i) Alterations to stainless steel Halfen brackets.
CASTLE have provided invoices for the above item but no reasons or locations for the necessity to carry out such alterations.
I am of the opinion however that if the modifications arise as a result of J&J's errors then the *contra*-charge would be valid.

ii) OB Contractors Ltd.
"Costs to carry out alterations to brickwork and blockwork to overcome pre-cast concrete defects."
A review of these *contra* charges lead me to conclude that in general they are valid.
"Various materials involved in alterations as described in item ii) i.e. bricks, cement, sand purchased in bulk say purchased in bulk no record kept of usage."
As stated by CASTLE no record of material usage has been kept. A review of the *contra*-charge items led me to consider that the material charge of £1,250.00 is excessive.
Most of the activities refer to "shot fixing" Abbey slots or drilling holes or cutting bricks thus little additional material (if any) would be required.

6.1.4.8 *Acceleration Cost:* CASTLE "Finishing Foreman lan Rolston from SITEC ..." "Provide additional site supervision to accelerate production by co-ordinating sub-contractors and directly employed labour."

CASTLE allege, in discussion that they would not have required a finishing foreman, thus this claim is not for an additional foreman.

Mr Rolston was not engaged upon the site until end of September 1996 when CASTLE were suffering the effects of delays against their revised programmes. At this time CASTLE were still forecasting completion by 14 December 1996.

On the basis of some of the "out-of-sequence" charges made by CASTLE the question arises as to the effectiveness of the finishing foreman's "co-ordination".

It is my opinion that these costs do not arise as a result of J&J activities.

6.1.4.9 *Labour & Material Costs*

a) "Increased material and labour costs as a result of Jones & Jones's 14-week delay in completion of their works."

An element of the works were planned to be carried out between August and December 1996 and no account of the costs arising from these has been taken.

No link or determination of the activities that were pushed into this period allegedly as a result of J&J's activities has been provided.

No dates of material purchases have been provided allowing a view to be taken as to the alleged additional costs.

The above observations apply to all the categories submitted by CASTLE under this head.

On the basis of my conclusions in previous sections of this report I disagree with the allegation that J&J were 14 weeks late. As such the claims cannot, in my view, be supported.

b) "Estimated increased costs incurred by delaying the commencement of the sub-contract works, due to Jones & Jones Limited's 14-week delay in the completion of their works."

These claims apparently cover all sub-contracts let after January 1996 where contract periods which took into account the relative site progress at that time were entered into.

As stated in Part V, the figures of CASTLE in this claim are incorrectly calculated. However, in reliance on the statement supporting these claims that J&J were 14 weeks late thus leading to those estimated increased costs, I am of the opinion that such claims cannot be supported.

6.1.5 SUMMARY & CONCLUSION OF REVIEW

To CASTLE's counterclaim The counterclaim as submitted by CASTLE relies upon a) the premiss that J&J were 14 weeks late in completing their works b) that the overrun of the contract completion date was as a direct result of J&J's late completion.

I am of the opinion, as set-out in previous sections that on both bases CASTLE are incorrect and therefore their counterclaim is ill-founded. In addition, having reviewed the detail of their counterclaim, I am of the opinion that the majority of the items submitted as resulting from J&J's alleged delay, even if J&J were found to be in delay, would not arise as a result of any delay by J&J.

With the exception of the items of *contra*-charges arising from section 6.1.4.7 it is my opinion that CASTLE's claim(s) as presented cannot be supported.

PART VII

7.0 *Review of Jones & Jones final account*

7.1 A number of meetings have taken place between Mr R Trett, the author of this report, retained as Expert Witness on behalf of the Plaintiff and Mr Bell retained as Expert Witness on behalf of the Defendant. The outcome of those meetings have been to agree:

a) The measured account of J&J at	667,960.72
b) Figures as Figures in respect of:	
1. Extra design costs	5,295.39
2. Craneage for erection of stairs	420.00
3. Increased costs	21,125.67
4. Interest Para 34a of the amended pleadings	4,923.99
5. Interest Para 34b of the amended pleadings	4,443.14

7.2 The outstanding item not agreed in principle or as figures relates to cleaning steelwork on site and applying one coat of paint.

7.2.1 Cleaning Steelwork on site and applying one coat of paint.
J&J Evaluation £3,768.50
CASTLE Evaluation £not valued

7.2.2 This item arises from the requirement for B & W to clean steelwork on site and apply one coat of paint as a result of the damage to the paintwork arising as alleged by J&J of site conditions, particularly the lack and fitness of storage areas provided by CASTLE.

7.2.3 CASTLE allege that the reason for the requirement was that the steelwork was brought to site too early.

7.2.4 J&J's quotation for the works excludes "site painting" and also states:

> *"Our tender does not include for cleaning down or removing adherent mud from the steelwork after erection where this is due to inadequate site conditions for the storage of our steel. Your attention is drawn to the need for providing a hard-cored and drained surface over the whole of our site working area. Steel which is laid at ground level before erection must not be used as a walkway or as a means of access by site personnel. Any effect on the primed steelwork surface caused by this action will not be the responsibility of Jones Structures."*

It is precisely these conditions that J&J allege led to the requirement to clean down and apply one coat of paint on site.

7.2.5 On the basis of the exclusion of site painting from J&J's quotation and the witness evidence substantiating that the above conditions resulted in the necessity for site painting I conclude that this item is valid in principle.

7.2.6 As to the evaluation of this item I do not have contemporary evidence to support the time utilised and at this point in time have not yet been able to identify in isolation the men or the hours involved. CASTLE Daily Reports identify steelwork painting commencing from 26-2-96 to 29-3-96 as follows:

DATE	DIRECT LABOUR	DESCRIPTION
26.2.96	11	Painting Steelwork/Cladding to Roof/General Making Good
29.2.96	12	Painting Steelwork/Roof Sheeting
1.3.96	10	Painting Steelwork/Roof Cladding General Making Good
2.3.96	10	Ditto
3.3.96	10	Ditto
4.3.96	10	Ditto
7.3.96	10	Ditto
8.3.96	4	Fix Para Bolts Courtyard Area/Paint Steel etc.
9.3.96	4	Paint Steel/Fix Para Bolts
10.3.96	4	Paint Steel/Fix Bolts
11.3.96	4	Paint Steel/Fix Bolts
14.3.96	4	Fix Missing Bolts
15.3.96	4	Fix Missing Bolts/Clean Steel
16.3.96	4	Fix Missing Bolts/Clean Steel
22.3.96	4	Fix Missing Bolts/Paint Steel
23.3.96	4	Fix Missing Bolts/Paint Steel
24.3.96	4	Paint Steelwork/and Timber
25.3.96	4	Paint Steelwork/and Timber
28.3.96	4	Fix Missing Bolts
29.3.96	4	Painting Steelwork/Trim Louvres

7.2.7 The above represents 141 man/days of which J&J allege 60 man/days or 42.5% equates to cleaning down and painting steelwork.

7.2.8 On the basis that 125 of the man days includes the activity of steelwork painting, combined with the recollection of the witness of fact that 4 men and 3 weeks were involved in painting I am of the opinion that J&J's assessment of 60 man days could be a reasonable assessment of the time.

7.2.9 In view of the fact that the steelwork would have been erected such standard factors of coating would not be appropriate as the labour force would be working in an environment not conducive to standard factors of output, as such any purported finite calculation would be subject to question.

7.2.10 As regards the cost of paint I have not been able to identify by invoice the separate cost of the paint or the quantity. J&J advise me that the paint was supplied by D.E.B. Industries, their (J&J) steelwork subcontractor, and the cost would have been included within D.E.B. final account, such costs are, as far as I can tell not separately identified. D.E.B. have since gone into liquidation making the determination of the actual cost impossible. However, a check with a manufacturer of zinc phosphate type paint confirms that the cost is £4.22/litre. Thus the evaluation of 15 gallons at 4.546 litres/gallons @ £4.22/litre

=	287.76
+25% =	71.94
	£359.70

On the basis that the price quoted is correct the sum of £328.50 in respect of the paint appears reasonable. Note the 25% mark-up is in accordance with J&J's quotation.

7.2.11 The hire of trestles and ladders for this work is not separately identified. P. Dawson (J&J's erection foreman) advises me that most of the work was undertaken off ladders and one tower. The sum scheduled by J&J is obviously an estimate and any attempt at final determination would be subject to question.

During the period in question J&J had "on site" hired plant items, excluding cranes, to the value of £1,320.28 of which £150.00 have been attributed to the painting requirements. I would consider this sum to be a reasonable evaluation in the circumstances.

7.3 *J&J Claim for Loss and Expense*

7.3.1 J&J's claim arises from their allegation that the works were delayed and disrupted and is based upon two scenarios:

a) That arising from a contract formed on or about the 26 March 1995.
b) That arising from a contract formed on the 7 October 1995

7.3.2 The respective claims as pleaded are, arising from:

a) above £82,015.54.
b) above £15,789.87.

7.3.3 Claim a) £82,015.54

7.3.3.1 This sum is made up of £29,382.64 for additional manufacturing costs and £52,632.90 additional erection costs.

7.3.3.2 J&J allege that due to the delay in finalisation of the design, brought about by reasons outwith their control, that the works, which were planned to produce the frame in the period of June and July 1995, were unable to do so. Similarly in addition to the delay in availability of drawings and the subsequent variations that the works were physically unable to manufacture the frame in the sequence planned or required, due to the manufacturing unit being committed to other work in the later period when information became available. As a consequence J&J were forced into sub-contracting part of the manufacture to a sub-contractor, Christie Stone.

7.3.3.3 The financial effect of the position imposed upon J&J was to increase their overall manufacturing costs.

7.3.3.4 The evaluation of these alleged additional costs has been based upon:

a) The direct production costs.
b) The costs of sub-contracting.

7.3.3.5 J&J Contract Cost Report (see Appendix 44) identifies a "factory" (direct production costs) of £117,093.00 of this the summary report shows that £39,525.00 equates to overheads thus making the direct production costs £77,568.00.

7.3.3.6 The Erection Cost Report (see Appendix 45) identifies under materials, Christie Stone, which sums are for the manufacture of beams, stairs etc. The total sum for Christie Stone = £39,070.00.

7.3.3.7 Thus the total cost of (concrete) frame manufacture

		£77,568.00
	+	£39,070.00
		£116,638.00

7.3.3.8 To determine the additional cost the original cost of manufacture plus any variations must be considered.

From J&J's estimate and the variations the following can be deduced:

Planned Production Costs (excluding overheads)

Column/Beams 490.95M3 @ £120.00		58,914.00
Roof Beams 2 × 2.67M3 L @ £140.00		747.60
Floor Beams 4 × 2.28M3 @ £146.00		1,276.80
Shear Walls 45 × 1.90M3 @ £120.00		10,260.00
Balcony Frame		350.00
		71,548.40
Variations		
Omit Shear Walls		10,260.00
		61,288.40
Add VO 11 3.34M3	@ £120.00	400.80
VO 12 5.30M3	@ £120.00	696.00
VO 13 12.42M3	@ £120.00	1,490.40
VO 14 10.44M3	@ £120.00	1,252.80
VO 15 21.33M3	@ £120.00	2,559.60
VO 16 23.328M3	@ £120.00	2,799.36
VO 17 1.36 M3	@ £120.00	163.20
VO 18 9.00M3	@ £120.00	1,080.00
VO 20 1.79	@ £120.00	214.80
VO 22	@ £120.00	120.00
		72,065.36

7.3.3.9 Shortfall

Shortfall	116,638.00
	72,065.36
	£44,572.64

However J&J had planned to sub-contract the stairs and landings to Christie Stone and as such the sub-contract value should be deducted to provide the resultant additional cost of the manufacturing that J&J had planned to undertake.

Therefore shortfall	44,572.64	
	15,190.00	(Sub-Contract stairs etc)
	£29,382.64	

7.3.3.10 *ERECTION* The erection claim of £52,632.90 is made up of the additional costs expended by J&J in erecting the concrete and steel frame. J&J allege that the factors dealt with in section 2.4.8 of this report contributed to and resulted in the additional expenditure:

a) Inclement weather.
b) Winter working.
c) Variations.
d) Site Conditions.
e) Restricted mobility.
f) Late foundations for stairs (thus denying the use of stairs as access).

7.3.3.11 Whereas J&J had planned to undertake erection with their own erection gang (3) due to these various matters their labour had to be supplemented by sub-contract labour.

7.3.3.12 J&J's erection cost report (Appendix 45) identifies a total of £135,523.37 of erection labour and plant.

This sum is made up of:

Direct Labour	29,123.75
Sub-Contractor J.C. Construction	14,820.00
W. Port	9,900.00
Surrey Steel	24,605.00
Redwood Construction	37,438.95
Plant Hire	25,459.37
	141,347.07

From this sum has to be deducted:

a) The planned erection costs.
b) The erection value contributed from variations.

Planned erection costs = £40,000.00

VOs		
10	42,570.00	
12	50.00	
13	300.00	
17	100.00	
20	60.00	
25	869.17	
30	420.00	
31	3,440.00	
32	900.00	48,714.17
		88,714.17

Therefore additional erection costs = £52,632.90

7.3.4 Claim b) £15,789.87

7.3.4.1 Claim b) deals with the additional costs of erection that arise from a contract formed on 7 October.

7.3.4.2 On the premiss that a contract was formed on 7 October the factors that contributed to the additional manufacturing costs would have been knowledge to J&J at that time and as far as I am advised would not then fall to be claimed as additional. The only potential claim arising would be for delays and disruption to the erection programme which became factors that were not in the knowledge or contemplation of J&J at 7 October.

7.3.4.3 Thus the heads of contribution referred to at 7.3.3.10 with the exception of the stairs slabs and the site conditions arising from the lack of the hardcored site would have been in the knowledge or contemplation of J&J.

7.3.4.4 Thus it is effectively alleged by CASTLE that J&J had agreed to a contract that they knew or contemplated would incur them additional costs to the value of approx £75,000 for which they would not be entitled to recover any additional monies. It is my opinion that such a position adds strength to J&J's view that no such contract was entered into.

7.3.4.5 Nevertheless, in dealing with the position of contract formation at 7 October the only heads of claim available, I am of the opinion, to J&J to pursue are:

a) Loss of productivity due to lack of stairs as access, and
b) Loss of productivity due to site conditions.

It is not possible from the records and costings to isolate such costs and any such assessment is arbitrary. However I am of the opinion that an assessment of 30% of the total erection costs to be realistic assuming the following % contribution.

a) Inclement weather	15%
b) Winter working	25%
c) Variations	15%
d) Site conditions	15%
e) Restricted mobility	15%
f) Lack of stairs for access	15%
	100%

7.3.4.6 Thus I evaluate J&J's claim at £52,632.90 × 30% £15,789.87.

7.3.5 Based upon the method of calculation above the figures of:

7.3.2 a) £82,015.54
b) £15,789.87 have been agreed as figures by the Experts.

7.4 *Interest Charges*

7.4.1 The Experts have agreed as figures the sums pleaded as follows:

Interest at 15% therefore

a) Interest on valuation No. 1 as at February 1996	£4,923.99
b) Interest on valuation No. 1.2.3 for the period 1 February 1996 to 18 March 1996	£4,443.14

7.4.2 The Experts have not agreed interest due on the balance of the J&J charges from 18 March to the date of the issue of the writ 27 October 1996.

I calculate these charges as follows:

Agreed measured account	667,960.92
Extra design costs	5,295.39
Craneage for erection of stairs	420.00
Increased costs	21,125.67
Painting costs	3,768.50
	698,570.48
Less amount paid	303,075.00
Amount outstanding	£395,495.48

7.4.3 Interest a) Contract Formed 26 March 1995

Add Loss and Expense claim a)

Amount Outstanding	395,495.48
	82,015.02
	£477,511.02

Interest b) Contract formed 7 October 1995

Add Loss and Expenses claim b)	
Amount Outstanding	395,495.48
	15,789.87
	£411,285.35

a) 477,511.02 × 15% p.a. @ 222 days = £43,564.70
b) 411,285.35 × 15% p.a. @ 222 days = £37,522.74

7.4.4 Total interest to date of writ:

a) 43,564.70	
4,923.92	
4,443.14	
	£52,931.76
b) 37,522.74	
4,923.92	
443.14	£46,889.80

7.4.5 Daily rate of interest

a) 395,495.48 × 15% 365 = £162.53
b) 477,511.02 × 15% 365 = £196.24
c) 411,285.35 × 15% 365 = £169.02

Part VIII

8.0 Conclusion

8.1 The preceding sections of this report deal with the events and the effects thereof upon the works undertaken by J&J for CASTLE. The report also considers the position as regards the four scenarios pleaded:

a) No Contract
b) Contract at 26 March 1995 (Simple).
c) Contract at 26 March 1995 (DOM 1 as amended by J&J conditions).
d) Contract at 7 October 1995.

8.2 As a result of my investigations I am of the opinion that:

a) Not in any of the scenarios were J&J responsible for the failure of CASTLE to meet the completion date.
b) On the basis that no formal contract exists that J&J are entitled to be reimbursed the sum of £395,495.48 plus interest from 27 October 1996 at £162.53 per day.
c) On the basis of a Simple contract, or a contract based upon DOM 1 conditions as amended, formed on or about the 26 March 1995, that J&J are entitled to be reimbursed the sum of £477,511.02 plus £52,931.76 interest to 27 October 1996, thereafter at £196.24 per day.

d) On the basis of a contract formed on 7 October 1995 that J&J are entitled to be reimbursed the sum of £411,285.35 plus £46,889.80 interest to 27 October 1996 and thereafter at £169.02 per day.

RT Trett
August 1990

Declaration

2.0 *The Expert—Mr Roger T Trett*

2.1 I am required to consider the sub-contract between the Plaintiff and the Defendant, the Pleadings and the Contemporaneous documentation and to report on my findings to the Court, particularly in relation to matters of time and *quantum*. A copy of my instructing solicitors' instructions are included at Appendix "A" to this report.

2.2 My *curriculum vitae* is incorporated at Appendix "B" to this Report.

2.3 In investigating the matter(s) in dispute I have had assistance from colleagues within Trett Consulting in preparing schedules etc. I have given instructions for the preparation of schedules and examined them for correctness upon completion. I am satisfied that they have been prepared from and accord with the contemporaneous documentation.

2.4 Mr .... Senior Consultant, Trett Consulting, provided assistance in the analysis of the records and inspection and preparation of the evaluation. Mr ....'s *curriculum vitae* is incorporated at Appendix "C" to this report.

2.5 I am the author of this Report and the statements made in this report are true and accurate to the best of my knowledge and belief, and the conclusions drawn and the opinions expressed herein are my own.

2.6 I have been provided with a copy of the Order for Directions dated 18 October 1996 and I understand my duties to the Court. I have read the list of duties and responsibilities of expert witnesses set out by Mr Justice Cresswell in the *Ikarian Reefer* case and I have endeavoured to follow those guidelines.

2.7 I believe that I have complied with the duty required of me in my role as an expert in relation to the production of this report and where necessary I have given details herein of any matter which might affect the validity of my report.

Mr Roger T Trett—September 1997

CHAPTER 5

THE EXPERT IN INSURANCE AND REINSURANCE CASES

Phillippa Rowe

INTRODUCTION

001 Cases in which insurance or reinsurance experts find themselves involved fall into two main categories: claims under insurance policies, and disputes as to the operation of insurance (and reinsurance) policies.

002 In the former, insurers have assumed the management and control of an underlying dispute or claim which will—if resulting in a settlement—be met from the sum insured available under an insurance policy. In most cases insurers will have assumed the defence of a third party claim against their insured, who has cover for some form of personal or professional liability. In others insurers will be standing in the shoes of a plaintiff, or be the plaintiff, in a subrogation or uninsured loss or third party recovery action. These claims, or cases, are meat and drink to the professional insurance claims manager. The subject matter of the case, however, will be related to the insurance cover provided and the expert, if any, will be expert in that subject matter—be it subsidence damage to neighbouring property from tree roots, medical negligence, a motorist's liability for personal injury or a host of other subjects. There will rarely be a need for an expert in insurance practice *per se*. Insurers usually prefer, nonetheless, that any expert they appoint is at least familiar with the basics of insurance law and practice, if only so that he will understand and sympathise with their particular position and perspective on the case, and grasp the possible differences from the insured's position and interests.

003 In a number of these cases there may be a separate argument as to whether the liability established to a third party properly falls to be met under the terms of the policy—perhaps because of breach of a policy condition—but these are a different class of dispute, and must not be confused with the question of the underlying matter to be resolved. (Practitioners and insurers with experience of USA actions will be aware that most USA jurisdictions insist on clear recognition of this difference, and insist that insurers appoint separate counsel for the policy dispute from those handling the original matter—and in some states also provide the insured his own independent counsel if there is any hint of a conflict of interest. Whether insurers might also have to pay for separate experts has not, as far as I know, been considered.) They more properly fall into my second category for the purposes of this chapter.

004 My second category of cases, disputes as to the meaning and operation of insurance policies and reinsurance wordings, and as to what is covered under them, are essentially contract construction disputes. There may be matters of fact to be established—such as whether a notice of claim provision was in fact complied with, or whether a material fact (assuming all parties agree it *was* material) was disclosed. Any expert evidence required or permitted, however, will be designed to assist in understanding the policy or contract. In general, therefore, expert evidence will concentrate on demonstrating that a particular interpretation should be favoured, on the basis of precedent, law or universal past practice—with the difficulty of course that the expert is not there to teach the court the law. Most experts will thus be chosen for the length and extent of their experience on a given class of insurance or reinsurance so that they can vouch authoritatively for a universal, or at least generally accepted, practice or interpretation.

005 The two case studies I have chosen for this chapter therefore attempt to illustrate these two different categories. The first is, at basics, a simple professional negligence, or professional indemnity, case. The subject matter, however, is the negligence or otherwise of a reinsurance underwriter, so the example should have useful indicators for both insurance and reinsurance experts, as well as for experts involved in other professional negligence cases. The case study is derived from the notorious Lloyd's Action Groups' litigation of the early 1990s, and is based on my expert report in one of those cases. (I gave similar evidence in other Action Group cases, but not all of them reached the courts before the overall Lloyd's settlement.) Because of the existence of various confidentiality orders affecting the evidence in these cases, I have not been able to reproduce my report *verbatim*. The version provided here does, however, closely follow the structure and style of the original, and still serves, I hope, to provide the same lessons for other experts as the real thing would.

006 The second case study is of a question of interpretation and construction of a reinsurance contract, and was produced for an arbitration hearing in North America. Apart from removal of the names of the parties, it is the original report which I provided.

007 Both cases, however, should be of interest to experts in many other fields since they both illustrate a dilemma faced by us all—how to avoid telling the court "the law" (with which, as experts we are probably very familiar, and on which we may also have strong feelings). This is because both examples involve the expert in playing essentially a legal game: in one case determining whether the defendant has been "negligent", and in the other the attempt at construction of a contract wording. Neither problem is unique to the insurance or reinsurance world and it is hoped that the approaches adopted here to the expert's dilemma will be of general assistance.

SOME BACKGROUND—AN OUTLINE OF INSURANCE AND REINSURANCE

008 Readers who are familiar with, even expert in, the fields of insurance or reinsurance may skip this section. For others, however, a brief explanation of the principles underlying these two case studies may be of assistance.

009 Insurance policies are essentially promises to pay agreed sums of money (agreed in amount or by reference to a pre-selected measure of cost or damages) in the event of a specified unwanted occurrence. Because the promised payment is both contingent and, if it is made, will occur at some unspecifiable future date, insurance policies are rarely read in detail by insureds unless and until a claim arises. Expectations, raised by marketing departments and agents, are frequently disappointed. Discussion of the terms of the policy therefore almost invariably takes place in the context of a dispute or potential dispute, when it becomes apparent that the cover provided does not exactly match the circumstances of the alleged claim.

010 Insurance contracts are contracts of utmost good faith which means, in particular, that severe duties of disclosure of all material facts and possibly material facts, and changes to them, fall on insureds. Insurers' rights in the event of misrepresentation or failure to disclose material facts are draconian—the policy is void *ab initio* and the premium returnable. There are other contractual considerations peculiar to insurance policies, such as the status of warranties and conditions, and the effects of breaches of them. (The law of insurance warranties is highly complex, and not for discussion here, but essentially an insurance warranty is the equivalent of a "condition" in any other form of contract, and *vice versa*.) In the UK, the operation of insurance contracts—including non-marine insurances, and reinsurance of all classes—is governed by the Marine Insurance Act 1906, interpreted and amended by a succession of judicial pronouncements. All this makes a fertile ground for contract construction and policy coverage disputes. In practice most personal lines insurance—"consumer insurances" in the current jargon—are regulated by the Consumer Contracts legislation and by various codes of conduct promulgated by, for example, the Association of British Insurers (ABI). Most personal lines policy interpretation disputes are handled by the Insurance Ombudsman's Bureau, an industry-funded scheme which produces decisions binding on subscribing insurers but not on policyholders ("consumers"), and which is—for those interested in the subject—a highly successful working example of ADR in practice. (At the time of writing the Insurance Ombudsman's Bureau faces two major changes. Its terms of reference have been changed to allow it, for the first time, to handle disputes with insurance brokers and agents and other non-insurers in the chain of supply of insurance; and the government has announced that it is to be merged with other consumer Ombudsmen's bureaux in a new "super bureau" under the aegis of the new Financial Services Authority. The effect of both these moves on the handling of insurance related disputes remains to be seen.) Most insurers who do not subscribe to the Ombudsman's Bureau (a minority of the industry) provide for arbitration of disputes with policyholders under the Chartered Insurance Institute's Personal Insurance Arbitration Scheme. The Scheme is similarly binding on insurers but not policyholders. The effect of both these, however, is that very few personal lines insurance policy interpretation disputes are heard in the courts. These two schemes are not available for dealing with commercial insurances, disputes under which are generally heard in the courts.

011 Reinsurance is the insuring at one further remove by insurance companies of the risks they have assumed. The best non-insurance analogy, although the insurance fraternity does not like it, is the laying off of bets by a bookmaker. The reinsurers are themselves also insurance companies, some dealing exclusively in reinsurance business.

012 The purposes of reinsurance, from the point of view of the reinsured company, are either to protect an insurer from suffering too great a loss, or the laying off, or passing on, of liability to another insurer. These two fundamental functions may sometimes overlap, but they are separate and distinct.

013 This is not the place for a reinsurance primer, but reinsurance is of two types—proportional or sharing, and non-proportional or excess of loss—and utilises two methods: "facultative" or specific to single risks, and "treaty" or based on a whole portfolio of risks. (But those to whom this is entirely new but who wish to go further could start with Chapter 1 (only six pages long) of RJ Kiln *Reinsurance in Practice*, Witherby, 3rd edn 1981.) Different *types* are predominantly intended to achieve the different functions of reinsurance. Proportional business is mainly designed to lay off liability while excess-of-loss business is mainly designed to protect against large losses. Either *method* can be applied to both types and both functions.

014 The point of all this in this chapter's context is that because of their different functions the two main types of reinsurance contain significantly different contract provisions designed to reflect their different purposes, and the different methods of reinsurance also produce different contract wordings reflective of their different structures—all of which might seem only to be expected.

015 The problem facing reinsurance practitioners—buyers and sellers—and their advisers is that until very recently the courts have refused to acknowledge, let alone give effect to, these critical differences, and even now some bad decisions and problematic rulings could still be considered universal precedents. Some but not all of the damage has been remedied by the three recent House of Lords reinsurance cases (*Axa* v. *Field*, *Hill* v. *M&G* and *Charter Re* v. *Fagan*, all reported in *Reinsurance Law Reports* 1996). In the most recent and major cases there has been a marked disinclination on the part of the courts to hear, and on the parties to evince, expert evidence as to either technical explanation of the purpose and type of reinsurance contract at issue or historic market custom and practice and understanding of similar contracts. It is not true that such evidence has never been called, but it has frequently caused problems.

016 It will surprise no-one that both reinsureds and reinsurers faced with a dispute will seek to hold fast to an interpretation of a contract, or an example of market practice, which best suits their particular current position. Equally, it will surprise no-one that expert witnesses can be found to espouse the cause demanded by their principals, and even to contradict what others would consider to be indisputable basic tenets of reinsurance theory and practice. However, reinsurance is all about spreading risk as far as possible, including geographically, and one of the consequences is that reinsurance is a global business. Another is that most companies are or at some time have been both reinsurers and reinsureds (on different pieces of business). There therefore exists, in my opinion, a core of agreed reinsurance knowledge unaffected by the exigencies of a particular contractual position, and a body of independent experts who can and should be relied on to assist the courts in these cases.

017 For the purposes of the Marine Insurance Act, regulatory considerations and court rulings, reinsurance is a form of insurance. However, both parties to a reinsurance contract are professional and informed players in the field, both can be assumed to have equal knowledge of the implications of the contract terms and equal authority and bargaining power. In disputes over interpretation of ambiguous or allegedly ambiguous contracts, the normal rules of *contra preferentem* therefore have to be applied with care and a simplistic approach will be dangerous. In particular, although reinsurers will usually indicate, at least in summary, the clauses or conditions they wish to see included in a reinsurance when offering premium quotations, it is quite usual for the final wording to be drafted by the reinsurance broker or intermediary on behalf of his client—the buyer—and accepted (after checking, one hopes, that it is correct) by the reinsurer, the seller.

EXAMPLE 1—PROFESSIONAL NEGLIGENCE AND REINSURANCE MARKET PRACTICE

018 This is essentially a case of alleged professional negligence—albeit of a reinsurance underwriter—and alleged failure of an agent in his duty to his principals. The defendants were to be indemnified, and the defence controlled, by professional indemnity insurers. The case is therefore both defence of a claim under an insurance policy and one involving expert evidence on insurance and reinsurance practice. It may therefore provide assistance and be of interest to experts in a wide range of fields. It arose in the context of the infamous and extensive "Lloyd's litigation" of the 1980s and 1990s which culminated in a massively complicated market-wide settlement including the creation of Equitas, a new reinsurance company to take on the liabilities of Lloyd's Names arising from old underwriting years. These liabilities predominantly arose from the underwriting in the 1950s and 1960s, by most members of the Lloyd's and London insurance company markets, of USA liability insurances against claims arising out of, for instance, asbestosis and related conditions, use of other pharmaceutical products, and environmental pollution. The total sums at issue were huge—estimated at one point as greater than the entire capital of the USA's energy and manufacturing industries and of their insurers. It was undoubtedly the size of these claims, as well as their surprising emergence 20 or more years later on policies thought to have long before expired, which gave rise to the extensive litigation surrounding them. This began with defence of the original claims in the USA on behalf of insureds by their USA and London insurers. In parallel were a large number of disputes between insurers and insureds—again taking place in the USA—as to the interpretation of these old policies and their applicability to the claims presented. Most of the decisions of the USA courts were unfavourable to insurers and tended to increase their liability for these claims rather than contain it. The results of these decisions, and the legal costs associated with them, in turn gave rise to two further classes of litigation. Reinsurers, also in the Lloyd's and London insurance company markets, sought to avoid meeting these claims on their reinsurances of fellow London insurers and of USA insurance companies, with further massive associated legal costs. The Lloyd's Names confronted with the final bills for all these claims, damages and costs, sought in turn to avoid meeting them by raising—*via* various Action Groups—a range of allegations of negligent underwriting of these policies, negligent record keeping, failure to disclose their existence to Names newly joining Lloyd's, and negligently assessing their impact on syndicates' final results with the effect that the syndicates were improperly closed.

019 A Lloyd's syndicate is a group of Names whose underwriting affairs are managed on their behalf by an underwriting agent, who employs an "Active Underwriter" to write insurances on behalf of the syndicate's Names. The active underwriter was usually also a member of the syndicate for whom he underwrote. A syndicate is not a going concern but an annual venture (or was at the time of this litigation, and still is at the time of writing, although there are indications that with new developments the days of the annual venture in the Lloyd's market might be numbered), because the constitution of the syndicate changes annually as members renew, or not, their membership, amend the amount of liability they contract to underwrite, die, or join as new members. In order to achieve a distribution of any profit or loss between the syndicate members each annual venture needs to be wound up. This was achieved in Lloyd's by means of a mechanism known as the "Reinsurance to Close", which normally takes place at the end of the thirty-sixth month of the underwriting year of the annual venture. This Reinsurance to Close—discussed more fully in the sample report below—is, briefly, an estimate of the ultimate cost of all outstanding and residual liability still attaching to the policies issued in the underwriting year in question. This estimate is expressed as a reinsurance premium, paid by the members of the syndicate seeking to close or wind up its affairs, to a successor syndicate. In consideration of this premium the successor syndicate accepts all the remaining liabilities of the closing syndicate.

020 In much of the Lloyd's litigation the plaintiff Names argued that their agents—the underwriting agents and the active underwriters—had been negligent in their assessments of the impact of the USA asbestos related and other third party claims on old policies. They therefore, it was alleged, failed to include adequate provision for them in calculating the Reinsurance to Close premiums with the results that Names on successor reinsuring syndicates received significantly inadequate consideration for the claims which they found themselves facing. It was alleged that some Names were induced to join such syndicates by the over favourable impression created by this under-reserving, and some of the cases included other pleadings of deliberate concealment, or of negligent handling of the original US insurance claims.

021 These allegations of negligence within Lloyd's, and the various claims and lawsuits surrounding the professional indemnity insurances of the underwriting agents (also written by Lloyd's underwriters), were at the centre of the eventual Lloyd's settlement, though not before some of the Lloyd's Action Groups had succeeded in their claims in the Commercial Court.

022 At the time of the Lloyd's negligence cases, the original underlying claims and lawsuits were far from settled. Claims and legal proceedings were still ongoing in the USA and in the UK reinsurance market, and there was therefore much concern to protect the privilege, in the US courts, of material relating to those original matters. Information on original policy wordings, insureds and their claims and the legal disputes surrounding them, all needed to be adduced in evidence in the English negligence proceedings. All this evidence was heard only subject to careful confidentiality agreements providing that all such evidence would remain private despite having been put before the UK courts, and barring all participants from relying on this evidence elsewhere or quoting it in the public domain.

023 As it happens, the report I gave which forms the basis of the example below did not include any detailed references to the underlying claims. Nonetheless, because the case was subject to a confidentiality agreement I have felt obliged to disguise the identity of the parties, and to alter the content of the report in some respects. The version below nonetheless follows closely the construction of the original, and I wrote very similar reports (in argument and structure, but not of factual basis) for several other Lloyd's Action Groups which were not heard in court before the market settlement. I have incorporated some elements of those other reports in this example.

024 In the matter below, the underwriter and the underwriting agent faced two pleadings of negligence—that they had been negligent in underwriting some reinsurances of other syndicates facing asbestos related claims without assessing the impact of these claims on the reinsurances written, and that they had been negligent in their approach to the calculation of their own syndicate's Reinsurance to Close premium with adverse consequences for Names subsequently joining the syndicate. The allegations pleaded related to a span of some five or six underwriting years.

025 As an expert I was asked to opine, not on the underwriting of the reinsurance contracts which was outside my area of expertise, but on the approach used to estimating the Reinsurance to Close premium, and on whether or not the defendants had been negligent in this approach. The reader will notice that the word "negligent" does not appear in the report. The report follows below after which I discuss its structure, and how I tackled the problems presented.

FIRST MODEL EXPERT'S REPORT

RE: RAINBOW NAMES ACTION GROUP (VARS) V. RAINBOW SYNDICATES LIMITED *ET AL*

REPORT OF MRS PHILLIPPA C ROWE

CONTENTS

I. Introduction

1 I, Mrs Phillippa Carne Rowe of 1G Castle Gardens, Stanhope, County Durham, England, have been asked to prepare a report describing the calculation and setting of a Lloyd's syndicate's Reinsurance To Close ("RITC") and in particular on the methods used by the Rainbow Syndicates. I have been asked to give an opinion on whether, in this context and given the series of "run-off" contracts which the syndicates have written, it was proper for the syndicates to have been "closed" by RITC as they were.

1A I have been asked to read certain comments of Mr Justice Cresswell in a case known as *the Ikarian Reefer*. I have also read the comments made by the Court of Appeal in the same case. I understand that these comments set out the duties and obligations of expert witnesses. I can confirm that the manner in which this report has been prepared complies with those duties and obligations.

My Qualifications and Experience

2 At *Appendix 1* to this report I provide a *curriculum vitae* with full details of my qualifications and of my experience in the Lloyd's market and of setting RITCs. After graduating in 1974 in Economics from New Hall, Cambridge I spent some fifteen years in Lloyd's employed by ABC & Others ("ABC"). In 1981 I qualified as a Fellow of the Chartered Insurance Institute by examination and I am a Chartered Insurance Practitioner. My time at ABC was spent almost entirely—but for two years on the underwriting box as part of my training—in the Claims Department where for most of my career I was Claims Manager and was responsible, *inter alia*, for the calculation of the RITC figures, including estimates for Incurred But Not Reported losses ("IBNR"). Since 1989 I have been practising independently as senior partner in my own firm, Phillippa Ross & Co, reinsurance consultants to the London non-marine market, including Lloyd's. In this capacity I have assisted clients with the

calculation of year-end reserves, akin in their statistical estimation to RITCs,[1] and have lectured to insurance company staff on reserve estimation.

3 While at ABC, although I did not personally see every file, I was ultimately responsible for settlement of all claims presented to the ABC syndicate, including those on the direct US Casualty account which the syndicate had written between 1963 and 1969. (The syndicate was formed in 1963; the casualty underwriter left in about 1969.) I was familiar with the workings of the office set up to handle asbestosis and similar claims for the market. I saw all the market circulars issued by the appropriate market committees, signed some of their authorities, read the instructed USA attorneys' reports circulated on individual losses or accounts and met several of the USA attorneys responsible. In the 1980s I made two or three trips to the eastern USA specifically to meet attorneys, ABC's reinsureds and their brokers, to discuss asbestosis and pollution claims at first hand with them. In particular in early 1985 I visited the USA with various insurance company executives, including Mr US Witness, to discuss reserving for asbestos claims. Since establishing my own firm I have inspected files on the same and similar claims at many other Lloyd's syndicates and London companies on behalf of their reinsurers.

Sources Used

4 I have read the Amended Statement of Claim in these actions and the statements of the executives and employees of, Multicoloured plc, and the various statements of partners of Add & Divide, the defendant auditors. In addition I have studied the various copy RITC files made available to me, in particular the so-called "pruned" RITC files which form Bundle A. I have also read the statements of Mr Witness and Mr WZ Attorney and the bundle of documents entitled "State of Market Knowledge" (Bundle B). It is not my intention to quote large passages from these documents, but rather to assume that they can be taken as read, and only to refer to specific short extracts. I have also read the defendants' Reports and Accounts for 1979 to 1991 and have read the draft reports of two of the underwriting expert witnesses, Messrs Penn and Ink.

5 In writing this report I also rely on my own knowledge of the Lloyd's and London market, the US Casualty business written herein, the problems surrounding asbestos, other latent disease and pollution related claims, my own expertise in and experience of calculating RITC values and my own recollection of events and developments during the period at issue.

II. The Nature of The Lloyd's Market

6 Lloyd's is a market of underwriting individuals ("Names") each of whom provides capital for the underwriting of insurance business. Names are sole traders and consequently have several and unlimited liability for the risks which each one undertakes. They nonetheless trade in groups known as syndicates, each represented by an Active Underwriter who, with his staff, carries out the actual underwriting on behalf of his fellow Names. The syndicate staff and the Active Underwriter are overseen by a Managing Agent, usually a limited liability company, formed for the purpose. Most, if not all, Names participate in more than one syndicate.

7 A Name's underwriting affairs at Lloyd's are managed for him by a Members Agent, who *inter alia* advises on syndicate selection, oversees his application for membership and manages his funds at Lloyd's. The Name's underwriting authority is delegated to his Members Agent. If the Members Agent is also a Managing Agent then that firm will also oversee the Name's underwriting. (Names in this position are commonly known as "direct Names".) Otherwise

1. But not in the accounting assumptions which must be followed—a company is a going concern and can add to its reserves year by year as matters develop: a Lloyd's syndicate is an annual venture and must attempt to reserve its outstanding liabilities to finality after three years for each year of account. In fact, however, as—for example—Exhibits UU and VV show, several US companies facing asbestos losses were able to "duck" the issue, reserving nowhere ". . . near ultimate anticipated losses". This option is not available in a proper RITC.

the Members Agent will in turn appoint one or more Managing Agents to underwrite on behalf of the Name.

III. Lloyd's Reinsurance to Close ("RITC")

8 A Lloyd's syndicate, in consequence of these arrangements, is an entity which exists for an annual life only. Each year, as Names change their underwriting arrangements—capital made available, syndicate choice, amount to be underwritten—so the syndicate changes. The Names belonging to each syndicate year are responsible for its liabilities, being those arising on insurance and reinsurance policies attaching to that year of account. The year of account to which a policy or piece of business attaches is determined by the calendar year in which it is "signed", i.e. entered into Lloyd's central records, by the Lloyd's Policy Signing Office. Each year of account is kept open for three years before its books are closed and a profit or loss declared and distributed. This delay in accounting in practice assists in a more accurate estimation of liabilities (claims) outstanding before a balance can be struck. The mechanism by which the closing of each syndicate year is achieved is the RITC. An estimate of future claims is drawn up, and based on this the Active Underwriter of the syndicate year to be closed arrives at a reinsurance premium for its closing. This premium, the RITC, is paid to the successor syndicate year which in exchange accepts all outstanding liabilities, known or unknown, of the closed syndicate.

9 If for any reason the Underwriter finds it impossible to arrive at a reasonable assessment of the remaining liabilities then it is not possible to effect an RITC and the syndicate must be left "open". Its existing Names must then remain liable for incoming claims until such time as either more information emerges and an RITC can be calculated, or all possible liability has been exhausted.

10 Implicit in this process is the requirement that any RITC premium so established must be equitable as between both the closing Names and the successor reinsuring Names. Any other arrangement will produce a profit for one set of Names at the expense of the other. This principle of equity between Names is now given enforcement in the Lloyd's Syndicate Accounting Byelaw No 11 of 1987.[2]

11 The decision as to the amount and acceptability of the premium to be charged to one syndicate year and paid to its successor for the RITC is formally that of the Active Underwriter of the syndicate. It must, however, have the approval of the Managing Agent to whom the Underwriter reports and will usually be discussed by the Board of that Managing Agent. The Managing Agent will commonly provide administrative assistance to the Active Underwriter and the syndicate staff—accounting, computing and sometimes actuarial facilities—but the responsibility rests formally with the Active Underwriter.

12 I shall discuss the detailed ways in which an RITC could be calculated in Section VII below, but, in general, in order to close a year of account and calculate an appropriate premium for the RITC a syndicate must examine the trends of past premiums, paid losses and incurred (paid plus outstanding) losses and use them to make, as far as possible, a statistical projection of future claims costs. It must also examine the actual settlement performance of previous RITC provisions to determine how far previous projections on the same basis have in fact been reliable. Such statistical exercises can be of varying levels of sophistication, with adjustments to the patterns for distortions arising from, for example, known unusually large claims, changes in underwriting decisions, or changes in reinsurance protections applying to the claims. The advice of an actuary may sometimes be sought, and the statistical projections can be made manually from graphs and arithmetical ratios, or more explicitly mathematically with the aid of computer programs. (It is fair to say that the use of neither actuaries nor computer models was common in Lloyd's before the mid 1980s, but that does not affect the underlying principles.)

13 All these methods, however, in common with all attempts at forecasting by statistical methods, assume that past figures are a reliable guide to future performance. As soon as anything occurs suggesting the opposite (any "discontinuity" in the figures or their pattern

2. Which in turn replaces the Syndicate Accounting Byelaw No 7 of 1984 and the 1983 Provisional Accounting Manual.

or any change in the nature of the underlying data or in the causes of the patterns the data exhibit) this assumption falls and so does any estimate made. Such discontinuities can be dealt with in different ways, depending on their nature. For instance, the effect of, say, an unusually large hurricane on original claims, or of the insolvency of a single reinsurer, can be removed from the figures before projections are attempted, and "added back" afterwards. Gradually changing trends in litigation awards or inflation can themselves be projected and estimated and the answers superimposed on the estimated results.

14 The larger and more fundamental in cause any discontinuity appears, the greater the uncertainty it creates in any prediction and the less reliable the mathematics become. All estimates contain a measure of uncertainty, and all statistical tools therefore produce a range of estimates. In calculating an RITC premium the syndicate must make a qualitative judgement of the impact of the causes of uncertainty in choosing a result from within the range presented. While it is difficult to conceive of a measure of uncertainty, there could well be something which creates uncertainty of such materiality that it is impossible to make any rational forecast. If this arises then it would not be possible to arrive at any RITC, and certainly not at any possibility of equity between sets of Names, and it will not be possible to close a syndicate year. In such circumstances a syndicate must be left open. The original Names will then remain responsible for the losses of that year and the successor Names receive no RITC premium, but are not left with the risk that it could prove inadequate (or excessive).

15 This problem is of particular concern to a Lloyd's syndicate, in contrast to the position of a typical insurance company. An insurance company draws up its accounts on the basis that it is a "going concern". While it will attempt as accurate an estimate as it can of future liabilities, it need only reserve amounts necessary to meet claims in the short or medium term, and can add to those reserves year by year as circumstances dictate and finances allow. Because a syndicate is an annual trading venture it is not a going concern and in order to release its members of all liabilities and "close" it must estimate and reserve those liabilities to finality.

16 In some circumstances, an underwriter might view events affecting a year of account as not being infected with uncertainty so material as to oblige him to leave it open, but nonetheless subject to some significant discontinuity from expected performance. In such cases, having regard to the paramount need for equity between Names, a prudent underwriter might still decide to leave the year open, perhaps hoping as he does so that it will be possible to close it in the near term as more information is established. It is common, for example, for an underwriter facing litigation on one very large claim, which he will either win or lose outright, to leave the year in which the litigation falls open until the outcome of the case is known.

17 I suggest that the market knowledge and warnings of the problems surrounding US asbestosis claims, the state of knowledge of the syndicate's own US Casualty underwritings exposed to asbestos claims,[3] the existence of the run-off contracts which multiplied the exposure to such claims and the lack of information on the policies covered by those contracts all combined to produce such a degree of uncertainty as to make it improper to have closed the syndicates at issue. In addition, the existence of other syndicate or company unlimited run-off contracts must multiply the existing uncertainty surrounding any estimated result. While a multiple of infinity is still infinity, if the capacity of a single syndicate's Names is effectively carrying the "tail" of several other syndicates or other unlimited run-offs, the chances of reaching too expensive a result, that is one of such material proportion and such financial impact on the Names that the impact of any error in its estimate will have a grave effect, are greatly increased for the reinsuring Names as is the speed with which it might arise.

18 I discuss each RITC and give my reasons in each case in Section VII of this report below.

3. Which appears from a memorandum to the Directors of Multicoloured (see Bundle C) to have been inadequate at least as far as records of claims were concerned. I do not know how complete their underwriting records on past business were.

IV. US Casualty Business

19 The term "casualty business" has no exact definition in the UK. It is of American usage and implies business roughly similar to that described in this country as "Accident" business. Casualty business is distinguished from Fire and related business, namely property insurance or first party coverage. It includes such classes of insurance business as all forms of third party insurance, surety and Bankers Blanket Bond business, Workmen's Compensation Act business, and some contingency and political risks business. Although "Accident Business" in the UK also usually encompasses personal accident and sickness business, "Casualty Business" usually does not. In the US there is frequently a third classification of non-life insurance in "Accident & Health" business which includes these classes as well as medical expenses insurance.

20 The term "Casualty Business" is commonly used in the Lloyd's market as a consequence of the large volume of US business placed at Lloyd's and here it is probably understood to mean third party liability and related business emanating from the United States. The allied phrase "Property and Casualty Business" is similarly used to indicate the non-life, or general, portfolios of American insurance companies reinsured in Lloyd's.

21 The Lloyd's market has traditionally written a considerable volume of US Casualty business—and still does, though not usually on the same bases as in the past. In particular, in the period of the 1950s to early 1970s, the market wrote a large volume of insurance of American manufacturers and producers in respect of public and products liability risks. Most of this insurance was not so-called "primary" coverage (meeting first dollar claims against the insureds) but insurance on an "excess" basis, responding only when claims—in the aggregate or individually—exceeded the limits of the primary policies. These policies were frequently arranged in "layers" of coverage, each layer responding only when the limits of the underlying policy were exhausted. The primary policies were usually written by domestic US insurance companies.

22 A large part of the business was placed at Lloyd's by means of binding authorities and brokers' line-slips, both facilities (similar but not identical)[4] allowing the broker to place risks with the agreement of only one or two leading underwriters whose acceptance would also bind following underwriters on the slip. This made life for the broker considerably easier and reduced the cost of placing such business in Lloyd's or London, but is partly responsible for some underwriters' paucity of records of what was written by their syndicates at the time.

23 Most of this US Casualty business was written on a so-called "losses occurring" basis—responding to claims, whenever they might be made, arising out of losses or events occurring during the period of the policy. Because US courts and insureds are now interpreting the dates of loss occurrence as including "exposure" to hazardous substances (such as asbestos) or to the dumping of waste materials on now polluted sites over long periods of time, claims being first intimated today as arising from the late 1970s onwards are now falling on these policies. Although this business has always been recognised as "long-tail", this tail was never historically estimated as much more than, say, ten years for public or third party liability and twenty years for products liability. That tail, however, has always been perceived as consisting largely of a delay in notifying, assessing and adjudicating claims from incidents at least suspected during or soon after the policy period. It is unlikely

4. A binding authority is an agreement to delegate specified underwriting authority, for a given class of business within predetermined limits and usually at predetermined rates of premium, to a third party usually known as a "coverholder". Premiums and claims are usually reported to the principal underwriters by the coverholder as block figures in account and, unless claims arise, underwriters subscribing to the binding authority will usually have no knowledge of the identity of their insureds whose coverage has been bound. A line slip is a similar arrangement, but the delegated underwriting authority is not complete and "declarations" under the line slip must be authorised by one or two leading underwriters on the line slip. Unless following underwriters on the slip insist on being kept informed, or the line slip broker is properly efficient, they could still be ignorant of the identity of risks underwritten on their behalf. It was quite common, in my experience, for Lloyd's underwriters in the 1960s, for example, not to keep records of all insurances bound under line slips, even if the broker gave them full details. An underwriter without full knowledge of the risks within his portfolio will be hampered when it comes to assessing his probable exposure to claims, present or future.

that anyone writing these policies in the 1950s and 1960s expected a thirty-year or longer tail, or the making of completely new claims after that length of time.

24 US Casualty business seems, in my experience, to have been written by a large part of the Lloyd's market. Certainly the major placing facilities used in the 1950s were subscribed to by many of the market. A large number of the claims currently being faced by the market fall on policies bound under these facilities. Marine syndicates frequently wrote this business as part of their "incidental non-marine account". Non-marine syndicates, naturally, also wrote it.

Reinsurance

25 There is also written in the Lloyd's market a large volume of reinsurance of American insurance companies. These reinsurances also covered Casualty business, and are an additional source of the same claims. The American companies frequently wrote the primary policies not placed directly in Lloyd's as well as participating in the excess business. These reinsurances continued to be written at Lloyd's after the direct business had become less commonly accepted, and were written in both the Marine and Non-Marine markets. Indeed, until the early 1980s these contracts were often placed on a so-called "Global" basis—covering all of the reinsured's combined marine and non-marine portfolios.

The position of Multicoloured plc in the market

26 The Rainbow marine syndicates were respected leading syndicates in the marine market, and Mr Rainbow himself was highly regarded. I do not know what is known about the business the syndicate was writing during the 1950s and 1960s, but it would certainly be expected that the syndicate would be shown virtually all available business and, by virtue of its size and leading position, write a considerable part of it. The allied non-marine syndicate, underwritten for by Mr Founder and then Mr Partner was equally highly respected and a leader in the non-marine market. Indeed it was especially an acknowledged leader in US Casualty classes, both insurance and reinsurance, borne out by its subsequent active participation in the various market claims committees.

Run-off reinsurances

27 Run-off contracts are a form of reinsurance contract. They provide protection in the aggregate for the reinsured's whole portfolio of business in respect of claims in excess of a predetermined level. They can be written with a finite limit to cover, or on an unlimited basis. They differ from other reinsurance contracts in that they protect a company not in respect of claims arising on business currently being written, or about to be written, but on business written in the past. They therefore provide protection against deterioration in the loss experience of an existing book of business, and are really a protection against the potential inadequacy of a reinsured's existing claims reserves. As a result, the most important underwriting consideration in rating them must be the projected or estimated future claims outcome, and this can only be assessed in the same way as the loss development for the reinsuring syndicate's own RITC. There will also need to be an estimated loss settlement, or cash-flow, pattern to be compared with the investment earnings which the premium can generate for reinsurers over time. They differ from an RITC in that they are arm's length contracts and no principle of equity applies. Indeed the price charged will presumably include an explicit element for the projected profit of the reinsurer. They are also subject to all the same conditions of utmost good faith as any other reinsurance contract.

28 Run-off reinsurances on a limited or finite basis, with varying details of terms, payment periods and price, can—and could in the 1980s—be obtained in a number of insurance markets, including the USA, Canada and Bermuda. They are sometimes written by reinsurance subsidiaries of captive insurance companies (companies owned by their principal insured) or of life insurance companies. As far as I am aware, the only market in which *unlimited* run-off reinsurance can be bought is Lloyd's itself.

V. Asbestos and Pollution—The London Market's Awareness 1981 to 1988

29 I have read the statement provided by Mr WZ Attorney on this subject and refer to the file of generally available reports and documents provided as Bundle D. I have no reason to dispute Mr Attorney's chronology of dissemination of information, and some of the documents produced or referred to are familiar to me from my time of employment on the ABC underwriting box.

30 I also refer here to the "Market Knowledge" Bundles of documents (Bundle B), some of which are again familiar to me from the past. I do not intend to reproduce quotations from these Bundles at great length, or from Mr Attorney's statement. I will assume that the documents are common knowledge.

VI. The RITC Process

31 The Reinsurance To Close is a financial mechanism whereby one annual entity, the closing syndicate, can be relieved of all outstanding liabilities for a consideration, the RITC premium, which is paid to another syndicate. This allows the members of the closing syndicate to receive any profit distribution and finalise all business affairs in respect of that syndicate year of account. The reinsuring syndicate accepts all further liabilities, of whatever sort, in return for the RITC premium. The reinsuring syndicate, by Lloyd's practice, is usually but not necessarily the succeeding year of account for the "same" syndicate—i.e. the successor syndicate, of the same identifying number and consisting of largely the same Names. Where this is not possible, for instance if the syndicate ceases to exist in substantially the same form or the Managing Agent ceases business, then the RITC can be effected into some other syndicate year.

32 The criteria for establishing the RITC are therefore those required on the basis of winding up the affairs of the syndicate to extinction. Reserves for, or estimates of, the ongoing liabilities must be calculated on a prudent basis. A syndicate is not an ongoing concern and future deterioration cannot be expected to be made up by later years of account or "syndicate years". From this follows the need to establish "equity" between closing and reinsuring Names—neither set of Names should make a profit at the expense of the other, or at least the RITC should not be set so as to make this certain or highly probable, or with the intention of achieving such a profit.

33 Until the Lloyd's Act of 1982 and the various ByeLaws promulgated under it, there was no formal requirement for the setting of the RITC. Lloyd's market practice certainly acknowledged the need for equity between Names. However it was fairly common, but not openly acknowledged, practice to err on the side of "over-reserving" in profitable years to help in increasing the creation of reserves likely to prove prudent in the long run. The principles of prudent reserving and equity between Names are now codified in the Syndicate Accounting ByeLaw Number 11 of 1987.

34 Until the creation of the Provisional Syndicate Accounting Manual in 1983, the only instructions from Lloyd's in respect of year-end provisions were the so-called "Instructions to Lloyd's Panel Auditors", issued annually. These were in fact concerned with calculation of Names' ability to meet the annual statutory solvency requirements in compliance with DTI regulations. They dealt predominantly with valuation of Names' assets—funds at Lloyd's, personal reserves, valuation of investments *et al.* As far as valuation of liabilities was concerned, the instructions annually included a statement that the syndicate's reserve for these should be the *greatest* of:

(i) a calculation made by applying percentages (agreed annually with the DTI and known colloquially as "audit percentages") to the syndicate's premium income divided into various major classes of business;

(ii) the sum of the syndicate's known and noted outstanding claims plus an estimate of IBNR claims; and

(iii) the RITC premium established by the underwriter.

35 In practice, large numbers of underwriters applied the "audit percentages" to their books of business, checked that the results exceeded known outstanding claims and added a "load" which was not mathematically calculated. In many cases, in my experience, it consisted of what the underwriter felt he could afford, possibly tempered by the limit which he felt the Inland Revenue would agree as a reasonable tax-deductible provision.

36 A proper RITC calculation, notwithstanding the lack of specific instruction from Lloyd's, requires and required much more than this. It is true that before the Syndicate Accounting ByeLaw codified the basis of the RITC and before the general deterioration in long tail accounts as a result of asbestos claims revealed serious deficiencies in earlier RITCs, almost no Lloyd's syndicates used highly sophisticated methods of analysis. Even then, however, professional underwriters were analysing their figures in considerable detail and attempting to make a sound estimate of future claims development. The forecasting and estimating techniques used for assessing the cost to run-off a portfolio were well known as tools for purposes other than providing an RITC basis—for example calculating the ultimate claims cost of a long tail reinsurance contract so that a renewal premium could be quoted, or assessing the profitability of an individual class of business. In particular, Mr Actuary, then employed by *RE Re Ltd* (and, I believe the first actuary to be employed by non-life insurers or reinsurers), had published a series of booklets on "chain ladder" techniques and the use of loss triangulations to assist in these calculations.

37 The first stage in the process—usually carried out by Claims Departments of syndicates—is and was to ensure that the figures on which the RITC was to be based are as accurate as possible. This involves a process of confirming with Lloyd's brokers that all notified claims figures are as up to date as possible, and then that those figures are accurately recorded in the syndicate's books. Most syndicates in the 1970s began this process in September each year, but some started in the summer. Today I suspect most syndicates need to begin in the late summer.

38 The syndicate must then subdivide its figures into reasonably homogeneous subsets of data, usually by major class of business. This subdivision will vary from syndicate to syndicate depending on the size and make-up of the portfolio, but at a minimum figures should be split into the various "audit categories" required by the solvency regulations (and certainly all syndicates hold their data so divided). For each category, for each historic year of account separately, it is necessary to examine the historical development of premiums, paid claims and incurred (paid plus outstanding) claims. The commonest way of presenting these figures is in the form of cumulative "development" triangulations. From the development pattern revealed by the earliest years of account it is possible to project forward the probable result of the newer, less historically developed, years of account including the one to be closed.

39 A range of methods can be used to make this projection. The simplest, especially in the absence of any mathematical sophistication, is to look at the ratios between claims figures at the date of closing an account and their ultimate outcome. This method assumes that the oldest data available have in fact reached their ultimate value and will not continue to develop. To allow for any further development a plot of the cumulative figures on a graph will allow a visual estimation of ultimate values and, with only extended arithmetic, an estimate of the probable range of outcomes (by calculating the variance of the data points from the line drawn on the graph). The visual estimate of the outcome can be improved on by mathematical calculation of the equation of the curve which best fits the data points and using that equation to predict the expected result at various future points.

40 These estimates can be made more reliable by, for example, using analysis of loss ratios to premium as well as loss figures. This will allow for general changes in rating levels from year to year. Known "odd points" such as the incidence of a single large claim can be allowed for by removing the figures for such claims before making a projection and adding back the removed figure after the exercise. Simultaneously, an analysis of expenditure on claims from previous RITCs to assess the adequacy of the reserves created in the past is essential. It has always been required by Lloyd's, so that auditors may report on the adequacy of such reserves for "old years" and also allows an assessment of the reliability of the projected patterns in estimating current years.

41 In my experience, these sorts of technique were being used to varying degrees by professional syndicates in Lloyd's by the end of the 1970s. The level of detail of analysis varied as did the explicitness of the underlying mathematics. These syndicates, however, did

more than arrive at what the underwriter could "afford" or "felt" was right. They also did more than rely simply on Lloyd's audit percentages, so-called.

42 From the mid-1980s onwards, the existence of off-the-shelf software packages and the arrival in the market of an increasing number of non-life actuaries meant that steadily the level of mathematics applied to this exercise increased. The underlying principles however have not really changed. What has changed is the degree of detail of subdivision of data, and an increased accuracy of original figures. The extent of use of modern tools still varies in the market, but the use of standard software packages is now commonplace.

43 All these methods and techniques, however, suffer from two problems. One is common to all statistical forecasting attempts—the reliance on the assumption that the past is a guide to the future. In mathematical terms this means an assumption that all the underlying relationships in the data remain constant. The second is that a large part of the data—the figures for outstanding claims—are largely subjective. These figures are themselves only estimates, albeit carefully made by professional loss adjusters, attorneys and claims managers.

44 In both cases, these problems can largely be overcome by "judgement". Individual claims reserve figures can be scrutinised by underwriters and their claims managers for "reasonableness". Most syndicates do, and did, carry out such an exercise, increasing the outstanding claims reserves with so-called "specific IBNR" where they deem it appropriate. Increasing the figures in this way increases the level of aggregate claims forecast as the ultimate and increases the tendency to prudence in the RITC figures. The patterns of development produced from one year of account to the next can be compared to see—assuming that the underlying portfolio of risks has not changed—that they are similar to each other, implying consistency of estimation and a degree of reliability. The exercise is subjective and a matter of judgement, but not impossible. It is akin to any other matter of commercial judgement.

45 A far greater problem is, potentially, presented by the assumption that past statistics are a guide to future claims costs. Some of the inherent difficulties—future inflation, cash flow and interest rate patterns and the like—can also be statistically forecast. To the extent that data for past claims are in "actual" rather than "real" values, and have not been deflated to allow for rising costs or prices (past inflation), then any forecast based on these actual values will already include an element of predicted inflation, at a rate equal to the average of past inflation in the data. Again the answers are only estimates and themselves uncertain. But, again, arriving at an answer is a matter of commercial judgement tempered by knowledge of the range of results produced by that part of the uncertainty which is statistically measurable. Most financial decisions about the future have to be based on some uncertainty and the fact that the answer chosen is unlikely ever to be arithmetically correct does not make the judgement impossible, or the decision invalid.

46 However, other changes from the conditions which produced the past patterns and projections may be so significant as to make any forecast impossible or nearly so. The advent of the first asbestos claims, and the predictions as to their future flow, were in my opinion just such a change. None of these claims formed part of the old statistics. Their effect could not therefore be forecast from them. Policies believed to have expired now produced claims. There was qualitative uncertainty as to which theories of liability would obtain, and therefore which policies would respond. Predicted and known numbers of claimants were large, and estimates of average claim varied. Medical evidence available to the market,[5] of a forty year latency period before the symptoms of asbestos related diseases might become apparent, implied the existence of a possible forty year "tail" for claims—it was both possible for new claims to arise on policies now forty years old and for current policies not be fully run-off for a possible further forty years. This should inevitably have thrown serious doubt on any RITC calculated as before.

47 For some syndicates, it would have been possible nonetheless to arrive at an RITC and still feel secure that the level of uncertainty in the process remained "manageable". In particular, any syndicate with accurate records of its US Casualty policies written in the appropriate period could attempt an assessment of its maximum exposure to claims (with some assumptions as to how many claims might be expected on policies with unlimited amounts of coverage). An assessment might be possible, based on known market share applied to the

5. See Bundle B.

overall predictions being put out by industry commentators. Asbestos claims first advised, including those on a precautionary basis, could be projected separately from other claims but in the same way to give a tentative first projection for comparison with exposure estimates.

48 However, all such approaches would, in the first two or three years of advice of asbestos claims in particular, have been very approximate indeed and unreliable. Unless a syndicate was in the fortunate position of having complete records of its writings on US Casualty business, and had good reason to believe that its susceptible portfolio was truly small in proportion to its book of business and its other reserves then—given the legal, medical and financial warnings being circulated in 1980 and 1981—it should probably have concluded that the uncertainty surrounding any RITC calculation was so material that the syndicate should not, in fact, be closed. The tenor of the Subtract & Multiply and DCL letters[6] circulated throughout the market certainly implied as much.

VII. The Rainbow Syndicates' RITCs

49 Later in this Section, I set out year by year my conclusions as to the methods and techniques utilised by Mr Rainbow in arriving at the RITCs, and why in the circumstances he could not properly have done so. There are, however, some general considerations applying to the Rainbow syndicates over all years which I discuss here.

50 The Syndicate Reports and Accounts for successive years make several statements to the Names to the effect that the RITC has been "calculated" by Mr Rainbow. However, in the various bundles of "RITC Files" provided to me I can find no evidence of any such "calculation". Various loadings seem to have been applied to outstanding claims figures, but there is no explanation or illustration or calculation to show how these loadings have been established. It is not consistently clear whether the figures before "loading" are "pure" outstanding claim figures as provided to the syndicate by external advisers, or whether they have themselves been amended to include any "specific IBNR". Where specific IBNR is mentioned there is no note in the files as to how the figures are arrived at, or by whom. There are no proper cumulative triangulations of historic figures, although these were frequently used in the market by 1982. The papers I have reviewed in the "RITC Files" seem all to be allocations of the underwriter's "loading" over various classes of business and years of account, reconciliations of investment figures, comparison with Lloyd's solvency test "audit minima" and drafts of syndicate accounts and balance sheets. In other words, they all relate to the detailed work which should be done, and obviously was done, by the Managing Agent, after the underwriter has arrived at his RITC. It would seem, on the basis of the evidence I have seen, that there was *no* proper attempt to calculate the RITC.

51 It is not therefore surprising that there seems to be no recognition, on a purely statistical basis, that the advent of asbestos claims represented a mathematical and qualitative discontinuity which made the old basis of closing the syndicate untenable. There seem to have been no proper analyses to make this apparent.

52 The position of Multicoloured plc in the market, running both a leading marine and a leading non-marine syndicate, and the involvement of the Agency in the various market claims committees put them in an almost unique position to realise the major impact which asbestos claims were going to have. Mr Partner was a market leader in US Casualty business, a founder member of the market committees and a member of the Agency board. I find it hard to believe that his knowledge of asbestos was not shared, however informally, with the in-house marine syndicate. If it was not, it should have been.

53 The syndicate's involvement in US Casualty business, *via* its incidental non-marine syndicate appears to have been extensive. In common with many incidental non-marine syndicates it appears not to have kept accurate records of its writings. It was therefore in no position to make any assessment of its probable exposure or its likely "market share" of any global figures predicted.

54 The various run-off contracts exacerbated this in several ways. No analysis of the estimated ultimate cost of these contracts seems to have been made before 1985 or 1986. No information as to the original US Casualty business protected under the contracts existed. Rainbow's own actuary reported in 1987 that the figures available for these run-off

6. See Bundle B.

contracts were not susceptible to actuarial analysis. The figures for asbestos within these run-off contracts were certain in one respect—they would accumulate with the syndicate's own involvement and make the scale of the problem significantly greater.

55 From a study of the figures, syndicate accounts and RITC files made available, I conclude that the syndicate made little or no attempt at proper calculation of its RITC, before the employment of its own actuary in 1984. Had such an attempt been made, and had the non-financial information on asbestos being circulated to the market by the group's non-marine syndicate been properly considered, it would have been apparent to the underwriter that the uncertainties surrounding the account were so great that equity between Names meant he could not properly close the account from the 1979 account onwards. Only when the syndicate's own actuary cast doubts on the uncertainty surrounding the run-off contracts, which aggregated with the syndicate's own writings, did the idea seem to be taken on board.

The Reinsurance to Close the 1979 a/c at 31.12.1981

56 Mr Rainbow, in the statement of his which I have read, gives no details of the processes carried out to arrive at the 1979 account RITC. Mr AN Actuary had not at this time joined Multicoloured plc, so I would not expect any so-called actuarial work to have been carried out. I have, however, studied the papers disclosed in the "pruned" Rainbow RITC files (Bundle A) and the Syndicate Report and Accounts for 1979 to 1981.

57 The 1979 and 1980 Accounts do not appear to make any comment or predictions for the 1979 account, then at the end of its first and second years of development respectively.[7]

58 In his underwriter's Report in 1981 Mr Rainbow says:

> "... there have been significant developments ... which have led us to increase the very substantial provision already made for claims as a result of asbestosis and other latent diseases. There has been a substantial increase in the losses advised, both in terms of total numbers and in the anticipated average settlement of such cases as may be proved ... With more information available, reinsurance claims are also higher.... Perhaps of greater significance has been the thrust of judgments in the United States courts [*re*: exposure/manifestation/other theories of date of loss].... It is too early to estimate (in public) what the consequences of the development of this approach might be."

59 It is clear from these remarks that the syndicate was already well aware of the problems surrounding the treatment of asbestosis and other similar claims on old years. This is not surprising since in 1980 the first market committee on this subject had already been set up, largely—from my recollection and his own evidence—at the instigation of Mr Claimsman of Multicoloured plc. Mr Claimsman also tells us that he was responsible for the management of non-marine claims falling on these syndicates. Mr Attorney's statement (paragraph aa, pages y) clearly outlines the views being expressed by US attorneys instructed by Lloyd's syndicates, some of those views being expressed directly to Mr Claimsman himself. I shall not requote them all here, but they all stress in common the uncertainty surrounding future developments in asbestos-related disease claims and the impossibility of predicting their outcome. They also include similar severe warnings on the impact of asbestos-related property damage claims, which are not mentioned by Mr Rainbow in his 1981 Underwriter's Report.

60 I do not know what the significance of the remark ("in public") made by Mr Rainbow in his Report to Names was supposed to be, but it is my belief (and, I contend, supported by the many Lloyd's circulars written by Mr Partner in his capacity as Chairman of the market committees and the number of times his views were sought by journalists and at market conferences) that Multicoloured plc were the best placed of all syndicates in Lloyd's to appreciate the *real* implications of the surge in asbestos litigation and the real impossibility of predicting the cost to the syndicate or the whole market.

7. At least, not in the version I have seen, which contains no narrative Underwriter's or Managing Agents' report.

61 A note to the 1981 Accounts for the syndicate says that the RITC for the 1979 year "... has been *calculated by* the Underwriter and complies with the requirements of the Committee of Lloyd's, as approved by the Department of Trade." (My emphasis.) With respect, I can find no evidence of "calculation" in the RITC files and papers which I have examined. A view seems to have been taken that an addition of 50 per cent to the amount of noted outstanding claims would be adequate to run-off the liabilities of the syndicate. The only calculations I can find in the papers are concerned with checking the adequacy to date of a similar provision for earlier RITCs and reconciling the amount of the RITC in separate years of account to the syndicate accounts.

62 This RITC, for the 1979 account, will have been carried out in the context of the market letter from the then Deputy Chairman of Lloyd's dated March 1982 (the "DCL letter"). Amongst other guidelines this letter dealt at length with the problems of reserving for asbestosis related claims and recommended that:

> "Where the reserve for Asbestosis represents a material proportion of the total reserves of the syndicate, Agents should consider whether or not to leave the account open."

At 31.12.1981 when the 1979 account was being closed, the syndicate had total noted outstanding asbestos claims of approximately US$5.2m and total noted outstanding losses on US business of some US$31m—in other words known outstanding asbestos losses were already approaching one sixth of total outstandings from American business. And this was before any addition was made for IBNR for asbestos losses, which, given all the warnings in existence as to possible numbers of claimants and the forty-year latency period for asbestos-related disease, was bound to be substantial. In the light of the depth of non-quantitative knowledge which Multicoloured plc had about the potential seriousness of both asbestos disease and asbestos property damage claims to come, this must in my view have been a significant and "material proportion" of known and IBNR reserves arising out of asbestos. If the DCL guidelines were to be followed, very serious consideration should have been given to leaving the account open.

63 In addition, the syndicate had already written the first of the unlimited run-off reinsurance contracts in its book—the reinsurance of the Simple Insurance Co, signed into the 1978 account. Although this was not a reinsurance of a Lloyd's syndicate, it was a reinsurance of a London market company co-insuring the same USA business as was written in Lloyd's and covered business written in 1968 and earlier—precisely the years worst affected by asbestos claims. All the same difficulties arise as in assuming the run-off of another Lloyd's syndicate on the support of the reinsuring syndicate's capacity. The DCL letter in paragraph 6 drew attention to the dangers of including run-off accounts and this warning, coupled with the recognition that the syndicate had taken on a second unlimited exposure to asbestos-related and other latent disease and property damage claims, meant that the 1979 account could not properly have been closed.

64 At the time, it was still unusual for a syndicate to be left open, and certainly in the Lloyd's culture of the time underwriters felt more pressure to close a syndicate, so that Names could finalise their liabilities and, for example, complete their tax affairs in respect of each year, than to leave it open. This made the strong recommendation in the DCL letter that consideration be given to keeping the 1979 year open all the more significant. Mr Rainbow in his statement (paragraph 75) says that:

> "An Agency is not entitled to leave a year open on the basis of nothing more substantial than speculation regarding any future unforeseen factors."

What we are looking at here, however, is not mere speculation regarding future factors, unforeseen or otherwise, but a substantial body of knowledge which the syndicate must have possessed to the effect that the future liabilities to be created by asbestos-related claims, both for bodily injury and for property damage, could not be estimated with any reliability and the year of account could not be closed. The position was compounded by the presence in the account of an unlimited run-off reinsurance of another similar account whose liabilities aggregated with those of the syndicate and would have to be met by the same Names.

The Reinsurance to Close the 1980 a/c at 31.12.1982

65 I have again not seen any specific evidence as to this RITC from Mr Rainbow. Nor, it seems, was Mr Actuary involved. Lloyd's instructions in respect of the 1982 end-of-year audit included a new statement reminding the Managing Agent that, in closing, it had responsibility to ensure that adequate funds were created to discharge "all liabilities" of the syndicate. In my view, and my view at the time, this was a further, albeit oblique, attempt to remind Underwriters and Managing Agents to look very carefully at the estimation of future asbestos and similar losses.

66 By 31.12.1982 known outstandings for the syndicate alone had risen to US$8m for asbestos claims and $2m for DES claims (previously deemed "negligible" for the syndicate) and for all other USA claims some $14m, so reserves for known latent disease claims were now over 40 per cent of the total. The file shows attempts at triangulations of loss settlement patterns and analyses of the adequacy or otherwise of earlier RITC values, but no evidence that the syndicate recognised that these analyses, based on past underwriting history and results, would be of no relevance to predicting the future for previously unknown latent disease and pollution claims. The other information which the syndicate was receiving, and which Messrs Partner and Claimsman were circulating to the Lloyd's market *via* the market committees, included warnings that numbers of asbestos claims advised continued to accelerate, that there was still uncertainty as to which policies should respond or how, and still an impossibility of predicting the ultimate global cost of asbestos claims. Again, the detailed knowledge held by senior members of Multicoloured plc must have meant that they, of all Lloyd's organisations, were best placed to appreciate the real import of these warnings.

67 By now the syndicate apparently had been advised that known asbestos and DES claims on the Simple Co Ltd run-off contract (previously not, it seems, mentioned by Simple) amounted to US$3.8m and that Simple's estimated total potential for asbestos claims was US$23m. This was a clear indication, if it had not been realised before, that this run-off was subject to identical problems with respect to latent disease claims as was the syndicate and that these claims would aggregate with the syndicate's own causing problems out of proportion to the premium quoted for the contract or the capacity of the original syndicate. By now also the syndicate had written, and senior personnel should have known it had written, a second unlimited run-off contract, reinsuring the Helpful Insurance Co. This seems to have covered an almost identical portfolio to Simple's and all the uncertainties of estimation and impossibility of arriving at a proper ultimate liability were further compounded in exactly the same way.

68 Again, I do not believe, given the information available to the syndicate, the proportion of its known reserves represented by asbestos and similar claims and the existence (now) of two other unlimited run-off contracts facing the same difficulties, that the syndicate's 1980 year of account should have been closed.

The Reinsurance to Close the 1981 a/c at 31.12.1983

69 I really repeat my comments, *mutatis mutandis*, on the 1981 close. I would add only that there are various RITC files I have seen suggesting that the full importance of the run-off contracts (of which there were now four) was beginning to be realised. Further, Mr Actuary in his statement says that in 1984, after the event, when he was asked to review the previous RITCs he found that the non-marine syndicate experience had not until then been used as a guide. This, if true, suggests that the syndicate failed to make use of all the information available within Multicoloured plc before reaching its decision to close the account. Mr Rainbow's statement does not specifically address this close.

The Reinsurance to Close the 1982 a/c at 31.12.1984

70 In his statement, Mr Rainbow says that for the syndicate the previous policy of adding 50 per cent to net noted outstanding losses for IBNR was continued. This policy had been followed for a number of years and always been found to be "conservative" (which I take to mean "adequate"). It was obviously recognised, however, that this past history would not

serve to predict latent disease and pollution losses since a further $12m was added for these. Mr Rainbow attempts to show that this $12m was not an arbitrary figure, but he states that the pollution element of this figure was set at three times the syndicate's worst possible loss for their largest single pollution claim, because pollution was regarded as the minor of the two problems. This created a pollution IBNR of $7.5m leaving only $4.5m for the presumably "major" problem of asbestos and other latent disease claims. However the need to establish substantial reserves for the run-off contracts was finally recognised (Mr Rainbow describes this as a "shock") and these were reserved in line with the non-marine syndicate's experience.

71 Mr Actuary supports this description of the processes used. He explains that the assumptions used by the non-marine syndicate for estimating ultimate asbestos losses was that they would run-off steadily from 1986, gradually reducing over a period of 15 years or more. It is not clear how these assumptions were arrived at, given that the other information being received from US attorneys and outside sources was still that the number of claims was increasing annually and that it was not possible to identify all possible sources of claims, or their outcome.

72 At this time the group purchased a "Time and Distance" contract to protect themselves against future deterioration of losses and took immediate full credit against their reserves for the US$51.65m cover bought. This presumably provided a measure of comfort in the face of steadily rising reserves, but it could not, in my view, even then have been expected to be adequate to cover the many unlimited accounts which the syndicate Names were now running-off. It did not in itself do enough to make it possible properly to close the syndicate.

The Reinsurance to Close the 1983 a/c at 31.12.1985

73 The syndicate continued to create reserves broadly in line with previous policies, although the files show an increasing amount of statistical and arithmetical work on historic loss development figures for major classes of business. It is probably still fair to say that Multicoloured plc was amongst the leaders in the Lloyd's markets in its approach to estimating reserves and the RITC. However, there still appears to be no logical rationale to its loadings for asbestos, latent disease and pollution. The letters written to the Inland Revenue in November 1986 illustrate this clearly. I suspect that they recognised that such a rationale could not be provided in the light of the extent of their involvement, especially on the run-off contracts. For these contracts they lacked the original underwriting information which would allow any estimate, however approximate, of the total potential exposure to these losses.

74 It was in this year that it was decided to leave a smaller parallel syndicate open, because of the effect of the run-off contracts on the syndicate's portfolio. Mr Rainbow lucidly describes in his statement and in his Underwriter's Report for the year the "gearing" effect which a small change in the results of these contracts would have on the overall result of the syndicate. He concluded, however, that this argument did not apply to the main syndicate because of its much greater underwriting capacity and greater reserves. The smaller syndicate had written fewer run-off contracts than the main syndicate's eleven. The greater uncertainty involved in running off eleven unlimited accounts in addition to the syndicate's own portfolio would make the predictable movements around any estimated outcome greater than that for the smaller syndicate and the likely effect on the total reserves could not therefore be dismissed as definitely much less than for that smaller syndicate. If the argument properly applied to one syndicate it also did to the other.

75 During 1985 the second market committee was established, again largely at the instigation of Mr Claimsman. This continues to suggest Multicoloured plc was in possession of more information than most of the Lloyd's market and was most aware of its implications. I again conclude, that as in prior years, they should have known that they could not properly close the syndicate.

76 Incidentally, in a memorandum written by Mr Bookkeeper of Multicoloured plc on early estimates of the results for the 1983 account he says of asbestos reserves that "... it is hoped

that the 1985 reserves will be within the IBNR provisions raised last year" and describes this as "encouraging". If the IBNR provisions previously raised had been in any sense a reasonable estimate of the *ultimate* liability to be met, then this remark would be superfluous and the fact that one year's "reserves" were contained by those provisions could not be described as "encouraging". This remark, made in an internal memorandum, coupled with Mr Rainbow's stated opinion that "All syndicates at Lloyd's are continuing business activities" (rather than annual ventures) suggests to me the possibility that in closing each successive year what the syndicate was actually trying to do was create short term reserves, adequate for the next one or two years' development, and not to create reserves adequate to discharge *all* liabilities as required by the Audit Instructions, and as implied by the need for equity between successive syndicates. Indeed, the loadings created by Mr Actuary for the 1983 close were based on short-term (three-year) forecasts of developments in asbestos, DES and pollution, giving further weight to my suspicion.

The Reinsurance to Close the 1984 a/c at 31.12.1986

77 The syndicate files for this RITC include a "Note" on the Reinsurance to Close for the syndicate by one of the Agency staff which includes a comment that the note does not cover the run-off contracts written by this syndicate and which warns:

> "Even on a syndicate the size of the . . . Syndicate these . . . run-off contracts can significantly affect the overall result."

78 Mr Rainbow in his statement says that the continued increase in asbestos claim numbers during 1986 and 1987 was a "source of surprise to the London Market and to me. We envisaged that the problem would start to decrease from 1985". Although new market initiatives were expected to reduce average claim costs and legal costs from 1985 onwards, it is my recollection supported by the selected papers in Bundle B that it was very much feared that claim numbers would continue to increase.

79 The syndicate's degree of sophistication of assessment of the possible outcome of its main account, excluding asbestos, pollution and the like, continues to show improvement in this year's RITC files. However Mr Actuary himself noted that for these problems the syndicate had "insufficient data to make a reliable statistical projection".

80 In my view nothing fundamental had changed to make closing the syndicate a proper option.

The Reinsurance to Close the 1985 a/c at 31.12.1987

81 During 1987 the new Syndicate Accounting ByeLaw was introduced, encoding the requirement that the RITC should achieve equity between successive syndicate memberships.

82 This is the first year for which the RITC files contain substantial evidence of attempts, particularly by Mr Actuary, to analyse the account, including asbestos and pollution claims, to determine the syndicate's ultimate liabilities. It is interesting that his conclusion was that this would not be possible and that the account should remain open. Mr Rainbow in his statement and when writing to the Names explains this by reference to "serious" concern as to the development of asbestos property damage claims and continued deterioration on the run-off contracts, several of which were now being disputed or re-negotiated. He concludes that he had to be certain that the losses were properly borne.

83 At this point a decision was finally made that the syndicate should be left open. The syndicate's real exposure to asbestos and pollution and related claims had not changed. Its involvement in the classes of business giving rise to them had always been extensive. The syndicate's position was made worse by the presence in the account of the eleven run-off contracts whose ultimate liabilities had also to be borne by the same Names. However, if the analysis attempted by Mr Actuary had been carried out in any of the earlier years under discussion, and the syndicate's detailed qualitative knowledge on the impact of these claims on the whole market been properly considered, then the defendant could only have concluded at any of the earlier RITC assessments that the level of materiality of these claims

and the degree of uncertainty surrounding their estimates were such that it was not possible to close the syndicate. In my opinion a competent underwriter acting on the knowledge in the market at the time and applying the analytical techniques in use elsewhere in the market at the time would not have closed the previous years of the syndicate.

APPENDIX 1

CURRICULUM VITAE: MRS PHILLIPPA ROWE

Mrs Phillippa Carne Rowe (née King) MA, FCII, MAE, Chartered Insurance Practitioner

Date of Birth:	21 March 1952	Married One child
Home Address	Allercleugh Farmhouse Wearhead, BISHOP AUCKLAND Co Durham DL13 1PU Tel 01388 537665	
Business Address	1G Castle Gardens Stanhope BISHOP AUCKLAND Co Durham DL13 2FJ Tel 01388 526111 Fax 01388 526333	

Education and Qualifications:

1963–71	Grangefield Grammar School for Girls, Stockton-on-Tees GCE A-Levels in English Literature (and S-level) Mathematics Further Mathematics General Studies
1971–74	New Hall, Cambridge BA in Economics (II.2) 1974 MA 1977
1978	ACII (Associate of the Chartered Insurance Institute)
1981	FCII (Fellow of the CII)
1989	Chartered Insurance Practitioner
1992	Associate of The Academy of Experts
1993	Member of The Academy of Experts

Career History:

1991 to date	Senior Partner, Phillippa Ross & Co, Reinsurance Consultancy and Reviews—a firm providing professional services to the non-marine insurance market.
1989–91	Sole Practitioner, Phillippa Ross & Co.
1974–88	ABC & Others, Lloyd's—a leading non-marine syndicate in the Lloyd's market, working primarily in the fields of claims management (including assessment of the RITC), wordings and treaty accounting.

Current professional activities include provision of technical consultancy, audit and inspection services on reinsurance and insurance matters to members of the Lloyd's and London insurance market, predominantly but not exclusively in the claims, contract wording and technical accounting spheres. All these are more fully described in the enclosed company brochure.

Mrs Rowe has been involved in litigation and litigation support in various ways, having twice been deposed as a witness/principal defendant in insurance cases in the USA, acted as a witness of fact in a London reinsurance arbitration and as expert witness in reinsurance litigation and arbitrations and provided investigative analysis and consultancy to parties contemplating reinsurance disputes. She is registered with The Academy of Experts as a Qualified Mediator.

She has recently acted as assistant/researcher for the expert witness in one Lloyd's Action Group case, and is currently acting for reinsurers as expert witness on claims and RITC aspects of a dispute in litigation between a Lloyd's syndicate and its Run-Off reinsurers.

In addition Mrs Rowe lectures at the CII College of Insurance on reinsurance subjects, and for the Council of Legal Education on ADR. Mrs Rowe is a member of the Council of The Academy of Experts and Chairman of its ADR Committee, and until September 1993 was Secretary of the London Region of the CII's Society of Fellows.

Mrs Rowe has published several articles, in *ReActions*, *Global Reinsurance* and the *Society of Fellows Journal*, and has been commissioned by Witherby's to write a book on claims reserving.

DISCUSSION ON FIRST MODEL EXPERT'S REPORT

026 First some explanatory background to my writing of this report. Other experts reading this might be surprised at the relative lack of discussion of factual evidence in a discussion such as this one. Normally I would agree. However, the main problem I faced in this case was that the defendant had done so very little—almost nothing—by way of calculating or estimating his RITC that there was little I could analyse. Questions of degrees of materiality and uncertainty occur throughout my argument, and I originally included some percentage analyses of, for example, asbestos claims to total claims and the like, but later removed them. Since the decision as to what was a material level of effect was ultimately one for the court I did not want to be led in cross-examination down the path of "If not 10 per cent, then why 11?" and the like. Nor did I want to fall into the trap of appearing to tell the court what level of uncertainty or impact was material.

027 I was also removed from any obligation to conduct laborious mathematical exercises, however, by the nature of the evidence I was asked to examine. I was instructed to act very late in the proceedings, even later than the cynical expert might find usual. The trial date was looming and I was "lent" at almost the last possible moment by solicitors for another Lloyd's case on similar lines whose trial was nothing like as imminent. As a consequence I was asked to provide my opinion on the basis of very limited documents, including so-called "pruned" syndicate files which were to form the basis of the trial bundles. Given the precise limits of my instructions, the documents I had seemed adequate to form an opinion, without the recital of facts which were generally accepted by all the parties, whose analysis might have opened the pitfalls of approach I wanted to avoid. (I do *not* mean that I think that this analysis, or sight of the fuller files, would have changed my opinion to one less favourable to my client. Had there been vital gaps in the papers I was given I would have had to act differently.) Readers will note that I was very careful in Paragraph 4 to set out the limited nature of the materials on which I based my opinion.

028 The structure of the report is, I hope, self-explanatory. I did not set out consciously to follow The Academy of Experts' *Model Form of Expert's Report,* though it should not be a surprise that there are distinct similarities. The *Model Form,* designed with assistance from The Academy's Judicial Committee, provides a logical order for presentation of an expert's opinion to the court and is intended to be "judge-friendly". Its most important points are that paragraphs should be numbered, text should whenever possible be arranged in short sentences and paragraphs, matters of fact should be kept separate from matters of opinion or deduction, as much supplementary and explanatory material as possible should be relegated to appendices, and there should clearly be an identifiable conclusion (for a copy of the *Model Form of Expert's Report,* see Appendix G to this book). The *Model Form* consists of a formal introduction; outline background to the dispute and the issues; description of any technical investigation or enquiry; facts on which the opinion is based; conclusions; signature and date. The 1998 revision of the *Model Form,* in response to Lord Woolf's *Access to Justice* also contains a declaration as to how the report has been prepared and confirming the expert's proper understanding of the nature of his duties to the court.

029 Not all sections of the model will be applicable to all reports, but since the scheme of the model is both simple and logical, leading from a statement of the problem, and the expert's instructions in assisting with it, through the evidence and argument to a conclusion as to the expert's findings, it is not surprising that most well-constructed reports will be very similar to the model—as is this example.

030 Paragraph 1A is worthy of brief explanation. The Commercial Court judge to whom almost all of the Lloyd's litigation was assigned was Cresswell J, of *Ikarian Reefer* fame, and it was at his insistence that all experts in all the Lloyd's cases were required to include this declaration (the wording is Cresswell J's). The instruction was handed down after the report was written, and I was not going to renumber all my paragraphs! This requirement in these Lloyd's cases is interesting since it foreshadowed the requirement from Lord Woolf in his final report on *Access to Justice* that all experts include in their reports a declaration of their understanding of their duties to act as impartial assistants to the court, and confirmation that they have prepared their reports on this basis and after an investigation of all relevant information. (Experts, particularly *via* The Academy of Experts, objected to this last provision, since the onus on them to trawl the world for all possible information in support of either side of the argument seemed unreasonable. It was altered in the declaration drafted by the Academy and approved by Lord Woolf which is incorporated in the revised edition of the *Model Form*.) Lord Woolf's proposed declaration was considerably longer than Cresswell J's. The final version drafted by The Academy of Experts and approved by Lord Woolf is somewhere between the two. Section I also sets out the basis, and limits, of my expertise, reserving a full CV to the Appendix. It demonstrates that I had had direct experience of the matters on which I give an opinion—handling the original claims, and calculating RITC premiums. Although obviously a necessary part of my report, these two paragraphs were to backfire somewhat, as will be revealed below.

031 Section I of the report needs no further comment. Sections II, III and IV set out the background to the dispute, putting the later analysis into context. The first of these, "The Nature of the Lloyd's Market", was deliberately brief. It was needed in order to establish some key underlying facts and definitions, but since earlier parts of the Lloyd's litigation (which, incidentally, was a superb example of litigation management on a major scale, with careful timetabling of individual cases involving solicitors for all the parties in the various cases, combined handling of preliminary issues common to all cases and recognition of evidence common to all cases whose repetition was, as far as possible, avoided) had dealt with the nature and structure of the Lloyd's market in deciding the preliminary issue, amongst others, of whether underwriting agents owed a duty of care to their Names at all, it would have been superfluous to repeat a lengthy description here. It was, at this stage, taken as common ground by all involved in the litigation.

032 Section V, "London Market Awareness", served several purposes. First, by general agreement of all involved, it removed the need to append large volumes of (the same) documents to each expert's report. Secondly, the Bundles referred to constituted an agreed *corpus* of evidence as to what was generally available (as information on the impact, handling and likely development of the original claims) in the London Market at the relevant time, avoiding considerable examination and cross-examination. Thirdly, it established, as common ground, the extent of the generally available information of which the defendants should have been aware, and therefore of which they should have taken note. We begin to tiptoe round the question of the defendant's negligence or otherwise, or at least, even if only by implication, whether an ordinarily competent professional in the field could have been expected to be aware of this information agreed to be generally available. (It remained a matter of evidence as to whether the defendants were aware of this information, had given due regard to it, or had good reasons for not doing so. But a picture is built, without my ever saying that the defendants had been negligent in not heeding the contents of these various publications and memoranda.)

033 Section VI, while ostensibly related to the four preceding ones, begins to deal with the meat of the matter. It sets out my opinion and description of the proper way that a professional underwriter (or his staff) in the market at the time should have approached the whole business of arriving at an RITC premium. It therefore sets the standard against which, I believe, the defendants' own practice was to be judged. I was careful, I hope successfully, not to use hindsight or try and attribute later more sophisticated practices to early years when such practices were not in common use. Although any statistician reading this section could take the view that the principles applied in later years were not new and could and should have been utilised earlier, the fact is that as a matter of general practice in Lloyd's they were not. If one standard of proper (non-negligent) professional behaviour is that adopted generally in the profession at the time (unless, of course, everyone can be shown to have been careless, unprofessional or negligent, so that a proper standard cannot be said to have been established), then the expert must be careful not to be "too clever" or too stringent in choosing standards to apply. I also tried not to suggest or state that my own practice had been perfect when measured against these standards, or that what I did at any given time should define the standard.

034 Finally in Section VII I describe my understanding, from the evidence, of what the defendants actually did and whether, in my opinion they met the standard I set and therefore the requirements of the regulatory principles underlying the whole RITC calculation process. Because I was required to do this several times, separately for each year in which the defendants allegedly were negligent, I have not produced a final "Conclusion" section—it would only have repeated most of Section VII.

035 I have already alluded to the requirement of an expert witness that he must not tell the court the law, which I assume is also common ground amongst readers of this book. The expert, as we are repeatedly told, is there to assist the court on technical matters, not to usurp its function, and deciding on whether a pattern of behaviour has been negligent is a legal decision. The expert must therefore strive not to conclude that a professional has, or has not been negligent. This is, of course, an artificial constraint since the whole tenor and subject matter of an expert report in a case such as this one is precisely to demonstrate that the defendant was or was not negligent. There are some techniques, however, for avoiding the pitfall and the wrath of the court. First, quite simply, do not use the words "negligent" or "negligence" ever, or any near synonyms for them. Ground your whole opinion in practice, both that generally to be adopted and that adduced in the evidence. Restrict your conclusions to whether or not the standard, or performance, you have observed meets that which you have laid down, or which has been codified or otherwise independently laid down, or which you believe would have been generally expected in the circumstances of the alleged negligence.

036 I hope this report demonstrates these techniques. It attempts to lay down the knowledge and discussion of the problem generally available at the time, the regulatory principles surrounding the exercise to be performed and my view of the general professional standards and methods pertaining at the time. It examines the defendants' actual practice at the time, compares it—in the context of the generally available information—with the suggested standard, and concludes that the defendants, given their failure to adopt the current good practice, should not have reached the conclusions they did in deciding on an RITC premium each year. Is that the same as being negligent . . .? Did it work? The court found in the plaintiffs' favour that the defendants had indeed conducted their affairs negligently, and failed in their duty of care to the plaintiffs. The judgment set out the standards which an underwriter should be expected to meet, never previously laid down.

037 However, notwithstanding my attempts to anchor the argument of my report firmly to generally prevailing practice and the defendants' own procedures, I faced several days of cross-examination on my own practice during my career at Lloyd's. My erstwhile employer's files had been produced under a *subpoena*, days before I was called to give evidence. Documents which I had thought when I left Lloyd's I would never see again were produced so that I could explain in detail the meanings of phrases in ten-year-old memoranda, and calculations presented for me to describe just how I had arrived at ancient conclusions. The aim was obviously to discredit my competence and therefore expertise, and my opinion. At this stage I was deeply grateful for experience gained as a witness in previous arbitrations, when being deposed in the United States; and for advice previously given by instructing, and instructed, lawyers and by Academy of Experts tutors: answer the question as asked. Don't volunteer especially long explanations, don't elaborate, speculate or try to be "helpful"; wait for a complete question before beginning an answer; don't be afraid to say you don't know or can't remember; if asked a hypothetical question phrase your answer appropriately; look at the judge when answering.

038 It is a fact of life that many more experts are asked to give expert opinions, or even produce final drafts of experts' reports for the courts than are ever called to appear to give evidence and be cross-examined on it. For those entering the witness box for the first time, advice such as this is essential. Cross-examination is not pleasant, and not designed to be, and it is important to master some of the techniques which help you to cope. One point, however, none of the advice covered: my greatest struggle, especially by day three of pedestrian questioning designed to trip me up and produce a self-contradiction, was not to lose my temper. At times I had to grip the edge of the witness's chair quite hard to remind myself to stay polite!

039 It was, it seems, worth it. The judgment said:

> "Although Mrs Rowe's evidence must be approached with care having regard in particular to the extent of her expertise and her limited consideration of the materials in the case, I formed the impression that she was a sincere and generally a reliable witness."
>
> "I was left with the impression that Mrs Rowe was thorough in her statistical analysis of [her] own book of business."

and

> "I find that the correct approach to reserving for the run-off contracts was stated by Mrs Rowe. . . . I prefer Mrs Rowe's evidence as above to that of Mr [. . . .]."

040 It is hoped that use of some of the techniques outlined above, and following some of the same precepts, can help other experts called upon to opine in professional negligence cases.

EXAMPLE 2—REINSURANCE CONTRACT INTERPRETATION

041 Example 1, as well as being essentially a professional negligence insurance claim, was taken from a case litigated in the High Court. This example, just by way of contrast and comparison, is based on a reinsurance arbitration. It must be noted, however, that from the point of view of the expert there is very little difference between the two processes. It remains true that the procedures are adversarial and that the expert will be appointed by one of the parties, but nonetheless has still been appointed to assist the arbitration tribunal and owes his primary duty to the tribunal. Proceedings may sometimes be less formal than in the courts, and preliminary proceedings handled differently, but in producing an expert opinion or report, and in facing examination in chief and cross-examination, the expert will find very little different from legal proceedings.

042 Most reinsurance contracts contain arbitration clauses, and most reinsurance disputes are therefore arbitrated. It is almost universal practice in the reinsurance market for the arbitration clause to specify a tribunal of three—either three arbitrators, or two and an umpire (each is equally common). Usually, the arbitration clause will specify that the tribunal be made up of active, or recently retired, reinsurance practitioners (most often "underwriters", occasionally a less restrictive description is used). Despite this, it is common, by agreement, for one of the tribunal, not always the chairman or umpire, to be a senior lawyer in the reinsurance field.

043 The other important characteristic of the reinsurance market is that it is international, although most worldwide practice is heavily based on that in London because of London's historic importance as the centre for the creation and development of reinsurance business. Perhaps because of this, very few reinsurance contracts contain a choice of jurisdiction or choice of law clause, although some arbitration clauses will specify the seat of the arbitration.

044 This arbitration took place in Canada, and some of the respondents were American, although the contract wording under dispute was closely based on a standard London wording. Because the arbitration was, of course, confidential, I have again disguised the names of the parties, and altered some of the underlying facts to preserve that confidentiality. The particular problem addressed, however—the interpretation of a so-called "hours clause" in construing the contract to define one "event", and whether two storms close together in time can be that "one event"—has been the subject of countless discussions, disputes and arbitrations to my own knowledge alone.

045 The reinsurance wording in dispute is of a so-called excess of loss reinsurance contract. Such contracts indemnify the reinsured in respect of single large, untoward, losses affecting a portfolio of business. The commonest example is all claims from a single hurricane but arising on hundreds of individual household and commercial property insurances. Another example could be a single air crash giving rise to a combination of original claims on aircraft hull, aviation liability, personal accident and travel policies. The essence of all these contracts is that they respond up to their limit of cover to "one loss" in excess of a pre-agreed amount (the "deductible") to be borne by the reinsured company. Most of the contract wording is therefore concerned to define and limit the concept of that one loss. Various terms are used, including "occurrence", "event", "catastrophe", "disaster" and the like. It is almost impossible to define any one of these without recourse to another. In consequence the main contracting clause of a wording will typically say something along the lines of: "... this reinsurance is to pay ... in respect of any one occurrence, which shall be defined as all losses arising out of or caused directly or indirectly by ... one event ...".

046 Countless pages of print have been devoted to the semantics of disentangling and distinguishing an occurrence and an event, or a happening and an occurrence, or a disaster and a catastrophe. In my view the exercise is largely futile, and I shall not attempt it here, nor do I in the report below. The main point to bear in mind, however, is that having defined the "loss" to the contract in terms such as those above, reinsurers then need to limit its impact on themselves (for losses "indirectly" caused by a hurricane, for example, could continue to arise for several weeks, or over several hundred square miles). Without such limitations they face unquantifiable results from each "event" and pricing their contracts would be even less exact an art than currently. Other clauses deal with other problems of definition of one loss to the contract—for example in respect of certain classes of liability policy—but the clause at issue here, which is designed to deal with weather losses and the like, is called the "hours clause". Read on:

SECOND MODEL EXPERT'S REPORT

IN THE MATTER OF AN ARBITRATION BETWEEN:

THE ALLWEATHER ASSURANCE COMPANY
APPLICANT

— AND —

ASSUMING REINSURANCE CORPORATION *ET AL*
RESPONDENTS

REPORT OF MRS PHILLIPPA C ROWE, MA, FCII, MAE, CHARTERED INSURANCE PRACTITIONER

INTRODUCTION

1. I, Phillippa Rowe of 1G Castle Gardens, Stanhope, Co Durham, England, have been instructed by my instructing solicitors ("XYZ"), acting for the Respondents, to provide my opinion on coverage in this matter. Specifically I am asked to discuss whether the losses sustained as a result of two hailstorms in Firstcity and Anytown on 16 July 1996 can in my opinion be aggregated by the Reinsured, the Allweather Assurance Company ("Allweather"), the Applicant in this matter, for the purposes of claiming indemnity under the reinsurance cover provided by the Respondents, Assuming Reinsurance Corporation *et al.* ("Reinsurers") under the wording of the treaty in effect for the calendar year 1996. I have also been asked to review the change in the treaty wording referred to in paragraphs 12 and 13 of Allweather's written submissions, and comment on the effect if any of this change on the treatment of losses of such nature.
2. Although I am familiar with such legal decisions as exist on the reinsurance issues pertinent to this arbitration, and specifically as to interpretation of reinsurance treaty definitions of "one event", "occurrence" and related terms, in addressing these questions and formulating my opinion I make no attempt at a legal analysis of the issues. Rather, I base my findings on my knowledge and understanding of general reinsurance market practice in this area and of the practical effect of such treaty wordings on claims disputes of this kind.
3. The documents with which I have been provided for the purposes of this Report are;
    1. The written submission of the Applicant, which contains—*inter alia*—copies of some advice as to the meteorological analysis of these hailstorms;
    2. The applicable treaty wordings for calendar year 1996.

I have based my conclusions on these documents and on my own general reinsurance and market knowledge, gained during twenty-three years' experience of reinsurance practice, and on my own general reinsurance reading and study during that period.

MY EXPERIENCE AND QUALIFICATIONS

4. My entire working career has been spent in the London market, or as a consultant to it, specialising in the fields of reinsurance claims assessment and management, and reinsurance wordings. On graduating from New Hall, Cambridge, with a BA degree in Economics in 1974 I joined the RJ Kiln group at Lloyd's where I spent fifteen years, mostly as claims manager, although with two years as an assistant underwriter as part of my training.
5. While at RJ Kiln I handled and made settlement decisions on a wide variety of non-marine insurance and reinsurance claims, in both property and casualty classes, but particularly specialising in property natural catastrophe claims, of which the hailstorms under discussion here are an example. The Kiln group were, and are, regarded worldwide as leaders in the field of property catastrophe reinsurance. The claims which I handled as representative of leading reinsurers included a large number of USA and Canadian reinsurance catastrophe losses. In 1981 I assisted Robert Kiln in production of his book *Reinsurance in Practice* by reading and reviewing the manuscript before publication. In addition I had considerable experience of drafting, checking and approving insurance and reinsurance wordings, including event-based reinsurance wordings similar to those which are the subject of this dispute.
6. In 1989 I left the Kiln group to establish my own firm which provides independent consultancy and litigation support services to the London reinsurance market. In that capacity I have inspected the claims records of a number of London market companies and Lloyd's syndicates and I have seen a range of presentations of such claims to reinsurers. I have had numerous and extensive discussions with reinsurers on reinsurance issues, and have remained familiar with general market practice in this field.
7. I qualified as a Fellow of the Chartered Insurance Institute by examination in 1981. I am a Chartered Insurance Practitioner and a Member of The Academy of Experts. My full *curriculum vitae* is provided as Appendix 1 to this report.

BACKGROUND TO THIS DISPUTE—THE ORIGINAL LOSSES

8. There appears to be no dispute between Allweather and Reinsurers as to the circumstances of the original losses, or that they were two separate hailstorms. From all the materials I have been shown, including the meteorological reports, it seems that on the day in question a hail and/or thunderstorm occurred in Firstcity producing some 513 claims for property damage. On the same day a hail and/or thunderstorm occurred in the City of Anytown producing some 822 claims for property damage. The total cost of these claims has not, at the date of Allweather's written submission, been finally determined but the parties agree that it will be sufficiently high to exhaust, at least, the first layer of reinsurance cover if treated as one loss. The total recovery available to Allweather is of course significantly reduced if the storms are determined to be two reinsurance losses to the treaty. (One reinstatement of the limit of each layer is available to Allweather.) The Firstcity storm took place approximately 91 minutes after the Anytown one.
9. In paragraph (5) of their written submission Allweather

   "acknowledge(s) that the Thunderstorms which occurred at Anytown and Firstcity within 91 minutes of each other were not the same thunderstorm. They arose out of two atmospheric disturbances."

10. The meteorological report written by Mr Smith of The Environment Department concludes, at Section 4.0,

    ". . . when the thunderstorms began at Firstcity and Anytown late in the afternoon of July 16/96, the two cities were under the influence of slightly different air masses"

    and

    ". . . two separate thunderstorms foundations were visible over Firstcity and over southern Anytown at roughly the same time. No significant activity was noticeable in between these two formations . . .".

11. All parties therefore agree that there were two storms, in two different places but on the same day. I find it interesting that no commentators describe these storms as "hailstorms". Instead, Allweather and the Environment Department describe them as "thunderstorms". I shall discuss the significance of this in my analysis of the correct operation of these reinsurances later in this Report (at paragraph 22 below).

THE REINSURANCE TREATY WORDINGS

12. I have been provided with, and reviewed, four treaty wordings for the calendar year 1996, reinsuring Allweather. Each wording appears to have been produced by, or to, a separate co-reinsurer of Allweather. The wordings are, in all material aspects connected with this dispute, identical and I shall therefore confine my discussion to the first wording in the bundle, namely that signed by the first Respondent, Assuming Reinsurance Corporation.

13. This reinsurance treaty protects the Reinsured, Allweather, in respect of Property and Automobile Physical Damage:

> "as respects loss sustained by the Reinsurer **as a result of occurrences taking place** (during the period of the agreement)". [Article I]

Coverage is granted for 100 per cent of the amount:

> "of loss **each occurrence** excess of $ (varying by layer) Subject to limits of $ (varying by layer) **any one occurrence".** [Article III]

There therefore seems no doubt that this reinsurance is "occurrence based" and designed to indemnify Allweather for the sum of all physical damage losses arising out of one occurrence in excess of that deductible *per* occurrence.

14. "Occurrence" is defined in Article VI of the treaty, and the important parts of that Article for this dispute are:

"DEFINITION OF OCCURRENCES. The word 'occurrence' shall have the following meanings:

(a) The word 'occurrence' shall mean the sum of all individual losses directly occasioned by **any one disaster, accident or loss** or series of disasters, accidents or losses **arising out of one event** which occurs within the area of one state of the United States or province of Canada and states or provinces contiguous thereto and to one another. However the duration and extent of any one 'occurrence' shall be limited to all individual losses sustained by the Reinsured occurring during any period of 168 consecutive hours arising out of and directly occasioned by the same event, except that the term 'occurrence' shall be further defined as follows:

1. **As regards windstorm, hail, tornado, hurricane, cyclone, including ensuing collapse and water damage,** all individual losses sustained by the Reinsured **occurring during any period of 72 consecutive hours arising out of and directly occasioned by the same event.**

However, the event need not to be limited to one state or province or states or provinces contiguous thereto."

15. It therefore follows that the nature and intent of this reinsurance is that it should respond to the sum of losses arising out of one occurrence, which in turn means losses arising out of one disaster (which might include one hailstorm, although the parties do not appear to be relying on this part of the definition) or out of a series of disasters, accidents or losses arising out of one event. In respect of the perils of windstorm, hail, tornado, hurricane and similar phenomena, an occurrence is further defined as the sum of all losses occurring during 72 hours and arising out of and directly occasioned by one event. The 72-hour period is essentially a limitation on the length of time over which individual losses arising out of the event created by the operation of these perils can be aggregated for the purposes of presenting a claim under the reinsurance.

16. The word "event" is not easy to define accurately in this context, and most practical attempts produce something very similar to a definition of "occurrence", making the interpretation of language such as this "Occurrence Definition" almost circular in result. However, an event must be something finite and something recognisable. My understanding of market practice is that an event has always been considered as something whose effect is limited in time and place. It must also have been the cause of the insured losses in order to give rise to a loss occurrence, or a reinsurance claim. In my opinion none of this conflicts with the few existing legal rulings on the meaning in reinsurance wordings of "event", and although over time there have been modifications to the exact language used, the proper operation of such treaties is clear. A loss under the treaty must be shown to have arisen entirely out of one discrete, observable, separate occurrence or event limited in time and place by the conditions of the hours clause, if any. The hours clauses have been developed historically to cope with situations where one clearly recognisable "event" or "occurrence"—such as a hurricane, an earthquake or a severe freeze—produces claims for damage which manifest themselves over an extended time or area, and which therefore at first sight appear not themselves to be a single event. If, however, all the individual claims can be shown to have "arisen out of or (been) directly occasioned by" an event, and to result from a reinsured peril, then it is reasonable—and the purpose of the reinsurance contract—that they should be aggregated for the purpose of making a reinsurance claim.

APPLICATION OF THE TREATY TO THE LOSS CIRCUMSTANCES

17. In this case it seems to me quite clear that there were two events, being two storms in two different places. All the parties agree that there were two storms, and the meteorological evidence is that they were caused by two separate weather systems. In my opinion as a matter of commonsense they were therefore two events, and my experience of reinsurance market practice, including in the North American continent, is that they must be treated as two separate events for reinsurance purposes and therefore bear two deductibles and create two reinsurance loss occurrences. There is nothing in the wording at issue here to lead me to find that this should not be the result in this case.
18. The function of the hours clause is not to allow the aggregation of claims "arising out of and directly occasioned by" different events into one claim just because they coincidentally occur within the same 72 hours' period. Its function is to provide a limiting envelope—both in time and place, despite being commonly named an "hours clause"—preventing the aggregation of losses occurring outside of the envelope even if arising from the original single event.
19. Allweather seek to argue in their written submission that the "event" within which they may aggregate 72 hours of losses is "hail". I disagree. "Hail" is not of itself an event. It is an insured **peril** which can, in the event of a hailstorm affecting insured properties, produce original claims to the reinsured's account. The peril of "hail" can operate during a clearly recognisable loss occurrence and so give rise to a reinsurance loss occurrence. Hail damage need not arise out of a single identifiable event, but may occur sporadically over an extended period of time. It is for precisely this reason that it is common to provide hail reinsurance cover on an annual basis, particularly in respect of hail damage to crops. This cover is available to reinsureds in many parts of the world, including the North American continent. The reinsurance at issue in this matter, however, is **not** an aggregate protection for hail insurance. It is an occurrence based catastrophe reinsurance, providing protection for an accumulation of claims from single identifiable happenings.
20. Allweather seek to justify their contention that hail is an "event" by asserting that:

> "... no hailstorm has ever lasted for 72 hours or more, nor has one ever travelled the 1,200 kilometres from Anytown to Firstcity."

I infer from this that they wish to argue that it would therefore be meaningless within the reinsurance treaty to attempt to limit losses from a single hail event to 72 hours, or to permit aggregation of hail losses in non-contiguous, or even contiguous, provinces. In my opinion they are wrong, and their argument, if I have correctly interpreted it, conflicts with consistent reinsurance market practice over several years.

21. This reinsurance wording, and I cannot recall ever having seen one which does the opposite, does not require that a 72-hour loss be made up **only** of hail, or only of wind or tornado *et al.* damage. The perils are listed without the use of any "ands" or "ors". The perils may operate separately or together, and are frequently associated with each other. The 72-hour limitation applies to any combination of any or all of them, which is why they are conventionally grouped together in one sub-paragraph of the hours clause—as they are here. There have been many reinsurance catastrophe losses in the past whose original constituent losses are a mixture of wind and hail; hurricane and tornadoes; hurricane wind damage and water damage from a surge from the sea; or tornadoes and hail. Any of these quite recognisable "events" could well last for more than 72 hours, and many have, particularly those associated with major hurricanes or—to take a famous historic example—the mid-west US tornadoes of April 1974.

22. Equally it is quite possible and has been known for US hurricanes to make landfall in one state, veer back out to the Atlantic and then make another landfall in a state not contiguous to the first one. The removal of the limitation of a reinsurance claim to contiguous provinces or states recognises this. These reinsurances are treaty reinsurances—this means that they cover whole portfolios of reinsured business. Equally they are designed to cover a variety of different circumstances, and the practical result of this is language such as that discussed here, designed to deal with a variety of similar or related circumstances. As a matter of practicality, and of market practice over time, they should not be read as applying wholly and in detail to a single peril included in those grouped together in the sub-paragraph. In this context, I find it interesting that all the parties refer to these two storms not as "hailstorms" but as "thunderstorms" or "hail/thunderstorms"—a precise demonstration of the way that the peril of hail need not operate in isolation from any other related weather phenomenon.

23. Allweather also appear to argue, or at least imply, that there is some significance to be extracted from the Reinsurers' changing of the treaty wording to delete the occurrence definition as "arising out of one atmospheric disturbance" and to replace it with the "event" wording which is subject of the dispute. In their written submission (paragraphs 12 and 13) they describe it as a "most significant change". Although they do not state their understanding of the effect of this change, the implication is that the use of "event" in some way opened up the possibility of aggregating losses from two distinct storms, which the previous language would not have done. I have been asked to comment on the abandonment of the same "atmospheric disturbance" language by the London market and to throw some light on the reasons for it.

24. This "atmospheric disturbance" language appeared in some wordings—at least in USA and UK reinsurance business—at least up to the 1970s. However, on occasions when reinsurers had recourse to meteorologists to assist in determining the extent of reinsurance losses, we were informed that the words "atmospheric disturbance" had no meaning in meteorology, and that a single such disturbance could not be identified, as the whole of the earth's atmosphere is in continual and widespread disturbance. Discussions of this nature were widespread following the major UK windstorms in January 1976 (which storms also extended to continental Europe and therefore beyond 72 hours), and following the USA-wide freeze, PCS Cat 24, in 1983. It was because "atmospheric disturbance" was thus demonstrated to be devoid of meaning that the phrase was gradually abandoned, and replaced in many cases by "event", which was considered more capable of definition, and was also already in common use for other perils. The reinsurance market moves very slowly in reacting to such changes, as shown by my personal recollection that the matter arose in 1976 and then again seven years later. RJ Kiln in *Reinsurance in Practice*[1] ascribes the same change to 1948, following a series of Texas, Kansas, Illinois and Indiana tornado, flash flood and hail (*sic.*) losses. He gives the same reason for the change as my recollection of several years later—that reinsurance contracts should not contain words not capable of definition.

25. I obviously cannot say why Reinsurers in this matter chose to make a similar change, or why they chose the time which they did. It would seem likely, however, that having taken over

1. See *Reinsurance in Practice*, Witherby 1981, p. 164.

the leading role in 1994, they reviewed the wording and resolved in December [Exhibit B to Allweather's written submission] to remove in the following calendar year some outdated language well known by then to be meaningless, and to replace it with more commonly obtaining language. Certainly I would not be surprised to discover that this was the case.

CONCLUSION

26. In my opinion, based on my knowledge of reinsurance market practice and understanding over several years, an insured, or reinsured, peril is not the same as an "event", and in the context of sub-paragraph A(1) of Article VI of this wording, "hail" in the phrase "windstorm, hail, tornado ... etc." is referring to a peril. To be recoverable under this reinsurance, claims must all form one occurrence, and in order to do so must arise out of or be directly occasioned by one event. An event in turn is a single identifiable happening which causes the insured damage.
27. The purpose of the hours clause is to limit and assist in the definition of loss occurrences arising out of events with extended consequences, and not to enlarge or override the nature of an event. The 72-hour limitation for these perils of wind, hail etc. is not meaningless in the context of hailstorms which can be of very short duration, but is a general limitation on loss occurrences arising out of any possible combination of the perils listed. The 72-hour period cannot therefore be read as requiring "hail" to have been intended as an event definition *per se* rather than a peril which could operate during a covered event alone or in conjunction with others to produce a loss hereon. Equally the 72-hours clause is not designed to negate the requirement that losses derive from one event by permitting the aggregation of original losses from clearly separate events. The event must be identified first; the hours clause applied afterwards.
28. In this case there are two clearly separate storms, some 1,200 kilometres apart and agreed to be the result of two clearly separate and distinguishable weather systems. In my opinion they are therefore clearly two separate events, both as common sense would determine and as reinsurance market practice would in my experience generally require. The coincidences of peril and of timing cannot logically mean that the meaning of the hours clause can be stretched to find that they are one event. The events must have been the two storms, or the two weather systems which produced the storms. I consider that this market practice based approach, and my understanding of the effect of the contract language, is in accord with the various legal determinations of an "event" which are available, although I have not, and could not, attempt any analysis of the legal arguments.
29. I therefore consider that there are two losses to this reinsurance, being the two separate storms, and that Allweather should therefore bear two deductibles. Were I still employed by a reinsurer I would have settled these claims on that basis, and so I believe would my colleagues in the reinsurance market.

Signed: Date:

APPENDIX 1
PHILLIPPA ROWE: *CURRICULUM VITAE*

[Not reproduced]

DISCUSSION ON SECOND MODEL EXPERT'S REPORT

047 Again, the structure of this report was not consciously based on The Academy's *Model Form*, but again it follows it fairly closely. Because the report is considerably shorter than that in Example 1, I have not provided a "Contents" page, and consequently not numbered the sections. In long reports both of these are of considerable help.

048 The formal Introduction sets out my instructions, and therefore sets the limits on what the report will discuss, and the material on which it will be based. Establishing these limits at the outset can be useful in more than one way. It tells the reader of the report what subject is being addressed and therefore what to expect. It also anticipates, and disposes of, the question "Why did you not consider/discuss ...?" by providing the answer "Because I was not asked/instructed to". (You cannot be blamed for answering only the question you are asked.)

049 Since this report was prepared for a Canadian arbitration tribunal I did not include a "Woolf-type" declaration that I had prepared the report with due regard to my position as an expert. (In any event, I take the view that that follows automatically from my membership of The Academy of Experts, and the requirement that I follow The Academy's guidelines—it should therefore be a superfluous declaration.)

050 My experience and qualifications are self-explanatory. Again a full CV is consigned to an Appendix. It should be noted, however, that I cite different aspects of my experience and expertise—the court (and your client) are interested in your expertise in the field of their problem. Anything else is irrelevant. Similarly, although I have not reproduced a second *CV* in this chapter it is worth recognising that it was not identical to that in Example 1. Not only had time moved on, but again different aspects of my career and experience needed to be emphasised. Note also my emphasis on having kept up to date—the "consultant" or "professional expert" can too easily be accused of being out of touch with "real practice" or "real work", and it is easier to deal with the challenge in advance than in cross-examination. Once the question is asked the impression, however unjustified, is created and the doubt raised.

051 The next Section, "Background", sets out the facts underlying the dispute, and the following one, "The Reinsurance Treaty Wording", reproduces and discusses the appropriate parts of the contract (for the purposes of this discussion, "treaty" can be taken as synonymous with "contract"). Then "Application of the Treaty to the Loss Circumstances" does just what it says, and contains my argument and justification for my opinion, which is summarised and repeated in "Conclusion".

052 The whole question of construction of contracts is even more of a purely "legal game" than establishing professional negligence, and has its own rules and principles particular to the legal analysis. This makes it even harder for the expert, asked after all to give an opinion as to what the contract means, to avoid the appearance or, worse, the fact of telling the court its own business. It is not possible for any professional expert, used to drafting, operating, and interpreting contracts as a normal aspect of working life not to have an understanding of and opinion on the meaning of those contracts, and it is not possible for that expert to be ignorant of court decisions and precedents as to what the law holds those contracts to mean. It is very easy, in the course of discussing a standard form or a specific clause therefore to slip into language such as "the courts have held ...", "the law says that this clause means ...", or "according to *Bloggs* v. *Rat* ...". All of these constitute a statement of what the law is.

053 The first technique to avoid this pitfall is simple: avoid any mention of any legal decisions or precedents at all, as well as statements as to what the law has said. I have found a simple statement, "that I am of course aware of the various pertinent legal pronouncements but do not intend to discuss them or refer to them", helpful. The second technique will also make sense of this statement—and that is to base your findings firmly on market or industry practice, rather than legal analysis. After all, your expertise is presumably founded on practice and practical knowledge, so to rely on it must be legitimate. When you cannot avoid interpreting a clause, phrase or sentence, emphasise that your interpretation is based on general practice and your understanding in the light of that practice of the effect of the particular words. Sometimes it can be useful also to call that elusive concept "common sense" to your aid—but beware of over-using it. It will appear that you cannot find any other intellectual or factual basis for your interpretation. The last sentence of the conclusion of this report is intended firmly to anchor the argument in market practice and practicality, and simultaneously to remind the tribunal that I do have that practical first-hand experience of interpretation of just such contract language as is at issue.

054 There are some general considerations to bear in mind when giving expert evidence on the meaning of reinsurance contracts—which do not apply just to this example. The expert acting in a contract interpretation dispute has to try and help by defining very carefully the line between technical interpretation of the contract and legal interpretation—not easy—and then stay on the nearer side of that line. In the reinsurance world there are several examples of clauses which have caused practical problems of operation, and real differences of opinion and which have had subsequently to be construed by the courts—and usually wrongly. For those who follow the reinsurance world, these include clauses crucial to defining the amount of a claim such as definitions of "an event"; clauses which go to the operation of the contract such as "follow the settlement" clauses; and disputes as to the meaning of the words "actually paid". You might find it hard to imagine what technical advice one could possibly give on the meaning of such a phrase, but the House of Lords and the two lower courts managed to produce—in my personal view—the wrong answer (that "actually paid" means neither "actually" nor "paid" but rather "agreed with reasonable certainty as likely to be paid", or something comparable). Their Lordships had recourse to lengthy discussion on what a claimants' wife might reasonably reply in response to a question on the price of her dresses (so much for the "modern" judiciary!), but no recourse to evidence on market practice, or on other existing forms of the clause in question designed to deal with different circumstances.

055 In my view the expert must adopt two strategies. The first is to explain to the court the nature and purpose (*not* the "intent" of the parties, which is quite different and possibly irrelevant since the wording should be taken as embodying the agreed intent, which is therefore precisely what the dispute is about) of the contract at issue, and the correct technical operation of the reinsurance which flows from that. This could and should include a demonstration of how a loss to the contract is properly to be determined, what an exclusion or a definition of a class of insurance business means, how a premium is calculated, or what the effect of a particular limitation is. In most cases this—although a matter of technical "opinion"—should not involve the expression of a personal bias or influence, but should be dictated by proper technical understanding. In doing this, remember that you are rendering *technical* assistance to the court. Try to set out your explanation of the operation of the disputed contract or clause or procedure by reference to first principles. Describe the purpose of reinsurance in general, differentiate the types of reinsurance and their different, but related, purposes. Point out the crucial distinctions between the type of reinsurance at issue, and others. Then describe how the type of reinsurance at issue should properly work, in the context of this introduction. Treat this explanation a little as if you were writing a practical textbook.

056 Secondly in attempting to base an interpretation on existing practice, the expert must show that this practice is sufficiently widespread and general as to be universal, or nearly so. It is not enough for the practice to be common, or one of several normal options; it must be shown to apply consistently. This can sometimes be demonstrated by showing that to achieve other effects or meanings the industry has (again, generally or consistently) used different contract language, and that the parties could therefore have chosen, but did not, that universally adopted language to achieve the result now being sought. Sometimes there may also exist industry or market agreements, protocols or understandings of varying formality setting out the purpose and meaning of a particular clause or contract.

057 How did this example succeed in these aims? The hearing was dealt with in a day and a half. Witnesses and experts were not allowed to hear any evidence before giving their own, so I do not know how cross-examination or examination of the opposing expert was conducted. This time my cross-examination was more directly to the point of my argument, and counsel tried hard to show a flaw in my logic, and make me concede that a "peril" or a "risk" might also be a "loss". Semantic arguments such as these are difficult to manage in the context of cross-examination, especially when centred on words whose common daily usage can encompass a range of meanings in different contexts. My aim was to attempt to keep returning firmly to the context at issue. I possibly succeeded. The tribunal's only comment on the oral evidence before it was that:

> "[The] ... witnesses, ... all with considerable experience within their respective fields ... gave their evidence in a forthright and articulate manner."

The tribunal, in its award, agreed almost exactly with my interpretation of the contract and the claims, so something went right.

CONCLUSION

058 Insurance and reinsurance experts are likely to find themselves appointed most usually in professional negligence cases, to opine on proper insurance professional standards, or in contract construction cases. In this respect they are probably faced with the same demands and difficulties as experts in many other disciplines, and need to adopt very similar approaches.

059 From the expert's point of view, there is, equally, little difference between litigation and arbitration, especially in the majority of cases where the expert's involvement ends with production of a report for the court or tribunal. The Academy of Experts' *Model Form of Report* provides a very useful and adaptable skeleton for those unused to writing such reports.

060 In all cases the main hazards are straying outside the bounds of the problem posed in instructions—or outside one's own precise expertise—and trying to do the court's or tribunal's job by giving, or appearing to give, legal analysis. Limiting one's argument strictly to technical explanation and demonstration of sufficiently wide industry practice should assist in both these. Again, in this respect the insurance or reinsurance expert is not unique.

061 In the few cases which proceed to a full hearing there may sometimes be differences in style between litigation and arbitration, in that the latter may be less formal. I have however experienced some extremely formal reinsurance arbitrations, so nothing should be taken for granted. Many experts may never, however long they practise, have to give evidence in person. The most important points for the expert facing cross-examination to bear in mind are: to remember to answer exactly the question answered and only the question answered; not to be over "helpful"; and to try and keep one's temper. Again, experts in other disciplines will find the same, so I hope some of my suggestions prove helpful to a large number of readers.

062 As this book goes to print, experts are faced with the new court Rules and procedures introduced (in April 1999) in consequence of Lord Woolf's *Access to Justice*. These, unsurprisingly, include new Rules as to the extent and nature of expert evidence and the role and duties of the expert witness. They should hold little fear for the conscientious expert, in that the emphasis—for example—of the expert's duty to the court as one that overrides any duty to his instructing party should not be seen as anything new. The feared, or eagerly anticipated, insistence always on a single court-appointed expert has not materialised, although the Rules do now give the courts explicit power to direct that there be a single expert, who can receive instructions from both parties. How an expert will handle such, possibly conflicting, instructions remains to be seen. I suggest that a clear focus on one's duties to the court to help it on matters within one's expertise will prove an essential support.

063 It is interesting that the first paragraph of the Rules, "35.1 Duty to restrict expert evidence" says that "Expert evidence shall be restricted to that which is reasonably required to resolve the proceedings", while the "Expert's Declaration" required by Rule 35.10, and whose wording has been approved by Lord Woolf, says that the expert has considered "all" matters which could or should have any bearing on the facts or opinions in his report. Leaving aside the impossibility of ever being sure that one has found "everything" which might have any relevance, this declaration seems to be in conflict with Rule 35.1. Doubtless a way will be found to reconcile the two. My personal preference would be to see that part of the declaration dropped—and replaced with a statement of what material has been relied on, such as I have suggested and used in the two examples above. The Rules require the expert to state the instructions on which his report is based—again any expert currently following The Academy of Experts' *Model Form* is doing so already, and I always find it helpful to have set out the question, in effect, which I hope my report is going to answer. While these new Rules formalise the position, duty and role of the expert they do not alter the position which any ethical and accredited expert should already be adopting. Moreover, since they do not—and cannot—address the subject of how the expert can best give his evidence and put his conclusions persuasively without usurping the court's job of deciding the case, the Rules will have little effect on how the expert can best tackle the drafting and production of his report. To that extent the new Rules should make very little difference indeed to the practising expert, and I do not consider that either of the two sample reports above would have been differently written if the Rules had then been in existence.

***Phillippa Rowe** is a leading independent consultant in the London reinsurance market and senior partner in Phillippa Ross & Co, a firm providing expert opinions and analysis, books and records inspections and technical assistance to Lloyd's syndicates and London Market reinsurance companies. Before setting up the firm she worked for fifteen years at R J Kiln and Others at Lloyd's, a leading reinsurance syndicate.*

Mrs Rowe has extensive experience of giving evidence, as both witness and expert, in litigation and in arbitrations, and in the UK and the US. She appeared in the High Court in 1995 as expert witness for the successful plaintiffs in Henderson and Others *v.* Merrett Syndicates Ltd and Others. *She has written several articles in professional journals on reinsurance and dispute resolution subjects. She is a Member of The Academy of Experts, a member of its Council and past Dean of its Faculty of Mediation and ADR. She is a member of the ARIAS (UK) Panel of reinsurance arbitrators. She is also an Accredited Mediator on The Academy's Register of Qualified Dispute Resolvers.*

CHAPTER 6

THE EXPERT WITNESS IN MARITIME DISPUTE CASES

Ron Vince

001 Maritime disputes occur in every facet of the marine industry where contracts relating to shipbuilding, carriage of cargo, charter parties, ship repairs, and ship sale and purchase exist, or where there are claims by shipowners upon their insurers.

002 The maritime expert exists to provide technical expertise and assistance to the party by whom he is instructed, and where a dispute continues through to litigation or arbitration, it is his function to provide assistance of a technical nature to the court judge or arbitration tribunal by oral evidence.

003 In the past, most maritime experts and consultants had a practical marine industry background, having sailed on merchant vessels up to the rank of master or chief engineer, and having also had experience in other facets of the industry such as ship management, superintendency, shipbuilding, ship repair and naval architecture. However, in recent years, with the advance of electronics and computers, highly qualified theorists are beginning to take the place of the marine expert with a practical marine background.

004 In paragraphs 005–080 I have provided an appraisal of the type of dispute in which the maritime expert is likely to become involved.

MARINE DISPUTES

Newbuilding disputes

005 Disputes often occur between the shipbuilder and the prospective owners of a new vessel under construction, either during the course of the building process, or at the time of, or shortly after, delivery, usually in respect of defects or deficiencies which were not considered, or catered for, in the terms and clauses of the shipbuilding contract, or fully covered by the terms of the shipbuilder's guarantee insurance. By way of illustration, I have referred below to a number of the disputes of this nature with which I have been involved.

006 A Far Eastern shipowner was in the process of building two 100,000 tonnes deadweight bulk carriers at a shipyard in the same area. During the outfitting of the first vessel the builders yard was affected by a severe tropical storm and the vessel broke adrift and was swept aground onto rocks. The vessel was refloated and drydocked whereupon it was found that the hull had sustained severe grounding damage. The damaged structure was renewed, but the potential owners refused to take delivery, alleging that the damaged and repaired vessel was no longer a new ship. This case was well on the road to litigation when a settlement was achieved. However, the vessel was sold "on the stocks" to eastern Mediterranean interests.

The owners for whom the vessel was built maintained their position that the ship was no longer a new vessel.

007 Another major shipbuilding claim which comes to mind concerned the machinery of a new vessel, the defects in which came to light during the guarantee period. The defects complained of by the owners of the new vessel concerned the seawater pipeline systems, and the vessel's structure in the upper engine room.

008 The seawater pipeline systems throughout the engine room were all intended to be internally lined with a polyurethane lining 2mm in thickness to prevent corrosion. It became apparent during the subsequent investigation into the claim that the shipbuilders' pipework outfitting department had little or no previous experience with this type of pipe lining and consequently the result was of very poor quality, with uneven thickness around the bore of the pipe sections, and a complete lack of lining in some pipeline bends, flanges and welded connections.

009 Within about three months following delivery and entry into service, operational problems became manifest. Initially, the freshwater generator, an important piece of equipment on a modern vessel, ceased to function. Investigation showed that the polyurethane lining in the seawater pipeline to the generator had become detached and had blocked the system, preventing the flow of water, and rendering the unit inoperable. In addition, there was rapid subsequent corrosion in sections of pipe where the polyurethane had become detached. As a result it was necessary for the vessel to take on fresh water at frequent intervals. The available storage capacity for fresh water on board was minimal as the vessel's design was dependent upon an efficient water generator.

010 Subsequent to the freshwater generator defects, other operational problems rapidly ensued involving the main and auxiliary engines, the ballast system and the bilge system.

011 As far as the main engine was concerned, there were sudden, and initially unexplained, incidents of power reduction due to overheating. Investigation showed that sections of torn polyurethane lining had become detached and had partially blocked the tube nests and seawater headers of the heat exchangers. A lot of time was spent out of service during the warranty period removing sections of pipeline and stripping out loose or defective polyurethane pipe linings.

012 A similar problem was experienced with the auxiliary engine heat exchangers, there being a number of instances where increases in cooling water temperature due to the blockage of the heat exchangers caused a sudden partial or complete loss of electrical power, and, as a consequence, a loss of propulsion and steerage. This could have been extremely hazardous had it occurred in confined waters when the vessel was entering or leaving port, or navigating a canal. Fortunately all such failures occurred at sea.

013 In the ballast system, the blockage of valves by torn and detached pipe linings caused serious delays at loading berths when attempting to deballast and load simultaneously. Bilge strainers and suction pipes became seriously choked with polyurethane debris.

014 In some instances, due to the inability to deballast completely, the vessel was unable to load a full cargo.

015 The dispute in this instance was concerned with whether the shipbuilder was liable only for the sections of pipe where lining failure had occurred, or whether the entire system was considered deficient and should have been replaced completely. At the guarantee repair period, the shipowner replaced all seawater pipework with galvanised pipelines, and the dispute as to the liability for the considerable cost involved continued for many months before an amicable settlement was subsequently reached without resorting to litigation.

016 I have referred above to an additional claim on the same vessel relating to the main engine, which was a high powered, slow speed, long stroke engine. Due to the length of stroke, the upper part of the engine frame required support from the surrounding upper structure in the engine room. The engine was designed with support brackets and girders equipped with friction pads to permit slight, restricted, movement to compensate for expansion. Shortly after delivery it was found that severe, structural fractures were occurring in the engine room upper casing. Investigation showed that, contrary to the design plans, the longitudinal and transverse support girders were not continuous, but were fabricated *in situ*, and many of the individual elements were misaligned, hence, instead of providing support to the engine, a stress couple was created in many areas, and structural failure eventually occurred due to fatigue. In this instance, the builders agreed to modify the engine support system and to add additional stiffening to the engine room upper casing, in order to rectify, or compensate for, the discrepancies which had occurred during the construction of the vessel.

017 Finally, before leaving newbuilding disputes, one extremely interesting case with which I was recently involved concerned the steering gear with which three, highly sophisticated, specialised newly built vessels were equipped.

018 The vessels required a high degree of manoeuvrability and were thus equipped with bow and stern transverse thrusters, a White Gill thruster with which the vessel could manoeuvre in any direction, and also a steerable nozzle surrounding the controllable pitch propeller. The steering gear with which the vessels were equipped was a specially designed, rotary vane type of gear. The steering gear rotor and stock was equipped with a large, heavy thrust washer to take the weight of, and support, the steering nozzle, the nozzle being a fabricated steel unit measuring approximately four metres in external diameter and three metres in length.

019 With the vessel pitching in heavy seas, it does not require much imagination to see that a partially buoyant steel section, with an area measuring three metres by four metres presented to the sea, would result in a considerable upward force on the nozzle stock and steering gear. Although the weight of the nozzle was adequately supported with a large lubricated bronze thrust ring, the only fitting with which the steering unit was equipped to accommodate upward thrust on the nozzle was a relatively thin bronze thrust ring secured by eight set bolts, each 20mm in diameter. It appears that the designers had limited practical knowledge of the effects of a vessel pitching heavily in a seaway, and had not designed for any upward thrust on the steering nozzle.

020 The end result was that, on the first of the three vessels, the thrust ring became detached in adverse weather, allowing the steering nozzle to move bodily upwards by 6cm to 8cm, resulting in the nozzle coming into contact with the propeller, causing severe damage to the propeller blades and immobilising the main propulsion unit. The immobilisation and time required for repairs resulted in the loss of lucrative charters worth millions of dollars and required the shipbuilders to completely redesign the unit to provide adequate support for upward thrust on the unit, as well as for the downward thrust resulting from the weight.

021 In my opinion, the design was so obviously wrong that it remains a mystery how it ever left the drawing board.

022 Before leaving the subject of shipbuilding disputes, I recall a series of interesting cases involving a Brazilian shipyard which was building four small bulk carrier/container vessels for eastern Mediterranean interests. The particular shipyard had previously built only for domestic owners or interests in other South American countries where supervision during building was minimal, the builders being generally left to their own devices as far as quality control was concerned.

023 When the builders commenced work on the four referred bulk carriers, the owners placed a team of supervisors in the shipyard whose function appeared to be to raise objections in writing to virtually every aspect of construction. Prolonged meetings ensued at the end of which it was generally proposed that the owners would accept a "commercial settlement" *in lieu* of any alterations to the construction.

024 My company was engaged and I attended the vessels periodically throughout the building period generally to assess the merits of the owners' claims and to advise the builders on what action should be taken. I found that certain claims were genuine and merited modification, but others were bordering on the outrageous as far as the owners' allegations were concerned. Finally, at delivery, it was possible to limit the owners to claims where there was a genuine, minor divergence from specification.

025 The above examples give an insight into the type of dispute which occurs as a result of errors in building, outfitting and designing of new vessels, and with which, from time to time, the maritime expert becomes involved. As can be seen from the brief details set out in the preceding paragraphs, such disputes can be extremely interesting for the technically minded expert, and can involve considerable investigatory work as well as recommendations as to alterations or amendments to designs or constructional procedures.

Sale and purchase disputes

026 Sale and purchase disputes involving the interpretation of the sale form Memorandum of Agreement (or MOA) are quite commonplace, and generally relate to alleged deficiencies in the vessel's structure, machinery or equipment which is alleged, by the buyer, to exist at the time of the delivery of the vessel by the seller.

027 Most sale and purchase contracts are made under the Norwegian Saleform, of which Clause 11 states that:

> "Condition on Delivery
> The vessel with everything belonging to her shall be at the Sellers' risk and expense until she is delivered to the Buyers, but subject to the conditions of this Contract she shall be delivered and taken over as she is at the time of inspection, fair wear and tear excepted.
> However she shall be delivered with present Class free of recommendations. The Sellers shall notify the Classification Society of any matter coming to their knowledge prior to delivery which, upon being reported to the Classification Society, would lead to the withdrawal of the Vessel's Class, or to the imposition of a recommendation relating to her Class."

028 Disputes in connection with sale and purchase contracts usually relate to the correct interpretation of the above clause, and what would constitute a condition of class had certain defects been reported to the classification society by the seller. This clause is often used by a prospective buyer as a lever to attempt to obtain a reduction in purchase price.

Charter party disputes

029 Disputes between owners and charterers are probably the most numerous of any category of maritime disputes, involving as they often do, disputes concerning a vessel's actual performance compared with the performance warranted in the contract. Other common disputes relate to the supply of bunkers by charterers in connection with time charters, and the seaworthiness of the vessel in respect of alleged damage to cargo. Some examples are discussed below.

Performance disputes

030 Time charter parties include a clause which is intended to set out the vessel's performance warranty, relating to speed and fuel oil consumption in good weather conditions. In my opinion it should be a relatively simple matter to specify, for example, that a particular vessel is warranted throughout the charter party to steam fully laden at say, 15 knots, burning 60 tonnes of fuel oil in weather conditions not excluding winds of Beaufort Scale force four. In my opinion, such a statement would restrict any discussion as to the vessel's performance to interpretation of weather conditions, and with the modern technology used in weather recording and forecasting, the assessment of a vessel's performance should be a relatively exact science.

031 However, this is not as simple as it would appear to be. For a start, the legal fraternity who have the task of drawing up such charter party contracts see fit to add the word "about" before both the speed warranty and the fuel consumption warranty, as a result of which it has become common practice to make an allowance, usually in favour of the owners, in respect of both the speed and fuel consumption when interpreting the "about" clauses in the charter party. Furthermore, the usually accepted allowances, which are a reduction in speed together with an increased percentage in fuel consumption, contravene all common sense, as, even the layman is aware that a reduction in speed will automatically result in a reduction in fuel consumption, all other things being equal. Despite this, there are many disputes which centre solely upon the interpretation and quantification of the term "about".

032 One further ingredient which is added to the melting pot in respect of performance disputes is the ability (or inability) of those navigating the relevant vessels to accurately interpret and record the weather conditions applicable to the vessel during the voyage. From experience, I find that it is remarkable how common it is for winds of Beaufort force five to be encountered by vessels on time charter, particularly when it is evident that the vessel, for reasons of limited engine power or fouling of the hull, is unable to maintain the charter speed even after the various adjustments in the owner's favour for the term "about" have been made.

033 Considerable reliance is nowadays placed on the analysis provided by Ocean Routes, a company which collects data worldwide and interprets weather conditions considered to have been encountered by a vessel on a daily basis throughout any particular voyage. However the information supplied to Ocean Routes also depends to a very large extent, upon the ability of the navigators on the vessels supplying the information to be able to accurately interpret the wind and sea conditions.

034 From the foregoing, it appears to be the case that the legal document which constitutes the Time Charter Party is a document which is designed to promote litigation and dispute.

Bad bunker claims

035 The charterers usually supply the bunkers to a vessel on time charter. Nowadays, the charter party often sets out the principal details of the vessel's machinery and also the details of the specification with which the fuel oil supplied to the vessel should comply.

036 Over the past 25 years, the quality of residual fuels supplied to ships as bunkers for use in diesel engines has deteriorated considerably, both as a result of the method of production and also the method and additives used to produce the blend and the viscosity required by the shipowner. Consequently, despite the fact that a full and detailed fuel specification may well be included in the charter party, it is often the case that the product supplied to the vessel can be unstable, or incompatible with fuels from other sources, or it can contain abrasive particles, all or any of which could result in damage to the vessel's machinery.

037 Two of the principal classification societies have now set up fuel testing facilities and have provided methods and equipment for sampling bunkers as they are pumped aboard the vessel. Lloyd's Register have formed FOBAS (Fuel Oil Bunker Analysis Service), and det Norske Veritas have their own Veritas Fuel Testing Services. A shipowner who contributes to one or other of these services is provided with special sampling equipment and instructions for its use. A drip sample is then drawn during bunkering at the ship's manifold, and is dispatched by the ship's agents to the appropriate, approved laboratory from where the analysis results will be sent to the vessel and her owners usually within about 48 hours. It is the intention that the ship should not use the new bunkers until given the green light to do so following analysis of the bunker sample.

038 Despite such precautions problems do occur. The sampling equipment flow rate can be adjusted whereby the samples obtained are not representative of the fuel, in particular, if the fuel is not correctly blended when pumped on board. A fuel, the analysis of which might appear satisfactory, can be unstable or incompatible with fuel already on board, resulting in sludge formation when heated and/or agitated, or exposed to pressure. As heating, agitation and exposure to pressure takes place in many parts of the engine fuel system (for example at heaters, purifiers and fuel injection pumps), an unstable fuel will be unsuitable for consumption, despite intensive use of the onboard fuel treatment equipment. Despite the accepted good practice of segregating bunkers from different sources, it is not always possible to do this with the limited number of fuel storage tanks found on many modern ships, thus mixing of fuels is sometimes unavoidable.

039 If a fuel contains abrasive particles which have remained in suspension following the catalytic cracking process, known as catalytic fines, and if these are not removed by purification on board the vessel, very expensive wear of engine components can occur involving the need to renew cylinder liners, pistons and piston rings, and fuel injection equipment.

040 It is generally the case that the bunker suppliers provide what are termed to be the sealed samples, the intention being that such samples represent the quality of fuel supplied to the ship. It is frequently the case however, that the contents of sealed samples bear no resemblance whatsoever to the fuel received on board the vessel, particularly when bunkers are supplied by barge.

041 Allegations concerning the poor quality of bunkers are also sometimes used by the unscrupulous shipowner, who will allege that off-specification bunkers have been supplied in an attempt to claim the cost of new engine components from charterers to replace items which are worn out as a result of normal wear and tear.

042 An example of the problems which can be experienced with bunkers is indicated below. In a recent case the particular vessel bunkered from a barge at a Far East port and the drip sample taken from the vessel's manifold was analysed and found to be seriously off-specification. The vessel was on passage from the Far East to Europe by way of the Cape of Good Hope and had sufficient existing bunkers on board without the need to resort to the use of the newly bunkered product. As it turned out, this was extremely fortunate. Upon arrival at a convenient South African port, the sealed sample supplied by the bunker barge, together with additional samples drawn from all accessible tanks on board the vessel, were sent ashore for analysis, and the results were somewhat horrific.

043 The sealed sample provided by the barge indicated a fuel oil product which was within acceptable limits as far as the required specification was concerned. However, each of the samples obtained from the vessel's tanks were severely contaminated with water and had extremely low viscosity and flash point. With regard to the latter, I should make it clear that a minimum flash point is stipulated for combustible or flammable fluids to be carried in the engine room on board merchant vessels, this being 60°C. The flash point of the samples analysed was, in some cases, below 45°C, which in certain circumstances could have given rise to a fire or explosion in the engine room. It was ascertained by the laboratory that the product supplied in the Far East contained crude oil slops. These had either been used by an unscrupulous bunker supplier during blending, or had come from the tanks on the barge which had not been cleaned prior to its use as a bunker barge. Furthermore, as the vessel was a small container ship, the fuel contaminants could not, in this instance, have had their origin on board the vessel, although the latter is sometimes found to be the case upon investigation.

Unseaworthiness

044 It is a warranty in charter parties that the vessel to be chartered shall be in a fit condition for the venture, and be properly manned and equipped. The precise wording differs between various charter parties and two examples are reproduced below.

SHELLTIME 4 CHARTER PARTY

045 This relates to oil cargoes and tankers and includes the warranty.

"Clause 1

At the date of delivery of the vessel under this Charter,

(a) she shall be classed;
(b) she shall be in every way fit to carry crude petroleum and/or its products;
(c) she shall be tight, staunch, strong, in good order and condition, and in every way fit for the service, with her machinery, boilers, hull and other equipment (including but not limited to hull stress calculations and radar) in good and efficient state;
(d) her tanks, valves and pipelines shall be oil tight."

046 The remainder of Clause 1 relates to the consumption of fuel, canal regulations and certificates. Clause 2 relates to personnel and prosecution of voyages. Section 2(a) includes the following relevant requirements.

"2(a) At the date of delivery of the vessel under this charter;

(i) she shall have a full and efficient complement of Master, officers and crew for a vessel of her tonnage, who shall, in any event, be not less than the number required by the laws of the flag state and who shall be trained to operate the vessel and her equipment competently and safely;
(ii) all shipboard personnel shall hold valid certificates of competence in accordance with the requirements of the law of the flag state;
(iii) all shipboard personnel shall be trained in accordance with the relevant provisions of the International Convention on Standards of Training, Certification and Watchkeeping for Seafarers 1978."

047 Paragraph i of Clause 3 relates to the maintenance of the vessel during the charter party and states as follows:

"Clause 3

(i) Throughout the Charter Service Owners shall, whenever the passage of time, wear and tear, or any event ... requires steps to be taken to maintain or restore the conditions stipulated in Clauses 1 and 2(a), exercise due diligence so to maintain or restore the vessel."

NEW YORK PRODUCE EXCHANGE

048 The New York Produce Exchange (NYPE) Time Charter Party includes the same warranty only in a more concise form as follows:

(Lines 6 to 9 inclusive) "... of ... tons gross register and ... tons net register having engines of ... horse power and with hull, machinery and equipment in a thoroughly efficient state, and classed ... ".

(Lines 41 to 50 inclusive) ... "Vessel on her delivery shall be ready to receive cargo with clean-swept holds, and tight, staunch, strong and in every way fitted for ordinary cargo service, having water ballast and with sufficient power to operate all cargo-handling gear simultaneously (and with full complement of officers and crew for a Vessel of her tonnage), to be employed in carrying lawful merchandise excluding any goods of a dangerous, injurious flammable or corrosive nature unless carried in accordance with the requirements or recommendations of the proper authorities of the state of the Vessel's registry and of the states of ports of shipment and discharge and of any intermediate states or ports through whose waters the Vessel must pass. ..."

049 A common charter party dispute involves the alleged, or actual, unseaworthiness of a vessel, as a result of which the vessel may be unable to complete the voyage, or performs badly due to repeated machinery failures. Disputes relating to seaworthiness are closely associated with claims by cargo interests and are therefore discussed in the following paragraphs.

050 Before considering cargo claims however, it is worth noting that claims relating to unseaworthiness have sometimes nothing at all to do with the condition of the vessel, but are related solely to commercial interests. One such case comes to mind and is mentioned briefly below. An elderly, and somewhat worn and dilapidated large bulk carrier was chartered to a Far Eastern concern and performed satisfactorily for a number of voyages carrying iron ore from North and South America to the Far East. It should be noted that at the time the vessel was chartered, rates were high and available tonnage was in somewhat short supply.

051 After operating for about a year, there was a slump in the market and charter rates were reduced, thus our elderly bulk carrier, which still had a considerable period of the charter to run, became expensive. Suddenly the charterers discovered that the vessel was unseaworthy and could not be traded without extensive repairs. As with many ships, and particularly elderly bulk carriers, it was not difficult to list many defects which technically or actually would render the vessel unseaworthy, although such defects had existed throughout the charter party. A rapid arbitration was arranged, and the charterers' position was upheld. They were able to rescind the charter without financial loss, and charter in alternative tonnage at a considerably reduced rate, despite the fact that the owners spent considerable sums of money in their attempts to rectify the defects which the charterers alleged rendered the vessel unseaworthy.

Cargo claims

052 Cargo claims are, in many instances, associated with charter party disputes, particularly where unseaworthiness is alleged. Cargo claims form a large percentage of marine disputes.

Shortage claims

053 Cargo shortage claims are generally associated with liquid cargoes such as crude oil, and oil products, where the difference in the quantity discharged, when compared with the agreed loading figure, is in excess of the normally acceptable carriage losses.

Damage during transit

054 Cargo claims and disputes can often arise as a result of damage or loss sustained during carriage due to defective equipment or fittings on the vessel (for example, leaking hatch covers), or due to structural failures. Some examples are discussed below.

055 Many disputes arise as a result of deficient hatch closing and/or sealing arrangements, mainly with regard to perishable cargoes such as grain or grain products. As wear and corrosion take their toll, particularly on large vessels, hatch covers, which may appear sound and properly sealed and secured, will flex and distort due to the working of the vessel in adverse weather, and the pressures of seas breaking on the deck and hatch covers. Consequently water enters the holds causing damage to cargo.

056 The use of grabs during discharge can also result in damage to hatch coamings, in particular, seal compression bars, where grab runners can create a "saw tooth" effect, destroying seals and permitting water ingress.

057 A number of large cargo disputes have occurred due to structural or equipment failures with regard to the vessel or its machinery. A number of such disputes with which I have been involved are mentioned briefly hereunder.

058 A large crude oil tanker loaded a full cargo in the Arabian Gulf and sailed eastward towards the discharge port. During the passage, adverse weather was encountered, although nothing abnormal for the area and the time of year. Approximately 36 hours prior to arrival at the discharge port, the bow of the vessel, as far aft as the collision bulkhead, parted and fell off. As the cargo tanks aft of the collision bulkhead were breached there was some pollution. The owners signed a Lloyd's Open Form of salvage contract, and, as is usually the case nowadays, the efforts of the media and local politicians succeeded in prolonging the salvage and increasing the risk of further pollution. As a result, the vessel had to be towed astern for a two-week period to a position approved by the authorities before a transshipment could be made. In this instance the disputes involved loss of cargo, pollution and general average, together with the question of the contribution by cargo interests to the salvage fund and transshipment costs.

059 Investigation into the cause revealed that extensive corrosion of deck plating and side shell structural members, which should have been known to owners, had resulted in the failure, and a settlement between the parties was concluded before the case reached litigation.

060 A large bulk carrier loaded iron ore on the American continent and sailed for Europe encountering normal winter weather in the Atlantic. During the voyage water ingress to one cargo hold occurred and salvage services were incurred. Most of the cargo was eventually discharged and was in sound condition. A dispute between cargo interests and owners ensued. Subsequent investigation revealed extensive wastage of the cargo hold internal structure.

061 A laden vessel was approaching a bunker port when a high bilge water alarm sounded in the engine control room. This was apparently not an unusual occurrence on this vessel, and the audible alarm was cancelled, the alarm light remaining lit. After about five minutes a crew member had cause to leave the engine control and was concerned to find that the engine room was flooding, and that water was above the lower floor plates at the after end of the engine room and was entering at a great rate. Unsuccessful attempts were made to close the sea injection and discharge valves. All available pumps were started in an attempt to contain the ingress but this was to no avail. All machinery was subsequently shut down and the engine flooded to sea level.

062 A Lloyd's Open Form salvage agreement was signed and the salvors' divers had to locate externally all openings in the hull.

063 After salvors had sealed all sea chest and ship's side valve openings externally, the engine room was pumped out and a corroded sea water pipe was found to be the cause of the ingress. In the subsequent dispute, the claim by cargo interests that the vessel was unseaworthy was defended by owners on the basis that the corrosion was internal within the defective pipe due to a partial failure of the lining and was therefore not discoverable. This was disputed by the cargo interests who pointed out that there would be a period of time prior to final failure when there would be evidence of increasing leakage from the pipe. The case was settled before reaching the point of litigation.

Refrigerated cargo claims

064 One specialised area of cargo carriage, where disputes and claims are on the increase, concerns the carriage of refrigerated foodstuffs, in particular fruit cargoes where the product has a limited shelf or storage life between harvest and marketing. One particular commodity which, in my experience, figures increasingly in disputes, is the banana cargo. Banana cargoes require accurate and detailed attention to carriage temperatures and to the condition of circulating air. Bananas also have a limited transit life, thus particular attention must also be paid to maintaining propulsion machinery in an efficient condition so that the voyage times are not extended to any great degree.

065 There are a number of reasons why refrigerated cargo claims and disputes are on the increase. Most shipboard refrigeration plants are nowadays fully automated, and some of these plants are becoming somewhat dated, thus spare components are difficult to come by. In addition, with the advent of full automation, it has become unnecessary to train or carry specialist refrigeration engineers on board ships. The operation of the refrigeration plant is usually left to engineers who themselves are becoming increasingly less well trained. The upshot is that, when automation failures occur, the engineers on board the vessels are often unable to operate the refrigeration plant manually, as they have not been instructed in the rudiments of refrigeration.

066 I have been involved in a number of cases where cargoes have been lost, partially or totally, because coolers have not been defrosted, or because a failed condenser tube has not been located and rectified before the complete charge of refrigerant has been lost and, in one instance, the entire system flooded with sea water.

067 The same criticism applies to voyage delays which occur as a result of propulsion machinery problems. Cargoes then arrive late, and in a condition which makes them unsuitable for marketing.

068 It is often the case that the shipowner, excluding some of the liner companies, is apparently not prepared to invest money in training personnel, but is concerned to obtain a crew as cheaply as possible so long as the resultant number, and their grades on paper, comply with the requirements of the Flag State in which the vessel is registered.

Damage claims against underwriters

069 Most claims against underwriters are dealt with by the markets' own appointed technical department, and are settled without resorting to litigation. However, certain major incidents, where a third party might be involved, or where there might be a question as to the condition of the vessel's structure or equipment, can result in litigation between owners and their insurers. Such incidents may involve structural failures, outbreaks of fire on board ship, groundings, collisions, and total losses in what might appear to be suspicious circumstances. I have been involved in a number of such cases.

Structural failures

070 Structural failures have been considered previously when they involve disputes between owners and cargo interests. It is sometimes the case, however, that there is evidence of corrosion and lack of maintenance which have played a large part in the structural failure. I have been involved in a large number of cases where structural sections of vessels, generally bulk carriers, have become detached. In such cases a dispute between owners and their hull and machinery underwriters often develops. Such failures occurred so often in the early 1990s that the classification societies revised their rules concerning the frequency and extent of inspections, particularly of cargo holds and ballast tanks.

Fire damage

071 The most frequent outbreaks of fire on board ship occur in the engine room, and the most common cause of engine room fires is the leakage of fuel oil, diesel oil or lubricating oil onto the hot surfaces of adjacent operating machinery. To add to the problem it is sometimes the case that the firefighting equipment installation on the vessel is operated incorrectly due to lack of knowledge, or is partially inoperative due to poor maintenance, whereby its use becomes ineffective.

072 In such instances, it is again the case that disputes arise between the owners and their underwriters concerning the maintenance of the vessel and its safety equipment, and also the competence of the crew.

073 One recent case with which I was involved, concerned an auxiliary diesel engine. The engine was equipped for operation in an unmanned engine room, thus high pressure fuel pipes were equipped with external shields to contain any leakage of fuel which might occur. The shield took the form of a flexible steel pipe fitted over the high pressure fuel pipe. The spacers between pipe and shield had been allowed to wear and become loose, and vibration between pipe and shield caused wear and eventual failure of pipe and shield. High pressure fuel sprayed onto the hot exhaust system causing the outbreak of fire. This was a case where improperly maintained devices designed to prevent fire were, in fact, the cause of a fire outbreak. Had the shield not been fitted, contact and vibration would not have occurred, thus no fuel leakage would have taken place.

Collision damage

074 One of the functions of the marine expert in respect of collisions is to determine the speed and angle between the two vessels at the time of the collision. This involves a detailed inspection, and measurements of the damage to each vessel, and the application of formulae to determine the force required to cause the deformation and rupture of the structure noted during the inspection. From this evidence, the relative speeds between the vessels can be calculated.

Total losses—underwater inspections

075 Where a vessel has foundered in circumstances which are considered questionable, and also where the prospective claim upon hull underwriters is going to be substantial, it is sometimes the case that the underwriters will commission an underwater survey using a remotely controlled vehicle to locate, investigate, and photograph or film the wreck in order to determine the cause of the incident.

076 In a casualty in the late 1980s, it was alleged that a vessel sank in the vicinity of the Arabian Gulf as the result of an explosion caused by a drifting mine. The casualty was photographed at length by an air-sea rescue aircraft sent out when the vessel's distress signals were received, and the actions of the crew, together with the attitude of the vessel before sinking, as depicted in photographs, raised doubts as to the alleged cause of the casualty.

077 An ROV (remotely operated vehicle) underwater survey was commissioned and the wreck was located in about 2,000 metres of water. Sand-jetting setting equipment was used to uncover certain areas of the vessel considered to be of importance in relation to the owners' allegations concerning cause, and no corroborative evidence was located. As a result the owners' claim failed.

078 With the increasing availability of underwater survey equipment, able to operate at ever increasing depths, it is probable that more use will be made of this type of equipment during future investigations.

Other disputes

079 In the foregoing paragraphs, I have set out the main categories of maritime dispute with which the marine expert usually becomes involved. There are other areas, for example salvage disputes involving the assessment of salvage awards, but the details set out above give the reader a general idea as to the complex and diverse nature of the maritime consultancy business.

080 As ships, together with navigational and propulsion equipment, and also cargo carrying and handling equipment have become more complex, and automation has generally superseded all aspects of manual control on board, so the field of maritime expertise has diversified to include metallurgists, chemists, fire experts, electronics experts and various other categories of specialists. However, my experience is that the specialists referred to above are generally instructed in conjunction with a marine expert in order to provide the specialist input as necessary in a particular case. For example, a fire expert may be instructed in connection with engine room fires, or a metallurgist where structural failure has occurred, but in each it would normally be together with a marine engineering expert.

CASE HISTORY

081 In the following paragraphs, I have set out details of an interesting case covering the following aspects:

(i) The case facts.
(ii) The appointment of experts.
(iii) The process of instruction.
(iv) The method of tackling the task.
(v) An example of the type of report prepared for such a case.
(vi) The outcome of litigation.

082 The contents of the following paragraphs are factual, although the name of the vessel and location of the casualty have been changed. The case is considered interesting as it sets out the type of bulk carrier failure which was not an infrequent event five or six years ago. It also demonstrates how many parties can become involved, and also the sums of money involved in providing guarantees to enable assistance to be given to a crippled ship.

The background facts of the case

083 The "BULK KARRIER" was an elderly dry bulk carrier, registered with one of the lesser known classification societies and managed by Far Eastern interests. The vessel was spot-chartered to load 93,000 tonnes of iron ore in South Africa for discharge in the Far East.

084 The vessel's problems commenced at the load port where an inspection by the port authorities revealed some structural defects which delayed the loading of the vessel.

085 The surveyor representing the port authorities required repairs to be carried out in accordance with the recommendations of the classification surveyor. Due to the type and extent of the defects, the classification surveyor was instructed by his head office to conduct a number of full surveys, no doubt because the general condition of the vessel was suspect.

086 However, despite such instructions, the repairs were restricted to a minimum and the vessel was provided with a certificate which satisfied the port authorities and the vessel was permitted to load a full cargo of iron ore. The vessel, like most large bulk carriers, was specially strengthened for heavy cargoes, thus the iron ore was loaded into alternate holds, leaving the remaining holds empty. The reason for this loading configuration was to reduce the metacemetric height (or GM) of the vessel, and thus reduce the violent rolling which might otherwise be encountered in adverse weather conditions. Such violent rolling would apply undue racking stresses to the vessel's structure. On completion of loading, the "BULK KARRIER" sailed towards the discharge port.

087 During the voyage, the vessel encountered adverse weather conditions, and commenced taking water into one of the empty cargo holds through a fracture in the ship's side shell plating. An inspection of the cargo holds by the Chief Officer, where accessible, revealed that some side frames had become detached, or partially detached, in Nos 2, 6 and 8 cargo holds. The vessel's operators were advised of the condition, but made no attempt to divert the vessel to the nearest port where a full inspection could be made. Instead the Master was instructed to go to a nearby anchorage where it was arranged that he would embark material and personnel to effect repairs. The Master reduced speed and sought shelter, where he anchored, and took on board materials, personnel, and equipment in order to carry out repairs to the damaged side shell structure. However, having taken the material on board, no immediate repairs were carried out, and the ship resumed the passage in the same defective condition.

088 Although the weather conditions improved the rate of water ingress gradually increased. Approximately three days before reaching the discharge port, a sudden failure of the side shell plating occurred causing flooding of the cargo hold and commencement of leakage through the transverse bulkheads into the adjacent holds which were filled with cargo. The Master sent out a May Day signal and the crew were lifted off the vessel by helicopter.

089 One interesting point arising from the abandonment was that the vessel was left with the auxiliary machinery in operation, the main engine running at dead slow ahead, and the automatic pilot in operation. The vessel, completely unmanned, continued on passage at five to six knots, and the chief engineer with assistants had to be dropped back on board the vessel by helicopter about 36 hours after abandoning the ship, in order to shut down the main engine and so curtail the vessel's progress which had been reported in the maritime press as a six knot "drift".

090 The vessel remained afloat and was subsequently taken in tow by local tugs, following a salvage contract signed between the tugs and the ship's owners. She was then towed to the discharge port and was anchored in the Roads. The first technical hitch in the salvage process occurred upon the arrival of the tug and tow at the anchorage. The salvage contract called for the vessel to be redelivered to the owners at a safe anchorage or berth at the discharge port. However, the salvors anchored the vessel outside the confines of the port and then proceeded with the tug to a berth, leaving the vessel abandoned at anchor with no watchman on board, no lights and no power. A dispute about redelivery immediately arose between salvors and owners. The port authorities took a hand and insisted that the vessel's machinery was mobilised. The senior officers and some crew members were placed back on board the vessel to reactivate the machinery. Meanwhile discussions and negotiations were held between all interested parties and the port authorities in order to obtain permission for the vessel to enter the port and discharge the cargo. One of the major concerns was the attitude of the port authorities and also of the cargo receivers. The receivers had their own terminal which received about 150,000 to 200,000 tonnes of ore per week, this being the quantity required to keep their plant in continuous operation. Furthermore, the discharge berth could only be reached by passing through the commercial port entrance channel. An inspection of the vessel upon arrival showed one hold flooded to a tidal condition and one other hold partially flooded. Fuelled by press comments, the opinion of the port authorities and the terminal owners was that neither wanted to take the risk of a crippled vessel sinking, either in the approach channel, or at the berth with the ensuing possibilities of the extreme financial losses which such an incident would incur.

091 Vast sums of money were suggested by the legal representatives of the port and of the terminal as a guarantee against such an eventuality, and lengthy discussions took place to try and resolve the problem.

092 It was whilst these discussions were taking place that the weather deteriorated and the owners ordered their agents to evacuate the crew from the vessel. At the time of the evacuation, the owners also sent a telex to the port authority advising that the ingress of water was increasing, and the vessel was in danger of sinking, despite the fact that such comments were without foundation. When the port authorities received this information, the harbour master ordered that the anchor cable be cut, and arranged for a tug to tow the vessel outside the 50-mile limit from the shore where is was initially stated that the vessel would be scuttled.

093 Further intensive discussions took place and it was subsequently agreed that professional international salvors would be employed in an attempt to recover the vessel, render it safe and bring it to the discharge berth. Further guarantees had to be provided to the salvors before the work could begin. Such work would only be attempted on a fixed daily rate to the salvors.

094 On reboarding the vessel, the salvors now found that the upper wing tank covers had been left open and water had entered other compartments including most of the upper wing ballast tanks such that the vessel was heavily trimmed by the head and was almost awash at the forward end. After a considerable number of days the water was pumped out and the draught reduced sufficiently for the vessel to be allowed to go alongside to discharge cargo, but only after fuel had been removed and the necessary guarantees had been provided by those representing both owners and cargo interests.

The appointment of the expert

095 There are a number of well known companies of maritime consultants whose senior members are frequently appointed as expert witnesses in the event that a particular case is likely to proceed to litigation, either by High Court trial or by arbitration. However, the appointment of a particular marine expert is very much a personalised business which is dependent upon the individual's reputation rather than that of the company for whom he works.

096 The marine expert should restrict himself to the particular field of maritime expertise of which he has personal experience and with which he is familiar. Thus an expert whose previous career was in shipyard, and/or marine engineering as a seagoing engineer, should restrict himself to cases involving machinery and ship's structure. He should not become involved with cases which relate solely to cargo or navigational aspects. These latter should be dealt with by nautical experts with a practical background as a master mariner or deck officer.

097 One method used by opposing counsel at the commencement of cross-examination of an expert witness, in order to discredit him or to undermine his confidence, is to question him on his own personal seagoing experience in relation to the particular subject upon which he has prepared his expert report. It is thus unwise, and damaging to the expert's reputation, to involve himself in particular aspects or subjects of which he has no previous practical experience.

098 The writer has already referred to the developments in the maritime industry which have taken place over the past 30 years. Such developments have seen the wholesale introduction of electronics, resulting in centralised control and automation both in the engineering and navigational aspects of ship operation. Due to the complexity of some equipment, it is often necessary for specialists in certain fields to be appointed as experts to assist the court or tribunal in aspects of the case which are beyond the expertise of the marine consultants.

099 I have also referred, in passing, to the fact that the developments noted above have had the effect of reducing the size and expertise of ships' crews, such that the marine expert, with an in-depth and detailed experience in operation and maintenance of shipboard machinery and equipment, is a dying breed. Future generations will have to rely upon an ever increasing number of experts who are specialists in their own particular field, and who have not had practical, "hands on", seagoing experience.

100 Reverting now to the specific case referred to at paras 083–094 above, I was instructed by the representatives of the charterers and cargo interests. I was known to the cargo and charterers representatives, having been appointed by them previously in cases where structural failures had occurred. Although not a naval architect by profession, my experience had included three to four years' "hands on" experience and survey work in one of the large southern European shipyards, where extremely large structural repairs and modifications were carried out, some cases involving thousands of tonnes of new steel, so structural failure investigation was and is well within my knowledge and expertise.

101 There were a number of other interests involved in the investigations, namely the shipowners, their protection and indemnity assurance, the hull and machinery underwriters, the salvors, the harbour authorities, and the classification society, all of whom appointed their own experts or consultants, and all of whom were either marine engineers or naval architects by profession. In addition, a number of metallurgists were involved to comment upon rates of corrosion and steel failures due to varying stresses.

The process of instruction

102 The process of instruction varies somewhat from case to case. In an ideal world, the method of instruction would take the following form.

103 A telephone call from the prospective client enquiring as to interest and availability of the expert, would be followed by the provision of the expert's *Curriculum Vitae* and an indication of the expert's daily charges, or a lump sum estimation of cost to prepare a report. If these were acceptable to the client, a formal letter of instruction would be provided, together with the documentation to be considered by the expert. The instruction would then be acknowledged in writing and the expert would proceed with the task in the agreed allotted time schedule.

104 It is often the case, however, that the prospective client requires immediate attendance at the site of, or on board, the casualty, which may have just occurred. In such a situation, a telephone call will be the only form of instruction and, if available to act, the consultant may find himself on board an aeroplane to a destination half way around the world within three or four hours of the initial receipt of the instructions. In such circumstances, there is often no formal letter of instruction at any time throughout the period of investigation or litigation.

105 In the circumstances of the incident referred to at paras 083 *et seq.* above, I was telephoned and asked if I was available to act and to attend on board the vessel upon its arrival, under tow, at the discharge port. The vessel was expected to arrive in approximately 36 hours, so the preparations and travel arrangements were relatively leisurely.

106 The instructions received were to investigate the cause of the structural failure on board the vessel, which had resulted in the abandonment by the crew and the necessity for salvage services. The writer was requested to ascertain whether the vessel was seaworthy at the time of loading the cargo, or whether defects existed which were, or should have been, known to a prudent owner, and if such defects existed, whether they were causative of, or contributory to, the casualty.

The task of investigation

107 The task of investigating a casualty can be made extremely difficult or relatively easy, depending, to a large extent, upon whose behalf or interest the consultant or expert has been appointed. An appointment upon behalf of the shipowner and/or their protection and indemnity association usually results in the assistance of the owners' agents, their superintendent, and the Master and officers of the vessel, as well as access to documents, log books, operational and maintenance records as applicable, and the relevant plans and drawings of the vessel. Furthermore, unrestricted access to all parts of the vessel, as requested by the consultant, is usually provided, and statements can normally be obtained from the crew.

108 The opposite conditions usually apply to a consultant appointed by those representing cargo and/or charterers' interests. It is often the case that a court order has to be obtained to gain access to the ship and then it is necessary for the order to specify the precise areas which the attending consultant wishes to examine. Furthermore, unless such areas are directly associated with the damage under investigation, a court application for access will usually be contested by those representing owners, as a result of which the court order will not normally be granted. Thus, even when provision is made for a consultant representing cargo interests to attend on board the vessel, inspection is limited to specific areas or items directly involved with the relevant incident and access to documents, log books and even plans is usually forbidden, although it is usually permissible to take photographs. The owners' lawyers, usually involved from the outset in such cases, generally prefer to withhold documents which, if available, could well assist in solving differences between the opposing parties at an early stage, until such times that pleadings have been served and document discovery is finalised.

109 One important thing for the consultant to bear in mind is that a detailed photographic record of the casualty, or the results of the incident, is of extreme value later when the casualty is being explained, either in report form, or verbally, to the layman, who in such instances will probably be a protection and indemnity association representative, an underwriters' representative, an instructing solicitor or counsel. It is furthermore of great importance that adequate, explanatory captions should be provided with the photographs. All too often, I have been presented with an envelope of photographs of a particular incident to which the attending surveyor has added absolutely no captions at all, so the end result is of little value to someone who has not had the advantage of actually attending on board the vessel.

110 The value of detailed, legible, handwritten notes made at the time of inspection is important, in particular when they are sometimes called for by the opposing solicitors involved in a case, often years after the event has taken place. The writing of detailed notes on site is often easier said than done in certain areas of a damaged vessel. An unlit, burned out engine room, or a damaged double bottom tank with an ambient temperature in excess of 40°C, are just two of the many places where, with the best will in the world, legible, detailed notes are virtually impossible.

111 Turning now to the case of the incident referred to above at paras 083 *et seq*., it will be recalled that I was instructed by those representing charterers and cargo interests in order to investigate the probable condition of the vessel at the time of loading cargo, and whether the vessel was seaworthy at that time.

112 As far as seaworthiness is concerned, under the terms of the contract entered into by the shipowners for the carriage of the cargo, it is the duty of the shipowner to make sure that, upon loading the cargo, the vessel is, in all respects, fit to load and carry the cargo, and is properly manned and equipped for the intended voyage.

The classification societies

113 Whilst considering the seaworthiness of a ship, it is perhaps relevant at this stage to look at the position of the classification society with regard to this aspect. After all, the classification societies were initially formed to set minimum standards with regard to the condition of merchant vessels and their crews.

114 The major classification societies, of which there are probably six which are recognised to be in this category, exist to ensure that a ship is designed, built and equipped to a certain standard, and, in general, it is reasonable to conclude that this condition is achieved in virtually all newbuildings. The writer emphasises the newbuilding aspect of the classification role, because an inspection of the classification Rule Books shows that in excess of 95 per cent of these voluminous documents relate to newbuilding standards, scantlings, machinery and equipment, and something less than 5 per cent to the standards of inspections and surveys after the new vessel has entered service.

115 The classification societies also exist to regulate the condition of the vessel throughout its operational life and this is done by requiring the structure and machinery to be fully inspected once every five years (special surveys), and, further, more superficial inspections to be carried out on an intermediate and annual basis.

116 A full, detailed inspection of hull and machinery every five years is inadequate to assure that a ship, its machinery and equipment is, at all times, fully seaworthy. For example, most items of machinery require full overhauls at intervals of time which are considerably less than five years. Thus an owner, or any other interests involved with shipping, and carriage of cargo by sea, cannot assume that, just because a vessel is fully classed by a reputable classification society, it is also seaworthy and fully equipped for a particular, or any, voyage.

117 The classification societies' Rule Books all cover the aspects referred to previously, including in the introduction to their rules, a requirement that the shipowner shall inform the classification society of any damage or defect with the vessel, its machinery or equipment which would render the vessel unseaworthy, and that such repairs as necessary should be carried out in accordance with the recommendation of the attending surveyor. This does not mean that an owner has to involve class every time that routine maintenance is carried out, or when defective components are replaced. The purpose of this particular rule is such that an owner is put on notice that he cannot continue to trade his vessel with damaged or defective structural or machinery items, which items would affect the classification of the vessel.

118 The prudent shipowner will normally comply with the classification rules, and will deal with any defect which emerges as a result of regular maintenance and inspections by qualified and diligent technical personnel. There are, however, an increasing number of unscrupulous owners who either omit to carry out routine maintenance and diligent inspections, or, having ascertained that defects exist, either ignore them, or attempt to effect repairs with unqualified personnel and without advising their classification society. The deterioration in the qualities of shipboard personnel also adds to the deterioration in the maintenance of the ship's structure, machinery and equipment.

119 Before leaving the classification-related aspects concerning the condition of a vessel, it is relevant to record that, in recent years, a considerable number of what are termed "minor" classification societies have appeared which, in the main, rely upon non-exclusive personnel to carry out the required surveys of vessels in the field. As the classification reports, and the certificates issued, only reflect the diligence and competence of the attending surveyor, it is often my experience that, according to the classification documents on board, a vessel may be fully classed without any condition, when inspections reveal clearly that structural wastage or machinery deficiencies exist in abundance, any one of which could result in withdrawal of class, or the imposition of a recommendation, unless dealt with immediately.

120 It has been due to the fact that the classification standards have been deteriorating over a number of years that the protection and indemnity assurance associations and also the hull and machinery underwriters' technical services have evolved their own set of standards and regular inspection of vessels in an attempt to reduce the number of claims.

121 Having expressed criticism of the classification societies, which in my opinion, is relevant to the incident under consideration, it should be pointed out that I am normally only involved with the "disasters", and am well aware that there are a vast number of vessels at sea which are well maintained and operated, and manned by competent and efficient officers and crews.

Inspection of the "BULK KARRIER"

122 Reverting now to the case of the "BULK KARRIER", I arrived at the vessel's discharge port to learn that, due to weather, the speed of the tow had been reduced and the vessel would not arrive for another 24 to 30 hours. The available additional time before arrival was spent in ascertaining the location of the ship's and salvor's agents, attending a meeting with the cargo receivers, investigating the facilities made, and available, for discharge of the cargo, and meeting the representatives of the other parties involved.

123 As the cargo receivers would have to rely heavily upon the goodwill of the port authorities to obtain permission for a large, damaged and partially flooded bulk carrier to enter the port, they asked that a court surveyor be appointed by the port authorities to assess the condition of the ship and to make certain that there was proper liaison between the technical representatives of the other interested parties. In this particular instance there were independent technical consultants appointed by a total of seven parties, namely the owners, the Protection and Indemnity Association, the owner's hull and machinery underwriters, the salvors, the classification society, the cargo underwriters and the cargo receivers. Each party, with the exception of the underwriters and classification interests, had legal advisors in attendance. Thus with seven separate interests having a total of about 32 people on site, and in particular, with the involvement of the port authorities, each day's operation was preceded by a meeting of all parties chaired by the court-appointed surveyors, at which time the up-to-date progress, and the future programmes, were fully discussed.

124 Although somewhat time-consuming, and, in many instances, repetitive, the fact that all inspections were preceded by such a meeting was advantageous for me in that there were no delays in gaining access to the vessel at any time, and all evidence relating to the casualty was available for inspection to all attending surveyors.

125 The initial meeting was convened by the court surveyors prior to the vessel's arrival. It was learned that the vessel had been stopped outside the port limits where an underwater inspection was carried out by the divers appointed by the court surveyors. The divers reported that sections of side shell plating and frames were missing from the starboard side of the flooded cargo hold. It was also reported that a second hold was partly flooded, although the source of this second ingress of water was not known. There was also some bulkhead leakage into holds adjacent to the flooded cargo holds, but the extent of such leakage could not be determined.

126 During the meeting, the function and field of inspection of each consultant and expert was discussed and agreed. As far as I was concerned, my instructions were to ascertain the structural condition of the vessel with regard to the cargo holds, and the request was made to inspect the following compartments:

- The laden cargo holds from the top of the cargo stowage.
- The flooded cargo holds from access ladders.
- The non-flooded and empty cargo holds.
- The upper wing ballast tanks.
- The main deck overall.
- The cargo holds throughout upon completion of discharge.

127 The initial five of the foregoing inspections were carried out during the first three days following the vessel's arrival, and the final inspection of the empty cargo holds was made about one month later, following the completion of the discharge of the vessel.

Value of the inspection

128 A site inspection on board the vessel is of great assistance to the expert. For reasons of economy, it is often the case that a local surveyor will be appointed whose report will then be made available to the expert. This is often false economy, as certain details relevant to the case may well be overlooked by the local man.

129 In the case of the "BULK KARRIER", I boarded the vessel together with the court surveyors on the evening of arrival at the anchorage. Although, as mentioned previously, the vessel had been anchored without lights or watchmen, and the tug had departed, an inspection of the deck with torch and camera revealed a number of things which were of considerable value in assessing proceedings on board prior to the abandonment by the crew. It was noted that oxy-acetylene burning equipment was on deck and leading down into cargo holds, together with electric welding leads. Furthermore, there were sections of steel on deck which corresponded in size to the vessel's side shell frames. It appeared from the evidence noted on the first evening aboard that steel renewals had been taking place at sea. The evidence referred to above had "disappeared" when the vessel was next attended a day later and would not have been known to me, had I been restricted in initial access to the vessel as would normally have been the case.

130 Subsequently, during the inspection of the cargo holds, it was noted that staging support angles had been welded to the frames in some cargo holds and wooden staging planks were found in each of the two flooded holds, which again supported the opinion formed that steel renewals were being carried out at sea.

131 Such first hand evidence was invaluable in forming an opinion as to the reason for the casualty and the condition of the vessel at the time of departure from the load port.

Reporting

132 On completion of the on-site inspection, a factual report setting out the findings was prepared and sent to the client, together with captioned photographs which demonstrated the conditions referred to in the report. Subsequently, as the case progressed towards litigation, and the relevant documents were provided by both parties, an Expert Report was prepared for use at the litigation.

133 Prior to the exchange of Experts' Reports between the parties, it is normal for counsel representing the clients to call for a conference where the case will be discussed and the content of the Expert Report analysed. It is usually the case that counsel will seek to direct the expert's attention and comments in a particular direction which is of assistance to the client. Whilst on paper this might appear to be reasonable, the expert must, at all times, bear in mind the fact that his credibility will be questioned if contents of the report cannot withstand cross-examination in the witness box.

134 It is my opinion that an Expert Report should stand on its own, and be understood by the reader without the need to refer to additional documents. In this respect, where the report refers to specific documents, it is advantageous for the expert to append such documents to his report.

135 The report should be preceded by an index relating to the specific contents of each section of the report, and a short section setting out the expert's conclusions should either precede the narrative section of the report or be included at the end of the report. It is not really of any consequence whether conclusions precede or follow the body of the report, as long as an index is provided whereby the reader can ascertain for himself where the expert's conclusions are set out.

136 The format for an expert report as used by myself, and which is apparently acceptable to instructing solicitors and counsel, is set out in the following manner.

Preamble

137 A short preamble setting out the source of the instructions, the location of the incident and, if applicable, the inspection of the vessel, and the intention of the Report.

Details of vessel

138 This section should briefly set out the details of the vessel, in particular, any structural details which might be applicable to the content of the Report.

Documents provided

139 It is my practice to include a section setting out brief details of the documents provided which have been used in the preparation of the Report.

Details of the incident

140 In this section details of the incident under investigation should be set out together with the findings of the expert during his inspection of the vessel.

Cause of the incident

141 The facts relating to the cause of the incident should be set out, together with the opinion of the expert concerning cause.

Conditions of structure/equipment

142 Where the condition of structure or equipment had contributed to or caused the incident, details should be set out clearly and precisely in a short section of the Report.

Cause of failure

143 Where structural failure has been causative of the incident, details should be included in a separate section.

The knowledge of the owner

144 In instances where a casualty has occurred as a result of deficiencies which should have been or were known to the owner, details should be set out in a separate report section.

The actions of a prudent owner

145 Following on from the reference to the knowledge of the owner, the expert should then set out separately, what, in his opinion, a prudent owner should have done to prevent the occurrence of the casualty.

The classification position

146 As most major casualties occur on vessels which are fully classed, or at least have on board the relevant documents which record that the vessel is fully classed, it is advantageous for the expert to set out what the classification position was at the time the incident occurred.

Measurements and calculations

147 If measurements and/or calculations are relied upon by the expert to support his opinion, these should be referred to in a separate section of the Report, and the actual calculations and measurements should be appended to the Report.

Witness depositions and/or statements

148 It is often the case that statements or depositions are taken from various factual witnesses who will normally be crew members, the owner's shore based staff or other personnel (for example stevedores), who were involved in the incident, or were in contact with, or on board, the vessel prior to the occurrence of the casualty. If such statements are provided, they should be referred to in the Report, and their relevance to the casualty should be discussed.

Discussion

149 The expert would normally include a discussion section in his Report, whereby the various relevant facts set out in preceding sections are drawn together and commented upon in order to demonstrate why certain conclusions have been drawn concerning the cause of the casualty.

Conclusions

150 Finally, a short conclusion section should be added whereby the expert sets out his opinion as to the cause of the casualty or incident, and brief comments upon why he has drawn such conclusions.

151 By way of an example, a sample report based upon these headings referred follows.

SAMPLE REPORT

REPORT

"BULK KARRIER"

At the request of Messrs Maritime Solicitors and Company, the Undersigned attended upon the "BULK KARRIER" whilst afloat at a Far Eastern discharge port, in order to investigate the cause of damage which led to the abandonment of the vessel by the Crew. Subsequently, relevant documents have been provided and this Report upon the structural condition of the Vessel at the time of loading has been prepared.

DETAILS OF VESSEL

The "BULK KARRIER" is an OBO built in 1968 by Far Eastern Shipbuilders Limited. The Vessel has nine cargo holds equipped with steel hatch covers, and the superstructure and machinery spaces are located aft.

Propulsion is by means of an eight cylinder turbocharged diesel engine rated at 17,000 Brake Horse Power giving a service speed of 14 knots.

The principal particulars of the vessel are as follows:

Length overall	:	250.00 metres
Length between perpendiculars	:	234.00 metres
Moulded breadth	:	36.00 metres
Moulded depth	:	19.50 metres
Summer draught	:	14.00 metres
Gross tonnage	:	48,000.00 tons
Net tonnage	:	38,000.00 tons
Deadweight to summer draught	:	98,500.00 tonnes

The Vessel is strengthened for carriage of heavy cargoes, with Nos 2, 4, 6 and 8 holds empty.

DOCUMENTS PROVIDED

The Undersigned has been provided with the following documents which have been referred to in the preparation of this Report.

The Pleadings.
Classification Documents.
Condition Survey Reports.
Various Coastguard Reports.
Reports prepared on behalf of the Vessel's Hull Underwriters.
Reports prepared by those representing Cargo Underwriters.
Reports prepared by Representatives of the Salvors.
Reports prepared by the Port Authorities at the discharge port.
Witness Statements.
Reports relating to various ultrasonic structural measurements.
Various Report Invoices.
Various Shipboard Records and Correspondence.

DETAILS OF THE INCIDENT AND THE UNDERSIGNED'S ATTENDANCE ON BOARD THE VESSEL

The "BULK KARRIER" loaded a full cargo of iron ore concentrate in South Africa for discharge at a Far Eastern port. The Vessel sailed on 11 July 1991, Nos 2, 6, and 8 holds being empty on departure.

During the passage, ingress of water to No. 6 hold occurred and conditions deteriorated until the decision was made by the Master to abandon the Vessel. The Vessel was taken in tow by Salvors and was towed to the discharge port where she was anchored awaiting the permission of the Port Authorities to go alongside the discharge berth. Shortly after the Vessel's arrival, Officers and Crew reboarded the Vessel and were able to restore power and lighting.

Subsequent to meetings and discussions with the Port Authorities, Surveyors representing various interested parties were permitted aboard together with the Port Authority Surveyor and inspections of the accessible cargo holds and upper wing tanks were carried out. An underwater inspection by divers revealed that the ingress of water to No. 6 cargo hold was the result of the failure of side shell plating, a section on the starboard side having become detached over an area of approximately 12 square metres.

After considerable negotiations with Port Authorities, Salvors, Cargo Interests and other interested parties, the Vessel was eventually permitted to enter the port and go alongside the discharge terminal where, upon completion of discharge, and the de-watering of flooded compartments, a further detailed inspection of the damaged cargo hold was carried out.

Summary of Cargo Hold Inspection

As recorded in my Original Factual Reports, and based upon the visible evidence on board the Vessel, I formed the opinion that "BULK KARRIER" was unseaworthy at and before the commencement of the voyage on the load port, with the knowledge of the Owners, and that this unseaworthiness was directly causative of the loss. My opinion has been strengthened and endorsed by the contents of documents subsequently provided and referred to earlier in this Report.

Summarising, the Vessel was unseaworthy prior to the voyage in question because:

> The Ship's side frames in Nos 3, 6 and 8 holds were heavily wasted beyond permissible standards and were partially detached from the side shell plating. This condition was discoverable by diligent inspection, and in my opinion, was known to the Owners.
>
> There was evidence that frames on the port side of No. 6 holds had been previously renewed after failure, as frame webs were shaped to fit the inward curvature of side shell plating, this curvature having been formed by external pressure when the original side shell frames had failed.
>
> The renewals were apparently carried out without reference to the Classification Society, as such renewals do not appear in Classification Documents.
>
> Evidence was found on board the Vessel that unauthorised and unclassified repairs were being carried out by the Crew, using uncertified welders.

CAUSE OF VESSEL'S ABANDONMENT AND SUBSEQUENT SALVAGE

In the following paragraphs, the Undersigned has documented the facts relating to water ingress, and has expressed an opinion as to the cause of such ingress. I have further set out the actions a prudent Owner would adopt to prevent the structural failures which were causative of such ingress.

The loading of "BULK KARRIER" was delayed due to the intervention of the Coastguard, who insisted that a fracture in the side shell plating was repaired to the approval of the Classification Society prior to permitting loading to commence.

During the laden voyage, ingress of water to No. 6 cargo hold commenced. Although the Owners/Managers were informed, the Master was not instructed to seek a Port of Refuge. Subsequently, the rate of ingress increased and an inspection by the Master of all cargo holds revealed that apart from hold No. 6, there was movement between side shell plating and frames in a number of other compartments. This condition caused the Master to fear that the Vessel might break up and thus resulted in his decision to abandon the Ship.

CONDITION OF CARGO HOLD STRUCTURE

The Undersigned carried out internal inspections of the cargo holds, both prior to, during, and subsequent to the discharge of the cargo. The conditions noted in the cargo holds were as follows.

No. 1 Cargo Hold

No major deficiencies noted.

No. 2 Cargo Hold

On the port side of No. 2 cargo hold, it was found that four frames were partially detached from the side shell plating immediately above the lower wing tank.

On the starboard side of No. 2 hold it was noted that all side shell frames, totalling nineteen in number, were detached from the side shell plating to varying degrees, the amount of detachment measuring between 0.5 metres and a maximum 3.5 metres at mid-length of the hold. Where detachment was extensive, the frame web plates were buckled. The detached condition of side shell frames was clearly visible from the tank tops and should have been discovered during routine inspections.

Nos 3, 4 and 5 Holds

No deficiencies noted.

No. 6 Hold

On the starboard side of No. 6 hold, an area of shell plating was missing, measuring approximately 12 square metres, the shell plate having fractured and broken away following the detachment of side shell frames. At each frame space, the frames remained partially in place but were heavily distorted. The remaining sections of frame web plates were found to be heavily wasted.

On the port side of No. 6 cargo hold, it was noted that sections of side shell frame had been recently renewed, the web plates of such frames having been shaped to align with the distorted condition of side shell plating. As stated above, these renewals do not feature in the Classification Records of the Vessel. There was evidence in No. 6 cargo hold that repairs or replacements appeared to have been in progress immediately prior to or at the time the ingress of water first commenced.

No. 7 Cargo Hold

No defects noted.

No. 8 Cargo Hold

On both port and starboard sides of No. 8 cargo hold, it was noted that a number of frames were partially detached, or had broken up and were part missing. It was further noted that partial flooding of No. 8 hold had occurred due to fractures in the side shell plating where fatigue had set in following the failure of the supporting side shell frames.

THE FLOODING MECHANISM

It was clear to the Undersigned that water ingress to both Nos 6 and 8 cargo holds occurred because of the failure of side shell plating due to severely corroded side shell frames which had become detached, leaving the side shell plating unsupported.

As a result, varying external pressures on the side shell plating caused by wave action and by the normal movement of the Vessel in a seaway, resulted in flexing or 'panting' of the unsupported side shell plating. Such flexing caused fatigue failure, in particular where support remained, that is in way of the connections to upper and lower wing tanks.

Once fractures occurred and water ingress commenced the dynamic effect of water 'sloshing' inside the cargo hold, caused by movement of the Vessel, accelerated the propagation of plate fractures and, in the case of No. 8 hold, the final loss of a section of shell plating.

In the case of No. 8 hold, the failure mechanism had not progressed to the same extent as that in No. 6 hold, hence only the commencement of side shell frame failures had occurred. Had the fractures in No. 8 hold continued to propagate as they undoubtedly would have done, leading to the complete flooding of that compartment, it is possible that the Vessel would have foundered.

CAUSE OF FRAME CORROSION AND DETACHMENT

Corrosion in the cargo holds of bulk carriers is to be expected, because of the nature of the cargoes carried, and the normal lack of, or damage to, protective paint coatings. Due to the density of certain cargoes and the need to attain acceptable stability, it is normal practice to load cargoes, such as iron ore, in alternate holds, provided the vessel is strengthened for such loading, as was the case on the 'BULK KARRIER'. In the loaded condition, transverse distortion of the structure takes place, as a result of which corrosion scale is periodically broken away, resulting in newly exposed steel being subjected to further corrosion.

Condensation occurs on the side shell plating due to the lower, external, sea temperatures, and water so formed can gravitate to the frame webs and lower brackets where it corrodes the steel work, leading to frame and bracket detachment from the side shell plating. The carriage of "corrosive" cargoes, such as, for example, coal with a high sulphur content, exacerbates the problem.

This corrosion is ongoing and, in the experience of the Undersigned, can seriously affect vessels less than ten years old. However, it should be monitored by close-up inspections of side shell frames and brackets. Whilst it is an accepted fact that, due to the lower hopper tank slope bulkheads, access to the side shell frames for inspection is difficult, access is possible for inspections by using ladders to climb the slope bulkhead. In any event, the condition of the wasted frames on the 'BULK KARRIER' particularly in Nos 2, 6 and 8 cargo holds, was clearly visible from the double bottom tank top. As corrosion problems in bulk carriers are well known, a prudent Owner would make certain that close-up inspections are carried out at least annually by competent staff in order to monitor the condition of side shell frames and brackets, corrosion rates can vary, and are often as rapid as 0.75mm to 1mm *per annum*, so that a frame web having an original thickness of 12mm can become wasted to the extent that it becomes detached in less than 10 years' service.

THE KNOWLEDGE OF THE OWNERS

The defects of the hull structure in way of the cargo holds, noted at the time of my Surveys, were in the opinion of the Undersigned, known to the Owners prior to the commencement of the relevant voyage. By 1993, a bulk carrier Owner or Operator would have been well aware of the potential structural problems in a 23-year-old vessel and should have instigated a regular close-up inspection of the side shell frames and welds in order to monitor the thickness of the remaining material.

Apart from documentary information available to Owners, it was evident to the Undersigned from my inspection of the Vessel, that the Owners were aware of the condition of the hull internal structure in the areas where failure had occurred because:

Internals had been recently renewed in cargo holds.

Preparations had been made for further renewals at sea.

Steel for frame renewals together with necessary ancillary equipment had been put aboard the Vessel.

Visual evidence and Witness Statements had confirmed that steel renewals were in progress prior to this voyage, and also shortly before the Vessel was abandoned.

It is therefore clear that Owners were well aware of the wasted condition of internal structure in Nos 2, 6 and 8 cargo holds prior to commencement of the voyage. Furthermore, and contrary to Classification Rule Requirements, there is no evidence that known structural defects had been reported to the Classification, and no evidence that the Classification Society had seen or approved recent structural renewals, some of which appear to have been carried out at sea.

THE ACTIONS OF A PRUDENT SHIPOWNER

It is normal practice for inspections of the cargo holds on commercial vessels to be carried out at periodical intervals by the Ship's Chief Officer together with other Crew members appointed by the Master. The results of such inspections would normally be reported to the Shipowners' Technical Department.

Such inspections are particularly relevant on bulk carriers, as structural damage is often sustained as a result of cargo operations by use of grabs, and it is necessary to inspect and prepare claims against Stevedores at the time such damage occurs. A prudent Shipowner would require periodical reports from the Master and from the Superintendent attending the Vessel, as to the structural condition of the Ship. The condition of frames and brackets can be ascertained by a visual inspection from the bottom of the cargo holds, using ladders, or, when cargo is loaded from the top of the cargo.

A prudent Shipowner would have heeded the published recommendations of the Classification Societies and carried out regular and frequent inspections.

CONCLUSIONS

Having surveyed the Vessel at the port of discharge and been provided with the documents discussed in this Report, I conclude as follows.

The Vessel was unseaworthy at the time of departure at the load port due to the fact that side shell frames were excessively wasted in Nos 2, 6 and 8 cargo holds.

The Owners were aware of this condition, and had, for the two to three months prior to the casualty, employed supernumerary technicians to carry out partial renewals at sea without notifying, or gaining the approval of, the Classification Society.

The Vessel's original Class Society withdrew Class in 1991, and the Owners' present Classification Society appears to have turned a blind eye to the defects which led to the original Class withdrawal.

Prior to loading the cargo for the last voyage, the Class Society Surveyor attended but did not carry out a full inspection of the hull as was instructed by the Class Head Office.

A prudent Shipowner, knowing that the structure of the Vessel in way of at least three cargo holds was prone to possible imminent failure, would have withdrawn the Vessel from service and carried out a full and detailed inspection of the structure in way of all nine cargo holds and in way of the ballast tanks. A specification would then have been drawn and the economics of repairs would have been assessed.

Summarising, it is the view of the Undersigned that the Vessel was clearly unseaworthy with the knowledge of both Owners and the Classification Society, at the commencement of the voyage and this unseaworthiness was the sole cause of the loss. It is also noteworthy that subsequent actions by the Owners almost resulted in the total loss of ship and cargo."

AWARDS

152 In the case of the "BULK KARRIER", the tribunal found for the charterers, concluding that the vessel was unseaworthy with the knowledge of owners when the cargo was loaded.

153 As an example of the reasoning behind an arbitration award, and the detail which has to be considered by the tribunal, I have set out below the reasons behind the award in a small case involving a charter party dispute relating to bunkers and consumption. For reasons of anonymity, the names of the vessel, ports and experts involved have been deleted.

1. The Vessel was fixed by her Owners on a "Shelltime 3" Form of Charter Party to the Charterers, who, in turn, Sub-Chartered her to the Oil Refining Company for seven consecutive voyages, on each of which she loaded residual fuel oil in the Arabian Gulf and discharged it in the Red Sea. After each laden voyage the Vessel returned in ballast to the load port for the next cargo, cleaning *en route* only sufficient cargo tanks as were necessary to contain the minimum safe quantity of clean ballast water which could be discharged overboard on arrival alongside the loading berth.
2. This Arbitration arose as a result of several claims made by Owners for bonuses due to them under Clause 24 of the Charter Party, the Owners claiming that the Vessel had performed better than warranted in the Charter Party during the course of the charter period. Charterers initially admitted most of the Owners' claims but counter-claimed against them for excessive consumption of fuel used for tank cleaning.
3. At the commencement of the Arbitration Owners decided not to pursue the major item in their claim, covering underconsumption of intermediate fuel oil under Clause 24, which reduced their claims to a total of $39,664.18. Charterers had previously accepted these claims in principle, subject to a minor complaint concerning the mathematics of the claim for underconsumption of diesel oil. Charterers' revised calculations produced an admitted claim against them of $38,292.81 and Owners in turn accepted this figure during opening submissions at the start of the hearing.
4. The Arbitration was therefore entirely concerned with the Charterers' Counterclaim which was basically for overconsumption of fuel oil under Clause 24, overconsumption of fuel oil for tank cleaning purposes during ballast passages and wrongful consumption of fuel oil for the purpose of heating cargo in the absence of any instructions from Charterers to do so.
5. Clause 24 of the Charter Party provided, *inter alia*, for financial compensation to be paid to Charterers in the event that the daily consumption of intermediate fuel oil at sea exceeded 62 long tons *per* day for all purposes except cargo heating, tank cleaning and pumping. Compensation under the terms of this clause was intended to reimburse Charterers for the cost of extra bunkers consumed, calculated by reference to the Texaco posted price at the load port. Both Owners and Charterers agreed that, for the purposes of any calculation to be made for the charter period, Texaco posted price of intermediate fuel oil at the load port could be taken as $183.36 *per* metric tonne.
6. Both Mr X on behalf of Charterers and Mr Y on behalf of Owners had difficulty in establishing exactly how much fuel was used during the charter period. It was agreed by both that the log book abstracts which had originally been produced by Owners to Charterers were false, at least in so far as the second half of the charter was concerned. Mr X went even further and alleged that the abstracts were inaccurate for all voyages except for the first laden passage, and suggested that even the scrap engine log books were a fabrication. These were admitted by Mr Y to be incomplete in that they contained no proper record of daily fuel consumption. He agreed that such a proper daily record was essential for the efficient operation of any ship but that none had been produced by the owners. However he believed that the scrap engine log books were an accurate record of that information which they did contain.

7. Both Mr X and Mr Y advanced methods of obtaining the daily fuel consumption of the main engine based upon readings of the fuel oil flow meter recorded in the scrap log book. Both these methods were admitted to be inaccurate to some degree because, despite repeated requests, Owners had failed to provide the flow meter calibrations which both Experts agreed were necessary in order to make a meaningful assessment of the readings. In the end we concluded that neither method was satisfactory without these calibrations.
8. A further method of assessing main engine fuel consumption was put forward by Mr Y in which the total quantity of fuel passing through the boiler fuel tank was subtracted from the total quantity of fuel supplied to the ship to leave the fuel consumed in the main engine. This method relied upon establishing accurately the total fuel consumption for all purposes and the total fuel consumption in the boiler and, although initially the basic data for calculating these quantities appeared to have been agreed, differences appeared between the experts at a later stage.
9. Both experts agreed that the total quantity of fuel on board when the Vessel was delivered into the charter was 1,055.63 metric tonnes. They also both agreed that the quantity of bunkers delivered to the Vessel during the course of the charter was 8,247.65 metric tonnes but there was some disagreement as to the quantity remaining on board at the end of the charter, which Owners, of course, were obliged to buy back from Charterers at Texaco posted price at the load port (Clause 14). The Master had certified that this quantity was no more than 412 metric tonnes but this was a unilateral declaration and was disputed by both Experts.
10. Mr Y contended for something more than 412 tons ROB on redelivery and Mr X for less. The only contemporaneous evidence put before us was the Off Hire Certificate signed by the Master showing that 412 tons remained on board. Since this was no doubt the figure used when the final hire statement was agreed, this was the quantity for which the Owners had to account to Charterers. We therefore decided to use this figure since to use another figure would require an adjustment to be made to the final hire statement which would cancel out any credit either party had obtained as a result of our having chosen a different figure. An overall consumption for the period of the charter of 8,891.28 m.t. for all purposes is thus provided.
11. Both Experts agreed that the log books showed that a total quantity of about 2,565 metric tonnes of fuel were transferred to the boiler fuel tank. Their respective figures were only three tonnes apart and we rounded both their individual quantities to this intermediate figure. Mr X suggested that the scrap log books might not be correct and that quantities of fuel recorded in them as having been transferred to the boiler fuel tank had subsequently been transferred into the main engine fuel system *via* the fuel oil drain tank. We were not impressed with this suggestion. We found that the scrap log books had the appearance of genuine log books, despite their cleanliness. The Vessel was constructed so that she could be operated with the machinery spaces unmanned for part or all of each day and, although not being operated in this way during the charter period, it is likely that most of the instrumentation was still working. It is therefore likely that the scrap engine log book was written up in the engine control room, a clean, air conditioned compartment, from readings taken from remote reading instruments in the control room. It would have been relatively easy in these circumstances to keep the log book clean. We were finally convinced by the argument put forward by Mr Y that, if the scrap log books had been falsified it is likely they would have been compiled so as to confirm the log abstracts, not contradict them.
12. If the boiler consumption of 2,565 metric tonnes is deducted from the overall consumption of 8,891.28 m.t. a quantity of 6,326.28 metric tonnes of fuel oil is produced which is the quantity which would have been consumed in the main engine during the period of the charter. Both Experts agreed that the maximum consumption permitted under Clause 24 of the Charter Party was 6,285.6 m.t. so that there was clearly an overconsumption of 40.68 m.t. in the main engine during the Charter.
13. However, Clause 24 specified the maximum fuel consumption for all purposes except cargo heating, tank cleaning and pumping. We deal with the exclusions later, but it is clear that fuel was used in the boiler during loaded passage Nos. 3, 5, 6 and 7 amounting to 52 tonnes for which Owners gave no explanation. This fuel could clearly not have

been consumed for tank cleaning or pumping during a laden passage and Charterers gave no orders to heat cargo at any time during the Charter. We therefore consider this amount to be an overconsumption of fuel oil within the terms of Clause 24.

14. We therefore found that the total overconsumption at sea for all purposes other than cargo heating, tank cleaning or pumping was excessive by an amount of 92.88 metric tonnes which, at the agreed Texaco Posted price at the load port of $183.36 *per* metric tonne, is equivalent to $17,030.48 and we therefore awarded Charterers this sum.

15. Turning now to fuel used for tank cleaning, there was considerable disagreement between the experts about how much fuel should have been used for tank cleaning on each voyage. Basically, they were agreed about the likely consumption of fuel *per* hour during tank cleaning operations and the difference between them lay in how many hours the operation should have taken on each voyage.

16. Both experts agreed that only one centre tank and two wing tanks should have needed cleaning ready for clean ballast which could be discharged into the sea when the Vessel arrived at her loading berth at the load port. Mr X argued that proper cleanliness could have been achieved in 18 hours of cleaning, followed by changing ballast and line washing, and calculated that this would have required a total consumption *per* voyage of 49.78 tonnes of fuel. However, he conceded in cross-examination that if the cleaning time was extended to 22 hours, as put forward by Owners in a telex dated 1 July 1983, he would not have considered this to be unreasonable.

17. Mr Y considered that, in order to properly clean one centre tank and two wing tanks so as to avoid any risk of oil pollution at the loading port when the clean ballast water in them was discharged overboard, a period of about 30 hours of tank washing would be required, followed by changing ballast, slop transfer and line washing. He calculated that a fuel consumption of 78.9 tonnes' power operation would be required but also took the view that the amount of cleaning required might vary with the condition of the tanks on each voyage and that the final responsibility for ensuring that there was no oil pollution at the loading port rested with those on board.

18. The Vessel was trading only between Port A and Port B, carrying intermediate fuel oil. On most occasions that intermediate fuel oil bunkers were supplied by the Sub-Charterers, they were drawn from the Vessel's own cargo tanks and pumped into her bunker tanks. It was agreed by both Experts that the average density of fuel supplied to the ship during the Charter was 0.95 and it is therefore reasonable to assume, as Mr X did, that the cargoes carried were good quality intermediate fuel oil. The laden voyages were of no more than about six days' duration and the longest period that the Vessel spent discharging at Port B was three weeks. There was no evidence that any of the cargoes was a "rogue" cargo which might have resulted in heavier deposits of sludge settling in the tank bottoms and which would have required more extensive cleaning than usual. We therefore concluded that the quality of fuel used for tank cleaning should have been reasonably constant for each voyage during the Charter, and should not have varied by as much as was recorded in the scrap engine room log book.

19. Both Mr X and Mr Y abstracted from the scrap engine room log books the actual boiler consumption for tank cleaning purposes during each of the ballast voyages. The figures put forward by Mr Y were generally lower than those of Mr X and the differences were thought to be due to differences in apportionment of fuel between port consumption and consumption at sea. The overall difference was only 19.5 tons during the whole of the charter period and we think that the true consumption probably lies somewhere between these two figures which were less than 3 per cent apart. We have therefore taken a figure of 677 tonnes as the overall consumption for tank cleaning purposes throughout the period of the Charter.

20. Only about 70 tonnes of fuel were used for tank cleaning and transfer of ballast on voyage No. 6 and, for the reasons given above, we can see no reason why any more should have been used on other voyages. In particular, on each of voyages 4 and 5, well over 100 tonnes were used for tank cleaning and no evidence was adduced by Owners to show why this should have been so. We therefore concluded that Owners were

cleaning more tanks than were necessary on some of the voyages, probably for their own reasons of maintenance.

21. We therefore decided that fuel consumption for tank cleaning and pumping purposes during ballast voyages performed during the period of the Charter should not have exceeded this figure of 70 tonnes on each voyage, giving an overall consumption for the whole of the charter period of 490 tonnes. We therefore decided that there had been an overconsumption of fuel oil for tank cleaning of 187 tonnes and that this fuel had been used for Owners' purposes.

22. Since all fuel was paid for by the Sub-Charterers, the Respondents had suffered no loss and they only asked for a declaration that they were entitled to an indemnity for liability to Sub-Charterers in the event that a claim was made against them. We therefore concluded that they were entitled to the declaration which they sought.

23. Finally, we deal with fuel used for cargo heating. Once again, this was a specific area of fuel consumption which was excluded from the warranty in Clause 24. Once again Charterers asked only for a declaration that they were entitled to an indemnity for liability for any claim which Sub-Charterers might make against them.

24. Cargo heating was performed only once, on the first laden passage performed under the Charter. Boiler fuel consumption during this voyage was 89 tonnes according to the engine scrap log book and this was all used for heating cargo.

25. Charterers contended that it was not necessary to heat this cargo and that no orders were given to the Master for it to be heated. They claimed that, in the absence of specific instructions to heat, the Master should either not have heated or should have requested specific heating instructions from Charterers. They pointed to the fact that heating did not commence until 25 January, some two days after the Vessel sailed from Port A, so that there was plenty of time for instructions to be obtained.

26. Owners were unable to produce any written instructions to the Master that cargo should have been heated on this particular voyage. Both parties agreed that no instructions had been carried out. Owners suggested that as the Charter contained a warranty that the ship was to be capable at all times, of heating cargo to 135°F, in the absence of specific instructions to the contrary it was reasonable for the Master to assume that heating was required.

27. We were not impressed with this argument. We think that if the Master had been in any doubt as to whether or not heating of the cargo was required by Charterers, he should have applied to them for definite instructions. We therefore decided that the heating of the cargo and the use for this purpose of 89 tonnes of bunkers was unreasonable.

28. We therefore made the declaration that Charterers were entitled to an indemnity in respect of any claim which their Sub-Charterers might make against them for consumption of 89 tonnes of fuel for unwarranted heating of cargo during voyage No. 1."

Ron Vince *completed an Engineering Apprenticeship and Technical College Education to Higher National Certificate level, and went to sea with Blue Star Line 1954. In 1959 he was promoted to Chief Engineer at the age of 26 and became an Assistant Superintendent with the Company in 1964. He joined consultants Casebourne and Turner in 1968 and subsequently, after two years with Verolme Cork Shipyard as a Repair Manager, spent four years (1972–1976) running the Casebourne Leach Abel office in Lisbon, during which time he was involved, generally on behalf of underwriters, in many massive structural ship repairs following explosions, groundings or collisions. After a short period in the Arabian Gulf, he returned to the UK in 1977 and from that date up to the present time has been involved in upwards of 220 cases which have either progressed to litigation or have settled immediately prior to commencement of litigation. In 1982 he joined Edon Liddiard, and his present consultancy Edon Liddiard Vince was formed in 1984.*

He has provided expert evidence on matters concerning all aspects of ships' hull and machinery litigation, and damage to refrigerated cargo.

CHAPTER 7

THE EXPERT WITNESS IN RENT REVIEW DISPUTE CASES

Lesley Webber and Peter Wainwright

001 Where commercial property is let by landlords to tenants for long periods at fixed rents there is a risk that the rent may fail to keep pace with current property values or with the current value of money.

002 In England unlike other parts of Europe, landlords and tenants have shown a marked reluctance to resolve this problem by linking rents to price indices, and turnover-related rents have found favour only in certain specialist fields, for example, licensed premises. The preference has been for upwards only rent reviews to open market value with some variations on this theme.

003 Rent reviews are often thought of as a relatively modern phenomenon: a creature of the period of inflation which beset England in the 1960s, 1970s and 1980s. In fact rent reviews have been found in legal documents for hundreds of years. To take just one example, leases of ecclesiastical property might contain 50-year or 100-year reviews tied to the open market price of corn, wheat or barley. So, in 1882, Lord Jessel MR was able to say without fear of contradiction: "We are all of us familiar with variable rents; I have seen a vast number of them myself" ((1882) 21 CRD 442 at 455).

004 It is, however, fair to say that leases of commercial property in the early part of the twentieth century tended to be at rents which were fixed throughout the term and were not subject to review.

005 The Landlord and Tenant Act 1954 was a milestone in English commercial property law, giving business tenants the right to extend their leases from the date on which they would contractually have expired for periods of up to 14 years, provided that the tenant complied with certain procedural requirements and provided that the landlord could not establish one of the limited grounds of objection, for example, an intention to redevelop.

006 The Act made no reference to rent review, but simply required the provisions of the new lease to have regard to those of the old. However, the case of *Re 88 High Road, Kilburn* ([1959] 1 WLR 279) saw a rent review clause included in a tenancy granted under the Act, and in 1969 the Act itself was amended so that the terms of the tenancy may include provision for varying the rent (see Landlord and Tenant Act 1954, s.34(3) which was added by the Law of Property Act 1969).

007 The modern form of rent review clause dates from, and achieved precedent status during, the 1960s and the interval between reviews has reduced since then from 14 through seven to what might reasonably be regarded as the industry standard of five years. Three-year intervals have been adopted in certain specialised sectors but have not found favour generally.

008 Although the general purpose of a rent review clause has been described by the courts as: "to keep the rent in line with current property values having regard to the current value of money" (per Sir Nicolas Browne-Wilkinson V-C in *British Gas Corporation* v. *Universities Superannuation Scheme* [1986] 1 WLR 398), the standard form of review clause remains upward only, that is, the landlord will still be entitled to the rent payable immediately prior to review even if the open market rent established at review is less and the property is therefore over-rented by comparison with the then current property values. During the course of the recession of the late 1980s and early 1990s there was therefore a marked falling off in rent reviews, the right to review either not being exercised or the reviews being settled at nil increases.

009 The standard review clause is therefore intended to enable the landlord to benefit from increases in open market property values and to compensate him for any falls in the value of money over a long term and not to bring the rent into line with open market values over that period.

010 With recession there also came a shortening of the length of new leases being granted. What had become known as the 25-year institutional lease with its five-year review pattern, rapidly reduced to ten-year or even shorter lease terms, sometimes to include break clauses in the tenant's favour linked with any rent reviews. Break clauses were generally seen by landlords as preferable to allowing for the possibility of a downward review on the basis that the tenant might choose not to break, notwithstanding the likelihood that he would do so if the property became over-rented.

WHAT MAKES RENT REVIEW DIFFERENT?

011 The feature of rent review which gives it its unique flavour from the point of view of dispute resolution in general and expert evidence in particular is that the standard review clause is invariably founded on a hypothesis. That hypothesis usually requires an assumption of a hypothetical letting of the property in the open market on the rent review date. In keeping with the courts' analysis of the purpose of a rent review clause the courts have held that it would be "wayward to impute to the parties an intention that the landlord should get a rent which was additionally inflated by a factor which has no reference either to changes in the value of money or in the value of the property but is referable to a factor which has no existence as between the actual landlord and the actual tenant" (*British Gas* v. *Universities Superannuation Scheme* [1986] 1 WLR 398).

012 This has become known, by the shorthand of the "presumption of reality", that is, that in the absence of clear words to the contrary there should be valued on review the interest which the tenant actually has in the circumstances prevailing at the review date.

013 However, in order to avoid the application of discounts or uplifts for sitting tenants, rent review clauses contain a number of assumptions and disregards which are to be applied when assessing open market value, the most usual being: vacant possession, a willing landlord and a willing tenant, a disregard of tenant's goodwill and occupation and of tenant's improvements. The more sophisticated the lease (and the more money involved) the more complex the hypothesis which may even extend to conjuring an entirely hypothetical building or location from the parties' negotiations to form the basis for review.

014 The effect, intended or unintended, of those assumptions which extend beyond matters necessary to achieve a genuine open market comparison, is to allow an increase in rent over and above what would have been obtained in the market or to reduce an increase which would otherwise have been obtained. The question of whether the wording used is sufficiently clear to overcome the presumption of reality and achieve such a result has exercised surveyors, lawyers and courts in a plethora of cases, the best known of these to date being the so-called "Headline Rent" cases (*Co-operative Wholesale Society* v. *National Westminster Bank*; *Scottish Amicable Life Assurance Society* v. *Middleton Potts & Co*; *Broadgate Square plc* v. *Lehman Brothers Ltd*; and *Prudential Nominees Ltd* v. *Greenham Trading Ltd*, together reported at [1995] 1 EGLR 97).

015 In rent review, open market value is normally assessed by reference to "comparables", that is lettings or other transactions in similar properties in similar locations as near to the review date as possible.

016 Adjustments are made to the rentals derived from the comparable evidence so that, so far as possible, like is being compared with like. During the recession, lettings in the open market were often achieved by means of incentives such as rent free periods or reverse premiums. The rent which the tenant who benefited from such incentives would pay would be expected to be higher because of those benefits. Rent review clauses require an assessment of the rent payable from the start of the relevant review period, without incentives, sometimes referred to as a "Day 1" rent. (In the absence of express direction in the rent review clause, an arbitrator is not entitled to award incentives or alternative structures for payment of the reviewed rent although these may be agreed between the parties.) The surveying approach is, therefore, to adjust the incentive-influenced comparable rents back to the rent which would have been paid without these benefits.

017 In the Headline Rent cases, four different sets of wording were argued to require the reviewed rent to be at the level of the unadjusted comparable rents. Only one set of wording (in *Broadgate Square plc* v. *Lehman Brothers Ltd* [1995] 1 EGLR 97) was held to achieve that result. The outcome was that the actual tenant in that case found itself paying a rent *per annum* some £1.75 million in excess of the open market rent. It is therefore perhaps unsurprising that landlords and tenants alike have looked to the wording of their rent review clauses to secure rental growth or restriction which would not necessarily otherwise be supported by rental values.

018 The formula adopted in the lease will cover all future reviews under that lease and its impact may differ substantially depending on the market conditions pertaining at each review date. By the later reviews in a lease term, the parties to the lease may have changed, possibly several times, as the freehold is sold and leasehold is assigned. The inevitable failure of the parties successfully to foresee the future over, say a 25-year term underlies much of the litigation on the interpretation of rent review clauses over the last three decades.

DISPUTE RESOLUTION

019 Some review clauses provide for the landlord to choose at the time the dispute arises which method he wishes to adopt. The essential differences between the two alternatives are summarised in the *Handbook of Arbitration Practice* (3rd ed, Bernstein, Tackaberry, Marriott and Wood).

020 By convention, the resolution of rent review disputes is dealt with either by arbitration or by independent expert determination. The choice between the two is usually made at the time the lease is drafted, although some review clauses provide for the landlord to choose which method he prefers at the time of each review. In the case of arbitration, the parties are able, under section 5 of the Arbitration Act 1996, to cover by agreement in the lease, how they wish any of the non-mandatory matters in that Act (other than liability for costs) to be dealt with in relation to their future rent review disputes.

021 As the lawyers who draft leases are rarely the same as those who deal with disputes under them, and indeed many rent review disputes are dealt with solely by surveyors without any need for legal involvement, such agreements are rare and agreements as to the procedure and evidence for the arbitration are reached, if at all, once the dispute has arisen.

022 The difference between the two forms of dispute resolution have acquired a special significance in rent review: expert determination being regarded as an investigative process, albeit conventionally allowing for some of the trappings of arbitration, such as directions and submissions, and arbitration requiring a decision on the evidence put before the arbitrator.

023 This has led to a view amongst rent review arbitrators that, whilst the independent expert is required to determine the "right rent", an arbitrator is required to award a rent which he knows to be "wrong" if an analysis of the evidence put before him leads inexorably to that conclusion.

024 The efforts of rent review arbitrators to avoid being driven to an award which they believed to be wrong can be seen in the reported cases of misconduct (under the pre-1996 law) on the grounds that the arbitrator has exceeded his remit, for example, by carrying on his own pedestrian counts (*Top Shop Estate* v. *Danino* [1985] 1 EGLR 9) or by applying his own valuation method (*Unit 4 Cinemas* v. *Tosara Investment* [1995] IRLR 243).

025 It is to be doubted whether arbitrators were as a matter of law prevented from taking their own steps to ascertain the true open market value prior to the Arbitration Act 1996; the misconduct in question arose from the unfairness inherent in not giving the parties an opportunity to comment on the approach the arbitrator intended to take and the information on which he intended to rely. However, the point has been clarified by the 1996 Act which permits the arbitrator (unless the parties agree otherwise) to take the initiative in ascertaining facts and law, provided always that he complies with his general duty under section 33.

026 Similarly doubts have been expressed by the courts as to the extent, if any, to which an expert must make his own inquiries for evidence when he has been provided with experts' submissions from both parties (*Wallshire* v. *Aarons* [1989] 1 EGLR 147 and *Zubaida* v. *Hargreaves* [1995] 09 EG 320(CA)) the conclusion being that he need only do so to the extent that a reasonable independent expert would feel it necessary to extend his search.

027 The effect has been to blur the sharp edges which the two alternatives had acquired in a rent review context, and thus has been compounded by doubts as to the finality of expert rent review determinations on legal issues (*National Grid* v. *M25 Group* [1999] 08 EG 169) and by the RICS Practice Statement for Surveyors Acting as Expert Witnesses (which is under review at the time of writing) which sets out the duties and responsibilities of such surveyors in the light of the decision of Cresswell J in *National Compania Naviera SA* v. *Prudential Assurance Co (The Ikarian Reefer)* ([1993] 37 EG 158) and provides that they apply to oral or written expert evidence which may be relied upon by courts, arbitrators or independent experts.

THE EXPERT WITNESS IN RENT REVIEW

028 A typical rent review arbitration will involve one witness of fact and one expert witness on each side.

029 Witness of fact and expert witness will generally be one and the same: the relevant party's retained surveyor. Each surveyor will produce one submission, in the form of a report covering the facts of the subject building, the provisions of the lease, the comparable evidence and his opinion of the state of the market at the relevant date together with an analysis of its application to the subject premises, and his rental valuation. Commonly these reports will be exchanged within four to six weeks with counter submissions being exchanged within a shorter period thereafter.

030 Hearings are rare and most cases settle before an award is reached. Similar procedures tend to be followed in independent expert determinations as a means of formalising the receipt of information from the parties by the independent expert.

031 In more complex rent review arbitrations, this procedure may be more drawn out, and interrupted by the resolution of legal issues usually concerning the interpretation of the lease, without which the arbitrator, and indeed the expert witnesses may be unable to reach any sensible valuation.

032 Such cases are sometimes accompanied by hearings and legal representation. The decision in *National Grid* v. *M25 Group* ([1999] 08 EG 169) to the effect that the interpretation of the assumptions and disregards in the rent review provisions of the lease in question were not within the exclusive remit of the independent expert and should be construed by the courts, indicates that such complications are not the sole preserve of arbitration.

033 In rent review, expert evidence is mainly required in relation to the state of the market for the relevant type of property at the rent review date, although from time to time expert evidence may also be required on particular aspects of the property which affect its value, for example, high maintenance costs in relation to the particular air conditioning system which do not apply to the comparables.

034 Where there are few provable facts, for example, during phases of the economic cycle where there is very little transactional evidence, the comparative depth of experience of the experts may itself become an issue. Where the market for the property is heavily dependent on its location, the arbitrator may well prefer the evidence of a surveyor who is also active in the letting of property in that area on matters of opinion about that market.

035 It follows that in rent review it is not uncommon for the most persuasive expert to be someone who has not given evidence before, but who is a letting agent involved in dealings with the specific type of property in that area on a day-to-day basis.

036 However, where there is sufficient factual evidence, an expert witness may not need to be directly involved in the local market but may be able to impress the arbitrator with the quality of his research and analysis.

037 For substantial properties, where good quality locational evidence is needed, but this also needs to be analysed in a broader, for example, regional, context, two experts, one from the agency side and the other a professional valuation expert, may be called upon.

THE VALUATION EVIDENCE

038 In *English Exporters* v. *Eldonwall* [1973] Ch 415 the court held that an expert valuation witness is entitled to:

- state his opinion of value based on his general experience (which will have been built up from his direct and indirect information obtained in the market);
- state as facts the details of transactions in which he was personally involved;
- support his opinion of value by referring to and analysing transactions which will be proved by other witnesses or agreed with his opponent.

039 Valuation is recognised by the courts as depending a great deal on experience or "feel". In *Abbey National Mortgages plc* v. *Key Surveyors* [1995] EGCS 79, the assistance of a court-appointed valuation expert was justified on the basis that such subjects are more difficult for a non-expert decision-maker and that valuations were "paradigmatic" examples of that category. Similarly, the court in the independent expert negligence case of *Wallshire* v. *Aarons* [1989] 1 EGLR 147 regarded the exercise which a valuer has to undertake as one of reaching a gut feeling and then testing it against the evidence.

040 The basis upon which expert opinion valuation evidence is relevant to the process has been explained by an eminent QC in this field (Kim Lewison QC) who noted that if he were to tell an arbitrator that the government were mismanaging the economy, that would only be evidence of his thought, but if an economist were to say this, it would be evidence that it was true that the government were mismanaging the economy. The lay opinion on this point is worthless, but an economist's opinion might be worth more. The same can be said of an expert valuer's opinion that one location is worth more than another. Although there may be no transactional evidence that this is or is not the case, this does not mean that the valuer's opinion is not evidence.

041 The lack of supporting factual evidence will go to the weight to be attached to that opinion evidence. Even a persuasive expert witness's opinion may be given very little weight if it differs inexplicably from factual evidence so, in *Dover* v. *Sherred* (1997) *The Times*, 5 February, it was held that whilst the judge could not substitute his own opinion for an expert's opinion without justification, however, he was not bound to follow expert opinion if it was unconvincing or if other evidence refuted it.

042 The *Eldonwall* decision was reached before the abolition of the hearsay rule by the Civil Evidence Act 1995. Prior to this legislation, the expert was not allowed to state as facts matters of which he had no direct knowledge, on the grounds that this information would be hearsay. In court and some other forms of arbitration, it was common practice to serve notices under the Civil Evidence Act 1968, to enable hearsay evidence to be introduced. In valuation arbitrations, this procedure was little known and too cumbersome to be adopted generally. The facts relating to the comparable evidence were therefore expected to be strictly proved unless the parties were able to agree them. If the expert witness had not acted in a comparable letting which he wished to put before the arbitrator, he would need to agree the facts with the opposing surveyor or to call as a witness someone who had been directly involved, usually an agency surveyor who had acted for one of the parties to the comparable transaction. Where the comparable evidence was particularly important to the case, the appropriate witness could be the subject of a subpoena (now known as a "witness summons" under the Civil Procedure Rules).

043 The 1995 Act applies to all civil proceedings "to which the strict rules of evidence apply, whether as a matter of law or by agreement of the parties". The issue of whether this should include arbitrations was left to be dealt with under the Arbitration Act 1996, which then, when enacted, made no specific reference to the point. Under the 1996 Act evidential and procedural matters can be agreed by the parties, failing which these are left for the decision of the arbitrator. These matters include whether the strict rules of evidence should apply or not. It is, therefore, not entirely clear how the 1995 Act applies to arbitrations. If the parties agree or the arbitrator decides that the strict rules of evidence will not apply it would appear that neither the 1995 Act nor the hearsay rule have any application. However, on one reading of the inter-relationship between the two pieces of legislation, if the arbitrator were to decide that the strict rules of evidence, including the hearsay rules, would apply, the 1995 Act would abolish the hearsay rule for that purpose substituting a requirement to give "such notice as is reasonable and practicable in the circumstances", and statutory guidelines as to the weight to be attributed to hearsay evidence. (This view is shared by the RICS Guidance Notes for Surveyors acting as Arbitrators and as Independent Experts in Commercial Property Rent Reviews 7th Edition, paras 3.7.4 and 3.7.12, also reproduced in Bernstein & Reynolds *Handbook of Rent Review.*)

044 A consensus of opinion is emerging in rent review that strict proof of comparables can still be required, either by agreement between the parties or at the direction of the arbitrator, and the requirement for notice imposed by the 1995 Act is largely ignored or treated as met by the procedure of serving written representations followed by counter-representations.

045 The possibility of introducing hearsay evidence of comparables is less attractive in rent review than in some other contexts because of the lesser weight it is likely to carry. However, the speed and simplicity of the witness summons as a means of overcoming the reluctance of those directly involved in comparable evidence to supply information has been complicated by the new requirement under the 1996 Act for the arbitrator's leave to be obtained before a witness summons is issued. Since the majority of arbitrations in rent review are quick and relatively inexpensive, the cost of pursuing recalcitrant witnesses may now be disproportionate to the overall costs of the process, and this procedure has lost much of its straightforward effectiveness.

046 It is generally accepted that the best evidence in a rent review arbitration will usually be open market lettings of similar accommodation to the subject property in the same general area provided that the specific terms of the comparable letting can be adjusted to compare with the hypothetical letting terms of the subject property. However, such evidence may be unavailable or too remote from the subject property, for example, because it is much earlier than the review date. Other types of evidence may then acquire a greater importance.

047 By way of broad guidance, the descending order of relevance of the most common types of evidence would look something like this, although the precise battle order is open to considerable debate amongst rent review practitioners:

- Open market lettings
- Negotiated rent reviews
- Negotiated lease renewals
- Rental value derived from reversionary sale
- Independent expert determination
- Arbitration awards
- Lease renewals under the Landlord and Tenant Act 1954 determined by the court.

048 In the absence of open market transactions, or where those transactions are not comparable to an open market letting of the subject premises at the review date, the expert witness may rely on rentals achieved on the rent reviews of comparable properties. In *Land Securities plc* v. *Westminster City Council* ([1992] 44 EG 193) Hoffman J expressed the view that rent review settlements were admissible on the basis that they were some evidence of what a landlord and tenant would agree as a rent for a comparable property although they had to be treated with caution because neither party was free to walk away. Similar considerations may apply to negotiated lease renewals, although the statutory basis for renewal under the Landlord and Tenant Act 1954 differs materially from the open market hypothesis on rent review, adding further cause for caution.

049 Attempts are sometimes made to analyse certain capital transactions so as to produce evidence of rental value. These are, however, likely to be of limited relevance, save where there is a dearth of better evidence or to provide limited support for opinion evidence as to the general state of the market.

050 In the *Land Securities* decision the High Court was asked to consider whether an arbitrator's award of the reviewed rent on a comparable property was admissible evidence in another rent review arbitration. The court concluded that it was not, on the grounds that it was:

(a) hearsay,
(b) the decision of another tribunal which as a matter of public policy was not admissible to prove a fact for another arbitration, and
(c) insufficiently relevant to the question which the rent review clause required to be answered.

The case did not deal with independent expert determinations, but the judgment of Hoffmann LJ in the Court of Appeal in *Zubaida* v. *Hargreaves* [1995] 09 EG 320 indicated that he considered an independent expert determination on a comparable to be equally inadmissible as evidence in a rent review arbitration.

051 As is pointed out in the RICS Guidance Notes (para 3.76) the Civil Evidence Act 1995 disposes of the hearsay rule (save for those arbitrations to which strict rules apply). The notes conclude that an independent expert determination is probably not excluded by the public policy rule concerning other tribunal decisions, but that it is still potentially excluded on the grounds of irrelevance.

052 Section 34(1)(c) of the Arbitration Act 1996 provides that it is for the arbitrator to decide (in the absence of agreement between the parties to the contrary) what rules of evidence will apply to the arbitration including rules relating to admissibility, relevance and weight. The question remains, therefore whether the arbitrator can, in effect, ignore the *Land Securities* decision and direct that arbitrator's awards will be treated as admissible and relevant. This argument is finely balanced between the arbitrator's powers under the 1996 Act to decide all matters of procedure and evidence which have not been agreed between the parties and Hoffmann LJ's view from the *Land Securities* decision that someone else's view of the value of a comparable property on a review is of so little relevance to the other reviews as to be not worth enquiring into.

053 In practice arbitrators who anticipate the introduction of awards or determinations are encouraged by the RICS Guidance Notes to invite the parties' agreement on whether these will or will not be admissible. Should the arbitrator have to decide this for himself and conclude that such decisions should be admissible, the question of the weight which they will carry will remain a matter for him. In the case of arbitrators' awards this weight is likely to be less because of the difficulty of knowing what information was before the arbitrator and what influenced him. The expert witnesses may, therefore, be better advised to seek out the comparable evidence and opinions which persuaded that arbitrator and put similar material before their own tribunal. In the case of independent expert determinations, which are frequently unreasoned, the expert will need to be asked to explain how he has reached his decision. Again the underlying facts on which he relied may be the better evidence.

054 In one particular circumstance it is generally thought that awards and determinations are admissible irrespective of the decison in *Land Securities*. This is where the award or determination had become known to the market at the review date and so formed part of the background material against which a tenant in the open market at that date would formulate his rental bid.

055 There are two other categories of evidence in rent review which the courts have ruled inadmissible on the grounds of irrelevance to the question which the rent review clause requires to be answered and so are similarly open to the question of whether an arbitrator could not rule them to be admissible:

- post review date events: *Industrial Properties (Barton Hill) Ltd* v. *Associated Electrical Industries*, 7 April 1976 (unreported). This category is to be contrasted with post review date comparables which are admissible: *Segama NV* v. *Penny Le Roy Ltd* (1984) 269 EG 322;
- trading accounts. The private trading accounts of the actual tenant have been held not to be admissible unless they would have been made available to hypothetical tenants in the open market. Public accounts are for this reason admissible: *Cornwall Coast* v. *Cardgrange* [1987] 1 EGLR 146.

056 The probability is that post review date events will continue to be treated as irrelevant by arbitrators on the grounds that they would not have influenced the market for the property at the review date, whereas applications for discovery of the tenant's trading accounts may be viewed with greater sympathy, particularly for those types of property where profit-earning capacity is central to rental value and would be difficult to estimate.

OBTAINING AND PROVING EVIDENCE

057 Facts relating to the property which is under review are normally the subject of a statement of agreed facts between the parties. Where there are relatively few comparables, the agreed facts relating to them may also be included. Where on the other hand, the comparable evidence is extensive, details of those comparables may be produced in an agreed schedule which also identifies those aspects which are not agreed.

058 The statement of agreed facts has been held to be a contract between the parties which is intended to be legally binding but to be one which the arbitrator has a discretion to refuse to enforce if (after hearing submissions from the parties) he considers that it would be inequitable to do so, for example, where it becomes clear that part of the agreement is subject to a fundamental factual flaw (*Techno* v. *Allied Dunbar* [1993] 22 EG 109). However, if minded to release the parties, the arbitrator must dispense with the statement of agreed facts as a whole rather than deleting the offending provisions. This is because the agreement will include elements of give and take on both sides and the other parts might have been dealt with differently had the flawed part been excluded.

059 The obtaining of comparable evidence may be made more difficult by confidentiality clauses. In some states in Australia, such clauses have been ruled to be contrary to public policy on the grounds that they distort market intelligence on which letting transactions will be made and valuation evidence given.

060 As a matter of English law, confidentiality is one factor to be taken into account in deciding whether or not to order disclosure and whether or not to set aside a witness summons under section 43 of the 1996 Act. However, this factor will be balanced against the evidential significance of the information sought, and such procedural considerations as whether there are other ways of obtaining the information, such as the arbitrator making his own inquiries.

061 In rent review arbitrations, arbitrators have traditionally been reluctant to make broad disclosure orders, particularly where these will substantially delay the generally swift timetable for written representations. Surveyors should therefore expect to be precise as to the documents they seek. However, wider orders may be obtained where the arbitrator is persuaded that either landlord (or occasionally the tenant) is withholding relevant rental evidence from its other premises which may be damaging to its case.

062 Government concern about certain elements of commercial rent review clauses, including confidentiality, led to the preparation of the Code of Practice for Commercial Property Leases in England and Wales. The government is monitoring and reviewing the effectiveness of the code in improving flexibility and transparency in the market.

063 This provides that "generally ... parties and their advisers should avoid unnecessary secrecy in transactions. This will help the availability of market data". It suggests careful consideration by parties to confidentiality agreements as to how long they should remain confidential, particularly if they are requested to disclose them for use at a rent review.

064 In the context of rent review disputes, the code warns surveyors that:

> "If there is a confidential side agreement, the transaction should only be used as a comparable in exceptional circumstances. Attention should be drawn to the existence of a side agreement, the contents of which cannot be disclosed."

065 This advice can, however, give rise to difficulty when the confidentiality agreement precludes any reference to its existence. Surveyors should exclude from any confidentiality agreement which they sign any requirements to disclose information made of them by a court or arbitrator. Should they not do so, they risk disqualifying themselves from giving evidence on which the confidential transaction might have a bearing.

066 Because solicitors are commonly not involved in rent review arbitration, difficulties may arise for an expert witness in claiming privilege for valuations he has given. Bernstein & Reynolds' *Handbook of Rent Review* refers to the potential vulnerability of the surveyor's initial valuation advice to a landlord client who is deciding whether or not to instigate a review. In practice rent review arbitrators have proved reluctant to allow these areas to be explored, whether by discovery or cross examination, and have preferred to rely on the surveyors' considered representations in the arbitration itself. It remains to be seen whether inquiries of this kind will be received with more sympathy in the light of the RICS Practice Statement and courts' strictures on impartiality.

THE ROLE OF THE EXPERT WITNESS IN RENT REVIEW

067 The majority of rent review arbitrations and independent expert determinations are dealt with without legal advice or advisors. The same expert witness may, therefore (and often does) perform three distinct roles.

068 As negotiator he is entitled, and expected, to be partisan; as advocate his role is one of presentation and persuasion and he is under no obligation to present a balanced case; but as expert witness his duty is to give his honest opinion "uninfluenced by the exigencies of litigation" (*National Compania Naviera SA* v. *Prudential Assurance Company (The Ikarian Reefer)*

[1993] 37 EG 158). Lord Woolf in his Final Report on Access to Justice concluded that most of the problems with expert evidence arise because the expert is initially recruited as part of the team which investigates and advances a party's contentions and then has to change roles and seek to provide the independent evidence which the court is entitled to expect. Experts needed clear guidance that when giving evidence their first duty was to the court and not to their client (see the new Civil Procedure Rules, Rule 35.3).

069 Ronald Bernstein QC, an eminent specialist in rent review as well as in arbitration generally, expressed some sympathy for the practical problems which this created for the expert witnesses, in an article in the *Arbitration Journal* in 1992:

> "It is a human tendency to want to please—to tell the client what he wants to hear, particularly if a great deal turns upon his opinion for the client . . . . Moreover, advising that he has no case may mean talking yourself out of what could be a lucrative case which someone else will take on if you won't. There is no easy solution to this difficulty. But it is by not grasping the nettle at this early stage that you can do maximum damage to your clients . . . . A significant proportion of disastrous cases result from the expert's failure to give a disinterested assessment at the outset."

070 In rent review this difficulty acquires a particular emphasis, because the competing claims which come before the arbitrator are as to what the open market rent for the property should be. It is in the nature of things unlikely that the arbitrator will find for one or other party's submitted figure and he is more likely to consider that the answer lies somewhere between the two. Ronald Bernstein QC has described the rent review process as not one which is likely to lead to customer satisfaction since at best there will be one winner and one loser and at worst there may be two losers.

071 There is a further consideration. Although case law (*Tramountana Armadora SA* v. *Atlantic Shipping Co SA* [1978] 1 Lloyd's Rep 391) requires a *Calderbank* offer (known as a "Part 36" offer under the Civil Procedure Rules) to "beat" the award so far as damages and interest are concerned if it is to have a bearing on costs, some rent review arbitrators apply a fractional or proportionate test to such offers, so that a *Calderbank* offer which is nearer the award may achieve a cost benefit. This approach can be argued to have some merit in valuation cases where there may be no practical difference between the figure awarded and a figure of up to perhaps 10 per cent either side of that figure. However, the possibility of narrowing the gap may encourage "outside edge" rental claims in submissions.

072 Valuation experts have not been immune from court criticism for "descending into the arena": *Wallshire* v. *Aarons* ([1989] 1 EGLR 147). In addition to the risk of being seen to be misguidedly partisan is the still graver risk of being seen to be prepared to say one thing on one side of any particular fence and something quite different from the other side.

073 In the *London & Leeds* v. *Paribas* ([1993] 2 EGLR 149) saga, the arbitration hearing had not long resumed after an issue in relation to fitting out and improvements had been decided by the Court, before the parties returned to the court in *London & Leeds* v. *Paribas No 2* [1995] 2 EG 134.

074 Paribas' expert witness had been the arbitrator in another rent review (*Delta Point*). London & Leeds' expert had then been representing British Telecom (BT) (the landlord). Paribas' expert told Paribas' lawyers that he thought London & Leeds' expert had said something then which was inconsistent with what he was saying now. A subpoena was issued against London & Leeds' expert to obtain his submissions from the *Delta Point* arbitration. A subpoena was also issued against Paribas' expert (as the *Delta Point* arbitrator) which he was of course willing to comply with. London & Leeds' expert applied to have both subpoenas set aside.

075 The court set them aside. Arbitration is a private process and the arbitrator should not have used information obtained from the *Delta Point* arbitration to assist Paribas. There was no evidence of inconsistency other than the arbitrator's improper hint.

076 Paribas did not however give up that easily on the *Delta Point* submissions. They went away and got better evidence from elsewhere of what was in the submissions. *London & Leeds* v. *Paribas No 3* considered a fresh subpoena against BT. BT were willing to provide the submissions, but the court allowed London & Leeds' expert to challenge the subpoena against BT on the grounds of his copyright in his document, and the confidential nature of arbitrations generally "which must be a consideration affecting the decision of an expert witness to testify in them".

077 However, the court rejected the application to set aside this time. They drew the inference that the expert's continued objection to produce the relevant section of his submissions in the *Delta Point* arbitration, even after BT had conceded, made it at least likely that there was an inconsistency. They relied, in particular, on a comment in a letter from the expert to BT: "I believe it wholly unfair for BT to provide a section of my proof to a third party to use against me when I have been loyal to BT and indeed very successful in the *Delta Point* case on their behalf."

078 The court thought it at least likely that the reason for this protest was that examination of the proof would disclose inconsistencies with his evidence in the *London & Leeds* arbitration.

079 The court endorsed the "powerful principle" that expert witnesses should be expected not only to be truthful, but also to resist any tendency to give views which were unduly favourable to those instructing them. The court concluded that:

> "If a witness were to prove to have expressed himself in a materially different sense when acting for different sides that would be a factor which should be brought out in the interests of the individual litigants involved and in the public interest."

080 Given that the court thought there was a real likelihood of such inconsistency the judge went on to conclude that whatever breach of confidentiality might be involved in upholding the subpoena, it should not be allowed to prevent the evidence from being disclosed.

081 Paribas' route would have a further hurdle to overcome under the 1996 Act. Section 43 would now require the consent of the arbitrator before a witness summons could be issued.

THE IN-HOUSE EXPERT WITNESS

082 It is a particular grievance of the corporate entities to be found amongst landlord and tenant consumers of the rent review service that their employed surveyors are not generally considered by arbitrators to have the requisite degree of independence to give credible expert evidence, and it is therefore necessary to retain a surveyor in private practice. For certain specialised industries, this may not merely work unfairly so far as one or both of the parties are concerned, but may deprive the arbitrator of useful opinion evidence to weigh in the balance. Examples include utilities, public houses and motorway services. An experienced surveyor-arbitrator may have little difficulty in separating the elements of such expert evidence which are given from the employer's perspective and those which are a reflection of a witness's long-standing experience in the relevant industry. However, in a highly specialised market, the arbitrator may have more difficulty identifying where that dividing line falls.

083 Where the in-house surveyor is a member of the RICS, it may be possible to improve his credibility by building into his terms of employment with his employer provisions which require compliance with the practice statement and impose internal disciplinary sanctions for non-compliance. Protection for the employee where compliance involves disclosure of confidential information or opinions which are otherwise contrary to the employer's interest can also be provided for.

084 Lord Woolf at a lecture to the Property Litigation Association on the new Civil Procedure Rules in April 1999 suggested that a particular advantage of the new emphasis on the substitution of a court-appointed expert for expert witnesses from each of the parties would be that parties with in-house surveyors could now use those surveyors to prepare their cases and to question the court-appointed expert without need to retain their own private practice surveyor. However, if the court-appointed expert is to consider parties' cases which in turn include or are based on parties' experts' reports, the issue of the credibility of the parties' own experts may still have a part to play in the formulation of the court-appointed expert's opinions. The CPR envisage that pre-action protocols will encourage parties to start by endeavouring to agree a single expert. If this operates to change the culture of the approach to expert evidence in valuation disputes over the long term, the issue of credibility for in-house surveyors may lose its present significance.

085 It might be thought that, in rent review, the process of referring a dispute to an independent expert had similarities with the court-appointed expert system. However, the fact that the RICS Practice Statement expressly applies to representations made to an independent expert in practice reinforces the difficulty of the in-house expert in terms of perceived lack of independence.

THE RICS PRACTICE STATEMENT AND GUIDANCE NOTES

086 In the light of judicial criticism of expert witnesses in cases such as *The Ikarian Reefer* and in the Woolf Report on Access to Justice the RICS has produced a Practice Statement and Guidance Notes for Surveyors acting as Expert Witnesses (Appendix C of this book). These apply "where any chartered surveyor agrees or is required to provide expert evidence, whether oral or in writing, which may be relied upon by any judicial or quasi-judicial body in the United Kingdom". Members of the RICS may depart from the requirements of the practice statement where special circumstances make it inappropriate or impractical to comply fully, but are required to make a declaration in writing giving reasons. A possible area for such declarations would be where the expert witness is subject to a confidentiality clause in relation to a comparable, or is unable to give full evidence of a transaction because the parties to it are themselves bound by confidentiality agreements.

087 The practice statement covers not only evidence to courts and arbitrators, but also to an independent expert (see the definition of "Judicial Body" in para 1.1). Mediation is excluded.

088 The duty of the surveyor is emphasised to be to the court, arbitrator or independent expert concerned and is to be "truthful as to fact, honest as to opinion and complete as to coverage of relevant matters" whether or not it is given on oath. This evidence must be independent, objective and unbiased, whoever is paying for it. The duty does not apply to professional advice to help his client to decide whether to commence or defend proceedings, but where such advice is given in contemplation of proceedings he must advise the client in writing if his advice would fall short of that necessary to enable evidence complying with the practice statement to be given.

089 The practice statement provides that if the surveyor expert witness is also acting as advocate the two roles "must be clearly distinguished and declared to the judicial body and to the opposing party".

090 The Guidance Notes remind surveyors to consider whether undertaking both roles is desirable and cites *Multimedia Productions Ltd* v. *Secretary of State for the Environment* ([1988] EGCS 83), a planning case, in which the court warned that "while there is no rule against someone combining the role of advocate and expert witness ... it is generally speaking undesirable practice. Someone who combines these conflicting roles must not be surprised if ... a court approaches his evidence with a degree of caution".

091 The Guidance Notes suggest that in written submissions, submissions and opinion evidence should be in separate documents or parts of a document and that at a hearing advocacy should be undertaken from a different position in the room from that at which evidence is given. An alternative would be to enlist the services of another member of the surveyor's firm to act as advocate.

THE EFFECT OF THE NEW CIVIL PROCEDURE RULES

092 The precise consequences of the CPR for civil litigation in relation to property disputes remain uncertain. Pre-action conduct will have to be considered by analogy with protocols for other areas of law which do not readily adapt themselves to the different considerations applicable to other fields, until tailor-made versions become available.

093 Similarly the operation of the court-appointed expert system in complex commercial property disputes will need to be considered against some worked examples. Response to reforms of litigation and arbitration procedures has traditionally proved unpredictable as can be seen from experience in relation to witness statement requirements, an entirely laudable reform whose effectiveness was substantially undermined by the way in which practitioners applied the process.

094 The CPR does not of course apply to arbitrations, although it will apply to court proceedings arising out of arbitrations, such as challenges for serious irregularities and appeals on points of law. In this it will not differ from its predecessors, the *White Book* (for the High Court) and the *Green Book* (for the county court). It is interesting to note that there are now two pieces of legislation concerned with dispute resolution, the CPR and the Arbitration Act which have different overriding objectives, and this may have particular implications for those powers and discretions which an arbitrator is required by law to exercise judicially.

095 For example, judicial decisions on costs under the CPR may be affected by that part of the overriding objective which requires the courts to take into account "the need to allot resources to other cases" which has no equivalent in arbitration. Does this mean that the arbitral approach may increasingly differ and be accepted by the courts as entitled to differ from the judicial approach? Similarly the Arbitration Act 1996 has entrenched the principle of party autonomy, under which the parties are entitled by agreement to dictate how they want their arbitration to be conducted. The case-management culture of the CPR entitles the court to override such agreements in the interests of efficiency and cost effectiveness whereas the arbitrator must abide by the parties' agreement or resign.

096 Some aspects of the CPR will be familiar to rent review arbitrators, for example, the mutual right to make *Calderbank* offers, which is standard in rent review, and the full statement of case, rather than pleadings. The influence of other new principles such as that of "ensuring that the parties are on an equal footing" will be a matter of debate.

097 Perhaps the most controversial aspect of the CPR from a rent review perspective will be its approach to expert evidence. Since the rent review arbitrator will, save in the most exceptional of cases, be himself a valuer, the benefits of the court-appointed expert as identified in *Abbey National* v. *Key Surveyors* are less pertinent. Similarly, the parties have the alternatives of independent expert determination, or arbitration on written representations alone, if they wish to avoid the cost and delay of hearing evidence and cross-examination of each sides' expert witnesses.

098 However, on issues which are peripheral to the main valuation arguments and outside the arbitrator's own expertise, for example, whether the air conditioning system of the premises carries a higher maintenance cost than those of the comparables, the arbitrator may wish to use his powers under sections 34 and 37 of the 1996 Act to encourage, or direct, a procedure which involves only one expert on that topic.

099 The rent review arbitrator may also wish to avoid an adversarial contest on legal issues where the legal issue can be identified without extensive legal submissions, for example, whether the hypothetical term is to be the same length as the original term or as the residue of the original term. In such cases the appointment of a legal assessor under section 37 may enable the parties to benefit from the reduced cost of a single legal opinion on that point.

100 Any such initiatives by the arbitrator could, of course, be vetoed by the agreement of the parties and are subject to the arbitrator's duty under section 33 not only to act fairly and reasonably as between the parties, but also to adopt procedures suitable to the circumstances of the particular case. The courts, by contrast, are entitled to refuse to allow the parties to call their own expert evidence and to appoint a court expert instead. In the case of technical assessors and court-appointed experts the role of the parties' own experts will become that of ensuring that the full facts are before the appointee and that his views are questioned and commented on so as to ensure that parties and tribunal have the benefit of the best possible evidence from the appointee. Where the technical assessor or court-appointed expert is a member of the RICS his evidence will, presumably, be subject to the Practice Statement and Guidance Notes.

101 The court's duty to manage cases under the CPR includes "encouraging the parties to use alternative dispute resolution procedures if the court considers that appropriate and facilitating the use of such procedure". In addition to mediation this would cover arbitration or independent expert determination.

102 The PACT initiative devised by the Joint RICS/Law Society Working Party on the Landlord and Tenant Act 1954 provides a framework for such an alternative in the case of disputes over business renewals. The draftsmen of the scheme had to work within the requirements of the 1954 Act which included a statutory requirement for the tenant to apply to the court for a new tenancy within the prescribed time limit, on pain of losing its rights. The scheme documents provide a *Tomlin* Order, staying the court proceedings, and an agreement to arbitrate or obtain an independent expert determination on the matters in dispute. The scheme is being revised by the Working Party draftsmen to bring it into line with the CPR. The format may prove adaptable to other forms of dispute where the parties agree that they would prefer to present the evidence of their own expert witnesses.

103 The Arbitration Act 1996 would enable the parties to agree between them on how they wish the expert evidence to be dealt with, whether there is to be a right to call a hearing, and whether the arbitrator is allowed to make his own inquiries, should they decide to resolve their disputes by arbitration instead of court proceedings.

RECENT DEVELOPMENTS IN THE LAW RELATING TO AN INDEPENDENT EXPERT DETERMINATION

Setting aside

The background

104 In order to challenge the decision of an independent expert itself, rather than to sue the independent expert for negligence, it is necessary to apply to set aside the determination. The relationship between the parties to an independent expert determination and the independent expert is purely contractual. An independent expert determination can be overturned where it is made fraudulently or for some form of improper motive, but what of the rights of the parties where the determination goes wrong, but the independent expert's behaviour is not quite as serious as this?

105 The law has been clear for some years that it is necessary to show that an expert has "departed from his instructions in a material respect" (*Jones* v. *Sherwood Computer Services* [1992] 1 WLR 277) before his decision can be set aside.

106 On points of law, the indication in rent review cases has been that the courts would not interfere to tell the independent expert how to decide these either before or after he had made his determination. However, in *Mercury Communications Limited* v. *Director General of Telecommunications* [1995] CLC 266 the House of Lords was faced with an agreement between BT and Mercury under which either could request the Director General of Telecommunications to determine whether the agreement should be amended. He was empowered to determine the terms necessary to secure payment of "fully allocated costs" taking into account "relevant overheads". The parties disagreed as to the interpretation of those expressions. The House of Lords (perhaps unsurprisingly given the importance of the agreement in question), concluded that the court had jurisdiction to review the determination of the Director General on the basis that if he had incorrectly interpreted those expressions he had not done what he had been asked to do.

107 In the rent review context, this opened up the possibility of arguing that if the independent expert had incorrectly interpreted the rent review clause, it might be said that he had failed to comply with his contractual instructions. However a shipping decision by Lightman J in *British Shipbuilders* v. *VSEL Consortium plc* [1997] 1 Lloyd's Rep 106 had re-emphasised how limited the circumstances in which an independent expert determination can be quashed are. The court summarised the legal position as follows:

> "The experts' jurisdiction and remit are a matter of construction of the contract under which he is appointed.
>
> If the independent expert is given the exclusive remit to determine a particular question, the jurisdiction of the court to determine that question is excluded because as a matter of contract the decision of the expert alone is relevant and any decision of the court is irrelevant. It is in particular irrelevant whether the court would have reached a different conclusion or consider that the expert is wrong because the parties have agreed to abide by the decision of the expert.

If the expert goes outside his remit, for example, by determining a different question from that remitted to him, or fails to comply with any conditions attached to the agreement, the court may intervene and set his decision aside. His decision in these circumstances is not a decision which the parties agreed would bind them and the court would intervene.

The court may set aside a decision of the expert where the agreement so provides if his determination discloses a manifest error.

The court can decide a question as to the rules which the expert is required to apply before he makes his decision, but will only do so in exceptional circumstances. This is because the question would ordinarily be hypothetical, only proving live if, after seeing the decision of the expert, one party considers that the expert got it wrong. To apply to the courts in anticipation of the expert's decision and before it is clear he has got it wrong, is to waste time and money, the saving of which would have been one of the objectives of going to an independent expert in the first place."

Morgan Sindall plc v. Sawston Farms (Cambs) Ltd [1997] 07 EG 135

The facts

108 The facts in the *Morgan Sindall* case were that the independent expert had been appointed to determine the price for the exercise of an option to purchase an industrial estate road. The independent expert reached his determination, which was given without reasons in the sum of £130,000.

109 When the purchaser began steps to complete the purchase, it was discovered that land adjacent to the industrial estate road (known as Deals Grove), which was now in the hands of the purchaser, had in fact had the benefit of a right of way over the road for all purposes. The purchaser refused to complete and applied to have the independent expert's determination set aside. He submitted that had the independent expert known of the existence of the right of way, this would have materially have reduced his valuation of the estate road.

110 The purchaser submitted that the valuer did not do what the contract said he should, because he did not value the interest which the vendor had to sell, namely an interest subject to the right of way for all purposes to the owner of the adjacent land, but something different, namely an interest not subject to such right of way. The vendor submitted that the independent expert had done what he was required to do, namely to value the property as defined in the option agreement. That property was the relevant strip of land subject only to what was specified in the schedule to the option agreement, which did not include a deed of grant of right of way. There was no evidence to suggest that the *valuer* made any mistake; any mistake there might be lay in the formulation by the option agreement of the task which was to be undertaken by the valuer.

The decision

111 In the High Court, the judge agreed with the vendor that the purchaser had failed to establish that the valuer had not made his valuation in accordance with the terms of the option agreement.

112 The judge saw it as "part of the irony of this case" that the purchaser's expert witness had originally made submissions to the independent expert that the existence of any rights of way had no relevance to the question of valuation. The judge was therefore less than impressed with an affidavit from the same expert witness saying that the valuer's decision must necessarily have been affected by the knowledge of the existence of the deed of grant of right of way.

113 The purchaser appealed on the grounds:

- that the independent expert had not done what he was supposed to do, namely to value on an open market basis, because he had valued the estate road as a ransom strip for development of the Deals Grove land and therefore had taken into account a special purchaser for the land in the form of the owner of Deals Grove;
- that the independent expert had not valued the right thing in that he had valued a roadway with limited rights of way over it when the actual roadway had unlimited rights of way over it.

114 The Court of Appeal upheld the independent expert's determination and rejected the appeal.

The reasons

115 The Court of Appeal was not impressed by the ransom strip argument which they regarded as "seeking, by a process of inference, to turn a non-speaking valuation into a reasoned valuation and then to attack the reasons". The court thought the basis argued by the purchaser for drawing their inference was very tenuous:

> "Even if the materials had been more substantial and the process of inference less speculative, the court should, in my view, turn its face against that sort of argument, except in wholly exceptional circumstances. The whole point of instructing a valuer to act as an expert (and not as an arbitrator) is to achieve certainty by a quick and reasonably inexpensive process. Such a valuation is almost invariably a non-speaking valuation with the expert's reasoning and calculations concealed behind the curtain. The court should give no encouragement to any attempt to infer, from ambiguous shadows and murmurs, what is happening behind the curtain."

116 In any event the court was not convinced about "the very sharp distinction" drawn by the purchaser between a limited and an unlimited right of way. Nor did it find RICS practice statements of assistance because their advice was not mandatory for independent expert determinations and because no clear dividing line was drawn between release of "marriage value" which the practice statement allowed a valuer to take into account on an open market valuation, and the extra bid of a special purchaser, which it did not.

117 So far as the second ground was concerned the Court of Appeal was not persuaded that the independent expert had valued the wrong thing. They agreed with the first instance judge that there was nothing to suggest that the valuer had not valued the "property" as defined in the option agreement. Any mistake was as to the attributes of the land being valued, not the identity of the land as to which there was no evidence that the valuer made any mistake.

DIRECTIONS TO INDEPENDENT EXPERTS ON LAW—NATIONAL GRID COMPANY PLC V. M25 GROUP LTD [1999] 08 EG 169

The background

118 It is perhaps unsurprising given the difficulty of challenging an independent expert determination once it has been made, particularly where no reasons have been given, that attempts have been made to obtain decisions from the courts in advance on any disputes as to the legal principles which the expert has to apply. Both parties may agree to seek such a declaration. But what of the position where only one party wishes to intervene?

119 In *Norwich Union Life Insurance Society* v. *P & O Property Holdings Ltd* [1993] 1 EGLR 164 the courts had shown themselves unwilling to give directions to the independent expert as to the answers to any points of law. In the earlier rent review decisions in *Nikko Hotels (UK) Ltd* v. *MEPC plc* [1991] 2 EGLR 103 and *Pontsarn Investments Ltd* v. *Kansallis-Osake-Pankki* [1992] 1 EGLR 148, the courts had concluded that the questions of construction of the leases concerned had to be decided by an independent expert as part of making his decision on the rent. The courts would not therefore intervene.

120 However, legal commentators (notably Jonathan Gaunt QC and Nicholas Cheffings in the *Estates Gazette*) have recently begun to doubt the correctness of the common assumption from these decisions that the courts would not intervene on the legal aspects of a determination, particularly in the light of the *Mercury* and *British Shipbuilders* decisions. That assumption was put to the test in the *National Grid* case.

The facts

121 A piece of land next to the Grand Union Canal in Ealing also adjoined a substantial electricity substation. The land was held by National Grid under a lease for 60 years from 24 June 1964. The original rent was £830 per annum which was increased on review on 23 June 1979 to £5,500. The next review was due on 24 June 1994.

122 An independent expert was appointed to review the rent. The parties' submitted figures were £25,000 in the case of the tenant and £914,925 in the case of the landlord.

123 The tenant applied to the court for a series of declarations:

- that the land was to be valued without any buildings or structures on it;
- what the nature and extent of the demised premises was;
- that any improvement carried out by the CEGB (as distinct from National Grid) was to be disregarded;
- what were the identity and extent of the improvements to be disregarded under the terms of the lease;
- what tenant's fixtures or chattels were to be disregarded (this was abandoned as being a matter of fact not law);
- what access the premises were assumed to have;
- that the National Grid were not to be treated as a potential hypothetical tenant;
- that the hypothetical lease would include a similarly restrictive alienation clause to that in the actual lease.

The decision

124 In the High Court, the tenant's application for declarations was struck out. The judge (whilst expressing considerable sympathy with the tenant's wish to obtain declarations from the court) applied the *British Shipbuilders* decision and decided that on a true construction of the lease the legal issues had been remitted to the expert to determine exclusively of the court: "they are questions of interpretation which the expert has necessarily to undertake along the way to determine the rent. . . . The expert must work out what the premises are; he must work out what the improvements are and when they were made. In order to make these determinations, he must decide for himself, in the light of the representations made to him, on the meaning of the words used". The judge did, however, go on to say that, had he considered that he had any discretion in the matter, he would have made the declarations. It is perhaps therefore unsurprising that the tenant appealed.

125 In the Court of Appeal, the court held that the application for declarations should not be struck out and that the court was entitled to give answers to the legal questions raised.

The reasons

126 The Court of Appeal concluded that the question of whether the court's jurisdiction was excluded was a matter of construction of the particular lease. In this case the lease provided that the parties should endeavour to reach agreement as to the reviewed rent. Failing agreement "the question of whether any and if so what increase ought to be made in the rent payable hereunder as from ... the expiration 30th and 45th year shall be referred to the valuation of a single valuer ...".

127 The court considered that if the clause had stopped there they would have agreed that they had no jurisdiction to entertain the proceedings. However, the lease went on to provide three categories of agreed contractual directions which the valuer should observe in determining the question referred to him:

- that he should value at the review date on an open market basis for the remainder of the terms as between a willing landlord and a willing tenant;
- that he should have regard to the terms of the lease other than those relating to rent;
- that he should disregard the occupation of the lessee, any goodwill attached to the premises and the effect on the rent of any improvement carried out by the lessee otherwise than in pursuance of an obligation to the landlord.

128 The Court of Appeal concluded that issues of construction of the lease were not within the exclusive authority of the expert and they did not become within his exclusive authority simply because he had to reach a conclusion on them in order to make his decision on valuation.

129 The assumptions and disregards were his contractual terms of reference. The limits to the powers conferred on him by the lease had to be ascertained by a process of construction of the lease. The terms of the lease did not confer on the valuer, either expressly or by implication the sole and exclusive power to construe the lease. It was the absence of such limits (the assumptions and disregards) in the *Norwich Union* decision which the Court of Appeal considered set that case apart from the one with which they were dealing.

The consequences

130 The Court of Appeal did not actually make the declarations sought; these could have been referred back to the High Court for a decision, although it is understood that the case has now been settled.

131 It appears that the court considered that it had concurrent jurisdiction over legal issues with the independent expert. The court could therefore give directions before the determination or deal with any application afterwards to set it aside for error of law, although then the parties may fall foul of the *Morgan Sindall* decision if the decision is unreasoned. It is not entirely clear whether an expert's decision which is clear on its face to have dealt with legal issues is a nullity or valid until successfully challenged (although the latter seems likely).

132 The assumptions and disregards which the Court of Appeal regarded as depriving the expert of jurisdiction over legal issues are commonplace in rent review clauses in leases (the *Norwich Union* decision did not concern a rent review clause), therefore lease draftsmen are likely to look at additional wording which makes clear that the independent expert has exclusive jurisdiction over all disputes arising out of the review provisions. Alternatively, with many more restrictive rights of challenge to an arbitrator's award for error of law, parties may turn instead to arbitration.

133 At an earlier stage of proceedings, the tenant, fearful that the independent expert might reach his decision before the Court of Appeal could rule, sought a stay of the determination, which was achieved by consent. In the proceedings for a stay it was made clear by the High Court (and subsequently confirmed by the Court of Appeal) that the courts have an inherent power to stay an independent determination and Pumfrey J also expressed the view that there was an implied term in the lease that the independent expert would not "race" the court whilst it was deciding whether it had jurisdiction and, if it did, what the legal answers were.

134 The effect of these two decisions is that it is likely to be all the more difficult to persuade the courts to overturn an independent expert determination on a rent review unless the expert gives reasons, but it is more likely that the courts will intervene to give the expert directions on points of interpretation before he reaches his decision, unless the lease makes it clear that these are to be left exclusively to the expert. In consequence, independent expert determination risks becoming lengthier, more expensive, and possibly even less final than arbitration.

CONCLUSION

135 The role of the expert witness has been the focus of much attention from the judiciary and the legislature in recent years and may well be revolutionised by the CPR, particularly through the role of the court-appointed expert. In rent review the speed and relative cheapness with which the majority of cases progress through arbitration or independent expert determination, especially where no hearing is involved, together with the valuation expertise of the decision-maker, may attract parties to other forms of property disputes who have previously been discouraged by the complexity of arbitration in other commercial contexts. It will be interesting to see whether the implementation of the CPR leads judicial decision-making to diverge from arbitration and independent expert determination, or whether the similarities between the court-appointed expert and the independent expert or arbitrator with inquisitorial powers may lead to greater convergence with the non-judicial routes in their approach to expert evidence.

Lesley Webber *is a Partner and Head of Property Litigation and Planning at solicitors Beachcroft Wansbroughs. She is an Honorary Member of Arbrix and a Member of the Property Advisory Group to the DETR. She is co-author of the PACT scheme for business tenancy renewals.*

Peter Wainwright *is a Chartered Surveyor, Chairman and Director of Lambert Smith Hampton (Manchester) and former President of the General Practice Division of RICS, Manchester. He specialises in landlord and tenant matters in arbitration and expert determination and as an expert witness.*

CHAPTER 8

INTERLOCUTORY AND HEARING PROBLEMS AND THE EXPERT WITNESS

D Mark Cato

GENERALLY

The facts

001 In a construction arbitration the claimant who is a small builder is representing himself and the respondent (employer) is represented by a solicitor and counsel.

002 At the preliminary meeting when the arbitrator asks the parties about their intention concerning witnesses which they wish to call at the forthcoming hearing the respondent requests consent to call three experts, one of whom is a quantity surveyor.

003 The arbitrator conducting this reference has a quantity surveying background and as a result the claimant objects to the respondent's request and suggests that such an expert is unnecessary in view of the arbitrator's own expertise and as such is wasteful of the parties' costs. He further requests that in the event of the arbitrator deciding to allow the claimant to call that quantity surveyor expert then any costs associated with the calling of this witness be disallowed should the respondent succeed with his counterclaim.

Question

004 In such a situation as this why is it necessary for one party to call a quantity surveying expert to give what seems to amount to technical evidence when the arbitrator is probably better qualified to deal with these technical issues from his own practical experience?

Course of action

005 This question was put to me by my pupil, Thomasina. I reminded her that under English law and certainly up to the enactment of the Arbitration Act 1996 (AA '96) the adversarial convention requires that each party can put its case as it sees fit—it is their prerogative.

006 I explained that it was first of all necessary to distinguish between witnesses of fact and witnesses of opinion. As she was well aware arbitrators are chosen for their expertise in the subject matter of the dispute.

007 No doubt she would also remember that the arbitrator can only normally determine the issues on the basis of the evidence which is adduced before him (leaving aside for the moment the possibility of the parties agreeing to vest the arbitrator with inquisitorial power under s.34(2)(g), AA '96). It is not for him to make one party's, or the other's, case for them. Thus, it is necessary for someone to put the issues in the context of the dispute to the arbitrator no matter what knowledge the arbitrator may have himself. This principle was well illustrated by the comments of Hoffman J in the case of *Land Securities* v. *City of Westminster* [1993] 1 WLR 286, where the issue was whether an arbitrator in a rent review case should allow as evidence of a comparable rent the decision in another case of another arbitrator.

008 The arbitrator in the other case may, by reason of his expertise, have known about matters which cast doubts upon points which went unchallenged in the arbitration. If he had been acting as an expert he would have been able to take this knowledge into account. As an arbitrator he would not. His position, in Hoffman J's judgment, was no different from that of a judge determining the rent of a new lease of premises under the Landlord and Tenant Act 1954. The admissibility of his judgment as evidence of value of the premises in proceedings between different parties could not depend upon whether he happened to have expertise in valuation.

009 Although legal advocates are generally very competent at dealing with technical issues, it is more effective to engage an independent third party to analyse those issues and to give his "unbiased" opinion on them. These independents are, in effect, there to assist the tribunal and through the medium of their reports and cross-examination, air the pros and cons of the various issues in dispute.

010 This led us to a discussion about the role of experts generally beyond the narrow confines of such specialist disciplines as construction and rent review disputes.

011 I commended Thomasina to read a paper written by Michael Reynolds, one of our leading authors on the subject. He had prepared this paper for the MSc students engaged on the Construction Law Course at King's College. However, in doing so I reminded her of the recent implementation of the new Civil Procedure Rules and suggested that we looked at the historic position first covering the principal duties, obligations and liability of an expert and then considered the Civil Procedure Rules, at the end.

012 From this short paper Thomasina gleaned the following:

> "The Concise Oxford Dictionary defines an expert as a person having special skill or knowledge. One of the earliest references to expert evidence being admitted was in *Buckley* v. *Rice-Thomas* (1554) 75 ER 182, which was confirmed by Lord Mansfield's judgment in *Foulkes* v. *Chadd* (1782) 99 ER 589, where he recognised that the courts would admit 'the opinion of scientific men upon proven facts'."

013 Mr Reynolds identifies the functions of experts as follows:

> "*Functions*
> (i) To advise the client on technical aspects of a case that may be contentious.
> (ii) To report to the client his conclusions and advice thereon.
> (iii) To assist the client in the conduct of litigation or arbitration both with preliminary reports, incidental reports and a final report for the purposes of exchange of expert opinion evidence."

014 Although Mr Reynolds highlights the expert's function from the client's viewpoint the whole point is that the expert is there to help the tribunal to understand complex or unfamiliar technical concepts of the case.

015 In addition there may be a host of other minor functions that the expert has to perform for counsel/solicitors, most of which are incapable of precise definition. (See Reynolds & King: *The Expert Witness and His Evidence*, BSP Oxford 1992.)

Credibility

016 In his book Mr Reynolds deals with the issue of credibility. He quoted Lord MacMillan in a lecture entitled "Law and Other Things":

> "I am not certain that any scientific man ought ever to become partisan of one side. He may be the partisan of an opinion but ought never to accept a retainer to advocate a particular view merely because it is the view which is in the interests of the party who has retained him to maintain. To do so is to prostitute science and practise a fraud on the administration of justice. The true role of the expert witness is to offer the court the best assistance it can by getting at the truth. It is in some form of consultative capacity that the abilities of professional men are best utilised in the public service."

017 In an article from the *New Zealand Law Journal*, 8 March 1888, Sir George Jessel MR expressed the public's general and natural suspicion of experts who were paid by one side:

> "having much distrust of expert evidence for several reasons ... the person knows he cannot be indicted for perjury who have not the authority of legal sanction .... Evidence of this kind is evidence of persons who sometimes live by business, but in all cases are remunerated for their evidence."

018 Mr Reynolds pointed out that in the English adversarial system the expert is employed by one side; he is paid by one side; he is called by one side; he is instructed by one side; receives the evidence from one side until discovery, and is, to all intents and purposes, the paid agent of one side.

019 Mr Reynolds suggests that this adversarial dilemma may possibly be reviewed in the light of practices in France, Germany and Scotland where the court appoints an expert witness. This has been given some recent attention by Lord Woolf and it may be appropriate in certain cases to appoint an expert in litigation.

020 Order 40 of the Rules of the Supreme Court provided a basis for a court-appointed expert although recently one official referee had certain practical difficulty with regard to the payment of the court expert's costs. In practice this Order was rarely used.

021 The proposition of the tribunal-appointed expert was explored at length in an article entitled "The Law and Practice of Court and Tribunal Appointed Experts" ([1993] ADRLJ 194).

022 In this article the authors say, *inter alia*:

> "By the very nature of the fact that the expert is instructed by one party and paid for his services by him, some slight element of subconscious bias is perhaps unavoidable in the circumstances, if only because the party appointed expert's view of the case is inevitably coloured by the information being 'fed' to him by his client. ...
>
> In addition, there is often a limited number of experts in any particular field (see *Boyle* v. *Ford Motor Co. Ltd* [1992] 1 WLR 476) and it is not impossible that, in any given dispute, one expert may well be approached by both sides to provide an opinion. This possibility suggests that the parties in a case may well be in agreement as to the choice of expert and the side for whom an expert eventually acts may well be an accident of chance, dependent upon the speed with which the expert is approached by one side, or the other.
>
> Given the above provision, the possibility therefore exists for the parties to agree upon the choice of expert, but only if his complete independence is accepted by all concerned and the particular scope and extent of his expertise is fully understood.
>
> ...
>
> The questions to be submitted to the ... tribunal appointed expert should obviously be agreed between the parties at the outset. ... the scope of his enquiries must be clearly defined, either by agreement between the parties ... or arbitrator. ... A report from an independent court expert may assist in reducing those issues which are the subject of ... arbitration, and which might subsequently

be put, if this remains absolutely necessary, as separate issues to experts appointed by each of the parties. This we believe would be cheaper and quicker than the current usual practice of each side's expert preparing his own report, meeting to prepare a joint report which is and is not agreed and then putting in a supplementary report dealing with what remains . . . .

. . . the use . . . of a tribunal expert appointed at an early stage would considerably reduce the needless duplication of huge amounts of evidence by experts for each party and establish a single expert view of the relevant facts and identify precisely which points are in issue. Any further use of separate experts by the parties would then be merely to oppose the views of the court expert and support the parties' respective positions on any points then remaining in dispute."

023 The utility of a court expert may save costs and time insofar as the court expert can be directed to deal with particular and precise questions of fact thus saving time on examination and cross-examination in court. It is felt that in certain cases this may be useful because in normal actions two experts have to exchange reports and hold "without prejudice" meetings which may or may not be fruitful and considerable time is spent in court dealing with their evidence.

024 The opponents of the court-appointed expert concept suggest that if this practice was adopted then each party would probably have to appoint its own experts to rebut the evidence of the court-appointed expert thus adding to the parties' costs rather than reducing them. In a letter in 1996 to the *Law Society Gazette* Mr Reynolds appeared to warn of any abolition of the right of the parties to choose their own experts possibly offending the rules of natural justice.

025 On the evidence itself Mr Reynolds had this to say:

"The evidence itself should be the independent evidence of the expert

Although the expert is instructed by one side and has the benefit of instructions from solicitors and the advice of counsel throughout the preparatory stages of the case, nevertheless his report must be his independent product. It must be uninfluenced as to form or content by the exigencies of the litigation. This was the key point in the case of *Whitehouse* v. *Jordan* [1981] 1 All ER 267 HL.

The expert must be qualified in his discipline, profession or calling

As a general rule, experts ought to be qualified in their profession or calling if they are giving evidence in that field. However, there is an exception in the case where there is, as Scottish lawyers say, a 'man of skill' or a tradesman who has practical experience of many years' standing. Another possible exception is that of the solicitor who in the case of *R* v. *Silverlock* [1894] 2 QB 766 was also a handwriting expert.

The expert must be a good witness

It is no use eminent professionals giving evidence in court or preparing reports unless they know the basic format the report should take or have an appreciation in the art of presenting their evidence simply, clearly and to the point. Very often eminent people can become bogged down in too much detail or sometimes feel they need to demonstrate their expertise in all subjects before the court. Such an approach is totally unnecessary. They are only there to assist the court, or the arbitrator, with their opinion and to help resolve difficult and complex matters of liability and tactical responsibility.

An expert is not an advocate

Advocates should be able to carry out their functions fearlessly and independently and not be afraid of putting their client's case. An expert cannot be an advocate because if he advocated his client's case in that respect he would not be impartial or independent.

Again, there are serious difficulties in non-lawyers acting as advocates in, say, arbitration where no legal privilege attaches to their role and function and any advice they give a client is disclosable in evidence; any report they make to a client is disclosable in evidence; and none of their expert reports in this particular context would be privileged from production.

Expert evidence should not be excessively adversarial

Mr Justice Garland, giving judgment in *University of Warwick* v. *Sir Robert McAlpine* (1988) 42 BLR 1 referred in his judgment to the excessively adversarial approach to expert evidence which could have been avoided if experts who had, at various times, expressed contrary or inconsistent views, had dealt with such views in their reports giving any necessary explanations. Also, where experts alter their views at a subsequent stage it would have been appropriate in that case, and indeed in all cases, for the change of view to be notified to the other side. Such failures resulted in further costs and further time being spent in court to the disadvantage of the parties.

Expert witnesses are professionally liable in contract and tort

An expert witness could be liable for breach of contract for failure to carry out an express or implied duty under his terms of engagement, e.g. for failure to produce an expert report in time which causes further delay, adjournment and costs thrown away, or he may be liable for breach of warranty insofar as he fails to use the appropriate standard of skill and care required of him in presenting his report or conducting himself as an expert witness should. [Author's note: or the expert does not have the experience or knowledge to deal with the issues.]

With regard to the law of tort, the expert witness ought to exercise that duty of skill and care commensurate with the ordinary standard of professional skill and care expected of a person in his profession or calling.

In *Bolam v. Friern Hospital Management Committee* [1957] 2 All ER 118 Mr Justice McNair stated that such was: 'The standard of the ordinary skilled man exercising and professing to have that special skill'.

In *Saif Ali* v. *Mitchell (Sydney) & Co (A Firm)* [1980] AC 198 Lord Diplock said:

> 'No matter what profession it may be, the common law does not impose on those who practise it any liability for damage resulting from what in the result turn out to have been errors of judgement, unless the error was such as no reasonably well informed and competent member of that profession could have made.'

In *Campbell* v. *Edwards* [1976] 1 Lloyd's Rep 522 Lord Denning MR said:

> 'The expert does not act in any arbitral or quasi-arbitral capacity and consequently has no immunity from suit on that basis.' "

026 More recently in 1991 it was held in *Palmer* v. *Durnford Ford (A Firm)* [1992] 2 All ER 122 that an expert witness could not claim immunity from suit by his clients for his action in the course of preparing evidence for a claim or a possible claim.

027 I told Thomasina that the only instance that I could recall of an expert being sued was a case to do with diesel engines. Under cross-examination, the so-called expert apparently admitted that he knew little about diesel engines. I believe that he admitted to never having seen one of the sort which was the subject of the dispute. Not surprisingly his client's case collapsed and the expert was subsequently sued for the wasted costs.

General responsibilities of expert witnesses

028 In the case of *National Justice Compania Naviera SA* v. *Prudential Assurance Company Ltd (The Ikarian Reefer)* [1993] 2 Lloyd's Rep 68 Cresswell J set out what he said to be the seven principal responsibilities of expert witnesses.

029 Anthony Speaight QC, in an article for the *New Law Journal* in July 1996 commented, *inter alia*, on these seven responsibilities as follows:

"i) 'Expert evidence presented at court should be and should be seen to be the independent product of the expert uninfluenced as to form or content by the exigencies of litigation.'

If Cresswell J simply meant to say that an expert ought to express the same opinion on a given issue irrespective of which side was calling him, then most of us would warmly agree . . . .

. . . both "form and content", he says, must be uninfluenced by "the exigencies of litigation". Consider form first. It is, with respect, nonsense to suggest that the form of an expert report should not be influenced by the fact that it is to be used in litigation. Litigation reports require quite a number of features which would not be found in reports issued for other purposes. Litigation reports ought to be the report of a named individual who will enter the witness box to speak to it . . . .

There are even more important respects in which the requirements of litigation ought to shape the form of a litigation report . . . .

. . . in my view it is not only proper but desirable for lawyers to identify for experts the issues on which their opinion is sought . . . .

The proposition that the content of the report should be uninfluenced by the exigencies of litigation may sound more reasonable.

The issue surfaced in the case of *Whitehouse* v. *Jordan* (see below).

When the case went to the House of Lords Lord Wilberforce said:

> 'While some degree of consultation between experts and legal advisers is entirely proper, it is necessary that expert evidence presented to the court should be, and should be seen to be, the independent product of the expert, uninfluenced as to form or content by the exigencies of litigation.'

Here, then, is the genesis of Cresswell J's first principle. There is surely a distinction to be drawn between lawyer involvement in the content of a report which is merely an extension of posing the questions and lawyer involvement which distorts the answer.

The Academy of Experts' Guidance Notes also consider it proper for counsel to ask an expert to clarify or develop material in a draft or 'to arrange it differently', provided the expert sees to it that the report remains a proper balanced account of the truth. Therefore, to the extent that the contents of expert reports should be confined to the questions posed to the expert, the content as well as the form may on occasions be influenced by the requirements of litigation.

ii) 'An expert witness should provide independent assistance to the court by way of objective, unbiased opinion regarding matters within the expertise of the expert witness. (See *Polivitte Ltd* v. *Commercial Union Assurance* [1987] 1 Lloyd's Rep 379 at 386.) An expert witness in the High Court should never assume the role of an advocate.'"

030 On this Mr Speaight, *inter alia*, had this to say:

"Experts should certainly provide objective unbiased opinions . . . .

However, the espousal of the giving of unbiased opinions is not quite the same thing as the expert providing 'independent assistance to the court' . . . .

Looking at the *Polivitte* case one finds that Garland J gave a rather more balanced picture of the expert's role:

> 'I have almost considered the role of an expert to be two-fold: first, to advance the case of the party calling him, so far as it can properly be advanced on the basis of information available to the expert in the professional exercise of his skill and experience:

and secondly, to assist the court, which does not possess the relevant skill and experience, in determining where the truth lies.'

iii) 'An expert witness should state the facts or assumptions upon which his opinion is based. He should not omit to consider material facts which could detract from his concluded opinion.'

This statement is fine, so long as the reference to not omitting what could detract from the opinion is limited to the questions actually posed to the expert. See discussion on the first principle above. As the late and greatly respected Official Referee, Judge John Newey QC wrote:

> 'since the procedure in both courts and arbitrations is adversarial, an expert is not obliged to speak out, or write in his report, about matters concerning which he has not been asked' (*Construction Disputes: Liability and the Expert Witness*—Butterworths 1989).

iv) 'An expert witness should make it clear when a question or issue falls outside his expertise.'

v) 'If an expert's opinion is not properly researched because he considers that insufficient data was available, then this must be stated with an indication that the opinion is no more than a provisional one. In cases where an expert witness who has prepared a report could not assert that the report contained the truth, the whole truth and nothing but the truth without some qualification, then that qualification should be stated in the report.' (*Derby* v. *Weldon (No 9)* [1991] 2 All ER 901.)

The remarks of Staughton LJ in *Derby* v. *Weldon (No 9)* are worth quoting more fully, because they introduce a different, and more realistic nuance:

> 'I do not think that an expert witness, or any other witness, obliges himself to volunteer his views on every issue in the whole case when he takes an oath to tell the whole truth. What he does oblige himself to do is to tell the whole truth about those matters which he is asked about.'

vi) 'If, after exchange of experts' reports, an expert witness changed his view on a material matter having read the other side's expert's report or for any other reason, such change of view should be communicated to the other side (through legal representatives) without delay and, when appropriate, to the court.'

This is a radical idea . . . .

. . . Cresswell J was not stating the existing practice . . . .

. . . In general a party to litigation is under no obligation to reveal to the other what his prospective witnesses will say. Quite the contrary: witness statements are privileged. However, rules of court have in practice modified the scope of that privilege by providing that leave to call experts may be made conditional on abiding by directions. The usual direction is that 'the substance of the evidence' shall be disclosed in the form of a written report. I can quite see that if an expert changed his mind on a significant matter between writing his report and its service, one should amend the report before service . . . .

. . . a party ought not to place an expert report before a judge to read unless at the time of doing so the report is still broadly accurate as to the witness's opinions, and unless that party genuinely intends to call that expert . . . .

. . . So, if an expert changes his mind on a matter after service of his report, is there any obligation to signal that to the other side over all the months that elapse between then and trial? I think not, and I am fortified that other respected lawyers share my view. (See Michael Ludlow *The Independent Expert* (1993) and Andrew Bartlett QC *Independence and Partisanship*.)

vii) 'Where expert evidence refers to photographs, plans, calculations, analyses, measurements, survey reports or similar documents be provided to the opposite side at the same time as the exchange of reports'."

031 After this brief summary I then referred Thomasina to an article which appeared in the May 1994 edition of the *Chartered Institute's Journal* (60, JCI Arb 2 94) written by Andrew Bartlett QC which dealt with the preparation of the expert's report.

032 I felt it important that Thomasina should understand what to expect from such reports and how they come to be prepared in the way that they are.

033 In effect Mr Bartlett took issue with the *dictum* of Lord Wilberforce in the case referred to above. Here counsel had assisted in the writing of a report by a medical expert. This involvement attracted judicial criticism both in the Court of Appeal and by Lord Wilberforce who said:

> "While some degree of consultation between experts and legal advisers is entirely proper, it is necessary that expert evidence presented to the court should be, and should be seen to be, the independent product of the expert, uninfluenced as to form or content by the exigencies of litigation. To the extent that it is not, the evidence is likely to be not only incorrect but self-defeating."

034 It was this *dictum* which Mr Bartlett suggests has caused confusion as to counsel's role. He says:

> "In practice, it is impossible to comply with it both in form and in content for the needs of the litigation. To the extent that a report is not influenced in form and content by the needs of litigation, it is likely to hinder the due administration of justice and to result in costs being wasted. Everyone involved in litigation sees this occur; lawyers and experts see it—and judges see it. Yet, like the crowd who saw the Emperor with no clothes, they seldom dare say that they see.
>
> Judges giving guidance on experts' reports have felt constrained to pay lip service to Lord Wilberforce's *dictum*. This is to be expected in view of the eminence and wide legal learning of its author, but has been unfortunate, since opportunities to dispel the confusion have been missed. Even Homer may nod. The *dictum* has no binding force. It was *obiter*—not forming any part of the reasons for the decision. Confusion would be reduced if judges, instead of citing the *dictum* as if they fully agreed with it, were to state plainly the true position, which is thought to be that:
>
> — the content of an expert's report must not be dishonestly or recklessly devised, slanted or 'massaged' for the purpose of supporting the case of the party calling him; but
> — within the limits of propriety, the expert is entitled—and indeed ought—to receive guidance from the party's legal advisers as to the form and content of his report."

035 As to the form of the report it is suggested that in all but the simplest of cases it should *not* be left to chance or to the personal views of the expert.

036 This is a point very much after my own heart. How often have I seen it left to experts to determine what is required and, as a result, they have produced voluminous reports at great expense which counsel cannot use and are not in a form which I find either helpful or easy to assimilate.

037 Mr Bartlett suggests the following format:

(i) The report should be signed and dated.
(ii) There should be a table of contents at the beginning.
(iii) The report should commence with an introduction of the author, and his CV should be contained either in the introduction or in an appendix.

iv) The report should be clearly laid out, preferably in short numbered paragraphs.
v) The contents should be presented in a logical order and broken down in whatever separate sections are appropriate for the particular case covering matters such as background facts, explanation of technical concepts, discussion of the material issues and conclusions.
vi) Supporting items such as calculation sheets, test results and the like should be contained in appendices.
vii) The report should be consecutively paginated throughout (including the appendices).
viii) Any photographs contained in the report should be properly reproduced (black and white photocopies are generally useless).

038 Returning to Lord Wilberforce's *dictum* about the report being "the independent product of the expert, uninfluenced as to form or content by the exigencies of litigation" Mr Bartlett's view is that in relation to the content of these reports lawyers have a very important function to perform.

"They should vet the report to ensure that it contains, and contains only, the material that it ought to contain.

Does it clearly indicate the scope of the expert's remit?

The expert should state exactly what he has been asked to report on by indicating the nature of his term of reference. [Author's note: He should also be asked if he has been instructed not to report on anything—*Whitehouse* v. *Jordan*.]

Does it adequately identify the material on which it is based?

Differences of opinion between experts often stem from their having been given different facts or assumptions from which to work. If the tribunal is to weigh conflicting opinions from different experts it is vital that it should know the factual basis of each opinon (cf. the remarks of Cresswell J in *The Ikarian Reefer*).

Is the report properly researched?

If the data available to the expert are insufficient for him to be confident of his opinion, he should indicate the areas of uncertainty and state explicitly that his opinion is provisional (*In Re J (A Minor) (Expert Evidence)* [1990] TLR 568, *The Ikarian Reefer, supra*).

Does the report properly acknowledge the limits of the writer's expertise?

The expert should make clear the extent to which questions considered by him fall within his special expertise. A report which incorporates argument or comment on facts outside his expertise is likely to provoke an adverse reaction from the judge (*Polivitte Ltd* v. *Commercial Union Assurance Co plc* [1987] 1 Lloyd's Rep 379, 387, *The Ikarian Reefer, supra*).

Is the report dependent upon the research or opinions of others?

Where the report is that of a leader of a team of investigators or research assistants who have acted under his direction or control, it may be sufficient merely to state that fact.

But in general, if the report contains evidence or expertise contributed by persons other than its apparent author, those persons and their contributions should be identified so that they can at the very least be tendered for cross-examination (*University of Warwick* v. *Sir Robert McAlpine* (1988) 42 BLR 1, 23).

Has there been any change of view by the expert which requires explanation?

Sometimes experts express one view in experts' meetings or in reports and subsequently change their minds and express a different opinion. Where this occurs this should be dealt with in their latest report, giving any necessary explanations. Otherwise they may lay themselves open to damaging cross-examination upon their inconsistencies (*University of Warwick, supra*).

Does the report go too far in usurping the role of the judge?

This can be a delicate matter. The traditional wisdom was that in no case was it competent for the expert to express his opinion upon any of the issues, whether of law or fact, which the judge had to determine (*per* Neville J in *Crosfield & Sons* v. *Techno-Chemical Laboratories Ltd* (1913) 29 TLR 379, still cited 80 years later in the *Supreme Court Practice 1993*, para 38/4/2. But times have changed. Today this rule is more honoured in the breach than in the observance. In a professional negligence case it is impossible for the expert to state his opinion without expressing a view on the very issue of negligence that the judge has to decide. [Author's note: Here I would respectfully take issue with Mr Bartlett. It is one thing to express a view on whether the respondent has conducted himself competently and exercised the degree of care and skill reasonably to be expected; it is another thing entirely to proclaim that the respondent was negligent—that, as is said, is for the judge, or arbitrator, to decide.]

Indeed, in *Whitehouse* v. *Jordan, supra*, counsel appears to have been criticised for deleting a passage in a report where the expert stated expressly that there had been no negligence (see the report of the proceedings in the Court of Appeal [1980] 1 All ER 650, 655f–g). [Author's note: There is a world of difference in counsel instructing a report then deleting a passage which they may consider is unhelpful to their client's case, and limiting, or carefully defining, the instructions in the first place. By pursuing the first of these options, imbalance in the report is inevitable.]

Nevertheless, judicial sensitivities remain. It is still advisable for the expert to tread warily and, if he can, to avoid giving the appearance of trespassing unduly into the province of the judge. Even in a professional negligence case, it may be wise for him, instead of saying (for example) 'the defendant was negligent', to say 'in my opinion the defendant adopted a course which no skilled practitioner acting carefully would have adopted'.

(Is this not the question? Is this what you would have done, Mr Expert, as a matter of good practice, acting with appropriate skill and care? Some arbitrators might find this approach helpful.)

Do the words of the report truly reflect the expert's views?

This may at first sight seem an odd question but engineers, scientists, doctors and other experts are not always accomplished craftsmen with words. Particular words or phrases used by the expert in his draft report may, when carefully examined, appear ambiguous or may not accurately reflect his real views carrying unintended meaning or erroneous implications.

To an expert the word 'possible' may denote something that is more likely than not, or something that is possible but unlikely. When proof of a fact depends on the balance of probabilities, the difference between these shades of meaning becomes fundamental.

Such words or phrases may have to be amended in debate between counsel and the expert until both are satisfied that the written words accurately convey the expert's true opinion.

Does the report adequately cover the pleaded allegations?

This is particularly likely to be a problem in complex cases. It is unfair to leave it to the expert to guess upon which allegations made in the pleadings he ought to comment. The lawyers know which allegations are for this expert to deal with; which should be left to another; and which should be matters solely for factual evidence. It is important that solicitors or counsel check that every allegation that ought to be dealt with by the expert is clearly covered in his report."

039 Mr Bartlett started his article by arguing that contrary to the well-known *dictum* of

Lord Wilberforce in *Whitehouse* v. *Jordan* it was the duty of lawyers conducting litigation to ensure that the experts' reports were suitable both in form and content for the needs of the litigation. He concluded this article by dealing with two further matters which cause concern in the preparation of experts' reports:

(i) How far can inconvenient facts or opinions legitimately be omitted from a report; and

(ii) Whether the duties of an expert witness included the advancement of his client's case.

On these two matters Mr Bartlett said:

"What can properly be omitted from the report?

This question often exercises counsel's conscience. Sometimes there are known facts which tend to weigh against the opinion the expert has formed and the question arises whether these should be omitted from the report. In *The Ikarian Reefer, supra,* Cresswell J said that the expert's report should state facts or assumptions on which his opinion was based, together with material facts which could detract from the concluded opinion. This is clearly right. If the expert's opinion is to carry proper weight he must show that he has already taken account of all facts which might tend to weaken his stated conclusions on the issues with which his report is concerned.

A more difficult situation arises where there are matters which might be used against the interests of the expert's client, but which are not directly relevant to the pleaded issues. Should these be included in the report?

The Rules of Court (RSC Order 38, rule 37(1) and Order 25, rule 8(1)(b)) provide for the disclosure of 'the substance' of the evidence of an expert whom a party proposed to call.

In *Kenning* v. *Eve Construction Ltd* [1989] 1 WLR 1189 an engineer, asked by the defendants to report on an accident, wrote a report refuting the allegations of negligence pleaded in the statement of claim. In a separate letter he drew attention to two points, not covered in the statement of claim or in his report, on which he considered the defendants were at fault. By mistake, the defendants' solicitors sent off not merely the report but also the letter, which was greeted with some interest, not to say glee, by the plaintiff's solicitors when they received it.

The defendants sought to prevent the plaintiff relying on the letter. The deputy judge acknowledged that it was a widespread practice that anxieties, qualifications or adverse views expressed by expert witnesses were very often communicated to their instructing solicitors by way of a confidential covering letter. He also acknowledged that the letter was privileged. But he held that, if the defendants wished to call the expert, they must disclose not only his report but also his letter, since otherwise they would not be complying with their obligation to disclose 'the substance' of his evidence.

This was a wrong decision. In effect, the deputy judge was misled by the simplicity of the case. He evidently felt that the report, which dealt only with the matters raised by the pleadings, concealed by omission the expert's views on what he called 'the overall issue of liability' (see [1989] 1 WLR 1189 at 1194). This was an understandable reaction in a simple case, but one only has to consider its application to a complex case for it to be exposed as fallacious. Suppose in a building case the plaintiff, based on advice from his own expert, pleads 47 criticisms of various parts of a defective structure.

The defendants' expert in the course of his investigation comes upon another 15 items where the defendants may be vulnerable to criticism. What should he say in his report? It is the duty of the defendants' lawyer to tell him that his report should not go beyond the pleaded issues.

This is the only logical and practical solution in an adversarial system of justice. The plaintiff may not be aware of the further 15 points, or he may have decided not to pursue them in order to avoid more complication or delay or expense or some adverse reflection on some of the 47 points already pleaded.

The defendants' expert should not raise in his report points against his own clients which have not been pleaded. Conversely, the plaintiff's expert's report should cover the allegations which are pleaded, and should not raise any additional criticisms, unless they are to be made the subject of an application to amend. Failure by the plaintiff's lawyers to restrict the contents of the report to issues which are pleaded leads to needless expense and confusion as both the judge and the defendants try to determine which passages in the report are relied upon by the plaintiff in support of the pleaded case and which are to be disregarded as irrelevant. The court's task under the adversarial system is to address the 'overall issue of liability' not in the abstract, but by considering the particular issues which the parties have chosen to raise on their pleadings.

The Court of Appeal had to consider a related situation in *Derby & Co Ltd* v. *Weldon (No 9)* [1990] TLR 712. In that case the defendants' expert accountant had prepared a report, which had been disclosed, on the plaintiff's 'initial conspiracy' claim. The report did not deal with an 'alternative initial conspiracy' which had been introduced into the plaintiffs' pleading by amendment. The court took the view that the rules for disclosure of expert evidence did not override legal professional privilege. Any report which the accountant might have prepared on the 'alternative initial conspiracy' was privileged, and, if the defendants did not wish to adduce evidence from him on that issue, they could not be ordered to disclose any report which he might have made upon it. The court confirmed that *Kenning, supra*, was wrongly decided. In the Rules of Court the 'substance' of the evidence refers only to the evidence it is intended the expert should give at trial; it does not mean all the evidence he could give.

Nevertheless, while in principle it is legitimate to exclude unfavourable matter by confining the report strictly to the issues raised on the pleadings, an expert witness must not mislead by omission (see *per* Cazalet J in *Re J, supra*). It is therefore appropriate, when something is omitted, for the barrister to help the expert avoid forms of expression which may be misinterpreted as carrying undue implications of a favourable view on a matter not expressly dealt with. It is important to remember also that the line dividing legitimate from illegitimate omissions is one which may depend on the character of the litigation. Where the proceedings are of an inquisitorial character, the expert's duty to disclose unfavourable material is a higher one.

The foremost example is wardship proceedings, where the interests of any adult parties are made subject to the paramountcy of the welfare of the child. In such cases there are no pleadings to limit the issues; the expert's task is to assist the court as best he can in a straightforward and objective manner, and he certainly must not omit to mention any factor which does not support his omission: In *Re J, supra.*

Is the report unduly partisan?

It is sometimes necessary to remind experts that they must not become advocates for their clients. In *Polivitte, supra*, Garland J made the somewhat Delphic statement:

> 'I have almost considered the role of an expert to be two-fold: first to advance the case of the party calling him, so far as it can properly be advanced on the basis of information available to the expert in the professional exercise of his skill and experience; and, secondly, to assist the court, which does not possess the relevant skill and experience, in determining where the truth lies' [1987] 1 Lloyd's Rep 379, 386.

The word 'almost' was well chosen. Everyone concerned in litigation knows that the purpose of employing an expert is to advance the case of the party calling him. Yet if that purpose is baldly stated, without suitable qualification, it gives an incorrect impression of the expert's true role and duties, which require objectivity and the exercise of independent professional judgement. He should write his report so as to advance his client's case without actually promoting it. He should assist his client, yet never assume the role of advocate (*The Ikarian Reefer, supra*). If he ventures into the arena as an advocate, his credibility and perhaps even his veracity will be attacked: *University of Warwick* (1988) 42 BLR 1, 22.

The Code of Conduct for the Bar (para 607.3) states, 'that a barrister must not rehearse, practise or coach a witness in relation to his evidence or the way in which he should give it'. The rule is directed to the making of illegitimate 'improvements' to a witness's evidence, and should not be taken to prohibit the barrister from helping the expert to fulfil his duties. When consulting with the expert, the barrister must not place him under any pressure to provide other than a truthful account of his opinions, but he may be failing in his duty to his client and making the task of the court more difficult if, *pace* Lord Wilberforce, he omits to give the expert proper guidance as to his duties and the form and content of his report."

040 The sentiments expressed in this article should be considered in the light of the comments made by Laddie J in *Cala Homes South Ltd and Others* v. *Alfred McAlpine Homes East Ltd* [1995] CILL 1083. In this case the witness admitted that his view of his task, of the expert witness, was set out in an article he had written for a professional journal from which the judge quoted him as having said:

> "How should the expert avoid becoming partisan in a process that makes no pretence of determining the truth but seeks only to weigh the persuasive effect of arguments deployed by one adversary or the other?
>
> ... the man who works the Three Card Trick is not cheating, nor does he incur any moral opprobrium, when he uses his sleight of hand to deceive the eye of the innocent rustic and to deny him the information he needs for a correct appraisal of what has gone on. The rustic does not have to join in: but if he chooses to, he is 'fair game'.
>
> If by an analogous 'sleight of mind' an expert witness is able so to present the data that they seem to suggest an interpretation favourable to the side instructing him, that is, it seems to me, within the rules of our particular game, even if it means playing down or omitting some material consideration. *Celatio veri* is, as the maxim has it, *suggestio falsi*, and concealing what is true does indeed suggest what is false; but it is no more than a suggestion, just as the Three Card Trick was only a suggestion about the data, not an outright misrepresentation of them.
>
> Thus there are three phases in the expert's work. In the first he has to be the client's 'candid friend', telling him all the faults in his case. In the second he will, with appropriate subtlety, be almost what the Honorary Editor's American counsel called 'a hired gun' so that client and counsel when considering the other side's argument can say, with Marcellus in *Hamlet* 'shall I strike at it with my partisan?'. The third phase, which happens more rarely than is acknowledged in much of the comment on expert witness work, is when the action comes to court or arbitration.
>
> Then, indeed, the earlier pragmatic flexibility is brought under a sharp curb, whether of conscience, or fear of perjury, or of fear of losing professional credibility. It is no longer enough for the expert, like the 'virtuous youth' in the *Mikado*, to 'tell the truth whenever he finds it pays': shades of moral and other constraints begin to close upon him."

041 The witness had confirmed in cross-examination that that was indeed his view of his task. In unreservedly condemning such an approach to the giving of evidence of opinion, Laddie J said:

> "No doubt it is currently fashionable to say that our legal system makes no pretence to determining the truth. I accept that some people not only say it but also believe it. If it were true then (the witness) would be right in thinking that anything short of outright misrepresentation is permissible in an expert's report and that not only the other party, but also the person trying to decide the issue, the 'rustics', are fair game. On reflection, if [the witness] were right, I am not sure that even outright misrepresentation should be avoided. If litigation is to be conducted as if it were a game of Three Card Trick, what is wrong with having a couple of aces up your sleeve? ...
>
> ... The whole basis of [the witness's] approach to the drafting of an expert's report is wrong. The function of a court of law is to discover the truth relating to the issues before it. In doing that it has to assess the evidence adduced by the parties. The judge is not a rustic who has chosen to play a game of Three Card Trick. He is not fair game. Nor is the truth. That some witnesses of fact, driven by a desire to achieve a particular outcome to the litigation, feel it necessary to sacrifice truth in pursuit of victory is a fact of life.

The court tries to discover it when it happens. But in the case of expert witnesses the court is likely to lower its guard. Of course the court will be aware that a party is likely to choose as its expert someone whose view is most sympathetic to its position. Subject to that caveat, the court is likely to assume that the expert witness is more interested in being honest and right than in ensuring that one side or another wins.

An expert should not consider that it is his job to stand shoulder-to-shoulder through thick and thin with the side which is paying him. 'Pragmatic flexibility' as used by (the witness) is a euphemism for 'misleading selectivity'. According to this approach the flexibility will give place to something closer to the true and balanced view of the expert only when he is being cross-examined and is faced with the possibility of being 'found out'.

The reality, of course, will be something different. An expert who has committed himself in writing to a report which is selectively misleading may feel obliged to stick to the views he expressed there when he is cross-examined. Most witnesses would not be prepared to admit at the beginning of cross-examination, as (the witness) effectively did, that he was approaching the drafting of a report as a partisan hired gun. The result is that the expert's report and then his oral evidence will be contaminated by this attempted sleight of mind. This deprives the evidence of much of its value. I would like to think that in most cases cross-examination exposes the bias. Where there is no cross-examination, the court is clearly at much greater risk of being misled . . . .

. . . In the light of the matters set out above, during the preparation of this judgment I re-read (the witness's) report on the understanding that it was drafted as a partisan tract with the objective of selling the defendant's case to the court and ignoring virtually everything which could harm that objective. I did not find it of significant assistance in deciding the issues . . . ."

042 It is said by some commentators for the reasons stated above that to engage claims consultants to prepare a claim will mean that this work is of little use if it goes to arbitration, as independent experts will then have to review the evidence afresh and prepare an objective, impartial report for the purpose of giving expert evidence of opinion at the hearing. The same commentators suggest that claimants who have gone down the route of the claims consultant would rarely have the stomach for changing horses when they proceed to the hearing with their partisan, with the risk that involves as was exposed in the *Cala Homes* case.

043 It is further said by the critics of the claims consultants that they are not "experts" in the legal sense and that the purpose of their trade is to sit in the party's place and to prosecute his claim on his behalf. Sometimes a claims consultant will not only prepare the claim but also prosecute the contractor's case as his advocate. Whilst at a hearing or trial he might also seek to give evidence of opinion, they conclude by suggesting that it would be a rare arbitrator or judge who gave much credibility to the opinion of a consultant whose overt task was to win his client's case, no matter what title he gave himself.

044 Whilst I have certainly experienced partisan claims consultants I cannot honestly say that they are invariably so. If an arbitrator is in any doubt on this score then he can do as Laddie J in *Cala Homes* and question the claims consultant's independence.

045 Having considered Mr Bartlett's article and the views expressed by the judge in *Cala Homes* Thomasina had a far better understanding of the role of the expert report in arbitral proceedings.

046 I had to admit that we had strayed some way from the original question as to why an experienced arbitrator with a Quantity Surveying (QS) background would find it necessary or desirable to allow one party or other to call a QS to express an opinion on quantity surveying matters. I hoped that Thomasina realised that although the arbitrator may well have even more expertise than the expert he cannot undertake the necessary research himself (unless the parties otherwise agree (s.34(2)(g), AA '96), which is scarcely likely).

047 In addition, the independent QS expert is in a position, if so authorised, to agree some issues or elements of issues during his meetings and exchanges with his opposite number—again a function which cannot normally be undertaken by the arbitrator, but it can be undertaken by the parties, or anyone acting on their behalf, without the need for them to be called to give evidence of opinion.

048 I cautioned Thomasina to remember that the Woolf Report on the Civil Justice System (June 1995) expressed concern that engaging experts was a source of excessive expense, delay and in some cases unnecessary complexity.

049 This comment from the Woolf Report brought me to the point which I had made many times before to Thomasina, of the necessity to give careful consideration to the form of instruction given to experts, as I have long believed that one of the primary reasons for arbitration having become as expensive as litigation is the misuse and abuse of the expert witness.

050 As to the reasons for this state of affairs, it may be due in part to a lack of precise instructions from the solicitor but equally by misrepresentations by experts holding themselves out to be able to do the job. The construction industry in particular attracts numerous professionals who have no particular experience. There are increasing numbers of so called "experts" writing to solicitors asking for work. Just because these people are members of an expert academy does not mean to say they are competent.

051 The blame for this might lie either with those instructing the experts or the so called experts themselves. Although any expert experienced in litigation/arbitration could at least offer some suggestions as to the form that his instruction should take when he is dealing with a solicitor not as well versed as he is not being regularly involved in litigation. Therefore, the solicitor, possibly in conjunction with the expert, will seek to define the issue, or issues, on which the expert's opinion is sought. He will not merely hand him the files and ask him to write a report which, as I have said on many previous occasions, is in effect saying to the expert "take this spade, dig a hole in your garden and pour my client's money into it".

052 Unfortunately some solicitors—inexperienced in litigation—appoint experts as a sort of "knee-jerk" response in certain disputes without giving serious thought as to whether an expert is necessary. A classic example of this occurred in the case of *R* v. *Strudwick* (1994) *The Independent*, 18 January, where the court held that a jury could reach its verdict on the plain facts of the issue rather than needing assistance from an expert.

The New Civil Procedure Rules

053 As at 26 April 1999, the familiar *White Book*—beloved of lawyers—will no longer lie in front of counsel (or solicitors) at trial in court. In any event in arbitration this *White Book* has never had significant relevance except perhaps in rare instances where an arbitrator, who is bound to act judicially, must take cognisance of the court's approach in, for example, a security for costs application (now a power granted to arbitrators under s. 38 of the Arbitration Act 1996).

054 In place of the *White Book* will be the *Brown Book* (?) encapsulating the new Court Procedures (emanating from the Woolf Reforms—*Access to Justice*). These new procedures eschew legal jargon and as a result, out go *pleadings, discovery, ex parte* and so on, to be replaced by *statement of case, disclosure* and *non-attendance of a party*. No bad thing except that all those concerned with litigation and arbitration understood what the former terms stood for.

055 Certainly these Civil Procedure Rules herald a dramatic change in the court's approach to attempt to achieve speedy cost-effective litigation. In this respect it is hard on the tracks of the Arbitration Act 1996 which gave to the arbitrator many of the powers that are now being vested in the judicature.

056 The big question is whether the judges will really be given sufficient time and resources to case manage in the manner that the new Rules now provide—time will tell.

057 So far as expert evidence is concerned, there are three parts of the new Rules which apply.

058 *Part 27—The Small Claims Track.* This is what it says, a small claims procedure which limits the costs that can be recovered in respect of a claim which has been allocated to this procedure. The only exception to the limit is in respect of expert evidence. However, clearly the intention is to avoid, wherever possible, using experts in this small claims track and the disputant can only do so with the consent of the court.

059 The next section of relevance is *Part 32—Evidence.* Of course, the entirety of this important part touches experts but the important provisions, so far as the expert witness is concerned, can perhaps be summarised as follows.

060 The court has power to decide on the nature of evidence and the way in which that evidence is placed before it. It may, for example, allow evidence through a video link. A court may limit cross-examination, either oral or written, again echoing what is now becoming commonplace in arbitration. The court has power to order evidence by affidavit as well as such things as notices to admit facts—all designed to reduce expensive hearing time.

061 The most important part of these new rules which affects experts is *Part 35—Experts and Assessors.*

062 As all three parts are reproduced in Appendix A/3 to this book it is suggested that the reader studies Part 35 in its entirety. However, the key provisions can be summarised as follows.

063 Named experts only can be used with the court's permission; then they have a duty to restrict their evidence to that which is reasonably required to resolve the proceedings. Having agreed the appointment the court may limit the amount of the expert's fees and expenses, which the appointing party may recover from the other.

064 Evidence is to be given by way of a written report and, where the claim is a "fast-track" one, the court will not direct him to attend the hearing unless it is necessary to do so in the interests of justice.

065 Rather in the same way I do arbitration, a party may put written questions to the expert, within a limited timescale from the receipt of his report, for the purpose of clarification, and the expert is obliged to answer these questions which will be treated as part of his report. In the event that he fails to answer them the court may order that a party may not rely on the evidence of that expert or that the party who called him may not recover the fees and expenses of that expert from the other party.

066 Possibly the biggest single change concerns the court's power to direct that evidence on a particular issue be given by a single joint expert only, who will be selected by the court (if the parties' cannot agree). Following appointment, each party may give instructions to that single expert. The court may give directions about the payment of fees and expenses to this single expert and, provided it is before he is instructed, limit the amount that can be paid to him and direct that the instructing parties pay that amount into court. In addition the court may give direction concerning inspection, examination or experiment, which the expert may wish to carry out.

067 The expert's report must comply with the requirements set out in the relevant *Practice Direction* and include a statement that says that he understands his duty to the court and has complied with it.

068 There is an interesting point concerning instructions to the expert which shall not be privileged against disclosure, but the court will not ordinarily order disclosure or permit any questions to be put to the expert in court by the other party concerning these instructions unless it is satisfied that there are reasonable grounds to consider the statement of instructions to be inaccurate or incomplete.

069 This is a different approach from that adopted in most arbitrations where parties are urged to agree joint instructions so far as possible, and where this proves not to be possible the arbitrator is to be informed on what differences there are between the parties concerning joint instructions and he will attempt to bring them together. If not, of course, then the different instructions are clearly "disclosed".

070 Once an expert's report has been disclosed any party may use that report as evidence at the trial. Where a party fails to disclose the report, this report may not be used at the trial and the expert who drafted it may not be called to give evidence orally unless the court gives permission.

071 There is an interesting new subsection concerning discussions between the experts where the court may direct such discussions to take place to identify the issues and agree on common ground etc. but the court may also limit the issues which the experts discuss and direct that they prepare a statement—as is common in most arbitrations—on the issues on which they agree and on those on which they do not, but the court also requires reasons to be given for their disagreement. Something which arbitrators could well adopt to advantage.

072 The content of the discussions between the experts shall not be referred to at the trial, unless the parties agree, and even if the experts reach agreement during their discussions, such agreement shall not bind the parties unless they expressly agreed to be bound by such agreement.

073 Compare this with His Hon Judge John Newey's judgment in *Richard Roberts Holdings Ltd* v. *Douglas Smith Stimson Partnership and Others (No 2)* QBD 31 July 1989, which dealt largely with instructions to experts and what was said (and disclosable) in their discussions. There was also a question concerning the effect of an expert's signature on a document agreed between the experts.

074 One of the most interesting points to come out of this case was the expert's personal position where the judge said that if an expert was persuaded of the correctness of the other expert's view and stated as much in writing, or even orally, he could not subsequently give evidence truthfully to the contrary, although it was accepted that he could not be cross-examined on it because the meeting, or discussions, were "without prejudice". The judge did say, however, that in such a case that expert might have sanctions invoked against him by his professional body.

075 This then appears to be unchanged in that under Part 35 the content of discussion shall not be referred to at the trial unless the parties agree.

076 Finally, a new provision giving an expert the right to file a written request in the court for directions to assist him in carrying out his function as an expert, and he may do so without giving notice to either party, i.e. not even his own!

077 I cannot see this particular right being invoked very often except, perhaps, by a single joint expert who may have nothing to gain from future patronage.

078 That concludes the main provisions of Part 35. Reference was made, when discussing the contents of the expert's report, that it had to comply with the requirements set out in the relevant *Practice Direction*. At the time of writing such *Practice Directions* are not yet available but there are various expert witness protocols in draft—for example, what was the Official Referees' Solicitors Association (ORSA) Expert Witness Protocol, version 1.0—now the TeCSA (the Technology and Construction Court) Protocol.

SO YOU WANT TO BE AN EXPERT WITNESS?

The facts

079 You receive a telephone call from a firm of solicitors asking if you are prepared to give expert evidence in a case concerning the manufacture of wigglepins and, if interested, what are your terms?

Question

080 What should the expert do next?

Course of action

081 First of all the expert should find out what aspect of the manufacture of wigglepins the case is concerned with. This is to ensure that the issue on which he is being called as an expert is the one on which he really *is* expert. Obvious, you might say, but, sadly, not invariably observed.

082 The Official Referees' Solicitors Association (ORSA) has drawn up a useful protocol, Version 1.0, which they published at the end of 1997. (The full text of this is reproduced in Appendix B at the end of the book.)

083 Tony Bingham wrote the following commentary on this valuable guide to solicitors and expert witnesses in *Building* (12 December 1997) where he said, *inter alia*:

> "[the expert] . . . must be given some idea of the time commitment involved. By the way, if you are an architect or surveyor or wigglepin expert ORSA is keen that you maintain, or are part of, an enterprise that still practises in the real world of wigglepins or whatever.
>
> Next, the solicitor provides a list of people involved, both for or against. This is to eliminate conflict of interest. So far, the expert has not been appointed. We still have to come to the business of money. If is usual for the expert to give the proposed basis for charging. At the same time, the solicitor is to be informed about relevant expertise and experience.
>
> There is an immediate balance to be struck here. The solicitor has to be careful about providing documentation and information to mere potential appointees. If no appointment is made, that expert is free to take an appointment with an opponent. He should be reminded that he cannot use the documentation previously given.
>
> Once appointed, the expert can expect a brief to be given by the solicitor. It will contain the timetable, current status, the pleadings or statements of case, details of other experts and the lead expert. Then there will be the list of specific issues on which the expert is to advise. Key documentation is to be included. Finally, the brief should explain the important legal principles of privilege and discovery.
>
> Ordinarily, the expert will produce a written report. ORSA suggests that this is issued to the solicitor as a draft for discussion. This is done only to consider format; the report shall remain the independent product of the expert. It is wise at this stage for the solicitor and expert to test the expert's opinion in the light of alternative facts contended for by the opponent. The final report is then exchanged by the solicitors.
>
> Confusion sometimes occurs regarding 'meetings of opposing experts'. ORSA says no standard format exists for such meetings, but it gives helpful guidance:
>
> - meet before exchange of reports, since this may avoid 'taking positions' prior to the meeting
> - formulate an agenda before the meeting. This is best done by the solicitors with the expert's assistance
> - lawyers and clients should not be present at the meeting

- usually, the meeting is for experts of 'like discipline'. But occasionally, a multi-disciplinary meeting may be necessary
- the expert immediately reports to the solicitor after the meeting
- a memo jointly signed by opponent experts is necessary when matters of opinion are agreed. Brief reasons for the agreement should be incorporated. Where some, but not all, experts agree, a limited agreement can be explored
- a solicitor should not instruct an expert to apply pressure on other experts
- ensure all notes of meetings are marked 'without prejudice' until agreed

ORSA points out that an expert has no authority to bind his client. Clearly, though, an agreement of experts may be binding on the experts.

An important duty of the expert is to remain impartial and be reminded that the overall duty is to the tribunal or court.

Finally, the matter of fees is discussed in the protocol. It has to be clearly decided whether the solicitor is responsible for the fees or is agent for the client. Important, too, is the timing of payments, together with the method of keeping accurate and contemporaneous records to justify the fees claimed. Legal aid work requires a careful eye; the solicitor must advise of any likelihood that the expert's fees may be reduced on legal aid taxation.

ORSA finishes with an appropriate warning about cancellation fees. I get the feeling these are unpopular. So, too, are minimum charges or commitment fees."

DISTINGUISHING BETWEEN EVIDENCE OF WITNESSES OF FACT AND EXPERT WITNESSES

The facts

084 In a construction dispute the claimant was represented by a project manager consultant whom the contractor claimant had engaged to run the project. The respondent was legally represented but his chief witness was the architect/surveyor named in the contract.

085 There was a substantial claim and a counterclaim of similar magnitude. Both sides wished to call experts to deal with *quantum* and quality of workmanship although both of these matters were dealt with on a day-to-day basis by the project manager for the claimant and the architect/surveyor for the respondent.

Question

086 How should the arbitrator direct the parties at the preliminary meeting to differentiate between fact and opinion evidence?

Course of action

087 The first point to make here is that neither the project manager nor the architect/contract administrator can give expert evidence. They both fail the test of independence. The arbitrator can inform the parties that these two witnesses would be witnesses of fact. Where, for example, an architect wishes to give evidence on the quality of the workmanship this would be evidence of fact and not of evidence as it would relate to what he said during the project.

088 During the hearing the arbitrator will have to be alert as to these witnesses of fact and to take care not to admit evidence of opinion.

089 It is one thing for an architect to express an opinion on quality during the progress of the works when as agent of the client he is seeking to ensure that this client gets what he is paying for and another thing in expressing an impartial and independent opinion as agent of the tribunal. His opinion given during the course of the works on quality is one of the facts in dispute—or rather that he gave his opinion reasonably.

090 An expert should not express an opinion in his disclosed report on any issues whether of fact, law or liability which the tribunal has to determine (*per* Neville J in *Crosfield & Sons* v. *Techno-Chemical Laboratories Ltd* (1913) 29 TLR 379). However, in practice, particularly in complicated construction cases the expert is often required for the purpose of the instructing solicitors to assist in finding relevant case law and in identifying potential and proportional liability. That advice, however, should not be contained in his disclosed report and, in the light of his privileged position it is important that the expert should not express his opinion on matters not within his technical expertise. Only an architect can give expert evidence of opinion on the duties of an architect and in *United States Shipping Board* v. *Ship St Albans* [1913] AC 623 PC it was held that a land surveyor could not give expert evidence of opinion of the position of ships involved in a collision at sea determined by means of photographs taken from a passing ship.

091 In another similar case the claimant objected to a job architect who was a witness of fact giving expert evidence. The grounds for that objection were that he was not qualified as an expert and therefore he should not be permitted to give his opinion evidence. What he should have objected to was the architect's lack of independence.

092 Either party can field whomsoever he wishes to give expert evidence—assuming that no agreement or restriction has been imposed on the number of witnesses which the parties are permitted to call. It matters not that the expert witness is an architect or even an ex-employee of one party. What matters is whether the expert is qualified either by experience or education or preferably both but most important of all is his objectivity. If a witness is an employee or consultant to one of the parties his credibility may need more careful scrutiny than it would if he were wholly and clearly independent of either side. In that case he cannot give expert evidence.

093 Finally, Thomasina drew my attention to a letter on the topic which appears in the *Chartered Surveyor Weekly*, 19 November 1992. This letter read as follows:

"When does an opinion turn into a fact?

Dear Sir: The recent High Court judgment that arbitration settlements can no longer be used as evidence in other rent-review disputes (CSW, 22 October) offers the prospect of some fascinating, if not contentious, discussions.

To quote parts of the judgment reported in your article: 'An arbitration award is an arbitrator's opinion after hearing the evidence before him the letting is hypothetical, not real. It is therefore not direct evidence of what is happening in the market.'

Expressed in such language the reasoning could appear compelling. But given this explanation, what now is the relevance of any rent-review settlement? Are not all such agreements simply reflections of the negotiating parties' opinions, and of their relative strengths and weaknesses in negotiating the outcome? All rent reviews are assessed on the basis of a letting which is 'hypothetical, not real'.

Maybe the only true market rental evidence is the open market letting. Yet even if this evidence were available it might nevertheless be flawed in open market terms since the transaction is essentially an agreement, unique to the parties involved.

Exactly when does a decision stop being an opinion and turn into fact?
Answers on a postcard, please.
Elisabeth Carter ARICS
Leicester"

THE RESPONDENT MAKES AN APPLICATION DURING THE HEARING TO HAVE HIS KEY WITNESS OF FACT CALLED AS AN EXPERT

The facts

094 At the preliminary meeting in a construction dispute the parties agreed to one expert each. The dispute was for loss and expense resulting from a severely extended subcontract and involved such issues as disruption, uneconomic working and loss of productivity, as well as prolongation.

095 The interlocutory stage proceeded normally until the point shortly before the hearing when the experts were due to meet "without prejudice" as directed by the arbitrator, to agree figures as figures and narrow the issues so far as possible. The experts had been instructed to prepare a joint report setting out those points on which they agreed and those on which they did not. Shortly before the hearing the respondent's solicitor contacted the advocate for the claimant and informed him that they would not be engaging an independent expert; instead they would rely on their in-house surveyor who had been an employee of the respondent's company for the last 20 years. He also attempted to talk the claimant out of using an expert saying that the nature of the dispute was such that it did not warrant one.

096 As a result of this late change of mind the claimant's expert's report was served on the other side and copied to the arbitrator only two days before the hearing.

097 The hearing proceeded until the claimant's expert was called and he concluded his evidence in chief. This coincided with the rest day and overnight the respondent's counsel faxed his response to the claimant's expert's report but not styled as such. This response was said to be the basis of argument on which the respondent's counsel intended to cross-examine the claimant's expert.

098 No objection was made to these exhibits at the resumed hearing and the cross-examination proceeded.

099 As the argument unfolded and the respondent's response was put to the claimant's expert, it became clear that it was not as asserted by respondent's counsel's logical argument deduced from the claimant's expert's figures but, in effect, points made in a report prepared for counsel by the respondent's in-house surveyor.

100 The claimant's advocate expressed his concern that this was opinion evidence being introduced through "the back door". He averred that it was opinion that could not be tested in cross-examination by the claimant as the questions derived from a report which was not being adduced in evidence. As such the principle of mutuality and fairness was not being observed.

Question

101 What reaction should the arbitrator make to the claimant's expressed concern?

Course of action

102 The claims consultant, advocate of the claimant, has missed the point. The respondent's counsel can ask the claimant's expert any questions he likes provided they are relevant to the points in issue. The fact that the questions result from a report from one of his client's witnesses is totally irrelevant. What is clear is that this is not as averred by the claimant's representative opinion evidence "through the back door".

103 Advance notice of matters on which it is intended to cross-examine the expert is *not* evidence. Here the last minute change of heart was unfortunate as it might have assisted the arbitrator to hear an opposing expert's opinion.

104 The arbitrator could perhaps have reminded counsel for the respondent that one of the purposes of having experts was to avoid the parties being taken by surprise as to the true nature of the dispute. The parties should proceed to a hearing in the knowledge rather than the ignorance of the strength and weakness of their respective cases. The principle was mutuality and fairness. With the experts concentrating on the controversies a great deal of wasted effort, labour, cost and expense could be saved and the hearing shortened.

105 In responding to the claimant's advocate's complaint the arbitrator, whilst admitting that arbitration proceedings were not bound by the same rules as those which govern proceedings in the High Court, took guidance from s.2(3) of the Civil Evidence Act 1972. He said that his understanding of this section was that the pre-trial disclosure of an expert's report was a precondition to that evidence being admitted or, in the event of non-compliance with a direction to the effect that the reports be exchanged, a party may be debarred from adducing oral evidence on the matter. (Note: this was before the Civil Evidence Act (CEA) 1995 became operative—see paras 374–408 below.) He emphasised again that the respondent's surveyor's report being used as the basis for cross-examining the claimant's expert was not an expert's report *per se*.

106 The arbitrator pointed out that irrespective of how counsel conducted his cross-examination he could not express opinions during this cross-examination, or if he did, that would not be opinion evidence. Advocates can never be experts (and *vice versa*) at the same time.

107 Had there been an expert on each side, *ab initio*, could the arbitrator have directed these experts to meet "without prejudice" in an attempt to further narrow the issues, albeit that the hearing was well advanced? As the arbitrator said in his submission to counsel and advocate he was not bound by the Rules of the Supreme Court but sought guidance from them.

108 Order 38, rule 38 provides:

> "In any cause or matter the court may, if it thinks fit, direct that there be a meeting 'without prejudice' of such experts within such periods before or after disclosure of their reports as the courts may specify, for the purpose of identifying those parts of their evidence which are an issue. Where such a meeting takes place, the experts may prepare a joint statement indicating those parts of their evidence on which they are, and those on which they are not, in agreement."

109 The note to the rule contains the following comment:

> "the major objective of the rule is to produce as wide an area of consensus between the experts (as possible), in which case, they should indicate in their joint statement those parts of their evidence on which they are agreed. Such agreement will have the effect of removing the protection of 'without prejudice' in respect of the matters agreed upon."

110 In *Richard Roberts Holdings Ltd* v. *Douglas Smith Stimson Partnership and Others (No 2)* (1989) 47 BLR 117, Newey J said that he

> "... respectfully disagreed with the proposition that an order that experts should agree a statement made in reliance upon rule 38 can confer upon them an authority to bind the parties instructing them and a joint written statement made at the conclusion of a 'without prejudice' meeting is automatically an 'open' statement.
>
> In my opinion there are no words in rule 38 which purport to confer upon experts power to bind anyone. If it did, then since the rule would not be dealing with procedure, but with the substantive rights of persons under the laws of agency, it would, I think, be *ultra vires*.
>
> ... Whether a court may direct that there be a meeting of experts after the trial has begun is a matter of conjecture."

111 Newey J went on to say that it may be that rule 38

> "is so widely expressed that a court could order a meeting of experts even after a trial has begun but in practice in the official referees' courts meetings are ordered on summonses for directions. Once a trial has commenced meetings only take place by agreement of the parties and this is so even if the court has expressed the view that a meeting would be desirable."

(See paras 574–587.)

112 In *Shell Pension Trust Ltd* v. *Pell Frischman & Ptnrs (a firm)* [1986] 2 All ER 911 Judge Newey had admitted the party's evidence as that of an expert witness on the grounds that provided that witness was sufficiently expert (*peritus*) then his evidence could be admitted.

AN EX-EMPLOYEE WISHES TO APPEAR AS AN EXPERT WITNESS FOR THE PARTY WHO PREVIOUSLY EMPLOYED HIM

The facts

113 A property company employed an architect on its staff and one of the projects entrusted to him ended up in dispute. The arbitration clause was invoked and eventually a hearing took place.

114 The claimant property company requested permission to call the architect who had by then left its employ as an expert witness on quality of workmanship.

Question

115 Should the arbitrator allow the claimant to call this person as an expert witness?

Course of action

116 The function of an expert witness of opinion is to furnish the judge with the necessary scientific criteria for testing the accuracy of his conclusions, so as to enable the judge to form his own independent judgment by application of those criteria to the facts proved in evidence (*Davie* v. *Magistrates of Edinburgh* 1953 SC 34). Also it is accepted that the expert witness has a number of other miscellaneous duties—to prepare reports, publish and exchange such reports, advise his client etc.

117 It is not the expert's function to act as advocate for his client, i.e. the party paying his fees, but to assist the tribunal by giving it the benefit of his knowledge and experience (see paras 084–093 above). He must be impartial and independent. An ex-employee may find difficulty in fulfilling this independent role but he is more independent than the project manager or architect/surveyor in paras 084–093 above. It is said that cogent evidence can only be given by someone who *is* independent. I see no reason to prevent the arbitrator from saying, when granting consent to call the architect as an expert, that such opinion evidence as he may adduce would carry more weight if it came from a witness who is seen to be totally independent.

118 The respondent objected to this architect being called as an expert witness on the grounds that witnesses with particular experience of the facts of the issues in dispute cannot give independent evidence of opinion simply because of their connection with the factual matrix. The arbitrator disagreed and said that his understanding was that witnesses of a fact may give opinion evidence in certain circumstances, for example an architect on quality of workmanship. This is not correct. The evidence of this architect is only his opinion at the time the work was done—after that it is evidence of fact on what he did at the time.

119 Having been given leave to adduce expert evidence the choice of expert is that of the party.

120 A statement by the arbitrator to the effect that the architect's opinion evidence will carry less weight than similar evidence from a totally independent expert is inadvisable. There is a presumption to be drawn from the arbitrator's statement that he will be biased against this witness merely because he avers some form of allegiance to the party who has engaged him to give evidence. Far better for the arbitrator to wait until he has heard the evidence and to leave any comment concerning weight afforded to any particular evidence until writing his award, i.e. "I prefer the evidence of 'X' because . . .".

IS A DOCTOR ANY DIFFERENT FROM ANY OTHER EXPERT WITNESS?

The facts

121 W was charged with rape, and a witness summons was served on the complainant's general practitioner requiring his attendance at the trial and further requiring him "to produce medical reports in your possession relating to the complainant". The doctor duly attended in compliance with the summons, but handed the records to W's solicitors.

Question

122 When a doctor is called as a witness of fact does his Hippocratic oath preclude him from giving evidence concerning intimate communications which the patient may have made to him?

Course of action

123 The facts of this example were drawn from *R* v. *Westcott* [1983] Crim LR 545.

124 In this case the trial judge refused an application by defending counsel to be allowed to cross-examine the complainant on her medical history.

125 After the jury had retired the judge indicated to both prosecuting and defending counsel that only in exceptional cases should a summons be issued for a witness to produce medical records relating to the complainant and only when it was shown that there were substantial grounds for thinking that such records contained relevant matters. Where such a summons was issued it should be absolutely clear to the witness that he was only to produce the documents to the court, and not to disclose them to the legal advisers for the prosecution or the defence, until the court has decided whether they should be disclosed.

126 A doctor who is called as an expert witness simply to give his opinion does not differ, in the eyes of the law, from any other expert witness. His communications, even where of an intimate nature, are not protected in the same way as a client's communications with his legal advisers.

127 Should a doctor called to give evidence refuse to testify as to what he has learned during a professional consultation, he may be held in contempt of court and sent to prison (*Nuttall* v. *Nuttall and Twyman* (1964) 108 SJ 605).

128 However, a court may exercise its discretion and allow a doctor to refrain from answering particularly embarrassing and confidential questions. In *Att-Gen* v. *Mulholland; Att-Gen* v. *Foster* [1963] 2 QB 466 Lord Denning MR said:

> "The only profession that I know which is given a privilege from disclosing information to a court of law is the legal profession and then it is not the privilege of the lawyer but of his client. Take the clergyman, the banker and the medical man. None of these is entitled to refuse to answer when directed to by a judge. Let me not be mistaken. The judge will respect the confidences which each of these honourable professions receives in the course of it, and will not direct him to answer unless not only is it relevant but also it is a proper and, indeed, necessary question in the course of justice to be put and answered. The judge is the person entrusted on behalf of the community to weigh these conflicting interests, to weigh on the one hand the respect due to confidence in the profession and on the other hand the ultimate interest of the community in justice being done, e.g. in the case of a tribunal such as this, in a proper investigation being made into these serious allegations."

129 However, it was made clear in *R* v. *Westcott* when a doctor has a witness summons served upon him, requiring his attendance at a trial and requiring him to produce medical reports in his possession relating to a patient, he should not disclose the medical reports to legal advisers for any party in the proceedings until the judge has ruled whether or not the documents are admissible.

THE CORRECT STANDARD IS NOT WHAT THE EXPERT WOULD HAVE DONE

The facts

130 The plaintiff was born on 27 December 1969 and was referred to Southend General Hospital in July 1986 with swellings on his neck. In September 1986 he was referred to University College Hospital for a second opinion and was diagnosed as suffering from a rare congenital condition known as plexiform neurofibroma.

131 In a negligence action against the two hospitals, as first and second defendants, expert medical evidence was adduced to the effect that the witness giving that evidence might have acted differently from the medical practitioner.

Question

132 Where does the expert's duty lie in a situation like this?

Course of action

133 The facts of the above example are taken broadly from *Sharpe* v. *Southend Health Authority and Another*, 25 April 1997, QBD; [1997] 8 Med LR 299.

134 In giving his judgment in favour of the first defendant (the claim against the second defendant was withdrawn in the plaintiff's counsel's closing speech), Cresswell J stated:

> "... the duties and responsibilities of expert witnesses in civil cases are set out in *The Ikarian Reefer* [1993] 2 Lloyd's Rep 68. I would add the following in relation to medical negligence cases. In such cases the defendant will not be held to have been negligent if he/she acted in accordance with a practice accepted as proper by a responsible body of practitioners skilled in the relevant field. There is seldom any one answer exclusive of all others to problems of professional judgement. A court may prefer one body of opinion to another, but that is no basis for a finding of negligence, although the question whether there was or was not negligence is at the end of the day one for the courts. An expert witness should make it clear in his/her report (if it be the case) that although the expert would have adopted a different/approach practice, he/she accepts that the approach/practice adopted by the defendant was in accordance with the approach/practice as proper by a responsible body of practitioners skilled in the relevant field ...."

135 On a related point, the Queen's Bench Division ruled in *Sanderson* v. *Liverpool Health Authority* (*The Expert*, June 1997 at p. 25) that if the case had not been pleaded or conducted on the basis that a hospital's facilities were inadequate or it was operating a negligent policy for procedures, there was no scope for experts to engage in comparing systems, "despite the surprise and misgivings expressed by some of the expert witnesses".

ONE PARTY APPOINTS AN EXPERT, THE OTHER PARTY FAILS TO DO SO

The facts

136 At the preliminary meeting in a maritime arbitration, the arbitrator directed on the application of the parties that one expert be allowed on each side and that expert reports were to be agreed so far as possible.

137 One side subsequently decided not to appoint an expert and as a result the other party refused to disclose its expert's report.

138 At the hearing, the party who had not appointed an expert objected to expert evidence being given by the other side, unless they were given time to consider it.

Question

139 Is the expert evidence admissible?

Course of action

140 The direction given by the arbitrator, by consent, following the preliminary meeting included, *inter alia*:

> **"9.00 EXPERTS**
>
> 9.01 Each party intends to instruct one expert. The parties will attempt to agree on joint instructions. A copy of the agreed instruction to be sent to me or, if no agreement, details of those points of instruction on which they do agree and details of those on which they do not.
>
> 9.02 These instructions to state whether experts will meet 'open' or 'without prejudice' and also what authority they have (if any) to bind their respective parties. In any event 'without prejudice' attaching to these discussions shall be removed in respect of matters agreed upon.
>
> 9.03 The experts to consider exchanging draft reports before they meet but, in any event, not later than eight weeks after the service of the last statement or reply to any request for further and better particulars thereof (see 7.06.6 of the Agenda) for the preliminary meeting and to meet within two weeks of this exchange.
>
> 9.04 The experts shall endeavour to narrow the issues and to agree facts as facts, figures as figures etc. as far as possible.
>
> 9.05 They shall prepare, date and sign a note of the facts and opinions upon which they are agreed and of the issues upon which they are not. A copy of such note to be exchanged and delivered to me within 14 days of their final meeting but, in any event, no later than 14 days before the hearing. Reports not exchanged will not be admitted."

141 Basically, here is a case of the parties having agreed on a procedural matter under s.34(1), AA '96. Having made this agreement it is quite unreasonable for one party unilaterally to change this arrangement. However, no one can force them to appoint their own expert. Equally, not having done so they should still be given reasonable time to consider the other side's experts' reports.

142 It is unfortunate that the arbitrator was not informed earlier of the failure of the defaulting party, as he would normally direct, otherwise he could have further directed that the sole expert report be disclosed to the other side in advance of the hearing. Indeed, it could be said that by not being on top of this case—he should have noted the failure of the parties to comply with his direction 9.05, some two weeks before the hearing—he is guilty of failing to avoid unnecessary delay under the duty imposed upon him by s.33.

143 As a general rule, unless disclosed to the other side prior to the hearing, expert evidence is inadmissible at the hearing, except by agreement between the parties or by leave of the arbitrator, which would only normally be given on terms, i.e. costs against the party seeking to adduce this previously undisclosed evidence.

144 The best the arbitrator can now do to resolve the situation is to try to persuade the parties to agree on a procedure which will not cause an adjournment of the hearing. He should order the party with the expert to disclose their expert's report forthwith and at the same time grant leave to adduce it and, if unavoidable, be prepared to grant an adjournment should it be requested in order to give the other side sufficient time to consider the expert's report.

145 It would do no harm for the arbitrator to point out to the party objecting to this expert's evidence that it could have raised this objection prior to the hearing and thus save the cost of the adjournment.

146 Although not bound by the *White Book*, the arbitrator could well follow the guidance given therein, *inter alia*, in RSC Order 38, rules 4, 35 and 36:

> **Rule 4** provides, *inter alia*:
> "In Admiralty actions, *Practice Direction (Admiralty: Evidence of Expert Witnesses)* [1968] 1 WLR 312; [1968] 1 All ER 447 applies. It sets out as follows:
>> 'Where a party intends to adduce expert evidence, he should produce to the other party his expert's statement of proposed evidence, together with any reports, plans, models, calculations etc. relevant to it, for agreement if possible. Failing such agreement, the other party should deliver to the first party a written statement setting out particulars of the matters not agreed. Failure by any party to follow this procedure may result in a special order as to costs'."
>
> **Rule 35/2** provides, *inter alia*:
> "The machinery for the pre-trial disclosure of expert evidence is intended to operate on the basis of fairness and mutuality as between the parties, and conversely neither party should be able or should be allowed to operate such machinery so as to overreach any other party, by obtaining the disclosure of the party's expert evidence before the trial without at the same time disclosing his own expert evidence to that party or being precluded from calling such expert evidence at the (civil) trial.
>
> To achieve such fairness and mutuality, the machinery is intended to operate so as to provide for the simultaneous exchange of experts' reports on or before a fixed date which it may be convenient to call the 'exchange date', and the parties will be expected and required, to carry out arrangements for the exchange of experts' reports in the sense of simultaneously disclosing their reports to each other."
>
> **Rule 36(2)** provides, *inter alia*:
> "The rule leaves it open to the parties to agree that all or any of them may adduce expert evidence at the trial without seeking a direction of the court whether or not there should be any pre-trial disclosure of such expert evidence. For this purpose, all the parties must agree on this course and such agreement should be explicit and precise . . . .
>
> On the other hand, the power to order the compulsory disclosure of expert evidence under r.37 or r.41 does not affect the right of any party voluntarily to disclose his own experts' reports to the opposite party in the negotiations before litigation is started, or thereafter at an earlier stage than the summons for directions. The voluntary disclosure of such reports makes it easier to demonstrate to the court that the relevant expert evidence on both sides is of a kind which is appropriate for an order for compulsory exchange; and in any event, the disclosure of such report is a condition precedent to its admissibility as of right as evidence at the trial.
>
> . . . the rule recognises that the sanction for the failure or refusal to comply with such orders or directions of the court could be the stay or dismissal of the action or the striking out of the defence, as the case may be.
>
> The court has an inherent jurisdiction to refuse leave to adduce expert evidence where prejudice to a party to the action would be caused by the need to seek an adjournment of the trial to deal with such evidence (*Winchester Cigarette Machinery Ltd* v. *Payne*, (1993) *The Times*, 19 October, CA)."

147 In this case the party who had previously decided that they would not appoint an expert then sought leave to appoint one to bring forward evidence to challenge the expert's report. The arbitrator should have granted leave with any costs thrown away to be borne by the applying party.

148 An interesting light was thrown on this issue by the Master of the Rolls, Lord Woolf, in *Beachley Property Ltd* v. *Edgar* [1996] CILL 1182, CA. In this case witness statements were served late and in contravention to the County Courts Rules. This required an application to the court for leave to adduce the evidence therein.

149 Order 20, rule 12A(10) of the County Court Rules provides:

"Where a party fails to comply with a direction for the exchange of witness statements he shall not be entitled to adduce evidence to which the direction related without the leave of the court."

150 Lord Woolf had this to say, *inter alia*, in this case:

"The explanation for the witness statements being served so late, and for the application being made at the relatively last moment for leave for those witnesses' evidence to be adduced at the hearing, is apparently that there was a change in the plaintiff's solicitors' office so that the same person was not dealing with the case throughout.

I would emphasise that I regard that as no explanation or excuse whatsoever for the non-compliance with directions with regard to witness statements.

The situation is that evidence which is contained in the statements does go to one of what may be the most important issues in this case. There can be no possible excuse for the plaintiff not adducing that evidence at an earlier stage.

In support of the appeal, Miss Bhaloo says that if that is right there is still no evidence that the defendants have been prejudiced in any way by that failure on their part.

It was submitted by Miss Bhaloo that unless there was some evidence of prejudice on their part which could be shown by the defendant, in these circumstances the court has no alternative but to allow the calling of the evidence in relation to which there has not been compliance with the orders of the court. I would like to make it absolutely clear that I do not accept that submission. The very reason why the order is drafted in the terms that it is is to ensure that unless there are circumstances which justify the court exercising discretion in favour of the party in default, that discretion will not be exercised and the party will be deprived of the evidence. It is no use the party coming forward and saying 'The evidence will help our case'. If this is the position, the rule may as well not exist. You have to consider the position not only from the plaintiff's point of view, but also from the point of view of the defendant, and with a view to doing justice between other litigants as well."

151 The learned author of CILL had this to say of this case:

"Although this is not a building case there seems no reason why it should not be a general application. In particular, it illustrates the new attitude of the Master of the Rolls—no doubt anxious to set the tone for his procedural reforms.

Prior to this case the conventional approach of the courts would be to let the evidence in. The general rule has been that, in the absence of prejudice that cannot be compensated for by a costs award, the court always allowed procedural omission to be made good.

Confident that this has been the approach, parties have very frequently served witness statements and experts' reports later than the date ordered.

The draconian order in this case, excluding the evidence altogether, will send shivers down many spines, although it remains to be seen whether the official referees will, as a matter of routine, start adopting the Woolf line."

IF AN EXPERT HAS BEEN CONSULTED BY ONE SIDE AND HAS GIVEN HIS OPINION TO THAT SIDE, CAN HE THEREAFTER BE CONSULTED AND SUBPOENAED BY THE OTHER SIDE TO GIVE HIS OPINION ON THE FACTS OF THE CASE?

The facts

152 A handwriting expert, who had had a consultation with those advising the plaintiffs in an action concerning a charterparty, was later approached by the solicitors acting for the defendants in the action. After giving them an opinion on certain documents the expert realised that they concerned the same matter on which he had already been consulted by the plaintiffs. He then informed the defendants' solicitors that he could not accept further instructions from them as it was not his practice, once consulted by one party to an action, to accept instructions from another party. The defendants, anxious to secure the expert evidence, served him with a *subpoena ad testificandum.*

153 The plaintiffs objected to the expert being allowed to give evidence and issued a writ, against the expert and the defendants in the main action for:

(1) An injunction restraining the expert from disclosing to the defendants:

(a) the nature or terms of any instructions given to him by the plaintiffs;
(b) the fact of, or nature of, any terms of any advice given by him to the plaintiff;
(c) any information given to him by the plaintiffs for the purpose of, or in connection with such advice;
(d) any information obtained by him when acting pursuant to those instructions.

(2) An injunction requiring the expert to apply to the court to set aside the subpoena served on him.
(3) An injunction restraining the defendant:

(a) from appearing voluntarily to testify on behalf of the defendants in the main action;
(b) from accepting or continuing to accept further instructions from the defendants;
(c) from advising or continuing to advise the defendants.

(4) An injunction restraining the defendants to the main action from procuring or inducing the expert to do anything it was sought to restrain him from doing under paragraphs (1) to (3).

Question

154 Was the judge right in refusing to set aside the subpoena or to refuse to exclude the expert from giving evidence?

Course of action

155 This was the situation in *Harmony Shipping Co SA* v. *Saudi Europe Line* [1979] 1 WLR 1380, CA, where Lloyd J did refuse the plaintiff's application.

156 The plaintiffs appealed against the judge's refusal to uphold their objection on the grounds:

(1) That the judge was wrong in law in holding that the defendants were entitled to consult and call a witness, Derek Davis, a forensic expert consulted and employed by the plaintiffs to advise them in connection with the litigation between the plaintiffs and the defendants.

(2) The judge was wrong in law in holding that the expert was entitled to accept instructions from, advise and give evidence for the defendants.
(3) The judge failed to exercise his discretion and/or exercised it on wrong principles in considering whether the defendants should be entitled to consult and call as a witness the expert.
(4) The judge was wrong in law in holding that there was not to be implied into a contract between the party to litigation and an expert employed by him a term that he will not accept instructions from an opposing party nor voluntarily appear to give evidence for that party.
(5) The judge was wrong in law in holding that there was no relevant distinction between an expert witness and a witness of fact.
(6) The judge was wrong in law in holding that there was an overriding public interest that a party should be free to call whatever witnesses, including experts, he desires.
(7) The judge was wrong in law in holding that such public interest overrode the public interest that a party to litigation should be free to consult and employ an expert to advise him in the litigation and be able in so doing to respose complete trust and confidence in him.
(8) The judge was wrong in law in holding that an express term of the contract between the party to litigation and an expert that he would not accept instructions from an opposing party or appear voluntarily to give evidence for that party was invalid as being against public policy.
(9) The judge was wrong in law and/or misdirected himself in not holding that the expert once consulted by a party to litigation could not thereafter act for an opposing party without the serious risk that he would use or disclose confidential information gained in connection with his consultation with the first party or otherwise would be placed or be seen to be placed in a position of conflict of interest.

157 The plaintiffs also appealed against the refusal of injunctions sought in the subsidiary action on the same grounds as in their notice of appeal in the main action and on the additional ground that the judge erred in law

(1) and/or failed to exercise his discretion on correct principles in considering whether to grant an interlocutory injunction and in failing to hold that on the balance of convenience an injunction should have been granted;
(2) in holding that there was no evidence on which to grant the injunction sought in paragraph (1) of the claim and in holding that public policy precluded him from granting an injunction in the terms of paragraphs (2) and (3) thereof; and
(3) in holding that to grant an injunction restraining the expert from giving evidence voluntarily would be either nugatory or have the effect of compelling him to disobey the subpoena.

158 It was held, in dismissing the appeal, that the general rule that there was no property in a witness of fact applied also to an expert witness, though such a witness could not give evidence as to communications, arising in the course of his being instructed by one party, which were protected by legal professional privilege; that, on the evidence, there was no contract, express or implied, between the plaintiffs and handwriting expert to the effect that he would not voluntarily assist the defendants; and that, accordingly, the defendants were entitled to subpoena him.

Per Denning MR. A contract by which a witness bound himself not to give evidence before the court on the matter on which the judge said he ought to give evidence would be contrary to public policy or would not be enforced by the court. We have it here.
Per Waller LJ. It is clearly undesirable that expert witnesses should be involved with both sides.
Per Cumming-Bruce LJ. It is not necessarily for the determination of the appeal to consider the situation of any other kind of expert in any other kind of situation; and the court decides only the obligations that arise from the very peculiar facts of the case.
Decision of Lloyd J affirmed.

159 As their Lordships, in this case, gave some seminal guidance on broader issues concerning the property in and the compellability of a witness, the full judgment of this case is reproduced hereto.

"LORD DENNING MR. Mr Davis is an expert in handwriting. He finds himself in an embarrassing position. He has been consulted by both sides in an action. The question is whether he should give evidence for one side without the consent of the other.

The plaintiffs in that action, Harmony Shipping Co SA, own a ship called the *Good Helmsman*. They allowed the defendants, a Saudi Arabian company, the use of that ship. Hire would be payable to the plaintiffs for the use of the ship during the time the defendants had it. The case involves the question of the charterparty. The defendants by one of their agents, signed a charterparty for the hire of the vessel in December 1976. The shipowners sue upon that charterparty. They say that the ship was delivered under it and that the charterers are liable for the hire accordingly. But the defendants seek to avoid their obligations under that charterparty. They say,

> 'It is a sham. It was never intended to be a real charterparty. It was only signed so that it could be taken to the bank in order that the plaintiffs could raise money from the bank on it.'

That is not a very laudable defence: but that is what the defendants say.

The question has arisen as to the validity of a particular document which appears to have come into being on 9 February 1977. It is a letter from the Harmony Shipping Co. to the master of the *Good Helmsman*. It says:

> 'Re Charterparty dated 3 December 1976. The Captain. Enclosed please find a copy of charterparty dated 3 December 1976, attached with *adendem* (sic) dated 22 January, 1977, between Harmony Shipping Co and Saudi Europe line. Please treat the charterers like owners and offer them the most possible facilities.'

If that is a genuine, good, authentic letter, it goes far to show that this was a genuine charterparty—intended to be acted upon by the master of the vessel. The defendants say that that is not a good, valid or genuine document, only carbon copies were produced of it: and one carbon seems to differ from an earlier one.

In order to prove that the latter was genuine and authentic, a firm of London solicitors, Messrs Holman Fenwick and Willan, acted for the plaintiffs decided to obtain the services of a handwriting expert. They approached Mr Davis.

Mr Davis is a very busy man. We had been told that he works on about 200 cases at any one time. He always does his best to avoid accepting instructions from more than one side in any particular case. That is one of his professional rules. He maintains a systematic index record of instructions which he has received.

When Messrs Holman Fenwick and Willan decided to consult Mr Davis, he happened to be engaged in another case in these courts and was waiting to be called as a witness. After communicating with his secretary, it appeared to Mr Davis that he had not been consulted by anyone else in this case. So he saw Mr Robinson of Messrs Holman Fenwick and Willan on 27 February 1979, outside Court 26 in this building. At that interview carbon copies of the letter were produced to Mr Davis. He expressed his opinion as to the genuineness and authenticity of one or other of them. At the same time there was discussion about his fee. There was communication between counsel and Mr Davis. He said that it was not his practice to accept instructions for one side once he had been instructed by the other side. Something was said to the effect that he would give his usual undertaking that he would not accept instructions from the other side.

I think it may be inferred that Mr Davis said that in his opinion the letters were not genuine. So his evidence would not help the plaintiffs, the clients of Messrs Holman Fenwick and Willan. Therefore, they told him that they would not be wanting his assistance again; but, if they did, they would let him know. That was on 27 February in 1979. That was all that Mr Davis heard about the matter from the plaintiff's side.

In April 1979, Mr Davis was being consulted by Messrs Thomas Cooper & Stibbard about another case. Then, on Friday, received a message from Messrs Thomas Cooper & Stibbard asking him whether he could give his opinion on some documents which had been brought in. He said he would. He saw one was from Mssrs Thomas Cooper & Stibbard. He examined the documents and gave his opinion of them. He probably said that they were not genuine. So his evidence would help the defendants, the clients of Thomas Cooper & Stibbard. But in the course of his conversation with a partner from Messrs Thomas Cooper & Stibbard something was said as a result of which, for the first time, it occurred to Mr Davis that he had already been consulted by the other side. So he referred to his file and realised it might be the same matter. Immediately he told the partner from Messrs Thomas Cooper & Stibbard:

> 'I cannot accept any further instruction in the matter since I have already been consulted by the other side.'

There it is. On 27 February he had given his opinion on some of the documents to the solicitors for one side and then on 6 April he had given his opinion on like documents to the solicitors for the other side. He had done it quite inadvertently. Having discovered that he had given his opinion to the other side, he said he could go no further.

Messrs Thomas Cooper & Stibbard wanted his evidence because they realised it would be helpful to the defendants. They attended at counsel's chambers. A decision was reached that they would subpoena Mr Davis to give evidence on their behalf. That is what they did. They issued a *subpoena ad testificandum* on Mr Davis so that he should give evidence in the case as to his opinion on the genuineness of these letters—to the effect that they were not genuine. The plaintiffs took objection. They said that Mr Davis should not have been subpoenaed. They said that the subpoena ought to be set aside because he should not give any evidence as he had already been consulted by them.

The trial has been going on for a long time. Lloyd J has been considering the case for some weeks. He has ruled that Mr Davis is compellable and ought to give evidence as to his opinion of these documents. He said that there was no reason for barring him from doing so, but, as it was a difficult point which had never arisen before, he adjourned the case pending the decision of the Court of Appeal as to whether he was right or wrong.

So we have before us a question of principle. If an expert has been consulted by one side and has given his opinion to that side, can he thereafter be consulted and subpoenaed by the other side to give his opinion on the facts of the case? That is the issue which the court has to decide.

So far as witnesses of fact are concerned, the law is as plain as can be. There is no property in a witness. The reason is because the court has the right to everyman's evidence. Its primary duty is to ascertain the truth. Neither one side nor the other can debar the court from ascertaining the truth either by seeing a witness beforehand or by purchasing his evidence or by making communication to him. In no way can one side prohibit the other side from seeing a witness of fact, from getting the facts from him and from calling him to give evidence or from issuing him with the subpoena. That was laid down by the Law Society in 1944 and published in the *Short Guide to Professional Conduct and Etiquette*. It was affirmed and approved in 1963 by the then Lord Chief Justice and the judges and was republished in the *Law Society's Gazette* for February 1963. It says:

> '... the Council will have always held the view that there was no property in a witness and that so long as there is no question of tampering with evidence of witnesses it is open to a solicitor for either party to civil or criminal proceedings to interview and take a statement from any witness or prospective witness at any stage of the proceedings, whether or not that witness has been interviewed or called as a witness by the other party.'

That principle is established in the case of a witness of fact for the plain, simple reason that the primary duty of the court is to ascertain the truth by the best evidence available. Any witness who has seen the facts or knows the facts can be compelled to assist the court and should assist the court by giving that evidence.

The question in this case is whether or not that principle applies to expert witnesses. They may have been told the substance of the party's case. They may have been given a great deal of confidential information on it. They may have given advice to the party. Does the rule apply to such a case?

Many of the communications between the solicitor and the expert witness will be privileged. They are protected by legal professional privilege. They cannot be communicated to the court except with the consent of the party concerned. That means that a great deal of communication between the expert witness and a lawyer cannot be given in evidence to the court. If questions were asked about it, then it would be the duty of the judge to protect the witness (and he would) by disallowing any questions which infringed the rule about legal professional privilege or the rule protecting information given in confidence—unless, of course, it was one of those rare cases which come before the courts from time to time where in spite of privilege or confidence the court does order a witness to give further evidence.

Subject to that qualification, it seems to me that an expert witness falls into the same position as a witness of fact. The court is entitled, in order to ascertain the truth, to have the actual facts which he has observed adduced before it and to have his independent opinion on those facts. It is interesting to see that it was so held in Canada in *MacDonald Construction Co Ltd* v. *Bestway Lath and Plastering Ltd* (1972) 27 DLR (3d) 253.

In this particular case the court is entitled to have before it the documents in question and it is entitled to have the independent opinion of the expert witness on those documents and on those facts—excluding, as I have said, any of the other communications which passed when the expert witness was being instructed or employed by the other side. Subject to that exception, it seems to me (and I would agree with the judge upon this) that the expert witness is in the same position when he is speaking as to the facts he has observed and is giving his own independent opinion on them, no matter by which side he is instructed.

In this particular case Mr Davis has been subpoenaed by the defendants. It seems to me that that is very right and proper. It was suggested that the subpoena should be set-aside. As far as I know, no *subpoena ad testificandum* has ever been set-aside except at the instance of the witness himself when he has claimed that it would be oppressive to make him answer that subpoena. Otherwise the *subpoena ad testificandum* must be obeyed by the witness. He must come to the court and be ready to give his evidence and answer such questions as the judge permits to be answered. He will be protected insofar as there is any proper claim for legal professional privilege or confidence. So, it seems to me, on principle that Mr Davis can be subpoenaed. He can be seen beforehand and give a proof on those limited matters I have mentioned, and give evidence accordingly.

Against this argument of principle, Mr Bathurst put forward this argument. He said that in this case there was an express contract: or, alternatively, an implied contract to the effect that Mr Davis would not voluntarily assist the other side. He analysed the evidence, and submitted that in the conversation, which I have mentioned, of 27 February, it was understood that Mr Davis would not accept instructions from the other side, however inadvertently. Mr Bathurst submitted that Mr Davis recognised [this]: because as soon as he realised what had happened, he said that he could not go on any further in the case at all.

To my mind no such contract, express or implied, is to be found. At least there was a statement by Mr Davis of his practice, namely, that, having been instructed by one side, he would not accept instructions from the other. That is a statement of a proper professional practice. It is no doubt very valuable in order to save embarrassment to him and others like him when they are placed in a situation like this as handwriting experts often are because there are not many of them. But it is not a contract. It is not a binding contract at law, express or implied. But I would go further. If there was a contract by which a witness bound himself not to give evidence before the court on a matter on which the judge said he ought to be giving evidence, then I say that any such contract would be contrary to public policy and would not be enforced by the court. It is the primary duty of the courts to ascertain the truth and, when a witness is subpoenaed, he must answer such questions as the court properly asks him. This duty is not to be taken away by some private arrangement or contract by him with one side or the other.

So on those two grounds (1) that there is no proof of any contract, express or implied, and (2) that it is against public policy, I would hold that the point raised by Mr Bathurst in this case is not a good one.

I would add a further consideration of public policy. If an expert could have his hands tied by being instructed by one side, it would be very easy for a rich client to consult each of the acknowledged experts in the field. Each expert might give an opinion adverse to the rich man—yet the rich man could say to each of the acknowledged experts in the field:

> 'Your mouth is closed and you cannot give evidence in the court against me.'

We were told that in the Admiralty courts, where there are a very limited number of experts, one side may consult every single one of them. Does that mean that the other side is debarred from getting the help of any expert evidence because all the experts have been taken up by the other side?

The answer is clearly No. It comes back to the proposition which I stated at the beginning. There is no property in a witness of fact. There is no property in an expert witness as to the facts he has observed and his own independent opinion on them. There has been no such property in the witness. It is the duty of a witness to come to court and give his evidence insofar as he is directed by the judge to do so.

I find myself in general agreement with the judgment of Lloyd J, and would dismiss the appeal.

WALLER LJ. I believe that Mr Davis has found himself in a difficult position in spite of all the steps he has taken to avoid such a position; and his first reaction when he realised what had happened was to say,

> 'I take no further part in this matter.'

But the field in which he's an expert is one in which there are not very many people of ability. Therefore, this situation has arisen where he has been subpoenaed by the defendants to give evidence although he has first been consulted by the plaintiffs.

As Lord Denning MR said, the general principle must be that no party has any property in the witness; and the argument before us has partly involved a discussion as to whether there is the difference between a witness of fact and an expert. In my view, there is no difference between these two kinds of witnesses as a matter of general rule. Were it otherwise, as Lord Denning MR has indicated, in the sphere of a small number of specialists it might be possible for one party to buy up all the possible experts and clearly such a situation is not right. On the other hand, it is clearly undesirable that expert witnesses should be involved with both sides, and Mr Davis has, very properly, a rule of conduct which he adopts for himself to use his very best endeavours to make sure that such a state of affairs does not happen. I say at once that I feel great sympathy with him in this case where his first involvement was in a hurried consultation during the midday adjournment whilst he was engaged in giving evidence in another case. That indicates how it was that his accident happened.

The safeguard against an expert witness giving evidence on more than one side is the existence of professional privilege, and it is clear that there is professional privilege for all the discussions which took place between Mr Davis and the plaintiffs outside the door of the court where the consultation took place; and whether or not Mr Davis is put in a situation of considerable embarrassment has been a matter for him to consider.

Mr McDonnell on his behalf has explained that, when he was subpoenaed, consideration was given as to whether or not he could apply to have the subpoena discharged. Mr McDonnell set out three grounds which might possibly have been grounds for setting aside the subpoena which he categorised, first, as convenience and secondly, whether it would be very difficult for Mr Davis to disentangle those matters which had been given to him as a matter of confidence from those which were not and, thirdly, whether it could be said that for him to give evidence would have been a breach of contract. Mr McDonnell, who very helpfully addressed the court about these matters, said that Mr Davis had come to the conclusion that it was quite impossible to sustain any of those grounds.

I need not deal any further with the ground of convenience or breach of contract because I shall return to contract in a moment but I will simply deal with the second of those three, whether or not Mr Davis would be in difficulty in separating out in his mind anything which had been given to him in confidence during that consultation from the rest of his evidence.

It is not surprising that Mr Davis is unable to make that objection. What he is required in the main is to give evidence about his examination of documents. It has been agreed that two out of the four are not carbon copies from the other two, and he is required to express an opinion as to whether or not it was probable or highly probable, I suppose, that the two that were not copies of the other two were in fact deliberately intended to look as though they were copies of the other two.

As it seems to me, that is not a matter which depends on confidential information at all. It depends entirely upon an examination by somebody expert in these matters looking at the documents and deciding from a number of factors—Mr Wilmers has said that there are 10 or 11 points which indicate deliberation—whether or not it must have been a deliberate imitation and not an accidental one. So I completely accept that it would be difficult for Mr Davis to make the case that he was oppressed by being subpoenaed in this case unless, of course, Mr Bathurst's argument about contract could be established.

Mr Bathurst has sought to get round the difficulty in this case—the difficulty I have just mentioned—by submitting that there was a contract either express or implied that Mr Davis should not voluntarily give assistance to the other side on the same or related matters and to use his best endeavours not to appear for both sides. Mr Davis willingly accepts that there is a principle by which he acts but does not accept that there was any contractual term to that effect. Mr McDonnell, in dealing with the particular facts of this consultation, posed the question: when was the contract made? Was it made when the telephone conversation making the appointment was made, or was it made at the moment when the consultation started outside the door of the court, Court 26, or was it made at some later stage? and arrived at the conclusion that whenever it was made it was certainly clearly made before Mr Robinson, the instructing solicitor, had left and before any observation had been made at all by anybody about Mr Davis's personal rules about trying to avoid being instructed by both sides. So I find no possibility of establishing that there was an express term in the contract arrangement between Mr Davis and the plaintiffs.

Was there then an implied term? Mr Wilmers has drawn attention to *Liverpool City Council* v. *Irwin* [1977] AC 239 where, taking the matter very shortly, both Lord Wilberforce and Lord Cross of Chelsea have indicated that a term should not readily be implied unless it is necessary to imply such a term, and it clearly is not necessary to imply such a term in this case, and I find myself quite unable to give such an indication.

In my view, although it cannot be a general rule and every case must depend on its own facts, in this particular case, Mr Davis, giving evidence of the nature I have indicated, having expressed the view that he does not willingly give evidence, would not be embarrassed in being compelled to give evidence to the court. For that reason I have given, in my view, there is no contract and therefore there would be no oppression on Mr Davis which would make it difficult for him to give evidence.

I should add this. It is significant, having arrived at the conclusion that Mr Davis cannot sustain such an objection, that the attempt to set aside the subpoena is made by the plaintiffs. I do not find it surprising that there is no such case where the objection is made by somebody other than the person subpoenaed. It seems to me that that is the natural result of the situation, and the case where somebody else can set aside the subpoena must be if not non-existent then very, very rare indeed.

I would dismiss this appeal.

CUMMING-BRUCE LJ. I agree. I would only add that the different kinds of expert witness are various, and this case is concerned with the particular functions, responsibilities and activities of a handwriting expert on the problems raised by the case, which arise from very unusual and peculiar facts.

When Mr Davis was first confronted with the plaintiffs' solicitors it was in the luncheon adjournment at a time when Mr Davis had been giving evidence in Court 26 in this building. He was then shown a couple of documents; and the solicitor concerned, having received a reaction from Mr Davis left after a mere 20 minutes.

Some six weeks later a partner in another firm who had been instructing Mr Davis in an entirely different matter happened to ask him if he will be good enough to give an opinion on some documents to another partner of that firm that same evening if that other partner brought the documents to him that night on his way home. Thus on the telephone, without the faintest idea about any details at all, Mr Davis agreed to do what he was asked to do; and at eight o'clock in the evening the other partner to whom I have referred, left some documents with him. Mr Davis proceeded to spend a couple of hours or so looking at the documents and thinking about them. Then he telephoned not the partner who first asked him if he would act but that second partner who was concerned in the case and left the documents, and he gave preliminary opinions upon the documents to that gentleman. Then, and only then, in the ensuing conversation something was said which enabled Mr Davis to realise that quite inadvertently he had got himself into a situation in which he had given an opinion to the defendants although six weeks earlier he had given advice to the plaintiffs. Mr Davis himself, in his affidavit, makes it perfectly clear that he is quite unaware of the risk of any disclosure of confidential information received by him from the plaintiffs' solicitors. Thus it will be seen on what very special facts these proceedings involving Mr Davis have reached this court.

For my part, I agree with Lord Denning MR and Waller LJ that the plaintiffs have failed to establish any express contract in the terms that they allege and they have also failed to establish that the implied terms which they seek to set up are necessary to the contract originally made when the plaintiffs' solicitors asked Mr Davis originally to help, as he did, outside Court 26.

It is not necessary for the determination of this appeal to consider the situation of any other kind of expert in any other kind of situation; and this court decides only the obligations that arise from the very peculiar facts that have been described in the evidence in this case.

I agreed that the appeal should be dismissed."

160 The appeals were dismissed with costs.

161 With the greatest respect to Cumming-Bruce LJ's reservations, I believe there is an object lesson for all experts in the judgment in this case as well as some interesting observations for practitioners concerning the subpoenaing of witnesses.

BOTH PARTIES WISH TO CALL SAME WITNESS—ONE AS A WITNESS OF FACT AND THE OTHER AS AN EXPERT

The facts

162 In an arbitration which arose from a building dispute governed by a JCT contract both parties had invited the same witness to appear for them and this witness had agreed. The person concerned had been named as supervising officer under the contract.

163 Each party then wrote to the arbitrator asking him to direct that the witness should not be allowed to give evidence for the other side.

Question

164 How should the arbitrator respond to these applications?

Course of action

165 Although this is not an ideal situation, there would seem to be no reason why the witness could not appear for both sides as one wished to call him as a witness of fact and the other as an expert witness. I would imagine that the witness and the lawyers representing the party for whom he was being called would be greatly concerned that there should be no statement in his proof of evidence which might conflict factually with something included in the proof of evidence that he prepared for the other party. This was a bizarre situation and a most unsatisfactory state of affairs.

166 There is no property in a witness. Either side can call the other's witness to give evidence for them, and indeed can even subpoena the other party's witness if necessary (and "secure the attendance of a witness", as it is now described in s.43, AA '96).

167 The arbitrator suggested that it might be preferable and less confusing if one party were to call the supervising officer and the other to rely on eliciting the evidence they wished to present by cross-examination. This suggestion did not find favour with the parties' representatives who said that to do so might turn him into a hostile witness and they preferred to do things in their way. The arbitrator saw this as "the right of the parties to agree on procedural and evidential matters" under s.34(1), AA '96 and therefore bowed to the parties' wishes and agreed to allow the witness to act in a dual capacity, but warned the parties that he would intervene if either party attempted to act improperly in examination or cross-examination of the witness.

168 The arbitrator did find it necessary to intervene on several occasions where lines of cross-examination became confused between fact and opinion.

169 This witness conducted himself very poorly as a witness of fact (and was subsequently sued by the employer, as supervising officer, for negligence) but performed very convincingly and professionally as an expert witness.

170 This curious state of affairs concluded with the arbitrator stating in his award that he preferred the evidence of the witness as expert to that of the same witness on the facts of the dispute.

USING A SECOND EXPERT WITNESS

The facts

171 In a rent review dispute a preliminary meeting was held at which both landlord and tenant were represented by solicitors and valuers. A timetable was agreed for the exchange of proofs by the valuers. A date for the hearing was set.

172 In due course after the exchange of proofs and only a few days before the hearing the tenant's solicitors indicated that they intended calling a second expert witness whose evidence they claimed was vital to the case. The landlord's solicitors informed the arbitrator that they objected to this, as it was not agreed at the preliminary meeting and they considered it was not necessary.

Question

173 Should the arbitrator allow the second witness to give evidence?

Course of action

174 The arbitrator wrote to the parties informing them that he would consider the situation over the weekend and give them a decision on the Monday morning, at the commencement of the hearing.

175 He decided, albeit with some reluctance, that he should allow this evidence to be given in case it might be crucial but that in fairness to the opposing party they must be allowed to respond with expert evidence of their own (but see paras 136 to 151 above, RSC Order 38, rules 4, 35 and 36).

176 At the commencement of the hearing he therefore indicated to counsel that he was minded to allow the second expert witness to give evidence, but offered three alternatives before this evidence was tendered (he also indicated that the introduction of a late witness could, in any event, have a bearing on his award of costs).

177 The three alternatives which the arbitrator offered were:

(a) That he abandon the hearing immediately, so as to allow the landlord to decide whether he wished to (i) challenge his view, or (ii) introduce a second expert.
(b) That he complete the hearing, allowing the tenant's second expert witness to give evidence and then reconvene at a later date with a second witness for the landlord, if the landlord considered that this extra evidence needed to be answered.
(c) That the landlord produce his additional expert witness—if possible—at the hearing, and both witnesses would then be examined and cross-examined without undue delay.

178 The arbitrator went on to indicate that alternative (c) was his preferred course of action as all the other witnesses, counsel and solicitors were available and it would be wasteful as to costs not to proceed immediately.

179 When I discussed this with Thomasina she questioned why it was necessary to appoint so many experts in what was a relatively straightforward matter for a surveyor arbitrator engaged in valuation work himself. If it was because he could not undertake the necessary research himself unless the parties so agreed (see paras 001 to 052 and paras 198 to 225) could he not suggest to the parties that he appoint one expert to advise him which would certainly show a considerable saving over the three experts currently envisaged. (See paras 198 to 225 for method of selecting that expert.)

180 This would be one solution which provided the parties agreed was very much in the spirit of AA '96—the duty laid on the arbitrator by s.33 to "adopt procedures suitable to the circumstances (and) avoid unnecessary expense".

THE TRIBUNAL APPOINTED EXPERT

The facts

181 An experienced arbitrator was appointed in a building dispute which included *inter alia* the not uncommon ingredients of claims for an extension of time and loss and expense.

182 When the Statement of Case was delivered to him the arbitrator noted that there were several A1 computer generated coloured bar charts on which there was a minutiae of information and symbols. These bar charts purported to demonstrate critical delays substantiating the claim for an extension of time.

183 Other than noting these the arbitrator did not attempt to study these charts at that early stage of the exchange of the parties' statements. Subsequently the arbitrator received a request for an extension time of three months to serve:

(a) A request for further and better particulars of the Statement of Case; eight weeks of this time was required for the respondent's expert to study the bar charts and to prepare a report on them.
(b) The defence.

184 The request was a result of a number of issues raised by the respondent's expert in a letter to his client a copy of which was also sent to the arbitrator.

185 The claimant objected vehemently to the proposed delay averring that the issues raised by the respondent's expert were not actually relevant to the "pleading" stage but were matters which they would expect to be dealt with at the "without prejudice" meetings of the experts.

186 The respondent did not agree and requested an oral hearing to make submissions in respect of his application for the three-month extension of time. At the same time the respondent requested the arbitrator to study the charts and the supporting documentation in preparation for the interlocutory hearing to consider his request.

187 The arbitrator did as he was requested in preparation for the interlocutory meeting and found the bar charts far too complex to comprehend in so short a time. Beyond anything else he realised that they were so comprehensively annotated with symbols and other presumably relevant information that it would take him a considerable amount of time at a substantial cost to the parties to unravel them.

Question

188 How should the arbitrator react to this request?

Course of action

189 Assuming the reference is governed by AA '96, the arbitrator probably has discretion as to whether he "hears" the parties or invites them to deal with the matter by written submissions (s.34(2)(h)).

190 If he does decide to hear the applicant, and having studied the bar charts and supporting documentation, he is still totally baffled by them, what next?

191 There are three possible options.

(1) The arbitrator waits until the hearing proper for the parties' respective experts to take him through the charts, however long this takes for him to understand what they purport to represent.
(2) If he really is concerned about these charts and they are more sophisticated than his experience stretches then he could seek some technical assistance from an independent programmer ideally sitting in with him and the other experts representing the parties outside the full hearing.

This arrangement would require carefully drafted instructions for the parties' experts in terms of what they were allowed to agree and what was reserved for the hearing proper. This arrangement would also be dependent upon the arbitrator having power to appoint this technical adviser under s.37, AA '96 and perhaps, to be most efficacious, the power to act inquisitorially under s.34(2)(g), AA '96. Although the arbitrator's adviser is an added expense it should only represent a fraction of the cost of dealing with this discrete issue at a full hearing with counsel and solicitors on both sides, as well as the parties' experts.

(3) A tribunal appointed expert.

192 In this present example it may be too late for the parties to grasp this option as the whole problem over the extension of time has only arisen because of the respondent's expert's queries on the claimant's bar charts. Presumably the claimant engaged an expert to prepare these charts in the first place so each party has an expert in place. However, even if this were so, I believe that it is not too late to go down this route.

193 If the parties agreed that it was sensible for one independent expert to advise the arbitrator, provided both parties were made aware of that advice and given the opportunity to comment on it, then this would undoubtedly be the most cost-effective method of determining this particular issue. The arbitrator put this proposal to the parties and in doing so, drafted terms of reference for them to consider and comment on (see the Annex to this example).

194 It will be seen from these terms of reference that there is still a role to play for the party appointed programmer who will not assume the role of the parties' advocate in cross-examining the tribunal appointed expert, rather than attempting the difficult task of divorcing himself from the client paying his fees and giving the tribunal independent advice.

195 In an article on the subject entitled "The Law and Practice of Court and Tribunal Appointed Experts" [1993] ADRLJ 194, the authors say:

> "By the very nature of the fact that the expert is instructed by one party and paid for his services by him, some slight element of subconscious bias is perhaps unavoidable in the circumstances, if only because the party appointed expert's view of the case is inevitably coloured by the information being 'fed' to him by his client. Indeed, 'shopping around' for a favourable view has been witnessed by one of our number.
>
> In addition, there is often a limited number of experts in any particular field and it is not impossible that, in any given dispute, one expert may well be approached by both sides to provide an opinion. This possibility suggests that the parties in a case may well be in agreement as to the choice of expert and the side for whom an expert eventually acts may well be an accident of chance, dependent upon the speed with which the expert is approached by one side, or the other. Given the above provision, the possibility therefore exists for the parties to agree upon the choice of expert, but only if his complete independence is accepted by all concerned and the particular scope and extent of his expertise is fully understood.
>
> The questions to be submitted to the court or tribunal appointed expert should obviously be agreed between the parties at the outset. In order to do this, the scope of his enquiries must be clearly defined, either by agreement between the parties or by the court, or arbitrator. It is to be hoped that the issues to be examined would then be self-evident. It is in this context that early consideration of the use of a court or tribunal appointed expert could assist in pin-pointing the matters to be examined. A report from an independent court expert may assist in reducing those issues which are the subject of litigation or arbitration, and which might subsequently be put, if this remains absolutely necessary, as separate issues to experts appointed by each of the parties. This we believe would be cheaper and quicker than the current usual practice of each side's expert preparing his own report, meeting to prepare a joint report of what is and is not agreed and then putting in a supplementary report dealing with what remains in dispute.
>
> . . .

> ... the use of a court or tribunal expert appointed at an early stage would considerably reduce the needless duplication of huge amounts of evidence by experts for each party and establish a single expert view of the relevant facts and identify precisely which points are in issue. Any further use of separate experts by the parties would then be merely to oppose the views of the court expert and support the parties' respective position on any points then remaining in dispute.
> ..."

196 At paragraph 9–08 on page 67 of Edgar Fay's book *Official Referees' Business* published by Sweet & Maxwell, 1988, the author records as follows, under the heading "Joint independent reports":

> "It was at one time the practice of the official referees in a suitable case to persuade the parties to agree to retain an independent expert jointly. From articles contributed by Sir Francis Newbolt (official referee 1920–36) to the *Law Quarterly Review* in 1923 and 1926 ('Expedition and Economy in Litigation' (1923) 39 LQR 427 and 'Avoidable Waste' (1926) 42 LQR 52) it is clear that at that time very many of the official referees' cases were dealt with in this way. The independent expert was jointly appointed and jointly paid by the parties and his report usually concluded the dispute.
>
> If not, he could be cross-examined by both sides. It is not known when the practice fell into desuetude but it has not been employed within the memory of those now connected with the court. Perhaps it lost vitality when formalised in the Rules of the Supreme Court, as mentioned in the next paragraph. Perhaps it should be revived. Sir Francis Newbolt summed up its advantages in the following passages.
>
> > 'By a simple scheme one of the main difficulties of the costly traditional fight between partisan experts can often be got rid of. In the commonest type of case a lawyer had to decide between conflicting specialists, equally competent and confident, and the expense was of course enormous. In rare cases the (official referee) may still have to do this, but it nearly always happens that in a discussion in chambers on date and mode of trial both parties agree that one expert engaged and paid by both sides is preferable [at p. 436 of the 1923 article].
> >
> > An independent witness surveys the subject matter unbiased and estimates the amount due before any of the great expense of the trial is incurred, with any necessary reservations where questions of law may arise, and he gives a proof to both sides and receives half his fee from each, both halves being made costs in the cause. He may be cross-examined by both parties if either calls him at the trial, which he attends only if required; and both parties retain the right to call any amount of evidence to contradict him, a right which in practice however is not often exercised.' "

197 Assuming that the parties had made no agreement under s.34, AA '96, could the arbitrator unilaterally make the decision to have a tribunal appointed expert instead of two party appointed experts as a function of his duty under s.33 "to avoid unnecessary expense" and "to adopt procedures suitable to the circumstances of the particular case", even in the face of the parties' opposition? I think not. If he really felt strongly about it and believed that considerable savings in time and money could be effected by this means, then he should make his feelings clear to the parties and if they insisted on going down the more expensive route of parties' experts he could invite them to show in their cost submissions that they had cost no more than his proposal, and if they were unable to do so he could reflect this when allocating the parties' costs or limiting recoverable costs following his determination of the substantive issues. If he is inclined this way he must warn the parties at an early stage that he will consider so restricting the recovery of the experts' costs of the winning party.

ANNEX

TYPICAL ALTERNATIVE AGENDA ITEMS FOR THE OPTION OF A TRIBUNAL APPOINTED EXPERT

Consider a tribunal appointed expert for appropriate issues.
In which case the parties are:

1 To define the scope of the tribunal's expert's enquiries and, in the absence of agreement, this matter is to be decided by the arbitrator taking into account the parties' submissions.
2 To agree who the tribunal's expert should be, in consultation with the arbitrator.
3 To agree on the wording of the issue(s) to be submitted to the tribunal's expert and in the absence of agreement the arbitrator will decide on this wording.

Not later than 28 days of the close of pleadings the tribunal appointed expert is to deliver a draft report to each party.

Within 14 days of the delivery of this report a representative of the parties is to meet with the tribunal's expert to discuss his draft report. The discretion as to whether to amend this draft report, following submissions from the parties' representatives, to be entirely at the discretion of the tribunal's expert.

Not later than 14 days after the meeting between the tribunal's expert and the parties' representatives the tribunal's expert shall deliver a copy of his final report to the tribunal, copied to the parties.

Should either party wish to cross-examine the tribunal's expert on any matter contained in his final report (on any issue within the tribunal's expert's terms of reference, whether or not covered by his final report) then, not later than seven days before the hearing notice must be given in writing of the matters on which the cross-examination is desired to be delivered to the tribunal's expert, copied to the arbitrator and the other side.

At the hearing any cross-examination of the tribunal's expert may be conducted by a party appointed expert rather than the party's general advocate if that is the party's preference.

EXPERT APPOINTED BY THE ARBITRATOR

The facts

198 In a dispute involving copyright of computer software the appointed arbitrator is himself a leading figure in this rapidly evolving world.

199 The arbitrator invited each party at the preliminary meeting to paint an informal picture of the dispute between them and he learned that it comprised claims and counterclaims on over 50 instances of alleged infringement.

200 Each side sought and was granted the right to call three experts covering different aspects of programming. In drafting his order for directions following this preliminary meeting the arbitrator included his "usual clause" concerning the experts; their meeting together; exchanging draft reports and sending him a note of what they agreed upon and what not etc.

201 Some months later the arbitrator received his copies of the experts' reports, the totality of which ran into several hundred pages of highly technical and complex detail.

Question

202 What is the most cost-effective way for the arbitrator to deal with this evidence?

Course of action

203 Was it evidence? Thomasina asked. Surely it only became so when it was admitted by the experts under oath—assuming that there is a hearing and this is not a "documents only" procedure.

204 I agreed that this was the usual practice but it is possible, with the parties' agreement, to treat the experts' reports as evidence at the point of exchange. I have been given to understand that this device has been used by His Hon Judge John Newey but have been unable to confirm this.

205 However, we are straying from the point. When the arbitrator gave his initial direction he did not devote sufficient time to thinking it through. Although experienced in this particular field he had not fully appreciated how complex were the issues until he had received and read the experts' reports—six in all—in which each side put forward what seemed on first reading to be a perfectly plausible case.

206 The arbitrator realised that he would spend a great deal of time attempting to analyse and sift out the bones of the alternative submissions. There were obscure technical areas with which he was unfamiliar and following this analytical exercise would come the subsequent cross-examination of these experts, leaving him with the problem of deciding which of these experts to believe. He could take the usual course and plump for the most plausible. He realised that the outcome of this case was of such significance that whoever lost was almost certainly bound to appeal, and this was the type of case which could well end up in the House of Lords. The amount at stake in this case ran into tens of millions of pounds.

207 Bearing all of this in mind the arbitrator decided to appoint his own expert to analyse the six reports and produce a single summary report for his consideration.

208 The rules of the administered scheme governing this reference gave him power to seek legal and technical assistance without consent but after consultation with the parties.

209 He felt that this rule alone was probably sufficient for him to make this appointment even if the parties objected. However he was experienced enough to know that to impose this solution on the parties without at least attempting to persuade them that it was the most sensible, expeditious and therefore most cost-effective procedure would be unwise.

210 He invited the parties and their representatives, including the six experts, to an interlocutory meeting where he explained his thinking. He reminded the parties that he had a duty under s.33 of AA '96 to adopt procedures suitable for the circumstances of the case, and to avoid unnecessary delay and expense, all of which he considered would be achieved by his proposal. He further told them that if they would agree to his proposal for an independent tribunal appointed expert, he would consider one name from each party to which he would add one name of his own. He then proposed that all three candidates be interviewed by a committee of three which he would chair with the other two places being filled by a nominee from each side. Following the interviews if there was not a unanimous choice then the casting vote would be his.

211 The arbitrator suggested that instead of the "usual" direction concerning the meeting and exchange of reports for the experts, he would like to adopt a Standard Direction to Experts developed by a former Chief Justice for New South Wales, His Hon Sir Laurence Street. (See the Annex to this example.)

212 I pointed out to Thomasina that, in drafting his proposals, Sir Laurence Street had acknowledged that the normal constraints, inherent in the conventional procedures of examination-in-chief, cross-examination and re-examination, do not always enable the experts to give of their best. Thus, his standard direction includes the provision, which I have tried on occasions with great success, of swearing in both experts at the same time and dealing with them in the form of a discussion as set out in iii(c) of this standard direction.

213 Sir Laurence, quite rightly, sounds a note of caution as follows:

> "1 It is not a direction to be arbitrarily imposed in every case involving conflicting expert opinion. It provides, however, a basis for discussion at the interlocutory hearing as to how best to approach the question of expert evidence. Whether any direction at all, and if so what precise form it should take, will be a matter for consideration in relation to the particular dispute in hand.
>
> 2 Paragraph (iii) involves a procedure not to be lightly entered into. In particular it is necessary to ensure that the representatives of the parties are comfortable with the procedure. Experience indicates that the latter portion of sub-paragraph (d) or paragraph (iii) is usually accepted as a sufficient reassurance in that regard. It is also necessary to preserve an ongoing flexibility in relation to following through this procedure at the hearing.
>
> Due to a variety of factors it may be perceived not to be working satisfactorily. In that event it may be appropriate to revert to the conventional process of examination-in-chief, cross-examination and re-examination. I should add that, although this prospect is always a matter to keep in mind, I have not myself, on any occasion, encountered the need to revert to the conventional process."

214 Even accepting Sir Laurence Street's reservation, the arbitrator felt that the provisions of the standard direction for sitting down experts of the same discipline to hold a discussion on their reports, chaired by the arbitrator, would save a considerable amount of hearing time.

215 The arbitrator proposed that the chosen tribunal appointed expert be permitted to sit in on this discussion and advise and assist him during his questioning of the experts. In seeking the parties' consent to this arrangement the arbitrator stressed the direction specifically provided in (iii)(d) of the Annex for the parties' representatives to intervene in the discussion and question the opposing experts themselves.

216 After hearing these proposals the parties' solicitors then asked if they could meet briefly on their own to discuss what the arbitrator had put to them. This they did and returned shortly afterwards agreeing with all aspects of the arbitrator's proposal.

217 This anecdote prompted Thomasina to draw my attention to the *Access to Justice Report 1996*, which was drafted under Lord Woolf's chairmanship. In this Report Lord Woolf bemoaned the fact that "the power under Order 40 has been rarely used in the past" and recommended that more use be made of court appointed experts.

218 Having said that, this initiative has been taken by the Official Referees' Court on at least two occasions. It is thought that Judge Hicks made the first of the appointments in February 1995 in the case of *Abbey National Mortgages and Others* v. *Key Surveyors Nationwide and Others* [1996] 1 WLR 1534. The case involved a dispute over the valuation of 29 houses in the UK in which the defendants sought leave to call 29 experts.

219 The appointment made by Judge Hicks was done on the application of the plaintiff and was appealed by the defendants. The appointment was upheld by the Court of Appeal in February 1996.

220 The second appointment in June 1995 was made by Judge Newman, where the court appointed expert was in addition to the parties' own experts in another construction case. In this action the efficacy of a proposed remedial scheme was an important apparently discrete issue in the proceedings.

221 The court appointed expert (or tribunal appointed expert) should not only reduce the overall number of experts required but narrow the scope for disagreement and therefore save valuable hearing time.

222 In making such an appointment the tribunal should give very clear and concise instructions as to the *modus operandi* to be adopted by their appointed expert.

223 Judge Newman in his order defined the questions the court appointed expert should answer, the date when the report should be served and the terms of payment. The parties were then required to agree the detailed terms of the appointment and the identity of the expert.

224 Further terms of the appointment were agreed and set out in a schedule. This provided that the court appointed expert would receive representations from the parties' experts before serving his report and would ensure that any documentation made available by the parties would be copied to all the other parties.

225 The court appointed expert was prohibited from taking legal advice and a ceiling was placed on the amount he could spend producing his report. The person was chosen by a voting system which awarded points to each of the seven candidates, with each party being allowed one vote.

ANNEX
STANDARD DIRECTION ON EXPERT EVIDENCE

(developed by His Hon Sir Laurence Street—former Chief Justice for New South Wales)

Direct that:

(i) On or before ________ the parties exchange the names, fields of expertise and witness statements of the experts whose opinions will be advanced as evidence.

(ii) (a) Thereafter the parties arrange for their respective experts in each field of expertise to meet together as soon as reasonably practicable and on as many occasions as may be necessary to prepare the report referred to hereafter;

(b) it will be the purpose of the meeting and the responsibility of the experts to strive to reach agreement on as much as possible of the expert opinion relevant to the dispute;

(c) the meeting of experts is encouraged to call by unanimous agreement of the parties or either of them to obtain and provide any additional data or information the experts may need with a view to reaching agreement, a copy of any such call to be lodged by the claimant with the arbitrator/referee;

(d) either party shall be at liberty to apply for a direction that such call be complied with;

(e) the experts shall prepare a condensed joint report stating in the first part the matters upon which they have finally been able to reach agreement and stating in the second part the matters upon which they have not been able to reach agreement;

(f) the report shall be accompanied by annexures prepared by each expert stating in condensed form the opinion of the expert on each matter of disagreement including the reasons why the expert does not agree with the opinions of the other experts;

(g) the original report shall be sent to the claimant on or before ________ who shall forthwith lodge it with the arbitrator/referee and send a copy to each other party;

(h) evidence may not be received from an expert who has without adequate reason not participated in such meeting and report.

(iii) At the hearing

(a) as each field of expertise arises for consideration each expert in that field will verify by affirmation his/her witness statement, the joint report and his/her annexure to the joint report. After these documents have been admitted into evidence all the expert witnesses in that field shall participate in a continuation of their meeting at which they will discuss with each other the matters of disagreement;

(b) for the purpose of such discussion the experts will be seated facing each other at a table placed between the arbitrators/referee's table and the bar table;

(c) the discussion will be chaired by the arbitrator/referee who will guide the discussion and will intervene with the object of the matters of disagreement being examined and analysed so as to enable the arbitrator/referee to reach a determination upon them;

(d) the representatives of the parties will be at liberty with the permission of the arbitrator/referee to intervene in the discusssion and, prior to the arbitrator/referee reaching a determination on any matters of disagreement, they will be permitted to question the experts and make submissions to the arbitrator/referee.

EXPERT OPINION MUST BE FOUNDED ON FACT

The facts

226 The defendant, who was charged with murder, admitted that he had killed his girlfriend by hitting her with a hammer but pleaded that he had been provoked by her statement that she had had affairs with other men and that he was not the father of her expected child.

227 The defence sought to call a psychiatrist to give his opinion, based on information from medical records, the defendant and his family and friends, that the defendant was not suffering from a mental illness, that he was not violent by nature but that his personality was such that he could have been provoked in the circumstances and that he was likely to be telling the truth.

228 The defendant had not put his character in issue and the Crown sought to have the psychiatric evidence excluded on the ground that it would put the defendant before the jury as having a character and disposition which, in the light of his previous record of violence, he had not got.

Question

229 Was that expert evidence from the psychiatrist admissible?

Course of action

230 The facts of this case are drawn from *R* v. *Turner (Terence)* CA (1975) 60 Cr App R 80. The judge of the first instance thought not and refused to admit it. The defendant was convicted. He appealed.

231 In dismissing the appeal Lawton LJ said:

> "Before a court can assess the value of an opinion it must know the facts upon which it is based. If the expert has been misinformed about the facts or he has taken irrelevant facts into consideration or has omitted to consider relevant ones, the opinion is likely to be valueless."

232 The judge went on to say that in the judgment of the Court of Appeal, counsel calling an expert should, in examination-in-chief, ask his witness to state the facts upon which his opinion is based, and it is wrong to leave the other side to elicit the facts in cross-examination.

233 Lawton LJ reiterated that the foundation of these rules was laid down by Lord Mansfield in *Foulkes* v. *Chadd* and was well laid, i.e. the opinion of scientific men upon proven facts may be given by men of science within their own science.

234 Thus, it was held that:

(1) that, since the question whether the defendant was suffering from a mental illness as defined by the Mental Health Act 1959, was not in issue, the psychiatric evidence that the defendant was not suffering from a mental illness although admissible, was not relevant and had been rightly excluded;

(2) that not withstanding that the opinion evidence, if relevant and not based on hearsay, was admissible to furnish a court with scientific information likely to be outside the experience of a judge or jury, there was no general rule that, in the absence of mental illness, psychiatric evidence was admissible to prove that the defendant was likely to be telling the truth, and that accordingly, since the defendant's veracity and likelihood of having been provoked were matters within the competence and experience of the jury, the psychiatric evidence was rightly excluded.

235 From this case it can be seen that the facts on which psychiatrists base their opinions must be proved by admissible evidence and counsel calling an expert should in examination-in-chief ask the witness to state the facts upon which his opinion is based.

EXPERT OMITS TO DEAL WITH MATERIAL FACTS

The facts

236 In a case involving defective machinery the expert presenting his report failed to deal with two key issues of the claimant's case.

237 The claimant alleged that the lift mechanism was of defective design for various reasons including the choice of the wrong material and that while the lift was being installed the engineer failed to attend site and inspect. Whilst the expert dealt with the engineer's attendance at the works where the plant was manufactured he did not deal with the more direct issue of the engineer's attendance at the installation stage.

238 It became clear to the claimant's advocate that his expert had failed to deal with an issue which the opposing counsel was making much of. After a brief adjournment and taking instructions from the claimant's solicitor he made a formal application for his expert's report to be amended to cover the installation stage.

239 The hearing was due to last another two or three weeks and claimant's counsel undertook to have the amended report available to the respondent and the arbitrator within 24 hours should leave be given.

Question

240 Should the arbitrator give leave and if so on what terms?

Course of action

241 The claimant's advocate—who was a claims consultant—having explained that he did not anticipate that the opposing party would be making such an issue of the installation stage respectfully suggested that it would not be unreasonable for the arbitrator to grant consent to amend provided that respondent's counsel convinced him that this was an important issue. To do this, the arbitrator should invite respondent's counsel to explain why he felt that this installation stage was so important when the claimant's advocate had submitted that the problem stemmed from a defect in manufacturing and no matter what degree of supervision was carried out at the installation stage this defect would not necessarily have been exposed.

242 The first point to make here is that it would not be appropriate to amend the expert's report at this late stage. The more usual procedure would be to give leave to submit a supplementary report. The arbitrator should not rush into granting consent for such a supplementary report with the inevitable delaying effect, unless he is convinced, by the parties' advocates' arguments of the necessity to amend to further the case. This must be weighed in the balance of his duty to avoid unnecessary expense and delay under s.33, AA '96.

243 If the arbitrator gave leave to amend it would be on the terms that the party submitting the supplementary report pays the other side's costs thrown away including the arbitrator's costs, e.g. if an adjournment was necessary, the wasted costs of that adjournment, while the expert amended his report.

244 Whatever order the arbitrator gave he should always keep the parties' costs in mind and introduce whatever flexibility he can persuade the parties to adopt to keep such costs to a minimum.

EXPERT WITNESSES UNABLE TO AGREE ON ANY MATTERS OF FACT IN DISPUTE

The facts

245 At the preliminary meeting the parties asked if the arbitrator would agree that they would each call an expert to deal with *quantum*. Accordingly, the arbitrator directed:

> **"Experts**
>
> 1 Each party intends to instruct an expert. The parties will attempt to agree on joint instructions. These instructions to state whether experts will meet 'open' or 'without prejudice' and also what authority they have (if any) to bind their respective parties. The 'without prejudice' nature attaching to these discussions shall be removed in respect of matters agreed upon.
>
> 2 The experts to meet and attempt to narrow the issues and in particular the number of items on the Scott Schedule. They shall prepare, date and sign a note of the facts and opinions upon

which they are agreed and of the issues upon which they are not. A copy of such note to be exchanged and delivered to me within 14 days of their final meeting, but in any case, not later than 14 days before the hearing."

246 At the pre-hearing review the arbitrator reviewed all matters on which he had given directions including those given to the experts. He was told that the experts had met but had not been able to agree on anything, but they were scheduled to meet again before the hearing.

247 At the end of the first day of the hearing the arbitrator asked counsel if the experts had met again and, if so, whether they had managed to reach any measure of agreement. Counsel confirmed that the meeting had taken place but said that the experts still did not apparently agree on any points.

248 The dispute was for a relatively small amount of money and the costs of the action were getting out of proportion to the matters in dispute. The area of expertise to be addressed by the experts was that in which the arbitrator himself was expert and able to take an informed view.

Question

249 How can the arbitrator break this deadlock?

Course of action

250 The arbitrator was very experienced in the field of the dispute and he realised that if he allowed the lack of agreement between the experts to run on, the costs would be out of proportion to the issues. If he adjourned the hearing and issued further directions that the experts should meet again the risk was that no progress would be made.

251 The arbitrator pointed out his concern about costs to the parties and said that in the absence of agreement between them he was empowered under s.34, AA '96 to direct what procedure would be followed. Bearing in mind the small amount of money at stake he had decided that he would adjourn the hearing so that the experts could meet on a "without prejudice" basis in his presence to see what progress could be made.

252 At the end of a relatively short meeting substantial progress was made which enabled the experts to take fresh instructions from their respective parties and avoid the waste of time and costs which would otherwise have resulted in additional days on the hearing with all the parties and their representatives present.

253 The role of an expert witness in an arbitration is twofold. First, to explain technical and scientific issues which the arbitrator may not understand without assistance which are material to the substantive issues in dispute. Secondly, where applicable, to give evidence on *quantum* issues and attempt to reduce the hearing time by agreeing with the other side's expert amounts which each is prepared to accept as fair and reasonable albeit in a spirit of compromise.

254 Although the arbitrator may be sufficiently well-versed in the field of the dispute to dispense with the first category of expert evidence, it is frequently useful for him to have the services of the experts to deal with the second element. Without these independent opinions of *quantum* the arbitrator would be in danger of entering the arena of conflict and leaving himself open to the accusation of being a valuer for one party or the other on *quantum*.

255 Used properly, experts can affect considerable savings in costs for their parties particularly in hearing time which tends to be the most expensive element of any reference.

256 To ensure that the value of these experts is maximised, the sort of direction given by the arbitrator in this example should be considered. The parties should be asked to agree—possibly at the preliminary meeting—whether their experts should meet "open" or "without prejudice" and what authority they have to agree matters, or elements of those matters, in dispute. The parties should attempt to agree on identical instructions to their experts.

257 There was an interesting case before His Hon Judge Newey QC in the Official Referees' Court (*Richard Robert Holdings Ltd* v. *Douglas Smith Stimson Partnership and Others (No 2)* (1989) 47 BLR 117) which dealt with this issue. He said, *inter alia*:

> "If a meeting is 'without prejudice' while an agreement between the experts is not binding on the parties unless ratified by them, a party who does not wish to accept what his expert has agreed is in a far more difficult position than if the trial had not begun. He would be most unlikely to obtain leave to call a further expert witness at that stage and particularly not if their only reason for applying is disagreement with the opinion of his present expert.
>
> I think that in deciding whether a meeting held after a trial has begun is 'without prejudice' and, whether an agreement reached between experts at it, is 'open' and binding on the parties, the position during earlier meetings ordered by the court may be taken into account, but that in respect of the latter the difficulty of a party's position if he is not minded to accept the agreement, is much more important. Obviously the facts as a whole have to be considered; just as they have to be in deciding whether the experts actually reached agreement."

258 Judge Newey also said:

> "It may be that rule 28 [of RSC Order 38] is so widely expressed that a court could order a meeting of experts even after a trial has begun, but in practice in the official referees' courts meetings are ordered on summonses for directions. Once a trial has commenced a meeting only takes place by agreement of the parties and this is so even if the court has expressed the view that a meeting would be desirable."

259 That may be so in the courts but many arbitrators in the absence of agreement to the contrary between the parties are masters of their own proceedings and continue to use the experts throughout their hearings setting them tasks to agree specific matters as issues become clearer.

260 All of this is very much in the parties' interests and is a pragmatic use of experts by the experienced arbitrator.

261 It is not uncommon for the experts to arrive at different conclusions because they began from different facts.

262 Bernstein (1992) 58, JCI Arb 1–9, says of this:

> "Experts should not allow conflicts of this class to reach a hearing because it is now almost invariable practice, in both litigation and arbitration, for them to be directed to meet before the hearing to agree facts and narrow issues. At that meeting differences as to the facts (often arising from differing instructions) should be identified and noted. In arbitration, I consider that the arbitrator should ask them to produce, before the hearing, a Statement of Agreed Facts, and he should—still before the hearing—study this Statement to ensure, so far as he can, that they have made a genuine effort to ensure that each of them is proceeding from the same factual premises.
>
> If this kind of conflict does reach a hearing, it is usually resolved at a relatively early stage in it, leaving no residual problems for the tribunal, and only the embarrassment for each expert of explaining to his client why the facts were not identified at a much earlier, and much less costly, stage. Even this embarrassment is manageable, for each expert will undoubtedly tell his client that it was all the other expert's fault."

ADMISSIBILITY OF EXPERT EVIDENCE

The facts

263 In a reference involving a dispute over a commodity contract the claimant's counsel requested consent to call two experts.

264 The respondent, who was also represented by counsel, strongly objected to this on the grounds of unnecessary expense. Counsel, with the greatest respect, pointed out that should the arbitrator admit the evidence of these two expert witnesses, there would be a case for claiming that he had failed under the duty imposed upon him by s.33, AA '96, to adopt the most cost-effective procedure and would be open to an action for failing or refusing to properly conduct the proceedings.

Question

265 How should the arbitrator react to this request and the subsequent objection?

Course of action

266 The respondent's counsel was absolutely correct in pointing out the duty laid upon the arbitrator to follow a cost-effective procedure. In the absence of agreement between the parties, the arbitrator has absolute discretion (s.34, AA '96) but, like all such discretion invested in arbitrators, it must be exercised judicially. Thus, the arbitrator initially invited the parties to cite any authority they could in support of their respective submissions.

267 The respondent referred the arbitrator to *Regina* v. *Stockwell* (1993) *The Times*, 11 March, CA. He accepted that this was a criminal case but the principles evinced by that case, counsel submitted, were as applicable to arbitration as to litigation or criminal proceedings. The Times Law Report which counsel submitted to the arbitrator read as follows:

> "The Lord Chief Justice (Lord Taylor of Gosforth), giving the reserved judgment of the court, said that on 27 April 1990 at about 12 noon a man robbed the Leeds Building Society in Catford. A video film taken by a security camera recorded the crime.
>
> On 5 September 1990 someone attempted to rob the Woolwich Building Society in Beckenham High Street. Photographs were also taken of that crime by a security camera.
>
> The appellant denied involvement in either incident. The issue at this trial was one of identification. The trial judge ruled that the evidence of Mr Richard Headley Neave, a facial mapping expert, could be adduced by the Crown to assist the jury in determining whether the appellant appeared in the photographs during the robbery and attempted robbery.
>
> Mr Clegg submitted that the admission of the expert evidence was not justified; the jury was capable of deciding from their own observations whether the photographs were that of the defendant in their charge.
>
> He argued that there were only two classes of case in this context: (i) those that raised questions of fact, on which expert evidence was inadmissible and (ii) those that raised questions which depended on specialist knowledge, where the jury could form no view without expert evidence, which was therefore not only admissible but necessary. He admitted of no middle ground.
>
> Reliance was placed on what Lord Justice Lawton had said in *R* v. *Turner (Terence)* ([1995] QB 834, 841):
>
>> 'An expert's opinion is admissible to furnish the court with scientific information which is likely to be outside the experience and knowledge of a judge or jury.

If on proven facts a judge or jury can form their own conclusions without help, then the opinion of an expert is unnecessary.'

The reference to the jury forming 'their own conclusions without help' was to be noted. Where, for example, there was a clear photograph and no suggestion that the subject had changed his appearance, a jury could usually reach a conclusion without help.

Where, as here, the accused admittedly had grown a beard shortly before his arrest and it was suggested, further, that the robber might have been disguised by spectacles and a wig, a comparison of photograph and defendant might not be straightforward.

In such circumstances, their Lordships could see no reason why expert evidence, if it could provide a jury with information and assistance they would otherwise lack, should not be given. But in which case it was for the judge to decide whether the issue was one where the jury could be assisted by expert evidence and whether the expert tendered had the expertise to provide the assistance.

Mr Clegg submitted next that Mr Neave, an artist working in the field of medicine and life science at Manchester University, was not an expert of facial mapping.

The judge ruled that, on the basis of his experience and by the nature of the assistance he could give, Mr Neave's evidence was admissible. In their Lordships' judgment the judge was entitled to come to that conclusion.

It was submitted, further, that even if Mr Neave was allowed rightly to state his findings, he should not have been allowed to give his opinion on the very issue before the jury.

Whether an expert could give his opinion on what had been called the ultimate issue has long been a vexed question.

If there was such a prohibition, it had long been more honoured in the breach than the observance: see for example, *DPP* v. *A and B C Chewing Gum Company Ltd* ([1968] 1 QB 159, 164) and the cases cited at p. 501 of *Cross on Evidence* 7th edition (1990).

The rationale behind the supposed prohibition was that an expert should not usurp the functions of the jury. But since counsel could bring the witness so close to opining on the ultimate issue that the inference as to his views was obvious, the rule could only be a matter of form rather than substance.

In their Lordships' view, an expert was called to give his opinion and he would be allowed to do so. It was, however, important that the judge should make it clear to the jury that they were not bound by the expert's opinion and that the issue was for them to decide.

The trial judge had done just that and he had put Mr Neave's evidence in its proper perspective. None of the grounds of appeal was well founded, and accordingly the appeal was dismissed."

268 Counsel specifically drew attention to the two classes of expert evidence which William Clegg QC submitted were inadmissible:

(i) straightforward questions of fact, and
(ii) where questions were raised which required specialist knowledge where the tribunal could form no view without expert evidence.

269 He submitted that some of the evidence which the claimant's counsel wished to adduce through their experts, in this reference, came under (i) above and there was nothing in the dispute which could possibly fall under (ii).

270 Claimant's counsel's response was that the *Stockwell* case clearly showed that it was for the tribunal to decide whether it would be assisted by expert evidence or not and therefore the final question of admissibility depended upon the tribunal's view of matters in the light of its own experience and the facts of the case.

271 The arbitrator accepted the claimant's counsel's argument and having decided that he would not be assisted by the expert evidence refused permission to the claimant to call his two experts.

IS EVIDENCE FROM ANOTHER UNRELATED DISPUTE ADMISSIBLE IN THE SUBJECT DISPUTE?

The facts

272 In a major rent review an expert witness was called to give evidence on behalf of the claimant, the lessee.

273 Both sides were represented by counsel. In cross-examination the expert was confronted by counsel who produced a proof of evidence provided by the expert in another quite unrelated hearing involving a not dissimilar property. The only line was that counsel in the present dispute had also appeared in the other one.

274 Counsel for each side addressed the arbitrator on this issue, with counsel for the respondent vehemently insisting that such evidence was inadmissible.

275 The expert was also asked for his opinion and he said that he would be most reluctant to give evidence on the proof as it was a document confidential to his client in the previous dispute.

Question

276 Faced with the opposition of both respondent's counsel and the expert witness, would the arbitrator be correct in admitting this evidence?

Course of action

277 The arbitrator should admit it as there is good authority for him to do so.

278 In *Percy Bartram Ltd* v. *Standard Life Assurance Co* [1990] NPC 57, involving renewal proceedings under the Landlord and Tenant Act 1954, the plaintiff's expert witness was requested to admit that he had acted as witness in an arbitration for other premises in the same street. In that case the arbitrator had fixed a rent of £74 per sq. ft. where in that arbitration the party had offered "without prejudice" to settle at £70 per sq. ft. In the current case he was contending for £55.

279 The judge ruled that the evidence was admissible. It was also held that the witness as agent for the other tenant with different landlords could claim no privilege for that negotiation in the present proceedings.

280 In *Rush & Tompkins Ltd* v. *Greater London Council* [1988] 3 All ER 737 the House of Lords held that in general the "without prejudice" rule made inadmissible, in any subsequent litigation between the same parties connected with the same subject matter, any admissions made with a view to reaching a settlement. In *Percy Bartram* the parties to the rent review of the adjacent premises were not parties to the litigation in which the alleged "without prejudice" statement was sought to be put in evidence. The rule in *Rush & Tompkins* therefore did not extend to those circumstances.

281 There is authority for the use of evidence filed in the public domain in subsequent proceedings: affidavits, writs and evidence given publicly in the course of a trial. The general common-law position was outlined by Atkin LJ in *British Thomson-Houston Co Ltd* v. *British Insulated and Helsby Cables Ltd* [1924] 2 Ch 160. In that case it was stated that unless the same witnesses would give exactly the same evidence in the second action it would not be possible to use in the second action evidence given only in the first without breaking the rule about hearsay.

282 However, some of the issues in that case were complicated by matters relating to using admissions to prove knowledge and witness "agency" and material as to "issue estoppel".

283 The courts have allowed reliance to be placed on admissions contained in affidavits of witnesses previously relied on by a party (see *Evans* v. *Merthyr Tydfil Urban District Council* [1899] 1 Ch 241).

284 The Civil Evidence Act 1968, s.2 expressly provides that in civil cases, statements made in previous proceedings are admissible. Section 2(1) reads:

> "In any civil proceedings statements made either orally or in a document or otherwise by any person, whether called as a witness to those proceedings or not, shall, subject to this section and to the rules of court, be admissible as evidence of any fact (or matter) stated (or dealt with) therein, but from which direct oral evidence by him would be admissible."

285 With specific regard to previous proceeedings, there is a proviso to s.2(3), which reads:

> "Provided that if the statement in question was made by a person while giving oral evidence in some other legal proceedings (whether civil or criminal) it may be proved in any manner authorised by the court."

286 The Rules of the Supreme Court, Order 38, rule 28 provides the mechanism for this evidence to be adduced. It enables any party wishing to give evidence on a statement made in other proceedings to apply to the court for directions as to whether (and if so on what grounds) the person desiring to advance the statement in evidence will be permitted to do so, and the Master or Registrar will also give directions as to the manner in which the statement may be proved. The application is by summons (or a notice under the summons for directions) and this must be served on every party in the action.

287 The Master has very wide powers to exclude a statement even though it fulfils the necessary requirements of admissibility, or the court may impose conditions on the admissibility of the statement made in previous legal proceedings. The Master may also give directions as to how the statement should be used. This is basically to stop a party leaving out passages not favourable to his own case. If the court directs that a statement together with more evidence given in formal proceedings was approved by a transcript made by the shorthand writer at the trial or arbitration, secondhand hearsay will also be admissible.

288 See also *Shearson Lehman Hutton Inc and Another* v. *Maclaine Watson & Co Ltd and Others* [1989] 1 All ER 1056 where it was held that documents produced voluntarily in a private arbitration were not privileged from disclosure in subsequent public litigation between different parties, since, in view of the fact that such documents had been disclosed voluntarily and not compulsorily pursuant to a court order, there was no significant risk that parties to an arbitration would, contrary to the interests of justice, be discouraged from making full and frank disclosure of confidential documents used in the arbitration by their possible use in subsequent litigation between different parties. Accordingly, there was no policy reason which would justify the court in protecting the documents from further disclosure.

289 A general principle is that the arbitrator must receive all admissible evidence which is relevant to the issues in question (unless the parties have agreed otherwise—s.34(2)(f), AA '96) and a failure would amount to serious irregularity affecting the proceedings (s.68(3), AA '96) in consequence of which there is a substantial risk that the award would be remitted or set aside by the court. (But see Rule 32.1(2) of the CPR, where in litigation the court may exclude evidence which would otherwise be admissible.) This is the case even where the arbitrator (who undoubtedly will be an expert in his own field) considers himself better informed than the person giving the evidence.

290 One possible exception to this would be where the arbitrator believes that he is so sure of a particular fact or matter that he requires no further evidence on the subject—although it would be unsafe to apply this exception during the claimant's case, because at such stage the arbitrator would not have heard the respondent's evidence in rebuttal, which might prove to be even more compelling than the claimant's evidence.

291 Another exception might be where the amount and nature of the evidence was disproportionate to the sum involved, although in such circumstances the arbitrator might be well advised to make the point in question to the party adducing the evidence before excluding it. If such party nevertheless insisted on introducing it there would be little that the arbitrator could safely do. In such circumstances he could reflect his concern at this unnecessarily wasteful exercise in his award on costs.

292 Had the parties, on the other hand, made no agreement under s.34, AA '96, the arbitrator could exclude this evidence, albeit normally admissible, on the ground that the cost involved in adducing such evidence was disproportionate with the sum involved etc. He could do this by virtue of his power under s.34 and his overriding duty to avoid unnecessary expense.

293 Arbitrators must realise that they have no power (unless the parties to the arbitration expressly agree to the contrary) to act on evidence which would be inadmissible in a court of law. If an arbitrator admits inadmissible evidence, it amounts to an error of law which may be appealed against. If an arbitrator deliberately accepted evidence which was obviously inadmissible he would be guilty of serious irregularity and it is highly likely that any award he made would be set aside. The situation might, however, be different where the reception of the evidence was due to an honest mistake or where the wrongly admitted evidence had no substantial bearing on the outcome of the case.

294 What about an award in another arbitration, would that be admissible? asked Thomasina. She said that she had in mind a rent review case in which Charley's pupil master had been involved. In this case comparables were submitted to the arbitrator by the parties' representatives. Three of these were included in the statement of agreed facts. One included by the lessor's representative was an arbitration award of the arbitrator's.

295 The lessee's representative, in his submissions, said that the inclusion of the arbitration award by the lessor's representative was not good evidence as open market evidence is "top of the rankings". Thomasina said that Charley's pupil master decided that the lessees' representative's claim that the award was not good evidence was meaningless as it was unspecific in the context of well-understood questions of admissibility. Anything in the "valuation picture" is relevant and therefore admissible. It is for the arbitrator to decide the weight to be attached to the evidence having considered the surrounding circumstances, taking care to restrict his findings solely to the factual and expert opinion evidence adduced. It should be remembered that an agreement of facts does not admit the relevance or admissibility of them.

296 Just what Charley's pupil master meant by the "valuation picture" I am not sure. Presumably it had to do with direct comparables. This was borne out in a case with similar facts, *Land Securities plc* v. *Westminster City Council* [1993] 1 WLR 286, where on the landlord's application to the High Court under s.2(1), AA '79 with the tenant's consent the parties asked for a determination of the question whether the interim award was admissible as evidence of the rental value of a comparable property.

297 It was held in this case that an arbitration award determining the market rent of a property represented an arbitrator's opinion of the rent at which the premises could reasonably have been let and it was not direct evidence of the rents at which comparable properties were actually let in the open market at about the same time. Accordingly it was not admissible evidence in other proceedings between different parties to prove a fact in issue in, or relevant to, the issue in those proceedings.

298 I ventured to suggest to Thomasina that in other circumstances an arbitration award could be admissible. It is all a question of relevance because generally, subject to the accepted exclusions, all relevant evidence is admissible. In general the parties to an arbitration are subject to an implied undertaking that documents obtained in other proceedings will not be used in these proceedings without leave of the court or arbitrator in the previous proceedings. This will be a situation encountered in two scenarios—when acting as arbitrator in proceedings brought as a result of documents obtained in other proceedings, and where the arbitrator is told that documents obtained in these proceedings will be used to bring other proceedings. This is sometimes the case where proceedings brought against the contractor produce documents showing that the real culprit is one of the professional team.

299 Relevant authorities: *Home Office* v. *Harman* [1983] AC 280 HL; *Sybron Corp* v. *Barclays Bank plc* [1985] Ch 299.

300 In *Home Office* v. *Harman* the House of Lords were asked to decide *inter alia*:

> "Whether a solicitor was released from an implied undertaking not to use documents for a purpose other than the present action because those documents had been quoted in court in that action and, in disclosing them, whether the solicitor was guilty of contempt of court?"

301 It was held in this case (Lord Simon and Lord Scarman dissenting) that it was the duty of the solicitor of a party to civil litigation, who obtained possession of copies of documents belonging to the other party by way of discovery, to refrain from using the advantage enjoyed by such possession for some collateral or ulterior purpose of his own which was not reasonably necessary for the proper conduct of the action on his client's behalf.

302 The implied undertaking given by a solicitor to the court, that he would not use or allow documents made available to him on discovery to be used for any collateral or ulterior purpose of his own, his client's or anyone else's, did not terminate when the document was read out in open court, in the course of the litigation for which it had been produced, because if that were the case full and frank discovery of documents before trial would be discouraged and the proper administration of justice would be impeded by the parties attempting to ensure that particular documents were, or were not, read out in court. It follows that the appellant had been guilty of contempt of court, and the appeal was accordingly dismissed.

303 In exceptional circumstances the court may allow the relaxation of this rule, see *EMI Records* v. *Spillane* [1986] 1 WLR 967.

304 While it may be that s.41(5), AA '96 gives the arbitrator power to restrain the improper use of these documents by peremptory order, the widening of the arbitrator's powers under the AA '96 and the restrictions on the power of the court to intervene makes this a potentially difficult area for arbitrators. It is also an area where arbitrators should be astute to the parties' obligations—to do otherwise is to risk devaluing the whole discovery process. The application for leave to use the documents should be made to the tribunal in which discovery was given, and the party from whom they were obtained should have the right to make representation as to why the undertaking should not be relaxed. That tribunal is entitled to exercise its discretion in reaching a view and is allowed to attach conditions to the release of the undertaking. Since s.34(2)(d), AA '96 gives the arbitrator a general power in relation to discovery, the arbitrator might sensibly adopt the following approach.

- Does a party to this arbitration propose using documents obtained upon discovery in other proceedings?
- Does the party from whom those documents were obtained object to that course, and if so why?
- What prejudice will that party suffer if use of the documents is permitted, and how is that balanced against any prejudice which will be caused by preventing their use?
- Would any confidentiality issue be dealt with by undertakings as to form and use to which those documents would have been put?

305 The final consideration is that the party against whom it is proposed that the document be used does not have the right to be heard. Since the undertaking exists as between the parties to the original arbitration, that has nothing at all to do with the third party. This is apparent from the authorities cited above. While this may appear to produce an unfair result, the reality is that if the arbitrator did otherwise he would be devaluing the undertaking which was being debated in the first place.

IN A NEGLIGENCE ACTION, IS EXPERT EVIDENCE FROM ANOTHER PROFESSION ADMISSIBLE?

The facts

306 The plaintiffs instructed the defendant surveyors to undertake a structural survey of a property they wished to purchase. The plaintiffs argued that the surveyors had not drawn attention to a crack in the wall. The judge held that the crack had been present, and that it had been overlooked by the surveyors. The judge further found that a competent surveyor would have called in a structural engineer who would have advised that the wall was defective. The surveyors appealed, arguing that the judge should also not have attempted to decide whether he preferred the expert evidence of an engineer to a surveyor. The surveyors maintained that the judge should have asked whether the plaintiffs had proved that the surveyor had fallen short of the required standard.

Question

307 Should evidence from the structural engineer be inadmissible in this action against the surveyor?

Course of action

308 The Court of Appeal held not, in the case from which the facts of this example are drawn *Sansom and Another* v. *Metcalf Hambleton & Co, The Times*, 29 December 1997, CA.

309 A court should not find a chartered surveyor professionally negligent upon the evidence of a structural engineer unless the case was so obvious that there was no room for two views.

310 The Court of Appeal (Lady Justice Butler-Sloss, Lord Justice Hutchinson and Sir John Vinelott) so held on 17 December in allowing an appeal by the defendant, Metcalf Hambleton and Co, chartered surveyors, from Judge Overend who, at Exeter County Court, had given judgment for the plaintiffs, Miss Denise Sansom and Mr John Monaghan. The court set aside the judgment and dismissed the action.

311 Lady Justice Butler-Sloss said that a court should be slow to find a professionally qualified person guilty of a breach of his duty of skill and care without evidence from those within the same profession as to the standard expected on the facts of the case and the failure of the professionally qualified person to measure up to that standard.

312 While it was not an absolute rule, unless it was an obvious case, in the absence of the relevant expert evidence, the claim would not be proved. As the instant case was not an open and shut case the evidence of the structural engineer was not expert evidence admissible in accordance with s.3 of the Civil Evidence Act 1972 on the issue of the chartered surveyor's negligence.

313 The engineer had not been aware of the situation and whether it would have been reasonable or not to call him in. Therefore, there was no admissible evidence before the court, and the plaintiffs had not proved their case.

ADMISSIBILITY OF FRESH MEDICAL EVIDENCE

The facts

314 Steven Martin Jones appealed against conviction at Caernarfon Crown Court of the murder of his wife, Madallin, by striking her forehead with a 4½lb lump hammer, fracturing her skull and putting her body partly immersed in a stream beside a faked motor accident.

315 On hearing the appeal the court decided, for reasons of convenience, to receive the evidence *de bene esse* of Professor Bernard Knight, a Home Office pathologist and professor of forensic pathology at the Wales Institute of Forensic Medicine and two other Home Office pathologists.

Question

316 Was this fresh medical evidence admissible at this late stage?

Course of action

317 The facts of this example are drawn from *R* v. *Jones (Steven Martin)* [1997] 1 Cr App R 86, CA.

318 In a reserved judgment the court dismissing the appeal gave guidance on the court's approach to the admission and consideration of fresh expert medical evidence in the light of 1995 amendments to the Criminal Appeal Act 1968.

319 Section 2 of the 1968 Act, as amended by s.2(1) of the Criminal Appeal Act 1995, provides:

"(1) Subject to the provisions of this Act, the Court of Appeal—

(a) shall allow an appeal against conviction if they think that the conviction is unsafe: and
(b) shall dismiss such an appeal in any other case."

320 Section 23 of Part 1 of the 1968 Act, as amended by s.4 of the 1995 Act, so far as relevant, provides:

"(1) For the purposes of this Part of the Act the Court of Appeal may, if they think it necessary or expedient in the interests of justice ....

(c) receive any evidence which was not adduced in the proceedings from which the appeal lies.

(2) The Court of Appeal shall, in considering whether to receive any evidence, have regard in particular to

(a) whether the evidence appears to the court to be capable of belief;
(b) whether it appears to the court that the evidence may afford any ground for allowing the appeal;
(c) whether the evidence would have been admissible in the proceedings from which the appeal lies on an issue which is the subject of the appeal; and
(d) whether there is a reasonable explanation for the failure to adduce the evidence in those proceedings."

321 The Lord Chief Justice, giving the judgment of the court, initially referred to the Act.

322 Section 23 as amended made it plain that, in the exercise of its discretion whether to receive evidence or not the court had to be guided above all by what it considered necessary or expedient in the interests of justice.

323 Section 23(2)(d) did, however, acknowledge the crucial obligation on a defendant in a criminal case to advance his whole defence and any evidence on which he relied before the trial jury. He was not entitled to hold evidence in reserve and then seek to introduce it on appeal following conviction.

324 While failure to adduce the evidence before the jury was not a bar to reception of the evidence on appeal, it was a matter which the court was obliged to consider in deciding whether to receive the evidence or not.

325 The court had in the past accepted that s.23 might apply to expert evidence, and their Lordships would not wish to circumscribe the operation of a statutory rule enacted to protect defendants against the risk of wrongful conviction. But it seemed unlikely that the section was framed with expert evidence prominently in mind.

326 The requirement in subs.(2)(a) that the evidence should appear to be capable of belief applied more aptly to factual evidence than to expert opinion, which might or might not be acceptable or persuasive but was unlikely to be thought to be incapable of belief in any ordinary sense.

327 The giving of reasonable explanation for failure to adduce the evidence before the jury, again applied more aptly to factual evidence of which a party was unaware, or could not adduce, than to expert evidence, since if one expert was unavailable to testify at a trial a party would ordinarily be expected to call another, unless circumstances prevented that.

328 Expert witnesses, although inevitably varying in standing and experience, were interchangeable in a way in which factual witnesses were not, it would clearly subvert the trial process if a defendant convicted at trial were to be generally free to mount on appeal an expert case which, if sound, could and should have been advanced before the jury.

329 If it was said that the only expert witness in an established field whose opinion supported a certain defence was unavailable to testify at the trial, that might be thought, save in unusual circumstances, to reflect on the acceptability of that opinion.

330 On reading Professor Knight's report, and despite his great eminence in the field, the court had great doubts whether his opinion could displace the very clear conclusions reached by the other pathologists, who had had the advantage of inspecting the wounds which led to the death of Mrs Jones.

331 The court did not conclude that Professor Knight's evidence appeared to be other than capable of belief. It appeared to the court that the evidence, if accepted, would afford a ground for allowing the appeal.

332 Clearly the evidence would have been admissible at the trial on an issue which was the subject of the appeal.

333 While the court fully appreciated that the appellant could not have adduced Professor Knight's evidence before the jury on the date when the trial took place, it could see no good reason why application could not have been made for vacation of the trial date if evidence to the same effect could not be obtained from any other source; and, if the evidence could have been obtained from some other source, then in their Lordships' opinion it should have been obtained and no reasonable explanation had been given for failure to obtain it.

334 Although the case made out for receiving that evidence on appeal was not strong, on balance the court concluded that it was expedient, if not necessary, in the interests of justice that it should receive that evidence.

335 Their Lordships, therefore, treated the reports of Professor Knight and the other two Home Office pathologists as received in evidence. All the witnesses were examined and cross-examined before their Lordships, and they received the oral evidence also.

336 It seemed plain on the language of s.2(1) and as ruled in *R v. Callaghan (Note)* ((1988) 88 Cr App R 40) that the court was obliged to exercise its own judgment in deciding whether, in the light of the new evidence, the conviction was unsafe.

337 Their Lordships considered the evidence and continued that, even if the expert medical evidence stood alone, they would not regard the conviction as unsafe. But, if the evidence of Professor Knight had raised a doubt in their minds, as in the event it had not, such doubt would have been dispelled by the cumulative effect of the evidence in the case.

338 Their Lordships considered the other evidence and concluded that, despite the new evidence which they had received, they did not think the conviction of the appellant was unsafe. They had, accordingly, to dismiss the appeal.

WHETHER THE OPINION OF AN EXPERT ON THE ULTIMATE QUESTION OF NEGLIGENCE IS ADMISSIBLE

The facts

339 A firm of surveyors (KFR) were instructed by a mortgagee and the receivers of a company in receivership to market a property.

340 KFR gave specific advice to these mortgagees and to the receivers concerning the marketing of this property.

341 Part of this present action involved a claim for negligent marketing by KFR.

342 During the case, a Mr Ames was called, as an independent expert, by the parties bringing the action against KFR.

343 Mr Ames was pressed on the number of occasions, both by the judge and by counsel, to say that KFR fell below the standards of any competent valuer or estate agent.

Question

344 Is opinion on the ultimate question (of negligence) inadmissible?

Course of action

345 The facts of this example are drawn from *Routestone Ltd v. Minories Finance Ltd and Another* [1997] 21 EG 148.

346 Here Jacob J said on this issue:

> "I must also consider an important question of the law of evidence. Is an expert's opinion on the 'ultimate question' admissible? In this case the ultimate question is the *Whitehouse* question. Now it is clear that an expert's opinion as to what the legal test is must be inadmissible. As Oliver J observed in *Midland Bank Trust Co Ltd* v. *Hett, Stubbs & Kemp* [1979] Ch 384 at p. 402:
>
> > 'The extent of any legal duty in any given situation must, I think, be a question of law for the court.'
>
> It is by no means self-evidence that an expert's opinion on whether or not that test is satisfied is also inadmissible. Section 3 of the Civil Evidence Act 1972 provides:
>
> > '(1) Subject to any rules of court made in pursuance of Part 1 of the Civil Evidence Act 1968 or this Act, where a person is called as a witness in any civil proceedings, his opinion on any relevant matter on which he is qualified to give expert evidence shall be admissible in evidence.
> >
> > ...
> >
> > (3) In this section "relevant matter" includes an issue in the proceedings in question.'
>
> I think this provision makes the opinion admissible. It by no means follows that the court must follow it. On its own (unless uncontested) it would be 'a mere bit of empty rhetoric' (Wigmore, *Evidence* (Chadbourn rev) para 1920). What really matters in most cases is the reasons given for the opinion.
>
> As a practical matter a well constructed expert's report containing opinion evidence sets out the opinion and the reasons for it. If the reasons stand up the opinion does, if not, not. A rule of evidence which excludes this opinion evidence serves no practical purpose. What happens if the evidence is regarded as inadmissible is that experts' reports simply try to creep up to the opinion without openly giving it. They insinuate rather than explicate. And there is this further consideration, of considerable significance in this case. Suppose the expert is *not* prepared to say that the conduct complained of fell short of the *Whitehouse* test? It would be bizarre for the case to go to court at all. I think it is a good thing for an expert to have given to him the legal test and the facts as alleged by the plaintiff. If his own expert is not prepared to say that the defendant fell short of the relevant standard, then the plaintiff knows where he is. And the expert himself will be faced directly with what he is doing—saying another fell below an acceptable standard and knowing that he himself will be challenged on that opinion. If the expert merely says he would have done things differently the case may yet end up in court when it should not, as this one has, and I suspect others do.
>
> The point is of significance here precisely because Mr Ames was not prepared to say (despite being pressed a number of times in his evidence in chief both by me and Mr Trace) that KFR fell

below the standards of any competent valuer or estate agent. He thought other marketing strategies should have been followed in the sense that he would have done something different. He thought there were matters of criticism but no more. Oliver J described that sort of evidence in *Midland Bank*:

> 'Evidence which really amounts to no more than an expression of opinion by a particular practitioner of what he thinks he would have done had he been placed, hypothetically and without the benefit of hindsight, in the position of the defendants, is of little assistance to the court.'

Because Mr Ames would not say that what KFR advised fell below the standard of any reasonably competent valuer Mr Trace was driven to argue that opinion evidence on the ultimate question was inadmissible. I have already said that I think it is (as opposed to evidence of what the legal test is) but I should deal with the cases suggested to show otherwise. Only one of them refers to section 3 of the 1972 Act. And as it seems to me they are not dealing with the precise point. Thus, in *Midland*, Oliver J was dealing with evidence as to the legal test (inadmissible) and evidence as to what a particular expert would have done (admissible but of 'little assistance'). He was not dealing with an opinion as to whether particular conduct satisfied the legal test. That is surely an 'issue in the proceedings in question' within the meaning of the statute.

Again, in *Liddell* v. *Middleton* unreported, CA (Stuart-Smith, Gibson and Hutchinson LJJ) 7 July 1995, a traffic accident case, the Court of Appeal made it clear that there was over-use of expert evidence in road traffic cases, when the question is essentially whether or not the defendant was negligent. In that sort of case, where the court had its own experience to go by, the expert can only help when considering things like inferences to be drawn from tyre marks. You do not need an expert to tell you whether or not someone should have sounded their horn or driven slower.

And in *Bown* v. *Gould & Swayne*, unreported CA (Leggatt, Simon Brown and Millett LJJ) 24 January 1996, expert evidence (in a claim for professional negligence) as to what a solicitor should do was excluded. Such evidence would be evidence as to the legal test to be applied and was plainly inadmissible. All the matters of evidence sought to be admitted 'proves, on analysis, to involve either a question of law or a question of fact' *per* Stuart-Smith LJ. *Bown* does not assist either side, though both sought to rely upon it.

By way of contrast, and in support of the conclusion that an expert opinion on whether a legal test has been complied with is admissible is what was said by Sir Donald Nicholls V-C giving the judgment of the Court of Appeal in *Mölnlycke AB* v. *Proctor & Gamble No 5* [1994] RPC 49 at p. 113:

> In applying the statutory criterion (i.e. as to whether an alleged inventive step was obvious) and making these findings (i.e. as to obviousness) the court will almost invariably require the assistance of expert evidence. The primary evidence will be that of properly qualified expert witnesses who will say whether or not in their opinions the relevant step would have been obvious to a skilled man having regard to the state of the art.'

Further, the current edition of *Cross and Tapper on Evidence 1997* at p. 552 is clearly of the view that opinion evidence relating to the ultimate question is admissible by virtue of the 1972 Act. It is noteworthy that the Act was passed following the 17th report of the Law Reform Committee 1970 Cmnd 4489 which specifically recommended that an expert opinion on the ultimate question should be made admissible. Mr Trace submits that *Cross* is irrelevant because it was published before *Liddell* and *Bown* but as I have indicated, I do not think those decisions are on the point. As to the Law Reform report, Mr Trace is driven to say it is irrelevant even though it is clearly the basis upon which the 1972 Act was passed.

So I think the fact that Mr Ames was prepared to criticise but was not prepared to say that KFR fell short of the standard of any competent estate agent is itself fatal to *Routestone*'s case. But that is far from an end of the matter. I next observe that Mr Ames did not give any evidence of a kind recognised by Oliver J as admissible:

> 'Clearly if there is some practice in a particular profession, some accepted standard of conduct

> which is laid down by a professional institute or sanctioned by common usage, evidence of that can and ought to be received.'
>
> So all I have is that Mr Ames would, with hindsight, have advised differently. That is far from proving that KFR were wrong or negligent. This is again a clear further reason for rejecting the claim. Mr Trace says that having heard what KFR did and what Mr Ames would have done I can use my common sense. I suppose there may be cases where that would be enough to establish a case of negligence, but they would have to be so plain that they would probably never come to court. Here I am dealing with a fairly specialised field—the sale of investment properties of a rather unusual kind (very unusual in the case of SGE and GR). I do not think my 'common sense' provides any light as to what would amount to going about things the best way, still less, whether a particular way fell below an acceptable standard."

347 In the course of his judgment, Jacob J made the following interesting comments:

> "Interesting though complex legal argument may be for some lawyers, it is not the function of the court to hear it at great expense to the parties if it can be avoided. I therefore inquired of the parties whether or not, for the purposes of this case only, sensible concessions could be made. It is to the credit of all that they were."

348 The judge then went on to record those concessions made solely for the trial before him. An object lesson to arbitrators in the exercise of their s.33 duty under the Arbitration Act 1996 to

> ". . . adopt procedures suitable to the circumstances of the particular case, avoiding unnecessary . . . expense . . . "

349 Later, in the same judgment, Jacob J, commenting on the unacceptable partisan approach of one of the independent witnesses, said this:

> "I have to say that I found Mr Robinson's evidence did not remotely support the factual allegations made in the pleadings which I have summarised above. Although I acquit him of any intention deliberately to mislead the court, I do not think that his whole thinking about the case—from very early on—was coloured by an over-zealous passion for his clients' causes."

350 Again, an object lesson to all so-called independent expert witnesses.

351 Finally, it is worth repeating what the judge reiterated, i.e. the relevant legal standard in negligence cases.

> ". . . to show that the advice given . . . was more than erroneous—it had to amount to an error of the sort that would not have been made by a reasonably competent estate agent professing himself to have the standard and type of skill that KFR held themselves out as having, and acting with ordinary care, *per* Lord Fraser in *Whitehouse* v. *Jordan* [1981] 1 WLR 246 at p. 263."

352 On another case where the issue of the expert's opinion on the ultimate question arose, *R v. Doheny* [1997] 1 Cr App R 369, CA; *The Times*, 14 August 1996, one commentator, B Mahendra, in *NLJ Practitioner* (28 November 1997), said this:

> "As the Court of Appeal in *Doheny*, NLJ 25 October 1996, re-asserted the traditional view that an expert forensic scientist presenting DNA profile evidence should not encroach on the province of the jury. All he could do was to adduce the evidence of DNA comparisons together with his calculations of the random occurrence ratio, and, provided he had the necessary statistical expertise, he could say how many individuals with the matching characteristics might be found in defined

areas and defined groups of individuals. The scientist was not to be asked his opinion on the likelihood that it was the defendant who was the author of the incriminating stain—this remained firmly a matter for the jury. It was the judge—not some statistician armed with Bayes' theorem or any other device—who would explain to the jury the niceties of statistical terms.

In civil cases, these problems should not arise, at any rate in theory. Section 3 of the Civil Evidence Act 1972 allows the expert to give his opinion on all relevant matters including the ultimate issue. But in *Re M and R* (1996) NLJ Digest page 1425, the Court of Appeal discovered a lower court had taken a heavy hand to experts, denying them the opportunity to give an opinion as to whether the child witnesses were telling the truth on the grounds that it was a matter for the court, not the expert. The Court of Appeal held the decision made on that basis were *per incuriam*. Experts can properly have their say on these matters and it was for the court to weigh the evidence."

(See paras 444 to 461 below for full details of *R* v. *Doheny*.)

AN EXPERT INCLUDES EVIDENCE IN HIS REPORT FROM ANOTHER EXPERT

The facts

353 An arbitrator was appointed in a dispute which concerned certain technical valuation matters and he had directed that each side could call one expert.

354 The parties agreed the appointment of their respective quantity surveying experts and their reports were exchanged.

355 In the report of the respondent's expert quantity surveyor reference was made to the report and advice of a firm of geotechnical engineers such that this was clearly the expert evidence of another person and dealt with an area outside the permitted expert's field of expertise.

356 The claimant requested a hearing before the arbitrator and sought an order that the respondent be debarred from relying upon the offending section of his report in evidence.

357 The respondent opposed the application on the grounds that the arbitrator had not defined the discipline of the expert to be appointed and their expert quantity surveyor could give evidence on whatever technical issues he wished.

Question

358 What order should the arbitrator make?

Course of action

359 This issue goes to credibility. The opinion of someone who has no experience in the field is worthless and experts should only give evidence on matters within their experience.

360 If it is clear to the arbitrator that the principal issue relates to the geotechnical matters included within the respondent's expert's report then rather than debarring the respondent from relying on the section of his expert's report to which the claimant objects it would be more appropriate to give the claimant the time and opportunity to address these matters by allowing the claimant the opportunity of appointing a geotechnical expert himself if he so desires.

361 If one expert's report contains another expert's report then the second expert's report must be inadmissible. The second expert should produce a separate report which the first expert can refer to but the primary evidence in the second report should be given by the second expert himself. Thus, the logical solution would be to give leave to both sides to call a geotechnical expert. This would be achieved in practice by inviting submissions from both sides as to the relevance of the geotechnical issue.

362 It may also be necessary for the arbitrator to consider whether the geotechnical evidence was outside his terms of reference as this would mean that he did not have jurisdiction to decide the issue. If this did prove to be the case the arbitrator could suggest that the parties enter into an *ad hoc* arbitration agreement enlarging the reference to include this issue.

363 Alternatively this may be a case where the arbitrator can rule on his own jurisdiction (s.30(1)(c), AA '96).

364 What if an expert cites passages from a report prepared by the arbitrator when he was acting as an expert in another reference, Thomasina asked? She went on to say that this had actually happened to Charley's pupil master. In that case he (as arbitrator) had disclosed at the time of his appointment that he had acted as expert witness at some time in the past for a party (not involved in the current arbitration) represented by the solicitors for the claimant in the reference that he was now conducting as arbitrator. Neither party took issue with this disclosure.

365 Subsequently the arbitrator ordered exchange of the experts' reports in the current arbitration and copies were sent to him.

366 Previously the arbitrator has ascertained the parties' views with regard to what documentation he should read before the hearing. In this pre-hearing reading, the arbitrator found that the claimant's report quoted extensively from one which the arbitrator had prepared for the previous arbitration. When he drew this to the attention of the parties the respondent's solicitor respectfully suggested that he should consider standing down as it would appear, as a result from the quotation from his report, that he might be biased in the claimant's favour. The arbitrator declined to stand down on the grounds that it was not in the parties' interests that he should do so. He went on to say that he would determine this present case on its facts which were materially different from the previous arbitration. If the respondents wished to seek to have him removed he would stay proceedings for 14 days for the respondent to produce evidence that he had made the necessary application to the High Court, after which, failing receipt of such evidence, he intended to proceed.

367 The only possible ground, today, on which the respondent on the facts of this example would be removed is s.24(1)(a), AA '96:

> "that circumstances exist that give rise to justifiable doubts as to his [the arbitrator's] impartiality."

368 Having said that I believe that taking the facts as presented here it would be unlikely to lead to a judge having the arbitrator removed. (See also paras 428 to 443.)

WHETHER OPINIONS ON VALUES BASED ON HEARSAY ARE ADMISSIBLE

The facts

369 In the course of an arbitration concerning the rent review of business premises, as is the normal practice, a number of comparables were adduced. Some of these comparables turned out to be supported only by hearsay evidence or by evidence that was, in the judge's words, "... in other respects less than cogent".

Question

370 Is opinion evidence on values based on hearsay admissible?

Course of action

371 This arose in *English Exporters (London) Ltd* v. *Eldonwall Ltd* [1973] Ch 415.

372 On this point Megarry J said this:

"There was no formal process of a ruling being made to exclude those comparables which were supported only by hearsay evidence; but I was discouraging, and in the event Mr Ibbotson, though rueful, did not seriously argue the point, or press it. I nevertheless think that I ought to make more explicit the reasons for my having been discouraging for in my experience the status of hearsay evidence of comparables in valuation cases is a matter that is often misunderstood, and not only by valuers. For all I know, that misunderstanding may in recent years have been fostered by a passage in Woodfall's *Landlord and Tenant*, 27th ed (1968) p. 1350, to which Mr Lightman very properly referred me. There the editors take the view that when a valuer is giving his opinion on rental value under the Act of 1954:

> 'he should speak his reasons for holding that opinion even if this involves a reference to comparisons of which he only knows at second-hand, that surely going to weight rather than admissibility'.

There are further passages amplifying that view, but I think that this is a sufficient indication of the general import of a paragraph which seems to contend that valuers are entitled to give hearsay evidence of comparables.

Let me put on one side the cases in which exceptions to the rule excluding hearsay evidence have grown up, whether by case law or by statute (and sometimes almost by a side-wind; see, for example, *In re-Koscott Interplanetary (UK) Ltd* [1972] 3 All ER 829); and in particular I exclude cases in which, subject to observing the statutory safeguards, hearsay evidence has been made admissible under the Civil Evidence Act 1968. Let me further ignore cases in which questions in cross-examination may have let in evidence that otherwise would be inadmissible, and confine myself to the admissibility of hearsay in chief and in re-examination in these valuation cases. In such circumstances, two of the heads under which the valuers' evidence may be ranged are opinion evidence and factual evidence. As an expert witness, the valuer is entitled to express his opinion about matters within his field of competence. In building up his opinion about values, he will no doubt have learned much from transations in which he has himself been engaged, and of which he could give first-hand evidence. But he will also have learned much from many more sources, including much of which he could give no first-hand evidence.

Textbooks, journals, reports of auctions and other dealings, and information obtained from his professional brethren and others, some related to particular transactions and some more general and indefinite, will all have contributed their share. Doubtless much, or most, of this will be accurate, though some will not; and even what is accurate so far as it goes may be incomplete, in that nothing may have been said of some special element which affects values. Nevertheless, the opinion that the expert expresses is none the worse because it is in part derived from the matters of which he could give no direct evidence. Even if some of the extraneous information which he acquires in this way is inaccurate or incomplete, the errors and omissions will often tend to cancel each other out; and the valuer, after all, is an expert in this field, so that the less reliable the knowledge that he has about the details of some reported transaction, the more his experience will tell him that he should be ready to make some discount from the weight that he gives it in contributing to his overall sense of values. Some aberrant transactions may stand so far out of line that he will give them little or no weight.

No question of giving hearsay evidence arises in such cases, the witness states his opinion from his general experience.

On the other hand quite apart from merely expressing his opinion the expert is able to give factual evidence as well. If he has first-hand knowledge of a transaction, he can speak of that. He may himself have measured the premises and conducted the negotiations which led to a letting of them at £x, which comes to £y per square foot; and he himself may have read the lease and seen that it contains no provisions, other than some particular clause, which would have any material effect on the valuation; and then he may express his opinion on the value. So far as the expert gives factual evidence, he is doing what any other witness of fact may do, namely, speaking of that which he has perceived for himself. No doubt in many valuation cases the requirement of first-hand evidence is not pressed to an extreme: if the witness has not himself measured the premises, but it has been done by his assistant under his supervision, the expert's figures are often accepted without requiring the assistant to be called to give evidence.

Again, it may be that it would be possible for a valuer to fill a gap in his first-hand knowledge of a transaction by some method such as stating in his evidence that he has made diligent enquiries of some person who took part in the transaction in question, but despite receiving full answers to his enquiries, he discovered nothing which suggested to him that the transaction had any unusual features which would affect the value as a comparable. But, basically, the expert's factual evidence on matters of fact is in the same position as the factual evidence of any other witness. Further, factual evidence that he cannot give himself is sometimes adduced in some other way, as by the testimony of some other witness who was himself concerned in the transaction in question, or by proving some document which carried the transaction through, or recorded it; and to the transaction thus established, like the transactions which the expert himself has proved, the expert may apply his experience and opinions, as tending to support or qualify his views.

That being so, it seems to me quite another matter when it is asserted that a valuer may give factual evidence of transactions of which he has no direct knowledge, whether *per se* or whether in the guise of giving reasons for his opinion as to value. It is one thing to say:

> 'From my general experience of recent transactions comparable with this one, I think the proper rent should be £x';

it is another thing to say

> 'Because I have been told by someone else that the premises next door have an area of x square feet and were recently let on such-and-such terms for £y a year, I say the rent of these premises should be £z a year.'

What he has been told about the premises next door may be inaccurate or misleading as to the area, the rent, the terms and much else besides.

It makes it no better when the witness expresses his confidence in the reliability of his source of information: a transparently honest and careful witness cannot make information reliable if, instead of speaking of what he has seen and heard for himself, he is merely retailing what others have told him. The other party to the litigation is entitled to have a witness whom he can cross-examine on oath as to the reliability of the facts deposed to, and not merely as to the witness's opinion as to the reliability of information which was given to him not on oath, and possibly in circumstances tending to inaccuracies and slips. Further, it is often difficult enough for the courts to ascertain the true facts from witnesses giving direct evidence, without the added complication of attempts to evaluate a witness's opinion of the reliability, care and thoroughness of some informant who has supplied the witness with the facts that he is seeking to recount.

It therefore seems to me that details of comparable transactions upon which a valuer intends to rely in his evidence must, if they are to be put before the court, be confined to those details which have been, or will be, proved by admissible evidence, given either by the valuer himself or in some other way. I know of no special rule giving expert valuation witnesses the right to give hearsay evidence of facts: and notwithstanding many pleasant days spent in the Lands Tribunal while I was at the Bar, I can see no compelling reasons of policy why they should be able to do this. Of course, the long-established technique in adducing expert evidence of asking hypothetical questions may also be employed for valuers. It would, I think, be perfectly proper to ask a valuer:

> 'If in May 1972 No 3, with an area of 2,000 sq. ft. was let for £10,000 a year for seven years on a full repairing lease with no unusual terms, what rent would be appropriate for the premises in dispute?'

But I cannot see that it would do much good unless the facts of the hypothesis are established by admissible evidence; and the valuer's statement that someone reputable had told him these facts, or that he had seen them in a reputable periodical, would not in my judgement constitute admissible evidence.

On principle, therefore, I would not accept the proposition in *Woodfall* p. 1350; and in this I do not think I would be alone. To the end of the passage in question *Woodfall* very properly appends a footnote which reads:

> 'See, however, *Wright* v. *Sydney Municipal Council* (1916) 16 SR (NSW) 348.'

The case cited seems to me to provide much support for the views that I have expressed; and *Woodfall* does not attempt to discuss or refute the decision. In *Wright* v. *Sydney Municipal Council*, much the same sort of point came before Sly J, Gordon J and Ferguson J. The case concerned a sale and not a tenancy, but that seems immaterial. It was contended (see p. 359) that an expert valuer

> 'was entitled to state what sales he had knowledge of, even from hearsay, and to give the details of such sales, including price etc. in evidence . . .'

but this contention was rejected. Sly J said that the expert could, in addition to giving direct evidence of sales of other comparable land, provided there was legal evidence of these, testify that, *inter alia*, he had kept in touch with sales not made by himself in the district, to show that he was competent to give evidence of values in the district. Sly J added, at p. 359:

> 'But he had no privilege beyond any other witness to speak in detail of the prices realised for other lands unless he can give legal evidence of such sales, or that evidence has already been given by the witnesses.
>
> It would be a most dangerous thing to allow an expert to speak of the details of sales of which he really knows nothing, and see the difficulty the plaintiff in a case like this would be in if he had to answer such evidence not knowing whether the sales were really existent or not. I think the same principle applies whether the evidence is given in chief or in reply.'

At p. 365 Gordon J took a similar view, and at p. 366 Ferguson J rejected the contention that the witness could 'give hearsay evidence of the particulars of the transactions in question': see also *Phipson on Evidence*, 11th ed (1970) p. 518. Bramwell B, I may say, apparently would have put matters on an even narrower basis, saying that a valuer may state his opinion of the value of land, but that he must not in chief add that he says this because some other land sold for such-and-such a price, although he may say this in cross-examination: see *Sheen* v. *Bumpstead* (1862) 1 H & C 358, 365. However, this, I think, was an *obiter* remark in a dissenting judgment (although *Phipson* at p. 519 does not reveal this), and for many years now such evidence has not been rejected in chief when the witness has been speaking from his first-hand knowledge.

Putting matters shortly, and leaving on one side the matters that I have mentioned, such as the

Civil Evidence Act 1968 and anything made admissible by questions in cross-examination, in my judgement a valuer giving expert evidence in chief (or in re-examination):

(a) may express the opinions that he has formed as to values even though substantial contributions to the formation of those opinions have been made by matters of which he has no first-hand knowledge;
(b) may give evidence as to the details of any transactions within his personal knowledge, in order to establish them as matters of fact; and
(c) may express his opinion as to the significance of any transactions which are or will be proved by admissible evidence (whether or not given by him) in relation to the valuation with which he is concerned; but
(d) may not give hearsay evidence stating the details of any transactions not within his personal knowledge in order to establish them as matters of fact. To those propositions I would add that for counsel to put in a list of comparables ought to amount to a warranty by him of his intention to tender admissible evidence of all that is shown on the list.

I have spent some little time in dealing with this matter of evidence as it appears to be the subject of no direct modern authority, and experience suggests that it is a matter upon which there is considerable misunderstanding. When a list of comparables is being prepared for the trial, as is usual and convenient, it is all too common to include in the list transactions upon which there will be no admissible evidence but only hearsay of a greater or lesser degree of reliability. If the parties exchange lists of comparables at an early date, often much time and money can be saved by the experts on each side agreeing such of the transactions in each list as, after any necessary inquiry, they feel they can accept as being reliably summarised; and in this way the additional expense of proving a favourable comparable not within an expert's own knowledge can be avoided. But if the other side will not accept the facts, then either the transaction must be proved by admissible evidence or it must be omitted as a comparable."

(But see also the Civil Evidence Act 1995—paras 374 to 408 below.)

373 Thus what Megarry J said in answer to this question was, in essence, that although an expert valuer may in evidence express his opinion on values even though substantial contributions to the formation of those opinions have been made by hearsay, he cannot give hearsay evidence as to the fact of transactions which lie outside his personal knowledge.

IS REFERENCE BY AN EXPERT TO A THIRD PARTY'S DIARIES HEARSAY AND THEREFORE INADMISSIBLE?

The facts

374 A construction arbitration approaches the scheduled hearing date. Hearing bundles are prepared by both sides as they have been unable to settle on an agreed bundle.

375 In sending his bundle to the arbitrator, the claimant includes a complete copy of the clerk of works' site diaries which are referred to by the claimant's expert in his report. The respondent immediately writes to the arbitrator objecting to the inclusion of these diaries, on the ground that as the claimant does not intend to call the witness they are hearsay evidence and therefore inadmissible. It is clear that the respondent has no interest in having this witness called himself.

376 The claimant counters this objection, averring that the evidence is relevant but that he is not in a position to call this witness. He points out that under the Civil Evidence Act 1995 (CEA '95) hearsay evidence is now admissible. He then formally gives notice under s.2(1) of that Act that he proposes to adduce this hearsay evidence.

377 The respondent then requested, under s.2(1)(b), CEA '95, that the claimant explain

(a) why it was so important this evidence is adduced, and
(b) if it is that important why he cannot call the witness?

378 The claimant responded that the clerk of works' evidence went to the root of one of the substantive issues and he could not call this witness because the local authority who employed the clerk of works refused to release him.

Question

379 What action should the arbitrator take following this exchange?

Course of action

380 Evidence at the hearing may be proved by the testimony of witnesses. This testimony is offered as truth of what that witness asserts. It is evidence of facts which he has perceived for himself—it is fundamental evidence, which the party against whom it is given has a right to test in cross-examination.

381 The general rule in common law was prior to the CEA '95 that hearsay evidence was not admissible—for example in this case the written statements by the clerk of works who is not being called as a witness.

382 The procedure for introducing this type of evidence, in the event that the maker of the statement is not available for some good reason, is clearly established by CEA '95.

383 This Act:

1. Abolishes the rule against hearsay evidence which it defines as anything other than direct oral evidence.
2. Requires those who wish to introduce hearsay to give the other side "such notice as is reasonable and practicable in the circumstances".
3. Gives guidelines on the weighing of hearsay evidence.

384 Failure to comply with the notice requirement will not affect the admissibility of the evidence, but may be taken into account on procedure and costs, and as a matter "adversely affecting weight".

385 The tribunal is required to have regard to "any circumstances from which any inference can reasonably be drawn as to the reliability or otherwise of the evidence", and to weigh hearsay evidence taking account of whether:

(a) it was reasonable and practicable to produce the maker of the original statement;
(b) the statement was contemporaneous with what happened;
(c) the statement involves multiple hearsay;
(d) there was any improper motive;
(e) the account is edited or results from collaboration;

(f) the circumstances in which the evidence is produced are such as to suggest an attempt to prevent proper evaluation of its weight.

386 Section 34(2)(f) of AA '96 deals with the question of the strict rules of evidence as follows:

> "34 (1) It shall be for the tribunal to decide all procedural and evidential matters, subject to the right of the parties to agree any matter.
> (2) Procedural and evidential matters include—
> ...
> (f) whether to apply strict rules of evidence (or any other rules) as to the admissibility, relevance or weight of any material (oral, written or other) sought to be tendered on any matters of fact or opinion, and the time manner and form in which such material should be exchanged and presented."

387 Thus, the parties can agree between them whether or not strict rules will apply. If they do not agree, the arbitrator will be entitled to decide for them. If strict rules do not apply neither will the Civil Evidence Act. This means that hearsay will be admissible without the notice and weight safeguards, which will only have any bearing insofar as they form part of the general duty to act fairly between the parties.

388 The parties have followed the procedures laid down in this Act and it is now at the discretion of the arbitrator to give leave to call the clerk of works should he be convinced by the respondent's argument as to why he wishes to have this witness cross-examined on his diaries. Assuming the arbitrator is to convinced then he should issue a direction granting his consent.

389 This provision for cross-examination is covered by s.3, CEA '95 which states:

> "Rules of court may provide that where a party to civil proceedings adduces hearsay evidence of a statement made by a person and does not call that person as a witness, any other party to the proceedings may, with the leave of the court, call that person as a witness and cross-examine him on the statement as if he had been called by the first-mentioned party and as if the hearsay statement were his evidence in chief."

390 Thomasina then asked what happened if the clerk of works simply could not be called (or subpoenaed) because he had died or was working overseas? I explained that hearsay evidence can be admitted in these circumstances (or indeed in any circumstances provided the parties agreed), and then it all comes down to a question of weight.

391 This is covered by s.4, CEA '95, which states:

> "(1) In estimating the weight (if any) to be given to hearsay evidence in civil proceedings the court shall have regard to any circumstances from which any inference can reasonably be drawn as to the reliability or otherwise of the evidence.
> (2) Regard may be had, in particular, to the following—
> (a) whether it would have been reasonable and practicable for the party by whom the evidence was adduced to have produced the maker of the original statement as a witness;
> (b) whether the original statement was made contemporaneously with the occurrence or existence of the matters stated;
> (c) whether the evidence involves multiple hearsay;
> (d) whether any person involved had any motive to conceal or misrepresent matters;
> (e) whether the original statement was an edited account, or was made in collaboration with another or for a particular purpose;

(f) whether the circumstances in which the evidence is adduced as hearsay are such as to suggest an attempt to prevent proper evaluation of its weight."

392 Basically, what this Act is all about is weight. Where hearsay—even multiple hearsay—is *prima facie* now admissible, under the old '68 and '72 Acts it had not been. Now the main consideration is not admissibility but what weight to attach to it. As is seen from the list of matters to which the court must have regard, these are all fairly commonsense things which would, in any event, be taken into consideration. What this, by no means exhaustive, list emphasises is that hearsay will have varying degrees of weight given to it. This section is also intended to prevent the abuse of secondary hearsay evidence rather than calling a potentially unimpressive witness to give direct evidence.

393 Other parts of this Act deal with competence and credibility. Hearsay by a person who would not normally be accepted as competent is inadmissible, i.e. the mentally insane, inebriated persons *et al.*

394 An important condition concerning hearsay in documents is contained in s.8, CEA '95 which provides:

"(1) Where a statement contained in a document is admissible as evidence in civil proceedings, it may be proved—
(a) by the production of that document, or
(b) whether or not that document is still in existence, by the production of a copy of that document or of the material part of it, authenticated in such manner as the court may approve.
(2) It is immaterial for this purpose how many removes there are between a copy and the original."

395 This means that photocopies are now clearly acceptable and this avoids the sort of problem that the arbitrator faced in *Fairclough Building Ltd* v. *Vale of Belvoir* (1990) 59 BLR 74. Computer buffs will be pleased to learn that "document" in the sense of this section includes computer generated information.

396 Under the '68 Act public and business records relied on a chain of duty which linked the supplier of information to the record. In addition it required the compiler of the record to have personal knowledge of the subject-matter of the record. As with other hearsay, records of business or public authorities will be admissible, subject to the notice and weight provisions of CEA '95.

397 Section 9(1) provides:

"A document which is shown to form part of the records of a business or public authority may be received in evidence in civil proceedings without further proof."

398 The Act recognises that there are exceptional cases where such records should not automatically be admitted and s.9(5) provides this dispensation. It reads:

"The court may, having regard to the circumstances of the case, direct that all or any of the above provisions of this section do not apply in relation to a particular document or record, or description of documents or records."

399 I recalled an arbitration governed by CEA '68 where the respondent produced a building research leaflet on which he wished to rely, and the claimant objected on the ground that his expert fundamentally disagreed with the findings in this leaflet.

400 The respondent asserted that as it was an official quasi-government publication the arbitrator was entitled to take judicial notice of it.

401 While it was correct, at that time, that the arbitrator could take judicial notice of certain documents, this was generally restricted to Acts of Parliament, European Community treaties and the like, and would not extend to cover publications such as the one in dispute. Again either the author of this leaflet would have to be called, or the evidence given less weight, as with the clerk of works' diaries above.

402 Under CEA '95 the admission of this document would now be covered by section 9 as above.

403 Whether or not CEA '95 applies to this reference is for the arbitrator to decide in the absence of agreement to the contrary by the parties (see s.34(2)(f), AA '96).

404 In another pre-CEA '95 arbitration concerning a game damage valuation, the landlord's valuer, acting as advocate and witness, submitted a claim which was acceptable to the landlord. The game damage had not actually been observed by the valuer himself but by two assistants who had now left his employ. The game damage occurred some years before the hearing. The arbitrator rightly refused to accept this evidence of the damage unless one of the two assistants with first hand knowledge was prepared to give testimony on it.

405 At the request of the landlord, the arbitrator agreed to adjourn the hearing to enable him to call one or both of these assistants. He directed that the costs thrown away by the adjournment be paid by the landlord.

406 If this reference was under AA '96 and the parties had not agreed to waive the strict rules then the arbitrator would be thrown back on to the provisions of CEA '95. If the landlord was reluctant to call one of the assistants, then he could give the other party notice, under s.2(1), that he cannot or will not call these witnesses and leave the tenant to apply to the arbitrator under s.3 to give consent to call them. In the normal way this exchange would have occurred long before the hearing and thus avoided the costs thrown away by the adjourned hearing.

407 The whole tenor of CEA '95 is to bring common sense to bear on what has been a perennial problem. Far better to hear evidence and then reject it or afford little weight to it than to have to refuse to admit it at all because it is hearsay.

408 Reverting to this present example then, in the absence of agreement between the parties, the arbitrator may admit the clerk of works' site diaries but warn that in doing so he will have to attach less weight to them than he would be able to do if the clerk of works was called and was able to be cross-examined on them.

USE OF HEARSAY EVIDENCE FROM ASSISTANTS OF EXPERT WITNESSES IN CRIMINAL PROCEEDINGS

The facts

409 J appealed against his conviction of assault occasioning actual bodily harm following the acquittal of a co-accused.

410 The appellant and two other youths, Neil Hannington and John Caffrey, were charged with attacking Graham Taylor who was punched and kicked until he lost consciousness. Caffrey and the appellant were convicted but Hannington was acquitted by direction of the judge. Caffrey had not applied for leave to appeal.

411 Bloodstains were found on the appellant's shoes and the lower edge of his jeans. A forensic scientist, Mr Martin Whittaker, gave evidence that by reference to STR typing, a form of DNA analysis, there was:

> "strong evidence to support the assertion that Taylor's blood was on the appellant's jeans"

but

> "the distribution of the blood ... provided no evidence to assist in assessing whether the appellant kicked Taylor".

412 Mr Whittaker provided similar evidence with respect to blood found on Caffrey's trousers. The appellant admitted he had approached Mr Taylor while he was being attacked, so acquiring the blood on his own trousers, but that that was with a view to stopping the attack.

413 The problem founding the appeal arose thus: for the purposes of committal, witness statements, including that of Mr Whittaker, were served on the defendants. Mr Whittaker stated that he had been assisted by six other laboratory staff in the STR typing and that a full record of the work carried out could be prepared from the other staff involved provided sufficient notice was given.

414 There was no reaction from the defendants' advisers with respect to that statement. In opening, prosecuting counsel made use of the content of Mr Whittaker's statement without any objection.

415 Before the close of the prosecution there was no request by the Crown to the defendants to make admissions as to fact pursuant to s.10 of the Criminal Justice Act 1967.

416 None of the submissions of "no cases" made on behalf of the three defendants was based on Mr Whittaker's professed interpretation of that which had not been directly proved.

417 It was not until after Jackson had given evidence that counsel for Caffrey, Mr CJ Hart, drew the attention of other counsel and then the court to the lack of evidence as to that which Mr Whittaker had interpreted and cited a decision of the court *R* v. *Abadom* [1983] 1 WLR 126, the headnote of which at (1983) 76 Cr App R 48 read:

> "Where an expert witness relies on the existence or non-existence of some fact which is basic to the question on which he is asked to express his opinion, that fact must be proved by admissible evidence.
>
> Further, where the existence or non-existence of some fact is in issue a report made by an expert who is not called as a witness is not admissible as evidence of that fact merely by the production of the report, even though it was made by an expert."

418 As Mr Hart submitted to the judge, Mr Whittaker did expressly rely on the existence of facts which had not been proved and it followed that there was then no evidential foundation for his opinion. Miss Tedore adopted that submission.

Question

419 Is such hearsay evidence admissible?

Course of action

420 The facts of this example are drawn from *R* v. *Jackson (Terry Paul)* (1996) *The Times*, 21 May, CA.

421 In this case the Crown made a belated application to provide the necessary evidence by serving statements as additional evidence and by then calling the witnesses.

422 By way of a conspicuously thorough ruling the judge ruled in favour of the Crown who called two of the witnesses from the examination schedule, recalled Mr Whitaker and secured the admission of a set of documents with the aid of another careful ruling from the judge. The trial proceeded normally thereafter to verdict.

423 Their Lordships then made the following observations about that sequence of events.

424 Whereas individually they had not previously encountered a statement from an expert containing a paragraph similar to that cited, their Lordships believed that the device was not uncommon.

425 Preparation of statements by everyone named in the examination schedules might be time-consuming and therefore costly. Given that more often than not such statements once served did not give rise to factual issues (the situation here) and were either read or made the foundation for an admission, it was tempting in the interests of the public purse not to put preparation in train unless and until the defence flagged up an issue.

426 Their Lordships made no comment about that practice not having received submissions about it, but did comment on the consequences of its adoption as follows:

1. Mr Whittaker's statement was fatally flawed because the primary facts upon which his opinion was based were not proved by him: he had no personal knowledge of such and his expertise could not extend to establishing their existence.
2. It was for the Crown to identify and fill the evidential gap. Had the point been identified at the appropriate time, that is on a first reading of Mr Whittaker's statement, perhaps ways of saving costs and time could have been explored.

   The *Report of the Royal Commission on Criminal Justice 1993* (Cm 2263) raised the same concern in paragraph 78 of Chapter 9:

   > "It seems to us that this rule (as to expert witnesses giving hearsay evidence) is badly in need of change and we recommend that it be considered by the Law Commission . . . .
   >
   > Meanwhile, although the defence must have the right to examine the assistants of expert witnesses if it so chooses, we look to the courts and to the parties to make maximum use of the facility to present the evidence of assistants in written form until such time as the law is changed. Any unreasonable exploitation of the system should be met by sanctions against the counsel concerned if he or she is found to be responsible."

   That passage was cited in full in *Consultation Paper of the Law Commission, No 138 on Evidence in Criminal Proceedings: Hearsay and Related Topics* (1995, p. 210).

   Their Lordships drew attention to the scope for some alternative cost and time saving approach, encouraged by the use of admissions and by perusal of s.81 of the Police and Criminal Evidence Act 1984, the Crown Court (Advance Notice of Expert Evidence) Rules (SI 1987 No 716 (L2)) and ss.30 and 31 of the Criminal Justice Act 1988.

   As Mr McGrail had pointed out, a plea and directions hearing offered an excellent opportunity for any such problem to be identified and resolved.

3. Granted that the Court of Appeal was in a position to review the case with the advantages of hindsight and experience, their Lordships could not be other than critical.

   Not only did all counsel fail to identify the evidential gap until very late in the day. Once the point had emerged it was thereafter dealt with over two days without obvious regard for costs, for time or for patience of respectively the judge and, more importantly, the jury: all this when this appellant was admitting contact with the victim's blood and when Caffrey's denial of such contact had given rise to no earlier challenge of the data on which Mr Whittaker had advised.

   If inexperience accounted for much of the foregoing, their Lordships hoped that this case and these comments would serve rapidly to supplement such.

   The evidential gap could have been simply dealt with by the use of admissions. Indeed, if the defence had been minded to refuse to make such, that refusal would have triggered a helpful inquiry into what issues were real so as to command the subsequent attention of the court and the jury.

   The grounds of appeal criticised the judge's exercise of his discretion to allow the Crown belatedly to close the evidential gap by adducing evidence after the close of the prosecution case but their Lordships could not fault his exceptionally careful exposition properly based as it was upon the guidance in *R* v. *Francis* [1990] 1 WLR 1264.

   The judge had no hesitation in dismissing the appeal.

427 Thus, this holding by the Court of Appeal was summarised in the TLR as follows:

> "Although an expert witness was not, strictly speaking, permitted to give an opinion in court based on scientific tests run by assistants unless all those assistants were called upon to give supporting evidence in court, savings of time and money could be made by the maximum use of the facility to present such evidence in written form or, even more simply, by the use of admissions."

EXPERT DID NOT PRODUCE HIS OWN BACKUP MATERIAL

The facts

428 During the course of giving evidence the respondent's expert admitted that he had not carried out preliminary investigations into the facts and had delegated the initial survey of building premises in question to his assistant. He stated that this was common practice amongst experts in such cases where the junior acted according to his instructions as a partner in the practice and under his supervision. He said he had studied the survey carefully and had taken the opportunity of attending site on several occasions to ensure that the survey had been conducted properly.

429 The claimant's counsel interjected at this point and asked the arbitrator to strike out this expert's evidence as hearsay and therefore inadmissible. Counsel asked the arbitrator to afford this expert's evidence less weight than he would had he personally carried out the survey.

Question

430 How should the abitrator react to claimant's counsel's application?

Course of action

431 As a general rule the evidence given up by an expert witness must be the evidence of that person as to fact and opinion evidence on those facts that he adduces. It is a matter for the arbitrator to determine admissibility of such evidence and for him to consider the weight and importance he will attach to it in considering and in determining his award on the issues.

432 In such cases it would be appropriate for experts to state whether or not and to what extent they were assisted in their task.

433 As, generally, expert evidence is not subject to the hearsay rule in the same way as a witness of fact (see *R* v. *Abadom* [1983] 1 All ER 364). If an expert refers to the results of research published by a reputable journal the court or tribunal will ordinarily regard those results as supporting any inferences fairly to be drawn from them unless or until a different approach is shown to be correct (see *H* v. *Schering Chemicals Ltd* [1983] 1 All ER 849).

434 In the *Schering Chemicals* case, the plaintiffs in two separate actions claimed damages for personal injuries and wished to introduce evidence being copies of certain specified documents. The documents included summaries of results or research, articles and letters. By analogy to this case reliance was being placed on that evidence.

435 Experts are entitled to draw and rely on materials produced by others in the area in which they—the expert giving evidence—have expertise. As stated above statistical records compiled by the weather office, authoritative books, papers consisting of the summary of the results of research, or articles published in reputable journals.

436 Such material may form part of the body of the report and if it does the arbitrator must admit it in evidence and give the factual assertions in it such weight as is thought fit (see note to Order 38, rule 41).

437 In *The Ikarian Reefer* Cresswell J categorised the duties and responsibilities of expert witnesses and ruled that the expert should state that his report contains the truth and nothing but the truth. This duty would be breached in the contributor's view if the expert did not disclose his reliance on his colleague's work. The colleague should be identified so that he may be called to give evidence of fact if necessary.

438 It has been common practice for many years for experts in construction cases to rely upon the work of in-house assistants without whom heavy cases could not be undertaken. Care must be taken by experts to ensure insofar as is practically possible that the adoption of others' evidence is limited to what is necessary, because the report must ideally be the work of the expert himself and not others. Reference to other authorities and published papers etc. is quite usual but the adoption of evidence can present difficulties of credibility and weight.

439 Section 4(1) of the Civil Evidence Act 1968 provides that in any civil proceedings a statement contained in a document could be admissible as evidence of any facts stated therein of which direct oral evidence would be admissible if the

> "document is, or forms part of, a record compiled by a person acting under a duty from information which was supplied by a person (whether acting under a duty or not) who had, or may reasonably be supposed to have had, personal knowledge of the matters dealt with in that information and which, if not supplied by that person to the compiler of the record directly, was supplied to him to the compiler of the record indirectly through one or more intermediaries each acting under a duty."

440 Commenting on this section Bingham J, as he then was, said:

> "I believe to admit in evidence records which a historian would regard as original or primary sources, that is, documents which will either give effect to a transaction itself or which contain a contemporaneous register of information supplied by those with direct knowledge of the facts."

441 Bingham J went on to say:

> "That the plaintiffs in that case were in his judgment entitled by means of expert evidence to incorporate the contents of those articles in that evidence in that case and to give it such weight as in the light of any other evidence and of any cross-examination appears to be proper."

(See King & Reynolds, *The Expert Witness and His Evidence*, BSP Oxford, 2nd Edition at pp. 125–127.)

442 Here the first thing the arbitrator should do is to invite the respondent's representative's comments on the application. Hopefully, he will make the point about it being common practice to use assistants etc. and emphasise the degree of supervision exerted by the expert giving evidence. He might, perhaps, apologise for the fact that his expert's report should have made it clear that he was assisted and state what was the extent of that assistance, emphasising perhaps there was no deliberate intention to mislead the tribunal.

443 Assuming the parties had made no agreement to exclude hearsay evidence under s.34(2)(f), AA '96, as the expert attended the site on several occasions and has assured the arbitrator that the survey had been conducted properly the arbitrator could say that he will admit the evidence but will give it slightly less weight than he would had the expert carried out the survey himself.

THE LEGITIMATE USE OF DNA EVIDENCE

The facts

444 D appealed against conviction for offences in which the prosecution relied on the comparison of DNA profiles obtained from a sample of blood provided by each appellant. The grounds of appeal were that the verdicts were unsafe due to the misleading and inaccurate manner in which forensic evidence was presented, in particular the way in which the random occurrence ratio, the frequence with which the match characteristics were likely to be found in the population at large, was expressed.

445 D was convicted of rape and buggery after a 65-year-old widow was attacked at her home. The expert witness for the prosecution used two different test methods to examine samples and his results were undermined by fresh expert evidence on appeal.

Question

446 Was it legitimate for the prosecution's expert to multiply the result of one test with the results of the other?

Course of action

447 The facts of this example were drawn from *R* v. *Doheny (Alan James)* (1996) *The Times*, 14 August. This case was joined in the Court of Appeal with *R* v. *Adams (Gary Andrew)*.

448 In this latter case A was convicted of buggery and sentenced to five years' imprisonment which he served after a 32-year-old woman was attacked in her home by a man she claimed to have spoken to on the telephone when she rang the Samaritans. A was a volunteer worker for the Samaritans and a chair cushion found at the complainant's home bore traces of semen which, after A provided a blood sample, showed a DNA match. A's grounds of appeal were that the DNA evidence presented to the jury was inappropriate and erroneous, the jury should have been directed that he may have visited the complainant's home to participate in a sexual activity other than buggery, the judge misdirected the jury on corroboration and alibi and should have given a direction on lines following *R* v. *Lucas* (1981) 73 Cr App R 159; [1981] CLY 400.

449 It was held, allowing D's appeal but dismissing A's, that:

(1) in D's case the approach demonstrated by the prosecution's expert was not legitimate and the conviction was unsafe and was quashed. In A's case the complainant's identification of him was considered as well as the DNA evidence and the judge was under no duty to put before the jury the possibility of facts which were at odds with the evidence adduced by both the prosecution and defence; it was desirable that a corroboration direction should have been given but it was not necessary that the jury should have been directed that there should be corroboration of every element of the complainant's evidence, and
(2) when adducing DNA evidence in a criminal trial the expert should also provide his calculations of the random occurrence ratio and the prosecution should provide the defence with the means of calculation to allow adequate scrutiny of the results.

450 The expert should explain the match between the DNA samples, but should not give his opinion on the chances of the defendant having left the crime stain.

451 The trial judge should make clear to the jury other evidence which either pointed to or away from the defendant being responsible for the crime stain in the content of the random occurrence ratio and direct them that it was their task to decide, on all the evidence, whether they were satisfied that it was the defendant who left the crime stain.

452 Phillips LJ, delivering the reserved judgment of the court, said that the cogency of DNA evidence made it particularly important that DNA testing was rigorously conducted so as to obviate the risk of error in the laboratory, that the method of DNA analysis and the bases of subsequent statistical calculation should, so far as possible, be transparent to the defence and that the true import of the resultant conclusion was accurately and fairly explained to the jury.

453 When a scientist gave evidence in relation to DNA it was important that he should not overstep the line which separated his province from that of the jury. He should properly explain to the jury the nature of the match between the DNA in the crime stain and the DNA in the blood sample taken from the defendant.

454 He should properly, on the basis of empirical statistical data, give the jury the random occurrence ratio, the frequency with which the matching DNA characteristics were likely to be found in the population at large.

455 Provided that he had the necessary data, and the statistical expertise, it might be appropriate for him then to say how many people with the matching characteristics were likely to be found in the United Kingdom, or perhaps in a more limited relevant sub-group, such as, for instance, the Caucasian sexually active males in the Manchester area.

456 That would often be the limit of the evidence which he could properly and usefully give. It would then be for the jury to decide, having regard to all the relevant evidence, whether they were sure that it was the defendant who had left the crime stain, or whether it was possible that was left by someone else with the same matching DNA characteristics.

457 A scientist should not be asked his opinion on the likelihood that it was the defendant who left the crime stain, nor when giving evidence should he use terminology which might lead the jury to believe that he was expressing such an opinion.

458 When the judge came to sum up, the jury were likely to need careful directions in respect of any issues of expert evidence and guidance to dispel any obfuscation that might have been engendered in relation to areas of expert evidence where no real issue existed.

459 The judge should explain to the jury the relevance of the random occurrence ratio in arriving at their verdict and draw attention to the extraneous evidence which provided the context which gave that ratio its significance, and that which conflicted with the conclusion that the defendant was responsible for the crime stain.

460 Insofar as the random occurrence ratio was concerned, a direction along the following lines might be appropriate, although any direction had always to be tailored to the facts of the particular case:

> "Members of the jury, if you accept the scientific evidence called by the Crown, that indicates that there are probably only four or five white males in the United Kingdom from whom the semen stain could have come. The defendant is one of them. The decision you have to reach, on all the evidence, is whether you are sure that it was the defendant who left that stain or whether it is possible that it was one of that other small group of men who share the same DNA characteristics."

461 In *Adams* (1996) *The Times*, 9 May (see also NLJ 13 December 1996), the Court of Appeal dismissed the idea that it would be proper to allow an expert to present to the jury the workings of Bayes' Theorem, a statistical device to determine probability, stating:

> "Jurors evaluated evidence and reached conclusions not by means of a formula, mathematical or otherwise, but by the joint application of their individual common sense and knowledge of the world to the evidence before them."

WHETHER THE ARBITRATOR HAS POWER TO ORDER THE DISCLOSURE OF AN EXPERT'S REPORT

The facts

462 An architect was appointed for a project under the conditions and fees as set out in the "Architect's Appointment" as published by the Royal Institute of British Architects.

463 Clause 3.25 of these conditions referred any dispute or difference arising out of the appointment which cannot be solved by reference to one of three named bodies to fall to be decided by arbitration.

464 A dispute over non-payment of the architect's fees arose and experts were directed by the arbitrator to meet without prejudice and agree so far as they could on abatement of the percentage fee applicable to each work stage as defined in the "Architect's Appointment" booklet.

465 The experts met but were unable to agree. In the course of the meeting the expert for the claimant disclosed that the other side had not yet begun to see the strength of their case. He had prepared a very detailed report for his client which he had neither exchanged with the respondent expert nor intended to do so. In addition, he said that there were a number of supporting documents which would be produced at the hearing by his client.

466 At a pre-hearing review meeting, the respondent repeated the claimant's expert's admission to the arbitrator and asked for a direction ordering disclosure of the full expert's report and discovery of the supporting documentation to which the expert referred at his meeting with the respondent's expert.

Question

467 What sort of order for directions can the arbitrator make in these circumstances?

Course of action

468 Dealing first with the supporting documents, if they are relevant and are admissible evidence on which the claimant intends to rely the respondent is entitled to see them before the hearing. The English legal system does not countenance the surprise element as depicted in American movies. Accordingly, the arbitrator would be entitled to order specific discovery of these documents.

469 The expert's report is not quite so straightforward. In *Ollett* v. *British Aerojet Ltd* [1979] 3 All ER 544, a case concerning an industrial accident, Ackner J said:

> "I would like to make two observations with regard to experts' reports. The first point I make is this. There has been in the past some suggestion that, when an order is made under RSC Order 38, rule 38(1), that the substance of the experts' reports be exchanged, then that order is satisfied by the experts merely setting out factual descriptions of the machine and the alleged circumstances in which the accident happened and leaving out any conclusions as to the defects in the machine, the system of work or other relevant opinion evidence.
>
> This seems to me to be a total misconception of the ordinary meaning of the word 'substance'. It is also a misconception of the function of an expert. An expert, unlike other witnesses, is allowed, because of his special qualifications and/or experience, to give opinion evidence. It is for his opinion evidence that he is called, not for a factual description of the machine or the circumstances of the accident, although that is often necessary in order to explain and/or justify his conclusions.
>
> When the substance of the expert's report is to be provided, that means precisely what it says, both the substance of the factual description of the machine and/or the circumstances of the accident and his expert opinion in relation to that accident, which is the very justification for calling him.
>
> Secondly, there appears to be a tendency to make orders which do not involve any obligation to disclose experts' reports, other than medical reports. It is true that the court has to be satisfied that it is desirable for experts' reports to be exchanged but, as the *Supreme Court Practice* indicates, the court will ordinarily make such an order.
>
> The whole purpose of Order 38 is, in relation to expert evidence, to save expense by dispensing with the calling of experts when there is in reality no real dispute and, where there is a dispute, by avoiding parties being taken by surprise as to the true nature of the dispute and thereby being obliged to seek adjournments."

470 Rule 38 provides:

"In any cause or matter the court may, if it thinks fit, direct that there be a meeting 'without prejudice' of such experts within such periods before or after disclosure of their reports as the court may specify, for the purpose of identifying those parts of their evidence which are in issue. Where such a meeting takes place, the experts may prepare a joint statement indicating those parts of their evidence on which they are and those on which they are not, in agreement."

471 In *Carnell Computer Technology Ltd* v. *Unipart Group Ltd* (1990) 16 Con LR 19, it was reported that:

"The judge said that the note to the order in the *White Book* merited consideration. He said that rule 38 took a significant step towards the open system of pre-trial procedure.

It empowered the court in any cause or matter other than actions for personal injuries to direct that the experts of the parties must meet, though under the protection of 'without prejudice' for the purpose of identifying those parts of the evidence which are in issue. At such a meeting they can prepare a joint statement indicating those parts of their evidence on which they are and those parts on which they are not in agreement.

His Honour said that the power under the rule might be exercised without the prior consent of the parties. The experts of the parties are required to meet, albeit 'without prejudice'. The rule assumed that the experts of the parties may wish to decide to remain in a state of 'confrontation' on all or some of the matters, issues or questions, and in such case they should prepare a joint statement.

This statement should say either that they are not in agreement on the whole of their joint statement, or indicate those parts on which they are in agreement. Such agreement then has the effect of removing the protection of 'without prejudice' in respect of the matters agreed upon.

His Honour said that by this machinery, the parties will know before the trial the rationale and extent of the agreement or disagreement between their experts and this may well promote a settlement between them, which will be arrived at on a fairer basis in the sense that they will be proceeding in the knowledge rather than the ignorance of the strength or weakness of their respective cases.

His Honour said that if the action should proceed to trial, the parties would be able to concentrate on the real controversies between them in the areas on which the experts will have indicated that they are unable to agree, and in that way a great deal of otherwise wasteful effort, labour, cost and expense could be saved. The process of the trial itself should be made more smooth and its length significantly shortened.

His Honour said that in the experience of many solicitors practising in construction litigation, 'without prejudice' meetings have often proved very beneficial. Partial or complete settlement has resulted from such meetings.

The judge said that an important element is the creation of mutual trust between the experts, and that such trust can only be achieved over a number of meetings.

He also said that orders for the preparation of such joint statements had been made extensively only in recent times. After a slow implementation, experts under guidance from the parties' solicitors were becoming active in preparing such a joint statement.

In a recent action before the judge, *Allen-Fox Construction Ltd* v. *Transhaven Ltd* (which in the event settled) experts for three parties produced a masterly signed joint statement, which greatly reduced the time that would have otherwise been spent on various matters of fact and opinion."

472 However, in *Derby and Others* v. *Weldon and Others (No 9)* [1991] 2 All ER 901, the question before the court was, did it have jurisdiction to order one party who had prepared a report on an alternative claim to disclose that report if the party did not wish to adduce evidence on it at the trial?

473 Before 1972, it had been settled by three Court of Appeal decisions that reports of potential expert witnesses made on behalf of either party on the advice of legal advisers and for the purposes of preparing their case for trial were privileged from disclosure. Section 2(3) of the Civil Evidence Act 1972 enabled important changes to be made with respect to the procedure affecting the evidence of expert witnesses. It provided that:

> "Notwithstanding any rule of law by virtue of which documents [are] privileged from disclosure, provision might be made by rules of court enabling a civil court to direct that each party should disclose to the other 'in the form of one or more expert reports the expert evidence on matters of that class which he proposed to adduce as part of his case at the trial'."

474 The opening words of s.2(3) expressly recognised the existence of privilege from disclosure enjoyed by reports of expert witnesses prepared for the purposes of pending or contemplated civil proceedings. The statutory provisions did not remove the principle regarding such documents or require them to be produced on discovery. What was contemplated by s.2(3) was a procedure whereby, as a condition of being permitted to adduce expert evidence at trial, a party might be directed to make a pre-trial disclosure of his expert's report and, in case of non-compliance with such a direction, might be prohibited from adducing oral expert evidence on the matter specified in the direction.

475 RSC Order 38, rule 36(1) provided that expert evidence may not be called except with leave of the court or where the parties agreed:

> "unless the party seeking to adduce the evidence (a) had applied to the court to determine whether a direction should be given under rule 37".

476 Rule 37 enabled the court to give directions that experts' reports should be disclosed. It provided that where an application was made under rule 36(1) in respect of oral expert evidence:

> "then, unless the court considers that there are special reasons for not doing so, it shall direct that the substance of the evidence be disclosed in the form of a written report".

477 The plaintiffs' primary submission was that by a combination of s.2(3) of the Civil Evidence Act 1972 and RSC Order 38, rules 36 and 37 the court had jurisdiction to order a party to disclose in the form of a written report expert evidence on an issue even though that party did not wish to adduce expert evidence on that issue at the trial. An obstacle in the way of that submission was the privileged status of an expert's report as recognised in the three Court of Appeal cases decided before the 1972 Act and in the opening words of s.2(3) of the Act.

478 Counsel for the plaintiffs attempted to surmount the obstacle. While agreeing that privilege attached to draft documents embodying an expert's evidence for consideration by a party with his solicitors, he contended that privilege never attached to a report of an expert witness which had been communicated to solicitors for disclosure to the other side, or if it did attach it was lost when a disclosure order pursuant to Order 38, rule 37 was sought or made or acted upon.

479 Mummery J was not convinced by those arguments. The privilege enjoyed by documents prepared for the purpose of pending or contemplated civil proceedings, or in connection with the obtaining or giving of legal advice, was strong. It meant that a party or witness had a right to refuse to disclose documents or information falling within the scope of the privilege. Neither s.2(3) of the 1972 Act, nor RSC Order 38, rules 36 and 37 expressly or impliedly removed or modified the privilege from production enjoyed by such documents under the pre-existing law of evidence and discovery of documents. There was nothing in those procedural provisions which empowered the court to direct a party to bring into existence a privileged document embodying an expert's evidence on an issue, or to disclose it to the other side, when that party had no intention of adducing expert evidence on the issue. Rules 36 and 37 applied only to a case where a party sought to adduce expert evidence on an issue. So long as the defendants did not want to adduce expert evidence on the issue they were entirely within the rules if they do not submit an expert's report.

480 Accordingly, his Lordship held that the court had no jurisdiction under the 1972 Act or Order 38 or by way of inherent jurisdiction or under s.37(1) of the 1981 Act to make the order sought.

481 The plaintiffs appealed.

482 The Court of Appeal, in dismissing the appeal, held that the court had no power to call for the disclosure of expert evidence on an issue which the party did not intend to adduce at the trial (although see now Appendix A/3 for the changes made by the CPR). That is not the current position, however, since the procedure in both the courts and arbitration is adversarial. An expert is not obliged to speak out or write in his report about matters concerning which he has not been asked either by his client's opponent's counsel or by the judge or arbitrator.

483 However, as the judge observed in *Cala Homes*:

> "There is a world of difference between not volunteering evidence on topics on which you have not been asked to express a view and giving misleading answers on topics where you have."

484 If the matter comes to court or arbitration, then the expert may present his opinions to the court or tribunal as evidence in the case. It is for that reason that he must maintain his impartiality. An expert who departs from the rule of impartiality renders his opinions worthless and is likely to have his evidence dismissed (*Cala Homes*).

485 In this present example it seems that the claimant does intend to adduce evidence on this expert's report and therefore on this authority the arbitrator would not be entitled to order disclosure of the report.

486 Finally, it should be remembered that no one has property in an expert—the other side could have subpoenaed him to give evidence if his own side did not wish to call him.

THE DUTY OF PROSECUTION EXPERTS TO MAKE FULL DISCLOSURE

The facts

487 Appellants in the Court of Appeal had all been convicted of knowingly having in their possession or under their control an explosive substance, namely nitro-glycerine, under such circumstances as to give rise to a reasonable suspicion that they did not have it in their possession for a lawful object.

488 The appeals followed a reference to the court by the Home Secretary, pursuant to s.17(1)(a) of the Criminal Appeal Act 1968. Section 17 of this Act provides:

> "(1) Where a person has been convicted on indictment . . . the Secretary of State may . . .
> (a) refer the whole case to the Court of Appeal and the case shall then be treated for all purposes as an appeal to the court by that person . . . ."

489 The appellants argued that the failure of the prosecution to inform the defence of three tests carried out by forensic scientists who were prosecution expert witnesses which were relevant to the defence constituted a material irregularity in the course of the trial.

490 Neither prosecuting counsel nor those instructing them knew of the tests. The question, in considering the prosecution's duty of disclosure, therefore was who was embraced by the word "prosecution"?

Question

491 Is a forensic scientist who was an adviser to the prosecuting authority under a duty to disclose material which he knew might have some bearing on the offence charged and the surrounding circumstances of the case?

Course of action

492 The court were of the opinion that the answer to the question was in the affirmative in the case of *R* v. *Maguire and Others* (1991) *The Times*, 28 June.

493 In this case the appeals were allowed on the ground that the convictions were unsafe and unsatisfactory because the possibility of innocent contamination of the appellants' hands could not be excluded.

494 It was held that failure by a prosecution expert witness to disclose the results of certain tests was capable of constituting a material irregularity in the course of the trial, even though prosecuting counsel was unaware of the existence of those results.

495 Further, the Court of Appeal had power under s.17(1)(d) of the Criminal Appeal Act 1968 to consider a reference by the Home Secretary of the case of a person who was dead.

496 The Court of Appeal, Criminal Division, so held in a reserved judgment allowing the appeals and quashing the convictions of the appellants.

497 Their Lordships giving the judgment of the court said of the duty of the forensic expert to disclose, that the disclosure would be to the authority which retained him and which must in turn, subject to sensitivity, disclose the information to the defence.

498 There was no cause to distinguish between members of the prosecuting authority and those advising it in the capacity of a forensic scientist.

499 Such a distinction could involve difficult and contested enquiries as to where knowledge stopped, but most important, would be entirely counter to the desirability of ameliorating the disparity of scientific resources as a between the Crown and the subject.

500 One of the appellants, Mr Conlon, had died while still serving his sentence and their Lordships went on to consider Mr Conlon's position should the other appellants' convictions be quashed.

DUTY OF EXPERTS TO DISCLOSE ALL RELEVANT RESEARCH MATERIAL

The facts

501 On 8 November 1992 the child, then 10 weeks old, suffered what his parents described as an apnoeic attack. After resuscitating him by allegedly shaking and smacking him the parents called the doctor who sent him to hospital. There he was found to have multiple fractures and some brain damage. The evidence was that the fractures were recent and had occurred on two or three separate occasions and that the brain damage had occurred some days before 8 November 1992. At the hearing to determine the cause of the injuries, the paediatric consultant at the hospital and two consultant paediatric radiologists called by the local authority and the guardian *ad litem* all took the view that the injuries had been non-accidental. The opinion of the medical expert called by the parents was that, taking into account the absence of bruising and the fact that nothing untoward had been noticed by the health visitor, grandparents or others, the injuries were due to some form of brittle bone disease which, as he accepted that the baby had never suffered from *osteogenesis imperfecta,* he categorised as "temporary brittle bone disease".

502 The parents accepted that view and vehemently denied any responsibility for the injuries, insisting that the brain damage and fractures had been caused by their attempts to resuscitate the baby.

503 The medical expert called by the parents specialised in research into what he described as "temporary brittle bone disease" and had written articles in medical journals on the subject. The body of medical opinion, and in particular that represented in the instant case, did not acknowledge the existence of temporary brittle bone disease in young infants.

Question

504 Does an expert owe a duty to the tribunal to indicate when his theory of causation is a matter of controversy and disclosure credible material which contradicts his view?

Course of action

505 The facts of this example are taken from *Re AB (Child Abuse: Expert Witness)* [1995] 1 FLR 181 where it was held that on the facts, taking into account the nature and timing of the injuries and the evidence of the experts, it was clear that the baby's injuries were entirely consistent with non-accidental injury and inconsistent with anything else. The conflicting evidence of the expert called by the parents had to be discounted since he had failed to take into account or to explain the brain damage; research showed that the absence of bruising did not have the significance he had placed on it; and he had not only failed to disclose the controversial nature of his research into temporary brittle bone disease, but appeared to have assumed the role of advocate to promote his belief in it. The court therefore found that the child had suffered multiple non-accidental injuries while in the care of his parents.

506 *Per curiam*: the duty of an expert witness in children's cases is to form an assessment and express his opinion within the particular area of his expertise. The judge, having no medical training, decides particular issues in individual cases on the basis of all the evidence. It follows that the dependence of the court on the skill, knowledge and, above all, the professional integrity of the expert witness cannot be over-emphasised. In particular:

(a) Where an expert advances a hypothesis to explain a given set of facts, he owes a very heavy duty to explain to the court that what he is advancing is a hypothesis, that it is controversial (if it is), and to place before the court all the material which contradicts the hypothesis.
(b) The expert must also make all his material available to the other experts in the case.

(c) Where the medical evidence points overwhelmingly to non-accidental injury, any expert who advises the parents and the court that the injury has an innocent explanation has a heavy duty to ensure that he has considered carefully the available material and is expressing an opinion that can be objectively justified.

507 The parents and the child are ill-served by an opinion which wrongly exonerates the parents. The objective of the lawyers and the experts should always be to limit the ambit of disagreement to a minimum. A misleading opinion from an expert may well inhibit a proper assessment of a case by the non-medical professional advisers, is likely to increase costs, may lead parents to false views and hopes and may help to lead the judge to a false conclusion.

508 Guidelines in *Re R (A Minor) (Experts' Evidence)* and *National Justice Compania Naviera SA* v. *Prudential Assurance Co Ltd* were followed.

509 It is worth repeating what Wall J had to say in his judgment concerning the duties of experts in children's cases.

> "Before I turn to the detail of my findings on the medical evidence, I propose to summarise my understanding of the duties owed by medical experts in giving evidence in children's cases. It is against that background that I must judge their evidence.
>
> The *locus classicus* for the exposition of the duties of experts in children's cases is the decision of Cazalet J in *Re J (Child Abuse: Expert Evidence)* [1991] FCR 193 at 226, also reported as *Note: Re R (A Minor) (Experts' Evidence)* [1991] 1 FLR 291. The latter report contains only the judgment given in open court; the former gives both the chambers' and the open court judgments. I respectfully endorse and adopt every word of the latter judgment as being of general application in all cases in which expert evidence is involved.
>
> . . .
>
> In my judgment it is of critical importance in discussing the role of the expert witness in children's cases to bear in mind throughout the respective functions of expert and judge. The expert forms an assessment and expresses his opinion within the particular area of his expertise. The judge decides particular issues in individual cases. It is therefore not for the judge to become involved in medical controversy except in the extremely rare case where such a controversy is itself an issue in the case and a judicial assessment of it becomes necessary for the proper resolution of the proceedings. The reason for this is obvious. Whilst the judge has knowledge and experience from practice and previous cases, he or she rarely has more medical knowledge than the intelligent lay person: the judge, almost by definition, is not an expert in the field about which the witness is giving evidence.
>
> The judge brings to the inquiry forensic and analytical skills and has the unique advantage over the parties and the witnesses in the case that he or she alone is in a position to weigh all its multifarious facets. This process, of course, involves an evaluation of the expert opinion in the context of a duty to make findings of fact and assessments of the credibility of witnesses. It follows that the dependence of the court on the skill, knowledge and, above all, the professional and intellectual integrity of the expert witness cannot, in my judgement, be over-emphasised. The judge's task is difficult enough as it is in sensitive child cases. To have, in addition, to resolve a subtle and complex medical disagreement or to make assessments of the reliability of expert witnesses not only adds immeasurably to the judge's task but, given his fallibility and lack of medical training, may help to lead him to a false conclusion.
>
> It is partly for this reason that the current practice of the courts in children's cases is to require disclosure of all medical reports and to invite the experts to confer pre-trial. By these means the ambit of agreement and disagreement can be defined.
>
> Mr Kennerley, for the local authority, referred me to an article in *Archives of Diseases in Childhood*, vol. 68 at p. 712 in which the author, discussing expert evidence in cases of child abuse, says:
>
> > 'Experts obviously are involved in pursuing theories, in research, and in trying to persuade the rest of the medical profession of the validity of their conclusion. However, a court is not a suitable forum in which to advance untested hypotheses. The place for that kind of debate is in

the medical literature and in conferences and meetings, where others, who are eminently well qualified to do so, may challenge any findings. Judges and magistrates are not in such a position. They must take much of the expert evidence presented to them on trust. As Cazalet J stated:

"Outside the legal field the court itself has no expertise and for that reason frequently has to rely on the evidence of experts."

Consequently, if an expert believes that current medical opinion on, for example, the occurrence of fractures in babies, is subject to challenge, he or she should present their arguments to medical peers for scrutiny. Only after there has been such scrutiny, followed by acceptance of the validity of the expert's argument, should evidence be presented in a court.'

Having referred to comments made in *Report of the Inquiry into Child Abuse in Cleveland* 1987, Cm 441 (1988) ('the Cleveland report') the author then quotes a letter from the then President of the British Paediatric Association which is in these terms:

'The regulation of medical practice is achieved best when it is accomplished within the medical profession. New stances based on a new awareness of clinical signs, or new significance being attached to them, require first to be established within the profession. This takes some time and requires persuasion and scientific evidence of validity, based on the accepted method of communication to professional journals or scientific meetings. It is the dedicated research worker and the pioneering enthusiast who so often change medicine for the better and uncover deficiencies in medical practice and the understanding. In the end, however, any new development has to be fitted into the complex jigsaw which constitutes balanced medical practice. As well as the benefits, the possible adverse effects of any revision of accepted practices have to be taken into account.'

I respectfully agree with the broad thrust of what is being asserted in these two passages. My only *caveat* is that there are sometimes cases in which there is a genuine disagreement on a scientific or medical issue, or where it is necessary for a party to advance a particular hypothesis to explain a given set of facts. Where that occurs, the judge will have to resolve the issue which is raised. Two points must be made. In my view, the expert who advances such a hypothesis owes a very heavy duty to explain to the court that what he is advancing is a hypothesis, that it is controversial (if it is) and to place before the court all the material which contradicts the hypothesis. Secondly, he must make all his material available to the other experts in the case. It is the common experience of the courts that the better the experts the more limited their areas of disagreement, and in the forensic context of a contested case relating to children, the objective of the lawyers and the experts should always to be to limit the ambit of disagreement on medical issues to the minimum.

In *Note: Re R (A Minor) (Experts' Evidence)* [1991] 1 FLR 291 at 292H–293B, Cazalet J said this:

'It should be borne in mind that a misleading opinion from an expert may well inhibit a proper assessment of a particular case by the non-medical professional advisers and may also lead parties, and in particular parents, to false views and hopes.

Furthermore, such misleading expert opinion is likely to increase costs by requiring competing evidence to be called at the hearing on issues which should in fact be non-contentious.

In wardship cases the duty to be objective and not to mislead is as vital as in any case because the child's welfare, which is a matter of extreme importance, is at stake, and his/her interests are paramount. An absence of objectivity may result in a child being wrongly placed and thereby unnecessarily put at risk.' "

510 Later in his judgment Wall J said this:

"There is uniformity of view across the various Divisions of the High Court in relation to the duties of experts. In *National Justice Compania Naviera SA* v. *Prudential Assurance Co Ltd* [1993] 2 Lloyd's

Rep 68, Cresswell J, sitting in the Commercial Court, said that the duties and responsibilities of expert witnesses included the following:

> '1) expert evidence presented to the court should be and should be seen to be the independent product of the expert uninfluenced as to form or content by the exigencies of litigation;
> 2) an expert witness should provide independent assistance to the court by way of objective unbiased opinion in relation to matters within his expertise . . . . An expert witness in the High Court should never assume the role of advocate;
> 3) an expert witness should state the facts or assumptions on which his opinion is based. He should not omit to consider material facts which detract from his concluded opinion . . .;
> 4) an expert witness should make it clearer when a particular question or issue falls outside his expertise;
> 5) if an expert's opinion is not properly researched because he considers that insufficient data is available then this must be stated with an indication that the opinion is no more than a provisional one . . .;
> 6) if after exchange of reports, an expert witness changes his view on a material matter, such change of view should be communicated . . . to the other side without delay and when appropriate to the court;
> 7) where expert evidence refers to photographs, plans, calculations . . . survey reports or other similar documents these must be provided to the opposite party at the same time as the exchange of reports.'"

511 And, towards the end of his judgment Wall J said:

> "Whilst the courts of course accept that there may be cases where there is a divergence between judicial and clinical findings, I regard as worrying in the extreme Dr Paterson's failure to record in his research material of cases of proven brittle bone disease judicial findings to the contrary. In my judgment this is a factor which must cast the gravest doubts on his findings.
>
> None of these matters were discussed in Dr Paterson's report. He gives no indication that his theory of causation is a matter of controversy and he ignores credible material which contradicts his views.
>
> I set Dr Paterson's report and oral evidence against the guidelines laid down by Cazalet J in *Re R* at [1991] 1 FLR 291."

512 The judge then went on to set out a catalogue of criticism against this medical expert concluding that he

> "assumed the role of advocate to promote his belief in temporary brittle bone disease.
> In *Re R*, Cazalet J said this of Dr Paterson:
>
> > 'He accepted that he has been criticised in certain previous cases for developing particular theories as to causation. In the present case, I think he may have developed a theory of causation rather than a diagnosis.'
>
> Mr Kennerley, for the local authority, invited me to make the same finding in the instant case. I regret to say that I think such a finding justified."

513 Interestingly, what the judge said of the current practice of the courts in children's cases to require disclosure of all (medical) reports, and invite the experts to confer pre-trial in order to define areas of agreement and disagreement, is commonplace in litigation and arbitration of construction disputes.

DUTY OF MEDICAL EXPERT TO DISCLOSE ALL REPORTS

The facts

514 The plaintiff was awarded a total of £1,333,231 as damages for nervous shock and psychiatric injury caused when he witnessed unsuccessful attempts to rescue his two daughters from a car driven into a river by the children's nanny. The defendant appealed on the grounds that the plaintiff's post traumatic stress disorder, as opposed to his extreme grief reaction, was caused by events unconnected with the accident. After the Court of Appeal had given a draft judgment reducing the damages, but before the final order of the court was drawn up, defence counsel received from an anonymous sender copies of the judgments of the county court and Court of Appeal in family proceedings in which the plaintiff had sought a residence order in respect of his surviving child. From those judgments it appeared that the same medical experts had given evidence in both cases as to the plaintiff's psychiatric condition and the prognosis.

Question

515 Should the medical expert be obliged to disclose a report from another action if it gives a better prognosis?

Course of action

516 The facts of this example were drawn from *Vernon* v. *Bosley* [1997] 1 All ER 614 CA.

517 The medical experts' evidence for the purposes of the family litigation was that the plaintiff's health had improved dramatically so that he was substantially recovered. That view was contrary to the view expressed by them for the purposes of the personal injury litigation. The defendant successfully applied for discovery and inspection of the relevant reports in the family proceedings and for a rehearing of the appeal.

518 Stuart-Smith LJ said that the existence of medical reports, notes of evidence and the judgment in the family proceedings should have been disclosed to the defendant's advisers before judgment was given in the personal injuries case. It was the duty of every litigant not to mislead the court. The plaintiff sought to rely on the distinction between actively misleading and passively standing by and watching the court be misled. But where a case was conducted on the basis of certain material facts which were an essential part of the case (in this case the plaintiff's condition at the trial and the prognosis, which were discovered before judgment to be significantly different), the court was being misled by a failure to correct an incorrect appreciation which the court would otherwise have. Moreover, where there was a danger that the court be misled, it was counsel's duty to advise his client that disclosure should be made. If he refused it was not as a rule for counsel to make disclosure himself, but he would have to withdraw from the case.

519 In this case the Court of Appeal was clear on the strictures placed on the conduct of the experts.

520 Thorpe LJ, commenting in his judgment on the manifest bias demonstrated by the experts, said this:

> "In my judgement on the appeal I commented upon the unsatisfactory contribution of the mental health professionals at the trial."

521 There is little doubt that the partisan performance of experts on both sides threatened not merely injustice to the defendants but an assault on the integrity of the legal process and the standing of all experts.

THE COMPETENCE OF A WITNESS TO GIVE EXPERT EVIDENCE

The facts

522 One of the many Lloyd's underwriting cases heard in the early 1990s was *Deeny and Others* v. *Gooda Walker Ltd* (1993) QBD 4 October 1994; (1994) *The Times*, 7 October.

523 In this case a question arose as to the competence of the witness to give expert evidence.

Question

524 How would a judge decide a witness was, or was not, competent to give expert evidence?

Course of action

525 In this case there were two witnesses whose competence was, or may have been, questioned: Mr Von Eicker, about whom a submission was made that he was not competent to give expert evidence in this case; and Mr Jewell, who was called as the witness of fact but ended up giving valuable expert evidence.

526 It was argued, in the light of Mr Von Eicker's evidence, that he had no personal experience of LMX business, and in particular no experience of writing XL on XL cover.

527 For that reason, it was said that he was not qualified to comment on the principles that should be applied by the reasonable competent underwriter in that market.

528 Mr Von Eicker, who was employed by the Munich Re-insurance Company for 35 years, in the judge's words:

> "... would not accept that there were special principles to be applied to the writing of LMX business. His constant theme was that LMX business was subject to the same basic principles as all reinsurance, indeed all insurance, and that he was highly qualified to speak to those principles."

529 Later it was argued that as Mr Von Eicker had deliberately kept out of that market (the spiral business market) he was not competent to express opinions about the conduct of those practising within it. However, the judge reached the conclusion that:

> "Mr Von Eicker is qualified to express an opinion as to the principles that should be followed when writing excess of loss business. He is also qualified to express an opinion as to whether those principles are compatible with the writing of spiral business."

530 Before he turned to the expert evidence, the judge said that it was only right that he should state the impression made on him by those who gave it. Of Mr Von Eicker he said this:

"Mr Von Eicker was not an ideal expert witness. He showed a keen appreciation of his own abilities and a contempt for any challenge to his views. This attitude was not justified, for in his report leak Mr Von Eicker had, in places, made sweeping statements of underwriting principle which could not be justified. He adopted, throughout, a vigorously partisan approach and could scarcely ever be induced by ... to make a concession, however clear it might be that a concession was due.

Mr Jewell was not called by the plaintiffs as an expert ....

... Mr Jewell was called by the plaintiffs to give factual evidence ....

... Mr ..., however, chose to cross-examine him at length on matters of expert evidence. I am glad that he did, for Mr Jewell impressed me as a witness of high standing, ability and experience in the field of excess of loss reinsurance. I found the evidence that he gave in relation to the practice of excess of loss reinsurance more compelling than that of the witnesses who had been called specifically to give expert evidence on this topic."

(See also paras 601 to 612 below.)

EXPERT EVIDENCE AS TO A WITNESS'S COMPETENCE

The facts

531 A man was convicted of two offences of indecent assault for which he was sentenced to a two-year supervision order.

532 He appealed and the issues were, *inter alia*:

(1) whether the child witnesses were competent;
(2) whether expert evidence should have been admitted to assist in determining the question of competence; and
(3) whether the recordings of the children's evidence should have been admitted.

Question

533 To what extent then is expert evidence admissible on the question of a witness's competence?

Course of action

534 The facts on this case were drawn from *Gibson* v. *DPP*, 12 December 1996, QBD.

535 Here Phillips LJ held, dismissing the appeal, that:

(1) the court had been correct in determining the competence by following the test set out in *R* v. *Hampshire* [1995] 2 All ER 1019;
(2) it does not require expert evidence to determine whether a child is capable of giving intelligible evidence and the court was correct to decline to hear expert evidence;
(3) video-taped interviews should not be admitted if to do so would be contrary to the interests of justice. The court was right to exercise its discretion in deciding not to hear the expert evidence on the issue of whether to admit the video interviews of the children.

536 If a child suffered a particular abnormality then it was right for there to be expert evidence, otherwise it was for the jury or the judge to assess the reliability of the evidence.

WHETHER AN EXPERT CAN BE COMPELLED TO GIVE EVIDENCE

The facts

537 In a commercial dispute referred to arbitration, the claimant maintained that there was only one person who could confirm his version of events—the chairman of the respondent holding company.

538 The holding company was a multi-national conglomerate and the chairman was rarely in this country. To make himself available on a specific day or date, with no great certainty that he would be called at a specific time, would have caused him great inconvenience and have been grossly disruptive to his work schedule. Counsel for the defendant made these points in objecting to the claimant's application to have this witness called.

Question

539 Has the judge power to compel this chairman to attend as a witness for the claimant?

Course of action

540 The facts of this case are similar to those in *Society of Lloyd's* v. *Clementson (No 2)* (1996) *The Times*, 29 February, CA, where the plaintiff, in the lower court, sought to subpoena the chairman of Lloyd's.

541 Before we considered whether the judge had the power to compel a witness, I suggested to my pupil Thomasina that we first considered the general position in arbitration.

542 Thus, I explained that all competent persons (with a few exceptions such as the diplomatic corps) are compellable but not all persons are competent (for example, some children or mentally defective persons). Thus, if the facts of this example occurred in an arbitration, the claimant could make it clear to the chairman of the holding company that if he continued to refuse, the claimant would apply to the courts, under the provisions of s.43, AA '96 (the old *subpoena ad testificandum*). If the court granted the *subpoena* and the witness then failed to appear he would be liable to a penalty imposed by the court. Section 43 of AA '96 provides:

> "(1) A party to arbitral proceedings may use the same court procedures as are available in relation to legal proceedings to secure the attendance before the tribunal of a witness in order to give oral testimony or to produce documents or other material evidence.
>
> (2) This may only be done with the permission of the tribunal or the agreement of the other parties.
>
> (3) The court procedures may only be used if—
>
> (a) the witness is in the United Kingdom, and
>
> (b) the arbitral proceedings are being conducted in England and Wales or, as the case may be, Northern Ireland.

(4) A person shall not be compelled by virtue of this section to produce any document or other material evidence which he could not be compelled to produce in legal proceedings."

543 The Department Advisory Committee (DAC), in their report on what was then the Arbitration Bill in 1995, had this to say of section 43:

"213 This Clause (which corresponds to Article 27 of the Model Law, and is derived from section 12(4) and (5) of the 1950 Act) is also designed to provide court support for the arbitral process. It will be noted, in particular, that the agreement of the parties or the permission of the tribunal is required. The reason for this is to make sure that this procedure is not used to override any procedural method adopted by the tribunal, or agreed by the parties, for the arbitration. Thus, for example, if the tribunal has decided that there shall be no oral evidence, then (unless all parties agree otherwise) this procedure cannot be used to get round that decision."

544 Harris, Planterose and Tecks in *The Arbitration Act—A Commentary* (hereafter *Harris/Planterose/Tecks*), *inter alia*, say this:

"**(43C) Availability—Subs (2)**

...

The arbitrators should not unreasonably refuse permission for a writ of subpoena to issue, bearing in mind the s.33 duty to afford each party a reasonable opportunity to put its case.

(43D) Procedures

The relevant High Court procedures, set out in Order 38, Rule 19 of the Rules of the Supreme Court, provide for the form, issue and service of a writ of subpoena, and the notes give guidance as to the basis on which writs of subpoena may be challenged and set aside.

(43E) Privilege—Subs (4)

As in legal proceedings, a witness cannot be compelled to produce evidence which is protected by privilege. For example, advice given to a party by is lawyers; communications between a party (or his lawyers) and witnesses concerning the arbitration: and 'without prejudice' correspondence between the parties, need not be disclosed."

545 Merkin, in *Arbitration Act 1996—An Annotated Guide* (hereafter *Merkin*), at p. 69, adds this about subsection (3) of s.43:

"Section 43(3) restricted the power in section 43(1) to witnesses within the jurisdiction: evidence can be obtained from a witness outside the jurisdiction by means of application to the court under section 44(2)(a), although if the witness is a party the matter can probably be dealt with by the arbitrators themselves under section 41 by the making of a peremptory order requiring evidence to be given. The proceedings must also be conducted in England and Wales or Northern Ireland under section 43(3)(b) but it is specifically stated by section 2(3) that section 43 can be used whether or not the seat of the arbitration is in England. The phrase 'conducted in' in section 43(3)(b) must therefore, necessarily mean something different to the proposition that the arbitration has its seat in England, and it may be that it simply refers to a transitory phase of the arbitration which happens to have been held in England.

It would seem, therefore, that an arbitration with its seat abroad but requiring the attendance of a witness who happens to be in the United Kingdom, can reconvene in England and Wales or

Northern Ireland—so that the arbitration is at that point being conducted within the jurisdiction—and a party is thereby empowered to seek the court's assistance for the attendance of that witness.

The court does, however, have the discretion under section 2(3) to refuse its assistance where granting assistance would not be appropriate, and it may be that in the circumstances outlined above the court would take the view that, while it possesses the necessary jurisdiction there is not sufficient connection between the arbitration and England and Wales or Northern Ireland to make such an order."

546 Finally, Rutherford and Sims, in *Arbitration Act 1996—A Practical Guide* (hereafter *Rutherford/Sims*), *inter alia*, say this of s.43:

> "43.3 The legal jargon of *subpoena ad testificandum subpoena duces tecum* and, even worse, writ of *habeas corpus ad testificandum* have been left out of the Act for the greater understanding of laymen and foreign users. Apart from that, however the effect is the same as the 1950 Act provisions, i.e. the court would act in respect of normal witnesses required to give oral evidence or produce documents or other material evidence by way of *subpoena* and the power would include that of having a prisoner brought from prison to give evidence (an arbitrator having no jurisdiction in criminal matters, would have no power to do this himself)."

547 Having compelled a witness to give evidence, it may be that that witness fails to prove the facts for which the claimant called him. This is the risk that the calling party runs and he cannot attempt to recover the situation by cross-examination of that witness. If, on the other hand the compelled witness is adjudged to be hostile or adverse and not desirous of telling the truth at the instance of the party calling him, then the arbitrator may give leave to treat this witness as hostile and allow leading questions by the party calling him.

548 Previously, the arbitrator had no power to call witnesses himself. (See *Re Enoch and Zaretsky, Bock & Co* [1910] 1 KB 327.) Now I am not so sure. Provided the parties agree (s.34(1)) I can see no reason why an arbitrator should not call a witness and indeed proceed to cross-examine him, i.e. act inquisitorially, provided the parties have not removed that power under s.34(2)(g).

549 Indeed, I had a case once where I could not understand why a clerk of works was not called by one party or the other. He would certainly have greatly assisted me in my determination and given me, at least, a semi-unbiased view of what really went on on site. (The clerk of works, who was freelance, had since moved on to another local authority so would not be concerned that any evidence adverse to his former employer would influence his work prospects.) Presumably his site diaries would have been available. However, neither party seemed keen to call him and, this being prior to AA '96, I had no powers myself.

550 I also remember one particular case when each party produced one witness each at a meeting on site where I had agreed to take evidence. These two witnesses violently disagreed with each other and there was a third person in attendance who was well-known to me and whom I knew would greatly assist me to get to the truth if he were called. Both parties were against this witness being called. Even with the new powers under AA '96, if the parties are not happy about an arbitrator calling a witness of fact and that arbitrator cannot persuade them of the value to him of that witness, then I believe he should probably not call him. In any event, if the parties felt strongly enough about it they could indicate their agreement in writing to the arbitrator that they did not wish him to call any particular witness and that, I believe, would be the end of the matter.

551 Has the arbitrator power to limit the number of witnesses that a party wishes to call?

Thomasina asked. It would depend, I said, on what agreement, if any, the parties had made under s.34. If the default clauses prevailed then certainly the arbitrator could restrict the number of witnesses. Indeed, he could restrict the amount of oral evidence as well (s.34(2)(h)).

552 If, however, the parties agreed that they would not limit the number of each other's witnesses and the number of witnesses is totally disproportionate to the size of the dispute, and the arbitrator is satisfied, after hearing the party who wishes to call his large number of witnesses, that many of them are unnecessary, his remedy lies in costs. He should accede to the party's request but make it clear that if he is still of the same mind after hearing all these witnesses, he will award the costs of and incidental to hearing these superfluous witnesses to the other side—either under his power to cap recoverable costs (s.65, AA '96) or, if the parties have not given the arbitrator this power, then, when he comes to settle the costs, by discounting the cost of the excessive number of witnesses as being costs unreasonably incurred.

553 Thus, reverting to this example, it was held that an expert can be subpoenaed to attend court even if there is no contractual relationship; but there has to be good reason.

554 For example, in the *Lloyd's* v. *Clementson* case, the judge refused the application to subpoena the chairman of Lloyd's on the ground that there were other experts available and that the expert chosen held an important office and was a very busy man. (See also the example at paras 152 to 161 above regarding the subpoenaing of an expert witness.)

CAN AN EXPERT BE COMPELLED TO PRODUCE HIS PROOFS OF EVIDENCE FROM PREVIOUS ARBITRATIONS?

The facts

555 In the course of a rent review arbiration the landlord's expert (Mr Main) gave evidence about the changes in the office market in relation to the review date and was asked questions in cross-examination concerning evidence he had given on behalf of a tenant in an earlier and separate arbitration.

556 Following the cross-examination the respondent tenant issued two *subpoenas duces tecum*, one to the landlord's expert to produce his proofs of evidence from the two earlier unrelated arbitrations and the second subpoena was issued for the respondent's own expert (Mr Jones) to produce the landlord's expert's evidence for one of these earlier arbitrations, where, in that case, the respondent's expert had acted as arbitrator.

Question

557 Can an expert be compelled, in circumstances such as these, to produce proof of their evidence, or indeed, any proof of evidence in his power or possession?

Course of action

558 This was the question the court had to decide in *London & Leeds Estates Ltd* v. *Paribas Ltd (No 2)* [1997] 1 EGLR 102.

559 Some very important issues were aired in the course of the judgment given in answer to the landlord and the landlord's expert's application to set aside both subpoenas. These included, *inter alia*:

(a) The privacy/confidentiality in arbitration proceedings;
(b) Breach of arbitral duty;
(c) Breach of copyright (in a proof of evidence);
(d) The interests of individual litigants and public interest if a witness should be proved to have expressed himself in a materially different sense when acting for different sides;
(e) The duty to tell the truth.

560 The issues in this case are of such seminal importance to expert witnesses generally—both in arbitration and litigation—that the full text of the relevant passages from the judgment of Mance J (as he then was) are reproduced herewith.

> "It was common ground that a *subpoena duces tecum* may be issued only in circumstances where the fair disposal of the current proceedings justifies it and that the onus is on the person issuing the subpoena to demonstrate that this is the case. Such a subpoena is not a means of obtaining documents which are no more than relevant to issue in a sense which would make them discoverable *inter partes*.
>
> Authority for these propositions is to be found in the Court of Appeal decision in *Macmillan Inc* v. *Bishopsgate Investment Trust plc* [1993] 1 WLR 1372. Normally any objection for a subpoena comes from the person to whom it is addressed: see *Boeing Co* v. *PPG Industries Inc* [1998] 3 All ER 839 *per* O'Connor LJ at 842 H–J where he said:
>
> > 'The fact that in the ordinary course of events the opposite party cannot and does not apply to the court to set aside a subpoena means that the party's right course there is to object to the production and admissibility of the documents when the subpoena is complied with in court.'
>
> However, there are circumstances in which a third party, that is someone other than the party issuing the subpoena or to whom it is directed, may apply to set it aside. An example is the owner of documents who has been subpoenaed while the documents are being held in somebody else's hands. See *Marcel* v. *Commissioner of Police of the Metropolis* [1992] Ch 225 *per* Dillon LJ at 253B–C. In that case the police had seized and held documents belonging to the plaintiffs. Dillon LJ said:
>
> > 'It has been submitted that only a person served with a *subpoena duces tecum* can apply to set it aside. But for my part I can see no reason why if a *subpoena duces tecum* is served on A to produce documents in his possession which are actually B's documents, B should not have the right, just as much as A to apply to set aside the subpoena or prevent the production of the documents if B has valid grounds for doing so.'
>
> Dillon LJ also said at 259A–B:
>
> > 'Even where a subpoena has been served, the police should not disclose seized documents to the advisers of a party to civil proceedings in advance of the attendance at court required by the subpoena, unless at the least the police have first given to the true owner of the documents notice of the service of the subpoena *and* of the wish of the police to produce the documents in advance of the attendance at court required by the subpoena, *and* have given the true owner a reasonable opportunity to state his objections, if any, to that course.'
>
> On the facts of *Marcel* any objection failed because the owners could not establish any valid

ground on which they themselves could have resisted a subpoena had the documents been in their own hands. It would of course have been different if the documents had been privileged in their hands. Another situation in which it seems to me that the third party may intervene is where confidential or private documents are subpoenaed. The existence of confidentiality is not an absolute bar to the enforcement of the production of documents by subpoena. However it is a relevant consideration in deciding whether such a subpoena is necessary for the fair resolution of the proceedings and should be permitted: see *Hassneh Insurance Co of Israel* v. *Mew* [1993] 2 Lloyd's Rep 243 *per* Colman J at 250–251, citing *Science Research Council* v. *Nasse* [1980] AC 1028, at 1065, 1077 and 1089.

It might be of no interest to a person subpoenaed to raise considerations of confidentiality or privacy and in a proper case I would think that the person entitled to the confidentiality or privacy may therefore be permitted to intervene. In this connection, I note that in *Sphere Drake Insurance plc* v. *Denby*, an unreported decision on 28 July 1991 of Judge Kershaw QC, sitting as a deputy judge of the High Court, subpoenas were addressed by the defendants to the DTI and the Corporation of Lloyd's in respect of statements made by four potential witnesses for the plaintiffs. The DTI and Lloyd's as the persons subpoenaed objected themselves. The interviews, which they had had with the DTI inspectors and with those conducting a Lloyd's inquiry, took place in circumstances which involved at least qualified undertakings of confidentiality and privacy towards the witnesses.

The present applications raise the question whether a witness may claim a like interest in respect of a proof of evidence given and used by him in the course of a previous arbitration. There is no doubt that the parties to such a previous arbitration owed each other a duty of confidence and privacy in respect of the course of and evidence given during it: see *Hassneh Insurance Co of Israel* v. *Mew*, cited above.

There is also no doubt that an expert such as Mr Main owes to those instructing him, in the case of the previous arbitrations here, BT, a duty to keep confidential the evidence which he gave in such previous arbitrations. The confidential nature of a private arbitration means, in my judgement, that Mr Main must also owe a like duty to the other party to such an arbitration.

The present issue however, is whether the parties to an arbitration owe any duty of confidence or privacy to a witness such as Mr Main. On this no authority directly in point was cited. Mr Price for Mr Main relied heavily on the words in the evidence showing that Mr Jones and Mr King of DTZ Debenham Thorpe understood that they were given sight of part or all of Mr Main's *Euston Tower* proof by BT's in-house surveyor and Chestertons on the basis that no use would be made hereof in the present arbitration without further consent from them and Mr Main. The attitude of BT's in-house surveyor or Chesterton's is not, however, a very sure guide to the boundaries of confidence or privacy or of great assistance to Mr Price's submissions, since they were in each case prepared to release the material

(a) without the consent of the other party, both being on different sides in the *Euston Tower* arbitration and
(b) without Mr Main's consent. Further the authorities are full of statements relating the element of confidentiality in cases of private arbitration to implied agreement between the parties. See, for example, *Oxford Shipping Co Ltd* v. *Nippon Yusen Kaisha, The Eastern Saga* [1984] 2 Lloyd's Rep 373 at 379; *Dolling-Baker* v. *Merrett* [1990] 1 WLR 1205 at 1213F–1214A; and *Hassneh* (*supra*) at 246–247.

None of these authorities deal with the need to consider the rights of a witness which could arise if duties of confidentiality or privacy were owed to him or her. Despite this I see some force in the submission that it is implicit in the nature of private consensual arbitration that witnesses who give evidence, even paid and professional experts, will within certain limits be accorded the benefits of the privacy which overall attaches to this type of arbitration. The privacy of arbitration is likely to be a factor in persuading many witnesses to give evidence and a factor in encouraging them to speak, or in the case of experts enabling them to obtain permission from other principals to speak, about matters within their experience about which otherwise they might be hesitant or unable to speak. Further, in the case of Mr Main's proofs there is another factor since it is common ground that he retains copyright in his proofs. Mr Fancourt pointed out that the Copyright, Designs and Patents Act 1988, s.45(1) creates an express exception to copyright protection in the case of anything done for the purposes of 'judicial proceedings'. Mr Price retorts that judicial proceedings do not include arbitration proceedings. I doubt whether Mr Price is right in this since judicial proceedings are defined by section 178 of the Act as including

> 'proceedings before any court tribunal or person having authority to decide any matter affecting a person's legal rights or liabilities'

which on its face embraces arbitration. I also note that the predecessor section 48(1) of the Copyright Act 1956 referred to

> 'any court, tribunal or person having by law power to hear, receive and examine evidence on oath'

which, in the light of section 12(3) of the Arbitration Act 1950 would include an arbitrator.

But even assuming that Mr Main cannot directly complain of breach of copyright by persons proposing to copy and use his previous proofs in connection with the present arbitration, it seems to me, that Mr Main's general copyright interest, coupled with the generally private nature of the previous arbitration in relation to which he gave his proofs, does confer on him a sufficient interest to enable him to intervene and complain if he sees that a subpoena is being issued, which is, on the face of it, designed to compel the production and admission of one of his proofs in different proceedings. The position would be *a fortiori*, of course, if there had been, or would be, a breach of copyright involved in the circumstances leading up to the subpoena.

There must however, be limits to any such right of privacy in the witness as well, I think, as to any copyright which Mr Main may claim in his proofs, just as it has been regarded as necessary to put limits on the confidentiality or privacy upon which the parties to an arbitration may insist: see again *Hassneh* (*supra*). An expert witness must, for example, accept that one or other of the parties to the arbitration may either be compelled, or in its own interests, may require to deploy, in other contexts, proofs or other material deriving from the arbitration; see *Hassneh* at 248–9. The witness's interest must necessarily be subsidiary to such considerations.

The other issue raised by the present applications is whether *London & Leeds Estates Ltd* as claimants in the present arbitration have standing to object to the subpoenas addressed to Mr Main and Mr Jones. They can claim no confidentiality or privacy in respect of the previous arbitrations or in respect of Mr Main's proofs. Their objections are sought to be made solely in their capacity as opposite parties in the present arbitration. They say that the subpoenas addressed to Mr Main and Mr Jones are irregular and fishing; that they will, or may, introduce into the present arbitration material which will, or may, add unnecessarily to its length and complexity and that they are not necessary for its fair disposal.

In relation to these objections the starting point is that the subpoena process gives no opportunity to the opposite party to litigation to review the propriety of a subpoena. Further, if a general right were recognised in an opposite party to raise such objections, it would encourage ancillary litigation in relation to subpoenas, whether in aid of arbitration or court proceedings. A party to litigation is generally exposed to whatever material the other party can procure and deploy in evidence or in cross-examination. The subpoena adds relatively little to this exposure. The arbitration tribunal or court hearing the substantive dispute will permit only the use of material which can properly be deployed in accordance with the rules governing evidence and cross-examination. These appear to me in general, at least, sufficient safeguards.

Approaching the present applications in the light of these conclusions, first, there is no doubt about Mr Main's standing to object to the subpoenas addressed to him in respect of his *Euston Tower* and *Delta Point* proofs.

Second, I accept Mr Main's standing to object to the subpoenas addressed to Mr Jones in respect of Mr Main's proof in the *Delta Point* arbitration and, so far as necessary, I shall order that he be joined as a party to the present applications before me under Order 15, r.6(2).

Third, I do not accept that *London & Leeds Estates Ltd* have any standing to object to the subpoenas addressed to either Mr Main or Mr Jones.

I turn therefore, to consider the merits of the objections raised in relation to the subpoenas. They involved a number of submissions.

First, there was no basis upon which Mr Main's proofs would be or could become admissible in evidence.

Second, the subpoenas represented pure fishing expeditions in that:

(a) in the case of the *Delta Point* proof there was no clear indication as to what it said;
(b) in the case of the *Euston Tower* proofs there was no basis for supposing that Mr Main had contradicted or would contradict it and
(c) on the contrary Mr Main had 'readily assented' to such part of its contents as had already been adverted to in his cross-examination.

Third, the subpoenas were not in any event necessary for the fair disposal of the present arbitrations having regard in particular to:

(a) the issues in the present arbitration;
(b) the evidence already given by Mr Main;
(c) the desirability of retaining the sphere of investigation and documentation in any arbitration within appropriate bounds;
(d) the desirability of preserving the privacy and confidentiality of the previous arbitrations; and
(e) the circumstances in which *Paribas* had obtained information about the *Delta Point* proof and copies of an extract and the whole of the *Euston Tower* proof.

Fourth, in respect of the *Delta Point* proof any challenge to the subpoenas by Mr Main's summons dated 8 July 1994 (London & Leeds Estates Ltd's summons is dated 12 July 1994) was too late, having regard to the fact that Mr Jones had attended with the documents subpoenaed on 26 May 1994 and given them into the arbitrator's custody then.

As to the first submission, Mr Fancourt, for Paribas Ltd referred to the proofs as capable of use in three ways:

first, as evidence demonstrating what Mr Main had previously said and presumably believed and was very relevant to credit:
second, as evidence insofar as he accepted their contents in the present arbitration; and
third, as potentially admissible relative to an issue in the present arbitration and evidence if Mr Main gives answers inconsistent with their contents.

As to the first basis, what Mr Main said or believed previously is not in issue in this arbitration and material going to credit *alone* is not admissible in evidence. It may be mentioned to the witness but his answers are final. As to the second basis, this is not strictly correct in that, if Mr Main in this arbitration accepts as accurate, statements made by himself in the previous arbitration, the relevant evidence is his evidence repeating or endorsing the previous statements not the previous statements themselves. The third basis was thus a major plank in Mr Fancourt's case during the argument before me. It relies on, and refers to, sections 4 and 5 of the Criminal Procedure Act 1865 and section 3(1)(a) of the Civil Evidence Act 1968. Mr Fancourt says that a subpoena may be issued to compel production of a document produced in cross-examination in civil proceedings with a view to putting its contents to a witness as a prior inconsistent statement and if he does not 'distinctly admit' then putting the document and proving that he did, in fact, make the statement. Mr Fancourt then relies upon section 3(1)(a) of the 1968 Act whereby:

'Where in any civil proceedings

(a) A previous inconsistent or contradictory statement made by a person called as a witness in those proceedings is proved by virtue of sections 3, 4 or 5 of the Criminal Procedure Act 1865 . . .

that statement shall by virtue of this subsection be admissible as evidence of any fact stated therein of which direct oral evidence by him would be admissible.'

Mr Fancourt referred me to *Macmillan Inc* v. *Bishopsgate Investment Trust plc* [1993] 1 WLR 1372, cited above, where the issue was whether the plaintiffs, who were in the course of cross-examining a Mr Haas, were entitled by a *subpoena duces tecum* addressed to Mr Haas to obtain transcripts of his private examination by the defendant's liquidators under section 236 of the Insolvency Act 1986. The attempt to obtain such transcripts failed on the basis that it was 'fishing' since it was pure speculation whether the transcripts contained any answer upon which the plaintiffs would wish to rely in any way.

Certain points appear, which are, in the present case of particular interest.

First, after discussing the authority of *R* v. *Cheltenham Justices ex parte Secretary of State for Trade* [1977] 1 WLR 95, the Court of Appeal, while rejecting any suggestion that a *subpoena duces tecum* could be used as means of obtaining discovery against third parties, adopted as applicable a broad test whether the production of the document sought by such a subpoena was shown to be necessary for the fair disposal of the proceedings in which the subpoena was issued.

Second there is the following discussion in Dillon LJ's judgment on the basis on which the transcripts might have been subpoenaed if the plaintiffs had shown that they were likely to contain helpful answers. He said at p. 1375H:

> 'Then there was some discussion about the possibility of the transcript being admissible under the Civil Evidence Act 1968. The judge said that there was no reason for supposing that Mr Haas had made inconsistent statements or that he had made any statements helpful to the plaintiff which the plaintiff had not thought of extracting from him in the course of cross-examination. On that it is plain that, in the judge's view, it was not shown that the order for the production of the transcripts was necessary for disposing fairly of the cause or matter.'

At 1377E to 1378A–B Dillon LJ also considered the prior decision of *R* v. *Clowes* [1992] 3 All ER 440, where Phillips J upheld a witness summons by Mr Clowes seeking to obtain transcripts of interviews with liquidators by persons who were due to be called and had given witness statements to the prosecution in the criminal proceedings against Mr Clowes. Phillips J upheld the witness summons on the basis that there were significant matters in at least two transcripts which had been seen by Mr Clowes's advisers, upon which the defence would wish to rely at the trial in one way or another. Phillips J referred to an argument which had apparently found favour with Henry J in *R* v. *Saunders*, an unreported decision on 9 February 1990, to the effect that use under sections 4 and 5 of the Criminal Procedure Act 1865 to contradict evidence could itself and alone constitute a legitimate basis for distinguishing *R* v. *Cheltenham Justices*. Phillips J did not have to say whether he agreed with this argument although Dillon LJ's judgment in the *Macmillan* case may not be altogether favourable to it: see 1378B.

In *R* v. *Clowes* the documents were not required for contradiction of the witness, but primarily to put to the witness in order to elicit his agreement to the statements they contained. Phillips J found, however, that

> 'it was not inconceivable that circumstances might arise in which parts of the transcripts might themselves be adjusted in evidence'.

For example, if one of the witnesses professed no recollection of a particular incident in the transcript, in which case it could be proved under section 24 of the Criminal Justice Act 1988 as a statement in a document created by the liquidator in the course of his profession or occupation. On either basis Phillips J regarded *R* v. *Cheltenham Justices* as sufficiently distinguishable. Both in *R* v. *Clowes* and in the *Macmillan* case itself (see *per* Dillon LJ at 1375A cited above) there are therefore indications that it is no absolute objection to a subpoena that its aim is to obtain a document the contents of which there is reason to believe will constitute additional matters which, if they can be ascertained and put to a witness, will add to or put a different complexion on his evidence even if the hope is that this will be achieved by his agreeing with them. *A fortiori* if there is a prospect that he will not agree with or remember the contents, and they may then be adduced in evidence:

(a) in a criminal case in circumstances within section 24 of the Criminal Justice Act 1988; or
(b) if they are statements of fact, in a civil case under section 2(1) of the Civil Evidence Act 1968; or

(c) at least in a civil case, if they may be put to a witness under sections 4 and 5 of the Criminal Procedure Act, and proved and then adduced in evidence under section 3(1)(a) of the Civil Evidence Act 1968.

R v. *Cheltenham Justices* is also distinguished in another case to which Mr Fancourt referred me, decided in 1991, but not reported. That is *Sphere Drake Insurance plc* v. *Denby* to which I have already referred. In that case Judge Kershaw explained *R* v. *Cheltenham Justices* as limited in two ways:

(i) to attempt 'to obtain a document for use in cross-examination where the cross-examination is to make evidence only that a witness has made a previous inconsistent statement and is cross-examination which goes only to credit and not to an issue between the parties' (in this connection I note that he does not appear to have been referred to Henry J's decision in *R* v. *Saunders* or indeed to Phillips J's decision in *R* v. *Clowes*); and
(ii) to witness statements as distinct from High Court procedures for the production of documents.

The criteria for issue of a witness statement are defined by section 77 of the Magistrates' Courts Act 1952 in the following way:

> 'Where a justice of the peace . . . is satisfied that any person . . . is likely to be able to . . . produce any document or thing likely to be material evidence . . . .'

This provision is in language not found in any of the Rules of the Supreme Court governing production of documents and has been regarded as defining the jurisdiction of magistrates: see *R* v. *Lewes Justices ex parte Secretary of State for the Home Department* [1972] 1 QB 232 referred to in *R* v. *Cheltenham Justices*.

The broad test adopted in relation to subpoenas by the Court of Appeal in the *Macmillan* case indicates that there is force in the distinction drawn by Judge Kershaw although no doubt *R* v. *Cheltenham Justices* identifies certain policy considerations which are also relevant in the context of production of documents under the rules.

Reverting to the first basis on which Judge Kershaw distinguished *R* v. *Cheltenham Justices*, he considered that a reasonable possibility that a prior inconsistent statement would become evidence under section 3(1)(a) of the Civil Evidence Act 1968 could justify issue of a subpoena for its production. Further, he considered that there would be no reason to await the trial or the eliciting by cross-examination of an apparently inconsistent statement before such a subpoena could be issued.

I agree with both his conclusions. On the facts of *Sphere Drake* the subpoena was once again set aside as fishing because there was no basis for expecting to find any discrepancy whether major or minor.

Mr Barnes QC, who represented London & Leeds Estates Ltd and whose submissions were adopted generally by Mr Price in addition to his own, submitted that there could on the facts of this case be no question of Mr Main's previous proofs being deployed under sections 4 and 5 of the Criminal Procedure Act, let alone becoming admissible as evidence under section 3(1)(a) of the Civil Evidence Act 1968. The only prior inconsistent statement to which these sections referred were, according to him, statements put in use with a view to showing that a witness was deliberately lying in his current evidence. Indeed, all cross-examination as to credit or creditability was, according to Mr Barnes, confined to challenges to truthfulness. While counsel could always suggest to a witness that he had forgotten some matter or was plain wrong, it was only if he were challenging the witness's current honesty that counsel could put and prove the contents of a prior inconsistent statement. Since there was no express challenge to Mr Main's truthfulness it would not therefore, according to Mr Barnes, be possible to use any contradictory statement in his prior proof during his cross-examination.

These were somewhat remarkable propositions which, if correct, would alter the nature and practice of much cross-examination and deprive courts of what is frequently very useful material to assist in identifying the real factual position. Where a witness gives evidence what is of direct concern is whether his evidence is accurate and not whether the witness is lying or has genuinely come to believe some version other than what is accurate, whether by some version other than what is accurate, whether by some process of erroneous reconstruction or wishful thinking or whatever. The usefulness of a prior inconsistent statement does not depend on any investigation into, or consideration of, his current truthfulness.

The purpose of putting to a witness any prior inconsistent statement, assuming of course that it does not immediately lead him to change his evidence so as to agree with the cross-examiner, is to have him admit that he made it and, if he does not admit this, prove this under section 4 of the Criminal Procedure Act.

In this event, the statement also becomes admissible evidence under section 3(1)(a) of the Civil Evidence Act 1968. Mr Price himself sought to introduce another restriction on the operation of the Criminal Procedure Act and Civil Evidence Act. He referred to the reference in sections 4 and 5 of the former Act to cross-examination as to a former statement made by a witness 'relative to the subject matter of the indictment of proceeding'. According to Mr Price the subject matter of the present arbitration proceedings is simply the proper rent valuation of the premises at 33 Wigmore Street, as at 8 August 1991. This is, indeed, the ultimate issue, but there are numerous very important subsidiary issues being litigated, as the extracts from Mr Main's proofs, which I have quoted demonstrate, in the course of determining and with a view to assisting determine this ultimate issue. One of these subsidiary issues—essential background to the determination of the open market rental value of 33 Wigmore Street, itself at 8 August 1991—concerns the state of the West End property market at the relevant time.

The passages which Mr Price emphasised in sections 4 and 5 of the Criminal Procedure Act embrace all such issues arising in the arbitration, not merely the ultimate issue. Mr Price's submissions to the contrary were again contrary to practice and policy.

I turn therefore to the defendant's other submission. It is convenient at this point to consider the *Euston Tower* proof first. The second submission raised was that the subpoena represented in respect of this proof a mere fishing expedition. It was said that it contained nothing which Mr Main had contradicted or was likely to contradict. On the contrary he had readily assented to such part as had already been adverted to in his cross-examination. Mr Barnes pointed out that the state of the property market is not capable of being measured with exact or mathematical precision. If necessary it can be measured only by generalities or adjectives. There would always be differences of language and nuance. Two witnesses would never say precisely the same thing.

However, here we are concerned with one and the same witness. Comparison of the market sections in Mr Main's present proof and in is *Euston Tower* proof indicate that they start off virtually identically. The present has been copied from the former or there exists a master draft. His *Euston Tower* proof then moves to a passage on world events covering the period October 1990 to October 1991 and containing this colourful and forceful paragraph which I have already set out.

> 'This unique cocktail of events led to great uncertainty and a general lack of business confidence as a true recession became a harsh reality. In the property market there was choice, the tenant was at last king and rent and capital values were falling.'

His present proof, on the other hand, speaks of his experiencing 'several periods of economic difficulties which have affected the property market' and then identifies the four phases which he says are characteristic of such periods. Starting by saying that the market on 8 August 1991 (five months further down a falling market than the *Euston Tower* review date) 'was moving' into stage (ii) Mr Main amended this to 'had moved'. Even after this amendment I see force in the submission that the two proofs take noticeably different lines and give significantly different impressions. I can see good reason why counsel for Paribas Ltd should wish and be entitled to put *Euston Tower* proof to Mr Main in relation to the state of the property market in August 1991 and seek to have him either agree, without qualification, with his previous views or, if necessary, put the document and prove that Mr Main expressed them.

Such cross-examination as there has already been does not dispel this conclusion. It is said that Mr Main 'readily assented' to what he previously said. If he did then Phillips J's decision in *R* v. *Clowes* suggests and indeed the Court of Appeal's *dicta* which I have set out in the *Macmillan* case, suggest that that may not be inconsistent with the purpose of a subpoena. If there is a good reason to believe that a witness has, in a previous statement, said something additional to, or different from, what he now puts in his proof there is, as I have already concluded, much to be said for the document being made available to enable its contents to be used to obtain the witness' full account, whether or not it is necessary actually to put and prove the document.

In the present case, however, I also think that 'ready assent' is not an entirely accurate description of what happened. The likelihood in the case of an inconsistent statement recorded in a document is not that the witness will, or will continue to, deny making the statement outright, but is that he will seek to modify or qualify rather than simply admit. Mr Main's reaction to the suggestion that by March 1991 tenants regarded themselves as being king in the market-place was 'Did I say that?' and after reference to the *Euston Tower* arbitration 'I shall have to look it up, but if you say I gave that evidence I gave it'. (I note in parenthesis in this connection Lord Esher's words in *North Australian Territory Co* v. *Goldsborough Mort & Co* [1893] 2 Ch 381 at 385.)

In the end, after much argument, the question was repeated:

> 'In purely general terms is it or is it not your view that in March 1991 a few months earlier, when it came to negotiations of substantial lettings, at any rate, the tenant was king of the market place?'

Mr Main answered,

> 'If you were negotiating 50,000 sq. ft. in Euston Tower the answer is yes.'

So Mr Main is not in fact assenting to his previous proof in terms. He is dividing the market. He is qualifying the language of the *Euston Tower* proof to apply only to buildings of 150,000 sq. ft. or so. This may, of course, prove to represent a correct distinction. But the important point which can at present be made, on the material before me, is that the passages about the state of the West End market in both proofs are entirely general. The market is not, for example, split into different commercial markets dependent on whether the premises are large or very large. Paribas Ltd can, in my view, say 'arguably and on reasonable grounds' that there appear to be potential inconsistencies between the approach in the previous and present proofs: see *Sunderland Steamship P & I Association* v. *Gatoil International Inc 'The Lorenzo Halcoussi'* [1988] 1 Lloyd's Rep 180 *per* Steyn LJ at 184, cited in the *Sphere Drake* case.

Turning to the third submission, is the subpoena in respect of the Euston Tower proof necessary for the fair conduct of the present arbitration? I have referred to the central importance of property market conditions in 1991 in the West End to the present arbitration. Mr Main is obviously a weighty witness although not the only witness on the subject. I, of course, bear in mind the desirability of retaining the present arbitration within appropriate bounds. No doubt the present arbitrator will seek to ensure this also. But the intention is cross-examination on a previous proof so far as it summarises general market conditions in the West End. This will not, in my judgement, unduly overinflate an already expanded arbitration. It will not call for invesetigation of all the other evidence given in the previous arbitration. Further, of course, he has already gone into one aspect of the previous proof although it has not been possible to put it to him. If Mr Main changed or qualified his description of general West End market conditions when he came to give his oral evidence in the *Euston Tower* arbitration he can say this and I have little doubt that he can, probably without much difficulty, demonstrate it by obtaining a transcript.

He can also develop the point that the Euston Tower premises were so much larger as to constitute, in effect, part of a different market, if that is his explanation. It is worth bearing in mind that, if instead of acting as expert in the previous arbitration Mr Main had written articles or given previous evidence about the West End property market in court proceedings there could be no obstacle to cross-examining him on his previous statements.

As to privacy and confidentiality, the fact that Mr Main's previous proof is required on a single issue of general market conditions, in my view, means that these factors carry relatively little weight as arguments against upholding the present subpoena. The circumstances in which first some pages of the proof were obtained from one party and then a copy of the whole proof from the other party, without in either case approaching Mr Main, can justly be viewed as unsatisfactory, but both parties to the previous arbitration have indicated a readiness to allow Paribas Ltd to get to know of the relevant contents, even though Mr Main has not done so himself and the contents of the whole proof have, in fact, been deployed in evidence before me. Mr Price said that Mr Main was contemplating separate proceedings based on breach of confidence and/or copyright, but these are not before me and would also appear to strike new ground in terms of injunctive relief since this case is not concerned with any question of privilege. The usual principle is that unprivileged material is admissible even if it can be seen to have been procured in circumstances involving breach of confidence.

The evidence of the contents of the proof is, in fact, before me and I cannot ignore it. I can take into account the circumstances in which, and even on their own view limited, the basis on which Paribas Ltd obtained the proof in determining whether, as a matter of discretion, the subpoena should be upheld as necessary for disposal of the matter, but in deciding whether Mr Main's objection to the production and use of his proof should prevail, there is, in my view, another powerful principle at play. To introduce it I will refer to a cogent passage in *Bernstein & Wood's Handbook of Arbitration Practice*, 2nd edn. 1993 at para. 21.2.1:

> 'Duty to tell the truth
>
> There are surprising differences of opinion between professional men as to the principles they should observe when preparing, and ultimately giving evidence before a court or an arbitrator. It has been said by a professional man of great standing, that an expert witness is under no duty to bring out facts which do not advance the case that his client is putting forward; that that is the duty of the expert on the other side. This view has been repeated recently.'

Then there is a reference to an article in *Arbitration* of August 1990:

> 'Many rent review valuers take the view that, having regard to the margin of error inherent in any valuation, if the best estimate of rental value that anyone could make for a particular building is £10,000–£11,000 per annum it is wholly legitimate for the valuer to value the building at £10,000 per annum if instructed by the tenant and at £11,000 per annum if instructed by the landlord, putting forward different arguments and sometimes different evidence in each case.
>
> This view is misconceived. A witness who states in evidence (whether or not on oath is irrelevant) that his opinion of value is 100, when his opinion in truth is that the value is a figure between 100 and 110 as to which he cannot be more certain, is not telling the truth; he is shading the truth, presumably because he thinks it will advance his client's interests. It cannot be right that two valuers who in truth agree (as they so often do) that the right answer is a figure between 100 and 120 should give evidence, on different sides, one saying that his opinion is 100 and the other that his is 120. Of course, while a case is being prepared, the expert owes a duty to his client to assist by every proper means in preparation of the case and, if requested, in negotiation. But once the witness begins evidence (and this includes submitting a proof or report before the hearing, as well as the oral evidence given during the hearing) his duty to his client is no more than that he shall use a reasonable level of professional skill and care. Subject to that duty, he owes a duty to himself, to tell the truth, the whole truth and nothing but the truth. He also owes a duty to the arbitrator to assist him to arrive at a just decision. No greater tribute can be paid to a professional man than to have it said of him that his opinion remains the same whoever is paying for it.'

This passage focuses on the issue of truthfulness which is, of course, fundamental. But similar observations, in my judgement, apply with respect to the need to resist any subconscious tendency for an expert to become a member of a team and as a result to proffer views unduly favourable to the position of the party instructing him. As I have said, it is evident that Mr Main's two proofs start off down a common path and then diverge at least somewhat. It does not seem to me that Mr Main has legitimate ground to object to cross-examination about his previous statements on the general subject of West End property market conditions in 1991. If a witness were proved to have expressed himself in a materially different sense when acting for different sides, that would be a factor which should be brought out in the interests of individual litigants involved and in the public interest.

Thinking as I do, that there is at least a legitimate basis for admitting the *Euston Tower* proof in the present arbitration, I have come to the conclusion that the arguments in favour of upholding the subpoena outweigh such objections as there are on grounds of privacy and confidentiality.

I turn therefore to the *Delta Point* proof. The circumstances here are quite different. No one, save Mr Jones under subpoena, has released it to anyone. There has been no discussion of it during the arbitration. The only information about it is cryptic in the extreme and comes in plain breach of confidence from Mr Jones as arbitrator in the *Delta Point* arbitration. His statement that some of the views expressed by Mr Main are 'relevant' to the 33 Wigmore Street arbitration does no more than reflect a test which would be applicable on discovery *inter partes* and says nothing which would enable me to judge whether any use can be made of the proof in the present arbitration. His statement to Miss Di Lorio, that Mr Main's present proof is 'not what Mr Main said in *Delta Point*', gives no particulars as to the respects in which the two might differ or, if it be the case, might be positively inconsistent.

Delta Point appears, unlike *Euston Tower*, to be outside the West End property market. If one surmises that Mr Main's *Delta Point* proof may have said the same as his *Euston Tower* proof, that, to my mind, simply confirms that it is not necessary to go into the *Delta Point* arbitration at all. One instance of inconsistency would appear as good as two in the present context. All these factors lead me to the conclusion that the *Delta Point* subpoena was, first, no more than a fishing expedition and, second, in any event not an exercise which the court should in its discretion regard as necessary for fairly disposing of the present arbitration.

That leaves me, however, to consider the final point, whether the summons to set aside the subpoena addressed to Mr Jones should be regarded as too late in the light of Mr Jones' production of the proof to the arbitrator on 26 May 1994. Assistance on this point is in my view provided by *Marcel* v. *Commissioner of Police of the Metropolis* [1992] 2 Ch 225 at 231C–D and 239B–C *per* Sir Nicolas Browne-Wilkinson V-C. There, documents 'were left in the custody of the court under an informal arrangement' and not looked at or read. Thereafter proceedings were begun for an injunction to restrain their use, later amended to include a claim to set aside the subpoena: see 231F–G. The Vice-Chancellor rejected the submission that it was too late to set aside the subpoena saying at 239B:

> 'Mr Serota takes two preliminary points. First, he says it is to set aside the subpoena: the police officer has lodged the papers with the court and therefore the subpoena is spent. I reject this submission. All that has happened is a convenient arrangement whereby, by consent, the documents have been lodged with the court. The police officer has not gone into the witness box to prove them: they are not in evidence in the main action and, save by the consent of the company, will not become so unless and until the police officer has gone into the witness box.'

By parity of reasoning, nothing having happened in this case save the formal consignment of the documents to the custody of the arbitrator under a degree of protest from the landlord's side, it is not too late to apply to set aside the subpoena. In the circumstances I consider that Mr Main has sufficient standing to intervene on valid grounds to make this application which, in my judgement, succeeds.

I therefore dismiss the summons dated 12 July issued by London & Leeds Estates Ltd relating to both proofs as well as Mr Main's summons dated 18 May 1994, so far as it relates to the *Euston Tower* proof. I grant Mr Main's application by summons dated 18 May 1994 to set aside the subpoena addressed to Mr Jones in respect of the *Delta Point* proof."

561 The valuable commentary by Sandi Murdoch, in the *Estates Gazette*, on this case (28 January 1995), included, *inter alia*, the following:

"(It should be noted that the arbitrator who had tipped the wink to his current team was roundly criticised by the judge for acting in breach of his duties of confidentiality with regard to the earlier arbitration.)

Not surprisingly, Paribas wished, at the very least, to be able to force the expert to explain why the evidence which he was now giving as the Landlord's expert differed from that which he had given when acting for a tenant.

Having failed to elicit this explanation by cross-examination which, in the absence of the earlier proof, was necessarily allusive, Paribas issued two *subpoenas duces tecum*. These sought production of these proofs by the expert witness and one of the arbitrator's and were being challenged by the expert and the landlords in the current arbitration. Mance J had to deal with two basic questions.

Did either the expert or the Landlords have the standing to seek to have these subpoenas set aside? If so, should they be set aside? The case raised some very technical questions on the law of evidence. What follows is, necessarily, over-simplified.

There was no doubt that the expert could seek to resist the subpoena issued against himself. Mance J was also satisfied that he was entitled to challenge the subpoena issued against the arbitrator since, as the author of the proof in question, he had an obvious interest. The judge was equally satisfied that the landlords did not have any legal right to object; they could claim no confidentiality in respect of the earlier proceedings in which they were not involved and had no rights in respect of the proofs themselves. Their only interest was as a party to the current arbitration and this was not sufficient.

The judge then turned to the substantive question which was, whether the expert could establish any legal basis on which the subpoena issued against himself in respect of one of the proofs, and that issued against the arbitrator in respect of the other proof, could be set aside.

While the *subpoena duces tecum* process bears some resemblance to that of discovery, it is rather stricter. It is not enough to show that the documents to be produced are relevant to the issues between the parties; it has to be shown that they are necessary for the fair disposal of those issues. Mance J decided that the proof in respect of the previous arbitration involving another property in the West End must be produced. Comparing the earlier proof with that in the present proceedings the judge made this comment:

> '. . . it is evident that [the] two proofs start off down a common path and then diverge at least somewhat. It does not seem to me that [the expert] has legitimate ground to object to cross-examination about his previous statements on the general subject of West End property market conditions in 1991. If a witness were proved to have expressed himself in a materially different sense when acting for different sides, that would be a factor which should be brought out in the interests of individual litigants concerned and in the public interest'.

However, he ruled that the other subpoena should be set aside. There was no clear indication that the proof to which it applied contained discrepancies over and above those which would already be put to the expert.

Duties of an expert witness

The above litigation arose out of the central dilemma facing any expert witness in a valuation dispute. He is being paid by one of the parties and is often, at the very least, one of that party's team of advisers and negotiators. Clearly when acting purely as an adviser to a client, a surveyor should warn the latter of the strengths and weaknesses of his case and should give an honest opinion of value. If and when negotiating for that client the surveyor is perfectly entitled to ignore the weaknesses of his case; its strengths can be exaggerated and any flaws are for the other side to point out. To a large extent, a similar approach can be adopted when acting as an advocate. It is when the expert witness hat is donned that partiality must disappear.

In *Ikarian Reefer* [1993] 37 EG 158 Cresswell J provided a useful summary of the duties of an expert witness, which included the following points.

> 'Expert evidence presented to the court should be, and should be seen to be, the independent product of the expert uninfluenced as to form or content by the exigencies of litigation . . . . An expert witness should provide independent assistance to the court by way of objective unbiased opinion in relation to matters within his expertise . . . . An expert witness . . . should never assume the role of an advocate . . . he should not omit material facts which could detract from his concluded opinion.'

In the *Paribas* case the judge quoted at length with approval from *Bernstein & Wood's Handbook of Arbitration Practice*. The following bears repetition:

> 'A witness who states in evidence . . . that his opinion of value is 100, when his opinion in truth is that the value is a figure between 100 and 110 as to which he cannot be more certain, is not telling the truth; he is shading the truth, presumably, because he thinks it will advance his client's interest. It cannot be right that two valuers who . . . agree . . . that the right answer is a figure between 100 and 120 should give evidence, on different sides, one saying that his opinion is 100 and the other that his is 120 . . . . Once the witness begins evidence (and this includes submitting a proof or report before the hearing . . .) his duty to his client is no more than that he shall use a reasonable level of professional skill and care. Subject to that duty, he also owes a duty to himself to tell the truth. He also owes a duty to the arbitrator to assist him to arrive at a just decision. No greater tribute can be paid . . . than to have it said of him that his opinion remains the same whoever is paying for it.' "

Commentary

562 The decision in the *Paribas* case turned upon ss.4 and 5 of the Criminal Procedure Act 1865. These state:

> "4. If a witness, upon cross-examination as to a former statement made by him relative to the subject matter of the indictment or proceeding, and inconsistent with his present testimony, does not distinctly admit that he has made such statement, proof may be given that he did in fact make it; but before such proof can be given the circumstances of the supposed statement, sufficient to designate the particular occasion, must be mentioned to the witness, and he must be asked whether or not he has made such statement.
>
> 5. A witness may be cross-examined as to previous statements made by him in writing, or reduced into writing, relative to the subject matter of the indictment or proceeding, without such writing being shown to him; but if it is intended to contradict such witness by the writing, his attention must, before such contradictory proof can be given, be called to those parts of the writing which are to be used for the purpose of so contradicting him: Provided always, that it shall be competent for the judge, at any time during the trial, to require the production of the writing for his inspection, and he may thereupon make such use of it for the purposes of the trial as he may think fit."

563 Although they are in an Act governing criminal procedure, the above sections apply also to civil cases—CPA 1865, s.1. They had to be read subject to s.3(1) of the Civil Evidence Act 1968 by which:

> "Where in any civil proceedings—
>
> a previous inconsistent or contradictory statement made by a person called as a witness in those proceedings is proved by virtue of section 3, 4 or 5 of the Criminal Procedure Act 1865; or
> (b) . . .
> that statement shall by virtue of this subsection be admissible as evidence of any fact stated therein of which direct oral evidence by him would be admissible."

564 This s.3(1) has been repealed by s.15(2) of the Civil Evidence Act 1995, but the Criminal Procedure Act has been left unscathed.

565 The present position concerning the issues raised in the *Paribas* case is now found in s.6(3) of the Civil Evidence Act 1995 which provides that:

> "(3) Where in the case of civil proceedings section 3, 4 or 5 of the Criminal Procedure Act 1865 applies, which make provision as to—
>
> (a) . . .
> (b) the proof of contradictory statements made by the witness, and
> (c) cross-examination as to previous statements in writing,

this Act does not authorise the adducing of evidence of a previous inconsistent or contradictory statement otherwise than in accordance with those sections."

566 The legal position is thus the same after the 1995 Act as it was when the *Paribas* case was decided.

WHETHER AN EXPERT CAN GIVE EVIDENCE CONCERNING THE CREDIBILITY OF A WITNESS GIVING VIDEO EVIDENCE

The facts

567 In a case of alleged sexual abuse of a minor, the plaintiff sought to have video evidence admitted. The defendant objected on the grounds that this was hearsay evidence.

568 Following consideration of submissions from both parties, the judge admitted the video evidence stating that it was for him to decide its weight and credibility.

569 In the course of these submissions, the defendant's counsel said that he would call expert evidence to show that the party shown on the video was not telling the truth.

Question

570 Can an expert give evidence concerning the credibility of another witness?

Course of action

571 This issue that was raised *Re N (A Minor) (Child Abuse Evidence)* reported in *The Times* 25 March 1996. Here the judge said that he would receive expert evidence to explain and interpret the video. It was for him to separate admissible from inadmissible expert evidence. Proper evidence from an expert would be couched in terms that a particular fact was consistent or inconsistent with sexual abuse, and that it rendered the child's evidence capable or incapable of being accepted by the judge as true.

572 The *New Law Journal* (12 April 1996) commenting on this case said that the received wisdom is that the expert may not assert the truthfulness of a witness or reporter of events which are in dispute.

> "The debate suggests something of a power struggle between judges and expert witnesses, one which ultimately the judges must win. The question must be how far they will allow the expert witness to go, while never reaching the position where it is the expert who decides the case. That must depend on the confidence they have in the expert."

573 Ward LJ commented:

> "Evidence of a diagnosis of sexual abuse called for a very high level of expertise. For the court to rely on opinion evidence, even to admit it, the qualifications of a witness must extend beyond experience gained as a social worker and require experience as or akin to a child psychologist or child psychiatrist."

NEITHER EXPERT'S EVIDENCE PREFERRED BY THE ARBITRATOR

The facts

574 At the hearing, experts appeared for each side. After hearing the evidence the arbitrator was unable to prefer one to the other. He had his own view of the matters in dispute on which the experts had given evidence.

Question

575 Is it permissible for the arbitrator to reject both the experts' evidence in favour of his own view of this matter?

Course of action

576 Although I was convinced that I had dealt with this situation with Thomasina on more than one previous occasion, I directed her to *Davie* v. *Magistrates of Edinburgh* 1953 SC 34, where it was said that the function of an expert witness:

> "is to furnish the judge with the necessary scientific criteria for testing the accuracy of his own conclusions so as to form his own independent judgement by the application of those criteria to the facts proved in evidence."

577 Experts frequently lose sight of this and sometimes display a tendency to act like an advocate of their client's case. This has been criticised in *The Ikarian Reefer* [1993] 2 Lloyd's Rep 68 *per* Cresswell J:

> "Expert evidence should be, and should be seen to be, the independent product of the expert, uninfluenced as to form or content by the exigencies of litigation."

578 In a reference where the arbitrator is clearly knowledgeable about the subject-matter and has firm opinions of his own which he is unable to ignore in weighing the experts' evidence and which do not match those of either expert, he should inform the parties of his own view, and invite them to address him on it. After he has heard the parties, if he still prefers his own view, he should so inform the parties and he is then free to find on the strength of that view.

579 When I was discussing this with Thomasina, Charley dropped into the office and I asked him how rent review arbitrators deal with this conflict, which cannot be an unusual situation for them.

580 Charley told us that there is a reasonable expectation that in a rent review award, recognising it is a declaration of the amount of value usually based on expert opinion evidence, an award wholly in favour of one party is unusual if experts for both sides recognise their duties as clearly set out in *The Ikarian Reefer.* Experience shows that many experts have difficulty in adapting to the true role of an expert witness. The training and day-to-day practice of valuers as negotiators and advisers centres on conducting the case to the client's best advantage or as a member of a team with a similar remit. As an expert witness the valuer's role changes. Mance J in *London & Leeds Estate Ltd* v. *Paribas Ltd (No 2)* [1995] 2 EG 134 at 141, para 1 said:

> "The issue of truthfulness is fundamental and, in my judgement, [applies] with respect to the need to resist any subconscious tendency for an expert to become a member of a team and, as a result, to proffer views unduly favourable to the position of the party instructing him."

581 The Court of Appeal in *Kemp Properties (UK)* v. *Dentsply Research and Development Corporation* [1991] 2 EGLR 197 at 200 highlighted the position:

> "It is a sad feature of litigation that expert witnesses, particularly in valuation cases, instead of giving evidence of their actual views as to the true position, enter into the arena and, as advocates, put forward the maximum or minimum figures as best suited to their side's interests. If experts do this then they must not be surprised if their views carry little weight with the judge. In this case, such evidence rightly led the judge to reject the expert evidence of both sides."

582 But Cresswell J in *The Ikarian Reefer* said

> "An expert witness in this High Court should never assume the role of an advocate."

583 By way of example, Judge Bowsher QC, in *Shortlands Investments Ltd* v. *Cargill plc* [1995] 1 EGLR 51 (a dilapidations case), at 55, weighed up the evidence of the two opposing experts as follows:

> "[Mr L's] evidence was strongly argumentative without always having the support of logic. He was very ready to draw inferences adverse to the [other side]. Mr [B], on the other hand seemed to be a very honest witness as to the facts of which he had first hand knowledge and he gave his evidence of opinion modestly and with a willingness to make proper concessions and his evidence appeared logical and sensible."

584 There is always conflicting opinion evidence in rent reviews in varying degrees and the arbitrator is left to weigh that evidence.

585 As Diplock LJ said in *R* v. *Deputy Industrial Injuries, ex parte Moore* [1964] 1 All ER 81 at 94:

> "He must not spin a coin or consult an astrologer; but he may take into account any material, which as a matter of reason has some probative value, the weight to be attached to it is [for him to decide]."

586 What if this conflicting evidence is made in written submissions in a "documents only" reference which appears to contain a number of untruths? Thomasina asked. Should the arbitrator call a hearing to allow their statements to be tested in cross-examination, or if requested by the other party to hold a hearing, should the arbitrator accede to this request?

587 I suggested that in such circumstances a short hearing was probably the only satisfactory way forward. If the other party made a request for such a hearing and the arbitrator refused that request he would be at risk of removal for misconducting the proceedings (s.24(1)(d)(i), AA '96) (see *Faure Fairclough Ltd* v. *Premier Oil & Cake Mills Ltd* [1968] 1 Lloyd's Rep 237).

WHEN A JUDGE MAY DISSENT FROM AN EXPERT'S OPINION

The facts

588 The defendant, aged 52, pleaded not guilty to assault occasioning actual bodily harm by conducting a four-year obsessive pursuit of the victim, causing injury to her mental and physical health.

589 After a two-week trial he was convicted. Psychiatric reports put forward the view that, if he were at liberty, he would not present a continuing threat to her.

590 The sentencing judge, having been present throughout the trial, expressed a different view and imposed a 2½ years' sentence of imprisonment. The defendant appealed.

Question

591 Under what circumstances is it likely that a judge will dissent from an expert's opinion?

Course of action

592 The facts of this example were drawn form *R* v. *Smith (Leonard)* [1997] Crim LR 614 CA.

593 Lord Bingham of Cornhill CJ, giving the judgment of the court, said that the threshold of detention having admittedly been crossed by the offender, the judge was entirely justified in taking the view he had taken, even if it meant some divergence from the psychiatric opinions before him.

594 A judge would be unlikely to dissent from an opinion on technical questions turning on medical expertise, but the judge had correctly held that he was much better placed than the doctors on the question whether the defendant was likely, if at liberty, to represent a continuing threat to the victim.

595 The defendant experiencing his first sentence of imprisonment, there was reason to hope that it might have the effect of bringing him to his senses. A significant custodial sentence was called for and a sentence of 21 months would be substituted for the 2½ years.

596 Another case where it was made clear that a judge is not bound to accept an expert's evidence was *Dover District Council* v. *Sherred* (1997) *The Times*, 11 February. The Court of Appeal reiterated the point that expert evidence may be rejected if it is in conflict with other evidence, it lacks credibility or if, for whatever reason, the courts find it unconvincing—the judge should decide issues of fact in accordance with the evidence before him.

597 There were no special rules governing the receipt of expert evidence in such cases. The standard that he had to consider was that of the "ordinary user" raised in *Morgan* v. *Liverpool Corporation* [1927] 2 KB 131.

598 The Court of Appeal so stated in a reserved judgment in *Dover.*

599 *The Times*, reporting on the *Dover* case, said:

> "Lord Justice Evans said that Mr Arden had opened the appeal as one which raised a question of general importance, namely, whether the county court judge should adopt what he called a 'commonsense, lay, factual approach' in cases of the present sort or whether such cases depended

upon technical issues which the judge decided in accordance with the expert evidence and was not free, on those technical matters, to substitute his own opinion.

His Lordship would prefer to stick to the general rule that issues of fact were for the judge to decide in accordance with the evidence given before him.

Where expert evidence was admissible in order to enable the judge to reach a properly informed decision on a technical matter then he could not set his own lay opinion against the expert evidence that he had heard.

But he was not bound to accept the evidence even of an expert witness, if there was a proper basis for rejecting it in the other evidence that he had heard, or the expert evidence was such that he did not believe it or for whatever reason was not convinced by it.

That was the effect of *Patel* v. *Mehtab* (1980) 5 HLR 78 and was wholly consistent with leading authorities such as *McLoughlin* v. *O'Brian* [1983] 1 AC 410, 432–3.

The appeal fell to be decided in accordance with general principles with two aspects raising issues of some general importance.

Standard to be applied

His Lordship agreed that the appropriate standard in accordance with the statutory language was objective, but it did not follow that the experience or even the wishes of current occupiers must necessarily be disregarded in assessing what the standards of ordinary user were: see Lord Atkin's test in *Morgan* (at p. 145).

The question was whether the approach to section 604(1) of the Housing Act 1985, as amended by section 165(1) of the Local Government and Housing Act 1989, still depended upon the standards of ordinary use, as defined by the evidence but taking account also of the judge's knowledge of contemporary affairs, and his Lordship would unhesitatingly answer that it did. The Atkin test of 'ordinary user' still applied.

Status of expert evidence

His Lordship did not consider that there were special rules that governed the receipt of expert evidence in cases such as the present.

The challenge would fail."

600 The point for experts to note from this case is that the judge cannot set himself up in opposition to properly admitted expert evidence.

EXPERT IS CLEARLY PARTISAN

The facts

601 In a reference involving a dispute over the installation of a chemical plant the specialist arbitrator was sufficiently knowledgeable about the intricacies of the process to know that the claimant's expert's report was heavily weighted in his client's favour. As a result the report was less credible than it might otherwise have been.

602 The respondent's expert, on the other hand, had offered a balanced view—admittedly concluding in his client's favour, as might be expected.

603 The arbitrator had only read the expert's report in the days preceding the commencement of the hearing so there was no time to take any action on this report prior to the hearing.

Question

604 What action, if any, should the arbitrator take concerning this clearly biased and unhelpful expert's report?

Course of action

605 There is little the arbitrator can do at this late stage. He will have to rely on the oral examination of the expert who prepared this unhelpful report and trust that the opposing advocate will expose its deficiencies.

606 If the hearing is scheduled over several days or weeks and therefore the experts are not due to be heard until sometime later, it might do no harm to draw attention to the claimant's representative what Mr Justice Laddie had to say in *Cala Homes* v. *Alfred McAlpine Ltd* [1995] CILL 1083 where he held that an expert

> "should not consider that it is his job to stand shoulder to shoulder through thick and thin with a side which is paying his bill".

607 He went on to state that if the court forms the view that the expert has approached the drafting of his report as a "partisan hired gun" the result would be that

> "the expert's report and then his oral evidence will be contained by this attempted sleight of mind".

608 With such a broad hint the claimant might well instruct his expert to amend his report and produce a copy to the other side for consideration prior to the experts being examined.

609 Ronald Bernstein classified partisan experts under two heads—subconscious and deliberate. Of these two classes he says this:

> **"One or both of the experts has become partisan**
>
> Partisanship by one or both experts accounts for eighty to ninety per cent of the cases in which I have been concerned.
>
> In his perceptive article in *Arbitration*, August 1990, p. 159 Francis Goodall says
>
> > 'We fool ourselves if we imagine that the expert in a legal action can hold himself uncommitted.'
>
> He also says:
>
> > 'The great part of the expert's report goes into the earlier stages; into advice at the very outset and into the subsequent preparation of a report whose persuasive arguments will play a significant part in the negotiating process whereby, in so many instances, an actual trial or arbitration is avoided altogether.'
>
> Whether the expert takes an oath or not, his duty once he becomes a witness is the same: to tell the truth, the whole truth and nothing but the truth. But—to quote from Bacon's Essay:
>
> > 'What is the truth? said jesting Pilate—and would not stay for an answer.'

Consider these statements by an experienced valuer contained in a letter to his client which I read recently:

> 'I can't find evidence to support a rental value for this property of more than £12,000 *per annum*.
> I believe I could get £15,000 a year if I had it for letting.
> I am asking for £20,000 a year.'

He negotiates; he will ultimately offer to settle at £13,500 or thereabouts to avoid the risks and cost of a hearing. But if his offer is refused, what value will he ascribe to the premises in the report which he exchanges with his opponent and delivers to the arbitrator? In all too many cases he states as his opinion that the market value of the premises is £20,000. Is he lying, or has he persuaded himself that the market value is really £20,000? And if the latter, how has an experienced professional man so easily persuaded himself that his earlier, considered opinion was 33 per cent wrong?

The difficulties arise from the fact that (as Francis Goodall points out) within the normal sequence of events leading to arbitration or litigation the expert performs three different roles: the expert giving an opinion to his client; the expert as negotiator; and the expert as witness.

The role of adviser to the client in theory presents no problem; you assess the problem and state your opinion. But in practice this stage often raises the greatest difficulty. It is a human tendency to want to please—to tell the client what he wants to hear, particularly if a great deal turns upon his opinion for the client.

If a prospective lawsuit is likely to mean, for the client, the difference between riches and bankruptcy, it requires strength of character to tell him that in your opinion he has no case. Moreover, advising that he has no case may mean talking yourself out of what could be a lucrative case—which someone else will take on if you won't. There is no easy solution to this difficulty. But it is by not grasping the nettle at this early stage that you can do the maximum harm to your client. For if you yield to the temptation to tell the client that he has a strong case when you believe he has a weak case or none at all, it becomes impracticable to retreat later from an untenable position. A significant proportion of disastrous cases result from the expert's failure to give a disinterested assessment at the outset.

One expert has become deliberately partisan

There has been much fine argument on this question, but my mind is clear on it. Anyone who goes into the witness box and states as his opinion something other than his honest opinion, is a liar. Moreover, if he is giving his evidence under oath he is a perjurer. An expert who knowingly 'shades' his opinion according to which side employs him is a liar. A man (or woman) who believes that the value of a picture on the open market is anything between £100,000 and £150,000 cannot, in honesty, state as his expert opinon of its value £100,000 if called for one party or £150,000 if called for the other.

And that is true whether or not he is giving evidence on oath, and whether he is making the statement in the witness box or in a report or proof intended to be received as evidence, e.g. in an arbitration on written representations only.

But this paper is concerned with the efficacy, not the ethics, of lying, or 'shading' as it is sometimes called, when giving an opinion in litigation or arbitration. In my experience it is usually easier for a judge or arbitrator to spot a liar than to detect that an expert witness has become partisan, so that the opinion he is expressing in evidence is one of which he has persuaded himself. It follows that an expert who lies to further his client's case may increase the prospects of a favourable settlement of the case; but he also greatly increases the chances that if the matter proceeds to a hearing his lies will be detected and his client will lose the case at the most expensive stage, and thereby suffer the maximum harm."

610 Another lawyer who found experts to be partisan was Richard Southwell QC sitting as a Deputy Judge in the Queen's Bench Division in *Burroughs Day* v. *Bristol City Council* [1996] 1 EGLR 167; where, referring to the seven duties and responsibilities of expert witnesses as set out in the judgment in the Court of Appeal decision in *The Ikarian Reefer* (see paras 001 to 052 above), he had this to say:

"It is unfortunate that in the current 1995 edition of the *Supreme Court Practice* (the *White Book*) there is no reference to *The Ikarian Reefer* for example, in the notes to the relevant part of Order 38 (rules 35–44) and no reference to any of the principles or guidance relating to the preparation of experts' reports. *The Ikarian Reefer* is mentioned only in note 104/13/1 (on p. 1569) in relation to Order 104, rule 13 concerning experts in patent and other intellectual property proceedings.

My judicial experience in the High Court is that of a Deputy Judge, and therefore less frequent than the experience of a full-time High Court judge. I have found, when sitting as a Deputy Judge, little appreciation on the part of litigators, advocates and expert witnesses of these elementary requirements governing the production of expert evidence.

In the present case, as I have indicated,

(1) Some of the expert witnesses were not independent, being employees or ex-employees of the council.
(2) Some of the expert witnesses apparently thought that it was an essential part of their function as experts to act as supplementary advocates for their clients, the council.
(3) Each of the expert witnesses, who were architects or town planners, took it upon himself to reach conclusions as to the interpretation of the statutory provisions, a matter of which expert opinion from a non-lawyer is neither admissible nor helpful.

I hope that in the next *Supplement to the White Book*, or by some other means, it will be possible to bring to the attention of the legal profession the simple requirements to be met by expert witnesses as summarised in *The Ikarian Reefer.*"

611 Fine, said Thomasina, but what if an expert is being paid a fee contingent on the success of the case? Clearly in such circumstances this expert would be partisan. Of course, she was absolutely right. If it came to my attention that an expert was engaged on such terms I would draw the attention of the party's representative who produced this expert to the *Guidance Note on Contingency Fees* issued by the Judicial Committee in 1995.

612 This note reads as follows:

"It has come to the Judicial Committee's attention that there is increasing pressure for expert witnesses involved in litigation to be paid on a contingency fee basis. This causes the Judicial Committee concern.

It is clearly established law that expert witnesses in adversarial proceedings must give the court, or tribunal, their independent, objective and unbiased opinions on the aspects of the case that comes within their expertise. The expert witness is not an advocate employed on behalf of a party.

An expert witness' written report and oral evidence must genuinely reflect his independent opinion. An expert must not mislead a court or tribunal by placing undue emphasis on points that favour his client, whilst omitting or understating legitimate points that he believes go against his client.

The Judicial Committee considers that any form of contingency fee arrangement for expert witnesses is incompatible with the experts' duty of independence and impartiality. A contingency fee means that the expert witness has a direct financial interest in the outcome of the case. Such a direct financial interest must increase the pressures on expert witnesses to give evidence that favours their client. Even if an expert witness resists this pressure, his independence may still be compromised. An expert witness must not only be independent, but must be seen to be independent.

The Judicial Committee considers that a contingency fee arrangement, in this context, is an arrangement that leads to the expert witness having a financial interest in the outcome of the particular case. Examples of such an agreement include:

- an agreement that the expert witness will be paid a percentage of any damages recovered by his client;
- an agreement that the expert witness will be paid a basic fee together with a bonus if his client wins; and
- an agreement that the expert witness will be paid a percentage of his fee in advance, but will not bill the client for the rest of the fee if the client loses.

The Judicial Committee also understands that solicitors sometimes place undue pressure on expert witnesses. For example, there are instances when a solicitor has indicated to an expert that if he agrees to the solicitor's terms, he will be placed on the firm's approved list of experts. The clear implication being that the expert will then receive further referral work from the solicitor. The Judicial Committee considers that this practice is objectionable and does compromise the expert's independence and impartiality.

If an expert feels that a solicitor has attempted to exert improper pressure on him or her, the expert should report the matter to the Academy.

Council at its meeting on 14 June 1995 adopted the Guidelines."

(All of the references in the above extract to The Academy, The Council and the Judicial Committee relate to The Academy of Experts.) (See also paras 001 to 052 above.)

EXPERT DEVIATES FROM HIS REPORT AND ARGUES MERITS OF HIS PARTY'S CASE

The facts

613 In the course of giving evidence for the claimant who averred that the design of roof trusses for the building were inadequate, the expert structural engineer after stating why the measurements of the trusses were inadequate went on to argue that in so finding as fact it must be the case that the respondent's (engineers) were in breach of their duty under the terms of their engagement/appointment and further in breach of their duty of care in negligence (an issue which had not been pleaded in the statement of case).

614 Counsel for the respondent vehemently objected to the claimant's expert's unsolicited opinion pointing out, respectfully, to the arbitrator that this was not a pleaded issue and as such they requested this evidence be struck out as any issue of negligence was in excess of the arbitrator's jurisdiction.

Question

615 What action, if any, could or should the arbitrator take?

Course of action

616 The fundamental role of the expert witness is to give the arbitrator and his client's legal advisers the benefit of his opinion evidence whether by way of a report to be used in evidence or by advice to the client about the technical merits of the case. In stating that the roof trusses were inadequate the expert structural engineer was proferring an opinion not stating a fact.

617 In the course of giving evidence an expert witness has no duty to act as an advocate of his client. This expert cannot specifically be an advocate, for in putting his client's case he destroys his impartiality or independence (see para 025). The client will already have retained an advocate in most cases, albeit in some construction cases claims consultant quantity surveyors are retained as advocates. If they are so retained they must be very careful not to confuse the role of advocate and expert. To do so is improper and undermines the impartial and independent role of the expert witness (paras 601–612 above).

618 In categorising the duties and responsibilities of expert witnesses Cresswell J in *The Ikarian Reefer* said:

> "An expert witness should provide independent assistance to the court by way of objective unbiased opinion in relation to matters within his expertise."

619 See *Polivitte Ltd* v. *Commercial Union Assurance Co* [1987] 1 Lloyd's Rep 379 at 386 *per* Garland J and *Re J* [1990] FCR 193 *per* Cazalet J. An expert witness in the High Court should never assume the role of an advocate.

620 An expert who becomes adversarial will lose credibility. Lord Macmillan once said:

> "The true role of the Expert Witness is to offer the court the best assistance he can at getting at the truth. It is in some form of consultative capacity that the abilities of professional men are best utilised in the public service."

621 In *Lord Abinger* v. *Ashton* (unreported) Sir George Jessel MR said:

> "Undoubtedly there is a natural bias to do something serviceable for those who employ you and adequately remunerate you. It is very natural and it is so effective that we constantly see persons, instead of considering themselves witnesses, rather consider themselves the paid agents of the persons who employ them."

622 Here the arbitrator would be acting perfectly reasonably in acceding to the respondent's counsel's application. As an unpleaded issue he has no jurisdiction to hear or determine it.

623 The arbitrator could do well to remind the expert that his primary function was to assist him and not to act as an advocate even for the pleaded issues. So far as the issue of negligence was unpleaded he would formally strike it from his note.

624 When Thomasina and I were discussing this Charley happened to drop into the office and told us of a similar experience that he and his pupil master had in a recent rent review arbitration where a surveyor who was the claimant's only representative in giving evidence on oath was clearly arguing his client's case.

625 The arbitrator explained the duties of an advocate and the duties of an expert witness to the surveyor and cautioned him to observe this distinction when giving evidence as an expert.

626 The arbitrator told the surveyor that an advocate's duty is to present and argue a party's case both generally and specifically. This extends to all relevant propositions of law appropriate to the issues. Advocates do not give evidence. This is dependent on professional etiquette rather than exclusionary rules. An advocate has a duty to a tribunal to introduce relevant authorities irrespective of whether or not an authority assists a party.

627 The arbitrator also reminded the parties' representatives that his knowledge and experience was limited to understanding the parties' contentions. These representatives must not suppose that he will do their work for them. He is expected to receive the evidence of witnesses and the submissions of advocates and to be guided by them in reaching his conclusions (see *Fox* v. *Wellfair* [1981] 2 Lloyd's Rep 514 CA).

628 The arbitrator went on to explain that he was not appointed to investigate the truth of the matter but to say who had adduced the heavier evidence and/or the most convincing arguments as to law. An arbitrator does not develop rival arguments or fill deficiencies. The conduct of the party's case is in the hands of the party. These principles derive from the adversarial system in the English jurisdiction.

629 The arbitrator pointed out that under s.34(2)(g), AA '96, unless the parties agreed otherwise, the arbitrator may take the initiative in ascertaining the facts and the law. Accordingly the arbitrator may adopt an inquisitorial role by asking questions on matters introduced. This may save considerable time. However, the arbitrator could ensure that if he procures evidence/submission he must give the parties a reasonable opportunity to comment—reflecting the provisions of s.33, AA '96.

630 Lord Bingham in *Abbey National Mortgages plc* v. *Key Surveyors Nationwide Ltd* [1996] 33 EG 88 CA pointed out that a court would not block reasonable attempts to mitigate the defects of established practice provided that a fair procedure cannot be compromised.

WHEN AN EXPERT'S REPORT CONSISTS MAINLY OF HEARSAY, ADVOCACY AND SUBMISSIONS, CAN IT BE STRUCK OUT IN ITS ENTIRETY?

The facts

631 The Official Receiver commenced proceedings under the Company Directors Disqualification Act 1986.

632 The directors concerned engaged independent accountants to give evidence on their behalf.

633 Each of these accountants commenced their reports with the words:

> "The report has been prepared for the purpose of supporting the defence of Mr X."

634 The judge said that this was not a promising start.

635 The reports went on in advocacy terms, attempting, in one instance, to discredit one of the other directors and, in another, extolling the business acumen of the director at whose behest he had been called.

Question

636 In such a blatant exhibition of advocacy by an expert could the accountants' affidavits be struck out and, if so, on what grounds?

Course of action

637 The brief facts of this example are drawn from *Re Oakfame Construction Ltd* (1995) unreported before R Reed QC, sitting in the Chancery Division as a Deputy High Court Judge.

638 The court struck out the affidavits sworn by the two accountants on the grounds that they were irrelevant and oppressive under RSC Order 41, rule 6.

639 In order to understand the court's reason for taking this seemingly draconian line, it is necessary to refer to Mr Reed QC's judgment where, *inter alia*, he said this:

> "I have before me a summons by which the official receiver, in proceedings under the Company Directors Disqualification Act 1986, seeks to strike out all or part of the affidavits of two accountants who have put in affidavit evidence on behalf of the respondents to the summons, Mr Peteranna and Mr Howe.
>
> The summons is under Ord. 41, r.6 of the Rules of the Supreme Court, which, in its present form reads as follows:
>
> > 'The court may order to be struck out of any affidavit any matter which is scandalous, irrelevant or otherwise oppressive.'
>
> The notes to that rule read as follows:
>
> > 'An affidavit must be pertinent and material and may be ordered to be taken off the file if scandalous and irrelevant matter is inserted (*Rossage* v. *Rossage* ...) or the scandalous matter may be expunged (*Warner* v. *Moses* ...). The court will only strike out matter that is both scandalous and irrelevant, or is otherwise oppressive (*per* Buckley LJ *Re Jessop* [1910] WN 128, a case in which the CA refused to strike out extracts from letters marked "without prejudice"). The court is not bound to strike out such matter (*Re J* ...).'
>
> The note as it stands is misleading because the authority cited (*Re Jessop*) related to the rule Ord. 38, r.10, which permitted the striking out of affidavits only in relation to scandalous material. As Peter Gibson J pointed out in *Savings and Investment Bank Ltd* v. *Gasco Investments (Netherlands) BV* [1984] 1 WLR 271, in a passage at 277, the rule as it presently stands is disjunctive, so it is possible for material to be struck out if it is irrelevant or otherwise oppressive, even if it is not also scandalous.
>
> In the present case it is said that the affidavits are irrelevant or otherwise oppressive because the exhibited reports forming the substance of the evidence contain hearsay, advocacy and submissions rather than expert opinion. It is said they simply comment on matters without expressing the opinion of an expert.
>
> When looking at evidence sought to be adduced on matters of opinion, one must start from the position that opinion evidence is not generally admissible. However, by way of exception the opinion of an expert may be admissible. The general principle is that evidence of opinion, that is conclusions drawn from received facts, is not admissible but an expert called as a witness in civil proceedings can give evidence of his opinion upon relevant matters.
>
> For the purposes of the summons before me, I assume that the two deponents in question can properly be called experts though I have to say that there might have been some argument or doubt about it in the light of the paucity of material in their respective *CV*'s. It may well be that a fuller statement of their qualifications would have cleared up any doubt on that topic but at present the statements of those qualifications are skeletal at best.
>
> **What is the function of an expert witness?**
>
> An expert witness is not an advocate. The duty of an expert witness is to record the facts and state what in his expert opinion are the implications. The duty of an advocate is to persuade the court as to the construction, legal or otherwise, that it should place not only upon the facts but also upon the implications as indicated by the expert witness. The *locus classicus* now in relation to the functions and duties of experts is in the judgment of Cresswell J in *The Ikarian Reefer* [1993] 2 Lloyd's Rep 68 in a passage beginning at 81. I need for present purposes read only the first three heads of what he says:

'(1) Expert evidence presented to the court should be, and should be seen to be, the independent product of the expert uninfluenced as to form or content by the exigencies of litigation (*Whitehouse* v. *Jordan* [1981] 1 WLR 246 at 256 *per* Lord Wilberforce).

(2) An expert witness should provide independent assistance to the court by way of objective unbiased opinion in relation to matters within his expertise (see *Polivitte* v. *Commercial Union Assurance Co plc* [1987] 1 Lloyd's Rep 379 at 386 *per* Garland J and *Re J* [1990] FCR 193 *per* Cazalet J). An expert witness in the High Court should never assume the role of an advocate.

(3) An expert witness should state the facts or assumption upon which his opinion is based. He should not omit to consider material facts which could detract from his concluded opinion (*Re J supra*).'

I should add although he must state the facts and assumptions on which he forms his opinion, and will usefully state the sources from which he derives those facts and assumptions, he cannot himself introduce hearsay evidence. The authority for that is the well known decision of *English Exporters (London) Ltd* v. *Eldonwall Ltd* [1973] Ch 415, a decision of the former Vice-Chancellor, Sir Robert Megarry.

In the present case against that background I must look first briefly at the issues. This is a directors disqualification application and for present purposes all I need do is look at p. 33, at the beginning of para. 81, of the affidavit and Mr Titherington to set the scene of what is alleged to show unfitness. He there says:

'With regard to the affairs of *Oakfame*'—that is the company in question—'the following, in my opinion, are matters by reference to which the respondent is unfit to be concerned in the management of the company:

82. That the respondents failed both to ensure the accounting records of *Oakfame* maintained were sufficient to comply with s.221 and/or they were preserved under s.222 of the Companies Act 1985, and/or failed to deliver up the accounting records maintained.'

He then gives a reference to the paragraphs where that is substantively dealt with in his evidence.

'83. The respondents caused the failure of *Oakfame* and the detriment of creditors by:

84. Knowingly continuing its business beyond a date when there was no reasonable prospect of all creditors being paid (paras 37–50); and/by

85. Financing its business with'—he then gives a large sum of money—'retained from revenues collected on behalf of the Crown (paras 57–62); and/by

86. Tendering cheques to creditors and sub-contractors without due regard to the prospect of their being honoured on presentation (paras 30–31); and/by

87. Preferring themselves, by reducing the bank overdraft which they had guaranteed (paras 66–69).

88. Transferred a valuable asset to the first respondent to the detriment of the creditors (paras 51–56).

89. The first respondent failed to comply with his obligations in the proceedings to supply information to the official receiver and liquidator regarding the various assets and transactions (paras 70–81).'

That is a summary of what might inaccurately be called the charges laid, and it is to deal with those that the two experts were called upon to provide in their evidence.

The first point that must be made about that evidence is that it is in a form which makes it clear that each of them is putting himself forward not as an independent and unbiased expert, doing his best to assist the court, but as an advocate. Paragraph 2 of the report of the expert whose evidence is filed on behalf of the first respondent, Mr Peteranna, says:

'This report has been prepared for the purpose of supporting the defence of Mr Peteranna.'

The second paragraph of the expert instructed on behalf of the second respondent is in similar terms:

> 'This report has been prepared for the purpose of supporting the defence of Mr Howe.'

That is not a promising start.

I then turn to look and see what it is that they put in their respective reports. The first five paragraphs of the first respondent's expert are introductory. The tenor of his report, however, can be gained from the first two sentences of para. 6, under the heading 'General'.

> 'The applicant's identification of the potential error in the statement of affairs dated 12 June 1991 is an initial attempt to discredit the first respondent. We feel that this has been done on the basis of inaccurate and insufficient documentary proof.'

As discussed, it goes on in more detail in this report:

> 'the applicant has not made sufficient attempts to justify his claims and figures.'

That clearly is not either a statement of sources or a necessary lead into, or statement of expert opinion of, a matter to which expert evidence properly relates.

The following paragraphs 7 and 8, state facts derived from documentation which is in evidence. Paragraph 9 reads as follows:

> 'We consider that the above noted level of salaries and profit indicates the directors intended to operate the business on a profitable basis, whilst only drawing a level of income that could be sustained from the profits of the company. We do not consider that these figures would indicate that the directors were looking to draw a high level of income to the detriment of the creditors.'

In my judgement, that cannot possibly be considered proper expert evidence from an accountant.

When one goes on through the report exhibited with the affidavit, one sees, for example, at para. 11:

> 'The respondents had been working together for 20 or more years, until the incorporation of *Oakfame*. Throughout their business relationship the first respondent has always, we understand, been in a position to clear his business liabilities and we are not aware of any instances of insolvent action being taken against Mr Peteranna, or of any county court judgments being issued against him as a result of his business activities.'

Again, that is clearly a matter which is not appropriate to include in what is intended to be an expert accountant's report dealing with issues in the proceedings.

The first point at which one comes to something which might be regarded as being an expert accountant's view is at para. 13. That paragraph is in these terms.

> 'Having reviewed the audited accounts, we estimate the following profile of the amount due to HM Inspector of Taxes for PAYE and subcontractors' taxes may, in fact, reflect the actual position for each year. Estimated taxes due: year ended 31 October 1987, £56,306; year ended 31 October 1988, £92,715; year ended 31 October 1989, £128,146. Estimated amounts paid: year ended 31 October 1987, £46,298; year ended 31 October 1988, £74,268; year ended 31 October 1989, £62,336.'

That, in some other context, or if it were placed in the proper context, might be a valuable expert's assessment of the matter in issue. Stated simply in that form with no proper explanation and no workings, I find it difficult to see that can be relevant and proper material to be placed before the court. One might have expected the report to go on to set out some workings, why it was, for example, the review of the audited accounts produced these estimates. It does not. It goes on in these terms:

> '14. It can be seen from the early years of trading that the company was maintaining a satisfactory level of payments to HM Inspector of Taxes of PAYE and subcontractor taxes. In fact we understand that, prior to incorporation, amounts due to HM Inspector of Taxes maintained a satisfactory profile.'

That last sentence, in particular, causes considerable difficulty. How a company could have had a satisfactory profile prior to its incorporation is a little difficult to see. Paragraphs 15–23 are a mixture of hearsay and advocacy, and at least in the case of para. 16, a statement of self-inconsistent fact because in para. 16 the deponent says that his review of the statutory accounts reveals that HM Customs and Excise were a debtor to the company in, amongst others, the year ended 31 October 1988, in the sum of £9,263. He then goes on:

> 'in the year ended 31 October 1988 the company owed HM Customs & Excise £40,556.'

Going through to para. 23, we then come to what does appear to be an expression of an expert's opinion, in these terms:

> '... we consider that it is not unusual for a small proprietor managed business, such as *Oakfame*, to send cheque books, paying-in books, invoices and receipts to their accountants, who would be operating on instructions to maintain books and records on behalf of the company and to assist in the preparation of VAT returns for submission to HM Customs & Excise.
>
> 24. It is our experience that such businesses place reliance on the professional standards of their accountants in assisting in maintaining proper books and records as required under s.221 of the Companies Act 1985. In situations where the company directors do not have the relevant book-keeping and accounting expertise the services of outside accountants are employed, as would appear to have been the case in this instance since the incorporation of the company.'

That might form a passage in a properly constructed report if the deponent were seeking to show that, as a matter of his expert judgment, the way these proprietors, these shareholders and directors had managed their business, was a standard and approved method of doing so. It appears, however, stuck in a long series of submissions and hearsay evidence. I think it would be undesirable simply to strike out all around that and leave a couple of paragraphs of that sort standing on their own.

Going on, then, to para. 26 which is under a heading 'Specific comments on the applicant's affidavit', para. 26 points out what is said to be an error of arithmetic. Paragraphs 27 and 28 make some assertions of fact as to the cause of the failure of the company and repeat statements made by the second respondent in his questionnaire. Paragraph 29, under the heading 'Failure to preserve accounting records', retells the fact that Mr Peteranna says that some of the accounting documents of the company, as well as his briefcase, were stolen from his car. It goes on to express the view that it would have been possible to prepare accounts notwithstanding the difficulties that the loss had caused. Paragraph 30 goes on to say that there was a sales day book in which the final entry is generally headed 'September 1990' because he understands that no invoices were raised after that date.

That is confirmed by the second respondent in answer to his questionnaire. Paragraph 31 refers to it being a normal accounting practice for accountants to maintain a debtors' ledger although the first respondent had stated that no debtors' ledger was maintained by the company. Again, it is difficult to see how that is a matter of expert opinion relevant to the case.

Paragraph 32 makes some assertions of fact. It contains passages such as:

'We do not believe we have a complete document reference "PT18".'

—and some beliefs as to the deponent's statement of facts:

'we believe that the £400,000 is calculated by reference to ...'

—certain matters, and so on, down to para. 35 where the deponents appear to be expressing an opinion. That paragraph is in this form:

> 'It is our experience that in small proprietor managed companies, personal injections of funds by either director, or withdrawal thereof, is normally well known to each of them. Such transactions would not normally form part of the normal course of business of the company and accordingly it is our experience that directors are always aware of these transactions especially when relying on the professional assistance of accountants. ...'

That is hardly a matter of expert accounting evidence. If it is intended to be prefacing a view that it was the fact that the directors of a small company would know about personal injections of funds or withdrawal of funds by either director, and therefore would not see if they were recorded in the books, that is something which perhaps should be spelled out in far greater clarity and detail.

Then the report goes on through a variety of matters which are mainly derivations of statements of fact from elsewhere in the evidence; there is one further expression of opinion as to the level of petty cash not being material for the size of the company. Again, that is hardly a matter which, standing alone, would form a proper subject of expert evidence, still less as a throwaway line seven-eighths of the way through a report. There then follow comments on trading with knowledge of insolvency which expressed no experts' opinions. There is a quibble about the *quantum* of retention of Crown moneys, asserting that there is double counting, though this deponent does not give any sort of indication of how he reaches that conclusion, and an assertion that the deponent considers that the statement of affairs is wrong by an estimated sum of £138,400.03. There then follows a comment on the misuse of the bank account and some assertions of fact exhibiting the particulars of claim by a building society in a possession action against the first respondent and his wife. The assertions of facts relate to allegations of misfeasance and misconduct during the course of the liquidation.

The difficulty, when one looks at the report annexed to the affidavit overall is that it does not state clearly the basis on which the expert is purporting to draw expert opinions. It does not identify what the expert opinions are supposed to be, or to what issues they are supposed to go. I respectfully suggest it had not been thought through by reference to any consideration of what might usefully be the role of an expert in this particular case.

In my judgement, the vast bulk of this report, and hence the affidavit of which it forms the only substantive part, is irrelevant in that it is advocacy, hearsay evidence, and comment. It is not what can properly be regarded as being a proper expert's report for the purpose of this litigation, aimed at specific matters on which expert opinion could properly be sought and on which expert opinion evidence would properly be admitted.

I therefore take the view that the whole of the affidavit sworn by the expert instructed on behalf of the first respondent ought to be struck out.

I turn to the second expert's report, that exhibited to an affidavit sworn on behalf of the expert instructed on behalf of the second respondent. It was accepted very realistically in the course of argument before me that the first two heads of this expert's report, headed '(1) The purchase of *Oakfame Construction Ltd* of a property at 20 Wick Lane, Bow' and '(2) A transaction involving a Rover motorcar' comprised matters which were not properly expert evidence and no effort was made to suggest those parts ought to be retained. As to the third part, headed 'Inland Revenue', that contains at the third substantive paragraph of that section—it is not, I am afraid, numbered—a reference to an appendix in which the summary of information is set out and which is undoubtedly a useful document. In my judgement, useful though this is, it is not a matter for expert evidence from an accountant. It is not an expression of his opinion about anything. It is simply a useful exercise in collation. The remainder of the report deals with such matters as difficulties through inability to find documents that had been mislaid, matters which have been related to the deponent by the second respondent and so forth. In my judgement, none of the remainder of that can properly be regarded as expert opinion evidence. There then follow three subheads under the heading 'Other matters', one relating to VAT which boils down to this; there is an assertion that the records kept by the company were sufficient to comply with their obligations to Customs & Excise in respect of VAT, even if they did not comply with s.221 of the Companies Act; then, the subheading, 'The Hawksmill Development Company Ltd', which does no more than exhibit some searches and retell one or two matters set out elsewhere in the evidence; and, thirdly, the subheading 'Bank of Ireland', which contains comment, no doubt useful for cross-examination but not a matter for expert evidence. I will read it to show the flavour of it:

> 'The applicant at para. 69 suggests the two respondents chose to use moneys received by the company to reduce the overdraft to their ultimate benefit. This statement is clearly in conflict with the statement made in para. 44 where the applicant identifies 118 separate occasions when the Bank of Ireland returned cheques. The second respondent has confirmed that he understood the Bank of Ireland from time to time set overdraft limits within which the company had to maintain its borrowings.'

One simply has to read it to demonstrate that it is not appropriate material for an expert's opinion report.

In my judgement, therefore, this report too should be struck out and with it the affidavit which exhibits it, because that affidavit has no other useful purpose. It does not mean that useful material cannot be gleaned from the work those two accountants have done, which will assist counsel and solicitors in their preparation of the case. They have pointed up, for example, various prospective deponents on matters of fact. They have pointed up various matters on which comment might be made. They have pointed up areas on which cross-examination might be directed at Mr Titherington, the principal deponent, and one of the joint liquidators of this particular company. But the fact that such assistance may be rendered to counsel and to their instructing solicitors does not mean that those reports are appropriate reports to be put in as expert opinion evidence before the court. In my judgement, they quite clearly are not. I would suggest that if there is going to be any further effort to adduce expert evidence to replace that which I have now struck out, it would behove those acting on behalf of the two respondents to think carefully as to what areas there are in relation to which expert opinion could be useful in this particular case. They should bear in mind the distinction between material useful for priming themselves for making submissions and for cross-examining deponents, and material which can properly be placed before the court as expert testimony. They should not try to put in as expert evidence what is better described as preparatory work to help in the preparation of argument or cross-examination.

I am not suggesting that it is inappropriate to have expert evidence in director disqualification cases. It depends on the particular case. Nor am I suggesting that it is inappropriate for the Legal Aid Fund to authorise expenditure on an accountant to assist in analysing accounts and assist solicitors and counsel in the preparation of their case. But what does appear from the attempt to put evidence in in this case is that there are those who have not appreciated either what the true role of the expert witness is, or the circumstances in which expert evidence can be adduced and may be of assistance to the court.

It follows that I give the relief sought by the summons and I strike out both of those affidavits on the primary ground that they are irrelevant but also on the basis that, as they stand, they are oppressive."

640 So what is the lesson for experts to learn from this case? In the words of Tony Bingham, reporting on this case (*Building*, 27 February 1998),

"Root but don't toot."

641 What Tony says is this:

"First, if you give evidence in arbitration or litigation, the tribunal will shut you up if you start expressing an opinion. Opinion evidence has a starting point of being inadmissible. A witness is there to testify to the facts as he or she knows them. That is the formal position. However, by way of exception, the opinion of an expert may be admissible.

The rules for expert opinion are important, which brings me to my second point. The courts have got fed up with terrorist experts and hired guns. This kind of expert confuses everyone since he becomes part of the mob that wants to win. The loud and clear message from a case five years ago was that the expert's evidence has to be independent and uninfluenced by the 'pressures' of litigation. Moreover, the expert is to give objective, unbiased (ouch) opinion and not fail to consider material facts that could detract (ouch) from his concluded opinion.

Oakfame gets to grips with a problem that frequently arises in construction disputes, which is when the expert wants to do my job and be the advocate. The message was clear: the judge simply slung out the evidence of the two expert witnesses. And, what is more, he threw out the good parts (the parts that were proper admissible opinion) with the bad. It was baby and bath-water stuff. It is a judgment with a message. It explains, I think, how the expert can be independent and objective and also be part of my team. Experts can root but not toot."

642 Then, after discussing some of the judge's findings, Tony concluded thus:

"Undeniably, the expert is part of the team. Undeniably, he has to give evidence that is objective, independent, impartial, whole and complete. And, undeniably, he can help his client's legal team by suggesting to them lines of enquiry about his client or about the opposing party or the opposing party's witness, whether expert or mere fact. A gem of an expert will assist the advocate, telling him which parts of the other side's evidence are doubtful, wrong or daft.

Do not become confused by the role. But do recognise that the expert has been the target of change. The gunslinging, rooting, tooting cowboy has gone—but rooting is still in."

643 So, the position in court is quite clear. A judge can strike out such affidavits under Rules of the Supreme Court, Order 41, rule 6, but what of arbitrators who are not governed by the *White Book* rules?

644 There is no power under the Arbitration Act 1996 to strike out evidence on the ground that it is oppressive so, rather than striking out, I believe the arbitrator should make it clear that he will afford the advocacy element of the experts' reports little or no weight, provided that is, that the parties have made no agreement as to procedural and evidential matters under section 34 and the discretion therefore rests with the arbitrator.

645 Under s.34(2)(f) for example, the arbitrator can decide on:

"admissibility, relevance or weight of any material."

646 Thus, if he was so inclined, the arbitrator could have the best of both worlds. He could give little or no weight for those parts of the experts' reports which he considered irrelevant and admit, with some weight, those parts which the judge suggested

"... might form a passage in a properly constructed report if the deponent were seeking to show [something] as a matter of his expert judgement".

647 This message was reinforced in an article by Jeremy Williams and Peter Garcia in the *Chartered Surveyor Monthly* (April 1998) entitled "Giving expert witness? What the judge might throw out".

648 The authors gave examples of the distinction between the opinion of an expert that could be declared inadmissible, and a factual statement from which a judge will draw a conclusion.

"'The windows do not fit the openings and obviously let in water.'

'The windows have a 5 mm gap to all edges and are not sealed at the reveals. Moisture meter readings to the reveals shows saturation of the plaster.'

The former is the expert's conclusion, which a judge may well discount as such while the latter states facts upon which the judge can easily draw his own conclusion that the gap to the edges of the windows has caused a leak.

The statement of facts used in the second instance does not call into question the expert's technical skills or his professional conduct when compiling a report on behalf of his client.

How then do experts tailor their reports to be useful to legal advisers while satisfying their professional duty of care?

Initially, the expert must ensure that the letter of appointment either from the client or his legal adviser is sufficiently detailed to allow the expert to establish his or her remit properly. In many instances it is, in fact, the initial solicitor's brief which is lacking in detail, and therefore the expert's report does not focus on the points in issue. Before making his inspection of the premises, documents or whatever, the expert should clarify with the instructing solicitor which points are to be covered and what the issues are.

This is not to suggest that the expert and legal adviser should collude in the drafting of the report. That would be quite wrong, and leave both parties open to claims of professional negligence. It is, however, a waste of time and money to examine parts of a building or documents that do not relate to the claim or defence.

A typical scenario is that a report is requested within 28 days. The report duly arrives, but does not deal with the salient points, and experts have to be contacted in order to clarify the issues in dispute. This process then takes a further two weeks or more, during which time the client cannot make or take offers in respect of the proposed action—which could be critical at a later stage if the issues proceeds to court.

Having clarified the scope of the report, the expert must then produce a factual account of his findings. For example, if costings are being examined by a quantity surveyor he must identify which elements are allowable and which are not. Subsequently, he will need to provide some form of authority, showing why he believes such items would fall into either category.

Similarly, if a building is being inspected for defective works such as leaking windows, it must be established that the windows actually leak; then the expert may seek to establish whether this is a design fault or a fault of workmanship. Any such conclusion must be based on facts and capable of being supported by relevant authority, which in this case might be technical manuals, codes of practice or agreement certificates.

An expert should never assume that he will be called as a witness to explain the content of his report, and should therefore prepare it as a stand-alone document that can be presented to the tribunal and clearly understood by all parties to the proceedings.

For this reason it is unacceptable that a report be full of technical prose yet not provide the reader with conclusions which can be easily appreciated by either counsel or judge.

It is the expert's duty to:

- clarify his brief;
- act in an impartial and professional manner;
- establish the relevant facts; and
- provide conclusions that will help the court."

649 The very title of this article, "What the judge might throw out", gives strength to my suggestion that the arbitrator (or, indeed, the judge, if he feels so inclined) can select the good and reject the bad provided there is not so much of the latter, as in the *Re Oakfame* case, that the judge had no choice but to reject the totality of the experts' evidence.

WHEN A JUDGE IS HIGHLY CRITICAL OF EXPERT EVIDENCE

The facts

650 In a Lloyd's underwriting case, mainly concerned with run-off contracts, a large number of the experts were called. However, the judge in that case had cause to criticise many of these experts, in one way or another, in connection with the evidence they sought to adduce.

Question

651 What weight should the judge give to expert evidence?

Course of action

652 It must be remembered that the function of an expert is to assist the tribunal and not to act as advocate for the party calling him (see paras 001 to 052 above).

653 Whilst the facts of this case are irrelevant in the context of this example, the language used by Cresswell J in this case (*Henderson* v. *Merrett* (1995) QBD 31 October) is relevant and of some considerable interest to all witnesses and expert witnesses in particular.

654 The judge made the following comments concerning the expert evidence:

> "... I regret to say that I have serious reservations about many aspects of Mr Merrett's evidence .... Mr Merrett's ... explanation for the inconsistency (is) unconvincing ....
>
> ... After making full allowance for the difficulties that Mr Randall faced ..., I have a number of reservations about his evidence. In particular I consider that Mr Randall was at times inclined to go further than was justified in seeking to defend the approach of the Merrett defendants.
>
> ... I have marked a reservation about Mr Ringer's witness statement, save where the statement contains matters that are agreed between the parties. The statement contains numerous assertions which should have been qualified so as to make it clear that the opinions expressed were based upon research and not on any contemporary experience.
>
> ... Mrs Rowe was expert in claims handling and managing but made no claim to have expertise in underwriting decisions. Mrs Rowe based her report on a reading of limited material.
>
> ... Although Mrs Rowe's evidence must be approached with care having regard, in particular, to the extent of her expertise and her limited consideration of the materials in the case, I formed the impression that she was a sincere and generally a reliable witness.
>
> ... I accept Mrs Rowe's evidence that there are a number of relevant materials missing from the files relating to the ... Syndicate. I was left with the impression that Mrs Rowe was thorough in her statistical analysis.
>
> ... I have carefully considered the contemporary documents relating to ... and with these in mind I have given appropriate weight to Mrs Rowe's evidence in relation to ....
>
> ... I do not accept without reservation the totality of Mrs Rowe's evidence.
>
> A number of paragraphs in Mr Neil's witness statement are open to criticism .... To his credit he was ready to withdraw criticisms if they could not be justified and to acknowledge errors.
>
> ... I found Mr Neil's evidence in relation to the run-off contracts far more compelling than Mr Rome's evidence on that subject ....
>
> ... It is, of course, most unusual for an expert witness to have a financial interest in the result of the case. I do not suggest that it consciously affected Mr Rome's evidence. I have, however, a number of reservations about his evidence for other reasons. In my view Mr Rome's evidence about the writing of the run-off contracts was unrealistic and unreasonably defensive.

I was very impressed with the candid manner in which Mr McNamara gave his evidence. He responded frankly to detailed questioning.

... Mr Attwood was an extremely impressive witness. He has very considerable professional standing and knowledge. He was prepared to withdraw a criticism if it was not justified or supportable.

... I was left with the firm impression that Mr Attwood's evidence was soundly based by reference to appropriate professional standards.

... I regret, however, that I have serious reservations about Mr Whiter's evidence. It seemed to me that he was concerned to defend, without reservation, everything that E & W did in years 4 to 6. I consider, that at times, Mr Whiter's answers were evasive. Some of this evidence was unrealistic.

... I consider at times Mr Whiter's approach was not logical."

655 In making these comments, mainly about the expert witnesses in this case, Cresswell J invariably gave reasons by citing passages of the witnesses' testimony. For this reason the full judgment in this case makes instructive reading for any expert witness.

AN EXPERT SHOULD NOT DISPLAY INTELLECTUAL ARROGANCE

The facts

656 In a multi-party action between a number of the major oil and gas exploration companies, three experts were called.

657 All three were distinguished in their own fields. However, the judge said of these three experts that:

"The quality of their evidence was made more difficult to assess by the manner in which it was given. It was not always apparent to two of them that there is a difference between giving evidence in court and lecturing a class of students."

Question

658 Is it likely that the weight given to an expert's evidence is influenced by that expert's manner?

Course of action

659 The judge's comment given in the facts above comes from *Conoco UK Ltd and Others* v. *Phillips Petroleum Company and Others* (1995), [1997] ADRLN 21.

660 Morison J went on to say this of the two experts of whose evidence he was critical:

"I have had to be careful in making my assessment of their worth to avoid being unduly put off by their manner and demeanour, which from time to time might have strained the patience of leading counsel less courteous or benign than Mr Tomlinson QC, who represented the first three defendants. Without criticising their undoubted competence, I did not find, in general terms, the evidence of either Dr A ... or Dr B ... as helpful as that of Dr N. The evidence of the last-named expert was, frankly, much superior to either of the other two. I thought Dr N was balanced in his approach and did not display the intellectual arrogance which the other two showed from time to time. His evidence was well-reasoned and researched and he ultimately emerged as one of the more impressive expert witnesses whom I have seen in court. In the most general terms, I should say at this stage that whenever the evidence of the experts conflicted, there is no issue on which I did not prefer to accept what Dr N said in preference to the evidence, whether in harmony with each other or not, of the other two."

661 Morison J expanded later in his judgment why he preferred Dr N's evidence to that of the other two experts.

"The adversarial process often requires the judge, where there is a conflict of factual evidence or opinion, to indicate a preference for the evidence of one person as opposed to another. I hope that nothing I say about their worth as witnesses will be thought by Dr A ... or Dr B ... to be a reflection on their academic integrity or capabilities. The reasons why I preferred the evidence of Dr N to either of them may be summarised thus:

1. He showed an obvious detachment; whereas they did not. The transcript will show that they both adopted the role of advocate. They were, therefore, too partisan and their views were often extremely expressed and lacked balance. It was Mr Tomlinson's final submission that both of them were 'arrogant, intransigent, opinionated and oblivious to the possibility that the contrary view of others could conceivably have merit'. In the context of them as witnesses, and in no other context, I would tend to agree with that description.
2. Dr A ... was, I think, wrong to maintain that he had understood how Enclosure 17 had been calculated. His first report was based upon a misunderstanding, and it would have been more impressive if he had accepted that he had made an error.
3. They both persisted, especially in the case of Dr B ... in attributing to ERC base motives in relation to the blanked out square on Enclosure 17 and the words written there. Dr A's rather dramatic characterisation of what he thought had happened seemed to me to show a lack of balance and thoughtfulness. Dr B ... returned to the theme time and time again. He implied that there had been something sinister in ERC's work, yet it became clear that he had not properly checked before making the innuendoes of lack of integrity on ERC's part. Neither of them could give any explanation as to why ERC would go to the trouble of concealing what they had done when Enclosure 17 showed excessively high velocities on it. I was, frankly, rather surprised that these two distinguished experts should have persistently and unjustifiably maintained this assault on ERC's work.
4. Both of them sought to dismiss Dr N's reports in terms seldom used in litigation by one expert of another. I was sufficiently concerned at the lack of respect being shown by them for a different point of view that I felt it necessary to ask them to consider whether there might not be just a genuine disagreement between men of science. Again, this showed, I think, a lack of balance."

662 An object lesson, surely to all experts when giving evidence before any tribunal, arbitrator or court.

EXPERT EVIDENCE IN COMPLETE CONTRADICTION

The facts

663 A commercial dispute had gone through its interlocutory stage and reached the hearing which was scheduled to last ten days.

664 Expert witnesses had met but had been unable to agree on very much. They had subsequently exchanged their reports as directed.

665 On the fourth day of the hearing the first of the experts was to be heard.

Question

666 Is there any action that the arbitrator can take at this late stage to avoid hearing evidence from experts whom he knows are in conflict and then have to decide between these conflicting views?

Course of action

667 In the present reference, at the adjournment at the end of the third day the arbitrator asked the experts to meet again before the hearing resumed the following day. He asked them to reconsider whether in the light of submissions and evidence made so far there were not areas where they were now in agreement. (The arbitrator had in mind his duty under s.33, AA '96 to "adopt procedures suitable to the circumstances of the particular case, avoiding unnecessary delay or expense".)

668 The experts returned at the beginning of the next day with a measure of agreement which shortened the overall hearing by one day.

669 It is not totally unknown for the arbitrator in such circumstances to meet with the experts alone (of course, with the parties' consent) to try to ascertain the reasons for their failure to agree on so little. If solicitors for each side object to such an arrangement unless they themselves are present the arbitrator should accede to their request, counselling them to refrain from involving themselves in the discussion so far as possible. (See *Town & City* v. *Wiltshier* (1988) 44 BLR 109.) The solicitors could play a useful role in instructing their experts at various stages of the discussion, if there were matters on which the experts required direction.

670 The objective of the meeting would not be to attempt to agree matters in issue—or indeed part thereof such as liability or *quantum*—but to attempt to unlock any fundamental difference of approach. The experts are there to assist the tribunal and this assistance will not be of much value of the experts cannot agree on anything.

671 There are two ways that the arbitrator and the parties can approach such meetings. Much depends upon the ability of the parties to agree procedure and evidential matters binding the arbitrator to their agreement or in the absence of such agreement, the arbitrator deciding of his own volition on a particular procedure (s.34, AA '96).

672 If the first option is pursued the arbitrator should make it quite clear to all present that the meeting was of an informal nature. He would treat it very much like the preliminary meeting to clarify issues for his benefit. Nothing either expert said would be evidence and therefore could not be adduced subsequently by the other side. The arbitrator himself would take no note of the meeting.

673 Even if the parties were unwilling to allow the arbitrator to meet informally with their experts—and it would be wrong for the arbitrator to order such a meeting in the face of opposition from one or both parties—sending them away for a further meeting particularly as in this instance they will have had the benefit of hearing three days' evidence can often bear fruit and consequently shorten the hearing time.

674 That's all well and good, Thomasina said, when she read this course of action, but where does that leave the arbitrator where two experts hold diversely opposed views? She cited the rent review dispute where her boyfriend Charley had been involved. His pupil master had been appointed arbitrator to determine the rental upon the first rent review of a series of leisure properties located throughout England.

675 At the preliminary meeting the parties did not disclose any problems relating to legal interpretation or to the agreement of fact and it was agreed that the matter was to proceed by written representations.

676 Following initial submissions, cross-representations and the arbitrator's inspection of the properties, it became obvious to him that there was a total lack of co-operation between the parties. The landlord has adopted a valuation related to his estimated turnover of each property whereas the tenant has adopted a rate per square foot utilising comparables from a wide geographic area.

677 In their counter-representations there was no criticism of the other side's case. Neither party wished to appear to acquiesce to the other side's basis of valuation by putting forward any criticism.

678 The arbitrator recognised that he needed to exercise great care in this situation. He knew that in practice it was very likely that if he drew the parties' attention to his difficulties they would likely respond with a request to him to make further submissions on the other side's valuation method. Despite the inevitable delay which further submissions would cause this was what the arbitrator decided. He felt it important to give each side a further opportunity to respond on the other side's submissions.

679 In the unlikely event that the parties were unwilling to respond to the invitation made by the arbitrator he should prior to publishing his award inform the parties of his dilemma, indicating that in the absence of any further submissions he might be minded to find for a figure between the two contentions. The danger of so doing is exposure to an allegation from the aggrieved party of relying on a method not contended by either party. The award would be based on evidence not introduced in the arbitration. The arbitrator is chosen for his skill and experience in understanding the evidence. He must not rely upon his own experience or specific knowledge in making his award. Providing the award is appropriately worded as to the procedural details and the arbitrator's invitation it is suggested the arbitrator could reasonably find for a figure between the two contentions in the exercise of his valued judgment on the evidence. This is supported by the view that the dispute is the amount of the rent. The method of calculation of the amount of the rent is an issue within the dispute.

680 What if there is a genuine difference of opinion between the experts? Thomasina asked. This is the only class that ought to come to a hearing between a judge or arbitrator, said Ronald Bernstein QC in an article in *Arbitration* (February 1992) entitled "How to Lose Cases and do the Maximum Harm to Your Client".

681 Here Mr Bernstein said:

> "... and in most cases they are better decided by a technical arbitrator, or by a judge sitting with a technical assessor, than by a judge alone. I was once asked, as Official Referee, to decide a genuine difference of opinion between experts as to whether a landslip had or had not been caused by periglacial solifluction. When the issue had been explained to me, by the eminent expert for the plaintiff through the mouth of his counsel who understood it less than perfectly, I announced that I felt like a rather unintelligent first-year undergraduate asked to decide a difference of opinion between his two professors. (The parties settled during the lunch adjournment.) Unhappily I had not dealt with the preparations for trial; if I had, I would have acquainted myself with the issue much earlier and then, probably, invited the parties to agree to my sitting with a technical assessor.

An arbitrator is always in a position to shape the hearing in this way, because he is personally in charge of the preparations for hearing. If he fails to take charge, costs will be wasted—sometimes massively.

In my experience conflicts of this class—where the core of the dispute is a genuine difference of opinion between experts—account for less than one case in ten that come before the courts or arbitrators. When they do occur, an arbitrator of like discipline will usually be a more appropriate tribunal than a judge or lawyer if—and this is an important qualification—he can approach the evidence of the experts with an open mind. The intellectual discipline that this requires can be achieved by training as an arbitrator; without such training its presence is problematical. In major disputes a tribunal containing both lawyer and expert, or a lawyer sitting with an expert as assessor, is probably best.

Avoiding judgments based on demeanour

A very wise judge once said:

> 'I question whether the respect given to our findings of fact based on the demeanour of the witnesses is always deserved. I doubt my own ability, and sometimes that of other judges, to discern from a witness's demeanour, or the tone of his voice, whether he is telling the truth. He speaks hesitantly. Is that the mark of a cautious man, whose statements are for that reason to be respected, or is he taking time to fabricate? Is the emphatic witness putting on an act to deceive me, or is he speaking from the fullness of his heart, knowing that he is right? Is he likely to be more truthful if he looks me straight in the face than if he casts his eyes on the ground perhaps from shyness or a natural timidity? For my part I rely on these considerations as little as I can help.
>
> This is how I go about the business of finding facts. I start from the undisputed facts which both sides accept. I add to them such other facts as seem very likely to be true, as for example, those recorded in contemporary documents or spoken to by independent witnesses like the policeman giving evidence in a running down case about the marks on the road. I judge a witness to be unreliable if his evidence is, in any serious respect, inconsistent with these disputed or indisputable facts, or of course if he contradicts himself on important points. I rely as little as possible on such deceptive matters as his demeanour. When I have done my best to separate the true from the false by these more or less objective tests, I say which story seems to me the more probable, the plaintiff's or the defendant's.'

A judge or arbitrator should where possible avoid basing his decision on the demeanour or dress of the witness. Nor is the certainty with which an expert expresses an opinion a very reliable guide to its validity. Another judge once said:

> 'The courts are full of honest witnesses whose memory as time passes becomes more and more certain and less and less accurate.'

You surely know, from your own experience, how often you find that beliefs of which you are certain are in fact unfounded.

The passages cited above relate to deciding between opposing witnesses of fact. Deciding conflicts of evidence between two experts is more difficult. These are the most important matters I consider:

a. the extent of his experience with problems of this kind;
b. whether he has done his homework on the problem;
c. whether his evidence conflicts with opinions he has previously expressed;
d. whether he has lost his objectivity; and generally
e. whether I believe that his opinion would have been the same if he had been instructed by the other party."

EXPERT EVIDENCE CONTRADICTS EVIDENCE THAT THE EXPERT GAVE IN A PREVIOUS ARBITRATION

The facts

682 An expert appeared on behalf of a landlord in a rent review dispute. As it happened the same expert had appeared before the same arbitrator in another arbitration but at that time he was acting for the tenant on a property quite close to the property which was the subject of the current arbitration. In the small world of valuation surveyors in the provincial city in which the arbitration was taking place, the arbitrator and the expert were well known to each other.

683 The landlord's expert, in the course of giving his expert testimony on the review rent, expressed a view which was diametrically opposed to that set out in his report adduced as evidence in the arbitration when he had come before the arbitrator in the previous arbitration. This expert refused, under cross-examination by the tenant's counsel, to change testimony or admit that there could be any contrary correct view.

Question

684 Should the arbitrator draw the parties' attention to what that expert said previously?

Course of action

685 The issue raised by the question is one of the expert's credibility. See *Shearson Lehman Bros* v. *Maclaine Watson & Co Ltd (International Tin Council intervening) (No 2)* [1988] 1 All ER 116, which is authority for the proposition that documents arising out of a private arbitration can be disclosed in subsequent court proceedings where they are relevant to the issues in the court action. It is therefore at least arguable that such documents can be disclosed in a subsequent arbitration.

686 There is also the more recent case of *London & Leeds Estates Ltd* v. *Paribas Ltd* [1995] 2 EG 134. In this case Mance J held:

> "Having regard to sections 4 and 5 of the Criminal Procedure Act 1865 and section 3(1)(a) of the Civil Evidence Act 1968 a prior inconsistent statement, which is not admitted by a witness in cross-examination may be put in evidence and is admissible. If a witness were proved to have expressed himself in a materially different sense when acting for different sides, that would be a factor which should be brought out in the interest of individual litigants involved and in the public interest. There is a legitimate basis for admitting the *Euston Tower* proof of M, which outweighed objectives on grounds of privacy and confidentiality."

(See paras 558–561 above for further detail of the judgment in *London & Leeds Estates Ltd* v. *Paribas Ltd.*)

687 In an example such as this the arbitrator should disclose the fact of knowledge of this matter from a previous arbitration and having discussed that knowledge invite the parties to address him on it. No doubt this would embarrass the landlord's expert but he has created this problem for himself and gets all that he deserves.

688 Had the arbitrator not disclosed his knowledge of the facts from the previous arbitration and this had come to the notice of the tenant at a later stage that tenant could have challenged the award on the grounds that it was influenced by secret knowledge of the arbitrator's on which he had not given the parties the opportunity to address.

689 This point was well illustrated in *Zermalt Holdings SA and Nu-Life Upholstery Repairs Ltd* (1985) 275 EG 1134 where there was an application to remove the arbitrator for misconduct.

690 The complaint made by the applicants against the award was that, as reasons given for the award were alleged to show, the arbitrator had been influenced in his decision by matters which had not been raised by the parties and had not been put to the parties for their observations.

691 Bingham J, as he then was, held that the landlords' case against the award had been made out. Matters likely to form the subject of the decision, insofar as they are specific matters, should be exposed for the comments and submissions of the parties. Importantly, the judge drew the distinction between the use of the arbitrator's expertise in respect of general matters and the specific matters which must be put to the parties. An order was made to set aside the award and to remove the arbitrator.

692 In his judgment Bingham J said, *inter alia*:

> "I fully accept and understand the difficulties in which an expert finds himself when acting as an arbitrator. There is an unavoidable inclination to rely on one's own expertise and in respect of general matters that is not only not objectionable but is desirable and a very large part of the reason why an arbitrator with expert qualifications is chosen. Nevertheless, the rules of natural justice do require, even in an arbitration conducted by an expert, that matters which are likely to form the subject of decision, insofar as they are specific matters, should be exposed for the comments and submissions of the parties. If an arbitrator is impressed by a point that has never been raised by either side then it is his duty to put it to them so that they have an opportunity to comment. If he feels that the proper approach is one that has not been explored or advanced in evidence or submission then again it is his duty to give the parties a chance to comment. If he is to any extent relying on his own personal experience in a specific way then that again is something that he should mention so that it can be explored. It is not right that a decision should be based on specific matters which the parties have never had the chance to deal with, nor is it right that a party should first learn of adverse points in the decision against him. That is contrary both to the substance of justice and to its appearance."

(See also paras 809 to 837 below on the subject of the arbitrator's own knowledge.)

WHETHER AN EXPERT'S REPORT IN CHILD CARE PROCEEDINGS IS EXEMPT FROM DISCLOSURE BY LEGAL PROFESSIONAL PRIVILEGE

The facts

693 A child was admitted to hospital having consumed a quantity of methadone. Her mother's explanation was that the child had accidentally drunk the substance from a beaker left carelessly in the kitchen.

694 Having obtained an emergency protection order from the magistrates' court, the local authority instituted care proceedings in the county court pursuant to s.31 of the Children Act 1989.

695 The mother was given leave, by the district judge, to disclose the court papers to a consultant chemical pathologist, who was to give her an independent opinion as to whether the child's medical condition, when admitted to hospital, was consistent with the mother's account of events.

696 The district judge's order required the report to be filed with the court. The area police authority, having learned of the report's existence, issued a summons in the High Court for leave to be given access to the report to assist in their investigation as to whether a criminal offence had been committed.

Question

697 Did the judge have jurisdiction to order the disclosure of the report or was it protected by legal professional privilege?

Course of action

698 In *Re L (A minor)* (1996) SJ 140, LB16, the case from which these facts were drawn, the judge held that she had jurisdiction to order disclosure to non-parties and exercised her discretion to make an order for disclosure. The Court of Appeal, dismissing the mother's appeal, held that she could not resist disclosure on grounds of legal professional privilege or privilege against self-incrimination. The mother appealed.

699 The case was heard in the House of Lords on 21 March 1996, when Lord Jauncey of Tullichettle said that the mother had argued that the absolute nature of the privilege attaching to the solicitor–client relationship extended equally all other forms of the legal professional privilege. However, there was a clear distinction between the privilege attaching to communications between solicitor and client and the litigation privilege that attached to reports by third parties prepared on the instruction of a client for the purpose of litigation.

700 Litigation privilege was an essential component of the adversarial process. Care proceedings under Part IV of the 1989 Act were primarily non-adversarial and investigative and were so far removed from normal actions that litigation privilege had no place in relation to reports obtained by a party thereto, which could not have been prepared without the leave of the court to disclose documents already filed.

701 Litigation privilege was excluded by necessary implication from the terms and overall purpose of the Act. That did not, of course, affect the privilege arising between solicitor and client. There was no need for the House to decide whether the privilege against self-incrimination arose since, on the facts, the mother had waived any such right. There were no grounds for interfering with the judge's order for disclosure.

702 Lord Lloyd of Berwick and Lord Steyn agreed.

703 Lord Nicholls of Birkenhead, dissenting, said that the crucial question was not whether proceedings were inquisitorial rather than adversarial, but what was required if they were to be conducted fairly. Parties to family proceedings were as much entitled to a fair hearing as were parties to other court proceedings. That included the right to legal professional privilege.

704 A party had to be able to obtain advice in confidence from an expert.

705 Lord Mustill agreed with Lord Nicholls of Birkenhead.

706 The appeal was dismissed.

PRIVILEGE IN A "DOCUMENTS ONLY" RENT REVIEW ARBITRATION

The facts

707 The parties were in dispute over a rent review and resorted to arbitration in accordance with the terms of the lease.

708 At a preliminary meeting it was agreed that the arbitrator should conduct the reference by "documents only" but should keep his options open, in the event that, after seeing written submissions from each side, if he felt that a short oral hearing would be helpful he could so direct.

709 The arbitrator made no specific direction concerning discovery but made it clear, at the preliminary meeting, that each party should append all principal relevant documents to their written statements and that if either party was aware of a relevant document, or class of documents, in the power or possession of the other, which had not been disclosed, then he would be prepared to consider an order for specific discovery.

710 Following the exchange of written submissions the claimant wrote to the arbitrator saying that he was aware of a valuation which had been prepared for the respondent's landlord which he had failed to disclose with his statement. The claimant requested a direction for specific discovery.

711 The respondent, in acknowledging the valuation to which the claimant referred, claimed privilege on the grounds that this valuation had only been commissioned because of the prospect of litigation over the rent review.

Question

712 How should the arbitrator respond to the claimant's application?

Course of action

713 He must satisfy himself what was the "dominant purpose" for which the valuation was produced by inviting a written submission from the claimant—copied to the respondent—and then allow a brief period of time for the respondent's comments on that submission before giving his decision.

714 If he concluded that the "dominant purpose" for the valuation was the anticipated litigation, then he would be right to uphold the respondent's claim for privilege.

715 The important test is that litigation is in prospect and was not a mere vague anticipation.

716 In discussing this with Charley, he pointed out that reports were often commissioned in anticipation of rent reviews arbitration. He referred to the judgments in *M and W Grazebrook Ltd* v. *Wallens* [1993] 2 All ER 868 and *Alfred Crompton Amusement Machines* v. *Cmrs of Customs & Excise (No 2)* [1972] 2 All ER 353.

717 He went on to point out why the initial advice of the valuer on review is vulnerable. It may meet the requirement of having been produced in anticipation of a rent review arbitration but it is unlikely to meet the dominant purpose test.

718 Charley told us that the way they satisfy this test and avoid embarrassing initial opinions coming out is to ensure that valuation advice from the earliest stage of considering a review is given by surveyors through lawyers expressly for the purpose of enabling those lawyers to advise their clients.

719 He told us that far more common, in rent reviews, were problems associated with "without prejudice" documents. Generally, these documents, between the parties or those representing them, are privileged and cannot be referred to at all in arbitration.

720 In rent review they tend to fall into two categories:

(i) "Without prejudice" communications made for the purpose of attempting to settle a dispute and not to be referred to on any aspect of the rent review arbitration (except to interpret terms on which the review has settled). These do not have to be offers, they can include "opening shots".

(ii) "Without prejudice save as to costs"—these are dual-purpose documents. They are offers capable of acceptance and, as such, attempts to settle, but they are also intended to influence the arbitrator on costs and therefore to bring pressure on the other side to settle.

721 This is similar to the situation in construction cases—where such offers have little to do with the merits of the arbitration and refer specifically to costs.

722 I told Charley and Thomasina that the important thing to remember was that "without prejudice" documents are privileged provided they are genuine attempts to settle a genuine dispute. This is so in all forms of arbitration on the grounds of public policy.

723 Even when no dispute has arisen, an "opening shot" or a letter initiating negotiation which does not actually constitute an offer would be privileged, if marked "without prejudice". This was so held in *South Shropshire District Council* v. *Amos* [1986] 2 EGLR 194.

724 I further explained that something a lot of people do not seem to understand is that the question of whether a document is without prejudice is one of substance not form. Just because a document is headed "without prejudice" does not automatically make it so nor, indeed, if the words are missing does that prevent it from being a privileged document.

725 Generally "without prejudice" documents between parties to a particular review are privileged from discovery as well as from production. The parties, of course, know of their existence and do not need to have them listed, as the fact that negotiations had taken place may itself be prejudicial if disclosed. However, as I pointed out, listing itself does not normally present such a problem in construction cases.

726 What if, Thomasina asked, the "without prejudice" documents arose not out of the particular rent review arbitration but out of another rent review of the same property or, indeed, a comparable one?

727 I know little of rent review cases but was able to mention a leading construction case which illustrated the point: *Rush & Tompkins* v. *GLC* [1988] 2 WLR 939. In this case, the litigation was between a developer and the main contractor and subcontractor. The case between the developer and the main contractor settled but the subcontractor's counterclaim against the developer did not. The subcontractor knew what the settlement was but wanted a breakdown but the court refused to allow him to see the "without prejudice" documents which gave this breakdown. In this case it was held that the parties' "without prejudice" documents had to be protected from production to the other parties in the same litigation (and possibly also in subsequent litigation on the same subject matter).

728 Thomasina asked how far this extended in rent review. Charley explained that rent review arbitration is not normally multi-party but suggested that the question may arise in the following types of situation.

(i) Review of an underlease where there are negotiations on the headlease review.
(ii) Review of a lease where there are negotiations on a comparable property which has the same landlord.
(iii) Review of a lease where there are negotiations on a comparable property with an unrelated landlord and tenant.

729 He cited a relatively recent county court decision, *Percy Bartram* v. *Standard Life* [1990] NPC 57, where the tenant's expert on a 1954 Act renewal had also acted as expert witness, for a different tenant, on the rent review of a comparable property. It was believed, by the landlords of the first property, that the tenant's expert had offered to settle the comparable review at a much higher figure than he was contending for on the renewal. The comparable had not in fact settled; the arbitrator had given an award. It was argued by the tenant that the negotiations on the comparable review were protected by "without prejudice" privilege and that the expert could not be cross-examined on them.

730 In this *Percy Bartram* case the court held that the privilege which attached to "without prejudice" negotiations did not extend this far. Although the decision is not reported it appears that the essential difference from the fact in *Rush & Tompkins* was that the parties to the renewal were different from those on the comparable review and the comparable review did not form part of a chain of litigation/arbitration which included the renewal. It may also be significant that the comparable review had concluded.

731 Charley told us that his pupil master is apparently of the opinion that this case is very weak authority and may well have been wrongly decided. It is his view that had the case been concerned with documents rather than oral evidence, discovery would have had to be refused because discovery is not available against a third party. A subpoena could have been issued, but questions of relevance and the weight to be attached to the evidence would then have been material to any challenge. The decision appears to suggest that the expert's offer might be relevant to the credibility of the expert witness, but the expert would have been representing his clients whose commercial interest in settlement might well have led to instructions to achieve a sensible compromise even if this was at a figure higher than that recommended by the expert. It might well have been a different matter if the expert's submitted figure, in a proof of evidence, had been sought.

732 According to Charley the report of the decision also said that the privilege which attaches to "without prejudice" negotiations belongs to the parties to those negotiations not to their expert. He told us that again doubt is cast on this point and raises the question of what would have happened if the tenant of the comparable property had been served with a subpoena.

733 Clearly this case was worth looking at on the issue of whether, and if so where, the line should be drawn in relation to the *Rush & Tompkins* approach. I asked Thomasina to dig out the full judgment for us to read when we had more time. It clearly has relevance to both construction and rent review cases.

734 The distinction, it seems, lies in whether there is a close connection between the parties, the proceedings or the properties. The closer the relationship, as in the headlease/underlease situation, and possibly the group of comparable properties with a common landlord, the more likely it is that *Rush & Tompkins* will apply, making the documents inadmissible. If the properties and parties are unrelated and the comparable review has been concluded, *Percy Bartram* v. *Standard Life* [1990] NPC 57 suggests that the court might allow the material to be admitted.

735 Of course, in construction cases, a close relationship exists between employer, contractor, subcontractor, sub-subcontractor, supplier etc.

736 Finally, Charley spoke of "open documents" from comparable reviews—not something we would meet in construction cases. Apparently this is now not quite so clear-cut as it may have appeared. Charley quoted the case of *Dolling-Baker* v. *Merrett* [1991] 2 All ER 890 which deals with the point and confirms that although arbitration is confidential as between the parties, this does not automatically prevent documents from one arbitration being used in other proceedings.

737 However, the case goes on to say that since there is an implied obligation that documents in a comparable review will not be disclosed unless the parties consent or the court orders, the arbitrators must have regard to this in making an order which would effectively override that obligation.

738 An arbitrator must also assess relevance and the question of whether the documents are necessary, to dispose fairly of the matter, and then weigh these considerations against the undesirability of overriding the privacy of arbitration.

739 What is "necessary" is largely up to the arbitrator to decide as, indeed, "fairly" gives him some leeway as to how the parties prove their case.

PRIVILEGED MATERIAL REFERRED TO AT A PRELIMINARY MEETING

The facts

740 At a preliminary meeting reference was made to matters which had been discussed in the course of a series of meetings which had taken place earlier between the parties' experts.

741 Shortly before the hearing was due to commence the respondent's solicitor wrote to the arbitrator complaining of the privileged information which the arbitrator had been made privy to at the preliminary meeting. He maintained that it was common ground that the meetings between the experts, which were referred to, had been held on a "without prejudice" basis.

742 As a result the respondent's solicitor invited the arbitrator to withdraw from the arbitration or, alternatively, to give his consent to have the issue determined by the High Court.

Question

743 What action should the arbitrator take in these circumstances?

Course of action

744 Presumably, what the respondent's solicitors had in mind was to seek to have the arbitrator removed under s.24(1)(a), AA '96—

> "that circumstances exist that give rise to justifiable doubts as to his impartiality"—

having been prejudiced against the respondent by being made privy to matters discussed at the "without prejudice" meetings of experts; or, possibly, under s.24(1)(d)—

> "that he has failed
> (1) to properly conduct the proceedings . . .
> and that substantial injustice has been . . . caused to the applicant"

(although this alternative must be very tenuous on the facts of this example).

745 Following the invitation to the arbitrator to withdraw, he adjourned the hearing for 21 days to enable the respondent to apply to the High Court for his removal. The respondent's solicitor objected to this approach and then invited the arbitrator to withdraw forthwith.

746 The arbitrator's response was to invite the parties to make written submissions on the proposal to submit the matter to the High Court for a decision. The parties failed to do so and subsequently the arbitrator discussed the matter by telephone with the claimant's solicitors. He reported the conversation to the respondent but subsequently refused either to withdraw or to consent to having the issue determined by the court.

747 In the case of *Ian Keith Brown* v. *CBS Contractors Ltd* [1987] 1 Lloyd's Rep 279, with similar facts, Hawser J concluded:

> "I am not satisfied that this is a case where it would be in the interests of justice, or of the parties, for me to remove the arbitrator but I do think the arbitrator should reconsider the situation and give the parties the opportunity of making their representations on the issue as to whether the arbitration should continue with this particular arbitrator."

748 Elsewhere in his judgment Hawser J said:

> ". . . the arbitrator was entitled to reach the conclusion that he could properly continue and ignore the references to the 'without prejudice' discussions. The decision on that matter was one for him."

749 It seems to me that the arbitrator was altogether too heavy handed over this matter. Firstly, what was he doing even listening to what appears to have been privileged material at the preliminary meeting? Normally, these meetings are fairly informal and nothing either side says in explaining what the dispute is all about should be taken by the arbitrator as evidence.

750 If something did inadvertently slip out, as appears to be the case here, and the respondent objects, then provided the arbitrator himself was not compromised, after inviting submissions from the parties concerning the respondent's request for him to withdraw and presumably having rejected the proposition, he should proceed with the reference leaving the respondent to make his own application for his removal if he saw fit. This seems to be borne out by Hawser J in the *Brown* case (see above).

TO WHAT EXTENT, IF AT ALL, ARE PARTIES BOUND BY "WITHOUT PREJUDICE" MEETINGS BETWEEN THEIR RESPECTIVE EXPERTS?

The facts

751 In an action against an architect for damages for breach of contract in respect of improvements to a dyeworks, the judge ordered, by consent, that:

> "Experts be limited to three per party . . . to meet 'without prejudice' to endeavour to narrow issues and agree facts . . . ."

752 Subsequently, meetings took place between the experts which resulted in some agreement.

753 In the trial which followed the judge determined liability and laid down some issues of principle as to damages. A few months later the same judge began a detailed assessment of damages. As part of that assessment the judge inquired whether the parties' respective experts had met to agree the estimate of remedial works and was told that this had not been possible due to other commitments.

754 During these early stages of the second trial, a request was made for a further meeting between experts to clarify some confusion between them and attempt to resolve some of their differences. The judge agreed and adjourned.

755 During the adjournment the experts reached agreement on one of the important technical issues and one of them recorded the terms of what he believed had been agreed, under the heading of "Agreement by Experts re Effluent tank"—all three experts signed this document. However, in the subsequent written statement produced as part of his evidence-in-chief, one of the experts stated his intention to raise considerable reservations when he returned to the witness box.

Question

756 What is the effect of this "Agreement" and, in particular, the signature of the expert now expressing reservations?

Course of action

757 The facts of this example are precisely those of the milestone case on expert evidence, that of *Richard Roberts Holdings Ltd* v. *Douglas Smith Stimson Partnership and Others (No 2)* (1989) 47 BLR 117, before His Honour Judge John Newey QC.

758 Although key points of the judgment have been quoted in two other examples in this book (paras 094 to 112 and paras 245 to 262) despite the overlap, the judgment is well worth reproducing in full.

759 Judge Newey's judgment picks up from the first meeting between the experts following the request of the parties for an adjournment on the second day of the damages trial.

> "It is clear that no one gave any instructions to the experts, but that everyone expected them to do what had been mentioned in court—to meet and to talk. Mr Andrews, who had had ten to fifteen

years' experience as an expert, Mr Bray with experience extending over more than twenty years, and Mr Otter, retired to the consultation room next to the court and began to discuss the technical question of whether a manifold were needed and an associated question of fact, namely whether Mr Otter's price included the cost of a sludge pump. Everyone else concerned went out for lunch.

Mr Otter's role at the meeting was to explain what his company could do: it was not for him to agree or disagree about anything.

After half an hour or more Mr Bray and Mr Andrews reached what, according to Mr Bray and Mr Otter, was an agreement to the effect that a manifold would not be needed and that the pump was included in the price. Mr Bray wrote the terms of what he believed to have been agreed under a heading of 'Agreement by Experts re Effluent Tank' and he, Mr Otter and Mr Andrews each signed the paper. In a written statement produced as part of his evidence-in-chief Mr Andrews stated that it was still his intention to raise his considerable reservations when he returned to the witness box and in oral evidence he told me that he said as much at the meeting.

Second Meeting of Experts on 21 March

By the time the experts emerged from the consultation room, counsel and solicitors had returned. Mr Bray handed the document recording the alleged agreement to Mr Gowan and said in substance that the meeting had gone well and that he thought that further progress could be made in agreeing other aspects of Mr Otter's scheme. Mr Gowan indicated that he was fully in favour of the meeting continuing and that Mr Bray should agree as much as possible with Mr Andrews. All or part of the conversation was in the presence of Mr Darling and Mr Sheridan and without objections from anyone the meeting was resumed.

According to Mr Andrews on resumption Mr Bray said 'They want us to look at the other items' and by 'they' he understood Mr Slater and Mr Darling. At two o'clock Mr Slater and Mr Darling came to see me in my room, showed me the document which had been signed and, at their request, I agreed not to sit until 4.15. Refreshments were, I am glad to say, supplied to the experts and to Mr Otter in the consultation room.

At the second meeting Mr Andrews' 'Revision of Costs' document was treated as an agenda and the experts worked through it item by item. The matters discussed included: what work was covered by Mr Otter's estimate; whether his charges were reasonable; whether more work would be needed; and if more was required, what would be the extra cost involved.

At about 4.15 I returned to court when Mr Darling told me that the afternoon had been useful, that discussions were still going on, that they had been more frutiful in some areas than in others and that the experts wished to continue with them. He said, according to the transcript, 'We hope that it will obviously lead to a considerable saving in time, because at the very least the respective positions of the parties will be established'. I agreed to adjourn until the following day and said words to the effect that discussion was often better than conflict and Mr Slater said 'I am sure that they will narrow the issues and possibly agree. As Your Honour has seen already there is a considerable saving on one document alone.' The parties have never disputed that the first meeting disposed of the manifold and sludge pump question.

The meeting continued, but a little while later Mr Hayes called Mr Andrews out of it and had a conversation with him, at first alone and then in the presence of Mr Darling and Mr Sheridan. Mr Hayes had been surprised at Mr Andrews having withdrawn from his earlier position at the first meeting. He was plainly concerned that Mr Andrews should, because of pressure of numbers or of time, concede too much at the second meeting.

Mr Hayes told Mr Andrews that he did not want him to agree anything in writing and that he should write down anything which he was inclined to agree, think about it overnight and discuss it with Mr Hayes and others next morning. At one stage Mr Darling thought that Mr Hayes was saying that Mr Andrews was merely to listen and not to participate in the discussion and he intervened to say that Mr Andrews had to be able to participate. Mr Andrews himself said that he told Mr Hayes that he had, I quote, 'to commit my statement and I have got to acknowledge their point of view'. Neither Mr Darling nor Mr Sheridan mentioned what Mr Hayes had said to Mr Andrews to Mr Slater or to Mr Gowan, and Mr Andrews did not report it to Mr Bray and Mr Otter.

According to Mr Otter and to Mr Bray, as they and Mr Andrews worked their way through Mr Andrews' 'Revision of Costs' Mr Bray and Mr Andrews agreed as to items listed as 2, 3, 4, 5, 6, 7, part of 8, 9 and 10. The result was to be no increase in cost in respect of 2, 3, 4, 9 and 10, described as 'Zero Items', but increases in connection with 5, 6, 7 and part of 8, which together would raise Mr Otter's estimate to £122,855.96. On that evidence both experts had made concessions, but no agreement was reached as to another part of 8 (referred to as '8a'), as to 9 or as to contingencies.

Mr Andrews in written and oral evidence-in-chief and at first in cross-examination denied that he had at any time agreed with Mr Bray. When Mr Fernyhough, leading Mr Darling, asked him about what were alleged to be zero items he said:

> '... those were outstanding items. They were saying it was nil; I was saying it was something, and we just could not agree the principle of it. But I had to accept that Mr Otter said it was in his price.'

Asked what he expected would happen, he said:

> 'I expected that subsequently every one of these items that we had discussed, I would give my opinion in this witness-box in the same way I had given my opinion and been cross-examined on every other matter which the experts had discussed at previous meetings, and either confirmed or nor that we had an agreement.'

The meeting lasted about three and a half hours and during it both Mr Andrews and Mr Bray made notes. After they had gone through the whole of Mr Andrews' 'Revision of Costs', Mr Bray wrote out in Mr Andrews' and Mr Otter's presence a document which he headed 'Basis of Costs from Experts' Meeting', which purported to record what had been agreed and disagreed. The word 'agreement' does not appear in it, but on its face it is a revision of Mr Andrews' 'Revision of Costs'.

Mr Bray, Mr Otter and Mr Andrews each signed the document. Mr Bray and Mr Otter said that they signed it as a record of what had been agreed. Mr Andrews in evidence which was not always easy to follow denied that that was so. Later, first in cross-examination and then in answer to me, when I was trying to be sure as to the final effect of his evidence, Mr Andrews said that he had agreed to individual items with Mr Bray.

The experts left the consultation room and produced the 'Basis of Costs' document to counsel and solicitors and then everyone left the court building, which was about to be closed. Mr Andrews travelled by train to Manchester and on the way made further notes. They were put in evidence in cross-examination and I have looked at them but without gaining any material assistance from them.

On the following day, 22 March, counsel asked me to deal only with the items which had specifically not been agreed by the experts, including contingencies, and I did so, giving yet another judgment. Questions relating to the manifold and sludge pump were treated as resolved, but I was told that the status of the 'Basis of Costs' document was in doubt.

Issues

I am now asked to decide two more issues, which have been reduced to writing. They are:

(1) Whether the document entitled 'Basis of Costs' from experts' meeting ... constitutes an agreement binding upon (Richard Roberts) as to the amount of the reasonable repair costs recoverable by them in the action and
(2) If the answer to the first question is in the negative, what is the effect of the document and in particular is the signature of Mr Andrews thereon binding upon him as to the figures contained therein.

Defendants' Submissions

Mr Slater has submitted to me that the matrix to the second meeting on 21 March included the pre-trial meeting held pursuant to orders of the court. He said that, because of the wording of Order 38, the experts at that meeting could by entering into a written agreement have bound the parties on whose behalf they were instructed. He said that when further meetings were held after the trial had begun, since neither party informed the other that there was to be a change in the experts' positions they had, at the very least, apparent or ostensible authority to conclude agreement on the parties' behalf. He said that agreements as to floor size and edge detail made at post-trial earlier meetings and as to the manifold and pump at the first meeting on 21 March had all been accepted as binding.

Mr Slater submitted that even if he were wrong as to the powers of experts at meetings under Order 38 or even if pre-trial meetings should be disregarded in considering later ones, so far as Douglas Smith was concerned Mr Andrews had ostensible authority to bind Richard Roberts. He submitted that on the facts Mr Andrews had plainly reached a concluded agreement with Mr Bray.

Plaintiffs' Submissions

Mr Fernyhough agreed with Mr Slater that pre-trial meetings of experts ordered by the court formed a background against which the status of any later meetings and the powers of experts attending them could be judged. He said that everything which was said, or written, at meetings pursuant to court orders was 'without prejudice' and that that included any agreement reached between the experts. He said that, while Order 38 encouraged experts to prepare joint statements of their conclusions, they were not binding on the parties unless expressly ratified by them. He said that all the post-trial agreements in the case were 'without prejudice', that in view of what Mr Hayes said to Mr Andrews there could be no question of his having actual authority to bind Richard Roberts and that, since the second meeting was no different from earlier ones, there was no basis on which Douglas Smith could have believed that Mr Andrews had authority.

Evidence of Practice

Mr Bray was both examined and cross-examined at length as to what generally happens at meetings of experts and as to his opinions, with regard to the role of experts, when they can bind the parties instructing them and their personal position. I was particularly interested by his statement that if an expert has a limitation upon his authority, for example to discuss freely, it is customary for him to mention it at the beginning of the meeting. Mr Gowan and Mr Sheridan also expressed views as to the authority ordinarily conferred upon experts. Mr Andrews was not asked about practice at meetings as he said that he had not been to many.

Meetings Held Pursuant to Court Order

I take first the position of experts and parties when a meeting is held in fulfilment of a court order requiring that the parties' experts should meet.

I was the first official referee to make orders for meetings of experts. I did so in the summer of 1981, after experimenting with them when sitting as a planning inspector in the previous year. My brethren were quick to follow. At first parties were suspicious of such orders and reluctant to agree to them, but, as it was made plain that all meetings were to be entirely 'without prejudice' and as they seemed to result in shorter trials and even settlements, meetings gradually gained the acceptance of most practitioners. Orders of the type which I made in this case became usual.

There remained, however, a few cases in which consent to an order was withheld and in 1982 and again in 1984 the official referees proposed that the rules be altered to allow them to require 'without prejudice' meetings of experts.

The new rule of 1986 is now contained in RSC Order 38, rule 38. It applies to all courts and reads:

> 'In any cause or matter the court may if it thinks fit, direct that there be a meeting "without prejudice" of such experts within such periods before or after the disclosure of their reports as the court may specify, for the purpose of identifying those parts of their evidence which are in issue. Where such a meeting takes place the experts may prepare a joint statement indicating those parts of their evidence on which they are, and those on which they are not, in agreement.'

The notes to the rule at paragraph 38/37–39/6 in the *Supreme Court Practice* contain the comment:

'... the major objective of the rule is to produce as wide an area of consensus between the experts (as possible), in which case, they should indicate in their joint statement those parts of their evidence on which they are agreed. Such agreement will have the effect of removing the protection of "without prejudice" in respect of the matters agreed on.'

No authority was cited in support of the latter proposition.

In *Carnell Computer Technology Ltd* v. *Unipart Group Ltd* (1988) 45 BLR 100 on the summons for directions orders were made, not only that the experts should meet, but that they should produce a joint report. The parties had expressly agreed terms of reference for the experts before they met and at the trial the parties conceded that if the parties had produced a report it would not have been privileged. Judge Fox-Andrews QC, Official Referee, held that in fact the experts never agreed a report, but he said, no doubt *obiter*, at 108:

'The only authority the experts had to reach agreement ... was vested in them by my directions.

I find that an expert had no implied or ostensible authority to agree facts orally or in any form other than in a joint report where an order such as the one I made here exists.'

In *Murray Pipework Ltd* v. *UIE Scotland Ltd* (1988) unreported, a case concerned with whether a party should be allowed to call an expert at trial, Judge Fox-Andrews said, *obiter*, of what is now rule 38:

'... the major objective of the rule is to produce as wide an area of consensus between the experts in which they should indicate in their joint statement those parts of their evidence on which they are agreed. Such agreement will have the effect of removing the protection of "without prejudice" in respect of the matters agreed on.'

I respectfully disagree with the propositions that an order that experts should agree a statement made in reliance upon rule 38 can confer upon them an authority to bind the parties instructing them and that a joint written statement made at the conclusion of a 'without prejudice' meeting is automatically an 'open' statement.

In my opinion there are no words in rule 38 which purport to confer upon experts power to bind anyone. If it did, then since the rule would not be dealing with procedure, but with the substantive rights of persons under the law of agency, if would, I think, be *ultra vires*.

The first sentence of the rule empowers the court to direct 'without prejudice' meetings of experts; it does not confer power to require 'open' meetings. The second sentence does not authorise experts to do anything; it is, I think, no more than a sensible reminder to experts that it may be useful for them to reduce the results of their discussions to writing. There is nothing in the second sentence to state that joint statements should be 'open'.

I think it would be quite alien to the role of expert witnesses that they should have an automatic power to bind parties at the conclusion of 'without prejudice' meetings. An 'expert' does not represent a party in the way that a solicitor represents his client; he is principally a witness and his duties are to explain to the court (and no doubt to those who instruct him) technical matters and to give objective 'opinion' evidence.

If every order for a meeting of experts were likely to result either in an agreement disposing of all or part of the case without either a party or his legal advisors being consulted, orders for meetings would be likely to be strongly opposed.

Expert's Personal Position

If of course, during or at the conclusion of a meeting an expert is persuaded of the correctness of another expert's views and states as much in writing or even orally he cannot subsequently give evidence truthfully to the contrary. The only exception to this is when fresh information, such as the result of new laboratory tests, or a growth in scientific knowledge, has caused him again to change his mind.

If, in the absence of any new development, an expert were to give evidence contrary to that which he had agreed, he could not be cross-examined about what had happened at the meeting because it was 'without prejudice', but other sanctions might be invoked against him. If he is a member of a profession, complaint might be made to its governing body; further or alternatively if he is a member of an association of consultants or of experts he might be reported to it.

In practice a party whose expert witness has at a 'without prejudice' meeting held before trial agreed matters which are contrary to that party's case, is in a difficulty. He can either accept as binding upon himself the agreement made by the expert, or he can replace the expert. If a party adopts the latter course, he will have to apply to the court to order a further experts' meeting and will almost certainly be ordered to pay the costs of the first one.

Meetings Held After Commencement of Trial

It may be that Rule 38 is so widely expressed that a court could order a meeting of experts even after a trial has begun, but in practice in the official referees' courts meetings are ordered on summonses for directions. Once a trial has commenced meetings only take place by agreement of the parties and this is so even if the court has expressed the view that a meeting would be desirable.

Ideally when parties agree to a meeting of their experts they should also agree expressly whether the meeting is to be 'open' or 'without prejudice' and what authority (if any) the experts should have. In the absence of express agreement the parties' intentions have to be inferred.

If, however, a meeting is 'without prejudice' while an agreement between the experts is not binding on the parties ratified by them, a party who does not wish to accept what his expert has agreed is in a far more difficult position then if the trial had not begun. He would be most unlikely to obtain leave to call a further expert witness at that stage and particularly not if his only reason for applying is disagreement with the opinion of his present expert.

I think that in deciding whether a meeting held after a trial has begun is 'without prejudice' and, whether an agreement reached beween experts at it is 'open' and binding on the parties, the position during earlier meetings ordered by the court may be taken into account, but that in respect of the latter the difficulty of a party's position if he is not minded to accept the agreement is much more important. Obviously the facts as a whole have to be considered; just as they have to be in deciding whether the experts actually reached agreement.

Conclusions

In this case I think that the pre-trial meeting between Mr Andrews, Mr Bray and other experts held in accordance with my orders of 18 February and 16 October 1986, was 'without prejudice' and that if any agreement had been made at it, the agreement would also have been 'without prejudice' and not binding on the parties. The two meetings between Mr Andrews and Mr Bray during the trial were arranged by the parties and there is insufficient information before me to enable me to decide what was their status, but they disposed of the matters discussed.

During the hearing on the morning of 21 June last I encouraged the parties to agree matters of financial detail and at lunchtime counsel decided that Mr Andrews, Mr Bray and Mr Otter should meet to deal with technical questions concerning the manifold. The experts were not given any express instructions, but I have no doubt that the parties' representatives intended that they should, if possible, reach agreement with regard to the manifold. Despite Mr Andrews' evidence to the contrary, I am certain that he agreed with Mr Bray as to both the manifold and the pump; if he had not done so he would not have signed the document headed 'Agreement' and he would also have reported his 'reservations' with regard to it to Mr Darling and to Mr Sheridan without delay. The parties accept that without further consideration by them the experts' agreement ended disputes concerning both manifold and pump; at 2 pm counsel showed me the agreement and at 4.15 pm Mr Slater referred to the saving in time which it had achieved, without protest by Mr Darling.

Two matters having been disposed of by the experts, the parties' representatives by their words and/or conduct encouraged the experts to consider other matters in issue, which all concerned money, and they proceeded to do so. In the late afternoon Mr Hayes effectively withdrew any authority which Mr Andrews had to commit Richard Roberts in writing without prior consultation on the following morning, but this was not brought to the attention of Mr Bray,

Mr Otter or anyone representing Douglas Smith. Mr Andrews continued to discuss as before and he eventually signed the 'Basis of Costs' document.

I think that perhaps to a small extent because the pre-trial meeting ordered by the court had set a pattern, but to a very much larger extent because if discussions or negotiations are to have any prospect of success they need to be held under the cloak of privacy, the talks between Mr Bray, Mr Andrews and Mr Otter leading up to an agreement were all 'without prejudice'.

I think that in view of the statements made in court before the luncheon adjournment and at 4.15 pm and the way in which the manifold and pump agreement was treated as binding, both Richard Roberts and Douglas Smith held out their respective experts as having legal authority to make an agreement on their behalf after full discussion concerning the matters committed to them. In practice they had little alternative for if the experts had agreed, neither could have given evidence of opinions which were contrary to the agreement and a court would have been most unlikely to have allowed either party to call a new expert at that stage.

I found Mr Andrews' earlier evidence to the effect that he did not reach agreement with Mr Bray very unconvincing and I am glad that he later admitted that he had done so. I think that Mr Andrews' embarrassment at having entered into a written agreement when Mr Hayes had told him not to do so helps to explain his early denials.

Ultimately there was no conflict between Mr Otter, Mr Bray and Mr Andrews as to there having been a concluded agreement, but, if there had been, I should have unhestitatingly (*sic*) preferred the evidence of Mr Otter and Mr Bray, who were both very clear and impressive witnesses, to that of Mr Andrews, who at best seemed to be thoroughly confused.

My conclusions upon the issues are:

(1) The 'Basis of Costs' document constituted an agreement binding upon Richard Roberts.
(2) This issue does not arise, but Mr Andrews could not honourably have given evidence contrary to that which he had agreed."

PARTY PROMPTS OWN EXPERT WHILE GIVING EVIDENCE

The facts

760 The principal expert witness for the respondent was undergoing cross-examination by counsel for the claimant and matters were not going well for the respondent.

761 When the difficulty arose and objection was made by cross-examining counsel the arbitrator was taking a detailed written note of the evidence and was thus unaware of the attempts being made by the respondent to "instruct" his expert by means of hand signals and the "mouthing" of replies.

Question

762 How should the arbitrator rule on the objection?

Course of action

763 The arbitrator should remind counsel and instructing solicitors for both sides, that although arbitration is a flexible process and there is inevitably some informality in the proceedings, it was nevertheless incumbent upon them to control the activities of the participants both inside and outside the arbitration room in accordance with customary conventions particularly during the course of their evidence.

764 He should also remind the parties that expert witnesses were there to assist him and to give an independent opinion, based on their own knowledge and experience, and they should not be prompted or guided by the party retaining them in giving their evidence.

765 The problem arose due to the somewhat cramped accommodation in the arbitration room and was resolved by resiting the witness table so that the parties themselves at least were behind it.

766 The arbitrator could, in an extreme case, exclude the offender during the expert's evidence particularly in a case like this where the offending party is legally represented.

767 A more difficult situation arises where the offending party is representing himself, as a party to a reference has the right to be present throughout the proceedings. In such a case the arbitrator could make it clear that if the expert is prompted again he will either ignore that expert's evidence entirely or give it little weight. Alternatively, or in addition, he could warn the respondent that if he persisted in prompting his expert then his conduct could be reflected in any award on costs.

PROBLEM OF HEARING EXPERT EVIDENCE ON LENGTHY SCOTT SCHEDULE

The facts

768 In a construction dispute a Scott Schedule was ordered by the arbitrator. This resulted in a document comprising over 100 items and despite the experts having met and agreed so far as they were able virtually all of the items were contested as to liability or *quantum* or both.

769 There were two experts on each side: a building surveyor and a quantity surveyor.

Question

770 How could the arbitrator most effectively hear evidence on the Scott Schedule items?

Course of action

771 It appears that the most satisfactory way to deal with the Scott Schedule is to tackle the items individually with the arbitrator deciding to hear the appropriate experts for each side one after the other. This would mean that all of the evidence applicable to a particular item was clear in the arbitrator's mind, enabling him to form his conclusions on that item as he proceeds. The parties would also be encouraged to settle and agree as much of the schedule as possible.

772 The alternative of working through the entire list with one set of experts followed by the same procedure hours if not days later with the opposing party's experts would mean a great deal of to-ing and fro-ing with the documents. This would introduce a grave risk of confusion as well as stretching the arbitrator's memory as to what was said precisely in relation to a particular item by the first set of experts.

773 The arbitrator could swear all four experts together and seat them in a row at the witness table. He could then take the evidence on the Scott Schedule item by item—evidence in chief, cross-examination and then re-examination—of each of the four experts in turn. This method has been used in recent arbitration and the benefits were immediately obvious. The evidence was clear and seen in the round on each item. Progress was rapid.

774 Counsel for both sides had to be persuaded before they agreed—although in the absence of a prior agreement to a different procedure it is hard to see how they could have refused to co-operate if the arbitrator decided, albeit unilaterally, to proceed in this manner—but they were soon convinced when they saw how efficacious this method really was. The arbitrator is master of the proceedings to the extent that the parties do not agree to the contrary (s.34, AA '96).

775 An alternative procedure would be to adopt His Hon Sir Laurence Street's method at the hearing. (See Annex following para 225 above.) This avoidance of formal examination, cross-examination and re-examination on each of the 100 Scott Schedule items would undoubtedly result in a very substantial saving in hearing time.

CAN AN EXPERT ENTER INTO A "NO-WIN, NO-FEE" ARRANGEMENT?

The facts

776 An expert is approached by a firm of solicitors and asked if he is prepared to accept instructions on the basis of a "no-win, no-fee".

777 They point out that they are on a conditional fee basis themselves and therefore require their expert to share the risk of success.

Question

778 Can, or should, an expert accept instructions on this basis?

Course of action

779 This issue was discussed in an article for *The Lawyer* (25 November 1997) by Dr Christopher Pamplin, editor of the *UK Register of Expert Witnesses*.

780 Dr Pamplin, in this article, said:

> "As solicitors generally consider expert witnesses to be part of the litigation team, this widening of conditional fee arrangements for lawyers will put pressure on expert witnesses to accept instructions on the same basis. If the proposals are adopted, solicitors—now financially obliged to ensure their case is strong—will put pressure on experts to advise on the strengths and weaknesses of the case much earlier in the litigation process.
>
> These pressures bring the role of the expert witness into sharp focus. The solicitor's view of the witness as a member of the team is not shared by the judiciary, which sees the expert as an independent adviser to the court.
>
> An agreement by an expert witness to be paid on a conditional basis would infringe the

maintenance and champerty rule. There is a fundamental difference between lawyers and experts that argues against payment of the experts' fees ever being conditional on the outcome of the case.

Experts are in a unique position in the UK legal system: they are the sole source of opinion evidence that the courts will consider.

It is generally the case that the expert for the plaintiff will express an opinion favourable to the plaintiff, while the expert for the defendant expresses one that is favourable to the defendant. It is for the court to decide which evidence it prefers.

How would the knowledge that experts might be working under a conditional fee agreement influence the weight the court placed on their testimony? In a no-win, no-fee arrangement, the expert would only be paid if his or her opinion wins the day. The implicit risk to the just operation of the litigation process is obvious.

The Bar has already experienced this. Barristers initially argued that conditional fees should not be applied to them, since a financial interest in the outcome of the case might lead to the temptation to "over-egg the pudding" in favour of the client's case.

Lord Irvine's proposals make a definition of the expert's position crucial. If the government allows experts to take on conditional fee instructions, their independent position would immediately be compromised. Yet preservation of their independent status demands prohibition of conditional fee arrangements.

If we learn anything from the Bar's experience it is that the Lord Chancellor may not see it as his duty to prevent expert witnesses being employed on a conditional fee basis. If the Lord Chancellor's Department was to outlaw it, then barristers would have been excluded from the existing conditional fee system.

In the worst-case scenario, the changes will be implemented without any prohibition of experts' fees being made conditional. In this event, expert witnesses will come under inevitable pressure to agree to no-win, no-fee terms.

An insurance scheme to cover experts' fees would help to alleviate fears of 'biased' expert evidence. It is a parallel solution to that proposed by Lord Irvine to ensure that the client is able to pay the other side's costs should he or she lose.

There is a precedent for experts arranging favourable insurance cover in the *UK Register of Expert Witnesses'* Professional Indemnity Scheme. This scheme provides professional indemnity cover for expert witnesses in the event of their being sued for negligence in their expert witness work. It is likely that terms could also be negotiated to cover conditional fee situations.

Another outcome might be that expert witnesses unite to resist conditional fees. Both of the expert witness organisations have expressed their opposition to such arrangements.

Unfortunately, the majority of expert witnesses are not members of any organisation. In such circumstances, it seems unlikely that those who do belong to such a body will agree to be bound by a voluntary code that rejects conditional fees and, as such, places them at a competitive disadvantage to the rest."

781 Let us speculate for a moment and assume that an expert can enter into such an arrangement and he is prepared to accept that the tribunal may well afford his evidence less weight than it would if the expert were truly independent.

782 How is success to be determined? If a claim is for £50,000 and the claimant succeeds to recover £5,000, is that a "win" so far as the expert and his fees are concerned?

783 What about the client's role in all of this? With solicitor and expert, and possibly counsel, on a "no-win, no-fee" basis, the solicitor is not likely to allow his client the luxury of pursuing poor points, or matters of principle.

784 Under our current system a successful party can expect to receive a substantial amount of its costs from the losing side, but this is unlikely to be the case if he is involved in a successful fee arrangement.

785 On all counts then there is much to be said for the expert maintaining his traditional role of providing truly independent assistance to the tribunal for a proper fee, win or lose.

DETERMINATION/TAXATION OF INCOMPETENT EXPERT'S COSTS

The facts

786 In the course of the proceedings it became evident that the expert architect for the respondent had failed to properly consider the real technical merits of his client's amended case.

787 His report effectively dealt with the respondent's counterclaim and specifically covered liability and *quantum* of defective work.

788 Although he had taken some of the points into consideration when drafting his final report he failed to deal with the allegations of breach of the architect's obligations as project manager in the development of a nine-screen multiplex cinema and associated leisure developments on the site in Southend-on-Sea.

Question

789 When the arbitrator was determining the respondent's solicitor's costs (the respondents being successful in the case), the claimant's solicitors objected to the fees of the expert on the ground that he had been unable to give evidence on the points that the respondents had in fact won.

Course of action

790 The respondent was awarded less than he might otherwise have recovered due to the failure of his expert to come up to proof.

791 Why should the respondent be further penalised by having his incompetent expert's costs disallowed or partially disallowed?

792 When an expert does not know whether the pleaded case coincides with his technical allegations of fact there is something wrong. In such cases an arbitrator may disallow the costs of an expert who has given evidence which is not to the point, or allow only a proportion of the cost (see *Mitchell* v. *Mulholland* (1973) 117 SJ 307).

793 That is not the case here. The expert has simply not adequately covered an issue despite which the respondent has enjoyed a measure of success on this issue. Provided the expert has not actually wasted the tribunal's or the other party's costs and his only fault is incompetence, I see no reason for acceding to the claimant's objection. Presumably the expert's report, so far as it went, assisted the respondent's case to some extent. After all he did turn out to be the net winner—in which case, to the extent that the expert's charges are reasonable, they should be allowed.

794 The arbitrator's duty in "taxing" the successful party's costs is to allow "reasonable costs, reasonably incurred". In this case costs would normally follow the event—the event being it seems, the respondent's overall success. Merely because he has not been as successful as he might have been with a more competent expert, is not a good ground for "taxing" down that expert's costs, or in the language of AA '96, making an award allocating costs of the arbitration as between the parties and in doing so allow less than the full amount of the expert's costs (s.61, AA '96).

795 That is not to say that a serious failure by an expert in some area of his evidence cannot or should not be reflected in an award of costs.

796 There was a recent example given by Richard Pughe (*The Lawyer*, 21 May 1996) of a plaintiff's costs being reduced in a personal injury case as the result of unpleaded evidence by expert witnesses:

> ". . . in a recent county court personal injury case, the firm's instructing solicitor, who was acting for the plaintiff, had provided the firm with pleadings in respect of the case. In the pleadings, the plaintiff set out a claim for gratuitous care but did not quantify the number of hours of care per week given by the plaintiff's wife since the accident.
>
> Prior to issue of our report, we contacted the provider of the care and orally ascertained the number of hours of care provided by the wife. We incorporated this into our report without expressing an opinion.
>
> The difficulty with the case was that both the plaintiff and the provider of care were killed in another car accident before further statements could be taken. So the only evidence was hearsay and could not be incorporated into the court's pre-trial bundle of papers.
>
> To avoid this problem, the expert should be involved in the case sooner so any discovery can be included in the pleadings. Further evidence should also be exchanged by way of supplemental statements or an exchange of documents.
>
> Effective communication is required between the solicitor and the expert. This is particularly important when the new evidence forms a crucial part of the expert's case. The aim is to avoid a situation in which the *quantum* of a plaintiff's claim is reduced as a result of insufficient preparation or unavoidable events outside the control of the solicitors."

EXPERT WITNESS DIES JUST BEFORE THE HEARING

The facts

797 In a complex dispute an expert witness for the respondent had prepared and exchanged his report with the other side's expert.

798 The report, which was 200 pages long, comprised facts drawn from the background to the dispute and the expert witness's conclusions/opinions on those facts.

799 The expert had been engaged to give his opinion of the competence of another professional in the subject-matter of the dispute and to ascertain what proportion of the professional's quoted fee would be fair and reasonable in view of his having failed to complete his assignment.

800 Counsel had relied heavily on this expert's evidence in preparing late and amended pleadings. Shortly before the hearing the expert witness died.

801 The respondent applied to the arbitrator for consent to adjourn the hearing to allow him to instruct a second expert.

802 The claimant objected on the ground that his specialist counsel was booked to take a local enquiry following the conclusion of the arbitration which was set down to take 12 months. He also argued that as the expert evidence had been exchanged it would take little time for someone else to familiarise himself with the contents of the report and give evidence on it. In the alternative, the claimant asked if the arbitrator was minded to grant the postponement requested by the respondent, for the costs thrown away to be paid by the respondent in any event.

Question

803 How should the arbitrator react to the application and subsequent objection?

Course of action

804 The arbitrator, in expressing sympathy to the respondent for the untimely demise of his expert witness, agreed that he could instruct another expert to give the evidence. In doing so, he made it clear that in deciding on the admissibility of such evidence he would apply the tests laid down by Megarry J in *English Exporters (London) Ltd* v. *Eldonwall* [1973] 1 All ER 726 where Megarry J said:

"A valuer giving expert evidence in chief (or re-examination) may

1 express the opinions he has formed as to values even though substantial contributions to the formation of those opinions have been made by matters of which he has no first hand knowledge;
2 give evidence as to the details of any transaction within his personal knowledge, in order to establish them as matters of fact;
3 express his opinions as to the significance of any transactions which are or will be proved by admissible evidence (whether or not given by him) in relation to the valuations with which he is concerned; but
4 may not give hearsay evidence stating the details of any transactions not within his personal knowledge in order to establish them as matters of fact."

805 In addition, the arbitrator would consider Mr M Turner's judgment in *Town Centre Securities Ltd* v. *Wm Morrison Supermarkets Ltd* [1982] EGLR 435, 31 July 1982, where it was held that

"evidence of which the expert witness does not have first hand knowledge is inadmissible as hearsay even where that evidence is given in support of opinion evidence".

806 The arbitrator agreed to allow the postponement requested with costs thrown away to be paid by the respondent. He expressed his regret at having to make this order as the result of such unfortunate circumstances, but the claimant could not be expected to underwrite the respondent's misfortune.

807 The arbitrator also regretted that the adjournment might mean the loss of the claimant's counsel. He would leave the question of the additional costs incurred as a result to be determined by him if and when he was requested to make such determination if costs were not agreed.

808 The respondent was able to instruct a new expert who would be able to use the original expert's report as part of his investigations amending any conclusions in that report as he in his opinion saw fit. Such amendments would have to be exchanged with the claimant's expert sufficiently in advance of a reconvened hearing for him to consider them and prepare his response.

ARBITRATOR HOLDS CONTRARY VIEW TO EXPERTS—HOW FAR CAN HE USE HIS OWN KNOWLEDGE?

The facts

809 In an insurance arbitration experts were instructed by each side. They prepared and presented a joint report in which they were agreed on one aspect of the dispute. The arbitrator, being a very experienced insurance man, knew from his own personal knowlege that what they had agreed was incorrect.

Question

810 Should the arbitrator tell the experts what was on his mind and invite them to address him on it; and, if so, what happens if the experts maintain their original stance?

Course of action

811 This was the question that I put to Thomasina which inevitably led us to examining the proposition from first principles.

812 The first thing that I impressed upon Thomasina was the difference between general knowledge and special knowledge of the facts of the issues in dispute.

813 An arbitrator is chosen for the very reason that he has formal knowledge of the subject-matter of the dispute which he is expected to use. This then is the exception to the rule that the arbitrator must decide the issues solely on the evidence which is being adduced before him. For example, if a wall is so obviously out of plumb that it is clear to all who see it, then expert evidence is not required to prove the point. Arbitrators clearly have a right, and indeed a duty, to use their own knowledge in appropriate cases, as was borne out by Bingham LJ in *Zermalt Holdings SA* v. *Nu-life Upholstery Repairs Ltd* [1985] 2 EGLR 14 where he said:

> "in respect of general matters that is not only not objectionable, but is desirable and a very large part of the reason why an arbitrator with expert qualifications is chosen."

814 An arbitrator is therefore chosen for the very reason that he has expert knowlege that he is expected to use in resolving a dispute. As Ronald Bernstein QC says:

> "No one ever chooses an arbitrator for his inexperience."

815 Indeed, it is said that one of the principal reasons for going to arbitration rather than litigation is the very fact that the parties can choose their tribunal on the basis of their experience of the matters in dispute.

816 The key to the arbitrator's dilemma lies in our old friend "natural justice"—let the parties know what you are thinking and give them the opportunity of telling you their views on this. In that way an arbitrator is unlikely to be open to criticism later, should one or other party attempt to have him removed for misconduct on the grounds that he gave himself "secret evidence".

817 Secret evidence in this context means no more than the arbitrator using his expert knowledge, without telling the parties and therefore without inviting them to address him on it.

818 I commended Thomasina to read the case of *Fox and Wellfair (Fox* v. *PG Wellfair* (1982) 263 EG 589).

819 In this case O'Connor LJ said:

> "Nothing that I say in this case must impugn the right of arbitrators to use their own knowledge in appropriate cases; that is essential to arbitration in very many cases."

820 Lord Denning said in the same case:

> "[The arbitrator] can and should use his special knowledge so as to understand the evidence that is given—the letters that have passed—the usage of the trade—the dealings in the market—and to appreciate the worth of all that he sees upon a view."

821 His Lordship attempted to show where to draw the line between general knowledge, which the chosen arbitrator would be expected to have and to use without especially drawing it to the attention of the parties, and knowledge of special facts related to the dispute.

822 In this regard he said:

> "The arbitrator cannot use his special knowledge—or at any rate he should not use it—so as to provide evidence on behalf of the defendants which they have not chosen to provide for themselves . . . at any rate he should not use his own knowledge to derogate from the evidence of the parties' experts—without putting his own knowledge to them and giving them a chance of answering it and showing that his own view is wrong."

823 Charley intervened at this point, and said that although *Fox and Wellfair* was a construction case, it was frequently referred to in rent review cases, as the judgment contained some fundamental principles which were equally applicable to his discipline.

824 I suggested that the rent review arbitrator was probably in an even more difficult position than one conducting a construction dispute. In my arbitrations I have absolutely nothing to do with the building in dispute or, generally, with either of the parties. However, in rent review, where an arbitrator may be chosen for his expertise in a particular type of property, perhaps even a property in a relatively isolated location, the likelihood of such complete detachment is rare. For this reason, and the special problems that I was aware that rent review arbitrators face (see paras 838 to 871 below), I felt I could best illustrate the difference between general and special knowledge by giving some examples.

825 First, we considered the situation where the arbitrator has special knowledge concerning, or clearly allied to, the facts in issue. The case I had in mind involved an eminent expert for the claimant who had given technical evidence which included an opinion that it was not possible to comply with specification requirements in the particular material occurring on-site. The arbitrator had in the past supervised a similar operation in almost identical material which had met similar problems. By the use of different methods the problems were successfully overcome. The arbitrator had written a paper for the ICE proceedings which included a description of the methods used to overcome the problem.

826 The dilemma that the arbitrator faced was should he disclose the existence of his paper on the subject?

827 Of course, the answer was "yes". At the end of the day's hearing, while the expert was still being cross-examined, the arbitrator should have informed the expert of his experience and handed counsel for each party a copy of his paper and then offered to let both sides address him on it if they wished the following day.

828 Another example I quoted was a dispute concerning a house which had suffered from subsidence as a result of inadequate foundations.

829 The arbitrator would not be able to take into account his knowledge of the fact that deeper foundations are generally required in clay soils to counter the possible effect of heave that such a point had not been raised and argued by the parties. However he could and indeed should tell the parties what he has in mind concerning problems associated with clay soils and invite them to address him on the point.

830 This sort of situation was dealt with by Darling J in *British Oil & Cake Mills Ltd* v. *Horace Battin & Co Ltd* (1922) 13 Ll L Rep 443 where he said:

> "The people who go to arbitration desire to have arbitrators or umpires who will not decide on evidence alone, but will bring to the consideration of cases a great deal of special knowledge, and they beyond everything want the matter decided one way or another without delay, so they can devote all their attention to their business and not to litigation in the courts."

(See paras 872 to 879 below.)

831 An arbitrator owes a duty to decide an arbitration on the facts and the law as he finds them to be. If he takes a view of the facts or law which does not accord with the submissions of either party, he should inform the parties of his provisional view so that they may deal with it. In *Thomas Borthwick (Glasgow) Ltd* v. *Fairclough Ltd* [1968] 1 Lloyd's Rep 16, Donaldson J said:

> "A trade arbitral tribunal is fully entitled to use its own knowledge of the trade. Indeed, the fact that it has this knowledge is one of the reasons why it exists and performs a most useful purpose. Experience, however, dictates that this knowledge shall never be used in such a way as to take a party by surprise. If, therefore, a tribunal considers that both parties have missed the point—this sometimes happens both in litigation and in arbitration—it should invite the parties to deal with this point and, if the point arises for the first time in the course of deliberations after the hearing, should offer the parties a further hearing if either wish to avail themselves of the opportunity.
>
> Equally, if the tribunal has knowledge of the facts which do not appear to be known to either party, it is only fair to reveal this knowledge to the parties, giving them an opportunity of putting those facts into different perspective or of persuading the tribunal that they are irrelevant."

832 Such a course is not only fairer to the parties; it also enables the tribunal to have additional assistance from the parties in arriving at a just decision.

833 We then returned to consider the original proposition, the situation where an arbitrator might find that he does not agree with either expert when those experts themselves have agreed, say in a joint report, on one of the matters in dispute.

834 In the normal course of events the arbitrator should tell the parties why he differs from their experts and invite them to address him on these differences. This would quell any charge of secretly using personal knowledge. However, in this example we have agreement between both sides on one point on which the arbitrator holds contrary views.

835 The arbitrator is in a dilemma as he is convinced that the experts are wrong. The best he can do is to explain to them why he believes them to have come to the wrong conclusion and hope that by doing so they will see the error of their ways and revise their joint agreement.

836 If, after that, they still hold to their original views, then it appears that the arbitrator will be quite safe in awarding on the basis of his own knowledge even where this is contrary to the views held by the experts.

837 Authority from this comes again from *Fox* v. *Wellfair* where Dunn LJ said:

> "it seems to me that an expert arbitrator should not in effect give evidence to himself without disclosing the evidence on which he relies to the parties . . . he should not act on his own private opinion without disclosing it. It is undoubtedly true that an expert arbitrator can use his own expert knowledge. But a distinction is made in the cases between general and expert knowledge and special facts relevant to the particular case.
>
> If the expert arbitrator, as he may be entitled to do, forms a view of the facts different from that given in the evidence which might produce a contrary result to that which emerges from the evidence, then he should bring that view to the attention of the parties so that they may have an opportunity of dealing with it. This is especially so where there is only one party and the arbitrator is, in effect, putting the alternative case for the party not present at the arbitration."

ARBITRATOR'S PERSONAL KNOWLEDGE OF A RECENT RELEVANT RENT AGREEMENT

The facts

838 An arbitrator was appointed to settle a rent review dispute. The parties agreed on a written representation procedure. When proofs were submitted the arbitrator noticed that neither party had referred to a rent on a nearby property of which he had personal knowledge of the terms of settlement. He considered the settlement to be relevant to the award of rent on the subject property.

Question

839 Should the arbitrator disclose details of this recent transaction?

Course of action

840 The arbitrator realises he would find it very difficult to shut this transaction out of his mind in arriving at his decision. He therefore draws to the attention of the parties the details of the settlement and invites them to make further submissions to him on it and its relevance or otherwise to the property in dispute. (See *Top Shop Estate Ltd* v. *Danino* (1984) 273 EG 197.)
841 Also in *Fox* v. *Wellfair Ltd* [1981] 2 Lloyd's Rep 514, Ackner J said:

> "... if the result of my judgment is that arbitrators in general are obliged to give to the parties an opportunity to deal with any major points, be they matters of fact or law, which the arbitrator alone is finding difficulty in accepting, then it is not a result which should cause any anxiety at all. It is of the very essence of a fair hearing that the parties should have an adequate opportunity of dealing with any substantial criticism of their claim or defence, whether the source of that criticism comes from the opposing party or the tribunal who makes the decision. It must, however, always be a question of fact and degree, whether or not such an opportunity has been denied."

842 Charley was with us when we discussed the course of action in this case. He then took the floor and told us that this personal knowledge of property was a very common problem in rent review cases and that in contrast to construction they have any number of reported cases on the subject. He referred us to an excellent paper delivered jointly to RICS Surveyors Arbitration Club (Arbrix) in May 1994 by the well-known solicitor/speaker Lesley Webber and the equally renowned chartered surveyor Robert Dean.
843 Here the authors set out the test which an arbitrator should apply which came from Bingham J in the *Zermalt* decision.

> "i) If an arbitrator is impressed by a point that has never been raised by either side, then it is his duty to put it to them so that they may have an opportunity to comment.
> ii) If he feels that the proper approach is one that has not been explored or advanced in evidence or submission, then again it is his duty to give the parties the chance to comment.
> iii) If he is to any extent relying on his own personal experience in a specific way, then that again is something that he should mention so that it can be explored.
>
> It is not the right that a decision should be based on specific matters which the parties have never

had the chance to deal with, nor is it right that a party should first learn of adverse points in the decision against him.

If the arbitrator alerts the parties to the special knowledge which he has or to his reasons for being minded to contradict the evidence put before him and allows them full opportunity to comment, his views may favour one party and may be adopted by it.

However, it is, of course, possible that both parties will argue against the arbitrator. In such circumstances the arbitrator should, in effect, be prepared to answer questions in relation to the special knowledge he seeks to apply, in particular in relation to facts on any new comparable evidence which he is introducing. If having given a fair opportunity to the parties, the arbitrator's faith in his own view has not been shaken, the court's approach would, in our view, allow the arbitrator to rely on his own expert knowledge (provided that it is otherwise admissible), notwithstanding that this goes beyond or contradicts the evidence of the parties.

The courts are not concerned with the correctness or otherwise of the decision in valuation terms (there are, of course, remedies for errors of law) but they are concerned that a fair route was followed in getting there."

844 As Charley said, we have heard from Lord Denning that an arbitrator can and should use his special knowledge to understand the evidence. Where this special knowledge may involve matters unknown by either party or not agreed by either, then he must not add to the evidence adduced before him without telling the parties.

845 Charley then told us of the situation where the arbitrator believes that the parties have set out their cases incorrectly, as occurred in *Techno Ltd* v. *Allied Dunbar Assurance plc* [1993] 22 EG 109.

846 In this case the surveyors agreed in a statement of agreed facts that the notional premises were of a similar age, height, construction and layout as the existing property. In his award, the arbitrator decided not to follow the statement of agreed facts. However, the court decided that it could only be departed from with good reason and after giving the parties the opportunity to comment on this departure. Again, this is an illustration of where the arbitrator is entitled to bring his experience to bear upon the facts of a case to form a view which is at variance with one or both parties' view but made it clear that he could not substitute his own view without reference to the parties.

847 On a similar tack we then considered the decision in *Amego Litho Ltd* v. *Scanway Ltd* [1994] 2 EG 110 when leave to appeal was given on the grounds that the award contradicted the only conclusion that could properly be drawn from the findings of fact which the arbitrator had made. The judge accepted that such circumstances could constitute an error of law entitling an appeal.

848 Charley then dealt with a problem which was common in rent review, that of the arbitrator inspecting the premises.

849 Although the arbitrator may be familiar with the property and its location it is not uncommon for him to carry out an inspection to see if there have been any changes which could have a bearing on the issue since he last saw the property. In such circumstances it is sensible to inform the parties that he is intending to inspect and, most important of all, let them know subsequently of the effect of that inspection on his ultimate determination so as to give them an opportunity of addressing him before making that determination.

850 The best known example of the rent review arbitrator failing to observe this simple rule and as a result being removed for misconduct was in the case of *Top Shop Estate Ltd* v. *Danino* (1984) 273 EG 197 where the arbitrator carried out a pedestrian count at the subject property and noted the findings in his award but failed to ask the parties to comment on those findings before doing so.

851 In another Top Shop inspection case, *Top Shop Centres Ltd* v. *Bellhaven Ltd* (1992), unreported, an arbitrator noted that a subtenant had ceased trading and assumed that this was because he could not afford the rent but, in reflecting this in his award, failed to invite the parties' views on it. Not surprisingly this award was also set aside.

852 Charley then referred us to two specific examples from the Webber/Dean paper peculiar to rent review.

> "The first was where the arbitrator departed from the agreed analysis of comparables. In the *Zermalt* decision the arbitrator said, in his award, that he believed it was for him to decide, as an arbitrator with experience in the matter, whether the equated Zone A rental which the parties had agreed as the appropriate way of analysing the comparables was reliable evidence upon which to base the valuation of other properties. He went on to say that he knew of two schemes where key lettings were achieved prior to reviews which were settled on a Zone A basis, following which when the units came on to the market they could not be let even with incentives. Clearly this sort of evidence was too much for the courts who overturned the award."

853 The second illustration from the Webber/Dean paper that Charley cited concerned the selection of the valuation method and the arbitrator's difficulty of trying to find a compromise between the parties' differing contentions as a result of these different methods of valuation. It is clear from the cases that Webber/Dean cited that the arbitrator is given considerable latitude over making relatively minor technical adjustments to the analysis of comparables.

854 He showed support for this view by citing *Secretary of State for the Environment* v. *Reed International plc* [1994] 6 EG 137. Here the authors said:

> "The Secretary of State was the subtenant under two leases of two adjoining multi-storey blocks occupied by the Department of the Environment. In making his award the arbitrator stated that in his opinion when assessing the rent under each sublease and faced with the reality of a large organisation occupying the other half of the building and appearing to be a potentially active bidder, the hypothetical tenant would have made a small overbid of £1 per sq. ft. The arbitrator was challenged on the basis that
>
> (a) there was no evidence to support this finding which constituted an error of law and grounds for leave to appeal; and
> (b) that neither party in their written submission had suggested the route to allowing an uplift which was ultimately selected by the arbitrator.
>
> This route was his own and the award should therefore be set aside for misconduct.
>
> The court was not persuaded that the absence of evidence to support a finding of fact was grounds for granting leave to appeal, but decided in any event that there was evidence on which the arbitrator could have based his conclusion. The department's occupation of the adjoining premises, their relationship to the subject premises, and the department's search for premises were admitted and could be relied on by him."

855 On the application to set aside for misconduct in choice of route the judge said:

> "It seems to me that what the arbitrator was here doing was the exercise of pure valuation experience on his part. The point with which he was dealing was a pure valuation point and what the arbitrator was doing was really partially accepting the submission . . . that there should be an uplift, but not accepting it in full . . . . It seems to me, in these circumstances, that where I am in doubt as to whether one of the parties can justly complain that he has not had an opportunity to make submissions with relation to a particular, and not very important, point in the arbitration, I should resolve that doubt by leaving the arbitrator's award to stand."

WHERE ARBITRATOR'S SPECIAL KNOWLEDGE NOT ABLE TO BE USED

The facts

856 The dispute was over a rent review on a superior flat in the West End of London.

857 The landlord produced comparable rental evidence on two flats only but these were known to the arbitrator to be in more superior residential blocks than the subject property. The tenant also correctly averred that these two comparables were of an entirely different nature and therefore were of limited assistance. The tenant produced no specific rental evidence however and expressed only general opinions.

858 The abitrator had a good knowledge of rental values in the area around the subject property; this knowledge was gleaned from his experience in private practice and from a number of other arbitrations he had conducted over similar rent review disputes.

Question

859 As the arbitrator's general knowledge was wider than that of either of the parties or their experts, how far could he use this knowledge in determining the correct level of rent on the subject property?

Course of action

860 In view of the lack of relevant comparable evidence offered to the arbitrator, he suggested that he should produce some evidence known to him for the parties to consider and address him on.

861 The landlord said that he would only agree to this if he was allowed to carry out internal inspections of the properties of which the arbitrator had this special knowledge. This was not a practical suggestion as the information on these properties had come to the arbitrator's notice through his privileged position as an expert witness in another arbitration, and thus such an inspection would have required the consent of a third party which was not likely to be forthcoming. In any case, neither of the landlord's two comparables was available for the arbitrator's internal inspection.

862 The arbitrator decided that he had no choice but to proceed on the basis of the landlord's evidence but making substantial deductions for the differences between the two cases and the subject properties.

863 The percentage deductions applied by the arbitrator were very much a matter within the arbitrator's judgement and not something which the parties had seriously addressed. However, the arbitrator is the absolute judge of the facts and can only make his best assessment from the evidence available to him, having been precluded, by the circumstances related above, from using better evidence.

864 Ironically, the decision in this case was quoted to the arbitrator as relevant evidence in a subsequent arbitration where he had to disclose to the parties in that arbitration how tenuous this was as market evidence.

865 The case of *Ravenseft Properties Ltd* v. *Boots Properties Ltd*, QBD, [1997] ADRLN 23 gives clear authority for the arbitrator to use his own expertise and make an award based on but adjusted from the figures provided by experts.

866 In this case the applicant, Boots Properties Ltd, was the tenant of a shop with two street frontages under lease from the respondent landlord, Ravenseft Properties Ltd. The lease provided for rent reviews and for arbitration in the event that a revised rent could not be agreed. The parties were unable to agree a rent for the period from 25 March 1996, the passing rent being £90,700 *per annum*, and an arbitrator was appointed to determine it.

867 The parties agreed to an arbitration based on written submissions, but the arbitrator gave a number of directions as to how matters were to proceed. Each party was required to make representations of their honest and sincere opinions of the rental value of the premises in accordance with the lease, setting out assumptions made in arriving at that valuation. When each side's representations were in, they were both given the opportunity to make counter-representations, confined to comments on points made in the opposing party's initial representations. Further comment was not to be entertained and the arbitrator was to issue his valuation as soon as possible thereafter. The arbitrator also reserved the right, if the need arose, to call a meeting with the parties to clarify any points in their representations.

868 The parties complied with these directions, their respective experts adopting different approaches to the valuation. The respondent's expert contended for a rent based on a separate assessment for each of the shop's two frontages, less a 10 per cent discount. The applicant's expert assessed the rent on the basis of the frontage associated with the main entrance, with a 5 per cent uplift for the second frontage.

869 In his award, the arbitrator adopted the approach taken by the applicant's expert, but stated that he did not consider a 5 per cent adjustment for the second frontage to be adequate. Instead, he adopted a 20 per cent adjustment. In applying this uplift, he arrived at a rent of £95,026, a figure which, it was common ground, should have been £96,000 but for a miscalculation made by him.

870 The applicant sought remission on the ground that the arbitrator was in breach of the rules of natural justice by rejecting, or substantially qualifying its evidence that the uplift should only be 5 per cent, thus substituting his own view, without giving the parties an opportunity to deal with what he was proposing to do. A second application to remit the award because of the mathematical error was withdrawn.

871 In this case, Tuckey J held that the arbitrator had not adopted a new approach. Rather, he accepted the approach adopted by the applicant's expert. The fact that he used a different percentage to reflect the location of the unit did not alter this approach, but was a simple matter of quantification. What he was doing was substituting his own valuation experience for that of the expert whose approach he had accepted. Since the parties had chosen the arbitrator for his own expertise, he was entitled to use his expertise in this way and it was not a breach of natural justice to do so.

IMPORTANT TO MAKE PARTIES AWARE OF WHAT IS IN THE ARBITRATOR'S MIND

The facts

872 An eminent expert for the claimant had given technical evidence which included an opinion that it was not possible to comply with the specification requirements in the particular material occurring at site.

873 The arbitrator had in the past supervised a similar operation, in almost identical

material which had met similar problems. By the use of different methods the problems were successfully overcome. The arbitrator had written a paper for the ICE proceedings which included a description of the methods used to overcome the problem.

Question

874 Should the arbitrator disclose the existence of his paper on the subject?

Course of action

875 Yes. At the end of that day's hearing, while the expert was still being cross-examined, the arbitrator should inform the expert of his experience and hand counsel for both parties a copy of his paper, then offer to let both sides address him on it the following day.

876 See, as in para 830 above, *British Oil & Cake Mills Ltd* v. *Horace Battin & Co Ltd* (1922) 13 Ll L Rep 443, where Darling J said:

> "The people who go to arbitration desire to have arbitrators or umpires who will not decide on evidence alone, but will bring to the consideration of cases a great deal of special knowledge, and they beyond everything want the matter decided one way or another without delay, so that they can devote all their attention to their business and not to litigation in the courts. It may be that they do things quite differently from what would be done in these courts, but that is because they desire to do so and so agree."

877 An arbitrator owes a duty to decide an arbitration on the facts and the law as he finds them to be. If he takes a view of fact or law which does not accord with the submissions of either party he should inform the parties of his provisional view so that they may deal with it (see Donaldson J's remarks with reference to a trade arbitral tribunal in *Thomas Borthwick (Glasgow) Ltd* v. *Faure Fairclough Ltd* [1968] 1 Lloyd's Rep 16 (see para 831 above)).

878 See also Lord Denning MR's remarks in *Fox* v. *Wellfair* when he drew attention to an important distinction between arbitrations in the construction industry and the special type of arbitrations—sometimes called "look-sniff" arbitrations—arising from disputes which are very different from those in the construction industry. His judgment included the following:

> "There are some arbitrations in which the arbitrator is expected to form his own opinion and act on his own knowledge without recourse to evidence given by witnesses on either side: such as an arbitrator who is to decide as to whether the goods are the sample, see *Mediterranean & Eastern Export Co* v. *Fortress Fabrics (Manchester) Ltd* (1948) 64 TLR 337. But there are other arbitrations in which the arbitrator is expected to receive the evidence of witnesses and the submissions of advocates and to be guided by them in reaching his conclusion: such as arbitrations on shipping contracts or building contracts. In such cases the arbitrator is often selected because of his knowledge of the trade, so that he can follow the evidence and submissions, but he must act judicially.
>
> He must not receive evidence in the absence of the other parties, and so forth. In the present case, if the defendants had been represented, I have no doubt that the plaintiffs' experts would have been cross-examined so as to throw doubt on their findings and on their opinions: and the defendants would have called experts to support the line of cross-examination. The arbitrator would then have been able to form a judgment—based on evidence other than his own."

879 But see also the judgment in *Ravenseft Properties Ltd* v. *Boots Properties Ltd* in paras 856 to 871 above.

IMMUNITY FROM SUIT OF AN EXPERT WITNESS—WHETHER LIABILITY CAN ARISE FOR CONCESSIONS MADE IN THE COURSE OF PREPARING A JOINT STATEMENT OF EXPERTS

The facts

880 Mr and Mrs Stanton consulted Mr Callaghan, a surveyor, after their property suffered subsidence and partial underpinning, undertaken with the agreement of their insurers, failed to stabilise the property. Mr Callaghan advised that partial underpinning has been the wrong solution and rather than remedying the problem had given rise to the risk of further movement, so that full underpinning would now be required to overcome the problem.

881 On the basis of that report, the plantiffs claimed against the insurers for the cost of the total underpinning of the building, which claim was rejected. They commenced proceedings against insurers and Mr Callaghan was retained to provide expert advice in support of the claim.

882 A direction was given in the proceedings that expert evidence be agreed where possible. Mr Callaghan was instructed to meet with the other expert within two weeks "with a view to agreeing as much as possible and making a list of those areas where a dispute really does exist".

883 The experts met and prepared a joint statement in which it was accepted that the partial underpinning gave rise to a risk of movement. This statement identified a cheaper, alternative solution to total underpinning involving the creation of a gap between the partial underpinning and the foundation. This would, in effect, have returned the foundations to their original state and therefore overcome the insurers' objection that total underpinning would represent a degree of betterment.

884 Having provided a copy of the joint statement to the solicitors for Mr and Mrs Stanton, Mr Callaghan subsequently incorporated the alternative solution in his expert's report.

885 In the light of these events the claim was settled prior to trial following an increased payment into court by the insurers, and the property was sold without any remedial works being carried out.

886 Mr and Mrs Stanton brought proceedings against the defendants. It was their primary case that the alternative solution was not feasible or effective and that Mr Callaghan's advice was thereby negligent and in breach of implied terms of his contract of retainer. They also alleged that, even if the alternative solution was viable, Mr Callaghan's concession breached the implied terms of his retainer, that, if he changed his opinion as to the merits of the case he would obtain express authority to disclose that change of view and that his view would be uninfluenced by the prospect of reaching agreement with the insurers.

887 The defendants claimed immunity from suit and sought to have the plaintiffs' claim struck out on the grounds that it disclosed no cause of action or was an abuse of the process of the court.

Questions

888 These were:

(1) Did the expert breach the terms of his contract of retainer when he reached agreement with the insurer's solicitors without his client's consent?
(2) If negligence was proven, was the expert in any event immune from suit in relation to the concession?
(3) Was the immunity lost if the expert did not subsequently give evidence?

Course of action

889 The facts of this example came from the case of *Stanton* v. *Brian F Callaghan & Associates* [1998] CILL 1409–1420, CA.

890 The short answers to the above questions, from the judgment in this case, are:

(1) No. In agreeing the joint statement the defendant was doing just what he had been instructed to do which was to agree as much as possible. It followed from the expert's role, in assisting the court, which required him to be free to make proper concessions, that there was no duty to inform the lay clients or the solicitors or to seek instructions before recording the concession in the joint statement.
(2) Yes. The public interest in facilitating full and frank disclosure between experts before trial in order to assist the court in resolving the issues and reaching a just solution, requires that each should be free to make proper concessions without fear that any departure from advice previously given to the party who has retained him will be seen as evidence negligence.
(3) No.

Extracts from the judgment

891 Chadwick LJ:

"I turn, therefore to the primary claim that Mr Callaghan's advice that the gap solution would resolve the subsidence problem and restore the property to its full market value was wrong, as pleaded in paragraph (a) in the particulars under paragraph 11 in the statement of claim. On this application to strike out the court must assume that that is an allegation which could be established at trial . . . .

What then, is the position in relation to expert reports? It seems to me that the following propositions are supported by authority binding in this court:

(i) an expert witness who gives evidence at a trial is immune from suit in respect of anything which he says in court and that immunity will extend to the contents of his report which he adopts as, or incorporates in, his evidence;
(ii) where an expert witness gives evidence at a trial the immunity which he would enjoy in respect of that evidence is not to be circumvented by a suit based on the report itself; and
(iii) the immunity does not extend to protect an expert who has been retained to advise as to the merits of a party's claim in litigation from a suit by the party by whom he has been retained in respect of that advice, notwithstanding that it was in contemplation at the time when the advice was given that the expert would be a witness at the trial if that litigation were to proceed. What, as it seems to me, has not been decided by any authority binding in this court is whether an expert is immune from suit by the party who has

retained him in respect of the contents of a report which he prepares for the purpose of exchange prior to trial—say, to comply with directions given under Order 38, rule 37 RSC—in circumstances where he does not, in the event, give evidence at the trial; either because trial does not take place or because he is not called as a witness.

If there is to be immunity in such circumstances, it must be founded on some, identifiable, ground of public policy. As Lord Wilberforce points out in *Saif Ali* v. *Sydney Mitchell & Co* [1980] AC 198, 214H

> "... account must be taken of the counter policy that a wrong ought not to be without a remedy".

Further, it must be recognised that the report prepared for the purposes of exchange prior to trial is likely to contain, or reflect, the initial advice as to the merits of the claim—advice which, as Sir Thomas Bingham, Master of the Rolls, pointed out in *M (a Minor)* v. *Newham London Borough Council* [1995] 2 AC 633, 661F, did not itself attract immunity.

In my view, the only ground of public policy that can be relied upon as a foundation for immunity in respect of the contents of an expert's report, in circumstances where no trial takes place and the expert does not give evidence, is that identified by Lord Morris of Borth-y-Gest in *Rondel* v. *Worsley* [1969] 1 AC 191, at 251G and referred to by Lord Diplock in *Saif Ali* v. *Sydney Mitchell* [1980] AC 198 at 222B:

> 'It has always been the policy of the law to ensure that trials are conducted without avoidable strains and tensions of alarm and fear.'

The other grounds mentioned in the authorities—the need to ensure that potential witnesses are not deterred from coming forward and the need to avoid a multiplicity of actions—appear to me to have little or no relevance in the present context. The claim for immunity in a case like the present must, as it seems to me, be tested against the criteria: is the immunity necessary for the orderly management and conduct of the trial which is in prospect.

I am not persuaded that experts who, as part of their professional practice and for reward, offer their services as potential witnesses on matters within their expertise are prone to 'strains and tensions of alarm and fear' at the stage at which they are preparing reports for exchange. I would not, myself, subscribe to the view that experts' reports would be any more or less helpfully drawn than they now are if the authors were or were not immune from suit by those who retain them in respect of the contents of those reports. But there does come a point at which the expert begins to take part in the management and conduct of the trial in advance of proceedings in court. In *Landall* v. *Dennis Faulkner & Alsop & Others* [1994] 5 Med LR 268 Mr Justice Holland referred at paragraph 13 in the report of his judgment, to the well known observation of Mr Justice Tomlin in *Graigola Merthyr Co Ltd* v. *Swansea Corporation* [1928] 1 Ch 31 at page 38 that:

> 'Long cases produce evils .... In every case of this kind there are generally many "irreducible and stubborn facts" upon which agreement between experts should be possible, and in my judgement the expert advisers of the parties, whether legal or scientific, are under a special duty to the court in the preparation of such a case to limit in every possible way the contentious matters to be dealt with at the hearing. That is a duty which exists notwithstanding that it may not always be easy to discharge ....'

Mr Justice Holland took the view that:

> '... given the importance to the court of agreements such as that evidenced by the impugned report, the public importance of immunity from suit for such is underlined.'

I respectfully agree. It is of importance to the administration of justice, and to those members of the public who seek access to justice, that trials should take no longer than is necessary to do justice in the particular case; and that, to that end, time in court should not be taken up with a consideration of matters which are not truly in issue. It is in that context that experts are encouraged to identify, in advance of the trial, those parts of their evidence on which they are, and those on which they are not, in agreement. Provision for a joint statement, reflecting agreement after a meeting of experts has taken place, is made by Order 38, rule 38, RSC. In my view, the public interest in facilitating full and frank discussion between experts before trial does require that each should be free to make proper concessions without fear that any departure from advice previously given to the party who has retained him will be seen as evidence of negligence. That, as it seems to me, is an area in which public policy justifies immunity. The immunity is needed in order to avoid the tension between a desire to assist the court and fear of the consequences of a departure from previous advice.

In the present case, as in *Landall* v. *Dennis Faulkner & Alsop* [1994] 5 Med LR 268, the expert's report was made after, and as a result of, a meeting between the experts on each side. The report incorporated what had been agreed. On that ground, I agree with the judge's conclusion that Mr Callaghan and the other defendants are immune from suit by the plaintiffs in respect of the alleged negligence in agreeing the viability of the gap solution on 14 December 1989 and incorporating that agreement in the report delivered on 18 December 1989."

892 Otton LJ:

"[Not] only does this principle cover evidence given at trial, over the years the protection has extended to cover certain pre-trial actions thought to be deserving of immunity from suit (*Evans* v. *London Hospital Medical College (University of London)* [1981] 1 WLR 184). Immunity has been held to cover not only witnesses giving evidence, but also to extend to the preliminary examination of witnesses (*Watson* v. *McEwan)* and also to other pre-trial work in preparing the case (*Marrinan* v. *Vibart: Rondel* v. *Worsley* [1969] 1 AC 191; *X (Minors)* v. *Bedfordshire County Council* [1995] 2 AC 633). This extension of immunity is important because it illustrates the courts' recognition that the smooth administration of justice, commonly given as a reason for granting immunity, and one to which I shall return, relies on not only what happens in the courtroom, but also what goes on before. The hearing cannot be neatly divorced from the prepratory work it depends on.

The immunity for pre-trial work is not indiscriminate. Not all work done prior to a hearing will be covered. It is a tailored immunity, and whether or not immunity exists in respect of pre-hearing conduct rests on an assessment of whether the work in question can be said to be

> 'So intimately connected with the conduct of the case in court that it can fairly be said to be a preliminary decision affecting the way the cause is to be conducted when it comes to a hearing',

McCarthy P of the New Zealand Court of Appeal in *Rees* v. *Sinclair* [1974] 1 NZLR 180, at 187, which test was adopted by a majority of the House of Lords in *Saif Ali*.

The issue of whether this protection should properly be applied to pre-hearing work done by an expert, such as Mr Callaghan, came before the courts only recently in *Palmer* v. *Durnford Ford* [1992] QB 483. In that case, the facts of which are set out in the judgment of Lord Justice Chadwick, Mr Simon Tuckey QC, as he then was, cognisant that he was dealing with a novel situation and referring to the House of Lords' decision in *Saif Ali* as set out above, said, at p. 488H:

> 'Immunity would only extend to what could fairly be said to be preliminary to his giving evidence in court judged perhaps by the principal purpose for which the work was done. So the production or approval of a report for the purposes of disclosure to the other side would be immune but work done for the principal purpose of advising the client would not.
>
> Each case would depend upon its own facts with the court concerned to protect the expert from liability for the evidence which he gave in court and the work principally and proximately leading thereto.'

The position of experts had been considered in subsequent cases, but I do not think anything has been said to disturb these principles as stated in *Palmer* v. *Durnford Ford*.

Thus there is clear authority that, provided the test of 'principal and proximate connection' is satisfied, the pre-hearing work of an expert will come within the protective circle of the witness immunity principle. What remains to be considered is whether it is appropriate to draw the circle narrower so that some experts, say lawyers and police officers, are admitted, while others, such as surveyors and architects, are not. Are there circumstances or a guiding principle which would permit of such a distinction?

... the case is best approached by asking the simple question:

Would it serve the interests of the administration of justice to grant immunity?

To answer this question we need to examine the role and place of an expert in the legal system ...

The role of an expert witness was recently considered by Cresswell J in the case of *'The Ikarian Reefer'* [1993] 2 Lloyd's Rep 68. At pp. 81–82 (citations omitted), he said:

> '1. Expert evidence presented to the court should be, and should be seen to be, the independent product of the expert uninfluenced as to form or content by the exigencies of the litigation.
> 2. An expert witness should provide independent assistance to the court by way of objective unbiased opinion in relation to matters within his expertise. An expert witness in the High Court should never assume the role of an advocate.
> 3. An expert witness should state the facts or assumption upon which his opinion is based. He should not omit to consider material facts which could detract from his concluded opinion.
> 4. An expert witness should make it clear when a particular question or issue falls outside his expertise ....
> 6. If, after exchange of reports, an expert witness changes his view on a material matter having read the other side's expert's report or for any other reason, such change of view should be communicated (through legal representatives) to the other side without delay and when appropriate to the court. ...

What these comments demonstrate is that although expert witnesses have duties to their clients, they have also another, overriding, duty to the court, to assist the court in resolving the issues and coming to a just conclusion. This also is the understanding of the role of an expert witness as expressed in chapter 13 of Lord Woolf's *Access to Justice Report* ....

It is clear to me that in order to enable the court to arrive at the fair and just result in the way set out by Lord Morris of Borth-y-Gest, expert witnesses must be given full opportunity to uphold their duty to the court, and achieve it in the way set out by Cresswell J and Lord Woolf, in an atmosphere free from threats of suit from disappointed clients.

Against the analysis I consider the particular circumstances of this case. On any basis the defendant when attending the meeting with his opposite number enjoyed the immunity. It is true that he did not do so pursuant to Order 38, rule 38 but the purpose of the meeting was to identify those parts of the evidence and the other's opinion which they could agree and those which they could not. It was in the public interest to do so. The duty to the court must override the fear of suit arising out of a departure from a previously held position. The expert must be able to resile fearlessly and with dignity. In the instant case both experts resiled from more extreme positions. In theory, at least, the defendants could have sued their expert for placing them in a more adverse position. It must follow that there was no duty to inform the lay clients or the solicitors or to seek instructions before recording the concession in the joint statement."

893 Nourse LJ:

"The extent of an expert witness's immunity from suit is still in course of development. No doubt it can and will be developed on a case by case basis.

Nevertheless it is desirable that it should so far as practicable be governed by a general rule, just as in the case of a witness of fact. The rule cannot be quite the same because the expert witness usually has the dual capacity of advising the client as well as giving evidence in support of his case.

That said, I see no justification for distinguishing between an expert and a lay witness, either on the ground that the expert is usually remunerated for his services or on the ground that he may be less likely than a lay witness to be deterred from giving evidence. Nor would I make any distinction between civil and criminal proceedings. An immunity founded on a requirement of public policy that witnesses should not be inhibited from giving frank and fearless evidence cannot afford to make distinctions such as these. If they were allowed, it could never be certain that the public policy would not sometimes be put at risk ....

[The] suggested analogy with the advocate's immunity from suit led Mr Tuckey [in *Palmer* v. *Durnford Ford, supra*] into propounding, though tentatively, a principal purpose test for pre-trial work. While I doubt that the distinction will often be material, I am not certain that this is the correct test. If the object of the immunity is to be achieved, it might well be said that a substantial purpose test should be preferred. That question does not, however, arise here. It is clear that Mr Callaghan's draft report of 11 December 1989, the joint statement which followed his meeting with Mr Kelsey on 14 December and his final report on 18 December or thereabouts were all prepared for the principal, if not the sole, purpose of his giving evidence in court at the trial fixed to start on 11 January 1990. Moreover, it is to my mind obvious that the immunity was not lost by Mr Callaghan's not subsequently giving the evidence he was expected to give."

Commentary

894 This case restates the overriding function of the expert witness to provide independent assistance to the court as emphasised in the *The Ikarian Reefer*. The issue of immunity did not arise in relation to advice given by the expert prior to the joint statement and his report. However, *obiter* statements of the Lord Justices in this decision indicate that there would not have been any such immunity. It would appear that the test as to whether or not an expert would benefit from immunity depends upon the primary purpose of the advice. For example, if the primary purpose of an expert's advice is to advise upon the merits of a particular issue prior to the issue of proceedings there would probably be no immunity. Where advice has dual purposes, Lord Justice Nourse has indicated that it may be sufficient to establish immunity if a substantial, but not necessarily a principal purpose of the advice is to be the giving of evidence at trial. To avoid the difficulties that Mr and Mrs Stanton faced in this case it is advisable that a party instructing an expert ensures that the expert is aware of the extent of his authority and that matters which the expert agrees in any note of a meeting may be binding upon him. This course is recommended in the ORSA Expert Protocol (reproduced as Appendix B of this book).

(The above example is reproduced almost *verbatim* from the *Construction Industry Law Letter*, September 1998, with the kind permission of the joint editors Robert Fenwick Elliott and Tony Francis.)

PART II

EXPERT DETERMINATION

CHAPTER 9

INTRODUCTORY ARTICLES

CHAPTER 9/1

EXPERT DETERMINATION

Review of John Kendall's book by
Alan Redfern, Barrister

001 If an expert, in the celebrated phrase of a former President of Columbia University, is someone "who knows more and more about less and less," then we are all experts now. The medical profession, of course, has long had its specialisations, some more esoteric than others. The major firms of lawyers and accountants now have their specialist departments—experts in mergers and acquisitions, debt financing, intellectual property, tax planning, forensic accounting and so on—who guard their mysteries and tend their own particular sacred flame. Nor is this development confined to the professions: even the better class of supermarkets has its specialist sectors, its delicatessens, bakeries, and cheese counters.

002 It should come as no surprise then if the peaceful resolution of disputes, which used to be the work of judges and arbitrators, is now becoming separated into a series of different, specialised procedures, ranging from mediation and conciliation at one end of the spectrum to full scale litigation at the other. In his new edition of this excellent book, John Kendall sets out to show how the decision of an expert may be of crucial importance, both in avoiding disputes before they arise and in resolving disputes once they have arisen.

003 The traditional role of an expert was, of course, that of a valuer or assessor: he or she would be asked to assess the worth of a house or a block of flats; or to put a price on shares in a private company or a professional partnership; or to certify the value of work done by a building or engineering contractor. This work of valuation is clearly but succinctly explained in the opening chapters of this book, which are full of sensible comment and advice. They will be of great value to the busy practitioner, looking for a quick but authoritative answer to a particular problem.

004 However, what will be of particular interest to many readers is the way in which the role of the expert has developed—whether he or she be an accountant, an architect, a surveyor, an engineer or a lawyer. The work of valuation continues, of course; but increasingly the expert is seen as a "decision-maker"—someone whose determination of a dispute may well put an end to it. This new role for the expert goes well with new technologies. As the author explains:

> "The 20th Century has seen the growth of new technologies and of the power of organised professions which have assisted the expansion of the role of the referee from valuer to expert. The energy and computer industries are obvious examples: applications of expert determination in the energy and computer industries are set out in the following sections. There are many new technologies, and expert determination may be appropriate to many more applications than these instances."

005 When the expert becomes an adjudicator, then the process of expertise itself begins to resemble more closely that of arbitration. Nonetheless, there is a difference and it is an important one. There are two main reasons. First, an arbitrator, unlike an expert, has traditionally been regarded in English law as being immune from liability for negligence in the carrying out of his or her functions, and this immunity is now confirmed by statute in the Arbitration Act 1996. Secondly, the award of an arbitrator is enforceable as such, both nationally and internationally under such treaties as the New York Convention of 1958, whereas the decision of an expert is only binding contractually and will need to be enforced by proceedings in court if it is not carried out voluntarily.

006 One formula which is conventionally used in the appointment of an expert is the phrase that he should act "as an expert and not as an arbitrator". However, this formula of itself (which the author tells us first appeared in the Law Reports in *Dean* v. *Prince* [1953] Ch 590 at 591, where it is misquoted!) is not in itself determinative of whether, in a particular case, the decision-maker is in fact acting as an expert or as an arbitrator. How to distinguish between them is a problem which perplexed at least two of the five judges in the House of Lords in *Arenson* v. *Casson Beckman Rutley & Co* [1977] AC 405. The case concerned the liability of accountants who had carried out an expert valuation of shares in a private company, "acting as experts and not as arbitrators". The issue was whether or not they were entitled to the same immunity from being sued for professional negligence as an arbitrator would enjoy. Lord Kilbrandon said: "The question which puzzled me as the argument developed was, what was the essential difference between the typical valuer (the auditor in the present case) and an arbitrator . . . ."

007 Lord Kilbrandon looked at the traditional tests for distinguishing the two roles (which the author also discusses in this book) but attached little or no weight to them. Lord Fraser shared his doubts: "It does not seem possible, therefore, to distinguish between mutual valuers and arbitrators on the ground that the former are experts and the latter are not. I share the difficulty of Lord Kilbrandon in seeing why arbitrators as a class should have immunity from suit if mutual valuers do not".

008 Perhaps the essential difference, as the author points out, is that arbitrators have judicial functions to perform, and they must observe the basic rules which govern judicial proceedings.

009 The increasing use of experts to resolve disputes once they have arisen can be seen in some of the major international constructions projects carried out in recent years. In the Channel Tunnel project, for example, any dispute had to be referred to the Panel of Experts and then, if either party so requested, to arbitration under the rules of the ICC. In the Boston Central Artery/Tunnel project—one of the most complex highway projects ever undertaken, involving many hundreds of contracts and sub-contracts—any disputes have to be resolved first by "partnering" (a form of mediation); if unsuccessful, by an "authorised representative", who gives a decision; and then by a Disputes Review Board, which may by agreement with the parties refer the dispute to any form of ADR that is acceptable to them, before issuing its findings and recommendations. Again, in the Hong Kong Airport Core programme, four steps were contemplated. These are the submission of the dispute for decision by the engineer, followed (if either party is dissatisfied at any stage) by mediation, adjudication and then arbitration. These complex procedures, consisting like a wedding-cake of three or four tiers, are a reflection of the amounts of money likely to be at stake and of a reluctance to trust in one decision-maker.

010 One of the problems involved in setting up a panel or a committee of experts is the problem with which this review began. What specialist qualifications are required of the experts who are to constitute the committee? In a major construction project, it is easy to suggest that the experts should be engineers. But from what precise disciplines should they be drawn? An expert who is highly qualified in one discipline (for instance, runway construction) may not necessarily be the right expert for a dispute which arises over the efficiency of the air traffic control system. It may be that for long-term engineering projects involving different disciplines, there should be a wider list of experts from whom to draw, so as to establish a suitably qualified panel for each particular dispute.

011 One final service which this book renders to its readers is that it contains a series of excellent precedents relating to expert determination. It is not intended by the author that these should be followed word for word, but they are packed with useful guidance and information. The layout of this book is admirable, with careful and intelligent cross-referencing. Separate topics are covered in separate chapters, so that the busy practitioner can go straight to the relevant chapter for information and advice. Inevitably there is some repetition, but this is a price which is well worth paying for the clarity with which the separate chapters are written and the mastery with which the text is marshalled.

***Alan Redfern** was for many years the senior litigation partner at Freshfields. He transferred to the Bar in May 1995 and joined the Chambers of Lord Grabiner QC at 1 Essex Court, where he specialises in international commercial arbitration.*

CHAPTER 9/2

EXPERTLY HANDLED?

Andrew Tugwell

001 What steps can an independent expert take to avoid a negligence action, and what remedies are available to a dissatisfied party?

002 Arbitrators have limited personal liability under section 29 of the Arbitration Act 1996, unless they are shown to have acted in bad faith. An independent expert, however, can be sued in negligence although this can be notoriously difficult to prove. From the dissatisfied parties' perspective, whilst an arbitrator's award can be challenged in court, the independent expert's determination remains binding even if negligence is proved save in very exceptional circumstances.

003 *Lewisham Investment Partnerships Ltd* v. *Morgan* [1997] 51 EG 75 concerned an action for negligence against an independent expert who it was alleged wrongly undervalued an M&S supermarket using the overall method of valuation instead of zoning. For reasons discussed below, this independent expert was held not negligent, but independent experts and arbitrators do occasionally get it wrong.

004 In practice, there are few successful negligence actions brought against independent experts. In *Lewisham* Neuberger J said: "If it were for me to decide how to assess the market rent of [the unit], I would have thought it right to give more weight to the zoning method than to the overall method." But this was not enough for him to find the independent expert negligent.

STANDARD OF CARE

005 The standard of care to be adopted by an independent expert is the same standard as that imposed upon any fellow professional. An independent expert must exercise reasonable care and skill in carrying out his or her professional task to the standard of an ordinary skilled man or woman exercising and professing to have that particular skill. Such skill does not have to be the highest independent expert skill, just competent. The test applied in *Lewisham* was whether the determination was so low to be below the figure which a reasonably competent and careful surveyor could have determined.

006 If the independent expert's practice is called into question, the independent expert's care and skill in adopting that practice will be measured against whether an ordinary competent valuer would so adopt the independent expert's methodology under the same circumstances as faced by the independent expert at that time.

007 It is not sufficient to prove, for example, that a reasonably competent valuer might have used a different valuation method but, instead, that the valuation method used was such that no competent valuer, under the circumstances, could have adopted it. Neuberger J's preference for the zoning method was therefore, as he himself pointed out, "strictly irrelevant" to the matter of negligence.

008 Even if the independent expert was negligent, it must be shown that the resultant valuation falls outside the non-negligent values accepted by the court. Regardless of negligent practice, therefore, an independent expert can be found not to have acted negligently by luck rather than judgement. It is not sufficient to show that an independent expert's valuation methodology was negligent in itself if the resultant valuation is shown to be the same or nearly the same as the figure produced by a non-negligent valuation approach.

ADVICE TO THE INDEPENDENT EXPERT

009 In contrast to arbitration awards, independent determinations are rarely reasoned. As a result, it is not easy for a dissatisfied party to follow the methodology used by the independent expert in reaching his or her valuation. If a dissatisfied party is to issue proceedings, however, the independent expert's files (including notes of deliberations, inspections and comparables) will be disclosed. A defence to a claim in negligence will often depend upon the careful and contemporaneous notes made by the independent expert and the court will be reluctant to infer what is happening in the independent expert's mind (*Morgan Sindall plc* v. *Sawston Farms (Cambs) Ltd* [1997] 07 EG 135).

010 An independent expert is free to make use of valuation evidence or legal matters known to him or her. An independent expert is not, however, under a duty to take submissions, unless the lease or appointment so provides. Nevertheless, an independent expert who does not take submissions will be exposed to a far greater prospect of a claim arising and the parties' submissions should therefore not be dismissed without carefully noted reasons.

011 In dealing with a complicated legal issue, the reasonable standard of enquiry relating to the issue is that of a reasonable surveyor and not a lawyer. The independent expert should, however, take legal advice if unsure of legal issues submitted by the parties and give the parties further opportunity to make representations or apply to the court if necessary, for example, to seek a declaration on a point of construction. Having taken legal advice, this should be followed. This principle was summarised by Neuberger J in *Lewisham*:

> "One particular circumstance which could result in the surveyor not escaping liability is where he ought, bearing in mind the facts surrounding his determination, [to] have sought independent legal advice and/or have reverted to the parties for further submissions. Although the [parties] had agreed in the Lease that they were entrusting the assessment of the Market Rent to a surveyor, this would obviously not exonerate him if he erred in law when making his determination, if it can be shown that he did not seek independent legal advice and/or he did not discuss the matter with the parties, and that a competent careful surveyor would have done so."

012 In *Lewisham*, Neuberger J criticised the Court of Appeal decision in *Iceland Frozen Foods plc* v. *Starlight Investments Ltd* [1992] 1 EGLR 126 CA, which was relied upon by the independent expert to ignore the prospect of subletting. If taken into account, this would have favoured the zoning method of valuation. The independent expert, however, was found to have acted properly by taking legal advice and giving the parties an opportunity of making representations.

013 An independent expert's standard should always be measured against the benchmark of a body of reasonable valuers. If an independent expert uses new valuation practices which might not be recognised by the profession, then care should be taken to cross-check the valuation by recognised methods and a record should be kept of the independent expert's justification for using non-standard practices, such as in dealing with an unusually sized shop.

014 It may be significant if the parties to comparable transactions have agreed the basis of devaluation including the method adopted by both parties such as an agreed value *per* square foot ITZA but that is not to say that the independent expert is bound to follow that approach. There should, however, always be a consistency of valuation approach between the devaluation of comparables and the subject property. This does not mean that each comparable has to be relevant, only that each comparable should be considered. Neuberger J observed that:

> "It is frequently difficult to reconcile all of [the comparables] satisfactorily . . . he [the independent expert] based his valuation on . . . two comparables. It seems to me that that was something he was entitled to do, particularly as he considered all the comparables put to him before he reached that conclusion."

015 Every independent expert's personal checklist should include, as a minimum, the following guidelines:

- Take care in accepting the appointment. Check that there are no conflicts and that you have sufficient experience for the task both generally and to satisfy any requirements in the lease.
- Proceed promptly and diligently, checking any stipulated timetable in the lease.
- Check the lease for any procedural steps to be followed and do not set out to determine issues beyond your remit.
- Consider very seriously whether there is any good reason not to invite the parties to make written submissions to you.
- Give due consideration to all comparables submitted to you by the parties and all legal issues raised by the parties.
- Follow the RICS Guidance Notes for Surveyors acting as Arbitrators and Independent Experts. For example, consider whether there are any legal issues or issues of construction which are fundamental assumptions and comply with your duty to make independent investigations.
- Only take into account material and relevant facts/matters/information.
- Take legal advice if necessary, but try to get the parties to agree to be bound by the advice, and give the parties an opportunity to make their own submission on the issue.
- Adopt a consistent valuation approach.
- Take accurate notes at all times including the reasons for all decisions. Remember that your files may be disclosed.
- Do not give reasons for your determination unless the lease requires them.

ADVICE TO THE DISSATISFIED PARTY

016 A dissatisfied party may wish to have the determination set aside by the court as an alternative to an action in negligence. This will only be possible in exceptional circumstances.

Broadly speaking, the court will only set aside a determination if it agrees that the independent expert has not performed the task assigned, for example, if the independent expert has answered the wrong question as opposed to answering the right question but in the wrong way. For an excellent review of the law, see the article by Jonathan Gaunt and Nicholas Cheffings in *Estates Gazette*, 18 January 1997, reproduced in this book as Chapter 9/3.

017 On appeal, the court will not decide any question which falls to be decided by the independent expert under a lease and, generally, the court will only set a determination aside, even in the case of a manifest error, if the lease does not confer exclusive jurisdiction on the independent expert.

018 Another option is to seek a declaration from the court regarding an issue in dispute before a determination is made, although the court is likely to decline to interfere with issues concerning matters of fact (but may rule on matters of law or fundamental assumptions (*National Grid Co plc* v. *M25 Group Ltd* [1999] 08 EG 169)).

019 If the parties wish to ensure that they reserve the ability to refer such matters as important legal issues to the court rather than leaving this in the hands of the independent expert, they should agree that the independent expert must bring to the attention of the parties any conflicting legal interpretations as soon as these become apparent. The independent expert should then be required to obtain a legal ruling on the interpretation which could be made not immediately binding on the parties unless the parties fail to make an application to court within, say, 21 days of receipt of the ruling.

020 As a matter of tactics, it is sometimes argued that making an objection to an appointment should be avoided because of the risk of upsetting an independent expert but it is surely not logical for a party to agree to an appointment which it believes is likely to lead to an unsatisfactory determination in any event. Such a passive acceptance is likely to prohibit the possibility of an objection at a later stage, and even if the objection is over-ruled, the independent expert will be put on notice of the concern.

021 I suggest that a party to a reference for determination by an independent expert should, as a minimum, consider the following matters:

- Take care to investigate the proposed independent expert. Does the independent expert have experience in the relevant field and satisfy any requirements under the lease? Check whether the independent expert has published works or articles which might indicate a particular line of thinking. Ask for details of the independent expert's experience and object if necessary, even if the appointment is to be made by a third party such as the President of the RICS.
- Take care to agree, if possible (which it may not be at this stage), the procedures to be adopted, including the ability of the parties to make submissions and counter-submissions and further submissions if necessary regarding legal issues. If possible, agree that any legal ruling made by the independent expert will be decided as a preliminary issue and that the parties are able to appeal the ruling if necessary.
- After the determination, consider whether the terms of the independent expert's appointment have been met? Has there been a material procedural error which has resulted in an erroneous valuation?
- If the determination appears unreasonably low or high, take independent advice as to whether a competent valuer, under the same circumstances at the time of the determination, would have come to the same, or nearly the same, valuation.

THE OPTION TO ARBITRATE

022 It has been suggested that, in light of the potential personal liability faced by the independent expert, an indemnity should be sought from the parties before an independent expert undertakes an instruction.

023 In practice, it is doubtful that such a arrangement would be acceptable to the parties, let alone to the RICS. Why should the parties settle for less than a reasonable standard of care and skill from the independent expert?

024 A more practical suggestion for a recalcitrant valuer to put forward prior to accepting an appointment as an independent expert might be that the parties make an appointment as an arbitrator under the Arbitration Act 1996. Under the provisions of this Act, an arbitrator can be given, or will have by default, much greater powers of independent investigation than was the case before. Further, the parties may agree to forfeit any rights of appeal as will be the natural consequence of the parties agreeing that the arbitrator should make an award without reasons.

CONCLUSION

025 It is in the nature of a third party valuation determination that, more often than not, one of the parties, and sometimes both parties, will be unhappy with the result but this rarely means that the independent expert has acted negligently. No amount of prior preparation or management of the independent determination procedure will eliminate this dissatisfaction. However, careful consideration of the matters discussed above should make the process less painful and a dissatisfied party could be satisfied at least that every precaution had been taken to ensure a fair outcome.

026 From the independent expert's perspective, some comfort might be drawn from the absence of decided cases holding that independent experts have been negligent. However, this should not lead to a false sense of security. A significant factor in *Lewisham* was, no doubt, the fact that Neuberger J was impressed by the independent expert as a careful surveyor, both by the copious and detailed notes he made and by his evidence. Others should take note.

Andrew Tugwell *is a litigation solicitor with Nabarro Nathanson specialising in property related disputes and is experienced in general landlord and tenant matters, rent review, dilapidations, property management and surveying issues such as valuation, arbitration and negligence. He is also a Fellow of the Royal Institute of Chartered Surveyors and the Chartered Institute of Arbitrators and is a trained mediator, formerly practising with DTZ Debenham Thorpe plc and on his own account. He has published various articles and given talks relating to arbitration, independent experts and estate agency issues.*

The original of this article first appeared in the Estates Gazette *dated 17 January 1998 (p. 133) and has been updated for the purpose of this book.*

CHAPTER 9/3

EXPERT DETERMINATIONS—FINAL AND BINDING?

Jonathan Gaunt QC
and Nicholas Cheffings

INTRODUCTION

001 This article concerns

(a) whether a determination by an independent expert on an issue referred to him by two parties in dispute, such as a rent review, is always binding upon those parties or whether it can ever be challenged through the courts and
(b) whether the courts have jurisdiction to determine such an issue before, or pending, its reference to the expert.

002 The learned authors of *Woodfall on Landlord and Tenant Law* (at para 18–030, footnote 71) wrote that a decision in the House of Lords appeared to have overruled the earlier cases, which had suggested that, save in exceptional circumstances, the expert's decision could not be set aside. In a recent case, Lightman J observed that this suggestion was wrong. In their latest edition, the editors described themselves as not "wholly persuaded" of this.

003 This issue is obviously of fundamental importance to parties in dispute and, by reviewing the cases, we attempt in this article to remove some of the uncertainty.

THE OLD CASES

004 *Dean* v. *Prince* [1954] Ch 409 concerned the articles of a company and the price at which a member's share should be purchased by the directors on his death, which was to be certified by the auditor to be, in his opinion, the fair value of the shares.

005 The Court of Appeal took as settled law a judgment in *Collier* v. *Mason* (1858) 25 Beav 200 that the court must act on the valuation unless there was proof of some mistake or some improper motive, for example if the valuer had valued something not included or had valued it on a wholly erroneous principle or if the price was so excessive or so small as only to be explicable by reference to some such cause. Denning LJ said that a valuation could be impeached not only for fraud but also for mistake or miscarriage, for instance, if the expert had interpreted the agreement wrongly. The Court of Appeal upheld the auditor's valuation but made it clear that they would have held the valuation to have been a nullity if they had agreed with the judge that it had been made on the wrong basis. This principle was applied in two reported cases at first instance: in one, the error was held to be immaterial (*Wright* v. *Frodoor* [1967] 1 WLR 506) and in the other the valuation was declared invalid (*Jones* v. *Jones* [1971] 1 WLR 840).

SPEAKING AND NON-SPEAKING AWARDS

006 There were then developments in the general law of negligence which caused Lord Denning to change his views. The reason for this was that, whereas in 1954, there had been an established line of cases to the effect that a valuer could not be sued in negligence, by 1976, the House of Lords had overturned those authorities (*Arenson* v. *Casson Beckman Rutley & Co* [1977] AC 405—decided in 1975). Lord Denning reviewed the circumstances in which an expert's determination could be set aside in the light of this development and laid down a stricter rule as follows:

> "It is simply the law of contract. If two persons agree that the price of property should be fixed by a valuer on whom they agree, and he gives that valuation honestly and in good faith, they are bound by it. Even if he has made a mistake, they are still bound by it. The reason is because they have agreed to be bound by it. If there were fraud or collusion, of course, it would be very different. Fraud or collusion unravels everything."
> (*Campbell* v. *Edwards* [1976] 1 WLR 403 (which concerned the price to be paid for the surrender of the lease of a flat in Mayfair).)

007 That decision was endorsed by the Court of Appeal in *Baber* v. *Kenwood Manufacturing Co Ltd* [1978] 1 Lloyd's Rep 175, another shares valuation case, where the court did, however, point out that a valuation would not be binding if the valuer had valued the shares of the wrong company or the wrong number of shares, because such a valuation would not accord with the express terms of the contract.

008 Both of those cases concerned what are known as "non-speaking" determinations, that is decisions given without reasons. In the case of *Burgess* v. *Purchase & Sons (Farms) Ltd* [1983] 1 Ch 216, Nourse J observed that the question of what remedy the plaintiff might have against the valuer had no relevance to the question of what was his remedy against the other party to the contract and summarised the state of the law as depending upon whether the determination was speaking or non-speaking. If it was non-speaking, it could not be impugned by the parties provided it was made of the right property by the right man and in good faith. On the other hand, a speaking valuation could be impugned if it was made on a fundamentally erroneous basis.

THE MODERN LAW

009 The next significant case was *Jones* v. *Sherwood Computer Services plc* [1992] 1 WLR 277 (decided in 1989) in which the Court of Appeal disapproved *Burgess* v. *Purchase* and held that no distinction was to be drawn between determinations with or without reasons.

010 This case concerned the acquisition of shares in a company; in the event of accountants being unable to agree the amount of sales of products sold by two subsidiaries of the company, the matter was to be referred to a third accountant who would determine the amount. The accountant's determination, given as an expert, was to be conclusive and final and binding for all purposes. Having considered the facts, the Court of Appeal concluded that the experts had done precisely what they had been asked to do and accordingly their determination of the amount of the sales could not be challenged by the parties (at 288G).

011 Dillon LJ did, nevertheless, make clear that if the evidence established that the expert had departed from his contractual instructions in a material respect, then either party would be able to say that his certificate was not binding, because the expert had not done what he was appointed to do (at 287A). The ability to challenge the award would not depend on whether the expert had given reasons but on whether the necessary evidence was available from whatever source.

THE RENT REVIEW CASES

012 In *Nikko Hotels (UK) Ltd* v. *MEPC plc* [1991] 2 EGLR 103, an accountant had been required to determine the average room rate of a hotel for insertion in a formula for deciding the rent. The tenant sought to have the determination declared a nullity on the basis that he had misconstrued that expression. Applying *Jones* v. *Sherwood*, Knox J held that, if the parties agree to refer to the final and conclusive judgment of an expert an issue which either consists of a question of construction or necessarily involves the solution of a question of construction, the expert's decision will be final and conclusive and therefore not open to review unless it can be shown that the expert has not performed the task assigned to him. Knox J summarised it thus: "If he has answered the right question in the wrong way his decision will be binding. If he has answered the wrong question, his decision will be a nullity".

013 In *Pontsarn Investments Ltd* v. *Kansallis-Osaki-Pankki* [1992] 1 EGLR 148, His Honour Judge Paul Baker held that the interpretation of the expression "fit for immediate occupation and use" was a matter for the expert to determine. The fact that he might be patently wrong did not mean that he had not done what he was appointed to do nor that he had asked himself the wrong question. Accordingly, his determination could not be set aside.

Comment

014 In our opinion, the "has he asked the right question?" test is unsound and based on a misunderstanding of *Jones* v. *Sherwood*. In a rent review case, the question referred to the expert is typically "what is the rental value of certain premises assessed according to certain prescribed valuation criteria?". If he fails to apply those criteria, whether because he ignores them or misunderstands them, the expert is not valuing in accordance with the parties' contract. For example, suppose there is a direction to ignore certain tenant's improvements, but the valuer values those improvements. He has not performed the valuation that the parties contracted for but has valued a different thing. According to the *Nikko Hotels/Pontsarn* approach, his award would be inviolable even if he had plainly misinterpreted the direction. Decided rent review cases, of course, illustrate many much more obtuse points of construction than that. If the evidence clearly establishes that the expert has applied his valuation expertise in the light of a misapprehension as to what he has to do, then he would surely be seen to have "departed from his instructions in a material respect" (in the words of Dillon LJ) and either party ought to be able to say that his award is not binding.

015 Ultimately, it comes down to a question of construction of the agreement to refer the matter to the expert. That entails asking whether the parties, on the true construction of their agreement, were agreeing to take the risk not only of the expert making a mistake in the application of his own expertise as a valuer/accountant or whatever but also the risk of his misunderstanding what he was to value or how he was being asked to value it? Few parties, surely, would accept that they had agreed the latter.

A NEW TWIST—CAN THE COURT GRANT DECLARATORY RELIEF?

016 Nevertheless, it was now apparent (our doubts aside) that it would be extremely difficult to set aside an expert's determination provided that he had "answered the right question" and had done so in good faith. In *Postel Properties Ltd* v. *Greenwell* [1992] 2 EGLR 130 a rent review had been referred to a surveyor, acting as expert and his decision was to be final on all matters referred to him. Before he had made his determination, however, a question of construction arose as to the user restrictions to be assumed for the purpose of the valuation.

017 The judge concluded that the issue of construction between the parties was clearly within the jurisdiction of the courts and its resolution might assist in the determination of the rent. It did not follow that, because the court would not upset a determination once made, even if convinced that it was made on a wrong basis as a matter of construction, it should not make a ruling preliminary to a determination yet to be made.

018 By contrast, in the case of *Norwich Union Life Insurance Society* v. *P&O Property Holdings Ltd* [1993] 1 EGLR 164, the Vice-Chancellor refused to grant an injunction to restrain an expert from proceeding with the determination of a dispute under a funding agreement pending the decision of the court on a question of construction. He held that, as a matter of principle, the issue on which a determination by the court is being sought is either within the matters remitted to the expert for his decision or it is not; if it is, then the court will not intervene either before or after, unless there has been fraud or collusion.

019 The Vice-Chancellor's decision was upheld by the Court of Appeal but in terms which make it clear that it turned on its own facts. The issue referred to the expert was the date which was to be regarded as "the completion date" for the purpose of the agreement. That turned on the standard of completion required and the identification of the design documents. Those were matters dependent entirely on the facts and were thus the very matters which had been remitted to the expert.

Comment

020 We suggest that it would be wrong to regard this case as laying down any general principle that an issue of interpretation concerning the basis upon which an expert is to conduct a valuation is excluded from the jurisdiction of the court.

THE HOUSE OF LORDS

021 The decision which has caused the recent uncertainty and the difference of opinion between commentators is that of *Mercury Communications Ltd* v. *Director General of Telecommunications* [1996] 1 All ER 575.

022 The case concerned a reference by British Telecom and Mercury to the Director General for a decision on the amounts to be charged for connection and the conveyance of calls.

023 A dispute arose as to the validity of the Director General's determination. Mercury alleged that he had misinterpreted phrases relating to "fully allocated costs attributable to the services to be provided" and "relevant overheads". British Telecom disagreed. There was no issue before the House of Lords as to whether Mercury was right in its interpretation of the phrases in dispute. The sole issue was whether Mercury could question the interpretation of the Director General.

024 Having regard to the decided cases, the Court of Appeal found, by majority, in favour of British Telecom on the ground that these matters had been remitted to the Director General for his determination and it was not for the court to take over that function.

025 Delivering their Lordships' judgment, Lord Slynn of Hadley said that what had to be done by the Director General depended upon the proper interpretation of words in the original agreement. He held as follows:

> "If the Director misinterprets these phrases and makes a determination on the basis of an incorrect interpretation, he does not do what he was asked to do. . . . The parties did not intend him simply to apply such meaning as he himself thought they should bear. His interpretation could therefore be reviewed by the court."

Comment

026 It has been suggested that there is a conflict between this decision and that in the *Norwich Union* case, but in truth there is none. The question is simply whether, *on the true construction of the agreement*, a particular matter falls within the exclusive remit of the expert. Matters which involve investigations of the facts (as in *Norwich Union*) and the application of the expertise of the expert almost certainly will do so. Questions of law and construction (as in *Mercury*) will usually not.

027 Lord Slynn went on: "There is no provision expressly or impliedly that these matters were remitted exclusively to the Director . . . . Nor is there any provision excluding altogether the intervention of the court."

028 It is, of course, perfectly possible for the parties to remove issues of construction from the court's jurisdiction as a matter of contract but we do not consider that this is *necessarily* achieved simply by expressing the expert's award to be "final and conclusive". Even where these words are used, it must remain overwhelmingly unlikely that the parties intended to take the risk that the expert would misapprehend his instructions and conduct his valuation on a basis for which they had not provided (as opposed, of course, to accepting the risk of the expert arriving at a wrong or wayward valuation on the correct basis).

BRITISH SHIPBUILDERS

029 In *British Shipbuilders* v. *VSEL Consortium plc* (1996) *The Times*, 14 February, Lightman J was faced by an agreement which provided that an expert's decision should, in the absence of manifest error, be final and binding on the parties. The matter came before him before the expert had been appointed in order that the parties could, with a view to saving time and costs, clarify the respective roles of the court and the expert.

030 The key issue before Lightman J was whether "upon the true construction of the Agreement", the court or the expert had jurisdiction (alternatively exclusive jurisdiction) to resolve disputes between the parties.

031 In answering this question, the judge observed that five principles govern the status of decisions of an expert, as follows:

1. questions as to the role of the expert, the ambit of his remit (or jurisdiction) and the character of his remit (whether exclusive or concurrent with a like jurisdiction vested in the court) are to be determined *as a matter of construction of the agreement* (our emphasis);
2. if the agreement confers upon the expert the exclusive remit to determine a question, the jurisdiction of the court to determine that question is excluded because the determination of the expert alone is relevant and any determination by the court is irrelevant; it is irrelevant whether the court would have reached a different conclusion or whether the court considers that the expert's decision is wrong, for the parties have in either event agreed to abide by the decision of the expert;
3. if the expert in making his determination goes outside his remit, the courts may intervene and set his decision aside; such a determination by the expert as a matter of construction of the agreement is not a determination which the parties agreed should affect the rights and duties of the parties;
4. likewise the court may set aside a decision of the expert *where the agreement so provides* (our emphasis) if his determination discloses a manifest error (service charge clauses often provide for a certificate to be final and binding except in cases of "manifest error");
5. the Court has jurisdiction ahead of the determination of an expert to determine a question as to the limits of his remit or the conditions which the expert must comply with in making his determination but (as a rule of procedural convenience) will (save in exceptional circumstances) decline to do so.

032 The judge rejected the suggestion in *Woodfall* that the House of Lords in *Mercury* v. *Director General* had overruled *Jones* v. *Sherwood* and *Norwich Union* v. *P&O*. He said: "The suggestion ... that the court has jurisdiction to correct an error in the construction of an agreement by an expert *in all cases* [our emphasis] is wrong."

CONCLUSION

033 We agree with Lightman J that *Mercury* does not overrule *Jones* v. *Sherwood* and *Norwich Union* (if the House had meant to overrule those cases it would have said so. In fact, Lord

Slynn's judgment carefully *distinguishes* them on their own facts at 58C–F.) It simply shows, as Dillon LJ made clear in *Jones*, that there can be cases where the court will

(a) entertain proceedings for a declaration as to the meaning of a provision which is to be applied by an expert and
(b) declare a decision of an expert to be a nullity because he is shown to have misinterpreted what he had to do.

034 As we have said above, it comes down ultimately, to a question of the correct construction of the agreement to refer the matter to the expert. If the parties wish to exclude the jurisdiction of the Court *entirely*, it is open to them to do so. If that is what the parties to a lease wish to achieve then they must draft their leases accordingly and this may well require wording beyond simply describing the expert's decision as final and binding or conclusive. In the absence of clear wording in the lease or other agreement the courts can, and will, intervene. We hope that the editors of *Woodfall* are now "wholly persuaded".

Jonathan Gaunt QC *has been the Joint Head of Falcon Chambers since 1992, having taken silk in 1991. He specialises in property law and is one of the editors of the Landlord and Tenant Volume of* Halsbury's Laws of England *(Vol 27). He is also the joint editor of the 1996 Edition of* Gale on Easements. *He has appeared four times in the House of Lords and has conducted over 50 cases in the Court of Appeal.*

Nicholas Cheffings *is Head of Property Litigation at Lovell White Durrant. He sits as a mediator and also as a Legal Assessor to Rent Review Arbitrators and Independent Experts. He specialises in all aspects of contentious work relating to property in England and Wales, a leader in his field. He has published a number of articles and papers on a range of topics and is a regular speaker at seminars and conferences.*

The original of this article first appeared in the Estates Gazette.

CHAPTER 9/4

LEFT TO THE EXPERT—WHAT HAVE WE DONE? A COMMENTARY ON NATIONAL GRID CO PLC v. M25 GROUP LTD

Jonathan Gaunt QC
and Nicholas Cheffings

001 In our earlier article (Chapter 9/3), we tried to make sense of the law concerning the relationship of independent experts and the courts. We were concerned with the questions:

(i) Is a determination by an independent expert on an issue such as the amount of the rent under a rent review always binding on the parties?
(ii) Do the courts have jurisdiction to determine an issue of law which affects the reference to the independent expert before or pending the reference and, if so, can the independent expert be restrained from determining the rent pending the determination of the court on the point of law?

002 We reviewed the authorities and concluded

(a) that there is no general principle that an issue of interpretation concerning the basis upon which an independent expert is to conduct a valuation is always excluded from the jurisdiction of the court;
(b) that whether this is so is a matter of construction of the individual contract or lease;
(c) that parties to a lease are most unlikely to have intended to take the risk that the independent expert would misapprehend his or her instructions and conduct the valuation on a basis for which they had not provided;
(d) that parties to a lease may expressly exclude the jurisdiction of the court; and
(e) that if they do not do so expressly, rent review clauses ought generally to be construed as entitling the courts to intervene either by granting declaratory relief in advance or by declaring the determination a nullity if the independent expert had departed from his or her instructions in a material respect.

003 We posited an example where there is a direction to ignore certain tenant's improvements but the valuer values those improvements. We argued that in such a case the valuer would not have performed the valuation that the parties contracted for but would have valued a different thing and that such a situation fell squarely within these dicta of Dillon LJ (*Jones* v. *Sherwood Computer Services plc* [1992] 1 WLR 277 at 287A):

> "If the mistake made was that the expert departed from his instructions in a material respect, e.g. if he valued the wrong number of shares or valued shares in the wrong company . . . either party would be able to say that the certificate was not binding because the expert had not done what he was appointed to do."

004 In real property terms, the analogue to valuing the wrong company is to value the wrong property.

005 This very situation arose for decision by the High Court in *National Grid Co plc* v. *M25 Group Limited* [1998] 32 EG 90. A lease provided for rent review every 15 years and for the question whether any and, if so, what increase ought to be made to be referred to a valuer appointed by the President of the RICS in default of agreement. The review date was June 1994. A valuer was appointed in December 1995 and an originating summons for declarations as to the interpretation of the review clause issued by the tenant in September 1997.

006 The matter came before Pumfrey J on an application to strike out and the judge duly struck out the proceedings on the basis that they raised: "questions which by their nature must be decided by the expert on his way to reaching his determination of the new rent".

007 What were these questions? They included:

(i) whether "the demised premises" meant the land without any buildings or structures thereon;
(ii) whether certain works fell to be disregarded as tenant's improvements;
(iii) what access to the premises was to be deemed to exist; and
(iv) whether the position of the actual tenant (which would give rise to a substantial ransom element in the value) was to be disregarded.

008 One can readily think of cases in which the courts have been perfectly happy to rule on precisely these questions. In the light of their differing answers to these questions, the tenants valued the premises at £25,000 a year and the landlords at nearly £915,000 a year. The passing rent was £1,925 (fixed in 1979) and the review was upwards only with the next review falling in 2009.

009 The judge accepted that all these questions raised serious issues of construction of the lease and were seriously arguable and central to the question of valuation. He also expressed sympathy for the view that the effect of provisions which have an enduring effect, such as rent review provisions, is something which should be open to consideration by the courts and observed that, had the parties foreseen that the property might have a ransom value at ten years purchase of £10m, "they might well have provided for a more elaborate form of review".

010 He concluded his judgment by stating that the questions should, in his view, have been decided by the court and that (if he had had a discretion) he would have exercised it to permit the originating summons to proceed, staying the rent review proceedings if necessary. Nevertheless he held that, on a true construction of the lease, the questions raised had been remitted to the expert to determine *exclusively* of the court and struck the proceedings out. Why?

011 The fallacy in his reasoning appears to us to be found in the word "exclusively". It does not follow from the fact that an expert may well have to decide questions of construction of the lease in order to complete his valuation task that, in remitting the valuation job to him, the parties necessarily intended to exclude the jurisdiction of the court. This was recognised by Lightman J in the first of his five "principles" in the *British Shipbuilders* case (*British Shipbuilders* v. *VSEL Consortium plc* [1997] 1 Lloyd's Rep 106) (discussed in Chapter 9/3 and which Pumfrey J purported to follow) and is implicit in the principle that, if the expert departs from his instructions in a material respect, his decision can be declared a nullity.

012 It is a question of construction whether the parties intended to exclude the court's jurisdiction (see *Mercury Communications Ltd* v. *Director General of Telecommunications* [1996] 1 WLR 48 at 58C–59B). The factors identified by the judge which caused him to express sympathy with the view that the points in question should have been open to decision by the court, could have been invoked by him to support the view that the parties had no such intention, namely:

(a) the fact that these were provisions which would have enduring and repeated effect; and
(b) the fact that it was readily foreseeable that the adoption of an erroneous basis of valuation might have a spectacular effect on rental value.

013 Indeed, this was not even a case where the parties had provided that the valuer's decision was to be "final and binding".

014 Turning to the cases referred to in the judgment, the decision of the House of Lords in *Mercury Communications* is a clear example of the courts interpreting a clause providing for reference to an expert as *not* conferring *exclusive* jurisdiction on the expert, despite the fact that the agreement provided that the parties were to be "bound forthwith" by the expert's determination in the absence of any appeal. Dillon LJ in *Jones* v. *Sherwood* (see above) explained on what basis the courts can interfere, thus showing that the expert's jurisdiction is not exclusive in certain respects. The Court of Appeal in *Norwich Union* v. *P&O* ([1993] 1 EGLR 164) plainly regarded the questions there as being primarily ones of fact peculiarly suited to investigation by the expert and not, therefore, matters for the court.

015 Pumfrey J seems to have read Dillon LJ in *Norwich Union* as saying that the courts *never* have jurisdiction to grant a declaration in advance of a reference but that is not said and would be contrary to the fifth principle stated by Lightman J in the *British Shipbuilders* case:

> "The court *has jurisdiction* ahead of a determination by the expert to determine a question as to the limits of his remit or the conditions with which the expert must comply in making his determination but (as a rule of procedural convenience) will (save in exceptional circumstances) decline to do so." (Our italics.)

016 To Pumfrey J seeking to apply Dillon LJ's words, the issue was simply whether it was the function of the expert to answer the questions on his way to determining the rent. He concluded that it was and that, *therefore*, the jurisdiction of the court was excluded. The judge appears, whilst purportedly following the decision in *Mercury Communications*, not to have given any weight to Lord Slynn's observations. In that case that the parties intended the expert:

> "to deal with such matters and such principles as correctly interpreted. They did not intend him simply to apply such meaning as he himself thought they should bear. His interpretation could therefore be reviewed by the court. There is no provision expressly or impliedly that these matters

> were remitted exclusively to the [expert], even though in order to carry out his task he must be obliged to interpret them in the first place for himself. Nor is there any provision excluding altogether the intervention of the court."

017 We do not see why that approach should not be applied to the interpretation of rent review clauses.

018 It appears from the report of *National Grid* that the case was argued on the basis that *Norwich Union* and *Jones* v. *Sherwood* were overruled by *Mercury Communications*. As Lightman J held in *British Shipbuilders* and as we argued in our earlier article (to which the judge does not appear to have been referred), that argument is misconceived. Those cases are readily reconcilable. In *Mercury Communications* it was held that the expert's jurisdiction was not exclusive and the two Court of Appeal cases were decided on their own facts. They do not tell us what the outcome would have been if the expert's alleged mistakes had been more fundamental and had involved pure questions of law.

019 That brings us to the real crux. When does a question answered by the expert constitute an actual or potential "departure from his instructions in a material respect" (to use the words of Dillon LJ) or go to "the limits of the expert's remit" (to use the words of Lightman J)? A very helpful analysis of this problem is to be found in the dissenting judgment of Hoffmann LJ in the Court of Appeal in *Mercury Communications* ((1994) *The Times*, 3 August; (1994) *The Independent*, 19 August; 138 SJ LB 35). (Hoffmann LJ was in the minority in dismissing the appeal but Saville LJ agreed with him that the court had a discretionary jurisdiction to grant a declaration but felt that it was not a case for exercising the discretion. The House of Lords, of course, allowed the appeal, thus vindicating Hoffmann LJ.)

020 Hoffmann LJ posited an agreement requiring a parcel of shares to be valued by a firm of accountants. He then distinguished between a case where no principles of valuation are prescribed and a case where principles of valuation have been agreed. In the former case, the court will not intervene in advance of the valuation or afterwards; the parties have agreed to accept the valuation and are bound by it, whatever it is, in the absence of fraud or collusion. In the latter case, however, if it can be shown that the accountants have valued on a basis other than that prescribed, the court will set aside the valuation. Even in this case, however, the application of the prescribed principles may involve questions of judgment which the parties have left to the accountants (e.g. what is to count as net profits) and again, the courts will not interfere with the accountants' judgment on such a question (Hoffmann LJ explains the decision in the *Norwich Union* case on this basis: the question of what amounted to "completion" and which were "the design documents" were questions which, on the true construction of the agreement, the parties had intended to be decided by the expert). An expert, however, who acts upon what, in the court's view, is the wrong *meaning* of his instructions exceeds his decision making authority and his decision is not that contracted for (when a judge at first instance Hoffmann J appears to have applied this approach in *SB Property Co Ltd* v. *The Chelsea Football & Athletic Co Ltd and Alexander Tatham & Co* [1990] NPC 86 where he held that an auditor was not expected to determine a question of construction but that his certificate was binding on questions such as the amount of the relevant receipts and on matters of apportionment).

021 This distinction between matters of judgment and opinion which are to be left to the expert and the failure by the expert to carry out his instructions was also drawn by the Court of Appeal in *Macro* v. *Thompson* [1997] 1 BCLC 626. In that case, the valuer had valued the company's shares by reference to the assets of another company and the court held that his valuation was not binding upon the parties.

022 In the *National Grid* case, some at least of the questions before the expert went to what it was the valuer was to value. One cannot get much more fundamental than that.

023 What are the practical implications of this decision?

024 First, it may cause landlords, tenants and their lawyers to re-appraise the choice of arbitrator or expert: with an arbitrator, the parties can require the right to make submissions, insist that the arbitrator makes use of a legal assessor and with consent, apply to the court for the determination of a preliminary point of law (Arbitration Act 1996, s.45); one also has at least the possibility of an appeal if the arbitrator errs in law. By contrast an independent expert may be able to proceed without any assistance and get it fundamentally and spectacularly wrong without either party having any recourse—it is quite possible to be wrong but not negligent, especially if the expert has brought in a legal adviser (see, for example, *Lewisham Investment Partnership* v. *Morgan* [1997] 2 EGLR 150).

025 Secondly, if an independent expert is preferred, it is worth the parties considering writing in words to make it clear whether or not his or her jurisdiction is to be exclusive on questions of construction or law.

026 Thirdly, if the expert is not required to give reasons, it will be very difficult either to impugn the determination or to sue for negligence. The Court of Appeal has held, in *Morgan Sindall plc* v. *Sawston Farms (Cambs) Ltd* [1999] 1 EGLR 90, that, in the case of a non-speaking valuation, the court will not favour any attempt to infer "from ambiguous shadows and murmurs" the reasons behind the valuation.

027 Fourthly (even now that appeal in *National Grid* has been allowed), Lightman J was surely right to warn that it will only be in exceptional cases that the courts will (in the teeth of one party's objection) entertain an application for a declaration in advance of the determination (in saying this, Lightman J was summarising a similar statement by Hoffmann LJ in the Court of Appeal in *Mercury Communications*)—there will often be matters of fact which need to be investigated and, in the course of a review, some legal issues often vanish while others surface. Preliminary legal issues are often misconceived.

028 The Court of Appeal's decision ([1999] 1 EGLR 65) has now confirmed that the question of whether the rent review provisions in a lease exclude the jurisdiction of the court to construe the lease turns on the construction of the provisions in the particular lease. Where the lease gives exclusive power to the expert to determine the question of valuation, it does not follow that the expert has a completely free hand in approaching that task. In this case, the terms of the lease did not confer on the valuer, either expressly or by implication, the sole and exclusive power to construe the lease because limits were set on the expert's power to determine the increase in rent (because he was required to have regard, for example, to the contractual assumptions and disregards). Thus, the court will intervene if the expert has given the wrong meaning to those limitations. This is because the parties have not agreed to give to the expert the exclusive jurisdiction to decide anything other than the ultimate valuation.

Jonathan Gaunt QC *has been the Joint Head of Falcon Chambers since 1992, having taken silk in 1991. He specialises in property law and is one of the editors of the Landlord and Tenant Volume of* Halsbury's Laws of England *(Vol 27). He is also the joint editor of the 1996 Edition of* Gale on Easements. *He has appeared four times in the House of Lords and has conducted over 50 cases in the Court of Appeal.*

Nicholas Cheffings *is Head of Property Litigation at Lovell White Durrant. He sits as a mediator and also as a Legal Assessor to Rent Review Arbitrators and Independent Experts. He specialises in all aspects of contentious work relating to property in England and Wales, a leader in his field. He has published a number of articles and papers on a range of topics and is a regular speaker at seminars and conferences.*

CHAPTER 10

EXPERT DETERMINATION IN COMMERCIAL CONTRACTS

Doug Jones

INTRODUCTION

What is expert determination?

001 Expert determination is a process whereby two parties agree to submit an issue for the determination of a third party. It is commonly used in a wide variety of commercial contracts. For example, the parties to a lease may agree that the amount of rent to be paid under the lease will be determined by a third party. The parties to a share purchase agreement may agree that the price to be paid will be determined by a third party. The parties to a construction contract may agree that the price for varied work performed under the contract will be determined by a third party. In each of these three scenarios, and in countless others, the third party is known as an "expert", although the name given to the process varies with the particular application of the concept.

The new wave of expert determination

002 The types of issues traditionally referred to experts have been narrow in scope, typically involving the expert only in a process of valuation. The three examples given above, namely rent review, share valuation and certification under construction contracts, all fall into this category. An expert's terms of reference in situations such as these are clear and narrow.

003 There is, however, a new type of expert determination clause in contemporary commercial practice. Such clauses provide for the reference of entire disputes or differences to experts for determination. They appear in commercial contracts in the place of and sometimes in substitution for an arbitration clause.

004 Throughout this chapter, the phrases "traditional expert determination" and "expert dispute determination" are used to distinguish these two types. The distinction is crucially important, since the differences between the two types of expert determination are quite radical. While the legal position in relation to the enforceability and reviewability of traditional expert determinations is relatively well settled as a result of well over a century of litigation, the legal position in relation to expert dispute determination is characterised by considerable uncertainty. This is because expert dispute determination is a new phenomenon, and the courts have not yet had sufficient opportunities to clarify its legal effect.

Other categories of expert determination

005 To distinguish between traditional expert determination and expert dispute determination does not tell the whole story. A third category of binding expert determination can be identified. This is where expert determination is used as an intermediate level of appeal from the decisions of a certifier. The determinations of such an expert are subject to further appeal, usually to arbitration. A three-tiered process of dispute resolution is not uncommon in construction contracts.

006 Expert determinations of this kind have almost never been the subject of litigation. The principles of law relevant to such expert determinations will depend on the wording of the relevant clauses. They will share some characteristics with traditional expert determination and others with expert dispute determination.

007 Non-binding expert appraisal is a popular form of alternative dispute resolution. Here the parties engage an expert to appraise an existing dispute and suggest an outcome. Although the suggested outcome is non-binding, it is used to further negotiations thus assisting the parties to reach their own agreed solution to the dispute. As this chapter is concerned with binding expert determination, this is not the place to do other than recognise the existence, and importance, of the non-binding process.

Purpose of this chapter

008 The main purpose of this chapter is to provide a summary of the current state of the law in relation to expert determination. This covers key issues, such as:

- the expert's jurisdiction;
- the enforceability of an expert determination clause where court proceedings are brought in breach of it;
- the capacity of the courts to facilitate the expert determination process;
- the enforceability of expert determinations;
- the extent to which an expert determination can be attacked and reviewed by a court; and
- the liability of an expert for negligence.

009 The differences between traditional expert determination and expert dispute determination are sometimes so dramatic that they need to be dealt with separately.

010 A subsidiary purpose of this chapter is to highlight some of the drawbacks in using expert determination as a dispute resolution technique. To this end, pertinent comparisons with arbitration are made.

EXPERT DETERMINATION AND ARBITRATION COMPARED

011 Expert determination is not a new phenomenon. For hundreds of years, contracting parties have agreed to submit issues for determination to third parties with expertise in particular areas. Arbitration is even more ancient. It has been practised for thousands of years as a means of generating binding solutions to mercantile disputes. As a consequence, the distinction between the two processes is well known. Lord Esher MR explained it as follows in *Re Dawdy* (1885) 15 QBD 426; 54 LJQB 574; 53 LT 800:

> "... An arbitration [is] to be conducted according to judicial laws, where the person who is appointed arbitrator is bound to hear the parties, to hear evidence if they desire it and to determine judicially between them. He must have a matter before him which he is to consider judicially. As a consequence of this, it has been held that if a man is, on account of his skill in such matters, appointed to make a valuation, in such a manner that in making it he may, in accordance with the appointment, decide solely by the use of his eyes, his knowledge and his skill, he is not acting judicially; he is using the skill of a valuer, not of a judge."

012 As was outlined in paras 001–010 above, arbitration and expert determination have in recent times begun to compete in exactly the same market, i.e. that of dispute resolution. It was once a matter of course that contracting parties wanting to make provision for some final and binding dispute resolution process other than litigation would put an arbitration clause into their contract. This is no longer so. Such parties now have the option of inserting an expert determination clause instead. Furthermore, vast numbers have taken up this option.

013 What has motivated so many commercial parties to substitute expert determination for arbitration? No doubt it is the fact that arbitration has developed a reputation for being incapable of delivering cheap and speedy dispute resolution. Although this reputation is somewhat undeserved, it is easy to see how it developed. Due to the temptation in arbitration to mimic traditional court procedure, parties have failed to take advantage of what arbitration has to offer. In many instances the arbitrator's fear of criticism by a court has resulted in arbitration procedures being more cumbersome than the foreshortened procedures available even in the commercial courts.

014 As a consequence of the essentially consensual nature of arbitration, arbitral proceedings can be as simple and quick as the parties agree, subject of course to any relevant legislation. If a dispute reaches arbitration, the parties, and particularly their advisers, should look carefully at ways of simplifying the process. In the past there has been too little advantage taken of the opportunity to agree upon a simplified procedure at the commencement of an arbitration. This may be attributed to:

- a perception that it is to the commercial advantage of one party to lengthen, delay and increase the expense of the process; and
- a lack of preparedness on the part of lawyers confidently to advise their clients of the advantages (and risks) of simplified arbitration procedures due to a fear of leaving stones unturned in the path to victory.

015 Ways of modifying or eliminating various procedural steps should be part of an active consideration by lawyers and their clients, and by arbitrators, at the commencement of the arbitration. Methods of simplifying the arbitral proceedings include:

- "papers only" arbitration where the arbitrator decides issues of contract construction or technical interpretation on written submissions from both parties without the need for any pleadings or (sometimes) any hearing;

- limitations on discovery of documents, a process which can bury both parties in mountains of paper only some of which has any relevance to the issues;
- "look and sniff" arbitrations where the issue is quality of work and the arbitrator looks at the work in question and makes a binding determination within days of the dispute arising;
- simplified pleadings and statements of the matters at issue;
- presentation of evidence in writing rather than orally with (sometimes) a limited time for cross-examination;
- exchanges of expert reports prior to hearing with or without a requirement for the experts from the opposing sides to confer and isolate for decision in an appropriate way only those issues on which they cannot agree.

016 The arbitration process can be as streamlined as the parties wish. This is one of the major advantages of arbitration. And it is principally due to a failure to recognise this advantage that the perceived need for expert determination as a method of dispute resolution has arisen.

017 It will become apparent throughout this chapter, as expert determination and arbitration are compared as techniques of dispute resolution, that expert determination has a number of drawbacks. These need to be considered by any commercial party thinking of joining the expert determination bandwagon.

018 It must be stressed that these arguments relate only to expert dispute determination. Traditional expert determination is a well established commercial practice, without which all sorts of markets would grind to a halt. Expert dispute determination, however, is still suffering from teething problems.

THE EXPERT'S JURISDICTION

The parties' agreement

019 The expert's jurisdiction comes from the agreement of the parties. Unless one can clearly identify an agreement between the parties to submit an issue for determination by an expert, then the expert has no jurisdiction, and therefore no right to proceed.

020 Ascertaining whether or not the parties have agreed to an expert determination is a matter of contract law. Naturally it is not possible here to discuss all of the relevant principles. Only the most important issues will be mentioned.

Oral or written agreement

021 There is no requirement for expert determination agreements to be in writing. An oral agreement can provide the basis for an expert to proceed. In practice, however, this is very rare in commercial contracts.

022 Usually, the expert determination agreement is contained in an expert determination clause which forms part of a written contract. In such a case, the expert should read the clause carefully, to ensure that he or she is entitled to act. For example, if the clause requires one of the parties to issue certain notices in order to activate the expert determination process, then the expert should ensure that these have been complied with.

Expert determination, not arbitration

023 The distinction between expert determination and arbitration was discussed above (in paras 011–018). It is important to ensure that the process referred to in the agreement is actually expert determination. If it is arbitration, then it will be subject to the supervision of the courts under the Arbitration Act 1996.

024 Most expert determination clauses use the phrase "acting as an expert, not an arbitrator", or something similar, to put the nature of the process beyond doubt. Nevertheless, ambiguities sometimes occur, and in such cases it is necessary to consider the *nature* of the process provided for by the contract. The *name* given to the process cannot be regarded as conclusive.

025 In this respect, the following table compares the expert determination and arbitration processes. It can be used as a guide to determine whether the parties' true intentions are for expert determination or for arbitration.

Table 1

EXPERT DETERMINATION	ARBITRATION
An expert is less likely to be required to give **reasons**	The requirement of a **reasoned judgment** is persuasive of the process being an arbitration (*Arenson* v. *Casson Beckman Rutley* [1977] AC 405 *per* Lord Simon at 424; *Sport Maska* v. *Zittrer* [1988] 1 SCR 164 *per* L'Heureux-Dubé J at 596)
A person whose decisions are **reviewable** by an arbitrator is unlikely to be an arbitrator itself (*Sutcliffe* v. *Thackrah* [1974] AC 727 *per* Lord Morris at 744)	**Finality** suggests an arbitration (see *Sport Maska, supra per* L'Heureux-Dubé J at 589)
An expert is less likely to receive **rival contentions**	The reception of **rival contentions** is persuasive toward the process being an arbitration (*Arenson, supra per* Lord Simon at 424)
An expert is **not necessarily bound to hear the parties**	The parties to an arbitration have the **right to be heard** if they wish (*Hammond* v. *Wolt* [1975] VR 108 at 112 *per* Menhennitt J, and the cases cited therein)
A decision based on **personal expertise**, especially if the tribunal possesses **professional status**, suggests that the process is an expert determination (see *Sport Maska, supra* at 589–590 *per* L'Heureux-Dubé J)	An arbitral award must be based on the **submissions** made by the parties, and is governed by the **dispositive rule**, whereby the arbitrator's choice is "limited by fixed options determined by the opposing arguments of the parties" (*Sport Maska, supra per* L'Heureux-Dubé J at 596)

Ousting the jurisdiction of the courts

026 There is a rule of public policy which renders void any contractual provision purporting to oust the jurisdiction of the courts on a question of law. This rule is in place so that all people are able to enjoy the protection of the courts. If a contract confers a right, but then provides "You may not sue on this right", then that provision is void.

027 Naturally, it is crucial for the parties and the expert alike to ensure that their expert determination clause does not violate this rule. If it does, then the expert has no jurisdiction to proceed, because the clause is void.

028 It is often said that expert determination clauses violate the rule because they prevent recourse to the courts. Surprisingly, however, there are very few cases in which such clauses have actually been held to violate the rule. The only example known to the author is *Baulderstone Hornibrook* v. *Kayah Holdings* (unreported, Supreme Court of Western Australia, Heenan J, 2 December 1997). That case concerned an expert determination clause, not unlike many others in contemporary contracts, which provided that the expert's decision would be "final and binding" upon the parties. Heenan J considered that it purported to oust the jurisdiction of the courts (and was therefore void) because of this "final and binding" stipulation.

029 The *Baulderstone Hornibrook* v. *Kayah Holdings* decision is, with respect, rather difficult to reconcile with a number of other decisions which have upheld "final and binding" expert determinations. It will probably not be widely followed.

030 It is suggested that the rule avoiding agreements which oust the jurisdiction of the courts will only apply to expert determination clauses which provide for such cumbersome or impractical procedures that they seriously hinder parties from enforcing their contractual rights.

Severability of expert determination clause

031 An expert determination clause will usually form part of a wider contract (such as a lease or a construction contract). Occasionally, this wider contract will for some reason not be enforceable. The wider contract may, for example, have been procured by duress, it may be illegal, or it may simply be too uncertain to be enforced. What becomes of the expert determination clause in such a case? Does it become unenforceable too?

032 This issue has not yet been settled by the courts in relation to expert determination. But it has been settled in relation to arbitration. The courts have held that an arbitration clause is regarded as "severable" from the wider contract of which it forms part, so that if the wider contract is unenforceable, the arbitration clause will nevertheless survive.

033 For example, in *Harbour Assurance* v. *Kansa General International Insurance* [1993] QB 701, a dispute arose under a re-insurance contract. It was alleged that the re-insurers under the contract were not registered or approved to carry on insurance business in Great Britain under the relevant legislation and that, as a result, the re-insurance contract was void for illegality. Court proceedings were initiated in breach of an arbitration clause contained in the re-insurance contract. The defendants applied for a stay of these proceedings on the basis that the arbitration agreement should be enforced. The plaintiffs argued that the arbitrator could not have jurisdiction to determine the dispute because a finding that the contract was void for illegality would destroy the arbitrator's jurisdiction.

034 The Court of Appeal upheld the defendant's argument. The arbitration clause, as a matter of construction, was wide enough to cover disputes as to the initial illegality of the contract and, since the particular type of illegality alleged had nothing to do with the arbitration clause itself, the arbitration clause remained operative. Even were the rest of the contract to fall, this would not bring down the arbitration clause, because the illegality alleged did not affect it.

035 In the result, a stay of the court action brought in breach of the arbitration clause was granted.

036 It has been suggested that the courts would hold an expert determination clause to be severable in an appropriate case: J Kendall, *Expert Determination*, 2nd ed (1996), p. 77.

Coverage of expert dispute determination clauses

037 Contractual provisions for the resolution of disputes by expert determination commonly use words such as this: "... Any dispute or difference which arises out of or in connection with the contract or the project shall be referred to expert determination ... ."

038 The question arises: what is the coverage of such a clause? What disputes would have to be submitted to the expert if such clause were to be activated?

039 Again, there is little guidance from the courts as to the meanings of such words when found in expert determination clauses. But in cases relating to the jurisdiction of arbitrators, such words have often been considered. They have been held to confer jurisdiction over a wide variety of claims and disputes. For example, the Court of Appeal has held that a claim in tort for negligence resulting in a collision between two vessels during unloading arose "out of the contract": *Aggeliki Charis* v. *Pagnan (The Angelic Grace)* [1995] 1 Lloyd's Rep 87. Indeed, an arbitrator will generally have power under such clause to decide all claims in tort if those claims are sufficiently connected with the contract: e.g. *Ashville Investments* v. *Elmer Contractors* [1988] 2 Lloyd's Rep 73. A wide variety of other disputes have been held by the courts to fall within the ambit of such an agreement, including:

- release, estoppel, waiver or set-off: *Kathmer Investments* v. *Woolworths* [1970] 2 SA 498;
- internal rectification of the contract: *Ashville Investments* v. *Elmer Contractors* [1988] 2 Lloyd's Rep 73; *Overseas Union Insurance* v. *AA Mutual Insurance* [1988] 2 Lloyd's Rep 63;
- in Australia, claims for civil remedies under the Trade Practices Act 1974 (Cth): *National Distribution Services Ltd* v. *IBM Australia Ltd* (1991) ATPR 41–077.

040 There seems no reason why phrases such as these should not confer a similarly wide jurisdiction upon an expert.

Limiting the jurisdiction of the expert

041 In comparison to arbitration, expert determination is an abbreviated form of issue resolution. It is fast, it involves less argument, and its results are usually absolutely final. As a result, parties often attempt to limit the expert determination to small matters appropriate for the speedy resolution which it provides. Such parties regard larger matters as warranting a more extensive process.

042 Accordingly, phrases such as the following are sometimes used: "... The expert shall have exclusive jurisdiction in respect of disputes valued at less than $100,000 ...". However, it is suggested that provisions such as this may be productive of almost insoluble disputes. The question arises whether a given claim encompasses one dispute of a large value or many disputes of a small value. Since construction disputes are notorious for the myriad tangled chains of causation which characterise them, this question easily breaks down into nonsense.

043 An alternative to this form of drafting is to provide that the determination will only be final and binding if it awards less than some maximum figure. This does not seem, however, to be any more satisfactory, since it is likely to place pressure on the expert artificially to alter the amount he or she is awarding if it is approaching the ceiling figure. For example, if the correct outcome was to award $105,000, the expert may feel obliged to award $99,000 to ensure finality.

COURT PROCEEDINGS BROUGHT IN BREACH OF AN EXPERT DETERMINATION CLAUSE

044 Where a commercial contract provides that an issue is to be determined by an expert, one party may become unwilling to submit to the expert determination process and may instead seek to have the issue determined by a court. This involves commencing court proceedings in breach of the expert determination clause.

045 In such circumstances, the other party has two options. One option is to choose not to enforce the expert determination clause, but rather submit to the court proceedings as a means of resolving the issue. On the other hand, it may seek to enforce the expert determination clause. This would involve requesting that the court grant a stay of proceedings so as to enable the expert determination process to continue. We therefore need to ask: in what circumstances will the court grant a stay of proceedings so as to enable the expert determination process to continue?

Traditional expert determination

046 This question very rarely arises in the case of a traditional expert determination clause. It is simply not within the jurisdiction of the court to entertain proceedings commenced in breach of such a clause.

047 Suppose, for example, that a lease provided for expert determination as a means of reviewing the rate of rent to be paid after renewal of the lease. Suppose that the lessee refused to submit to the expert determination but instead commenced court proceedings, asking the court to set the rate of rent. The court would refuse to do this. Consequently the lessee would be forced to submit to the expert determination process.

Expert dispute determination

048 The issue is more likely to arise in relation to clauses providing for full scale dispute resolution by expert determination. It is well illustrated by *Cott UK Ltd* v. *F E Barber Ltd* [1997] 3 All ER 540. That case concerned a dispute which had arisen out of a contract for the bottling and packaging of soft drinks. Any disputes or differences arising out of the contract were to be referred to a final and binding expert determination.

049 Rather than submitting to the expert determination, one party chose to commence court proceedings in respect of a dispute which had arisen under the contract. The other party then applied for a stay of these proceedings, arguing that the parties had agreed to submit the dispute to expert determination. Judge Hegarty QC refused to grant such a stay. As a result, the court proceedings continued and the expert determination was supplanted.

050 Judge Hegarty QC held that the court did have the power to stay court proceedings brought in breach of an expert determination clause, but in his discretion decided not to grant a stay in this case. There were a number of reasons for this decision.

- First, the organisation which was supposed to be conducting the expert determination had no rules governing any form of dispute resolution.
- Secondly, the expert who had been appointed under the clause had no experience in dispute resolution.
- Thirdly, the clause laid down no rules or principles for the determination of the dispute.
- Fourthly, Judge Hegarty QC perceived some potential problems in the interpretation of the clause.

051 The *Cott* v. *Barber* decision, if correct, enables us to draw some conclusions in relation to the circumstances in which a court will grant such a stay. It appears that a court will *usually* grant a stay *unless* there is some good reason for allowing the court proceedings to continue and the expert determination to be supplanted.

052 *Cott* v. *Barber* shows that where the expert determination clause is unclear and uncertain in operation, or where the expert has no experience in dispute resolution, the court may consider that good enough reasons exist to decline to grant a stay. The practical advice to take from the case is that expert determination agreements should be clearly and comprehensively drafted so as to have the maximum chance of being given judicial effect.

Comparison with Arbitration

The availability of a stay of legal proceedings commenced in breach of an arbitration agreement is, unlike that in relation to an expert determination agreement, not governed by the common law. It is governed by ss.9 and 86 of the Arbitration Act 1996.

Under s.9(4), which relates to international arbitration agreements, the court *must* grant a stay unless it is satisfied: "that the arbitration agreement is null and void, inoperative, or incapable of being performed".

This provision is very strongly in favour of upholding arbitration agreements. The grounds on which Judge Hegarty QC refused to grant a stay in *Cott* v. *Barber* would not be valid reasons under s.9(4).

Section 86(2) relates to domestic arbitration agreements. It provides that the court *must* grant a stay unless satisfied:

"(a) that the arbitration agreement is null and void, inoperative, or incapable of being performed, or

(b) that there are other sufficient grounds for not requiring the parties to abide by the arbitration agreement."

This provision is not as strongly in favour of upholding arbitration agreements as is s.9(4), because it provides an additional ground for refusing a stay, i.e. "other sufficient grounds for not requiring the parties to abide by the arbitration agreement". This provision is still, however, more strongly in favour of arbitration than its counterpart under the previous Arbitration Act, because the grant of a stay is mandatory rather than discretionary.

If *Cott* v. *Barber* is a good indication, then it seems as though court proceedings brought in breach of an expert determination clause will be stayed in similar circumstances as would apply in relation to a domestic arbitration agreement.

Expert determination clause in Scott v. Avery form

053 According to the rule in *Scott* v. *Avery* (1856) 5 HLC 811, an arbitration agreement can effectively provide for reference to arbitration to be a condition precedent to the accrual of a cause of action in respect of a matter the subject of the agreement. The effect of such a clause is that unless the parties first submit their dispute to arbitration and get an award, they will not be permitted under the contract to commence proceedings in court. This means that a court has no power to entertain proceedings commenced in breach of such a clause.

054 The question arises whether an expert determination clause can successfully be placed in *Scott* v. *Avery* form. If it could, then a stay of proceedings brought in breach of the clause would in effect be made mandatory.

055 Apparently there are no decided cases dealing with expert determination clauses truly in *Scott* v. *Avery* form. There is, however, the case of *Amoco* v. *Amerada Hess* [1994] 1 Lloyd's Rep 330, where the expert determination clause was very similar to a *Scott* v. *Avery* clause. It provided that: "... [the parties] agree that no action or other legal proceedings shall be brought in respect of any matters in dispute which may be referred to the expert for decision in the course of the redetermination, or in respect of or arising out of any decision of an expert ... until all the key steps in that redetermination have been completed ... ."

056 One party commenced legal proceedings, seeking a determination from the court as to which evidence the expert was permitted to consider. Morritt J stayed this action, because it was in breach of the agreed prohibition on legal proceedings.

057 The clause considered in this case was not a *Scott* v. *Avery* clause, because it did not place a condition precedent on the *accrual* of a right to litigate; it merely placed a condition on the *exercise* of the right to litigate. As a result, the court had a discretion either to grant or refuse a stay. Nevertheless the clause had its desired effect because the court in its discretion granted the stay.

Comparison with Arbitration

It must be noted that, by virtue of s.9(5) of the Arbitration Act 1996, placing an arbitration clause in in *Scott* v. *Avery* form will not be effective to deprive the court of its discretion to assume jurisdiction in respect of a dispute covered by the arbitration clause. As a result, the final outcome as to whether the dispute is arbitrated or litigated does not turn on whether the arbitration clause is in *Scott* v. *Avery* form, but on the court's discretion whether or not to grant a stay of court proceedings brought in breach of the clause.

Expert determination followed by arbitration

058 Some contracts, particularly large commercial contracts, contain elaborate dispute resolution procedures. Such a procedure may, for example, provide that any dispute or difference arising under the contract is to be referred to expert determination, and, if either party is dissatisfied with the result thereof, then the dispute is to be referred to arbitration.

059 Where court proceedings are commenced in breach of such a provision before or during the expert determination process, the question arises whether the court proceedings can be stayed. This situation arose in *Channel Tunnel Group* v. *Balfour Beatty Construction* [1993] AC 334 in which a stay was granted. Lord Mustill said:

> "My Lords, I also have no doubt that this power [the inherent power to stay court proceedings] should be exercised here. This is not the case of a jurisdiction clause, purporting to exclude an ordinary citizen from his access to a court .... The parties here were large commercial enterprises, negotiating at arm's length in the light of a long experience of construction contracts .... It is plain that clause 67 was carefully drafted, and equally plain that all concerned must have recognised [its] potential weaknesses. Having made this choice I believe that it is in accordance, not only with the presumption exemplified in the English cases cited above that those who make agreements for the resolution of disputes must show good reasons for departing from them, but also with the interests of the orderly regulation of international commerce, that having promised to take their complaint to the experts and if necessary to the arbitrators, that is where the appellants should go."

060 This position has now been confirmed by the Arbitration Act 1996, s.9(2) of which provides:

> "An application [for a stay of legal proceedings] may be made notwithstanding that the matter is to be referred to arbitration only after the exhaustion of other dispute resolution procedures."

061 This provision expressly contemplates the type of provision which makes expert determination part of a dispute resolution process which culminates in arbitration. It makes clear that, subject to the fulfilment of certain conditions outlined in s.9, a stay of legal proceedings commenced in breach of such a dispute resolution clause will be granted.

FACILITATION OF THE PROCESS

062 An expert determination clause sets up contractual machinery for the determination of issues or disputes. This machinery consists of a number of components. The most important is, of course, the *expert* himself or herself, on whose appointment the parties must agree. Other components include the *parties*, whose co-operation is often required for the viability of the expert determination process. Apart from that, the expert determination process requires *rules* to enable it to proceed on a certain basis.

063 What happens when this contractual machinery breaks down? The expert may die or fail to act, one party may refuse to co-operate, or the contract may not contain any rules for the conduct of the process. Expert determination clauses frequently make no provision for what is to happen in this event. The consequences can be quite serious, especially where the purpose of the expert determination is to determine an essential term of the contract, such as price (which is of course the most common purpose of expert determination).

Traditional expert determination: contract for sale of property at valuation

064 A contract for the sale of goods at a price to be determined by an expert will be unenforceable if the expert for some reason or another fails to act: Sale of Goods Act 1893, s.9(1). This reflects the common law position in relation to the sale of goods, and probably all personal property.

Sudbrook Trading Estate Ltd v. Eggleton

065 In *Sudbrook Trading Estate Ltd* v. *Eggleton* [1983] AC 444, the lessee of a parcel of land had been granted an option to purchase the parcel outright at the expiration of the lease. The purchase price was to be determined by a process which involved the lessor and the lessee each appointing a valuer. If these valuers could not agree on a price, then they were to appoint an umpire who would make the final determination. The lessee purported to exercise the option, but the lessor refused to appoint a valuer. The situation appeared to be a deadlock, because there was no way of determining the purchase price for the land. Without curial intervention, the option agreement would have been unenforceable.

066 The House of Lords ordered that the contract should be specifically performed, with the purchase price to be determined by the court on the principle of a fair and reasonable market value. According to Lord Diplock, damages would not, as far as the lessee was concerned, have been an adequate remedy for the lessor's failure to appoint a valuer, because they would have been assessed as the difference between the market value of the land and the purchase price, which difference was by definition zero. It followed, therefore, that the contract must be specifically performed. The court substituted its own machinery for the failed contractual machinery in order to determine the price.

067 It is unclear how widely this case will be followed. There are at least three possible limitations on the application of the case's reasoning:

- It may only apply where the property being sold is of such a kind as to warrant specific performance of the contract. Contracts for the sale of land and unique items such as paintings are normally specifically enforced. Contracts for the sale of non-unique items, such as shares, are not specifically enforced without some good reason.
- The result in the case was that the court substituted its own machinery for the failed contractual machinery of the parties, i.e. it determined the purchase price because the expert determination process had failed. In order to do this, the court had to be able to discern from the contract an objective basis on which the valuation was to be made. The court was able to discern such a basis only because the contract made clear that the purchase price was to be a reasonable market price. If the contract had disclosed no objective basis for the calculation of the price, the contract would have been void for uncertainty.
- The contractual machinery had broken down because the lessor (the would-be vendor) was refusing to co-operate. The House of Lords was particularly concerned to prevent the lessor from benefiting from this wrongdoing. Accordingly, it ordered the contract to be specifically performed, which was the result that the lessor had been trying to prevent. Thus the reasoning of the House of Lords would not apply in the case where the machinery broke down without wrongdoing on the part of either party, e.g. the expert died and the parties, acting in good faith, could not agree on a new expert.

068 In summary, the position after *Sudbrook* is that the court is still unable to *appoint an expert* where the parties' contractual machinery to do so has failed. However, the court may be able to *substitute its own machinery* to determine the question that the expert was supposed to have determined, but this is only possible if the contract contains an objective statement of what the expert was supposed to have determined and the basis on which he or she was supposed to have determined it. This is instructive for drafters. It suggests that an expert determination clause should ideally contain an objective statement of the parties' entitlements, separate from the provision for this entitlement to be determined by an expert.

Expert dispute determination

069 *Sudbrook* was concerned with a traditional expert determination, i.e. where the expert was charged with the narrowly defined task of determining the price for a sale of land. What of the clauses which provide that all disputes or differences arising under a contract are to be referred to expert determination? What if the expert fails to act?

070 Although there are no decided cases on this point, it seems fair to assume that in such circumstances the expert determination clause would fall down and the dispute would have to be resolved by litigation.

071 A good illustration of some of the problems which can arise is the case of *Triarno Pty Ltd* v. *Triden Contractors Ltd* (unreported, Supreme Court of New South Wales, Cole J, 22 July 1992). In that case, a construction project deed obliged the contractor to provide a bank guarantee to the owner. Any claims by the owner were to be paid out of the bank guarantee. In the event of disputed claims, the owner was not entitled "to any amount of his claim in dispute until it received a determination from an independent expert agreed upon by the parties or failing agreement, appointed by the chairperson of the Institute of Arbitrators Australia, New South Wales Chapter, whose decision shall be final and binding".

072 Unfortunately, however, as Cole J observed: "The deed made no express provision for payment of the independent expert, for the procedures to be followed by the independent expert in reaching his determination, or for any rights or obligations upon Triarno [the owner] or Triden [the contractor] in relation to such expert determination." Cole J refused to make a declaration as to the rules and procedures for the conduct of the expert determination and he also refused to order the contractor to submit to and co-operate with the expert determination. He said: "If the parties have not by their deed agreed the procedures to be followed upon an expert determination, that is not a void the court can fill".

073 The problems which arise when the parties cannot agree on the identity of the expert need not be serious, if drafters follow the common practice of providing that in this situation some appointing authority (such as a professional association) will make the appointment. In the event that circumstances subsequently come to light which indicate that there are reasonable grounds for suspecting the expert to lack impartiality or independence, it would seem necessary for there to be contractual provision for the procedures to be followed. Many expert determination agreements fail to make such provision.

Comparison with Arbitration

Situations may often arise in arbitrations where exercises of discretion and/or coercion by courts are required in order for the arbitration to proceed. Courts are empowered to provide such assistance. For example, under the Arbitration Act 1996 the parties to an arbitration may apply for the following assistance:

- Appointment of an arbitrator in the case where the parties cannot agree on one: ss.16, 18.
- Decisions on challenges made to the appointment of arbitrators and on applications for their removal: s.24.

- Assistance in taking evidence in any way which the court is competent to take: s.43; e.g. the issue of subpoenas or the ordering of discovery.

The wealth of curial assistance available to parties involved in arbitrations contrasts starkly with the dearth of such assistance for expert determinations. The courts are unable either to appoint experts, to remove them or to assist them in the taking of evidence. All that a court can do if an expert determination process breaks down is either:

- declare the contract to be unenforceable for uncertainty; or
- where the issue to be determined by the expert is sufficiently well defined in the contract, the court *may* be able to determine that issue itself.

For example, if an expert is biased, a court is unable to remove it, although of course the expert's decision would ultimately prove to be unenforceable.

ENFORCEMENT OF EXPERT DETERMINATIONS

074 Where an expert determination agreement provides that the determination will be final and binding on the parties, the courts will generally enforce determinations made under it, subject to their limited power to open it up and ensure that it is not contaminated by fraud or a serious error of law (see paras 080 *et seq.* below). But it must be emphasised that the enforcement mechanism is purely contractual in nature. This means that a party faced with non-performance of an expert determination has no course but to sue on the contract at common law.

075 Historically, when the only option open to a party faced with non-performance of an arbitral award was to sue on it, considerable difficulties were faced. It was found that the law of contract was a weak and cumbersome enforcement mechanism indeed. It was for this reason that provisions for the summary enforcement of awards were introduced into arbitration legislation, both domestically and, later on, at the international level. From an enforceability viewpoint, expert determination is where arbitration was over a century ago. Two consequences flow from this position.

Foreign arbitral awards v. foreign judgments

076 The first problem arising from the purely contractual nature of the enforcement mechanism for expert determinations relate to those expert determinations with an international dimension. In addition to the difficulties of suing on the determination, this introduces the even more serious difficulty of enforcing foreign judgments. This is governed by the Brussels and Lugano Conventions which operate within the European Community, as well as reciprocal enforcement treaties with various other countries. In many situations the enforcement of a foreign expert determination will require reliance on the conflict of laws rules of individual countries. These may operate in a cumbersome and unpredictable way.

077 These problems of course only occur where the party seeking enforcement needs to extract money from the other. This is not always the case, as disputes often arise where one party withholds payment from the other, alleging a wrongful act or omission. If, under the expert determination, the party withholding the money wins, it may be that no money will need to change hands. In this case, of course, the problems with enforcing an expert determination are not serious.

> **Comparison with Arbitration**
>
> By comparison with the treaties relating to foreign judgments, the New York Convention on the Recognition and Enforcement of Foreign Arbitral Awards is very widely observed. Arbitral awards are therefore easier to enforce internationally than are expert determinations. One must not discount the effectiveness of goodwill, reputation, and a desire to avoid conflict as mechanisms for the enforcement of any kind of dispute resolution outcome. But where there is no such co-operation a wide gulf separates the enforceability of an arbitral award and that of an expert determination.

Remedies

078 The second problem is that the remedies available from an expert are limited. Without express contractual provisions to the contrary, an expert cannot award any remedy except a sum of money. Whether or not the parties can agree to confer on the expert the power to issue injunctions and the like is not yet clear.

079 This problem is not generally a live issue in traditional expert determination, where the role of the expert is limited to valuation. But in expert dispute determination, it may reduce the expert's flexibility, because such entire formulated disputes often cover a wide range of contractual and extra-contractual claims. To deal with many of these claims properly, there is a need for the expert to have at its disposal a number of remedies apart from the power to order that one party pay a sum of money to another.

> **Comparison with Arbitration**
>
> By comparison, under the Arbitration Act 1996, s.48, arbitrators have powers to:
>
> - make declarations;
> - order the payment of money in any currency;
> - order a party to refrain from doing anything;
> - order specific performance of a contract; and
> - order rectification of a deed or other document.

ATTACKING AN EXPERT DETERMINATION

080 The extent to which an expert determination can be attacked for fraud or error is of enormous importance to disputing parties, but it exhibits a tension. On the one hand, an expert determination not subject to attack and review by the courts is desirable in that it provides fast and cost effective dispute resolution. On the other hand, however, there is a greater risk of capricious results.

081 Attacks on expert determinations occur only in the context of the successful party suing on the decision. An advantage flowing from this is that the determination need only be acceptable to the courts of the jurisdiction in which it is sought to be enforced (unless the local judgment is sought to be enforced in another jurisdiction). By contrast, under the UNCITRAL Model Law, Article 34, an arbitral award is subject to scrutiny in two jurisdictions: the jurisdiction where the award is made as well as the jurisdiction where it is sought to be enforced.

082 On the other hand, there is a disadvantage in that enforcement of an expert determination is "all or nothing". The court cannot remit it to the expert: all it can do is either grant or refuse enforcement, with the latter course of action often placing the parties in a particularly sticky situation because there may be nothing with which to replace the determination.

083 As noted in paras 074–079 above, a contractual provision purporting to render an expert determination final and binding on the parties will generally be given effect by the courts. The starting point, therefore, for any discussion as to what will render an expert determination susceptible to attack, is the relevant agreement. Thus, in the context of valuation for rent review purposes, it has been said that

> "In each case, the critical question must always be: Was the valuation made in accordance with the terms of a contract? If it is, it is nothing to the point that the valuation may have proceeded on the basis of error or that it constitutes a gross over or under value. Nor is it relevant that the valuer has taken into consideration matters which he should not have taken into account or has failed to take into account matters which he should have taken into account. The question is not whether there is an error in the discretionary judgment of the valuer. It is whether the valuation complies with the terms of the contract": *Legal and General Life of Australia Ltd* v. *A Hudson Pty Ltd* (1985) 1 NSWLR 314 at 336 *per* McHugh JA.

084 Bearing this in mind, it is proposed to consider the susceptibility of an expert determination to attack on three bases: fraud, error of fact and error of law.

Fraud

085 It is well accepted that an expert determination procured on the basis of fraud will not be given effect by the courts. As Lord Denning MR said in *Campbell* v. *Edwards* [1976] 1 All ER 785 at 788, "fraud or collusion unravels everything".

086 What if the contract expressly provides that the expert determination shall remain binding despite fraud? Amazingly, this situation was considered in *Tullis* v. *Jacson* [1892] 3 Ch 441. Chitty J held that a provision in a building contract providing that the decisions of the architect were to be final even in the event of fraud or collusion would be given effect by the court.

087 This decision may be incorrect. But even if it is correct, the only situation in which a fraudulent expert determination will stand is in the extremely unusual case where the contract expressly provides for that result.

Error of fact

Generally, determination still binding

088 In the absence of express provision to the contrary, the parties to an expert determination are regarded as agreeing to be bound by the determination even if it is based on an error of fact: *Campbell* v. *Edwards* [1976] 1 All ER 785; *Baber* v. *Kenwood* [1978] 1 Lloyd's Rep 175. An expert determination, by its nature, is an arrangement whereby an "expert" is employed to ascertain an objective fact. Although differences of professional opinion are possible, it proceeds on the assumption that there is one "correct" outcome. Thus, as Megaw LJ said in *Baber* v. *Kenwood* [1978] 1 Lloyd's Rep 175 at 179, where the parties agree to be bound by the decision of someone whom they recognise as being an expert not an arbitrator: "[I]t would . . . be entirely wrong in principle that one party, having so agreed, should be entitled in law to frustrate the agreement by alleging mistake in the expert's opinion".

089 These principles are well illustrated by *Campbell* v. *Edwards* [1976] 1 All ER 785. In that case, a tenant surrendered her lease to her landlord. The tenant and the landlord agreed that a particular firm of surveyors would determine the price to be paid. The surveyors determined a price of £10,000, which the landlord duly paid, but it was subsequently discovered that the value of the lease was no more than £4,000. The landlord therefore argued that it was not bound by this valuation. The Court of Appeal rejected this argument, holding that the parties were bound by the expert determination even though it may be incorrect. The only relief available to the party being asked to pay more than it should is to sue the valuer himself or herself.

When will an error of fact render a determination non-binding?

090 There are three situations in which an error of fact may result in an expert determination being held not to be binding on the parties.

091 The first is where the mistake of fact is such as to render the expert determination contrary to the agreement under which it was made. Thus

> "If the mistake made was that the expert departed from his instructions in a material respect—e.g. if he valued the wrong number of shares, or valued shares in the wrong company, or if . . . the expert had valued machinery himself whereas his instructions were to employ an expert valuer of his choice to do that—either party would be able to say that the certificate was not binding because the expert had not done what he was appointed to do": *Jones* v. *Sherwood* [1992] 1 WLR 277 at 287.

092 The second is where an expert determination is infected by a mistake which produces a result so harsh that it justifies equitable intervention by the court. As McHugh JA put it in *Legal and General* v. *A Hudson* (1985) 1 NSWLR 314 at 336: "When a party seeks the assistance of equitable remedies to enforce an agreement to abide by the valuation of the third party, mistake . . . can be a defence to the action in certain circumstances." Equitable intervention for mistake in this context has not yet occurred in any decided case, but remains a theoretical possibility.

093 The third situation is where an expert determination is given with reasons. Lord Denning MR suggested that "if a valuer gives a speaking valuation—if he gives his reasons or his calculations—and you can show on the face of them that they are wrong it might be upset": *Campbell* v. *Edwards* [1976] 1 All ER 785 at 788. This suggestion has received both approval and disapproval, and as such awaits authoritative resolution. It is suggested, with respect, that the idea that a "speaking valuation" is inherently more susceptible to review for errors of fact is contrary to principle. The question will always be whether the valuation complies with the terms of the contract.

Error of law

The public policy rule

094 The position with respect to errors of law in expert determinations is complicated by the fact that the parties' agreement is not necessarily paramount. Although the question whether the determination complies with the terms of the agreement is still highly relevant, there is a rule of public policy which may operate to limit the autonomy of contracting parties in framing their issue resolution procedures. This rule, which is also discussed above (in paras 026–030), renders void any contractual provision purporting to oust the jurisdiction of the courts on a question of law.

095 As a practical matter, modern courts have tended to refrain from opening up expert determinations for review, even though they may be infected by error of law. However, the rule provides the courts with a justification to set aside an expert determination (even though it may comply with the parties' contract) if it is based on a particularly serious error of law resulting in unfairness to a party.

096 Aside from the public policy rule, the agreement pursuant to which an expert determination has been made again assumes paramountcy. An expert determination will be enforceable provided it is clear from the agreement that the parties have agreed to be bound by it. For example, if the agreement provided that no expert determination would bind the parties if it contained a serious error of law on the face of the record, then a determination infected by such an error would not be enforceable.

Mercury Communications

097 The remarks of Lord Slynn of Hadley, with whom the other Lords agreed, in *Mercury Communications* v. *Director General of Telecommunications* [1996] 1 WLR 48 are relevant in this context. The case concerned the re-negotiation of an agreement between British Telecommunications and Mercury Communications for telephony interconnections. The parties, considering it unlikely that they would be able to reach agreement on the issue of price, referred this issue to the Telecommunications Director pursuant to an earlier agreement into which they had entered together. The task of the Telecommunications Director in making his determination included interpreting certain phrases found in Mercury's licence. Mercury alleged that the Telecommunications Director misinterpreted some of these phrases, causing him to arrive at a price prejudicial to Mercury's interests. The Telecommunications Director argued in reply that the meaning of these phrases was for him to determine and not the courts. Lord Slynn dealt with this argument in the following way:

> "What has to be done in the present case ... depends on the proper interpretation of the words 'fully allocated costs' which the defendants agree raises a question of construction and therefore of law, and 'relevant overheads' .... If the Director misinterprets these phrases and makes a determination on the basis of an incorrect interpretation, he does not do what he was asked to do .... [The parties intended the Director] to deal with such matters and such principles as correctly interpreted. They did not intend him simply to apply such meanings as he himself thought they should bear .... There is no provision expressly or impliedly that these matters were remitted exclusively to the Director .... Nor is there any provision excluding altogether the intervention of the court. On the contrary, clause 29.5 contemplates that the determination shall be implemented 'not being the subject of any appeal or proceedings'. In my opinion, subject to the other points raised, the issues of construction are ones which are not removed from the courts' jurisdiction by the agreement of the parties."

098 It will be noted that His Lordship's analysis does not proceed on the basis that the court's jurisdiction as to a question of law cannot be ousted. On the contrary, he assumes that it can be so ousted, at least to some extent, but finds that the parties' agreement had not achieved this result. It is therefore suggested that this decision does not represent an application of the rule that a clause ousting the jurisdiction of the court is void. The decision simply gives effect to the parties' contract.

Drafting issues

099 *Mercury Communications* indicates that clear words will be required to render an expert determination final and binding even though contaminated by an error of law. It shows that the courts are prepared to open up expert determinations if this can be justified according to terms of the contract. In this context, it is relevant to consider two provisions commonly found in expert determination clauses.

100 "... the parties agree to give effect to the expert's determination unless and until it is appealed, reversed or overturned in subsequent litigation proceedings ...." Lord Slynn, in *Mercury Communications,* saw such a clause as a request by the parties for the courts to open up the expert determination. Some expert determination clauses specifically contemplate review by arbitration in the event of an appeal from the expert determination within a specified period. In such cases it is clear that the decision is not final until the time period expires. This is however a different issue to that of judicial review, but may assist the conclusion that the parties intended it to be excluded.

101 "... the expert must take all relevant considerations into account in coming to his or her determination ...." Again, this may be seen by the courts as an invitation for judicial review of the determination. Cases on administrative law demonstrate the extent to which the relevance or irrelevance of factors considered by a decision maker can easily be a justification for opening up the decision.

102 Even if the parties want an expert determination to be reviewed by the courts, the utility of a clause of this kind is limited, considering that the courts do not possess the flexibility in reviewing expert determinations as they do in reviewing arbitral awards. Essentially all they are able to do is either to refuse to give effect to a determination contaminated by an error of law, or (in some cases) to provide declaratory relief. In short, if the parties desire a judicially reviewable expert determination, they may be well advised to opt for an arbitration instead.

LIABILITY OF EXPERTS

Generally

103 The question whether an expert is liable in respect of a determination negligently made is a multifaceted legal question involving inquiries into:

- the *basis* of liability (e.g. tort or implied term of contract);
- the *standard of care* that the expert was bound to observe;
- *breach* of duty;
- *causation* of damage;
- *remoteness* of damage; and
- *measure* of damages.

104 These issues are beyond the scope of this chapter, and it is proposed here to deal with only one issue; namely, whether an expert is *immune* from an action for negligence. See also Chapter 1/8.

Immunity

105 It is well established that an arbitrator is so immune, and it was once thought that, by analogy with this immunity, an expert, such as a property valuer or architect, also enjoyed immunity from suit for negligence. The principle upon which this immunity was granted has been explained as follows: "... where a third party undertakes the role of deciding as between two other parties a question, the determination of which requires the third party to hold the scales fairly between the opposing interests of the two parties, the third party is immune from an action for negligence in respect of anything done in that role": *Arenson* v. *Arenson* [1973] Ch 346 at 370 *per* Buckley LJ.

106 The old cases use the term "quasi-arbitrator" to refer to an expert who would receive an arbitrator's immunity from suit due to his or her obligation to act fairly between the parties.

107 The "quasi-arbitrator" principle was narrowed considerably by two cases in the House of Lords, *Sutcliffe* v. *Thackrah* [1974] AC 727 and *Arenson* v. *Casson Beckman Rutley and Co* [1977] AC 405, in which it was held that, to enjoy an arbitrator's immunity from suit, a person whose determination will bind the parties to a contract must be obliged to afford the parties more than mere fairness.

Traditional expert determination

108 These two House of Lords cases have clearly reduced the class of quasi-arbitrators: at the very least, architects, engineers and accountants (in most circumstances) are no longer quasi-arbitrators. Broadly speaking, therefore, traditional experts are no longer quasi-arbitrators. They are now vulnerable to being sued by parties to whom they cause loss.

109 The case of *Campbell* v. *Edwards* [1976] 1 All ER 785, which was also discussed above (in paras 088 to 089), illustrates this principle. In that case, expert quantity surveyors ordered a landlord to pay £10,000 to a tenant for the surrender of a lease when the proper amount would have been no more than £4,000. Although the landlord was bound to pay the over-inflated amount to the tenant, it was open to him to sue the expert for the loss he thereby incurred.

Expert dispute determination

110 The concept of a quasi-arbitrator was not entirely repudiated in these cases. Thus, there might still be a class of third parties who are not arbitrators for the purposes of the Arbitration Act 1996, but who still enjoy an arbitrator's immunity from suit. If such a category of quasi-arbitrators still exists, then the experts involved in expert dispute determination would probably fit into this category, considering that they are quite similar in role to arbitrators.

111 It has never been denied that both experts and arbitrators are obliged to be fair to the parties. The two landmark House of Lords decisions established the principle that the mere obligation to be fair to both the parties is not sufficient to ground an immunity from suit. The basic thrust of the cases is that an obligation of fairness *plus something else* is required; however, this something else was not clearly spelt out.

112 The most widely held view in practice is that experts engaged in expert dispute determination are not immune from suit. As a result it is common for the expert's retainer to contain a release from liability. Contracting parties preparing to sign such releases must be aware that they have minimal recourse in the event of being disappointed with the expert's decision.

CONCLUSION

113 Traditional expert determination is a proven method of defining contractual relations in a complex commercial world. On the other hand, the broadened concept of expert dispute determination, although a reaction to the cost and delay of arbitration, is a poor substitute indeed for arbitration as a means of resolving disputes in commercial contracts in a binding way.

114 There are many necessary laws facilitating and assisting arbitration. The use of binding expert determination for the resolution of existing disputes enjoys few of these.

115 Those who seek to use expert determination for this purpose run the real risk of taking a journey back to the stone age of dispute resolution from which there may be no escape.

116 It would be far safer to ensure that arbitration is used in an abbreviated and amended form, rather than take what in many cases is an uninformed risk for fear of a process which is both extremely flexible and well supported by established domestic and international laws.

Doug Jones *is a partner in Clayton Utz, Sydney—one of Australia's leading firms of solicitors. He specialises in construction disputes and is widely recognised as a leading figure in that field.* *He gratefully acknowledges the assistance that he received from Andrew Schmidt, solicitor of Clayton Utz, in the preparation of this chapter.*

CHAPTER 11

EXPERT DETERMINATION IN CONSTRUCTION DISPUTES

Tony Ensom

EXPERT DETERMINATION: A PRACTICAL EXAMPLE

001 Each President of the Royal Institution of Chartered Surveyors would expect during his year to appoint five to six thousand members as arbitrators or independent experts. The majority of these appointments are made in connection with commercial rent reviews, but a significant number are made in connection with agricultural tenancies and construction disputes. In the case of the construction disputes the appointments are limited to arbitrators, since independent expert determination is rarely used in construction disputes. However, the statutory adjudication provisions in the Housing Grants, Construction and Regeneration Act 1996 are producing the need for adjudicators, who in some respects have a similar role to independent experts.

002 In addition to these three principal areas in which disputes arise the President receives applications to appoint arbitrators and independent experts to resolve disputes in a wide range of other areas. Many of these disputes arise out of leases, agreements for lease, development agreements and the like. These often involve matters of building construction. They may relate to, for example, boundaries, building defects, dilapidations, disrepair, rent cessation, completion of building works and service charges. Where the dispute relates to one of these areas the building surveyor will often be the best person to deal with them. As a building surveyor myself, I am often appointed as independent expert in these situations, sometimes by Presidential appointment, but often by agreement between the parties.

003 Service charge agreements within leases are a common source of dispute particularly where the charges relate to building works carried out by the landlords. This is an area of work in which I have often been involved and is how I came to be involved with Fairoaks Lodge, a large detached Edwardian house in a rather nice residential area on the outskirts of a home counties town. It was converted many years ago into four self-contained apartments, the main entrance hall and staircase having been retained as a common access for three of the apartments, but with the fourth having its own separate entrance at ground floor level.

004 The house was originally built in 1902 by a well-known writer of the time and was used as the family house until about 1938, by which time the family had grown up and left home, leaving the now elderly writer and his wife as the sole occupants. They died suddenly and in tragic circumstances and the house was left to the writer's spinster sister. She had been secretary for many years to Mr Wynthrop of Wynthrop Smyly and Smith, solicitors. Almost immediately after her brother's death she married Mr Wynthrop, an elderly widower. He already owned a number of properties and they decided to convert Fairoaks Lodge into apartments which were then let. Mr Wynthrop died shortly after the Second World War, leaving his wife very well provided for.

005 Over the years various relations of Mr Wynthrop had fallen on hard times and so, as and when tenants moved on and flats became vacant, Mrs Wynthrop gave three of them apartments, each granted on a 99-year lease. However, the property was neglected and poorly managed and the three original family members had little money. Mrs Wynthrop was getting old and took no interest in the house. Eventually the last tenant left and the fourth apartment (on the first floor) was sold to a businessman, Reginald Cornish and his excitable Spanish wife, Maria.

006 Mr and Mrs Cornish obviously spent a great deal of money on their apartment and were concerned at the poor state of the rest of the house. They persuaded the other lessees that they should collectively offer to purchase the freehold from the now elderly Mrs Wynthrop and manage it themselves. She agreed and the freehold was transferred to Fairoaks Lodge Residents Limited. This however did not solve the problem. The remaining family members dominated, but had no money, and they resisted all efforts by Mr and Mrs Cornish to carry out the repairs which were now essential to the house. Mr and Mrs Cornish decided that the only way out of the dilemma was to buy out the other leases. They all initially agreed but at the last moment one family member, Alistair Brown who had the top floor flat, changed his mind. The other sales went through in 1993 with one apartment being purchased by Mr Cornish and the other by Mrs Cornish.

007 Mr and Mrs Cornish were now effectively in control, with only Mr Brown, who was a pleasant but rather eccentric man, left from the original family.

008 Mr and Mrs Cornish embarked on major repairs to the house, organised largely by Mrs Cornish. During this time demands were made on Mr Brown for rent and insurance premiums and his share of the cost of repairs through the service charge agreement which formed part of his lease. He made substantial payments over a four-year period, but resisted some demands. Mr and Mrs Cornish eventually took legal advice and commenced proceedings for forfeiture in the High Court. However, Mr Brown's lease contained provisions that any disputes concerning demands under the service charge provisions should be referred to an independent expert and the court stayed the proceedings to allow an independent expert to deal with the matter. This is where I came in.

009 It was clear from the start that this would not be an easy case. To say that Mr and Mrs Cornish and Mr Brown were not on friendly terms would be an understatement. Mr and Mrs Cornish constantly referred to Mr Brown as "that man" and, in turn, Mr Brown referred to Mr and Mrs Cornish as "they" or "them".

010 My first contact with the case was a telephone call from Mrs Cornish who explained that she was secretary of a company which was the landlord of a house converted into flats and that the company was owned by the four lessees. She said that the company was in dispute with one of the lessees concerning the non-payment of service charges. She explained that the lease required disputes to be determined by a surveyor appointed by the landlord and that her husband had been given my name by a solicitor friend, Mr Johnson. I remember that Mr Johnson had been involved in another case a few years ago in which I was the arbitrator. Mrs Cornish clarified for me that, according to the lease, the appointed surveyor was to act as an expert and not as an arbitrator.

011 Before going any further, I asked Mrs Cornish who the lessee was and whether either party had instructed solicitors. I wanted to be sure that there would be no conflict of interest. She said that she would not want to instruct solicitors, unless absolutely necessary, because she and her husband would have to finance the expert determination and had little money to do so. (I was later to discover that they were not, of course, as hard up as Mrs Cornish suggested in this initial telephone conversation.) As far as she was aware Mr Brown had also not consulted a solicitor. Of course I had not previously come across either Mr Brown or Mr and Mrs Cornish and I therefore decided that I could accept the appointment, provided terms could be agreed.

012 Although Mrs Cornish had assured me that there was a provision for the landlord to appoint the surveyor without the agreement of the lessee I wanted to be quite sure that this was the case and asked Mrs Cornish to let me have a copy of the clause in the lease, which she did the following day, together with a full copy of the lease. The relevant clause read as follows:

> "14. PROVIDED ALWAYS AND IT IS HEREBY AGREED that if any dispute or difference shall arise between the Lessor and the Lessee under or in connection with the provisions of Schedule 3 (the Service Charge Agreement) the Lessor shall appoint an independent Chartered Surveyor to determine the matter and who shall act as an expert and not as an arbitrator and whose decision shall be final and binding. The fees and expenses of the Surveyor shall be borne by the Lessor and Lessee in such proportions as the Surveyor shall determine."

013 The wording was in most respects similar to clauses I have seen in many leases and other agreements. The provisions were typically brief but contained the essentials; the surveyor was to act as an expert and not an arbitrator and his decision was to be final and binding. It also helpfully dealt with the question of the surveyor's fees, a provision often lacking in leases and which causes immediate further dispute between the parties. Although the choice of expert was the lessor's and might on the face of it lead to debate on his independence I have found that it rarely does so. It does seem to be a commonly accepted way of choosing an independent expert or even an arbitrator in property related agreements. I was quite satisfied in my own mind that I could act independently and that in this case I would be seen to be independent of the parties. I therefore decided to take on the task, provided I could agree satisfactory terms.

014 Independent expert determination, unlike arbitration or litigation, is not subject to a legislative framework. The independent expert is dependent on the parties for his jurisdiction and powers. The agreement in Mr Brown's lease would give me jurisdiction over the dispute (providing it was in connection with the service charge agreement) and obliged the parties to accept my determination. It is helpful, however, to have the parties' agreement to the procedure to be followed and to the terms of my appointment. If these details cannot be agreed between the parties and by me, I could, nevertheless, proceed, but I would then have to rely on the common law as it applies to independent expert determination. The courts have in the past been supportive of this method of resolving disputes and have been reluctant to interfere in the process unless absolutely necessary. They have generally taken the view that, if parties have agreed to resolve their disputes by putting them to an independent expert and are contractually bound to accept his determination, he should be allowed to get on with his task without interference from the courts. In many cases independent experts have proceeded without more than a simple agreement between the parties and have had no difficulty. However, I would always prefer to have an agreement with the parties setting out the matters to be determined, the terms of my appointment and the procedure to be followed.

015 Having seen the dispute clause in Mr Brown's lease, I contacted Mrs Cornish and told her that the lease clause appeared satisfactory, but that I wished to have a written agreement with both parties. She was, at first, reluctant to involve Mr Brown and wanted the agreement to be confined to the lessor and me on the basis that the lease provided for them to appoint the independent expert. I explained that any agreement with me went beyond the agreement in the lease and persuaded her that a three-way agreement would be a more sensible option. She nevertheless wanted to see my standard terms before they were sent to Mr Brown and I agreed to this. I therefore sent her my standard terms for a dispute of this sort and asked her in return to summarise for me the matters in dispute and which I would be asked to determine. My terms (as subsequently amended to include for a reasoned determination) are set out in Appendix 1 of this chapter.

016 Mrs Cornish responded almost immediately by telephone saying she wanted to discuss my terms. She firstly wanted to know whether there could be any appeal against my determination and also how it could be enforced. I sensed that she and her husband had been discussing what options would be open to them when they received my determination depending on whether they "won" or "lost". Lay clients often ask questions like this which are really requests for advice on how they should deal with matters which arise during the course of the process. Independent experts have to be cautious and not allow themselves to become either party's adviser. On the other hand one does not wish to be unhelpful in these circumstances and I therefore decided to give her some basic information. I told her that the lease provided for my determination to be final and binding on the parties and that there was therefore no appeal mechanism. I did say, however, that if she felt that my determination was not confined to the issues in dispute agreed between the parties she should take legal advice. I also suggested that she should take legal advice if she was herself unable to enforce my determination (assuming of course that I determined that money was due from Mr Brown).

017 She then turned to the question of reasons and asked why, in my terms I stated that reasons would not be given. I frequently have queries on this point. There are two schools of thought on the subject. Some say that parties are really only interested in the actual determination and not the reasons behind it. They also say that a reasoned determination costs more and simply gives the losing party unnecessary encouragement to challenge it, when in reality it is almost impossible to do so. On the other hand, supporters of reasons say that the parties are surely entitled to know how the independent expert has reached his decision and that, in any case, reasons are now required in arbitrator's awards and judges give reasons for their judgments and so why should the same principle not apply to experts' determinations.

018 The first point to make is that expert determination is neither litigation nor arbitration and so judgments and awards have no direct bearing on the question. Also the need for reasons in judgments and awards arises from the legal system within which they are made. They are also "reasons" rather than "reasoning" which is what I think parties often expect in expert determination. My own view is that reasoned determinations can be considered quite independently of procedures and requirements of litigation and arbitration. Having said that, however, I do think that parties are entitled to know, if they wish, how the expert reached his conclusions. The "winners" may not be bothered because the decision is in their favour, but "losers" may well find an adverse decision more acceptable if they know why they lost.

019 In some types of dispute it may be also extremely helpful to both parties if an explanation of the decision can be given and in my experience service charge disputes fall into this category. In these cases the parties will have a continuing relationship and will need to administer the contractual provisions of their lease for long after the dispute has been settled. It may, therefore, be helpful to them if they have an explanation of the expert determination for future reference. I discussed these points with Mrs Cornish and agreed to give "reasons" for my determination.

020 Finally Mrs Cornish queried my payment terms, asking me to reduce my hourly rate and why security of my fees was necessary when this was a very simple dispute which she was sure I could sort out in a matter of days once I had seen the papers which she would be passing to me. She also objected to the landlord being required to pay these interim fees when, as she put it "he is the one who is in the wrong" (a reference, of course, to Mr Brown). I was able to persuade her that my hourly rate was reasonable and she agreed to this. The question of security of my fees was rather more difficult. My experience has been that service charge disputes where building works are involved are rarely simple and it often takes some time to assemble and investigate all of the facts. It is also usually the case that time has to be spent considering the construction of the lease and its service charge provisions. I also see no reason why someone acting as independent expert should not have some assurance that they will be paid. Experience has also taught me that however reasonable people appear at first sight there are some who will find any excuse not to pay, particularly when a decision is not in their favour. I assured Mrs Cornish that I believed both she and her husband, and indeed Mr Brown, were the sort of people who would never welch on their responsibility to pay, but explained that unfortunately there were others who were not so scrupulous and that it was therefore my normal practice to seek security for my fees. I also explained that it was only practical to ask for payment from whoever initiated that expert determination process and that who was to finally pay my fees would be a matter for my determination. After a long discussion, during which I began to realise that Mrs Cornish might be a difficult person to deal with, she agreed to my terms with one amendment regarding reasons.

021 Having cleared my terms with Mrs Cornish I asked her to forward a summary of the matters in dispute so that I could add these to my Terms and Conditions of Appointment before they were sent to Mr Brown for his agreement. A few days later I received a letter from Mrs Cornish setting out the issues. This is often a difficult task for a lay person and I was, therefore, pleasantly surprised that she made such a good job of it. She wrote:

> "Fairoaks Lodge Residents Limited claim payment of two demands sent to Mr Brown as follows:
> 1. A letter dated 24 June 1995 demanding payment of £2,410.00 for emergency repairs.
> 2. A letter dated 24 June 1994 for £115.25 for building insurance premium.
>
> We also claim interest on the money due at a rate of 6% above Barclays Bank base rate."

She attached copies of the letters.

022 I was able to set out the issues in my Terms and Conditions of Appointment and send them to Mr Brown who within a few days returned them signed and without any amendment or comment. This surprised me, but as I later discovered was consistent with his attitude throughout my dealings with him: he simply wanted the matter settled as soon as possible. My Terms and Conditions of Appointment were then signed by Mrs Cornish on behalf of Fairoaks Lodge Residents Limited. She also sent me a cheque for £500.00 as an advance payment. This was from her personal account which seemed odd but I accepted it and it was in due course credited to my clients' account. I was now able to begin my task.

023 I decided, firstly, to examine the lease. As is often the case the relevant provisions were rather complicated.

024 There was a large number of schedules and a great deal of cross-referencing to these and to the clauses in the lease. This style of drafting is traditional, but not easy for the layman to follow. I highlighted those clauses which appeared to be relevant to the dispute and worked out in my own mind how they related to each other. The clauses which in the end were relevant were set out later in my determination.

025 Having gained some idea of the way in which the lease provided for the service charges and payment by the lessee, I turned to the two letters demanding payment by Mr Brown. I wanted to satisfy myself, first, that the demands (at least on the face of it) fell within the provisions of Schedule 3 because clause 14 of the lease limited my jurisdiction to matters under or in connection with that Schedule and I would not be able to deal with items falling outside its provisions.

026 It could be argued that I should perhaps have looked into this question before agreeing to my appointment. My experience has been that if there is a question of jurisdiction the non-appointing party will mount a challenge at the time of appointment and one is therefore put on notice to deal with it at that time. However where, as in this case, neither party raises the matter then it may be better to simply accept the appointment and then look into the question of jurisdiction oneself rather than unnecessarily alerting the parties to what may be a red herring. It is also often the case that it is difficult to tell whether or not the matters in dispute are covered by the lease provisions until the issues become clear. It is however important for independent experts to check that they have jurisdiction to deal with the disputes put to them, otherwise their determination may prove to be invalid, at least in part.

027 The letters provided very little detail, but on the face of it the items claimed did appear to fall within the service charge schedule and so I decided to proceed to look into them in detail, but to check again later that this was the case.

028 It was obvious that in all cases I would need further information on the items claimed by the lessor and I therefore decided to obtain these, if I could, from Mrs Cornish and then, armed with this information to ask Mr Brown for his reasons why he disputed them. I realised that I might have to ask for further information later, but this seemed a reasonable approach to the problem of getting to the heart of the matter. The immediate question was whether to ask Mrs Cornish to send me the information or to have a meeting with her and go through the claims item by item and ask for the specific information which I needed. Where parties are represented by a solicitor or a surveyor I have found that a request for information to be sent to me usually works well, even if I sometimes have to ask for further detail later. Lay clients who represent themselves, however, generally have no idea what papers to send and a meeting is more productive and saves a great deal of time in the long run. In this case it had already become clear to me that a meeting with Mrs Cornish might be a long and frustrating experience and I was reluctant to suggest it unless really necessary. It was also the case that, although aggressive and extremely voluble she did seem to have a grasp of the issues and so I took the coward's way out and wrote to her asking for the information which I needed.

029 She telephoned as soon as she received my letter and said that she took her appointment as secretary of Fairoaks Lodge Residents Limited very seriously, that the best thing would be for me to come along and read all her files, which she assured me were in "apple pudding" order, and that tomorrow would be convenient to her. This, of course, was just what I did not want! I explained that her files would probably contain all sorts of correspondence and documents which were entirely irrelevant to the matters in dispute. I said that, for example, I was not interested in correspondence with the other lessees and that even correspondence relating to Mr Brown probably dealt with all sorts of other things which had nothing to do with the items in dispute. She then told me, for the first time, that she and her husband were the other two lessees. She gave me what seemed to be the complete history of the house and the entire Wynthrop family. When I finally managed to get a word in, I explained that it would be a waste of time for me to read all of her files in order to find what was wanted and that since she knew what was in them it would be better and quicker if she went through them and extracted the relevant documents. The conversation continued for some time, but having discussed a couple of examples, I felt that she probably understood what I required and left her to her task, which she said would take a couple of weeks or so.

030 I confirmed the important points of our conversation in a letter to her and also wrote to Mr Brown telling him what I was doing. Copies of each letter also went to the other party. Mrs Cornish responded with yet another telephone call to ask whether, if she did not let me have the information in two weeks, she would be penalised in some way. I told her that the reference in my letter to two weeks was simply confirmation of what she had told me and not a time limit. I said that if it became clear that two weeks was insufficient to let me know, but to do her best. Mr Brown's response was brief; merely an acknowledgment of my letter and that he looked forward to hearing from me again in due course.

031 Two weeks later, to the day, a parcel arrived through the post from Mrs Cornish. I opened it with some trepidation, but to my surprise I found, firstly, a bundle of documents concerning the emergency repairs with a little explanation of each of the items obviously prepared by Mrs Cornish. Her English was not always perfect, but I could certainly understand what she was saying. The second bundle of documents clearly related to insurance premiums, although she seemed to have included correspondence covering at least five years rather than just the one in dispute. A third bundle contained a list of payments of ground rent and insurance premiums by Mr Brown from 1993 to 1997 with copies of cheques which, to my surprise, were made out, not to Fairoaks Lodge Residents Limited, but to Mr and Mrs Cornish. Mrs Cornish had attached to this bundle a note stating that this was the information I would need to calculate the interest due to her and her husband in respect of payments made by them which in effect was money borrowed from other lessees.

032 A quick look through these three bundles of documents suggested that Mrs Cornish had indeed understood my request and had provided a comprehensive set of documents, with the exception of interest payments where I would need proof of payment for work and the insurance premium by Mr and Mrs Cornish. I called Mrs Cornish and she confirmed that she would be able to obtain all relevant information within a day or so.

033 I then called Mr Brown and suggested a meeting with him. He readily agreed and asked if one day the following week would be convenient because he would be in London that day and could come to my office. I was free that day and if Mr Brown came to my office it would save my time and the expense of travelling to the property. We therefore agreed to meet.

034 I decided to tackle first, with Mr Brown, the emergency repairs. The first item under this heading was the cost of installing a Yale lock and letter plate to the front entrance door for which reimbursement of one third was claimed. Mr Brown explained that in his view this was not a repair but an improvement. He explained that the lock and letter plate had been installed at Mrs Cornish's request because the door had originally only a dead lock and the front door had been left open to allow postal deliveries and the like which she thought was a security risk. Mr Brown said that he had not agreed to the new lock and letter plate and that he should not be asked to contribute to the cost. I had shown him Mrs Cornish's notes and he pointed out that this confirmed what he was saying, which indeed it did.

035 The second item concerned a new telephone entry system which had been installed to the front door and Mr Brown's argument was much the same. The third item was more complicated. Apparently Mr and Mrs Cornish discovered dry rot in the floor between Mr Brown's flat and the flat below when they took over the lease of that lower flat. They claimed the whole cost of eradication on the basis that Mr Brown had refused access to his flat for the work to be carried out and that it had as a result cost more to carry out the repairs. Mr Brown first queried whether the repair was to the flat itself or to the structure and suggested that the floor was part of the lower flat. He also disagreed that the work cost more because he would not allow access.

036 The fourth and fifth items were very similar. Mrs Cornish had suspected a gas leak and called in the gas board. They had confirmed that there was a leak in one of the supplies to one of the flats and that in fact all of the gas supplies were very old and should be replaced. They had however insisted that the meters, which were in each flat, should be relocated in the common entrance hall. As a result Mrs Cornish had also contacted the electricity board and been told that the mains supplies to each flat were in a dangerous condition and should be replaced, but again with meters relocated from the flats to the common entrance hall. Mr Brown agreed that the replacement of the gas and electricity mains was a repair and that he should contribute his share of the cost. What he was objecting to was what he said must be additional costs in relocating the meters.

037 Finally under this heading was a claim for replacing a night storage heater in the ground floor of the common hallway with three separate heaters, one on each floor. Although Mr Brown acknowledged that in theory the single heater should have been sufficient to heat the whole of the common staircase he agreed that it had not been effective in heating the area outside his flat on the top floor. He accepted that the old heater had become defective and that the three new heaters did now provide a better solution. He thought that three heaters instead of one was bound to be more expensive and argued that this solution was an improvement rather than a repair.

038 The second head of claim was for a proportion of the insurance premium for the year commencing 24 June 1994. The letter dated 24 June 1994 requesting payment also contained a request for ground rent, but this did not form part of the lessor's claim in the expert determination. I asked Mr Brown why he thought he should not pay the premium, particularly when he seemed to have paid all subsequent demands. To my surprise he said that he had paid. He explained that this was the first demand for payment sent to him by Mrs Cornish in her capacity of secretary to Fairoaks Lodge Residents Limited and that he had handed Mrs Cornish a cheque made out to the company for the full amount of the rent and insurance premium. However, it appeared that soon after Mr Brown had done so Mrs Cornish had closed down the bank account of the company and decided that all payments by Mr Brown should be made to her and her husband. Mr Brown said that he had objected to this arrangement at a board meeting but had been outvoted. Mr and Mrs Cornish had never paid the cheque into the company account and had subsequently demanded that Mr Brown issue a new cheque made out to them. He then told me that, although the action in the county court had been stayed in respect of the claims under the service charge agreement, the court had dealt with the allegation of non-payment of rent and had ruled that Mr Brown had discharged his obligation by giving Mrs Cornish the cheque made out to the company which at the time had a bank account. He was able to show me a copy of the judgment.

039 I then showed Mr Brown a copy of the list of payments which Mrs Cornish claimed had been made by him. He agreed to check this against his records during the next few days. He responded a few days later to confirm his agreement to Mrs Cornish's list.

040 Mrs Cornish called me shortly after my meeting with Mr Brown and asked if I needed any further information. I suspected that she really wanted to know how I had got on with Mr Brown and on the spur of the moment decided to go through the items with her on the telephone. It was a long conversation but I succeeded in getting her reaction to Mr Brown's points, even if it was to dismiss them without any logical argument. It quickly became clear that she would not concede any points and that what she really wanted was for me to come up with the answers.

041 I was careful in my conversations with both Mrs Cornish and Mr Brown to relate what the other had said on the various points each had made and concluded after my telephone conversation with Mrs Cornish that I had all the information I needed. I therefore wrote to them both and told them that I would now make my determination. They both wrote back saying they looked forward to receiving it.

042 Like so many of these disputes it was easy to make up my mind on some points and rather more difficult on others. However I concentrated on the task one afternoon and produced a draft determination. I immediately put it aside and returned to it the next day. I find that rereading a draft a day or so later is helpful in approaching it with a fresh eye. I did not on this occasion make any substantial changes but merely corrected some typing errors. The final decision which I had to make was who should pay my fees. The lease clearly left me with total discretion and I suppose that whatever I did could not be challenged. However I decided to follow the normal convention of costs following the event and determined that the lessor had "won" and therefore that the lessee should pay my fees. My determination (reproduced as Appendix 2 of this chapter) was sent off the following day to both parties with my invoice for the balance of my fees to Mr Brown who, thankfully, paid it by return.

043 This was a very small dispute between private individuals and any method of resolving their differences needs, in my view, to be quick and cost effective. In this case my fee was £650.00 plus VAT and I had dealt with it in a total period of five weeks from start to finish. Mr Brown wrote a short but courteous letter enclosing his cheque thanking me for dealing with the matter. Mrs Cornish on the other hand telephoned to say that she was disappointed with parts of my determination but accepted it. She could not however resist one last swipe at Mr Brown by suggesting that he would probably not honour it and that they would continue to "have trouble with him".

***Tony Ensom** is a Chartered Building Surveyor with 40 years' experience acting for private and public sector clients. He has particular expertise in construction law, contract administration and dispute avoidance and resolution. He is Customer Services Director of Citex Consulting Limited in London and frequently provides expert evidence and acts as an arbitrator, independent expert and adjudicator.*

He a leading member of his profession and a member of the RICS Construction Contracts Group and the President's Advisory Group on Dispute Resolution. He has also represented the RICS on the Joint Contracts Tribunal for the last 14 years.

APPENDIX 1

A DISPUTE BETWEEN FAIROAKS LODGE RESIDENTS LIMITED AND MR ALASTAIR BROWN

Terms and Conditions of the Appointment of Mr A C Ensom FRICS FCIArb MAE as Independent Expert Surveyor

We (1) Fairoaks Lodge Residents Limited and (2) Alastair Brown jointly and severally agree:

A that Mr A C Ensom has been appointed as the Independent Expert Surveyor to determine the issues in dispute between us arising under or in connection with a Lease dated 26 April 1952;

B that Mr Ensom's Determination shall be given in writing and shall be final and binding upon us; and

C that the following Terms and Conditions shall apply to Mr Ensom's appointment:

1 Mr Ensom shall with reasonable dispatch carry out his duties as Independent Expert Surveyor and shall make his determination as soon as reasonably practical.

2 Mr Ensom shall act impartially, set his own procedure and at his absolute discretion may take the initiative in ascertaining the facts and the law as he considers necessary in respect of the issues referred to him, including the following:
   - (a) using his own knowledge and/or experience;
   - (b) requiring information and documents from us which we agree to provide promptly;
   - (c) obtaining such information as he considers necessary from any third party, subject to giving us notice of his intention to do so;
   - (d) obtaining from others such information and advice as he considers necessary on technical and/or legal matters, subject to giving us notice of his intention to do so and informing us of his estimate of the cost involved.

3 Mr Ensom shall give reasons for his decision.

4 Mr Ensom shall not be liable for anything done or omitted in the discharge or purported discharge for his functions as Independent Expert Surveyor, unless the act or omission is in bad faith.

5 Mr Ensom shall be paid fees at a rate of £100.00 per hour for all his time engaged in acting in his capacity as Independent Expert Surveyor, together with VAT thereon.

6 Mr Ensom shall be reimbursed any expenses which he incurs in connection with his appointment, together with VAT thereon.

7 Mr Ensom's fees and expenses shall be borne by the parties in such proportions as Mr Ensom directs in his Determination (in accordance with Clause 14 of the Lease).

8 Mr Ensom shall be entitled to advance payments from time to time on account of fees which he estimates he is likely to incur. All advance payments shall be made by Fairoaks Lodge Residents Limited within 7 days of written demand by Mr Ensom and shall be held by Mr Ensom in his client's account. Any advance payments shall be credited against Mr Ensom's fee invoices issued from time to time.

9 Payment of Mr Ensom's fees and expenses and the VAT thereon shall be made within 7 days of the date of his invoices.

Agreed by or on behalf of Fairoaks Lodge Residents Limited

....

Date: ....

Agreed by or on behalf of Alastair Brown

....

Date: ....

I, A C Ensom FRICS FCIArb MAE, agree to my appointment as Independent Expert Surveyor subject to the above terms and conditions.

....

A C Ensom FRICS FCIArb MAE
Date: ....

APPENDIX 2

A DISPUTE BETWEEN FAIROAKS LODGE RESIDENTS LIMITED AND MR ALASTAIR BROWN

Expert Determination

By a lease dated 26 April 1952 (the Lease) the Lessor Amelia Geraldine Wynthrop demised Flat D, part of Fairoaks Lodge, St. Peter's Avenue, Leicesterfield, to the Lessee Alastair Brown for a period of 99 years from the date of the Lease. The Lessor's interest in the property was transferred to Fairoaks Lodge Residents Limited on 02 August 1991.

In November 1997 proceedings were commenced by the Lessor against the Lessee in the Leicesterfield County Court for possession of Flat D and for the sum of £2,580.50 alleged to be due under the Lease together with interest and costs. On 21 May 1998 the Court made an Order staying the proceedings and requiring the Lessor to make the appointment of an Independent Expert in accordance with the terms of the Lease to determine the disputes arising under or in connection with the Lease.

On 30 July 1998 the Parties appointed me Anthony C Ensom FRICS FCIArb MAE as Independent Expert on terms and conditions agreed with them.

I have made enquiries of the parties, received oral and written submissions from them and considered documents provided to me at my request. Having done so **I NOW MAKE THIS MY DETERMINATION** on the matters in dispute.

The background to the dispute between the Parties is as follows:

The property Fairoaks Lodge comprises a detached Edwardian house built in 1902. It is constructed of brick under a tiled roof and is divided into four flats. Leases on all four flats were granted between 1947 and 1952 and are for 99 years.

Mr Brown's Lease contains a number of provisions and covenants which are relevant to the matters in dispute as follows:

2. *The Lessee hereby covenants with the Lessor .... that the Lessee will at all times throughout the said term hereby granted:*

    (4) *participate to the extent of a one quarter share in keeping the common areas where appropriate swept clean tidy mown weed free and generally in good household order,*

    (5) *observe and perform the Management Rules* (these are contained in the Second Schedule),

    (8) *pay to the Lessor forthwith upon demand one quarter of any sum expended by the Lessor pursuant to the covenants contained in Clause 4 hereof provided for or referred to in the Third Schedule hereto but to pay one third of the costs incurred by the Lessor in heating and lighting the staircase and one third of the costs incurred by the Lessor in maintaining the common parking area and in the event of the Lessee not so paying on demand resulting in the Lessor having to borrow money from other Lessees or the bank to pay third parties then to pay in addition to the Lessor interest on this sum so borrowed (from the date of the borrowing to the date of the payment of the sum demanded and its interest) at the rate of 6% above Barclays Bank base rate calculated on a daily basis,*

    (14) *at all reasonable times during the said terms permit the Lessor with or without workman and others upon giving 7 days' previous notice in writing (or in the case of emergency without notice) to enter into and upon the flat or any part thereof for the purposes of performing its obligations under Clause 4 hereof and without prejudice to the generality thereof of inspecting repairing and renewing any parts of the entire property and for the purpose of supporting all other structures belonging to serving or used by any part of the entire property making good all damage occasioned thereby to the flat.*

4. *The Lessor hereby covenants with the Lessee as follows:*

    (4) *that the Lessor will insure and keep insured the Property for its full reinstatement value such insurance to be with a reputable insurer and the Lessor shall pay the premiums demanded by the insurer and shall provide on demand by the lessee at any time proof of payment of the said premium,*

    (6) *that so far as the same are not liable to be repaired by the Lessee or by the other lessee owner or occupier of the other flat the Lessor will*

        (i) *maintain and keep in good and substantial repair and condition the main structure of the Building and its foundations roofs chimney stacks down pipes from the roof, external main walls pipes and wires and water system (including water storage tanks) and drainage and other systems and services (other than the pipes wires and systems serving the flat alone or the other flats alone) and the common areas in good and substantial repair and condition (except as regards damage caused by or resulting from any act or default of the Lessee).*

The Second Schedule

Management Rules

12. *The owner shall comply at the owner's expense with all security regulations made by the Lessor and concerning the lagging of pipes and the switching or turning on and off of services all with the intent of minimising burglary fire and flooding.*

The Third Schedule (Service Charge Agreement)

Costs, expenses outgoings and matters in respect of which the Lessee is to contribute:

1. *All costs and expenses incurred by the Lessor for the purpose of complying or in connection with the fulfilment of its obligations under Clause 4 hereof.*
3. *The costs of management of the entire property.*

The Fifth Schedule

There is excepted and reserved out of this Lease to the Lessor

3. *The right with servants workmen and others at all reasonable time upon giving seven days' previous notice in writing (except in cases of emergency) to enter into and upon the flat for the purpose of repairing or renewing any such cables and wires repairing and maintaining and carrying out permitted alterations or other building works to the entire property giving subjacent or lateral support to the entire property in either case causing as little disturbance as possible and making good any damage caused.*
4. *Power for the Lessor and its surveyor or agents with or without workmen and others at all reasonable times on notice (except in case of emergency) to enter upon the flat for the purpose of carrying out its obligations under Clause 4 of this Lease.*

The Lessor claims against the Lessee under the Lease.

The Lessor says that Lessee is in breach of various covenants in the Lease and claims under the terms of the Lessee's Lease as follows:

1. The sum of £2840.59 in respect of emergency repairs to the Property;
2. The sum of £120.50 in respect of an insurance premium; and
3. Interest as defined in the Lease.

The Lessee denies that the sums claimed are due.

I shall deal with each element of the claim in turn.

Claim 1—The sum of £2,840.59 in Respect of Emergency Repairs to the Property

The total sum claimed is made up as follows:

1. £44.36 (being one third of £133.08) for the installation of a Yale lock and letter plate.
2. £250.28 (being one third of £750.83) for the installation of a telephone entry system.
3. £1,116.25 for the repair of a floor.
4. £398.03 (being one third of £1,592.12) for the replacement of gas service pipes.
5. £861.54 (being one quarter of £3,442.16) for the replacement of electrical wiring.
6. £170.13 (being one quarter of £510.38) for the replacement of a nightstore heater.

Item 1

This item concerns the installation of a Yale lock and letter plate to the common front doors to flats B, C & D. The total cost to the Lessor was £133.08 and the request is for reimbursement of 1/3rd i.e. £44.36.

The Lessor says that the Lessee's liability to pay the amount requested arises under Clause 2(8) of the Lease, Clause 12 of the Second Schedule and Clause 3 of the Third Schedule. The Lessee says that the work does not constitute repair works under the terms of the Lease.

I determine that Clause 12 of the Second Schedule and Clause 3 of the Fifth Schedule are not relevant to this issue.

By Clause 2(8) of the Lease the Lessee covenants to pay the Lessor a defined proportion of any sums expended by the Lessor pursuant to the Lessor's repairing covenants in Clause 4 or referred to in the Third Schedule and in heating and lighting the staircase and maintaining the parking areas. The only sub-clause in Clause 4 which it seems to me might have some relevance is Clause 4(6) the Lessors repairing covenant. There is no evidence that the installation of the lock and letter plate was a repair and indeed the Lessor has stated in its submission that the work was carried out for security purposes. I find that neither the remainder of the Clause 2(8) nor remainder of Clause 4 or the Third Schedule are relevant to this issue.

I THEREFORE DETERMINE THAT ITEM 1 OF THE CLAIM FAILS.

Item 2

This item concerns the installation of a telephone entry system to the common front door to flats B, C and D. The total cost to the Lessor was £750.83 and the request is for reimbursement of 1/3rd i.e £250.28.

The Lessor says that the Lessee's liability to pay the amount requested arises under Clauses 2(5), (8) and 4(6) of the Lease, Clause 12 of the Second Schedule and Clauses 1 and 3 of the Third Schedule. The Lessee says that the work does not constitute repair works under the terms of the Lease.

I find that Clause 2(5) of the Lease, Clause 12 of the Second Schedule and Clause 3 of the Fifth Schedule are not relevant to this issue. Clause 1 of the Fifth Schedule merely repeats the first part of Clause 2(8).

By Clause 2(8) of the Lease the Lessee covenants to pay the Lessor a defined proportion of any sum expended by the Lessor pursuant to the Lessor's repairing covenants in Clause 4 and referred to in the Third Schedule and in heating and lighting the staircase and maintaining the parking areas. The only sub-clause in Clause 4 which it seems to me might have some relevance is Clause 4(6) the Lessor's repairing covenants.

There is no evidence that the installation of the telephone entry system is in any way a repair and indeed the Lessor has stated in its submission that the work was carried out for security purposes. I determine that neither the remainder of Clause 2(8) nor the remainder of Clause 4 or the Third Schedule are relevant to this issue.

I THEREFORE DETERMINE THAT ITEM 2 OF THE CLAIM FAILS.

Item 3

This item concerns the strengthening of the floor structure beneath the bathroom in Flat D. The Lessee refused the Lessor, their surveyor and workmen access to inspect the floor and carry out the works which were subsequently carried out by the Lessor from the flat below. The total cost to the Lessor was £1,116.25 and the request is for reimbursement of the whole amount.

The Lessor says that the Lessee's liability to pay the amount requested arises under Clauses 2(14) and 4 of the Lease, Clause 3 of the Third Schedule, Clauses 3 and 4 of the Fourth Schedule and Clauses 1 and 3 of the Fifth Schedule. The Respondent says that the work was solely to Flat C and that under the terms of the Lease the Lessee is not obliged to contribute towards the cost.

I determine that Clause 3 of the Third Schedule and Clause 3 of the Third Schedule are not relevant to this issue.

Clause 4 of the Lease contains the Lessor's repairing covenant. Clause 2(14) is the Lessee's covenant to allow access to Flat B to the Lessor in order to carry out his obligations under Clause 4 of the Lease and Clause 4 of the Fourth Schedule gives the Lessor the right to access. Clause 3 of the Fourth Schedule gives a similar right to the Lessor in order to repair and maintain the structure of the property. Clause 1 of the Fifth Schedule defines costs incurred by the Lessor in complying with its repairing obligations under Clause 4 and costs in respect of which the Lessee is to contribute under the provision of Clause 2(8).

The relevant provisions of Clause 4 of the Lease are contained in Clause 4(6) in which the Lessor covenants to maintain and keep in good and substantial repair and condition the main structure of the building. I find that the floor structure is part of the building, that it was defective and that the strengthening works were a repair which fall within the Lessor's obligations. I also find that the costs of the work reasonable.

By Clause 2(8) of the Lease the Lessee covenants to reimburse the Lessor 1/4 of the costs expended in carrying out its repairing obligations in Clause 4. However the Lessor is claiming the full cost from the Lessee based on the Lease and Schedule Clauses quoted above. There appear to be two Clauses which have possible relevance. The first is Clause 4(6) of the Lease and in particular the exception at the end of the general repairing covenant which reads "except as regards damage caused by or resulting from any act or default of the Lessee". There is a question as to whether this exception applies to the whole Clause or to repairs only to common areas but leaving that aside I find that the strengthening work to the floor was not necessary as a result of damage caused by or resulting from any act or default of the Lessee.

The other Clause which appears relevant is 2(14). I find that the Lessee was in breach of his covenants to permit access to the Lessor. It is clear to me that the Lessor was put to additional cost due to the Lessee's breach of the covenant in Clause 2(14) of the Lease and it would be reasonable to require the Lessee to bear that additional cost. I find that the additional cost was £200.00.

If the total cost is reduced by £200, i.e. to £916.25 then I find that under Clause 2(8) of the Lease the Lessee is liable for one quarter of the cost.

I THEREFORE DETERMINE THAT THE LESSEE IS LIABLE UNDER THE TERMS OF THE LEASE TO PAY TO THE LESSOR £429.06 (BEING 1/4 OF £916.25 PLUS £200.00).

Item 4

These bills concern the replacement of gas service pipes to the building and to the flat and the consolidation of the gas meters in an area on the lower ground floor. The total cost to the Lessor was £1,592.12 and the request was for reimbursement of 1/4 i.e £398.03.

The Lessor submits that the Lessee's liability to pay the amount requested arises under Clauses 2(8) and 4(6)(i) of the Lease, Clause 12 of the Second Schedule and Clauses 1 and 3 of the Fifth Schedule. The Lessee submits that the works do not fall within the repairing covenant in Clause 4(6), that the gas meter to Flat D was not in disrepair and that it was moved against his wishes.

I find that Clause 12 of the Second Schedule and Clause 3 of the Fifth Schedule are not relevant to this issue and Clause 1 of the Fifth Schedule merely repeats the covenant in Clause 2(8) of the Lease.

I find:

1. that the gas service pipes were in disrepair;
2. that the replacement of the gas service pipes were a repair within the terms of Clause 4(6)(i);
3. that as part of the replacement works it was reasonable for the gas meters to be consolidated;
4. that the costs claimed were incurred by the Lessor;
5. that the cost of the work was reasonable;
6. that under Clause 1 of the Fifth Schedule the costs are those in respect of which the Lessee is to contribute; and
7. that under Clause 2(8) of the Lease one quarter of the costs are payable by the Lessee to the Lessor.

I THEREFORE DETERMINE THAT THE LESSEE IS LIABLE UNDER THE TERMS OF THE LEASE TO PAY TO THE LESSOR £398.03 (being 1/4 of £1,592.12)

Item 5

These bills concern the replacement of electrical mains, wiring and switchgear to all flats, consumer units to Flats A, B & C, consolidation of the electrical meters in an area on the lower ground floor, the replacement of the landlord's supply and lighting installation and provision of the door closer to the main entrance door to Flats B, C & D. The total cost to the Lessor was £3,442.16 and the request was for reimbursement of 1/4 i.e. £861.54.

The Lessor submits that the Lessee's liability to pay the amount requested arises out of Clauses 2(8), (14), 4(6)(i) of the Lease, Clause 12 of the Second Schedule, Clause 3 of the Fourth Schedule and Clause 1 of the Fifth Schedule. The Lessee denies liability.

I find that the Clause 12 of the Second Schedule is not relevant to this issue.

I find:

1. that the electrical mains, wiring and switchgear and the landlord's supply and lighting were in disrepair;
2. that their replacement was a repair within the terms of Clause 4(6)(i);
3. that as part of the replacement works it was necessary for the electricity meters to be consolidated and the consumer units replaced;
4. that the costs claimed were incurred by the Lessor;
5. that the cost of the works was reasonable;
6. that under Clause 1 of the Fifth Schedule the costs are those in respect of which the Lessee is to contribute; and
7. that under Clause 2(8) of the Lease one quarter of the costs are payable by the Lessee to the Lessor.

So far as the door closer is concerned there is no evidence that this was provided by way of replacement for an existing closure in disrepair and I therefore find that the works were not a repair within the terms of Clause 4(6)(i). The sum of £50.00 should be deducted in respect of the door closer before the total of these bills is apportioned.

I THEREFORE DETERMINE THAT THE LESSEE IS LIABLE UNDER THE TERMS OF THE LEASE TO PAY TO THE LESSOR THE SUM OF £848.04 (being 1/4 of £3,392.16).

Item 6

This item concerns the replacement of a night storage heater in the hallway with three similar small heaters on the landings of the common staircase to Flats B, C & D. The cost to the Lessor of the wiring to the heaters was £350.15 and the request was for reimbursement of 1/4 i.e. £87.54. The cost to the Lessor of the heaters themselves was £510.38 and the request was for reimbursement of 1/3 i.e. £170.13.

The Lessor submits that the Lessee's liability to pay the amount requested arises out of Clauses 2(8) and 4(6)(i) of the Lease and Clauses 1 and 3 of the Fifth Schedule. The Lessee denies liability for the costs claimed.

I find that Clause 3 of the Fifth Schedule is not relevant to this issue.

I find:

1. that the original night storage heater was defective;
2. that its replacement was a repair within the terms of Clause 4(6)(i);
3. that in all the circumstances it was reasonable to replace the one defective heater with three small heaters;
4. that the costs claimed were incurred by the Lessor;

5. that the cost of the work was reasonable;
6. that under Clause 1 of the Fifth Schedule the costs were those in respect of which the Lessee is to contribute.

The Lessor has claimed one third of the cost of the heaters themselves on the basis that under Clause 2(8) the Lessee is responsible for one third of the cost of heating the staircase, but only one quarter of the cost of wiring on the basis that under Clause 2(8) the Lessee is responsible for one quarter of the cost of repairing wiring under the terms of Clause 4(6). I accept this analysis. I therefore find that under Clause 2(8) of the Lease one quarter of the cost of wiring and one third of the cost of the heaters themselves are payable by the Lessee to the Lessor.

I THEREFORE DETERMINE THAT THE LESSEE IS LIABLE UNDER THE TERMS OF THE LEASE TO PAY TO THE LESSOR THE SUM OF £257.67.

Claim 2—Insurance Premium

This item concerns the premium paid on 24 June 1994 by the Lessor for insurance of the building for the year 1994/95. The total cost to the Lessor was £461.00 and the request was for reimbursement of one quarter i.e. £115.25.

The Lessee admits liability and alleges that the payment was made on 26 June 1994. The Lessor denies that the payment was made on this date or at all.

It is common ground that the Lessee handed a cheque to the Lessor on 26 June 1994. The cheque was payable to Fairoaks Lodge Residents Limited. It was not paid into a bank account.

I DETERMINE THAT ON 26 JUNE 1994 THE LESSEE DISCHARGED HIS RESPONSIBILITY TO PAY THE SUM OF £115.25 IN RESPECT OF A PROPORTION OF THE INSURANCE PREMIUM DUE FOR THE YEAR 1994/95.

Claim 3—Interest

The Lessor claims interest on the sums in Claim 2 in accordance with the provisions of Clause 2(8) of the Lease from 01 July 1996 until the date of payment. The Lessee makes no pleading in respect of this claim.

Clause 2(8) contains a Lessee's covenant that in the event that the Lessee does not pay on demand sums due under the first provision in Clause 2(8) and as a result the Lessor has to borrow money from other Lessees to pay third parties the Lessee is to pay interest on the amount borrowed from the date of borrowing to the date of payment at the rate of 6% above Barclays Bank base rate calculated on a daily basis.

The total amount which I determine the Lessee is liable to pay to the Lessor is £2,265.16. Under Clause 2(8) of the lease interest is due from 01 July 1996 until the date of this determination.

I find:

1. that the total amount payable in accordance with Clause 2(8) is £2,265.16;
2. that £2,265.16 was properly demanded by the Lessor from Lessee;
3. that the Lessor borrowed £2,265.16 from other lessees to pay third parties prior to 01 July 1996;
4. that the amount of interest on £2,265.16 from 01 July 1996 to the date of this determination is £553.85;
5. that interest will accrue at the rate of £0.84 per day from the date of this determination until payment.

I DETERMINE THAT THE LESSEE IS LIABLE UNDER THE TERMS OF THE LEASE TO PAY TO THE LESSOR THE SUM OF £553.85 IN RESPECT OF INTEREST AND A FURTHER SUM OF £0.84 PER DAY IN RESPECT OF INTEREST FROM THE DATE OF THIS DETERMINATION UNTIL PAYMENT OF THE SUM OF £2,265.16 DETERMINED IN RESPECT OF CLAIM 1 AND THE INTEREST OF £563.42 AWARDED IN RESPECT OF CLAIM 3.

Costs

Clause 14 of the Third Schedule in the Lease states that my fees and expenses for acting as Independent Expert and in making this Determination shall be borne by the Lessor and Lessee in such proportions as I shall determine.

I DETERMINE THAT MY FEES FOR ACTING AS INDEPENDENT EXPERT AND IN MAKING THIS DETERMINATION SHALL BE PAID BY THE LESSEE.

IN SUMMARY MY DETERMINATION IS AS FOLLOWS:

1 THAT THE LESSEE IS LIABLE UNDER THE TERMS OF HIS LEASE TO PAY TO THE LESSOR THE SUM OF £2,819.01 IN RESPECT OF CLAIM 1 AND THE INTEREST THEREON AND

2 THAT THE LESSEE IS LIABLE UNDER THE TERMS OF HIS LEASE TO PAY TO THE LESSOR £0.84 INTEREST PER DAY FROM THE DATE OF THIS DETERMINATION UNTIL PAYMENT OF THE SUM OF £2,819,01 IN 1 ABOVE AND

3 THAT THE LESSEE SHALL PAY MY FEES FOR ACTING AS INDEPENDENT EXPERT AND IN MAKING THIS DETERMINATION.

THIS DETERMINATION IS MADE IN LONDON ON ....

A C Ensom FRICS FCIArb MAE
Independent Expert

CHAPTER 12

EXPERT DETERMINATION IN RENT REVIEW DISPUTES

Tim Cooper

001 For ease of reading the independent expert (not to be confused with an expert witness) is referred to as the "Expert".

002 The use of an Expert to make a rent review determination arises from a belief by the parties to a lease or their solicitors that a determination of a rent at review should be by an "expert" who should be "independent" of the parties. Provisions in leases for such determinations vary considerably and there is little consistency in terminology. He may be described as an independent valuer, independent surveyor, but it is usually a common feature that the provision goes on to distinguish between his status as an Expert, not an arbitrator.

003 In the event that there is doubt whether his status is an Expert or an arbitrator, on a true construction of the provisions in the lease, he should obtain the parties' agreement to his status. If they cannot agree he should invite them to take appropriate steps to resolve the issue, e.g. by obtaining a declaration from the court. If the appointee has been appointed by a nominating body, e.g. the RICS, the Expert is well advised to check his status by reference to the lease as the status described by the appointing body would not be conclusive. It is the provisions in the lease which determine his status. The distinction between an Expert and an arbitrator is fundamental. An Expert determination is a means of obtaining an independent valuation of the reviewed rent when the parties are unable to agree the rent themselves, and the Expert has no judicial immunity and will always be liable in negligence, whereas an arbitrator enjoys immunity under the Arbitration Act 1996, s.29 unless bad faith is shown.

004 In distinguishing an Expert from an arbitrator the following are important points:

- The Expert is not governed by legislation on his appointment or procedure.
- The Expert can consider any information which he decides is relevant to the determination and the rules of law on admissibility of evidence do not apply.
- The Expert has no power to order disclosure.
- The Expert has a duty to carry out his own investigations including verification of evidence presented to him.
- The Expert's determination is based on his own skill, knowledge and investigations.
- The Expert's determination does not have to be within the range of the parties' contended figures.
- The Expert does not usually and is under no obligation to give reasons for his determination unless the lease requires him to do so or he has agreed to do so under the terms of his appointment.
- The Expert has no power to apportion responsibility for payment of his fees nor a power to determine recovery of a party's costs unless the lease expressly provides otherwise.

- Strictly speaking the slip rule does not apply to an expert determination, save that there is some support for being able to implement the slip rule in *Wallshire Ltd* v. *Aarons* [1989] 1 EGLR 147, Ch.
- The Expert's determination cannot be enforced as a judgment; a separate action would have to be brought based upon it.
- The Expert's determination may only be challenged on the sole ground of a material mistake. Questions of immaterial mistake and the Expert's liability in negligence are dealt with elsewhere.

005 The source of the Expert's appointment is the lease. If the lease provides that, in the absence of agreement, the Expert shall be nominated/appointed, e.g. by the RICS, *United Co-operatives Ltd* v. *Sun Alliance & London Assurance Co Ltd* [1987] 1 EGLR 126 inferentially held that the appointing body has a contractual relationship with the applicant and the power to appoint stems from the application to appoint, not from the parties' agreement in the lease to refer the rent to an Expert. Accordingly it is important to check the validity of an Expert's appointment to avoid the determination being a nullity, as an invalid appointment could be made.

006 The basis of the Expert's powers are always contractual whether through the lease or by the subsequent agreement of the parties. The lease will say how the rent is to be reviewed. Accordingly the lease is a set of directions on how the Expert is to reach his determination. He, therefore, must comply with those directions subject to a subsequent agreement between the parties which would create a consensual variation estoppel. The lease may include procedural requirements, e.g. inviting the parties to provide a valuation. An Expert must follow the procedural requirements. Some provisions contain a timetable which may or may not be expressed to be "time of the essence". However, this will be subject to consensual variation estoppel.

007 The Expert is well advised to agree remuneration terms with the parties in the early stages. In the absence of such agreement it is an implied term of the contract of his appointment that he is entitled to reasonable remuneration. It is also generally accepted that the parties are jointly and severally liable for his remuneration.

008 In the absence of provisions to the contrary in the lease the Expert has no powers in relation to the parties; he has a duty to proceed to his determination but must not depart from his instruction in a material respect. Instructions may include a requirement to invite the parties to make representations.

009 Questions on his role are a matter of construction of the provisions of the lease. If the Expert goes outside his remit in making his determination he has not complied with the provisions of the lease and his determination may be set aside.

010 The duty of a rent review Expert is the *Bolam* test (*Bolam* v. *Friern Hospital Management Committee* [1957] 1 WLR 582). It is well recognised that valuation is not an exact science and that within a band of figures valuers may differ without one of them being negligent. Nevertheless, to resist an allegation of negligence, the Expert may be required to show that he has acted in accordance with practices which are regarded as acceptable by a respectable body of opinion in his profession. This includes a requirement to make inquiries to that extent. It may reasonably be argued that the standard of care expected of an Expert determining a rent review for a particular type of property is a higher standard than a valuer, as a general practitioner, providing advice to a client. The standard is judged by the standards of a specialist. This is particularly important in accepting a nominated appointment as the parties are likely to have little or no say in who is being appointed. Prior to appointing an Expert the

RICS Dispute Resolution Service requires a prospective appointee to confirm his expertise, including that he has real market knowledge of the type of property concerned or the area in which the property is located or both. It is unlikely that the subtlety of the market and, perhaps, its direction in an underlying sense, can be accurately perceived by someone who is not actively engaged in carrying out transactions. It is essential that the Expert is able to demonstrate that he is regularly involved in the marketplace appropriate to his declared area of expertise.

011 The extent of inquiries the Expert should make is a question of fact in the particular case. The question arose in *Zubaida* v. *Hargreaves* [1995] 1 EGLR 127 at 129E, CA:

> "Mr Zubaida [the plaintiff landlord] also complains that Mr Hargreaves [the independent expert] did not find any further comparables of his own. Having rejected the . . . comparable upon which Mr Zubaida relied, [Mr Hargreaves] did not go off looking for others. . . . [Mr Hargreaves] says that he had a general feel for values in the area. Consequently, he did not think it necessary to search out more comparables than he already had. The judge [in the court below] dealt with this matter by reference to the case of *Wallshire Ltd* v. *Aarons* [[1989] 1 EGLR 147, QB] where he said it was stated in the headnote that there was no obligation on an independent surveyor to make inquiries of his own in regard to comparables, other than those presented to him. The learned judge said that he thought that was putting the matter too broadly. In his view, one has regard to the facts of a particular case in deciding whether the defendant acted reasonably in taking the view that he had sufficient comparables in the submissions of the parties to make it unnecessary for them to make further inquiries. On the facts of this case, the judge came to the conclusion that Mr Hargreaves had acted reasonably and there seem no grounds for upsetting that finding."

012 Following an appointment, the Expert will normally advise the parties and their representatives (if any) of his appointment, seeking confirmation of the correct names and current addresses of the parties, seeking confirmation that any representative has conduct of the matter, referring to the documents received, communications to the Expert to be sent simultaneously to the opposing party, basis of fees. As the appointment of a rent review Expert is often a tactical move by one party to encourage early settlement many Experts introduce a short time delay (say seven days) to allow an opportunity for agreement and/or an opportunity to make a joint request to defer the procedure to allow further time for agreement.

013 Until relatively recently the usual basis of remuneration has been a fixed fee or a percentage of the average of the contentions of the parties. In the latter case there is clearly difficulty if neither party makes representations or one party does and the other party does not. More recently, recognising the prevalence of itemised billing, there has been a greater use of hourly rate. An hourly rate, in the author's view, is preferable and, if possible, a without prejudice indication should be given on the likely actual amount of fees.

014 The letter to the parties setting out the procedure will clearly depend upon the method of appointment, the requirements of the lease which must, of course, be followed as a matter of contract. It has already been indicated that best practice for the Expert, following a nominated appointment, ought to be to invite the parties to jointly agree a deferral of the procedure to allow time for a settlement. If there is no joint agreement to a deferral an example of a letter notifying the parties of the Expert's procedure when nominated by the RICS is set out below. Notes in explanation are given where appropriate in italics after each paragraph. Paragraphs should be numbered for ease of reference. Whilst some may argue that the detail is too great it is important that the parties should not be expecting the Expert to be doing something different from that which he intends to do—hence the detail.

MODEL STANDARD LETTER TO PARTIES

Sir/Madam,

RENT REVIEW DETERMINATION
PROPERTY:
LANDLORD:
TENANT:

1. I have received [*name*] letter dated [*date*]. The parties have not jointly requested a time delay. Accordingly I am proceeding as set out in the following paragraphs and I invite you to respond as appropriate. *This should refer to previous correspondence which does not create joint agreement to a deferral of the procedure.*
2. **Acknowledgement:** Please acknowledge receipt of this letter and if you are a representative of a party confirm that you have conduct of the matter for that party. A representative should respond to the matters I introduce as if the party. *The Expert needs to know that the parties/representatives have received the letter so he can deal with any matters arising. A representative should understand the burden placed on him as representative of his client.*
3. **Appointment/Lease:** I have previously referred to my appointment and the Lease. Please disclose any other documents relevant to my determination. *The first letter from the Expert should have referred to his appointment, the Lease and any other documents sent to him. Enquiries should be made on whether there are any other relevant documents, within the Expert's duty to investigate.*
4. **Implementation of the Review:** I infer there is no dispute about the procedures relating to implementation of the rent review and that there is no challenge to my appointment. If I am wrong please advise me immediately with your contentions. *Any challenges to the appointment of the Expert should be raised at the earliest opportunity.*
5. **The Parties:** Please confirm the correct full name(s) and address(es) of the current parties. I remind you that if the name of a party changes during my determination procedure I must be notified of any change prior to my determination; otherwise my determination will be in the names of the current parties confirmed to me. *Attention to detail is essential. If a party wishes to bring an action based upon the determination the importance of the correct name is obvious.*
6. **Determination:** I infer from my appointment by the President as independent expert that the matter I am to determine is the amount of [*state the word(s) used in the Lease*] as at [*date*] pursuant to clause [*number*] of the Lease. Please confirm that I am correct. *It is prudent to ensure the parties know what the Expert believes is referred to him for determination.*
7. **Fees:** My fees will be on the basis of £ *per* hour calculated upon the time I personally spend in respect of the matter. Additional charges for disbursements will be made. In the event of the amount of the rent being agreed by the parties prior to my determination my fees will be on the hourly rate I refer to reflecting time involvement. All fees will be subject to the addition of VAT. **Will the parties please confirm my basis of fees is acceptable.** *The basis of fees should be agreed at an early stage to avoid misunderstandings. If the Expert's appointment is conditional upon agreement of fees the Expert is entitled to say he will not proceed unless there is an agreement. If the Expert has been appointed unconditionally without agreement on fees he should seek agreement at an early stage to avoid a conflict. If there is no agreement it is suggested he should still proceed with the determination relying on an implied joint and several contractual term that he is entitled to reasonable remuneration.*
8. **Amount of Fees:** I estimate, solely as a guide, my time involvement is unlikely to produce total fees exceeding £ plus VAT for my determination on the amount of the rent. This is, of course, a without prejudice indication of my fees and assumes there are no unusual issues to be resolved requiring significant time involvement. *It should be helpful to the parties to know the approximate amount of the Expert's fees in considering settlement terms, e.g. if the amount of the total costs are disproportionate to the difference between the parties on the amount of the rent.*
9. **Nature of Appointment:** Clause [*number*] of the Lease provides that my appointment is that of a [*use the word(s) in the Lease*]. Accordingly my status is that of an independent expert and is not subject to the provisions of the arbitration acts. If the parties jointly wish my status to be changed to that of an arbitrator they should inform me accordingly, immediately. *The Expert should make his status clear to the parties to avoid any misunderstanding.*

10. **My Duties, Assumptions:** In making my determination I shall not carry out a structural or building survey and services will not be tested.
My determination will be made on the following assumptions:

(a) That all documents affecting the subject property and my determination have been disclosed to me.
(b) That no deleterious or hazardous materials or techniques were used in the construction of the property or have since been incorporated.
(c) That my determination would be unaffected by any matters which would be revealed by a local search and replies to usual enquiries, by investigations on any electromagnetic fields, by any statutory notices.
(d) That inspection of those parts that are not inspected by me would not reveal matters material to my determination.
(e) That no contaminative or potentially contaminative uses have ever been carried out on the property and that there is no potential for contamination of the subject property from past or present uses of the property or from any neighbouring property.

I shall be under no obligation to verify the assumptions I make. *The parties should be clear on what the Expert is and is not doing. Any objection by a party could then be raised at an early date. In the event of any suggestion of negligence the Expert may be able to rely upon the limitations introduced.*
11. **Procedure:** To give the parties an opportunity to bring any relevant matters to my attention: I invite both parties to submit relevant written statements, in duplicate, to be lodged with me within **TWENTY-EIGHT DAYS** from the date of this letter.
When I have received written statements I will send a copy of each party's statements to the opposing party.
Any written statements in reply should be lodged with me, in duplicate, within **FOURTEEN DAYS** after that party receives from me the written statements of the other party; after which I will send the duplicate to the opposing party.
Whilst I shall consider and be entitled to have regard to parties' statements I shall not be in any way limited or fettered thereby and shall determine the reviewed rent in accordance with my own judgment. *If the Lease contains terms on the parties' right to make representations the Expert must follow the procedural terms. If the rent review clause does not contain procedural requirements the Expert nevertheless has a duty to investigate, adopting the* Bolam *test. It is submitted that the duty to investigate includes making enquiries of the parties on whether they wish to bring any matters to the attention of the Expert which are relevant to the determination. It is also submitted that once the invitation is made and a party makes representations natural justice requires that the other party should be given the opportunity to reply. The Expert should avoid any suggestion that he is limited by the parties' representations by stating he will not in any way be limited or fettered by representations.*
12. **Endorsement of Statements:** Please ensure that all duplicate statements delivered to me are endorsed as follows: the original endorsed "Original", the copy endorsed "Confirmed a true copy" and signed to that effect. *This saves the Expert checking that the copy is a true copy of the original.*
13. **Content of Statements:** Written statements shall be made by a named person with confirmation that he/she is, in fact, the author of them. They should state whether there is any dispute on the interpretation of the Lease or on any other legal matters. If statements contain an opinion on value the valuation assumptions upon which the property has been valued should be clearly stated. Any written statements in reply should be limited to matters arising out of the opposing party's statements. *In considering the weight to be attached to representations the Expert is entitled to know the author of them. If there is an issue of law that should be identified at an early date.*
14. **Mensuration:** I request you to ensure that measurements are consistently imperial or metric as agreed by you. *Consistency in mensuration must be desirable.*
15. **Agreed Statement of Facts:** It may help you and me to identify and narrow the issues. This may be done by you jointly agreeing a Statement of Facts, (e.g. floor areas) and further jointly agreeing that I can accept the agreed Statement of Facts without the need to undertake my own enquiries. *If the parties do agree facts this should raise an estoppel and may avoid unnecessary Expert's costs.*
16. **Extension of Time Limits:** I trust the parties will endeavour to comply with the time limits I have imposed. In the event of an extension being requested the parties should, in the first instance, endeavour to agree any such extension themselves and inform me accordingly. *To avoid*

unnecessary expense and delay it is better for the parties to agree extensions of time rather than one party applying for an extension when the Expert should, applying natural justice, invite comment from the other party before granting/dismissing the application.

17. **Disregarded Matters:** Clause [*number*] of the Lease requires me to disregard the matters set out therein. Pursuant to this requirement will the parties please advise me of any such matters which I should disregard in making my determination. *This is within the duty to investigate.*

18. **Variations:** Will the parties please advise me as to whether there have been any variations/deeds of variation altering the terms of the Lease and whether there are any outstanding notices affecting the property, its use or occupation, which would be proper matters for me to take into account in making my determination. *This is within the duty to investigate.*

19. **Issue of Law:** If a point of law arises which is likely to affect my determination I reserve the right to take legal advice on the point, the costs of such legal advice to be borne by the parties. *Subject to the surrounding circumstances a lay person (the surveyor Expert) could be vulnerable to an allegation of negligence if appropriate legal advice is not taken. In* Lewisham Investment Partnership Ltd and Another *v.* Morgan *[1997] 2 EGLR 150, Ch, at 158L Neuberger J said:*

> *"Clearly there could be various reasons, in light of the facts of a particular case, why a surveyor determining a reviewed rent could be negligent even though he honestly applied what he believed was the reasoning in a reported case. One particular circumstance which could result in the surveyor not escaping liability is where he should, bearing in mind the facts surrounding his determination, have sought independent legal advice and/or have reverted to the parties for further submissions. Although the plaintiffs [the parties] had agreed in the lease that they were entrusting the assessment of the market rent to a surveyor, this would obviously not exonerate him if he erred in law when making his determination, if it can be shown that he did not seek independent legal advice and/or he did not discuss the matter with the parties, and that a competent, careful surveyor would have done so."*

There are several authorities on the question whether an issue of interpretation, concerning the basis upon which the Expert is to conduct a valuation determination, is excluded from the jurisdiction of the court. The whole question, with reference to several authorities, is addressed in a paper by Jonathan Gaunt QC and Nicholas Cheffings FCI Arb, Estates Gazette, *18 January 1997, [1997] 03 EG 128. They conclude that there can be cases where the court will retain jurisdiction but that turns on the correct construction of the agreement to refer the matter to the Expert. They submit that, in the absence of clear wording in the agreement to refer, the courts can, and will, intervene; and that wording beyond describing the determination as final and binding or conclusive may well be required to exclude the court's jurisdiction.*

In the event that the Expert decides the issue of law himself it is submitted that as the parties have referred the determination to a FRICS rather than, say, counsel the Bolam *test is by reference to a specialist surveyor.*

20. **Without Prejudice Matters:** I direct that no without prejudice correspondence or negotiations shall be disclosed to me. For the avoidance of doubt I regard any part of a *bona fide* negotiation for a settlement whether or not marked "without prejudice" as privileged unless expressed with clarity as an open offer. I also regard any "opening shot" as privileged if marked "without prejudice". **I stress the importance of this direction.** *Despite some commentators' view that the law of evidence privilege does not apply to an Expert's determination it is submitted that public policy, which dictates that parties should always be encouraged to settle their differences, overrides the proposition. Accordingly the parties should be advised that the Expert will apply the privilege rules.*

21. **Costs Discretion:** My discretion on the costs of my determination shall be restricted to my costs and exclude parties' costs. In the absence of an application to me to publish an interim declaratory determination on the amount of the rent (with costs reserved if not agreed) I shall publish a determination final on all matters including costs. *If the lease does not provide for the Expert to determine costs he must not do so. Most leases that provide for the Expert to determine costs refer to the costs of the determination. In the absence of wording to the contrary this means the Expert's costs. For the avoidance of doubt this should be stated to the parties. They should be reminded that if a party wishes to make costs representations the Expert must be asked to reserve costs to a further determination after representations on costs have been made.*

22. **Inspection of the subject property:** I shall inspect the subject property in detail. I will advise you when I would like to inspect it. *The date of inspection will usually be after completion of parties' statements. The parties should be invited to attend and to point out any features they wish to draw to*

the Expert's attention. The Expert should not inspect in the presence of one party alone without securing agreement to that effect from the absent party; save that if the tenant/an employee of the tenant is in occupation the Expert will infer that no objection will be raised.

23. **Inspection of comparable properties:** Each party shall identify in the written statements which comparable properties (if any) I am requested to inspect. In the event of no such request I shall inspect those comparables which within my discretion and judgement I decide will be of assistance to me. If either party wishes me to inspect any of the comparable properties introduced in detail, I am to be advised and I shall expect that party, in due course, to make the necessary arrangements for my inspection. If no request is made to me to make a detailed inspection of a comparable property I shall look at such areas of it as may be regarded as "public areas" normally seen by visitors to the property. *The parties should be told what the Expert intends to do as part of his investigations. He has no power to inspect a property which is not the subject of his determination.*

24. **Enquiries:** I reserve the right to make enquiries of either party on any facts relevant to my determination. *The Expert is maintaining his duty to investigate.*

25. **Communications:** I remind the parties of my direction on communications that all communications to me shall be in writing with confirmation that a copy has been sent simultaneously to the opposing party. *This requirement should appear in the first letter to the parties but a reminder is a good idea as many parties often forget.*

26. **Informal Meeting:** I reserve the right to call an informal meeting if I believe such a meeting would be of assistance to me or the parties. *If a meeting is likely to reduce costs or is necessary to clarify relevant matters the parties should be told of this reservation; and they should be aware of the Expert's willingness to hold a meeting.*

27. **Parties' Agreement:** If, at any stage, the parties reach a settlement the parties should notify me, immediately. Any settlement should be comprehensive to include all matters referred for determination and must include agreement on who is to pay my fees and costs (apportioned, if appropriate). *The parties should be reminded that they can agree the rent at any time—because parties should be encouraged to settle their differences—but if so, agreement should be made on the Expert's fees.*

28. **Party/Representative:** Reference to a party includes a party's representative having conduct of the matter. *This helps to ensure a representative realises the obligations placed on him.*

29. I trust you find these terms acceptable and I await hearing from both parties in due course.

Yours faithfully,

[Name]
INDEPENDENT EXPERT

Distribution: *List the names and addressees of the letter.*

015 The rules of evidence do not apply to an Expert's determination; save that, as has been submitted previously, the Expert is recommended to apply the privilege rule against seeing privileged documents.

016 Sometimes issues to be decided by the Expert include issues of construction. Readers are reminded of *Lewisham* (at para 19 of the letter above). If, having regard to the surrounding circumstances, the Expert does not obtain legal advice he will have to decide the issue himself. Modern judicial authority, in construing a contract, says that is now established law that contracts are not construed in a vacuum. A court is entitled to know the surrounding circumstances which prevailed when the contract was made. A court is looking for the common intention of the parties in that both parties are entitled to know or to have the means of knowing what the contract meant when it was made. However, surrounding circumstances should be confined to what the parties had in mind and what was going on around them at the time when they were making the contract. Subjective evidence of intention by either party is not admissible; neither is evidence of negotiations. Until a contract is made, negotiations represented what one party or the other hoped to achieve, not what the contract actually meant. These propositions are supported by *Scottish Power plc* v. *Britoil (Exploration) Ltd and Others* (1997), *The Times*, 2 December 1997 CA—see the Appendix to this chapter.

017 It is most unusual for a lease to give the Expert a power to determine interest on outstanding rent, consequent on a determination after the date of review.

018 It is submitted that after the inspection(s) and if parties have made representations, the Expert should ensure the parties do not wish to make further relevant representations before proceeding to his determination. A letter to that effect can be sent to the parties: advising them that the Expert now regards the representations procedure as completed and is proceeding to his determination.

019 A rent review Expert's determination does not normally contain reasons and there is no requirement to provide reasons unless there is a contractual provision to provide reasons in the Lease.

MODEL EXPERT DETERMINATION

The following is an example of an Expert's rent determination.

WHEREAS:

1. By a lease (the "Lease") dated [*date*] made between [*landlord*] (1) and [*tenant*] (2) [*address*] (the "Property") was let from [*date*] for a term of [*number*] years.
2. The present landlord is [*name*]. The present tenant is [*name*].
3. The parties have been unable to agree the amount of the [*use the exact rent wording in the lease*] (the "Rent") on [*date of review*] pursuant to clause [*number*] of the Lease.
4. By letter dated [*date*] I, [*name*] of [*address*], was appointed by the President of the Royal Institution of Chartered Surveyors as independent expert to determine the Rent pursuant to the Lease. My status in the Lease is that of [*use the exact wording in the Lease*]. It is agreed that my status is an independent expert, not an arbitrator.

I HEREBY PUBLISH THIS MY FINAL DETERMINATION

5. I have invited the parties to bring to my attention matters they consider relevant to my determination. Both parties [, through their representatives,] have made written representations. That procedure has been completed [by an agreed timetable]. I have read the copy of the [counterpart] Lease supplied to me and considered all matters therein. I have read the representations made to me by the parties [' representatives] but recognise that as an expert, not acting as an arbitrator, I shall consider the representations made to me, but I shall not be limited or fettered thereby and shall determine the Rent in accordance with my own judgement. I have inspected the Property and looked at the comparables introduced by the parties [' representatives]. I have obtained such additional information as is necessary for me to make my determination based upon my own judgment and calculations.

[6. Clause [*number*] provides that my fees shall be payable as between the Landlord and the Tenant in such proportions as I shall direct [*use the exact wording in the Lease*]. Neither party has requested me to reserve my decision on the apportionment of my fees to a further determination. My determination on my fees, determined herein, follows the principle that costs follow the event. Neither party has been successful [*if neither party has been successful*]. Accordingly each party shall pay one half of my total fees [*the determination on fees should follow settled legal principles, including that, save in special circumstances, costs follow the event*].]

8. That the amount of the Rent pursuant to the Lease was, on [*the review date*] £ [words] *per* year.

[9. That the Landlord and the Tenant shall each pay one half of my total fees of this my determination.]

10. This is my final determination.

Date:
[name]
INDEPENDENT SURVEYOR.

020 In the event that the Expert reserves costs, usually limited to the apportionment of the Expert's fees, to a further determination (if unagreed) the following is a letter inviting sequential submissions. The party applying for a costs determination makes the first submission.

MODEL LETTER INVITING COSTS SUBMISSIONS

Date
Sir/Madam,

Rent Review Determination Costs
Property:
Landlord:
Tenant:

1. [*Refer to the application (the tenant in this case) to determine costs—assumed in this case to be limited to the Expert's costs, not the parties' costs*] I invite you to proceed as follows:

   Representations on the costs of my determination shall be made by written documents only with liberty to either party to apply for a hearing.

   The representative having conduct of a party's case shall respond as if the party.

   The tenant's Statement of Case on costs shall be delivered to the landlord and to me on or before [*date*].

   The landlord's Reply to Statement of Case shall be delivered to the tenant and to me not later than **seven** days after the landlord's receipt of Statement of Case.

   Any reply by the tenant to the landlord's Reply to Statement of Case shall be delivered to the landlord and to me not later than **seven** days after the tenant's receipt of Reply to Statement of Case and shall be restricted to issues of law only.

2. I request you to acknowledge receipt of this letter.
3. Liberty is given to either party to apply in respect of the procedure I have invited. I recommend that the applicant party, in the first instance, discuss the application with the opposing party and seek to agree an application. An agreement will save time and costs.
4. My costs in determining the allocation of my costs of my determination will be on the basis previously notified to you in my letter dated [*date*].

Yours faithfully,

[name]
INDEPENDENT EXPERT

Distribution: *List names and addressees of the letter.*

021 Detailed considerations of the principles of costs allocation are outside this chapter. Readers in doubt on settled principles in the exercise of discretion on costs, acting judicially, are recommended to read Michael O'Reilly, *Costs in Arbitration Proceedings*, (2nd ed). The following is a suggested form of a determination, with reasons, when the tenant has made a successful *Calderbank* offer.

MODEL DETERMINATION OF THE ALLOCATION OF THE COSTS OF THE INDEPENDENT EXPERT

DATED DAY OF 19 .

DETERMINATION OF THE ALLOCATION OF THE COSTS OF THE INDEPENDENT EXPERT

RELATING TO THE RENT DETERMINATION OF [*ADDRESS*]

AS AT [*DATE*]

WHEREAS:

1. By my determination (the "First Determination") dated [*date*], I, [*name*] of [*address*] determined the amount of the [*use the exact rent wording in the Lease*] (the "Rent") pursuant to a lease (the "Lease") dated [*date*] made between [*landlord*] (1) and [*tenant*] (2) of [*address*] (the "Property") on [*date*] (the "Date") at £ (including vat £) *per* year. I reserved to my further determination my decision on my costs of my First Determination (the "Costs") if not agreed.
2. The present landlord is [*name*] (the "Landlord") [, represented by [*name of representative*]]. The present tenant is [*name*] (the "Tenant") [, represented by [*name of representative*]].
3. The Costs in the amount of £ (including vat £) have been paid to me by the parties in equal half shares. The allocation of the Costs has not been agreed. Upon the application of the Tenant I am requested to determine the allocation.
4. I have invited the parties to make representations to me. Written representations have been made and that procedure has been completed. I have read all the representations made to me.

I HEREBY MAKE MY FINAL DETERMINATION ON THE ALLOCATION OF THE COSTS

5. My First Determination of the Rent was £ *per* year.
6. The Landlord contended for the Rent at £ pa; the Tenant at £ pa.
7. The Tenant's representations set out events prior to my appointment by the President of the RICS on [*date*]; an offer (for which both parties have expressly waived privilege) made by the Landlord (the "Landlord's Offer") dated [*date*] at £ pa; a *Calderbank* offer (the "*Calderbank* Offer") from the Tenant dated [*date*] at £ pa, open for acceptance for 28 days, on terms that each party shall pay one half of the Costs.

8. The Tenant says the necessity to proceed with my determination was wholly due to the Landlord's unwillingness to settle or accept the *Calderbank* Offer at a rent greater than the Rent. Accordingly the Landlord should pay the Costs together with my costs of this my final determination.
9. The Landlord confirms the Landlord's Offer and the *Calderbank* Offer should be taken into account. The Landlord says that every effort had been made to settle the matter prior to my appointment, evidenced by the Landlord's Offer; the Tenant only made an increased offer after the Landlord's application for my appointment; the Landlord should not be penalised by the Tenant's reluctance to make a compromise offer save at the eleventh hour; the closeness of the respective offers should be taken into account in that one party will be unfairly treated should that party be responsible for the Costs; accordingly the Costs should be split equally between the parties, and the Tenant should pay my costs of this my final determination.
10. In the exercise of my discretion I hold that I shall adopt the principle that, save in special circumstances, costs follow the event. The event is the amount of the Rent in my First Determination.
11. I find and hold that:

    It is not disputed that the Landlord's Offer and the *Calderbank* Offer are valid.

    As the Landlord's Offer is at a rent greater than the Rent determined by me that offer is of no effect and I disregard it.

    The Tenant's *Calderbank* Offer is at a rent greater than the Rent; the Landlord has unreasonably failed to accept the *Calderbank* Offer; the *Calderbank* Offer is a special circumstance to depart from the principle that costs follow the event; the Landlord shall pay the Costs after the date the *Calderbank* Offer ought reasonably to have been expected to have been accepted.

    The *Calderbank* Offer was dated [*date*]. The date of my appointment was [*date*]. I find the date when the Landlord ought reasonably to have accepted the *Calderbank* Offer was [*date*].

    As public policy is that parties shall be encouraged to settle their differences I derive no assistance from evidence of compromise negotiations, other than the *Calderbank* Offer.

    The closeness of the Landlord's Offer (which I have decided is of no effect) and the closeness of the *Calderbank* Offer are not matters I should take into account.

    Neither party has been successful on its contentions relative to the Rent.

    On the issue of the costs of this my final determination the Tenant has been successful.

12. Accordingly I find and hold that the Landlord and the Tenant shall each pay one half of the Costs to [*date: the date the Expert finds is the date on which the* Calderbank *Offer ought reasonably to have been expected to have been accepted*]; and the Landlord shall pay the Costs after [*date: when the* Calderbank *Offer should have been accepted*].
13. I have not set out all the evidence and submissions but have considered them and for the reasons I have given:
14. I HEREBY DETERMINE that the Landlord and the Tenant shall each pay one half of the Costs to [*date: the date the Expert finds is the date on which the* Calderbank *Offer ought reasonably have been expected to have been accepted*] which proportionate part of the Costs to [*date*] I determine at £ ; and the Landlord shall pay the Costs after [*date: when the* Calderbank *Offer should have been accepted*] which proportionate part of the Costs after [*date*] I determine at £ ; and to the extent that either party has paid to me more than the amount for which it is liable as determined by me the other party shall reimburse that party with the excess within 10 days from the date of this my final determination.
15. I FURTHER DETERMINE that the Landlord shall pay the whole of my costs of this my final determination and if in the first instance the Tenant shall have paid to me the whole or

any part of my costs of this my final determination the Landlord shall pay to the Tenant such amount within 10 days of this my final determination.

16. This is my final determination.

Date:
[name]
INDEPENDENT EXPERT

***Tim Cooper, BSc FRICS FCIArb** has over 20 years' experience as an independent expert making determinations, primarily in rental and capital property valuation references. He has similar experience as a valuation expert adviser to disputants and as an expert witness to judicial bodies including the courts. He is a practising Registered Arbitrator, regularly accepting consensual and nominated appointments from the RICS and the CIArb. He is Vice-President (since 1988) of the West Midlands Rent Assessment Panel, entailing acting as Chairman Member of Leasehold Valuation Tribunals with,* inter alia, *leasehold enfranchisement and service charges jurisdictions. He is also a visiting lecturer and tutor to the College of Estate Management Diploma in Arbitration. His professional experience dates from 1965 in London with subsequent experience in the Midlands for 25 years. He is a joint senior partner in Charles Butters & Sons, an independent practice of Chartered Valuation Surveyors in North Staffordshire.*

APPENDIX

Construing contract in its factual context—*Scottish Power plc* v. *Britoil (Exploration) Ltd and Others* (1997) *The Times*, 2 December.

Before Lord Justice Staughton, Lord Justice Otton and Lord Justice Robert Walker (judgment 18 November).

The factual matrix to which a court was to have regard in construing a contract meant the immediate context of the contract. Consideration of the surrounding circumstances should be confined to the facts which both parties would have had in mind and known that the other had in mind when the contract was made.

A wide definition of surrounding circumstances tended to add to the cost of litigation but contributed little to the understanding of the contract.

The Court of Appeal so stated, allowing the appeal of the plaintiff buyer, Scottish Power plc, from a decision of Mr Justice Colman of 14 May 1997 on the extent of the sellers' rights to sell gas to other customers under five contracts for the sale of natural gas made between Scottish Power plc and five defendant sellers, Britoil (Exploration) Ltd, Lasmo (TNS) Ltd, MOC Exploration (UK) Ltd, Clyde Petroleum (Andrew) Ltd and Talisman North Sea Ltd.

A declaration was granted in terms sought by Scottish Power plc, but an injunction to restrain the sellers from selling gas to other customers was refused.

Mr Richard Wilmot Smith, QC, Mr Stephen Males and Mr Sean Wilkin for Scottish Power: Mr Anthony Grabiner, QC and Mr David Toledano for the sellers.

Lord Justice Staughton said that it was established law that contracts were not construed in a vacuum. The court was entitled to know the surrounding circumstances which prevailed when the contract was made.

Subjective evidence of intention by either party was not admissible. The court was looking for the common intention of the parties. Both parties were entitled to know, or to have the means of knowing, what the contract meant at the moment it was made.

Evidence of negotiations was not admissible. Until a contract was made, negotiations represented what one party or the other hoped to achieve, not what the contract actually meant.

What was comprised by the surrounding circumstances or the factual matrix? There was little authority.

His Lordship had tried to summarise established principles in *New Hampshire Insurance Co* v. *MGN Ltd (No 1)* ((1995) *The Times*, 25 July) and a later appeal in the same case on 6 September 1996, echoing his earlier comments in *Youell* v. *Bland Welch and Co* ([1992] 2 Lloyd's Rep 127, 133):

> "... what the parties had in mind, and the court is entitled to know, [is] what was going on around them at the time when they were making the contract. This applies to circumstances which were known to both parties, and to what each might reasonably have expected the other to know."

In *Investors Compensation Scheme Ltd* v. *West Bromwich Building Society* ([1997] CLC 1243, 1258) Lord Hoffmann, referring to the matrix of fact, said:

> "Subject to the requirement that it should have been reasonably available to the parties ... it includes absolutely anything which would have affected the way in which the language of the document would have been understood by a reasonable man."

No authority was cited for that proposition and it was not possible to tell whether it was the subject of argument. There did not appear to have been any dispute as to what matrix should be taken into account.

It was often difficult to restrain counsel from producing a great deal of evidence under the heading of matrix, which on examination contributed little or nothing to the true understanding of the parties' contract.

All, or almost all judges were now concerned about the huge cost of litigation. Such a wide definition of surrounding circumstances, background or matrix seemed likely to increase the cost to no very obvious advantage.

Since the *Investors Compensation* case, Lord Justice Saville in *National Bank of Sharjah* v. *Dellborg* (9 July 1997) wrote about surrounding circumstances and so did Lord Justice Judge.

His Lordship would add a plea that surrounding circumstances should be confined to what the parties had in mind, and what was going on around them at the time when they were making the contract.

Lord Justice Otton agreed and Lord Justice Robert Walker delivered a concurring judgment.

(The above is reproduced in its entirety from *The Times* Law Report.)

CHAPTER 13

EXPERTISE V. EXPERTS: THE EXPERIENCE OF THE COMMODITY SECTOR

Graham Perry

GENERALLY

001 In the era of the travelling caravan when traders fell out over the quality of spices they approached the *eminence grise* of the trade, presented their respective arguments and deferred to his decision. This decision was accepted and in this way the earliest form of dispute resolution was implemented. At that time there were few laws, no concept of private international law or jurisdiction and trades involved the sale of goods and not the sale of documents of title to the goods. Traders or businessmen—for that is what they were—sought the view and opinion of a respected colleague and allowed his decision to prevail. Today the simplicity of the past cannot be resurrected. Commerce is more complicated. Laws now grant rights and enshrine principles and the conduct of dispute resolution has similarly acquired new layers of precedent and procedure.

002 In the world of commodity trading today there remains a strong determination to ensure that experienced traders and businessmen of the trade sit in judgment on disputes and in this sense they are implementing the basic principles of arbitration practised in the meandering caravans. Traders—not lawyers—must prevail. Traders have the knowledge of the trade; their lifetime commercial experience is steeped in metals or oils or grains or feeding stuffs. They are familiar with the day-to-day contract problems that arise, having experienced them themselves at some stage of their business careers. Lawyers have a role to play. They are the first port of call when a dispute arises and they are learned and knowledgeable in the legal principles that govern the resolution of a dispute. They can also bring clarity and logic and assist the parties and the arbitrators in concentrating their attention on the essential elements of the argument. But, whatever acknowledged skills lawyers possess, they can never rival the man of the trade in his accumulated knowledge and experience of the trade. The trader may lack legal training but that can be acquired. The lawyer, however, regardless of the amount of time he spends in the company of traders, can never imbibe the traders' spirit. The lawyer has never had to book currency, go long on 1,000mts of tapioca, speculate on a downturn in the market for edible oils, or sell short. The lawyer will know all about the legal principles that will govern the resolution of arbitrations arising from such commercial positions but he will always be one step removed from the front line. In the world of international commodity trading it is right that the commercial man and not the lawyer should be the arbitrator.

003 Arbitrators in this sector are selected for their expertise and they need to graft onto their unquestioned commercial experience a thorough knowledge of the principles of natural justice and undergo arbitration training before they can sit in judgment on disputes from their particular trade. Some may struggle with the required training but most businessmen do possess the necessary ability and determination to reach the required grade and become experienced arbitrators and thereby make a considerable contribution to their trade. These men—and increasingly women—of the trade will be selected for their expertise. They will never sit as experts and only rarely will they be called to give evidence as expert witnesses.

004 The burgeoning role of expert determination springs from the increasing commercial need for precise judgments on specific issues. A rent review or a share valuation or a highly technical dispute about the implementation of a construction contract—where precise principles govern the application of the relevant law—offer increasing opportunity to practitioners to apply their skills. They are the acknowledged experts. They know about rental values and discounts for sitting tenants or adjusted repairing obligations, or the strengths and weaknesses of a minority shareholder or the quality and execution of a construction contract. Their precise skill blends with the need for precise judgments on the issue in dispute.

005 In the commodity sector the position is quite different. History and tradition have passed on a system which continues to maintain the fundamental principle that the trade itself will determine its dispute by arbitration. The individual trades are controlled by their respective trade associations—LME for metals, GAFTA for grain and feeds and FOSFA for oils for example—and within the associations the power lies with the users to determine policy and practice. The secretariat may have influence and the arbitrators may settle disputes—often running into many millions of dollars—but it is the big international traders and their competitors of all sizes who have repeatedly re-affirmed their commitment to the arbitral process and to London. Arbitration London has prevailed for more than 100 years as the traditional and preferred option of the commodity traders for the resolution of commercial disputes and it should be noted that 80 per cent of the participants in London arbitrations are from overseas. It is the international trade that has committed itself first to arbitration and secondly to arbitration in London. The London aspect is rooted in history and is explained by the mercantile leadership of the United Kingdom during the eighteenth and nineteenth centuries and, whilst of interest on its own, is not the topic for consideration in this essay. It is the continued strong preference for arbitration over expert determination that requires our attention. How has arbitration survived the competition? Why have the parties not made the switch to expert determination? Why do they persist in signing contracts that require disputes to be referred to "Arbitration", London? The pre-eminence of arbitration is not a surprise to members of the trade but to outsiders familiar with the principles of expert witness and expert determination it might appear that the commodity sector has become mired in old fashioned ways and procedures. Not so. Arbitration works. Expert determination has no future in the world of commodity arbitration for three principal reasons.

RECOGNITION OF THE ROLE OF ARBITRATORS

006 There is worldwide acceptance of the individual expertise of the arbitrators. Traders know the arbitrators. Often they are one and the same. A trader will work at his desk one day, sit in judgment the following day and return to his trading on the third day. In this way arbitrators are not divorced from the cut and thrust of day-to-day trading activity. They are immersed in it and bring their own commercial experiences into play when contributing to the reasoning process.

007 Of course an arbitrator must possess integrity. He must be free of prejudice and bias and treat every arbitral assignment with a completely open mind. He cannot come with animosity or preconceived ideas. He must be prepared to explore all the issues in a rational manner and with an enquiring mind. He must weigh the evidence fairly and be prepared to be persuaded by the arguments of his fellow arbitrators. These are topics that form part of arbitration training but, assuming that he fully understands the meaning and significance of natural justice and possesses the necessary personal skills of honesty and integrity, an experienced trader will be an ideal candidate for commodity arbitrator. The knowledge of the trade comes first and if his business experience shows he is rooted in the trade then, and only then, can he turn his attention to acquiring the indispensable arbitral skills. If he knows arbitration but not the trade he will forever be an outsider. The trade must control the process and for this vital reason ongoing training of arbitrators is a high priority of the commodity trade associations.

FEWER LOOK-SNIFF ARBITRATIONS

008 The origin of arbitration lay in quality/condition complaints and, returning to our travelling caravan, it was the buyer's complaint about the texture of the silk or the taste of the spices or the feel of the garments that initiated the dispute process. It was a question of look and sniff and touch and feel and it was the opinion of the experienced old man of the trade that prevailed. In the modern era goods are sold by description and rarely by sample and the description is further specified by the quality characteristics which opened the door to look-sniff arbitrations. Under this procedure arbitrators—one from each side and a third appointed by the two or by the trade association—would examine the disputed goods and make an award on the basis of allowances agreed in the contract between the parties that provided, for example, a reduction of US$5 for each density specification in excess of an agreed viscosity or a similar calculation due to excess moisture in the goods on arrival at destination. To this extent the men of the trade would apply their technical knowledge to assess the extent to which the goods have, if at all, departed from the agreed contractual specification and make the appropriate finding and award; but even in this limited area of quality/condition assessment the arbitrators worked as arbitrators and not as experts. Their specific expertise may have brought about their appointment as arbitrator but it was as arbitrator they carried out their duties and not as expert.

009 In part the explanation is that the concept of expert determination reached maturity only after the commodity trades had found a more suitable solution to the look-sniff arbitration. With the improvement in world transport facilities and the increase in demand for goods and cargoes caused by a burgeoning population and greater prosperity, a more scientific solution was needed for the problem of quality disputes and it came in the form of superintendents who added quality evaluation to their list of available skills. Hitherto the superintendents had provided staff to supervise the loading and discharge of goods. They would—as they continue to do today—be present and watch the manner of loading and check the quantities but now they added the important ability to test the goods at the port of loading and/or the port of destination and to provide certificates for the quality and condition of the goods. In this way the potential "expert" function of the trade arbitrator was made redundant by the employment by the parties to the contract of technical experts whose knowledge and sophisticated equipment enabled them to provide the parties with independent evidence of the technical specifications of the goods. They set up laboratories to provide investigation and examination for specifications such as moisture, fibre, protein, broken grains and foreign material. Some trade associations went further and set up schemes to encourage the superintending companies to become members of the associations and to publicise and promote their testing procedures and update the trade on new matters relating to technical examination of commodities. In this way the responsibility for assessing quality and condition moved from the arbitrator to the superintendent and, where a contract now provides for quality final at loading as per SGS (one of the leading international superintendent companies), it is the SGS certificate that the arbitrators will rely upon for making a decision on a quality dispute. (That is not quite the end of the story for the buyer who receives damaged goods, as he may still be able to maintain a claim against the vessel for faulty stowage or unclean holds/tanks.) Some trade associations maintain a watching brief to ensure that the superintending companies do uphold their high professional standards to justify their continued inclusion on the trade association list of approved superintendents.

MOST ARBITRATIONS ARE UNRELATED TO QUALITY/CONDITION

010 Whereas in the days of the caravans the buyer and seller dealt in goods, their modern counterparts deal in documents and the buyer buys title to the goods, and not the goods themselves. The documents entitle him to take delivery of the goods but first he must ensure that he receives the correct set of documents and many arbitrations in the commodity sector arise out of disputes over the movement of documents. In this sense the overwhelming majority of arbitration cases are technical and unrelated to quality or condition.

011 Many arbitrations stem from disputes about the documentation, especially the letter of credit (l/c)—a document made available by the buyers' bank which guarantees to the seller payment of the contract amount provided specified documents are presented by the sellers to the bank within specified dates. At this point the dispute can become quite technical. Was the l/c opened in time? Was it contract conforming? Were amendments requested by buyers' bank made within the proper time? Were the amendments proper? Were there preconditions to be observed by the seller prior to the opening of the l/c—such as the provision of a performance bond—and were the contract deadlines met; and if not, was the failure the fault of buyer or seller? Were the proper documents presented? Were they originals? Were they presented to the appropriate bank if such a bank was specified in the contract? These are just a sample of the documentary issues which give rise to commodity arbitrations and they are clearly far removed from the quality/condition issues assumed by the non-commodity world to be at the heart of most commodity arbitrations.

012 An example of the degree of precision that must be observed by the parties in carrying out their documentary obligations is provided by a dispute that arose from the failure of the master of the vessel carrying the goods to place his signature over the official stamp on the bill of lading confirming that he was the master. The requirement was specific; the signature had to be across the stamp and in this instance—entirely through oversight—the master's signature, although immediately alongside the stamp, was not actually over it. The document was faulty and unless the defect could be corrected the whole cargo could be rejected. The pressure was on the seller, who had only 48 hours within which to re-present the corrected bill of lading at the counters of a bank in Geneva and correction meant that the master had to re-sign the bill of lading directly over the official stamp. One hundred phonecalls later established that the vessel was approaching Port Said and that with reasonable tides and no changes in the berthing priority at the port it might be possible to make contact with the master. The seller was in London. The documents were in Switzerland. The master was in

Egypt and the clock was ticking. A senior executive arrived at his office in London to be told to return home to collect his passport and make his way to Port Said without delay. He caught the first flight to Geneva to pick up the offending document and made his way post haste to Cairo and thence by car to the quayside where he boarded the vessel and—the master having been notified of his error—was able to secure a fresh signature over the stamp. He then made the return journey to Geneva and was able to present the buyer with the proper documents with just 90 minutes to spare, thereby compelling the buyer to make full payment under the letter of credit. The seller was obliged to take such Phileas Fogg-type manoeuvres because the market had fallen and the buyer was looking for any legal right to reject the documents and free himself of the contractual responsibility to take delivery of a cargo which he could then only sell on at a considerable loss.

013 The bulk of commodity arbitrations are market driven. If the market has fallen between the date when the contract was signed and the date when the documents are presented the buyer will be looking for a loophole to escape his obligations. He will scrutinise the documents in the hope that he will find an error that will entitle him to reject and avoid having to take expensive goods. But the corollary is also true—if the market has risen between the date when the contract was signed and the date when the documents are presented the seller will be looking for a mistake by the buyer that will enable him to claim that the buyer is in breach of contract thereby allowing the seller to sell to another buyer at a higher price. This is not an issue of morality but of légality. The contract defines the mutual obligations and the parties' attitude to the contract is governed by the price movement in the intervening period. If the market has moved significantly then both parties—if they are experienced and knowledgeable—will pay the closest attention to all aspects of the documentation process and companies which overlook the need to employ quality personnel in these positions pay handsomely for such shortsightedness.

014 Many commodity disputes spring from alleged variations to the written contract made by the parties during their oral and written exchanges. Traders trade. They are businessmen not lawyers and, whilst some are alert, knowledgeable and wily and know well how to take advantage of a series of exchanges to blow their counterpart off course, the majority of traders are reacting to the needs of the moment without a full awareness of the long-term consequences of their actions. Often in situations where the written exchanges leave unanswered questions about the parties' obligations, the arbitrators are called upon to determine what they believe the parties intended at the time they entered into the contract. In these cases they have to pay regard to the written evidence, the often conflicting versions of oral conversations and the interpretations placed on the evidence by the parties' respective solicitors. Was there a contract? What were the terms? And in cases where both parties and possibly the broker too issued a note of agreed terms but where no one document contains the signatures of both buyer and seller, the arbitrators again have to make findings about the terms of the contract as a preliminary step to making findings about the substantive issue in dispute.

015 The list of topics that regularly arise in commodity arbitrations include the following.

WAS THE ARBITRATION PROPERLY COMMENCED?

016 A frequent problem occurs when the parent company of a trading house executes the contract as a seller and then passes to another associated or subsidiary company the responsibility for the actual execution of the contract or for the opening of the letter of credit. Is this an assignment of the contract or merely an administrative convenience? It becomes an issue when the contract breaks down and action is taken by the buyer against the parent company or the administering company but not both, and the respondent to the action alleges that the buyer has initiated the proceedings against a party with no status or involvement in the dispute. A prolonged argument then ensues about whether the tribunal has jurisdiction to hear the dispute.

017 A further issue arises as to whether the action was commenced within the relevant time limits which are clearly set down in the Trade Associations' rules of procedure. Different time limits apply to different types of dispute. In the case of a GAFTA Monies Due dispute the arbitration must be commenced not later than the 90th consecutive day after the dispute has arisen and an argument regularly arises as to the date when the dispute actually arose—what constitutes a dispute? At what point in the exchanges can it be said that the differences between the parties crystallised into a dispute?

018 Were arbitrators appointed within the necessary time limits and was action taken by the claimant to avoid the allegation that the claim has lapsed? Parties will commence an arbitration to protect their position and put it to one side, overlooking the need to take specific steps within the first 12 months. Sometimes a step is taken but a dispute arises as to whether the step is sufficient within the rules of the association to ward off a successful application that the claim has lapsed. Lengthy argument will be presented to the arbitrators by the respective parties' representatives for and against such an application.

DEMURRAGE

019 Demurrage is a sum of money paid by the charterer of a vessel to its owner to compensate the owner for the extended number of days that the vessel has remained at berth. Disputes invariably arise as to when the vessel arrived at the port or at the berth. Was the seller responsible for delaying the vessel by not having goods ready for loading or was that responsibility shared with other parties also supplying cargo to the same vessel; or alternatively was the buyer responsible by failing to arrive at the port in time or, if the vessel did berth at the correct time, was the vessel not properly cleansed from its previous cargo, thereby delaying the commencement of loading? And there are cases where there is no dispute about who is liable for the demurrage but a dispute arises as to the actual figure. Was it properly calculated bearing in mind the normal exceptions included in a demurrage clause? Did the rain fall in sufficient strength to make loading impossible and what evidence is adduced in support of such an argument?

020 An associated area of dispute relates to extensions of the period within which the buyer is to provide a vessel upon which the goods are to be loaded. Contracts often give to the buyer the right to extend the contract, but on certain terms, and disputes often arise as to whether the terms of the extension have been agreed. Again the arbitrators will be required to decide in the light of conflicting accounts what the parties did and did not agree at the time the exchanges occurred.

DAMAGES AND DEFAULT PRICE

021 The above list of examples is not exhaustive but merely illustrative of the disputes that account for the majority of commodity arbitrations. They are deemed to be "technical" in nature and arbitrators are called upon to use their own expertise to reach conclusions on the basis of the evidence as to what happened in a given situation. The disputes are contractual and relate to interpretations of actions by the parties within the context of their legal obligations under the contract. And yet there is one area that comes within the scope of expert determination but remains within the province of arbitration—the estimated value of the goods on the day of default. This becomes a matter for consideration by the arbitrators only after they have reached a conclusion that the claimant is entitled to damages; for example a buyer may have put in a vessel during the shipment period to take delivery of cargo from the seller. The seller fails to make the goods available for loading and is put in breach of contract by the buyer who then goes into the market and buys replacement goods at a higher price (known as the default price) than the contract price because the market has moved up between the date of the contract and the date of the default. The buyer claims the difference from the seller who refuses to pay because he claims that the buyer could have purchased the replacement goods at a lower price. The arbitrators will be called upon to decide the price on the day of default and award damages accordingly. In this case the arbitrators may possess some specific knowledge of the particular commodity, but this is unlikely. The arbitrators are drawn from the trade but the trade covers a large number of goods and it is very difficult to select an expert with detailed knowledge of price movements on such a range of products. The arbitrators therefore invite the parties to submit their evidence of price, which usually consists of evidence from brokers of their view of the price on the specific day coupled with published information from the commodity exchanges. The best evidence is of trades in the same goods on the same day on the same terms. Such information is rarely available and it is the task of the arbitrators to scrutinise the evidence and assess the relevance and importance of each piece of information. Their own commercial training and expertise will guide them in reaching a specific figure upon which their award of damages will be based. It would be quite possible to assign this function to an expert but this does not occur because the rest of the arbitration practice of the commodity trade is based on members of the trade with expertise sitting as arbitrators and not as experts.

022 Expert determination is a tried and trusted form of dispute resolution. Its non-application within the commodity sector is not an adverse comment on this form of process but a recognition that the system of arbitration practised within the sector has been shown to be accepted by the overwhelming majority of the trade. For the future it is possible to predict with confidence that, provided trade associations continue to attach a high priority to ongoing arbitral training and ensure that their arbitrators are well versed both in the business of the trade and in the implementation of the arbitration process, expert determination will continue to lack a role and function in the commodity sector.

Graham Perry *studied History and Economics at Churchill College, Cambridge. He qualified as a solicitor in 1973 and was a partner with Clinton-Davies & Co until 1977 when he joined London Export Corp Ltd and concentrated on trade in commodities with China. Since 1990 he has linked his legal and commercial career as an international arbitrator with the London Metal Exchange, the Grain and Feed Trade Association and the Federation of Oils, Seeds and Fats Association. He is a Fellow of the Chartered Institute of Arbitrators and a member of the panel of arbitrators of the China International Economic and Trade Commission (CIETAC). He is also a Justice of the Peace and a football referee.*

CHAPTER 14

INTERLOCUTORY AND TRIAL/HEARING PROBLEMS

D Mark Cato

INDEPENDENT EXPERT OR ARBITRATOR?

The facts

001 The President of the Royal Institution of Chartered Surveyors received an application from one party to an agreement to appoint an independent expert. The RICS Disputes Resolution Service, on his behalf, requested details of the agreement between the parties authorising him to make such an appointment. In response the applicant stated that although unable to produce a copy of the agreement he was able to confirm that there was such an agreement. On the basis of this assurance the President appointed a chartered surveyor to be the independent expert.

002 Following his appointment, the independent expert made contact with both parties and requested a copy of the agreement which was sent to him by the non-applicant party with an objection to his appointment on the grounds that the agreement between the parties was that disputes should be resolved by arbitration and not by independent expert determination.

003 The relevant clause in the agreement provided:

> "Any dispute arising out of this agreement shall be determined by an independent surveyor agreed between the parties or in default of such agreement by a surveyor nominated by the President of The Royal Institution of Chartered Surveyors to arbitrate on the dispute."

Question

004 How should the surveyor proceed from that point?

Course of action

005 Unlike an arbitrator under the Arbitration Act 1996 (AA '96) (s.30), unless specific power is given to him by the parties, an independent expert has no power to determine his own jurisdiction. The matter must therefore be resolved elsewhere and the surveyor should immediately make this clear to both parties. The question arises, however, whether having been appointed as independent expert he is under a duty to begin his task. If, at this stage, he has not yet agreed his terms of appointment and his fees with the parties he will clearly be at risk if he continued and would be wise not to do so until the question of the validity of the appointment has been resolved. There is no statutory duty requiring him to continue nor does there appear to be any common law duty although this has not been tested in the courts.

006 It may help the surveyor to make a decision, particularly if he is under pressure from the other party to continue on the basis that the objection has no merit and is merely a delaying tactic, if he briefly considers the agreement. He would, in any case, be advised to check the terms of the agreement to ensure his appointment is valid.

007 The facts in this present example are very similar to those in *North Eastern Co-operative Society Ltd* v. *Newcastle upon Tyne City Council* [1987] 1 EGLR 142; (1987) 282 EG 1409. In that case the court decided that where the surveyor was appointed by the parties he was an independent expert but where he was appointed by the President of the Royal Institution of Chartered Surveyors he was an arbitrator.

008 It is often difficult to determine whether or not the wording of an agreement indicates an intention to appoint an independent expert or an arbitrator.

009 A guide as to how a court would consider such an agreement can be deduced from case law.

010 Titles are not always helpful. References to "an arbitrator" or to "arbitration" will usually indicate that arbitration was intended. However in *Norwich Union Life Insurance Society* v. *P&O Property Holdings Ltd* [1993] 13 EG 108 the finance agreement referred to an "arbiter". Although this is the Scottish law equivalent to an English arbitrator the agreement made it clear that the person appointed was to act as an independent expert and not as an arbitrator.

011 The terms "surveyor" or "valuer" are often even more unhelpful since on their own they do not indicate the capacity of the person appointed. An appointment by the President of the RICS or indeed any other appointing body is again of little assistance since both arbitrators and independent experts can be so appointed.

012 In the case of *Safeway Food Stores Ltd* v. *Banderway Ltd* (1983) 267 EG 850 the rent review clause provided that the revised rent should be determined by each party appointing a qualified valuer to negotiate on its behalf but, in the event that no agreement was reached between the valuers within the time limit, an umpire should be appointed to settle the question whose decision should be final and binding on the parties. In this case, the court found that the umpire was to act as an expert to determine the revised rent.

013 An agreement which indicates that the appointee can act in the absence of a dispute would be a strong indicator that he is to act as an independent expert (see paras 069 to 075 below).

014 A clear indication is often given by the description of the nature of the exercise to be performed. The essential difference between an arbitrator and an independent expert determination is that the former exercises a judicial function of determining a dispute on the evidence and submissions of parties but the latter has a duty of investigation and discovery of the facts and determines the issues on the basis of his own knowledge and experience. The courts will be looking to the agreement for some clear indicator in the wording of the role of the appointee and thus to distinguish between an arbitrator and an independent expert (see paras 021 to 033 below for distinction between arbitrator and independent expert, and also the Table at 10–025 above).

015 This distinction was further illustrated in the case of *Cott UK Ltd* v. *F E Barber Ltd* [1997] ADRLN 21, a case concerning a dispute over a contract for bottling and packaging of soft drinks.

016 Clause 14 of their agreement (which was headed "Arbitration") provided that any dispute or difference arising from the construction or performance of the agreement should be referred to the decision of a person to be appointed by the Director General of the British Soft Drinks Association and that "The person chosen or appointed shall be an independent consultant and shall act as an expert and not as an arbitrator and his decision shall be final and binding on the parties".

017 In 1996, each side alleged a breach of the minimum obligations accepted by the other under clause 3 and the defendants wrote to the Director General, invoking the clause 14 procedure. The Director General thereafter appointed D (who was highly experienced in the soft drinks industry, but who had no experience of arbitration or dispute resolution) as an expert for the purposes of resolving the dispute.

018 The plaintiff considered that the Association was not the appropriate forum for the claim and issued High Court proceedings against the defendant claiming damages. The defendant immediately issued a summons to stay the action on the ground that the parties had (by clause 14) agreed to refer to an expert for determination the matters in respect of which the action was brought.

019 The plaintiff contended that, having regard to the hearing of clause 14, it was uncertain whether the clause contemplated arbitration, or expert determination. It was therefore inappropriate to grant any form of stay.

020 In *Cott UK* it was held

1. That when construing a clause in any agreement, the heading of the clause (which amounted to a catchword, or form of identification inserted for convenience of reference) could not prevail over the express wording of the clause, or create ambiguity where no ambiguity was already present. In this case, clause 14 was clear and unambiguous. Accordingly, notwithstanding the heading "Arbitration", the only proper construction of the clause was that it was not an arbitration clause and that the appointee was to act as an expert and not as an arbitrator.
2. That the court has power under its inherent jurisdiction to stay any action arising out of an agreement, not only where that agreement contains an arbitration clause, but also where it contains a clause providing for some alternative form of dispute resolution, such as expert determination. Where such a clause exists, the burden lies on the person opposing the stay to show grounds for refusing it. In this case, such grounds existed, since the Association had no rules of its own governing arbitration, or any other form of dispute resolution, D had no experience in those areas and the clause itself neither laid down nor incorporated any rules or principles, pursuant to which D was to approach or determine the dispute. A stay would therefore be refused: *Channel Tunnel Group Ltd* v. *Balfour Beatty Construction Ltd* [1993] AC 334 considered.

WHETHER PERSON IS APPOINTED AS AN ARBITRATOR OR INDEPENDENT EXPERT

The facts

021 In a contract for sale of property the vendor was contractually bound to dispose of it to a named purchaser at a price which, in the event of a dispute, should be determined by an independent valuer.

022 An appointment was made and the appointee called for a copy of the contract.

023 The wording of the dispute clause was such that it would appear that the intention of the parties was that the person appointed should determine any dispute or difference between them, not prevent disputes arising.

Question

024 Was the appointee an arbitrator or an independent expert?

Course of action

025 Even where parties agree to be bound by the decision of another, this does not necessarily constitute an arbitration agreement. It may be that the parties intended the third party to determine the value of some specific matter which is not in dispute.

026 If the parties intended some form of judicial enquiry to be determined on the basis of evidence submitted by them, then this would amount to an arbitration agreement.

027 In determining the intention of the parties, consideration must be given not only to the wording of the agreement but also to the subject-matter of the dispute.

028 The distinction between an arbitrator and an independent expert (or valuer) can be summarised generally as follows:

1. If the object is to prevent a dispute arising, then this would be a valuation; if it is the determination of a dispute which has arisen or which may arise in the future, then the agreement would be for arbitration.
2. If the appointee acts on his own experience and knowledge without taking evidence, then this would be a valuation; if evidence is taken in the form of a judicial enquiry (i.e. with both sides having a reasonable opportunity to present their evidence and make submissions) and the determination is based on the evidence adduced, then this would be arbitration.
3. The award of an arbitrator can be remitted or set aside by the courts, but the determination of a valuer cannot.
4. The arbitrator's award can be enforced by the courts under s.26, AA '50/s.66(1), AA '96, but a party wishing to enforce a valuer's determination must do so by an action for breach of contract.
5. An independent expert is liable for his actions in negligence and/or breach of contract (see the Table at 10–025 above), but it is thought that an arbitrator is not.

029 See *Sutcliffe* v. *Thackrah and Others* [1974] 2 WLR 295, HL, where Lord Reid said:

> "The undoubted rule, based on public policy, is that a judge is not liable in damages for negligence in performing his judicial duties. The next step is that those employed to perform duties of a judicial character are not liable to their employers for negligence. This rule has been applied to arbitrators for a very long time. It is firmly established and could not now be questioned by your Lordships. It must be founded on public policy but I am not aware of any authoritative statement of the reason for it. I think it is right but is hardly self-evident. There is a general rule that a person employed to

perform duties of a professional character is liable in damages if he causes loss to his employer by failure to take due care or to exercise reasonable professional skill in carrying out his duties. So why should he not be liable if the duties which he is employed to perform are of a judicial character?

The reason must, I think, be derived at least in part from the peculiar nature of duties of a judicial character. In this country judicial duties do not involve investigation. They do not arise until there is a dispute. The parties to a dispute agree to submit the dispute for decision. Each party to it submits his evidence and contention in one form or another. It is then the function of the arbitrator to form a judgement and reach a decision.

In other forms of professional activity the professional man is generally left to make his own investigation. In the end he must make a decision but it is a different kind of decision. He is not determining a dispute: he is deciding what to do in all the circumstances. He may go wrong because he has at some stage failed to take due care and that may not be difficult to prove. But coming to a wrong but honest decision on material submitted for adjudication is rarely due to negligence or lack of care, and it is seldom due to such gross failure to exercise professional skill as would amount to negligence. It is in the vast majority of cases due to error of judgment and there is so much room for differences of opinion in reaching a decision of a judicial character that even the most skilled and experienced arbitrator or other person acting in a judicial capacity may not infrequently reach a decision which others think is plainly wrong.

But a party against whom a decision has been given that is generally thought to be wrong may often think that it has been given negligently, and I think that the immunity of arbitrators from liability for negligence must be based on the belief—probably well-founded—that without such immunity arbitrators would be harassed by actions which would have very little chance of success. And it may also have been thought that an arbitrator might be influenced by the thought that he was more likely to be sued if his decision went one way than if it went the other way, or that in some way the immunity put him in a more independent position to reach the decision which he thought right.

But whatever be the grounds of public policy which have given rise to this immunity of persons acting in a judicial capacity, I do not think that they have anything like the same force when applied to professional men when they are not fulfilling a judicial function."

030 A case where the distinction was drawn between an arbitrator and an expert was *Jones and Others* v. *Sherwood Computer Services plc* [1992] 2 All ER 170. Here an accountant was appointed to act as an expert between two other accountants to determine the volume of sales in a company transaction. This expert was to provide a determination which was to be "conclusive and binding for all purposes".

031 The umpire (expert) submitted a report which, although it gave no reasons for its findings, was alleged by the plaintiffs to contain mistakes. Accordingly the plaintiffs sought to obtain a declaration from the court that they should not be bound by the report. In this case Dillon LJ said that the Court of Appeal was bound by the decision in *Campbell* v. *Edwards* [1976] 1 All ER 785 and the statement in that case by Lord Denning was as follows:

"It is simply the law of contract. If two persons agree that the price of property should be fixed by a valuer on whom they agree, and he gives that valuation honestly and in good faith, they are bound by it. Even if he has made a mistake, they are still bound by it. The reason is because they have agreed to be bound by it. If there were fraud or collusion, of course, it would be different."

032 Dillon LJ went on to say that it was permissible to look not only at the report but also at the contract and the letter of instruction to the expert. In this case, the expert did precisely what he was asked to do and his determination could not be challenged.

033 When both parties have agreed to be bound by the determination of an expert, there is only a limited right of recourse to the court. However, the expert could probably be successfully sued for negligence if it could be proved that he had failed in his duty of care to one party and caused that party loss as a result.

THE INDEPENDENT EXPERT NOT BOUND TO ACT JUDICIALLY

The facts

034 An agreement between the parties provided that in the event of a dispute arising between them under the contract it shall be determined by an independent expert appointed by agreement between the parties or, failing agreement, on the application of either party by the President of the Royal Institution of Chartered Surveyors. The agreement stated that the independent expert's determination should be final and binding on the parties and that the independent expert's fees should be paid equally by the parties.

035 A dispute arose and the parties failed to agree on an independent expert and, following an application by the claimant, an independent expert was appointed by the President of the RICS. The respondent was generally unco-operative, often failing to respond to the independent expert's letters and was tardy in providing information requested by the independent expert or provided it in a piecemeal fashion, or not at all.

036 The claimant was anxious to have the matter resolved as soon as possible and requested the independent expert to meet him so that he could make submissions and provide oral evidence.

Question

037 What action should the independent expert take?

Course of action

038 The independent expert's powers derive from the parties and any agreements between them. In this case there are no specific provisions regarding the procedure which the independent expert is to adopt nor are any specific powers given to him.

039 However, some guidance can be established from case law to assist the independent expert.

040 He is not required to act judicially, i.e. to receive and consider submissions from both sides. Instead he makes his own investigations. Lord Reid made the following comments in *Sutcliffe* v. *Thackrah* [1974] AC 727:

> "In this country judicial duties do not involve investigation. They do not arise until there is a dispute. The parties to a dispute agree to submit the dispute for decision. Each party to it submits his evidence and contentions in one form or another. It is then the function of the arbitrator to form a judgement and reach a decision."

041 Lord Reid went on to say:

"In other forms of professional activity, the professional man is generally left to make his own investigation. In the end he must make a decision but it is a different kind of decision. He is not determining a dispute: He is deciding what to do in all the circumstances."

042 In making his investigation the independent expert is expected to use his own expert knowledge.

043 In *Safeway Food Stores Ltd* v. *Banderway Ltd* (1983) 267 EG 850 Goulding J had to consider whether a surveyor had been appointed as arbitrator or independent expert. The provisions for rent review provided:

"It is hereby agreed and declared by and between the parties hereto that if during the continuance of this demise the Lessor shall not earlier than six months nor later than three months immediately preceding the expiration of the twenty-first, forty-second, sixty-third and eighty-fourth year of the term hereby granted serve upon the Lessee a notice in writing requiring a review of the yearly rent first hereby reserved then within ten days thereafter each party shall appoint a duly qualified valuer to negotiate and endeavour to reach agreement with the valuer of the other party as to the fair market rack rent of the demised premises at that time for a Lease for a term equivalent to the then unexpired residue of the said term.

In the event of such valuers not having reached such agreement by the expiry of a period of four weeks next following the date of the service of the said notice they shall agree upon an umpire to settle the question whose decision shall be final and binding upon both parties and if within the beforementioned period of ten days either party shall not have appointed a valuer as aforesaid or if within the said period of one week next following the said period of four weeks the said two valuers shall not have agreed upon such umpire or such an umpire shall not have been appointed then in the first contingency the other party and in the second contingency either party may request the President for the time being of the Royal Institution of Chartered Surveyors to appoint a member of that Body (but not the valuer appointed as aforesaid by either party) to settle the question and the parties hereto shall be bound as aforesaid by the decision of the person so appointed."

044 Goulding J concluded:

"In the context in which it occurs I think it is pretty plain that this umpire, as he is called, was intended to be a valuer who was to use his own knowledge and make such investigations as he, a qualified surveyor, would think fit, not to act as a quasi-judge upon evidence and arguments of the parties or their representatives. I say that for four reasons, none of which is conclusive in itself but which, taken together, seem to me to be a clear pointer."

045 He then sets out four reasons, one of which was: "First of all, the whole question is one of expertise in arriving at a fair market rack rent at a particular date. It is in its essential nature one of valuation rather than a question with two clearly defined sides to be argued and decided."

046 While the independent expert's duty is to make his own investigations there seems to be no reason why he should not receive submissions from the parties orally or in writing although he is not required to take these into account in his determination.

047 Bernstein, p. 12 (at 14/5), states:

"Whether an independent expert should invite representations (that is to say, arguments) as distinct from factual information is a matter for his discretion. In some circumstances—for example where the parties are grossly unequal in financial or technical resources, and the weaker party asserts that he does not wish to incur the expense of a professional valuation—it might be justifiable for him to invite factual information only, and to say that he will pay no attention to valuations, submissions or other representations. But he should not refuse to accept factual information that either party wishes to put before him. As to how far he should rely upon factual information put before him by an obviously interested party, this is a problem that may face any professional man instructed to give an expert opinion whether for a single client or as an independent expert, and it clearly calls for greater caution in ensuring that the full facts have been disclosed to him and that they were wholly accurate. This is because he has a duty to make his own investigations into all matters which he considers might be relevant."

048 In the present example, a sensible fair-minded independent expert would undoubtedly decide to invite the respondent to attend any meeting with him requested by the claimant. If the invitation is declined then there is no reason why he should not meet the claimant without the respondent being present.

049 If at the meeting, the claimant raised issues which the independent expert felt required answers or comment from the respondent in order to complete his investigations and have a clear understanding of the issues, he would, no doubt, invite the respondent to answer or comment as appropriate.

THE EXTENT TO WHICH A SURVEYOR ACTING AS AN INDEPENDENT EXPERT VALUER NEEDS TO MAKE HIS OWN INQUIRIES

The facts

050 A surveyor is appointed by the President of the Royal Institution of Chartered Surveyors (RICS) to determine the rent of a lock-up shop with a maisonette above, situated at 107 Mill Hill Broadway, London.

051 The appointment was for an independent surveyor acting as the expert, not an arbitrator.

052 The surveyor invited both parties to submit a valuation and statement of reasons as required by the lease, which they did. As a result the surveyor determined the annual rental at £6,600, up from £3,850.

053 The landlord did not accept the new rental and commenced an action in the High Court against the surveyor who he averred had arrived at a rent which was too low and had been arrived at negligently.

054 The landlord's basic complaint concerned the surveyor's failure to make inquiries regarding comparables other than those presented to him.

Question

055 As a matter of principle, is an independent expert obliged to make inquiries of his own?

Course of action

056 The facts of this example are drawn from *Wallshire Ltd* v. *Aarons* [1989] 02 EG 81. In this case the defendant Mr Aarons was the surveyor appointed as an independent expert by the

President of the RICS. Valuations and statements of reason were prepared and delivered by the parties' experts—Mr Ward for the landlord and Mr Roberts for the tenant.

057 The judge in this case cited the RICS note which summarised the duties of the surveyor acting as an expert, rather than an arbitrator.

058 These notes included, *inter alia*:

> "The Independent Expert has the duty of investigation to discover the facts and/or relevant transactions (though he may receive evidence of facts and/or transactions from the parties)....
>
> The Independent Expert must decide upon his own knowledge and investigations, but he may be required by the instrument under which he is appointed to receive submissions from the parties.
>
> ...
>
> The parties, through their surveyors or otherwise, may jointly agree to submit to the Independent Expert an agreed statement of facts covering, for example, such matters as floor areas, the existing use of the various parts of the premises, etc.
>
> Each party may also decide to send to the Independent Expert details of transactions of which they wish him to be aware, representations as to the matters which he should take into account, or even their own valuations. Nevertheless, it is still the duty of the Independent Expert to ensure that he has any additional information that is necessary for him to arrive at his own conclusions based on his own opinions and calculations. In a valuation dispute this may include data relating to planning restrictions, restrictive covenants, the condition of the premises as found and as they are to be valued under the terms of the lease, the adequacy and efficiency of the services and allied matters."

059 Mr Aarons received submissions from Mr Ward and from Mr Roberts, copies of which he sent to the other and thereafter he received comments on the submissions, which he did not exchange. He subsequently inspected the premises.

060 In giving judgment, the judge was referred to the decision in *Belvedere Motors Ltd* v. *King* (1981) 260 EG 813, where the judge, in that case, usefully summarised the "straightforward legal principles which I have to apply and ... adopt ...". The passage the judge cited was as follows:

> "Fortunately the law is wholly straightforward. The defendant did owe to the plaintiff a duty of care and that duty is adequately set out in *Charlesworth on Negligence*, 6th ed, para 945, where it says 'Nature of Duty. The duty of architects, surveyors, building contractors and engineers is to use the reasonable care and skill of such persons of ordinary competence measured by the professional standard of the time'. That was the duty of care which the defendant owed to the plaintiff and that is the duty of care which it says he has breached. It is obvious that in an assessment such as this a reasonable element of expert judgement must be employed. Experts using care are likely to arrive at different decisions, but those decisions one would expect to fall within a bracket."

061 The judge said that there was a reference to *Singer & Friedlander* v. *John D Wood & Co*, (1973) 243 EG 212, which he omitted. He then continued to cite the judgment as follows:

> "In this case the defendant can only be found guilty of negligence if it can be shown that he has omitted to consider some matters which he ought to have considered or that he has taken into account some matter which he ought not to have taken into account, or in some way has failed to adopt the procedure and practices accepted as standard in his profession and has so failed to exercise the care and skill which he, on accepting the appointment, held himself out as possessing. I wish to stress, as I am doing repeatedly in the course of this case, that it is not my task here to assess the rent. It is not my task in any way to seek to replace the defendant's figure with some other figure which I have determined. It is in a very real sense no part of my duty to decide whether the defendant's figure was right or wrong. The only relevance of the correctness or otherwise of his assessment is as possible evidence of negligence; that is, the correctness of his assessment becomes relevant only if it is shown that it is so significantly below what would have been a correct assessment that it leads to

the conclusion that he must have been guilty of one of the acts of omission or commission which would constitute negligence on his part."

062 The judge continued:

"In fact the report reads 'omission of commission', but I feel certain that that ought to read 'omission or commission'. As I have said, I find that passage useful in summarising the law and I adopt it.

I have already said what Mr Aarons' determination was, that is that he determined the rent at £6,600. I have also heard evidence as to how he reached that decision and part of that evidence was in written form. How he reached his decision emerges fairly clearly from his notes....

It is clear that Mr Aarons correctly understood the assumptions which he was required by the lease to make."

063 In dealing with the question of whether Mr Aarons should have made his own inquiries, the judge said, *inter alia*:

"In reaching that calculation, Mr Aarons took into account the valuations and statements of reasons of Mr Ward and Mr Roberts:

He made one further enquiry concerning a property at 111 The Broadway, but otherwise relied entirely on the comparables referred to in the two submissions and on the statements of reason submitted to him by Mr Ward and Mr Roberts. It is alleged by the plaintiffs that he was negligent in doing so, that he ought to have inquired further and that had he done so he would have discovered four other comparables, one of which, 98, the plaintiffs say would have indicated to him that Mr Roberts's comparables were far too low."

064 He then dealt, *inter alia*, with the following questions:

"... whether Mr Aarons should have made further inquiries concerning the goodwill which he found probably attached to 109 The Broadway (one of Mr Ward's comparables).

... whether he should have made any inquiries concerning further comparables.

... there was a consensus among the valuers who gave evidence that valuation entails the exercise of judgement. The procedure or thought process of a valuer is, first of all, a feel for the right rental and then to cast around for the evidence of comparable cases to see whether his feel is right or wrong. He can then get a feel of the right rental from his own knowledge or by looking at the comparables themselves. Valuation is not an exact science ....

I deduce from that that one does not determine the ITZA ('in terms of zone A') by looking at comparables; rather the comparables are of assistance to the valuer in order to enable him to decide whether his feel, his judgement, is right or wrong."

065 In discussing comparables, the judge said that there were ten in The Broadway, in eight of which Mr Aarons had acted himself.

"The plaintiff complains that Mr Aarons should have made further inquiries to investigate that goodwill and that had he done so he would have discovered that the premises had been empty for a year, that they were in a dilapidated condition when they were let, and that therefore a deduction for goodwill or so much deduction was not justified."

066 Beyond inspecting the premises which were the subject of the rent review, and measuring them up, Mr Aarons has made no other inquiries. In summing up the judge gave a useful illustration to Independent Experts or Arbitrators alike as to how to deal with conflicting evidence and different modes of presenting it. He said of the evidence adduced by the parties' experts and of Mr Aarons himself.

> "I have heard expert evidence from three witnesses. Mr Aarons himself, Mr Eric Shapiro (BSc FRICS) the plaintiff's expert, and Mr I C Hayward, the defendant's expert.
>
> They are all Fellows of the Royal Institution of Chartered Surveyors and they are all well qualified both academically and by experience, and there was a large measure of agreement between them. Mr Aarons was, of course, not an independent expert. He gave evidence of fact and of opinion. In giving his evidence of fact I find him to be entirely truthful and I accept his evidence on the facts without any hesitation. So far as his opinions were concerned, they accorded, to a substantial extent, with the opinions of Mr Hayward, and to the extent that they did so, I accept them entirely. Mr Hayward is a very experienced valuer and he was a very impressive witness. Mr Shapiro is also extremely well qualified and very experienced. He had the advantage over Mr Hayward in that he gave his opinion very forcefully and very eloquently, Mr Hayward's evidence being in some respects rather difficult to understand. But Mr Shapiro's theories evidence suffered from the defect that he tended to descend into the arena.
>
> I detected a tendency to argue the plaintiffs' case rather than to give entirely objective evidence of his opinion. He was forced on some occasions during the course of his evidence into making concessions which were not immediately apparent from his report or from his evidence in chief. He had moreover acted before for Mr Ackerman. I am not therefore persuaded that Mr Shapiro's evidence was in all respects entirely objective. I certainly do not dismiss his evidence of opinion, but I tended to prefer the evidence of Mr Hayward on those matters and in those areas in which he disagreed with the evidence of Mr Shapiro. It is against that background that I consider the outstanding issues to which I now turn."

067 The judge continued to consider the question of whether Mr Aarons should have made his own inquiries.

> "I have to ask myself what facts would have been discovered had the surveyor made further inquiries concerning 109 [The Broadway]. I found the opinion of Mr Hayward on this point persuasive. His opinion was, first of all, that a reasonable surveyor would not have asked the previous tenant because, on the basis of the evidence given by Mr Ackerman, he had in fact disappeared without paying the dilapidation's claim which he owed the plaintiff company. He would have discovered nothing, therefore, had he made inquiries of the previous tenant. Mr Hayward was of the opinion that a reasonable surveyor, or a reasonable valuer, would not have approached the landlord, because he would not have wished to appear unobjective and he would have to run the risk, had he made the inquiry, of not getting an objective answer. Neither would he have asked any neighbour because of the risk of getting an incorrect answer. . . .
>
> . . . What impressed me most, however, was the opinion of Mr Hayward that any answer which might have been given to any further inquiries which might have been made would not have been helpful or would have been unlikely to have been helpful.
>
> The plaintiffs' [one expert's] only criticism was that Mr Aarons failed to make further inquiries concerning that goodwill. In my view, that point is adequately dealt with by Mr Hayward in his conclusion that even had further inquiries been made they would not have produced anything of assistance in valuing the rent.
>
> The next issue . . . was whether Mr Aaron's ought to have made further inquiries concerning other comparables. It was urged upon me by the plaintiffs' counsel . . . that faced with two anomalies arising from the open market lettings of 109 and 111 Mr Aarons ought not to have accepted Mr Roberts' comparables (being negotiated settlements) without making further inquiries and the plaintiffs' case was that Mr Aarons should have made further inquiries by, in particular, telephoning the valuers to see what other comparables were available.
>
> By doing so, it was said, he would have discovered four further comparables which would have led him to the conclusion that the Roberts' comparables were too low. . . . I am not persuaded that had those inquiries been made Mr Aarons would have gained anything useful from any of those comparables.

. . . I was most impressed by Mr Hayward's proposition that a reasonable surveyor would have felt that he had sufficient comparables already in those which were presented to him by Mr Roberts and by Mr Ward. I come to the conclusion that a reasonable surveyor would have been satisfied with the number of comparables presented to him, and would have taken those comparable as providing a sufficient check on his judgement. A reasonable surveyor would not, in my view, have researched any further. Mr Aarons therefore, in my view, acted reasonably in taking the view that he had sufficient comparables already to make it unnecessary for him to make further inquiries."

068 This then succinctly answers the question posed by this example. The judge then concluded

"... that none of the criticisms of Mr Aarons are justified. Another valuer might well not have reached the same conclusion, but it does not follow that because another valuer, and Mr Hayward in particular, might have reached a different conclusion that therefore Mr Aarons was negligent in reaching the conclusion that he did and then the way that he did. In those circumstances I dismiss the claim against him."

DETERMINATION IN THE ABSENCE OF A DISPUTE

The facts

069 In a design and build contract for an office block which had been forward sold to an insurance company based on a price per square foot of net lettable floor area, an independent expert was named in an agreement "to determine the net internal area of the building on completion. The measurements are stated to be made in accordance with the RICS Code of Measuring Practice 4th Edition".

070 On completion the insurance company requested the independent expert to take measurements and make a determination.

Question

071 Should the independent expert ascertain whether or not there is a dispute between the parties before agreeing to act?

Course of action

072 Unlike an arbitrator, an independent expert can be appointed to make a determination either in respect of a dispute which may arise, or has arisen, or on any other matter which is capable of determination and which the parties agree should be determined by a third party.

073 In the present example, the parties could have left the matter of determination of the floor area for agreement between themselves or their surveyors and provided for an independent expert to make that determination only in the event that a dispute arose.

074 However, probably because they anticipated that a dispute would arise, they had provided for the contingency by agreeing that an independent expert would determine the matter so that no dispute on the issue need arise between them.

075 Clauses are often found in leases appointing an independent expert valuer to determine the rent under a rent review clause in a lease where either side has contended for a particular rent or not. This provision is common where the parties wish to avoid a dispute and leave the matter to be determined by an independent third party.

CAN AN INDEPENDENT EXPERT UNILATERALLY DECIDE TO DETERMINE A PRELIMINARY ISSUE?

The facts

076 An independent expert had been appointed to determine matters in dispute between the parties.

077 Having made some investigations and received written submissions and copies of relevant documents relating to the matters in dispute the independent expert concluded that it might be helpful to determine as a preliminary issue one of the matters in dispute in the belief that this may limit the extent of the remaining issues in dispute or possibly lead to an agreed settlement between the parties.

Question

078 Can the independent expert take this course of action?

Course of action

079 All the independent expert's powers derive from the parties and he therefore cannot unilaterally follow the course of action he has in mind. He should suggest to the parties what he has in mind and ask for their agreement. Unless both agree he must determine all issues at the same time.

080 When parties agree to the independent expert making an interim determination there needs to be a clear agreement as to whether this is to be a final determination of this issue or whether it is merely an interim decision which is to be subject to final determination at a later date.

081 In the latter case, there also needs to be agreement where relevant as to whether it is intended that the interim decision should be binding pending final determination.

082 The terms of such an agreement will need to be carefully worded, both for the benefit of the independent expert who will need to understand the status of his interim decision and for the benefit of the parties who may need to enforce that decision.

SHOULD AN INDEPENDENT EXPERT GIVE REASONS FOR HIS DETERMINATION?

The facts

083 An independent expert, having completed his investigations, was about to consider the results of those investigations and make his determination. He received a request from the respondent to give reasons within his determination for all his decisions. He invited comments from the claimant on the respondent's request. The claimant's response was that the determination should consist of a simple written statement of his decisions without reasons, which he argued were unnecessary and would add needlessly to the parties' costs.

Question

084 Should the independent expert accede to the claimant's request?

Course of action

085 There is no general requirement in law for an independent expert to give reasons for his determination. A straightforward agreement between the parties that an independent expert should determine matters in dispute between them clearly requires the independent expert to make his determination known to the parties but does not imply that he has to explain how he reached his decisions.

086 However, if the parties agree between themselves and, more importantly, make this part of their instructions to the independent expert before his appointment, then he would be obliged to give reasons for his determination. Most independent experts would prefer not to give reasons and if asked to do so, when invited to accept an appointment, would simply decline the appointment. (Although this appears to be the case, why an expert should be so reticent to committing his reasons to writing is hard to understand.)

087 Where one party requests, after his appointment, that an independent expert should issue a reasoned determination and the other party states that reasons are not required, then he should not do so. (Unlike under AA '50, if one party requested reasons and the other said not, then reasons should be given—*Warde* v. *Feedex* [1984] 1 Lloyd's Rep 310. In arbitration, reasons are now the norm, unless it is an agreed award or the parties have agreed to dispense with reasons—s.52, AA '96.)

088 The difficulty arises when after his appointment the independent expert is asked by both parties to give reasons. One way of avoiding this problem is for the independent expert to agree with the parties as a term of his appointment that no reasons will be given for his determination.

089 *Healds Foods Ltd* v. *Hyde Dairies Ltd,* 6 December 1996, CA, was a case which also dealt with experts' reasons. The facts of this case were broadly as follows.

090 The terms of an agreement for the sale of the defendants' businesses and assets to the plaintiffs provided that in the event of a dispute an independent chartered accountant should be appointed. It was part of the independent accountant's mandate that in calculating net profit for the purpose of his determination he was bound to consider the effect of taxation as the agreement required. The vendors claimed that the independent accountant had not done so and accordingly they were not bound by his determination.

091 The trial judge found that the fact that the independent accountant did not set out any intermediate calculations and/or figures in a completion statement re-stated to take into account the judgements that he made, did not demonstrate that the independent accountant had failed to apply his mind to the matter of tax. It could well be that he considered no adjustment for tax was necessary.

092 On appeal it was held that it was impossible to fault the judge's reasoning. Although he agreed that at first blush it might appear that the exercise had not been performed, there were strong countervailing considerations. Here was an expert who should be presumed to have carried out his task carefully and correctly. It was inconceivable that the independent accountant was not aware of the effect upon the net profit of reworking the figures in a manner which he did.

093 An expert is not obliged to set out his reasoning. The fact that he does not do so does not of itself give rise to an implication of error, let alone manifest error. "All errors are manifest when discovered; but such clauses as those referred to here are intended to be confined to oversights and blunders so obvious as to admit of no difference of opinion"—*Lindley on Partnership* (16th ed) p. 162. The error alleged by the defendants may or may not have been made but it was certainly not manifest that it was made. The defendants also failed to show that on the balance of probabilities the expert departed from his instructions. There is a presumption that an experienced accountant, qualified for his task, has carried out the task properly and correctly.

094 In summary then, manifest error must be proved in order to succeed in challenging an accountant's determination when appointed by the parties as an expert.

095 The court in this case could not be satisfied that the independent accountant had departed from his mandate and accordingly Waller, McCowan and Gibson LJJ upheld the decision of the judge at first instance.

A VALUER IS NOT NEGLIGENT MERELY BECAUSE HE REJECTS A COMPARABLE

The facts

096 A surveyor was appointed by the President of the Royal Institution of Surveyors, as an independent expert, in accordance with the provisions of the rent review clause and following the notice served by the landlord of some restaurant premises seeking a substantially increased rent.

097 Following submissions by both parties, the surveyor determined what he considered was the fair rack rental value of the premises.

098 The landlord claimed that the surveyor acted negligently in arriving at his rack rental value contending that he placed too much reliance on retail comparables and that he had not only wrongfully rejected the rent determination of another restaurant but had failed to make his own inquiries and had wrongly valued the upper parts.

Question

099 Did the valuer act negligently in rejecting a comparable included in the landlord's submission?

Course of action

100 The facts of this example are drawn from *Zubaida* v. *Hargreaves* [1993] 2 EGLR 170, where it was held that the defendant (valuer) acted in accordance with a practice accepted by competent, respected professional opinion in the field of property valuation when he used, as comparables, rents of similar shop units.

101 The defendant's reasons for rejecting the 32–34 Thurloe Street rent determination—i.e. the property was an unusual shape; the relevant date was two years earlier and it was not an open market letting—were questions of judgement about which different surveyors may well come to different conclusions; the defendant was not negligent in rejecting its transaction.

102 Although there may be circumstances when an expert should seek his own comparables, no evidence was produced of any comparable not provided by the parties in the submission to the defendant before his determination which could in any way suggest that the defendant's valuation was outside any permissible bracket.

103 The defendant carried out his duty as an independent expert with competence and without negligence.

104 On the criticism that the independent expert did not make any enquiries as to rental value of any other restaurants in the vicinity not referred to by either party the judge had this to say:

> "That criticism is partly met by my finding that Mr Hargreaves could rely on retail comparables. It may, however, be taken as a general criticism that Mr Hargreaves should have sought other comparables. I have already referred to Mr Hargreaves' evidence that he considered that Mrs Walker and Mr Zubaida had provided him with sufficient information in respect of possible comparables in the circumstances.
>
> I have been referred to the report in *Wallshire Ltd* v. *Aarons* [1989] 1 EGLR 147, in which it is stated, in the head note, that the learned judge ruled in a similar case to this one that there was no obligation on the independent surveyor to make enquiries of his own in regard to comparables, other than those presented to him.
>
> That statement is perhaps couched in terms which might be considered too wide. The learned judge, in that case, held, that on the facts of that particular case, the defendant acted reasonably in taking the view that he had sufficient comparables in the submissions by the parties to make it unnecessary for him to make further enquiries.
>
> Whether an independent surveyor should make inquiries of his own in regard to comparables other than those presented to him must, again, be a matter of judgement in the particular circumstances of the case. Where the parties are professionally represented by surveyors it is unlikely to be necessary. It may be different where one or both are not so represented. However, it must be borne in mind that not all comparables subsequently produced when an independent expert's valuation is challenged might have been discovered by him on an enquiry conducted with reasonable diligence."

105 For a further fuller discussion of this point and *Wallshire Ltd* v. *Aarons* see paras 050 to 068 above.

106 The landlord appealed, contending that the defendant should not have paid attention to comparables other than restaurants. The plaintiff also sought leave to adduce additional evidence relating to a comparable relied on by the defendant which showed that the rent determined was an aberration because the tenant later surrendered the lease and took a further lease at a much lower rent.

107 The Court of Appeal dismissed the appeal and held that in an action for negligence against an expert, it is not enough to show that another expert would have given a different answer. Valuation is not an exact science; it involves questions of judgement on which experts may differ without forfeiting their claim to professional competence.

108 Although the hypothetical landlord of premises in a parade of shops may have to accept a discount if he lets one as a restaurant, it does not follow that lettings of some of the premises for other uses are irrelevant. It is up to the notional landlord as to whether, in all the circumstances, he would prefer to let the premises with the covenant for use as restaurant only or not. The defendant's regard to retail comparables was supported by a respectable body of professional people.

109 The plaintiff's application for leave to adduce the additional evidence was dismissed.

WHEN CAN A DETERMINATION BY AN EXPERT BE SUCCESSFULLY CHALLENGED?

The facts

110 In a rent review dispute concerning a hotel, the rent was to be based on a formula using "average room rate". The dispute arose because the tenant calculated his figure on the actual income achieved, whereas the landlord contended that the formula for calculating the rent should be based on the room prices available to members of the general public, i.e. published prices.

111 In accordance with the review provisions in the lease, the matter in dispute, although a question of construction and therefore of law, was referred to a chartered accountant who sat with a Queen's Counsel as legal adviser.

112 The expert found in favour of the landlord's interpretation. The tenant took out an originating motion challenging the expert's determination maintaining it was a nullity based on a misconstruction of the expression "average room rate".

Question

113 How successful is the tenant likely to be in challenging such an expert's determination?

Course of action

114 The case of *Nikko Hotels (UK) Ltd* v. *MEPC plc* [1991] 28 EG 86, sheds some light on this point. In that case Knox J said that the first question that he had to decide was whether it was open to the tenant to challenge the expert's determination by proceeding in court. He explained that the law on challenging an expert's decision had undergone some changes over the years but was now governed by the Court of Appeal decision in *Jones* v. *Sherwood Computer Services Ltd* [1989] EGCS 172 which disapproved the earlier case still quoted in text books of *Burgess* v. *Purchase & Sons (Farms) Ltd* [1983] Ch 216.

115 The decision in *Jones* v. *Sherwood* provided for a contractual analysis of the expert's task. The position is that if the parties agree to refer to the final and conclusive judgement of an expert an issue which either consists of a question of construction or necessarily involves the solution of a question of construction, the expert's decision will be final and conclusive, and therefore not open to review or treatment by the courts as a nullity on the ground that the expert's decision on construction was erroneous in law, unless it can be shown that the expert has not performed the task assigned to him. If he has answered the right question in the wrong way his decision will nevertheless be binding. If he has answered the wrong question his decision will be a nullity.

116 Applying these principles to the *Nikko* case, the question was whether the expert had assessed the wrong subject-matter as a result of a mistake or whether he carried out the very task which was entrusted to him (even if he reached an erroneous conclusion as a result of that assumed mistake).

117 The tenant submitted that the expert's mistake was that of assessing the average published room rate instead of the average charged room rate, a mistake comparable with valuing the wrong number of shares (an example shown by Dillon LJ in *Jones* v. *Sherwood*).

118 Knox J rejected this criticism, holding that the expert answered the questions entrusted to him with the result that his decision was binding on the parties whether it was right or wrong. The judge went on to consider the cases of *Absalom* v. *Great Western (London) Garden Village Society* [1933] AC 592 and *Re Davstone Estates Ltd's Leases* [1969] 2 Ch 378 cited on behalf of the tenant, but did not find that they affected his conclusion. In the event, the declaration sought by the tenant was refused and the summons dismissed.

119 The law governing challenges to decisions of experts has therefore now been considered and clarified by the Court of Appeal initially by *Jones* v. *Sherwood* and now by *Nikko*.

120 In *Jones* v. *Sherwood* an attempt was made to challenge the decision of an expert who had been appointed to resolve what sales should be taken into account when fixing the price to be paid for a company. The Court of Appeal held that the decision could not be set aside on the basis that so long as an expert does not depart from his instructions in a material respect his award is binding on the parties even if the evidence discloses that he has made an error of law. The proper approach, as Dillon LJ put it, is as follows:

> "On principle the first step must be to see what the parties have agreed to remit to the expert, this being a matter of contract. The next step must be to see what the nature of the mistake was, if there is evidence to show that. If the mistake made was that the expert departed from his instructions in a material respect, e.g. if he valued the wrong number of shares, or valued shares in the wrong company either party would be able to say that the certificate was not binding because the expert had not done what he was appointed to do."

121 In coming to this conclusion the court expressly disapproved the decision in *Burgess* (above) which had ruled that, where an expert gives a reasoned decision which discloses an error of law, that decision is open to challenge.

122 The full ambit of *Jones* v. *Sherwood* was explored in *Nikko*, where the judge made a number of points which will be of great interest to those seeking to find ways of challenging expert decisions. These were:

(1) If parties agree to refer to the final and conclusive judgement of an expert, an issue which either consists of a question of construction or necessarily involves a solution of a question of construction, the expert's decision will be final and conclusive and therefore not open to review or treatment by the courts as a nullity on the ground that the expert's decision on construction was erroneous in law.

(2) In deciding what has been referred to the expert (a matter which will henceforth be crucial when deciding whether the expert has done what he was required to do) the issue is not what precise question has been formulated by the parties for answer by the expert after the dispute has arisen but what it is that the contract between the parties under the deed had agreed should be the subject-matter of the expert's

determination. The judge was not satisfied that the parties' dealings leading up to the hearing were such as to effect an alteration in the contractual agreement between them as to the subject-matter of the expert's determination. It seemed to him that the parties' contractual rights have to be determined in accordance with what they provided in the document that they—or their predecessors in title—put their names to, rather than in the light of the procedural manoeuvrings that perfectly properly took place before the argument was heard by the expert.

(3) There is no "rule of public policy that prevents parties from referring to the conclusive decision of an expert any question of construction or other similar question of law". In reaching this conclusion the judge significantly eroded the ambit of the decision in *Davstone* which is frequently cited as authority for the proposition that an expert's decision cannot be binding on a point of law.

(4) Furthermore, Knox J went on to reject the narrower point that the courts lean against excluding the courts from deciding questions of law:

> "I do not accept that there should be in today's climate any such leaning. It seems to me that, if there is a leaning to be discerned, it is in favour of allowing the parties to do what they wish and keeping parties to their agreement, if they make one, that an expert, as opposed to the courts, should decide particular issues.
>
> The parties may well have all sorts of very justifiable reasons for preferring an expert's decision in such a matter over the decision that might be reached in the courts and I do not, myself, discern any particular policy of the law as being likely to lead to any different result in that regard."

(5) While he accepted that, in the case of a non-speaking award, it is more difficult to deduce exactly what the expert has done, he did not believe that this in itself meant that such awards have to be treated any differently from reasoned awards. The court has to grapple with the problem "of what was it that parties entrusted to the expert" and with whether the expert has carried out the required task.

123 These two cases not only mark a distinct shift to the finality of expert decisions, but also a new emphasis on the contractual basis of an expert's jurisdiction, even on a question of law.

WHEN THE DETERMINATION OF AN INDEPENDENT EXPERT IS BINDING, NOTWITHSTANDING AN ERROR ON HIS PART

The facts

124 A landowner exercised an option to acquire a narrow strip of land adjacent to his property over which he had previously been granted a right of way to afford access to the highway.

125 The option agreement provided for an independent valuer to act as an expert and not as arbitrator to determine the option price in the event of the parties being unable to agree.

126 When the option was exercised the parties failed to agree and an independent valuer was appointed who subsequently determined the value of the strip of land. In doing so no specific mention was made of an earlier grant of a right of way over this strip to the then owners of the land to which access would be gained.

127 This earlier grant only came to light when the vendors' solicitors produced a copy of the relevant deed in response to the routine requisitions on title.

128 As a result the purchasers of the strip sought a declaration from the court that he was not bound by the award and the price should be determined afresh.

Question

129 Was the purchaser correct in assuming that the valuation was not binding because of the expert's apparent error in overlooking the earlier grant?

Course of action

130 The facts of this case are a drawn from *Morgan Sindall plc* v. *Sawston Farms (Cambs) Ltd* [1997] EGCS 118, where a judgment was given for the vendor (the defendant in this case) and it was held that:

1. The award of a contractually appointed valuer, acting as an expert, was binding on the parties notwithstanding an error on his part, unless the error was such that he had failed to carry out the task prescribed by the agreement: See *Jones* v. *Sherwood Computer Services plc* [1992] 1 WLR 277 and *British Shipbuilders* v. *VSEL Consortium plc* [1997] 1 Lloyd's Rep 106. Since the valuer had valued the property as defined in the contract by reference to a plan, the plaintiff could not contend that what he ought to have valued was not so much the strip as the interest of the defendant therein.
2. Moreover, it was far from clear, the award being a non-speaking one, whether a mistake had, in fact, been made; there being no evidence either way as to what allowance, if any, had been made for encumbrances.

131 See paras 110 to 123 above for a detailed discussion on *Jones & Sherwood* and paras 132 to 141 below for detailed discussion of the effect of manifest error or fraud.

WHEN THE EXPERT'S DECISION IS FINAL AND BINDING

The facts

132 The parties concluded an agreement concerning gas in the Audrey Field. Under that agreement, the gas estimated to be in that field ("the initial gas in place") was apportioned between them, the percentage proportion which each party owned being its "tract participation". The agreement also provided for three re-determinations of the parties' respective tract participation as the gas was exploited and further data about the field became available. If the parties were unable to agree a re-determination, then an expert was to be appointed to carry it out on their behalf. The agreement concerning the expert (referred to in the case as Exhibit D) set out the rules and procedures to be followed by the expert and provided that the expert was to give his decision in writing with fully detailed reasons and that it would be final and binding on the parties.

Question

133 Under what circumstances could a party challenge the expert's determination?

Course of action

134 In *Conoco (UK) Ltd* v. *Phillips Petroleum Company and Others* (1995), [1997] ADRLN 21, 23 December 1997, whence came the facts of this example, the decision was said in the agreement to be final and binding on the parties save in the event of fraud or manifest error.

135 The parties were unable to agree the third re-determination and it was carried out by ERC Tigress Ltd ("ERC") as expert. The plaintiffs later brought proceedings in court, claiming that ERC's decision was not binding on the parties because ERC had failed to carry out its work in accordance with the contractually agreed procedure and had made manifest errors in its work.

136 Phillips, the defendant in this case, *inter alia* made the following submission.

1. The expert is required to resolve the matters in dispute in strict compliance with the terms of Article III as amended, and Exhibit D. The decision of the expert is final and binding on all the interest owners save in the event of fraud or manifest error.
2. As originally drafted Exhibit D was not intended to provide a series of procedures to be followed by a third party expert; rather it was intended to inform the deliberations of the unit interest owners in their attempts to agree the re-determinations. Therefore, the court should take account of the original purpose for which the document was created.
3. There has been a sea-change in the attitude of the courts to the ouster of its jurisdiction from *Czarnikow* v. *Roth Schmidt* [1922] 2 KB 478, through *The Nema* [1981] 2 Lloyd's Rep 239 to the judgment of Neill LJ in *The Glacier Bay* [1996] 1 Lloyd's Rep 370 at 377–378 (one might add, also, in the court's attitude to alternative dispute resolution).
4. Expert determination is now a clearly defined and understood system of dispute resolution with its own characteristic features. The first step is to identify what the parties have agreed to remit to the expert:

   > "On principle, the first step must be to see what the parties have agreed to remit to the expert, this being . . . a matter of contract. The next step must be to see what the nature of the mistake was, if there is evidence to show that.
   >
   > If the mistake made was that the expert departed from his instructions in a material respect, e.g. if he valued the wrong number of shares or valued shares in the wrong company, or . . . the expert had valued machinery himself whereas his instructions were to employ an expert valuer of his choice to do that, either party would be able to say that the certificate was not binding because the expert had not done what he was appointed to do", *per* Dillon LJ, *Jones* v. *Sherwood Computer Services plc* [1992] 2 All ER 170 at 179.

5. It is only if the expert has departed from his instructions in a material respect that there has been a breach of contract entitling the court to intervene. A departure from

the contract is not material unless it is likely to have a significant impact on the ultimate result towards which the expert determination is directed: *Wright* v. *Frodoor* [1967] 1 WLR 506 at 529. The burden of showing materiality rested on the party seeking relief. And reliance was placed on what Potter J said in an unreported decision given on 21 December 1989 in the matter of *Amoco* v. *Shell*.

6. An "error" which the plaintiffs must show is different in quality from a "mistake" which was the word used in the *Amoco* case. Error means, effectively, a departure from the prescribed course. "Mistake" is a more generalised word. Where an outcome is dependent upon a judgement, it cannot be said that there has been any error in the determination, which is partly a product of that judgement, unless it can be shown that the expert has failed to do that which he was contractually obliged to do.
7. For an error to be "manifest" it must be apparent from the determination itself. Reliance was placed on another unreported decision of Potter J in *Healds Foods Ltd* v. *Hyde Dairies Ltd and Another* delivered on 1 December 1994. There the judge had to consider the words "the Independent Accountant's Certificate (if any) shall be final and binding on the parties hereto (save in respect of manifest error)". At p. 12 he said:

> "So far as the question of 'manifest error' is concerned, I consider that the defendants have failed to discharge the burden which rests upon them. . . . As Lord Lindley observed in another context (a stipulation as between parties that the annual accounts, once approved and signed, should be regarded as conclusive, save in respect of manifest error): 'All errors are manifest when discovered; but such clauses as those referred to here are intended to be confined to oversights and blunders so obvious as to admit of no difference of opinion'."

137 Morison J said that he was invited to adopt this approach, and, in particular, to the finding by the Judge that: "The error alleged by the defendants may or may not have been made, but it is certainly not manifest that it was made; therefore the defendants fail upon that aspect of the case."

138 He then continued setting out Phillips's submissions:

8. On analysis the criticisms which were made of the experts in this case are allegations that they blundered in the method they used, whether in relation to the unacceptably high velocities or the addition of slabs of depth. Therefore, on a proper analysis, the contention that there was a manifest error and a departure from the agreed procedure are one and the same: it was the departure from the agreed procedure which involved the manifest error; without the one there would not be the other.
9. There are strong grounds of policy for respecting the parties' autonomy in cases of expert determination. Such a contractual provision is usually to be found in long-term contractual arrangements, as here, and is a means by which parties can settle disputes which will affect their long-term relationship without recourse to the courts. The agreed choice of an expert on complex matters of this sort will give greater comfort to the parties than if the matters are referred to the judge to decide. In carrying out his work the expert will almost certainly be able to take account of matters which rules of evidence prevent the judge from considering. The expert can fashion a solution to a problem which would be beyond the court's powers and his decision may be obtained more speedily "and economically" than from the court.

Finality and certainty are of particular importance to the parties. Allowing the judge to second-guess experts in a field on which he probably knows nothing leads to the very risk of abuse which characterised the case stated procedure in arbitrations prior to the 1979 Act.

139 Morison J then set out the court's approach to construction.

"There is a dispute between the parties as to the relationship between the obligation on ERC to make their re-determination in strict compliance with the procedures laid down, and the parties' right to challenge the re-determination only in the event of manifest error [I have left out fraud]. If the expert did not strictly comply with the provisions of Exhibit D, in the sense that there was a minor or trivial breach [but not to be characterised as so small that it could be ignored—*de minimis*] of a part of the procedure, would the re-determination be binding on the parties? Would it make any difference to the answer if the breach did not materially affect the result? And which party assumes the burden of showing that the breach did or did not make have any material effect? If there is a substantial departure from the procedure but, objectively, the re-determination itself could not be faulted, what then?

... the parties were entitled to and did tie the hands of the expert as to how he should approach his task, and at some point the parties are entitled to the court's protection to achieve the performance of their bargain. There is a balance to be struck between respecting what Mr Tomlinson referred to as the parties' autonomy, on the one hand, and acknowledging their rights to a determination by the court of their contractual entitlements, on the other.

Ultimately, as it seems to me, striking the balance is not a matter of policy but of contract, and a proper understanding of what the parties have entrusted to the expert and what they have left for the court. To this extent, some of the authorities to which I have been referred are not of great assistance, since they were decided on the basis of the contractual provisions then before the court. For example, in the *Amoco* case there appears not to have been a clause restricting the right of a party to challenge the determination for 'manifest error' and although the court was concerned with a similar type of agreement to this case, the agreements were different as were the facts. In the *Amoco* case, ERC's equivalent were a party to the litigation.

I seek to apply, therefore, the conventional canons of construction in ascertaining what ERC were required to do by virtue of the Expert Agreement.

In *The Glacier Bay*, Lord Justice Neill reviewed the limitations of the court's powers to intervene, across a wide spectrum of cases. He included within his review, as a partial exception to the current general rule of common law that an agreement wholly to oust the jurisdiction of the court is against public policy and void:

'cases where the parties have agreed to refer some matter to an independent expert. In *Jones* v. *Sherwood Computer Services plc* [1992] 1 WLR 277 the parties agreed to refer to independent determination the amount of "sales" made by the two subsidiaries of a named company and agreed that the determination was to be "conclusive and final and binding for all purposes". The Court of Appeal held that the determination made by the accountants was binding although it had involved considering as a matter of construction what transactions were included in the term "sales". The effect of the court's decision was summarised by Mr Justice Knox in *Nikko Hotels (UK) Ltd* v. *MEPC* [1991] 2 EGLR 103 at 108:

"The result ... is that if parties agree to refer to the final and conclusive judgement of an expert an issue which either consists of a question of construction or necessarily involves a solution of a question of construction, the expert's decision will be final and conclusive and, therefore, not open to review or treatment by the courts as a nullity on the ground that the expert's decision on construction was erroneous in law, unless it can be shown that the expert has not performed the task assigned to him. If he has answered the right question in the wrong way, his decision will be binding. If he has answered the wrong question his decision will be a nullity".'

This authority shows, I think, that the interpretation of the instructions given to the expert may be a matter for the expert rather than for the court.

In the instant case, it seems to me that ERC were required to place their own interpretation upon the language of Exhibit D having regard to the submissions made to them by the parties as to the approach which they should take. They were required to construe what Exhibit D meant. It was a necessary part of the determination that the procedures laid down should be followed, and to that end they needed to know how they should approach their task. ERC were entrusted with the task of construing Exhibit D. That, I think, was the intention of the parties to the agreements. Hence, the procedure allowed for the making of submissions by the parties, which ERC were obliged to consider.

It was submitted to ERC that within the procedure there was room for the exercise of discretion and judgement. ERC were entitled to have regard to that submission. If the conclusion they reached on the construction issue was obviously or plainly in error [manifest error] then the decision could be challenged on that account. Or, if it could be said that because of what they did, ERC effectively never performed the task allocated to them, that, too, would be a manifest error but would also, independently, I think, give a ground for challenge. It seems to me most unlikely that they intended the re-determination to be capable of challenge if there was a minor infraction of the procedure. Common sense demands, I think, that Mr Clarke's assertion that any minor breach which had no consequence would suffice for a successful challenge should be rejected.

Accordingly, it seems to me that the court is concerned to ask whether ERC have performed the task allocated to them, and if so, whether their re-determination was manifestly wrong, either because of the way they interpreted the procedural rules or on substantive grounds. That seems to me to be consistent with authority and consistent with the language which the parties used by their amendment to the Unitisation Agreement in May 1994, when the words 'save in the event of fraud or manifest error' were added. By this addition the parties were, as I think, restricting their right of challenge, whether on procedural or substantive grounds, to those two events, although it went without saying that no-one would be bound by a re-determination which could be said not to be a performance of the expert's task.

I agree and gratefully adopt Mr Justice Potter's approach to the question whether an error can be said to be manifest. Lord Lindley's statement succinctly expresses what it meant: 'oversights and blunders so obvious as to admit of no difference of opinion.' On that basis, it seems to me that there is no room for any debate as to whether the oversight or blunder would or would not have made any material difference to the result. If it could be shown that there was a manifest error, then in my judgement that would be an end of the case. The parties were entitled to have a re-determination without manifest error or fraud. If fraud was shown, I cannot accept that it would be open to debate as to whether the fraud did or did not affect the result; so also with manifest error."

140 The learned editors of the *Arbitration and Dispute Resolution Law Newsletter* summarised this point of the judgment as follows:

"... the court had to apply conventional canons of construction in ascertaining what the expert was required to do by virtue of the parties' agreement. Here, the parties had expressly agreed that the expert's decision would not be binding in the event of fraud or manifest error and had thereby restricted their right to challenge on procedural or substantive grounds to those two events; although it went without saying that no-one would be bound by a re-determination which could be said not to be a performance of the expert's task. Part of the expert's task in this case was to construe exhibit D, placing his own interpretation on what it meant, having regard to the submissions made to him by the parties, subject only to challenge on grounds of manifest error or fraud.

A manifest error did not simply mean one that had been discovered but, rather, oversights and blunders so obvious as to admit to no difference of opinion: *Healds Foods Ltd* v. *Hyde Dairies Ltd*, 1 December 1994 (unreported) followed. If such an error or, for that matter, fraud was shown, then it would be irrelevant whether or not it would have made any material difference to the result. The parties were entitled to have a re-determination without error or fraud.

In this case, however, there was, on the evidence, no obvious procedural or substantive error in the work performed by ERC. In consequence, its decision was binding on the parties."

141 See also paras 110 to 123 and paras 124 to 131 above.

WHEN THE COURT'S JURISDICTION OVER AN EXPERT'S DETERMINATION IS EXCLUDED

The facts

142 Through an originating summons, British Shipbuilders sought determination of its entitlement to documents over the purchase between it and the defendant, VSEL of Vickers Shipbuilding and Engineering Limited.

143 The contract provided for an initial payment and a further sum to be certified by reference to the profits of VSEL and its subsidiaries over a specific six-year period.

144 Clause 5.3 of the agreement provided:

> "If any disagreement arises between [accountants appointed by BS and VSEL] in connection with the certification [of those profits, it was to be referred ultimately to a firm of chartered accountants (or person) ... ('the expert') [whose] decision shall, in the absence of manifest error, be final and binding ...."

145 Clause 5.5(a) provided, *inter alia*,

> "... that each party should provide appropriate instructions to their respective accountants to certify under clause 5.2; and clause 5.5(b), that 'VSEL shall ... procure that the accountants appointed by BS will ... be allowed reasonable access to the [relevant] accounting records of each member of the new group'...".

Question

146 On the dispute between the parties as to the entitlement to documents under clause 5.5(b), had the court, or the expert, exclusive jurisdiction?

Course of action

147 The facts of this example are drawn from the case of *British Shipbuilders* v. *VSEL Consortium plc* (1996) *The Times*, 14 February.

148 Questions as to the role of an expert had to be determined as a matter of construction of the relevant agreement and if that conferred on him the exclusive remit to determine a question, the jurisdiction of the court over it was excluded; but if he went outside his remit the court could intervene and set his decision aside.

149 Likewise the court could set his decision aside, where the agreement so provided, in case of manifest error; the court had jurisdiction ahead of him to determine the limits of his remit or the condition with which he had to comply but would, save in exceptional circumstances, decline to do so.

150 Lightman J so held in the Chancery Division, on the authority of *Mercury Communications Ltd* v. *Director General of Telecommunications* ([1996] 1 WLR 48), *Jones* v.

Sherwood Computer Services ([1992] 1 WLR 277) and *Norwich Union Life Assurance Society* v. *P&O Property Holdings Ltd* ([1993] 1 EGLR 164).

151 In his Lordship's view, the role of the accountants did not extend beyond the certification process. They had no role in resolving disputes between *BS* and *VSEL* under clause 5.5(b); the experts, likewise.

152 That view was reinforced by:

1. Absence from the agreement that the expert had a role in resolving disputes between BS and VSEL as to their rights *inter se*.
2. VSEL's obligation under clause 5.5 was *prima facie* enforceable by specific performance on injunction; the expert had no jurisdiction to grant such relief.
3. One would expect clause 5.5 to precede clauses 5.2 and 5.3 if the expert was to have jurisdiction.
4. VSEL had conceded that the court was intended to retain jurisdiction over the ambit of clause 5.5 unless and until the accountants disagreed on that issue.

153 The defendant's counsel submitted that "in connection with" meant "not unrelated to" and had urged that disagreement of the accountants was not unrelated to the certification process; but in the instant context such a construction seemed inappropriate.

154 Plaintiff's counsel vigorously contended that clause 5.5 was for BS's benefit and, truly construed, obliged VSEL to give access to all documents which BS's accountants *bona fide* or reasonably said fell within it, thus achieving parity of access to what might prove vital information.

155 His Lordship said that the construction of clause 5.5 involved rewriting it, or at least reading in what was not there. The correct view was, therefore, that the court had exclusive jurisdiction to resolve disputes under clause 5.5(b).

156 The parties had also asked his Lordship to determine whether one, or more than one reference could be made under clause 5.3.

157 In response his Lordship held its language apt to embrace recurrent references to the expert.

WHERE THERE IS AN ISSUE BETWEEN THE PARTIES AS TO THE ASSUMPTIONS IN DETERMINING THE NEW RENT ON A RENT REVIEW, CAN THE COURT INTERFERE BEFORE THE DETERMINATION?

The facts

158 A lease of premises provided that if no agreement could be reached between the parties as to the reviewed rent six months before the review date, the landlord could require an independent surveyor to determine the new rent. In respect of the review, no agreement having been reached, an independent surveyor was appointed.

159 Following submissions made to the surveyor it became clear that there was an issue between the parties as to the assumptions to be considered in determining the rent. The surveyor invited counter-submissions but had not made any determination by the date of the present hearing.

160 The issue raised by the originating summons, issued by the plaintiffs, was whether the assumption to be made as to the terms of the hypothetical lease for rent review purposes, was subject to the same restrictions as to user as the actual lease.

161 By a notice of motion the defendants sought to strike out the originating summons, or to stay all proceedings on it, contending that by the lease the parties had made the surveyor the final arbiter of the question of construction and the court could not interfere even if it was clear that he had adopted a mistaken construction.

Question

162 Although a court is generally excluded from interfering with an independent expert's determination, can it do so before such determination?

Course of action

163 The facts of this example were drawn from *Postel Properties Ltd and Another* v. *Greenwell and Another* [1992] 2 EGLR 130. Here Mr Timothy Lloyd QC, sitting as a deputy judge, dismissed the motion and held that the real issue of construction between the parties was plainly within the jurisdiction of the court. It was no argument to say that, because the court could not interfere after the surveyor had made a determination, it followed that the court should not interfere before the determination.

164 Judgment was given for the plaintiffs on the originating summons with declarations accordingly.

165 The parties had made express provision for the user of the premises under the hypothetical lease, which was inconsistent with the general guide for the interpretation of rent review clauses in *Basingstoke and Dean Borough Council* v. *Host Group Ltd* [1988] 1 WLR 348 that the surveyor valuing should value that which the tenant has rather than something which he does not have.

166 Mr Lloyd QC referred to the judgment in *Nikko Hotels (UK) Ltd* v. *MEPC plc* [1991] 2 EGLR 103 where the judge decided, following *Jones* v. *Sherwood*, that the tenant was not entitled to this. After citing *Jones* v. *Sherwood*, at 99 Knox J said:

> "This decision of the Court of Appeal in *Jones* v. *Sherwood Computer Services* is, of course, binding on me, as counsel on both sides before me accepted. In my judgement it provides for a contractual analysis of the tasks set for the expert to perform, and it gives full effect to the parties' agreement regarding with what it was that the expert should be entrusted.
>
> The result, in my judgement, is that if parties agree to refer to the final and conclusive judgement of an expert an issue which either consists of a question of construction or necessarily involves the solution of a question of construction, the expert's decision will be final and conclusive and, therefore, not open to review and treatment by the court as a nullity on the ground that the expert's decision on construction was erroneous in law unless it can be shown that the expert has not performed the task assigned to him. If he has answered the right question in the wrong way, his decision will be binding. If he has answered the wrong question, his decision will be a nullity."

167 Mr Lloyd QC went on to say that there was a submission in that case that the contract should not be presumed to have ousted the court's jurisdiction to decide legal issues. On that the learned judge said, referring again to *Jones* v. *Sherwood* at 100:

> "It should be recorded that Mr Gaunt did not put his case that high, no doubt wisely seeing some of

the difficulties involved in doing so. He did, however, submit that the courts do lean against excluding the courts from deciding questions of law. I do not accept that there would be in today's climate any such leaning. It seems to me that if there is a leaning to be discerned, it is in favour of allowing the parties to do what they wish and keeping parties to their agreement, if they make one, that an expert, as opposed to the courts should decide particular issues.

The parties may well have all sorts of very justifiable reasons for preferring an expert's decision in such a matter over the decision that might be reached in the courts, and I do not, myself, discern any particular policy of the law as being likely to lead to any different result in that regard. One could gain support of much more eloquent nature for that approach in the speech of Lord Diplock in *Pioneer Shipping Ltd* v. *BTP Tioxide Ltd* [1982] AC 724 at 736."

168 And, later in his judgment, Mr Lloyd QC said this:

"I note that it seems logically to follow from the decision in *Jones*, that even if there were a court decision binding on the parties on a relevant point of construction, and if that point of construction is inherent in the process of the expert's determination, such a determination could not be challenged even if the expert expressly declined to follow the court ruling. Maybe that is more of a theoretical than a real possibility.

It seems to me that there being, so far as I can see, a real issue of construction as between the parties which is plainly within the jurisdiction of the court and the resolution of which may, to put it at its lowest, assist in the determination of the rent on the current and future rent reviews, it is a case in which it cannot be said on a preliminary basis that the court must decline to enter upon a consideration of the point, and must inevitably refrain from exercising its jurisdiction to grant declaratory relief on the question of construction."

169 The question posed by this example was further considered in *Norwich Union Life Insurance Society* v. *P&O Property Holdings Ltd and Others* [1993] 13 EGLR 108.

170 In the Chancery Division, the Vice-Chancellor, Sir Donald Nicholls, said, *inter alia:*

"In my view, the key question on this application is whether the society is entitled to have the court, rather than Mr Reilly [the arbitrator] determine the matters raised by the originating summons. If yes, then an injunction will follow, subject always to questions of the so-called balance of convenience. If not, not. Whether the society is so entitled in turn depends on what, as a question of interpretation of the funding agreement, is the ambit of the matters entrusted by the parties to the nominated arbiter for determination by him. This accords with the approach enunciated by the Court of Appeal in the leading case of *Jones* v. *Sherwood Computer Services plc* [1992] 1 WLR 227. Dillon LJ at 287 said this regarding the principle:

'The first step must be to see what the parties have agreed to remit to the expert, this being as Lord Denning said in *Campbell* v. *Edwards* [1976] 1 WLR 403, 407G, "a matter of contract".'

If, on the proper construction of the agreement, the question sought to be put to the court is an issue within the scope of the matters remitted to the nominated arbiter, then (by definition) the parties have chosen, for better or for worse, to have that question determined by a tribunal other than the court.

In answering that question of interpretation, I must apply the ordinary principles of construction. I must have regard to the language used and interpret that in the context of the funding agreement and its provisions as a whole. I must have in mind the commercial background to the agreement.

Miss Williamson submitted that the parties are not to be taken to have intended to submit to the nominated arbiter jurisdiction to determine a question of the proper interpretation of the funding agreement such as that raised by the first question, as I have described it, in the originating summons. Authority to the expert to determine an issue of fact does not necessarily carry with it authority to determine, at any rate to the exclusion of the court, questions of interpretation which are prerequisite to determining the issue of fact.

...

Parties to a contract such as this enter into a clause ... with the object of obtaining a speedy and conclusive determination on the matter in dispute by the tribunal they have chosen. They are not readily to be taken to have intended that any necessary prerequisite to that determination, which raises a question of law, is to be outside the matter so remitted. On the contrary, they are unlikely to have intended that fine and nice distinctions were to be drawn between factual matters which fall within the expert's remit and questions of law or questions of mixed law and fact which do not."

171 And further in the judgment:

"Miss Williamson sought to draw a distinction between the position before the expert makes his determination and the position afterwards. Afterwards, the court will not intervene, partly because it will often be impossible to know what is the basis on which the expert has made his award, and partly because, by proceeding with the hearing and arguing the issue in front of the expert, the parties have impliedly clothed him with authority to determine that issue. By their conduct and whatever they might say, they have elected to have the matter determined by him. Beforehand, however, those considerations do not apply.

I do not think that a distinction between before and after drawn in this way is satisfactory. This analysis does not get to the heart of the matter. As a matter of principle, the issue on which a determination by the court is being sought is either within the matters remitted to the expert for his decision or it is not. If it is, then the court will not intervene either before or after, unless there has been fraud or collusion.

...

I was also referred to the unreported decision of Mr Timothy Lloyd QC, sitting as a deputy judge of the Chancery Division, in *Postel Properties Ltd* v. *Greenwell* [1992] 2 EGLR 130, given on 17 July 1992. There the judge had before him an originating summons raising questions on the proper interpretation of a rent review clause. Certain assumptions had to be made by the independent surveyor and a dispute had arisen over the meaning of the assumptions. The judge refused to strike out the summons and proceeded to determine those questions.

As I read that case, counsel for the respondents did not contend that the jurisdiction of the court to entertain those questions had been excluded by the provisions of the lease. In that case it seems, therefore, not to have been argued that on the proper interpretation of the lease the questions raised by the summons were within the remit of the surveyor and, therefore, not open to determination by the court. The matter seems to have proceeded on the basis that the court had a discretion. That being the basis on which the case proceeded, it does not assist in the present case, nor does it assist on any question of general principle.

...

Finally, reference was made to a *dictum* of Judge Paul Baker QC, sitting as a judge of the High Court, in *Pontsarn Investments Ltd* v. *Kansallis-Osake-Pankki* [1992] 1 EGLR 148. At 152 the learned judge made an observation on which Miss Williamson placed some reliance. In that case the judge was concerned to address, and in his judgment he rejected, a submission that, if an expert went wrong in law, he exceeded his jurisdiction and his determination was a nullity. The judge rejected a suggested analogy with inferior courts and tribunals. He rejected a submission that the principles applied by the High Court in exercising control over inferior courts and tribunals should be applied to the determinations of experts, even though they operated in the field of private law. The judge gave several reasons for rejecting this submission. He gave, as one of his reasons:

> 'Second, if it is thought that some question of law requires resolution, either party can seek a declaration from the court.'

He stated that as a general proposition concerning a possible course available in the case of references to an expert. As I read the learned judge's judgment, that was a very general comment, and I do not understand it to have been directed at the point now under consideration.

Miss Williamson also submitted there was a distinction to be drawn between a case where the arbitrator or expert has jurisdiction to decide a matter and a case where the arbitrator or expert has been given exclusive jurisdiction to decide a matter. Only in the latter case will the court decline to intervene in advance of a determination. The difficulty I have with this submission is that in the normal way, when agreeing to refer a matter to a third party for his decision, parties must intend that he and he alone should decide the matter. It is, I suppose, theoretically possible to have a case where the parties intend that the expert's jurisdiction shall cover certain matters, but so that this should not exclude the court's jurisdiction to decide some of those matters as well. That would be a very strange and unusual arrangement. Clear language would be required before a court could safely conclude that the parties intended the expert's jurisdiction to be of this non-exclusive character. . . ."

172 In the Court of Appeal, Dillon LJ said, *inter alia*:

"I respectfully and entirely agree with the Vice-Chancellor in what he there said for the reasons he has given.

We were referred also to a decision of Hoffmann J in a case of *Royal Trust International Ltd* v. *Nordbanken* decided on 13 October 1989, but unreported. At p. 6F of the transcript he said:

> 'I do not think it is right that the court has no jurisdiction to make declarations in advance of an expert's determination except with the consent of the parties.'

He considered that the court had a discretion whether or not to grant such declarations and to stay the proceedings, if necessary, pending the making of such determination.

But with all respect I do not agree. The function of the expert is to make the decision and that is not the function of the court where the decision has been entrusted to the expert. It is otherwise if both parties agree—as they often do—to get a ruling from the court to determine the basis on which an expert is to proceed, and if it is practical to assist the court will do so. But here there is no such agreement."

APPENDICES

APPENDIX A

THE WOOLF REPORT

APPENDIX A/1

EXTRACT FROM "ACCESS TO JUSTICE"—THE WOOLF REPORT

(Reproduced with kind permission of the Lord Chancellor's Department)

CHAPTER 13 EXPERT EVIDENCE

Introduction

1. It was a basic contention of my interim report that two of the major generators of unnecessary cost in civil litigation were uncontrolled discovery and expert evidence. No-one has seriously challenged that contention.

2. A large litigation support industry, generating a multi-million pound fee income, has grown up among professions such as accountants, architects and others, and new professions have developed such as accident reconstruction and care experts. This goes against all principles of proportionality and access to justice. In my view, its most damaging effect is that it has created an ethos of what is acceptable which has in turn filtered down to smaller cases. Many potential litigants do not even start litigation because of the advice they are given about cost, and in my view this is as great a social ill as the actual cost of pursuing litigation.

3. It was to meet these concerns that, in chapter 23 of the interim report, I recommended that the calling of expert evidence should be under the complete control of the court. Within that framework, I argued for a wider use of "single" or "neutral" experts who would be jointly selected and instructed by the parties, or, if the parties could not agree on a single expert, appointed by the court. I also put forward a number of other recommendations designed to achieve a more economical use of expert evidence in cases where opposing experts were involved, by narrowing the issues between them as early as possible.

4. In the second stage of the Inquiry I issued an issues paper on expert evidence, in which I reviewed the approach adopted in the interim report and its underlying objectives, and sought views as to the best way in which arrangements for experts could be improved to meet my overall aims. In particular, I invited responses from those with experience of the use of expert evidence in areas of litigation which were not considered in any detail in the interim report, such as intellectual property, housing, and construction cases, as well as of expert evidence in personal injury which was my main focus of attention in the interim report.

5. There is widespread agreement with the criticisms I made in the interim report of the way in which expert evidence is used at present, especially the point that experts sometimes take on the role of partisan advocates instead of neutral fact finders or opinion givers. My detailed proposals on experts, however, have provoked more opposition than any of my other recommendations. Most respondents favour retaining the full-scale adversarial use of expert evidence, and resist proposals for wider use of single experts (whether court-appointed or jointly appointed by the parties) and for disclosure of communications between experts and their instructing lawyers.

Expert evidence within an adversarial framework

6. In the interim report I made it clear, in general terms, that I wanted to retain what was best in the English adversarial system. Any substantial curtailment of the parties' rights to adduce the expert evidence of their choice would certainly be a significant move away from the adversarial tradition. For that reason alone, many contributors to the Inquiry regard it as unacceptable. My concern, however, is with access to justice, and hence with reductions in cost, delay and complexity. The argument for the universal application of the full, "red-blooded" adversarial approach is appropriate only if questions of cost and time are put aside. The present system works well for lawyers and judges, but ordinary people are being kept out of litigation. Where commercial litigants are concerned, the English courts are becoming uncompetitive because of unacceptable cost and delay.

7. The purpose of the adversarial system is to achieve just results. All too often it is used by one party or the other to achieve something which is inconsistent with justice by taking advantage of the other side's lack of resources or ignorance of relevant facts or opinions. Expert evidence is one of the principal weapons used by litigators who adopt this approach. The present system allows them to withhold from their opponents material which may be damaging to their own case or advantageous to their opponents'. This practice of non-disclosure cannot be justified, because it inevitably leads to unnecessary cost and delay, and in some cases to an unfair result.

8. The traditional English way of deciding contentious expert issues is for a judge to decide between two contrary views. This is not necessarily the best way of achieving a just result. The judge may not be sure that either side is right, especially if the issues are very technical or fall within an area in which he himself has no expertise. Nevertheless, he hopes to arrive at the right answer. Whether consciously or not, his decision may be influenced by factors such as the apparently greater authority of one side's expert, or the experts' relative fluency and persuasiveness in putting across their arguments.

9. In continental jurisdictions where neutral, court-appointed experts are the norm, there is an underlying assumption that parties' experts will tell the court only what the parties want the court to know. For the judge in an inquisitorial system, the main problem is that it may be difficult for him to know whether or not to accept a single expert's view. There is no suggestion, however, that he is inevitably less likely to reach the right answer than his English counterpart.

10. Less adversarial forms of dispute resolution are not, in any event, completely alien to our tradition. The various Ombudsman schemes have for a number of years provided a valuable service based on an impartial investigation by a neutral third party. Within the court system itself there are precedents for limiting the scope of expert evidence, in particular in the Family Division, where no expert evidence may be adduced without leave of the court and there is considerable emphasis on use of single experts.

Court control of expert evidence: a flexible approach

11. The basic premise of my new approach is that the expert's function is to assist the court. There should be no expert evidence at all unless it will help the court, and no more than one expert in any one speciality unless this is necessary for some real purpose.

12. I do not recommend a uniform solution, such as a court-appointed expert, for all cases. My overall objective is to try, from the start, to foster an approach to expert evidence which emphasises the expert's duty to help the court impartially on matters within his expertise, and encourage a more focused use of expert evidence by a variety of means. We should avoid mounting a contest between opposing experts where justice (in the widest sense) can be achieved between the parties without it. The key to achieving this is flexibility: above the fast track, there is no single answer that would apply to all cases.

13. Under the system of case management which I proposed in the interim report, the court will have complete control over the use of evidence, including expert evidence. The new rules will say that no expert evidence may be adduced without the leave of the court, which may be given as part of its own directions or specifically on application. There will be a range of options which the court will have a discretion to apply according to the type of case, or to the circumstances of an individual case. The options for limiting the scope of expert evidence will be:

(a) directing that no expert evidence is to be adduced at all, or no expert evidence of a particular type or relating to a particular issue;
(b) limiting the number of expert witnesses per party, either generally or in a given speciality;
(c) directing that evidence is to be given by one or more experts chosen by agreement between the parties or appointed by the court (this will extend the court's existing power under RSC Order 40, which permits the appointment of a court expert only on application by one of the parties);
(d) requiring expert evidence to be given in written form without the expert's attendance at court.

14. In cases where opposing experts are involved, the court already has power to direct the parties' experts to meet, before or after the experts have disclosed their reports, so as to identify and reduce areas of difference. Under the new rules the experts will be required (not simply authorised, as at present) to produce a report identifying matters agreed and outstanding areas of difference after such a meeting.
15. In fast track cases the exercise of the court's discretion will be more restricted. For the vast majority of cases falling within the financial limits of the track (that is, cases up to £10,000) the principle of proportionality of cost dictates that the scope of expert evidence must be limited. The rules on expert evidence on the fast track will therefore limit the parties generally to one expert per side in any single speciality (with an overall limit of two per side) with no oral evidence. Single experts will be used wherever possible. These proposals are explained in greater detail in chapter 3.

Single experts

16. Since the publication of the interim report, resistance to my proposals on single experts has remained particularly strong, and it is clear that the idea is anathema to many members of the legal profession in this country who are reluctant to give up their adversarial weapons.
17. It needs to be understood that a neutral expert, under the system I am proposing, would still function within a broadly adversarial framework. Wherever possible, the expert would be chosen by agreement between the parties, not imposed by the court. Whether appointed by the parties or by the court, he or she would act on instructions from the parties.

The appointment of a neutral expert would not necessarily deprive the parties of the right to cross-examine, or even to call their own experts in addition to the neutral expert if that were justified by the scale of the case. Anyone who gives expert evidence must know that he or she is at risk of being subjected to adversarial procedures, including vigorous cross-examination. This is an essential safeguard to ensure the quality and reliability of evidence.
18. The consultation process I have carried out has, at least, revealed a measure of agreement that single experts would be acceptable in certain types of cases or in certain limited circumstances, particularly on issues of *quantum*. Acceptance of a single expert on liability issues is generally limited to cases where the amount in issue is very small, or where there is little scope for disagreement. This is a helpful start, but without further measures it is unlikely to have any significant impact on cost.
19. I do not think it would be appropriate to specify particular areas of litigation where a single expert should or should not be used. There are in all areas some large, complex and strongly contested cases where the full adversarial system, including oral cross-examination of opposing experts on particular issues, is the best way of producing a just result. That will apply particularly to issues on which there are several tenable schools of thought, or where the boundaries of knowledge are being extended. It does not, however, apply to all cases. As a general principle, I believe that single experts should be used wherever the case (or the issue) is concerned with a substantially established area of knowledge and where it is not necessary for the court directly to sample a range of opinions. The expert's duty to the court will require him to set out in his report his view of the range of possible opinions. Too often under the present regime the experts are in fact agreed upon the range of opinion, but their reports only set out the extreme positions.
20. Given the strength of opposition to my proposals, it would not be realistic to expect a significant shift towards single experts in the short term. What is needed to initiate such a shift is a clear statement of principle in the rules, coupled with procedures to ensure that parties and procedural judges always consider whether a single expert could be appointed in a particular case (or to deal with a particular issue); and, if this is not considered appropriate, that they indicate why not.
21. A single expert is much more likely to be impartial than a party's expert can be. Appointing a single expert is likely to save time and money, and to increase the prospects of settlement. It may also be an effective way of levelling the playing field between parties of unequal resources. These are significant advantages, and there would need to be compelling reasons for not taking them up. It is certainly not sufficient to say that a party is entitled to adduce separate expert evidence provided he is willing to pay for it.
22. It has been suggested to me that by the stage at which case management starts, it will be too late for the court to control the scope of expert evidence because parties will already have appointed their own experts. There are of course circumstances in which a party will need to consult an expert before proceedings have started, sometimes even before legal action is in contemplation. It does not, however, follow that each party is entitled to rely on its own expert evidence for the purposes of litigation. Once litigation appears likely, the use of experts will be subject to different considerations: impartiality is of

paramount importance, and because of the costs shifting rule, parties need to be protected against the extravagant use of experts by their opponents.

23. The use of experts before litigation has started cannot be directly controlled by the courts, but pre-action protocols of the kind that I am recommending in chapter 10 can help to encourage the parties to agree on a single expert. Failure to comply with the protocol should normally have consequences in costs. There will of course be cases where either party would be justified in not adhering to the protocol requirements, especially in relation to experts on liability rather than *quantum*, but the onus will be on the party to justify his decision.

24. I have said that in some cases there are good reasons for each side to appoint its own expert or experts. That need not, however, preclude a co-operative approach between the opposing experts, which should ideally start as soon as they are instructed. It should wherever possible include a joint investigation and a single report, indicating areas of disagreement where these cannot be resolved.

Impartiality

25. There is wide agreement that the expert's role should be that of an independent adviser to the court, and that lack of objectivity can be a serious problem. This may sometimes arise because of improper pressure on experts from solicitors, as was found in a survey of clinical and educational psychologists, the results of which were reported in the May 1996 issue of *The Psychologist*.

26. The present system has the effect of exaggerating the adversarial role of experts, and this helps neither the court nor the parties. As the Court of Appeal has recently remarked:

> "For whatever reason, and whether consciously or unconsciously, the fact is that expert witnesses instructed on behalf of parties to litigation often tend . . . to espouse the cause of those instructing them to a greater or lesser extent, on occasion becoming more partisan than the parties" (*Abbey National Mortgages plc* v. *Key Surveyors Nationwide Ltd and Others* [1996] EGCS 23).

27. The clear implication of this is that a new approach is required which emphasises experts' impartiality. In cases where the option of a single expert is not pursued, it is particularly important that each opposing expert's overriding duty to the court is clearly understood. This is partly a matter of good practice on the part of instructing solicitors, who may themselves need guidance as to the appropriate form of instructions to experts. In my view, clarification in the rules of court is also needed.

28. Contributions to the Inquiry from experts themselves suggest that there is a degree of uncertainty among them as to their duties, and a perceived conflict between their professional responsibilities and the demands of the client who is paying their fee. Experts would welcome some formal recognition of their role as advisers to the court rather than advocates of the parties.

29. The rules will provide that when an expert is preparing evidence for potential use in court proceedings, or is giving evidence in court, his responsibility is to help the court impartially on the matters within his expertise. This responsibility will override any duty to the client. The rule will reaffirm the duty which the courts have laid down as a matter of law in a number of cases, notably *Whitehouse* v. *Jordan* [1981] 1 WLR 246, when Lord Wilberforce said:

> "It is necessary that expert evidence presented to the court should be and should be seen to be the independent product of the expert uninfluenced as to form or content by the exigencies of litigation" (cited by Cresswell J in *The Ikarian Reefer* [1993] 2 Lloyd's Rep 68).

30. There was wide support for the proposal in my interim report that an expert's report intended for use as evidence in court proceedings should be addressed to the court. I now propose that there should be a requirement to this effect in the rules of court to apply whenever litigation is contemplated. This is a formal but important requirement. It does not imply that the expert is to be instructed by the court, but is intended to concentrate the expert's mind as he writes the report on his paramount duty to the court.

31. One of the recommendations in my interim report was that, once an expert had been instructed to prepare a report for the use of a court, any communication between the expert and the client or his advisers should no longer be the subject of legal privilege. My intention was to prevent the suppression of relevant opinions or factual material which did not support the case put forward by the party instructing the expert. There is, I believe, no disagreement with that intention, but it has been put to me very strongly that waiver of legal privilege is not the way to achieve it. The point has been made that experts must be free to submit drafts to clients and their legal advisers, so that factual misconceptions can be corrected. A further objection is that a great deal of time could be wasted if all these documents were disclosable, because the opposing party would have to comb through the various versions of a report to identify any changes, the reasons for which would not always be clear in any event. Another possibility is that lawyers and experts might begin to subvert the system by avoiding written communication in favour of off-the-record conversations.

32. I accept, in the light of these arguments, that it would not be realistic to make draft experts' reports disclosable. I do not, however, consider that privilege should apply to the instructions given to experts. The Chancery Working Group has pointed out that major problems can arise when opposing experts are working from different instructions, which leads to reports that are hard to compare and use. Joint or agreed instructions would meet this specific point, but even a single expert's report may be unclear or open to misinterpretation unless the instructions on which it is based are known.

33. Under the new system, transparency of instructions to experts will be particularly important. The effectiveness of pre-action protocols will depend on it. On the fast track, in cases where there are diverging opinions in two reports, it will be absolutely essential for the parties and the judge to know the basis on which the experts have been instructed. I therefore recommend that expert evidence should not be admissible unless all written instructions (including letters subsequent upon the original instructions) and a note of any oral instructions are included as an annex to the expert's report.

34. A further recommendation in the interim report was that any expert's report prepared for the purpose of giving evidence to a court should end with a declaration that it includes everything which the expert regards as being relevant to the opinion which he has expressed in his report and that he has drawn to the attention of the court any matter which would affect the validity of that opinion. That recommendation was widely supported on consultation, and I have come to the conclusion that a declaration along the lines I have proposed, coupled with the requirement for instructions to be disclosed, should be sufficient to meet my concerns about the disclosure of all relevant material.

35. The Working Group on Intellectual Property has proposed a form of declaration which would include statements that the expert:

(a) understands that his primary duty is to the court, both in preparing his report and in giving evidence;
(b) has endeavoured in his report to be accurate and complete, and to mention all matters which he regards as being material to the opinions he has expressed;
(c) has drawn the court's attention to any matter of which he is aware which might adversely affect the validity of his opinions;
(d) has indicated the source of his factual information if he has based an opinion on facts of which he has no personal knowledge;
(e) has not included anything in the report which has been suggested to him by anyone (including particularly his instructing lawyers) without forming his own independent view on the matter;
(f) will notify his instructing lawyers immediately in writing if for any reason he considers that his existing report requires any correction or qualification; and, if the correction or qualification is significant, will prepare a supplementary report as soon as possible; and
(g) understands that
  (i) his report will form the evidence he will give under oath, subject to any corrections he may make before swearing as to its correctness;
  (ii) he may be cross-examined on his report by a cross-examiner assisted by an expert; and
  (iii) if the court concludes that he has not fairly tried to meet the standards set out in the declaration, he is likely to be the subject of public adverse criticism by the judge.

36. I should like to see added to this a statement that where there is a range of reasonable opinion, the expert has indicated the extent of that range in his report.

37. Some elements in the working group's suggested declaration may be controversial; in particular, it might be argued that a reference to the possibility of adverse criticism could deter competent experts from giving evidence. I believe, however, that the outline broadly sets out the points which should be included in an expert's declaration. It should usefully form the basis of discussion between the Law Society, the Academy of Experts and any other interested bodies, with a view to drawing up a standard declaration for use in experts' reports.

Access to evidence: inequality of resources

38. One of the fundamental principles of my approach to civil litigation is that there should, so far as possible, be a level playing field between litigants of unequal financial or other resources. A particular problem arises when one party, often the defendant or potential defendant, has an easily available source of expertise to which the other party does not have access. This happens, for example, in medical negligence, where a health authority or hospital trust can use its own doctors; or in actions against large companies with in-house technical experts. The potential claimant, on the other hand, may not even know whether he or she has a case worth pursuing without paying for an independent expert to carry out an investigation.

39. I suggested in the issues paper that one way of redressing this imbalance would be to introduce a new procedure enabling claimants to apply to the court (either before or after proceedings have started) for an order requiring the defendant to provide an in-house expert's report on a particular situation. It seemed to me that such a procedure would be particularly helpful to claimants who did not qualify for legal aid, although it could also save money for the legal aid fund. The provision of an in-house report would not prevent the opposing party from instructing his or her own expert at a later stage if it emerged that there was a case worth pursuing.

40. This proposal was generally opposed by respondents to the consultation paper. Prospective defendants considered it unfair, and claimants' representatives questioned whether an in-house report could be accepted as impartial and independent, because of the fear that an in-house expert would come under pressure to report in favour of the defendant. In the light of this reaction, I have considered whether there may be a more acceptable way of acheiving my objective than a specific power to direct a prospective defendant to carry out investigations or tests.

41. I have concluded that the court should have a wide power, which could be exercised before the start of proceedings, to order that an examination or tests should be carried out in relation to any matter in issue, and a report submitted to the court. Any such order would indicate by whom the examination or tests were to be carried out, and at whose cost. This will cover a wider range of situations than I originally had in mind, and can be applied flexibly by the courts to meet particular circumstances.

Narrowing the issues: experts' meetings

42. Among the criticisms I made in my interim report was that the present system does not encourage narrowing of issues between opposing experts, or the elimination of peripheral issues. There has been widespread support for my suggestion that experts' meetings were a useful approach to narrowing the issues. In areas of litigation (such as Official Referees' business) where experts' meetings are already the usual practice, there is general agreement that they are helpful. In areas where they are not at present widely used, including medical negligence, the majority of respondents accept that they could be helpful. (This is not, however, the view of the Intellectual Property Working Group, which believes that sequential disclosure of reports may be a better way of narrowing the issues in some cases, or that each expert might usefully be asked to take the opposite side's report and underline the passages with which he or she disagrees.)

43. Two principal reservations have been expressed, even by those who support experts' meetings in principle. The first (mentioned in my interim report) is that meetings can be futile because the experts are instructed not to agree anything; or, alternatively, are told that any points of agreement must be referred back to their instructing lawyers for ratification. This subverts the judge's intention in directing the experts to meet, because the decision as to what to agree becomes a matter for the lawyers rather than the experts. I recommended in the interim report that it should be unprofessional conduct for an expert to be given or to accept instructions not to agree, and this has been widely supported.

44. On the basis of the consultation I have carried out, it is far from clear whether these are widespread problems, although there is certainly evidence that they do happen on occasions. The solution lies in a clear requirement that the experts must produce for the court, at the end of their meeting, a written list of agreed matters of professional opinion and issues still in dispute. It must be made clear that the discussion is to cover only matters within the experts' professional competence, and that it is for the parties and their legal advisers to consider the effect of any agreement or disagreement on the future conduct of the case.

45. At least in the heaviest cases where expert issues are likely to be most complex, the agenda for the experts' meeting should be set by the court. Narrowing the issues to be put before the court, including issues of expert opinion, is one of the fundamental purposes of the system of case management I have proposed. The procedural judge conducting a case management conference should not only direct an experts' meeting but define (with the help of the parties and their legal advisers) the subject matter to be covered.

46. The second reservation about the need for experts' meetings relates to cost. It is said that meetings are expensive to set up, especially if they are attended by the parties' legal advisers. My answer to this point is that, provided a clear agenda is set and the meeting is properly conducted, the investment, in the vast majority of cases, will be well worthwhile. Where the meeting does not lead directly to settlement, it will reduce the scope of further work on the case and either facilitate settlement at a later stage or ensure that the trial focuses on the essential issues. In any event, the net result should be a saving of costs.

47. It is also worth pointing out that, at least in the more straightforward cases, it may be possible to hold a "meeting" by using telephone conferencing and video conferencing technologies, at less expense than bringing the experts physically together. The important point is that they communicate with each other.

48. It is important, too, that experts communicate at the earliest possible stage in the case, to establish that they are answering the same questions or addressing the same issues. A useful starting point for discussions between experts would be to prepare an agreed chronology and statement of facts, with a summary of important or disputed points. This should be done as soon as possible after submission of the defence, with a view to identifying non-contentious points from the outset so as to define the scope of the experts' reports. In some cases, the first meeting may be only after the exchange of experts' reports. At that stage, in any event, the reports themselves will provide a clear and agreed basis for the discussion.

49. In areas of litigation where the use of experts' meetings is well established, it seems to be accepted that there is no difficulty in allowing them to be conducted in private, with no-one present apart from the experts themselves. In other areas, it has been suggested that experts' meetings should take place only in the presence of the parties' lawyers, or of a neutral third party such as an independent lawyer or the procedural judge. In medical negligence, for example, it is thought that such an arrangement would be needed to overcome the traditional attitude of suspicion between the parties. In particular, it is said that private meetings between experts would not be acceptable to patients, because of the common perception that doctors "hang together".

50. In the majority of cases I see no reason why the experts should not meet alone, but I accept that there are circumstances in which this will not be appropriate. When the court directs a meeting, I suggest that the onus should be on the parties to apply for any special arrangements. In considering any such application, the court should bear in mind the expense of attendance by the parties' lawyers. When the lawyers do attend, it must also be made clear that they are present simply as observers to ensure fair play, and not to participate in the discussion or inhibit legitimate agreement between the experts.

51. Given the potential advantages, and the flexibility of the possible arrangements, it is difficult to see why there should not be at least one experts' meeting in all cases where opposing experts are involved. Certainly, I would not expect to see any substantial case come to trial under the new system without at least one such meeting having taken place.

Improving the quality of experts' reports

52. Since the publication of the interim report an appreciable level of concern has been expressed about the quality and reliability of experts' reports. This can relate to the problem of partisan reports which I have already discussed, or to the inclusion of irrelevant material, a tendency to stray beyond the expert's field of professional competence, or failure to address the real issues.

53. There are a number of ways of tackling these problems, of which training for experts is one. Some people would like to see a compulsory system of training and accreditation of experts in particular fields, along the lines of what is already provided by bodies such as the Acadeny of Experts. This would mean that only fully qualified and accredited experts would be permitted to appear before the courts or prepare reports for forensic use. (Special arrangements would have to be made to meet the situation in some areas of litigation such as intellectual property, where experts commonly act on a "one-off" basis. For example, experts could be permitted to act in up to, say, three cases before accreditation was required.) Such a system would include the exercise of sanctions against experts who failed to meet the required standard.

54. I certainly support the provision of training for experts, both through attendance at courses and through the dissemination of published material such as the model form of expert's report which has been produced by the Academy of Experts. Professional people who take on responsibilities as expert witnesses need a basic understanding of the legal system and their role within it. They also need to be able to present their evidence effectively, both in written reports and orally under cross-examination. Training in presentational skills, however, should never lose sight of the fundamental point that the expert's duty is to assist the court. Otherwise it is not in the interests of justice because it may result in the truth being concealed.

55. I do not recommend an exclusive system of accreditation. Such a system could exclude potentially competent experts who choose for good reasons not to take it up. It might, in fact, narrow rather than widen the pool of available experts. It could foster an uncompetitive monopoly, and might encourage the development of "professional experts" who were out of touch with current practice in their field of experience.

56. Another way of improving the quality of experts' reports is by ensuring that experts are given adequate instructions. From the comments I have received on this point it appears that solicitors' instructions vary from detailed to perfunctory. "Please provide your usual report" is an example that has been mentioned to me, and it may well be that this is adequate for an experienced expert who is frequently instructed by the same solicitor. Many experts have, however, indicated that they would welcome more detailed and explicit instructions, and I have no doubt that solicitors would benefit from guidance in this area.

57. The Law Society has already published *pro forma* instructions in its *Directory of Experts*, and, jointly with the British Orthopaedic Association, a model letter of instruction to medical experts. A number of other initiatives which have begun in the course of the Inquiry will help to take this work forward under the new system. These include a working group set up by the ABI to develop a protocol for the instruction of experts, and an APIL/ABI working party on pre-action protocols for the fast track which has produced a model letter of instruction.

Expert assessors

58. In the interim report I recommended that the courts should make wider use of their powers to appoint expert assessors to assist the judge in complex litigation and, in appropriate cases, to preside over meetings between the parties' experts and help them to reach agreement.

59. There has been some resistance to those proposals, largely on the grounds that an assessor would usurp the role of the judge. I do not agree that this would necessarily be the case: where there are complex technical issues the assessor's function would be to "educate" the judge to enable him to reach a properly informed decision. In the most complex cases this function could be performed by two assessors, one instructed by each party.

60. Clearly the use of an independent assessor in addition to the parties' experts and the judge will not be cost-effective except in the heaviest cases. In smaller cases, such as boundary disputes or complaints about domestic appliances, there may also be technical issues which are not agreed between the parties. In these circumstances I see no objection to appointing an independent expert as adjudicator. This may well be the most economical way of disposing of the case, and the result is no less likely to be satisfactory to the parties than a decision by the judge who has little or no expertise in the subject matter of the dispute. The county courts already have a power (albeit rarely used) to appoint outside arbitrators for small claims.

Recommendations

My main recommendations are as follows.

(1) As a general principle, single experts should be used wherever the case (or the issue) is concerned with a substantially established area of knowledge and where it is not necessary for the court directly to sample a range of opinions.

(2) Parties and procedural judges should always consider whether a single expert could be appointed in a particular case (or to deal with a particular issue); and, if this is not considered appropriate, indicate why not.

(3) Where opposing experts are appointed they should adopt a co-operative approach. Wherever possible this should include a joint investigation and a single report, indicating areas of disagreement which cannot be resolved.

(4) Expert evidence should not be admissible unless all written instructions (including letters subsequent upon the original instructions) and a note of any oral instructions are included as an annex to the expert's report.

(5) The court should have a wide power, which could be exercised before the start of proceedings, to order that an examination or tests should be carried out in relation to any matter in issue, and a report submitted to the court.
(6) Experts' meetings should normally be held in private. When the court directs a meeting, the parties should be able to apply for any special arrangements such as attendance by the parties' legal advisers.
(7) Training courses and published material should provide expert witnesses with a basic understanding of the legal system and their role within it, focusing on the expert's duty to the court, and enable them to present written and oral evidence effectively. Training should not be compulsory.

APPENDIX A/2

EXPERTS ON TRIAL (OPEN LETTER TO LORD WOOLF)

John Ellison

Experts figured prominently throughout Lord Woolf's consultative process culminating in "Access to Justice". He expressed concern that the use of experts was a source of delay and expense; also that some experts failed to maintain their independence from the party by whom they had been instructed.

The costs problem is often greatest in medical negligence. The research into 673 cases undertaken for the enquiry shows that here experts' fees averaged 15 per cent of the total bill; in commercial cases the average was only 4 per cent. This may be why several of Lord Woolf's recommendations apply solely to doctors.

The importance of independence

Lord Woolf draws attention to the tension that exists between the roles of an expert. On the one hand, the expert will be instructed by and advise one party. He has legal duties in contract to his client. He has no right to waive his clients' privilege by disclosing information before trial without consent and the system requires he be part of the adversarial process.

On the other hand, the expert owes an overriding duty to the court. No expert should conceal material matters that might be to the disadvantage of his client. If further evidence comes to light, the expert should insist on modifying his opinions where necessary and material. The duties were summarised in a code of practice in *The Ikarian Reefer*[1] by Cresswell J to which Lord Woolf refers. In passing, it is worth noting that although that judgment was overturned by the Court of Appeal in December 1994, the code was largely upheld. The one area in which the Court of Appeal held a different view from Cresswell J was that an expert need not be unduly restrictive in the material he considers even if partially outside his expertise. It is not always possible for an expert to confine himself strictly to areas within his expertise and in certain circumstances an expert is entitled to weigh probabilities, make use of the skills of other experts and draw on his general knowledge.

As an auditor, this tension between the expert's roles does not worry me. One is well used to providing a high standard of client care on administrative and service issues, whilst nevertheless being very firm with management when discussing audit opinions for a company's shareholders or even resigning.

Where appropriate, an expert should decline to act. This is nothing new: in the last century no less than 68 experts were approached in one case[2] before one was found who would assist. We frequently turn down cases where we disagree with the pleadings; sometimes in cases of the nature of "My bank made the mistake of lending me money" and sometimes spurious negligence claims aimed at avoiding paying bills or at the wrong party.

It has always seemed to me that a good question for counsel to put to an expert is "Would your report have arrived at the same conclusions had you been instructed by the other side?" No judge would listen further to an expert who said "no" and it would wonderfully concentrate the minds of those experts who do not understand their duties.

I was involved as an expert in one case involving loss of profits, where a report was received from the other side's expert, extremely favourable to his client. Following a reply report from me pointing out, in restrained language, the logical flaws, that expert withdrew his report at 10.30 a.m. on the first day of the trial. His work had been positively counterproductive for his client—who proceeded to lose the case.

The Academy of Experts does valuable work in setting standards and running training courses. The evidence to Lord Woolf from some members stressed the desirability of accreditation. However, many unaccredited experts in highly specialised fields would still have valuable and relevant experience. The court can judge their reputation, expertise, and the probative value of their evidence.

The dangers of court-appointed experts

Lord Woolf has wisely not wholly agreed with those who proposed that all experts should be appointed by the court. At present this procedure is permitted[3] but is exceedingly rare. There must be cases, particularly smaller ones, where one expert is enough. If one doctor thinks a patient has a 5 per cent chance of recovery and another 10 per cent, it is doubtful that it is necessary to call both.

A recent survey undertaken by Herbert Smith showed limited support for court-appointed experts. In large commercial cases, each side would probably want to appoint its own expert in addition, if only for advice, which could lead to an undesirable *increase* in costs. There is also a danger that such an expert would in practice take over the judicial role; the court itself has no expertise and therefore frequently has to rely almost entirely on the evidence of experts. There is dissatisfaction with court-appointed experts on the Continent as pointed out by the Bar Council and the Law Society in their submissions to the enquiry.

In some cases, particularly professional negligence, widely differing views are strongly but genuinely held about appropriate standards. Many litigants would dislike leaving it all to one expert whose views might be inappropriate—for example a standard of perfection rather than of reasonable competence—even though Lord Woolf proposes that court-appointed experts could be cross-examined. In such cases, particularly where great sums of money and even personal livelihoods are at stake, it would be wrong to forbid a defendant from calling an experienced and reputable expert. For example, in the recent *Gooda Walker* case, the experts included Mr Outhwaite and Mr von Eichen, whose views were well known from previous litigation to be diametrically opposed. Neither would have been acceptable to the other party as a sole court-appointed expert.

As a further example, if a doctor is accused of professional negligence but the best surgeon in the land is prepared to state that what he did was entirely correct, it must be unjust to say that that surgeon could not be called by him to give evidence.

Privilege

The proposal of loss of privilege on communications with experts is interesting and may have a profound effect on practice. It will strengthen the hand of a client whose opponent has given his expert restricted or inappropriate instructions and of an expert in dealing with difficult clients. In practice its effect may be diminished in that more will be communicated orally, as already happens in the USA where much more is discoverable. Presumably (and in the interests of cases settling early) discussions involving the expert about settlement and payments into court would still remain privileged. This issue is not addressed in the report.

If an expert's report has been served but he subsequently changes his opinion, perhaps because of further scientific tests or new factual evidence, he has no power to ensure the court and the other side is made aware of this before he is called. The privilege is that of the client, not the expert (or even the solicitors). Loss of privilege on communications with experts means that such matters are likely to come to light at an early stage. Indeed, under RSC Order 24, the continuing discovery obligation on litigants means that arguably all correspondence with experts will have to be disclosed as soon as it is created, so that in effect experts will perhaps always be writing to both sides. If the draft report is unhelpful, this may mean that the *opposing* side will call the expert instead under the principle that there is no property in an expert.[4] Experts would be well advised to draft their engagement letters so that if this happens the first party still pays their fee.

The courts have already been moving towards requiring further disclosure. In *Kenning* v. *Eve Construction*[5] the expert sent his instructing solicitors a supportive report but accompanied it with a private letter expressing concerns about the case. The solicitors' assistant erroneously forwarded both documents to the other side. It was held that privilege was deemed waived, if the expert were called, since the court was entitled to "all the evidence he can give". However, this was slightly restricted by the Court of Appeal in *Derby & Co* v. *Weldon (No 9)*[6] where it was held that the expert's views do not need to be disclosed if the party has decided not to call evidence on those issues at trial.

Experts await with interest clarification of the law on whether they can (or should) refer to the opposing parties' witness statements. Judges are presently taking different views on this and the law is unclear.[7] The problem is that the *White Book* states that the mere service of a witness statement does not waive privilege in the statement until the statement is put in evidence during the trial. However, some commentators have suggested that the *White Book* is incorrect. Furthermore, it is surely unhelpful to the court if experts cannot comment on the factual background to the case until the witnesses are called and the date for service of experts' reports has long since passed.

Conclusion

Most of Lord Woolf's proposals are highly desirable. Some will strengthen the hands of those experts who are trying to stand up to lawyers. Some will save time and costs. The aim of litigation must be the prompt resolution of disputes and steps such as requiring experts to refuse instructions not to reach agreement are to be strongly welcomed. The one word of caution I have concerns court-appointed experts where, in large or important cases, care should be taken to ensure that the proposals do not increase costs or risk treating litigants unfairly.

End Notes

1 [1993] 2 Lloyd's Rep 68.
2 *Thorn* v. *Worthing Skating Rink* (1876) LR 6 ChD 415.
3 RSC Order 40.
4 *Harmony Shipping Co SA* v. *Saudi Europe Line* [1979] 1 WLR 1380.
5 [1989] 1 WLR 1189.
6 [1991] 1 WLR 652, 660.
7 See for example *Fairfield-Mabey* v. *Shell* [1989] 1 All ER 576; *Comfort Hotels* v. *Wembley Stadium* [1988] 3 All ER 53; *Youell* v. *Bland Welch (No 3)* [1991] 1 WLR 122; and *Balkanbank* v. *Taher (No 1)* (1994) *The Times*, 19 February.

John Ellison FCA, FBAE, *is Chairman of KPMG Forensic Accounting. A shortened version of this article originally appeared in the* Solicitors' Journal *on 28 July 1995. This article accordingly does not reflect the coming into being of the Civil Procedure Rules.*

THE CIVIL PROCEDURE RULES, PARTS 27, 32 AND 35

PART 27: THE SMALL CLAIMS TRACK

Contents of this Part

Scope of this Part

27.1 (1) This Part—

(a) sets out the special procedure for dealing with claims which have been allocated to the small claims track under Part 26; and
(b) limits the amount of costs that can be recovered in respect of a claim which has been allocated to the small claims track.

(Rule 27.14 deals with costs on the small claims track)
(2) A claim being dealt with under this Part is called a small claim.

(Rule 26.6 provides for the scope of the small claims track. A claim for a remedy for harassment or unlawful eviction relating, in either case, to residential premises shall not be allocated to the small claims track whatever the financial value of the claim. Otherwise, this small claims track will be the normal track for—

- any claim which has a financial value of not more than £5,000 subject to the special provisions about claims for personal injuries and housing disrepair claims;
- any claim for personal injuries which has a financial value of not more than £5,000 where the claim for damages for personal injuries is not more than £1,000; and

- any claim which includes a claim by a tenant of residential premises against his landlord for repairs or other work to the premises where the estimated cost of the repairs or other work is not more than £1,000 and the financial value of any claim for damages in respect of those repairs or other work is not more than £1,000.)

Extent to which other Parts apply

27.2 (1) The following Parts of these Rules do not apply to small claims—

(a) Part 25 (interim remedies) except as it relates to interim injunctions;
(b) Part 31 (disclosure and inspection);
(c) Part 32 (evidence) except rule 32.1 (power of court to control evidence);
(d) Part 33 (miscellaneous rules about evidence);
(e) Part 35 (experts and assessors) except rules 35.1 (duty to restrict expert evidence), 35.3 (experts—overriding duty to the court) and 35.8 (instructions to a single joint expert);
(f) Part 18 (further information);
(g) Part 36 (offers to settle and payments into court);
(h) Part 39 (hearings) except rule 39.2 (general rule—hearing to be in public).

(2) The other Parts of these Rules apply to small claims except to the extent that a rule limits such application.

Court's power to grant a final remedy

27.3 The court may grant any final remedy in relation to a small claim which it could grant if the proceedings were on the fast track or the multi-track.

Preparation for the hearing

27.4 (1) After allocation the court will—

(a) give standard directions and fix a date for the final hearing;
(b) give special directions and fix a date for the final hearing;
(c) give special directions and direct that the court will consider what further directions are to be given no later than 28 days after the date the special directions were given;
(d) fix a date for a preliminary hearing under rule 27.6; or
(e) give notice that it proposes to deal with the claim without a hearing under rule 27.10 and invite the parties to notify the court by a specified date if they agree the proposal.

(2) The court will—

(a) give the parties at least 21 days' notice of the date fixed for the final hearing, unless the parties agree to accept less notice; and
(b) inform them of the amount of time allowed for the final hearing.

(3) In this rule

(a) "standard directions" means—

(i) a direction that each party shall, at least 14 days before the date fixed for the final hearing, file and serve on every other party copies of all documents (including any expert's report) on which he intends to rely at the hearing; and
(ii) any other standard directions set out in the relevant practice direction; and

(b) "special directions" means directions given in addition to or instead of the standard directions.

Experts

27.5 No expert may give evidence, whether written or oral, at a hearing without the permission of the court.

(Rule 27.14(3)(d) provides for the payment of an expert's fees.)

Preliminary hearing

27.6 (1) The court may hold a preliminary hearing for the consideration of the claim, but only—

(a) where—

(i) it considers that special directions, as defined in rule 27.4, are needed to ensure a fair hearing; and
(ii) it appears necessary for a party to attend at court to ensure that he understands what he must do to comply with the special directions; or

(b) to enable it to dispose of the claim on the basis that one or other of the parties has no real prospect of success at a final hearing; or
(c) to enable it to strike out a statement of case or part of a statement of case on the basis that the statement of case, or the part to be struck out, discloses no reasonable grounds for bringing or defending the claim.

(2) When considering whether or not to hold a preliminary hearing, the court must have regard to the desirability of limiting the expense to the parties of attending court.
(3) Where the court decides to hold a preliminary hearing, it will give the parties at least 14 days' notice of the date of the hearing.
(4) The court may treat the preliminary hearing as the final hearing of the claim if all the parties agree.
(5) At or after the preliminary hearing the court will—

(a) fix the date of the final hearing (if it has not been fixed already) and give the parties at least 21 days' notice of the date fixed unless the parties agree to accept less notice;
(b) inform them of the amount of time allowed for the final hearing; and
(c) give any appropriate directions.

Power of court to add to, vary or revoke directions

27.7 The court may add to, vary or revoke directions.

Conduct of the hearing

27.8 (1) The court may adopt any method of proceeding at a hearing that it considers to be fair.
(2) Hearings will be informal.
(3) The strict rules of evidence do not apply.
(4) The court need not take evidence on oath.
(5) The court may limit cross-examination.
(6) The court must give reasons for its decision.

Non-attendance of parties at a final hearing

27.9 (1) If a party who does not attend a final hearing—

(a) has given the court written notice at least 7 days before the date of the hearing that he will not attend; and
(b) has, in that notice, requested the court to decide the claim in his absence,

the court will take into account that party's statement of case and any other documents he has filed when it decides the claim.

(2) If a claimant does not—

(a) attend the hearing; and
(b) give the notice referred to in paragraph (1)

the court may strike out the claim.

(3) If—

(a) a defendant does not

(i) attend the hearing; or
(ii) give the notice referred to in paragraph (1); and

(b) the claimant either—

(i) does attend the hearing; or
(ii) gives the notice referred to in paragraph (1),

the court may decide the claim on the basis of the evidence of the claimant alone.

(4) If neither party attends or gives the notice referred to in paragraph (1), the court may strike out the claim and any defence and counterclaim.

Disposal without a hearing

27.10 The court may, if all parties agree, deal with the claim without a hearing.

Setting judgment aside and re-hearing

27.11 (1) A party—

(a) who was neither present nor represented at the hearing of the claim; and
(b) who has not given written notice to the court under rule 27.9(1), may apply for an order that a judgment under this Part shall be set aside and the claim re-heard.

(2) A party who applies for an order setting aside a judgment under this rule must make the application not more than 14 days after the day on which notice of the judgment was served on him.

(3) The court may grant an application under paragraph (2) only if the applicant—

(a) had a good reason for not attending or being represented at the hearing or giving written notice to the court under rule 27.9(1); and
(b) has a reasonable prospect of success at the hearing.

(4) If a judgment is set aside—

(a) the court must fix a new hearing for the claim; and
(b) the hearing may take place immediately after the hearing of the application to set the judgment aside and may be dealt with by the judge who set aside the judgment.

(5) A party may not apply to set aside a judgment under this rule if the court dealt with the claim without a hearing under rule 27.10.

Right of appeal under Part 27

27.12 (1) A party may appeal against an order under this Part only on the grounds that—

(a) there was serious irregularity affecting the proceedings; or
(b) the court made a mistake of law.

(2) On an appeal the court may make any order it considers appropriate.
(3) The court may dismiss an appeal without a hearing.
(4) This rule does not limit any right of appeal arising under any Act.

Procedure for making an appeal

27.13 (1) A party who wishes to appeal must file a notice of appeal not more than 14 days after the day on which notice of the order was served on him.
(2) Notice of appeal—

(a) must be filed at the court which made the order; and
(b) must set out the grounds for the appeal with particulars of the serious irregularity or mistake of law alleged.

Costs on the small claims track

27.14 (1) This rule applies to any case which has been allocated to the small claims track unless paragraph (5) applies.
(Rules 44.9 and 44.11 make provision in relation to orders for costs made before a claim has been allocated to the small claims track.)
(2) The court may not order a party to pay a sum to another party in respect of that other party's costs except—

(a) the fixed costs payable under Part 45 attributable to issuing the claim;
(b) in proceedings which included a claim for an injunction or an order for specific performance a sum not exceeding the amount specified in the relevant practice direction for legal advice and assistance relating to that claim;
(c) costs assessed by the summary procedure in relation to an appeal under rule 27.12; and
(d) such further costs as the court may assess by the summary procedure and order to be paid by a party who has behaved unreasonably.

(3) The court may also order a party to pay all or part of—

(a) any court fees paid by another party;
(b) expenses which a party or witness has reasonably incurred in travelling to and from a hearing or in staying away from home for the purposes of attending a hearing;
(c) a sum not exceeding the amount specified in the relevant practice direction for any loss of earnings by a party or witness due to attending a hearing or to staying away from home for the purpose of attending a hearing; and
(d) a sum not exceeding the amount specified in the relevant practice direction for an expert's fees.

(4) The limits on costs imposed by this rule also apply to any fee or reward for acting on behalf of a party to the proceedings charged by a person exercising a right of audience by virtue of an order under section 11 of the Courts and Legal Services Act 1990 (a lay representative).
(5) Where—

(a) the financial value of a claim exceeds the limit for the small claims track; but
(b) the claim has been allocated to the small claims track in accordance with rule 26.7(3),

the claim shall be treated, for the purposes of costs, as if it were proceeding on the fast track except that trial costs shall be in the discretion of the court and shall not exceed the amount set out for the value of the claim in rule 46.2 (amount of fast track trial costs).
(Rule 26.7(3) allows the parties to consent to a claim being allocated to a track where the financial value of the claim exceeds the limit for that track.)

Claim re-allocated from the small claims track to another track

27.15 Where a claim is allocated to the small claims track and subsequently re-allocated to another track, rule 27.14 (costs on the small claims track) will cease to apply after the claim has been re-allocated, and the fast track or multi-track costs rules will apply from the date of re-allocation.

PART 32: EVIDENCE

Contents of this Part

Power of court to control evidence

32.1 (1) The court may control the evidence by giving directions as to—

(a) the issues on which it requires evidence;
(b) the nature of the evidence which it requires to decide those issues; and
(c) the way in which the evidence is to be placed before the court.

(2) The court may use its power under this rule to exclude evidence that would otherwise be admissible.
(3) The court may limit cross-examination.

Evidence of witnesses—general rule

32.2 (1) The general rule is that any fact which needs to be proved by the evidence of witnesses is to be proved—

(a) at trial, by their oral evidence given in public; and
(b) at any other hearing, by their evidence in writing.

(2) This is subject—

(a) to any provision to the contrary contained in these Rules or elsewhere; or

(b) to any order of the court.

Evidence by video link or other means

32.3 The court may allow a witness to give evidence through a video link or by other means.

Requirement to serve witness statements for use at trial

32.4 (1) A witness statement is a written statement signed by a person which contains the evidence which that person would be allowed to give orally.
(2) The court will order a party to serve on the other parties any witness statement of the oral evidence which the party serving the statement intends to rely on in relation to any issues of fact to be decided at the trial.
(3) The court may give directions as to—

(a) the order in which witness statements are to be served; and
(b) whether or not the witness statements are to be filed.

Use at trial of witness statements which have been served

32.5 (1) If—

(a) a party has served a witness statement; and
(b) he wishes to rely at trial on the evidence of the witness who made the statement,

he must call the witness to give oral evidence unless the court orders otherwise or he puts the statement in as hearsay evidence.
(Part 33 contains provisions about hearsay evidence)
(2) Where a witness is called to give oral evidence under paragraph (1), his witness statement shall stand as his evidence in chief unless the court orders otherwise.
(3) A witness giving oral evidence at trial may with the permission of the court—

(a) amplify his witness statement; and
(b) give evidence in relation to new matters which have arisen since the witness statement was served on the other parties.

(4) The court will give permission under paragraph (3) only if it considers that there is good reason not to confine the evidence of the witness to the contents of his witness statement.
(5) If a party who has served a witness statement does not—

(a) call the witness to give evidence at trial; or
(b) put the witness statement in as hearsay evidence,

any other party may put the witness statement in as hearsay evidence.

Evidence in proceedings other than at trial

32.6 (1) Subject to paragraph (2), the general rule is that evidence at hearings other than the trial is to be by witness statement unless the court, a practice direction or any other enactment requires otherwise.
(2) At hearings other than the trial, a party may, in support of his application, rely on the matters set out in—

(a) his statement of case; or
(b) his application notice,

if the statement of case or application notice is verified by a statement of truth.

Order for cross-examination

32.7 (1) Where, at a hearing other than the trial, evidence is given in writing, any party may apply to the court for permission to cross-examine the person giving the evidence.

(2) If the court gives permission under paragraph (1) but the person in question does not attend as required by the order, his evidence may not be used unless the court gives permission.

Form of witness statement

32.8 A witness statement must comply with the requirements set out in the relevant practice direction.

(Part 22 requires a witness statement to be verified by a statement of truth.)

Witness summaries

32.9 (1) A party who—

(a) is required to serve a witness statement for use at trial; but
(b) is unable to obtain one,

may apply, without notice, for permission to serve a witness summary instead.

(2) A witness summary is a summary of—

(a) the evidence, if known, which would otherwise be included in a witness statement; or
(b) if the evidence is not known, the matters about which the party serving the witness summary proposes to question the witness.

(3) Unless the court orders otherwise, a witness summary must include the name and address of the intended witness.

(4) Unless the court orders otherwise, a witness summary must be served within the period in which a witness statement would have had to be served.

(5) Where a party serves a witness summary, so far as practicable, rules 32.4 (requirement to serve witness statements for use at trial), 32.5(3) (amplifying witness statements), and 32.8 (form of witness statement) shall apply to the summary.

Consequence of failure to serve witness statement or summary

32.10 If a witness statement or a witness summary for use at trial is not served in respect of an intended witness within the time specified by the court, then the witness may not be called to give oral evidence unless the court gives permission.

Cross-examination on a witness statement

32.11 Where a witness is called to give evidence at trial, he may be cross-examined on his witness statement, whether or not the statement or any part of it was referred to during the witness's evidence in chief.

Use of witness statements for other purposes

32.12 (1) Except as provided by this rule, a witness statement may be used only for the purpose of the proceedings in which it is served.

(2) Paragraph (1) does not apply if and to the extent that—

(a) the witness gives consent in writing to some other use of it;

(b) the court gives permission for some other use; or
(c) the witness statement has been put in evidence at a hearing held in public.

Availability of witness statements for inspection

32.13 (1) A witness statement which stands as evidence in chief is open to inspection unless the court otherwise directs during the course of the trial.
(2) Any person may ask for a direction that a witness statement is not open to inspection.
(3) The court will not make a direction under paragraph (2) unless it is satisfied that a witness statement should not be open to inspection because of—

(a) the interests of justice;
(b) the public interest;
(c) the nature of any expert medical evidence in the statement;
(d) the nature of any confidential information (including information relating to personal financial matters) in the statement; or
(e) the need to protect the interests of any child or patient.

(4) The court may exclude from inspection words or passages in the statement.

False statements

32.14 (1) Proceedings for contempt of court may be brought against a person if he makes, or causes to be made, a false statement in a document verified by a statement of truth without an honest belief in its truth.
(Part 22 makes provision for a statement of truth)
(2) Proceedings under this rule may be brought only—

(a) by the Attorney General; or
(b) with the permission of the court.

Affidavit evidence

32.15 (1) Evidence must be given by affidavit, instead of or in addition to a witness statement if this is required by the court, a provision contained in any other Rule, a practice direction or any other enactment.
(2) Nothing in these Rules prevents a witness giving evidence by affidavit, at a hearing other than the trial, if he chooses to do so in a case where paragraph (1) does not apply, but the party putting forward the affidavit may not recover the additional cost of making it from any other party unless the court orders otherwise.

Form of affidavits

32.16 An affidavit must comply with the requirements set out in the relevant practice direction.

Affidavit made outside the jurisdiction

32.17 A person may make an affidavit outside the jurisdiction in accordance with—

(a) this Part; or
(b) the law of the place where he makes the affidavit.

Notice to admit facts

32.18 (1) A party may serve notice on another party requiring him to admit the facts, or the part of the case of the serving party, specified in the notice.

(2) A notice to admit facts must be served no later than 21 days before the trial.

(3) Where the other party makes any admission in response to the notice the admission may be used against him only—

(a) in the proceedings in which the notice to admit is served; and

(b) by the party who served the notice.

(4) The court may allow a party to amend or withdraw any admission made by him on such terms as it thinks just.

Notice to admit or produce documents

32.19 (1) A party shall be deemed to admit the authenticity of a document disclosed to him under Part 31 (disclosure and inspection of documents) unless he serves notice that he wishes the document to be proved at trial.

(2) A notice to prove a document must be served—

(a) by the latest date for serving witness statements; or

(b) within 7 days of disclosure of the document,

whichever is later.

PART 35: EXPERTS AND ASSESSORS

Contents of this Part

Duty to restrict expert evidence

35.1 Expert evidence shall be restricted to that which is reasonably required to resolve the proceedings.

Interpretation

35.2 A reference to an "expert" in this Part is a reference to an expert who has been instructed to give or prepare evidence for the purpose of court proceedings.

Experts—overriding duty to the court

35.3 (1) It is the duty of an expert to help the court on the matters within his expertise.
(2) This duty overrides any obligation to the person from whom he has received instructions or by whom he is paid.

Court's power to restrict expert evidence

35.4 (1) No party may call an expert or put in evidence an expert's report without the court's permission.
(2) When a party applies for permission under this rule he must identify—

(a) the field in which he wishes to rely on expert evidence; and
(b) where practicable the expert in that field on whose evidence he wishes to rely.

(3) If permission is granted under this rule it shall be in relation only to the expert named or the field identified under paragraph (2).
(4) The court may limit the amount of the expert's fees and expenses that the party who wishes to rely on the expert may recover from any other party.

General requirement for expert evidence to be given in a written report

35.5 (1) Expert evidence is to be given in a written report unless the court directs otherwise.
(2) If a claim is on the fast track, the court will not direct an expert to attend a hearing unless it is necessary to do so in the interests of justice.

Written questions to experts

35.6 (1) A party may put to—

(a) an expert instructed by another party; or
(b) a single joint expert appointed under rule 35.7,

written questions about his report.
(2) Written questions under paragraph (1)—

(a) may be put once only;
(b) must be put within 28 days of service of the expert's report; and
(c) must be for the purpose only of clarification of the report;

unless in any case,

(i) the court gives permission; or
(ii) the other party agrees.

(3) An expert's answers to questions put in accordance with paragraph (1) shall be treated as part of the expert's report.
(4) Where—

(a) a party has put a written question to an expert instructed by another party in accordance with this rule; and
(b) the expert does not answer that question,

the court may make one or both of the following orders in relation to the party who instructed the expert—

(i) that the party may not rely on the evidence of that expert; or
(ii) that the party may not recover the fees and expenses of that expert from any other party.

Court's power to direct that evidence is to be given by a single joint expert

35.7 (1) Where two or more parties wish to submit expert evidence on a particular issue, the court may direct that the evidence on that issue is to be given by one expert only.
(2) The parties wishing to submit the expert evidence are called "the instructing parties".
(3) Where the instructing parties cannot agree who should be the expert, the court may—

(a) select the expert from a list prepared or identified by the instructing parties; or
(b) direct that the expert be selected in such other manner as the court may direct.

Instructions to a single joint expert

35.8 (1) Where the court gives a direction under rule 35.7 for a single joint expert to be used, each instructing party may give instructions to the expert.
(2) When an instructing party gives instructions to the expert he must, at the same time, send a copy of the instructions to the other instructing parties.
(3) The court may give directions about—

(a) the payment of the expert's fees and expenses; and
(b) any inspection, examination or experiments which the expert wishes to carry out.

(4) The court may, before an expert is instructed—

(a) limit the amount that can be paid by way of fees and expenses to the expert; and
(b) direct that the instructing parties pay that amount into court.

(5) Unless the court otherwise directs, the instructing parties are jointly and severally liable for the payment of the expert's fees and expenses.

Power of court to direct a party to provide information

35.9 Where a party has access to information which is not reasonably available to the other party, the court may direct the party who has access to the information to—

(a) prepare and file a document recording the information; and
(b) serve a copy of that document on the other party.

Contents of report

35.10 (1) An expert's report must comply with the requirements set out in the relevant practice direction.
(2) At the end of an expert's report there must be a statement that—

(a) the expert understands his duty to the court; and
(b) he has complied with that duty.

(3) The expert's report must state the substance of all material instructions, whether written or oral, on the basis of which the report was written.
(4) The instructions referred to in paragraph (3) shall not be privileged against disclosure but the court will not, in relation to those instructions—

(a) order disclosure of any specific document; or

(b) permit any questioning in court, other than by the party who instructed the expert,

unless it is satisfied that there are reasonable grounds to consider the statement of instructions given under paragraph (3) to be inaccurate or incomplete.

Use by one party of expert's report disclosed by another

35.11 Where a party has disclosed an expert's report, any party may use that expert's report as evidence at the trial.

Discussions between experts

35.12 (1) The court may, at any stage, direct a discussion between experts for the purpose of requiring the experts to—

(a) identify the issues in the proceedings; and
(b) where possible, reach agreement on an issue.

(2) The court may specify the issues which the experts must discuss.
(3) The court may direct that following a discussion between the experts they must prepare a statement for the court showing—

(a) those issues on which they agree; and
(b) those issues on which they disagree and a summary of their reasons for disagreeing.

(4) The content of the discussion between the experts shall not be referred to at the trial unless the parties agree.
(5) Where experts reach agreement on an issue during their discussions, the agreement shall not bind the parties unless the parties expressly agree to be bound by the agreement.

Consequence of failure to disclose expert's report

35.13 A party who fails to disclose an expert's report may not use the report at the trial or call the expert to give evidence orally unless the court gives permission.

Expert's right to ask court for directions

35.14 (1) An expert may file a written request for directions to assist him in carrying out his function as an expert.
(2) An expert may request directions under paragraph (1) without giving notice to any party.
(3) The court, when it gives directions, may also direct that a party be served with—

(a) a copy of the directions; and
(b) a copy of the request for directions.

Assessors

35.15 (1) This rule applies where the court appoints one or more persons (an "assessor") under section 70 of the Supreme Court Act 1981 or section 63 of the County Courts Act 1984.
(2) The assessor shall assist the court in dealing with a matter in which the assessor has skill and experience.
(3) An assessor shall take such part in the proceedings as the court may direct and in particular the court may—

(a) direct the assessor to prepare a report for the court on any matter at issue in the proceeedings; and
(b) direct the assessor to attend the whole or any part of the trial to advise the court on any such matter.

(4) If the assessor prepares a report for the court before the trial has begun—

(a) the court will send a copy to each of the parties; and
(b) the parties may use it at trial.

(5) The remuneration to be paid to the assessor for his services shall be determined by the court and shall form part of the costs of the proceedings.
(6) The court may order any party to deposit in the court office a specified sum in respect of the assessor's fees and, where it does so, the assessor will not be asked to act until the sum has been deposited.
(7) Paragraphs (5) and (6) do not apply where the remuneration of the assessor is to be paid out of money provided by Parliament.

APPENDIX B

OFFICIAL REFEREES' SOLICITORS ASSOCIATION EXPERT WITNESS PROTOCOL—VERSION 1.0

The Official Referee's Solicitors Association (ORSA) was formed to promote the interests of solicitors and their clients conducting business in the Official Referee's Courts and in related arbitration.

The Committee of ORSA believes that the relationship between solicitor and expert witness is of the utmost importance in view of the duties each owes to the court or other tribunal. This protocol has been prepared with a view to assisting clarity of communication and in order to provide a framework within which solicitors and experts are able to operate freely. It is not intended that this protocol should operate in a rigid way but it is hoped that reference to it will enable experts and solicitors to consider key areas at an early stage.

The publication of this protocol arises out of the ORSA Response to the Issue Paper on Expert Evidence released by the Access to Justice Team in January 1996. ORSA hopes that this protocol will encourage independence and impartiality of the expert.

Not all of this protocol will apply to every appointment and there will inevitably be areas which the protocol does not specifically cover. It is intended to keep this protocol under review and comments will be most welcome. ORSA supports the Code of Practice published by the Law Society and acknowledges comments made by many bodies and individuals as part of the consultation process.

PROTOCOL

A Selection

1 The solicitor shall provide sufficient information to the expert to enable the expert to confirm whether or not the issues, as identified by the solicitor, are matters on which the expert is competent to act as expert witness. The expert should be satisfied that he has the necessary resources to meet the requirements of the appointment, including the required timetable. ORSA encourages the appointment of experts who maintain active professional practices.

Conflict and confidentiality

2 The solicitor shall provide the expert with a list of relevant parties and the expert shall state whether or not he has any connection with any of the parties named or to be reasonably inferred from the list to enable the solicitor and the expert to consider whether any conflict of interest exists.

Information

3 The expert should normally expect to provide information about his expertise and experience and suitability for the role for which he is being considered together with details of his proposed basis of charge. If the solicitor intends to approach more than one person to discuss their potential suitability for appointment as an expert witness, he should inform each expert that he is one of a number under consideration.

Independence of expert

4 In any selection and appointment process the solicitor should remember that a witness who is not selected or whose appointment is subsequently terminated may be free to accept an appointment from other parties. The solicitor may wish to ensure that documentation and information made available as part of any selection process is carefully chosen, commensurate with the requirement to provide relevant information, and that documentation is retrieved at the end of the process or of an appointment. The expert should be reminded that any documentation provided to him is subject to the rules relating to privilege.

B Brief

5 As soon as possible after the expert has been appointed, the solicitor shall explain the client's commercial and legal objectives in a manner commensurate with the independence of the expert and prepare for the expert a brief which shall be in a form appropriate to the nature and complexity of the matter on which the expert is asked to form an opinion. The Brief will normally contain the following information:

- Party making appointment.
- Subject matter.
- Contacts.
- Nature of proceedings.
- Timetable fixed in any proceedings and current status.
- Pleadings in any action which has commenced.
- Details of other experts appointed by the party making appointment and others, if known, with field of expertise.
- In a large or complex matter the method by which experts are to co-ordinate their services. Is there to be a lead expert with whom other experts will liaise?
- Area in which the expert is called upon to give his opinion.
- Specific issues on which the expert is asked to advise. In an appropriate case the solicitor should prepare a detailed Statement of Issues for the expert.
- Timescale within which the expert is asked to prepare:
  —initial review and advice on technical issues pleaded or assistance in preparing the client's pleaded case;
  —draft report for discussion and review of brief;
  —report for issue.
- Details of key documentation and details of location of all relevant documents. In a straightforward case appropriately bundled documents should accompany the brief but in a complex case the expert may be required to review documentation and the brief itself will contain only limited documentation.
- The brief should outline the principles of privilege and discovery.

6 On receipt of the brief the solicitor and the expert should review the nature and extent of the brief with regard to the role of the expert and those of any other experts appointed by the solicitor. If the expert has been appointed prior to the solicitor's involvement, it is important that a brief is established jointly. The proliferation of experts should be avoided. The solicitor should be aware that there may be no need to appoint a separate expert in every relevant discipline and that a carefully selected expert may be able to cover more than one area.

7 The solicitor and the expert should keep the brief under review at all times and advise each other of any material changes to relevant issues. The expert should not undertake work outside the brief without the prior approval of the solicitor.

8 The scope of the expert's appointment should be defined and the expert should be appointed in a way that will avoid costs being wasted.

9 The solicitor may wish to discuss with those representing other parties the matters on which expert opinion is required in order to assist and refine the brief.

Timescale

10 The solicitor and the expert shall agree the overall timescale and the programme within which the expert shall work. If either the solicitor or the expert becomes aware of any matter likely to affect that timescale, they should advise the other. The exact timing and sequence will vary from case to case. Consideration should be given to the extent of the expert's required attendance at any hearing. These issues should be discussed at an early stage.

Hearing date

11 The solicitor should keep the expert advised of the timescale set in any litigation or arbitration or of any timetable which is to be met and of any changes that are likely to be made, including the expected length of or dates of any hearing or trial.

12 The expert when advised of any hearing or trial date on which he is likely to be required to attend or give evidence shall make that date available and inform the solicitor if there are any pre-existing commitments likely to affect the expert's ability to fulfil the appointment.

13 Where the expert has pre-existing commitments the solicitor and the expert shall work together in order that the interests of the client can best be served. The expert shall not take on new commitments which might interfere with his responsibilities under the appointment without first assessing the position with the solicitor.

C Reports

14 The report should normally be issued to the solicitor as a draft for discussion and should be accompanied by any documents not originally supplied by the solicitor to the expert. The solicitor and the expert should discuss the format of the report, provided that the report remains the independent product, of the expert. It is wise for the solicitor and the expert to test the expert's opinions in the light of alternative facts contended for by the client's opponent.

15 When the expert's report has been finalised it will normally be exchanged by the solicitor and not by the expert. Usually simultaneous exchange is appropriate, but in certain cases sequential exchange may be required. The expert and the solicitor should discuss this early in the appointment. The expert's report and any copyright in it will normally be the property of the client.

16 The expert and the solicitor will need to review the status of the report if the underlying facts change or if the expert's opinion alters.

D Without prejudice meetings

17 It is common practice for a tribunal to order the parties' expert witnesses to meet to identify those parts of their evidence which is in issue. There is no standard format for such meetings. What follows is intended as a guide.

18 Meetings of experts should normally take place before exchange of the experts' reports. The predominant view of ORSA is that, if exchange takes place first, it is more likely that "positions" are taken too early to the detriment of proper discussion at the meeting.

19 The meeting may be most effective if it is chaired by one expert and an agenda agreed in advance. It may also be of value for the experts to exchange key criteria which they wish to discuss, for example, Standards or Codes of Practice or methods of valuation. It is appropriate for the parties' solicitors in conjunction with their experts to identify matters in issue to order to determine items for the agenda. Lawyers and clients should not be present at the without prejudice meeting of experts. It is important that the meeting of experts addresses the matters of expert evidence that relate to the matters in issue in the proceedings. The meeting is not the place for the lawyer to "surprise" the other party's expert with a new theory or new documents.

20 Close liaison will be necessary between solicitor and expert and amongst experts in order to make best use of the meeting. Normally experts of like discipline will meet together. Occasionally it will be appropriate to have meetings of experts in more than one discipline, usually following the initial meeting. For example; Architect, Structural Engineer and

Quantity Surveyor, from all parties, might meet to discuss the nature and extent of remedial works contended for.

E Notes of without prejudice meetings

21 The expert should report to the solicitor promptly after the meeting and discuss any apparent agreement or narrowing of issues.

22 The expert should, in conjunction with other experts of like discipline, prepare a written note signed by each of them as to matters of opinion on which they are agreed. The note should, where possible, give brief reasons for the views held. It should be remembered that matters of fact are for the tribunal or the agreement of the parties and not matters for the experts to agree between them. Where not all experts can agree a particular point, limited agreements should be explored.

23 If areas of apparent agreement on matters of opinion emerge at a without prejudice meeting, it is good practice to record these promptly to ensure accuracy. It may be appropriate for the expert to reflect on the issues following the meeting. A solicitor should not instruct an expert to apply pressure upon the experts of other parties.

24 The expert does not normally have authority to bind the client, but the solicitor should make sure that the expert is aware of the extent of the expert's authority and that matters which the expert agrees in a note of the meeting may be binding on him. It is good practice for the expert to ensure that all written notes of the meeting are marked "without prejudice" until clearly agreed by two or more experts.

25 The solicitor shall never impede the expert in reaching agreement or forming an opinion but can give guidance to the expert in formulating the note to reflect the matters in issue in the proceedings.

F Expert's duty and reporting

26 The expert shall comply with the requirements of the brief and exercise the reasonable skill and care of a person of the expert's profession, occupation or experience in providing advice on the matters in issue. In giving evidence the expert shall act impartially and owes an overriding duty to the court or tribunal.

27 The expert shall not express a final concluded opinion until all relevant issues of fact have been considered by him. The expert will advise the solicitor if the brief appears incomplete or where the expert believes other information is likely to be available.

28 The expert shall advise and assist the solicitor generally, where appropriate, beyond the matters on which the expert is required to give a formal opinion. The expert's report should contain the substance of the expert's evidence which it is intended to give at the tribunal and should be prepared in a clear and succinct manner. The solicitor and the expert should discuss the format of the report. It is not the role of the expert to make a finding of fact which is in issue. Where an opinion depends upon facts which are in issue, this should be clearly stated.

29 The solicitor shall throughout the currency of the appointment keep the expert up to date with information and issues as they relate to the appointment. The expert shall keep any opinon under review and have regard to all relevant matters when advising and assisting the client and the solicitor. After reports have been exchanged the expert and the solicitor should consider the need for a supplemental report.

G Fees

30 Fees and terms and conditions should be clearly agreed at the outset of an appointment. An appropriate breakdown, daily rate and hourly rate equivalent should be provided. Fees shall be inclusive except where survey, laboratory or other costs are expressly stated separately.

Payment of fees

31 The expert and the solicitor should consider and agree whether the solicitor appoints the expert and is responsible for the expert's fees, or whether the solicitor acts as agent for the client by whom all invoices are to be paid.

Budget

32 The expert should normally provide a budget for various stages of any appointment where the work is identifiable. The solicitor and the expert should ensure that fees are proportionate to the value or importance of the matters in issue.

33 It should be made clear and agreed at the outset how regularly fee invoices are to be rendered, what degree of information they are to contain and whether they are to be sent to the solicitor or the client. The expert shall provide supporting information and keep accurate contemporaneous records sufficient to justify the fees claimed or as may be required in any taxation of costs or similar procedure.

Legal expenses insurers

34 The solicitor should always advise the expert in advance where the agreement and payment of the expert's fee is subject to the approval of legal expenses' insurers and should immediately notify his expert of any ceiling on fees.

Legal aid

35 If the expert is appointed in a case where the solicitor's client has a legal aid certificate in force the solicitor must advise the expert of the basis on which interim fees can be claimed from the legal aid fund and whether the expert is to be appointed on the basis that the expert's fees may be reduced on legal aid taxation. The solicitor shall advise the expert immediately of any change in the client's legal aid status.

Cancellation and commitment fees

36 Cancellation charges shall only apply if they have been discussed and agreed at the outset of the appointment and where the expert can establish that he has no other appropriate work to undertake. The expert should not normally charge a minimum or commitment fee. The level of charge, which may be on a sliding scale, should aim to compensate the expert for disruption and inefficiency in rearranging his diary at short notice and not aim to provide remuneration for the whole of the period cancelled.

Security

37 Where the solicitor has appointed the expert as agent for the client, the expert may request that the client lodge with the solicitor, or in a designated account, sufficient monies to provide reasonable security for the likely fees of the expert. The solicitor and the expert will have regard to the financial status of the client.

ORSA welcomes comment on this protocol. Write to Marcus Harling at:
Burges Salmon,
Narrow Quay House,
Narrow Quay,
Bristol BS1 4AH.
Tel: 0117 939 2000
Fax: 0117 929 4705

APPENDIX C

SURVEYORS ACTING AS EXPERT WITNESSES: PRACTICE STATEMENT AND GUIDANCE NOTES

FOREWORD

Having spent much of my professional working life on Expert Witness work, I am delighted that the Institution has produced this Practice Statement and these Guidance Notes. They relate to the conduct of chartered surveyors acting as Expert Witnesses in the United Kingdom. They apply whatever the circumstances in which the evidence is to be given: irrespective of the employment status of the surveyor, whether the evidence is in writing or given orally, and whether the Judicial Body is a Court or another Body or person established to determine a dispute.

The surveyor's primary duty when acting as an Expert Witness, irrespective of who may be paying the bill, is to give the Judicial Body an objective, unbiased opinion on all matters within his or her expertise relevant to the dispute. This is not always understood by clients.

This Practice Statement imposes an obligation upon the surveyor to make its existence known to the client upon accepting the role of Expert Witness. I hope that it will serve to reduce misunderstandings and remove the pressure upon surveyors to support their clients' cases irrespective of their honest professional opinions. It will also help surveyors to provide high quality, respected evidence in the interests of justice under the law.

Jeremy Bayliss
President

INTRODUCTION

1. This document is in two parts: a Practice Statement, and Guidance Notes which supplement and amplify the Statement. Both parts apply, with effect from 1 March 1997, where any chartered surveyor agrees or is required to provide expert evidence, whether oral or in writing, which may be relied upon by any Judicial or quasi-Judicial Body in the United Kingdom.
2. The attention of Members of the Institution is drawn to the requirement for them at all times to comply with the By-laws and Regulations of The Royal Institution of Chartered Surveyors.

   Under RICS By-law 19(7) and by virtue of Conduct Regulation 23 it is the duty of every Member to comply with the contents of the Practice Statements issued by the Institution from time to time. This Practice Statement is one such.

   When an allegation of professional negligence is made against a surveyor, the Court is likely to take account of any relevant Practice Statement published by the RICS in deciding whether or not the surveyor has acted with reasonable competence. Failure to comply with Practice Statements is likely to be adjudged negligent.

   In the opinion of the RICS, a Member conforming to the requirements of these Practice Statements should have at least a partial defence to an allegation of negligence by virtue of having followed those practices.

   A Member may depart from the requirements of these Practice Statements, where he considers there are special circumstances which render it inappropriate or impractical for the assignment to be undertaken wholly in accordance with them. Where the Member so departs, a clear declaration in writing must be given to this effect, with the details of and reasons for the departure, which the member may be required to justify to the Institution. If the Institution is not satisfied with the reason(s) advanced and/or the manner in which the departure is declared or evidenced, it is entitled to take disciplinary measures.

Where Members depart from the practice required by this Statement, they should do so only for good reason. In the event of litigation, the Court may require them to explain why they decided to act as they did.

In addition, Practice Statements are relevant to professional competence in that each surveyor should be up to date and should have informed himself of Practice Statements within a reasonable time of their promulgation.

3. The Guidance Notes in this document provide advice to Members of the RICS on aspects of the profession. Where procedures are recommended for specific professional tasks, they are intended to embody "best practice", i.e. procedures which in the opinion of the RICS meet a high standard of professional competence.

Members are not required to follow the advice and recommendations contained in the Guidance Notes. They should, however, note the following points:

> When an allegation of professional negligence is made against a surveyor, the Court is likely to take account of the contents of any relevant Guidance Notes published by the RICS in deciding whether or not the surveyor has acted with reasonable competence.
>
> In the opinion of the RICS, a Member conforming to the practices recommended in these Guidance Notes should have at least a partial defence to an allegation of negligence by virtue of having followed those practices. However, Members have the responsibility of deciding when it is appropriate to follow the Guidance. If it is followed in an appropriate case, the Member will not be exonerated merely because the recommendations were found in an RICS Guidance Note.
>
> On the other hand, it does not follow that a Member will be adjudged negligent if he has not followed the practices recommended in the Guidance Notes. It is for each individual surveyor to decide on the appropriate procedure to follow in any professional task. However, where Members depart from the practice recommended in Guidance Notes, they should do so only for good reason. In the event of litigation, the Court may require them to explain why they decided not to adopt the recommended practice.
>
> In addition, Guidance Notes are relevant to professional competence in that each surveyor should be up to date and should have informed himself of Guidance Notes within a reasonable time of their promulgation.

SURVEYORS ACTING AS EXPERT WITNESSES: *PRACTICE STATEMENT*

Principal Message: Expert evidence provided by Chartered Surveyors must be, and must be seen to be, the independent product of the Surveyor.

1. Application of this Practice Statement

1.1 This Practice Statement applies where any Chartered Surveyor (hereinafter described as "the Surveyor") agrees or is required to provide expert evidence (whether oral or in writing) which may be relied upon by any Judicial or quasi-Judicial Body in the United Kingdom. For the avoidance of doubt such Bodies include Courts, Tribunals, Committees, Inspectors, Adjudicators, Arbitrators and Independent Experts (hereinafter described as a "Judicial Body"), but not Mediators.

1.2 This Practice Statement does not apply to the provision of professional advice for the purpose of assisting a client to decide whether to initiate or defend proceedings. However, where the Surveyor accepts instructions to provide such advice in contemplation of Judicial or quasi-Judicial proceedings, he must advise the client in writing if his advice or investigations would fall short of that necessary to enable evidence complying with this Practice Statement to be provided.

1.3 Where the Surveyor considers that there are special circumstances which render it inappropriate or impractical for the assignment to be undertaken wholly in accordance with this Practice Statement, the details of and reasons for the departure must be immediately given to those instructing him. Any Surveyor who does depart from the Practice Statement may be required to justify the reasons for the departure to the Institution. The Institution is entitled to take disciplinary measures if it is not satisfied with the reasons given and/or the manner in which the departure has been notified or evidenced.

2. Duty in providing evidence

2.1 The primary duty of the Surveyor is to the Judicial Body to whom his evidence is given.

2.2 The duty is to be truthful as to fact, honest as to opinion and complete as to coverage of relevant matters. The duty is the same if the Surveyor is giving evidence to a Judicial Body, whether or not on oath.

2.3 The Surveyor's evidence must be independent, objective and unbiased. In particular, it must not be biased towards the party who is responsible for paying him. The evidence should be the same whoever is paying for it.

2.4 The duty applies as much to the preparation of a statement of opinion intended to be used as part of written representations in an Arbitration or elsewhere where oral evidence is not given, as to a statement intended to be used at a Hearing before a Judicial Body.

3. Acceptance of and changes to instructions

3.1 The Surveyor may accept instructions to act as an Expert Witness only in matters where he has:

(a) the knowledge, experience, qualifications and training appropriate for the assignment; and

(b) the resources to complete the assignment within the timescales and to the standard required.

3.2 The Surveyor must, prior to accepting instructions:

(a) advise in writing those instructing him that this Practice Statement will apply and offer to supply a copy of the Statement upon request;

(b) ensure that there is a written record, held by the Surveyor and sent to those instructing him, as to the matters on which expert evidence is required, whether upon the initiative of the Surveyor or those instructing him;

(c) obtain agreement in writing from those instructing him if the Surveyor proposes that any part of the assignment is likely to be undertaken by a person other than the individual Surveyor instructed;

(d) agree Terms of Business; and

(e) be satisfied that no conflict of interest arises. If the Surveyor has any doubt whatsoever in this respect any actual or potential conflict must be reported to those offering instructions as soon as it arises or becomes apparent. For the avoidance of doubt any potential conflict arising after instructions have been accepted must be notified immediately.

3.3 If the Surveyor's instructions are changed or supplemented, the Surveyor must ensure that there is a written record thereof held as required in 3.2(b) above.

3.4 The Surveyor must address the matters in 3.1 and 3.2, and comply with 3.2(a) where, in the course of the provision of other services, the need for the Surveyor to act as an Expert Witness is identified.

4. Inspection

4.1 Where an inspection of any property is required it must always be carried out to the extent necessary to produce an opinion which is professionally competent having regard to its purpose and the circumstances of the case.

5. Reports

5.1 The Surveyor's written evidence must, unless the rules or directions of the Judicial Body require otherwise, be presented in an organised and referenced way, with brevity, distinguishing, where possible, between matters of plain fact, expert observation and expert inferences.

5.2 The Surveyor must, in preparing any written evidence, consider all matters material to the assignment.

5.3 The Surveyor must, in providing written evidence:

(a) comply with any rules or directions of the Judicial Body to which the evidence is to be presented;
(b) personally sign and date the report or other written evidence;
(c) include a declaration, which may be qualified:
   (i) of belief in the accuracy and truth of the matters put forward;
   (ii) that the report includes all facts which the Surveyor regards as being relevant to the opinion which he has expressed and that he has drawn to the attention of the Judicial Body any matter which would affect the validity of that opinion; and
   (iii) that the report complies with the requirements of the Royal Institution of Chartered Surveyors, as set down in *Surveyors Acting as Expert Witnesses: Practice Statement.*
(d) The Surveyor must use plain language and explain any technical terms. The Surveyor must not use words, terms, and/or a form of presentation with the intention of limiting the ability of those likely to have sight of it from checking the correctness of any statement, calculation or opinion given.

6. Amendment of the contents of written evidence and/or reports

6.1 The Surveyor must, without delay, notify those instructing him and, through legal representatives if any, other parties to the dispute and, where appropriate, the Judicial Body, if after issue of the evidence he identifies a material inaccuracy or changes his view of a matter material to his stated opinion.

7. Agreeing facts and resolving differences

7.1 Where, at the direction or order of the Judicial Body, Expert Surveyors appointed in the matter are instructed to meet or correspond the Surveyor must comply with such direction or order and, where such direction or order requires:

(a) agree relevant facts and calculations wherever possible; and
(b) seek to identify the issues and reasons for any differences of opinion.

7.2 Where, for any reason, the Surveyor is unable to comply with any order or direction of the Judicial Body he must:

(a) prepare a written record of the reason for such non-compliance; and
(b) communicate such record to those instructing him and, through legal representatives if any, to the Judicial Body.

8. Advocacy

8.1 Where, in appropriate proceedings, the Surveyor also assumes the role of Advocate, the roles of Expert and Advocate must be clearly distinguished and declared to the Judicial Body and to the opposing party.

SURVEYORS ACTING AS EXPERT WITNESSES: *GUIDANCE NOTES*

1. Introduction

1.1 These are Guidance Notes for Chartered Surveyors acting as Expert Witnesses. They should be considered in conjunction with the foregoing Practice Statement for Surveyors acting as Expert Witnesses and are intended to provide further material and information on good practice considered to be generally appropriate where a Surveyor is required to give expert evidence. The definitions in the Practice Statement apply also in these Guidance Notes. References in these Guidance Notes to "PS" are to a paragraph in the Practice Statement.

1.2 The Practice Statement has been prepared against a background of *dicta* emanating from the Courts regarding the duties and responsibilities of Expert Witnesses. These responsibilities were re-affirmed in the *Access to Justice Report* prepared by the Right Honourable Lord Woolf, Master of the Rolls, and submitted to the Lord Chancellor in July 1996.

1.3 That report, the principal proposals of which the Institution supported, also recommended, in the interests of reducing the number, length and cost of proceedings, that reports prepared for the purpose of giving evidence to a Judicial Body should end with a declaration that the witness' report includes all facts which the Expert regards as being relevant to the opinion which he has expressed and that he has drawn to the attention of the Judicial Body any matter which would affect the validity of that opinion.

1.4 The draft Civil Proceedings Rules, submitted with the Woolf Report, include a requirement as to the statements which must be included in an Expert's report, including a statement that:

(a) the Expert understands his duty to the Court;
(b) he has complied with that duty;
(c) his report includes all matters relevant to the issue on which expert evidence is given; and
(d) he has given details in his report of any matters which might affect the validity of his report.

1.5 The adoption of the Practice Statement responds to these comments and recommendations, and it is intended that the obligation upon Surveyors to make the existence of the Practice Statement known to clients when accepting instructions to act as Expert Witnesses will help to reduce misunderstandings and remove pressures upon Experts to support their clients' cases irrespective of their honest professional opinions.

1.6 The leading case which sets out the duties and responsibilities of Expert Witnesses is *National Justice Compania Naviera SA* v. *Prudential Assurance Co Ltd* (*The Ikarian Reefer*) (1993), where Cresswell J said:

"The duties and responsibilities of Expert Witnesses in civil cases include the following:

(a) Expert evidence presented to the Court should be, and should be seen to be, the independent product of the Expert uninfluenced as to form or content by the exigencies of litigation (*Whitehouse* v. *Jordan* [1981] 1 WLR 246 at 256 *per* Lord Wilberforce).
(b) An Expert Witness should provide independent assistance to the Court by way of objective unbiased opinion in relation to matters within his expertise (see *Polivitte Ltd* v. *Commercial Union Assurance Co plc* [1987] 1 Lloyd's Rep 379 at 386 *per* Mr Justice Garland and *Re J* [1990] FCR 193 *per* Mr Justice Cazalet). An Expert Witness in the High Court should never assume the role of an Advocate.
(c) An Expert Witness should state the facts or assumptions upon which his opinion is based. He should not omit to consider material facts which could detract from his concluded opinion (*Re J supra*).
(d) An Expert Witness should make it clear when a particular question or issue falls outside his expertise.
(e) If an Expert's opinion is not properly researched because he considers that insufficient data is available, then this must be stated with an indication that his

opinion is no more than a provisional one (*Re J supra*). In cases where an Expert Witness who has prepared a report could not assert that the report contained the truth, the whole truth and nothing but the truth, without some qualification, the qualification should be stated within the report (*Derby & Co Ltd and Others* v. *Weldon and Others*, *The Times*, 9 November 1990 *per* Lord Justice Staughton).

(f) If, after exchange of reports an Expert Witness changes his view on a material matter having read the other side's Expert's report or for any other reason, such change of use should be communicated (through legal representatives), to the other side without delay and, when appropriate, to the Court.

(g) Where expert evidence refers to photographs, plans, calculations, analysis, measurements, survey reports or other similar documents, these must be provided to the opposite party at the same time as the exchange of reports (see 15.5 of the *Guide to Commercial Court Practice*)."

1.7 The Practice Statement is intended to encompass the above principles.

1.8 Members are advised to be mindful of the fact that when giving expert evidence in relation to any matter referred to and covered by the Institution's other Practice Statements and Guidance Notes, that material should be considered.

2. General duty and roles

2.1 Upon accepting an instruction of any nature a Member assumes a responsibility to the client and himself (and to the Institution) to provide sound professional advice. To that end a Member should be satisfied, prior to accepting the instruction that he has the knowledge and resources to adequately fulfil the task specified within any allocated time span. If he cannot fulfil those basic criteria he should decline the instruction (PS3) or, alternatively, advise the client of the possible need to employ additional expertise.

2.2 It is imperative that Members appreciate that, while an instruction may originate from a particular client, the duty to that client becomes secondary once the Member is instructed as an Expert to produce evidence for the Judicial Body. PS3.2(a) makes it obligatory to bring this to the client's attention.

2.3 In some cases this change of responsibility may not be acceptable to the client; in such instances instructions to act should be declined. The various roles which may be adopted as an Expert include:

(a) assisting a party to establish the facts and to assess the merits of a case and to assist with its preparation;

(b) giving to the Judicial Body, as evidence, expert opinion where opinion evidence apart from that of an Expert would not be strictly admissible;

(c) giving factual evidence on a subject, where because of particular expertise, evidence will have greater weight than that of an unqualified witness. This category includes the evidence which Surveyors sometimes give, in addition to their opinion evidence, as to measurements they have made or examinations which they have carried out; and

(d) conducting enquiries on behalf of the Judicial Body and report to that Body as to findings.

3. Duty to client

3.1 In many instances, a Member will be asked to provide initial advice to a client prior to being instructed to provide expert evidence for presentation to the Judicial Body. All such initial advice is given in the normal client/professional advisor relationship.

3.2 If the initial advice given is in relation to a dispute which may have to be finally resolved by the Judicial Body, then the Member is advised to give careful consideration as to whether the advice should be provided to the client or to the client's solicitor (rather than to the client), in case, at a later date, it is discovered in proceedings and might prejudice the interests of the client. If in doubt, legal advice should be sought.

3.3 When, either upon accepting instructions or at a later date, it becomes apparent to the Member that he may be required to give expert evidence, then he should immediately make clear to the client that, upon being instructed to prepare evidence for submission to the Judicial Body, his duty lies firstly to the Judicial Body (PS2.1).

4. Duty to the Judicial Body

4.1 The duties of an Expert Witness have been defined by the Institution as follows:

"(i) The primary duty of the Expert Witness is to the Court or other Tribunal to whom his evidence is given.
(ii) The duty is to be truthful as to fact, honest as to opinion and complete as to coverage as to relevant matters. The duty is the same whether or not the Expert is giving evidence in Court on oath, or to a Tribunal on oath or to a Tribunal not on oath.
(iii) The Expert's evidence must be independent, objective and unbiased. In particular it must not be biased towards the party who is responsible for paying him. The evidence should be the same whoever is paying for it.
(iv) The duty applies as much to the preparation of a Statement of Opinion intended to be used as part of written representations in an arbitration or elsewhere where oral evidence is not given, as to a statement intended to be used in a Hearing before a Court or other Tribunal."

4.2 Members will appreciate that the Institution's definition can be compared closely with the statement by Cresswell J concerning the duties and responsibilities of Expert Witnesses in *The Ikarian Reefer* case, referred to in the Introduction to these Guidance Notes.

4.3 Any Member who does not feel entirely confident that he can fulfil the duty to the Judicial Body, for whatever reason, should decline instructions (PS2.1).

5. Acceptance of instructions

5.1 The appointor and the client of the Expert Surveyor are defined in sample Terms of Engagement, in Annexe A to these Guidance Notes. The Expert, on receiving the proposed instruction from the appointor, must ascertain the identity of the parties in order to establish:

(a) the party whom the Expert is to advise; and
(b) whether any conflicts of interest might be perceived.

5.2 A conflict of interest may arise out of a previous involvement with any party, the dispute, or property which would cause the Expert to be unwilling or seen to be unable or unwilling to fulfil his responsibility to be independent. In such circumstances, the Expert Surveyor should either refuse the assignment or seek written confirmation of instructions following disclosure, and if the Surveyor considers that the Judicial Body would not attach weight to his evidence due to such circumstances, he has a duty to advise accordingly.

5.3 As to the requirements to establish clear instructions and Terms of Business, see PS3.2. If standard Terms of Engagement are used, they should be attached to the acceptance of instructions. If in a particular case the Expert's standard terms are varied, such variations should be explained at the time. Annexe A provides sample Terms of Engagement which may be used (i.e. copyright is not reserved).

5.4 Circumstances may exist or arise where part of the assignment should be undertaken by another expert. Where this need arises, the Expert should notify the appointor/client and may give the name(s) of the individual(s) recommended to be engaged, together with information as to his/their experience and qualifications (PS3.2(c)).

5.5 The Expert is recommended to indicate a likely reporting programme to the appointor/client. This programme will vary according to the assignment but might follow three phases:

(a) **Initial report.** The Expert Surveyor may provide a report setting out relevant opinions relating to the assignment. Should the Expert's opinions not be accepted then, assuming that the report is competent and researched, the Expert may wish to consider withdrawing from the assignment.

(b) **Proof of evidence.** This may also involve supplemental proofs or counter-proofs together with joint meetings of Experts.

(c) **Giving evidence to a Judicial Body.** This may include conferences with Counsel appointed by the appointor/client.

6. Purpose of evidence

6.1 The purpose of expert evidence is to assist the Judicial Body in forming its own independent judgment.

6.2 The evidence given must, therefore, give all the necessary detail from which conclusions have been drawn in order to enable the Judicial Body to judge the appropriateness of the conclusions based upon the facts submitted (PS5).

7. Evidence of fact

7.1 The Expert Witness is often required to assist the Judicial Body in establishing, clarifying and ordering logically the relevant facts and issues to be addressed.

7.2 All relevant facts to the case must be stated truthfully and fully whether or not they favour the appointing party (PS5).

7.3 The Expert should be aware that evidence to the Judicial Body takes precedence over any contractual, professional or other duty and this may, on occasions, conflict with confidentiality agreements (PS2.2).

7.4 Where an Expert is instructed to assume facts such instructions should be stated fully in his report (PS5).

7.5 It is usual for those instructing an Expert to provide him with facts which he may adopt at his discretion. These, and facts which the Expert establishes for himself and to which he has regard in forming any opinion, should be set in the same detail as the Expert required to form his opinion or by cross-reference to other documents which will be made available to the Judicial Body. Accordingly, any written report provided by the Expert in evidence should include a full schedule of the documents upon which he has relied and, where necessary, copies of such documents or the relevant portions thereof. (The originals of all documents relied upon need to be available for inspection by other parties to the dispute and, unless agreed by the parties, to the Judicial Body; the Expert should therefore be aware of the location of all such documents.) The Expert should give within his report the source of factual information relied upon (PS5).

7.6 The Expert must carry out such factual research as he considers necessary to fully discharge his obligation to the Judicial Body including, where appropriate, an inspection of any property involved.

7.7 The Expert should give a sufficient explanation of what he has done in ascertaining and checking facts to enable the Judicial Body to be satisfied that he has fully discharged his obligations (PS5).

7.8 When directed to do so either by the Judicial Body or by the appointor, the Expert should seek to agree facts and to clarify what is and is not in dispute. Experts are recommended to request from appointors a copy of any directions relating to such meetings. The Expert has a duty to comply with those directions notwithstanding any instruction to the contrary (PS7).

7.9 If the Expert is in doubt about the admissibility (possibly because it is privileged) of any fact or statement upon which he is relying he should seek legal advice. Similarly, if he believes any material would be hearsay evidence, he should consult with the client's solicitor. Hearsay evidence is admissible in civil proceedings, provided that certain rules are followed. See Annexe B to these Guidance Notes.

8. Evidence of opinion

8.1 The opinion given must be honest. It must be objective, independent, unbiased and non-partisan. Opinion should not be exaggerated or seek to obscure alternative views.

8.2 Where an opinion has been formed based on incomplete knowledge of facts, then such limitations should be stated fully in the evidence (PS5.3(c)(ii)).

8.3 Where an Expert gives an opinion he should clearly set out the reasoning and facts upon which it is based. Differences of opinion between Experts often occur due to the detail of facts and assumptions upon which they are relying being different; such differences need to be set out for the Judicial Body (PS5.3(c)(ii)).

8.4 When Experts are instructed to meet to agree facts they may be instructed also to endeavour to agree opinions and, in such instances where opinions are not agreed, the reasons for disagreement should be recorded and reported (PS7.2).

8.5 Where an Expert changes his opinion, for whatever reason, such change should be communicated immediately in writing to the appointor, with whom the responsibility will lie to communicate it to other parties and the Judicial Body (PS6). It is suggested that the Expert should seek confirmation as to when and as to whom the change is notified.

9. Documents

9.1 Any evidence given by an Expert will, almost invariably, be based upon documents either provided to him or held by him.

9.2 When accepting instructions the Expert ought to request details of all relevant documents and, if he considers it necessary, ask to inspect his client's files to satisfy himself to this effect.

9.3 Documents from the Expert's own resources often provide useful factual information upon which to rely. Such documents might include text, published material, photographs, plans, the opinions of others, codes of practice and RICS Practice Statements, Guidance Notes and Information Papers.

9.4 Documents provided to the Expert by third parties may need to be independently proved and if the Expert intends to rely upon such documents, he should seek legal advice.

9.5 During the course of his enquiries the Expert may be made aware that other documents exist which might be of relevance. In such circumstances he should seek legal advice.

10. Extent of evidence

10.1 The Expert is advised not to give evidence on matters that are outside his competence and ought to be wary of straying inadvertently beyond such limits. In particular, an Expert should not express, as his own opinion, an interpretation of statute or case law; he may, however, state an interpretation as a basis on which his conclusions on other questions are provided.

10.2 The Expert is recommended to avoid having to prove or give opinions upon the contents of any document that deals with matters outside the scope of his own expertise, even where he feels it may assist the Judicial Body.

11. Oral evidence

11.1 In most instances where an Expert is required to give oral evidence, such evidence will be given under oath/affirmation but, whether or not such oath/affirmation is required, oral evidence must always be truthful and the Expert's honest opinion (PS2.2). If the Expert does not know the answer to a particular question, he should say so rather than endeavour to give an answer which might prove to be incorrect or misleading.

11.2 Preparation is important and the Expert should ensure that:

(a) all relevant files and documents are taken to the Hearing. It is the Expert's responsibility to ensure that all documents necessary for proving his evidence are available; and

(b) he has reminded himself of the detail of any written evidence which he has previously submitted and also of the detail of the contents of files, as specific points may need to be addressed before and during the Hearing and even while giving evidence.

11.3 Where an Expert has to refer to bulky material in his evidence or to video, film or other screen based material, it is his responsibility to ensure that appropriate arrangements have previously been made to enable such material to be communicated to the Judicial Body.

11.4 When giving evidence witnesses will be questioned by advocates but all answers should be addressed to the Judicial Body. Concise answers are preferable but Experts should not allow advocates to prevent a full answer from being given.

11.5 Experts should never attempt to advocate the merits of their clients' case, when acting as Expert Witnesses (see Section 19).

11.6 Adjournments of the Hearing, either for lunch, overnight or for longer periods, can sometimes occur. While a witness is under oath/affirmation he is not permitted to discuss the case with anyone during those adjournments. This includes his client, advocates, and fellow Experts. Adjournments between Hearing dates can be lengthy and in such instances the Expert is advised to be alert to requesting that he be released from this restriction immediately before the Hearing is so adjourned.

12. Advising advocates

12.1 The Expert Witness will almost invariably be required to advise his client's advocate.

12.2 Immediately prior to any Hearing it is not uncommon for advocates of opposing parties to discuss between themselves aspects of the case, including possible compromise solutions. Expert advice is often needed during such negotiations and the Expert, therefore, needs to ensure that he is available well before the Hearing is due to begin.

12.3 During the Hearing the advocate may wish to consult with his client's Expert while he is cross-examining other witnesses and, particularly, the other party's Expert Surveyor. It is important that the Expert establishes whether the advocate wishes him to be available for such consultation. The Expert is often asked to sit immediately behind the advocate in order that he can be consulted directly during the proceedings.

12.4 Experts not under oath/affirmation are commonly required to discuss other matters relating to the case with advocates during adjournments. An Expert should not expect to have free time during adjournments (except to another day).

13. Written reports

13.1 This section provides an example of the structure and nature of the content of a typical report by an Expert Witness. Some variations to this structure will be appropriate on occasion, to take account of:

(a) any prior agreement between the parties as to the order in which the various issues are to be addressed (and possibly determined);
(b) any direction of the Judicial Body as to the procedure or as to the order in which the issues are to be considered; and
(c) any statutory material or official guidance as to procedure applicable in particular types of proceedings.

13.2 The front sheet should reveal, not obscure, the name of the Expert Witness, the proceedings and the nature of the evidence, the subject of the report, and the date of the report. It should be entitled "Report" not "First (or other) Report".

13.3 Thereafter, the report often takes the following form:

(a) *Introductory material.*

(i) a brief résumé of the qualifications and relevant professional experience of the Expert Witness;
(ii) the names of the persons to be referred to in the report, together with a short, uncontroversial description of their respective roles;
(iii) chronology as to the Expert's involvement in the case;
(iv) the factual or assumed background of the case; and
(v) the issues which the Expert addressed in the report. No opinions are expressed in this section.

(b) *Enquiries made by the Expert.*

This section is also factual only. The description should be given in itemised sub-paragraphs, with sub-headings as appropriate.

(c) *The facts upon which the Expert's opinion is based.*

This should distinguish between facts which the Expert has been told to assume, those provided which he has chosen to assume, and those he has established for himself. The various sources of facts and material provided to and derived by the Expert should be identified.

(d) *Reasons and conclusions.*

This should give the Expert's opinion on each issue and the reasons in full on each of them in turn. Facts should only be reported to the extent necessary for the exposition of the opinion.

(Sometimes the usual contents of this section can conveniently be disaggregated to follow immediately upon particular sets of facts.)

(e) *Certificate as to completeness, and signature.*

The statements required in the Practice Statement must be included, along with the signature of the writer and the date thereof.

14. Meetings between Expert Witness and client/solicitor/counsel

14.1 Meetings can be beneficial to assist the client and his advisers to understand the points being made and the person making them.

14.2 In particular, the bringing together of counsel and the Expert as early as possible is to be encouraged. This enables the strengths and weaknesses of an Expert's case to be evaluated, and may result in the Expert wishing to make changes.

14.3 It may also assist the client, solicitor, and especially counsel if the Expert is readily available, and if the Expert takes a close interest in the progress of the case.

15. Meetings between experts

15.1 Such meetings are extremely desirable to attempt to achieve a greater understanding of the issues. They should reveal the initial extent of agreements and disagreements and may result in changed opinions, resolving some of the differences. This process is likely to produce clearer, shorter reports and to save time, thereby reducing costs.

15.2 The usual purpose of the meeting (subject to any directions of the Judicial Body) is to pool relevant technical information, to narrow the technical issues, agreeing as many as possible and to identify clearly areas of disagreement. Such issues may also be narrowed on hypothetical "what if" bases. It is helpful if there are frank exchanges of theories and opinions.

15.3 It is advisable that Experts in the same disciplines meet and it can be useful for combined meetings to take place, including Experts for each side but from various disciplines. It is generally best if such meetings occur before reports intended to be disclosed are written, as Experts tend to be slow to alter opinions thereafter and time can be wasted.

15.4 Each Expert ought to approach the meetings with a willingness to listen, be co-operative and constructive. Otherwise the worth of such meetings can be severely devalued. It is generally expected that the Plaintiff's Expert is the convenor of such meetings—or the first one at least, and neutral territory or "on-site" may be preferred venues.

15.5 It is useful to pre-agree a broad agenda and later to agree and jointly sign minutes, to obviate misunderstandings later. Experts are reminded that whilst such meetings may be "without prejudice", i.e. "off the record", the outcome of such meetings is "on the record". For example, if one Expert agrees with another that an aspect of his case is weak, counsel for the other side could, legitimately, exploit such an admission in the witness box.

15.6 An Expert who is a Chartered Surveyor should:

(a) agree relevant facts established by him and calculations prepared by him wherever reasonably possible (PS7.1(a)); and
(b) identify the issues and reasons for any differences of opinion (PS7.1(b));

referring to those instructing him for authority where necessary.

15.7 With the consent of the appointer, Experts can come outside the Expert Witness remit to conduct "without prejudice" meetings to explore and possibly settle differences as to facts and opinions.

16. Basis of charging fees

16.1 The basis of charging may vary dependent upon the nature of the Expert's appointment.

16.2 In the case of an Expert appointed by a Judicial Body the level of fees may be determined by the rules of that Body, taxation and/or other statutory provisions and the Expert is advised to establish such a basis prior to accepting instructions.

16.3 When appointed by a party to the dispute, the Expert should set out clearly in writing the basis of his fees (PS3.2(d)). Such a basis may be by reference to agreed daily or hourly rates undertaken or an agreed fixed fee. Regard should be had to the possibility that the level of fee may be subject to taxation. Provision may also be made for additional payments in respect of:

(a) travelling time;
(b) expenses and disbursements;
(c) rates for attending Hearings; and
(d) late notice or cancellation or settlement after the Expert has been booked to attend a Hearing.

16.4 It is considered important for both the basis of fee charging and for possible taxation purposes, that careful and detailed time-sheets and records of tasks undertaken are kept.

17. Contingency fees

17.1 The Institution considers that any form of contingency fee arrangement is incompatible with the duty of impartiality and independence required of an Expert and that, accordingly, contingency fees should be avoided if at all possible.

17.2 The Institution, however, recognises that many of its Members practising in some surveying specialisms charge on a contingency basis as a matter of normal practice. Those Members are advised that, while the Institution would not expect any of its Members to allow the quality of their evidence to be influenced by the potential fee, should the Judicial Body become aware that such a fee basis has been agreed, that Body may consider that the evidence and opinion proffered is not entirely unbiased.

18. Responsibility for fees

18.1 The responsibility for payment of fees should be clearly incorporated in the Terms of Engagement entered into. They may identify the client as being solely responsible or perhaps, alternatively, consideration may be given to making solicitors, claims' consultants or similar parties jointly and severally responsible for payment.

18.2 It is recommended that the Expert should advise the appointing party that liability will exist for all fees and expenses properly incurred in accordance with the Terms of Engagement even though those fees and costs may subsequently be taxed by the Judicial Body or, alternatively, to the extent that they are not fully recovered from another party to the dispute.

19. The two roles of Expert and Advocate

19.1 Sometimes Chartered Surveyors appear in the two roles of Expert and Advocate before such Judicial Bodies as:

(a) Valuation Tribunals and/or Lands Tribunal;
(b) Planning Inspectors;

(c) Arbitrators;
(d) Independent Experts; and
(e) Rent Assessment Committees and Leasehold Valuation Tribunals.

19.2 These two roles are especially common when disputes are resolved by written submissions rather than being tested at a Hearing and Members are recommended to carefully consider the desirability of the two roles.

19.3 This fact was emphasised in the case of *Multimedia Productions Ltd* v. *Secretary of State for the Environment and Another* [1988] EGCS 83 following an Inspector's dismissal of a planning appeal when the Court warned "although there is no rule against a person combining the roles of Expert and Advocate before a Public Local Enquiry it was an undesirable practice. An Expert Witness had to give a true and unbiased opinion, the Advocate had to do the best for his client. The Expert who had also played the role as Advocate should not be surprised if his evidence was later treated by a Court with some caution".

19.4 When acting as an Advocate, the duty and role is to promote the client's case whereas when acting as an Expert the duty is to assist the Judicial Body and to be entirely impartial.

19.5 Members are, therefore, under a duty, when undertaking these two roles, to make it clear to the Judicial Body which aspect of the two roles they are fulfilling at each and every stage of any Hearing or written submission (PS8.1).

19.6 It is suggested that, at Hearings, in order to avoid the different aspect of the roles being confused, advocacy should be undertaken from a different position in the room to that from which evidence is given.

19.7 The two roles are even more difficult to distinguish where a matter is conducted by written submissions and, if the distinction is not obvious, it may be advisable to place submissions by way of advocacy in one document and expert opinion evidence in another document or, at least, in separate, clearly distinguishable parts of the same document.

19.8 Members undertaking the two roles and their clients ought to be aware of the severe disadvantage that might arise where, in a Hearing, the Surveyor is giving evidence under oath/affirmation in his capacity as Expert and an adjournment occurs. Under such circumstances, the Surveyor would be unable to discuss any aspect of the case with his client during that adjournment.

ANNEXE A. SAMPLE TERMS OF ENGAGEMENT OF AN EXPERT SURVEYOR TO ACT AS AN EXPERT WITNESS APPOINTED BY A PARTY INVOLVED IN A DISPUTE BEFORE ANY COURT OF LAW OR AT ARBITRATION OR BEFORE ANY OTHER FORM OF JUDICIAL BODY

1. Recital of appointment

1.1 The Appointor has appointed the Expert Surveyor to provide advice and services, in respect of

____

in accordance with these Terms of Engagement.

2. Definitions

Unless the context otherwise requires:

2.1 The "Appointor" means the solicitor, person(s), organisation or department instructing the Expert.

2.2 The "Expert Surveyor" means the person appointed hereunder to provide expert advice, including the giving of evidence.

2.3 The "Client" means person(s), firm, company, or government department(s) to whom the Expert has been instructed to provide such advice.

2.4 The "Assignment" means the matter(s), to which these Terms of Engagement apply, referred to the Expert Surveyor by the Appointor, in respect of which, advice is or has been required.
2.5 "Fees" means (in the absence of written agreement to the contrary) the reasonable charges of the Expert based on the Expert's agreed hourly rate. Time spent travelling and waiting may be charged in full. Value Added Tax will be charged in addition where applicable.
2.6 "Disbursements" means the cost, reasonably incurred, of all photography, reproduction of drawings, diagrams and the like, printing and duplicating, and all out-of-pocket expenses, including travel, refreshments and hotel accommodation. Value Added Tax will be charged in addition where applicable.

3. The Appointor

The Appointor will:

(a) provide timely, full and clear instructions in writing supported by good quality copies of documents within his possession;
(b) deal promptly with every reasonable request by the Expert for authority, information and documents;
(c) not settle alterations to the reports of the Expert Surveyor before they are submitted to the Judicial Body; and
(d) where possible, at the Expert's request, arrange access to the property or properties relevant to the assignment in order that the Expert Surveyor can inspect them and make relevant enquiries.

4. Fees and disbursements

4.1 The Expert may present invoices at such intervals as he considers fit and payment of each invoice is due on presentation.
4.2 For the avoidance of doubt, the Expert shall be entitled to charge fair and reasonable fees where, due to settlement of the dispute, or any other reason not being the fault of the Expert:

(a) the Expert's time has been reserved for a specific Hearing, meeting or other relevant engagement; and/or
(b) specific instructions have been given to the Expert for an inspection and report; and
(c) the reservation of time is not required and/or the instructions have been withdrawn.

4.3 The Appointor and the Client shall (if different) be jointly and severally responsible for payment of the Expert's fees and disbursements.
4.4 The Expert shall, at his discretion, be entitled to invoice and recover interest at . . .% per month (or part thereof) on all unpaid invoices and in addition the full amount of his administrative, legal and other costs of recovering unpaid invoices.

5. Disputes

5.1 In the event of a dispute as to the amount of the Expert's fees such sum as is not disputed shall be paid forthwith pending resolution of the dispute, irrespective of any set off or counter claim which may be alleged.
5.2 Any dispute relating to the *quantum* of the Expert's fees shall initially be referred by application by any party to this Agreement to the President of the Royal Institution of Chartered Surveyors for the appointment of a Mediator. Any dispute not thereby resolved by mediation shall be resolved on the basis of the law applicable in the country where the Expert trades or practises and the venue shall be the appropriate Court for that area.

ANNEXE B. HEARSAY EVIDENCE

The Civil Evidence Act 1995 contains provisions which supersede the previous hearsay rules. This Act does three things: it abolishes the rule against hearsay evidence in civil proceedings; it requires a party who wishes to adduce hearsay evidence to serve notice on the other party; and, it sets out guidance as to hearsay evidence.

Section 1(1) of the Act provides that in civil proceedings, evidence otherwise admissible shall not be excluded on the grounds that it is hearsay. "Civil Proceedings" means civil proceedings before any tribunal where the strict rules of evidence apply, whether as a matter of law or by agreement of the parties.

A party wishing to rely on hearsay evidence must first serve notice on the other party, giving particulars of this evidence. Failure to comply with this requirement will not, however, affect the admissibility of the evidence but it may be taken into account by the Judicial Body in the exercise of its powers in connection with the proceedings and costs, and by the Judicial Body as a matter adversely affecting the weight to be given to the hearsay evidence.

The change in the hearsay rule by the Civil Evidence Act 1995 is a change of emphasis from admissibility to weight. The Act therefore sets out guidelines as to the weight to be given to hearsay evidence. Generally, the Judicial Body is required to have regard to any circumstances from which any inference can be drawn as to the reliability of the hearsay evidence. Specifically, it is required to have regard as to whether:

(a) it is reasonable and practicable to produce the maker of the original statement;
(b) the statement was made contemporaneously with the occurrence or existence of the matter stated;
(c) the statement involves multiple hearsay;
(d) there is any motive as to concealment or misrepresentation;
(e) the statement is edited or is the result of collaboration; and
(f) the circumstances in which the evidence is produced are such as to suggest an attempt to prevent proper evaluation of its weight.

Reproduced by permission of The Royal Institution of Chartered Surveyors which owns the copyright.

APPENDIX D

PACT: PROFESSIONAL ARBITRATION ON COURT TERMS

FOREWORD BY THE PRESIDENT OF THE RICS AND THE PRESIDENT OF THE LAW SOCIETY

We are delighted that The Law Society and The Royal Institution of Chartered Surveyors have joined forces to provide this new service to determine disputes relating to lease renewals. The Law Society and The RICS have supported the development of alternative methods of dispute resolution over a number of years and we applaud the objectives of this new service. We believe that landlords, tenants and their advisers will see the scheme as an effective way of resolving unopposed lease renewals. The benefits of having a specialist in landlord and tenant matters who is also a trained dispute resolver will lead to informed decision-making that is much quicker and cheaper than through the Courts. This is in line with Lord Woolf's proposals as set out in "Access to Justice". We are confident that the scheme will be successful and offer our thanks to all the members of the joint working party of The Law Society and The RICS who have so effectively worked together to develop this valuable new service.

Phillip Sycamore President The Law Society	Peter McKendrick President The RICS

PROFESSIONAL ARBITRATION ON COURT TERMS ("PACT")
AN ALTERNATIVE TO LITIGATION

Introduction

1. The Royal Institution of Chartered Surveyors ("RICS") and The Law Society, supported by the Incorporated Society of Valuers and Auctioneers, now offer an extension to the existing Dispute Resolution Service and Arbitration Service by providing the services of surveyors and solicitors to determine lease renewal disputes as an alternative to litigation.

   The PACT scheme focuses on unopposed lease renewals under the Landlord and Tenant Act 1954 and offers opportunity for disputes to be resolved without the necessity of going to Court.

   The scheme provides opportunity for Landlords and Tenants to have the terms and rent payable under their new lease decided by a surveyor or solicitor acting as either an arbitrator or independent expert. The appointments will be made by the RICS or Law Society. The professionals to be appointed are experienced specialists who have been specifically trained under the PACT scheme.

Objective

2. The objective of the scheme is to increase the effectiveness and flexibility of the legal system and to give a greater choice to both landlords and tenants, and to their advisers. The scheme is in line with Lord Woolf's proposals in "Access to Justice", which encourages litigation to be viewed as a last resort, and is in line also with the provisions of the Arbitration Act 1996.

Advantages

3. Advantages of the scheme are:

- **Flexibility**—The parties will be able to adapt the rules to their specific requirements and choose whether the appointed professional should be a surveyor or lawyer and whether they should act as an arbitrator or independent expert.
- **Speed**—Delay is one of the main problems of court action.
- **Lower Cost**—although fees will be payable, streamlined and/or informal procedures will be available, potentially reducing the overall cost.
- **Quality of Decision**—Professionals have the expertise to make sound decisions on technical matters within their specialised practice area.
- **Adaptability**—The scheme will not be cast in stone and can be developed and adapted according to need.

Limitations

4. It is recognised that it may be appropriate for the Courts to handle some difficult legal issues. Beyond that, it is emphasised that reference to PACT will be purely voluntary and prospective participants should take advice on whether the scheme is suitable for their particular dispute. Helplines have been established by the promoting bodies to give assistance in this respect and enquirers may be eligible for up to half an hour of free advice from a surveyor or solicitor operating under the scheme (see paragraph 7).

The Scheme

5. The main features of this scheme are:

(i) It has been designed to deal mainly with unopposed renewals under the Landlord and Tenant Act 1954 where a determination is required to settle the terms of the lease, or the rent, or both. Valuation in many cases may usefully be based on an agreed form of lease, but where drafting is required this function will be covered by the terms of a consent order and will influence the choice of the professional who will make the determination.

(ii) Given the initial focus of the scheme, it has been necessary to produce a framework in the context of the 1954 Act and Court jurisdiction. This is however regarded as a pilot scheme and the service may be made available, in due course, for other property-related disputes which would otherwise be the subject of litigation and which can appropriately be decided by a surveyor or solicitor—or both sitting together. These additional issues may relate to such matters as opposed renewals, service charges, breach of repairing covenants, insurance and other matters arising out of leases or contracts for sale, including the application of the Landlord and Tenant (Covenants) Act 1995.

(iii) The professional will be appointed by the President of the RICS or the President of the Law Society, who will ask for sufficient information to enable the appointment of a suitably qualified person. The appointee will act either as an arbitrator or as an independent expert, as decided by the parties.

(iv) Reference will be made by way of consent order from the Court. Model consent orders are included in the papers and are capable of being adapted to meet the needs of the particular case. The agreed terms of the order will be binding and the extent of rights of appeal to the Court will be a matter for decision by the parties. Appeals, if permitted, would fall within the existing legal procedures.

(v) The consent order will preserve the existing right of tenants to reject a new tenancy within a specified period subject to payment of costs.

(vi) An essential part of the scheme will be the exclusion of the jurisdiction of the Court over the matters to be determined by the arbitrator or expert. Where it is necessary for protective steps to be taken to comply with the renewal provisions of the 1954 Act the tenant will first apply to the Court in the normal way and the parties will then consent to refer the dispute to arbitration.

Training

6. The RICS and The Law Society both recognise the need for training if their members are to offer this service. Both bodies have existing lists of appropriate members, well able to handle many of the matters which will arise under this scheme but specialist courses have been run to ensure the expertise of those to be appointed. As demand for the scheme increases further training courses will be held to widen the pool of those available to be appointed.

Implementation

7. The scheme will operate from July 1997.

Requests for application forms or for further details should be addressed to one of the following:

The RICS Dispute Resolution Service, Surveyor Court, Westwood Way, Coventry CV4 8JE
Telephone 020 7222 7000 Facsimile: 020 7334 3802
Helpline: 020 7334 3806

The Arbitration Service, The Law Society, 50–52 Chancery Lane, London WC2A 1SX
Telephone: 020 7242 1222 Facsimile: 020 7320 5918
Helpline: 020 7320 5698

The Incorporated Society of Valuers and Auctioneers, 3 Cadogan Gate, London SW1X 0AS
Telephone: 020 7235 2282 Facsimile: 020 7235 4390
Helpline: Main number. Ask for Professional Services.

USING "PACT"
A SUMMARY OF KEY ISSUES

- ➤ Decide with the other party whether it would be advantageous to refer aspects of the lease renewal to a third party solicitor or surveyor rather than a judge.
- ➤ Identify which aspects of the renewal (if any) are agreed.
- ➤ Decide which aspects to refer to the third party:
  - the interim rent
  - the new rent
  - other terms of the lease
  - the detailed drafting of terms
  - a combination of these
- ➤ Choose which aspects to be resolved by a third party solicitor and which by a third party surveyor.
- ➤ Choose third party's capacity—arbitrator or expert?
- ➤ Draft Court Application making use of or adopting PACT model orders.
- ➤ Apply to Court for consent.
- ➤ Apply for appointment of person adjudicating (if not agreed).
- ➤ Proceed with adjudication.
- ➤ Receive decision subject only to cooling off rights and, in arbitration, any right of appeal.

"PACT" GUIDANCE NOTES

These Model Consent Orders are designed to provide an adaptable framework for the referral, by agreement of both parties, of some or all of the issues involved in deciding the terms of the lease renewal of business premises under the 1954 Act to arbitration or to independent expert determination rather than to a Court. The procedure can be used where both parties have identified the issues between them and are prepared to adopt the procedure to resolve them.

The Model Orders are intended to be used after any objection by the landlord to the grant of a new tenancy has been disposed of. Disputes concerning grounds of objection could be the subject of arbitration or independent expert determination, this would require a form drafted to suit the particular circumstances.

The Model Orders have been drafted on the basis that any issues in connection with the renewal which are not to be referred to arbitration or to independent expert determination will have been agreed between the parties or decided through the Courts before the Consent Order is entered into.

To preserve its right to a new business tenancy under the 1954 Act, the tenant must first serve the appropriate notice or counter-notice and must then apply to the Court, in each case complying with the time limits laid down by the Act.

Issues which can be resolved under PACT include the duration, rent and other terms of the new tenancy, together with the amount of any interim rent payable for the period between the end of the contractual term of the old lease (or the landlord's application for interim rent, if made later) and the start of the new tenancy. Some or all of these issues can be referred to an independent professional person acting either as an arbitrator or as an independent expert. The Model Orders provide a mechanism for this. It is for the parties, by agreement, to select the capacity in which they want the professional to act. The issue of interim rent, which the Act requires to be decided on a basis which includes making a judgment of reasonableness as between the parties, is considered to be more appropriate for arbitration than for expert determination and the forms do not therefore provide the option of expert determination for this issue. Thus expert determination is provided only for determining the rent under the new tenancy and any pure drafting points (but not substantive points) on its text. The chosen form of Consent Order must be approved by the Court in which the application for a new tenancy was made.

Each form comprises an Order with a schedule setting out the agreement to refer outstanding issues to arbitration or independent expert determination. There is also a form of joint application which is designed to be used with any of the Orders. Solicitors for each party are required to certify when signing the application that they have advised their client on the suitability of the procedure.

There are four versions of Consent Order:

Model Order 1	For referring all outstanding issues to arbitration.
Model Order 2	For referring the initial rent to independent expert determination and interim rent to arbitration.
Model Order 3	For referring issues other than rent to arbitration before endeavouring to agree the rental issues, and then, failing agreement, referring the initial rent to independent expert determination and interim rent to arbitration.
Model Order 4	For expert drafting of the text of the lease.

Model Orders 1 and 2 are the basic forms which it is anticipated will be of most use to the parties and their advisors.

Model Orders 3 and 4 illustrate the extra flexibility which can be built into the basic approach. Form 3 adopts a two stage approach allowing time for agreement, which may avoid the need for the second stage. Form 4 selects one specific aspect of the process, namely drafting the new lease itself. The parties can therefore agree which matters should be decided by the Court and which by an independent professional.

Each model form proceeds on the basis that the terms which have already been agreed between the parties or determined by the Court will be incorporated into the new tenancy and that the outstanding terms will be referred to arbitration or independent expert determination.

The arbitrator or independent expert is required to apply the criteria set out in the appropriate sections of the 1954 Act in reaching his award so that:

(1) the duration of the new tenancy must be determined in accordance with Section 33;
(2) the rent for the new tenancy must be determined in accordance with Section 34;
(3) the other terms of the new tenancy must be determined in accordance with Section 35;
(4) the interim rent must be determined in accordance with Section 24A.

In the rare case where the extent of the premises to be comprised in the new tenancy is at issue, a paragraph may be added to the Consent Order requiring this to be determined by the third party in accordance with Section 32 of the Act.

A landlord's application for interim rent may be made either as a separate action, or as a counterclaim in the tenant's application for a new tenancy. If the landlord has chosen to make a separate application, the forms will need to be adapted to reflect this and the two actions may need to be consolidated or a Consent Order lodged in each action.

Once the Consent Order has been made, the Court proceedings are suspended whilst the outstanding matters are referred to arbitration or independent expert determination. Landlord or tenant will, however, be entitled to ask the Court to enforce the agreement to refer the specified matters to arbitration or independent expert determination if the other party fails to comply.

The model Orders give a period (to be chosen by the parties) within which they will endeavour to make a joint application for the appointment of the arbitrator or independent expert (as the case may be). After that period either party may apply to the RICS or the Law Society. This approach could be varied to meet the parties' particular requirements.

The parties will agree and specify in the Consent Order whether the deciding person will be a surveyor or solicitor. Both appointing bodies have panels of trained arbitrators and independent experts for this purpose and one form of application is available for application to either body. The Model Orders give the parties the choice of stipulating the extent to which they will continue to be bound by matters contained in the pleadings they have filed with the Court. Alternative provisions are supplied.

The tenant's right under Section 36(2) of the Landlord and Tenant Act 1954 to elect not to take up a new tenancy is preserved. In order to exercise this right the tenant would need to apply to the Court, following the decision of the arbitrator or independent expert, for an order for the grant of a new tenancy on the terms set out in the Consent Order together with those determined by the arbitrator or independent expert. The tenant would then have a period of 14 days after the making of the Court Order to apply for its revocation and the remaining provisions of section 36(2) and (3) would apply.

The Model Orders preserve the tenant's right to bring the application for a new tenancy to an end at any time by filing Notice of Discontinuance with the Court and also preserve the landlord's right to discontinue his interim rent application. In each case notice must be given to the arbitrator or independent expert and the other party, the third party proceedings will then cease. If only the tenant discontinues, any reference of the interim rent to arbitration will nevertheless continue. The model Consent Orders as drafted provide that the discontinuing party will be responsible for the abortive costs of the arbitrator and the other party in the case of arbitration and of the expert, with the option of also being responsible for the other party's costs, in the case of expert determination. An independent expert, unlike an arbitrator, does not have authority over the costs as between the parties unless this is expressly conferred on him. The obligation to meet abortive costs applies irrespective of any order of the arbitrator or direction of the independent expert to the contrary. Section 60 of the Arbitration Act 1996 provides that an agreement to pay costs in any event is only valid if made after the dispute in question has arisen. If and insofar as the relevant provision of the model Consent Orders falls within this section, the dispute will have arisen by the time that the Consent Order is entered into.

In cases referred to arbitration, either party would have the right to challenge the arbitrator's award. Under the Arbitration Act 1996, three grounds of challenge are available:

— challenge on the grounds of substantive jurisdiction (Section 67),
— challenge on the grounds of serious irregularity (Section 68),
— appeal on a point of law (Section 69).

The time limit for such challenges is 28 days from the date of the arbitrator's award although the Court can be asked to extend this time limit. The model Orders specify the point at which matters decided by the procedure are "finally determined" by reference to the time for, and consequences of, challenge to any arbitrator's award which decided those matters.

No such statutory right of challenge exists in the case of independent expert determination. The determination of issues decided by the expert is generally final at the date of his determination.

Once the terms of the new tenancy which have been referred to the arbitrator or independent expert have been finally determined, either party may under the terms of the Consent Order apply to a Court for the grant of a new tenancy under Section 29 of the 1954 Act.

Form 1

This records the terms which have been agreed between the parties or determined by the Court and then refers the remaining terms to arbitration.

Part 2 of the Schedule contains the agreement to arbitrate the outstanding issues which should be identified by selecting one or more of the alternatives set out in paragraph A.

Paragraph D specifies when the matters referred to the arbitrator are deemed to be finally determined. This cross-refers to each party's entitlement at paragraph (a) of the Consent Order to apply for a new tenancy to be ordered under Section 29 of the 1954 Act on the terms which have been finally determined together with those which have been agreed.

Paragraphs E and F contain suggested terms in respect of abortive costs which may be adapted to suit the requirements of the parties.

Form 2

This form provides for the initial rent to be referred to an independent expert and if necessary for the interim rent to be decided by the same person but acting as an arbitrator. It is to be used where the other terms of the new tenancy have been agreed. It could include expert determination on other individual lease terms, for example, duration.

One of the essential differences between independent expert determination and arbitration is that an independent expert is not required to abide by the rules of natural justice or to confine himself to deciding on the evidence put before him by the parties. Therefore, in the case of complex issues on the initial rent, the parties may prefer to consider Form 1 or Form 3.

The Schedule is in a similar format to Form 1, but there is no reference to appeals in respect of the initial rent because an expert's decision is not governed by the Arbitration Act. Paragraph E provides that the initial rent is finally deetermined on the date of the determination.

Form 3

This form provides for a two stage process for resolving outstanding terms. It is likely to be most appropriate where the main areas of dispute between the parties do not relate to rent and it is anticipated that the rental issues will be capable of agreement, or speedy resolution by an expert, once the other terms have been resolved. The non-rental issues are referred to arbitration, but following the arbitrator's award there is a breathing space in which the parties may attempt to agree the rent for a lease on the terms awarded by the arbitrator and agreed between the parties. Failing agreement, the initial rent is then referred to an independent third party who will give an expert determination on this issue, and, if necessary, arbitrate on the interim rent.

Form 4

The parties may be able to agree heads of terms for the new lease but may have difficulty in agreeing the detailed drafting. This may result in delay in finalising the new lease. This form provides for the drafting of the lease to be settled by an independent expert.

This alternative could be used as a further option where the terms of the lease are subject to arbitration or independent expert determination and it is agreed that the initial award or determination should be in the form of heads of terms rather than a draft lease. The parties may then wish to endeavour to resolve the detailed drafting themselves, but to have the right, failing agreement, to refer drafting issues to a third party.

VERSION 1: Arbitration

Case No.

IN THE COUNTY COURT

In the Matter of the Landlord and Tenant Act 1954

In the Matter of the Premises known as

BETWEEN:

TENANT

Applicant

– and –

LANDLORD

Respondent

CONSENT ORDER

UPON the joint application of the parties by their respective solicitors and upon reading the parties' agreed terms

AND BY CONSENT

IT IS ORDERED THAT:

1. The duration of the new tenancy shall be [a term commencing on the and ending on] [determined in accordance with Section 33 of the said Act, by a third party under the provisions of Part 2 of the Schedule hereto].
2. The terms of the new tenancy (other than as to the duration thereof and as to the rent payable thereunder) shall be [in the form previously agreed between the parties, and set out in Part 1 of the Schedule hereto] [such terms as have been previously agreed between the parties and are set out in Part 1 of the Schedule hereto together with such other terms as shall be determined in accordance with Section 35 of the said Act by a third party under the provisions of Part 2 of the Schedule hereto] [determined in accordance with Section 35 of the said Act by a third party under the provisions of Part 2 of the Schedule hereto].
3. The initial rent payable under the new tenancy shall be [£ per year] [determined by a third party under the provisions of Part 2 of the Schedule hereto in accordance with Section 34 of the said Act [and as if the new tenancy were to commence on the date of his determination]].[1]
4. Pursuant to Section 24A of the said Act, the rent payable from [date] for so long as the current tenancy continues by virtue of Sections 24 and 64 of the said Act shall be [at the rate of £ per year] [at the same rate as is agreed or determined in respect of the new tenancy under paragraph 3 above] [determined in accordance with Section 24A of the said Act by a third party under the provisions of Part 2 of the Schedule hereto].[1]

AND IT IS FURTHER ORDERED that all further proceedings in this action be stayed upon the terms agreed between the parties and set out in the Schedule hereto save that:

(a) either party shall have liberty to apply to the Court for the purpose of carrying the said agreed terms into effect;

1 If an interim rent application has been made as a separate action, this paragraph will need to be incorporated in a separate consent order with an amended Schedule.

(b) when all the terms for the new tenancy have been finally determined in accordance with the provisions of the Schedule hereto and/or agreed either party shall have liberty to apply for an order pursuant to Section 29 of the said Act for the grant of a new tenancy on those terms;
(c) on the filing of a Notice of Discontinuance by the Applicant the Applicant's tenancy shall cease and determine on the expiration of three months from the date of filing of the said Notice with the Court.

SCHEDULE

Part 1

[Agreed terms]

Part 2

(A) The matters referred to in paragraphs [1][2][3] and [4] of the Consent Order ("the Substantive Issues") shall be determined by an independent third party acting as an arbitrator in accordance with the Arbitration Act 1996. [Unless otherwise agreed the parties shall be bound by their respective Originating Application or Answer and pleadings lodged with the Court ("the Pleadings") [but the arbitrator shall have the power to allow either party to depart from its Pleadings].] [The parties shall not be bound by their respective Originating Application, Answer or pleadings lodged with the Court.]
(B) The parties shall endeavour to make a joint appointment of the arbitrator within [ ] days from the date of the Consent Order failing which either party may thereafter apply to the President for the time being of the [Royal Institution of Chartered Surveyors] [Law Society] to make the appointment.
(C) The arbitrator shall make a single award ("the Award") determining all the Substantive Issues and where any of the Substantive Issues are agreed between the parties during the course of the arbitration proceedings, the arbitrator will incorporate their agreement in the Award. The Substantive Issues do not include, for this purpose, any issue solely related to costs. The arbitrator will make a separate award on costs unless otherwise agreed by both parties.
(D) The Substantive Issues shall be finally determined on the earliest date by which the arbitration proceedings on the Substantive Issues (including any proceedings on or in consequence of any application or appeal under Sections 67, 68 or 69 of the Arbitration Act 1996) have been determined and any time for making any such application or appeal or further application or appeal has expired without an application for extension of that time having been made.
(E) If Notice of Discontinuance is filed by the Applicant with the Court, the Applicant will forthwith notify the Respondent and the arbitrator and any arbitration proceedings concerning the duration, terms or initial rent payable for the new tenancy will cease. The Applicant will be liable for the arbitrator's fees and the Respondent's costs (to be taxed if not agreed) in relation to the arbitration of these matters notwithstanding any order of the arbitrator to the contrary.
(F) If the Respondent discontinues its application for the determination of a rent payable pursuant to Section 24A of the Landlord and Tenant Act 1954, the Respondent will forthwith notify the Applicant and the arbitrator and any arbitration proceedings concerning this matter shall cease. The Respondent will be liable to pay the arbitrator's fees and the Applicant's costs (to be taxed if not agreed) of the arbitration of this matter notwithstanding any order of the arbitrator to the contrary.

VERSION 2: Expert Determination on Rent and, if necessary, Arbitration on Interim Rent

Case No.

IN THE COUNTY COURT

In the Matter of the Landlord and Tenant Act 1954

In the Matter of the Premises known as

BETWEEN:

TENANT

Applicant

– and –

LANDLORD

Respondent

CONSENT ORDER

UPON the joint application of the parties by their respective solicitors and upon reading the parties' agreed terms

AND BY CONSENT

IT IS ORDERED THAT:

1. The duration of the new tenancy shall be a term commencing on the and ending on
2. The terms of the new tenancy (other than as to the duration thereof and as to the rent payable thereunder) shall be in the form previously agreed between the parties, and set out in Part 1 of the Schedule hereto.
3. The initial rent payable under the new tenancy shall be determined by a third party under the provisions of Part 2 of the Schedule hereto in accordance with Section 34 of the said Act [and as if the new tenancy were to commence on the date of his determination].
4. Pursuant to Section 24A of the said Act, the rent payable from [date] for so long as the current tenancy continues by virtue of Section 24 of the said Act shall be [at the rate of £ per year] [at the same rate as is agreed or determined in respect of the new tenancy under paragraph 3 above] [determined in accordance with Section 24A of the said Act by a third party under the provisions of Part 2 of the Schedule hereto].

AND IT IS FURTHER ORDERED that all further proceedings in this action be stayed upon the terms agreed between the parties and set out in the Schedule hereto save that:

(a) either party shall have liberty to apply to the Court for the purpose of carrying the said agreed terms into effect;

(b) when all the terms for the new tenancy have been finally determined in accordance with the provisions of the Schedule hereto either party shall have liberty to apply for an order pursuant to Section 29 of the said Act for the grant of a new tenancy on those terms;

(c) on the filing of a Notice of Discontinuance by the Applicant the Applicant's tenancy shall cease and determine on the expiration of three months from the date of filing of the said Notice with the Court.

SCHEDULE

Part 1

[Agreed Terms]

Part 2

(A) The matter referred to in paragraph 3 of the Consent Order ("the Initial Rent") shall be determined [first] by an independent surveyor acting as an expert and not an arbitrator who shall give both parties a reasonable opportunity to make written representations to him which he shall take into account in reaching his determination but which shall not be binding on him. [The independent surveyor shall have power to decide how his fees shall be borne as between the parties but otherwise each party shall bear its own costs of the determination of the Initial Rent.] [The independent surveyor shall have power to decide how his fees and the parties' own costs shall be borne as between the parties.] [Each side shall bear its own costs and one half of the independent surveyor's fees of the determination of the Initial Rent.]

(B) [The matter referred to in paragraph 4 of the Consent Order ("the Interim Rent") shall then be decided by the independent surveyor acting as an arbitrator in accordance with the Arbitration Act 1996.]

(C) The parties shall endeavour to make a joint appointment of the independent surveyor within [ ] days from the date of the Consent Order failing which either party may apply to the President for the time being of the [Royal Institution of Chartered Surveyors] [Law Society] to make the appointment.

(D) [Unless otherwise agreed the parties shall be bound by their respective Originating Application or Answer and pleadings lodged with the Court ("the Pleadings") [but the independent surveyor shall have power to allow either party to depart from its Pleadings].] [The parties shall not be bound by their respective Originating Application, Answer or pleadings lodged with the Court.]

(E) The Initial Rent shall be finally determined on the date of the independent surveyor's determination. Unless the parties otherwise agree the independent surveyor will the proceed to make an Award on the Interim Rent. [The Interim Rent shall be finally determined on the earliest date by which the arbitration proceedings on the Interim Rent (including any proceedings on or in consequence of any application or appeal under Sections 67, 68 or 69 of the Arbitration Act 1996) have been determined and any time for making such application or appeal or further application or appeal has expired without an application for extension of that time having been made.]

(F) If Notice of Discontinuance is filed by the Applicant with the Court the Applicant will forthwith notify the Respondent and the independent surveyor and the independent surveyor will take no further steps to determine the Initial Rent. The Applicant will be liable for the independent surveyor's fees in respect of the determination of the Initial Rent [and for the Respondent's costs of the determination of the Initial Rent, such costs to be taxed if not agreed] notwithstanding any direction of the independent surveyor to the contrary.

(G) [If the Respondent discontinues its application for the determination of the Interim Rent, the Respondent will forthwith notify the Applicant and the independent surveyor will take no further steps to determine the Interim Rent. The Respondent will be liable for the independent surveyor's fees [and for the Applicant's costs] in relation to the arbitration of the Interim Rent [such costs to be taxed if not agreed] notwithstanding any direction of the independent surveyor to the contrary.]

VERSION 3: Arbitration on Terms followed, if necessary, by Expert Determination on Initial Rent and Arbitration on Interim Rent

Case No.

IN THE COUNTY COURT

In the Matter of the Landlord and Tenant Act 1954

In the Matter of the Premises known as

BETWEEN:

TENANT

Applicant

– and –

LANDLORD

Respondent

CONSENT ORDER

UPON the joint application of the parties by their respective solicitors and upon reading the parties' agreed terms

AND BY CONSENT

IT IS ORDERED THAT:

1. The duration of the new tenancy shall be [a term commencing on the and ending on] [determined in accordance with Section 33 of the said Act, by a third party under the provisions of Part 2 of the Schedule hereto].
2. The terms of the new tenancy (other than as to the duration thereof and as to the rent payable thereunder) shall be [in the form previously agreed between the parties, and set out in Part 1 of the Schedule hereto] [such terms as have been previously agreed between the parties and are set out in Part 1 of the Schedule hereto together with such other terms as shall be determined in accordance with Section 35 of the said Act by a third party under the provisions of Part 2 of the Schedule hereto] [determined in accordance with Section 35 of the said Act, by a third party under the provisions of Part 2 of the Schedule hereto].
3. The initial rent payable under the new tenancy shall be [£ per year] [determined by a third party under the provisions of Part 2 of the Schedule hereto in accordance with Section 34 of the said Act [and as if the new tenancy were to commence on the date of his determination]].
4. Pursuant to Section 24A of the said Act, the rent payable from [date] for so long as the current tenancy continues by virtue of Sections 24 and 64 of the said Act shall be [at the rate of £ per year] [at the same rate as is agreed or determined in respect of the new tenancy under paragraph 3 above] [determined in accordance with Section 24A of the said Act by a third party under the provisions of Part 2 of the Schedule hereto].[2]

AND IT IS FURTHER ORDERED that all further proceedings in this action be stayed upon the terms agreed between the parties and set out in the Schedule hereto save that:

(a) either party shall have liberty to apply to the Court for the purpose of carrying the said agreed terms into effect;

2 If an interim rent application has been made as a separate action, this paragraph will need to be incorporated in a separate consent order with an amended Schedule.

(b) when all the terms for the new tenancy have been finally determined and/or agreed in accordance with the provisions of the Schedule hereto either party shall have liberty to apply for an order pursuant to Section 29 of the said Act for the grant of a new tenancy on those terms;

(c) on the filing of a Notice of Discontinuance by the Applicant the Applicant's tenancy shall cease and determine on the expiration of three months from the date of filing of the said Notice with the Court.

SCHEDULE

Part 1

[Agreed terms]

Part 2

(A) The matters referred to in paragraphs [1] [and] [2] of the Consent Order ("the Substantive Issues") shall be determined by an independent third party acting as an arbitrator in accordance with the Arbitration Act 1996 ("the Arbitrator").

(B) The parties shall endeavour to make a joint appointment of the Arbitrator within [ ] days from the date of the Consent Order failing which either party may apply to the President for the time being of the [Royal Institution of Chartered Surveyors] [Law Society] to make the appointment.

(C) The Arbitrator shall make a single award ("the Award") determining all the Substantive Issues and where any of the Substantive Issues are agreed between the parties during the course of the arbitration proceedings, the Arbitrator will incorporate their agreement in the Award. The Substantive Issues do not include, for this purpose, any issue solely related to costs. The Arbitrator will make a separate award on costs unless otherwise agreed by both parties.

(D) The Substantive Issues shall be finally determined on the earliest date by which the arbitration proceedings on the Substantive Issues (including any proceedings on or in consequence of any application or appeal under Sections 67, 68 or 69 of the Arbitration Act 1996) have been determined and any time for making any such application or appeal or further application or appeal has expired without an application for extension of that time having been made.

(E) The parties shall endeavour to agree the matters referred to in paragraphs [3] [and] [4] of the Order ("the Rental Issues") within 28 days (or such longer period as they may agree in writing) from agreement or final determination of the Substantive Issues.

(F) In default of agreement on the Rental Issues within the time referred to above either party may apply to the President for the time being of the [Royal Institution of Chartered Surveyors] [Law Society] for the appointment of an independent surveyor ("the Surveyor") to determine the Rental Issues.

(G) The matter referred to in paragraph 3 of the Consent Order ("the Initial Rent") shall be determined by the Surveyor acting as expert and not as arbitrator who shall give both parties a reasonable opportunity to make written representations to him which he shall take into account in reaching his determination but which shall not be binding on him. [The Surveyor shall have power to decide how his fees shall be borne as between the parties but otherwise each party shall bear its own costs of the determination of the Initial Rent.] [The Surveyor shall have power to decide how his fees and the parties' own costs shall be borne as between the parties.] [Each side shall bear its own costs and one half of the Surveyor's fees of the determination of the Initial Rent.]

(H) The Initial Rent shall be finally determined on the date of the Surveyor's determination. Unless the parties otherwise agree the Surveyor will then proceed to decide the matter referred to in paragraph 4 of the Consent Order ("the Interim Rent") acting as an arbitrator in accordance with the Arbitration Act 1996. The Interim Rent shall be finally determined on the earliest date by which the arbitration proceedings on the Interim Rent (including any proceedings on or in consequence of any application or appeal under Sections 67, 68 or 69 of the Arbitration Act 1996) have been determined and any time for making any such application or appeal or further application or appeal has expired without an application for extension of that time having been made.

(I) In relation to the determination of the matters referred to in paragraphs [1] [2] [3] and [4] of the Consent Order [unless otherwise agreed the parties shall be bound by their respective Originating Application or Answer and pleadings lodged with the Court ("the Pleadings") [but the independent third party shall have power to allow either party to depart from its Pleadings]] [The parties shall not be bound by their respective Originating Application, Answer or pleadings lodged with the Court].

(J) If Notice of Discontinuance is filed by the Applicant with the Court, the Applicant will forthwith notify the Arbitrator or the Surveyor as the case may be and any arbitration proceedings shall cease, and any Surveyor who has been appointed shall take no further action, in relation to the matters referred to in paragraphs [1] [2] and [3] of the Order. The Applicant will be liable for the Arbitrator and the Surveyor's fees [and for the other party's costs to be taxed if not agreed] of determining these matters notwithstanding any Order of the Arbitrator or direction of the Surveyor to the contrary.

(K) If the Respondent discontinues its application for the determination of a rent payable pursuant to Section 24A of the Landlord and Tenant Act 1954, the Respondent will forthwith notify the Applicant and the Surveyor and any arbitration proceedings concerning this matter shall cease. The Respondent will be liable to pay the fees of the Surveyor and the Applicant's costs of the arbitration of this matter (such costs to be taxed if not agreed) notwithstanding any Order of the Surveyor to the contrary.

VERSION 4: Expert Determination on text of Lease

Case No.

IN THE COUNTY COURT

In the Matter of the Landlord and Tenant Act 1954

In the Matter of the Premises known as

BETWEEN:

TENANT

Applicant

– and –

LANDLORD

Respondent

CONSENT ORDER

UPON the joint application of the parties by their respective solicitors and upon reading the parties' agreed terms

AND BY CONSENT

IT IS ORDERED THAT:

1. The duration of the new tenancy shall be a term commencing on the and ending on
2. The terms of the new tenancy (other than as to the duration thereof and as to the rent payable thereunder) shall be in accordance with the heads of terms previously agreed between the parties as set out in Part 1 of the Schedule and shall be given effect in a form of lease which shall be agreed between the parties or determined in accordance with the provisions of Part 2 of the Schedule hereof.
3. The initial rent payable under the new tenancy shall be £ per year.
4. Pursuant to Section 24A of the said Act, the rent payable from [date] [for so long as the current tenancy continues by virtue of Section 24 of the said Act] [from to] shall be [at the rate of £ per year].

AND IT IS FURTHER ORDERED that all further proceedings in this action be stayed upon the terms agreed between the parties and set out in the Schedule hereto save that:

(a) either party shall have liberty to apply to the Court for the purpose of carrying the said agreed terms into effect;

(b) either party shall have liberty to apply for an order pursuant to Section 29 of the said Act for the grant of a new tenancy in a form of Lease which has been finally determined in accordance with the provisions of the Schedule hereto;

(c) on the filing of a Notice of Discontinuance by the Applicant the Applicant's tenancy shall cease and determine on the expiration of three months from the date of filing of the said Notice with the Court.

SCHEDULE

Part 1

[Heads of Terms]

Part 2

(A) The heads of terms set out in Part 1 of this Schedule shall be incorporated in a form of lease which shall be determined by an independent third party who shall be a solicitor and who shall act as an expert and not an arbitrator who shall give both parties a reasonable opportunity to make written representations to him which he shall take into account in reaching his determination but which shall not be binding on him. [The independent expert shall have power to decide how his fees shall be borne as between the parties but otherwise each party shall bear its own costs of his determination.] [The independent expert shall have power to decide how his fees and the parties' own costs shall be borne as between the parties.] [Each side shall bear its own costs and one half of the independent expert's fees of the determination.]

(B) The parties shall endeavour to make a joint appointment of the independent expert within [ ] days from the date of the Consent Order failing which either party may apply to the President for the time being of the [Royal Institution of Chartered Surveyors] [Law Society] to make the appointment.

(C) [Unless otherwise agreed the parties shall be bound by their respective Originating Application or Answer and pleadings lodged with the Court ("the Pleadings") but the independent expert shall have power to allow either party to depart from its Pleadings.] [The parties shall not be bound by their respective Originating Application, Answer or pleadings lodged with the Court.]

(D) The said form of lease shall be finally determined on the date of the independent expert's determination.

(E) If Notice of Discontinuance is filed by the Applicant with the Court, the Applicant will forthwith notify the Respondent and independent expert and the independent expert will take no further action. The party filing such notice shall be liable for the independent expert's fees [and for the other party's costs to be taxed if not agreed] notwithstanding any direction of the independent expert to the contrary.

JOINT APPLICATION

Case No.

IN THE COUNTY COURT

In the Matter of the Landlord and Tenant Act 1954

In the Matter of the Premises known as

BETWEEN:

TENANT

Applicant

– and –

LANDLORD

Respondent

JOINT APPLICATION

WE [tenant] and [landlord] jointly apply to the Court for an order in the terms of the draft Consent Order attached.

We have each taken independent legal advice before agreeing to the terms of the proposed order.

DATED this day of

SOLICITORS' CERTIFICATE

We certify that we have each advised the applicant whom we represent on the suitability of the proposed procedure and terms set out in the draft Consent Order.

Signature:	Signature:
Solicitors for Tenant	Solicitors for Landlord

TO: The District Judge of the Court

NOTE This procedure is suitable for those landlords and tenants who have decided, following the receipt of professional advice, that they wish to resolve certain matters relating to the tenant's application for a new business tenancy by arbitration or independent expert determination rather than through the Courts. Landlord and tenant must each receive independent legal advice on the consequences of these procedures and their lawyers must sign the certificate on the application form.

Professional Arbitration On Court Terms (PACT)

THE LAW SOCIETY

THE ROYAL INSTITUTION OF CHARTERED SURVEYORS

APPLICATION FOR THE APPOINTMENT OF AN ARBITRATOR/INDEPENDENT EXPERT BY THE PRESIDENT OF THE ROYAL INSTITUTION OF CHARTERED SURVEYORS OR THE PRESIDENT OF THE LAW SOCIETY

(For applications where the parties have agreed to refer matters arising under the Landlord and Tenant Act 1954 to third party determination)

(You are encouraged to type all details)

I/We **hereby request the President of the** ***Royal Institution of Chartered Surveyors/Law Society*** **to appoint a** **** Surveyor/Solicitor*** **to act as an** ****Arbitrator/Independent Expert*** **in the case described overleaf.**
***delete as appropriate.**

Landlord **(full name, address and reference)**	
Landlord's Representative **(name, address, telephone number and reference)**	
Tenant **(full name, address and reference)**	
Tenant's Representative **(name, address, telephone number and reference)**	
Details of any other party relevant to the dispute (i.e. guarantor, parent or subsidiary company whose details should be given to enable the arbitrator/expert to check for conflicts of interest).	

Continued Overleaf.

FORM DRS7 (July 1997)

Nature of Dispute
Please give the address of the premises, including type of property and brief particulars of the main areas of dispute (i.e. whether valuation and/or legal issues are involved). Continue on a separate sheet if necessary.

Specialist Knowledge/Experience
Please indicate and detail if you consider that specialist knowledge/experience is required, e.g. geographical area or type of property.

Conflicts of Interest and/or Special Requirements
Please state the names of any Surveyors/Solicitors who should not be considered for appointment, because circumstances exist that give rise to justifiable doubts as to his/her impartiality. Give full reasons supporting your views (continue on a separate sheet if necessary). It is emphasised that while the President will give careful consideration to any representations, he will reach his own decision as to who shall be appointed.

Agreement to Refer
A signed CONSENT ORDER from the Court must accompany this form.

In some circumstances the appointment will be made by the President through one of his duly appointed agents and this is the basis upon which this application is submitted to you and upon which the application will be entertained. In special circumstances (to be decided by the President) it may be inappropriate for the President to effect the appointment and in these circumstances the appointment may be effected by another member of the RICS/Law Society in his own name.

Fees
A fee of £180.00 (inclusive of VAT) must accompany all applications for the appointment by the President. The fee is non-returnable whether or not the President makes the appointment (e.g. if the matter is settled by agreement).

I/We enclose a cheque for £180.00 (made payable to either the RICS or Law Society as appropriate).

Signed ....

Dated ....

To be returned to: The RICS Dispute Resolution Service, Surveyor Court,
Westwood Way, Coventry, CV4 8JE
Tel 0171 222 7000 (or Local Calls : 01203 694757) Fax 0171 334 3802

OR

The Appointments Officer, Arbitration Service
The Law Society, 50-52 Chancery Lane,
London WC2A 1SX
DX 56 Chancery Lane
Tel 0171 242 1222 Fax 0171 320 5918

JOINT WORKING PARTY MEMBERS

Royal Institution of Chartered Surveyors:

(Joint Chairman)	Torquil Gyngell	— Hargreaves Newberry Gyngell
	John Edgcumbe	— Hillier Parker
	Peter Jones	— DTZ Debenham Thorpe
	David Marsh	— King Sturge
	Graham Plumbe	— Gooch & Wagstaff
	Denis Reeves	— Donaldsons
	David Richardson	— Weatherall Green & Smith
	Ian Padbury	— RICS
	Carol Goodall	— RICS

Law Society:

(Joint Chairman)	Margaret Anstey	— Tozers
	Katie Bradford	— Linklaters & Paines
	Steven Fogel	— Titmuss Sainer Dechert
	Philip Freedman	— Mischcon De Reya
	Christopher Harrison	— Herbert Smith
	Iain Travers	— Nabarro Nathanson
	Lesley Webber	— Beachcroft Stanleys
	Neil Gower	— Law Society
	Suzanne Burn	— Law Society

Incorporated Society of Valuers and Auctioneers:

	Ian Loncaster	— Ian Loncaster & Co
	Brian Grainger	— ISVA

©The Law Society and RICS, July 1997. Copyright in all or part of this publication rests jointly with the RICS and the Law Society, and save by prior consent of the RICS or the Law Society, no part or parts shall be reproduced by any means electronic, mechanical, photocopying, recording or otherwise, now known or to be devised. Permission has been granted for members of the Law Society, the RICS and ISVA to reproduce the text of the Orders on a word-processor with any desired amendments.

APPENDIX E

COURT OF INTERNATIONAL ARBITRATION AUSTRALIA: EXPERT DETERMINATION RULES

ARTICLE 1 PREAMBLE

These Rules provide for the application of expertise to decide or make findings in respect of disputes, differences between or requests from parties to a wide range of relationships.

The Rules are not limited only to transactions of a commercial nature but may be applied wherever reliance on expertise is perceived as being appropriate.

ARTICLE 2 DEFINITIONS

In these Rules

"Applicant" means the party initiating the process.
"appointing authority" means a person empowered under these Rules to appoint an Expert.
"determination" means a decision, finding or answer made or given by the Expert to the matter referred or part of it.
"days" means calendar days and excludes weekends and holidays.
"document(s)" means writings, photographs, films, drawings, information or the like and in any form.
"Expert" means the person, firm, partnership, organisation or corporation appointed to act as the expert pursuant to these Rules.
"CIAA" means Court of International Arbitration Australia.
"law" means the law

- (i) stated in any contract or agreement which incorporates or adopts these Rules; or
- (ii) where no law stated then the law of the nation state in which the parties are domiciled; or
- (iii) where no common nation state of domicile then the law having the closest relationship to the matter referred as determined in the sole discretion of the Expert and whether or not the law of a nation state.

"matter referred" means the dispute, difference or question submitted to the Expert for determination.
"party" means any person, firm, organisation or corporation being an applicant or respondent in proceedings governed by these Rules.
"person" means a natural person, firm, partnership or a corporation.
"President" means the President for the time being of the Court of International Arbitration Australia or any person duly authorised by the President to act in respect of these Rules.
"proceedings" means all of the steps or requirements of the Process leading to the determination.
"process" means all aspects of referring and deciding a matter by expert determination.
"Respondent" means the party answering the initiation of the process.
"Rules" means these rules and any change, revision or amendment in effect prior to the date of initiation of the Process.
"submissions" means any documentary or oral presentation or material put before the Expert pursuant to the Rules and includes supporting documents.

Words imputing male génder shall be read as including the female gender and *vice versa*.

Unless the context of their use does not allow words imputing the singular shall be read as including the plural and *vice versa*.

ARTICLE 3 SCOPE OF RULES

The proceedings and the process shall be governed by these Rules and where the Rules are silent any Rules which the parties agree or failing agreement those determined by the Expert pursuant to Art 14.

ARTICLE 4 NOTIFICATION

(a) All notifications shall be made to the last known address of a party.
(b) Notification shall be by facsimile transmission or mail or any other means that provides a record of transmission.
(c) A notification shall be deemed to have been made on the day it was received by a party or would have been received if made in accordance with (b) above.

ARTICLE 5 EFFECT OF AGREEMENT

By adopting or submitting to these Rules the parties jointly and severally agree and covenant without further endorsement to be bound by and implement all of the terms and conditions of the Rules.

ARTICLE 6 INITIATING PROCEDURES

A party seeking to initiate an Expert Determination under these Rules shall give written notice to the other party or parties. Such notice shall

(i) identity the dispute, difference, or question to be referred for determination;
(ii) propose one or more persons, firms, partnerships, or corporations as suitable for appointment as Expert;
(iii) request that within seven days the other party or parties agree to an appointee drawn from the proposals given in accordance with (ii) above or to propose other prospective appointees.

ARTICLE 7 APPOINTMENT IN DEFAULT OF AGREEMENT

(1) Where the parties have failed to agree upon an Expert within 14 days of the written notice of referral to the Expert Determination process, by written request to the CIAA by one or more of the parties the President shall appoint an Expert. The written request shall include
  (a) written notice of referral to the process issued pursuant to Art 4;
  (b) copy of the agreement of the parties empowering the President to appoint;
  (c) a statement of any particular qualifications or requirements agreed or perceived by the parties or one or more of them as being required of the Expert;
  (d) the names of those persons or entities upon whom agreement has not been reached;
  (e) the names and addresses of all parties;
  (f) a copy of the notice given pursuant to Art 4;
  (g) payment in the sum stated in Appendix A of these Rules as a non-refundable appointment fee.
(2) Notwithstanding the provisions of sub-paragraph (1) above the parties may, by mutual agreement in writing, extend the time for agreement between them upon the Expert.
(3) The President shall, within seven days or such longer period as may be reasonably necessary, advise the parties of the person appointed as Expert.

ARTICLE 8 NOTIFICATION OF APPOINTMENT

Where the parties have agreed upon appointment of the Expert or where appointment is made under the provisions of Art 4 respectively the parties or the appointing authority as relevant shall as soon as possible notify the Expert so appointed.

Such notification shall include

(i) the full names and addresses of the parties;
(ii) a copy of the agreement between the parties making the appointment of the Expert, or a copy of the appointment made by the appointing authority;
(iii) a copy of these Rules;
(iv) a copy of the notice given pursuant to Art 4(i).

ARTICLE 9 ACKNOWLEDGMENT OF APPOINTMENT

Within seven days of receipt of notification of appointment the Expert shall acknowledge in writing such notification and accept or reject appointment.

ARTICLE 10 NATURE OF APPOINTMENT

The appointment of the Expert, whether by agreement of the parties or by an appointing authority, shall be presumed to be a joint appointment by all of the parties.

ARTICLE 11 INDEPENDENCE AND IMPARTIALITY OF EXPERT

The Expert shall be independent of the parties and act impartially. If the Expert becomes or is made aware of any circumstance that effects, or may effect, such independence and impartiality, such circumstance shall be disclosed to the parties and the Expert shall, if requested by any party, withdraw.

ARTICLE 12 REPLACEMENT OF EXPERT

(a) Where the Expert rejects appointment, subsequently withdraws, or cannot or does not conclude the process, whether by death, illness or any other cause, unless the parties otherwise agree, the Expert shall be replaced in the manner prescribed in Art 6 or Art 7 hereof.
(b) Where an Expert withdraws or cannot or does not conclude the process the Expert shall not be liable to repay any fees, costs or expenses previously drawn by the Expert pursuant to Art 26, or the parties' costs or expenses.

ARTICLE 13 CONDUCT OF PROCEEDINGS

(a) Other than as provided in these Rules, in conducting the proceedings the Expert is not bound to
  (i) apply the Law;
  (ii) apply principles of procedural fairness.
(b) The Expert may
  (i) direct or receive submissions, documents, or information from a party independent of the other party or parties and whether oral or otherwise;
  (ii) make enquiries or seek opinions of the parties or third parties;
  (iii) conduct or direct investigations, tests, experiments, calculations or other procedures of his own initiative;

(iv) if requested by one or more of the parties or of his own volition make an interim determination on a discrete or separable issue of the matter referred.

(c) In arriving at a determination the Expert may place such weight upon any or all material, information, opinions or submissions before him, including his own investigations, experiments, tests, or calculations (including no weight) as the Expert thinks fit.

(d) Unless otherwise agreed by the parties in writing, the Expert shall make available to the other party or parties all submissions, documents, or information received from a party pursuant to Art 20 and allow a reasonable time for comment or rebuttal.

(e) A replacement Expert may adopt or rely upon any determination made by an Expert that is replaced.

ARTICLE 14 SERVICE OF NOTICES

All notices or communications shall be made to the last notified address of a party. Such notices or communications shall be made by any means of delivery that provides a record of sending.

ARTICLE 15 PERIODS OF TIME

Periods of time provided in these Rules shall start to run on the day following the date a notification or communication is deemed to have been made.

ARTICLE 16 AGREED FACTS

With their submissions to the Expert the parties shall, where relevant, include a statement of agreed facts (if any).

ARTICLE 17 COMPETING ALLEGATIONS OF FACT

Where for determination of the matter referred the Expert is required or perceives the need to rely or have regard to facts which are in contention as between the parties, the Expert may require the parties or one or other of them to provide in support of the alleged facts such evidence and in such form as the Expert may direct.

ARTICLE 18 LANGUAGE

(a) The language of the Process shall be
  (i) the language of the agreement between the parties adopting or incorporating these Rules; or
  (ii) such other language as the parties and the Expert agree.

(b) Any party submitting documents in a language other than the agreed language shall provide a translation.

ARTICLE 19 REPRESENTATION

A party may be represented for any purpose in relation to the process.

ARTICLE 20 CONFERENCE

The Expert may convene and conduct a conference for the purposes of the process. Failure by a properly notified party to attend a conference will not of itself be grounds for the conference not proceeding.

ARTICLE 21 PARTY SUBMISSIONS

(1) Unless otherwise agreed by the parties in writing or directed otherwise by the Expert
 (a) Within 14 days of acknowledgment by the Expert to the parties of the lodgment of the full amount of initial security directed pursuant to Art 19 or advice to the parties from the Expert that no initial security is required
  (i) the applicant shall submit to the Expert and the other party a statement in writing setting out details of the matter referred and the alleged or agreed facts relied upon; or
  (ii) the Applicant and the respondent shall submit to the Expert a statement setting out details of the matter referred and the parties' respective positions, the contended facts and the agreed facts relied upon if any.
 (b) Within 14 days of the submission made by the Applicant pursuant to (a)(i) above the respondent shall submit to the Applicant and the Expert a statement in writing responding to the Applicant's submission and the alleged facts relied upon.
 (c) Within seven days of the response of the respondent as made pursuant to (b) above the Applicant may provide a further submission in rebuttal.
(2) The parties shall make further submissions in the form and as may be directed by the Expert.

ARTICLE 22 REFUSAL OR FAILURE TO PARTICIPATE

Where a party has agreed to submit to the process but refuses or fails to participate, the Expert may proceed to determination.

ARTICLE 23 DETERMINATION OF LEGAL RIGHTS AND OBLIGATIONS

Other than as necessary by the obvious nature or express terms of the matter referred, the Expert shall not make any determination purporting to establish the legal rights, duties and obligations of the parties.

ARTICLE 24 APPLICATION OF LAW

Where the Expert is required by the obvious nature or express terms of the matter or referred to determine the duties, rights or obligations of one or other or all of the parties, such determination shall be consistent with the Law.

ARTICLE 25 INTEREST

Where a determination is in whole or in part a money sum or sums payable as between the parties, the Expert may include in such determination an amount or rate of interest as may be the subject of prior agreement between the parties or, absent such agreement, such amount or rate as the Expert deems appropriate.

ARTICLE 26 FORM OF DETERMINATION

Unless otherwise agreed in writing by the parties a determination by the Expert shall be in writing and give reasons.

ARTICLE 27 COSTS OF THE PROCESS

The Expert may direct the parties to lodge monies in escrow with CIAA as security for the fees and expenses of the Expert due or incurred by the Expert in the carrying out of this Process. The Expert may draw upon such security from time to time to the extent of such fees and expenses properly due at the time of drawing without further recourse to or approval of the parties. Each party will share equally the Expert's costs and expenses of the Process.

ARTICLE 28 COSTS OF THE PARTIES

Each party shall bear its own costs and expenses of the Process.

ARTICLE 29 CONFIDENTIALITY

(a) Other than as required by law, or by direction of an authority having competent jurisdiction, or by release of the parties, the Expert shall keep confidential both the existence of referral to the Process and the Determination.
(b) The provisions of (a) above shall not act to prevent the Expert making at any time limited disclosures where issues of conflict or potential conflict arise.

ARTICLE 30 POWER TO CORRECT DETERMINATION

Where the determination contains

(i) a material miscalculation of figures or a material mistake in the description of any person matter or thing;
(ii) a clerical mistake;
(iii) an error arising from accidental slip or omission

the Expert may correct any determination within 30 days of issue whether or not such matter requiring correction is identified by the parties or one or other of them.

ARTICLE 31 CONTRACTUAL OBLIGATIONS

Where implementation of the Process arises by virtue of direct or indirect incorporation of these Rules in a contract between the parties and where absent a determination of the Matters Referred, all or part of the respective duties and obligations of the parties under the contract can be carried out, the parties shall perform or continue to perform such duties and obligations.

ARTICLE 32 GENERAL PROVISIONS

(a) In all aspects not expressly covered by these Rules the Expert shall act in the spirit of the Rules to maintain integrity and outcome of the Process.
(b) Where a dispute arises between the parties as to any aspect of these Rules the Expert may incorporate such dispute as part of the matter referred to him.
(c) The Expert shall act with due expedition in the conduct of the proceedings and the making of the determination having regard to the nature and extent of the matter referred.

ARTICLE 33 EXCLUSION OF LIABILITY

Save where there is a finding of fraud or corruption against the Expert or CIAA in respect or touching upon the Process no liability whatsoever shall lie as between one or other or all of the parties and the Expert or the CIAA.

ARTICLE 34 WAIVER

Where a party becomes aware of circumstances where any of these Rules have been breached in the conduct of the proceedings and does not immediately raise with the Expert and the other party of this, that party shall be deemed to have waived its right otherwise to object to or take further part in the proceedings or object to or avoid any determination made.

ARTICLE 35 INDEMNITY

The parties jointly and severally indemnify and shall forever keep indemnified the CIAA and the Expert against all and any claims, costs, expenses or damages for any matter arising out of or touching upon the Process.

ARTICLE 36 ENFORCEMENT

Any party may take action for enforcement of a determination made under these Rules by application to a court having competent jurisdiction under the law.

APPENDIX F

THE ACADEMY OF EXPERTS' MODEL TERMS OF ENGAGEMENT FOR EXPERTS

Dr Roger J Maddrell

The new Model Terms of Engagement enable both appointor and expert to focus on the requirements of the case at an early stage, avoiding costly and time-consuming arguments later on

The full title of these terms of engagement is "Model Terms of Engagement for the employment of Experts, on behalf of a party involved in a dispute before any court of law or arbitration or any other tribunal", quite a mouthful! They have been around for a number of years and were recently updated under the guidance of John Kaye FAE, to whom we owe our thanks.

The new Model Terms (nothing to do with the Labour Party!) set out clearly the requirements of the parties under the headings of Recital of Appointment, Definitions, The Appointor, The Expert, Intellectual Property Rights, Fees and Disbursements and Disputes. They are particularly useful in the way they describe the requirements and there can be little doubt, as an expert or an appointor, where you stand. This is especially so in, for example, legal aid cases. I have used them in the past, though not in all my cases, but I believe in the future it will become standard as they are cost effective as everyone knows what is required of them.

The new Model Terms cover two pages of A4 and might be considered by some as too long. However, they have to be as comprehensive as practicable. It is far preferable to some terms of engagement developed by members over the years I have seen, which run into many many pages. While the latter may be considered watertight, they can be extremely difficult to follow, especially for non-legal people like myself and thus are off-putting. This is not the case with the new Model Terms—that is not to say the new Model Terms cannot be further improved, and they are kept under constant review. At the very least, use of them will stimulate consideration of the requirements, avoiding later arguments, which can be time consuming and expensive.

WHY ARE THEY NEEDED?

It may seem obvious, but the appointors and experts can have differing views on what is required. For example, a lawyer, very familiar with legal aid, may be employing an expert who is not and later will feel very aggrieved through no fault of his own or the appointor, when they find at the end that the fees are not paid in full. In all cases it is essential that the requirements of the parties are set out as clearly and as early as possible and the Model Terms do this. While they state that the appointor will "provide full instructions in writing supported by legible copies of all relevant documents", as all experts know, such full instructions are not always forthcoming. This is not necessarily anyone's fault as clearly the appointor cannot be expected to understand the technical nuances of the case at the outset. It may indeed be that soon after their appointment the expert has to withdraw, as the case hinges around a point which they are not expert in (this point is covered in the Model Terms).

Signing up to these Model Terms focuses people's minds on the requirements of the case. If the exact requirements for the expert are not precisely known then the instruction can be developed jointly early on. Other aspects can also be developed as a case progresses.

PRINCIPAL CHANGES

The main headings given above remain unaltered in the new version, the changes are mainly those in emphasis, for example:

- the definitions for "The Appointor" and "The Client" have been expanded;
- minor changes have been made to "Fees" and "Disbursements" to include, for example, business class air fares;
- the appointor will ascertain the availability of the expert for every hearing, rather than, as before, informing them in writing;
- the appointor's requirements in legal aid cases have been extended as this has always been a contentious area;
- the expert's requirements have also been extended. For example, they must deal only with areas they have adequate experience and qualifications in, attend meetings of experts and assist the appointor in obtaining their legal aid fees;
- the moral rights of the expert are included;
- the section on "fees and disbursements" has been extended and a new paragraph included in "Disputes" to cover the appointment of an arbitrator should mediation not be successful.

CONCLUSIONS

The Academy's new Model Terms of Engagement are to be recommended, whatever the size or complexity of the case. They enable both the appointor and expert to focus early on as to the requirements of the case and avoid time wasting and expensive arguments later. They are being continually improved and updated and a new draft is being prepared in order to incorporate the new Civil Court Procedure Rules that were brought in in April 1999. However, there is nothing like hands-on experience and The Academy would welcome helpful comments from both appointors and experts at any time to assist in the updating process. The new Model Terms, for inserting into the Handbook, have been provided to The Academy's members. The A4 version will, however, have to be purchased.

Dr Roger J Maddrell is a Chief Engineer with Consulting Civil Engineers, Halcrow. He specialises in the maritime field.

"MODEL TERMS OF ENGAGEMENT FOR THE EMPLOYMENT OF EXPERTS

On behalf of a party involved in a dispute before any court of law or at arbitration or any other tribunal

1. **Recital of Appointment**—The Appointor has appointed the Expert to provide advice and services in accordance with these Terms of Engagement.
2. **Definitions**—Unless the context otherwise requires:

    (1) **"The Appointor"** means the lawyer, insurer, Government department, local authority, firm, or other body or persons instructing the Expert.

    (2) **"The Expert"** means the person appointed hereunder to render expert advice and services, including the giving of evidence, but not formal advocacy.

    (3) **"The Client"** means the person(s), Government department, local authority, firm or company to whom the Expert has been instructed to provide such advice and services.

    (4) **"Fees"** means (in the absence of written agreement to the contrary) the reasonable charges of the Expert based on the Expert's normal hourly rate for work of the type instructed. A daily rate

shall be applied to any day or part of any day of a hearing, including preparatory work and waiting time. Unless otherwise agreed, time spent travelling may be charged at the full hourly rate. Value Added Tax or the equivalent tax will be charged where applicable.

(5) **"Disbursements"** means all reasonable expenses necessarily incurred in rendering expert advice and services, including the giving of evidence. By way of example, they include the costs of relevant photography, video recordings, computer software, reproduction of drawings and diagrams, printing and duplicating, the cost of obtaining published documents including those withdrawn, as well as all appropriate out of pocket expenses including car mileage, first class rail travel, business class air fares, reasonable refreshments and four star hotel accommodation where an overnight stay is necessary. Value Added Tax or the equivalent tax will be charged where applicable.

(6) **References** to the masculine gender shall be deemed to include the feminine.

3. **The Appointor**—The Appointor will:

(1) Provide full instructions in writing supported by legible copies of all relevant documents.

(2) Deal promptly with every reasonable request by the Expert for authority, information and documents.

(3) Not alter or permit others to alter the reports of the Expert.

(4) Ascertain the availability of the Expert for every hearing, meeting or other appointment at which the Expert's attendance will or may be required and give the Expert immediate written notification together with adequate notice.

(5) **In Legal Aid cases:**

(a) inform the Expert at the outset if the case is or is expected to be legally aided;

(b) provide the Expert with sufficient details of the case and promptly answer any queries that will enable the Expert to prepare any required estimate of charges;

(c) not require the Expert to provide any services before the grant of authority by the Legal Aid Board for his fees and disbursements;

(d) apply to the Legal Aid Board for prior approval of the Expert's anticipated fees and promptly inform the Expert accurately of the outcome of the application;

(e) apply as above for additional fees required by any further work not originally authorised;

(f) make timely application to the Legal Aid Board or to the Court for interim and final payments for the Expert's fees and disbursements as invoiced and promptly remit to the Expert all such payments upon receipt;

(g) use his best endeavours to ensure that the Expert's fees and disbursements are recovered in full by way of the Legal Aid Fund and in the case of the Crown Court from the Lord Chancellor's Department;

(h) so advise the Expert if he is a Legal Aid Franchisee with devolved powers in the relevant category of work and ensure prompt remittance of interim and final payments as invoiced;

(i) use his best endeavours to ensure that the Expert's fees and disbursements are promptly remitted in full in the event of termination or suspenson of a Franchise Agreement or of a Legal Aid Certificate. Where a taxation of costs is necessary it will be applied for, pursued or defended (as applicable) in a timely manner.

(6) In privately funded cases ensure that he is at all times in funds to discharge and promptly discharge the fees and disbursements of the Expert.

(7) Unless otherwise agreed, pay in full the Expert's fees and disbursements irrespective of the outcome of any taxation of costs.

4. **The Expert**—The Expert will:

(1) Undertake only those parts of a case in respect of which the Expert considers that he has adequate qualifications and experience.

(2) Use reasonable skill and care in the performance of the instructions received.

(3) Act with objectivity and independence with regard to his instructions and, in the event of a conflict between his duties to the Client and to the Court or Tribunal, will hold his duties to the Court or Tribunal paramount.

(4) Promptly notify the Appointor of any matter including a conflict of interest or lack of suitable

qualifications and experience which could disqualify the Expert or render it undesirable for him to have continued involvement in the case.

(5) Endeavour to make himself available for all hearings, meetings and other appointments of which he has received adequate written notice.

(6) Not without good cause discharge himself from the appointment as Expert.

(7) Preserve confidentiality save as expressly or by necessary implication authorised to the contrary.

(8) Not negotiate with an opposing party or advisor unless specifically instructed by the Appointor so to do. For avoidance of doubt this clause does not apply to any Order of a Court or Tribunal.

(9) Attend such Meetings of Experts as Ordered by the Court or Tribunal or as required by the Appointor. At any such Meeting adhere strictly to the terms of reference set down in writing.

(10) Provide all relevant information to allow the Appointor to defend the Expert's fees or disbursements at any taxation of costs.

(11) Promptly respond to any complaint of the Appointor and within a reasonable time provide a statement of explanation or a means of rectification.

5. **Intellectual Property Rights**—The intellectual property rights of all original work created by the Expert shall remain vested in the Expert unless otherwise agreed in writing. The Expert asserts all his Moral Rights.

6. **Fees and Disbursements**

(1) The Expert may present invoices at such intervals as he considers fit. Payment of each invoice is due on presentation, subject to any written waiver or indulgence granted by the Expert.

Note: The Judicial Committee's Guidelines make a) payment upon a contingency fee basis unacceptable and b) the placing of pressure upon the Expert by the Appointor to provide extended credit terms or any other arrangement for inclusion in the Appointor's approved list of Experts improper, as they compromise the Expert's independence and impartiality.

(2) For the avoidance of doubt, in the following circumstances the Expert shall be entitled to charge fees on such basis as he considers appropriate:

(a) where the Expert's time has been reserved by subpoena or otherwise for a specific hearing, meeting or other engagement, or

(b) where specific instructions have been given to the Expert for an inspection/examination and report,

and where, due to settlement of the dispute or any other reason not being the default of the Expert, the reservation of time has been cancelled and/or instructions have been withdrawn.

(3) The Appointor and the Client shall be jointly and severally liable for payment of the Expert's fees and disbursements.

(4) The Expert shall at his discretion be entitled to invoice and recover interest at 1.5% per month on all unpaid invoices after 30 days. The full amount of his administrative, legal and other costs of recovering unpaid invoices is chargeable.

7. **Disputes**

(1) In the event of a dispute over the amount of the Expert's fees such sum as is not disputed shall be paid forthwith irrespective of any set-off or counter-claim which may be alleged.

(2) Any dispute arising between the Appointor or the Client and the Expert shall be referred to Mediation in accordance with The Academy of Experts' Mediation Guidelines. Upon the application of any party the Faculty of Mediation of The Academy of Experts will appoint a Mediator.

(3) Any dispute or difference not resolved by Mediation as in (2) above within 30 days of the appointment of the Mediator shall be referred to a single arbitrator who, if not agreed upon by the parties within 14 days thereafter, shall be appointed upon the application of either party by the President of the Chartered Institute of Arbitrators."

APPENDIX G

THE ACADEMY OF EXPERTS' MODEL FORM OF EXPERT'S REPORT

INTRODUCTORY NOTE

1. Why a Model Form?

1.1 Some senior judges have expressed concern at the length of many experts' reports and at the tendency to mix matters of fact and opinion.

1.2 The Judicial Committee of the Academy has commented that the hallmarks of a good report include:

(a) A stand-alone, concise, user-friendly format, expressed in the first person singular by the person whose opinion has been given or who adopts as his own the opinion of others.
(b) Text which is arranged in short sentences and paragraphs.
(c) Judicious use of appendices.
(d) Matters of fact being kept separate from matters of opinion.

Conclusions should be given in the final section of the report before appendices. They should be cross referenced to the text which supports the Conclusions.

1.3 Each opinion expressed in the report must be the opinion of the writer whether it was formed by the writer or formed by others and adopted by the writer as his own.

1.4 The following must be identified separately and distinguished:

(a) facts which the writer is asked to assume;
(b) facts which the writer observed for himself e.g. the results of experiments, investigations, etc., carried out by the writer himself;
(c) facts which others, acting on behalf of the writer, observed, identifying the persons concerned;
(d) opinions of others upon which the writer relies in forming his own opinion.

1.5 The model form of report has been developed with these comments in mind and with the aim of assisting both experts and those instructing to address the relevant issues in the most direct way. The model is intended as a guideline only. There may be valid reasons for departing from it and/or introducing additional sections.

2. The Scheme of the Model Form of Report

The Model Form is written in 5 distinct sections with suggested headings: notes are given.

The Front Sheet—the *first visible sheet* should contain the items of keypoint information indicated by the model and should not be obscured by a cover. The first report prepared for disclosure should be entitled "Report" and not "First Report".

The Contents Page—may be omitted altogether in the case of a short report of say seven pages or less.

Section 1 Introduction—deals with all the formal matters and chronology. The text is largely standard. Most of the material is transferred to appendices.

Section 2 The Background to the Dispute and the Issues

This section of the report will normally include:

(a) a list of the people who will be referred to in the report with a short uncontroversial description of their role.
(b) the assumed or given factual background of the case.
(c) the issues, set out clearly and numbered, which the expert will address.

No opinion is expressed in this section.
Section 3 Description of the Technical Investigation or Enquiry—this section is, again, factual only. The description should be given in itemised paragraphs with sub-headings.
Section 4 The Facts on which the Expert's Opinion is based—distinguishing those facts which he was told from those he observed for himself.
Section 5 The Expert's Conclusions—with opinion and reasons in full on each issue in turn, set out clearly and numbered. In this section, there should only be such repetition of fact as is necessary for the exposition of the opinion.
Signing Block—the report must be signed by the writer and dated at the end of the Conclusions.
Appendices—each Appendix should be provided with a front sheet of the type indicated in the model.
Headers—each continuation page of a section should be provided with a header on the left hand side showing the number and short title of the section and a header at the right hand side with the information suggested by the model.
Presentation—the practice is growing of the Court directing that a copy of experts' reports be made available on disc to the judge or official referee. Where practicable, therefore, reports should be typed in double spacing and prepared on or readily transferable to Wordperfect 5.1. The report should be presented on A4 paper, already hole punched for use in a standard lever arch binder and in a format that can be copied readily on a photocopier with automatic feed.

3. Evaluation of the Expert Witness

The following passage taken from the *dicta* of Stuart-Smith LJ in *Loveday* v. *Renton* [1990] 1 Med LR 177 provides a clear description of the processes which the Court has to undertake in order to evaluate the Expert witness, the soundness of his opinion and the weight to be attached to it.

> "...This involves an examination of the reasons given for his opinons and the extent to which they are supported by the evidence. The Judge also has to decide what weight to attach to a witness's opinion by examining the internal consistency and logic of his evidence; the care with which he has considered the subject and presented his evidence; his precision and accuracy of thought as demonstrated by his answers; how he responds to searching and informed cross-examination and in particular the extent to which a witness faces up to and accepts the logic of a proposition put in cross-examination or is prepared to concede points that are seen to be correct; the extent to which a witness has conceived an opinion and is reluctant to re-examine it in the light of later evidence, or demonstrates a flexibility of mind which may involve changing or modifying opinions previously held; whether or not a witness is biased or lacks independence ...".

[SHORT TITLE OF ACTION]

[DRAFT]

REPORT OF

[EXPERT'S NAME]

DATED

[ ]

Specialist Field	:	[State title of specialism]
Assisted By	:	[State names of assistants]
On behalf of	:	[State party's name]
On instructions of	:	[State name and business of those instructing]
Subject Matter	:	[State briefly the nature of the dispute and the date when it arose]
Inspection Date(s)	:	[Give the dates or period of all inspections]

[Name Address and Occupation of the writer's
Firm (if any) and telephone, fax, DX and reference]

Report of :

Specialist Field :

On behalf of :

CONTENTS

[Change or omit as appropriate]

(1.00 Introduction)

Report of :
Specialist Field :
On behalf of :

REPORT

1.00 Introduction

1.01 Formal Details

[Note 1—state (as applicable) your full name. Give your status (e.g., partner of), the name of your firm, the nature of its business and its address.]
[Note 2—state your own specialist field; there is provision later on for you to deal with qualifications, experience etc.]
[Note 3—state on behalf of whom you were instructed and the name, address and business of those instructing you.]

1.02 Synopsis

[Note 1—Set out concisely the general nature of the dispute e.g. "In this case, Ambridge Cricket Club alleges faulty design and erection of a new cricket pavilion. The main areas of complaint relate to the roof and verandah. I am advising the engineers. There are also complaints against the architects."]

1.03 Instructions

[Note 1—State briefly what you have been asked to do e.g. "to identify the issues within my specialist field that arise in this case, to make a technical investigation and to express my opinion with full reasons on each issue."]

1.04 Disclosure of Interests

[Note 1—State any actual or potential conflict of interests that you may have, for example a connection with any of the parties or witnesses or advisers which might be thought to influence the opinions expressed in the report.]
[Note 2—State (if it is so) that you have no such connection with any of the parties, witnesses or advisers involved in the case.]

1.05 Appendix 1—contains details of my experience, qualifications, appointments and specialist field(s) [together with those of ( ) who has/have assisted me in (state the areas of assistance).]
[Note 1—every person who has been involved in the investigation or enquiry and who has formed opinions on which the writer of the report is relying must be identified here and their details provided at Appendix 1.]

1.06 Appendix 2—contains a list of some of the documents I have considered together with copies of only those documents which I regard as essential for the understanding of my report.
[Note 1—every effort should be made to limit the number of documents which are added to the report.]
[Note 2—where documents are bulky they should be listed shortly by reference to bundles and not individually.]

1.07 Appendix 3—contains a list of the texts and published material to which I have referred in this report. I have included some copies or extracts for ease of reference.

1.08 Appendix 4—contains a list and copies of the [photographs, drawings, laboratory reports, schedules etc.] which [name of assistant and/or] I have prepared for the purposes of this report.

1.09 Appendix 5—contains [a full chronology].

1.10 Appendix 6—contains [etc. as/if applicable].

(2.00 Background/Issues)

Report of :
Specialist Field :
On behalf of :

2.00 The Background to the Dispute and the Issues

2.01 The Relevant Parties

[Note 1—set out briefly in short itemised paragraphs the names of those to whom you will refer in this report, together with a short, uncontroversial statement of their role in the relevant events.]
[Note 2—Please avoid acronyms. For example, the firm name Smith Jones Brown & Co Limited may better be shortened to "Smith" than "SJBCL".]

2.02 The Assumed Facts

[Note 1—set out in short itemised paragraphs a background narrative of the facts you have been asked to assume.]
[Note 2—bear in mind that a full chronology, if appropriate, will be provided at Appendix 5.]

2.03 The Issues to be addressed

[Note 1—identify, in short itemised paragraphs, each of the allegations and issues that you will, in turn, address. Say where in the case papers it arises and which party has raised it.]
[Note 2—where practicable, keep the list of issues raised by one party separate from those raised by any other party.]
[Note 3—this part of the report is factual only; no opinion should be expressed here.]

(3.00 Investigation)

Report of :
Specialist Field :
On behalf of :

3.00 The Technical Investigation [Enquiry]

[Note 1—give in short itemised paragraphs the date(s), and time(s) of day you attended to investigate the factual position. State where you went, what you saw and did and who assisted you, who else was present and what you found.]
[Note 2—it is desirable to avoid reporting second or third hand hearsay; this is not, however, an inflexible rule. There may be occasions when reliable hearsay should be reported. State in each case the name of the person who relayed the hearsay.]
[Note 3—experiments, detailed surveys, measurements, audits etc. should be briefly described. The full report should appear as an Appendix.]
[Note 4—this section of the report is factual only; no opinion should be expressed.]

(4.00 Factual Basis)

Report of :

Specialist Field :

On behalf of :

4.00 The Facts on which the Expert's Opinion is based

[Note 1—Identify separately and distinguish between:

(a) Facts which the writer has been asked to assume;
(b) Facts which the writer observed for himself e.g. the results of experiments, investigations etc. carried out by the writer himself;
(c) Facts which others, acting on behalf of the writer, observed (and identify the persons concerned);
(d) The opinions of others upon which the writer relies in forming his own opinion.]

[Note 2—refer as convenient to any rules, regulations or other documentary guidance which you consider to be relevant. Where essential, these should be copied at Appendix 3.]

(5.00 Conclusions)

Report of :

Specialist Field :

On behalf of :

5.00 Conclusions

5.01 [Set out the first issue and your opinion on that issue with reasons in full.]

[Note 1—if practicable provide a sub-heading for each of the issues.]
[Note 2—provide cross references to the text or any published material which supports the Conclusions.]
[Note 3—only refer to matters of fact so far as may be necessary to the understanding of the opinion.]

5.02 [Continue to set out each issue in turn with opinion and full reasons following the notes given above.]

Signature ....Name in full ....Date ....

Report of :

Specialist Field :

On behalf of :

APPENDIX 1

CONTENTS

1. [ ]

2. [ ]

3. [ ]

4. [ ]

APPENDIX G

THE ACADEMY

The Academy of Experts was founded on 14 October 1987. It is a multi-disciplinary body established to ensure high professional standards amongst Experts and to promote their use in litigation, dispute resolution and advisory roles. By the time the TAE was launched in June 1988 the principal objective had been refined to "The promotion of Cost Efficient Dispute Resolution".

Promotion of higher Expert standards and the more efficient use of Experts is still of primary concern. The Academy's ExpertSearch service attracts requests for Experts from all around the world, from both Common and Civil Law countries.

The Academy adheres to a strict code of practice and members, all of whom are vetted before entry, are drawn from a wide range of disciplines.

The Academy has also been promoting ADR (Alternative Dispute Resolution) in the UK and elsewhere, with a particular emphasis on training and standards. Included in this initiative have been training courses in the Far East, mainland Europe and the Caribbean. The Register of Qualified Dispute Resolvers has been published to enable the community to have easier access to properly accredited practitioners.

The Academy also works closely with the Judiciary and many professional bodies including The Law Society, The International Chamber of Commerce, The Royal College of Nursing, The Association of Consulting Engineers of Australia, The American Arbitration Association and The British Marine Industries Federation.

In 1989 the Lord Chancellor approved the formation of the Judicial Committee consisting of seven senior Judges representing the English, Scottish and Northern Irish Benches.

The Judicial Committee is responsible for examining ways in which the Expert can be used more efficiently. With the increasing number of Meetings of Experts being held, a set of "Rules" for their conduct has been produced by the Committee.

The Model Form of Expert's Report has been prepared by The Judicial Committee to further assist Experts and their clients by indicating a format that the Judiciary would find of assistance. In other words a "judge friendly" format. It must be remembered that the form is for a Model rather than a Standard form.

The Academy has been undertaking consultation about the future developments of the form for individual disciplines. When the consultation process has been completed the results will be referred back to the Judicial Committee for their advice and directions.

The Judicial Committee members are:

The Rt Hon The Lord Slynn of Hadley PC
Lord of Appeal in Ordinary
President of The Academy of Experts
Chairman of the Committee

The Rt Hon Lord Justice Neill
Court of Appeal

The Rt Hon Lord Justice Saville
Court of Appeal

The Rt Hon Lord Justice McDermott
Supreme Court of Judicature Northern Ireland

The Hon Lord Prosser
Court of Session Scotland

The Hon Mr Justice Garland
Queen's Bench Division

His Honour Judge Bowsher QC
Official Referees' Court

Julian Cohen
Secretary to the Committee
Masons Solicitors

The Judicial Committee were assisted in their work by members of The Academy. In particular Robert Boyd MAE of Veale Wasborough, Solicitors gave outstanding assistance in the preparation and drafting of the Model Form.

President

The Rt Hon The Lord Howe of Aberavon, CH QC

Vice Presidents

Prof Dr jur Karl-Heinz Böckstiegel
Daniel R Fund, QC SC
Sir Donald Harrison, MD MS PhD FRCS FRSM
Prof Pierre Lalive, Lic.jur. Lic.Litt(Geneva) Ph.D.(Cantab)
His Honour Judge Esyr Lewis, QC
Sir Francis McWilliams, GBE BSc(Eng) F.Eng DCL
Rodger Pannone, MAE
Norman Royce, OBE FRIBA PPCIArb FAE
His Excellency Judge Stephen Schwebel
Anthony Scrivener, QC

Patron

The Master of the Rolls, The Rt Hon The Lord Woolf

Chairman

Michael Cohen, LLB, FIBA, FCIArb, QDR, FAE, Barrister

Further details of Services, Training and Membership can be obtained from:

The Secretary
The Academy of Experts, 2 South Square, Gray's Inn, London WC1R 5HP
Telephone: 0171-637 0333·Facsimile: 0171-637 1893

APPENDIX H

THE ACADEMY OF EXPERTS' CODE OF PRACTICE

1. Experts shall not do anything in the course of practising as an Expert, in any manner which compromises or impairs or is likely to compromise or impair any of the following:

   (a) the Expert's independence or integrity;
   (b) a person's freedom to instruct any Expert of his or her choice;
   (c) the Expert's duty to act in the best interests of the client;
   (d) the good repute of the Expert or of Experts generally;
   (e) the Expert's proper standard of work;
   (f) the Expert's duty to the Court.

2. An Expert who is retained or employed in any action, suit or other contentious proceeding shall not enter into any arrangement to receive a contingency fee in respect of that proceeding.
3. An Expert should not accept instructions in any matter where there is an actual or potential conflict of interests. Notwithstanding this rule if full disclosure is made in writing the Expert may in appropriate cases accept instructions when the client specifically acknowledges the disclosure.
4. An Expert shall for the protection of his clients maintain with a reputable insurer proper insurances for an adequate indemnity.
5. Experts shall not publicise their practices in any manner which may reasonably be regarded as being in bad taste. Publicity must not be inaccurate or misleading in any way.
6. The Academy's plaque may only be used on firm's stationery when all Principals of that firm are Members of the Academy. Individual members, who are also members of a firm or company may use the Academy plaque on their personal stationery provided no references to the firm or company is made.

APPENDIX J

THE ACADEMY OF EXPERTS' FORM OF EXPERT'S DECLARATION

THIS DECLARATION SHOULD BE INSERTED BETWEEN THE END OF THE REPORT AND THE EXPERT'S SIGNATURE.

I .... DECLARE THAT:
[INSERT FULL NAME]

1. I understand that my primary duty in written reports and giving evidence is to the Court, rather than the party who engaged me;
2. I have endeavoured in my reports and in my opinions to be accurate and to have covered all relevant issues concerning the matters stated which I have been asked to address;
3. I have endeavoured to include in my report those matters, which I have knowledge of or of which I have been made aware, that might adversely affect the validity of my opinion;
4. I have indicated the sources of all information I have used;
5. I have not without forming an independent view included or excluded anything which has been suggested to me by others (in particular my instructing lawyers);
6. I will notify those instructing me immediately and confirm in writing if for any reason my existing report requires any correction or qualification;
7. I understand that;

   (a) my report, subject to any corrections before swearing as to its correctness, will form the evidence to be given under oath or affirmation;
   (b) I may be cross-examined on my report by a cross-examiner assisted by an expert;
   (c) I am likely to be the subject of public adverse criticism by the judge if the Court concludes that I have not taken reasonable care in trying to meet the standards set out above.

8. I confirm that I have not entered into any arrangement where the amount or payment of my fees is in any way dependent on the outcome of the case.

APPENDIX K

MODEL FORMS OF DIRECTION FOR EXPERTS

SIR LAURENCE STREET'S STANDARD DIRECTION

STANDARD DIRECTION ON EXPERT EVIDENCE

Direct that:

(i) On or before ______ the parties exchange the names, fields of expertise and witness statements of the experts whose opinions will be advanced as evidence.

(ii) (a) Thereafter the parties arrange for their respective experts in each field of expertise to meet together as soon as reasonably practicable and on so many occasions as may be necessary to prepare the report referred to hereafter;

(b) it will be the purpose of the meeting and the responsibility of the experts to strive to reach agreement on as much as possible of the expert opinion relevant to the dispute;

(c) the meeting of experts is encouraged to call by unanimous agreement on the parties or either of them to obtain and provide any additional data or information the experts may need with a view to reaching agreement, a copy of any such call to be lodged by the claimant with the arbitrator/referee;

(d) either party shall be at liberty to apply for a direction that such call be complied with;

(e) the experts shall prepare a condensed joint report stating in the first part the matters upon which they have finally been able to reach agreement and stating in the second part the matters upon which they have not been able to reach agreement;

(f) the report shall be accompanied by annexures prepared by each expert stating in condensed form the opinion of the expert on each matter of disagreement including the reasons why the expert does not agree with the opinions of the other experts;

(g) the original report shall be sent to the claimant on or before ______ who shall forthwith lodge it with the arbitrator/referee and send a copy to each other party;

(h) evidence may not be received from an expert who has without adequate reason not participated in such meeting and report.

(iii) at the hearing

(a) as each field of expertise arises for consideration each expert in that field will verify by affirmation his/her witness statement, the joint report and his/her annexure to the joint report. After these documents have been admitted into evidence all the expert witnesses in that field shall participate in a continuation of their meeting at which they will discuss with each other the matters of disagreement;

(b) for the purpose of such discussion the experts will be seated facing each other at a table placed between the arbitrator's/referee's table and the bar table;

(c) the discussion will be chaired by the arbitrator/referee who will guide the discussion and will intervene with the object of the matters of disagreement being examined and analysed so as to enable the arbitrator/referee to reach a determination upon them;

(d) the representatives of the parties will be at liberty with the permission of the arbitrator/referee to intervene in the discussion and, prior to the arbitrator/referee reaching a determination on any matters of disagreement, they will be permitted to question the experts and make submissions to the arbitrator/referee.

Sir Laurence Street
former Chief Justice, New South Wales, Australia

ALTERNATIVE ORDER FOR DIRECTION TO EXPERTS TO EXCHANGE A WRITTEN QUESTION

13.00 EXPERTS

13.01 Each party is given leave to call experts. The parties will attempt to agree on joint instructions. A copy of the agreed instruction to be sent to me or, if no agreement, details of those points of instruction on which they do agree and details of those on which they do not.

13.02 These instructions to state whether experts will meet "open" or "without prejudice" and also what authority they have (if any) to bind their respective parties. In any event privilege shall be waived for any matter agreed at these meetings.

13.03 The experts are to meet not later than 28 days after the service of the last statement or satisfactory reply to any request for further and better particulars thereof.

13.04 The experts shall endeavour to narrow the issues and to agree facts as facts, figures as figures etc. as far as possible and to exchange reports no later than 21 days before the commencement of the hearing.

13.05 They shall prepare, date and sign a note of the facts and opinions upon which they are agreed and of the issues upon which they are not. A copy of such note to be exchanged and delivered to me no later than 56 days before the hearing.

13.06 Not later than 42 days before the hearing, each party may address written questions to the opposing expert, to which that expert will be required to give written responses not later than seven days after receipt of those questions.

13.07 Not later than seven days after receipt of these written answers the party who posed the question may serve a further written comment.

13.08 All of the above to be copied to me, not later than 21 days before the hearing, and I may send written question to the parties to which their experts should respond. Replies to be sent to me not later than seven days thereafter and rebuttals or comments on these responses may be sent to me, copied to the other side, not later than seven days before the hearing.

13.09 Oral examination of experts will be limited to the key issues in difference between them as evidenced by the note referred to in 13.05 above unless I direct either on my own volition that there need be no oral examination of experts, or the parties jointly so agree.

Extract from D Mark Cato's Order for Directions following a preliminary meeting.

APPENDIX K/3

D MARK CATO'S STANDARD AGENDA ITEM IN ARBITRATION

10.03.4 EXPERTS

10.03.4.1 If experts engaged, parties to attempt to agree joint instructions. Such agreement/non-agreement to be notified to the arbitrator.

10.03.4.2 Date for exchange of their reports/rebuttals.

10.03.4.3 Inspection access for experts—if necessary?

10.03.4.4 Experts will meet, "open"/"without prejudice" to endeavour to narrow the issues. What authority do they have? Privilege shall be waived for any matter agreed at these meetings.

10.03.4.5 The experts to meet not later than 28 days of the close of "Pleadings".

They shall endeavour to narrow the issues and to agree facts as facts, figures as figures etc. as far as possible.

The experts shall prepare, date and sign a note of the facts and opinions upon which they are agreed, and of the issues upon which they cannot agree. A copy of such note to be exchanged and delivered to the arbitrator within 14 days of their last meeting but in any event, no later than 56 days before the hearing.

10.03.4.6 Not later than 42 days before the hearing, each party may address written questions to the opposing expert on the content of that expert's report to which that expert will be required to give written responses not later than seven days after receipt of those questions.

Not later than seven days after receipt of these written responses the party who posed the question may serve a further written comment.

All of the above to be copied to the arbitrator, who may, not later than 21 days before the hearing, send written questions to the parties to which their experts should respond. These replies to be sent to the arbitrator not later than seven days thereafter and rebuttals or comments on these responses may be sent to the arbitrator, copied to the other side, not later than seven days before the hearing.

The intention is either, to avoid, if possible, oral examination of experts, or restrict it to the major issues in difference between them. Whether any oral examination of experts is allowed, will, in any event, provided the parties do not agree otherwise, be at the discretion of the arbitrator.

Alternatively:

10.03.4.7 Consider a tribunal appointed expert for appropriate issues.

In which case the parties are:

1 To agree who the tribunal's expert should be, in consultation with the arbitrator.
2 To agree on the wording of the issue(s) to be submitted to the tribunal's expert and in the absence of agreement the arbitrator will decide on this wording.
3 To define the scope of the tribunal's expert's enquiries and, in the absence of agreement, this matter is to be decided by the arbitrator taking into account the parties' submissions.

Not later than 28 days of the close of pleadings the tribunal appointed expert is to deliver a draft report to each party.

Within 14 days of the delivery of this report a representative of the parties is to meet with the tribunal's expert to discuss his draft report. The discretion as to whether to amend this draft report, following submissions from the parties' representatives, to be entirely at the discretion of the tribunal's expert.

Not later than 14 days after the meeting between the tribunal's expert and the parties' representatives the tribunal's expert shall deliver a copy of his final report to the tribunal, copied to the parties.

Should either party wish to cross-examine the tribunal's expert on any matter contained in his final report (on any issue within the tribunal's expert's terms of reference, whether or not covered by his final report) then, not later than seven days before the hearing notice must be given in writing, of the matters on which the cross-examination is desired, to be delivered to the tribunal's expert, copied to the arbitrator and the other side.

At the hearing any cross-examination of the tribunal's expert may be conducted by a party appointed expert rather than the party's general advocate, if that is the party's preference.

APPENDIX L

COMMERCIAL COURT GUIDELINES: APPENDIX 12

EXPERT EVIDENCE IN CASES IN THE COMMERCIAL COURT: REQUIREMENTS OF GENERAL APPLICATION

1. It is the duty of an expert to help the Court on the matters within his expertise (CPR 35.3(1)). This duty is paramount and overrides any obligation to the person from whom the expert has received instructions or by whom he is paid (CPR 35.3(2)).
2. Expert evidence presented to the Court should be, and should be seen to be, the independent product of the expert uninfluenced by the exigencies of litigation.
3. An expert witness should provide independent assistance to the Court by way of objective unbiased opinion in relation to matters within his expertise. An expert witness should never assume the role of an advocate.
4. An expert witness should not omit to consider material facts which could detract from his concluded opinion.
5. An expert witness should make it clear when a particular question or issue falls outside his expertise.
6. If an expert's opinion is not properly researched because he considers that insufficient data is available, then this must be stated with an indication that the opinion is no more than a provisional one.
7. In a case where an expert witness who has prepared a report could not assert that the report contained the truth, the whole truth and nothing but the truth without some qualification, that qualification should be stated in the report.
8. If, after exchange of reports, an expert witness changes his view on a material matter having read another expert's report or for any other reason, such change of view should be communicated in writing (through legal representatives) to the other side without delay, and when appropriate to the Court.

INDEX

All references are to paragraph number or Appendix number.

THE ACADEMY OF EXPERTS

In 1987 The British Academy of Experts was founded with the objective of providing, for the first time, a professional body for experts to establish and promote high objective standards.

The "British" was subsequently dropped, as The Academy of Experts became an International Centre of Excellence for experts with a substantial multi-disciplinary membership, acting as both an accrediting and professional body.

The Academy is now the UK representative in the European Union organisation for Experts and has an ever-increasing role in the formulation of standards in areas as diverse as Hong Kong and the USA. This has stimulated the demand for Academy-accredited experts.

The promotion of Cost Efficient Dispute Resolution became increasingly important and this resulted in The Academy becoming a major force in the introduction and development of Alternative Dispute Resolution (ADR).

THE JUDICIAL COMMITTEE

The Academy's Judicial Committee is chaired by a Law Lord, The Rt Hon Lord Saville of Newdigate and consists of three Lords Justice of Appeal and other Senior Judges from the United Kingdom. They have been responsible for:

- The Model Form of Expert's Report (as commended by Lord Woolf's *Access to Justice*);
- Guidance Notes on The Meetings of Experts;
- Guidance Notes on Contingency Fees for Experts.

The Academy is fortunate that its President, Lord Howe, and his distinguished predecessors have all taken an active role in promoting The Academy both in the United Kingdom and around the world.

ACCREDITATION OF MEMBERS

All applicants to The Academy who wish to become Accredited Practising Expert Witnesses undergo a rigorous vetting procedure to ensure standards of excellence are maintained. The Academy has introduced examinations as an additional safeguard. This is the process, which gives the officially recognised full accreditation as a Practising Expert. Those who achieve it are awarded the designatory letters MAE. Ethical and professional standards are underlined by Codes of Practice and enforced by a disciplinary committee.

TRAINING AND DEVELOPMENT

The Academy offers a comprehensive range of training programmes to enable members to develop their expert skills, and undertake continuous professional development activity. The Academy is also a training and accreditation body for ADR Neutrals, including Commercial Mediators, Family Mediators, Conciliators and Expert Determiners. It publishes *The Register of Qualified Dispute Resolvers* and awards the designatory letters QDR to those achieving the approved standard. Standards are enforced in exactly the same way as for experts.

RANGE OF SERVICES

The Academy provides a full range of services to its members including:

- a helpline;
- technical meetings;
- a quarterly magazine and regular newsletters;
- a detailed Expert's Handbook for Practical Guidance;
- an annual survey of experts' fees;
- regular meetings on matters of expert interest;
- social functions.

In addition it provides a number of services which assist both members and the legal profession including:

- ExpertSearch;
- finding and matching the right accredited expert to the case;
- a Mediator Appointment Service;
- finding the right accredited Mediator;
- a special class of membership open to the legal profession to enable input and involvement to the work and development of The Academy.

Further information about The Academy and its services can be obtained from:

2 South Square
Gray's Inn
London
WC1R 5HP

Tel: 020 7637 0333
Fax: 020 7637 1893

http://www.academy-experts.org/
E-mail:mail@academy-experts.org

